D0755779

# THE GOOD
# FOOD GUIDE
## 2008

"*You can corrupt one man. You can't bribe an army.*"

Raymond Postgate, founder of
The Good Food Guide, 1951

Distributed by Littlehampton Book Services Ltd
Faraday Close, Durrington, Worthing, West Sussex BN13 3RB

Copyright © Which? Ltd 2007

Base mapping by Cosmographics
Data management and export by AMA DataSet Limited, Preston
Printed and bound by Scotprint

A catalogue record for this book is available from the British Library

ISBN: 978 1 84490 036 7

Consultant Editor: Elizabeth Carter
Senior Project Editor: Caroline Blake

*The Good Food Guide* makes every effort to be as accurate and up-to-date as
possible. All *Good Food Guide* inspections are anonymous but every main entry
has been contacted separately for details. We have very strict guidelines for fact-
checking information ahead of going to press, so some restaurants were dropped
if they failed to provide the information we required. Readers should still check
details at the time of booking, particularly if they have any special requirements.

Please send updates, queries, menus and wine lists to:
goodfoodguide@which.co.uk

For a full list of Which? books, please call 01903 828557, access our website at
www.which.co.uk, or write to Littlehampton Book Services. For other
enquiries call 0800 252100.

To submit a report on any restaurant, please visit: www.which.co.uk/gfgfeedback

**FSC**

**Mixed Sources**

Product group from well-managed
forests and other controlled sources

Cert no. TT-COC-2217
www.fsc.org
© 1996 Forest Stewardship Council

# CONTENTS

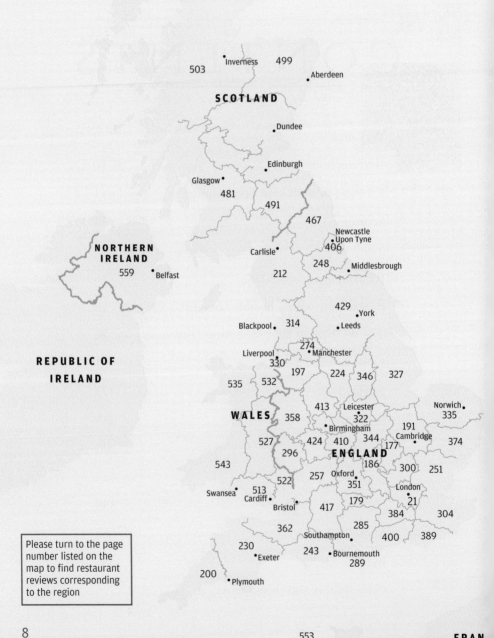

Inverness 503 499
Aberdeen
**SCOTLAND**
Dundee
Edinburgh
Glasgow
481
491
467
Newcastle
Upon Tyne
**NORTHERN IRELAND**
Carlisle 406
559 Belfast 248
Middlesbrough
212
429
York
Blackpool 314 Leeds
**REPUBLIC OF IRELAND**
Liverpool 274
330 Manchester
197 224 346 327
535 532
413 Leicester
Norwich
**WALES** 358 322 335
191
Birmingham Cambridge
527 424 410 344 177 374
296 186 **ENGLAND**
543
257 Oxford 300 251
522 351 London
Swansea 513 21
Cardiff Bristol 417 179 384 304
362 285
Southampton 400 389
230 243 Bournemouth
Exeter 289
200
Plymouth

Please turn to the page
number listed on the
map to find restaurant
reviews corresponding
to the region

553

FRAN

# Welcome

*The Good Food Guide* was first compiled by Raymond Postgate in 1951 and its ambition was simple: to inform people of places where '. . . the cooking, cellar and courtesy come up to proper standards'. More than 55 years later, the culinary world has changed beyond recognition. We enjoy cuisines from around the world, more people dine out regularly, and the standards of cooking are raising higher and higher.

And it's because of this evolution that *The Good Food Guide* is more important than ever before. All of its entries are based on genuine reader feedback; we have the most comprehensive reporting system of any publication in the field. We don't accept any sponsorship, advertising or free meals. And all of our reviewers conduct their inspections anonymously. It's because of this, and because the Guide will always be the voice of the consumer, not the catering industry, that *The Good Food Guide* remains the UK's most trusted, best-selling, best-loved restaurant bible.

And just as our culinary tastes have moved on, so it's time for *The Good Food Guide* to do the same with a respectful redesign. I'm excited about the changes to the 2008 edition. We have introduced county navigation, used full colour throughout and included a wider choice of restaurants. The 2008 edition includes more eateries than ever before, recommendations from you, the reader, and lots of interesting feature articles and interviews from across the culinary world.

The visual changes are dramatic; but the essence of the Guide – our independence, incisive writing and grading system – remains as important as ever. It is the start of a new era for Britain's favourite restaurant guide.

*Elizabeth Carter*

Consultant Editor

# Introduction

Raymond Postgate's assertion that, *'You can corrupt one man. You can't bribe an army.'* remains as true today as it was in 1951. Although much has changed since he published the first edition of the Guide in 1951 – both in terms of restaurants and publishing – the ethos of the original book remains. *The Good Food Guide* empowers diners, helping readers to find great places to eat, and encouraging restaurants to supply the best possible food, service and experience. And all of the content – every single entry – is based on a completely impartial assessment.

*The Good Food Guide* currently reports on over 1,200 top establishments, from à la carte and fine dining to bistros, pubs and ethnic cuisines. The Guide is completely rewritten every year, and it accepts no advertising or sponsorship. Critically, all of the inspections are anonymous. And, unlike some other guides, restaurants do not pay for inclusion in the book.

We encourage all of our readers to submit their reviews using the Which? website: www.which.co.uk/gfgfeedback. These reader submissions provide the basic list of restaurants for possible inclusion. The Guide's team of nearly 100 inspectors visit the recommended establishments reporting their findings and giving their professional thoughts on grading. Every successful entry is based on a mixture of independent inspection and reader feedback; *The Good Food Guide* does not accept any kind of payment or advertising for inclusion.

If you'd like to make a recommendation for *The Good Food Guide 2009*, please log on to: www.which.co.uk/gfgfeedback. We collect, read and count every bit of feedback – and we may well use some of your recommendations in next year's edition.

# Changes to The Good Food Guide

The essence of *The Good Food Guide* – our independence and integrity – is immoveable, but this year we've made a few aesthetic and content changes to make the Guide even more engaging and easy to use. Overleaf are sample pages, with an explanation of the changes, but here's a quick summary.

## County navigation
Having listened to feedback from many of our readers, we've introduced county ordering to make navigation much simpler. Each county has its own full-colour map showing the location of entries, in addition to the full-page maps at the back. Scotland, Wales and London are grouped in larger geographic regions, with relevant areas in alphabetical order contained within. Inevitably, some counties are stronger on entries than others; if you know a good, local restuarant that should appear in the Guide, please tell us by logging on to: www.which.co.uk/gfgfeedback.

## Full colour pages
We've introduced full colour throughout, with colour tabs and bars making navigation between towns and entries much easier.

## Reader recommendations
In addition to 1,200 full entries, the Guide includes around 300 additional entries, all recommended by our readers. These are local recommendations by local people, providing an insight into what's up-and-coming and what makes a great alternative when a main entry may be fully booked.

## Better symbols and headline information
We've introduced new, eye-catching symbols and headline information to help make information quick and easy-to-find. Restaurants that offer accommodation, special discounts or plenty of vegetarian options should be quick to spot, and the opening and closing details at the bottom of each entry are easier to find.

## Feature articles
The 2008 edition includes mini articles, interviews and features dropped-in throughout the book. So, whether you're hunting for a restaurant from the side of the road, or curled up on the sofa, flicking through the pages as you plan your next gastronomic delight, there should always be something to catch your eye.

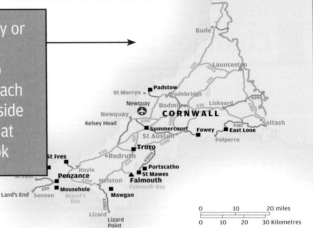

Organised by county or region, the Guide is faster and easier to navigate. Maps in each section work alongside the full-page maps at the back of the book

## ▌St Ives

### The A Restaurant
**Modern cuisine by the harbour**
1 The High Street, New Town, NT1 1AB
Tel no: 01234 567890
www.thearestaurant.co.uk
**Modern European | £43**
**Cooking score: 3**

If you want to secure the much-desired view over the harbour from this former lifeboat house, ask for a table by the window on the upper floor. The décor throughout is light, bright and minimalist, with white-painted walls and white napery. Dinner starts with an amuse-bouche – maybe creamed cauliflower and Stilton soup served in a tiny tureen – and 'excellent' home-made granary and tomato bread. Fish is a strong suit, as in a creamy nage of black bream or mackerel tempura with a sesame and soy dipping sauce which 'was an absolute *tour de force*' at inspection. Or you could start with a serving of duck with fig ... er selection of

chocloate, including a mould of dark chocolate and orange mousse, and banana and white chocolate ice cream. Plenty of wines are served by the glass from an international list. House Australian is £12.95
**Chef:** Graham Newton  **Open:** all week 11.30 to 2, 5 to 10 (6 to 9.30 low season)  **Closed:** 25 and 26 Dec
**Meals:** alc (main courses L £8-£15, D £14 to £20)
**Service:** not inc.  **Extra details:** No parking. Vegetarian meals. Children's helpings. No smoking.

## ALSO RECOMMENDED

### Café B
2 The Cresent, Old Town, OT1 1AB
Tel no: 01234 567890
Seaside café with a great position overlooking the beach and St Ives Bay. The lively menu offers simple stuff using the freshest seafood: crisp calamari or moules marinière (both £5.95) to start, followed by fish, chips and mushy peas in herb batter (£9.95) or whole local grilled lemon sole (£10.95). Breakfast and light lunches are also served (baguettes from £5.50). Wines from £10.95. Open all week, Apr to Oct.

Cuisine, price, score and symbols are quick to find

the content on these pages is sample text only

## The Restaurant C

**Spectacular alfresco beach dining**
10 The High Street, New Town, NT2 2BC
Tel no: 01234 567890
www.therestaurantc.co.uk
**Global/Seafood | £46**
**Cooking score: 4**

The position of this restaurant is rather special, with unbeatable views over the sea. It is closed over winter, so there's no opportunity to enjoy the view over the bay on the stormiest of days, but there's a large terrace for a truly Mediterranean experience in summer. Lunch can be a satisfying Cornish crab sandwich or crispy fried chilli squid with black spice, Thai salad and citrus white miso. In the evening, Jones pushes the boat out with scallop risotto with piquillo peppers, mascarpone and lemon vodka, followed by twice-cooked Barbary duck on braised salsify with seared foie gras and a gooseberry and Cointreau sauce. Finish with blood orange and Campari posset with a ginger glass biscuit.
**Chef:** George Jones **Open:** all week 12 to 3.45, 6 to 10 **Closed:** Nov to Mar **Meals:** alc (main courses L £7–£13, D £17 to £20) **Service:** not inc.
**Extra details:** 70 seats outside. Vegetarian meals.

### READERS RECOMMEND

### Bistro Number One
**Modern British**
Harbour Road, Old Town, OT2 2AB
Tel no: 01234 567890
**'Fantastic fish in a harbourside setting'**

### Café C
**Modern British**
20 The High Street, New Town, NT1 1AB
Tel: 01234 567890
**'Excellent food in a quirky, hippy-style setting'**

### The Restaurant D
**Fish**
Harbour Road, Old Town,
Tel no: 01234 567890
**'Fast, slick and stylish d**

Send your reviews

### A new start for Cornwall?

The Cornish fishing industry has suffered in recent years as diminishing fish stocks and EU quotas took their toll. Yet despite these problems, the industry is now quietly resurgent, and the growing demand for more sustainable food sources has led to a new take on fishing activity. There has been a recent enthusiasm in the industry to embrace more environmentally-friendly methods of fishing such as line-fishing for bass and pollack. And as reliance on depleted stocks of cod and plaice subsides, a new future for the fishing industry now looks possible. A county that relies so heavily on fishing and tourism for its income can now do so with ecological conscience.

## █ St Keyne

### Bistro Number Two
**Secluded splendour**
55 The High Street, New Town, NT1 1AB
Tel no: 01234 567890
www.bistronumbertwo.co.uk
**Modern British | £52**
**Cooking score: 3**

New owners have taken over this seclu... stone-built Victorian mansion overlook... Valley. However, there are few surprises in terms of combinations: a plate of roast goat's cheese and Parma ham comes with avocado, tomato and onion salad, while a meaty main course of fillet of beef might be teamed with mushroom and spinach fricassee and horseradish mash with a fish option along the lines of roast halibut and lime beurre blanc. For dessert, there's perhaps rhubarb fool tart with ginger ice cream. Mark-ups on the well-assembled wine list seem fair, with plenty of choice under £25.
**Chef:** Angela Williams **Open:** all week 12 to 1.30,

# Scoring

We should begin by saying that a score of 1 is actually a significant achievement. We reject many restaurants during the compilation of the Guide. Obviously, there are always subjective aspects to rating systems, but our inspectors are equipped with extensive scoring guidelines, so that restaurant bench-marking around the UK is accurate. We also take into account the reader feedback that we receive for each restaurant, so that any given review is based on severalmeals.

1/10   Capable cooking, with simple food combinations and clear flavours, but some inconsistencies.

2/10   Decent cooking, displaying good basic technical skills and interesting combinations and flavours. Occasional inconsistencies.

3/10   Good cooking, showing sound technical skills and using quality ingredients.

4/10   Dedicated, focused approach to cooking; good classical skills and high-quality ingredients.

5/10   Exact cooking techniques and a degree of ambition; balance and depth flavour in dishes, using quality ingredients.

6/10   Exemplary cooking skills, innovative ideas, impeccable ingredients and an element of excitement.

7/10   High level of ambition and individuality, attention to the smallest detail, accurate and vibrant dishes.

8/10   A kitchen cooking close to or at the top of its game – highly individual, showing faultless technique and impressive artistry in dishes that are perfectly balanced for flavour, combination and texture. There is little room for disappointment here.

9/10   At the moment, this is the highest mark in the Guide and it is not given lightly. This mark is for cooking that has reached a pinnacle of achievement, making it a memorable experience for the diner.

10/10 While it is extremely rare that a restaurant can achieve perfect dishes on a consistent basis (chefs are only human, after all), we live in hope.

# Symbols

Restaurants that may be given main entry status are contacted ahead of publication and asked to provide key information about their opening hours and facilities. They are also invited to participate in the £5 voucher scheme. The symbols on these entries are therefore based on this feedback from restuarants, and are intended for quick, at-a-glance identification. The wine bottle symbol, however, is an accolade assigned by the Guide's team, based on their judgement of the wine list available.

 Accommodation is available.

 It is possible to have three courses at the restaurant for less than £30.

 There are more than five vegetarian dishes available on the menu.

 The restaurant is participating in our £5 voucher scheme. (Please see the vouchers at the end of the book for terms and conditions.)

🍾 The restaurant has a wine list that our inspector and wine expert have deemed to be exceptional.

**£XX** This year, we have aligned the pricing for each restaurant in the book with our online feedback system: www.which.co.uk/gfgfeedback. The price indicated on each review represents the average price of a three-course dinner, excluding wine.

# Restaurant Awards 2008

*The Good Food Guide* has always recognised excellence and good service at restaurants throughout the UK. This year, we've introduced some new awards, designed to acknowledge the very best in modern dining, and to give our readers a stronger voice. So, for the first time, we introduced public nominations for an award called 'The Which? Good Food Guide Restaurant of the Year'. Members of the public were invited to nominate establishments for ten different regions, with the criteria that restaurants should be independently owned and offer regional or local produce. Nominations were submitted via our online feedback form (www.which.co.uk/gfgfeedback), by SMS text messaging, and by postal vote. We received thousands of nominations and *The Good Food Guide* team picked the overall winner from the list of regional winners.

## The Readers' Restaurant of the Year (2008 edition)
Yorke Arms, Ramsgill, North Yorshire

## Regional winners

1.  WALES - Tyddyn Llan

2.  SCOTLAND - Linen Room

3.  NORTHERN IRELAND - James Street South

4.  NORTH WEST - Ramsons

5.  NORTH EAST - Yorke Arms

6.  MIDLANDS - Perkins

7.  SOUTH WEST - Culinaria

8.  SOUTH EAST - The Plough, Bolnhurst

9.  EAST - The Swan Inn (Monks Eleigh)

10. LONDON - Canteen (Spitalfields)

Other awards in this Guide have been allocated by *The Good Food Guide* team and are as follows:

## Restaurant newcomer of the year
Restaurant Nathan Outlaw, Cornwall

## Pub newcomer of the year
Highwayman, Lancashire

## Wine list of the year
The Square, London

## Best chef
Jason Atherton, Maze, London

## Up-and-coming chef/s (joint award)
Peter and Jonray Sanchez Iglesias at Casamia, Bristol;
Chris Lee, Crown at Bildeston, Norfolk

## Most improved restaurant
West Stoke House, West Sussex

## Best fish restaurant
Cellar, Anstruther, Scotland

## Best value for money
Ottolenghi, London

## Best family restaurant
Felin Fach Griffin, Wales

## Best use of local produce
Sutherland House, Suffolk

# Restaurants with a notable wine list

## London

Almeida, N1
Andrew Edmunds, W1
Aubergine, SW10
Bacchus, N1
Bentley's, W1
Bibendum, SW3
Bleeding Heart, EC1
Bonds, EC2
Bradleys, NW3
Café du Jardin, WC2
Cambio de Tercio, SW5
The Capital, SW3
Le Cercle, W1
Chez Bruce, SW17
Club Gascon, EC4
The Don, EC4
Enoteca Turi, SW15
Eyre Brothers, EC2
Fifth Floor, SW1
Le Gavroche, W1
Glasshouse, TW9
Gordon Ramsay at
  Claridge's, W1
Gordon Ramsay, SW3
Great Eastern Hotel,
  Aurora, EC2
Greenhouse, W1
Greyhound, SW11
Hakkasan, W1
Kensington Place, W8
Ledbury, W11
L'Etranger, SW7
Lindsay House, W1
Locanda Locatelli, W1

Maze, W1
Metrogusto, N1
Odette's, NW1
Orrery, W1
Pearl, WC1
Pètrus, SW1
Pied-á-Terre, W1
Le Pont de la Tour, SE1
Ransome's Dock,
  SW11
Rasoi Vineet Bhatia,
  SW3
Restaurant Semplice, W1
Roussillon, SW1
RSJ, SE1
Square, W1
Tate Britain Restaurant,
  SW1
Tom Aikens, SW3
La Trompette, W4
Umu, W1
Wolseley, W1
Zuma, SW7

## Rest of UK

36 On The Quay,
  Emsworth
60 Hope Street,
  Liverpool
A Touch of Novelli at
  the White Horse,
  Harpenden,
Airds Hotel, Port Appin
Albannach, Lochinver
Aldens, Belfast
Angel Restaurant,
  Long Crendon,

Anthony's Restaurant,
  Leeds
Ardeonaig Hotel,
  Ardeonaig
Arundel House,
  Arundel
Arundell Arms, Lifton
Auberge du Lac,
  Welwyn Garden City
Balmoral, Number One,
  Edinburgh
Bath Priory, Bath
Bay Horse Inn,
  Kirk Deighton
Bell at Skenfrith,
  Skenfrith
Blue Lion, East Witton
Bodysgallen Hall,
  Llandudno,
Box Tree, Ilkley
Braidwoods, Dalry
Brasserie Forty Four,
  Leeds
Brian Maule at Chardon
  d'Or, Glasgow
Callow Hall, Ashbourne
Carlton Riverside,
  Llanwrtyd Wells
Castle Hotel, Taunton
Castle House, Hereford
Castleman Hotel,
  Chettle
Cayenne, Belfast
Cellar, Anstruther
Cherwell Boathouse,
  Oxford
Chester Grosvenor,
  Arkle, Chester
Clytha Arms, Clytha

Combe House,
  Gittisham
Corse Lawn House,
  Corse Lawn
Crooked Billet,
  Newton Longville
Crown at Whitebrook,
  Whitebrook
Crown Hotel,
  Southwold
Culinaria, Bristol
Curlew, Bodiam
Danesfield House,
  Oak Room, Marlow
Darroch Learg, Ballater
Devonshire Arms,
  Bolton Abbey
Dylanwad Da, Dolgellau
Fairyhill, Reynoldston
Fat Duck, Bray
Firenze,
  Kibworth Beauchamp
Fischer's Baslow Hall,
  Baslow
Forth Floor, Edinburgh
Fourth Floor Café
  and Bar, Leeds
Fox & Hounds,
  Hunsdon
Fraiche, Oxton
Gidleigh Park, Chagford
Gilpin Lodge,
  Windermere
Gravetye Manor,
  East Grinstead
Greens' Dining Room,
  Bristol
Greyhound, Stockbridge
Haldanes, Edinburgh

Hambleton Hall, Hambleton

Hart's, Nottingham

Holbeck Ghyll, Windermere

Horn of Plenty, Gulworthy

Hotel du Vin & Bistro, Bristol

Hotel du Vin & Bistro, Winchester

Hotel du Vin & Bistro, Tunbridge Wells

Hotel du Vin & Bistro, Henley-on-Thames

Hotel du Vin & Bistro, Brighton

Hotel du Vin & Bistro, Birmingham

Hotel du Vin & Bistro, Harrogate

JSW, Petersfield

Killiecrankie House, Killiecrankie

Kinloch House Hotel, Blairgowrie

Knockinaam Lodge, Portpatrick

La Cachette, Elland,

La Chouette, Dinton

La Luna, Godalming

Lake Country House, Llangammarch Wells

Le Champignon Sauvage, Cheltenham

Le Manoir aux Quat' Saisons, Great Milton

Le Poussin at Whitley Ridge, Brockenhurst

Le Vignoble, Aberystwyth

L'Enclume, Cartmel

Lewtrenchard Manor, Lewdown,

Lime Tree, Manchester

Linen Room, Dumfries

Linthwaite House, Bowness-on-Windermere

Little Barwick House, Barwick

London Carriage Works, Liverpool

Longueville Manor, St Saviour

Lowry Hotel, River Restaurant, Salford

Lumière, Cheltenham

Maes-y-Neuadd, Harlech

Magpies, Horncastle

McCoy's at the Tontine, Staddlebridge

Midsummer House, Cambridge

Mill Race, Leeds

Montagu Arms, Terrace, Beaulieu

Morston Hall, Morston

Mr Underhill's, Ludlow

Nantyffin Cider Mill Inn, Crickhowell

New Angel, Dartmouth

No. 6, Padstow

Northcote Manor, Langho

Oakley and Harvey at Wallett's Court, St Margaret's-at-Cliffe

Old Bridge Hotel, Huntingdon

Old Vicarage, Ridgeway

Olive Branch, Clipsham

Olive Tree at The Queensberry Hotel, Bath

Orestone Manor, Maidencombe

Penhelig Arms, Aberdovey

Penmaenuchaf Hall, Penmaenpool

Pheasant, Keyston

Pintxo People, Brighton

Plas Bodegroes, Pwllheli

Rampsbeck Country House Hotel, Watermillock

Ramsons, Ramsbottom

Read's, Faversham

Restaurant 22, Cambridge

Restaurant Martin Wishart, Edinburgh

Restaurant Nathan Outlaw, Fowey

Restaurant Sat Bains, Nottingham

Riverstation, Bristol

Rothay Manor, Ambleside

Sangster's, Elie

Sasso, Harrogate

Seafood Restaurant, St Andrews

Seafood Restaurant, St Monans

Seaham Hall, White Room, Seaham

Second Floor, Manchester

Sharpham Park, Charlton House Hotel, Shepton Mallet

Sharrow Bay, Ullswater

Shibden Mill Inn, Shibden, Halifax

Simpsons, Edgbaston

Sir Charles Napier, Chinnor

Sous le Nez en Ville, Leeds

Spire, Liverpool

St Tudno Hotel, Terrace Restaurant, Llandudno

Stagg Inn, Titley

Star Inn, Harome

Stravaigin, Glasgow,

Summer Isles Hotel, Achiltibuie

Sycamore House, Little Shelford

Tan-y-Foel Country House, Capel Garmon

The Anchor Inn, Sutton Gault

The Angel Inn, Hetton

The Boar's Head Hotel, Ripley

The Cross, Kingussie

The Dower House, Royal Crescent, Bath

The George in Rye, Rye

The Griffin Inn, Fletching

The Harrow at Little Bedwyn, Little Bedwyn

The Mirabelle at The Grand Hotel, Eastbourne

The Plough, Bolnhurst

The Vineyard at Stockcross, Newbury

Three Chimneys, Isle of Skye

Three Horseshoes, Madingley

Three Lions, Stuckton,

Tyddyn Llan, Llandrillo,

Ubiquitous Chip, Glasgow

Valvona & Crolla Caffé Bar, Edinburgh

Vintners Rooms, Edinburgh

Weavers Shed, Golcar,

Webbe's at the Fish Cafè, Rye,

Wellington Inn, Lund

West Stoke House, West Stoke

Westerly, Reigate

Whatley Manor, Easton Grey

White Moss House, Grasmere

Wildebeest Arms, Stoke Holy Cross

Winteringham Fields, Winteringham

Ye Olde Bulls Head, Beaumaris

Ynyshir Hall, Eglwysfach

Yorke Arms, Ramsgill

Ziba, Liverpool

# Top 40 2008

1. The Fat Duck (9)
2. Gordon Ramsay, Royal Hospital Road (9)
3. Le Manoir aux Quat'Saisons (9)
4. Winteringham Fields (8)
5. Le Champignon Sauvage (8)
6. Le Gavroche (8)
7. Pétrus (8)
8. Waterside Inn (8)
9. Vineyard (8)
10. Square (8)
11. Pied à Terre (8)
12. Restaurant Nathan Outlaw (8)
13. L'Enclume
14. Tom Aikens (8)
15. Restaurant Martin Wishart (8)
16. The Capital (7)
17. Restaurant Sat Bains (7)
18. Gidleigh Park (8)
19. Anthony's, Leeds (7)
20. Juniper (7)
21. Andrew Fairlie at Gleneagles (7)
22. Hambleton Hall (7)
23. Holbeck Ghyll (7))
24. Fischer's Baslow Hall (7)
25. Tyddyn Llan (7)
26. Harry's Place (7)
27. The Creel (7)
28. Mr Underhill's (7)
29. Bohemia, St Helier (7)
30. Castle Hotel, Taunton (7)
31. Chester Grosvenor (7)
32. Old Vicarage, Ridgeway (7)
33. Midsummer House (6)
34. Maze (6)
35. Club Gascon (6)
36. Simpsons (6)
37. Bath Priory (6)
38. Kitchin (6)
39. The Greenhouse (6)
40. Ledbury (6)

# Longest-serving restaurants

Connaught, London, 55 years
Gay Hussar, London, 51 years
Gravetye Manor, East Grinstead, 51 years
Porth Tocyn Hotel, Abersoch, 51 years
Sharrow Bay, Ullswater, 47 years
Rothay Manor, Ambleside, 39 years
Le Gavroche, London, 38 years
Summer Isles Hotel, Achiltibuie, 38 years
Miller Howe, Windermere, 37 years
The Capital, London, 37 years
Ubiquitous Chip, Glasgow, 36 years
Druidstone, Broad Haven, 35 years
Plumber Manor, Sturminster Newton,
    35 years
Waterside Inn, Bray, 35 years
White Moss House, Grasmere, 35 years
Isle of Eriska, Eriska, 34 years

Airds Hotel, Port Appin, 32 years
Farlam Hall, Brampton, 31 years
Corse Lawn House, Corse Lawn, 30 years
Hambleton Hall, Hambleton, 29 years
Pier Hotel, Harbourside Restaurant,
Harwich, 29 years
Grafton Manor, Bromsgrove, 28 years
Magpie Cafè, Whitby, 28 years
RSJ, London SE1, 27 years
Seafood Restaurant, Padstow, 27 years
Sir Charles Napier, Chinnor, 27 years
The Dower House, Royal Crescent, Bath,
    27 years
Kalpna, Edinburgh, 26 years
Le Caprice, London, 26 years
Little Barwick House, Barwick, 26 years
Moss Nook, Manchester, 26 years

# LONDON

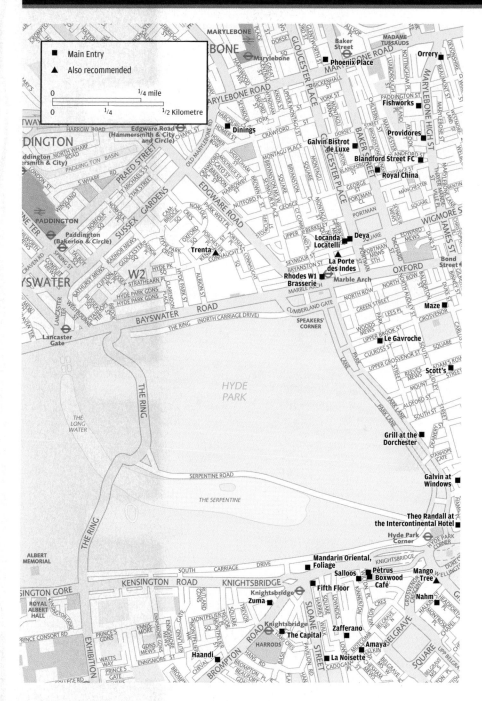

Legend:
- ■ Main Entry
- ▲ Also recommended

0 — ¼ mile
0 — ¼ — ½ Kilometre

Map labels:
MARYLEBONE, BONE, Marylebone, Baker Street, MADAME TUSSAUDS, Orrery, Phoenix Place, Fishworks, Dinings, Providores, Galvin Bistrot de Luxe, Blandford Street FC, Royal China, PADDINGTON, DINGTON, Paddington (Hammersmith & City) and Circle), Trenta, Locanda Locatelli, Deya, La Porte des Indes, Rhodes W1 Brasserie, Marble Arch, Maze, Lancaster Gate, Le Gavroche, Scott's, HYDE PARK, THE LONG WATER, THE RING, SERPENTINE ROAD, THE SERPENTINE, Grill at the Dorchester, Galvin at Windows, Theo Randall at the Intercontinental Hotel, Hyde Park Corner, ALBERT MEMORIAL, KENSINGTON ROAD, KNIGHTSBRIDGE, Mandarin Oriental, Foliage, Salloos, Pétrus, Boxwood Café, Mango Tree, Fifth Floor, Nahm, Zuma, Knightsbridge, The Capital, Zafferano, Haandi, Amaya, La Noisette, ROYAL ALBERT HALL, HARRODS

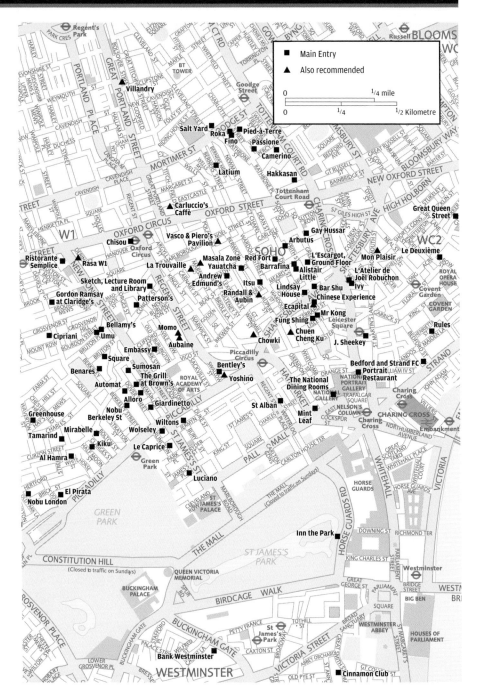

■ Main Entry

▲ Also recommended

0             ¼ mile

0       ¼       ½ Kilometre

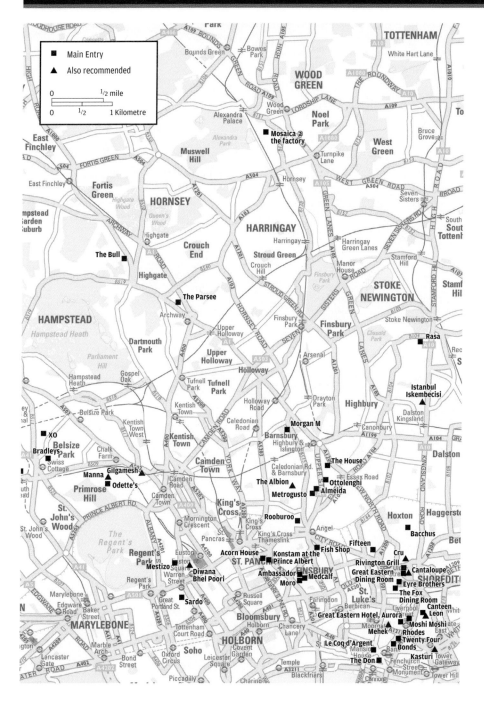

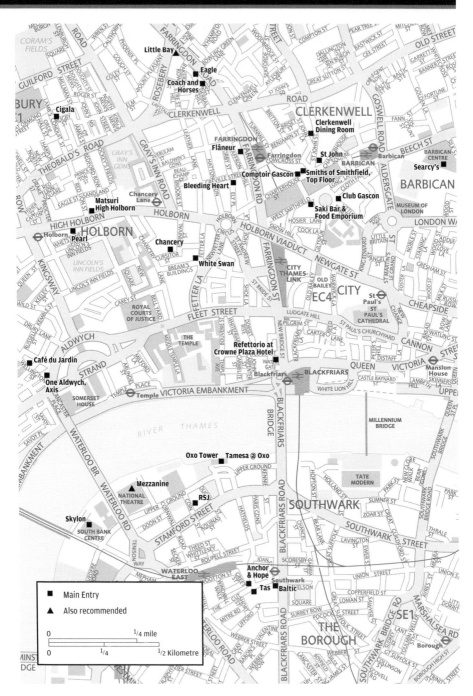

Little Bay
Eagle
Coach and Horses
Cigala
CORAM'S FIELDS
CLERKENWELL
Clerkenwell Dining Room
FARRINGDON
Flâneur
Farringdon
St John
Barbican
BARBICAN CENTRE
Searcy's
Comptoir Gascon
Smiths of Smithfield, Top Floor
Bleeding Heart
Club Gascon
BARBICAN
Matsuri
High Holborn
Chancery Lane
Saki Bar & Food Emporium
MUSEUM OF LONDON
LONDON W
Holborn
Pearl
HOLBORN
Chancery
White Swan
CITY THAMES-LINK
St Paul's
ST PAUL'S CATHEDRAL
CHEAPSIDE
EC4
CITY
ROYAL COURTS OF JUSTICE
FLEET STREET
CANNON
Café du Jardin
THE TEMPLE
Refettorio at Crowne Plaza Hotel
Blackfriars
BLACKFRIARS
QUEEN VICTORIA
Mansion House
One Aldwych, Axis
SOMERSET HOUSE
Temple
VICTORIA EMBANKMENT
WHITE LION HILL
RIVER THAMES
BLACKFRIARS BRIDGE
MILLENNIUM BRIDGE
Oxo Tower
Tamesa @ Oxo
Mezzanine
NATIONAL THEATRE
RSJ
TATE MODERN
SOUTHWARK
Skylon
SOUTH BANK CENTRE
STAMFORD STREET
SOUTHWARK STREET
WATERLOO EAST
Anchor & Hope
Southwark
Tas
Baltic
SE1
THE BOROUGH
Borough

■ Main Entry
▲ Also recommended

0     1/4 mile
0   1/4   1/2 Kilometre

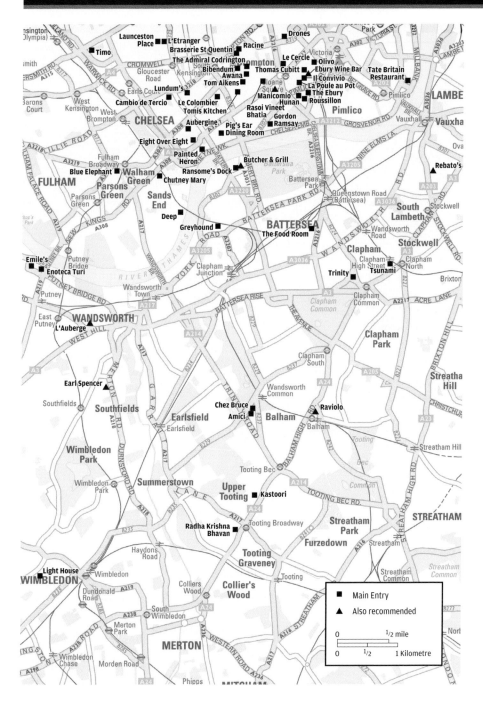

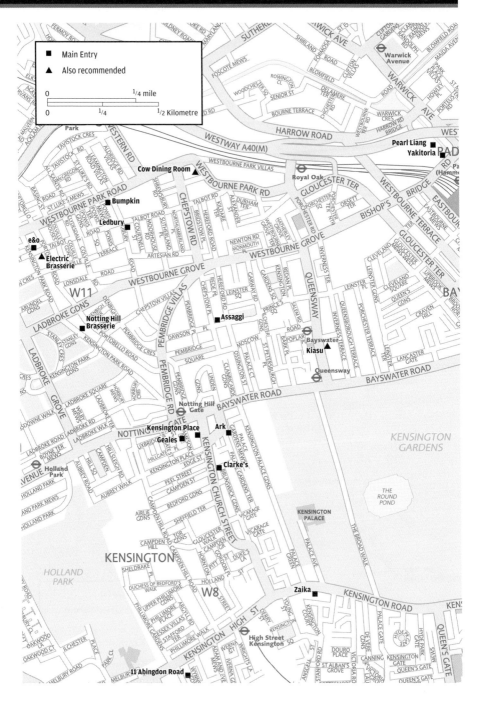

Main Entry

Also recommended

0 — ¹/₄ mile

0 — ¹/₄ — ¹/₂ Kilometre

Warwick Avenue

Pearl Liang

Yakitoria

Royal Oak

Cow Dining Room

Bumpkin

Ledbury

e&o

Electric Brasserie

W11

Notting Hill Brasserie

Assaggi

Bayswater

Kiasu

Queensway

Notting Hill Gate

Kensington Place

Geales

Ark

Clarke's

KENSINGTON GARDENS

THE ROUND POND

KENSINGTON PALACE

KENSINGTON

W8

Zaika

HOLLAND PARK

Holland Park

High Street Kensington

KENSINGTON ROAD

11 Abingdon Road

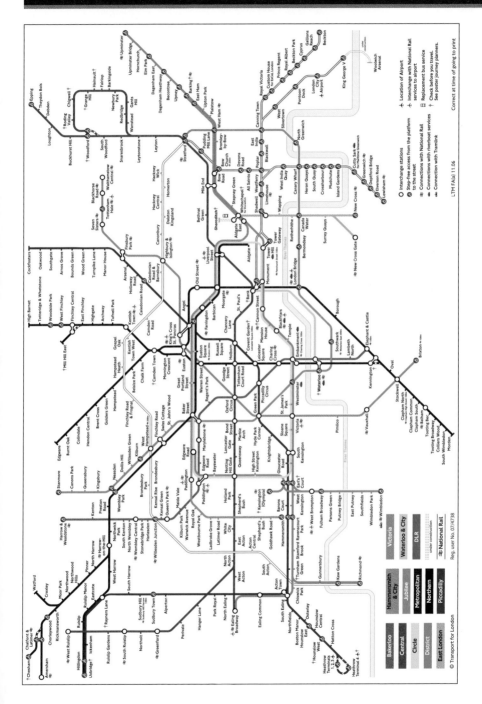

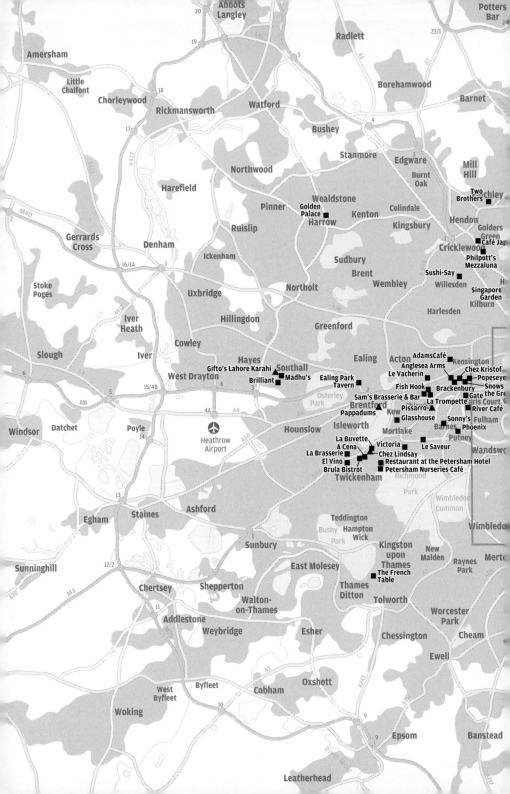

## ▌Belgravia

### Le Cercle

Imaginative French-style tapas
1 Wilbraham Place, SW1X 9AE
Tel no: (020) 7901 9999
⊖ Sloane Square
French | £34
Cooking score: 5

🍷 ✏

The younger sibling of Club Gascon (see entry), Le Cercle is in much the same business – tapas-sized portions of high-class, innovative cooking, loosely based on the traditions of southwest France. It's a windowless basement room off Sloane Street, cleverly done in neutral tones to mitigate the subterranean feel. Thierry Beyris is a formidable talent, both in imagination and in execution, as is witnessed by dishes such as cod with an artichoke emulsion and artichoke chips, wood pigeon with hazelnut mash and a rocket and truffle vinaigrette, or steamed brill with barley risotto, chorizo and spring onions. The menu, as at Club Gascon, is divided into French-titled categories, and you might want to play the game of sampling something from each, leaving space for the gourmandises of course. These include chocolate sorbet macaroon and redcurrant coulis, and 'luscious pears' with caramelised popcorn and sesame ice-cream. Every item on the menu has a suggested wine or other drink appended to it, and much is available by the glass. This encourages exploration of the lesser-known byways of French wine, such as the Jura, as well as the *sud-ouest* itself. Prices open at £18, with glasses from £4.50.
**Chef/s:** Thierry Beyris. **Open:** Tue to Sat 12 to 3, 6 to 11. **Closed:** Christmas to New Year. **Meals:** Meals: alc (main courses £4.50 to £35). Set L £15, Set D 6 to 7 £19.50. Bar menu available. **Service:** 12.5% (optional). **Details:** Cards accepted. 70 seats. Air-con. Music. Children's portions.

## Drones

Trademark mixture from Marco Pierre White
1 Pont Street, SW1X 9EJ
Tel no: (020) 7235 9555
www.whitestarline.org.uk
⊖ Victoria
French | £54
Cooking score: 4

✏

That particular Marco Pierre White blend of classical French and demotic British brings on dishes that soothe rather than challenge at this established Belgravia restaurant. The repertoire runs from croustade of poached egg served with a sauce hollandaise and, mushroom purée, via rillettes of duck with poivre vert and toasted Poilâne, to grilled lobster with sauce béarnaise. Another element at work is the comfort factor, which produces foie gras (parfait en gelée) for example, and classics like caramelised skate wing with clams, capers and jus à la parisienne, and grilled calf's liver with sauce diable, bacon and sage. Rice pudding with a compote of fruits or champagne gelée of red fruits and a syrup of passion fruit are alternatives to the famous lemon tart. Wines aim for the upper end of the market, for the rest of us there are a few choices in the £18 to £25 region, but a dozen by the glass.
**Chef/s:** Joseph Croan. **Open:** all week L 12 to 2 (3 Sun), Mon to Sat D 6 to 11. **Meals:** alc (main courses £13.50 to £24.50). Set L Mon to Sat £14.95 (2 courses) to £17.95, Set L Sun £22.50. **Service:** 12.5%. **Details:** Cards accepted. 96 seats. Air-con. Wheelchair access. Music.

### Please send us your feedback

To register your opinion about any restaurant listed in the Guide, or a new restaurant that you wish to bring to our attention, please visit the web address at the bottom of the page. Your feedback informs the content of the book and will be used to compile next year's reviews.

# Nahm
**Top-drawer Thai food**
Halkin Hotel, 5 Halkin Street, SW1X 7DJ
Tel no: (020) 7333 1234
www.nahm.como.bz
⊖ Hyde Park Corner
Thai | £47
Cooking score: 3

🛒 Y

A swish dining room in the Halkin Hotel provides a sleek, minimalist backdrop for David Thompson's highly personal take on Thai cuisine. After a taster of salted chicken and longan wafers, expect inventive salads such as poached chicken with banana blossoms ahead of cleansing soups. Other courses focus on intense curries including a 'green' version with braised salted beef, wild ginger, apple and pea aubergines. At lunch, the menu focuses on one-plate street dishes, with rice and noodles as the mainstays: look for chicken 'pilaff' with sweet chilli sauce or kanom kin (noodles) with rich fish and wild ginger curry. Prices on the pedigree wine list can seem intimidating; there is precious little below £30.

**Chef/s:** David Thompson and Matthew Albert. **Open:** Mon to Fri L 12 to 2.15, all week D 7 to 10.45 (10.30 Sun). **Closed:** bank hols. **Meals:** alc (main courses £8.50 to £16.50). Set L £26, Set D £49.50. Bar menu available. **Service:** 12.5% (optional). **Details:** Cards accepted. 90 seats. Air-con. Wheelchair access. Music. Children's portions.

★NEW ENTRY★
# La Noisette
**New addition to the Ramsay empire**
164 Sloane Street, London, SW1X 9QB
Tel no: (020) 7750 5000
www.gordonramsay.com/lanoisette
⊖ Knightsbridge
Modern European | £62
Cooking score: 4

By backing former Greenhouse chef Bjorn van der Horst, Gordon Ramsay is hoping to reverse the run of bad luck that has dogged

restaurants on this site. While it's hard to understand why a restaurant on this street has never succeeded, when you enter the brown, dimly lit dining room on the first floor you begin to see why. The kitchen cooks in the modern medium – think froth, espuma – and is undeniably talented, with pea velouté topped with a sabayon of ham, accompanied by a refreshing lollipop of mint sorbet. Techniques are varied: a starter of pan-seared foie gras comes with espresso syrup and Amaretto foam, while main-course milk-fed Somerset veal has pancetta, gnocchi and parmesan for company. A pre-dessert of mango sorbet placed over vanilla foam and a blackcurrant espuma visually resembled a dish of egg and bacon, and desserts take a cross-cultural road, with a honey and lychee ravioli, green tea and Japanese pepper cake. The highlight at inspection was an unusual red wine soufflé with a fromage blanc sorbet, shallot crystalline, and chives. The lengthy wine list is arranged by grape varietals, including the lesser-known Grüner Veltliner. Prices, starting at £20 or £7 for a glass, reflect the Knightsbridge location.

**Chef/s:** Bjorn van der Horst. **Open:** Mon to Fri L 12 to 2.30, Mon to Sat D 6 to 10.30. **Closed:** One week at Christmas. **Meals:** Set L £21 (up to 7pm) Set Dinner £55 to £65. **Service:** 12.5% (included). **Details:** Cards accepted. 55 seats. Air-con. Separate bar. No music. No mobile phones. Wheelchair access. Children allowed.

# Noura Brasserie
**Sleek venue serving authentic Lebanese food**
16 Hobart Place, SW1W 0HH
Tel no: (020) 7235 9444
www.noura.co.uk
⊖ Victoria
Lebanese | £36
New Chef

£5
OFF Y

Imported from Paris and now spreading its tentacles across central London, the Noura mini-chain aims to bring traditional Lebanese cooking to a wider audience by offering flexibility and all-day opening. The Hobart

Place original trades on sleek, minimalist elegance and offers an extensive menu of dishes with an authentic stamp. A vast assortment of hot and cold mezze is tailor-made to suit most dietary preferences: opt for a mixed platter or choose individually from a list that includes everything from hummus, kebbeh nayeh (lamb 'tartare' with cracked wheat) and moujaddara (lentils and rice topped with seared onions) to fatayer (pastry parcels of baked spinach) and samke harra (fish 'ratatouille'). Main courses are mostly high-protein chargrills and kebabs, ranging from marinated chicken to red mullet with tarator sauce, and there are some tantalising desserts to round things off. Heavyweight names from France and Lebanon hold centre stage on the concise wine list. Prices start at £23 for Château Ksara. See the website for details of other branches.

**Chef/s:** Yazbeck Yazbeck. **Open:** all week 12 to 12. **Meals:** alc (main courses £11.50 to £21). Set L £18 (2 courses), Set D £30 to £36. **Service:** not inc. **Details:** Cards accepted. 100 seats. Air-con. Wheelchair access. Music. Children's portions. Car parking.

## Olivo
**Lively Sardinian restaurant**
21 Eccleston Street, SW1W 9LX
Tel no: (020) 7730 2505
⊖ Victoria
**Italian | £30**
**Cooking score: 2**

The buzzy, convivial ambience generates the perfect atmosphere for the Sardinian-orientated food. Wooden floors, tightly-packed tables and a lack of napery help crank up the volume and lend an informal air to proceedings. Chargrilled stuffed baby squid with plum tomatoes and basil is a good way to start, or there's pasta, which comes in starter of main-course portions – try a Sardinian spaghetti dish with grated grey mullet roe as a second course before sautéed lamb's sweetbreads with white beans and artichokes. Desserts include the usual pannacotta, semifreddo or chocolate and almond tart. Staff

'have a passion for food'. Prices on the short but appealing patriotic all-Italian wine list open at £15.50.

**Chef/s:** Marco Melis. **Open:** Mon to Fri L 12 to 3, all week D 7 to 11 (10 Sun). **Closed:** bank hols. **Meals:** alc (main courses £13.50 to £15.50). Set L £18 (2 courses) to £20.50. Cover £1.50. **Service:** not inc. **Details:** Cards accepted. 45 seats. Air-con. No music.

## Pétrus
**Sublime, masterly food**
The Berkeley, Wilton Place, SW1X 7RL
Tel no: (020) 7235 1200
www.marcuswareing.com
⊖ Knightsbridge
**Modern French | £75**
**Cooking score: 8**

The Château Pétrus label is etched onto the front door handle, a sure sign that Marcus Wareing's ultra-exclusive restaurant means business. Nestling within the high-flown Berkeley Hotel and discreetly divided into three parts, the dining room exudes sexy warmth, style and class. Its walls are clothed in soft velvet and enunciated by a sensual claret colour scheme; elegant lampshades and petite chandeliers hang from the ceiling, and a smartly designed abacus replete with blown-glass beads guards the impressive wine store. Sink into one of the generously proportioned leather chairs to enjoy an appetiser of hummus while perusing the menu. To start, there is always something tantalising, perhaps warm mushroom velouté with cold cep foam, a dish that manages to deliver a 'clever interplay of hot and cold sensations'. The kitchen is never afraid to innovate, turning out an exquisite ballotine of tuna with spiced pineapple carpaccio alongside marinated mooli, mint and a cardamom foam, which resulted in a rare 'Umami' moment for one recipient. The sheer consistency and refinement of the food never fails to turn heads: one reporter's 'simply faultless' main course of entrecôte of veal with white asparagus, Jersey Royal new potatoes and morel mushrooms came topped with a dazzling piece of cromesquis made with the veal meat. Endorsements suggest that Wareing is at the top of his game: those who are analytically inclined note that flavours are pronounced, never too assertive; pristine ingredients and excellent technique are mobilised to conjure up dishes that lack nothing. Meals proceed at a measured pace, and napkins are changed before the final act: that signals the imminent arrival of an exquisite pre-dessert, perhaps a ravishing Sauternes jelly with vanilla yogurt and apple granita. Desserts here are amongst the best in class and they are Wareing's way of celebrating his Lancastrian roots. Few can resist the prospect of a supremely simple custard tart with vanilla and poached English rhubarb or a friable Eccles cake with Earl Grey tea cream, spiced prune and milk foam, before the irresistible bon-bon trolley appears. Service is impeccable, with much pampering and TLC dispensed with palpable largesse. Well-groomed courtesy extends to the sommelier, who proffers helpful advice without any hint of snobbery. The wine list itself is a shining model of care and grandiloquence, spread over 40 pages and brimming with superstars from every region. France takes centre stage but other countries are not ignored, and it's good to see Slovakia, Slovenia and Israel making an appearance among the wine world's veterans. Prices start from £20, with selections by the glass from £5, but since this restaurant is named after the world's most expensive wine, it is bound to be a magnet for financial big-hitters. Some 40 examples from the Château Pétrus dynasty are on show, going back to 1924 and including the legendary 1928 vintage for a mere £11,600.

**Chef/s:** Marcus Wareing. **Open:** Mon to Fri L 12 to 2.30, Mon to Sat D 6 to 11. **Closed:** 1 week Christmas. **Meals:** Set L £30 to £80, Set D £60 to £80. **Service:** not inc. **Details:** Cards accepted. 70 seats. Air-con. No music. No mobile phones. Wheelchair access. Children's portions.

# La Poule au Pot

**Rigorously authentic French restaurant**
231 Ebury Street, SW1W 8UT
Tel no: (020) 7730 7763
⊖ Sloane Square
French | £38
Cooking score: 2

Here is a little corner of provincial France on a smart London street. The décor features the kind of bistro clutter that others have long since chucked out in favour of blank minimalism, while the service is all old-school French bonhomie. Test your linguistic skills with a menu that offers simple cuisine bourgeoise, not excluding foie gras poelé with a glass of sweet Monbazillac. Other starters might be smoked salmon paupiette stuffed with crab, or nine snails, and then there is a wide range of fish or meat to choose from for main. Grilled daurade fillets in white wine and fennel, or rabbit in mustard, are likely to be the order of the day. Choose from the likes of crème brûlée, tarte Tatin or chocolate mousse to finish. Wines are of course exclusively French, with house Sauvignon and Merlot at £14.50.

**Chef/s:** Kris Goleblowski and Francisco Reis-Viela. **Open:** all week 12.30 to 2.30 (3.30 Sun), 7 to 11 (10 Sun). **Meals:** alc (main courses £14.75 to £21). Set L £16.75 (2 courses) to £18.75. **Service:** 12.5% (optional). **Details:** Cards accepted. 70 seats. 30 seats outside. Air-con. No music.

★NEW ENTRY★
# Thomas Cubitt

**Gastropub with grand designs**
44 Elizabeth Street, SW1W 9PA
Tel no: 020 7730 6060
www.thethomascubitt.co.uk
⊖ Victoria
Gastropub | £30
Cooking score: 3

Named after London's famous 19th-century master builder, this chic gastropub is inspired by Regency and Georgian design and draws the young and well-heeled from Belgravia's squares for quality modern European

cooking. Expect plenty of chatter and clatter in the buzzy downstairs bar, with its oak floors, open fires and big, roll-back windows that allow drinkers and diners to migrate to pavement tables when the sun shines. Tuck into traditional pub meals here, but head upstairs to the more formal restaurant – white-clad tables, muted colours, quirky *objets d'art* – for a more intimate dining experience. Careful buying of top-notch British produce is evident in starters like seared scallops with spiced sausage and celeriac purée and poached crayfish salad with saffron mayonnaise. Main courses take in 42-day aged Highland Black Angus sirloin with béarnaise, and Norfolk pork belly with braised black pudding stuffed trotter and white bean and apple purée. Desserts may include chocolate pot with summer berry salad and pistachio biscuits. Wines from £14.
**Chef/s:** Phillip Wilson. **Open:** Mon to Fri 12 to 3 and 6 to close. **Closed:** Christmas and New Year. **Meals:** Main courses £16 to £22. **Service:** 12.5%. **Details:** Cards accepted. 60 seats. Air-con. Separate bar. Music. Children's portions.

## Zafferano

**Top-notch seasonal food**
15 Lowndes Street, SW1X 9EY
Tel no: (020) 7235 5800
www.zafferanorestaurant.com
⊖ Knightsbridge
Italian | £39
Cooking score: 6
ɣ

From the outside, Zafferano still looks discreetly serious, but the interior has been lightened up of late with stone flooring, orange and brown banquettes and a 'capricious' bar. It feels reassuring and hospitable, with no designer-led frivolities to distract from the main business of the day. This is a 'very fine restaurant' and its enduring success hinges on Andy Needham's approach to thoroughbred Italian cooking. Much depends on sourcing, and Zafferano has an enviable, unchallenged reputation for garnering faultless raw materials that are at

their seasonal peak. First courses lay down a marker for what is to follow: having sampled a refreshing assemblage of spring vegetables with superb leaves and a light vinaigrette, one well-travelled correspondent noted that 'hardly a restaurant in the UK seems capable of producing a salad of this quality'. Homemade pasta is another star turn, impeccably fresh, perfectly timed and silky, with fascinating fillings and accompaniments (veal shank ravioli with saffron or linguine with bottarga, thyme and fresh tuna, for example); gnocchi are also 'a revelation'. Following the traditional four-course format and framework, centrepiece dishes prove their worth with up-front flavours and forceful simplicity, witness roast partridge with lentils and pumpkin cream, or red snapper with fennel and Taggiasche olives. There is a complete truffle menu in season, while desserts set out to tantalise with the likes of chestnut semifreddo, orange and pine nut tart with Cointreau cream or a near-legendary tiramisu. The wine list is an Italian gem aimed at those with plenty of disposable income. Premier-league names abound, with gilt-edged stuff from Piedmont and Tuscany in particular. Dessert wines venture into rarefied territory while, back on terra firma, house selections start at £17.50.
**Chef/s:** Andy Needham. **Open:** all week 12 to 2.30, 7 to 11. **Closed:** 24 Dec to 2 Jan, bank hol L. **Meals:** Set L £25.50 (2 courses) to £34.50, Set D £29.50 (2 courses) to £45. **Service:** 13.5% (optional). **Details:** Cards accepted. 75 seats. Air-con. No mobile phones. Wheelchair access. Music.

## ALSO RECOMMENDED

### ▲ Ebury Wine Bar

139 Ebury Street, Belgravia, SW1W 9QU
Tel no: (020) 7730 5447
www.eburywinebar.co.uk
⊖ Victoria

This long-standing wine bar (here for 40 years) offers a varied menu of Brit/Med influences to accompany an exciting wine list. Starters run to seared scallops with courgette blinis (£9.75) or Parmesan and herb-crusted sardines with tomato salad (£5.50). Steak and lamb grills are available from £16.50 or try a pavé of salmon with roasted fennel and tomatoes (£12.95). Finish with chocolate and black cherry truffle cake (£5.50). The extensive wine list starts at £12.80. Closed Sun L.

## ▲ Mango Tree
46 Grosvenor Place, Belgravia, SW1X 7EQ
Tel no: (020) 7823 1888
www.mangotree.org.uk
⊖ Victoria

Sophisticated Thai restaurant, a sibling to Awana (see entry), serving elegant 'exquisitely presented' dishes. The repertoire ranges from scallops with a garlic and sweet basil crust (£8) and seared tuna salad with dried chilli and lemongrass (£6.80) to main course slow-roasted pork belly with Chinese kale and an orange and chilli glaze (£15.50), and lobster pad thai with spicy sauce, bean sprouts and cashews wrapped in a pancake (£23.50). Desserts conform to a looser definition of Thai cuisine, and include both mango with coconut milk and sticky rice, as well as dark chocolate pudding with clotted cream (£6.50). House wine is £19. Open daily.

## ■ Bloomsbury
## Cigala
Fiery, intriguing Iberian
54 Lamb's Conduit Street, WC1N 3LW
Tel no: (020) 7405 1717
www.cigala.co.uk
⊖ Holborn
Spanish/Portuguese | £39
Cooking score: 1
Ⓥ £30

Immensely popular and buzzing, this no-frills Spanish restaurant with its picture windows, unadorned cream walls, rough-hewn wooden floorboards and chunky alfresco seating makes a great pit stop for tapas. Tuck into grilled chorizo, exemplary patatas bravas topped with a punchy sauce laced with red chilli and crushed coriander, chicken croquetas, or grilled quail with tomato and red onion salad.

On the restaurant menu, daily changing dishes incorporate imaginative ingredients, say cebreiro (traditional cow's milk mountain cheese) and there are two varieties of paella. Other robust mains might be grilled black bream with braised chard and anchovies, or roast pork belly with lentils and romesco sauce. A short, patriotic drinks list encompasses Cava, sherries and regional wines, around fifteen of which are available by the glass, priced between £3.50 to £8.
**Chef/s:** Johnny Murray and Jake Hodges. **Open:** Mon to Fri 12 to 10.45 (12.30 Sat, 12.30-9.30 Sun). **Closed:** D 24 Dec, 25 and 26 Dec, 1 Jan, Easter Sun. **Meals:** alc (main courses £12 to £18). Set L Mon to Fri £15 (2 courses) to £18, Set L and D Sun £10.50 (1 course). Tapas menu available. **Service:** 12.5% (optional). **Details:** Cards accepted. 60 seats. 20 seats outside. Air-con. Separate bar. No music. Wheelchair access. Children's portions.

## READERS RECOMMEND
## Norfolk Arms
Spanish/Portuguese
28 Leigh Street, Bloomsbury, WC1H 9EP
Tel no: 020 7388 3937
www.norfolkarms.co.uk
'Homely gastropub with a Spanish twist'

## Patisserie Deux Amis
French
63 Judd Street, Bloomsbury, WC1H 9QT
Tel no: 020 7383 7029
'A real neighbourhood secret'

## ■ Chelsea
## The Ebury
Evolving menu
11 Pimlico Road, SW1W 8NA
Tel no: (020) 7730 6784
www.theebury.co.uk
⊖ Sloane Square
Modern European | £30
Cooking score: 5

The Ebury seems to have evolved into a fully fledged restaurant, albeit one with a lively bar attached. Natural light pours in through windows ribboning round this imposing corner building. Downstairs, the bar-cum-dining room buzzes informally as the Sloane set rub shoulders with office workers stopping off for a drink before heading home. Upstairs, in the chandeliered clubroom a jazz trio provides a smooth backdrop to classy dining. Peter Woods's seasonal menu is mainly British inspired, but with a nod to mainland Europe, so expect a 'flawless' starter of soft poached egg, sautéed oyster mushrooms and brioche 'soldiers' served in neat lidded bowl, lamb's tongue salad teamed with pickled beetroot, or foie gras parfait, chicken livers and cured duck. For mains, seared gilthead bream with fennel reveals moist, flakey fish beneath a crispy skin, otherwise there could be lamb with potatoes boulangère and caramelised onion purée, and ribeye beef with bone marrow and Lyonnaise onions. Date and vanilla tart with nutmeg Chantilly cream is an appealing way to finish, with the all-French cheeseboard a savoury alternative. Service is cheerful and fast. Wines by the glass start with a Carignan Vieilles Vignes at a reasonable £3.50.

**Chef/s:** Peter Woods. **Open:** all week 12 to 3.30pm (4pm Sat and Sun), 6 to 10.30pm (10pm Sun). Dining room: Mon to Sat D only 6 to 10.30pm. **Closed:** 25 and 26 Dec. **Meals:** alc (main courses £10.95 to £16.50). **Service:** 12.5% (optional). **Details:** Cards accepted. 65 seats. Air-con. Wheelchair access. Music.

# Hunan

**Well-executed Chinese regional cooking**
51 Pimlico Road, SW1W 8NE
Tel no: (020) 7730 5712
⊖ Sloane Square
Chinese | £34
Cooking score: 3

The home-style Hunanese cooking on offer at this restaurant is in neat contrast to the plutocrats' paradise in which it sits. Pimlico Road's idea of 'home-style' is soft furnishings in four figures in the nearby shops. The 'leave-it-to-us' menu is one way of going about it, with Michael Peng gladly accepting free rein

to bring you a whole series of novel and unexpected dishes. Otherwise, there are various fixed-price menu options that take in dishes such as steamed monkfish and salmon rolls, whole prawn and spinach dumplings, and – unusually in Chinese cooking – lamb stir-fried with garlic shoots. Unusual bits of pig (ear and tongue) might turn up in a salad, while cuttlefish is labour-intensively stuffed and grilled. Finish with sweet red bean pancake and almond jelly. A much more extensive wine list than is the norm with Chinese food begins with nine house wines from £14, and there's Corton-Charlemagne if you want it.

**Chef/s:** Michael Peng. **Open:** Mon to Sat 12.30 to 2.30, 6.30 to 11.30. **Closed:** 25 Dec, Easter, bank hols. **Meals:** Set L from £24.80. Set D from £33.80. **Service:** 12.5% (optional). **Details:** Cards accepted. 44 seats. Air-con. Music.

# Il Convivio

**Contemporary flavours in a convivial setting**
143 Ebury Street, SW1W 9QN
Tel no: (020) 7730 4099
www.etruscarestaurants.com
⊖ Victoria, Sloane Square
Italian | £34
Cooking score: 2

Dante reputedly coined the term 'il convivio', and the poet's words are embossed on the deep-red walls of this cool Belgravia Italian. A sought-after conservatory with cedarwood decking and an electric roof provides alfresco dining all year round, while a skylight lends pleasant natural illumination to the main body of the restaurant. Contemporary themes and trends colour most dishes on the stylish menu, which might open with seared scallops, cauliflower purée, beetroot and hazelnut infusion or a risotto with chicory and suckling pig confit. Centrepieces could range from balsamic-caramelised black cod with grilled asparagus and Muscat grapes to milk-fed baby lamb with 'pappa al pommodoro' and a sauce of preserved lemons. Finish with Gianduia semifreddo, polenta crumble and blood oranges or explore the organic Italian cheeses.

Italy and France share most of the honours on the wine list, which includes a few bargains among the pricier stuff. House Colonnara is £13.50 (£3.95 a glass).
**Chef/s:** Lukas Pfaff. **Open:** Mon to Sat 12 to 2.45, 7 to 10.45. **Closed:** bank hols. **Meals:** alc L (main courses £8.50 to £21). Set D £27.50 (2 courses) to £39.50 (4 courses). **Service:** 12.5% (optional). **Details:** Cards accepted. 65 seats. Air-con. Music.

# Painted Heron
**Accomplished Indian with radical ideas**
112 Cheyne Walk, SW10 0DJ
Tel no: (020) 7351 5232
www.thepaintedheron.com
⊖ Sloane Square
**Modern Indian | £28**
**Cooking score: 3**

Hailed as an Indian restaurant for the twenty-first century when it opened, the Painted Heron is still going strong opposite the houseboats near Battersea Bridge. The décor aims for contemporary minimalism and the daily menu eschews most Indian names and terminology in favour of plain English (black tiger prawns in pickled lime marinade served with pomegranate chutney, for example). Some ideas are founded on the traditions of the subcontinent, witness spiced chick peas with raita and fried bread or diced mutton in slow-cooked Pakistani 'haleem' curry with wheat 'kernels'. But the kitchen also breaks the rules when it comes to wild Alaskan black cod in samphire marinade with tamarind rice noodles and coconut curry or Kashmiri-style venison with kohlrabi. The creative urge extends to the roll-call of side dishes, which calls into play asparagus, sugar snap peas and broad beans as well as a curry of strawberries and mini 'kumquat' oranges; naan bread flavoured with mango, coconut and pistachios simply adds to the unpredictability of it all. A dozen wines by the glass (from £4) head the racy global list.

**Chef/s:** Yogesh Datta. **Open:** Sun to Fri L 12 to 2.30, all week D 6.30 to 10.30. **Closed:** 25 and 26 Dec, 1 Jan. **Meals:** alc (main courses £11 to £18). Set menu £27.50. **Service:** 12.5% (optional). **Details:** Cards accepted. 75 seats. 20 seats outside. Air-con. Music.

# Pig's Ear Dining Room
**A versatile gastropub**
35 Old Church Street, SW3 5BS
Tel no: (020) 7352 2908
www.thepigsear.co.uk
⊖ Sloane Square
**Gastropub | £30**
**Cooking score: 2**

A perfectly contemporary London eating-place, the Pig's Ear is a gastropub that features a lively ground-floor bar and upstairs dining-room. It's Chelsea, but not as we used to know it. Hang loose with menus that deal in the likes of roast bone marrow with ginger salt and salad leaves, or smoked haddock kedgeree, to start. Then gather pace with crackled Tamworth pork belly with cabbage, carrots and apple purée, or roast cod with brown shrimps, spinach and gremolata. Sweet treats include ice cream and cookies, as well as banana Tatin with crème fraîche. Wines are predominantly French, with just a handful of southern Europeans and New Worlders. Prices open at £15, or £3.50 for a standard glass.
**Chef/s:** Chris Sharpe. **Open:** all week L 12.30 to 3 (12 to 4 Sat and Sun), D 7 to 10 (7 to 9.30 Sun). **Closed:** Between Christmas and New Year. **Meals:** alc (main courses £10.50 to £18.50). **Service:** 12.5% (optional). **Details:** Cards accepted. 35 seats. Separate bar. Wheelchair access. Music. Children allowed.

# Roussillon

**French gem goes from strength to strength**
16 St Barnabas Street, SW1W 8PE
Tel no: (020) 7730 5550
www.roussillon.co.uk
⊖ Sloane Square
French | £46
Cooking score: 6
🍷 ⋎

The well-worn description 'understated elegance' is for once fully merited at this French restaurant in a quiet corner of Pimlico. Alexis Gauthier starts as he means to go on, offering excellent breads baked in-house, and containing anything from cumin to black pudding. Nibbles come in waves, and then the main menu business begins. Like the décor, the style is deceptively simple, with much use of superb raw materials. A straightforward seafood salad stops being straightforward when its principal components – a pair each of scallops and langoustines – are so great, their sea-fresh savour enhanced by note-perfect timing. Potato gnocchi are texturally spot-on, served with an array of seasonal vegetables, with a finely judged sherry vinegar reduction and a Roquefort tuile. Fish may be as uncomplicated as roasted monkfish with chicory both raw and braised, or the sea bass that came with ('slightly over-chewy') girolles. At inspection, meat options included a properly timed piece of superlative beef fillet, garnished with purple artichokes and slivers of olive. Cheese service is highly knowledgeable, and the French cheeses themselves top-notch, while the show-stopping dessert is the Louis XV praline creation, a textural marvel that uses brilliant Weiss chocolate from St-Etienne. An alternative might be plum and almond tartlet with plum compote. The lunch deal at £35, including half a bottle of wine, water and coffee, remains one of the great London bargains. Eighteen wines by the glass head up an expansive list that is most assured in France, especially the lesser-known southern appellations (remember the restaurant's name). Elsewhere, it looks a little more haphazard. Bottles start at around £18.
**Chef/s:** Alexis Gauthier. **Open:** Mon to Fri L 12 to 2.30, Mon to Sat D 6.30 to 10.30. **Closed:** Christmas, New Year, Easter, bank hols, last 2 weeks Aug. **Meals:** Set L £35 (inc ½ bot wine), Set D £48. Tasting menus £55 to £65. **Service:** 12.5% (optional). **Details:** Cards accepted. 42 seats. Air-con. No music. Wheelchair access. Children allowed.

## READERS RECOMMEND

# Cheyne Walk Brasserie

French
50 Cheyne Walk, Chelsea, SW3 5LR
Tel no: 0207 3768787
www.cheynewalkbrasserie.com
'Compact and classy, with a great river view'

# Manicomio

Italian
85 Duke of York Square, Chelsea, SW3 4LY
Tel no: 020 7730 3366
www.manicomio.co.uk
'Fine Italian restaurant and deli'

# ▌Chinatown

# Chinese Experience

**Sound reputation in Chinatown**
118 Shaftesbury Avenue, W1D 5EP
Tel no: (020) 7437 0377
www.chineseexperience.com
⊖ Leicester Square
Chinese | £23
Cooking score: 2
⋎ £30

On the touristy fringes of Soho Chinatown, this sleek-looking restaurant puts on a contemporary show with muted primary colours and pots of paper orchids. Daytime dim sum are one of the high spots, and the long list extends well beyond the usual steamed dumplings into the esoteric realms of Szechuan duck tongue with 'green bean sheet', deep-fried cuttlefish with sweetcorn and lychee 'snow balls'. 'Lai min' noodles are also worth ordering. Elsewhere, the kitchen plays to the gallery with a full quota of Cantonese favourites (aromatic crispy duck, steamed sea bass with ginger and spring onion, pork chop with garlic), but it's worth homing in on chef's specials such as air-dried beef in spiced honey sauce, stir-fried lamb with leeks and baked pak choi with milky cream.

**Chef/s:** Gun Leung. **Open:** all week 12 to 11.
**Meals:** alc (main courses L £8 to £10, D £10 to £15). Set L £19.90 to £23 (all min 2). **Service:** 10%.
**Details:** Cards accepted. 130 seats. Air-con. Music.

## Fung Shing

**Acclaimed Cantonese cuisine in Chinatown**
15 Lisle Street, WC2H 7BE
Tel no: (020) 7437 1539
www.fungshing.co.uk
⊖ Leicester Square
Chinese | £31
Cooking score: 2

Held in high regards for over 30 years both inside and outside London's Chinese community, Fung Shing continues to be popular with everyone who appreciates authentic Cantonese cooking, appealing to a broad mix of Westerners and Chinese. The dining room is calm and restful with Chinese paintings, neat aqua-marine tablecloths and smart-suited waiters. Dishes on the long and wide-ranging menu may read fairly similarly to their Chinatown neighbours, but what arrives on the plate is far better – sizzling, spicy prawns, crispy aromatic duck, crab with ginger and spring onion and sweet and sour chicken are among a selection which includes familiar favourites. The chef's specials list should tempt the more adventurous, perhaps braised sea cucumber with meat balls, squid stuffed with seafood, or ostrich with yellow bean sauce. The wine list is a decent selection and opens at £15.

**Chef/s:** Chun-Fat Cheung. **Open:** all week 12 (6 bank hols) to 11.10. **Closed:** 24 to 26 Dec, bank hol L.
**Meals:** alc (main courses £8 to £30). Set L and D £17 to £30 (all min 2 or more). **Service:** 10%.
**Details:** Cards accepted. 100 seats. Air-con. Music.

## Mr Kong

**An unorthodox Oriental adventure**
21 Lisle Street, WC2H 7BA
Tel no: (020) 7437 7341
⊖ Leicester Square
Chinese | £33
Cooking score: 2
V

A fire in the kitchen shortly before the Guide went to press closed this restaurant temporarily – the owners taking the opportunity to upgrade the three-tiered restaurant 'substantially'. The menu, we are assured, will remain the same, offering much that is out of the ordinary, while the well-prepared likes of sweet-and-sour pork and crispy aromatic duck will continue to keep this place busy with tourists. It is for the recherché list of 'chef's specials' and 'manager's recommendations' that regulars rate this place so highly: a couple of soft-shell crabs encased in light, crisp batter and scattered with chillis, followed by deep-fried pig's intestine stuffed with minced prawn. Duck wrapped with yam is less adventurous but no less delicious, while a side plate of crunchy pak choi points, like all the dishes, to fresh ingredients. Hotpots, such as pork belly with preserved vegetables and chicken with salted fish, are another speciality well worth trying here. House wine is £8.90.
**Chef/s:** K Kong and Y W Lo. **Open:** all week 12 to 2.45am (1.45am Sun). **Meals:** alc (main courses £6 to £16). Set L and D £9.30 (2 courses) to £22 (all min 2 to 8). **Service:** 10%. **Details:** Cards accepted. 110 seats. Air-con. Music.

## ALSO RECOMMENDED
## ▲ Ecapital
8 Gerrard Street, Chinatown, W1D 5PJ
Tel no: (020) 7434 3838
⊖ Leicester Square

Essentially London's first entirely Shanghaiese restaurant. Generally sweeter and richer than Cantonese cooking, the traditional Shanghai options are highlighted in pink on the menu. To start try the cold combination platter (£6.50), which includes marinated meats, smoked fish and a crisp serving of what is known as vegetarian goose – dried tofu. Steamed dumplings with pork and a tasty soup stock (xiao long bao) are a Shanghai speciality that come served with a knowing smile. Main courses range from scallop, prawn and tofu hotpot (£8.50) and roast belly pork (£9.75) to fish dishes such as sea bass 'West Lake style' (£16.95). House wines are £11. Open all week.

# ▌Covent Garden

## Café du Jardin
**Long-standing theatreland favourite**
28 Wellington Street, WC2E 7BD
Tel no: (020) 7836 8769 and 8760
www.lecafedujardin.com
⊖ Covent Garden
Modern European | £31
Cooking score: 2

♦ ✌

A bastion of Covent Garden's theatreland scene for almost two decades, this veteran brasserie is driven by chef/proprietor Tony Howorth's enthusiasm. The fun-loving venue is spread over two floors, with a street-level, conservatory-style area providing the best views of the action and a live pianist playing below stairs in the evening. Brasserie stalwarts like confit of duck or calf's liver with 'cream whipped' potatoes and caramelised onions tend to be eclipsed by more contemporary ideas with an eclectic slant: tartare of blue fin tuna with sesame seed tuile could figure ahead of tempura of shrimps with chorizo and lime-scented rice. The international wine list is stuffed with gilt-edged drinking, especially from France, Italy and Australia, while the separate list of 'fine wines' ought to attract aficionados. Prices start at £11.50 (£3.85 a glass) for house vins de pays. Le Deuxième is part of the same stable and Tony Howorth recently added the Forge at 14 Garrick Street, WC2 to his portfolio.
**Chef/s:** Tony Howorth. **Open:** all week 12 to 3, 5.30 to 12 (12 to 11 Sun). **Closed:** 24 and 25 Dec.
**Meals:** alc (main courses £10 to £17.50). Set L £11.95 (2 courses) to £15.50 (3 courses), Set D £11.95 (2

courses) to £15.50 (3 courses). **Service:** 15% (optional). **Details:** Cards accepted. 100 seats. 20 seats outside. Air-con. Wheelchair access. Music.

## Le Deuxième
**Lively brasserie with eclectic overtones**
65A Long Acre, WC2E 9JH
Tel no: (020) 7379 0033
www.ledeuxieme.com
⊖ Covent Garden
Modern European | £32
Cooking score: 2

Like its elder brother Café du Jardin (see entry), Le Deuxième is in the heart of Covent Garden's cultural maelstrom, within earshot of the Royal Opera House. It copes efficiently with the crowds, offering a range of attractive fixed-price deals at peak times. European brasserie food with a few Oriental flashes is the order of the day, and the kitchen moves easily between escargots bourguignon and freshwater shrimp tempura with sweet Thai dressing. Pasta has its say and main courses are a lively assortment ranging from fillet of veal with Mozzarella, rösti and red pepper chutney to rare, grilled tuna with choi sum, water chestnuts and sesame glaze. Desserts are in the classic mould of lemon tart or warm chocolate fondant. The auspicious wine list is packed with quality drinking, especially from the French regions, Italy and Australia. Further treasures are on the 'fine wine list'; house recommendations start at £12.50. (The recently opened Forge at 14 Garrick Street, WC2 is from the same stable).
**Chef/s:** Geoffrey Adams. **Open:** Mon to Fri 12 to 3, 5 to 12, Sat 12 to 12, Sun 12 to 11. **Closed:** 24 and 25 Dec. **Meals:** alc (main courses £13 to £16.50). Set L and D £11.95 (2 courses) to £15.50 (3 courses). **Service:** 15% (optional). **Details:** Cards accepted. 60 seats. Air-con. No music. Wheelchair access.

### Average price

The average price listed in main-entry reviews denotes the price of a three-course meal, without wine.

## ★NEW ENTRY★
# Great Queen Street
**Scrupulously seasonal British brasserie**
32 Great Queen Street, WC2B 5AA
Tel no: 020 7242 0622
⊖ Covent Garden
Gastropub | £25
Cooking score: 4
£30

More gastro than pub, this is the epitome of moderately priced good eating with integrity: a scrupulously seasonal Brit brasserie in a former down-at-heel pub in Covent Garden. In an area where sound cooking is curiously scarce, it's a dream team, with The Eagle, The Anchor and Hope, and St John in its lineage. Notably, the head chef is Tom Norrington-Davies, the serving staff are equally committed, brimming with knowledge and enthusiasm. The short, daily changing menu is wholly appealing, and items such as the own-made potted shrimps with a piquant lemony edge set the tone. Invariably there's soup, perhaps wild garlic, and a salad starter. The roast beetroot, mint and delectable goat's cheese curd with textural toasted crumbs is scrape-the-plate moreish. Impeccable sourcing defines the main dishes, as found in the cod with roasted tomatoes on the vine and garlic aïoli, duck confit of impeccable crispness with braised lettuce and peas. Desserts all come in at under £5, including lemon pots and fabulous caramel custard with muscat. The well-chosen, mostly lesser-known French appellation wine list includes 375ml carafes and house wines from £10.
**Chef/s:** Tom Norrington-Davies, Al McKenna. **Open:** Mon 6 to 11, Tue to Sat L 12 to 3, D 6 to 11, Tue to Sat. **Closed:** Sun. **Meals:** alc (main courses £9 to £18). **Service:** 12.5% optional. **Details:** 70 seats. No music.

## ★NEW ENTRY★
# L'Atelier de Joël Robuchon
**Beautifully crafted dishes**
13-15 Well Street, WC2H 9NE
Tel no: (020) 7010 8600
www.joelrobuchon.co.uk
⊖ Leicester Square
French | £66
Cooking score: 6

It looks fittingly discreet from the outside, inside it's a show-stopper – Joël Robuchon's London outpost seduces most who cross its threshold. It's arranged on three levels: the unabashedly luxurious fine diner on the ground floor (where counter seating grandstands the kitchen), the monochrome first-floor dining room 'La Cuisine' (similar menu, less atmosphere), and a top-floor bar. There's a broad range of dishes in the repertoire, all carried off with the same sure touch and stunning presentation. While prices on the à la carte will make you gasp, it's the equally expensive list of small tasting plates that is the main draw and there was not a dud note among the beautifully crafted dishes tried at inspection. Fresh mackerel on a thin tart with Parmesan shavings and olives came bursting with flavour, while finely chopped pig's trotter spread on parmesan toast was refined and gutsy at the same time. A sense of comfort pervades the menu, exemplified by dishes such as a pair of exquisite miniature beef and foie gras burgers served with lightly caramelised bell peppers, and Robuchon's signature truffle mashed potato, a small dollop of which came with quail stuffed with foie gras (well worth ordering as a side dish). Green chartreuse soufflé with pistachio ice cream, or chocolate fondant with fresh ice mint sorbet, are both worth the 15-minute wait. Service can be a lottery; pedestrian at times, effortlessly accomplished at others. Wine selections open at £18.
**Chef/s:** Frederic Simonin. **Open:** Daily, ground floor L 12 to 2.30 D 5.30 to 10.30, La Cuisine L 12 to 2.30 D 7 to 10.30. **Closed:** Summer closed Sat L and Sun La Cuisine. **Meals:** alc (main courses £15 to £36) Set menu L £35 (four courses, small portions) D pre-

theatre £35 (as before). **Service:** 12.5%.
**Details:** Cards accepted. 101 seats. Air-con.
Separate bar. Wheelchair access. Music.

## One Aldwych, Axis

Urban hotel dining
Aldwych, WC2B 4RH
Tel no: (020) 7300 0300
www.onealdwych.com
⊖ Covent Garden
Modern European | £35
Cooking score: 3

A curving stone staircase winds down to a
large basement dining space with a full-length
mural of soaring tower blocks; all very
masculine and urban, this is a trendy take on
the hotel dining room. In a similar vein, the
food has modern British additions to a
brasserie/haute-cuisine mix. At inspection,
delicious soft little pieces of black pudding
came with small endive and chicory leaves,
while a main course lamb chop was pink as
requested, with strands of lamb shank that
spilled peas and rosemary scents when forked
– 'very attractive'. Basquais tart, a custard-
filled pastry topped with almonds and icing
sugar, was doughy and less refined. The wine
list is not bold enough, particularly in the
New World range and there are too few bottles
under £25. However, if you're prepared to
spend more than £30, options include the
delicious, minerally, fresh Riesling Kabinett
2004 from Armand Reichsrat von Buhl,
which is also available by the glass.
**Chef/s:** Jens Folker. **Open:** Mon to Fri L 12 to 2.30,
Mon to Sat D 5.45 to 10.30 (11.30 Sat). **Closed:**
Christmas, New Year, bank hols. **Meals:** alc (main
courses £14.40 to £43) Set L and D (before 7.15pm
and after 10pm) £17.50 (2 courses) to £20.50.
**Service:** 12.5% (optional). **Details:** Cards accepted.
110 seats. Air-con. Wheelchair access. Music.
Children's portions.

## Rules

Welcoming and resolutely British
35 Maiden Lane, WC2E 7LB
Tel no: (020) 7836 5314
www.rules.co.uk
⊖ Covent Garden
British | £43
Cooking score: 3

This time-honoured restaurant is reputedly
the oldest restaurant in London. It boasts a
priceless décor, the erstwhile design fit for
King George III, who ruled the country when
the restaurant first opened. Reassuringly, you
may find yourself being seated next to a bust
of Lord Nelson, but this historic setting is far
from stuffy, possibly due to the relaxed co-
existence of visitors and business suits, and the
welcoming service, straight from the school of
politesse. The cooking is utterly, traditionally
British (puds, pies, game), but it is not old-
fashioned. Start with a delicious pancake filled
with lobster and asparagus and served with
field mushrooms. The restaurant supports
'Keep Britain Farming', and has its own estate
in the High Pennines, so not surprisingly one
main course featured an exemplary roast
saddle of Wiltshire rabbit paired with foie gras
and a summer truffle risotto. Warm Eccles
cakes with butterscotch sauce is a sure way of
putting you in a positive mood to tackle the
modern world. Wines, mainly sourced from
France, and notably strong in the Rhone
Valley, start from £17.95, with a wide
selection by the glass or in jugs of 50cl.
**Chef/s:** Richard Sawyer. **Open:** all week 12 to 11.30
(10.30 Sun). **Closed:** 24 to 27 Dec. **Meals:** alc (main
courses £16 to £20). Post-theatre menu 10 to 11.30
(exc Dec). **Service:** 12.5% (optional). **Details:** Cards
accepted. 93 seats. Air-con. No music. No mobile
phones. Wheelchair access. Children's portions.

## ALSO RECOMMENDED

## ▲ Bedford and Strand

1a Bedford Street, Covent Garden, WC2E 9HH
Tel no: 020 7836 3033
www.bedford-strand.com
⊖ Covent Garden

First impressions might suggest that this relatively recent arrival to Covent Garden is owned by the corporate big-boys. However, this is a one-off that's owned by a team of young wine enthusiasts, a passion that's evident in a short, keenly priced (three house bottles for £12.50) list that offers a genuinely eye-opening selection – anyone for Brazilian Chardonnay? On the food front, starters kick off with bistro classics such as soupe de poisson (£5.95), while mains range from a fillet of sea bass with ratte potatoes, rocket salad, lemon and smoked paprika aïoli, to pork and leek sausages (£9.95) and shepherd's pie (£8.95). To finish, there's chocolate fondant (£5.50) for pud. Closed Sun.

## ▲ Mon Plaisir

21 Monmouth Street, Covent Garden, WC2H 9DD
Tel no: (020) 7836 7243

For 35 years, Mon Plaisir has stood like an outpost of France in Covent Garden, and remains a popular choice for pre-theatre meals before 8pm. Those with more time to enjoy their meal can choose from the full repertoire of French classics, ranging from onion soup (£6.75) to steak tartare (£17.45) and coq au vin (£14.50), as well as more inventive offerings such as crab and cauliflower pannacotta with curry (£8.50), or lamb rump with confit garlic and truffle bread-and-butter pudding (£16.95). Finish with raspberry crème brulée or floating islands. House wines are £12.75 a bottle, or £8.75 for a 50cl carafe.

## ▋ Fitzrovia

## Camerino
Good-value Italian plays to its strengths
16 Percy Street, W1T 1DT
Tel no: (020) 7637 9900
www.camerinorestaurant.com
⊖ Tottenham Court Road, Goodge Street
Modern Italian | £33
Cooking score: 3

Just off the bottom of Charlotte Street, Camerino attracts a less touristy crowd than the row's other eateries, with local media execs appreciating the well-spaced tables for quiet business lunches. Red drapes, spherical glass lights and swirly patterns on the walls might suggest modern Italian on the menu, but the cooking is straightforward. You're as likely to find a classic lasagne as roast salmon with spinach and balsamic sauce on the fixed-price menu (excellent value for this part of town). Strong, earthy flavours are in abundance – witness a starter of smoked duck breast with marinated mushrooms – while home-made pasta is the highlight of a meal here, whether a light fettuccine with tomato sauce and basil or a more substantial penne with mussels, garlic and tomato sauce. Desserts continue the theme of well-prepared simplicity with pears poached in red wine, tiramisu or Italian cheeses. House Chardonnay is £17.50 on a reasonably priced, all-Italian wine list.
**Chef/s:** Valerio Daros. **Open:** Mon to Fri L 12 to 3, Mon to Sat D 6 to 11. **Meals:** alc (main courses £18.50 to £20.50). Set L and D 6 to 7 £19.50 (2 courses) to £23.50. **Service:** 12.5% (optional).
**Details:** Cards accepted. 70 seats. 8 seats outside. Air-con. Wheelchair access. Music. Children's portions.

## Fino

**Modern tapas served in style**
33 Charlotte Street (entrance in Rathbone Street),
W1T 1RR
Tel no: (020) 7813 8010
www.finorestaurant.com
⊖ Tottenham Court Road, Goodge Street,
**Spanish/Portuguese | £30**
**Cooking score: 2**

The Hart Brothers' Charlotte Street restaurant is a tapas joint in the loosest sense of the word, bearing little relation to either the British 'sun, sea and sangria' or Spanish spit-and-sawdust model. There is a counter by the semi-open kitchen where one can order a caña and tortilla from an extensive menu of tapas standards, but nearly all opt for a sit-down tapas feast in the somewhat corporate looking basement dining room. Tapas are largely successful, with a range of basics, e.g. Pa amb Tomaquet, £3.50, or tortilla £5, supplemented by seasonal treats. Be warned, it soon adds up once you hit the good stuff like Jamon Jabugo, £16.50, or tiger prawns, £4.50 each. The wine list is exclusively Iberian with lesser-known regions like Utiel Requena and Toro represented, as well as a super sherry list, much of which is available by the glass. House wines kick off at £16.00
**Chef/s:** Jean Philippe Patruno. **Open:** Mon to Sat 12 to 2.30, 6 to 10.30. **Closed:** Christmas, bank hols. **Meals:** alc (main courses £7 to £16.50). Set L £17.95 to £30 (inc wine; all min 2 or more), Set D £17.95 to £28 (min 2). **Service:** 12.5% (optional). **Details:** Cards accepted. 90 seats. Air-con. No music. Wheelchair access. Children allowed.

### Symbols

🛏 Accommodation is available.

£30 Three courses for less than £30.

Ⅴ More than five vegetarian dishes.

£5 OFF £5-off voucher scheme.

🍾 Notable wine list.

## Hakkasan

**Resurgent Chinese culinary experience**
8 Hanway Place, W1T 1HD
Tel no: (020) 7927 7000
⊖ Tottenham Court Road
**Chinese | £70**
**Cooking score: 6**
🍾 Ⅴ

In the back alley off Tottenham Court Road, slip past sharp-suited greeters and descend down dark-green stone stairs lit by red lights to enter a surreal world in blue glass and shiny chrome. This is Alan Yau's cavern of cool, populated by staff dressed in Issey Miyake. The menu is far removed from the typical Cantonese format in nearby Chinatown: a short rack of baby spare ribs, for example, is marinated and tea smoked before being grilled so that the meat falls off gently with a slight push of the chopstick, while soup may be a simple broth with a traditional base of wild mushrooms, bamboo and woodberry, but it is studded with so many pieces of contrasting fungi that it becomes a stunning exploration of textures. The Hong Kong-style Chilean sea bass comes with glistening soft flakes covered with thin slithers of sliced pork, dates and mushrooms, to give a meaty intensity. Elsewhere, morning glory is stir-fried with dried bean curd and chilli, while pork dishes 'are usually the highlight'; worth exploring is Hakka ribs, a new addition to the repertoire, which are marinated in, and braised with, preserved cabbage. For one regular, this is food that brings 'memories of Chinese home cooking, a rare accolade, of beautiful soft textures and a pickled, sweet, sour glow'. With a range of cocktails, single malts and Japanese whiskies, you might almost overlook the opulent wine list. This opens at £28 before rocketing skywards.
**Chef/s:** Tong Chee Hwee. **Open:** all week 12 to 3.30 (4.45 Sat and Sun), 6 to 11.30 (12 Wed to Sat). **Closed:** 24 and 25 Dec. **Meals:** alc (main courses £12.50 to £68). Set L £30 to £50, Set D £50 to £70. **Service:** 13%. **Details:** Cards accepted. 200 seats. Air-con. Separate bar. Wheelchair access. Music. Children allowed.

## Latium

**Regional food in sleek surroundings**
21 Berners Street, W1T 3LP
Tel no: (020) 7323 9123
www.latiumrestaurant.com
⊖ Goodge Street
Italian | £30
Cooking score: 2

Maurizio Morelli's sleekly attired, minimalist restaurant takes it name from the Italian region of Lazio (Latium), and his food has a strong regional bias. The kitchen flaunts its 'passion for ravioli' with a full menu devoted to these stuffed morsels: among the possibilities might be a version filled with Taleggio, Swiss chard and walnuts or veal with courgette and Pecorino. The regular seasonal carte could open with foie gras terrine and Morello cherry bread or pea soup with chervil and Ricotta, while main courses might range from grilled tuna with braised baby lettuce, red wine vinegar, capers and shallot dressing to poached beef fillet with spinach, pickled baby carrots, toasted hazelnut and tomato broth. Regional cheeses are alternatives to desserts such as chocolate and almond tart with Amaretto sauce. The all-Italian wine list has plenty of good stuff from Piedmont and elsewhere. Prices start at £14.50 and around a dozen are available by the glass.

**Chef/s:** Maurizio Morelli. **Open:** Mon to Fri L 12 to 2.45, Mon to Sat D 6 to 10.30 (11 Sat). **Closed:** bank hols. **Meals:** Set L and D £24.50 (2 courses) to £32.50. **Service:** 12.5% (optional). **Details:** Cards accepted. Air-con. Wheelchair access. Music.

## Passione

**Sassy southern-Italian food**
10 Charlotte Street, W1T 2LT
Tel no: (020) 7636 2833
www.passione.co.uk
⊖ Goodge Street
Italian | £41
Cooking score: 4

Trendy Charlotte Street throngs with bustling restaurants and informal eateries and Gennaro Contaldo's intimate restaurant, hidden behind a narrow, unassuming shop-front flanked by potted bay trees, draws a loyal crowd for simple, modern Italian food. Lightwood chairs and a dark wood floor create a clean, convivial ambience, and the contemporary regional Italian cooking echoes this feeling. The menu is a sensible length, with a balance between meat, fish and vegetables, the carefully sourced ingredients include wild produce where possible, and dishes look good. They range from the robust and hearty, such as a main course of rabbit with pistachios, sun-dried tomatoes, black olives and sautéed potatoes, a simple risotto (wild sorrel, butter and parmesan) and pasta dishes (ribbon pasta with truffle sauce), to the sophisticated, perhaps pan-fried turbot with parmesan, asparagus and pea shoots. Flavours are paramount throughout. Desserts include liquorice pannacotta with berry sauce, a classic tiramisu, or round off with the aged-pecorino cheese served with chestnuts, honey and crispy Sardinian bread. The all-Italian wine list starts at £14.50, with little choice by the glass.

**Chef/s:** Mario Magli. **Open:** Mon to Fri L 12.30 to 2.15, Mon to Sat D 7 to 10.15. **Meals:** alc (main courses £21 to £26). **Service:** 12.5% (optional). **Details:** Cards accepted. 42 seats. 6 seats outside. No music.

## Pied-à-Terre

**Meticulously rendered French food**
34 Charlotte Street, W1T 2NH
Tel no: (020) 7636 1178
www.pied-a-terre.co.uk
⊖ Goodge Street
French | £58
Cooking score: 8

🍸 Ⅴ

Design makeovers continue to proceed at a stately pace at Pied-à-Terre, in what has always felt a rather womb-like interior. The narrow space could easily feel cramped, and yet doesn't because of some clever mirroring, artfully directed lighting and a large skylight. Staff are supremely capable and courteous, the sommelier knowing what you have ordered and making apposite, sensible suggestions. This contributes to the sense of a quality restaurant firing on all cylinders. Nibble an olive or two, glance at the menus, recline into the wine list, and all seems right with the world, an impression reinforced when the excellent breads and row of canapés arrive. Shane Osborn's cooking has pursued an interesting trajectory in recent years. He is one of those chefs who has journeyed out to the wilder shores, picked up some ideas and then headed back to safe harbour again, combining modern juxtapositions with classical technique. This results in dishes like slices of bluefin tuna wrapped in Parma ham, topped with soft-boiled quail eggs, and encircled with new season's broad beans and a parsley purée. Impressive, both for the standard and the timing of the tuna. A main course of blackleg chicken from Landes reminds us that chicken doesn't have to be the less exciting option. It came as a beautifully tender breast served with English spring vegetables, a smooth-textured garlic purée, well-made gnocchi and a top-notch reduction of the cooking juices. Kid goat has often cropped up on the menu here, perhaps with caramelised endive and roasted shallots, or there may be Devon venison loin, roasted and poached, served with Savoy cabbage, bacon, quince purée and walnuts. Excellent French cheeses are the alternative to the fiendishly inventive desserts, which might take in mandarin parfait with toasted marshmallow, citrus filo, fromage frais sorbet and blood orange foam. There is an incredibly good wine list, or rather lists, a volume each for reds and whites. Growers are carefully selected, and the range is as inspiring in the New World as in the Old. California and Australia are both sensational, there are pedigree Italians and Germans, and lovers of classical French stuff will be in clover. Prices start at £22 for a Rueda white, with glasses from £5.

**Chef/s:** Shane Osborn. **Open:** Mon to Fri L 12.15 to 2.35, Mon to Sat D 6.15 to 10.45. **Closed:** Last week Dec. **Meals:** Set L £24.50 (2 courses) to £30, Set D £49.50 (2 courses) to £62.50. **Service:** 12.5% (optional). **Details:** Cards accepted. 46 seats. Air-con. Wheelchair access. Music.

## Best food markets

**Borough Market**, London
The most celebrated of all food markets, and still going from strength to strength.

**Bridport Farmers Market**, Dorset
This market has a dedicated following, made famous by Hugh Fearnley-Whittingstall.

**City Food and Garden Market**, Belfast
Set in a sandstone hall, the market includes fish from Portavogie and beef from Armagh.

**Edinburgh Farmers Market**, Castle Terrace
Situated beneath the Castle, the market sells everything from duck eggs to water buffalo.

**Haverfordwest Market**, Pembrokeshire
With a mouth-watering list of primary producers, this market is authentically local.

**Leicester Market**, Market Centre
A thriving daily market providing a genuine alternative to supermarket shopping.

**Queen's Market**, London
This East End Market has been selling ethnically diverse produce for over a century.

**Slow Food Market**, Bristol
The first UK market organised by the Slow Food movement has been hugely popular.

**Swansea Food Market**, Oxford Street
This friendly market hall features cockles, laverbread and a range of local cheeses.

**York Farmers Market**, Parliament Street
Farmers sell produce direct to the public.

# Roka

**Terrific Japanese food**
37 Charlotte Street, W1T 1RR
Tel no: (020) 7580 6464
www.rokarestaurant.com
⊖ Goodge Street
**Japanese | £35**
**Cooking score: 4**

An open aspect on this stylish corner site ensures a generous amount of foot traffic and helps to maintain the bustling atmosphere, but sound effects 'can reach soprano levels'. The izakaya concept is taken a step further here, with a small army of chefs working on the robata grill. The DNA connection with Roka's older sibling, Zuma, is also evident when it comes to the menu, which is divided into snacks, sashimi and Roka dishes. Although underpinned by Japanese influences, the cooking has a distinct cross-cultural slant. A delicate maki roll of king crab leg tempura is a sensible way to kick things off, then flame-grilled tofu, artfully arranged, made special by a piquant dip of crushed yuzu and barley miso. Tasty baby pork ribs, which had been slowly pre-cooked with citrus fruit and spices before being placed on the grill, hit all the right notes, too. Finish with honey chawan mushi (egg custard) served with a medley of fruits. The erudite service is pleasant, helpfully guiding you through the menu. Wines and sake, in tune with the style of food, start high at £21.
**Chef/s:** Nicholas Watt and Rainer Becker. **Open:** Mon to Sat L 12 to 2.30, all week D 5.30 to 11.15 (10 Sun); summer all week 12 to 11.15. **Meals:** alc (main courses £7 to £55). Set L £15 to £25, Set D £50 to £75. **Service:** 13.5% (optional). **Details:** Cards accepted. 88 seats. 20 seats outside. Air-con. Wheelchair access. Music.

# Salt Yard

**A vibrant sweep of the Med**
54 Goodge Street, W1T 4NA
Tel no: (020) 7637 0657
www.saltyard.co.uk
⊖ Goodge Street
**Spanish/Portuguese | £25**
**Cooking score: 2**

£5 OFF  £30 ▼

Billed as a 'charcuterie bar and restaurant', Salt Yard, which takes inspiration from Italy as well as Spain, is not your average tapas joint. Kick off with 18-month cured Serrano ham and a selection of three Pecorinos with truffle honey, say. Hot dishes range from respectful treatments of crowd-pleasers such as crisply battered, squeaky fresh squid with a gentle aïoli to creative spins on classic tapas such as morcilla croquetas and dishes that are effectively mini main courses: try the meltingly tender, braised beef cheek with farro, peas and broad beans. Special mention must go to the signature dish of courgette flowers stuffed with Monte Enebro cheese and drizzled with honey one of several notable vegetarian options. Good-value prices draw a lively young crowd, though popularity means that table turning can operate, something that is handled with tact by the brisk staff. Sit for preference on the ground floor, higher on atmosphere if lower on space than the somewhat stark basement where an open kitchen forms the focal point. A snappy Spanish and Italian wine list offers eight sherries by the glass. House wine is £14.50.
**Chef/s:** Benjamin Tish. **Open:** Mon to Fri L 12 to 3, Mon to Sat D 6 to 11 (Sat 5 to 11). **Closed:** Bank holidays. **Meals:** alc (tapas £3 to £8.50, charcuterie £7.50 to £13). **Service:** 12.5% (optional).
**Details:** Cards accepted. 70 seats. 12 seats outside. Air-con. Separate bar. Wheelchair access. Music. Children allowed.

## Sardo
**Unsung hero of the London scene**
45 Grafton Way, W1T 5DQ
Tel no: (020) 7387 2521
www.sardo-restaurant.com
⊖ Warren Street
Italian | £30
Cooking score: 4

Don't be deceived by this Sardinian specialist's off-the-beaten-track location and pleasantly rustic interior: the family-run restaurant is one of the unsung heroes of the London restaurant scene and a first meal here can feel like stumbling across a well-kept secret, though with booking advised even early in the week, Sardo obviously has a considerable number of fans. A terrific bread basket (including the moreish olive focaccia) and a smashing bowl of juicy olives set the tone for simple cooking with an emphasis on unfussy flavour and top-quality ingredients. At inspection, sun-dried fillet of tuna made a memorable starter, the pungency of the fish nicely offset by French beans and sun-dried tomatoes. To follow, pasta parcels filled with pecorino cheese and potatoes with a sauce of fresh tomatoes and mint was fresh tasting and light; for something heartier, there are deftly handled meat and fish grills. Desserts take in the classics – lemon tart, pannacotta, tiramisu. Charming, knowledgeable service. The bulk of the Sardinian bottles on the wine list are under £30, with more elevated – but still reasonable – prices for big hitters from the rest of Italy. House wine is £14.
**Chef/s:** Roberto Sardu. **Open:** Mon to Fri L 12 to 3, Mon to Sat D 6 to 11. **Closed:** 25 Dec, bank hols. **Meals:** alc (main courses £12 to £16.50). **Service:** 12.5% (optional). **Details:** Cards accepted. Air-con. Wheelchair access. Music.

### Also recommended

An 'also recommended' entry is not a full entry, but is provisionally suggested as an alternative to main entries.

## ALSO RECOMMENDED
### ▲ Carluccio's Caffé
8 Market Place, Fitzrovia, W1W 8AG
Tel no: (020) 7636 2228
www.carluccios.com
⊖ Oxford Circus

Opened in 1991, and bustling and popular since day one, Antonio Carluccio's flagship continues to thrive, serving up simple, traditional Italian cooking in a friendly and lively environment. Choose from a selection of breads and pastries (from £1.30 for focaccia) and order antipasta massimo for two (£9.95). Calamari fritti (£5.95) is fresh and crispy with lemon and green leaves. Tortellini filled with ham and served with a cream sauce (£6.75) might be among main courses, as should sea bass with tomato salsa and sautéed potatoes (£11.75). Finish with the likes of tiramisu (£4.50) or affogato (ice cream with an espresso or liqueur poured over the top, £3.95 to £6.50). A decent Italian wine list starts at £11.25 Open all week.

### ▲ Villandry
170 Great Portland Street, Fitzrovia, W1W 5QB
Tel no: (020) 7631 3131
www.villandry.com
⊖ Great Portland Street

The steady encroachment of dining tables as the retail grocery side is scaled down finds the denizens of Fitzrovia mourning the loss of their much-loved food emporium – vociferously, if our reader feedback is anything to go by. For everyone else, casual all-day dining ranges from coffee and croissants to plates of charcuterie and salads, with a large bar serving food at lunch and dinner. In the more formal, light, spacious dining room, fried organic egg with Toulouse sausage and sautéed wild mushrooms (£9.50), fillet of sea bass with artichoke and salsify lyonnaise and truffle dressing (£22.50) and tarte Tatin with vanilla ice cream (£5.75) typify the pricey, French-led menu. House wine is £13.50. Closed Sun D.

## READERS RECOMMEND

### Ikkyu
Japanese
67A Tottenham Court Road, Fitzrovia, W1T 2EY
Tel no: (020) 7636 9280
'Basement café offering authentic sushi'

### Pescatori
Seafood
57 Charlotte Street, Fitzrovia, W1T 4PD
Tel no: (020) 7580 3289
'Rustic cooking focusing on fresh fish'

# ▌Green Park

## Al Hamra
Mezze in the market
3133 Shepherd Market, W1J 7PT
Tel no: (020) 7493 1954
⊖ Green Park/Hyde Park Corner
Middle Eastern | £28
Cooking score: 2
Ⅴ £30

There's a relaxed, continental feel to this popular Lebanese restaurant. Meat and vegetarian mezze dishes, include hummus, tabbouleh and arayes al Hamra, a speciality dish of minced lamb made with onion, sesame seeds and pine nuts on a pizza-style dough base. Mains incline more towards meat eaters: skewered lamb chunks and whole boneless baby chicken, say. Desserts are less numerous with a Lebanese milk pudding topped with crushed pistachios the only one on offer at inspection. The restaurant serves French wine from £15 a bottle and Lebanese wine at £21.50. But note the minimum charge of £20 per person, so it's not the place to go if you are after a light bite. Alfresco seats fill up quickly in the summer, so book ahead.
**Chef/s:** Mahir Abboud and A Batah. **Open:** all week, 12 to 11.30. **Closed:** 10 days at Christmas. **Meals:** alc (main courses £13 to £22.50). Set L £20 to £25, Set D £25 to £30. Cover £2.50. **Service:** not inc. **Details:** Cards accepted. 65 seats. 24 seats outside. Air-con. Wheelchair access. Music. Children's portions.

## Greenhouse
Finely tuned French gastronomie
27a Hays Mews, W1J 5NY
Tel no: (020) 7499 3331
www.greenhouserestaurant.co.uk
⊖ Green Park
Modern European | £67
Cooking score: 6
🍾 Ⅴ

The name is misleading: though reached via a fairy-lit decked walkway lined with elegantly clipped trees, The Greenhouse is a warm-toned dining room that is the height of sophisticated urbanity. Lyon-born Antonin Bonnet used to be the private chef for Marlon Abela, who also owns Umu (see entry), and one can only say that Mr Abela has shown the utmost generosity in sharing the Frenchman's talent with a wider public. Bonnet's repertoire includes a seven-course tasting menu and a seasonal menu based around a theme ('Crustacean & Shellfish', at inspection), alongside an à la carte that might start with a dish that has the smooth-textured sweetness of pan-fried scallop set off by the crunch of salted, toasted almonds and the juiciness of golden raisins scattered in a celeriac couscous. To follow, Bresse pigeon breasts served just the right side of rare served on top of a pungent cream made from the giblets and almonds, the legs served confit on the side, a ravioli filled with pigeon liver and cool cucumber relish acting as a palate cleanser amid the richness. Desserts, many based vogueishly around ice cream, might include pineapple carpaccio with crunchy cereals and coconut ice cream, but at inspection the intermittent wafts from a passing cheese trolley proved irresistible, the predominantly French board kept in tip-top condition. A 100-page wine list showcases one of the world's finest cellars, with a by-the-glass selection that would be the entire wine list of a lesser establishment. House wine is £21.00 and swiftly accelerates in price.
**Chef/s:** Antonin Bonnet. **Open:** Mon to Fri L 12 to 2.30, Mon to Sat D 6.45 to 11. **Closed:** Christmas, 31 Dec, bank hols. **Meals:** Set L £30 (2 courses) to £85,

Set D £60 to £85. **Service:** 12.5% (optional).
**Details:** Cards accepted. 60 seats. Air-con. No
music. Wheelchair access.

# ▋Haymarket

## Mint Leaf
**Indian food goes untamed**
Suffolk Place, SW1Y 4HX
Tel no: (020) 7930 9020
www.mintleafrestaurant.com
⊖ **Charing Cross**
**Modern Indian | £52**
**Cooking score: 4**

In the evenings, this restaurant can feel like
one hell of a party, prompting a reader to
proclaim that its 'worth going for the
experience'. DJs are often booked and the
atmosphere sometimes veers towards a club, as
opposed to a restaurant. The interior is
stunning, the design of this impressively sized
subterranean space simply outstanding. An
elevated catwalk connects the entire space, and
walnut louvres are cleverly positioned to sub-
divide the room into intimate sections. The
menu is kept sensibly short, segregated into
grilled, roasted or steamed dishes and curries.
Unlike the design, the cooking has not been
gentrified for Western palates; lightly battered
crab claws, teased into life with coriander and
chilli, were 'like some exquisite finger food'. A
mixed tandoori grill included 'delectable'
grouper fish as well as 'tender' lamb cutlets. A
curry of smoked aubergine with green pea
played nicely against the delicate flavour of
cumin. Naan bread is outstanding, but skip
desserts, a mango cheesecake was decidedly
ho-hum, and service can be out of step with
the sleek design. The wine list, commencing
from £19, works hard to match the style of
food, and there are some classy Burgundies
and clarets.
**Chef/s:** K.K. Anand. **Open:** Mon to Fri L 12 to 3, all
week D 5.30 to 11. **Meals:** alc (main courses £9 to
£32). Set L £15 (2 courses). Bar menu available.
**Service:** 12.5% (optional). **Details:** Cards accepted.
200 seats. Air-con. Separate bar. Wheelchair
access. Music.

# ▋Holborn

## Chancery
**European cuisine for London's legal eagles**
9 Cursitor Street, EC4A 1LL
Tel no: (020) 7831 4000
www.thechancery.co.uk
⊖ **Chancery Lane**
**Modern European | £30**
**Cooking score: 4**

The restaurant's name is a clue to its location,
just off Chancery Lane in the moneyed
backwaters of central London's 'lawyerland'.
Inside, the fabric of the high-ceilinged
building has been brought up-to-date with
mahogany parquet floors, brown leather chairs
and abstract oils on dark brown walls. It is a
place of fluctuating moods, veering from the
frenzied hubbub of power lunches to more
genteel, informal intimacy at night. Terse dish
descriptions suggest that the kitchen is
familiar with the prevailing culinary *lingua
franca*, and influences from the Mediterranean
loom large. Crisp red mullet with beetroot
carpaccio or rabbit beignet with quinoa, blood
orange and cardamom dressing lay down
colourful markers, ahead of Manuka smoked
monkfish and tiger prawns with Puy lentils
and confit tomato ravioli or fillet of pork
wrapped in Parma ham with pearl barley and
salsify. The kitchen's light touch and eye for
clear presentation extends to desserts such as
retro banana split with chocolate ice cream
and a boozy 'B52' parfait blitzed with Kahlua,
Baileys and Grand Manier. The concise wine
list offers a sharp selection of international
names with a sound pedigree. House
recommendations start at £15 (£5.50 a glass).
Andrew Thompson and Zak Jones also run the
Clerkenwell Dining Room (see entry).
**Chef/s:** Andrew Thompson. **Open:** Mon to Fri 12 to
2.30, 6 to 10.30. **Closed:** 22 Dec to 2 Jan, bank hols.
**Meals:** Set L and D £15.50 (2 courses) to £20.50, Set
D £32. **Service:** Service: 12.5% (optional).
**Details:** Cards accepted. 50 seats. Air-con.
Wheelchair access. Music.

## Matsuri High Holborn

**Modern design and traditonal Japanese cooking**
71 High Holborn, WC1V 6EA
Tel no: (020) 7430 1970
www.matsuri-restaurant.com
⊖ Holborn
Japanese | £45
Cooking score: 3

Matsuri stands out from the crowd in busy mid-town, thanks to its well-appointed interior design. Natural light from the lofty floor-to-ceiling windows helps to illuminate the main dining room, and the space is both attractive and functional. In contrast to its modern design, Matsuri continues to serve traditional Japanese dishes, and the menu here covers many of the classics, including teppanyaki, which can be enjoyed in the rather austere basement room. A typical meal could start with dobinmushi, a clear vegetable soup served in an earthenware teapot, followed by a platter of sushi or sashimi, brimming with scallops, 'so fresh it tasted velvety', and firm, tasty pieces of o-toro, salmon and turbot. For main course, beef teriyaki made with excellent quality ribeye, and to finish a rather workmanlike raspberry sorbet. Moderate prices, especially at lunchtimes, ensure a loyal following from nearby offices, and service has been singled out as being 'particularly courteous'. There is a fair selection of wines as well as hot and cold sakes with prices starting from £16. The original branch in St James is on 15 Bury Street, London SW1Y 6AL, tel (020) 7839 1101.
**Chef/s:** Hiroshi Sudo. **Open:** Mon to Sat L 12 to 2.30, D 6 to 10. **Closed:** Christmas, bank hols. **Meals:** alc (main courses £16 to £35). Set L £8.50 (2 courses) to £22, Set D £35 (4 courses) to £70. **Service:** 12.5% (optional). **Details:** Cards accepted. 100 seats. Air-con. Wheelchair access. Music.

## Pearl

**Insightful cooking and a sumptuous interior**
252 High Holborn, WC1V 7EN
Tel no: (020) 7829 7000
www.pearl-restaurant.com
⊖ Holborn
Modern French | £50
Cooking score: 5

Connected to an elegant hotel in a striking landmark building built originally for the Pearl Assurance Company, Pearl's opulent dining room, with its stylish bar, is a thoughtful blend of modern furnishings and Edwardian architecture. The cooking here is far from precious, and good technique is used to mobilise a trio of excellent amuse-bouche – rabbit rillette, imam bayaldi, hummus – served with olive ciabatta, and a vivacious starter of warm, fleshy mackerel fondant with à la grecque vegetables. Jun Tanaka's adventurous ideas are enhanced on the plate by skilful cooking, fine presentation and interesting variations of flavour and texture, but appear to work best when not preoccupied with multiplicity of flavours: an osso buco raviolo with Jerusalem artichokes plus a foam, jus and oil, was packed with so much meat that it was trying to burst out. To finish, a delectable prune custard tart with walnut ice cream put the meal firmly back on course. The enthusiastic service team is young and relaxed, but a little green. The stellar wine list includes a fine collection from the USA and starts at £18, but is marred by the high pricing policy – for example, 30 wines come by the glass and start at £5, but more than half are over £10.
**Chef/s:** Jun Tanaka. **Open:** Mon to Fri L 12 to 2.30, Mon to Sat D 6 to 10. **Closed:** Christmas to New Year, Easter, last 2 weeks Aug. **Meals:** Set L £25 (2 courses) to £28, Set D £29.50 (2 courses) to £55. **Service:** 12.5% (included). **Details:** Cards accepted. 70 seats. Air-con. No mobile phones. Wheelchair access. Music.

## White Swan

**Multi-faceted dining experience**
108 Fetter Lane, EC4A 1ES
Tel no: (020) 7242 9696
www.thewhiteswanlondon.com
⊖ Chancery Lane
Gastropub | £34
Cooking score: 3

Tom and Ed Martin's flagship city dining pub continues to thrive, drawing in drinkers to the buzzing groundfloor bar, and diners up the big, mirror-lined staircase to the more formal dining room above. The latter is a stylish space: polished wooden floors are reflected back from a mirrored ceiling along with the white-clad tables. Appealing, crowd-pleasing menus come bolstered by daily specials, the kitchen looking to Britain and Europe for inspiration. Start with Denham Estate venison carpaccio with caramelised apples, watercress and parsnip cream, or scallops with bacon blini, pea purée and truffle oil. The main course repertoire extends to line-caught sea bass with Jerusalem artichoke purée, sun-dried tomato and fennel foam, and roast duck breast with Bordelaise jus. Desserts embrace banana and toffee cheesecake as well as milk and white chocolate mousse with raspberry jelly. The international wine list is pretty extensive, with a dozen good-quality bottles served by the glass. Prices by the bottle open at £14.50.

**Chef/s:** Grant Murray. **Open:** Mon to Fri 12 to 3, 6 to 10. **Closed:** Christmas, New Year, bank hols. **Meals:** alc D (main courses £13 to £19.50). Set L £20 (2 courses) to £25. Bar menu available.. **Service:** 12.5% (optional). **Details:** Cards accepted. 40 seats. Air-con. Music. Children's portions.

## READERS RECOMMEND

## The Terrace

**Caribbean**
Lincolns Inn Fields, Holborn, WC2A 3LJ
Tel no: 020 7430 1234
www.theterrace.info
'Hidden café in a city oasis'

## ▮ Hyde Park

★NEW ENTRY★

## Grill at the Dorchester

**Talented chef attracting industry attention**
The Dorchester Hotel, 53 Park Lane, W1A 2HJ
Tel no: 020 7629 8888
www.thedorchester.com
⊖ Hyde Park Corner
Modern British | £60
Cooking score: 5

It appears we are witnessing a mini-stampede of leading chefs to this exclusive corner of Park Lane. Aiden Byrne has breathed new life into the Grill's previously outmoded menu (though the same can't be said for the new décor – a riot of tartan and murals of burly Highlanders). Highlights at inspection included a serving of Dublin Bay prawns, some pan-fried, another in tempura, brilliantly paired with a purée of broccoli and gnocchi filled with a little ricotta cheese. Every dish seems to be accompanied by a second instalment, in this case a glass filled with alternating layers of broccoli purée and ricotta topped with langoustine caviar. While the menu descriptions intrigue for their intricacy and imagination, the 'ambitious and restless' cooking doesn't always deliver. Experimentation can go astray, as in the case of a John Dory, its skin rubbed with almonds and red pepper, served with a courgette fritto, along with a chorizo risotto, red pepper tuile and parmesan. With so many competing flavours, this one failed to make its point. Nevertheless, this is a chef to watch. When the ideas do work, the results can be thrilling, and a banana and peanut crumble, accompanied by a 'divine' palm sugar ice cream and pineapple roasted with Malibu, was a case in point. The wine list, as substantial as the dining room, matches the Park Lane location in price. France takes centre stage, but other countries are equally well represented, including an impressive flight of Harlan. The section entitled '30 under 30' does provide refuge for more modest pockets.

Chef/s: Aiden Byrne. Open: all week 12 to 2.30 (12.30 to 3 Sun), 6.30 to 11 (7 to 10.30 Sun). Meals: alc (main courses £19.50 to £30) Set L £25 (2 courses) to £27.50. Service: 12.5% (included). Details: Cards accepted. 75 seats. Air-con. No music. Wheelchair access.

## Mandarin Oriental, Foliage
**Modern food in serene surroundings**
66 Knightsbridge, SW1X 7LA
Tel no: (020) 7201 3723
www.mandarinoriental.com/london
⊖ Knightsbridge
Modern European | £62
Cooking score: 5

🛏 Y

Glide past the marble foyer of this opulent Knightsbridge hotel to reach the verdantly-themed Foliage restaurant, which soothes visitors with its mood of calming serenity. Subtle peppermint hues complement the cream leather chairs and varnished walnut, floor-to-ceiling windows provide stunning views of Hyde Park and the 'foliage' motif is completed by leafy patterns encased in glass. Meals begin on a positively appetising note with, say, a 'wispy' horseradish and potato velouté with beef carpaccio. Dish descriptions are concise and accurate: a starter of crab, langoustine and fennel is exactly that – a pile of crabmeat placed in the middle of a confit of fennel with a langoustine bisque. This is intricate and inventive food, with more than enough to stimulate the senses. Occasional touches of 'over extemporation' may dull the impact, but when everything gels, the results are 'stupendous': a picture-perfect dish of sea bass ingeniously paired with a blood orange purée, red pepper confit and a sensational cucumber foam has been 'as refreshing as a puff of fresh oxygen'. Elsewhere, chicken cooked 'sous vide' and partnered by broccoli purée, gem lettuce and Gewürztraminer creates a suitably 'evanescent' impression. By and large, the carbohydrate count is kept low, which should enable the ladies-who-lunch to squeeze into their little black numbers from nearby Harvey Nicks. Desserts, such as a

fragile coffee pannacotta with hazelnut and frangelico, are exquisitely crafted, the nimble pastry work shining right through to the petit fours. Service is 'fantastic', unfailingly cordial and guaranteed to lift the most elegiac mood. France is the focus of the patrician, 40-page wine list, but other countries are not ignored and the 'Super Tuscans' get special coverage. Prices start at £17, choice by the glass (from £5.50) is commendable and lovers of sweet wines will find plenty to smile about.
Chef/s: Chris Staines. Open: all week 12 to 2.30, 7 to 10. Closed: 25 Dec, D 26 Dec, 31 Dec, 1 Jan. Meals: Set L £27 to £75, Set D £55 to £75. Service: 12.5% (optional). Details: Cards accepted. 46 seats. Air-con. Wheelchair access. Music.

# ▌Knightsbridge

## Amaya
**Stylish restaurant pulls out the stops**
15 Halkin Arcade, Motcomb Street, SW1X 8JT
Tel no: (020) 7823 1166
www.realindianfood.com
⊖ Knightsbridge
Indian | £44
Cooking score: 3

Few restaurants can boast such a captivating interior, 'a hedonistic mix of informality and style' and in the evening, the atmosphere simply rocks with a decidedly fashionable crowd. But it's worth concentrating on the grazing menu, which offers Indian street food elevated to Belgravia. Delivered from an open-plan kitchen and based on three different cooking methods (tandoor, charcoal grill, iron skillet), much of the cooking is enticing. Subtle spicing helped to elevate a pair of grilled lamb chops delicately imbued with ginger, lime and coriander, fresh spotted grouper came with a mustard, chilli, peanut mix and was served with pandan leaves, and staples – naan, basmati rice – are praise-worthy. If there is a niggle, it's the small portions 'which may be helpful for achieving size zero' but can result in having to order more 'leading to a surprising uplift to the final bill'. Service is well-mannered and fleet-

footed. Wines, thoughtfully assembled, start from £18.50 but rise steeply, although there are 35 by the glass from £6.10.
**Chef/s:** Karunesh Khanna. **Open:** all week 12.30 to 2.30 (to 3 Sun), 6 to 11 (10.30 Sun). **Meals:** alc (main courses £8.50 to £25) Set L £16.50 (2 courses) Set D £25 (2 courses). **Service:** 12.5%. **Details:** Cards accepted. 99 seats. Air-con. Wheelchair access. Music. Children allowed.

## Boxwood Café
**Swish brasserie with prices to match**
Berkeley Hotel, Wilton Place, SW1X 7RL
Tel no: (020) 7235 1010
www.gordonramsay.com
⊖ Knightsbridge
Modern British | £45
Cooking score: 3

With its own entrance at the Berkeley Hotel, the Boxwood sits on a spacious corner plot just below street level. The split-level dining room exudes an urbane air and is modern in design, with art deco lighting, shimmering gold effect walls and muted brown colours. The bustling atmosphere from a cosmopolitan crowd effortlessly captures that Knightsbridge buzz, and, while it may be one of the least prominent restaurants of the Gordon Ramsay group, it can still pack a punch. Highlights of its brasserie-style menu have included a starter of plump-baked queen scallops paired with a silky sea urchin butter, decorously presented over a cast-iron skillet filled with rock salt. Mains might feature moist chicken, grilled and then poached, and enhanced by a fragrant broth infused with thyme. To finish, perhaps a bulls-eye carpaccio of pineapple and roasted mango befittingly accompanied by a fine Campari and blood orange granita. The well-constructed wine list starts from £20, though there are some 30 on offer by glass from £5 for the more budget conscious.
**Chef/s:** Stuart Gillies. **Open:** all week 12 to 3 (4 Sat and Sun), 6 to 11. **Meals:** alc (main courses £10.50 to £28). Set L £25, Set D £55. **Service:** 12.5%. **Details:** Cards accepted. 140 seats. Air-con. No mobile phones. Wheelchair access. Music. Children's portions.

## The Capital
**Refined haute cuisine**
22-26 Basil Street, SW3 1AT
Tel no: (020) 7591 1202
www.capitalhotel.co.uk
⊖ Knightsbridge
French | £55
Cooking score: 7

Hidden away down a side street behind Harrods, The Capital makes a virtue of discretion, going about its business with cool aplomb. Two grand chandeliers hang from the lofty ceiling of the wood-panelled dining room, although it feels remarkably cosy, with just nine well-spaced tables. Over the years, Eric Chavot has become a grand master of refined French haute cuisine, bringing the best out of top-drawer ingredients and allowing flavours and textures to do their work cohesively. A single plump seared scallop sits on a pool of foaming tomato and lemon 'sauce vierge', garnished with a slice of Melba toast and intense tapenade, while unctuous foie gras terrine arrives in a little jar topped with apple foam, all accompanied by a pool of apple compote on the side, some celeriac rémoulade and a slice of gingerbread. By contrast, an inspector who has always viewed The Capital as 'a bastion of reliability' found little to applaud when it came to a main course involving 'seriously overcooked' sea bream. That said, the kitchen has more than proved its worth on other occasions with exemplary roasted lobster with tagliolini pasta and sauce vierge. The cheeseboard is an absolute stunner, comprising 17 species from arguably 'the best affineur in France', Bernard Antony: choice, quality and ripeness are beyond reproach, from two-year-old aged Comte to rarities like Tomme de Carayac. Desserts have displayed plenty of top-end technique and execution, as in homemade yoghurt with an intense red fruit and prune compote and a silky Jivara chocolate ice cream embellished with a thin stick of chocolate or a neatly balanced assemblage of Calvados jelly, apple jelly and hot caramelised apple contrasting with a

textbook crème brûlée. Coffee is excellent, although petits fours seem to have moved into fashionable Spanish territory, with variable results. The wine list is a very grand affair covering the classic French regions in exhaustive detail and providing some seriously fine alternatives from Italy, Australia and Germany. Expect to pay at least £30 for even the humblest offerings, although there are also plenty of half-bottles and a few options from £6 a glass.
**Chef/s:** Eric Chavot. **Open:** all week 12 to 2.30, 6.45 to 10.30. **Meals:** Set L £29.50 to £68, Set D £55 to £68. **Service:** 12.5% (optional). **Details:** Cards accepted. 34 seats. Air-con. No mobile phones. Music.

## Fifth Floor
**Harvey Nic's flagship brasserie**
Harvey Nichols, 109-125 Knightsbridge, SW1X 7RJ
Tel no: (020) 7235 5250
www.harveynichols.com
⊖ Knightsbridge
**Modern British | £42**
**New Chef**

🖢 ⋎

The fifth-floor food court at Harvey Nichols offers a sushi bar, wine boutique, food hall, café and bar, but the culinary centre of gravity remains with the restaurant. Helen Puolakka has left to take over the stoves at Skylon (see entry), but it is unlikely that the style of uptown brasserie cooking for which the place has always been renowned will change. A starter of scallops, for instance is teamed with pea purée, Bayonne ham and apple and hazelnut salad, while watercress velouté is delivered with a mayo tartine. Main courses may include a saddle of new season's lamb served with pickled lamb's tongue and rose harissa jus. While simple Mediterranean ideas have their place too: risotto primavera, or wild sea bass fillet served alongside a warm salad of fennel, confit tomatoes and olive jus. Expect caramel mousse and walnut sponge with sautéed pear, puff pastry and cider sorbet, or chocolate fondue for two for dessert. Harvey Nichols' own-label house wine starts at £14.

**Chef/s:** Jonas Carlson. **Open:** all week L 12 to 3 (3.30 Fri, 4 Sat/Sun), Mon to Sat D 6 to 11. **Meals:** alc (main courses £14.50 to £19.50). Set L £19.50 (2 courses) to £24.50. Set D £19.50 (2 courses) to £39.50. Bar menu available. **Service:** 12.5% (optional). **Details:** Cards accepted. 45 seats. Air-con. Wheelchair access. Music. Children's portions.

## Racine
**Authentic French bistro**
239 Brompton Road, SW3 2EP
Tel no: (020) 7584 4477
⊖ Knightsbridge, South Kensington
**French | £33**
**Cooking score: 4**

A chirpy 'Bon Soir' greets you as you enter Racine thus setting the tone for an unremittingly gallic experience. Chef Henry Harris's unpretentious Knightsbridge 'bistro deluxe' remains – five years later – ahead of the competition with classic dishes like soupe a l'oignon, or steak tartare often bettering what you mght find in Paris. With its wooden floor, dark brown leather banquettes, and light walls, it's a serious, smart looking spot, nicely in keeping with the straightforward cuisine. The generously priced prix fixe menu is on at lunch and dinner until 7.30pm, with house wines on the all-French list starting at £15.50. There are daily specials too, usually simple seasonal dishes like new season's asparagus with hollandaise, or ris de veau aux champignons sauvages. The carte offers all the bistro favourites – choucroute alsacienne, tête de veau, sauce ravigote – rendered with true flavours and the minimum of dressing-up. Service from black and white clad waiters is professional yet jolly, and refreshingly unparsimonious. When refills of tap water, baguette and pats of foil-wrapped Echiré butter arrive unbidden, you sense they know that such small things make all the difference. **Chef/s:** Henry Harris. **Open:** all week 12 to 3 (3.30 Sat and Sun), 6 to 10.30 (10 Sun). **Closed:** 25 Dec. **Meals:** alc (main courses £13.25 to £20.75). Set L £17.50 (2 courses), Set D £19.50 (3 courses).

**Service:** 14.5% (optional). **Details:** Cards accepted. 70 seats. Air-con. No music. Wheelchair access. Children's portions.

## Salloos
**Subtlety and spice from the subcontinent**
62-64 Kinnerton Street, SW1X 8ER
Tel no: (020) 7235 4444
⊖ Knightsbridge
Indian/Pakistani/Bangladeshi | £34
Cooking score: 3

Tucked away in a quiet corner of Knightsbridge (yes, they do exist), Salloos is a long-standing south-Asian restaurant that offers comfort, carefully cooked dishes and consistency. That last asset is borne out by the fact that Abdul Aziz has now entered on his fourth decade at the stoves here. At the stoves, and at the tandoor, for there is fine clay-oven cooking here too. The tandoori prawns are usually great. Lamb cooked with spinach, fenugreek and ginger, or chicken karahi, are reliable main courses, and might be preceded by a bowl of chicken and almond soup. Spicing tends to be fiery, so have plenty of water on hand. Haleem akbari is a recommended speciality – shredded lamb in wheatgerm, lentils and spices. Round things off with cool pistachio kulfi. House wines from Corney and Barrow are £15.50, or £4.50 a glass.
**Chef/s:** Abdul Aziz. **Open:** Mon to Sat 12 to 2.30, 7 to 11. **Closed:** 25 and 26 Dec. **Service:** 12.5% (optional). **Details:** Cards accepted. 65 seats. Air-con. No music. Children allowed.

## ▊ Leicester Square

### The Ivy
**The galactico of the London scene**
1-5 West Street, WC2H 9NQ
Tel no: (020) 7836 4751
⊖ Leicester Square
Modern British | £40
Cooking score: 4

The fame of this quintessential celebrity restaurant remains undimmed and, should you not find yourself sitting next to an Oscar

Antonio Carluccio OBE

*Why did you become a chef?*
Passion and greediness.

*Who was your main inspiration?*
My mother and Pellegrino Artusi.

*Where do you eat out?*
Mainly in ethnic restaurants and sometimes Italian ones.

*Where do you source your ingredients?*
Italy for authentic items and Britain for meat and fish.

*Who is your favourite producer?*
Mother (or Father) Nature.

*What's the best dish you've ever eaten?*
Pasta with truffles made with 40 egg yolks and one kilo of flour that I ate in an Italian town called Bra, the HQ of Slow Food.

*Do you have a favourite local recipe?*
Bacon and eggs.

*What's your guilty food pleasure?*
Tinned sweet condensed milk (or in a tube).

*If you could only eat one more thing, what would it be?*
My wife's soufflé.

*Which are your proudest achievements?*
The Neal Street Restaurant, Carluccio's, my OBE and Commendatore (Italian Knighthood).

winner or A-lister, the consistent quality of cooking, deferential service and infectiously upbeat atmosphere guard against any disappointment. The menu never changes but its length and variety ensure there's always something you'll want to eat whatever your mood: bang-bang chicken or Thai-baked sea bass with fragrant rice and a soy dip, say, or smoked haddock and salmon kedgeree, even a shared dish of roast poulet des Landes with Madeira jus and dauphinoise potatoes. At inspection, perfectly poached eggs Benedict atop soft folds of ham, a crisp muffin and a well-balanced hollandaise sauce was followed by a fine piece of battered haddock with proper chips and minted pea purée (aka mushy peas) with a tangy Welsh rarebit to finish. You won't, however, get to eat any of it unless you are prepared to book months ahead or eat off-peak: at pre-theatre, say, or a late weekend lunch (when a set menu is offered). House Chilean Sauvignon is £15.25 but the rest of the global wine list offers slim pickings until you've passed the £30 mark.

**Chef/s:** Alan Bird. **Open:** all week 12 to 3.30 (4 Sun), 5 to 12. **Closed:** 25 and 26 Dec, 1 Jan, Aug bank hol. **Meals:** alc (main courses £12 to £35). Set L Sat and Sun £21.50. Cover £2. **Service:** not inc. **Details:** Cards accepted. 100 seats. Air-con. No music. No mobile phones. Wheelchair access. Children's portions.

## J. Sheekey
**A venerable seafood establishment**
28-32 St Martin's Court, WC2N 4AL
Tel no: (020) 7240 2565
www.j-sheekey.co.uk
⊖ Leicester Square
Modern Seafood | £34
Cooking score: 4

It might have a lower profile than its nearby sibling The Ivy but this theatreland fish specialist pulls off the same trick of making ordinary mortals feel like A-list stars, from the welcome of the unfailingly polite liveried doormen and the graciousness of the staff within to the mirrored windows guarding the wood-panelled dining room from prying

eyes. Menus offer an undemanding mix of simply prepared fish and shellfish, British comfort food and classic matches from around the world. Starters could be one of several things on toast (potted shrimps, herring roe or crab pâté), a plateau de fruits de mer, or an Arbroath smokie with endive salad and soft-boiled quails' eggs. Follow, perhaps, with fish pie or fillet of cod with a crab risotto and tarragon dressing. Fishcakes with sautéed spinach and sorrel sauce, in which the salmon:potato ratio was firmly in favour of the fish, impressed at inspection. Puds include the sweet and tart Ivy classic, Scandinavian iced-berries with a hot white chocolate sauce. The wine list has a strong bias towards France, with cheaper bottles of white from the south and south-west for under £30 giving way to a strong showing from Burgundy. House wine is £15.25 and there are 20 available by the glass, mostly around the £7.50 mark.

**Chef/s:** Martin Dickinson. **Open:** all week 12 to 3 (3.30 Sun), 5.30 (6 Sun) to 12. **Closed:** 25 and 26 Dec, 1 Jan, Aug bank hol. **Meals:** alc (main courses £11 to £35). Set L Sat and Sun £21.50. **Service:** not inc. **Details:** Cards accepted. 106 seats. Air-con. No music. No mobile phones. Wheelchair access. Children's portions.

## National Portrait Gallery, Portrait Restaurant
**Picture-perfect British cooking**
Orange Street, WC2H 0HE
Tel no: (020) 7312 2490
www.searcys.co.uk
⊖ Leicester Square, Charing Cross
Modern British | £29
Cooking score: 2

£5 OFF 🍸 £30

Ask for a window seat when booking a table at the National Portrait Gallery's rooftop restaurant: the reward is fine views over Trafalgar Square and over London landmarks. The venue attracts a mixed clientele, from business lunchers to tourists, who are drawn not only by the view but by an eclectic menu of sparky modern British cooking. Pressed game confit typically opens proceedings, partnered with a rhubarb and sultana chutney with fig, red wine and nut bread, or you might opt for smoked black pudding with a poached egg on a spinach and bacon salad. To follow, monkfish is wrapped in bacon and served with buttered marsh samphire, while daily specials could include braised lamb shank with honey-roasted root vegetables, garlic and parsley mash and a rosemary and port jus. Caramelised citrus tart with kumquat syrup and Valhrona chocolate sorbet rounds things off nicely, and house wines are £15. **Chef/s:** Katarina Todosijevic. **Open:** all week L 11.45 to 2.45 (11.30 to 3 Sat and Sun), Thur and Fri D 5.30 to 10. **Closed:** 25 Dec. **Meals:** alc (main courses £15 to £32). Brunch, lounge and pre-theatre (Thur and Fri 5.30 to 6.30) menus available. **Service:** 12.5% (optional). **Details:** Cards accepted. 120 seats. Air-con. No music. Wheelchair access. Children's portions.

## ▌Marble Arch

### Deya
Contemporary Indian cooking
34 Portman Square, W1H 7BY
Tel no: (020) 7224 0028
www.deya-restaurant.co.uk
**Indian/Pakistani/Bangladeshi | £33**
**Cooking score: 4**

A fashionable, sophisticated affair, located just north of Oxford Street close to Marble Arch, Deya is set in a grand room with lofty decorative Georgian ceilings, dark-wood floors and subdued modern lighting. It is a swish, stylish set-up with a mellow Indian theme, decked out with substantial mirrors, murals of Indian figures and a central cocktail bar. Tables come suitably dressed in their best whites, while seating is on banquettes or low-slung, variously coloured modern chairs. The menu takes an appropriately modern approach – with the occasional nod to familiar classics – and comes driven by tip-top quality produce and an eye for detail, with well-handled spicing and attractive presentation. Take a main course of tilapia fillets marinated in fresh ginger, garlic, yoghurt and carom seeds, glazed in the tandoor, then served with a

tomato, dill and black mustard seed sauce, or perhaps a chilli and coconut prawn curry, its tiger prawns poached in coconut and lime leaf sauce and served with steam basmati rice. The excellent globetrotting wine echoes the cooking's approach, with classic and modern names. Prices step out at £15.50, while a dozen by glass start with Indian Sauvignon Blanc at £5.75. 192
**Chef/s:** Sanjay Dwivedi. **Open:** Mon to Fri L 12 to 2.45, Mon to Sat D 6 to 11. **Closed:** Christmas and New Year. **Meals:** alc (main courses £10.50 to £15). Set L £14.95 (2 courses), Set D £25.50 to £38.50. Bar menu available. **Service:** 12.5% (optional). **Details:** Cards accepted. 70 seats. Air-con. Music. Children's portions.

### Locanda Locatelli
A peerless reputation for seasonal food
8 Seymour Street, W1H 7JZ
Tel no: (020) 7935 9088
www.locandalocatelli.com
⊖ Marble Arch
**Italian | £56**
**Cooking score: 6**
🍷 ❤

Part of the Churchill Hotel, but clearly a separate operation, Locanda Locatelli is smartly swanky, with plenty of wood, leather and spotlights. It can be difficult to book a table here, and with good reason, as the Guide receives a steady stream of praise for Giorgio Locatelli's 'true Italian cuisine' and the restaurant's 'excellent service'. Although Locatelli could be described as a 'celebrity chef' (the book, the TV series . . .), his reputation was built and continues to be maintained in the kitchen (using the finest ingredients) and he delivers a menu that is laid out along traditional Italian lines. After antipasti, start with perfectly cooked fresh linguine with delicate langoustines, garlic and sweet chilli in a tomato sauce, say, or with pappardelle, broad beans and fresh peppery rocket. At inspection, a main course of chargrilled rolled pork was 'bursting with fresh herbs', and came with meat jus and deep-fried courgettes in batter, while a dish of grilled tuna with rocket salad and tomatoes, simply served with a wedge of lemon, showed off the freshness and quality of the raw materials. Side orders could include roast potatoes pungent with the scent of rosemary, while the foccacia and breadsticks are repeatedly pronounced 'excellent'. A chocolate tasting dessert, including everything from parfait to ice cream, gave Amadei chocolate the attention it deserves, while a perfect vanilla pannacotta with berries, red fruit sauce and stracciatella (chocolate chip) ice cream on a biscuit base also hit the spot. Coffee is 'as good as you would expect', and comes with a chocolate truffle and an 'outstandingly good' Amaretto biscuit. The wine list is all-Italian, apart from champagne. Whites and reds are arranged by region, and feature well-known growers such as Gaia and Antinori. There is a good range of wines by the glass, priced from £3.50 to £18. **Chef/s:** Giorgio Locatelli. **Open:** all week 12 to 3 (3.30 Sun), 7.00 to 11 (11.30 Fri and Sat, 10.00 Sun). **Closed:** bank hols. **Meals:** alc (main courses £12 to £29.50). **Service:** not inc. **Details:** Cards accepted. 70 seats. Air-con. No mobile phones. Wheelchair access. Music. Children's portions.

☆NEW ENTRY☆
## Rhodes W1 Brasserie
**Best-of-British brasserie**
Cumberland Hotel, W1A 4RS
Tel no: (020) 7479 3838
www.garyrhodes.com
⊖ Marble Arch
Modern British | £23
Cooking score: 3
♈ £30

The Gary Rhodes-accented dishes are exactly what you would expect from this longstanding TV chef. The vibrant, unfussy modern British cooking with a European twist here and there delivering the likes of 'beautifully presented' mackerel rillette on soft potato with dill, spring onion and a radish salad. There's a tempting grill section for mains, offering a variety of fish or steaks, such

as the thick slab of hake smothered in Montpellier butter tried at inspection, otherwise there could be calf's liver in a rich gravy with a side of 'smooth and very moreish' mash. A tangy lemon curd tart was 'flawless', brilliantly matched by a scoop of cocoa sorbet. Friendly, efficient and well-trained staff lift the experience, although the dimly lit surrounds (plush red velvet banquettes and dark wood tables) give the place a nightclub feel and the music from the adjacent bar can get loud and might not be to everyone's taste. A surprisingly reasonable and concise wine list starts at £3.50 a glass and £16.00 a bottle. **Chef/s:** Gary Rhodes. **Open:** Daily, L 12 to 2.30, D 6 to 10.30. **Meals:** alc main courses £13 to £22. **Details:** Cards accepted. 142 seats. Separate bar. Wheelchair access. Music. Children allowed.

## ALSO RECOMMENDED
## ▲ La Porte des Indes
32 Bryanston Street, Marble Arch, W1H 7EG
Tel no: (020) 7224 0055
www.pilondon.net

Exotic and evocative, with dark red wooden floors, colourful draped fabrics, huge murals of jungle scenes, spectacular flower arrangements and a cascading waterfall, it is perhaps the grandest setting of all London's Indian restaurants. Conventional dishes such as a classic chicken tandoori (£11.90) and pork vindaloo (£12.90) share the billing with colonial French (Creole) inspired dishes, including a starter of parsee fish (sole fillets encased in a mint and coriander chutney and lightly steamed in banana leaves; £9.50) or, for main course, chumude karaikal (seared beef tenderloin with roasted cinnamon,

### Average price

The average price listed in main-entry reviews denotes the price of a three-course meal, without wine.

aniseed, cloves and black pepper sauce). Good house menus plus global wines from £18. Closed Sat L.

## ▲ Trenta
**30 Connaught Street, Marble Arch, W2 2AF**
**Tel no: 020 7262 9623**

This pint-sized Italian restaurant, formerly Al San Vincenzo, occupies the ground floor and basement of a narrow terraced house not far from Marble Arch. Dark wooden floors and modern artwork on red-painted walls set an intimate scene for some accomplished cooking, the set-price two-course lunch (£13.50) and dinner (£19.50) menus are traditionally laid out and offer a good choice. From antipasti such as mixed seafood platter and interesting pasta options, say, spaghetti with clams, chilli and garlic, the menu extends to lamb steak with garlic and rosemary, and grilled prawns with balsamic mayonnaise. Desserts include chocolate pannacotta. Wines from £14.50.

## ▌Marylebone

## Blandford Street
**Sophisticated food in an upmarket setting**
**5-7 Blandford Street, W1U 3DB**
**Tel no: (020) 7486 9696**
**www.blandford-street.co.uk**
**⊖ Bond Street, Baker Street**
**French | £32**
**Cooking score: 2**
🍷 Ⅴ

Hidden behind a glass frontage on a quiet street off bustling Marylebone High Street, Blandford Street is smart, bright and cosmopolitan. Walls are hung with bold modern artwork and big mirrors, and widely spaced tables on wooden floors laid with crisp linen. The food takes a broadly European perspective, blending old ideas with new and drawing inspiration from a host of countries. The emphasis is on quality of ingredients and the short, seasonal carte may open with brandade of salted cod with grilled courgettes and herb oil, or chicken and foie gras terrine

with mustard leeks. To follow, there might be bouillabaisse with saffron potatoes and rouille, aged rib-eye steak with shallot and red wine jus, and asparagus and pea risotto. For dessert, try the Valhrona chocolate mousse with hazelnut praline and Cointreau anglaise. The daily changing set menu is excellent value. Wines are almost evenly divided between France and the rest of the world, with house French at £16.
**Chef/s:** Martin Moore. **Open:** Mon to Fri L 12 to 2.30, Mon to Sat D 6.30 to 10.30. **Closed:** Christmas, bank hols. **Meals:** alc D (main courses £11 to £22). Set L £19.95 (2 courses) to £22.95. **Service:** 12.5% (optional). **Details:** Cards accepted. 50 seats. Air-con. Wheelchair access. Music. Children's portions.

## ★NEW ENTRY★
## Dinings
**Tiny restaurant in an unlikely backstreet**
**22 Harcourt Street, W1H 4HH**
**Tel no: 020 7723 0666**
**⊖ Marylebone**
**Japanese | £36**
**Cooking score: 3**

This 'really titchy' newcomer, located in an anonymous backstreet, provides little in the way of creature comforts. The sushi bar on the ground floor is snug at best, but the achingly hard wooden chairs and harsh concrete floor in the basement dining room will not please everyone. However the cooking from ex-Nobu chef, Tomanari Chiba, is vibrant and delicate. The menu is neatly divided into cold or hot tapas and the cooking punches well above its weight, with high quality sushi and tempura – tuna belly and freshwater eel sushi, in particular, were considered 'exemplary' at inspection. Contemporary dishes are equally successful: the interplay of flavours of a saver fish sashimi served with a spring onion and horseradish ponzu sauce was well managed, and from the hot section, a slow roasted Iberian pork shoulder was cunningly paired with a piquant dressing of coriander, tomato and lemon yuzu. Even dessert, never the strongest aspect of an Oriental menu, did not disappoint with a textbook crème brulée made

with macha green tea. Sweet natured service hits the spot, and the brief wine list provides a selection of shochu and sake. House wine from Porter Mill is £14.50 a bottle, £4.20 a glass or alternatively try a glass of Umeshu plum wine at £3.80.
**Chef/s:** Tomanari Chiba. **Open:** Mon to Fri 12 to 2.30. Mon to Sat 6 to 10.30. **Closed:** 25 & 26 Dec. **Meals:** alc (main courses (£4 to £16). **Service:** 10% (included). **Details:** Cards accepted. 32 seats. Music.

## FishWorks

**Marylebone branch of strong seafood chain**
89 Marylebone High Street, W1U 4QW
Tel no: (020) 8994 0086
www.fishworks.co.uk
⊖ Marylebone
Seafood | £30
Cooking score: 2

There's now a whole shoal of FishWorks restaurants across London, with branches in Fulham, Chiswick, Islington, Notting Hill, Parsons Green, Primrose Hill and Richmond as well as Marylebone, all swimming smoothly along to Mitch Tonks' tried-and-tested formula of wet fish counter out front and stylish brasserie out back. It's all very lively, simple and unfussy, letting the fresh fish and its straightforward treatment speak for themselves. Selection depends on the day's intake of fish – it's a broad menu but dishes do run out and you may have to forsake your first choice. A fresh-tasting taramasalata served with bread, pesto and tapenade or whitebait with aïoli gets things off to a swinging start. Mains range from fresh Isle of Lewis langoustines to more substantial grilled swordfish with Moroccan spices and tomato salad, and a fulsome zuppa del pescatore with saffron and thyme. Service can occasionally be shaky, with staff sometimes slow to take orders and clear between courses. Choose from around a dozen house wines starting at £3.75 a glass; otherwise European whites dominate the list, with a clutch of fish-friendly reds also suggested.

**Chef/s:** Jack Scarterfield. **Open:** Tue to Sun L 12 to 2.30, Tue to Sat D 6 to 10.30. **Closed:** 24 Dec to early Jan, day after bank hols. **Meals:** alc (main courses £12 to £25). **Service:** not inc. **Details:** Cards accepted. 48 seats. Air-con. Music. Children's portions.

## Galvin Bistrot de Luxe

**Elementary French food on Baker Street**
66 Baker Street, W1V 7DH
Tel no: (020) 7935 4007
www.galvinbistrotdeluxe.co.uk
⊖ Baker Street
French | £38
Cooking score: 5

With its reasonable prices, simple food and informal atmosphere, brothers Chris and Jeff Galvin have made such a success of this formerly ill-fated site on Baker Street that their family name is in danger of upstaging that of Sherlock Holmes. Everything about this place feels so right: the bentwood chairs, starched white tablecloths and wood-panelled walls are absolutely *comme il faut*. There's 'excellent', well-timed service and a menu so stuffed full of good things that you're planning a return visit before you've even ordered. From a dream line-up of bistro dishes cooked with skill come six escargots bourguignonne, which slip from the shell, dripping garlicky juices, a chunkily chopped steak tartare topped with a quivering egg yolk, six fines de claire oysters accompanied by stubby sausages of cigar-shaped chorizo. There's an element of comfort food to the cooking but the brothers' respect for provincial French recipes prevents things from getting too cosy: veal brains may be roasted and served in beurre noisette or, à la forestière, as part of a flavourful assiette of veal that also includes roast rump and melt-in-the-mouth braised cheek. Desserts set out to delight, especially an oeufs a la neige, which skims the surface of the lightest of crème anglaises. A commitment to good value means that South and Southwest France are the strengths of the wine list, while offering four beers specifically chosen to match the food is typical of the democratic feel of the place. House wine is £13.95 a bottle, with a dozen available by the glass. **Chef/s:** Jeff and Chris Galvin. **Open:** all week 12 to 2.30 (3 Sun), 6 to 11 (10.30 Sun). **Closed:** 25 and 26 Dec, 1 Jan. **Meals:** alc (main courses £9.50 to £18.50). Set L £15.50, Set D 6 to 7 £17.50. **Service:** 12.5% (optional). **Details:** Cards accepted. 90 seats. Air-con. No music. No mobile phones. Wheelchair access. Children's portions.

## Orrery
**Light touch from a new kid on the block**
55 Marylebone High Street, W1M 3AE
Tel no: (020) 7616 8000
www.orrery.co.uk
⊖ Baker Street, Regent's Park
French | £50
New Chef

🍷 𝖸

The long, narrow first floor dining room with banquette seating down one side, windows overlooking a churchyard along the other, continues to give out an air of quiet restraint and well-drilled staff are 'exemplary'. Yet another new chef arrived in summer 2007 and was in the process of making big changes as the Guide went to press. Tristan Mason's opening menus fizz and pop with bright ideas, an early lunch revealing a light, modern touch, sound materials, unquestionable technical skill and safe handling. A 'revelatory' confit duck and foie gras roulade was rich and intense but well-balanced by the sweetness of red onion marmalade and orange powder. A 'dazzlingly good' sea bream came with perfect crisp, edible skin and a foamy saffron velouté. A pre-dessert of melon and watermelon soup with mint granita and a textbook raspberry soufflé, with a scoop of pistachio ice cream inserted by the waiter, made a fine way to finish. Similarly, dinner could bring roasted scallops with beetroot purée, Alsace bacon and sauce bordelaise, then fillet of beef, oxtail pastilla, onion purée and potato fondant. The impressively comprehensive wine list is now organized stylistically, but continues to offer some 14 or so 'sommelier's choices' by the

bottle (from £25) or by the glass (from £7). While it is too early to award a cooking mark, especially with changes still taking place in the kitchen, we feel confident in flagging up this young chef as one to watch. More reports please. **Chef/s:** Tristan Mason. **Open:** all week 12 to 2.30, 6.30 to 10.30. **Closed:** Christmas, 1 Jan, 17 April. **Meals:** alc (main courses £18 to £28). Set L £23.50 to £55, Set D £55. **Service:** 12.5% (optional). **Details:** Cards accepted. 80 seats. Air-con. No music. Wheelchair access.

## Phoenix Palace
**Opulent surroundings**
3-5 Glentworth Street, NW1 5PG
Tel no: (020) 7486 3515
⊖ Baker Street
Chinese | £25
Cooking score: 2

𝖸 £30

Just around the corner from Baker Street tube station, this busy, bustling restaurant is one of central London's best venues for reliably good Chinese cooking. The large dining room, patrolled by brisk staff wearing snazzy gold uniforms, is smarter and more elaborately decorated than most of those in Chinatown. A comprehensive (and bewilderingly long) Cantonese menu ranges from crowd-pleasers such as sesame prawn toast, crispy chilli beef and sweet and sour pork to more unusual (to western eyes) dishes such as kung po spicy hare, one of several game options. The quality of cooking is accomplished throughout and lotus root with minced pork, prawns and salted fish, and roast chicken stuffed with mashed prawns both impressed at inspection. The daytime dim sum is held in justifiably high regard and is particularly popular at the weekend with families, making Phoenix Palace even noisier than it is normally. House wine is £10. **Chef/s:** Mr Tan. **Open:** all week 12 to 11.30 (10.30 Sun). **Meals:** alc (main courses £6 to £28). Set D £15.80 (2 courses) to £26.80. **Service:** 12.5%. **Details:** Cards accepted. 250 seats. Air-con. Music.

# Providores

Marylebone's foremost Oceanic eaterie
109 Marylebone High Street, W1U 4RX
Tel no: (020) 7935 6175
www.theprovidores.co.uk
⊖ Baker Street, Bond Street
Fusion/Pan-Asian | £50
Cooking score: 4

The ground floor operates variously as a tapas bar, café and meeting place while Providores, the main dining room, is on the first floor. Peter Gordon's grasp of the complexities of the world larder and his juggling of contrasting flavours – none of his dishes has fewer than six ingredients – make for food that is 'entertaining on the plate'. Straightforward cooking techniques – grilling, roasting and frying – are at the heart of the cooking, and the kitchen's sound culinary sense keeps everything on track: for example, crisp, spiced nori soft-shell crab with avocado sesame purée, pickled tomato, hijiki and peanut sprout salad with wasabi-tobikko ginger dressing, proved to be 'very fine' at inspection. Brown shrimp and coconut-crusted sea bass, which came with fennel, orange, green olive, smoked eel and dill salad, ponzu dressing and soy tapioca, had a fresh and vibrant appeal, while accompanying steamed sugar snaps, sweet potato and miso mash were full of flavour. To finish, a banana and pecan charlotte filled with lime custard and topped with slices of cooked pears seemed positively homely. The wine list is almost exclusively from New Zealand with prices starting at £14.50 a bottle.
Chef/s: Peter Gordon, Michael McGrath, Jeremy Leeming. Open: all week 12 to 2.45, 6 to 10.30 (10 Sun), tapas room all week 9 to 10.30 (10 to 10 Sun). Closed: Easter Sun and Mon. Meals: alc (main courses £18 to £24.50). Service: 12.5% (optional). Details: Cards accepted. 86 seats. 6 seats outside. Air-con. No music. Wheelchair access.

# Royal China

An expanding family of Cantonese masters
2426 Baker Street, W1M 7AB
Tel no: (020) 7487 4688
www.royalchinagroup.co.uk
⊖ Baker Street
Chinese | £29
Cooking score: 3
V £30

The opening of a Fulham outpost in early 2007 brought the number of London branches of this well-respected mini chain to five. Though each restaurant has its own character – Bayswater and Baker Street are large and bustling, Riverside has a notable Thamesside terrace while St John's Wood and Fulham have a neighbourhood vibe – each follows the same glitzy design template of golden geese taking flight on black lacquered walls and offers the same menu of classic Cantonese cooking. Dim sum, is famously good for textbook versions of the likes of steamed prawn dumplings, roast pork puffs, fried turnip paste with dried meat and braised noodles with ginger and spring onion. It takes some time to fully peruse the evening à la carte – soups alone take up two pages – from which a meal might begin with spicy smoked shredded chicken ahead of chicken with yellow bean sauce, honey-roasted pork or the chain's speciality of seafood: steamed eel with black bean sauce. Faster (and more unusual) ordering can be facilitated by turning to the page of 'chef's favourites', such as stewed pork belly with preserved cabbage, or one of several set menus, including a vegetarian option. House French is £15. Other branches in St John's Wood, Bayswater and Canary Wharf.
Chef/s: Man Yuk Leung (executive chef). Open: all week 12 (11 Sun) to 10.45 (11.15 Fri and Sat, 9.45 Sun). Meals: alc (main courses L £8 to £15, D £10 to £25). Service: 15% (optional). Details: Cards accepted. 200 seats. Air-con. Wheelchair access. Music.

## READERS RECOMMEND

## Star Polska
Polish
69 Marylebone Lane, Marylebone, W1U 2PH
Tel no: (020) 7486 1333
'Cosy location for hearty, traditional food'

# ■ Mayfair

## Alloro
Top spot for business lunches
19-20 Dover Street, W1S 4LU
Tel no: (020) 7495 4768
www.alloro-restaurant.co.uk
⊖ Green Park
Italian | £50
Cooking score: 2

🍷 ⋎

Alloro caters for a well-heeled rather than hip crowd, and, as such, the décor is stylish, the service attentive and the cooking confident, though not attention-grabbing. A daily special might be roast lamb, while on the menu, prawns cooked with saffron and artichokes looks an adventurous choice. For starters, borage soup with sautéed red mullet fillets and Sicilian olive oil sounds more interesting than it was, while the pan-fried sea bream on a spinach salad tasted sprightly and fresh. The cheese board offers a diverse selection, and the sweet-toothed will enjoy an untraditional banana mousse. Less pleasing are the supplements sprinkling the set menus, which start at £26 for two courses. A reader praised the sommelier's guidance on the excellent wine list, which favours northern Italian producers. The mark-ups are on the high side, but there are eight decent house wines, from £18, which are also available by the glass.
Chef/s: Daniele Camera. Open: Mon to Fri L 12 to 2.30, Mon to Sat D 7 to 10.30. Closed: Bank hols, Christmas. Meals: Set L £26 (2 courses) to £29, Set D £28.50 (2 courses) to £36. Service: 12.5% (fixed). Details: Cards accepted. 66 seats. 4 seats outside. Air-con. No music. Children allowed.

## ★NEW ENTRY★
## Automat
Quality American diner
33 Dover Street, W1S 4NF
Tel no: (020) 7499 3033
www.automat-london.com
⊖ Green Park
American | £40
Cooking score: 1

Two years after opening, this all-day diner continues to pack customers in at an impressive rate. The three separate dining areas include a high turnover overspill zone by the front door, a stunning railway carriage mock-up section and the restaurant proper, which is an airy split-level eatery, with tiled walls and open kitchen. Superb steaks go against the current trend towards local produce, as all are imported from the US, with other main courses taking in roasted black cod, or baked lobster with cauliflower cheese, but prices are more Mayfair restaurant than American diner. If you want to keep the bill in check, visit for lunch and stick to soft-shell 'po boys', a burger (with good chips), or perhaps 'a positively sinful' macaroni cheese. Desserts, such as New York cheesecake, are equally well made. The succinct wine list is well thought-out though pricey; house French is £14.
Chef/s: Shaun Gilmore. Open: brasserie Mon to Fri 12pm to 1am, breakfast 7am to 11am, Mon to Fri L 12pm to 3pm, Mon to Sat D 6pm to 11pm, weekend brunch 11am to 4pm. Meals: Breakfast, Brunch, Lunch, Dinner. Service: 12.5% (inc). Details: 90 seats. Air-con. Wheelchair access. Children allowed.

## Bellamy's
Classy French brasserie in a discreet mews
18-18a Bruton Place, W1J 6LY
Tel no: (020) 7491 2727
⊖ Green Park
French | £37
Cooking score: 5

Its dark green canopies and outside planters pick this French brasserie-cum-deli out from the crowd in its quiet Mayfair mews just off Berkeley Square. Walking through the well-

stocked shop (where there is a new eight-seater oyster bar) really whets the appetite and heightens anticipation, while the dining-room itself comes classily decked out with dark leather banquettes and matching chairs. The atmosphere is buzzy and relaxed, and service generally friendly and enthusiastic, while the cooking is fittingly classic French brasserie, driven by well-sourced produce, intelligent simplicity and assured execution. The menu divides up comfortably into entrées, caviar, salads, fish and meat options, so maybe opt for lobster bisque or a terrine of foie gras to start (there is also Beluga caviar for the Mayfair-smart), while to finish, a tarte au citron or crêpes aux griottines could catch the eye. In between, perhaps try the John Dory à la planche with tomato and tarragon, or sliced entrecôte of beef with pommes frites. The short patriotic French wine list starts out life at £22, with a good selection by glass, before accelerating up to £650 for those wanting to push the boat out. (The Oyster Bar option delivers open sandwiches like lobster or salmon roe, or cold dishes such as potted shrimps alongside its namesake mollusc and a variety of shellfish.)
**Chef/s:** Stéphane Pacoud. **Open:** Mon to Fri L 12 to 2.30, Mon to Sat D 7 to 10.30. **Closed:** Bank hols. **Meals:** alc (main courses £18 to £28.50). Set L and D £28.50 (3 courses). Oyster bar menu available. **Service:** 12.5% (optional). **Details:** Cards accepted. 80 seats. Air-con. No music. Wheelchair access. Children's portions.

# Benares

**East meets West in glamorous surroundings**
12A Berkeley Square House, Berkeley Square, W1J 6BS
Tel no: (020) 7629 8886
www.benaresrestaurant.com
⊖ Green Park
Modern Indian | £40
Cooking score: 3

ᵛ

This supremely swish restaurant and cocktail bar would not disgrace one of India's Oberoi hotels, the luxury chain where Benares's

talented chef-proprietor Atul Kochhar did his training. Many of the subtly spiced dishes display a prominent European influence, but flavours are always balanced and ingredients intelligently paired. Chicken tikka with foie gras and smoked duck breast, for instance, might be followed by a bouillabaisse-style Indian fish stew with saffron and potatoes made with whatever's freshest at market. More traditional tastes are accommodated by a rogan josh. High prices are commensurate not only with the skill of the kitchen but the Mayfair location and glamorous sheen of the décor. Lunch and weekend menus provide a cheaper way in and, although choice is restricted to three options per course, the £29.95 price commendably includes a glass of wine, coffee and petits fours. The lengthy wine list requires proper consideration, not only for its selection of aromatic grapes from Europe's cool-climate regions (German Riesling especially), but for a handful of quirky inclusions such as Domaine Roxane Matsa 2004 from Greece at £28.00. At the other end of the scale, big money can be blown on 10 or so Super Tuscans.
**Chef/s:** Atul Kochar. **Open:** Sun to Fri L 12 to 2.30, all week D 5.30 to 11 (6 to 10.30 Sun). **Meals:** alc (main courses £16 to £38). Set L and D £20. Bar menu available. **Service:** 12.5%. **Details:** Cards accepted. 160 seats. 15 seats outside.

# Le Caprice

**Classy brasserie continues to shine**
Arlington House, Arlington Street, SW1A 1RJ
Tel no: (020) 7629 2239
www.le-caprice.co.uk
⊖ Green Park
Modern British | £45
Cooking score: 4

For twenty-seven years Le Caprice has been a perennial favourite of London's café society and its popularity remains undiminished despite an ever-expanding restaurant scene. The L-shaped room is predominately monochrome with lots of glass and mirrors placed strategically so that you can see most of the people in the room. The atmosphere shimmers and when it comes to service there are few slicker operations in town. An inspection meal found the kitchen on top form, happy to see that among the calf's liver and fish and chips, current trends are not ignored. An innovative starter of sea trout and foie gras tempura, shaped as a maki roll, placed over a banana leaf, proved a complex of contrasting textures and flavours. The main course saw a return to the classics with a superb roast Goosnargh duck, cep pithiviers ('excellent pastry work') and a fine Madeira sauce. This was classy stuff. For dessert, a rhubarb crumble was singled out for particular praise, and so, too, the sourdough bread. The wine list is well thought out, though prices reflect the swanky St. James location, starting at £18.50 for the house variety.

**Chef/s:** Paul Brown. **Open:** all week, L 12 to 3 (5 Sun); D 5.30 to 12. **Closed:** 25 and 26 Dec, 1 Jan, Aug bank hol. **Meals:** alc (main courses £13.25 to £26.50). Cover £2. **Service:** 12.5% (included). **Details:** Cards accepted. 90 seats. Air-con. No mobile phones. Wheelchair access. Music. Children's portions.

## Chisou

**Accomplished Japanese food**
4 Princes Street, W1B 2LE
Tel no: (020) 7629 3931
⊖ Oxford Circus
Japanese | £33
Cooking score: 4

Not all Japanese eating in the capital comes at arm-and-a-leg prices in designer surroundings. Chisou has the ambience of a simple Tokyo eatery, the kind of place you might stop off at on the way home from work. The menu is easily navigated, the appetisers including good sunomono (vinegar-dressed) seafood, or more recherché items such as monkfish liver in ponzu, spring onions and grated daikon. Sashimi and sushi include a full roll-call of tuna preparations, and there are the usual teriyaki dishes, which take in mackerel as well as chicken and beef. Set-price lunches look good value, and there is a handful of standard rice-bowls with toppings such as

### Rebirth of a legend

The Good Food Guide's 'longest-serving' restaurant, the Connaught, is closing for six months for a multi-million pound overhaul. After 54 unbroken years in the Guide, we're quite excited about the prospective changes afoot and already have our inspectors on standby. The re-opening is being described as, 'intensive restoration and (whisper it) renovation', so we suspect the new venture might ruffle the feathers of the regular Mayfair clientele. Chef patron Angela Hartnett is taking a sabbatical to open the latest Ramsay venture in Florida, but is planning to return to the Connaught helm, bringing her trademark mixture of classicism and European influences to the revamped hotel kitchen.

And to give you a flavour for how the menus – and prices – have changed, here's the original entry from 1953....
*'Exceptionally good international cooking in the atmosphere of a comfortable, rather Edwardian hotel. Three genuine "specialities" in the sense that they are probably unique: Crepes de volaille Connaught, Sole Carlos and Oeufs poché en surprise. Its service is excellent, it is usually crowded, and it is as well to telephone. Lunch 15/6 to 18/6; tea from 4/6; dinner, 18/6 to 25/–; menu unusually varied. Wine list of over 100 items, all but one (Beaujolais '49, 18/6) over £1, including some very interesting items – e.g. Ch. Pavie 1924, magnums of Ch. La Mission Haut Brion '45 and eleven 1927 ports at 65/–.'*

barbecued eel, or prawn and vegetable tempura. A full list of sakes complements the brief listing of grape wines, which start with Chilean house wines at £13.70 (£3.70 a glass). **Chef/s:** Kodi Aung. **Open:** Mon to Fri 12 to 2.30, Sat 12.30 to 3, Mon to Sat 6 to 10.15. **Closed:** Christmas and bank hols. **Meals:** alc (main courses £7 to £23.50). Set L £11.50 to £18. **Service:** not inc L, 12.5% D. **Details:** Cards accepted. 54 seats. Music.

## Cipriani

**An elegant slice of Venice**
23-25 Davies Street, W1K 3DE
Tel no: (020) 7399 0500
www.cipriani.com
⊖ Bond Street
Italian | £50
**Cooking score: 4**

This Mayfair spin-off from the Ciprianis – the people behind Harry's Bar in Venice – has proved a big hit with the glitterati ever since it opened in 2004 in a swanky location just off Berkeley Square. The modern glass-front conceals an opulently appointed dining room modelled on its Venice original – spacious and stylish, it oozes class and Art Deco style. Think Venetian chandeliers, chequered white marble floors, teak panelling and dark brown leather seating. An equally smart bar adds further buzz to the upbeat proceedings, while an army of white-jacketed waiting staff offer slick, knowledgeable Latin service. It is contemporary yet clubby, with 'bags of experience factor' and a high-price tag to match. The lengthy repertoire of straightforward, accomplished, classic Italian cooking comes driven by tip-top ingredients and peppered with Cipriani flashes. Take main-course beef medallions alla Rossini, or perhaps wild sea bass served with cherry tomatoes and black olives. The dessert trolley offers a selection of Cipriani cakes, or perhaps crêpes a la crème, while the heady prices continue with the predominantly all-Italian wine list that steps out at £26, though 'a Bellini for aperitifs should not be missed'.

**Chef/s:** Giuseppe Marangi. **Open:** all week 12 to 3, 6 to 11.45 (11 Sun). **Meals:** alc (main courses £15 to £38). Set L £29.40 (3 courses) to £36.80, Set D £36.80 (3 courses) to £42. **Service:** 12.5% (optional). **Details:** Cards accepted. 120 seats. Air-con. No music. Wheelchair access. Children's portions.

## ★NEW ENTRY★
## El Pirata

**Authentic tapas hidden away in Mayfair**
56 Down Street, W1J 7AO
Tel no: (0207) 491 3810
www.elpirata.co.uk
⊖ Hyde Park Corner
Spanish/Portuguese | £27
**Cooking score: 1**

Located in a quiet Mayfair back street, this welcoming bar and restaurant offers authentic Spanish cooking at good-value prices. The cheerful ground floor dining room with its crowded tables and walls bright with Picasso and Miro reproductions, is preferable to the basement. The tapas menu has a good balance of meat and seafood, with staples from the Spanish repertoire such as a 'silky and rich' arroz negro, piquillo peppers stuffed with seafood, meat balls, chicken croquettes, and bean stew with chorizo sausage and pancetta. Look to the specials list for main courses of roasted suckling pig with patatas a la pobre, or a zarzuela (casserole of seafood). The wine list is a well-chosen, all-Spanish affair and opens with good everyday drinking at £15.
**Chef/s:** Ramon Castro. **Open:** Mon-Fri 12pm-11.30pm, Sat 6pm-11.30pm. **Closed:** Sundays, Christian Holidays. **Meals:** alc (£1-£20 per dish, approx £20 per head ex wine) Set L £9 Set D £14-£18.. **Service:** 10% optional. **Details:** Cards accepted. 85 seats. 16 seats outside. Air-con. Separate bar. Wheelchair access. Children allowed.

## Embassy

An ambassador for British seafood
29 Old Burlington Street, W1S 3AN
Tel no: (020) 7851 0956
www.embassylondon.com
⊖ Green Park, Piccadilly Circus
Modern British | £40
Cooking score: 4

Readers of the tabloids might know Embassy as a late-night club where C-list celebs are snapped by the paps falling onto the pavement in the small hours of the morning. But there's more to the place than drinking and dancing: there's also a chandelier-lit dining room that's especially pleasant when the sun shines, whether on the alfresco pavement terrace or through the full-length windows. Fish and seafood are particular strengths of the modern menu, from starters such as a salad of roast scallops with walnuts and piccalilli to main courses like Cornish hake with caramelised chicory, garlic and Merlot jus. The Mayfair location dictates a fair number of top-end ingredients for top-end prices and the kitchen is adept at pairing them intelligently, so that roast foie gras with rhubarb and raisins might be followed by Iberico pork with spinach and goats' cheese gnocchi, piquillo peppers, sage and brown butter. Finish with something sweet such as spiced pecan pie with maple syrup ice cream before heading on down to the dance floor. House French is £16.50 on a surprisingly short global wine list, about half of which is surprisingly priced under £30.
**Chef/s:** Garry Hollihead. **Open:** Tue to Sat D 6 to 11.30. **Meals:** alc (main courses £14 to £28). Set D £17 (2 courses) to £20. **Service:** 12.5% (optional). **Details:** Cards accepted. 120 seats. Air-con. Wheelchair access. Music.

---

### Readers recommend

A 'readers recommend' review is a genuine quote from a report sent in by one of our readers. We intend to follow up these suggestions throughout the year to come.

## Galvin at Windows

French cuisine hits great heights
Hilton Hotel, 22 Park Lane, W1Y 4BE
Tel no: (020) 7208 4021
www.hilton.co.uk/londonparklane
⊖ Hyde Park Corner, Green Park
French | £58
Cooking score: 6

🍴 Y

Galvin at Windows is the special occasion restaurant to beat all others. From its 28th floor perch atop the Hilton Park Lane, it offers glorious wraparound views over London and even Her Majesty's back yard. Since May 2006, it's had the additional draw of two of London's best-regarded chefs, Chris Galvin and André Garrett, in the kitchen. Their modern French menu displays both a light touch and a classical bent, an approach that gives prime seasonal ingredients a real chance to show off. A glossy slab of pork knuckle, foie gras, cured ham and black pudding terrine arrived prettily presented and at a perfect temperature but no amount of cute salad leaves or artful dots of apple purée could conceal its wonderful bold rusticity. Main courses – maybe a tranche of pearly white halibut with crushed Jersey Royals and crab or Anjou Pigeon with petit pois a la française and pommes cocotte – are somewhat more refined, yet still generous and bursting with vibrant flavours. Perhaps inevitably, perhaps unfairly, this skyscraping destination takes a knocking for its conservative interior, its extensive but expensive wine list (take your pick from £22 a bottle), and the tourist-friendly appeal of its views. But if it's only for mugs and the expense account set, how else do you explain the terrific set-lunch deal, at just £45 for three courses, two glasses of wine, coffee, and petits fours?
**Chef/s:** Chris Galvin and André Garrett. **Open:** Sun to Fri L 12 to 2.30, Mon to Sat D 6 to 10.30. **Meals:** alc (main courses £15 to £29.50). Set L £28, Set D £65. **Service:** 12.5% (optional). **Details:** Cards accepted. 108 seats. Air-con. No music. Wheelchair access.

# Le Gavroche

**Peerless cuisine from a Mayfair legend**
43 Upper Brook Street, W1K 7QR
Tel no: (020) 7408 0881
www.le-gavroche.co.uk
⊖ **Marble Arch**
**French | £95**
**Cooking score: 8**

🍷 ⋎

The opulent basement dining room hasn't changed over the years: it remains a 'masculine refuge', with luxurious drapery, plush velvet chairs and dark green walls busily covered with paintings. The whole operation runs on ultra-smooth casters, thanks to legions of meticulous staff who tour the tables discreetly, attending to every need. Old-school, special-event dining doesn't come more assured than this, and the whole experience is gilded with trappings and protocol from a bygone era – the silver domes, the tactfully unpriced menus for ladies, the regimented dress code for gentlemen. Michel Roux Jnr wears the mantle with confidence and – judging by recent feedback – the food has moved up a gear of late. Technical finesse has never been in doubt here, but the kitchen is now able to match the standard of its high-art desserts right across the board. There are also signs of a lighter touch and clarity, which helps to temper the prevailing mood of luxury-laden richness: a two-part crab starter involves a refreshing salad with premier-cru tomatoes and a perfectly balanced lime and coriander dressing, plus fried soft-shell crab totally devoid of greasiness. By contrast, lightly seared scallops are served around a few leaves with an outer ring of carrot 'spaghetti', all resting in a mustard tarragon sauce that keeps its primary flavours persuasively in check. Main courses really highlight what the kitchen is capable of in terms of sheer technique, timing and professional élan. Turbot is cooked on the bone, its 'tremendous' flavour enhanced by a textbook butter and chive sauce, plus a courgette roll filled with ratatouille and some chickpea chips. Likewise, fillet of beef (again of faultless quality) is served with a dazzling port sauce reduced to glorious thickness and intensity; its hand-picked companions are a slab of über-rich foie gras and some macaroni. Then came a staggeringly accomplished assiette of raspberry desserts: a peerless soufflé, a sorbet bursting with fruity intensity, a gossamer mille-feuille and – best of all – an extraordinary beignet, with a pot of raspberry coulis and a white chocolate tuile for dipping. The wine list is a French aristocrat, running to 42 pages of top-notch wines from the finest growers in all the major regions. Rarefied vintages are covered 'in loving depth', including Romanée Conti going back to 1971; also note the glorious Gewürztraminers, the fabulous selection from Languedoc Roussillon and the choice of dessert wines. Prices are unrelenting, although there is – apparently – 'one obscure bottle of white at just £20'. Wines by the glass are not advertised, but some can be provided on request. In a novel move, the restaurant has also introduced its own beer menu.

**Chef/s:** Michel Roux. **Open:** Mon to Fri L 12 to 2, Mon to Sat D 6.30 to 11. **Closed:** Christmas and New Year, bank hols. **Meals:** alc (main courses £26.50 to £46.50). Set L £46 (inc wine), Set D £86. **Service:** 12.5% (optional). **Details:** Cards accepted. 70 seats. Air-con. No music. Jacket and tie required.

# Giardinetto

**Upmarket Italian food**
39-40 Albemarle Street, W1S 4TE
Tel no: (020) 7493 7091
www.giardinetto.co.uk
⊖ **Green Park**
**Italian | £49**
**Cooking score: 3**

Money has been lavished on this upmarket Italian restaurant and Maurizio Vilona's classic Genovese and Ligurian cooking certainly lives up to the swish Mayfair address. With buzzers to be pushed to gain access, you expect to find a stylish interior and the minimalist, split-level dining area, with its light plank flooring, copper and terracotta walls and linen-clothed tables provide the backdrop for some honest and passionate Italian cooking. The intention is to create a liaison of traditionalism and modernity, as is apparent in a main course of duck breast with caramelised oranges and ribiola cheese. Precede with an antipasto of steak tartare Piedmont style or traditional Ligurian ravioli filled with ham, spinach, eggs, herbs and beef fillet ragu. Finish with a classic apricot tart. The lighter lunch menu is excellent value. The all-Italian wine list is extensive and expensive, but a Puglian white starts proceedings at £17 and there's over 20 wines by the glass.

**Chef/s:** Maurizio Vilona. **Open:** Mon to Fri L 12 to 3, Mon to Sat D 7 to 11. **Meals:** alc (main courses £18 to £27.50). Set L £22. **Service:** 12.5% (optional). **Details:** Cards accepted. 54 seats. Air-con. Wheelchair access. Music.

## Gordon Ramsay at Claridge's
**Consistent standard at this Art Deco jewel**
Brook Street, W1A 2JQ
Tel no: (020) 7499 0099
www.gordonramsay.com
⊖ Bond Street
French | £72
Cooking score: 5
🍸 𝖸

Claridges just the mention of the name conjures up a sense of bygone days, when aristocratic hotels ruled the social fabric of London. Walking into the lobby, you may think that things have not changed all that much, but the dining room divides opinion with its pink and peach walls, purple chair covers and oversized layered lamp fittings. Mark Sargeant cooks in a diligent and decisive manner, his modern cooking has a strong classical foundation, so doesn't take too many risks. An amuse of celeriac velouté with Granny Smith apple and horseradish, for example, may precede a starter of perfectly seared scallops with sweetcorn purée, spring truffles and beurre noisette. Dishes are labour-intensive and since combinations are generally tried and tested, rely for effect on finesse: for example, a salt marsh lamb, rubbed with crystallised walnuts and cumin, turned round

a lining of parsnip purée, which in turn was paired with sweetbreads, roasted with thyme, and a superb filo pastry enveloping a confit of the lamb. When this energetic approach is applied to desserts it yields a 'faultless' lime-roasted pineapple, partnered with mascarpone cheese, served with pain perdu and a shot glass filled with alternating layers of pineapple jelly, cream and granite. Fresh-faced service, 'high in count', is polite but at inspection lacked attention to detail. The outstanding wine list, with limited choices under £30, can 'bling it with the best of them', starts at £20, and swiftly moves swiftly to £10,000 for a 1900 Ch. Lafite Rothschild. All the major wine regions are fully represented, with superb vintages from Italy and Spain as well as France, and there are three pages devoted to sweet wines.

**Chef/s:** Mark Sargeant. **Open:** all week 12 to 2.45 (3 Sun), 5.45 to 11 (6 to 10.30 Sun). **Meals:** Set L £30 to £75, Set D £65 to £75. **Service:** 12.5% (optional). **Details:** Cards accepted. 100 seats. Air-con. No music. No mobile phones. Wheelchair access. Children's portions.

## The Grill at Brown's
**A very British menu**
30 Albemarle Street, W1S 4BP
Tel no: (020) 7518 4060
www.roccofortehotels.com
⊖ Green Park
British | £40
Cooking score: 4

It's appropriate that London's oldest five-star hotel is home to some of the capital's most traditional British dishes. That's not to say that there's anything fuddy-duddy about The Grill at Brown's: the nineteenth-century effect of the sombre wood-panelling, huge fireplace and carving trolleys is tempered by modern fabrics and crisp blinds. Simple dishes made from sound ingredients is what the kitchen does best: potted Morecambe Bay shrimps ahead of calf's liver and bacon from the grill, say. More elaborate dishes, such as Atlantic sea bass with grilled baby fennel, tarragon and vermouth cream are available, too, and it's worth some forward-planning to co-ordinate your visit with a dish of the day: boiled brisket of Scottish beef with dumplings and horseradish for Monday lunch, say. The brevity of the dessert list – Eton mess is among the five on offer – suggests that huge portions defeat all but the most determined diner. Burgundy and Bordeaux lead the wine list with some vertiginously priced vintages, but the rest of the predominantly French selection is not nearly so stiff. House Chardonnay and Cab Sav from the Languedoc is £25, while a dozen by the glass and half bottle underscore The Grill's business lunch credentials.

**Chef/s:** Laurence Glayzer. **Open:** all week 12 to 2.30, 7 to 10. **Meals:** alc (main courses £13 to £28). Set L Mon to Sat £25 (2 courses) to £30, Set L Sun £27 (2 courses) to £35, Set D £45. **Service:** not inc. **Details:** Cards accepted. 80 seats. Air-con. No music. Wheelchair access. Children's portions.

# Kiku

**A long-standing Japanese stalwart**
17 Half Moon Street, W1J 7BE
Tel no: (020) 7499 4208/4209
www.kikurestaurant.co.uk
⊖ Green Park
Japanese | £31
Cooking score: 4

This venerable Mayfair institution marks its 30th anniversary in 2008, and though the culinary landscape has changed greatly since it first opened, Kiku has not been left behind. Its décor keeps pace with the contemporary fashion for clean lines and natural materials, and it remains one of the prime spots for first-rate Japanese cuisine in London. The long menu is a comprehensive run through the repertoire, opening with a page of nigiri and hand-rolled sushi from salmon through to razor clam, whelks and sea urchin. Seafood figures strongly throughout the menu, whether it's a salad of marinated mackerel, yellow tail sashimi, deep-fried lemon sole, or grilled eel on rice with miso soup. Meat and vegetable dishes are also well represented, including teriyaki beef, and chicken and

aubergine casserole. Various set dinner menus provide a good way to sample a range of dishes, while lunchtime brings a choice of noodles, zosui (Japanese porridge) and donburi. Wines from Corney & Barrow open with house French red and white at £14.50, with green tea, hot or cold saké and Japanese beer providing alternative options.

**Chef/s:** H. Shiraishi and Y. Hattori. **Open:** Mon to Sat L 12 to 2.30, all week D 6 to 10.15 (5.30 to 9.45 Sun). **Closed:** Christmas and New Year. **Meals:** alc (main courses £10 to £40). Set L £13.50 to £23, Set D £46 to £65. **Service:** 12.5% (fixed). **Details:** Cards accepted. 90 seats. Air-con. Wheelchair access. Music. Children allowed.

# Luciano

**Italian food served with trademark gusto**
72-73 St James's Street, SW1A 1PH
Tel no: (020) 7408 1440
www.lucianorestaurant.co.uk
⊖ Green Park
Italian | £38
Cooking score: 4

Marco Pierre White's chic, clubby St James's restaurant has been decorated with some new artwork since last year, seeing things take a decidedly adult turn. Glossy prints by Bob Carlos Clarke – the photographer who captured White's *enfant terrible* era so memorably in 'White Heat' – are on all the walls, with the more outré ones tucked away in the private dining room. The food at Luciano isn't exactly shy and retiring either. Undainty antipasti – a tennis ball sized burrata pugliese, and a Cornish crab salad with pane carasau, speak of full-on flavours and fuss-free presentation. Primi of oxtail fettuccine and a risotto alla milanese with osso buco ragu, were similarly straightforward. There are also more upscale (and pricey) dishes like fillet of beef with foie gras and truffle, presumably there to please the moneyed local crowd that demands such things. The presence of lots of champagne on what is otherwise a largely Italian wine list (starting at £14.95) says a lot. Prices overall aren't low, but given the glamorous surroundings and the postcode, aren't so unreasonable. **Chef/s:** Marco Corsica. **Open:** Mon to Sat 12 to 2.45, 5.30 to 11.15. **Closed:** 25 and 26 Dec. **Meals:** alc (main courses £12.50 to £26). Set L and D £42 to £45. **Service:** 12.5%. **Details:** Cards accepted. 50 seats. Air-con. Music. Children's portions.

★ BEST CHEF ★ JASON ATHERTON ★

## Maze
**Cutting-edge metropolitan cooking**
10-13 Grosvenor Square, W1K 6JP
Tel no: (020) 7107 0000
www.gordonramsay.com
⊖ Bond Street
French | £45
Cooking score: 6

Since it opened in 2005, Gordon Ramsay's pace-setting restaurant has never lacked for enthusiastic, solid support. That is partly what lends it its air of confidence and assurance – that, and having been at the cutting edge of metropolitan food fashion from its inception. The space is slick and classically unadorned, with creams and browns being the predominant colours. The focus of Jason Atherton's menu is tapas-sized portions; the recommendation being for around five to eight per head. Just about everything on the menu sounds fascinating, the combinations unusual but sensible and the kitchen can deliver some real treats. For example, roasted sea scallops teamed with a slick of pea purée, a fried quail's egg and potato with Yorkshire ham and maple syrup giving an extra flavour dimension. None of this would work if the raw materials weren't so classy. Witness just-seared Landes foie gras anointing honey and soy roasted quail, the accompanying spiced pear chutney further deepening the savour of the dish. Or roasted rack of lamb served with a melting nugget of braised shoulder and four ways with onions, including mini-battered rings. That same level of complexity is maintained for desserts that might include an outstanding Madagascan vanilla rice pudding

served with raspberry and lemon thyme jam, a dollop of mascarpone and pecan ice cream added at table, or peanut butter and cherry jam sandwich with salted nuts and cherry sorbet. Wines are a star turn. The list shimmers with class and convinces in all regions. In France, Bordeaux and Burgundy are complemented by a great range from the Loire, some Rhône heavyweights and the estate du jour of regional France. Elsewhere Italy and the Antipodes shine brightest and there's a good global selection by the glass. House wines start at £20.
**Chef/s:** Jason Atherton. **Open:** all week 12 to 2.45, 6 to 11. **Meals:** alc (main courses £16.50 to £18.50). Set L and D £37 to £60. **Service:** 12.5% (optional). **Details:** Cards accepted. 90 seats. Air-con. No mobile phones. Wheelchair access. Music. Children's portions.

## Mirabelle
**Vintage elegance, with a classic menu**
56 Curzon Street, W1J 8PA
Tel no: (020) 7499 4636
www.whitestarline.org.uk
⊖ Green Park
French | £50
Cooking score: 4

Any fan of Art Deco will be impressed by the Mirabelle's stylish décor. Sweep down the staircase, through the smart bar and beneath a huge glitzy mirrored ball to enter the classy dining room bright and light, dotted with vases of vibrant flowers. The kitchen sticks to a classic French repertoire, the heavyweight carte opening with the likes of a terrine of foie gras with green peppercorns in a gelée de Sauternes, or perhaps an omelette Arnold Bennett served with a Mornay sauce. Main courses might feature grilled lobster teamed with herbs, garlic and sauce béarnaise, or maybe roast duck à l'orange with a three-liqueur sauce. The set lunch offers 'fantastic value', with one reporter's ginger and lemon mousse, accompanied by pineapple carpaccio, proving an equally 'notable hit', and all dishes winning praise for presentation. The comprehensive wine list comes divided by region, with a reasonable selection in the £18 to £25 bracket. Wines by the glass from £6.50.

**Chef/s:** Igor Timchishin. **Open:** all week 12 to 2.30, 6 to 11.30 (10.30 Sun). **Meals:** alc (main courses £16.50 to £27.50). Set L £19.50 (2 courses) to £23, Set L Sun £23.95. **Service:** 12.5% (optional). **Details:** Cards accepted. 120 seats. Air-con. Separate bar. Music. Children's portions.

## Nobu Berkeley St
High-end Japanese chain
15 Berkeley Street, W1J 8DY
Tel no: (020) 7290 9222
www.noburestaurants.com
⊖ Green Park
Japanese | £55
Cooking score: 5
ᐺ

Chain restaurants don't come much cooler than the Berkeley Street branch of Nobu, which has supplanted its Park Lane sibling as the venue of choice for paparazzi-eager celebrities. It's consequently popular with a moneyed international crowd, for whom Nobu is as globally recognisable a luxury brand as Louis Vuitton. Fortunately, there's substance behind the style. Sushi rolls – each grain of rice glistening separately – might be filled with the sweet crunch of tempura prawn or melt-in-the-mouth tuna with a spicy sauce. It's prettily presented, too: asparagus spears shoot out of the prawn tempura sushi, while the signature dish of black cod marinated in miso, the fish firm-fleshed and pearly, is served on a banana leaf. Elsewhere, the long menu might yield duck breast with wasabi salsa cooked in the wood oven, pan-fried Chilean sea bass with jalapeño dressing, tuna sashimi salad, salmon teriyaki donburi, and spicy seafood udon noodles. Glum staff, sadly, are a big let-down: at inspection 'we weren't offered the daily specials suggested to a neighbouring table, spilt soy sauce was not wiped away and we were served starters and main courses out of the door in under an hour', not the sort of meal pacing commensurate with the high-scoring bill (including 15% service) and it's

this kind of attitude that has led another reporter to label Nobu Berkeley 'overpriced and a pale imitation of the original'. House Muscadet is £20 while an über-glam downstairs bar is notable for its sake-based Martini cocktails.

**Chef/s:** Mark Edwards. **Open:** Mon to Sat L 12 to 2.15, all week D 6 to 12.30 (10 Sun). **Meals:** alc (main courses £9.50 to £29.50). Set D £60. Bar menu available. **Service:** 15%. **Details:** Cards accepted. 180 seats. Air-con. Wheelchair access. Music.

## Nobu London
Godfather of new-wave Japanese cooking
19 Old Park Lane, W1K 1LB
Tel no: (020) 7447 4747
www.noburestaurants.com
⊖ Hyde Park Corner
Japanese | £60
Cooking score: 5
ᐺ

Nobu London opened in 1997, and since that time we have seen an explosion of new wave Japanese restaurants. It is a testament to Nobuyuki Matsuhisa that his ground-breaking cuisine still sets the culinary benchmark today, and the restaurant continues to be the dining choice of the A-list. All this glamour comes at a hefty price tag, but the first-floor dining room is surprisingly modest, with pale wood tables and green leather banquettes. The 'In & Out' bento box lunch can provide a worthy glimpse into some of the signature dishes, such as the black miso cod or rock shrimp tempura with ponzu, and at a fraction of the price. At inspection, a yellowtail sashimi 'any fresher you will have to catch it yourself', was cunningly enhanced by jalapeño peppers to provide a hot and sexy undertone, and sushi in the form of sea bream, salmon and prawn nigri, as well as tuna maki, were top notch. A spicy Anti-Cucho tea-smoked lamb partnered by a sublime aubergine and miso purée, revealed finely-balanced flavours, as did a dessert of Satandagi doughnut filled with warm dark chocolate and served with caramelised pistachios and an almond ice cream. Amenable service comes without any hint of snobbery 'and so it should, given the 15% service charge'. The appealing wine list starts from a towering base of £23 and includes an extensive selection of hot or cold sakes from £7.50.

**Chef/s:** Mark Edwards. **Open:** Mon to Fri 12 to 2.15, 6 to 10.15 (11 Fri), Sat 12.30 to 2.30, 6 to 11, Sun 12.30 to 2.30, 6 to 9.30. **Meals:** alc (main courses £11.50 to £29.50). Set L £25 to £60, Set D £70 to £90. **Service:** 15% (included). **Details:** Cards accepted. 150 seats. Air-con. No music. Wheelchair access.

★NEW ENTRY★
# Ristorante Semplice
**Simple, small-but-sassy establishment**
10 Blenheim Street, W1S 1LJ
Tel no: (020) 7495 1509
www.ristorantesemplice.com
⊖ Green Park
Italian
Cooking score: 5
🍶

Semplice is an intimate *ristorante* off Bond Street, the new venture of business partners chef Marco Torri and manager Giovanni Baldino, ex Locanda Locatelli. It certainly lives up to its name. Relying on exceptional ingredients often imported directly from Italy, the kitchen has the self-confidence and skill to prepare them very simply, bringing out their full, remarkable flavours. The prosciutto of duck breast is home-cured; the carpaccio of beef comes from *Fassone* all-female Alba cattle for extra tenderness. Original pasta dishes are a delight: try the Campanian *paccheri* penne with lamb ragù and a touch of red chilli, or spaghetti *alla chitarra* with Italian rabbit and black olives. Fish courses sensibly may rely on Cornish cod served with a beetroot sauce or wild sea bass with chick peas. From the prix fixe menu, the Piedmontese roast baby chicken with spinach or Herwick shoulder of lamb with fennel, followed by a plate of prime Italian cheeses makes a great £15 lunch. Fresh, simple

desserts like panna cotta with chocolate sauce and fresh raspberries. Giovanni, who comes from Franciacorta really knows his wines. The house *bianco* and *rosso* from top Sicilian estate Borgo Selene are first-rate value at £13.50. For something special, the Barbera d'Alba Conca Tre Pile, Aldo Conterno 2003 is a great bottle at under £50. Service is professional yet natural and warm-hearted. Outstanding espresso (Haiti Comet, Extra Superieur).

**Chef/s:** Marco Torri. **Open:** L Mon to Fri 12 to 2.30; D Mon to Sat 7 to 10.30. **Closed:** Sunday. **Details:** Cards accepted. 70 seats. Air-con. No music. Wheelchair access.

★NEW ENTRY★
# Scott's
**Cosmopolitan glitter**
20 Mount Street, W1K 2HE
Tel no: (020) 7495 7309
www.scotts-restaurant.com
⊖ Green Park
Seafood | £50
Cooking score: 3

Occupying a smart address, Scott's relaunch has brought a well-stocked shiny seafood bar, acres of dark wood, big contemporary artwork, and slightly cramped white-clad tables. The burst of enthusiasm that characterised its early output seems to have settled down to a gentle simmer, but it still delivers modern dishes with varying degrees of input from the British repertoire: dressed crab at one end, roast saddle of rabbit with langoustines and barba di frate at the other and wood pigeon on toast with hedgehog mushrooms somewhere in between. Seafood is plentiful, with a range from caviar to oysters, to clams, to sea bass with scallops and wild chervil. The kitchen's output, and hence reports, are mixed, however, but highly rated dishes include potted shrimps, gutsy cods' tongues and ceps bordelaise (perfectly complemented by three unadvertised little bone marrow), and an excellent, creamy rhubarb ripple ice cream 'with lovely rhubarb compote'. The wine list covers the whole spectrum of style but some of the prices may

raise an eyebrow. Wines under £20 can be found, however, and 23 types are available by the glass.
**Chef/s:** Mark Hix, Kevin Gratton. **Open:** Mon to Sat 12 to 10.30, Sun 12 to 10. **Closed:** Christmas Eve D, Christmas Day, Boxing Day, New Year's Day, August Bank Hol. **Meals:** alc (main courses £13 to £39.50). **Service:** optional. **Details:** Cards accepted. 120 seats. 12 seats outside. Air-con. No mobile phones. Wheelchair access. Children allowed.

## Sketch, Lecture Room and Library
**Controversial, imaginative and expensive**
9 Conduit Street, W1S 2XG
Tel no: (0870) 777 4488
www.sketch.uk.com
⊖ Oxford Circus
French | £90
Cooking score: 6
ᛦ

Sketch offers a myriad of dining options: Parlour, Gallery, Glade and the fine dining restaurant, Lecture Room and Library. The concept is a cavalcade of colours and designs, ranging from marble staircases to science fiction pods. The Lecture Room sits on the first floor, its dining room a celebration of comfort and flamboyance, matched by a menu predisposed to exuberance; stray away from the affordable lunch menu and 'you may need a defibrillator − the first two courses from the carte can easily take you past the £100 mark'. Following the outstanding breads, the opening act arrives in different vessels: cream of tuna, a jelly made with a few drops of Jack Daniel's and dusted with dark chocolate, 'sensational' tartlet of cuttlefish and a spoon of sea bream carpaccio. To follow, another flurry of small dishes, including a superb warm mousseline of chicken with green beans, a confit of salmon with caviar. The cooking can be cerebral, and there is no denying that Pierre Gagnaire is a culinary genius. However, without his presence, the intricate cuisine can get lost in translation, but when the techniques come together, the results can be breathtaking. Simmenthal beef, for example,

first poached in port bouillon and served with braised lettuce, and paired with beef marrow and pochas beans, accompanied by a 'sublime' carmine sauce made from tomatoes, mustard and white wine, and rounded off by the second installment of consommé of vinegar and wild mushrooms. To finish, a plate of textured desserts, 'resembling a small child's perfect birthday treat': a huge bowl filled with marshmallow, loukhoum, sable biscuit, crystallised and caramelised fruits as well as iced parfait of raspberries and pineapple pulp. The service is hard to fault, making you feel pampered and welcomed. France is the centerpiece of the lengthy wine list, particularly strong in Bordeaux, Burgundy and Rhone. Prices start from £19 but the list doesn't really get going until you reach £40.
**Chef/s:** Pierre Gagnaire and Pascal Sanchez. **Open:** Lecture Room/Library Tue to Fri L 12 to 4, Tue to Sat D 6.30 to 12. **Closed:** Bank hols, 21 Aug to 4 Sept, 25 to 30 Dec. **Meals:** (main courses £39 to £52). Set L £30 to £35, Set D £90. **Service:** 12.5% (optional). **Details:** Cards accepted. 50 seats. Air-con. No mobile phones. Wheelchair access. Music.

★ WINE LIST OF THE YEAR ★

## Square
**Exemplary French cuisine**
6-10 Bruton Street, W1J 6PU
Tel no: (020) 7495 7100
www.squarerestaurant.com
⊖ Green Park
French | £70
Cooking score: 8
🍶

The Square is a sure-fire gastronomic experience, rock-like in the consistent excellence of the ingredients and the reliably assured technique in the kitchen. The dining room has everything a serious restaurant should: high ceilings, full drop windows (looking out onto Bruton Street) and generously spaced tables. A few large, goodish pieces of abstract art adorn the walls. Lighting is excellent, with plenty of carefully directed ceiling spots and a few side lamps. Waiters and waitresses in smart black suits are extremely good, attentive and friendly; wine and water topped up effortlessly. The menu – nine starters, eight main courses and a couple of specials – is classical French, nicely balanced without too much elaboration. To start with, comes a little tray of delicious nibbles like anchovy bread stick, a warm broad bean savoury beignet, and a slice of lovely smoked salmon and asparagus terrine flavoured with dill and a little pickled cucumber. For one inspector, dinner began with three roast langoustine tails of excellent flavour, each resting on a Parmesan gnocchi; the gnocchi had 'lovely soft texture and strong Parmesan flavour'. The renowned lasagne of Devon crab was then served in a soup bowl with a fluffy cappuccino of shellfish and champagne foam; the silky mousse had a positive flavour of langoustine and lobster. For main course came a real highlight: a particularly tender, aged Ayrshire fillet of beef resting on a bed of spinach and a pool of superb demi-glace reduction of the cooking juices. The beef was exceptionally good, and the spinach just about perfect. The epic cheese board featured very fine St Felician and Epoisses. Pre-dessert was an old Square classic: sugar beignet with vanilla yoghurt and a passion fruit and mango coulis and mandarin mousse. Irish coffee baba managed a reasonably moist baba and an intensely flavoured espresso crème brulée topped with Drambuie ice cream, and a good cocoa and vanilla trifle. The superb wine list, is the passionate hobby of owner Nigel Platts-Martin, a man with a nose for the finest burgundy and champagne from the best growers. Alsace has a whole page, Germany, gets two, with the splendid Egon Müller Scharzhofberger Kabinett 1998 at £45, a good buy. Australia has a host of different vintages of Grange.

**Chef/s:** Philip Howard. **Open:** Mon to Fri L 12 to 2.45, all week D 6.30 to 10.45 (10 Sun). **Closed:** 25 Dec, 1 Jan, L bank hols. **Meals:** Set L £25 (2 courses) to £30, Set D £65. **Service:** 12.5% (optional). **Details:** Cards accepted. 75 seats. Air-con. No music. No mobile phones. Wheelchair access.

## Top food websites

**Egullet**
www.egullet.org
An online culinary society for gourmands, covering all interests and locations.

**Chez Pim**
www.chezpim.typepad.com
Pim Techamuanvivit blogs on her envy-inspiring, global visits to restaurants.

**Chocolate and Zucchini**
www.chocolateandzucchini.com
Clotilde Dusoulier has recorded her daily food observations and recipes since 2003.

**Noodlepie**
www.noodlepie.com
Relocated from Saigon to Toulouse, this blog covers food issues entertainingly.

**101 Cookbooks**
www.101cookbooks.com
An attempt to cook through every cook-book owned by the author.

**Dos Hermanos**
www.majbros.blogspot.com
Punchily written and stylishly designed, recording two food lovers' experiences.

**Moveable Feast**
www.moveable-feast.com
One of the few blogs written by a chef.

**The Tracing Paper**
www.tracingpaper.org.uk
Discusses local, forgotten foodstuffs such as Jack-by-the-hedge and alexanders.

## Sumosan

Intimate modern Japanese
26 Albemarle Street, W1S 4HY
Tel no: (020) 7495 5999
www.sumosan.com
⊖ Green Park
Japanese | £40
Cooking score: 4

More intimate than other restaurants operating at this level, such as Nobu and Zuma, Sumosan attracts a well-heeled European crowd who like to eat late: things don't really get into full swing here until after 9pm. As at many modern Japanese restaurants, there's little that's authentically oriental about many of the dishes, so you'll find roasted leg of wild rabbit in girolle mushroom sauce sitting next to chicken yakitori and, this being Mayfair, high-end ingredients such as wagyu beef and poached oysters with foie gras and sea urchin. Some very creative sushi rolls are a highlight of a meal here, including the Albemarle, a textural treat glistening with flying fish roe and filled with a crunchy mix of salmon, avocado and chunks of tempura batter. Various set menus make choosing easier and, priced between £60 and £80, indicate how much going à la carte is likely to cost; a surprise, then, to find a truly excellent value set lunch menu. House wines are £18 on a global list that isn't as expensive as you might expect. Alternatively, a lengthy selection of saké merits investigation.

**Chef/s:** Bubker Belkheit. **Open:** Mon to Fri L 12 to 3, all week D 6 to 11.30 (10.30 Sun). **Closed:** bank hols. **Meals:** alc (main courses £8 to £55). Set L £19.50. **Service:** 12.5% (optional). **Details:** Cards accepted. 140 seats. Air-con. Wheelchair access. Music. Children's portions.

## Tamarind

Basement restaurant with lofty notions
20 Queen Street, W1J 5PR
Tel no: (020) 7629 3561
www.tamarindrestaurant.com
⊖ Green Park
Modern Indian | £47
Cooking score: 4

ᐯ

Hopes rarely rise when descending to a basement restaurant, but from the charming greeting at street level to the sight of the smart and classy dining room below it's clear that Tamarind is in the premier league of London restaurants. Well-spaced tables fill a room decorated in warm sandy colours, with cleverly placed mirrors creating a sense of space, despite the lack of windows. Poppadoms with a superior range of chutneys foster high expectations, which are more than matched by a palate-awakening starter such as a cold salad of spicy minced prawns with peppers, pomegranate, coriander and ground spices with mixed leaves. The north-west Indian influence of cooking in the tandoor means that due prominence is given to a range of fragrant kebabs, such as supreme of corn-fed chicken marinated with yoghurt, cream cheese and saffron. Otherwise, main courses might include vibrantly flavoured tiger prawns tossed in a spicy gravy of browned onions, tomatoes and ginger with a blend of Chettinaad spices. House vin de pays d'Oc is £16.50.

**Chef/s:** Alfred Prasad. **Open:** Sun to Fri L 12 to 2.45, all week D 6 to 11.15 (10.30 Sun). **Closed:** 25 and 26 Dec, 1 Jan. **Meals:** alc (main courses £13 to £28). Set L £16.50 (2 courses) to £24.50, Set D £48 to £65. **Service:** 12.5% (optional). **Details:** Cards accepted. 85 seats. Air-con. Music. Children allowed.

## ★NEW ENTRY★
## Theo Randall at the InterContinental

Sublime Italian cooking

InterContinental London Hotel, 1 Hamilton Place, W1J 7QY

Tel no: (020) 7318 8747

www.theorandall.com

⊖ Hyde Park Corner

Italian | £41

Cooking score: 6

Theo Randall's decision to up-sticks from the River Café and move to the InterContinental Hotel was one of most-awaited openings of 2007. Initially, the choice for showcasing his inimitable talent appeared a strange one. The decoration of the ground-floor dining room is of the kind favoured by most modern business hotels – but what the space lacks in soul, it makes up for with high comfort-levels. And Randall's cooking certainly manages to encapsulate what makes Italian food so special. 'Incredible' fresh crab made an impressive opener at inspection, with herb aïoli and garlic-brushed bruschetta ably demonstrating the virtue of simplicity. A sureness of touch with richer dishes coaxed astonishing depth of flavour out of cappelletti stuffed with slow-cooked veal, artichoke and pancetta, and main courses never missed a beat. A fleshy sea bass (roasted in the wood-fired oven), partnered with contrasting red and yellow peppers delivered 'flavours finely balanced on a tightrope', while meat was treated with equal respect and came in the form of a meltingly tender slow-cooked shoulder of lamb with wet polenta. Among well-reported desserts have been chocolate and hazelnut ice cream, and soft chocolate cake with mascarpone cream. Early reports have commented on the cost of it all, but the lunch menu provides exemplary cooking without denting the wallet. However, there is much vacillation over the wine list, which is eclectic in style but seemingly out of kilter with the culinary aspirations, and ultimately let down by over-zealous pricing. House wine is £16.

Chef/s: Theo Randall. Open: Mon to Fri L 12 to 3 D 6 to 11, Sat D 6 to 11, Sun L 12 to 3.30. Meals: alc main courses £20 to £28, full menu available in bar area. Service: 12.5%. Details: Cards accepted. 124 seats. Air-con. Separate bar. Wheelchair access. Music. Children allowed.

## Umu

Expensive but authentic Japanese cooking

14-16 Bruton Place, W1J 6LX

Tel no: (020) 7499 8881

www.umurestaurant.com

Japanese | £55

Cooking score: 5

Tucked down a quiet Mayfair side street, the discreet frontage is easily missed; inside, the contemporary, pared-down interior exudes an air of exclusivity, not dissimilar to a private members' club. Welcome to Britain's first Kyoto-style restaurant, headed by Ichiro Kubota who has brought his native city's own venerable culinary tradition and a stream of authentic Japanese ingredients with him. It all comes at a price. A range of fixed-price kaiseki menus – which may be taken with pre-selected sakes or wines – starts at expensive, rising to the special Kyoto sushi kaiseki menu for which the old maxim applies – if you have to ask the price you can't afford it; or you might just choose to graze through the carte. Not all dishes impress at these prices, but standouts have included sweet shrimp with sake jelly, fried oysters with lemon vinaigrette, chives and ginger, an alluring clear soup with grilled sea bass, marinated grilled salmon with yuzu citrus-flavoured soy sauce, and the famed wagyu beef in hoba leaf with seasonal vegetables. Chilled green tea soup with pumpkin ice cream is an interesting way to finish. Sake is a speciality, at all levels of age and weight, but there is also a long French-dominated wine list. Pricing is unrestrained and the number of bottles under £25 is statistically insignificant.

Chef/s: Ichiro Kubota. Open: Mon to Fri L 12 to 2.30, Mon to Sat D 6 to 11. Closed: Christmas, 30 July to 14 Aug, bank hols. Meals: alc (main courses

£8 to £45). Set L £22 to £44, Set D £60 to £165 (inc wine). **Service:** 12.5% (optional). **Details:** Cards accepted. 60 seats. Air-con. Wheelchair access. Music.

# Wiltons

**Antique eatiere with an English ethos**
55 Jermyn Street, SW1Y 6LX
Tel no: (020) 7629 9955
www.wiltons.co.uk
⊖ **Green Park**
**British | £53**
**Cooking score: 4**

One of the capital's oldest restaurants and one of its best-known, Wilton's is a restaurant of the old school, discreetly opulent and offering a clubby Edwardian ambience and old-fashioned solicitous service at immaculately set tables. As a refuge from the modern world it could hardly be bettered. Just like the surroundings, the classic menu is steeped in tradition and remains little-changed, specialising in fish and game and keeping well at bay the whims and vagaries of fad and fashion. This is the place to come for avocado with crab, potted shrimps, lobster bisque and a plate of oysters for starters. Equally time-honoured main dishes include simple grills, from fillet steak to lamb cutlets, baked Dover sole, poached or grilled fish – may be wild turbot or halibut and daily dishes like Irish stew, roast rack of lamb, and braised ox tongue with Madeira sauce. It also takes its savouries seriously, serving anchovies on toast as an alternative to apple and rhubarb crumble. Prices on the far-reaching wine list are high, with little under £30, although ten are served by the glass from £6.50.
**Chef/s:** Jerome Ponchelle. **Open:** Mon to Fri 12 to 2.30, 6 to 10.30. **Closed:** Christmas, bank hols. **Meals:** alc (main courses £18 to £50). Set D Fri £50. **Service:** 12.5% (optional). **Details:** Cards accepted. 100 seats. Air-con. No music. No mobile phones. Wheelchair access. Jacket and tie required.

# Wolseley

**A dazzling setting for all-day dining**
160 Piccadilly, W1J 9EB
Tel no: (020) 7499 6996
www.thewolseley.com
⊖ **Green Park**
**Modern European | £36**
**Cooking score: 3**

This art deco beauty – once a car showroom – makes a spectacular setting for Chris Corbin and Jeremy King's take on continental café culture. From the suits in for a Full English at 7am to the post-theatre crowd still teeming in after 11pm, there is no typical Wolseley customer: think tourists, children, celebs, businessmen, ladies who lunch or couples. Given that up to 1000 people pour through the door each day, the service remains remarkably consistent. The menu is an 'all things to everyone' selection from around the globe. There are 'kaffeehaus' classics – sachertorte or the always-reliable wiener Holstein; French brasserie favourites – steak tartare or choucroute alsacienne; even some American options – salt beef on rye or a hamburger; and don't forget the lovely afternoon tea. The all-European wine list (with all but the reserve selection available by the glass), begins at £16.
**Chef/s:** Julian O'Neill. **Open:** all week 12 to 3, 5.30 to 12 (11 Sun). **Closed:** D 24-25 Dec and 31 Dec-1 Jan. August Bank Holiday. **Meals:** alc (main courses £9.75 to £39.50).. **Service:** 12.5% (optional). **Details:** Cards accepted. 140 seats. Air-con. No music. Wheelchair access. Children's portions.

## ALSO RECOMMENDED
### ▲ Aubaine
4 Heddon Street, Mayfair, W1B 4BS
Tel no: (020) 7440 2510
www.aubaine.co.uk
⊖ **Piccadilly Circus**

Old Paris comes to Mayfair in the shape of this fashion-conscious boulangerie-cum-bar-cum-brasserie. The whole set-up is spread over two floors and customers can call in for drinks, order bread and pastries to take out, or enjoy sit-down meals from the all-day restaurant menu. Dishes are in the classic bourgeois mould of salade niçoise (£5.85), coq au vin (£13.50) and grilled fillet of sea bass with carrot mousseline and orange vinaigrette, followed by crème brûlée or lemon tart. Great-value 'petit déjeuner' snacks from £2.50. Wines from £16.50 (£4.50 a glass). Open Mon to Sat. Aubaine's elder brother is at 262 Brompton Road, London SW3 2AS.

## ▲ Momo
25 Heddon Street, Mayfair, W1B 4BH
Tel no: (020) 7434 4040
www.momoresto.com

Momo does not trade in the Morocco of street food; rather, the evocatively decorated dining room recalls the expensive riad restaurants of Marrakech and draws a similarly well-heeled international crowd to its party atmosphere. The cooking is mostly made up of large portions of well-spiced, traditional Moroccan dishes – pastilla of pigeon (£10) followed by lamb tagine (£17.50) – plus 'modern Maghrebine cuisine' in which there's a fainter scent of north Africa, say veal cutlet with saffron baby fennel, spinach and wild mushrooms (£12). DJs rock the kasbah in basement bar Kemia or, for something more sedate, there's Mô, a tea room-cum-gift shop next door. House wine is £18.

## ▲ Yoshino
3 Piccadilly Place, Mayfair, W1J 0DB
Tel no: (020) 7287 6622
www.yoshino.net
⊖ Piccadilly Circus

The menu changes daily as only the freshest fish is served at this simple Japanese restaurant off Piccadilly. The formula remains the same however: sushi, sashimi, grilled or fried fish and side dishes like edamame (green soy beans) and homemade tofu. Rice and miso soup are provided with all set meals. Bento boxes can be as basic as deep-fried fish with omelette and pickle (£5.80), or a more elaborate combination including sashini, tofu,

pickle and edamame (£9.80). Sashini and nigiri sushi are also available by the piece from £2, or you can go for a trio of sushi rolls from £2.95. Evenings bring wider choice. Finish with tofu ice cream or green tea sorbet. Closed Sundays.

## READERS RECOMMEND
### The Café at Sotheby's
British
3435 New Bond Street, Mayfair, W1A 2AA
Tel no: (020) 7293 5077
www.sothebys.com
'You have to try the lobster club sandwich'

### Rose Bakery
Modern European
17-18 Dover Street, Mayfair, W1S 4LT
Tel no: (020) 7518 0680
www.doverstreetmarket.com
'Informal surroundings for a fresh lunch'

## ■ Piccadilly
### Bentley's
A revitalised seafood institution
11-15 Swallow Street, W1R 7HD
Tel no: (020) 7734 4756
www.bentleys.org
⊖ Piccadilly Circus
Modern Seafood | £43
Cooking score: 5
🍷

Richard Corrigan can do creative fine-dining (see Lindsay House) but he's also got a respect for good old-fashioned classics. His venture at this refurbished Piccadilly seafood institution is the perfect showcase for the latter. Upstairs, the various clubby yet comfortable dining rooms look chic in blue and white with handsome navy chairs and dark wooden flooring. Ordering classics is a good strategy: Dover sole meunière, shellfish cocktail or beef tartare never fail. But dishes like tiger prawns with chickpeas and olive oil or an Asian-inspired lobster with chilli, garlic, and coriander show Corrigan is not afraid to introduce some diverse international notes. Impeccably fresh seafood is Bentley's raison d'être, but there's no shame in hitting the meat entrées. The glorious mixed grill (sausage, beef sirloin, pork belly and lamb chop) and steamed Elwy Valley Lamb Pudding are hardly second best. Puddings are of the 'proper' variety: apple tart, Valhrona chocolate pot or bread-and-butter pudding. For a less buttoned-up experience, head for the jolly crustacea bar downstairs – fun even for solo diners. Grab a stool at the white marble bar and get to work on a plate of plump native oysters or Frank Hederman's smoked salmon over a glass of Ruinart and a chat with one of the friendly oyster shuckers. The strong wine list makes proceedings even more diverting: from only £14.95, there's a super range – heavy on the seafood-friendly whites and sherries too – with a slew available by the glass to maximise tasting opportunities.

**Chef/s:** Brendan Fyldes. **Open:** Sun to Fri 12 to 2.45, all week D 6 to 11. **Meals:** alc (main courses £11 to £29). **Service:** 12.5% (optional). **Details:** Cards accepted. 200 seats. Air-con. No music. Wheelchair access. Children's portions.

★NEW ENTRY★

## St Alban

**A modern Mediterranean outlook**
**Rex House, 4-12 Lower Regent Street, SW1Y 4PE**
**Tel no: (020) 7499 8558**
**www.stalban.net**
**⊖ Piccadilly Circus**
**Modern European | £42**
**Cooking score: 5**

This newcomer started life in November 2006, the latest venture from Chris Corbin and Jeremy King, who could have easily repeated the formula of their previous successes – latterly at The Wolseley (see entry). Instead they have deviated from the script, admirably refusing to be typecast. St Alban is set on the ground floor of an anonymous office block, boasting a contemporary and slightly edgy design, while the cooking shows affinity to the Mediterranean. Inside, the spacious dining room may suffer from a lowish ceiling, but is smartly furnished with curvy tomato red and green banquettes, while 'take it or leave it', larger-than-life etchings of household items cover all the windows. The room can feel a little 'corporate' and lacks intimacy at times, but the food is superb. The kitchen, with Franco Mazzei at the helm, cooks with distinction, utilising superior produce and keeping a tight rein on seasoning to deliver sophisticated dishes. Flavours are finely balanced, as demonstrated by a main course of flawless slow-roasted Norfolk pig served with Spanish marrow and perfect crackling, a blueberry soufflé dessert was worth the 20-minute wait. Service, from the well-groomed team, is affable and solicitous. The well-considered wine list is full of interesting options, with Italy, Spain and Portugal taking centre stage, while gentle mark-up encourages exploration. Prices start from £15.50.

**Chef/s:** Francesco Mazzei. **Open:** all week 12 to 3, 5.30 to midnight (11 Sun). **Closed:** Bank Hols. **Meals:** alc (main courses £9.25 to £27). **Service:** 12.5% (included). **Details:** Cards accepted. 120 seats. Air-con. No music. Wheelchair access.

# Soho

## Alastair Little

**Top-quality ingredients and modern flair**
**49 Frith Street, W1D 4SG**
**Tel no: (020) 7734 5183**
**⊖ Tottenham Court Road**
**Modern European | £37**
**Cooking score: 2**
**V**

At one time, this compact Soho restaurant stood at the forefront of a culinary trend, where chef Alastair Little was one of the first to introduce modern European cooking to the UK. It is many years since Little's departure and Juliet Peston has taken command in the kitchen. The décor is looking more than a little tired around the edges these days and casually attired waiting staff add to a general lack of crispness, though they deal efficiently with a full dining room. One set menu (at £40 for three courses) at dinner, proffers some

high points, but also a few inconsistencies. Highlights at inspection included a top-quality, tender chicken breast on a bed of leeks, mash, wood sorrel and morel sauce, and a decent asparagus and wild mushroom risotto with a seasonal salad. Well-presented desserts – an intensely flavoured baked chocolate mousse with Irish coffee liégeois, and pannacotta with rhubarb and pistachio praline – were spot on. The wine list opens at £18.50.
**Chef/s:** Juliet Peston. **Open:** Mon to Fri L 12 to 3; Mon to Sat D 6 to 11.30. **Closed:** bank hols. **Meals:** Set L £33, Set D £38. **Service:** not inc. **Details:** Cards accepted. 60 seats. Air-con. No music. Children's portions.

## ★NEW ENTRY★
## Andrew Edmunds
Long-standing Soho favourite
46 Lexington Street, W1F 0LW
Tel no: (020) 7437 5708
⊖ Oxford Street, Piccadilly Circus
Modern European | £25
Cooking score: 3
♠ £30

Antiquarian print dealer and wine-buff Andrew Edmunds' eponymous restaurant in the backstreets of Soho has a loyal following. There's a distinct touch of the Dickensian about the dark, candle-lit interior. Cramped pew-style seating and tables both upstairs and down are covered in paper cloths; seasonal flowers adorn the tables, but while the basement dining room is a touch gloomy, upstairs offers prime viewing of the passing pedestrians outside. Food is rustic both in flavour and presentation, but has a lightness of touch and a strong emphasis on seasonality. A beef fillet and ginger salad with peanuts, cucumber and bean sprouts, for example, was fresh and clean-tasting at inspection. A flavorsome pan-fried tuna with arborio puttanesca and tomato and chilli salsa followed, with dessert a crumbly brown bread ice-cream, an original Victorian recipe. It is, however, the predominately old world wine list – virtually no other alcohol is on offer –

that is the talking point. Edmunds' love of wine is evident in the exhaustive selection of punctually cellared, reasonably priced vintages that include a detailed sweet wine list. A blackboard menu of wine specials often features unusual and boutique wines. House wine starts at around £11. Service is as quirky and unpretentious as this little gem of a restaurant.
**Chef/s:** Rebecca St John Cooper. **Open:** Mon to Fri 12.30 to 3, (Sat 1 to 3, Sun 1 to 3.30), Mon to Sat 6 to 10.45 (Sun to 10.30). **Closed:** Easter, Aug bank hol mon, Dec 23 to Jan 2. **Meals:** alc (main courses £9.50 to £15.50). **Service:** 12.5% (optional). **Details:** Cards accepted. 60 seats. 2 seats outside. Air-con. No music. No mobile phones. Children allowed.

## Arbutus
Sophisticated cooking continues to excite
63-64 Frith Street, W1D 3JW
Tel no: (020) 7734 4545
www.arbutusrestaurant.co.uk
⊖ Tottenham Court Road
Modern European | £35
Cooking score: 6

Arbutus embodies everything you could wish for in a modern bistro – the cooking is sophisticated, the prices no higher than the nearby tourist traps and it is the perfect antithesis to some of the needlessly complicated dishes in town. Anthony Demetre's menu takes in half a dozen dishes per course, punctuated with superior ingredients – wild halibut, organic beef – and the cooking style is unpretentious, not bloated by appetizers or pre-desserts. Start with smoked eel paired with beetroot and given a touch of extravagance by horseradish cream, the flavours are clear and concise. Meat dishes can be memorable, especially a short rib of beef accompanied by English snails, which will have you mopping up the remnants. The kitchen seems able to keep flavours separate and eloquent, the star at inspection, a poached sea bass served with crushed Jersey Royals and parsley vinaigrette, was brought to life by a sublime matelote sauce. Momentum is not lost

The Good Food Guide 2008

at the dessert stage with rice pudding mousse served with Alphonso mango 'a marriage made in heaven', albeit only a short one given the fruit's notoriously short season. Warm chocolate soup with caramelised milk ice cream 'will guarantee sighs of satisfaction', too. Service has improved, showing willingness to explain the dishes and to make sure your meal is an enjoyable one. The wine list, which starts at £12.50, has always been an interesting one, and helpfully most are also available in 250ml carafes. As we went to press, the team at Arbutus opened a second restaurant in London. Wild Honey is located in the former Drones Club site, at 12 St George Street, W1. Tel (020) 7758 9160.

**Chef/s:** Anthony Demetre. **Open:** Mon to Sat 12 to 2.30, 5 to 11, Sun 12.30 to 3.30, 6 to 9.30. **Closed:** 25 and 26 Dec, 1 Jan **Meals:** alc (main courses £12.50 to £15.50). Set L and D Mon to Sat 5 to 7 £13.50 (2 courses) to £15.50. **Service:** 12.5% (optional). **Details:** Cards accepted. 75 seats. Air-con. No music. Wheelchair access. Children's portions.

## Bar Shu
**Fiery and uncompromising Szechuan cooking**
28 Frith Street, W1D 5LF
Tel no: (020) 7287 8822
⊖ Leicester Square
Chinese | £35
Cooking score: 4

Bar Shu stands alone against the uniformity of restaurants in London's Chinatown nearby. You won't find any traces of crispy aromatic duck on the extensive menu and unsurprisingly most of the customers are oriental. The interior 'seems tame enough', with well-appointed dining rooms adorned with rich wood carvings and sturdy dark wooden furniture. The Szechuan cooking here remains the 'real deal' and is ruthlessly authentic, none more so than a blisteringly rich braised beef paired with superbly textured but rarely seen, dried, wild bamboo shoots (although some dishes have been removed due to difficulties in sourcing the ingredients from Chengdu). Bean curd, normally so mild mannered, arrives in puckered 'bear's paw

form with a splendid spicy sauce, and assorted offal with duck's blood can still guarantee a 'sortie into your senses'. Portions are preposterously large, but save room for the unusual desserts such as deep-fried sweet potato ingots filled with sweet red bean paste. The willing service team is on hand to guide people through the impenetrable menu with its helpful illustrations. The lengthy wine list starts from £14, but it is not easy to find anything to match the fiery nature of the dishes.

**Chef/s:** Fu Wenhong. **Open:** all week 12 to 11.30. **Closed:** 25 and 26 Dec. **Meals:** alc (main courses £7 to £68). Set L £19.50 to £22.50, Set D £22.50 to £24.50 (all min 2). **Service:** 12.5% (included). **Details:** Cards accepted. 150 seats. Air-con. Wheelchair access. Music.

## ★NEW ENTRY★
## Barrafina
**Queue for the best tapas in town**
54 Frith Street, W1D 4SL
Tel no: (020) 7813 8016
www.barrafina.co.uk
⊖ Tottenham Court Road
Spanish/Portuguese | £28
Cooking score: 4

There's no doubt that Sam and Eddie Hart's homage to Barcelona's premier tapas bar, Cal Pep, is quite the hippest thing in Frith Street these days. Unlike their tapas restaurant Fino (see entry), it's all rollickingly informal, from the mirrored and marbled interior to the no-booking system, but nonetheless runs like a well-oiled machine thanks to excellent staff and fast-paced chefs cooking in full view behind the counter. Queuing is not necessarily de rigueur for the 23 bar stools – if you get your timing right – but it is worth the wait and you can order drinks and nibble such things as pimientos de padron while doing so. The simple and uncluttered presentation of the dishes highlights the sourcing of materials. Ingredients are all – sweet shavings of Jabugo ham, gambas al ajillo, simply grilled quail with aioli, chorizo perfectly partnered by watercress , or a mini cooked-to-order tortilla– but while the core of the menu doesn't change, daily specials keep regulars interested, whether it's grilled langoustine or a plate of crisp-skinned, succulent suckling pig. Bread is excellent and Santiago tart for dessert is also worth a punt. But note, portions can be small, neighbouring dishes tempting, and the bill quickly inflated. The short all-Spanish wine list opens at £15.

**Chef/s:** Nieves Barragan. **Open:** Mon to Sat 12 to 12. **Closed:** Sun. **Service:** optional. **Details:** Cards accepted. 23 seats. 10 seats outside. Music.

## Gay Hussar

**The obvious choice for hungry Hungarians**
2 Greek Street, W1D 4NB
Tel no: (020) 7437 0973
www.gayhussar.co.uk
⊖ Tottenham Court Road
Eastern European | £28
Cooking score: 1

£5 OFF  ✓  £30

This legendary restaurant has a cosy, old-fashioned feel, its dark, wood-panelled walls covered with caricatures of the leading lights in Westminster's political world. The Hungarian menu (with English translation) is heavily meat-orientated but includes some fish and vegetarian options. A fish terrine flanked by cucumber salad and delicious beetroot sauce and Bulgár saláta provided a light start to an inspection meal. Main courses are predominantly more robust – goulashes, pancakes and meat dishes. Kacsa sült is a huge leg portion of roasted duck served with apple sauce, red cabbage and potatoes, and leek and potato cake accompanies grilled sea bass. Finish with somloi galuska – a rum-soaked sponge filled with walnuts and coated with piped cream and chocolate sauce. House wine is £14.25.

**Chef/s:** Carlos Mendoca. **Open:** Mon to Sat 12.15 to 2.30, 5.30 to 10.45. **Closed:** Bank hols. **Meals:** alc D (main courses £9.50 to £16.50). Set L £16.50 (2 courses) to £18.50. **Service:** 12.5% (optional). **Details:** Cards accepted. 70 seats. Air-con. Wheelchair access. Music. Children's portions.

## L'Escargot, Ground Floor

**Urban brasserie with dependable cooking**
48 Greek Street, W1D 4EF
Tel no: (020) 7439 7474
www.lescargotrestaurant.co.uk
⊖ Tottenham Court Road, Leicester Square
French | £32
Cooking score: 3

This long-running restaurant, a Soho institution, was the first to serve the 'slow-mo' molluscan in the country. Inside, the alluring dining room is a showcase for artwork from the likes of Miro and Chagall, which can be admired against a backdrop of cut-glass mirrors and Art Nouveau lamps. In recent times L'Escargot has become less of a destination restaurant – the Franglais menu can appear outmoded and lacking in sparkle, the cooking 'seemingly lacking excitement' and service occasionally 'patchy and uncommunicative'. Nonetheless, the cooking under the helm of Simon Jones is far from complacent, although at inspection a tian of crab with shrimps and avocado was somewhat clouded by a gummy citrus mayonnaise. Reliable technique came to the fore, however, with a pork fillet, tantalisingly succulent, boldly served on the safe side of pink, and flattered by a silky 'au poivre' sauce, as well as a textbook blackberry soufflé with Bramley apple sorbet. Pricing is even-handed, with particular praise for the lunch and pre-theatre menu. Recent reports indicate that the ground floor brasserie can be more rewarding than the upstairs Picasso room. Wines start at £16.

**Chef/s:** Simon Jones. **Open:** Mon to Fri L 12 to 2.15, Mon to Sat D 6 (5.30 Sat) to 11.30. **Closed:** D 25 and 26 Dec, 1 Jan. **Meals:** alc (main courses £12.50 to £15). Set L and D (not after 7) £15 (2 courses) to £18. **Service:** 12.5%. **Details:** Cards accepted. 70 seats. Air-con. Music.

### Also recommended

An 'also recommended' entry is not a full entry, but is provisionally suggested as an alternative to main entries.

# Lindsay House

**A fine showcase for Irish cooking**
21 Romilly Street, W1D 5AF
Tel no: (020) 7439 0450
www.lindsayhouse.co.uk
⊖ Leicester Square
Modern Irish | £55
Cooking score: 6

🍷 V

Rather quaintly, you have to ring a doorbell to enter this townhouse restaurant. Dining itself takes place on two separate floors; the ground floor is the epitome of calm, exuding a warm glow, with green flourishes from the floral wallpaper to the carpets enhanced by some striking artwork. At inspection, a first course of duck served five ways included the gizzards and a croûton of its own liver, every component working like clever little soundbites. Not to be outdone, a roasted fillet of sea bass found empathy with caramelised endives, potato blinis and some lardoons. Flavours were clear and concise; sauces made only the briefest of appearances so as not to overshadow the ingredients. Flaky plum tart with pain d'épices served with vanilla ice cream provided a fitting finale. The standard of craftsmanship was high (an appetiser of salmon fishcake with tomato relish, and a pre-dessert of apple granita with buttermilk were both excellent) but the cooking lacked that little bit of sparkle – Richard Corrigan may not be as peripatetic as some of his peers, but his absence was nonetheless felt at inspection. Service lagged a few steps behind the cooking. The outstanding wine list, full of intrigue, was arranged in an idiosyncratic manner, mostly by weight, followed by sections devoted to Pinot Noir, Bordeaux, Italy and Iberia, and one for 'rare and forgotten grapes', such as Vin Jaune, Gringet and Provignage. Lovers of dessert wines will be impressed. Prices start from £12.50 but there is plenty of choice between £20 and £40.

**Chef/s:** Richard Corrigan. **Open:** Mon to Fri L 12 to 2.30, Mon to Sat D 6 to 11. **Closed:** bank hols L. **Meals:** Set L £27 to £56, Set D £56 to £68. **Service:** 12.5% (optional). **Details:** Cards accepted. 50 seats. Air-con. No music. Children's portions.

# Red Fort

**Long-standing, modern Indian restaurant**
77 Dean Street, W1D 3SH
Tel no: (020) 7437 2525/2115
www.redfort.co.uk
⊖ Tottenham Court Road
Modern Indian | £35
Cooking score: 3

V

One of Amin Ali's earliest ventures into the world of contemporary Indian cuisine, the Red Fort has reinvented itself over the years and currently looks in good shape. Below stairs is Akbar (a groovy evening venue for drinks and snacks), while the main dining room is sleek, cool and unashamedly plush. The kitchen's focus is the cuisine of Lucknow and Hyderabad, although it makes impressive use of native British produce from Devon lamb to Scottish lobsters (perhaps cooked with saffron and garlic). Seafood is a strength and the menu also lists monkfish tikka, spicy kingfish flavoured with curry leaves, and 'smoked' chunks of dorade with mint, garlic and green chillies. Elsewhere, corn-fed chicken breast might appear might appear in a creamed tomato and dill sauce or with brown onions, coriander and red chillies. Among the vegetables, look for kaddu channa (white pumpkin and Bengal chick peas) or the five-lentil panchrangi dhal. Desserts cover everything from Alphonso mango kulfi to chocolate fondant with pistachio ice cream. House wines are £22 (£6 a glass). **Open:** Mon to Fri L 12 to 2.15, all week D 5.45 to 11.15 (5.30 to 10.30 Sun). **Meals:** alc (main courses £12.50 to £30). Set L £12 (2 courses) to £25, Set D 5.45 to 7 £16 (2 courses) to £45. **Service:** 12.5% (optional). **Details:** Cards accepted. 77 seats. Air-con. Wheelchair access. Music.

## Yauatcha

**Fashionable next-generation dim sum**
15-17 Broadwick Street, W1F 0DL
Tel no: (020) 7494 8888
⊖ Tottenham Court Road
Chinese | £28
Cooking score: 4

Ⴘ

Alan Yau's trendy Soho dim sum and tea
parlour is a far remove from the standard
trolley and tea Chinatown joint in every way,
including price. But what you get is a stylish
venue, and glamour in spades. There's
substance as well as style, thanks to exquisitely
executed dim sum – asparagus cheung fun;
sparkling scallop shumai, and well-made
venison puffs – while at the upper end of the
menu, you'll find luxury ingredients like
Dover sole or Wagyu beef. Four years on,
Yauatcha's still packing in a trendy crowd
meaning even late afternoon tables are hard to
get. The draconian reservation system doesn't
ensure seamless service, however; long
waiting times and speedy turnaround
occasionally raise hackles. The street-level
pastel, white and neon all-day parlour – once
just for tea and beautiful cakes – is now used in
addition to the large shared tables in the
moodier ambience of the basement restaurant
proper. The wine list (from £23) is a whistle-
stop world tour of old and new that leans
sensibly towards white to aid food matching.
Tea-lovers will thrill to the lengthy, largely
Chinese, tea list.
**Chef/s:** Cheong Wah Soon. **Open:** Mon to Fri 12 to 3,
5.30 to 11.45, Sat and Sun 11.45 to 11.45 (10.30 Sun).
**Meals:** alc (main courses £3.50 to £38).
**Service:** 13%. **Details:** Cards accepted. 110 seats.

## ALSO RECOMMENDED
### ▲ Chowki

2-3 Denman Street, Soho, W1D 7HA
Tel no: (020) 7439 1330
⊖ Piccadilly Circus

Cheerful, busy, and inexpensive Indian diner
off Piccadilly Circus where customers sit at
traditional wooden tables ('chowki') and

choose from monthly changing menus that
draw on regional recipes. The northwest
Frontier could supply chargrilled fish skewers
(£3.95), chicken and turnip cooked in
mustard oil (£9.95) recalls Lucknow, while
Goa brings a yam and black gram curry
(£7.95) to the table. Three-course regional
feasts are £12.95; house wines from £10.95.
Open all week.

## ▲ Chuen Cheng Ku

17 Wardour Street, Soho, W1V 3HD
Tel no: (020) 7437 1398
www.chuenchengku.co.uk
⊖ Leicester Square

Three storeys of Chinese expertise draw the
crowds from Oxford Street and Leicester
Square to this long-established Chinatown
haunt. With over 100 dim sum on offer and an
extensive menu, choosing something to suit
all tastes is relatively easy. From staples such as
crispy aromatic duck (£9 to £29.50), via
deep-fried prawn dumplings (£4.50), to the
tasty seafood and coriander soup (£4.50),
starters are varied and interesting. Follow up
with fried beef with pickled ginger and
pineapple (£7.80). There are various set meals,
plus plenty of rice and noodles dishes. Wines
from £10.25. Open all week.

## ▲ Itsu

103 Wardour Street, Soho, W1F 0UQ
Tel no: (020) 7479 4790
www.itsu.com
⊖ Tottenham Court Road

Now a familiar name in the capital thanks to
its three restaurants and ten shops, Itsu's blend
of slick modernity, fresh food and helpful staff
is clearly a winning combination. Sit at the
kaiten and take your pick from the dishes that
pass by – perhaps salmon sushi; crab
California roll; chilli crab crystal roll or new-
style Asian seared tuna. Alternatively, press
your red button to summon a waiter and
request made-to-order sashimi, crispy
handrolls (perhaps with warm Teriyaki
chicken or prawn tempura with salmon).
Pudding might be crème brûlée, fresh fruit on

white chocolate yogurt, or the Itsu chocolate dessert. Drink-wise, there are cocktails, champagne by the bottle or the glass and wines from £15.95. Open daily. Other branches are situated in Chelsea and Canary Wharf.

## ▲ Masala Zone

9 Marshall Street, Soho, W1F 7ER
Tel no: (020) 7287 9966
⊖ Oxford Circus

Everything about this cheap and cheerfully decorated restaurant encourages a relaxed approach to Indian dining. Starters are based on traditional street food and include puri, bhajia and samosas (all £3.95). Grills, noodles and curries are offered as mains (mostly for between £7 and £8), say lamb curry braised with spinach and garlic or one with fresh vegetables flavoured with green herbs. For a more substantial meal, pick the grand thali: your choice of curry served with the vegetable, potato and dhal of the day with sides of raita, rice and chapatti (approximately £10). House wine is £10.95. Open daily. Additional branches in Islington and Earls Court.

## ▲ Randall & Aubin

14-16 Brewer Street, Soho, W1R 3FS
Tel no: (020) 7287 4447
www.randallandaubin.com
⊖ Piccadilly Circus

Set in one of the racier quarters of Soho, this former butcher's shop has an air of gallic charm. The high stools won't suit everyone (nor will the dance music that kick-starts most evenings) but window seats still remain highly coveted by locals. A rôtisserie offers some diversity in the menu, but the real star of the show is the silver, tiered presentation of fruits de mer (£27 per head). Wines from £13.50. Closed Sun L. A second branch is at 329-331 Fulham Road, SW10; tel: (020) 7823 3515.

## ▲ La Trouvaille

12A Newburgh Street, Soho, W1F 7RR
Tel no: (020) 7287 8488
⊖ Oxford Circus

An inventive take on classic French bistro cooking is what to expect at this Soho dining room. Start with quail and foie gras terrine, or snails bourguignon, before moving on to pan-fried veal loin with Camargue rice, crayfish and squid ink sauce, or perhaps fillet of Galloway beef with seasonal vegetables, parsley jus and wasabi gratin, with hot chocolate fondant and ginger ice cream to finish. Also available are bar snacks ranging from croque monsieur to onglet steak with French fries and béarnaise. Wines from the south of France are a speciality, starting with vins de pays d'Oc at £13.50. Closed Sat L and Sun.

## ▲ Vasco & Piero's Pavilion

15 Poland Street, Soho, W1F 8QE
Tel no: (020) 7437 8774
www.vascosfood.com
⊖ Oxford Circus

Traditional Umbrian dishes are a speciality of this long-established Italian restaurant. Lunchtime starters at around the £7 mark might include roast beetroot with egg, anchovies and tomatoes, while a typical main is calf's liver and sage with grilled polenta and asparagus. Three courses on the daily-changing evening set (£28) brings watermelon and goat's cheese salad with breast of guineafowl with wild mushrooms and lentils, then Robiola cheesecake or panacotta with strawberries. The mainly Italian wine list starts at £14.50 and includes some interesting regional choices, including an oak-conditioned Chardonnay from Umbria and a Salice Salentino (Riserva) from further south which would go well with one of the more robust offerings, such as lombetto (cured pork loin). Closed Sat L and Sun.

## READERS RECOMMEND

### Kulu Kulu Sushi
Japanese
76 Brewer Street, Soho, W1F 9TX
Tel no: (020) 7734 7316
'Quick-fix quality food'

### Mother Mash
British
26 Ganton Street, Soho, W1F 7QZ
Tel no: 020 7494 9644
www.mothermash.co.uk
'Comfort food served in wooden booths'

### Spaccanapoli
Italian
101 Dean Street, Soho, W1D 3TG
Tel no: (020) 7437 9440
www.spaccanapoli.co.uk
'Neopolitan specialties'

## ▌St James's Park

### Inn the Park
Fantastic views
St James's Park, SW1A 2BJ
Tel no: (020) 7451 9999
www.innthepark.com
⊖ St James's Park
Modern British | £30
Cooking score: 2

There can be few finer places to lunch on a summer's day than the terrace of Inn the Park, as the swans glide past on the lake of St James's Park and with the grand buildings of Whitehall visible through the swaying trees. Inside, the stripped wood ceiling and floors, full-length windows and angular modern furniture lend an almost Scandinavian feel to this most English of settings which, in the best café tradition, is open all day, from breakfast and elevenses through to lunch, afternoon tea and dinner. Lunch on crab on toast and trout fillet with artichokes and pea shoots, while dinner could be rabbit terrine with baby chard and grain mustard, grilled Herdwick lamb cutlets with a salad of spelt, chicory and grapes and pear and almond tart with vanilla ice

cream. Australian house red and white is £14.50 while there are canapés and platters of smoked meat and fish to graze on as accompaniment to a short selection of cocktails.
Chef/s: Oliver Smith. **Open:** all week L 12 to 3 (4 Sat and Sun), D 5 to 10.30. **Meals:** alc (main courses £10.50 to £22.50). Set L Sat and Sun £19.50 (2 courses) to £24.50. Bar menu available 5pm onwards. **Service:** 10% (optional). **Details:** Cards accepted. 100 seats. 70 seats outside. Wheelchair access. Music. Children's portions.

## ▌Trafalgar Square

★NEW ENTRY★
### The National Dining Rooms
Fine dining and afternoon tea
The Sainsbury Wing, The National Gallery, WC2N 5DN
Tel no: (020) 7747 2525
www.thenationaldiningrooms.co.uk
⊖ Leicester Square
Modern British | £25
Cooking score: 4
£30

Set within the National Gallery's Sainsbury Wing, the stylish National Dining Rooms boast high ceilings and vast windows framing views over neighbouring Trafalgar Square. Catering to the hungry hordes that descend on the Gallery at all times of the day is no mean feat, but Oliver Peyton's latest venture manages the neat trick of satisfying all appetites, tastes and whims while never losing sight of its goal to champion fine British cooking. Thus visitors can opt for a full meal, afternoon tea (smoked salmon sandwiches, buttermilk scones), or traditional savoury pies and tarts from the bakery; a separate children's menu also gets the thumbs-up. Each month head chef Jesse Dunford Wood offers an interesting regional menu alongside the carte. On a spring lunch it was Suffolk's turn: warm asparagus with a silky chervil butter, steamed skate with buttered cockles, welks and baby

leeks and Suffolk Gold cow's milk cheese with apple chutney to finish. A good, varied wine list starts at £15.
**Chef/s:** Jesse Dunford Wood. **Open:** Mon to Sun, 10 to 5. **Meals:** Set D £24.50 (2 courses) to £29.50. **Service:** optional. **Details:** Cards accepted. 100 seats. Children's portions.

# ■ Westminster

## Bank Westminster
**Lively, contemporary brasserie and bar**
45 Buckingham Gate, SW1E 6BS
Tel no: (020) 7379 9797 (centralised number)
www.bankrestaurants.com
⊖ St James's Park
**Modern European | £43**
**Cooking score: 3**
£5 OFF  V

Pass one of the longest bars in town the Zander Bar to reach Bank's airy, modern conservatory-style dining room, situated at the rear of the Crown Plaza Hotel. Its huge glass windows overlook a grand, flowery Victorian courtyard – quite a draw for fair-weather dining. The food is as cosmopolitan as the surroundings, the kitchen's modern brasserie style playing to the gallery with a something-for-everyone approach. The lengthy repertoire puts classics with dishes with modern spin, say cod and chips with mushy peas and tartare sauce alongside Szechuan peppered tuna and wok-fried Asian greens. On the meaty side, classics win supremacy, perhaps grilled ribeye with béarnaise, or maybe Gloucestershire Old Spot sausages served with creamed mash and onion sauce. Finish with a chocolate fondant teamed with pistachio ice cream, or the ubiquitous sticky toffee pudding and butterscotch. The international wine list offers a lively selection, with strength in Bordeaux and Burgundy but sees other regions stand their ground too, with prices starting out at £14.50.
**Chef/s:** Stuart Dring (Westminster). **Open:** Mon to Fri L 12 to 2.45, Mon to Sat D 5.30 to 11. **Meals:** alc (main courses £11 to £25). Set L £13.50 (2 courses) to £16, Set D 5.30 to 7 and 10 to 11 £13.50 (2 courses) to £16 (Aldwych), £15.95 (2 courses) to £17.95 (Westminster). Bar and (Aldwych only) breakfast menus available. **Service:** 12.5% (optional). **Details:** Cards accepted. 230 seats. Air-con. No music. Wheelchair access. Children's portions.

## Cinnamon Club
**Governing Indian gourmet**
Old Westminster Library, Great Smith Street, SW1P 3BU
Tel no: (020) 7222 2555
www.cinnamonclub.com
⊖ Westminster
**Modern Indian | £41**
**Cooking score: 4**
V

The twenty-first century role of the former Westminster Library (a fine Grade II listed building) is as the host to a top-drawer Indian restaurant. The Cinnamon Club keeps its heritage alive with a classy décor that blends old books, leather banquettes and white-clothed tables with splashes of India. The large airy bar and the modern English club feel to the dining room draw the suits from the nearby Houses of Parliament, as does the inventive Indian menu – the cooking is as far from curry-house as you can get. Expect a modern take on traditional dishes, with unusual ingredients and big flavours evident in such main dishes as smoked rack of lamb with Rajasthani corn sauce, seared rump of water buffalo with Goan spices, and Cumbrian milk-fed goat cooked three ways. Appetisers take in Bombay spiced vegetables with cumin pao, and baked chicken with cracked pepper and thyme, while the pudding choice extends to ginger toffee pudding and semolina halwa with caramelised pineapple. The international wine list complements the food, starting at £18 for house selections.
**Chef/s:** Vivek Singh. **Open:** Mon to Fri L 12 to 2.45, Mon to Sat D 6 to 10.45.. **Closed:** 26 Dec, 1 Jan, bank hols. **Meals:** alc (main courses £11 to £29). Set L and D before 7 £19 (2 courses) to £22. **Service:** 12.5%. **Details:** Cards accepted. 150 seats. Air-con. No music.

## Rex Whistler Restaurant at Tate Britain

Up-market eating for art lovers
Millbank, SW1P 4RG
Tel no: (020) 7887 8825
www.tate.org.uk
⊖ Pimlico
British | £30
Cooking score: 2

🍷 ⋎

This classic dining room with soaring columns, white tablecloths and a famed Rex Whistler mural takes its artistic surroundings seriously. Knowledgeable staff glide across the parquet floor to deliver Richard Oxley's faithfully British menu to a mature clientele, unsurprisingly made up of well-to-do tourists and arty Brits alike. Choose from starters such as lamb's kidney Turbigo on toasted sour dough or pickled mackerel with shaved fennel, lemon and salted capers. Brunch-type dishes include salmon, haddock and new potatoes with a poached duck egg and hollandaise, or archetypal fish and chips served in a stiff batter. Desserts including a rather boozy chocolate and amaretti tart served with clotted cream, elderflower sorbet or a selection of British cheeses. But the true talking point is the award-winning wine list compiled by sommelier Hamish Anderson. Presented in an educational folder, it includes a huge selection of New and Old World wines broken down into regions, notably featuring over 80 half bottles. House wine starts at £15. **Chef/s:** Richard Oxley. **Open:** all week L only 11.30am to 3pm (10am to 5pm Sat and Sun). **Closed:** 24 Dec. **Meals:** alc (main courses £14.95). **Service:** 12.5% (optional). **Details:** Cards accepted. 80 seats. 20 seats outside. Air-con. No music. Wheelchair access. Children's portions.

Heston Blumenthal

**Why did you become a chef?**
Aged 16, my father took us to the restaurant l'Oustau de Baumaniere in Provence. I was captivated by the sights, the smells, the sounds, the whole dining experience.

**Who was your main inspiration?**
Harold McGee.

**What's your favourite cookery book?**
At the moment I am reading *The Encyclopaedia of Practical Cookery*, published in 1895 and edited by Theodore Francis Garrett.

**What's the best dish you've ever eaten?**
Shopping for, preparing and cooking barbecues with the kids.

**Do you have a favourite local recipe?**
Eton Mess, a dessert we serve at the Hinds Head, from our local Eton College tuck shop.

**What's your guilty food pleasure?**
Tomato ketchup.

**If you could only eat one more thing, what would it be?**
A menu I discovered recently from the court of King James, comprising of 174 courses; one included 48 desserts and another 12 puffins. And that was just for two people.

**What's coming up next for you?**
The development of the Fat Duck historic British menu.

# ▌Belsize Park

★NEW ENTRY★
## XO
**Slick, modern pan-Asian restaurant**
29 Belsize Lane, NW3 5AS
Tel no: (020) 7433 0888
www.rickerrestaurants.com
⊖ Belsize Park
Fusion/Pan-Asian | £25
Cooking score: 2
🍶

–The latest outpost of Will Ricker's pan-Asian empire, XO – named after a Chinese pork and dried shrimp sauce – dutifully mimics the successful high-fashion formula of its sister restaurants: Notting Hill, E&O and Chelsea's Eight over Eight (see entries). Dark wood, white tables and strategically angled look-at-me mirrors make for a slick, minimalist dining room. The menu has a good selection of dim sum, Asian salads, tempura, futo maki rolls and sashimi, and dishes tried at inspection included 'refreshing' salmon and green papaya betel leaves, a soft-shell crab maki roll, and a whole sea bass 'flaky and fresh' that walked a fine line between chilli, sweet and savoury. The wine list stays true to the restaurant's pan-Asian roots, with plenty of aromatic grape varietals and an emphasis on New World wines. House wines start at £13. Given that Belsize Park is strangely devoid of decent upmarket restaurants, it's no surprise XO has been welcomed by affluent locals when it opened in early 2007. But while XO has shaken the foundations of Belsize Park's frumpy dining scene, it unfortunately lacks the sassy edge of its sister restaurants.
**Chef/s:** John Higginson. **Open:** all week 12 to 3; (4 Sat to Sun) 6 to 10.30 (10pm Sun). **Meals:** alc (small dishes £3.50 £6.50, mains). **Service:** 12.5% (optional). **Details:** Cards accepted. 90 seats. Air-con. Separate bar. Wheelchair access.

## ALSO RECOMMENDED
## ▲ Gilgamesh
The Stables, Chalk Farm Road, Camden, NW1 8AH
Tel no: (020) 7482 5757
www.gilgameshbar.com
⊖ Chalk Farm

Named after an ancient Mesopotamian hero, Gilgamesh is a vast and lavishly decorated restaurant in the heart of Camden. The interior replicates that of a palace built in Babylonian times, combining the history with contemporary and modern art, so the hand-carved Indian furnishings, Middle Eastern bas reliefs and ambient Arabesque music are impressively over the top. Ian Pengelly's menu trawls through Thailand, Hong Kong and Japan for inspiration, so expect a dim sum, a team of sushi chefs preparing sashimi (£4 to £14) and nagiri dishes (£3.60 to £6.20), tempura dishes such as lemon sole with ponzu (£16), and speciality main courses like beef rending (£14). Wines from £18. Open Mon to Sun, 11 to late.

# ▌Euston

★NEW ENTRY★
## Mestizo
**A ray of Mexican sunshine**
103 Hampstead Road, NW1 3EL
Tel no: (020) 7387 4064
www.mestizomx.com
⊖ Warren Street/ Euston
Mexican | £30
Cooking score: 2

An unassuming entrance on the Hampstead Road opens onto a dining scene as hot and lively as Mestizo's own green 'tomatillo' salsa. In two short years this authentic cuisine has gathered something of a following – delegates from the Mexican Embassy were spotted lunching eagerly at inspection, it wasn't their first visit either. Newcomers might wish to explore Mexico's vibrant flavours through the tapas-style 'antojitos' menu. Dishes like flautas (crispy chicken-stuffed tortillas topped with sour cream and piquant green salsa), panuchos (refried beans and pork on soft tortillas), and jaladas (cream cheese-stuffed jalapeño peppers), deliver complexity, texture and a sheer flavour explosion seldom found on the capital's Mexican scene. From the main menu, traditional chocolate-based mole sauce enlivens poussin or pork cutlets, while hot stone bowls sizzle with chicken, beef and cheese. Turn the heat up even higher with fiery tequilas, at £4.40 a glass.

**Chef/s:** Dalcy Aguilera and Miguel Bennetts. **Open:** Mon to Wed 12 to 12, Thu to Sat 12 to 1, Sun 12 to 4, 5 to 11. **Closed:** 25 Dec, bank hol Mons. **Meals:** alc (main courses £9.50 to £18.50. **Service:** not inc. **Details:** Cards accepted. 80 seats. Air-con. Wheelchair access. Music. Children allowed.

## ALSO RECOMMENDED
### ▲ Diwana Bhel Poori
121 Drummond Street, Euston, NW1 2HL
Tel no: (020) 7387 5556
⊖ Euston

For southern-Indian vegetarian food, the two adjoining eateries that make Diwana have been the pick of the crop for more than 30 years. Choose from nine coconut-laden 'dosas of the coral coasts. Bombay-style dishes include aloo papri chat, bhel puri, and dahi vada (all £3). For a main course try sag aloo, a vegetable curry and puris, or dosai pancakes served with chutney and sambhar (£5.95). The lunchtime buffet is good value at £6.50 for all you can eat. The restaurant is unlicensed, so BYO. Open all week.

## ▮ Finchley
### Two Brothers
**Deluxe fish and chips**
297303 Regents Park Road, N3 1DP
Tel no: (020) 8346 0469
⊖ Finchley Central
**Seafood | £30**
**Cooking score: 1**

The Manzi brothers' policy of not taking bookings does not deter people from this renowned fish and chip shop and it's not

unusual during busy periods to see the queue stretching round the block. The light and welcoming dining room appeals to families with children and couples alike, and the service is quick without being hurried, but it's the food that's the main draw. Starters include excellent Arbroath smokies, jellied eels and rock oysters, while a good selection of fish, from battered cod and haddock to trout, plaice and sea bass make up the main courses, which are served with chips. Sides such as mushy peas are also available, but the homemade tartare sauce left much to be desired. Puddings are fun and hearty – the knickerbocker glory and the rhubarb strudel did not disappoint. Two Brothers is probably the only fish shop where the owners also produce their own wine, which starts at £11.10 a bottle.

**Chef/s:** Leon and Tony Manzi. **Open:** Tue to Sat 12 to 2.30pm, 5.30 to 10.15pm. **Closed:** bank hol Mon. **Meals:** alc (main courses £9 to £18.50). **Service:** not inc. **Details:** Cards accepted. 90 seats. Air-con. Music. Children's portions. Children allowed.

## ALSO RECOMMENDED
### ▲ Rani
7 Long Lane, Finchley, N3 2PR
Tel no: (020) 8349 4386
www.raniuk.com

A gleamingly spick-and-span Indian restaurant offering a varied menu of traditional home-style vegetarian cooking based on the region of Kathiawar in Gujerat. Among the cold starters are bhel poori (£4.20) and chola papri chat (£4.10), while hot options include mixed bhajias (£3.80) and bhakervelli (spiced vegetables served with date chutney; £4). Speciality main courses range from chana (chick peas cooked with onions, tomato and tamarind; £5.10) to bhindi (deep-

| Average price |
| --- |
| The average price listed in main-entry reviews denotes the price of a three-course meal, without wine. |

fried okra delicately spiced and cooked with onions; £6). All-in-one set meals offer good value. Drink lassi, falooda or wine from £10.

# ∎ Golders Green

## Café Japan

**Animated sushi joint**
626 Finchley Road, NW11 7RR
Tel no: (020) 8455 6854
⊖ Golders Green
Japanese | £22
Cooking score: 4

£30

Simple, unaffected charm and good-value food bring the crowds to Koichi Konnai's animated Japanese eating house on Finchley Road. Queues regularly form outside, but there's a rapid turnover in the canteen-style dining room with its buzzy counter and rows of lacquered tables. Top-drawer, ultra-fresh sushi is the restaurant's trump card and the range of species is extensive, taking in octopus, sea urchin, flying fish roe and razor shells in addition to the more familiar tuna, eel and sea bass. 'Delux' sets are a good way of sampling the range and chirashi specialities (sliced fish on sushi rice) are also worth noting. Beyond raw fish, the kitchen delivers familiar cooked specialities such as salmon teriyaki, grilled eel and salt-grilled yellowtail neck. To finish, opt for one of the ice creams or try dorayaki (Japanese pancakes filled with sweet red bean paste). Wines are limited to white or red at £8.50 (£2.50 a glass), otherwise drink plum wine, saké, beer or green tea. Note that it's cash only at lunch.

**Chef/s:** Koichi Konnai. **Open:** Sat and Sun L 12 to 2, Wed to Sun D 6 to 10 (9.30 Sun). **Closed:** 3 weeks Aug  Meals: alc (main courses £4.50 to £20). Set L £8.50 (2 courses), Set D £12 (2 courses) to £18. **Service:** not inc. **Details:** Cards accepted. 39 seats. Air-con. Music.

## Philpott's Mezzaluna

**Neighbourhood Italian doesn't skimp on portions**
424 Finchley Road, NW2 2HY
Tel no: (020) 7794 0455
www.philpotts-mezzaluna.com
Italian | £42
Cooking score: 4

£5 OFF V

This is what is meant by a neighbourhood restaurant, a convivial, welcoming place that has a good local following, and looks after its customers well with unfashionably large portions of Italian-influenced food. Seared calf's tongue makes a diverting opener, garnished with celeriac and grape salsa, while a spring dinner menu featured grilled asparagus with olive oil, balsamic, pine-nuts and shaved Parmesan. You might opt for an intermediate pasta course in the Italian way – perhaps fusilli with mushrooms – or else just steam straight into the main courses, where involtini of pesto-crusted plaice, or hearty bollito misto, await. If you get to the finishing line with room left, there's mango ice-cream with poached berries, or chocolate tart, in store. The wine list does a commendably thorough job in Italy, sourcing wines from all regions of the boot, in amongst offerings from other countries. The bidding opens at £14 (with glasses from £3.50).

**Chef/s:** David Philpott. **Open:** Tue to Fri and Sun L 12 to 2.30 (3 Sun), Tue to Sun D 7 to 11. **Closed:** Christmas and New Year's Day. **Meals:** Set L £17 (2 courses) to £20, Set D £24.50 (2 courses) to £29.50. **Service:** 12.5% (optional). **Details:** Cards accepted. 60 seats. 10 seats outside. Air-con. Wheelchair access. Music. Children's portions.

## Highgate

### The Bull

Comfort cooking in Highgate
13 North Hill, N6 4AB
Tel no: (0845) 456 5033
www.inthebull.biz
⊖ Highgate
French | £32
Cooking score: 2

'The Bull' achieves a stylish informality that embraces the service as much as the food, a formula that attracts full houses. Much is made of the careful sourcing of ingredients with reassuring specifics such as Loch Fyne smoked salmon, Goosnargh chicken or Elwy lamb. Imaginative daring, which often works, takes dishes way beyond the meat and two veg approach; smoked haddock gets welsh rarebit crust and leeks and bacon, scallops have cauliflower fritters and almonds and sultanas and bass meets potatoes with porcini, créme fraîche and onion gravy. Buttermilk pudding or apple tart and roast rhubarb exemplify simpler desserts – you can even have tea and homemade biscuits. Wines, and beers, come from all over and show discrimination; a few are available by the glass and bottles start at £13.50

**Chef/s:** Jeremy Hollingsworth. **Open:** Tue to Sun L 12 to 2.30, all week D 6 to 10.30. **Meals:** alc (main courses £13.50 to £24.50). Set L £14.95 (2 courses) to £17.95. **Service:** 12.5% (optional). **Details:** Cards accepted. 70 seats. Air-con. Wheelchair access. Music. Children's portions. Car parking.

### The Parsee

Popular Indian regional fare
34 Highgate Hill, N19 5NL
Tel no: (020) 7272 9091
www.the-parsee.com
⊖ Archway
Indian | £23
Cooking score: 2

Opposite the Whittington Hospital, in an area of north London more famous for its late-night kebab shops than good restaurants, this modern, sparsely decorated dining room is something of a surprise. A sibling of Café Spice Namaste in the City, it specialises in the cuisine of India's Parsee community which, in its liberal use of herbs and low-fat cooking methods, bears the hallmarks of its Persian heritage. The richness of pan-fried chicken livers is balanced with a masala of cumin, coriander, garlic and ginger, with roti on the side to mop up the offal juices. A main course arrives as a plate of steamed rice accompanied by two gleamingly white bowls, one containing a moreish and deeply flavoured dhal, the other a colourful jostle of good-sized prawns cooked with red onions, red masala, tamarind and jaggery. Other dishes that display a similarly satisfying balance of flavour include fried potato cakes filled with curried beef mince, peas and coriander and served with a cinnamon-flavoured tomato gravy. Staff are kind and welcoming. House wine is £13.90.

**Chef/s:** Cyrus Todiwala. **Open:** Mon to Sat D only 6 to 10.40. **Closed:** 25 Dec to 1 Jan, bank hols. **Meals:** alc (main courses £10 to £13). Set D £25 to £30. **Service:** 10% (optional). **Details:** Cards accepted. 50 seats. Air-con. Wheelchair access. Music.

## Readers recommend

A 'readers recommend' review is a genuine quote from a report sent in by one of our readers. We intend to follow up these suggestions throughout the year to come.

# Islington

## Almeida

**Theatre crowds meet French tapas**
30 Almeida Street, N1 1AD
Tel no: (020) 7354 4777
www.conran.com
⊖ Angel, Highbury & Islington
French | £40
Cooking score: 4

🍷

Almeida functions both as a civilised Islington local and a convenient pit-stop for the Almeida Theatre opposite. It's a smart-casual sort of place, where large, well-spaced tables are set in a stylish dining room decorated in neutral tones, with an open kitchen at one end and a sunken bar area to one side. Cooking from a set-price menu mixes trad French bistro with sunnier Mediterranean dishes, so that you might construct a meal from escargots, oysters or terrine de foie gras followed by honey-glazed breast of duck or a rib-eye steak with mustard crust, or you could equally go for a salad of seared tuna, chervil and parsley followed by poached sea bass with mussels and saffron velouté. Sweet and savoury trolleys bearing charcuterie and tarts appear at the beginning and end of meals, and there is a cheeseboard and classic puddings such as crème brûleé. The food is soundly prepared: a splendid main course of spit-roast rack of pork with ceps and Madeira jus impressed on a recent inspection. The succulent meat edged with a ruff of terrific crackling and set off by the musky mushrooms. A lengthy wine list is particularly strong on Languedoc-Roussillon and south-western France and offers around 15 bottles by the glass or pot lyonnais. House wine is £15.95.
**Chef/s:** Ian Wood. **Open:** Mon to Sat 12 to 2.30, 5.30 to 10.45, Sun 1 to 9. **Closed:** Christmas, Easter Mon. **Meals:** alc (main courses £12.50 to £25). Set L and D 5.30 to 7 £14.50 (2 courses) to £17.50. Bar tapas menu available. **Service:** 12.5% (optional). **Details:** Cards accepted. 100 seats. Air-con. No music. Wheelchair access.

## The House

**A cut above your average gastropub**
63-69 Canonbury Road, N1 2DG
Tel no: (020) 7704 7410
www.inthehouse.biz
⊖ Highbury & Islington
Modern European | £30
Cooking score: 2

Pre-gentrification, this was a rough Islington pub. How times have changed. Although a sign swinging outside suggests that The House is your typical tarted-up gastropub, it's a little more polished than that: a smart-ish bar and restaurant where dinner might be preceded by a mojito and concluded with an espresso martini. The menu, however, is gastropub through and through, offering a mix of hearty Sunday lunch-style dishes interspersed with shafts of Mediterranean sunlight. So devilled kidneys and ceps on toasted brioche with smoked bacon, might be followed by shepherd's pie or, for more gloss, sea bass with braised fennel and a ragout of borlotti beans and baby onions. Finish, perhaps, with banoffee pie or British cheeses from La Fromagerie up the road in Highbury. The wine list has been assembled with humour and passion with house French £13.50. Another break from the norm: there's a weekend breakfast sourced from the local farmers' market.
**Chef/s:** Rob Arnott. **Open:** Tue to Sun L 12 to 2.30 (3.30 Sat and Sun), all week D 6 (6.30 Sat and Sun) to 10.30. **Closed:** Christmas. **Meals:** alc (main courses £9.50 to £22.50). Set L Tue to Fri £14.95 (2

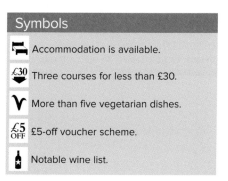

### Symbols

🛏 Accommodation is available.

£30 Three courses for less than £30.

V More than five vegetarian dishes.

£5 OFF £5-off voucher scheme.

🍷 Notable wine list.

courses) to £17.95. **Service:** 12.5% (optional). **Details:** Cards accepted. 40 seats. Wheelchair access. Music. Children's portions.

## Metrogusto
**Fine food with a fiery Silician streak**
13 Theberton Street, N1 0QY
Tel no: (020) 7226 9400
www.metrogusto.co.uk
⊖ Angel
Italian | £32
Cooking score: 3

🍷 ∀

High ceilings, white walls covered with bright and bold contemporary paintings, and chunky furnishings set the cool, idiosyncratic scene at this modern Italian restaurant off Upper Street. Cooking is described as 'progressive Italian' with an emphasis on regional foods although there is a definite Sicilian slant to the menu, which is laid out in traditional style with risottos and pastas following starters like Sicilian mussel soup with garlic bruschetta, or sea bream carpaccio with grilled fennel. Main courses range from grilled lamb cutlets with red wine and peach sauce and steak with apple and gorgonzola sauce to lemon sole fillets with roasted pepper coulis. Desserts take in the trendy (poached pear with pecorino ice cream) and the traditional (pannacotta with caramelised lime sauce). The all-Italian wine list concentrates on good producers, with around 15 by the glass from £4.50 and bottles starting at £15.50.
**Chef/s:** Antonio Di Salvo. **Open:** Fri to Sun L 12 to 2.30 (Sun and bank hols 12.30 to 4.30), Mon to Sat D 6.30 to 10.30 (11 Fri and Sat). **Closed:** 25 and 26 Dec, Easter Sun and Mon. **Meals:** alc (main courses £11.50 to £17.50). **Service:** 12.5% (optional). **Details:** Cards accepted. 65 seats. Air-con. Wheelchair access. Music. Children's portions.

## Morgan M
**Entente cordiale in Islington**
489 Liverpool Road, N7 8NS
Tel no: (020) 7609 3560
www.morganm.com
⊖ Highbury & Islington
French | £39
Cooking score: 5

∀

A recent makeover has helped this modest, corner dining room to project a warmer outlook, with plush burgundy walls and oak panelling accented by the chef's own paintings. Well-spaced tables highlight the modest but comforting appeal of the place. New cutlery and crockery add lustre, too, and the repertoire now includes two multi-course menus, one catering for vegetarians, along with an increased selection of French farm cheeses. What hasn't changed are the glowing reports with consistent applause for the very high quality food and polished service. While the cooking can appear conventional, Morgan Meunier's distinctive flair elevates it to a high standard. First to arrive at inspection, for example, was a 'delightful' amuse bouche of beetroot soup with Roquefort foam. Next, a ravioli of Burgundian snails in Chablis, served with poached garlic, followed by a main course of grilled Anjou squab pigeon, parsnip purée and braised pear, then a pre-dessert of rice pudding wrapped in orange tuile with a strawberry sorbet and raspberry coulis. But the highlight of the meal was the 'superb' warm strawberry tarte with fresh basil and olive oil ice cream, which had to be ordered at the start of the meal. The Francocentric wine list has also been improved, with some fine older vintages, and starts at the foothills of £15 and climbs to a pinnacle of £1,200 for a Château Pétrus 1983.
**Chef/s:** Morgan Meunier and Sylvain Soulard. **Open:** Wed to Fri and Sun L 12 to 2.15pm, Tue to Sat D 7 to 10.30pm. **Closed:** 24 to 30 Dec. **Meals:** Set L £23.50 (3 courses), Set D £34, Tasting menu £43.
**Service:** 12.5% (included). **Details:** Cards accepted. 48 seats. Air-con. No mobile phones. Wheelchair access. Music. Children's portions.

# Ottolenghi

**Bold fresh flavours**
287 Upper Street, N1 2TZ
Tel no: (020) 7288 1454
www.ottolenghi.co.uk
⊖ Angel, Highbury & Islington
Global | £23
Cooking score: 3
V £30

Queues often stretch out of this inventive café/ deli at weekends, but this isn't a chore – it's an opportunity to eye up the fresh salads, breads and cakes on display in the shop (takeaway if you don't fancy the wait). The minimalist dining area at the back takes in two long refectory tables with tight-packed chairs as well as cramped tables for two. Not a place for a lingering meal, then, but the food aims high nevertheless with the cooking taking inspiration from all over. Inspection was in time for a breakfast dish (served until 1pm) of perfect poached eggs and spinach, homemade muffin and blood orange mayo, while rare roast beef with mixed herbs and mustard yoghurt sauce, from the lunch menu, came with two highly imaginative salads noted for 'big, bold, fresh flavours', the pick being roasted aubergine with chilli garlic yoghurt, pistachios, preserved lemon and parsley. There's more ambition at dinner with dishes served starter-size – three per person is recommended – and quail baked on cedar wood with pomelo and coriander salad and tamarind relish is a typical choice. Desserts from a selection on display have included an intensely rich chocolate fondant cake. The breads are first class, and service is swift and efficient. The short wine list opens at £13.50.
**Chef/s:** Tricia Jadoonanan and Ramael Scully. **Open:** Mon to Sat 12 to 10.00, Sun 9 to 7. **Closed:** 25, 26 Dec, 1 Jan. **Meals:** alc D (main courses £6.00 to £9.50). Set L £8.50 to £13.50. **Service:** not inc. **Details:** Cards accepted. 45 seats. 5 seats outside. Air-con. Wheelchair access. Music. Children allowed.

## ★NEW ENTRY★

# Rooburoo

**Inventive, all-day modern Indian**
21 Chapel Market, N1 9EZ
Tel no: (020) 7278 8100
www.rooburoo.com
⊖ Angel
Indian/Pakistani/Bangladeshi | £15
Cooking score: 3
£5 OFF  V  £30

Down-at-heel Chapel Market is an unlikely setting for this restaurant, given the pie'n'mash or greasy spoon offerings nearby. The clean, cream walls and wooden tables set the scene for some of the freshest home style Indian cooking a Brick-Lane-weary London has seen for a long time. The conservatively priced menu takes inspiration from across the sub continent, hamming up the Indian love affair for an all-day snacking culture. Choose from small dishes such as flavoursome gram flour pancakes with chicken for a purse-friendly £2.75. Main courses for under £10 are chosen from the comically named 'rooburoast' or 'rooby murray' sections. Fresh tuna bhuna was flawless, perfumed with ginger and garam masala and finished with crunchy green beans. Other dishes include monk fish tikka or lamb chops with lemon juice and herbs. Desserts include gajjar halwa (Indian carrot cake) or sweet baked Indian yoghurt. Background music flits between modern tabla and Bollywood style drum and bass, while service is snappy but falls on the right side of casual. A cursory wine list features just four red and four white starting at £11.95.
**Chef/s:** Michael Tarat. **Open:** all week 12pm to 11pm (D 6pm to 11pm Mon). **Closed:** n/a. **Meals:** alc (main courses £5.75 to £9.95). **Service:** 12.5% optional. **Details:** Cards accepted. 60 seats. 8 seats outside. Air-con. Wheelchair access. Music. Children's portions.

## ALSO RECOMMENDED
## ▲ The Albion
10 Thornhill Road, Islington, N1 1HW
Tel no: (020) 7607 7450
www.the-albion.co.uk
⊖ Angel

Given the location of this pub, it's a wonder that it wasn't revamped years ago. A tattered old-man's boozer has been transformed into an elegant series of dining rooms, with a sophisticated garden that can seat over 100 Islingtonites at a time. Another Mark Hix-influenced menu offers a selection of well-executed dishes, such as broad bean and smoked ham-knuckle soup at £6; mains include roast mackerel with a gooseberry and fennel compote, and slow-roast Gloucester Old Spot with herb mash, both at £11. A sense of humour prevails, as news reaches us that diners in the garden were presented with sombreros on a particularly sunny Sunday afternoon. However, the party atmosphere means that weekends are best avoided if you have a tendency towards the quiet life. House wines start at £12.95. Reader reports please.

## READERS RECOMMEND
## Afghan Kitchen
Afghani
35 Islington Green, Islington, N1 8DU
Tel no: (020) 7359 8019
'Memorable food in stark surroundings'

## Elk in the Woods
Scandinavian
39 Camden Passage, Islington, N1 8EA
Tel no: (020) 7226 3535
www.the-elk-in-the-woods.co.uk
'Quirky eaterie with a nod to Nordic cuisine'

## ■ King's Cross

★NEW ENTRY★
## Acorn House
Eco-evangelists with a missionary zeal
69 Swinton Street, WC1X 9NT
Tel no: 020 7812 1842
www.acornhouserestaurant.com
⊖ Kings Cross
Modern British | £32
Cooking score: 2

Acorn House is the eco-friendly creation of ex-Fifteen chef Arthur Potts Dawson and manager James Grainger-Smith. The restaurant sits on a corner plot on a busy junction in the lower reaches of Kings Cross, an area in the throws of transformation, due to the impending arrival of Eurostar. The design is utilitarian and contemporary, with lime-green chairs, neat dark wooden tables and wooden banquettes (which can get uncomfortable after a while). The menu is well-formed, divided into soups, salads, cured meats, pastas and main courses. Our inspection comprised of earthy dishes such as Jerusalem artichoke and chestnut soup, along with a main course of roast shoulder of mutton with mint and quince. However, a venison taglietelle dish was fairly sloppy, causing one reader to raise an eyebrow towards the training kitchen. A poached rhubarb and custard dessert with sable stars was similarly disappointing. However, it is fair to say that Acorn House may well prove to be a seminal venture in the world of catering; an early adopter of standards that will undoubtedly become the norm. The concept is as sustainable as the restaurant's intentions, but the relentless brow-beating about the ethics of the operation can become a little wearing.

(Packet of seeds for you, sir? Biofuel cab, madam?). A tidy wine list includes some English offerings, with prices starting at £13. **Chef/s:** Arthur Potts Dawson. **Open:** B 8 to 11; L 12 to 3; D 6 to 10.30. **Meals:** Main courses, £12.50 to £18.50. **Service:** 12.5%. **Details:** Cards accepted. 50 seats. Wheelchair access. Music. Children allowed.

★NEW ENTRY★
## Konstam at the Prince Albert
**Seasonal food sourced within the M25**
2 Acton Street, WC1X 9NA
Tel no: (020) 7833 5040
www.konstam.co.uk
⊖ King's Cross
**Modern British | £26**
**Cooking score: 3**
£30

Starting in the inauspicious surroundings of King's Cross, Oliver Rowe, chef-patron of Konstam, had a mission. Not only did he elevate the humblest of eateries, the café, into a place where imaginative food could be bought at a reasonable price, but he sourced ingredients from local producers too. This quest and preparations for the ambitious Konstam at the Prince Albert were chronicled in *The Urban Chef*, the BBC2 documentary that made Rowe's name. The remarkable transformation of the Prince Albert is only apparent to diners once through the doors. It is now one of the most original dining rooms around. The menu is also a definite cut above; essentially Anglo-French, it is at turns both traditional and playful. Classic pork rillettes might come with pickled cauliflower and herb salad (£5.50). Mains generally include a choice of fish (the grilled Mersea brill with tarragon salad was excellent on a recent visit) and game. Puddings have a distinctly British feel, with gooseberries and Earl Grey tea featuring. A compact, well-chosen wine list includes English choices as well as continental offerings, is strong on dessert wines and complimented by a selection of beers and a wonderful cider. Konstam at the Prince Albert could be dismissed as modish, but that would

be unfair. The quality of the ingredients, subtle invention of the menu, good-natured service and solidity of the cooking set this establishment apart and make it somewhere to seek out. House wines start at £14. **Chef/s:** Oliver Rowe. **Open:** L Mon to Fri, 12.30 to 3; D Mon to Sat, 6.30 to 10.30. **Closed:** Christmas and New Year. **Meals:** Main courses, £12 to £16. **Service:** Optional. **Details:** Cards accepted. 50 seats. No music. Wheelchair access. Children allowed.

## READERS RECOMMEND
## Camino
**Spanish/Portuguese**
3 Varnishers Yard, King's Cross, N1 9FD
Tel no: (020) 7841 7331
www.barcamino.com
'Spanish influence in a converted warehouse'

## ▌Primrose Hill

★NEW ENTRY★
## Odette's
**Rejuvenated stalwart**
130 Regents Park Rd, NW1 8XL
Tel no: (020) 7586 8569
www.odettesprimrosehill.com
⊖ Chalk Farm
**Modern European | £40**
**Cooking score: 5**
🍸 ✔

When the denizens of Primrose Hill heard Bryn Williams was the new chef at their beloved Odette's, they breathed a sigh of relief. The determined young Welshman shot to fame on the *Great British Menu* last year, when he punched above his weight and won the fish course for the Queen's 80th birthday banquet. At Odette's, he showcases the accomplished cooking skills that led to the breakthrough in his career – 'it's a dining experience not to be missed'. The décor is classic with modern undertones. White tablecloths, white painted brick and bright yellow chairs clash loudly with brown patterned wallpaper and blue carpet. But what the 'bijou' dining room lacks in harmony, the food makes up for in taste and presentation: delicate pan-fried foie gras 'rich and soft', perfectly paired with the earthy flavours of beetroot, for example, and seared blue fin tuna with a smear of avocado purée and fresh radish and apple salad. Mains include a roasted wild sea trout with a pea and mint purée, and braised shoulder of Elwy Valley lamb with pine nuts and courgette, while Valhrona chocolate fondant with milk ice cream for dessert, was pronounced 'exquisite' at inspection. Service is highly polished. The wine is a Francophile's dream, starting with house wines at £23.

**Chef/s:** Bryn Williams. **Open:** Tues to Sun 12 to 2.30 (Sun to 3), Tues to Sat 6.30 to 10.30. **Meals:** Set L £14.50 (2 courses), 17.95 (3 courses) Set D £35 (2 courses) to £40 (3 courses). **Service:** 12.5% (optional). **Details:** Cards accepted. 65 seats. 12 seats outside. Air-con. Separate bar. Wheelchair access. Music. Children allowed.

## ALSO RECOMMENDED

### ▲ Manna

4 Erskine Road, Primrose Hill, NW3 3AJ
Tel no: (020) 7722 8028
⊖ Chalk Farm

Heaven-sent to north London's vegan and vegetarian constituency, Manna, founded in the 1960s, describes itself as 'Britain's first vegetarian restaurant'. Its menu draws flavours from around the world, say Moroccan briouat (spiced filo triangles filled with kasha, porcini and tempeh served with salsa verde, £6.95) to start, followed by aubergine ganmodoki tempura (aubergine stuffed with tofu pâté in tempura batter with cashew rice, £12.25), topped off with a lemon meringue tower (£7.25) for dessert. Much of the food is organic and the menu also accommodates those with a gluten allergy. The French house wine is £10.50. Open daily.

## READERS RECOMMEND

### Oslo Court

**Modern European**
Prince Albert Road, St John's Wood, NW8 7EN
Tel no: (020) 7722 8795
**'Long-standing local favourite'**

## ■ Stoke Newington

### Rasa

**Keralan restaurant curries favour with veggies**
55 Stoke Newington Church Street, N16 0AR
Tel no: (020) 7249 0344
www.rasarestaurants.com
⊖ Finsbury Park
Keralan | £24
**Cooking score: 2**
V £30

This is the original vegetarian Keralan restaurant in the Rasa chain. The staff are all Keralan, exuding enthusiasm and charm, always ready to describe a dish in heartfelt detail as if they'd watched their mothers making it. 'The Kerala Feast' (£16 per person) allows the chef to present a well-balanced selection, starting with the unmissable crunchy fried nibbles served with six different fresh chutneys including sweet garlic spiked with fenugreek. An array of vibrant curries will follow, such as mango and plantains in gently spiced yoghurt, savoy cabbage thoran with freshly grated coconut, plus tamarind rice and fresh parathas. An 'auspicious rice pudding' is a delicately perfumed finale. Despite the fresh, light nature of the dishes, the sheer tastiness of it all makes it easy to overeat, so you are advised to order judiciously. House wine is £11.95. Other branches are based in Bond Street, Fitzrovia, Euston, King's Cross and Newcastle.

**Chef/s:** Rajan Karattil. **Open:** Sat and Sun L 12 to 3, all week D 6 to 10.45 (11.45 Fri and Sat). **Closed:** 24 to 26 Dec, 1 Jan. **Meals:** alc (main courses £3.50 to £5.95). Set L and D £16. **Service:** 12.5% (optional). **Details:** Cards accepted. 64 seats. Air-con. Wheelchair access. Music.

## ALSO RECOMMENDED
## ▲ Istanbul Iskembecisi

9 Stoke Newington Road, Stoke Newington,
N16 8BH
Tel no: (020) 7254 7291
www.istanbuliskembecisi.com

For Turkish food in informal surroundings, this family-run restaurant is worth considering. The menu is immediately appealing, confidently combining staple dishes of the generic Middle Eastern restaurant with more unusual Anatolian fare. Hot and cold mezzes range from hummus (£3) to Albanian-style liver with onions (£3.50). Main dishes such as baked diced lamb on white sauce and aubergine purée (£8.50) are to be had alongside stews, fish and plenty of vegetarian options (£8 to £11). House wine is £10. Open daily.

## ▌Swiss Cottage
## Bradleys

Anglo-French menu in North London
25 Winchester Road, NW3 3NR
Tel no: (020) 7722 3457
⊖ Swiss Cottage
French | £33
Cooking score: 3
£5 OFF ⎍

Handy for the cultural buzz generated by Hampstead Theatre, Bradley's is a fine neighbourhood restaurant. Stepping up to the mark for the Swiss Cottage set, it deals in straightforward Anglo-French cooking with an appreciable degree of polish. Crab ravioli with broad beans, spinach and a tomato and saffron sauce was a typical spring starter, and sat alongside a wealth of other seafood options, such as red mullet niçoise, fried scallops or Rossmore oysters. Main courses haul in fish from the Cornish day-boats, together with well-judged meat dishes like Barbary duck breast with turnip gratin, or Dales lamb with boulangère potatoes and creamed flageolets. A cornucopia of ice creams and sorbets pours forth to garnish desserts such as hot lemon and raspberry soufflé with raspberry ripple ice cream, or passion-fruit bavarois with fresh pineapple and a coconut sorbet. The wine list is a model of what a small restaurant can achieve when it puts its mind to it. Arranged by style, concisely annotated, and packed with great producers, it genuinely tries to offer something for everyone. Wine per glass starts at £3.50, bottles at £13.
Chef/s: Simon Bradley. Open: Tue to Sun L 12 to 3, Tue to Sat D 6 to 11. Closed: Christmas, bank hols. Meals: alc £12.00 to £17.95 (main courses). Set L Tue to Sat £10.95 (2 courses) to £14.95. Service: 12.5% (optional). Details: Cards accepted. 60 seats. Air-con. No mobile phones. Wheelchair access. Music. Children's portions.

## Singapore Garden

Far-East flavour in Swiss Cottage
83-83A Fairfax Road, NW6 4DY
Tel no: (020) 7328 5314
⊖ Swiss Cottage
Fusion/Pan-Asian | £30
Cooking score: 2
Ỵ

Stylish floor-to-ceiling glass and tables laid with pristine white cloths and fresh roses lend an elegant, contemporary feel to this Swiss Cottage dining room. It is a popular spot for families at weekends, drawn by the friendly service and authentic Singaporean cooking. Familiar favourites include starters of charcoal-grilled satay beef, or chicken in filo pastry 'money bags' with a chilli dip. The rest of the long-ish menu is divided into sections, such as fish and seafood – where you'll find claypot prawns and scallops with glass noodles, or pan-fried mackerel in spicy sambal sauce – while chicken, duck and pork dishes stretch to braised pig's trotters infused with five-spice, and a page of Singapore and Malaysian specialities features squid in prawn chilli paste with crunchy sugar snap peas. Finish perhaps with soya beancurd with palm sugar. House selections from £15 open an uncomplicated wine list.

Chef/s: Mr Kok Sum Toh. Open: Mon to Sat 12 to 3, 6 to 11, Sun 12 to 11. Closed: 4 days Christmas. Meals: alc (main courses £7.50 to £20). Set D £23.50 to £38.50 (all min 2 or more). Service: 12.5% (optional). Details: Cards accepted. 85 seats. Air-con. Music.

## ▌Willesden
### Sushi-Say
Unpretentious sushi house
33B Walm Lane, NW2 5SH
Tel no: (020) 8459 2971
⊖ Willesden Green
Japanese | £31
Cooking score: 3

Katsuhara Shimizu's likeable Japanese eating house fizzes with enthusiasm since the dining room has been remodeled. Natural colours blend with modern clean lines, counter seating and tables are simply laid and there's an appealing warm ambience. Eating options on a long, user–friendly menu range widely from sushi and sashimi to combinations of vegetables, meat or fish, which may be fried, boiled, grilled or served in soup. Plenty of set meals for one person at lunch and dinner make ordering easy (teriyaki, sushi and sashimi lunches, for example, all come with rice, pickles and miso soup). Familiar appetizers, from edamame beans to gyoza dumplings (filled with minced pork and vegetables) start the ball rolling, and grilled black cod with salt is a fine main course. Meals end simply with fresh fruit or ice cream – which can include wasabi and red bean flavours. House wine is £12, otherwise choose from a comprehensive list of cold sake 'the best fit for Japanese food' or hot sake for traditionalists, alongside beer and tea.

Chef/s: Katsuharu Shimizu. Open: Tue to Fri L 12 to 2.15, Sat and Sun L 1 to 3.15, Tue to Fri D 6.30 to 10.30, Sat D 6 to 11, Sun D 6 to 10. Closed: 25 and 26 Dec, 1 Jan, mid-Jan to mid-Feb. Meals: alc (main courses £8 to £20.50). Set L £8.80 to £13.50 (all 1 or 2 courses), Set D £19.50 to £30.30. Service: not inc. Details: Cards accepted. 40 seats. Air-con. No music. Wheelchair access.

Allegra McEvedy

**Why did you become a chef?**
I went into it because I was attracted by the food, excitement and creativity.

**Which of today's chefs do you admire?**
I admire nearly every chef out there, out of respect for the sheer graft it takes to succeed in our business.

**Where do you source your ingredients?**
At Leon we put a lot of time and resources into our suppliers; all our meat is free-range and British, all our fish is sustainable.

**Who is your favourite producer?**
Lloyd Maunder – our chicken people in Devon.

**What's the best dish you've ever eaten?**
Nova Scotia lobster poached in butter at Thomas Keller's restaurant in NYC.

**What's your guilty food pleasure?**
Haribo Tangfastics – the sour mix!

**What's the hardest thing about running a restaurant?**
Keeping on top of the training. The team are everything: the more love you give them, the better and happier they are.

**Which achievement are you most proud of?**
Not having spent any time in jail. Or when my Colour Cookbook won International Chef's and Restaurants' Book of the Year.

# ▌Barbican

## Searcy's
**A fitting pit-stop for arts lovers**
Level 2, Barbican Centre, Silk Street, EC2Y 8DS
Tel no: (020) 7588 3008
www.barbican.org.uk
⊖ Barbican, Moorgate
British | £30
Cooking score: 2
£5 OFF ¥

Situated on the second level of the Barbican Centre, Searcy's affords good views of this historic part of London, perhaps best enjoyed on a summer evening before taking in a play. Jane Collins offers a pre- and post-theatre menu, as well as the main carte, and it's all up-to-the-minute cooking that piles on the style. Stone bass accompanied by Jerusalem artichoke, fennel and broad beans is a typically robust main course, while meat eaters might be drawn to rosemaried Welsh lamb with spring greens, onion purée and sweetbread croquettes. Precede these dishes with salt cod ravioli, or a plate of Italian cured meats with pickles and truffled pecorino and, if time permits, conclude proceedings with ricotta and ginger tart, served with figs and 'honey crunch'. The single-page wine list offers a good mixture, with prices from £16.60, or £4.25 a glass.
**Chef/s:** Jane Collins. **Open:** Mon to Fri L 12 to 2.30, Mon to Sat D 5 to 10.30. **Closed:** 24 to 26 Dec, Easter. **Meals:** alc (main courses £14.50 to £24.50). Set D £24.50 (2 courses) to £28.50. **Service:** 12.5% (optional). **Details:** Cards accepted. 89 seats. Wheelchair access. Music. Children's portions.

### Please send us your feedback

To register your opinion about any restaurant listed in the Guide, or a new restaurant that you wish to bring to our attention, please visit the web address at the bottom of the page. Your feedback informs the content of the book and will be used to compile next year's reviews.

# ▌Bethnal Green

## Green & Red
**Welcoming and chilled-out atmosphere**
51 Bethnal Green Road, E1 6LA
Tel no: (020) 7749 9670
www.greenred.co.uk
⊖ Liverpool Street
Mexican | £25
Cooking score: 3
¥ £30

Green and Red is inspired by the cantinas and regional specialties of Jalisco – the home of tequila so you know what to drink. It's an easygoing place. Starters such as chorizo con papas, with shallots, potatoes and coriander are served in traditional eathernware pots, while mains might include the popular carne asada (chargrilled, aged ribeye with chipotle salsa and spring onions) or slow-roasted pork belly and ribs with pasilla chilli and orange salt. Watermelon served with crushed piquin chilli and lime is a refreshing way to finish, but churros served with a thick spiced hot chocolate dipping sauce are recommended, too. Young staff are friendly, passionate and knowledgeable about the food and drinks. South American wines start at £12.50 and there's a great range of cocktails.
**Chef/s:** Alberto Figueroa. **Open:** Sat and Sun L 12 to 5, all week D 6 to 11. **Closed:** 25 to 30 Dec. **Meals:** alc (main courses L £4.50 to £6.50, D £9.50 to £14.50). Bar menu available. **Service:** 12.5% (optional). **Details:** Cards accepted. 65 seats. 15 seats outside. Air-con. Wheelchair access. Music.

## Les Trois Garçons
**High-end dining in camp surrounds**
56 Redchurch Street, E2 7DP
Tel no: (020) 7012 1234
www.lestroisgarcons.com
⊖ Liverpool Street
French | £35
Cooking score: 3

Set in a drab and down-at-heel part of town Les Trois Garçons positively shrieks its high-end credentials, with alluring torches

flickering over its entrance and, inside, an outrageously camp décor of stuffed pitbulls decked out in fairy wings and giraffes swathed in jewels. Among such outlandish surrounds, you might fear garish offerings on the menu, but happily the kitchen has resisted the obvious temptation. Start with a 'tremendously smooth and richly flavoured' sweet potato and ginger velouté served with just the right amount of gnocchi and poured at the table 'with a delicate flourish'. For mains, try wild Scottish lobster on squid ink linguini with celeriac purée and lobster foam, while the 'wonderfully rich' dessert trio of chocolate opera, Marquise and Valhrona chocolate profiterole with vanilla ice cream is strongly recommended. Whispers of snooty staff seem unkind; at inspection service was charming and slick, if perhaps just a little too efficient during the first early evening weekend sitting. The wine list is predominantly French and prices are stiff, starting at £19.
**Chef/s:** Jerome Henry, Yuka Aoyama & Erol Defoe. **Open:** all week D 7-9.30. **Closed:** Christmas, bank hols. **Meals:** alc (main courses £17.50-£34.00) Set D £24 (2 courses) £28 (3 courses). **Service:** 12.5% (optional). **Details:** Cards accepted. 180 seats. Air-con. Music. Children allowed.

## ▌Canary Wharf

### Gun
**A gastropub loaded with French method**
27 Coldharbour, E14 9NS
Tel no: (020) 7515 5222
www.thegundocklands.com
Gastropub | £35
Cooking score: 3

Smack beside the Thames in the heart of the Docklands, a stone's throw from Canary Wharf, the Gun is a rejuvenated eighteenth-century dockers' pub with cracking views from it smart decked terrace across the Thames to the Millennium Dome. Tom and Ed Martin, who also own the White Swan and Empress of India (see entries), have painstakingly restored this once burnt-out boozer to make a classy drinking and dining venue. There's a splendid traditional bar with

reclaimed oak floors, a smattering of maritime artefacts and a dining area with white-clad tables, as well as a couple of snugs and private dining rooms. Versatile menus combine modern British pub food with French brasserie cooking, say, pea and mint soup or seared scallops with pancetta, polenta with black olive sauce, and pan-fried gilt head bream with oxtail ravioli or lamb rump with white bean purée and morel jus. The list of desserts may take in warm chocolate fondant with camomile tea ice cream. The wine list, arranged stylistically, is comprehensive but pricey, although Spanish wines kick off at £13.
**Chef/s:** Scott Wade. **Open:** Mon to Fri 12 to 3, 6 to 10.30, Sat and Sun 10.30 to 4.30, 6 to 10.30 (9.30 Sun). **Closed:** 26 Dec. **Meals:** alc (main courses £11 to £21). Bar menu available. **Service:** 12.5% (optional). **Details:** Cards accepted. 85 seats. Air-con. Wheelchair access. Music. Children's portions.

### Plateau
**The place to dock for good French food**
Canada Place, Canary Wharf, E14 5ER
Tel no: (020) 7715 7100
www.conran.com/eat
⊖ Canary Wharf
French | £43
Cooking score: 3
ᐯ

In the heart of Canary Wharf, on the fourth-floor of a striking steel and glass building with stunning views over Canada Square, this stylish and informal restaurant draws the suits for accomplished modern French cooking. The two contemporary dining areas are separated by a semi-open kitchen, there are floor-to-ceiling windows, and immaculately laid marble-topped tables. The seasonally changing menu may kick off with black truffle gnocchi with white pepper sauce, goat's cheese fondue with baby beetroot, or a plate of Falmouth Bat native oysters. Mains favour fish from Billingsgate, perhaps spice-crusted cod with curried artichoke and tamarind sauce or line caught sea bass à la plancha with mushroom broth. Carnivores are not forgotten, there may be roast pheasant with

braised red cabbage and wild rice, or beef fillet the celeriac and pear purée and remoulade. Puddings have included roasted fig with mulled wine jelly and ginger ice cream. Expect a simpler menu in the Bar & Grill and summer barbeques on the terrace. The well-constructed wine list opens at £21
**Chef/s:** Tim Tolley. **Open:** Mon to Fri L 12 to 3, Mon to Sat D 6 to 10.30. **Closed:** Christmas, Easter, bank hols. **Meals:** alc (main courses £17 to £27.50). Set D £24.75 to £48. Bar and Grill menus available. **Service:** 12.5% (optional). **Details:** Cards accepted. 124 seats. Air-con. No music. Wheelchair access.

## Ubon by Nobu
**High-impact Japanese cuisine**
34 Westferry Circus, E14 8RR
Tel no: (020) 7719 7800
www.noburestaurants.com
⊖ Canary Wharf
**Japanese | £48**
**Cooking score: 5**
Ⴗ

Ring the bell at the iron gates, journey through the landscaped gardens of the Four Seasons Hotel, then take the lift to the fourth floor. It is a tortuous trek but, once inside the über-cool dining room, all is dramatically revealed. Like its siblings, Nobu at Hyde Park Corner and Nobu Berkeley St (see entries), this is a restaurant fuelled by celebrity glamour. As with its near namesakes, the food is a curious symbiosis of Japanese cuisine old and new with some South American influences. Many dishes are common to all three establishments – the yellowtail sashimi with jalapeño and ponzu sauce, the much-vaunted black cod in sticky sweet miso, the toro tartar with caviar, and more besides. Raw fish is of dazzling freshness, whether it is high-art sushi or more modern inventions like 'new style' tofu and tomato sashimi. Cooked dishes set out to dazzle the senses and presentation is eye-poppingly sharp: there is beauty to behold in everything from the oysters in filo with five sauces to lobster salad with spicy lemon dressing. Various forms of ceviche and Anti-Cucho Peruvian-style grills represent

the Latin American constituency, while the specials list extends to asparagus with egg sauce and salmon roe, sea urchin tempura and even Dover sole with black bean sauce. Wagyu beef is sold in 50 gram portions. Desserts aim for full-on sensual impact, as in apricot and jasmine soup with peanut crumble and Nobu beer ice cream. Speciality sakes and champagnes claim pole position on the exclusive wine list, which promises quality at a price: bottles start at £27, selections by the glass from £7.
**Chef/s:** Mark Edwards. **Open:** Mon to Fri L 12 to 2, Mon to Sat D 6 to 10. **Closed:** bank hols. **Meals:** alc (main courses £5.50 to £29.50). Set L £45 to £55, Set D £70 to £90. **Service:** 15% (optional). **Details:** Cards accepted. 120 seats. Air-con. Wheelchair access. Music. Car parking.

# ▌City

## Bonds
**Light-handed contemporary cooking**
Threadneedle Hotel, 5 Threadneedle Street, EC2R 8AY
Tel no: (020) 7657 8088
www.theetoncollection.com
⊖ Bank
**Modern European | £45**
**Cooking score: 6**
£5 OFF ♦ ⊨ Ⴗ

Formerly the HQ of Citibank, the Threadneedle Hotel is another of those lordly, moneyed transformations much favoured by savvy developers in the Square Mile. Bonds occupies the old banking hall, an imposing high-ceilinged room with plushness and gravitas aplenty, but some light relief provided by contemporary murals and vases of greenery. The refined setting is perfectly in tune with Barry Tonks's modern French and European-biased menus, which might open with Dorset Bay crab, pea and pistachio bavarois with pink grapefruit jelly or chicken liver and foie gras parfait with quince purée and pain d'epice mousse. Main courses suggest that the kitchen is eager to cast its net wide for top-drawer ingredients: Label Rouge 'poulet fermier' is roasted and served with wild garlic

leaves, gnocchi, morel and Madeira juice, lamb comes from the Elwey Valley and fillet of line-caught sea bass could be accompanied by borlotti bean and basil minestrone; also look for the slow-cooked Baillet mountain pork with spring vegetables. After that, consider sharing a textbook tarte Tatin with Calvados crème fraîche or investigate the exotic possibilities of coconut rice pudding with Alphonso mango and sesame seed 'dentelle'. France and the rest of Europe are at the forefront of the heavyweight wine list, which brings together a classy assortment of oenophilic tipples, big-name superstar labels and tantalising options to match the food. Prices are in keeping with the location, although the page of house selections (from £5.75 a glass) should prevent the bill from spiralling skywards.
**Chef/s:** Barry Tonks. **Open:** All week B 6:30am to 10:30am. Mon to Fri L 12pm to 2.30pm, D 6pm to 10pm. **Closed:** 24 Dec to 3 Jan, bank hols. **Meals:** alc (main courses £15 to £22). Set L £14.50 (2 courses) to £19.50. Bar menu available all week. **Service:** 12.5% (optional). **Details:** Cards accepted. 80 seats. Air-con. Wheelchair access. Music.

## Club Gascon

**Perfect showcase for southern-French cooking**
57 West Smithfield, EC1A 9DS
Tel no: (020) 7796 0600
www.clubgascon.com
⊖ Barbican, Farringdon
French | £48
Cooking score: 6
🍷

For ten years Club Gasgon has stood beside St Bartholomew's Priory Church in Smithfield Square, yet Pascal Aussignac's cooking still feels as original and exciting as it did when it first opened. The dining room exudes conviviality, exotic flower displays enliven the marble walls and close-together tables, and service is 'charming and sure-footed'. Aussignac's grazing menu has strong roots in southwest France (from where many of the high class ingredients are sourced), and is divided into sections such as 'la route du sel' or

'les paturages' and so on, with centre stage reserved for items based on foie gras. Even those with high expectations find them fulfilled by the innovative style: superbly balanced morels and broad bean 'ragout' paired unusually with aromatic rice crispies, a pressed duck foie gras with king crab and hot tomato – 'a clever marriage of contrasting flavours and textures' – a thought-provoking glazed black cod served with verijuice, crunchy grapes and pomegranate. Timing is good, textures carefully considered and there is an appealing simplicity to much of the cooking, including, at inspection, a Charolais beef fillet with creamy morels. Among desserts a marinated rhubarb, partnered with an exceptional champagne sorbet and rose Chantilly has proved a perfect finish. The wine list, extending over 25 pages, starts from £18 (£5 per glass), and provides a roll call of the best makers from south-west France. Champagne and Bordeaux do feature but this is a place to sample wines from Irouleguy, Cahors, Madiran, Languedoc, Roussillon and Provence.
**Chef/s:** Pascal Aussignac. **Open:** Mon to Fri L 12 to 2, Mon to Sat D 7 to 10.30. **Closed:** 22 Dec to 8 Jan, bank hols. **Meals:** alc (main courses £5 to £55). Set L £35 to £42, Set D £42. **Service:** 12.5% (optional). **Details:** Cards accepted. 45 seats. Air-con. Wheelchair access. Music.

## Le Coq d'Argent

**Rooftop dining in the City**
No. 1 Poultry, EC2R 8EJ
Tel no: (020) 7395 5000
www.coqdargent.co.uk
⊖ Bank
Modern European | £47
Cooking score: 1

Two express lifts whisk diners from street level to this rooftop restaurant where there's a wow factor about the setting and the option of alfresco eating in fine weather increases the attraction. The predominance of wood, stone, steel and glass gives a masculine city edge, softened only by the roof terrace greenery. At inspection, a dish of thyme roasted stone bass fillet with white bean casserole and caper dressing demonstrated that the kitchen knows how to treat fish, while six roast salt marsh lamb cutlets (served with creamed ratatouille pesto, black olives and rosemary jus) were 'tender, tasty and served perfectly pink'. Highlight, though, was a warm bitter chocolate fondant exposing a rich runny middle, and a classic tarte Tatin served with the 'smoothest' calvados ice-cream. The star attraction, however, is the good value and extensive wine list with something for all pockets; house wines start at £15.

**Chef/s:** Mickael Weiss. **Open:** Mon to Fri L 11.30 to 3.00, D 6 to 10. Sat D only 6 to 10. Sun L only 12 to 3. **Meals:** alc D (main courses £18.50 to £25). Set L and D £24.00 (2 courses) to £28.50 (3 courses). **Service:** 12.5% (optional). **Details:** Cards accepted. 150 seats. 56 seats outside. Air-con. Music.

## The Don
**Versatile and intelligent destination diner**
The Courtyard, 20 St Swithin's Lane, EC4N 8AD
Tel no: (020) 7626 2606
www.thedonrestaurant.co.uk
⊖ Bank
Modern European | £32
Cooking score: 2

🍷 V

Named after the Sandeman Port 'Don' whose cellars occupied the premises for over 170 years, this chic City restaurant is set in a courtyard, like its sister restaurant Bleeding Heart (see entry). The striking very twenty-first century dining room is the setting for some refined modern European cooking that makes sound use of luxury and more humble ingredients. The shortish carte may open with baked scallops with asparagus, tomato and lime sauce, go on to main courses of roast duck with confit leg and glazed root vegetables, and finish with tarte Tatin of pineapple and black pepper with rhubarb ice cream. The bistro has a separate menu promising more straightforward dishes. Wines are given star treatment here, with big names peppered throughout the 50-page list. There are also

plenty of more modest bottles, with eight house wines from the proprietor's own Trinity Hill wines (from £16.95).

**Chef/s:** Matt Burns. **Open:** Mon to Fri 12 to 2.30, 6.30 to 10. **Closed:** Christmas to New Year, bank hols. **Meals:** alc (main courses £13 to £24). **Service:** 12.5% (optional). **Details:** Cards accepted. 70 seats. Air-con. No music. Wheelchair access.

## The Fox Public House
**City gastropub open for week-day dining**
28 Paul Street, EC2A 4LB
Tel no: (020) 7729 5708
www.thefoxpublichouse.com
⊖ Old Street, Liverpool Street
Gastropub | £25
New Chef

£5 OFF  V  £30

As former chef at The Eagle – London's original gastropub – and author of two defining cookbooks on gastropub cooking, Australian Trish Hilferty knows a thing or two about the genre. The Fox, too, has won plaudits for its simple, rustic cooking that puts the emphasis on seasonality and provenance. Away from the boisterous bar, the upstairs dining room is surprisingly dark, its chandeliers, wax-splattered candelabras and gloomy wood interior oddly reminiscent of a nineteenth-century Gothic novel. The set menu keeps things simple with a choice of five or so starters and mains. Descriptions are straight to the point and avoid the need to scream their sourcing credentials: a starter of smoked mackerel with pickled beetroot was exactly that – a great tranche of meaty fish unapologetically unadorned. Roast onglet with terrific fat chips and pungent aïoli was gargantuan in size and packed a great big meaty punch. Desserts reinforce the simplicity of approach and might include buttermilk pudding with poached rhubarb. A good, varied wine list starts at £13.50, with around half available by the glass.

**Chef/s:** Araldo de Vitas. **Open:** Mon to Fri 12 to 3pm, 6.30 to 11pm. **Meals:** Set L and D £16.50 (2 courses) to £21.50. Bar L menu available.

**Service:** 12.5% (included). **Details:** Cards accepted. 35 seats. 25 seats outside. Separate bar. No music. Children allowed.

## Great Eastern Hotel, Aurora

Stylish dining spot
Liverpool Street, EC2M 7QN
Tel no: (020) 7618 7000
www.aurora-restaurant.co.uk
⊖ Liverpool Street
Modern European | £50
Cooking score: 2

🍸 ⊑ ∀

As a major league dining establishment in the financial heartland, it's not surprising that comfort levels are high. The striking dining room sits below a 'bewitching' glass dome and is augmented by stately columns, corniced ceiling and marble flooring. Dominic Teague (ex-L'Escargot) has taken up the reigns in the kitchen, but inspection found performance uneven, only sound technique 'rescuing the ordinary ingredients'. Roasted langoustine with a salad of pear, walnut and cabernet sauvignon vinaigrette, opened that meal, the highlight of which was Barbary duck served with pommes salardaise and girolles. The wine list continues to impress with dignified labels stretching to 800 bins from 18 countries. Prices starts from £21 (£5.50 for a glass), and although margins are lofty, good bottles can be found under £30, including 20 wines by the glass.
**Chef/s:** Dominic Teague. **Open:** Mon to Fri 12 to 2.30, 6.30 to 10. **Closed:** 22 Dec to 2 Jan, bank hols. **Meals:** alc (main courses £20 to £40). Set L £23.50 (2 courses) to £28, Set L 12 to 2 and D 6.45 to 9 £50 to £75 (inc wine). Bar menu available.
**Service:** 12.5% (optional). **Details:** Cards accepted. 85 seats. Air-con. Wheelchair access. Music.

## Refettorio at The Crowne Plaza Hotel

An Italian yardstick for the City
19 New Bridge Street, EC4V 6DB
Tel no: (020) 7438 8052
⊖ Blackfriars
Italian | £37
Cooking score: 2

⊑ ∀

The minimalist interior of this darkly stylish dining room is somewhat disarming given the no-holds barred approach to the cooking, which is firmly Italian. The kitchen knows its techniques. Star attractions are the convivium selections of cheeses and cold meats designed for shared eating and the fresh, homemade pasta. Fish and meat are cooked with precision and excellent timing, say a first course of ox tongue with honey potato bread, served with marinated button onions, and Ligurain style halibut with grass peas and mild vinegar dressing. Sweet ricotta cheesecake with candied fruits is a good way to finish. Champagne apart, wines are a cleverly succinct range of entirely Italian bottles. Considering its location, prices start fairly modestly – a decent range of by-the-glass is available, and bottles open at £15, but extravagant tastes are well looked after, with top-end Chianti and Piemontese Nebbioli.

### Cooking score

A score of 1 is a significant achievement. The score in any review is based on several meals, incorporating feedback from both our readers and inspectors. As a rough guide, 1 denotes capable cooking with some inconsistencies, rising steadily through different levels of technical expertise, until the scores between 6 and 10 indicate exemplary skills, along with innovation, artistry and ambition. If there is a new chef, we don't score the restaurant for the first year of entry. For further details, please see the scoring section in the introduction to the Guide.

Chef/s: Mattia Camorani. Open: Mon to Fri L 12 to 2.30, Mon to Sat D 6 to 10.30 (10 Fri and Sat). Closed: 24 Dec to 2 Jan, bank hols. Meals: alc (main courses £9 to £22). Service: 12.5% (optional). Details: Cards accepted. 100 seats. Air-con. No music. Wheelchair access.

# Rhodes Twenty Four
**Quality cooking and capital views**
Tower 42, 25 Old Broad Street, EC2N 1HQ
Tel no: (020) 7877 7703
www.rhodes24.co.uk
⊖ Liverpool Street
**Modern British | £41**
**Cooking score: 5**

Once the escalators, lifts, security passes and air-port style checkpoints have been negotiated, diners are relieved to find that the designer of the high-flying Rhodes 24 has sensibly decided not to compete with the stunning views over London. Apart from a 'minimum of obligatory modern art', there's nothing to detract from the view through curving windows. You might think Adam Gray had his work cut out to match the cooking to theses rarefied surroundings, but reporters remain convinced that his interpretation of Gary Rhodes' colloquial English-style is much more than just surface gloss. There is real invention, for one thing: successful dishes have included potted duck with foie gras terrine and burnt orange salad, buttered organic salmon with smoked bacon and oyster champ, and rack of lamb, mutton and spring vegetable casserole and garlic cream potatoes. While a finger is kept firmly on the pulse of today's taste for robust combinations, desserts are almost nostalgic, with steamed spotted dick with honey ice cream and warm custard, raspberry Bakewell tart with raspberry ripple ice cream, and bread and butter pudding among the repertoire of heritage puddings. The imaginative wine list opens at £18, but don't waste time sniffing for bargains, mark-ups reflect the City location.

Chef/s: Adam Gray. Open: Mon to Fri 12 to 2.30, 6 to 9. Closed: Christmas, bank hols. Meals: alc (main courses £17.50 to £25). Service: 12.5% (optional). Details: Cards accepted. 75 seats. Air-con. Wheelchair access. Music.

★NEW ENTRY★
# Saki Bar and Food Emporium
**Sublime sushi in a stylish setting**
4 West Smithfield, EC1A 9JX
Tel no: (020) 7489 7033
www.saki-food.com
⊖ Farringdon
**Japanese | £29**
**Cooking score: 3**
🍶 V £30

The Saki food complex is divided into deli, bar and restaurant. The smart and stylish restaurant is in the basement, the concept based on the Kaiseki idea of ordering a number of courses made up of small dishes with the menu divided into categories such as nimono (braised), mushimono (steamed) and oshokuji ('carb-up' dishes). It is a nice idea but 'putting a meal together becomes rather complex'. At inspection, a platter of assorted sushi was outstanding, and brought the likes of mackerel, scallop and sea bass nigiri. Other stand-out dishes included a wispy light lobster tempura, and kakuni, a meltingly tender braised pork dish. There's an impressive list of sake and wines, starting at the £15 mark, and you can also order wine and sake sets to match the 'pricey' tasting menus, which start at £40 for six courses. Service is well-meaning.
Chef/s: Hiroyuki Saotome. Open: Mon to Fri, L 12pm to 2.30pm, Mon to Sat D 6pm to 10.30pm. Closed: Sundays, main holidays (opens in line with Smithfield meat market). Meals: alc (main courses £6.20 to £18.50). Set D £40. Service: 12.5% discretionary service charge added. Details: Cards accepted. 100 seats. Air-con. Separate bar. Wheelchair access. Music. Children allowed.

## ALSO RECOMMENDED

### ▲ Mehek

45 London Wall, City, EC2M 5TE
Tel no: (020) 7588 5043

This upmarket Indian restaurant in the heart of the City aims to make an impact with lavishly theatrical décor. The kitchen similarly hopes to impress with a menu that is broad in scope, dipping into the different regions of the Subcontinent for inspiration. King prawn puri (£5.70) lines up alongside sheek kebab (£3.70) and malai chops (£5.90) among starters, while a wide choice of main courses encompass tandoor-cooked spiced squab (£12.90), tender, cinnamon-infused lamb shank (£12.50) as well as familiar curry-house favourites such as chicken korma (£7.90). Traditional Indian desserts to finish and house wines from £15.

### ▲ Moshi Moshi

Unit 24, Liverpool Street Station, Broadgate, City, EC2M 7QH
Tel no: (020) 7247 3227

The conveyor belt defines proceedings in this elite mini-chain of casual Japanese eating places. The original kaiten kitchen in the UK is still regarded as the best and the setting is unique – high above Liverpool Street's platforms with views of trains coming and going. Sit at the counter and take your pick from colour-coded plates (£1.20 to £3.50) as they pass by; choose from a range of sushi sets (nigiri sushi; 10.50, temaki; £8.40, sashimi; £13), or opt for a hot seasonal dish, say, salmon teriyaki (£9), or the tempura selection (£8.50). Sake is £6 a flask and house wine is £13.80. Closed Sat and Sun.

## ▌Clerkenwell

★NEW ENTRY★

### Ambassador

**Confident, competent cooking stands out**
55 Exmouth Market, EC1R 4QL
Tel no: 020 7837 0009
www.theambassadorcafe.co.uk
⊖ Angel
**Modern British | £26**
**Cooking score: 2**
V £30

The Ambassador has made a fine job of the open house concept. It's unpretentious, informal, welcoming – all the things that mark out neighbourhood success stories – with smart, well-executed dishes from the kitchen and equally smart service out front. The seasonal menu is both elegant and comforting: the freshness of sea bream ceviche is perfectly accented with a celery and cucumber purée and pickled cucumber, rabbit loin comes with Alsatian bacon and a fresh burst of early summer pea purée, and pork belly is rendered of fat but not of juicy tenderness, and brightened with the flavours of orange and lovage. An adult chocolate pudding with marmalade ice cream is refreshingly bitter. The good wine list is comprehensive and comprises an eclectic mixture of Old and New World (from £14.50), with a wide selection available in carafes (from £9) or by the glass.
**Chef/s:** Tobias Jilsmark. **Open:** Mon to Fri 9am to 11pm, Sat 11am to 11pm, Sun 11am to 4pm. **Closed:** 24 December to 2 January. **Meals:** alc (main courses £10 to £14). Set L £12.50 to £16. **Service:** Optional. **Details:** Cards accepted. 60 seats. 25 seats outside. Air-con. Separate bar. Wheelchair access. Music. Children's portions.

## Bleeding Heart

A favourite for Francophile diners
The Cellars, Bleeding Heart Yard, Greville Street,
EC1N 8SJ
Tel no: (020) 7242 8238
www.bleedingheart.co.uk
⊖ Farringdon
French | £32
New Chef

🍷 ✓

The address is so named after a seventeenth-century *belle dame* who was rather gruesomely dismembered here by one of her rejected lovers. There is an inn and an informal bistro in the vicinity now, with a smart, ambitious French restaurant in the basement. Here, Christophe Fabre took over in 2007, but maintains the tone set by his predecessor. The bilingual menus deal in salmon confit with black olive coulis and cherry tomatoes, or venison fillet with cabbage and bacon in bitter chocolate sauce. Not all is textbook French, as is attested by a starter that dresses seared tuna salad with rice wine, soy and ginger, but terrine of foie gras with homemade brioche will reorientate you, as will desserts such as hazelnut praline with raspberry coulis or tarte au citron. The proprietors own the Trinity Hill vineyard in Hawkes Bay, New Zealand, so the list isn't as Francocentric as you may be expecting. Indeed, its broad and generous compass makes for fine worldwide drinking. New Zealand prices start at £16.95, or £4.50 a glass, for the Trinity Hill Sauvignon.
**Chef/s:** Christophe Fabre. **Open:** Mon to Fri 12 to 2.30, 6 to 10.30. **Closed:** Dec 21 to Jan 2, Easter, bank hols. **Meals:** alc (main courses £12.45 to £22.95). **Service:** 12.5%. **Details:** Cards accepted. 150 seats. 30 seats outside. Air-con. Separate bar. No music.

## Clerkenwell Dining Room

Bank on culinary dexterity
69-73 St John Street, EC1M 4AN
Tel no: (020) 7253 9000
www.theclerkenwell.com
⊖ Farringdon
Modern British | £32
Cooking score: 3

£5 OFF ✓

Andrew Thompson's confident modern British cooking sets this quietly civilised restaurant apart from its nearby rivals in trendy Clerkenwell – despite its unpromising location on the ground floor of an office block. The modern, simply decorated dining room with parquet flooring and cream and blue colour scheme is an elegant and comfortable space, while the kitchen delivers gutsy, bold dishes that are big on flavour through good handling of great raw ingredients. Expect starters in the modern vein, perhaps oxtail ravioli with red wine jus, ballontine of foie gras with fig jam, Muscat jelly and toasted brioche, or squid with polenta and spicy tomato and pepper sauce. Well-constructed main courses extend to pork belly with scallops, celeriac purée and walnut salsa, or perhaps sea bream accompanied with steamed mussels and orange velouté. Finish with hot chocolate fondant with black forest ice cream, poached pear tart with blackberry sorbet, or a selection of British and French farmhouse cheeses. The well-chosen wine list favours Europe over the New World, with prices from £15.
**Chef/s:** Andrew Thompson and Daniel Groom. **Open:** Mon to Fri 12 to 3, Mon to Sat D 6 (7 Sat) to 11. **Closed:** 25 Dec, bank hols. **Meals:** alc (main courses £15 to £16). Set L Sun £14.50 (2 courses) to £19.50 (3 courses). **Service:** 12.5% (optional). **Details:** Cards accepted. 110 seats. Air-con. Wheelchair access. Music. Children's portions.

## Coach and Horses

British cooking in a no-nonsense setting
26-28 Ray Street, EC1R 3DJ
Tel no: (020) 7278 8990
www.thecoachandhorses.com
⊖ Farringdon
Gastropub | £30
Cooking score: 2

The Coach and Horses is a no-frills pub that's deservedly popular with locals. The separate dining room can feel somewhat spartan but is run by friendly and knowledgeable staff and the kitchen knows how to treat high quality British ingredients. The techniques and presentation on display are simple but effective. To start, there is smoked mackerel from Mersea Island with a light but potent horseradish cream and chicory, or a salad of beetroot with fresh goat's curd and peppery watercress. A crisp potato cake filled with blue cheese is served with a poached duck egg, and leg of rabbit is roasted with tarragon. The real treats are on the dessert menu: rhubarb queen of puddings 'stickily sweet', served with a 'spectacular' marmalade ice cream and thick wedges of toasted brioche. There's a basic but tempting bar menu and an interesting wine list. House wine is £12.50. **Chef/s:** Scott Walsh. **Open:** Sun to Fri L 12 to 3, Mon to Sat D 6 to 10. **Closed:** 24 Dec to 2 Jan, bank hols. **Meals:** alc (main courses £10 to £14.50). Bar menu available. **Service:** 12.5% (optional). **Details:** Cards accepted. 60 seats. Wheelchair access. Music.

## Comptoir Gascon

Gutsy French cooking
61-63 Charterhouse Street, EC1M 6HJ
Tel no: (020) 7608 0851
www.clubgascon.com
⊖ Farringdon, Barbican
French | £27
Cooking score: 4

Ⅴ

Pleasingly, Comptoir Gascon continues to be a beacon of *cuisine terrior* and the laid back ambience of this deli-cum-bistro has a sense of *la bonne vie* about it with helpful service full of Gallic charm. The cooking, hailing from southwest France, is as gutsy as the interior (think rough walls and simple wooden furniture) and hard to ignore on the menu is a plate of piggy treats, featuring various parts of the porker. Duck, too, is celebrated, appearing in various guises from Gascony pie to the 'wicked' confit *a la diable*, and its fat is used to cook the irresistible fries. Veal comes in the form of the loin, head and deep-fried brains – the richness tamed by French cornichon to balance the flavours. Nor is seasonality ignored, a plate of white asparagus bolstered by basquaise (red pepper) dressing is a lighter option. Large portions mean that it's tempting to skip dessert, but the lemon tart is worth leaving room for 'prior to Herculean strength coffee'. It's all resolutely regional, right down to the wines, which start at £14. **Chef/s:** Julien Carlon. **Open:** Tue to Sat 12 to 2, 7 to 10. **Closed:** Christmas to New Year. **Meals:** alc (main courses £8.50 to £13.50). **Service:** 12.5% (optional). **Details:** Cards accepted. 30 seats. Air-con. Wheelchair access. Music.

## Eagle

Pioneering Farringdon gastropub
159 Farringdon Road, EC1R 3AL
Tel no: (020) 7837 1353
⊖ Farringdon
Modern European | £26
Cooking score: 2
Ⅴ £30

Michael Belben's ground-breaking East London gastropub virtually defined the genre and it continues on its merry way, serving food and drink in a bare-boarded room with deconstructed, mismatched furniture and abundant greenery. The short menu is chalked on a boards above the bar and it comprises around a dozen dishes with no conventional distinctions between 'starters' and 'mains'. Here you will find spring vegetable minestrone and Kirkham's Lancashire cheese with pickles sharing the bill with full-blooded dishes like Venetian-style calf's liver with onions, red wine vinegar, parsley and toast or roast pollack with purple sprouting broccoli, anchovy, chilli and aïoli. Bifeana (marinated rump steak sandwich) has been on the menu since the very beginning, likewise pasties de nata (Portuguese custard tarts). A modest choice of tapas is also available. Beer drinkers get their fill and everything on the minimal wine list is available by the glass. Bottle prices start at £11.75.

**Chef/s:** Ed Mottershaw. **Open:** all week L 12.30 to 3 (3.30 Sat and Sun), Mon to Sat D 6.30 to 10.30. **Closed:** 1 week Christmas, bank hols. **Meals:** alc (main courses £8.50 to £18.00). **Service:** not inc. **Details:** Cards accepted. 65 seats. 24 seats outside. Wheelchair access. Music. Children's portions.

## Flâneur

**Accomplished deli dining**
41 Farringdon Road, EC1M 3JB
Tel no: (020) 7404 4422
www.flaneur.com
♦ Farringdon
Modern European | £24.50
Cooking score: 2

This hybrid deli/restaurant is almost a foodie theme park. Oversized chairs (à la Mad Hatter's tea party) and blond wood barrel-like light fittings add to the surreal feeling of dining while surrounded by floor-to-ceiling racks of interesting food. The daily changing menu includes charcuterie, cured fish platters, and salads such as watercress, pear, almond and Roquefort. Mains take in pan-fried mackerel with smoked paprika, garlic and parsley, and a 'gutsy' fish stew, the accompanying rouille 'luxuriously flavoured with saffron'. Puddings are predominantly cakes – many displayed in the deli section. A hazelnut chocolate tart, for example, comes with sweet, crisp pastry. The wine list is largely French but includes some

New World names, with bottles from £13 and a good selection available by the glass from £4.

**Chef/s:** Simon Phelan. **Open:** all week L 12pm to 3pm, Mon to Sat D 6pm to 10pm. Brunch Sat, Sun and bank hols 10am to 4pm. Light Breakfast Mon to Fri 8.30am to 10.30am. **Closed:** 25 Dec to 2 Jan. **Meals:** Set menu 2 courses £19.50, 3 courses £24.50, sides approx £3. **Service:** 12.5% (optional). **Details:** Cards accepted. 65 seats. No music. Wheelchair access.

## Medcalf

**Straightforward subtle cooking**
40 Exmouth Market, EC1R 4QE
Tel no: (020) 7833 3533
www.medcalfbar.co.uk
♦ Farringdon
Modern European | £30
Cooking score: 4

Blurring the line between bar and restaurant, Medcalf's cool and casual vibe suits its buzzy Exmouth Market surrounds to a tee. Don't be fooled by the scruffy décor of wobbly chairs and scuffed tables: Medcalf might be somewhere that you can eat a sausage sarnie but it also serves simple and well-prepared cooking with a strong British flavour and an eye for the seasons – appropriate for premises that used to house a butcher's. Starters range from good things on toast – Welsh rarebit, say, or herring roes, the assertive fishiness tempered by a peppery salad and capers – to salads such as pigeon breast, watercress and beetroot that are typical of the gutsy nature of much of the menu: a winter main course might be pork belly stuffed with prunes. But the kitchen is capable of subtlety, too: there's whole lemon sole with samphire and hollandaise in early summer, for instance. British cheeses with oatcakes and chutney lead the dessert list, or there's chocolate mousse and lemon tart. Roasts of rib of beef and leg of lamb are served at Sunday lunch, followed by treacle tart and bread and butter pudding. House white is £13.50 on the short Franco-

Spanish wine list, and there are interesting beers, such as the sour cherry-flavoured Liefmans Kriek from Belgium.
**Chef/s:** Tim Wilson. **Open:** all week L 12 to 3 (4 Sat and Sun), Mon to Thur and Sat D 6 to 9.50. **Closed:** bank hols. **Meals:** alc (main courses £10 to £14). **Service:** not inc. **Details:** Cards accepted. 60 seats. 20 seats outside. Air-con. Wheelchair access. Music. Children allowed.

## Moro

**Buzzy, relaxed hotspot**
34-36 Exmouth Market, EC1R 4QE
Tel no: (020) 7833 8336
www.moro.co.uk
⊖ Farringdon
**Spanish/Portuguese | £27**
**Cooking score: 4**
V

More than a decade since it first opened, Moro still rocks, continuing to draw a savvy cosmopolitan crowd who crank up the decibels at this Exmouth Market champion. The laid-back, no-frills, open-plan space comes with few decorative flourishes and something of a canteen buzz, its hard surfaces doing battle with the sounds and aromas of an open-to-view kitchen, chatter from the long zinc-topped bar (where tapas is served throughout the day) and the hubbub of an upbeat dining room. Polished floorboards, serried ranks of informally set, closely packed tables, plain walls and round pillars all have their say too. But it is Sam and Sam Clarks' cuisine that really plays to the gallery. Its blend of Spanish and Moorish influences comes full of interest and big on flavour, though not without a few lapses. Driven by well-sourced produce and unfussy execution, the kitchen's wood-fired oven or charcoal grill inspires many dishes on the weekly changing menu. Take wood-roasted Middlewhite pork teamed with chard, new potatoes and romesco aïoli, or perhaps charcoal-grilled grey mullet served with lemon and bay butter and a broad bean, tomato and grilled red onion salad. To finish, perhaps the yoghurt cake with pistachios and pomegranates might catch the eye, while the

wine list is a resolutely Spanish-bias affair, headed by an impressive line up of sherries and house wine from £12.50.
**Chef/s:** Sam and Sam Clark. **Open:** Mon to Sat L 12.30 to 2.30, D 7 to 10.30. **Meals:** alc (main courses £14.50 to £17). Tapas menu available. **Service:** not inc. **Details:** Cards accepted. 96 seats. 12 seats outside. Air-con. No music. Wheelchair access. Children's portions.

## St John

**Nose-to-tail dining**
26 St John Street, EC1M 4AY
Tel no: (020) 7251 0848
www.stjohnrestaurant.com
⊖ Farringdon
**British | £30**
**Cooking score: 6**
V

Terse, sometimes eccentric descriptions make the twice-daily changing menu at St John a fun read: snails and oak leaf or brill, bread and green sauce, for example, are as described, but the results are magic: dazzling produce – often British – resplendently unadorned. Chef Fergus Henderson's 'nose-to-tail' culinary philosophy sees offal figure high, an approach that certainly appeals to the hardcore, dare we say macho, foodie. But it would be a shame to not to sample, say, ox heart and celeriac, chitterlings and chips, or the signature bone marrow and parsley salad. Excellent game, rare breed meats, and lesser-spotted cuts (Bath chaps, spleen etc) – all entirely in keeping for an establishment on Smithfield Meat Market's doorstep – are popular choices, but don't ignore the 'softer' options of seafood or salads. Old-fashioned puds like rhubarb trifle or burnt cream make a fitting climax. St John has legion admirers, but one reader (and self-confessed fan) reports disappointedly this year of 'brusque service' and second-best menu substitutions, bewailing the high price charged for 'a small piece of meat with some lukewarm beetroot'. Though portions aren't usually ungenerous, the line between no-frills presentation and parsimony might be too fine for some. Similar caveats should be raised about the décor; to some the former smokehouse's white walls and floors, and its schoolroom chairs will be the height of cool; to others it will be plain spartan. Wine on the all-French list starts at £15. Note that there's also a friendly bar and excellent in-house bakery.

**Chef/s:** Fergus Henderson and Trevor Gulliver. **Open:** Mon to Fri L 12 to 3, Mon to Sat D 6 to 11. **Closed:** Christmas, Easter. **Meals:** alc (main courses £12.50 to £21.50). **Service:** not inc. **Details:** Cards accepted. 105 seats. Air-con. No music. No mobile phones.

## ALSO RECOMMENDED
## ▲ Little Bay
171 Farringdon Road, Clerkenwell, EC1R 3AL
Tel no: (020) 7278 1234
www.little-bay.co.uk
⊖ Farringdon

Modern bistro-style food at low prices is the defining feature of this unpretentious restaurant on the edge of an increasingly fashionable part of London. A flat price for each course rises by a pound or two after 7pm, so starters become £2.95, main courses £7.95 and desserts £2.95. Imagination has not been entirely constrained by the budget, alongside familiar starters such as mussels marinière, expect duck, figs and cranberry terrine and salmon fillet served with spicy coconut potatoes, with pears in red wine with vanilla pannacotta for dessert. Roasts every Sunday. Other branches now operate across London in Battersea, Kilburn and Fulham. House wine £10.90. Open daily.

## READERS RECOMMEND
## Pho
Vietnamese
86 St John Street, Clerkenwell, EC1M 4EH
Tel no: (020) 7253 7624
'A plethora of flavours; a real gem'

## St Germain
French
89 Turnmill Street, Clerkenwell, EC1M 5QU
Tel no: 020 7336 0949
www.stgermain.info
'Classic French comfort food'

## ■ Limehouse

★NEW ENTRY★
## The Narrow
Ramsay's take on a British pub
44 Narrow Street, E14 8DP
Tel no: 020 7592 7950
www.gordonramsay.com
⊖ Limehouse
Gastropub | £23
Cooking score: 3
£30

Currently vying with the Ivy as London's hardest to book restaurant, Gordon Ramsay's first pub venture occupies a pretty Edwardian dockmaster's house overlooking the Thames. It's a good-looking pub, a useful venue for the local community of yuppies – decent pubs, or restaurants for that matter, not being thick on the ground in Limehouse. The spacious riverside terrace pulls the fair-weather drinking crowd from the large, basic bar, while pub classics such as ploughman's, sausage roll with HP sauce, or half a pint of prawns are among the offerings for anyone who gets peckish. Those lucky enough to have secured a reservation, head for the pretty, raftered dining room – the diminutive size explains the pressure on tables – for some robust, unfussy cooking of regional British food. At inspection that included potted Morecambe Bay shrimps, tasty, tender, braised Gloucester pig cheeks served with a pile of mashed neeps, and a very rich baked custard with Goosnargh cakes. Service is exemplary – the right mix of casual and on-the-ball – and reasonable prices extend to the wine list, where house French kicks off at £13.50. Good range of real ales and bottled beers, too.

**Chef/s:** John Colllin. **Open:** Mon to Fri L 11.30 to 3, D 6 to 10; Sat. 12 to 10; Sun, 12 to 9. **Meals:** Main courses £9 to £14.50. **Service:** 12.5%. **Details:** Cards accepted. 32 seats. 100 seats outside. Separate bar. Wheelchair access. Music. Children allowed. Car parking.

# ▌Shoreditch

★NEW ENTRY★

## Bacchus

**Global gastronomy lands in Hoxton**
177 Hoxton Street, N1 6PJ
Tel no: (020) 7613 0477
www.bacchus-restaurant.co.uk
⊖ Old Street
Global | 40
Cooking score: 6

Bacchus may be the god of wine but here in Hoxton he's also the deity of ambrosial food realised in the sublime cooking of Nuno Mendes. A widely travelled Portuguese, Nuno worked at El Bulli in Spain and Jean-Georges in New York before settling in London by way of Tokyo. His truly original touch combines the subtlest flavours of East and West, underpinned by a mastery of sous-vide, low temperature cooking techniques. To get a glimpse, the express lunch menu (Monday – Friday) is a good intro at £22. At dinner, the six-course tasting menu rises to a wholly different level. An appetiser of the most intensely flavoured sea-green English pea purée with hazelnut crumble and Enoki mushrooms is an indelible memory, so too the sous-vide pork jowl which is brilliantly partnered by langoustine and slivers of black radish. A great fish dish of obviously both Japanese and Iberian influence is the warm cod with 'paella paint' (squid ink?), tomato hearts, wafer-thin potatoes and garlic. Or as thoughts turn to red wine, the slow-cooked lamb shoulder with fragrant kappa curry leaf and goat's cheese is inspired by the chef's spell in Thailand. Finally, some heavenly desserts particularly those showing a mastery of sweet and savoury tastes, as in a classic financier cake

flavoured with black olive, served with roasted pear ice cream, fig purée and pine nuts reduced in milk and cream. Wines are suitably Bacchanalian: seriously good reds and whites by the glass from £5, and a deftly selective range of classic and new wave wines by the bottle, strongest for quality and value in Italy and Spain: the Clos de Torribas, Penedes, Crianza 2003 is a snip at £21 – for something special, the Hamilton Russell Chardonnay 2005 from South Africa (£40) is exceptional. Great informal atmosphere in this uncluttered make-over from a Victorian pub – linen jackets and jeans *de rigueur,* and charming staff who are knowledgeable and watchful.
**Chef/s:** Nuno Mendes. **Closed:** Sunday and Monday. **Meals:** Mon to Fri L £22 (2 courses). **Service:** 12.5%. **Details:** Cards accepted. 50 seats. Air-con. Wheelchair access.

## Eyre Brothers

**For elaborate Iberian, go East**
70 Leonard Street, EC2A 4QX
Tel no: (020) 7613 5346
www.eyrebrothers.co.uk
⊖ Old Street
Spanish/Portuguese | £52
Cooking score: 2

In an edgy but trendy corner of Shoreditch, this light, buzzy room with friendly, likeable staff points to an impressive start from the brothers who brought us The Eagle. This is, however, a step up from gastropub ambitions. On the menu could be white bean and pancetta soup to start, a 'finely executed' grilled veal chop, or 'three enormous and delicious' tiger prawns for mains, with montada of raspberries making a simple but 'stunning end'. The wine list is a relative bargain and Iberia happily dominates. There are several considered choices by the glass starting at £3.75, and for the more discerning there are informed additions from France and Argentina. An outstanding white Rioja 2001 seemed a steal at £24. Not surprisingly, the list is also strong in the sherry and port departments, again with a number available by the glass.

**Chef/s:** David Eyre and João Cleto. **Open:** Mon to Fri L 12 to 3pm, Mon to Sat D 6 to 11pm. **Meals:** alc (main courses £10 to £21). **Service:** 12.5% (optional). **Details:** Cards accepted. 75 seats. Air-con. Wheelchair access. Music.

## Fifteen
**Jamie O's bright take on Italian cooking**
15 Westland Place, N1 7LP
Tel no: (0871) 330 1515
www.fifteenrestaurant.com
⊖ Old Street
Modern European | £60
Cooking score: 3

𝖛

The urban warehouse setting is as bright and breezy as Jamie Oliver's TV persona. On the ground floor is an all-day trattoria where you can pop in for coffee, or tuck into the likes of linguine alla carbonara or rib eye with porcini butter. The main dining room is below. Here the menu makes a virtue of simplicity, offering prosciutto with Italian black figs and leaves, and even pasta dishes can be as straightforward as ravioli of Scotch beef in a light marjoram broth. An occasional braise, such as 12-hour cooked rare-breed pork with fresh cannelloni beans in a light tomato sauce takes its place alongside the principle cooking techniques: pan-frying (scallops wrapped in pancetta) and chargrilling (leg of lamb). To finish there may also be chocolate and orange parfait, while 'good service' creates 'a fantastic eating experience'. The wine list is a global, but pricey affair – bottles open at £21 – but there's fair choice by the glass from £6.

**Chef/s:** Andrew Parkinson. **Open:** trattoria all week L 12 to 3, D 6 to 10 (5.30 to 9.30 Sun); restaurant all week L 12 to 2.30, D 6.30 to 9.30. **Meals:** trattoria alc (main courses £15 to £18); restaurant alc L (main courses £17.50 to £23.50). Set D £60. **Service:** 12.5% (optional). **Details:** Cards accepted. 65 seats. Air-con. Wheelchair access. Music. Children's portions.

## Great Eastern Dining Room
**Gastronomic survey of a continent**
54-56 Great Eastern Street, EC2A 3QR
Tel no: (020) 7613 4545
www.greateasterndining.co.uk
⊖ Old Street
Fusion/Pan-Asian | £43
Cooking score: 3

The Hoxton outpost of Will Rickers's ever-expanding pan-Asian empire offers a buzzing introduction to the genre. The dining room is achingly hip, the atmosphere, convivial. The menu certainly adds to the feeling that this is group meal territory rather than dinner for two, but staff are friendly and keen to help those less familiar with the myriad choices. A selection of dim sum hits the ground running, being fresh and impressive, while a red curry comes deeply flavoured with beautifully tender beef, and salt and pepper squid is 'cooked perfectly'. The pan-Asian staple dessert of chocolate fondant with green tea ice cream rounds things off nicely. The wine list is fashionable, as you might expect, with some unusual selections such as Grüner Veltliner featured, and a wide selection of wines by the glass starting at £3 (£13 a bottle), as well a serious cocktail list.

**Open:** Mon to Fri L 12 to 3pm, Mon to Sat D 6.30 to 11pm. **Meals:** alc (main courses £7 to £19.50). Set L and D £22.50 (2 courses) to £45. Bar menu available. **Service:** 12.5% (optional). **Details:** Cards accepted. 65 seats. Air-con. Separate bar.

★NEW ENTRY★
## Rivington Grill
**No-frills British cooking**
28-30 Rivington Street, EC2A 3DZ
Tel no: (020) 7729 7053
www.rivingtongrill.co.uk
⊖ Old Street
Modern British | £31

From the Caprice Holdings stable, the Rivington comes tucked away in a one-time warehouse-style building in upbeat Shoreditch. A large bar, whitewashed walls and stripped-wood floors create an easy-going mood, while off to one side, the dining area is bright and well set out. The relaxed, buzzy, unbuttoned mood is picked up by the menu's theme; no frills, back-to-basics British cooking driven by quality seasonal produce. Think fish fingers and chips, lamb chop with bubble and squeak, or perhaps roast pork served with 'crisp' crackling and a 'tangy' apple sauce. There is no over complication or pretension here, just admirably straightforward, honest flavours. Desserts are equally comforting, perhaps a treacle tart or 'rich' chocolate moouse, and, while wines may nudge toward the expensive side, they kick off at a pocket-friendly £15 before plateauing off at £85. (There is also a Rivington sibling in Greenwich.)

**Chef/s:** Simon Wadham. **Open:** Mon to Fri, L 12 to 3, Mon to Sun D 6.30 to 11 (10.30 Sun). **Meals:** alc main courses £9.75 to £27.50. **Service:** optional. **Details:** Cards accepted. 120 seats. Air-con. No music.

## ALSO RECOMMENDED
## ▲ Cru
2-4 Rufus Street, Shoreditch, N1 6PE
Tel no: (020) 7729 5252
www.cru.uk.com
⊖ Old Street

Located in a warehouse, this eaterie is also home to the White Cube Gallery, but it's brunch that sees the Hoxton folk flocking in at weekends – try porridge with bananas and maple syrup (£4.50), or kippers with roasted potatoes and spinach (£6.75). At other times the restaurant serves starters of panfried scallops with tomato and chilli (£8.50), with mains ranging from Buccleuch ribeye steak (£16), via burger with chips (£11.75) to a shared platter such as pork cassoulet with seasonal roast (£39 for two). Finish with marzipan pannacotta with lavender biscuits (£5.50). The bar downstairs is a welcome stop for tapas and a beer. Wines from £15. Closed Mon.

## READERS RECOMMEND
## Hoxton Apprentice
Modern British
16 Hoxton Square, Shoreditch, N1 6NT
Tel no: (020) 7749 2828
www.hoxtonapprentice.com
'Training restaurant in listed Victorian building'

## ALSO RECOMMENDED
## ▲ Village East
171-173 Bermondsey Street, Southwark, SE1 3UW
Tel no: 020 7357 6082
www.villageeast.co.uk
⊖ London Bridge

This restaurant is the second outlet from the team behind the Garrison gastropub up the road. The warehouse-style conversion is well-suited to the local creative set, featuring a mezzanine and a private dining room. Starters included a parfait of foie gras with pear and tomato chutney at £7.50, and the star of the main courses is undoubtedly Chateaubriand with green beans and château potatoes (to share, £34.80). One report remarked on 'surly service' and our inspector was given a slightly patronising introduction to the grape varieties on the wine list. However, the general vibe is open and relaxed, much like the clientele. House wines start at £14. Open all week.

## Spitalfields

★ READERS' RESTAURANT OF THE YEAR ★
LONDON

## Canteen
Market setting for modern Brit classics
2 Crispin Place, E1 6DW
Tel no: (0845) 686 1122
www.canteen.co.uk
Modern British | £25
Cooking score: 3

There's something of the American artist Edward Hopper about the long stretch of plate glass through which you can see plainly laid out wood tables and booth seating – the style echoing the clean lines of 1930s American diners. But there's not a burger in sight. Right in the heart of Spitalfields Market, Canteen is one of those places that has creatively redefined what we expect of eating out. It's open all day for a flexible menu of modern Brit classics at great prices – no wonder there are queues at weekends. Eggs Benedict with 'perfect, rich hollandaise' from the all-day breakfast menu vies for attention with potted duck with piccalilli, and potted shrimps on the starters list. Gammon with plain boiled potatoes and parsley sauce is a well-praised main, or you could opt for the meat pie of the day. Deliberately saving room for dessert rewards with an apple crumble with 'amazingly rich, creamy vanilla flecked custard'. Service is on the ball, and a sound choice of wines by the glass opens a decent selection that's almost evenly divided between France and the rest of the world. Prices from £12. NB As we went to press, a second branch of Canteen opened at the Royal Festival Hall on the Southbank.

**Chef/s:** Cass Titcombe. **Open:** all week 11 (9 Sat and Sun) to 11. **Closed:** 25 and 26 Dec. **Meals:** alc (main courses £7 to £12.50). **Service:** 12.5% (optional). **Details:** Cards accepted. 50 seats. Air-con. No music. Wheelchair access. Children's portions.

## St John Bread & Wine
**The upper crust of City brasseries**
94-96 Commercial Street, E1 6LZ
Tel no: (020) 7251 0848
www.stjohnbreadandwine.com
⊖ Liverpool Street
Modern British | £30
Cooking score: 3

A spinoff of the original St John (see entry above), this venue is a bakery, wine shop and deli, as well as somewhere to eat, just opposite Spitalfields market. The atmosphere is as casual as its elder sibling, and the British food will warm the cockles of your heart. Smoked sprats and horseradish is a good way to start, or you might take the plunge and go for the potted squirrel (no, really). As the evening draws on, main dishes come into play,

perhaps beef forerib with celeriac and mustard, or black bream with cabbage. You might opt to wait 15 minutes at the end of it all, while the kitchen rustles you up a plate of madeleines (sold by the dozen or half-dozen, like oysters), or there are baked egg custard, or rhubarb fool, on offer. Cheeses are great too. Nothing could be more British than an all-French wine list, and here is one, starting with vins de pays at £15.20, and motoring up to a 1992 premier cru Puligny-Montrachet at £110.

**Chef/s:** James Lowe. **Open:** all week Mon to Thu 9am to 11pm (10am to 11pm Sat, 10am to 6pm Sun). **Closed:** Christmas and Easter. **Meals:** alc (main courses £13 to £14.30). **Service:** not inc. **Details:** Cards accepted. 56 seats. Air-con. No music.

## ALSO RECOMMENDED
## ▲ Leon
3 Crispin Place, Spitalfields, E1 6DW
Tel no: 020 7247 4369
www.leonrestaurants.co.uk

Spitalfields outpost for this likeable mini-chain of central London eateries (also at Carnaby Street, The Strand, Brompton Road and Ludgate Circus), which offer Allegra McEvedy's appealing, fresh take on fast food. With a mix of North African and Mediterranean ideas, the predominantly fresh repertoire offers healthy, seasonal dishes that make good use of organic and free-range ingredients. Call in for power smoothies, organic porridge (£2) or a bacon sandwich (£2.40) for breakfast, savour Moroccan meatballs (£5.50), flatbread wraps, or a grilled chicken salad (£5.50) at lunch, while evening grazing and sharing menus take in hot mezzes (£1.50-£4.30) and daily specials like green pea curry and chicken tagine (£4.90).

### Average price

The average price listed in main-entry reviews denotes the price of a three-course meal, without wine.

## Tower Hill

### Café Spice Namaste
**A sweep of opulent Asian flavours**
16 Prescot Street, E1 8AZ
Tel no: (020) 7488 9242
⊖ Tower Hill
Indian/Pakistani/Bangladeshi | £45
Cooking score: 2

£5 OFF

Cyrus Todiwala's modern, vibrant pan-Asian cuisine is as fresh as ever. Start with beetroot and coconut samosa or cholya prawn chappati (a Nepalese-style dish of diced prawns with chopped shallots, ginger, chilli and tomato in a chapatti coated with date and tamarind chutney then pan-grilled). Main courses include a lengthy selection from the tandoor – from familiar chicken tikka to chargrilled marinated king prawns with garlic pulao and light, green coconut curry, and numerous vegetarian dishes  perhaps paneer tikka sagwala or water chestnut and sweetcorn masala. Wines start at £15.50.
**Chef/s:** Cyrus Todiwala and Angelo Collaco. **Open:** Mon to Fri L 12 to 3, Mon to Sat D 6.15 to 10.15. **Closed:** 25 Dec to 1 Jan, bank hols. **Meals:** alc (main courses £10.50 to £18.50). **Service:** 12.5% (optional). **Details:** Cards accepted. 110 seats. 45 seats outside. Air-con. Wheelchair access. Music. Children's portions.

## Wapping

### Wapping Food
**Ultra-hip culinary powerhouse**
Wapping Hydraulic Power Station, E1W 3ST
Tel no: (020) 7680 2080
www.thewappingproject.com
⊖ Wapping/Shadwell
Modern European | £29
Cooking score: 3

£5 OFF

Housed in a former hydraulic power station, Wapping Food is one impressive-looking restaurant, in a cavernous space where changing art installations are also on show. The menu offers a sprightly mix of Italian, Spanish, and Pacific Rim influences, delivering fresh, zingy flavours in unaffected, easy-to-like combinations. Buffalo mozzarella with anchovies, fennel, chilli, and garlic, or seared scallops, chickpeas, and aubergine, and chargrilled Welsh Black sirloin, parsnip purée and roast garlic, are typical. If you're amenable to something a bit different, the all-Australian wine list (from £16) is real delight; if you're not, you might get short shrift.
**Chef/s:** Cameron Emirali. **Open:** Mon to Fri 12 to 3, 6.30 to 11, Sat 1 to 3.30, 7 to 11, Sun 1 to 4. **Closed:** 23 Dec to 3 Jan and Bank Holidays. **Meals:** alc (main courses £12.50 to £17.50). **Service:** 12.5% (optional). **Details:** Cards accepted. 150 seats. 50 seats outside. Wheelchair access. Music. Children's portions. Car parking.

## ALSO RECOMMENDED

### ▲ Kasturi
57 Aldgate High Street, Whitechapel, EC3N 1AL
Tel no: (020) 7480 7402 / (020 ) 7481 0048
www.kasturi-restaurant.co.uk
⊖ Aldgate

Don't be put off by the the definition of 'kasturi' as a strong-smelling secretion found in rare musk deer; a glance at the menu reveals appetising Indian specialities from the northwest of India. Ginger-flavoured lamb chops (£5.50) and main courses such as mild chicken and cashew curry flavoured with saffron (£8.95) and knuckles of lamb cooked with cardamom (£9.95) are typical. Vegetarians are well served by a broad selection – baby aubergine with peanut and poppy seeds (£3.95), for example – with chicken tikka massala (£8.95) and chicken or lamb Madras or vindaloo (£7.95). House wine is £13.95. Closed Sun.

# ■ Balham

## Amici

**Family-friendly Italian venue**
35 Bellevue Road, SW17 7EF
Tel no: (020) 8672 5888
www.amiciitalian.co.uk
Italian | £27
Cooking score: 2

Ɣ £30

Celebrated gastro-diva Valentina Harris lends her considerable experience to this sociable 'bar and Italian kitchen' overlooking Wandsworth Common. Amici lives up to its 'friendly' name and it regularly plays to full houses. Crowds congregate under the shade of olive trees when the weather is kind; at other times, the spacious dining room provides an animated setting for robust food with sound credentials. The menu opens with starters like fennel and lemon soup with gremolata or octopus terrine, ahead of salmon baked 'in cartoccio' with dry Vermouth, basil and mint butter or corn-fed chicken breast with roast pepper gratin, pine nut and Vin Santo jus. Desserts are Italian standards such as tiramisu, sgroppino and coffee pannacotta with zabaglione. The drinks list is packed with glamorous cocktails, with support provided by some keenly priced Italian wines. House selections start at £13 a bottle (£9.25 for a 50cl 'pot', £3.50 a glass).
**Chef/s:** Paolo Zanca. **Open:** Mon to Fri 12 to 3, 6 to 10.30, Sat and Sun 11 to 4, 6 to 10.30 (9.30 Sun). **Closed:** 25 and 26 Dec. **Meals:** alc (main courses £8.50 to £15). **Service:** 12.5% (optional). **Details:** Cards accepted. 40 seats. Air-con. Music. Children's portions.

## Scores on the Doors

To find out more about the Scores on the Doors campaign, please visit the Food Standard's Agency website: www.food.gov.uk or www.which.co.uk.

## Chez Bruce

**Exquisite Anglo-French cooking**
2 Bellevue Road, SW17 7EG
Tel no: (020) 8672 0114
www.chezbruce.co.uk
⊖ Balham
Modern European | £45
Cooking score: 6

🍾 Ɣ

Bruce Poole's eponymous restaruant is a shining beacon of excellence in south-west London. The restaurant has its drawbacks: the room is cramped, particularly in the evening, with too many tables squashed into a small space; the chairs are uncomfortable and the decibel levels are brasserie-like – this is not a restaurant of hushed appreciation. However, the Guide's post bag is bursting with praise from appreciative diners. Poole's style of cooking marries classical French technique with the very best that the larder of England and Europe has to offer, be they pigs trotters or truffles. At a recent dinner, an elegant and restrained starter of English asparagus cooked just-so and enlivened by the addition of Joselito ham and parmesan was surprisingly overshadowed by a really gutsy melange of chicken wings, duck hearts and snails with parsley purée. Main courses which followed included an old-fashioned blanquette of pork, given the necessary lift with a pungent choucroute and a perfectly cooked roast cod with olive oil mash, served with grilled, marinated mediterranean vegetables. The prix-fixe menu formula makes a necessity of the dessert course and from a classic crème brûlée to a more adventurous millefeuille of pistachio and valhrona chocolates served with griottine cherries, they're exemplary. And so to the wine list: as befits the restaurant's status, the cellar is magnificent, with a huge global wine list touching top Meursaults and Bordeaux grands crus as well as magnificent Australian and American offerings. But where the menu pricing may look very reasonable, the wines seem rather more expensive, though the paucity of wines by the glass is relieved by a generous selection by the half bottle.

Chef/s: Bruce Poole and Matthew Christmas. **Open:** Mon to Fri 12 to 2, 6.30 to 10.30, Sat 12.30 to 2.30, 6.30 to 10.30, Sun 12.30 to 3, 7 to 10. **Closed:** 24 to 26 Dec, 1 Jan. **Meals:** Set L Mon to Fri £23.50, Set L Sat £27.50, Set L Sun £32.50, Set D £37.50. **Service:** 12.5% (optional). **Details:** Cards accepted. 75 seats. Air-con. No music. Wheelchair access. Children's portions.

## READERS RECOMMEND

### Balham Bar & Kitchen
**Modern European**
15-19 Bedford Hill, Balham, SW12 9EX
Tel no: (020) 8675 6900
www.balhamkitchen.com
**'A no-frills brasserie-style menu'**

### Lamberts
**Modern British**
2 Station Parade, Balham, SW12 9AZ
Tel no: 020 8675 2233
www.lambertsrestaurant.com
**'Legendary Sunday roasts and kid-friendly too'**

## ▮ Battersea

### The Food Room
**An admirable local**
123 Queenstown Road, SW8 3RH
Tel no: (020) 7622 0555
www.thefoodroom.com
**French | £44**
**Cooking score: 3**

This second restaurant of Eric and Sarah Guignard, following the unabated success of the French Table in Surbiton (see review), is a more muted, quieter affair, which doesn't seem to have caught the attention of locals in the same way. It's a shame, because this is a restaurant that deserves to be busy. Like its Alma Mater, The Food Room's cooking takes classical French food as a starting point, but the style here is simpler and less fussy. A starter of tuna carpaccio is set off with a light soy dressing, a fine dice of vegetables and mango adding a crunch and a contrasting sharpness; panfried cod offset with a saffron-laden seafood paella; carefully cooked pork fillet has

Hari Nagaraj

*Why did you become a chef?*
I had a genuine passion for food from an early age.

*Which of today's chefs do you admire?*
Heston Blumenthal.

*Where do you source your ingredients?*
Primarily small, specialist farms in the UK and some in Europe.

*Who is your favourite producer?*
We've recently started using water buffalo from Laverstoke Park in Hampshire, which has proved to be very popular with guests.

*What's your favourite cookery book?*
*Cooking Delights of the Maharajas* by Dharamjit Singh.

*What's the best dish you've ever eaten?*
I'm still working on finding that.

*Do you have a favourite local recipe?*
I do love a good bread and butter pudding.

*What's your guilty food pleasure?*
Apart from the bread and butter pudding? It has to be home-made chips.

*What's the hardest thing about running a restaurant?*
Finding the right balance between consistency and creativity.

a slab of pommes darphin to soak up the juices, an unctuous parsnip purée as a luxurious accompaniment. The kitchen lets itself down with its puddings which are more pedestrian affairs – stick to the excellent cheeses if you're still hungry. The wine list is well enough thought out and decently priced with plenty of wines by the glass, including the oh-so-fashionable Picpoul at £4.50 and Monbazillac at £4.25.

**Chef/s:** Eric Guignard. **Open:** Tue to Sat D 7 to 10.30. **Meals:** alc (main courses £9.50 to £15.80). **Service:** 12.5% (optional). **Details:** Cards accepted. 50 seats. Air-con. No mobile phones. Wheelchair access. Music. Children's portions.

# Greyhound
**Destination restaurant disguised as a pub**
136 Battersea High Street, SW11 3JR
Tel no: (020) 7978 7021
www.thegreyhoundatbattersea.co.uk
**Gastropub | £44**
**New Chef**
♦ ⋎

Holding onto its credentials as a public house by virtue of the big, open bar area at the front of the premises, The Greyhound leaves the awkwardly shaped extension at the rear to discerning diners. Best use is made of the space, with colour and clever lighting creating a certain uniformity, wallpaper and plants carving out more intimate spaces, the kitchen just visible at the end. Alessio Brusardin took over the stoves in March and has adjusted the menu to fit his style, but the ambition and intricacy of the dishes remain intact as does the gargantuan size of the portions: a starter of panfried scallops produces four fat, beautifully cooked bivalves divided by wafer thin croutons, served on brunoise cut peppers and a thick gaspacho sauce; a dish of black pork loin served fashionably pink arrives with accompanying pork belly and black pudding as well as sweet potato & spinach. Quality is high, but some of the combinations, like duck breast interlaced with foie gras are too rich for all but the most hardy. Quirky puddings like passionfruit tiramisu and chocolate tortellini

with black pepper ice cream are worth a look, but more important is the huge wine list. Wine is proprietor Mark Van Der Goot's passion and the wine list is encyclopaedic in length and global in concept, and starting at £3.10 for a decent sized glass of something drinkable, very affordable.

**Chef/s:** Alessio Brusardin. **Open:** Tue to Sun L 12 to 2.45 (3.30 Sun), Tue to Sat D 7 to 10. **Closed:** Christmas and New Year. **Meals:** alc L (main courses £7 to £12). Set D £27 (2 courses) to £31. **Service:** 12.5%. **Details:** Cards accepted. 55 seats. Wheelchair access. Music.

# Ransome's Dock
**Assured cooking beside the Thames**
35-37 Parkgate Road, SW11 4NP
Tel no: (020) 7223 1611
www.ransomesdock.co.uk
**Modern European | £32**
**Cooking score: 4**
£5 OFF ♦ ⋎

A fine-weather riverside terrace overlooking the old docks between Albert and Battersea Bridges is one of the major draws at Martin and Vanessa Lam's enduring neighbourhood restaurant. The kitchen is known for its loyalty to regional British produce, although most of its culinary inspiration comes from across the Channel. Warm Lincolnshire smoked-eel fillets are served with buckwheat pancakes and crème fraîche, Devon-reared Creedy Carver duck breast might appear with apple sauce, red cabbage and fondant potato, while noisettes of Rhug Estate organic lamb could be accompanied by a thyme and Syrah sauce. Daily fish specials are also worth noting: sea bass with asparagus, pea and broad bean risotto or medallions of monkfish with creamy lobster sauce and pennette, for example. Rhubarb fool is English nostalgia at its best; otherwise the kitchen roams around for prune and Armagnac soufflé (a fixture dessert) and labneh (strained yoghurt) with mango in orange blossom syrup. Saturday brunch attracts crowds of weekend tourists and chillout locals, while the style-conscious global wine list provides something to suit most palates and preferences. Top-notch labels from California, France and Italy grab the attention, along with expertly chosen 'Ransome's Dock Selections' from £13.95 a bottle. The list also provides some fine drinking by the glass (from £4). **Chef/s:** Martin and Vanessa Lam. **Open:** all week 12 to 5 (3.30 Sun), Mon to Sat D 6 to 11. **Closed:** Christmas, 1 Jan and Aug bank hol. **Meals:** alc (exc Sat and Sun L; main courses £10.50 to £21.50). Set L £15 (2 courses). **Service:** 12.5% (optional). **Details:** Cards accepted. 56 seats. 24 seats outside. No mobile phones. Wheelchair access. Music. Children's portions. Car parking.

## ALSO RECOMMENDED
### ▲ Butcher and Grill

3941 Parkgate Road, Battersea, SW11 4NP
Tel no: (020) 7924 3999
www.thebutcherandgrill.com
⊖ Battersea Park

Bullishly carnivorous in style, this Battersea young-blood combines a butcher's shop and deli with a laid-back bar and child-friendly restaurant. Meat from the owners' farm dominates proceedings, with everything from grilled steaks and new season's lamb cutlets (£19) to burgers and bespoke sausages. Alternatively, opt for the fish of the day or a main course like salt-and-pepper duck breast with crushed Jersey Royals and sweet black bacon sauce. Start with duck rillettes (£6) or tea-smoked quail with steamed aubergine salad, and finish with profiteroles or poached peaches and elderflower sorbet (£5). Keenly priced modern wines from £13.50 (£3.50 a glass). Open Mon to Sat 12 to 3.30 and 6 to 11, Sun 12 to 4.30

### Please send us your feedback

To register your opinion about any restaurant listed in the Guide, or a new restaurant that you wish to bring to our attention, please visit the web address at the bottom of the page. Your feedback informs the content of the book and will be used to compile next year's reviews.

## ▮ Bermondsey
## Le Pont de la Tour

**Stunning river views**
36d Shad Thames, SE1 2YE
Tel no: (020) 7403 8403
www.conran.com
⊖ Tower Hill, London Bridge
**Modern European | £35**
**Cooking score: 3**
♦ ⋎

Panoramic views of Tower Bridge and the London skyline will always come with a hefty price tag. Le Pont de la Tour certainly isn't cheap, but it manages to deliver the goods with enough finesse and old-fashioned elegance to warrant the bill. Pale yellow walls, white tablecloths and bow-tied waiters add to the French-style setting. The carpeted restaurant has an air of occasion, while the adjoining brasserie with its seafood bar is more of a relaxed, noisy affair. Accomplished French cooking with a British twist completes the continental experience. Starters included a fishy crab, tomato and avocado tian, or guinea fowl tortellini with wild mushroom and tarragon. Mains extend from poached skate, black rice and sauce vierge, to calf's liver, pomme purée and sauce vierge. Finish off with a signature dessert of champagne jelly, berries and crème Chantilly. The hefty 80-page wine list dedicates 22 pages to French varieties, but also takes in small wine-producing countries such as Slovenia and England (a lone Chapel Down Reserve is listed here). It notably features a good selection of rare and exceptional wines, some available in larger formats, such as jeroboams and imperials. Or, if you're budgeting, you could pick up a decent bottle starting at around £19.
**Chef/s:** James Walker. **Open:** all week 12 to 3, 6 to 11. Brasserie open all day at the weekends. **Meals:** alc D (main courses £17 to £26.50). Set L £30. Bar/grill menu available. **Service:** 12.5% (optional). **Details:** Cards accepted. 100 seats. 72 seats outside. Separate bar. Wheelchair access. Music. Children's portions.

# Tentazioni

**Modern cooking in an amiable atmosphere**
Lloyds Wharf, 2 Mill Street, SE1 2BD
Tel no: (020) 7237 1100
www.tentazioni.co.uk
⊖ London Bridge
Italian | £38
Cooking score: 3
£5 OFF 𝗩

Riccardo Giacomini's narrow warehouse restaurant close to Tower Bridge is a likeable place, from the modern paintings on vibrantly coloured walls via the amiable atmosphere to the modern Italian menu. The food may lack a little refinement, but that directness is part of its appeal. The repertoire opens with the likes of goat's cheese and roasted tomato ravioli with pesto sauce, and risotto matecato with foie gras, duck confit and port sauce. Among main courses, fine materials are evident in a robust dish of basil-roasted cod steak served with ratatouille wrapped in a puff pastry and a pepper sauce, while sound technique has produced a tender mint-crusted rack of lamb with potato timbale and button onions. Meals might end with wild berry pannacotta or a classic tiramisu. In addition, vegetarians are well catered for, and a five course 'degustazione' menu gives an edited version of the à la carte. A diverse bunch of Italian wines make up the intelligent list. In general, mark-ups are reasonable with a house selection opening at £15.

**Chef/s:** Riccardo Giacomini. **Open:** Tue to Fri L 12 to 2.45, Mon to Sat D 6.45 to 10.45. **Closed:** 23 Dec to 2 Jan. **Meals:** alc (main courses £12.50 to £19). Set L and D £28 to £38. **Service:** 12.5%. **Details:** Cards accepted. 75 seats. Wheelchair access. Music. Children's portions.

## Readers recommend

A 'readers recommend' review is a genuine quote from a report sent in by one of our readers. We intend to follow up these suggestions throughout the year to come.

## ALSO RECOMMENDED

### ▲ Arancia

52 Southwark Park Road, Bermondsey, SE16 3RS
Tel no: (020) 7394 1751
www.arancia-uk.co.uk
⊖ Bermondsey/Elephant & Castle

Locals show loyalty to Arancia (Italian for orange) for good reason – and its worth knowing about if you are in the neighbourhood. It has a warm décor, a busy atmosphere and a menu that changes weekly. Dishes such as rosemary-stuffed sardines (£4.75), home-made pumpkin gnocchi (£8.80) or delicate fishcakes with green bean salad and pesto (£8.80) can be followed by the likes of belly pork with borlotti beans (£9.75) and a range of desserts such as the popular and rich chocolate semifreddo (just £3) or Italian cheeses (£4.75). Italian wines from £10.50. Closed Sun and Mon.

## ▮ Blackheath

# Chapter Two

**Good value contemporary restaurant**
43-45 Montpelier Vale, SE3 0TJ
Tel no: (020) 8333 2666
www.chaptersrestaurants.co.uk
Modern European | £38
Cooking score: 4

The younger sibling of Chapter One (see entry, Farnborough, Kent) is set over two floors, the light and airy ground floor giving way to a larger, dramatically dark basement. Regulars are effusive in their praise, delighted with 'outstanding' cooking 'at prices you couldn't hope to imagine in the centre of the capital'. The set menu (which varies in price, but not content, between lunch and dinner) is comforting and modern. Trevor Tobin keeps the kitchen pretty well to a seasonal rhythm, in early June, for example, offering a salad of Kentish asparagus (with sweet and sour onions and sauce mousseline), and pea velouté with crushed peas and deep-fried haddock. Among main courses you might expect skate accompanied by oxtail ragu, beetroot, spinach and cauliflower purée , or braised shoulder of English lamb with spring vegetables, white bean purée and jus gras. To finish, go for mille-feuille of coconut pancake served with poached yellow peaches and nutmeg ice cream, or baked vanilla yoghurt with iced rhubarb crumble and citrus rum baba. A selection of eight wines by the glass, £4.15 to £4.75, is available from a pleasingly varied list starting at £16.

**Chef/s:** Trevor Tobin. **Open:** all week 12 to 2.30, 6.30 to 10.30. **Closed:** 2 to 5 Jan. **Meals:** Set L £15.95 (2 courses) to £19.95, Set D Sun to Thur £18.45 (2 courses) to £23.50, Set D Fri and Sat £24.50. **Service:** 12.5% (optional). **Details:** Cards accepted. 75 seats. Air-con. No music. Wheelchair access.

## READERS RECOMMEND
### Dark Horse
**Modern European**
16 Grove Lane, Camberwell, SE5 8SY
Tel no: (020) 7703 9990
www.barbarblacksheep.com
'Simple bar with a local feel'

## ▌Clapham

★NEW ENTRY★
### Trinity Restaurant
**New restaurant with serious ambition**
4 The Polygon, Clapham Old Town, SW4 0JG
Tel no: (020) 7622 1199
www.trinityrestaurant.co.uk
⊖ Clapham Common
**Modern European | £33**
**Cooking score: 2**

Chef-proprietor Adam Byatt's return to Clapham, where he first made his mark with the fondly remembered Thyme, has been greeted with almost universal delight. Rather than re-introducing haute grazing, whch was Thyme's trademark, dining is now strictly à la carte. Byatt is capable of good things: his charcuterie is impeccable and the choice of whole joints for sharing at Sunday lunch (prior booking by previous Thursday

required) suggests Byatt's fondness for meat is worth bearing in mind when ordering. Yet, though the menu invariably reads enticingly and ticks all the right fashionable boxes with its choice of modish ingredients and techniques, inspection found perfect balance is not always struck within the dishes. The highlight was a simple escabeche of mullet with saffron aïoli and basil from the light lunch menu, which had vibrant, well-judged flavour. Desserts mask beautiful ingredients such as Alphonso mango by playing too hard with myriad mousse and ice shots. The thoughtful, if relatively highly priced, wine list opens at £16.50.

**Chef/s:** Adam Byatt. **Open:** L Tue to Sun 12.30 to 2.30, D Mon to Sun from 6.30. **Closed:** L Mon. **Meals:** alc main courses £15 to £25. **Service:** optional. **Details:** Cards accepted. 60 seats. Air-con. Separate bar. Wheelchair access. Children allowed.

### Tsunami
**Reliable Japanese cooking**
5-7 Voltaire Road, SW4 6DQ
Tel no: (020) 7978 1610
www.tsunamirestaurant.co.uk
⊖ Clapham North
**Japanese | £34**
**Cooking score: 2**

ᛉ

Sitting cheek-by-jowl with Clapham's railway sidings, this well-liked restaurant does good business with its unflashy Japanese cooking. Appetisers and sharing plates head the lengthy menu: enjoy a succession of appealing, freshly prepared items including chicken and cabbage gyoza dumplings or Nobu-inspired yellowtail sashimi with jalapeño in yuzu ponzu sauce. Moving on there are oysters every which way (try the 'shooter' with sake, ponzu, momiji oroshi, quail egg and scallion), salads and tempura (including mixed vegetarian versions with sweet potato, lotus root and shiitake mushrooms). Main courses and specials feature 'toban' claypots as well as chargrilled lamb with wasabi pepper sauce and hira unagi (grilled marinated eel). Sushi

appears traditionally at the end of the menu, with nigiri and hand rolls involving everything from sea urchin to salmon skin. Beers and cocktails figure on the drinks list, along with assorted wines from £12 (£3.75 a glass).
**Chef/s:** Ken Sam. **Open:** Mon to Fri 6 to 11, Sat 12.30 to 11, Sun 1 to 9. **Closed:** 3 days Christmas, 31 Dec, 1 Jan. **Meals:** alc (main courses £6.50 to £16.50). **Service:** 12.5% (optional). **Details:** Cards accepted. 100 seats. Air-con. No music. Children's portions.

# East Dulwich

## Franklins

**Friendly one-time pub**
157 Lordship Lane, SE22 8HX
Tel no: (020) 8299 9598
www.franklinsrestaurant.com
**Modern British | £38**
**New Chef**

On a busy East Dulwich thoroughfare the blue-tiled frontage picks this buzzy, unbuttoned neighbourhood brasserie-cum-bar out from the crowd. Run the gauntlet of the bar to reach the airy dining room beyond, which is decked out with darkwood chairs, white paper-clad tables and bare-brick walls hung with large mirrors. The kitchen deals in carefully sourced seasonal produce (and some lesser-used ingredients) delivering a plain, unfussy, traditional style, its earthiness perfectly echoing the surroundings. Take chitterlings with chicory and snails as an opener, for instance, or tripe, saffron and mash, with Old Spot pork belly, beetroot and dandelion to follow. Puddings hit a homely nod too, with maybe Eton Mess, a chocolate pot, or strawberry tart to further strain the waistband. Menus come short on adjectives but not on flavour, with the carte backed by value fixed-price lunch, while the compact wine list has France in ascendancy and opens at £12.50.
**Chef/s:** Philip Greene. **Open:** Mon to Sat 12 to 10.30, Sun 1 to 10. **Closed:** 25 and 26 Dec, 1 Jan. **Meals:** alc (main courses £11.50 to £18.50). Set L Mon to Fri £12 (2 courses) to £15. Bar menu available.

**Service:** not inc. **Details:** Cards accepted. 66 seats. 8 seats outside. Air-con. Separate bar. No music. Wheelchair access. Music. Children's portions.

## The Green

**A versatile and lively brasserie**
58-60 East Dulwich Road, SE22 9AX
Tel no: (020) 7732 7575
www.greenbar.co.uk
**Modern European | £30**
**Cooking score: 2**

'Friendly, welcoming and contemporary' is how this Dulwich eaterie styles itself, a multi-mode establishment that functions as a bar, café and brasserie-style dining room, with a touch of modern art gallery thrown in for good measure. Eclectic cooking takes in everything from salmon, ginger and coriander fishcakes to glazed foie gras with black pudding, apple sauce and toasted brioche to start, followed by fillet of beef with red wine sauce, Cajun chicken Caesar salad, or pan-fried sea bass with sorrel and watercress sauce. Live jazz every Thursday evening adds to the buzz, and there's also a monthly opera night. House red and white at £10.50 a bottle, £4.25 a glass, open a straightforward, value-conscious wine list.
**Chef/s:** Damien Gillespie. **Open:** all week 12 to 4, 6 to 11. **Closed:** 1 Jan. **Meals:** alc (main courses £10 to £17.50). Set L £8.50 (2 courses). **Service:** 10% (optional). **Details:** Cards accepted. 120 seats. 40 seats outside. Air-con. Wheelchair access. Music. Children's portions.

## ALSO RECOMMENDED

## ▲ Le Chardon

65 Lordship Lane, East Dulwich, SE22 8EP
Tel no: (020) 8299 1921
www.lechardon.co.uk

Occupying a listed Victorian building with decorative thistle tiles, Le Chardon offers an authentic French bistro experience. The wide-ranging menu takes in starters of snails in garlic butter, moules marinière, and fishcakes with sweet chilli sauce, as well as classic cheese-topped French onion soup. Meat main courses might feature lamb shank with lemon and mint couscous, while fish dishes typically include roast sea bass with grilled fennel and an orange and lemon dressing. An open patio to the rear allows for alfresco dining. Wines are mostly French, as you'd expect, with house red and white at £10.95 a bottle, £3.85 a glass.

## ▲ Lobster Pot

**3 Kennington Lane, Elephant and Castle, SE11 4RG**
**Tel no: (020) 7582 5556**

Ring a doorbell to gain admittance to a tiny dining room hung with nautical knick-knacks where seagulls cry on the sound system. It sounds like the height of naff but somehow the effect is charming rather than kitsch. The menu is predominantly old-fashioned French, lightened by a few more modern dishes: gratinated oysters with a champagne sauce might be followed by grilled fillet of tuna with a tomato, garlic, chilli and coriander sauce, or, of course, lobster every which way. Grilled fillet of beef with green peppercorn sauce is one of five or so meat mains – while classic desserts include crêpes. A short wine list leans towards whites from Burgundy and the Loire; house wine is £12 a bottle. Note that between 8 and 10pm there is a minimum spend of £23 per person.

## ▌Greenwich

## Inside

**Local eatery with big ideas**
**19 Greenwich South Street, SE10 8NW**
**Tel no: (020) 8265 5060**
**www.insiderestaurant.co.uk**
**Modern European | £38**
**Cooking score: 1**

ᐯ

Close to Greenwich station, this converted former shop is the kind of friendly restaurant every neighbourhood should have. Simple décor and a lively atmosphere provide the ideal setting for some inventive modern cooking. An international outlook brings starters ranging from lobster and salmon cannelloni with broad beans, tomato and basil, to five-

spice chicken, coriander and coconut spring rolls, while mains take in seared Moroccan-spiced salmon with lemon couscous, and roast chump of lamb with Puy lentils, red cabbage, roast parsnips and rosemary jus. Spiced chocolate tart with roast almond ice cream is among original dessert ideas. Eight wines by the glass from £3.25 open an international list with house French red and white at £11.95.
**Chef/s:** Guy Awford and Brian Sargeant. **Open:** Tue to Sun L 12 (11 Sat) to 2.30 (3 Sun), Tue to Sat D 6.30 to 11. **Closed:** 24 Dec to 2 Jan. **Meals:** alc (main courses £11 to £17). Set L £14.95 (3 courses), Set D £16.95 (2 courses) to £19.95. **Service:** not inc. **Details:** Cards accepted. 38 seats. Air-con. Wheelchair access. Music. Children's portions.

## ▌Putney

## Emile's

**An enduring favourite**
**96-98 Felsham Road, SW15 1DQ**
**Tel no: (020) 8789 3323**
**www.emilesrestaurant.co.uk**
**⊖ Putney Bridge**
**Modern British | £34**
**Cooking score: 1**
£5
OFF

A well-known feature in the smart, sleepy streets of Putney, Emile's has been keeping the locals well-fed with its world-influenced, British based food for years. But as fashions move on, Emile's seems stuck in a timewarp and there are signs of fatigue. The furnishings are tired, the menu less exciting than it once appeared and the kitchen cooking by numbers instead of flair. Stick to the less adventurous dishes for the best results: a starter of Keens cheddar soufflé with a white wine beurre blanc was fine, but the Szechuan fillet of pork with Thai noodles that followed was less successful, delivering gloopy noodles and a withered accompanying salad. The wine list is a much happier experience and great value with house wine at under £12 a bottle and most of the eclectic selection offered under £20.
**Chef/s:** Andrew Sherlock and Matthew Johnson.
**Open:** Mon to Sat D only 7.30 to 11. **Closed:** 24 to 30 Dec, 2 Jan, Easter Sat, bank hols. **Meals:** Set D

£12.50 (2 courses) to £23.50. **Service:** not inc. **Details:** Cards accepted. 100 seats. Wheelchair access. Music. Children allowed.

## Enoteca Turi
**A truly epic wine List**
28 Putney High Street, SW15 1SQ
Tel no: (020) 8785 4449
⊖ Putney Bridge
**Italian | £35**
**Cooking score: 3**

The fashion of modern Italian cooking with its lightness of touch, deconstruction and simplification of classical dishes has certainly touched this smartish Italian, but the basis of the menu here is still rooted in regional Italy, with the use of really good raw ingredients and plenty of long, slow cooking when appropriate. A starter of antipasto Pugliese with roasted vegetables and a rich, flavoursome fava bean purée has all the beauty and colour of the former and makes a great contrast to the full old-fashioned potency of a ragu d'agnello served with papardelle. The cooking's perfectly competent, but what makes this restaurant really special is the wine list. Proprietor Giuseppe Turi has a passion for Italian wines and his 300-strong list, fully annotated and very fairly priced list is an education in itself. Wines start at £3.75 and each dish on the menu has its own recommendation, but if diners wish to make their own choice, the staff are only too happy to help.
**Chef/s:** Brian Fantoni. **Open:** Mon to Sat 12 to 2.30, 7 to 11. **Closed:** 25 Dec, 1 Jan. **Meals:** alc (main courses L £8.50 to £12, D £17.50 to £19.50). Set L £14.50 (2 courses). **Service:** 12.5% (optional). **Details:** Cards accepted. 70 seats. Air-con. Wheelchair access. Music. Children's portions.

### Average price

The average price listed in main-entry reviews denotes the price of a three-course meal, without wine.

## Phoenix
**A magnet for well-heeled locals**
162-164 Lower Richmond Road, SW15 1LY
Tel no: (020) 8780 3131
⊖ Putney Bridge
**Italian | £30**
**Cooking score: 4**

The Phoenix is a comfortable place to sit, with its generous tables, high ceilings and interesting modern-art collection indoors, but on warm days and especially warm evenings, most people want a table in the romantic, fairylit garden. Roger Brooks's Anglo-Italian menu has plenty to please, from potted shrimps to a fresh, seasonal broad bean, rocket and mint salad with pecorino to start and the likes of slow roast pork belly with beetroot and grilled halibut, sauce vierge to follow. Portions are generous, cooked with total competence and flair and served with grace by a team of cheerful, patient staff. The wine list is an eclectic affair, though there's plenty from Italy, including a decent prosecco and Vin Santo for those wanting to keep to the Italian theme, and at 11.95 for house wine to £60 for an Amarone Classico, fairly good value.
**Chef/s:** Roger Brooks. **Open:** all week 12.30 to 2.30 (3 Sun), 7 to 11 (10 Sun). **Closed:** 3 days Christmas. **Meals:** alc (main courses £11.50 to £17.50). Set L Mon to Sat £13.50 (2 courses) to £15.50, Set L Sun £19.50, Set D Sun to Thur £15.50 (2 courses) to £17.50. **Service:** 12.5% (optional). **Details:** Cards accepted. 100 seats. Air-con. Wheelchair access. Music. Children's portions.

## ALSO RECOMMENDED
### ▲ L'Auberge
22 Upper Richmond Road, Putney, SW15 2RX
Tel no: (020) 8874 3593
www.ardillys.com
⊖ East Putney

An intimate, much-loved asset to the local community, Pascal Ardilly's Putney restaurant serves classic French dishes. Start with frogs' legs with garlic purée and parsley jus (£6.25) or gratin of queen scallops (£7.90). Follow with pan-fried calf's liver with shallots and raspberry vinegar (£14.95) or grilled shark steak and hot tomato sauce (£14.95). Desserts are a must so save room for the lemon chocolate tart (£4.20). French wines from £12. Open Tue to Sat D only.

# ▌South Bank

## Anchor & Hope

**An urban gastropub**
36 The Cut, SE1 8LP
Tel no: (020) 7928 9898
⊖ Waterloo, Southwark
**Modern British | £30**
**Cooking score: 4**

You have to hand it to the team at the Anchor and Hope; this place is still on fire, as hot – nay, hotter – than it was when it opened four years ago: 'on a midweek lunch we had no choice but to perch at the bar'. It remains a credit to the word 'gastropub' as you'd expect of St John and Eagle alums: open kitchen, battered and bruised décor, and dressed-down service, yet it proves the formula isn't bankrupt. Flavours are unapologetically full-on. Snail, bacon, and laverbread on duck fat toast was a rich start, mains get even richer, in the form of a chicken, ham and morel gratin or slow-cooked Hereford beef, dripping potatoes and grass, with flourless chocolate cake to finish. It's worth spending a little extra on your wine choice (and not only for the sake of an upgrade to 'proper' glasses from the wretched thimble-sized tumblers): it's a well-chosen Francophile list, from £10 to just £65, with a few intriguing choices from elsewhere in Europe. Reservations are only taken for Sunday L. A new brasserie, Great Queen Street (see entry), is set for similar popularity levels.
**Chef/s:** Jonathon Jones. **Open:** Tue to Sat L 12 to 2.30, Mon to Sat D 6 to 10.30. **Closed:** Christmas, bank hols. **Meals:** alc (main courses £10 to £20). Bar menu available. **Service:** not inc. **Details:** Cards accepted. 80 seats. Wheelchair access. Music.

# Oxo Tower

**Perennial chic at high altitude**
Oxo Tower Wharf, Barge House Street, SE1 9PH
Tel no: (020) 7803 3888
⊖ Blackfriars, Waterloo
**British | £64**
**Cooking score: 4**

Ownership by Harvey Nichols ensures this eighth-floor dining room remains perennially chic, though it's arguably what's outside – a smashing view of St Paul's, the City skyline and the Thames – that's the main attraction, and a pre-dinner drink on the terrace is one of the capital's ultimate alfresco experiences. The high-rise location is matched by some very steep pricing, but the quality of cooking is generally sound and, although the menu is inevitably peppered with foie gras and lobster for corporate expense accounters, you'll also find creative, up-to-date assemblies such as tuna tartare with an enoki mushroom salad and a cucumber and lemon salsa followed by wild Scottish salmon with fennel gnocchi and baby vegetables. Gutsier tastes might be accommodated by roast fillet of beef with cep purée, oxtail and a truffle cream bon-bon. Finish with a spin on a classic dessert: lemon balm pannacotta with mango trifle, say. A shorter, less expensive menu is offered at lunch, while the next-door brasserie serves cheaper food (much of it with an Asian/Italian slant) in funkier surrounds. The 25-page wine list is a comprehensive tour of the world's major growing areas, with a strong selection of Champagne, Bordeaux and Burgundy underlining Oxo's celebration credentials. Elsewhere there's something for every budget, including house French for £16.50 and 20 by the glass.
**Chef/s:** Jeremy Bloor. **Open:** Restaurant Mon to Sat 12 to 2.30, 6 to 11, Sun 12 to 3, 6.30 to 10; Brasserie all week 12 to 3.15 (2.45 Sun), 5.30 to 11 (6 to 10.30 Sun). **Meals:** Restaurant alc D (main courses £16.50 to £25). Set L £33.50 to £35, Set D £33.50 to £70; Brasserie alc (main courses £14 to £18). Set pre-theatre D £16.50 (2 courses) to £21.50.
**Service:** 12.5% (optional). **Details:** Cards accepted. 80 seats. Air-con. No mobile phones. Wheelchair access. Music. Children's portions.

★NEW ENTRY★
## Skylon
**Capturing the spirit of the Festival of Britain**
Belvedere Road, SE1 8XX
Tel no: (020) 7654 7800
www.danddlondon.com/restaurants/skylon
⊖ Waterloo
**Modern British | £39**
**Cooking score: 4**

The reworking of the interior of this restaurant on level 3 of the Royal Festival Hall is 'a brilliant job', in particular the subtle connections with the building's 1950s origins, from the eye-catching bronze chandeliers right down to the stylish cutlery, a reprise of a classic fifties design by David Mellor. This vast space houses a bar, grill and restaurant with floor to ceiling windows providing a panoramic cityscape. Finnish-born Helen Puolakka, heads the brigade, her philosophy based on seasonality and exemplary ingredients. At a meal taken just after opening, it was felt that, for the most part, the kitchen 'cooked with distinction' – cold butter-poached Dorset lobster, paired with a broad bean salad, cashew nuts and pink grapefruit vinaigrette made an interesting start, while caramelised lamb shoulder came with its fillet pan-fried and a punchy piece of its kidney, cleverly offset with Swiss chard bolstered by Reggiano, Parmesan and girotte marmalade. Another classic, crêpe Suzette, flambéed at the table, made a good finish. The smartly assembled wine list spans various styles and budgets, and starts at £15. A section devoted to rare wines from the 1950s is, unsurprisingly, at prices as elevated as this restaurant.
**Chef/s:** Helena Puolakka. **Open:** Mon to Sun 12 noon to 2.30pm, 5.30pm to 10.45pm (bar 11am to 1am). **Meals:** Set L (1951) 2 courses £19.51, 3 courses £24.50. Set L & D 2 courses £29.50, 3 courses £34.50. Pre & Post Theatre 2 courses £24.50, 3 courses £29.50. **Service:** 12.5%. **Details:** Cards accepted. 92 seats. Air-con. Separate bar. Wheelchair access.

## ALSO RECOMMENDED
### ▲ Mezzanine
National Theatre, South Bank, SE1 9PX
Tel no: (020) 7452 3600

Buzzy eaterie attached to the National Theatre, popular for its stunning view across the River Thames and good value pre-show set deals (two-courses 19.95), so arrive early to bag a window seat or a table on the terrace. The post-show carte offers similar dishes along the lines of salad of wild rabbit and chorizo with broad bean hummus (£7), herb-crusted baked Pollack with spinach, tomato and saffron (£10.50), rump of lamb with roasted Mediterranean vegetables and basil (£12.95), with rhubarb and custard brûlée among the desserts. Wines from £13.25. Open Mon-Sat D and Sun L only.

## READERS RECOMMEND
### Benugo at the BFI
**Modern European**
Belvedere Road, South Bank, SE1 8XT
Tel no: (020) 7401 9000
www.benugo.com
'Stylish restaurant and bar at the British Film Institute'

## ▌Southwark
### Baltic
**Ultra-hip Eastern European restaurant**
74 Blackfriars Road, SE1 8HA
Tel no: (020) 7928 1111
www.balticrestaurant.co.uk
⊖ Southwark
**Modern European | £35**
**Cooking score: 3**

Opposite Southwark tube station, and within ambling distance of Tate Modern, Baltic combines a deeply cool and strikingly minimalist bar serving trendy vodkas, with a sumptuous airy dining space, all muted colours, modern art and mood lighting, and housed within an eighteenth-century building. The theme of the food is Eastern

European, the enticing menu taking in dishes familiar to the countries between the Baltic and the Black Sea, but mixed with modern British ideas. Start with Siberian Pelmeni – small beef and pork dumplings – barley and bacon soup, or pig trotter croquettes with pickled saffron cucumber salad. Then tuck into beef stroganoff with sour cream and pickles, roast pork shank with braised sauerkraut and bacon, or a less obvious Baltic dish like roast cod with lemon dumplings. Puddings extend to Ukranian rhum baba, and white chocolate cheesecake. House vins de pays at £13 kick off the wine list.

**Chef/s:** Peter Repinski. **Open:** all week 12 to 3, 6 to 11.15. **Closed:** 1 Jan. **Meals:** alc (main courses £10.50 to £18.50). Set L and D 6 to 7 £11.50 (2 courses) to £13.50. **Service:** 12.5% (optional). **Details:** Cards accepted. 100 seats. Wheelchair access. Music. Children's portions.

# Champor-Champor

**Riotous décor and bold Asian cooking**
62-64 Weston Street, SE1 3QJ
Tel no: (020) 7403 4600
www.champor-champor.com
⊖ London Bridge
Malaysian | £43
Cooking score: 3

The name roughly translates as 'mix and match', which applies equally to the food and the décor in this idiosyncratic restaurant. Diners sit in what looks like an anthropologist's den stuffed with tribal masks, carvings, a portly Buddha and other weird ethnic artefacts. The food is dubbed 'creative Malay-Asian': traditional village (kampong) cooking is the jumping-off point, but influences and ingredients are garnered from the Far East and beyond. Crabmeat and Asian chive toast with yellow pickled water chestnuts could open proceedings, alongside braised ostrich sausages in Szechuan pepper and miso. Next comes a palate-cleansing 'inter-course' granita before stir-fried kangaroo fillet in chilli oil, petai (an exotic legume) and egg noodles or cassava, ginko nut and preserved Chinese plum tagine with garlic

shoot pilau and parsnip crisps. Desserts are equally riotous concoctions like green tea jelly topped with coconut custard, warm pineapple and brandy pajery. The drinks list includes Asian-Pacific beers and spirits, plus a neat selection of global wines with bottles from unlikely sources including Georgia. Prices start at £14.

**Chef/s:** Adu Amran Hassan. **Open:** Mon to Sat D only 6.15 to 10; L by appointment for groups. **Closed:** 6 days Christmas, 4 days Easter. **Meals:** Set D £23.50 (2 courses) to £27.90 (3 courses). **Service:** 12.5% (optional). **Details:** Cards accepted. 46 seats. Air-con. Wheelchair access. Music. Children allowed.

# Delfina

**Inventive cooking and an art gallery**
50 Bermondsey Street, SE1 3UD
Tel no: (020) 7357 0244
www.delfina.org.uk
⊖ London Bridge
Global | £41
Cooking score: 4

A converted, one-time chocolate factory provides the colourful space for this Bermondsey restaurant-cum-art gallery. The vast white-walled, high-ceilinged, ground-floor (with artists' studios above) is a bright affair, with plenty of light from windows and skylight and large blocks of colour from modern art. Floors are honey-coloured wooden boards and the furniture is fittingly modern and stylish, with well-spaced tables decked out with lime-green tops. Opening times may be limited (lunchtimes and Friday evenings) but invention abounds, the ambitious modern approach peppered with some unusual ingredients and combinations. Take aubergine, cherry tomato, red onions and a mint-parsley salad with tahini dressing as the accompaniment for a main-course of chargrilled, smoked, paprika-marinated lamb, or maybe ginger-braised Puy lentils and roasted beetroot alongside pan-fried calf's liver. Desserts continue the theme, with a chocolate malva pudding teamed with frangelico ice cream, while the compact but

interesting wine list is also a global affair, with prices setting out at £13.50 to plateau at £58, and there are plenty on offer by glass too.
**Chef/s:** Maria Elia. **Open:** Mon to Fri L 12 to 3, Fri D 7 to 10. **Closed:** 23 Dec to 2 Jan. **Meals:** alc (main courses £10 to £14). **Service:** 12.5% (optional). **Details:** Cards accepted. 140 seats. Wheelchair access. Music.

## ★NEW ENTRY★
# Magdalen
**Lively newcomer showcasing honest British cooking**
152 Tooley Street, SE1 2TU
Tel no: (020) 7403 1342
⊖ London Bridge
**Modern British | £28**
**New Chef**

The double act of James and Emma Faulks pays dividends at this buzzy restaurant, which is spread over two floors on the site of the former Peruvian restaurant, Fina Estampa, just a short walk from London Bridge station. A laid back vibe, handsome décor and obliging service are what to expect, and the kitchen pumps out a short, daily changing menu of modern British dishes. It's simple, good value cooking with more than a nod to the influence of Fergus Henderson, but with some European influences at work, too, as in a starter of Spanish ham with stewed white asparagus. Potted crab and garlic soup share the stage with jellied rabbit, grain mustard and cornichons and the roll-call of dishes readers recommend include smoked eel, beetroot and horseradish, and a crisp-skinned salt duck leg with lentils and creamy mustard sauce. Venison and trotter pie (for two) is an outright winner, while desserts range from rum baba via treacle tart to baked yogurt and rhubarb. The French leaning wine list opens at £13.50.
**Chef/s:** James and Emma Faulks and David Abbot. **Open:** Mon to Fri 12 to 2.30, Mon to Sat 6.30 to 10.30. **Closed:** 23 Dec to 3 Jan. **Meals:** alc (main meals £13.50 to £17.50). **Service:** not inc. **Details:** Cards accepted. 90 seats. Air-con. Wheelchair access. Music. Children allowed.

## Martin Wishart

*Why did you become a chef?*
I left school at 15 and decided that I wanted to become a chef.

*Which of today's chefs do you admire?*
Anyone who is starting up on their own.

*Where do you source your ingredients?*
Primarily small, specialist farms in the UK and some in Europe.

*Where do you eat out?*
My favourite restaurant is The Wee Restaurant, North Queensferry.

*Who is your favourite producer?*
My gamedealer, Craig Stevenson is one of my favourite suppliers, and also my fishmonger, Stevie Fish.

*What's your favourite coookery book?*
Ham & Eggs. I like the repertoire. It is more of a reference book than a recipe book.

*What's the best dish you've ever eaten?*
Fresh grilled snapper in Puerto Esconditito, Pacific Coast of Mexico.

*What's your guilty food pleasure?*
Cheese.

*What's the hardest thing about running a restaurant?*
Making your suppliers understand what you require.

## Roast

**Fine dining in the middle of the market**
Floral Hall, Borough Market, Stoney Street,
SE1 1TL
Tel no: (020) 7940 1300
www.roast-restaurant.com
⊖ London Bridge
Modern British | £33
Cooking score: 4

Stylish and sassy, this modern British restaurant commands absorbing views of Borough Market, the railway line and the dome of St Paul's beyond. The buzz in the market outside is reflected by the kitchen's enthusiasm for well-sourced British ingredients. It's a versatile space - come for a relaxed brunch and enjoy a tattie scone with field mushrooms and Ayrshire bacon or the (recommended) full Borough cooked breakfast. From 11am you can savour more extensive all-day dining, featuring such home-grown delights as cold Yorkshire Dales beef, black pudding hash or grilled mackerel. And just to show how unstuffy Roast is, they'll cheerfully offer you your favourite British condiments, too, like Marmite on your toast, Coleman's with your sausages — even Bird's Custard if you follow the dessert route. Dinner takes itself more seriously (and at £22 for a 10oz rump, so it should). The latter was cooked beautifully, dripping in horseradish and mustard butter; grilled spring lamb chops with pease pudding and mint sauce were also a success. Starters on this packed spring evening included dressed Dorset crab with pickled cucumber and smoked haddock fishcake with rocket and lemon balm. Roast's wine list is by no means a snip (house starts at £18) but the global selection is interesting and around 15 are offered by the glass. Ask for a window table when you book.

**Chef/s:** Lawrence Keogh. **Open:** Sun to Fri L 12 to 2.30pm (4pm Sun), Mon to Sat D 5.30 to 10.30pm. **Meals:** alc (main courses £13.50 to £25). Set L £18 (2 courses) to £21. Set D (exc 6.45 to 9) £18 (2 courses) to £21. Breakfast and bar menus available. **Service:** 12.5% (optional). **Details:** Cards accepted. 110 seats. Air-con. Wheelchair access. Music. Children's portions.

## RSJ

**Sturdy restaurant with sound technique**
33 Coin Street, SE1 9NR
Tel no: (020) 7928 4554
www.rsj.uk.com
⊖ Waterloo, Southwark
French | £43
Cooking score: 3
🍷 ♈

This reliable, imaginative place, a stone's throw from the Old and Young Vics and the Southbank is as robustly unsusceptible to fashion as the steel joist it's named after. Clean minimalism and with everything from decent napkins and glasses to knowledgeable service done properly and without fuss, ensures RSJ's enduring and wide appeal. Sound francophile techniques emphasise the flavours of the ingredients straightforwardly: a smooth soup with beetroot and tomato finely balanced; accurately grilled salmon; classic puddings including excellent ice creams, epitomise the approach. Set two or three dish meals offering real choice are especially good value. A marvellous obsession with bottles from the Loire, virtually to the exclusion of all else, French or otherwise, makes doubters of the quality and range of wines offered from Muscadet to the Nivernais think twice. A wonderful stack of sweeties and halves completes the picture.

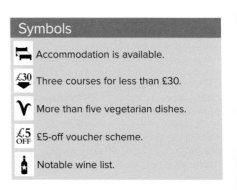

### Symbols

🛏 Accommodation is available.

£30 Three courses for less than £30.

♈ More than five vegetarian dishes.

£5 OFF £5-off voucher scheme.

🍷 Notable wine list.

Chef/s: Ian Stabler. Open: Mon to Fri L 12 to 2.30, Mon to Sat D 5.30 to 11. Meals: alc (main courses £13 to £18). Set L and D £15.95 (2 courses) to £17.95. Service: 12.5% (optional). Details: Cards accepted. 90 seats. Air-con. No music. Children's portions.

## Tapas Brindisa

**Outstanding tapas in packed surroundings**
18-20 Southwark Street, SE1 1TJ
Tel no: (020) 7357 8880
www.brindisa.com
⊖ Borough
**Spanish/Portuguese | £25**
**Cooking score: 3**
Ⅴ ₤30

This extremely convivial tapas restaurant on the edge of Borough Market is run by the renowned Spanish produce supplier Brindisa. Located in a potato warehouse, the curved building with its floor-to-ceiling windows, concrete floors and tightly packed bare wooden tables make for a light and airy dining room that becomes pleasantly boisterous during peak service. A changing menu features a superb choice of hot and cold tapas, that can either be eaten in the restaurant or standing at the bar. Choose from a selection of regional charcuterie, including Teruel serrano ham or salchichon de vich, a traditional Catalan recipe. Hot tapas include pungent prawns cooked in olive oil, garlic and chilli, or more adventurous dishes such as pan-fried sea bass with beetroot, orange and red onion salad. The exclusively Spanish wine list includes a fine selection of sherries and cava. Choose a bottle of house white Verdejo for £16, or a house Tempranillo for £13.20.
Chef/s: José Manuel Pizarro. Open: Mon to Thurs 11 to 11, Fri to Sat L 12 to 4, D 5.30 to 11. Closed: Christmas, bank hol Mon. Meals: alc (tapas £3 to £8). Service: 12.5% (optional). Details: Cards accepted. 40 seats. 9 seats outside. Air-con. Separate bar. Wheelchair access. Music.

## ALSO RECOMMENDED

## ▲ Rebato's

169 South Lambeth Road, Southwark, SW8 1XW
Tel no: (020) 7735 6388
www.rebatos.com
⊖ Vauxhall

Step into Rebato's and you step back into the 1970s as little has changed over the years at this traditional and much-loved tapas bar. In the dimly lit dark wood and tiled-front bar, tuck into some classic tapas dishes – boquerones (anchovies in olive oil and garlic), deep-fried squid, grilled sardines. More substantial traditional Spanish dishes are served in the light-filled formal dining room out back. Feast on fish soup Cantabrica (£4.95), chargrilled lamb cutlets served with garlic mayonnaise (£11.95) and finish with crème caramel (£3.95) from the trolley. Good value set lunch menus, cheerful, professional service and Spanish house wines from £10.50. Closed Sat L and Sun.

## READERS RECOMMEND

## Cafe One Seven One

**Modern British**
Jerwood Space, 171 Union Street, Southwark, SE1 OLN
Tel no: 020 7654 0100
'Great-value food in modern gallery space'

## The Table

**Modern European**
83 Southwark St, Southwark, SE1 OHX
Tel no: 020 7401 2760
www.thetablecafe.com
'Excellent canteen in an architectural practice'

### Which? Campaigns

To find out more about Which? food and drink campaigns, please visit:
www.which.co.uk

## Wright Bros Oyster and Porter Bar

**Seafood**
11 Stoney Street, Southwark, SE1 9AD
Tel no: (020) 7403 9554
www.wrightbros.eu.com
**'Fresh produce, straight from Borough Market'**

## ▌Tooting

### Kastoori

**Gujarati food with African influences**
188 Upper Tooting Road, SW17 7EJ
Tel no: (020) 8767 7027
⊖ Tooting Broadway
Gujarati Vegetarian | £21
Cooking score: 3

V £30

Dinesh and Manoj Thanki have been plying their trade in Tooting since 1987 and have made Kastoori a favourite destination for skilfully spiced Gujarati vegetarian food. Their restaurant is bright and cheerfully decorated, with Hindu sculptures adding an extra touch of exoticism. The family hails from the temperate region of Katia Wahd (the only part of the Sub-continent where tomatoes grow naturally) and also spent many years in Uganda. Both influences shine through on their menu, which moves from mainstay appetisers like samosas, bhel puris and dosas to intriguing vegetable curries and specials. The kitchen makes good use of aduki beans, cassava root, karela (bitter gourd) and other exotica: in particular, look for matoki (a green banana curry), kasodi (sweetcorn cooked in coconut milk with peanut sauce) and the family's 'sensational Euro-veg special' involving everything from leeks to rhubarb. Desserts are traditional stalwarts like

### Also recommended

An 'also recommended' entry is not a full entry, but is provisionally suggested as an alternative to main entries.

shrikhand, ras malai and khir (rice pudding 'like granny never made it'). House wine is £9.95.
**Chef/s:** Manoj Thanki. **Open:** Wed to Sun L 12.30 to 2.30, all week D 6 to 10.30. **Closed:** 25 and 26 Dec. **Meals:** alc (main courses £4.75 to £6.25). **Service:** not inc. **Details:** Cards accepted. 82 seats. Air-con. Wheelchair access. Music. Children's portions. Children allowed.

## Radha Krishna Bhavan

**Authentic Keralan food**
86 Tooting High Street, SW17 0RN
Tel no: (020) 8682 0969
www.mcdosa.com
⊖ Tooting Broadway
South Indian | £24
Cooking score: 1

£5 OFF £30

A life-size, traditional Kathakali statue and huge murals evoking the palm-fronded beaches of Kerala set the mood in this colourfully bedecked restaurant. The menu has its share of kurmas, dhansaks and other curry house stand-bys, but the real highlights are the specialities from the owner's beloved South Indian province. Skilfully prepared starters almost steal the show, especially the range of dosas with vegetable sambar and coconut chutney, uthappam (India's answer to a pizza, studded with chillies and tomatoes) and Mysore bonda (deep-fried spiced lentil and potato balls). The kitchen also focuses on exotic Cochin specialities such as lamb fry masala and kappa meen masala (boiled, spiced tapioca served with fish curry). Among the vegetable-based dishes look for avial and kalan (sweet mango and yam with coconut, yogurt and green chillies) or dry-cooked beetroot thoran. Drink lassi, juice or beer; workaday wines from £9.95.
**Chef/s:** Mr Terab Ali. **Open:** all week 12 to 3, 6 to 11 (12 Fri and Sat). **Closed:** 25 and 26 Dec. **Meals:** alc (main courses £2.50 to £8). **Service:** 10%. **Details:** Cards accepted. 50 seats. Air-con. Wheelchair access. Music. Children's portions. Children allowed.

## READERS RECOMMEND
### Rick's Café
**Modern European**
122 Mitcham Road, Tooting, SW17 9NH
Tel no: (020) 8767 5219
**'A well-kept secret for Tooting locals'**

## ▌Wimbledon
### Light House Restaurant
**Wimbledon's culinary bright light**
75-77 Ridgway, SW19 4ST
Tel no: (020) 8944 6338
www.lighthousewimbledon.com
⊖ **Wimbledon**
Modern European | £32
**Cooking score: 3**

Enormous windows let the light flood into this bright and breezy contemporary-styled neighbourhood restaurant, the pale wood floors and modern art-adorned walls adding to the airy and cheerful atmosphere. Informal and helpful service contributes to a laid-back feel that seems to suit the sunny food. There's a strong Italian influence to the menu, although dishes trawl all over the Mediterranean shores and further afield to Asia for inspiration, ensuring that there's something to please all tastes. Ingredients are confidently handled and dishes are rustic with robust flavours allowed to shine through. Devilled lambs' kidneys with pancetta and field mushrooms on toast, or seared scallops with Jerusalem artichoke puree and morcilla could be a good way to start, then follow with calf's liver accompanied by potato gnocchi, gorgonzola, roast sweet potato and crispy sage. Alternatively, opt for fish, perhaps pan-fried sea bass with carrot and ginger purée, bok choi and oyster mushrooms. Round off with white chocolate parfait with strawberry sorbet, or treacle tart. The wine list (house starts at £13.50) has a good selection by the glass and is well-judged, if not great value.
**Chef/s:** Chris Casey. **Open:** all week L 12 to 2.45, Mon to Sat D 6.30 to 10.30. **Closed:** 25 and 26 Dec, Easter Day. **Meals:** alc (main courses £11.50 to £17.50). Set L £14 (2 courses) to £16.50, Set L Sun

£18 (2 courses) to £23. **Service:** 12.5% (optional). **Details:** Cards accepted. 75 seats. Wheelchair access. Music. Children's portions.

## ALSO RECOMMENDED
### ▲ Earl Spencer
260-262 Merton Road, Wimbledon, SW18 5JL
Tel no: (020) 8870 9244
www.theearlspencer.co.uk
⊖ **Southfields**

This lively gastropub comes with a winter log fire and three cask-conditioned ales. Service is good 'once you have ordered and paid at the bar', and the menu changes daily. Start with grilled sardines and saffron potatoes (£6.50), or spinach and feta filo pastries with mint yoghurt (£5.50). For mains consider La Garbure smoked sausage, ham and white bean casserole (£10) or an above-average beer-battered whiting and cuttlefish with chips and minted peas (£10.50). Finish with sticky ginger pudding (£5) or apricot and frangipane tart with crème anglaise (£5). Wines start at £11. Open all week.

---

### Cooking score

A score of 1 is a significant achievement. The score in any review is based on several meals, incorporating feedback from both our readers and inspectors. As a rough guide, 1 denotes capable cooking with some inconsistencies, rising steadily through different levels of technical expertise, until the scores between 6 and 10 indicate exemplary skills, along with innovation, artistry and ambition. If there is a new chef, we don't score the restaurant for the first year of entry. For further details, please see the scoring section in the introduction to the Guide.

---

## ▌Chelsea

### The Admiral Codrington

**Not afraid to experiment**
17 Mossop Street, SW3 2LY
Tel no: (020) 7581 0005
www.theadmiralcodrington.com
⊖ South Kensington
Gastropub | £44
Cooking score: 3

Ⴘ

A blend of country-style décor – fussy floral banquettes and nautical knick-knacks – and well-informed, efficient and friendly staff makes this smart pub restaurant stand out from the crowd. You can't go wrong with the menu, which lists the kind of comfort food everybody likes to eat: fishcakes, roast lamb, roast chicken, steak and chips, and pork belly. There are occasional flourishes of ambition, too: artichoke salad is tossed with dandelion leaves and Valencia almonds, foie gras and chicken liver parfait comes with Vin de Constance jelly, and sausages are made with wagyu beef. Similarly, fluffy, rustic hand-made potato gnocchi is dressed with lusty, full-bodied tomato sauce crammed with sprightly spring vegetables and herbs. Puddings, like rich, dense chocolate and peanut butter parfait with pinot noir-glazed cherries, keep the comfort factor high. A fairly basic list of Old and New World wines starts at £13 a bottle, with around fifteen available by the glass.
**Chef/s:** Jon Rotheram. **Open:** all week 12 to 2.30 (3.30 Sat, 4.00 Sun), 6.30 to 12 midnight (7 to 10 Sun). **Closed:** Christmas Day, Boxing day. **Meals:** alc (main courses £10.95 to £17.50). Cover £1 at D. Bar L menu available. **Service:** 12.5% (optional).
**Details:** Cards accepted. 50 seats. Separate bar. No mobile phones. Wheelchair access. Music. Children allowed. Car parking.

## Aubergine

**Polished French cooking in a Chelsea backwater**
11 Park Walk, SW10 0AJ
Tel no: (020) 7352 3449
www.auberginerestaurant.co.uk
⊖ South Kensington
Modern French | £65
Cooking score: 5

🍷 Ⴘ

Little seems to change at this genteel Chelsea venue, which is discreetly tucked away in the affluent environs of SW10. William Drabble continues to deliver deft, technically skilled dishes from the bedrock of the modern repertoire and polished French cooking remains the order of the day. Diners can expect a generous smattering of luxury ingredients, from starters of sautéed foie gras served with figs in red wine and gingerbread crisps to poached lobster tail, which keeps company with a warm salad of asparagus, morels, artichokes and truffled potatoes. Frog's legs and a galette of pig's head (albeit with roasted langoustines) help to restore the earthy balance, while dishes such as chump of Lune Valley spring lamb with Provençal vegetables and rosemary jus suggest that the kitchen is happy to stay in the mainstream. Tradition also rules when it comes to classically inclined desserts such as apricot soufflé with dark chocolate sauce or caramelised apple with roasted almond ice cream. Almost everything here is ever-so-French, apart from the intriguing choice of world beers that is now a feature of the place. The lengthy wine list is a Francophile's dream, with stellar selections from the big-name regions backed up by serious contenders from the Italian new wave and California. Prices may seem financially challenging, but there are some attractive

### Average price

The average price listed in main-entry reviews denotes the price of a three-course meal, without wine.

bargains to be had – especially from Southwest France. House selections start at £17.

**Chef/s:** William Drabble. **Open:** Mon to Fri L 12 to 2.30, Mon to Sat D 7 to 11. **Meals:** Set L £34 (inc wine), Set D £64 to £77. **Service:** 12.5% (optional). **Details:** Cards accepted. 60 seats. Air-con. No music. No mobile phones. Wheelchair access. Children allowed.

## Awana

**A keystone of Malaysian cooking**
85 Sloane Avenue, SW3 3DX
Tel no: (020) 7584 8880
www.awana.co.uk
**Malaysian | £62**
**Cooking score: 1**

Ⴤ

The décor in Awana's long, rectangular dining room is inspired by the traditional Malaysian teak houses – all dark wood, glass screens and leather furnishings. The name means 'in the clouds' in Malay and the restaurant is under the same ownership as the Mango Tree (see entry). Typically, begin with a roti canai (flat bread) appetiser red curry sauce, move on to an assorted seafood satay starter, or, perhaps spicy crab and potato cakes with asian celery and coriander. High-quality ingredients are evident in the main courses, which take in a cumin-spiced curried lamb shank with pumpkin, sweet potato and lemongrass, whole grilled sea bass served with lime and lemongrass butter, and a good choice of stir-fries. The wine list has some exciting bottles, although mark-ups are a touch on the high side, with prices starting at £19.

**Chef/s:** Lee Chin Soon. **Open:** all week 12 to 3, 6 to 11.30. **Meals:** alc (main courses £9.50 to £24). Set L £12.80 (2 courses) to £15, Set D £36. Bar menu available. **Service:** 12.5% (optional). **Details:** Cards accepted. 80 seats. Air-con. Wheelchair access. Music. Jacket and tie required. Children's portions.

## Le Colombier

**Patriotic neighbourhood bistro**
145 Dovehouse Street, SW3 6LB
Tel no: (020) 7351 1155
⊖ South Kensington
**French | £28**
**New Chef**

Ⴤ £30

The 'entente' is decidedly 'cordiale' in Didier Garnier's dyed-in-the-wool Chelsea bistro, which is brimful of Gallic bonhomie. Blue and white colours set the tone in the opened-out dining room, which is a classic mix of wide floorboards, etched windows and Art Deco wall lights; a terrace out front attracts fair-weather crowds. No-nonsense French bistro food with a few Mediterranean flourishes is the kitchen's stock in trade, and the menu skips its way through potted goose rillettes, garlicky snails in puff pastry, veal kidneys with Dijon mustard sauce and fillet of wild sea bass with olive oil and lemon. Straightforward grills are a fixture, while desserts don't stray far from the realms of crêpes Suzette and crème brûlée. Frances rules emphatically on the big-hearted wine list, with bottle prices starting at £19.

**Chef/s:** Nigel Smith. **Open:** all week 12 to 3 (3.30 Sun), 6.30 to 10.30 (10 Sun). **Meals:** alc (main courses £13.50 to £23). Set L £16.50 (2 courses), Set L Sun £19. **Service:** 12.5% (optional). **Details:** Cards accepted. 42 seats. 30 seats outside. No music. Wheelchair access. Children allowed.

## Eight Over Eight

**Fusion meets fashion in this celeb hangout**
392 King's Road, SW3 5UZ
Tel no: (020) 7349 9934
www.eightovereight.nu
⊖ Sloane Square
**Fusion/Pan-Asian | £48**
**Cooking score: 2**

A converted Chelsea theatre pub is the setting for this branch of Will Ricker's in-vogue fusion group. Glitterati, media celebs and star-watchers throng the visually dramatic space, which has been done out with handsome furniture and ersatz oriental trappings. Food provides the accompaniment to serious socialising, and the menu is designed to make things as user-friendly as possible. Dishes are grouped into categories for grazing, and the kitchen delivers vibrant assemblages based on authentic ingredients: a glossary on the menu explains all. Dim sum and salads (duck with watermelon and cashews) share the billing with sushi and sashimi, tempura (soft-shell crab with ponzu and jalapeño), BBQs and curries (roast monkfish with choi sum). Specials such as Shanghai-style whole snapper provide extra choice, while desserts are flights of fancy such as chocolate pudding with green tea ice cream. Exotic cocktails fit the bill, and the wine list is a racy global affair. Prices start at £15 and there are numerous options by the glass.

**Chef/s:** Richard Francis. **Open:** Mon to Sat L 12 to 3 (4 Sat), all week D 6 to 11. **Meals:** alc (main courses £10 to £26). Set L £15 (2 courses). Bar menu available. **Service:** 12.5% (optional). **Details:** Cards accepted. 95 seats. Air-con. No music.

## Gordon Ramsay

**An unmissable experience**
68-69 Royal Hospital Road, SW3 4HP
Tel no: (020) 7352 4441
www.gordonramsay.com
⊖ **Sloane Square**
**French | £96**
**Cooking score: 9**

🍷 �🇾

Gordon Ramsay is now the proud owner of an international brand, fronting serious top-end restaurants in Dubai, New York and Tokyo (with Paris beckoning) in between hosting TV shows, running marathons and endorsing just about every product under the sun. He is also a consummate restaurateur and Hospital Road remains his treasured London flagship. Thanks to a £1m makeover from David Collins, this must-visit destination has been presented with a new suit of clothes. The result is a dining room that is more restrained than before, with simplified design gestures, predominantly cream and beige colours, long slim mirrors –

of course – GR-branded Royal Doulton crockery. This prevailing mood of calm simplicity allows the food to take centre stage, although there is a great deal of subtle orchestration along the way. Much depends on indefatigable maitre d' Jean-Claude Breton, who ensures that service comes complete with exactly the required amount of French polish. All of this comes at a price, although it is worth remembering that the admirable set lunch menu provides a tantalising and affordable glimpse of the kitchen's prowess. The whole culinary set-up is marshalled by executive chef Mark Askew, and regulars reckon that he has raised the bar of late when it comes to presentation: consider a ring of unctuous ballotine of foie gras filled with camomile jelly set alongside a row of baby pickled vegetables, with top-notch rosemary focaccia as an accompaniment. Breathtaking freshness and supremely good raw materials are the kitchen's hallmarks, coupled with 'peerless technique' and dazzling execution: an entrecôte of roast Gressingham duck breast, for example, is artfully arranged with honey-glazed onions and morels, offset by the bitter edge of a chicory tart and tempered with a limpid Madeira juice. Elsewhere, the kitchen works its magic with Northumbrian beef, cooked medium-rare, ringed by kohlrabi and finished with an infusion of root vegetables (which also appears in a cup ready to be drunk). Fish is no less impressive, whether it is a pair of scallops given the thinnest of Parmesan crusts then served with Parmesan velouté and octopus carpaccio or brilliantly timed fillet of line-caught halibut resting on rolls of pappardelle (one tinged green with coriander, the other red with ginger) with passion fruit butter sauce meticulously poured around it. Desserts remain as spectacular as ever: a star turn is Granny Smith parfait with honeycomb, bitter chocolate and Champagne foam – a 'complex labyrinth of sophisticated flavours'. By-pass coffee and you will miss the dramatic entrance of white chocolates filled with strawberry ice cream served in a silver dish with liquid nitrogen spilling out. Given the levels of expectation that are part and parcel of this rarefied culinary experience, there are bound to be occasional quibbles and lapses. Reporters are bemused by the fact that the kitchen seems unwilling to bake its own bread; some also find the 'wow' factor has faded a little of late, but the consistency of the kitchen still warrants plaudits. The awe-inspiring wine list is a cause for celebration, particularly if price is no option. One eagle-eyed oenophile observed that 'the number of bottles worth more than £10,000 exceeds the options under £20' which says a great deal about the restaurant's priorities. Rarities are sprinkled liberally throughout, with legions of mighty offerings from the classic French regions (as might be expected) but also some dazzling gems from Australia and the USA. The sommelier's advice is exemplary, and there is plenty to enjoy for around £30.

**Chef/s:** Gordon Ramsay. **Open:** Mon to Fri 12 to 2.30, 6.30 to 11. **Meals:** Set L £40 to £110, Set D £85 to £110. **Service:** 12.5% (optional). **Details:** Cards accepted. 44 seats. Air-con. No music. No mobile phones. Wheelchair access. Children's portions.

## Rasoi Vineet Bhatia
**A domestic approach to Indian cooking**
10 Lincoln Street, SW3 2TS
Tel no: (020) 7225 1881
www.vineetbhatia.com
⊖ Sloane Square
**Indian/Pakistani/Bangladeshi | £69**
**Cooking score: 5**

If you were looking for the kind of upscale Indian restaurant where you had to ring a doorbell to get in, Chelsea would be a good place to start. Look no further. Vineet Bhatia's singular establishment, not far from Sloane Square, is a little gem. Inside, the Lilliputian scale is compensated by vivid décor and a conservatory roof, and the feeling of domesticity is a world away from the last curry house you visited. As is the cooking. Bhatia brings a new-wave sensibility to dishes such as a wild mushroom starter that is comprised of rice- and lentil-based khichdi, tomato ice-cream, tandoori shiitakes and a mushroom-topped naan dressed in truffle oil. Variations on

crab encompass a masala crab cake, crab chutney and a crab and corn samosa. The vibrant, enlivening flavours continue through main courses like shredded duck confit in korma dressing with walnuts, potato, and apricot chutney, or in fish dishes such as herbed sea bass on crushed tandoori potatoes, with crispy okra and coconut sauce. If an agony of indecision overtakes you, there is a bells-and-whistles gourmand option of seven courses. The desserts are just as alluring as the rest, bringing on a samosa of marbled chocolate, chenna (crumbly cheese) and roasted almonds, with Indian tea ice cream. Wines are in keeping with the elevated tone. A generous page of half-bottles opens a list that is high on quality. The centre of gravity is France, and prices are not giveaway, but everything has been chosen with an eye to the food, as it should be. Glass prices start at £5, bottles at £20.

**Chef/s:** Vineet Bhatia. **Open:** Mon to Fri L 12 to 2.30, Mon to Sat D 6 to 10.45. **Closed:** Christmas. **Meals:** alc (main courses £15 to £39). Set L £24, Set D £75. **Service:** 12.5% (optional). **Details:** Cards accepted. 52 seats. Air-con. No music.

## Tom Aikens
**Superstar chef comes of age**
43 Elystan Street, SW3 3NT
Tel no: (020) 7584 2003
www.tomaikens.co.uk
⊖ South Kensington
**French | £59**
**Cooking score: 8**

As has been noted before in these pages, Tom Aikens' cooking has become more assured and less showy since his Pied-à-Terre days. The word 'simplicity' is not the first that springs to mind even now, but dishes are not quite as busy as they once were. Perhaps it's the effect of the interior design in this sober-looking restaurant, where even the flowers obey the black-and-white colour scheme. On arrival, you are greeted by 'excellent' staff who maintain well-paced service throughout, starting with an initial selection of nibbles,

which might include a crisp, intensely flavoured red pepper tuile; a poached quail's egg with a little Jabugo ham and a sliver of truffle; and a milk bottle from which you extract earthy celeriac foam and sweet Sauternes jelly with a long spoon. Fish shines out as fresh and correctly timed, from a starter of cod brandade with poached cod, cauliflower florets, two quail's eggs, a little mint oil and a few pea shoots and nasturtium leaves for colour, to a main course of Dover sole served with very good Jersey Royals, slices of baby cucumber, potato mousse, baby leeks and vichyssoise sauce, topped with a little caviar. Elsewhere, surf and turf combinations come into their own: poached native lobster teamed with virtually transparent ham, a few slices of summer truffle and pleasantly assertive langoustine oil, or a main course of roast pork cutlet and loin of pork with baby squid, a fine 'beignet' of pork meat and a mini lasagne of pork, while excellent caramelised baby onions and pork crackling filled out any missing elements of flavour or texture. One reporter grumbled that you needed a 'mouth like a vacuum cleaner' to successfully slurp a thick pre-dessert of plum jelly, plum foam and vanilla cream through the accompanying straw, but was cheered by the 'magnificent' chocolate fondant that followed it – where, it seems, the effort of restraint finally became too much. That said, the artiness serves well in the 'awe-inspiring' array of 22 petits fours – a gleeful jaunt from beignets and meringues to the playful sweetshop science of test tubes, jelly and lollipops. The wine list is a lengthy tome, presided over by a capable sommelier. It changes frequently but typically offers a smattering of German choices, some prime California and Australian wines, and a good covering of France, which takes in the lesser regions as well as the classics. Mark-ups are moderately stiff but not the worst in London, with the price of a bottle starting at £25.
**Chef/s:** Tom Aikens. **Open:** Mon to Fri 12 to 2.30, 6.45 to 11. **Closed:** 2 weeks Christmas to New Year, last 2 weeks Aug, bank hols. **Meals:** Set L £29, Set D £60 to £75. **Service:** 12.5% (optional).

**Details:** Cards accepted. 60 seats. Air-con. No music. No mobile phones. Wheelchair access. Jacket and tie required. Children's portions.

★NEW ENTRY★
## Tom's Kitchen
**New opening is drawing the crowds**
27 Cale Street, SW3 3QP
Tel no: (020) 7349 0202
www.tomskitchen.co.uk
⊖ **Sloane Square, South Kensington**
**Modern British | £33**
**Cooking score: 4**

This popular, lively and noisy dining room is the creation Tom Aiken who, rather than jump on the bandwagon and open a pub, opened this straightforward brasserie as his second string. It's a very trendy space with a soaring ceiling and neutral colour scheme and, if you're sitting in the right place, an open-to-view kitchen. But plainly laid wooden tables are inches apart, that's if you're not placed at a shared refectory table, and decibel levels are high at peak times. Thankfully, the food makes amends for any aural discomforts. The cooking looks to France for much of the inspiration – celeriac remoulade with Bayonne ham, bouillabaisse, roast rack of lamb with herb crust, mustard mash and confit garlic. An inspection meal found a few dishes requiring more attention to detail, but hits included sour dough bread, leeks with black truffles, lentils, parmesan and meat juices – a straightforward dish that made a big impact due to the quality of the ingredients – and a soup of butternut squash with sage and honey. Seriously good buttery mash accompanied spit-roast chicken with ceps and a side dish of savoy bacon with smoked bacon proved a 'brilliant combination'. Baked Alaska for two was a suitably retro finish. House wine is £13.
**Chef/s:** Tom Aikens. **Open:** Mon to Fri L 12 to 3 D 6 to 11, Sat B and L 10 to 3, D 6 to 11. Sun 11 to 3 6 to 11. **Closed:** Christmas. **Meals:** alc main courses £12 to £35. **Service:** optional. **Details:** Cards accepted. 70 seats. Separate bar. Wheelchair access. Music. Children allowed.

# Earls Court

## Cambio de Tercio

**Clearly proud of its Spanish accent**
163 Old Brompton Road, SW5 0LJ
Tel no: (020) 7244 8970
⊖ Gloucester Road
Spanish/Portuguese | £37
Cooking score: 2

White clothed tables are closely packed and there are a few pavement tables outside under an awning for fair weather dining – this warmly decorated restaurant positively throbs with activity and is popular with a young crowd. The cooking is modern Spanish in that it blends old ideas with new and offers the menu as a conventional starter/main/dessert combo or with every dish served tapas style (where three to four dishes per person is recommended). An inspection meal found a few dishes requiring more attention to detail but hits included 'brilliant' organic sobrasada, chorizo and El Suspiro goats' cheese caramelised served on toast, a well-judged plate of garlic prawns with baby chillies and lemon oil, deep-fried squid with ink and garlic mayonnaise, and arroz negro with baby squid and cockles. Desserts lack lustre – although chocolate fondant has impressed – and service, though good, can be rushed. An impressive range of sherries proudly heads up a patriotic modern wine list and mark-ups are not greedy.
**Chef/s:** Alberto Criado. **Open:** all week 12.15 to 2.30, 6.45 to 11.30. **Closed:** 2 weeks at Christmas. **Meals:** alc (main courses £14 to £17). **Service:** not inc. **Details:** Cards accepted. 45 seats. Air-con. Music.

# Fulham

## Blue Elephant

**Flamboyant Thai cooking**
3-6 Fulham Broadway, SW6 1AA
Tel no: (020) 7385 6595
www.blueelephant.com
⊖ Fulham Broadway
Thai | £45
Cooking score: 1

Part of an international chain that spreads from Brussels to Bangkok, the Blue Elephant offers a tourist's-eye-view of the Thai experience. Its dazzling interior comes complete with luxuriant, sub-tropical foliage, exotic flora, carp ponds and a sumptuous bar designed to resemble a royal barge. The kitchen deals in extravagant tours through the repertoire, with classics such as fishcakes and roast duck curry, lining up beside stir-fried crocodile with chilli, basil and palm hearts, or poached lobster 'swimming in a sea of vegetables, ginger and perfumed mushrooms'. Seared foie gras with tamarind sauce adds a touch of fusion, while desserts explore the native by-ways with jasmine cakes, steamed banana pudding and Thai mango with sticky rice. Sunday brunch is a lavish family affair. The wine list has a broad span and matches the incisive flavours of the food. Prices start at £17 (£5 a glass).
**Chef/s:** Sompong Sae-Jew. **Open:** Mon to Fri 12 to 2.30, (Sun 12 to 3.30), all week 7 to 12 (to 10.30 Sun). **Closed:** 4 days Christmas. **Meals:** alc (main courses £11 to £28). Set L Mon to Fri £10 (2 courses) Set D £35 to £53 (3 courses). **Service:** 12.5% (optional). **Details:** Cards accepted. 300 seats. Air-con. Wheelchair access. Music. Children allowed.

## Chutney Mary

**Respectable food and cosseting service**
535 King's Road, SW10 0SZ
Tel no: (020) 7351 3113
www.realindianfood.com
⊖ Fulham Broadway
Indian/Pakistani/Bangladeshi | £44
Cooking score: 2

Ⅴ

The scale of the dining room is impressive, it's smartly furnished and there's a conservatory filled with large plants creating a 'seductive enviroment'. An army of good-natured staff is on hand to ensure that all your creature comforts are catered for, making it feel as if you are a resident of a deluxe hotel not in an upmarket Indian restaurant on the King's Road. Not surprisingly, all this pampering comes at a high price, but judging by reporters enthusiastic comments, the standard of cooking has improved this year with the kitchen succeeding in its aim to provide refined, modern Indian cooking. At inspection chicken tikka was 'superb', made a bit more special by judicious seasoning. It was followed by a deeply flavoured, slow-cooked lamb osso bucco and carefully cooked bhindi dopiaza. Leave room for above average desserts, in particular a tasting plate with seasonal Alphonso mango used for the sorbet and kulfi, or try the crumbly rhubarb tart. The wine list is assembled with care to match the style of food, and starts from £17.25.

**Chef/s:** Nagarajan Rubinath. **Open:** Sat and Sun L 12.30 to 2.30 (3 Sun), all week D 6.30 to 11.30 (10.30 Sun). **Closed:** D 25 Dec. **Meals:** alc (main courses £14.50 to £31). Set L £20. **Service:** 12.5% (optional). **Details:** Cards accepted. 110 seats. Air-con. Wheelchair access. Music.

## Deep

**Stylish seafood by the Thames**
The Boulevard, Imperial Wharf, SW6 2UB
Tel no: (020) 7736 3337
www.deeplondon.co.uk
⊖ Fulham Broadway
Modern Seafood | £49
Cooking score: 4

Its location in the swanky new Thames-side development of Imperial Wharf may be a tad off-the-beaten track, but it certainly rewards with modern curb appeal and impressive seafood. Huge glass windows embrace the large, ultra-cool, minimalist space, perhaps recognisable to some as the venue for 'The F-Word' and 'The Great British Menu'. An open kitchen and sushi cabinet catch the eye, as do the side and front terraces for alfresco drinks or dining – both with glimpses of the Thames. The cooking suits the venue; equally clean cut and classy. Well-sourced produce, with seafood taking centre stage, cuts a tilt towards its Swedish owner's roots, while offering the occasional nod to carnivores. Take 'ocean fresh' steamed halibut topped with egg, prawns and horseradish in warm butter, or perhaps braised shoulder of lamb 'escargot' served with wild garlic and tomato. Save room for a 'cracking' chocolate fondant dessert with warm cherries and almond cream. The drinks list comes with a fine selection of aquavits and fashionable globetrotting wines varietally laid out, though with little under £20 but house South African at £14.75.

**Chef/s:** Christian and Kerstin Sandefeldt. **Open:** Tue to Fri and Sun L 12 to 3, Tue to Sat D 7 to 11. **Meals:** alc (main courses £13 to £22). Set L £15.50 (2 courses) to £19.50. Cover £1.. **Service:** 12.5% (optional). **Details:** Cards accepted. 40 seats. Air-con. Wheelchair access. Music.

# ▌Hammersmith

## Chez Kristof

**French food from a winning formula**
111 Hammersmith Grove, W6 0NQ
Tel no: (020) 8741 1177
www.chezkristof.co.uk
⊖ Goldhawk Road/Hammersmith
French | £31
Cooking score: 3

Having brought hearty Eastern European cooking to Southwark (Baltic, see entry), Jan Woroneicki now offers unpretentious, straightforward French regional cooking at this bustling brasserie. Peruse the flexible, seasonally changing menus over crudités at the bar, then tuck into some robust and gutsy dishes at closely spaced tables in the light and airy dining room, or dine alfresco under the front canopy when the sun shines. Start with devilled lambs' kidneys, sautéed prawns with white wine, parsley and garlic, or a plate of charcuterie, then follow with steamed hake with clams and peas, confit duck with potato and turnips, or braised shoulder of lamb with broad beans and garlic. Leave room for a classic apple tarte Tatin or rice pudding with caramelised oranges. Wines are all French, with prices to suit every budget and a good showing of top-value regional wines. Prices open at £14.
**Chef/s:** Jan Woroneicki. **Open:** all week 12 to 3 (4 Sat/Sun), 6 to 11.15 (10.30 Sun). **Meals:** alc (main courses £12.50 to £16.50). Set L and D before 7pm £12 (2 courses) to £15. **Service:** 12.5%. **Details:** Cards accepted. 85 seats. Wheelchair access. Music. Children's portions.

### Please send us your feedback

To register your opinion about any restaurant listed in the Guide, or a new restaurant that you wish to bring to our attention, please visit the web address at the bottom of the page. Your feedback informs the content of the book and will be used to compile next year's reviews.

## Gate

**Cosmopolitan vegetarian grub**
51 Queen Caroline Street, W6 9QL
Tel no: (020) 8748 6932
www.thegate.tv
⊖ Hammersmith
Vegetarian | £34
Cooking score: 2

℣

Perennially popular, this vegetarian haven seems to be going from strength to strength. Sit inside the sparsely furnished church or take advantage of the courtyard on sunny days to enjoy the innovative, full flavours that come out of the kitchen. Cooking styles and influences are wide-reaching: a light, creamy courgette and gorgonzola tart sits comfortably alongside a slightly tame Thai salad of green mango and paw-paw and Indo-Iraqi potato cake stuffed with spiced vegetables and served with a sweet tamarind sauce amongst the first courses, whilst a Thai flavoured laksa with pumpkin wontons features alongside simpler pastas and risottos to follow. The kitchen shows real ambition and happily dispels any sandal-wearing 'hippie' notions. A short, but decent, wine list starts at £3.50 a glass.
**Chef/s:** Jo Tyrell. **Open:** Mon to Fri L 12 to 2.45, Mon to Sat D 6 to 10.45. **Closed:** 23 Dec to 2 Jan. **Meals:** alc (main courses £7.50 to £13.50). **Service:** 12.5% (optional). **Details:** Cards accepted. 60 seats. 40 seats outside. Air-con. Music.

## River Café

**Fresh and thoughtful Italian cooking**
Thames Wharf, Rainville Road, W6 9HA
Tel no: (020) 7386 4200
www.rivercafe.co.uk
⊖ Hammersmith
Modern Italian | £65
Cooking score: 6

℣

There is no end of opinion about the River Café and not all of it good. It is famously difficult to get a booking, and it is awkward to get to. The tables and chairs are squashed in together and eaves-dropping on one's

neighbour is not so much a party game as a necessity given that the volume of noise is so great that it's often easier to hear your neighbour than your companion. Beyond that, there is the annoying demand on diners that comes with time slot dining and the eye-watering, seemingly unjustifiable prices. But once settled in, the brilliance of the place becomes clear. The daily changing menu is entirely seasonal, celebrating all that's good in England and Italy when treated with an Italianate hand – a spring dinner saw deep-fried anchovies as an antipasto, with a dish of fresh bright-green tagliorini served with delicate spring nettles to follow. A sublimely rich stew of veal shin was given vitality and lightness by a generous dosing of lemon zest and new season garlic. A tranche of turbot, on the other hand, makes the most of their searingly hot wood-fired oven, arrivingly perfectly cooked and slighty crispy, the flavours enhanced with the classic Italian combination of lemon, capers, olives and oregano. Portions are enormous but if possible save room for one of their classic Italian puds, including excellent tarts and pannacotta. The entirely Italian wine list (from £18.50 per bottle) is fairly impenetrable to all but the cognoscienti, so the habitually friendly and knowledgeable staff and wine waiters are an added bonus.
**Chef/s:** Rose Gray, Ruth Rogers and Theo Randall. **Open:** all week L 12.30 to 3 (12 to 3.30 Sun), Mon to Sat D 7 to 9.30. **Closed:** Christmas, bank hols. **Meals:** alc (main courses £25 to £31). **Service:** 12.5% (optional). **Details:** Cards accepted. 70 seats. No music. Wheelchair access. Children's portions. Car parking.

## READERS RECOMMEND

### Agni
Indian
169 King Street, Hammersmith, W6 0QU
Tel no: 020 8846 9191
www.agnirestaurant.com
'Genuine home-style cooking'

### Tosa
Japanese
332 King Street, Hammersmith, W6 0RR
Tel no: (020) 8748 0002
'Authentic Japanese food with friendly staff'

### William IV
Modern British
786 Harrow Road, Kensal Green, NW10 5JX
Tel no: (020) 8969 5944
www.elparadorlondon.com
'Excellent tapas in the garden'

## █ Kensington

### 11 Abingdon Road
Relaxed and informal atmosphere
11-13 Abingdon Road, W8 6AH
Tel no: (020) 7937 0120
⊖ High Street Kensington
Modern European | £31
Cooking score: 3

Tucked away down a little street off High Street Kensington, this light, simply decorated neighbourhood restaurant continues to prosper. It's owned by Rebecca Mascarenhas, who also operates Sonny's and the Pheonix (see entries). Young, friendly and casually dressed staff deliver three kinds of bread, including cinnamon, to the table, which precede soundly cooked modern European dishes. First-class materials underpin the operation, from starters of chargrilled sardines with lemon couscous and Sicilian dressing, or smoked eel with horseradish crème fraîche to successful main courses, like roast veal shin with spinach, artichokes, peas and gremolata, or seared skate wing on crushed potatoes with brown shrimps and capers. Finish with artisan cheeses or apricot and almond tart. The global wine list is compact but knowledgable, and starts at £12.75 for French house selections.
**Chef/s:** David Stafford. **Open:** all week 12 to 2.30, 6.30 to 11. **Closed:** bank hols. **Meals:** alc (main courses £11.50 to £17.50). Set L £13.50, Set D £17.50.. **Service:** 12.5% (optional). **Details:** Cards accepted. 80 seats.

## Popeseye
**Uncompromising steak house**
108 Blythe Road, W14 0HD
Tel no: (020) 7610 4578
⊖ Olympia
Steaks | £45
Cooking score: 1
£5
OFF

If steak is your thing, this no-nonsense west London eatery will be just the ticket, its sole raison d'etre being a celebration of prime grass-fed Aberdeen Angus beef from the Highlands, hung for a minimum of two weeks to ensure maximum flavour and tenderness. Occupying a corner site, the simply decorated dining room opts for modern prints on plain white walls, bare floorboards and tartan tablecloths, with the grill open to view in the corner. The menu takes an equally uncomplicated approach, listing a choice of popeseye (rump), sirloin or fillet, in cuts from 6oz up to 30oz, all served with chips, plus salad as an optional extra. And that's it. No vegetarian options, nor starters, and to finish there's a perfunctory choice of desserts or cheeses. But when the steak's this good, who's complaining? Wines focus on vintage clarets, with basic house red at £11.50.
**Chef/s:** Ian Hutchison. **Open:** Mon to Sat D only 6.45 to 10.30. **Meals:** alc (main courses £10 to £45.50). **Service:** 12.5% (optional). **Details:** Cash only. 34 seats. No music. Wheelchair access. Children allowed.

## Timo
**Made by Italians, for Italians...**
343 Kensington High Street, W8 6NW
Tel no: (020) 7603 3888
⊖ High Street Kensington
Italian | £52
Cooking score: 2
£5 OFF ⅄

It's reassuring when Italian restaurants are frequented by Italians; Timo is one such so the rest of us might be wise to take the hint. Each dish receives a useful translation, necessary since much will be unfamiliar. Wild boar with fresh broad beans, raviolini filled with braised guinea fowl with beetroot butter and thyme are not run of the mill. Dishes that look like old friends have a twist; asparagus with poached egg is topped with pancetta and a mustard dressing. Vigorous combinations such as monkfish with cream of pumpkin or bass with runner beans and dill show a kitchen in touch with imaginative, pragmatic, peasant cooking. Desserts touch standard territory, with tiramisu, a range of *sorbetti della casa* and panacotta scented with espresso. Wines, start at £16, proceed to astonishing heights and are exclusively Italian; there's a coda of a dozen or so grappa.
**Chef/s:** Franco Gatti. **Open:** Sun to Fri L 12 to 2.30, all week D 7 to 11. **Meals:** alc D (main courses £13.50 to £19.50). Set L £14.50 (2 courses) to £21.50. **Service:** 12.5% (optional). **Details:** Cards accepted. 119 seats. 4 seats outside. Air-con. Wheelchair access. Music. Children's portions.

## Zaika
**Excellent tasting menu**
1 Kensington High Street, W8 5NP
Tel no: (020) 7795 6533
www.zaika-restaurant.co.uk
⊖ High Street Kensington
Modern Indian | £34
Cooking score: 3
⅄

Zaika translates as sophisticated flavours and this is the driving force behind a menu that is a vivid take on the Europe-meets-West theme. But is this acclaimed contemporary Indian, once seen as daring and cutting edge, now in the danger of resting on its laurels? Opinion is divided, with some delighted by the whole operation, while others ask 'if it is time to overhaul the menu?' But there is still talent in the kitchen – puff pastry-crusted biryani, prolific use of curry leaves, several interpretations of single ingredients (like lamb or chicken) on the same plate, use of classic Gujarati and south Indian snacks as garnish and, of course, the chocolate samosas. The combining of old and new, with traditional dishes alongside original creations, has considerable appeal and the six-course tasting menu is a good introduction. The earthy-hued former bank building opposite Kensington Gardens is kitted out with ornate screens and stone carvings and continues to be a warm, pleasant place. A carefully chosen drinks list features spice-friendly wines from around the world, tropical fruit cocktails and spirits. **Chef/s:** Sanjay Dwivedi. **Open:** Sun to Fri L 12 to 2.45, all week D 6 to 10.45 (9.45 Sun). **Closed:** 25 and 26 Dec, 1 Jan. **Meals:** alc (main courses £14 to £19). Set L £15 (2 courses) to £19, Set D £38 to £88 (inc wine). Bar menu available. **Service:** 12.5% (optional). **Details:** Cards accepted. 80 seats. Air-con. Separate bar. Wheelchair access. Music.

## ALSO RECOMMENDED
### ▲ Cumberland Arms
29 North End Road, Kensington, W14 8SZ
Tel no: (020) 7371 6806
www.thecumberlandarmspub.co.uk
⊖ Kensington Olympia

The Mediterranean dominates the menu at this understated, well-worn dining pub. To start, try the antipasti – chicken liver purée on crostini with fried onions, pan-roast sea bass fillet with chicory, or a tomato, wild rocket and Parmesan frittata (£7). Mains might include grilled skewered marlin and tiger prawns with lemon rice, mint and sultanas (£12.50), and Tuscan lamb casserole (£11). For something different try the pheasant and merguez tagine with quince and saffron. Finish with apple and cinnamon crumble with cream (£4). Wines from £10.50. Open all week.

## READERS RECOMMEND
### Brunello
Italian
60 Hyde Park Gate, Kensington, SW7 5BB
Tel no: 020 7636 9709
www.brunellorestaurants.com
'Assured regional cooking'

### Nyonya
Malaysian
2A Kensington Park Road, Kensington, W11 3BU
Tel no: (020) 7243 1800
www.nyonya.co.uk
'Affordable cuisine'

## ■ Knightsbridge
### Haandi
Classy North Indian food near Harrods
136 Brompton Road, SW3 1HY
Tel no: (020) 7823 7373
www.haandi-restaurants.com
⊖ Knightsbridge
Indian | £33
Cooking score: 4
£5 OFF V

Situated directly opposite Harrods, this stylish Indian restaurant is one of an international quartet and it puts on a high-class show. Shades of brown, beige and yellow define the long dining room, where a glass-fronted kitchen is the main focus of attention. Behind the façade, a team of chefs gets to work on native specialities from the Punjab and North West Frontier. The tandoor gets plenty of use and its output ranges from chicken burra tikka to barbecued lobsters laced with garlic and tomato chutney. Other dishes are cooked – and served – in eponymous 'haandis' (wide-bellied, narrow-necked pots) and the choice extends from classic rogan josh and ubiquitous chicken tikka masala to chicken chennai (a South Indian speciality with coconut, curry leaves and mustard seeds). Goa contributes a fish curry and a pair of vindaloos, while the vegetarian contingent includes Punjabi aloo choley – a chick pea dish best eaten with fried batura bread. The lengthy international wine list offers plenty of suggestions for matching with particular dishes. House selections start at £12.95. A second London branch is at 301-303 Hale Lane, Edgware; tel: (020) 8905 4433.
**Chef/s:** Ratan Singh and Arjun Singh. **Open:** all week 12 to 3, 5.30 to 11 (11.30 Fri and Sat). **Closed:** 25 Dec. **Meals:** alc (main courses £6.50 to £16.50).

Set L £4.99 to £11.95 (all 1 course).. **Service:** 12.5% (optional). **Details:** Cards accepted. 95 seats. 8 seats outside. Air-con. Music. Children allowed.

## Zuma
**High fashion and seductive flavours**
5 Raphael Street, SW7 1DL
Tel no: (020) 7584 1010
www.zumarestaurant.com
⊖ Knightsbridge
Modern Japanese | £67
Cooking score: 5

🍷 ⋎

Designed to resemble a Japanese Zen garden in a Knightsbridge office block, Zuma exudes ultra-cool cosmopolitan style. The interior is homage to industrial chic: everywhere there are monumental unyielding surfaces, pink marble pillars, rough-hewn wood, steel, glass and concrete. It might seem hard-edged and architecturally primeval, but the place generates its own warmth and animated atmosphere. By day, Zuma is genteel and calming; at night it buzzes as the beautiful people come out to play. The overtly intricate menu divides up into appetisers and salads, tempura, fabulously fresh sushi and sashimi, plus offerings from the flaming robata grill. Exquisite miniature dishes arrive in waves and the idea is to share. Among the palate-arousing openers are fried soft shell crab with wasabi mayonnaise and mizuna or slices of yellowtail pointed up with green chilli relish, ponzu and pickled garlic. These are the prelude to skewers of yakitori and other grills ranging from ribeye steak with wafu sauce and garlic crisps to scallops paired with grated apple and sweet soy. There are also specialities and 'new dishes' including seared miso-marinated foie gras with a compote of umeboshi (fiercesome salted plums) or marinated langoustines with chilli, ginger and lime. Desserts turn westwards for European-inspired offerings like green tea and banana cake, hot chocolate fondant and intriguing sorbets. To drink, the vintage selection of aged sakes aims to seduce initiates and novices alike. Those who prefer the juice of the grape

should explore the exquisite compendium of fine wines – especially if price is no deterrent. Stellar selections shine out from every page, prices start at around £20, and there are a dozen good choices from £5.90 a glass.
**Chef/s:** Colin Clague. **Open:** all week 12 to 2.30, 6 to 11 (10.30 Sun). **Meals:** alc (main courses £12 to £30). Set L £21.80, Set D £96 (min 2). Bar menu available. **Service:** 13.5% (optional). **Details:** Cards accepted. 127 seats. Air-con. Wheelchair access. Music.

# ▌Notting Hill
## Ark
**An intimate Italian establishment**
122 Palace Gardens Terrace, W8 4RT
Tel no: (020) 7229 4024
www.ark-restaurant.com
⊖ Notting Hill Gate
Italian | £33
Cooking score: 2

£5 OFF ⋎

Generous portions and well-cooked, traditional dishes sum up the food at this neighbourhood favourite. A balsamic jus with pan-fried calf's liver and grilled figs, for example, is one of the few concessions to trendy cooking. Meals start with a homemade unsalted foccacia, ultra-thin grassini and pesto, and there is a good selection of home-made pastas, sorbets and ice creams. Main courses can include grilled yellow-fin tuna with salsa verde or lamb rump with canellini beans. Desserts have a retro feel with favourites such as raspberry fool with home-made lady-fingers. The long, narrow room, with its taupe walls, dim wall lighting and tealights, can be cozy and intimate, but has felt 'flat' with too many empty tables. The front terrace is inviting, but remember buses, cars and taxis pass a few feet away. Wines start at £4.75 with bottles from £15.
**Chef/s:** Alberto Comai. **Open:** Tue to Sat L 12 to 3, Mon to Sat D 6.30 to 11. **Closed:** bank hols. **Meals:** alc (main courses £11 to £21.50). **Service:** 12.5% (optional). **Details:** Cards accepted. 60 seats. 12 seats outside. Air-con. Separate bar. Wheelchair access. Music. Children allowed.

## Assaggi

**Simple and authentic**
The Chepstow, 39 Chepstow Place, W2 4TS
Tel no: (020) 7792 5501
⊖ Notting Hill Gate
Italian | £58
Cooking score: 4

In a terrace of large white houses, oddly situated above a perfectly ordinary pub, this boldly decorated restaurant has a rustic style of Southern-Italian cooking. It is lively and always full: book well in advance. The short menu is in Italian, but cheerful staff are ready with translations. A meal might start with grilled vegetables marinated in olive oil and herbs, or tartare of tuna, take in ravioli stuffed with ricotta as a pasta dish, then go on to simple main courses such as grilled sea bass, fritto misto, or fillet of pork with black truffle, with side dishes of new potatoes cooked with garlic, rosemary and tomatoes, with rucola and basil. The humble materials are sound as a bell. Flourless chocolate cake is a perfect way to finish. Some 30 Italian wines are fairly pricey, starting with Sardinian red and white at £21.95 or £5 by the glass.
**Chef/s:** Nino Sassu. **Open:** Mon to Sat 12.30 (1 Sat) to 2.30, 7.30 to 11. **Meals:** alc (main courses £17.50 to £20). **Service:** not inc. **Details:** Cards accepted. 35 seats. Air-con. No music.

★NEW ENTRY★
## Bumpkin

**Country life imported to the city**
209 Westbourne Park Road, W11 1EA
Tel no: 020 7243 9818
www.bumpkinuk.com
⊖ Westbourne Park, Ladbroke Grove
British | £35
Cooking score: 2

With a pastoral design taking in olive-green walls and floral wallpaper, tan leather chairs and satin pink blinds, this sprawling former pub is intended 'for city folk who like a little country living'. But any notion of a bucolic experience is short lived; the noise level generated by the well-heeled diners can reach fever pitch at peak times. The open-plan kitchen cooks in the British idiom with top-notch produce shining through in an appealing starter of seared tuna carpaccio with wild rocket, spiced up by lemon, capers and chili again, and in a juicy pork chop with cider and tarragon. Proper Bramley apple crumble with custard is a satisfying end. It's fun and relaxing, children are actively encouraged, and the service team is jovial and energetic. Wines start from £14, with 20 by the glass kicking off at £3.50, although 1997 Mersault, Coche Dury (£240) is not something you will see in a country inn outside W11. Whisky covers an entire page with some rarities such as a Springbank 1968 36 year at £392 a bottle or £28 for a 50ml shot.
**Chef/s:** Oliver Prince. **Open:** Tue to Fri 12 to 3 (11 to 3.30 Sat, 12.15 to 3.30 Sun), 6 to midnight (10.30 Sun). **Meals:** alc (main courses £12 to £16), Set L £22.50 (2 courses) on Sun. **Service:** 12.5% (included). **Details:** Cards accepted. 110 seats. 4 seats outside. Air-con. Wheelchair access. Music. Children's portions.

## Clarke's

**Where simplicity meets style**
124 Kensington Church Street, W8 4BH
Tel no: (020) 7221 9225
www.sallyclarke.com
⊖ Notting Hill Gate, High Street Kensington
British | £52
Cooking score: 4

After 24 years, Sally Clarke's vibrant, exciting and very delicious food continues to enthral at her eponymous restaurant, which is set amid the antique shops of Church Street. Eating takes place on two levels, a small ground floor area and the much more relaxing, low-lit basement room with its open-plan kitchen. She has waivered little from her tried and tested formula: using impeccable, seasonal ingredients to produce simple but perfectly executed dishes. The only change in recent years is that she now offers a choice of dishes in the evening, and it is no longer necessary to have all four courses. Lunch is a selection of four starters, three main courses, and either

cheese or a couple of puddings, and dishes are priced individually. Dinner often kicks off with a salad – perhaps peas, grilled spring onions and pea shoots with San Daniele ham and a crème fraîche dressing. To follow, there may be chargrilled Angus ribeye with parsley, lemon and garlic butter and hand-cut chips, or halibut baked 'en papillotte' with Jersey Royals, shallots and tarragon and served with roasted fennel and beetroot. First-class cheeses with oatmeal biscuits precede imaginative desserts: say, warm-baked cherry soufflé pancake with bay-leaf ice cream. The wine list is a pick and mix of good and prestigious bottles from around the globe. Prices climb steeply from the £15 starting point.
**Chef/s:** Sally Clarke. **Open:** Mon to Sat L 12.30 (11 Sat brunch) to 2, Tue to Sat D 7 to 10. **Closed:** 23 Dec to 5 Jan. **Meals:** alc L (main courses £14 to £16). Set D £43.25 to £49.50. **Service:** net prices. **Details:** Cards accepted. 80 seats. Air-con. No music. No mobile phones. Wheelchair access.

## e&o
**Stylish pan-Asian dining**
14 Blenheim Crescent, W11 1NN
**Tel no:** (020) 7229 5454
www.eando.nu
⊖ Ladbroke Grove
**Fusion/Pan-Asian | £30**
**Cooking score: 3**
ᐺ

A chic but sparse dining room forms the backdrop to this stylish pan-Asian eaterie from the Ricker stable. Slick but friendly staff serve a trendy, buzzy crowd at night and a laidback mix of families (children are welcome) and lunching groups during the day. The handy glossary helps navigate a menu built on plenty of choice. Sharing is de rigueur, recommended as a means of ensuring maximum coverage of the delicately flavoured dim sum – delicate prawn and chive dumplings, say, or baby pork spare ribs dressed in a sticky black bean sauce with fiery red chillies and generous flecks of ginger. Any sushi and sashimi worth its wasabi should be well presented, but e&o's excels, with

beautifully presented asparagus and avocado maki, and excellent seared tuna. Or try lamb redang curry with sweet potato or whole barbecued shredded duck. Traditional sweets get a Thai twist in the shape of ta koh pannacotta, but a chocolate fondue may prove hard to resist. A good, varied wine list opens with modest vin de pays at £13.50.
**Chef/s:** Simon Treadway. **Open:** all week 12.15 to 3 (4 Sat and Sun), 6.15 to 11 (10.30 Sun). **Meals:** alc (main courses £9.50 to £21.50). **Service:** 12.5% (optional). **Details:** Cards accepted. 84 seats. 20 seats outside. Air-con. No music. Wheelchair access.

## ★NEW ENTRY★
## Geales
**Posh fish and chips**
2 Farmer Street, W8 7SN
**Tel no:** (020) 7727 7528
www.geales.com
⊖ Notting Hill
**Modern Seafood | £30**
**Cooking score: 1**

It calls itself a neighbourhood fish and chip restaurant, but smart leather chairs and pristine cloth-clad tables (despite being crammed together) suggest there's more on offer than a quick fish supper. This legendary fish and chip shop (established in 1939) has been given a major revamp by new owners Mark Fuller and Garry Hollihead; even the menu has been overhauled, with starters such as dressed-crab and prawn cocktail marked by stylish presentation as strictly Notting Hill. Similarly, mains range from fish and leek pie to a token meaty sirloin steak with sauce béarnaise. Haddock was deliciously moist and concealed in super-crunchy batter, and although the accompanying chips and mushy peas are by separate price and order, the former delivered 'crunch then fluffiness', the latter 'bite and flavour'. Finish with jam roly-poly or rice pudding with strawberries. A glass of Sauvignon Grenache is £3.95. Bottles start at £12.95.

Chef/s: Gary Hollihead. **Open:** Tue to Sat L 12 to 2.30, D 6 to 11; Sun D 6 to 10.30. **Closed:** Mon lunch. **Meals:** alc main courses £9 to 16. **Service:** optional. **Details:** Cards accepted. 60 seats. 16 seats outside. Air-con. Wheelchair access. Children allowed.

## Kensington Place

**Modern British food in a buzzy space**
201-209 Kensington Church Street, W8 7LX
Tel no: (020) 7727 3184
www.egami.co.uk
⊖ Notting Hill Gate, Kensington High Street
**Modern British | £39**
**New Chef**

🍷 Y

Though Rowley Leigh, the man whose name is inextricably bound up with this seminal restaurant, may have moved on (to Les Café des Anglais in Bayswater, due to open after the Guide goes to press), the dining room is still as full as ever. Indeed, not everyone has twigged that the famous chef has left, the sense of continuity skilfully guided by 'efficient, relaxed and chatty' waiting staff. Under new chef Sam Mahoney, the longstanding foie gras with sweetcorn pancake still finds a place on the menu, but now there are fashionable nods to foraging, with ingredients like wild garlic and sorrel, paired with guinea fowl and John Dory respectively. A 'silky' starter of pappardelle embraced the trend with its tomato-herbed sauce and tender pieces of quail; a main-course of sliced pork belly was 'outstanding', topped with crisp crackling and served with mashed potato, sage-flecked carrots and light meat juices. An apple tart might make an appearance as a German strudel-style wedge teamed with vanilla ice cream. The choice of wines complements the food, the large selection (including 35 by glass) from quality winemakers across the globe, and offering a good choice under £20. **Chef/s:** Sam Mahoney. **Open:** all week 12 to 3.30, 6.30 to 11.15 (11.45 Fri and Sat, 10.15 Sun). **Meals:** alc (main courses £15.50 to £24.50). Set L Mon to Sat £19.50, Set L Sun £24.50, Set D Mon to Fri £24.50 to £39.50 (with glass of wine).

**Service:** 12.5% (optional). **Details:** Cards accepted. 140 seats. Air-con. No music. Wheelchair access. Children's portions.

## Notting Hill Brasserie

**A reassuringly local clientele**
92 Kensington Park Road, W11 2PN
Tel no: (020) 7229 4481
⊖ Notting Hill Gate
**Modern European | £59**
**Cooking score: 4**

The term 'brasserie' rather underplays the strikingly lit, enticing interior, where high-ceilinged dining rooms have intricate cornice work, well-spaced tables and impressive floral displays, and there's a jazz quartet in the front bar. Former sous chef, Karl Burdock, now heads the kitchen, but the broadly contemporary menu with Mediterranean influences remains the same. Among starters it offers well-reported cannelloni of lobster and prawns served with a cep purée and a 'frothed-up', nicely balanced shellfish velouté, and a single scallop classically paired with cauliflower purée but with the addition of chorizo, squid, black pudding and potato. Among meat main courses chateaubriand 'was of good quality and was correctly cooked in a salt crust' and came with béarnaise sauce and large chips. A typical fish dish was well-timed halibut with a sauce of morels, peas and broad beans. Amaretto cheesecake with a vanilla cake and cherry cream made a happy ending. The wine list of 70 bins is roughly half French with the rest given to a reasonably imaginative choice from around the globe. House wine is £15 and there's plenty of choice in the £25 to £40 range.
**Chef/s:** Mark Jankel. **Open:** all week L 12 to 3.30, Mon to Sat D 7 to 11. **Closed:** Christmas. **Meals:** alc D (main courses £19 to £24.50). Set L Mon to Sat £14.50 (2 courses) to £19.50, Set L Sun £25 (2 courses) to £30. Bar menu available. **Service:** 12.5% (optional). **Details:** Cards accepted. 110 seats. Air-con. Wheelchair access. Music. Children's portions.

## ALSO RECOMMENDED
## ▲ Electric Brasserie
191 Portobello Road, Notting Hill, W11 2ED
Tel no: (020) 7908 9696
www.electricbrasserie.com
⊖ Notting Hill Gate

Part of the Electric Cinema complex, this trendy bar/brasserie is lively on weekends, when the breakfast menu pulls crowds to munch on grilled sausage sandwich (£6), pancakes with blueberry compote (£7) or the deluxe hunger buster of smoked haddock, mushrooms, poached egg and hollandaise (£7.50) at the communal tables and benches. Elsewhere, brunch brings beef bourguignon (£12.50) and lobster and chips (£28), while for dinner there could be roast duck (£14.50). Small plates, sandwiches, burgers and salads are also available, as is a host of seafood (half-dozen oysters £9). Finish with white chocolate crème brûlée, or Sussex pond pudding (all £6). An international wine list starts at £3.75 per glass. Open all week.

## ▲ Kiasu
48 Queensway, Notting Hill, W2 3RY
Tel no: 020 7727 8810

Kiasu, a quintessential term in Singapore translates to 'fear of being second best', aptly describes the competitive spirit of this most successful Tiger economy. This newcomer, in a tightly packed space, resembles many simple cafes in South-East Asia. Blue/mauve walls with various connotations of the Kiasu theme help to brighten up the room. Service is cheery and fleet-footed. The restaurant has been a hit, thanks in part to the generous portions and reasonable prices. On a hot and humid evening, the bustling atmosphere can trick you into thinking that you are near the Equator. The menu features an extensive repertoire of street food from the Straits, although the popular Filipino dish of chicken and pork Adobo (£6.60) makes an appearance. Satay (£5.80) is acceptable, Penang style char kway teow (£6.50) (stir fried with rice noodles with prawns) is authentic. Hokkien mee (£6.70) (prawn and

noodle soup) comes with tasty pork ribs. Ice kachang (£4.80) (shaved ice with sweet corn and red aduki beans), is a good way to finish especially on a hot day, or you if you are brave try the infamous durian fruit, used for the ice cream. Wines, starting from £11.50 are inconsequential. Drink Tiger beer or tea tarik (stretched tea) instead.

## READERS RECOMMEND
## Fat Badger
**Gastropub**
310 Portabello Road, Notting Hill, W10 5TA
Tel no: (020) 8969 4500
www.thefatbadger.com
'Modern menu and friendly service'

## ■ Paddington

★NEW ENTRY★
## Pearl Liang
**Style and substance**
8 Sheldon Square, W2 6EZ
Tel no: (020) 7289 7000
www.pearlliang.co.uk
⊖ Paddington
Chinese | £31
Cooking score: 2

'A dead ringer for Hakkasan' mused one who managed to find this promising newcomer, tucked into the pedestrianised Paddington Central complex (do get directions). It's certainly drawing the crowds, including a fair proportion from the Chinese community, with a mix of fair pricing and stylish design, despite being in a 'culinary dead spot'. The spacious bar and dining room is expensively and attractively decorated with funky low chairs in pink fabric, dashes of mauve, with an outsized abacus and the flowery mural. Unlike the décor, the menu is rather more mainstream, based primarily on Cantonese cooking, although you can get lobster with belacan – a hot shrimp paste from Malaysia. But it's dim sum that steals the show, notably, at inspection, a dazzling zucchini and prawn dumpling. Deep-fried soft-shell crab has also

been singled out for praise, and fried sweet black sesame ball is a popular way to end. The service team, dressed in modish black, is cordial and attentive. Wines are hastily assembled, and start from £13.40.
**Chef/s:** Paul Ngo. **Open:** all week 12 to 11. **Closed:** 25 and 26 Dec. **Meals:** alc (main courses £6.80 to £24). Set Menus £20 to £65. **Service:** 12% (included). **Details:** Cards accepted. 150 seats. Air-con. Separate bar. Wheelchair access. Music.

## ★NEW ENTRY★
## Yakitoria
**Slick, canal-side modern dining**
25 Sheldon Square, W2 6EY
Tel no: 020 3214 3000
www.yakitoria.co.uk
⊖ Paddington
Japanese | £35
Cooking score: 3

V £30

Forget the Hogwart Express from platform nine and three-quarters at King's Cross the real magic is happening behind platform eight at Paddington Station. Yakitoria is flying the flag for exceptional contemporary Japanese cuisine, set amongst the new glass and steel structures of the Paddington basin redevelopment. Once you've managed to actually find the restaurant (take the ramp beside platform eight then hang a left along the canal) you're greeted with plenty of high-fashion, clean lines in an industrial setting. The airy L-shaped restaurant offers a calming water view, with a slick bar set back from the main room. An extensive menu includes the usual suspects like sushi and maki handrolls, modern fusion dishes, and some unexpected surprises. Push the boat out and try quail confit with wasabi ponzu, or green tea smoked rack of lamb with cucumber and bonito salad. Small dishes might include tamgo, fatty tuna or sea urchin nigiri, or sushi pancake with soy jelly and wasabi foam. An inventive cocktail list features Oriental-style cocktails with storybook names such as Tokyo Beauty, White Siberian, and Madame Butterfly. The well-

chosen wine list includes some unusual labels starting from £16, and an ample selection of sake and plum wines.
**Chef/s:** Ronald Laity. **Open:** Mon to Sat L 12 to 3pm; D 6 to 11pm. Sat D 6 to 11pm, Sun 12 to 10.30pm. **Meals:** alc (large dishes £14.50 to £25) Set L (bento boxes £14 to 17). **Service:** optional 12.5%. **Details:** Cards accepted. 120 seats. 30 seats outside. Air-con. Separate bar. Wheelchair access. Music. Children allowed.

## READERS RECOMMEND

### Fontana
**Lebanese**
10 Craven Terrace, Paddington, W2 3QD
Tel no: 020 8892 5417
'Above-average Lebanese cooking'

### Frontline
**British**
13 Norfolk Place, Paddington, W2 1QJ
Tel no: (020) 7479 8960
www.frontlineclub.com
'Dependable cuisine in a war reporters' club'

### Salusbury
**Gastropub**
50-52 Salusbury Road, Queens Park, NW6 6NN
Tel no: (020) 7328 3286
'Imaginative cooking with an Italian theme'

## ■ Shepherd's Bush
### Adams Café
**Arabic offerings**
77 Askew Road, W12 9AH
Tel no: (020) 8743 0572
⊖ Ravenscourt Park
North African | £24
Cooking score: 3

£5 OFF  V

'Very good North-African cooking, excellent service, incredible value for money' wrote one delighted reader after a visit to this long-established café whose revamped evening menu skips effortlessly from simple grilled meat and fish options, to earthy, aromatic

tagines. Among the starters are fish soup, grilled spicy lamb sausages, pastilla (Moroccan sweet chicken, almond and filo pastry pie), and chorba (a spicy Tunisian vegetable, lamb and pasta soup). Follow with one of seven different tagines (perhaps monkfish, tomatoes, peppers, saffron potatoes and coriander), a whole grilled sea bass with French fries and tastira sauce, or one of the kitchen's legendary couscous dishes. Desserts include tartelette au citron, an orange fruit salad with dates, cinnamon and orange blossom water, and crêpe berbère (a Moroccan-style pancake with a honey sauce). You can bring your own bottle (corkage is £3 per bottle) or order from the short, inexpensive wine list which opens at £9.
**Chef/s:** Sofiene Chahed. **Open:** Mon to Sat D only 7 to 11. **Closed:** Christmas to New Year, bank hol Mon. **Meals:** Set D £10.50 (1 course) to £15.50. **Service:** 12.5%. **Details:** Cards accepted. 60 seats. Wheelchair access. Music.

## Anglesea Arms
**Perennially popular gastropub**
35 Wingate Road, W6 0UR
Tel no: (020) 8749 1291
⊖ Ravenscourt Park
Gastropub | £25
Cooking score: 2
V £30

The Anglesea is all distressed wooden floors, exposed brickwork and battered furniture – the kind of enticing establishment that's cosy in winter and bright in summer. Drinkers sit on homely sofas by the bar (or under parasols out front in sunny weather). The open-plan kitchen bats well above its average for a gastropub and service is generally very well judged. Starters might be a fluffy twice-baked goat's cheese soufflé, while a spring Sunday lunch included plaice cooked just-so and complemented by brown shrimp, cucumber and new potatoes dressed in dill and crème fraîche. A standout was a generous portion of tremendous roast pork belly with perfectly crisp crackling, silky mash, sweet roasted apples and purple sprouting broccoli. Desserts

might be chocolate mocha tart or strawberry cheesecake. A decent and varied sheet of wines starts at £12.50, with a good clutch available by the glass (from £3). You can't book at this neighbourhood favourite so arrive promptly.
**Chef/s:** Henrik Ritzen. **Open:** all week 12.30 to 2.45 (3 Sat, 3.30 Sun), 7 to 10.30 (9.30 Sun, 10 Mon). **Closed:** 22 to L 31 Dec. **Meals:** alc (main courses L £8.50 to £13, D £12 to £23.50). Set L Mon to Fri £9.95 (2 courses) to £12.95. **Service:** not inc. **Details:** Cards accepted. 38 seats. Music. Children's portions.

## Brackenbury
**Simple elegant fare**
129-131 Brackenbury Road, W6 0BQ
Tel no: (020) 8748 0107
www.thebrackenbury.co.uk
⊖ Goldhawk Road
Modern European | £30
Cooking score: 4
£5 OFF  V  £30

An 'oasis in the heart of a tranquil village' is how one reader described this upbeat neighbourhood fixture, just a few minutes' away from the bustle of the Goldhawk Road. With soft lighting, mushroom-coloured walls, polished dark-wood tables, upholstered high-backed chairs and surprisingly comfy cushioned banquettes, the atmosphere and staffing is warm and welcoming. The sensibly compact, regularly changing menu is driven by quality seasonal produce, and, with a new chef onboard, comes intelligently less complicated than its predecessor. Take starters such as asparagus served with poached egg and lemon butter, or razor clams with lemon, garlic and parsley, their success a testament to accomplished simplicity. Mains like slow-roasted duck teamed with a rösti, braised endive and an orange sauce continue the theme, while 'attractively presented' desserts like a 'light, moist' chocolate cake with fresh cherries and fior de latte (vanilla ice cream to you and me) and 'exceptionally good' coffee round things off in style. A varied

international wine list starts at £12.95 with plenty to choose from under £20, and wines by glass from £3.50.
**Chef/s:** Matt Cranston. **Open:** Sun to Fri L 12.30 to 2.45 (3.30 Sun), Mon to Sat D 7 to 10.45 Sat,Sun Brunch from 10.00. **Closed:** 1st to 13th Jan. **Meals:** alc (main courses £10 to £18). Set L Mon to Fri £12.50 (2 courses) to £14.50. **Service:** 12.5% (optional). **Details:** Cards accepted. 60 seats. 20 seats outside. Air-con. Separate bar. No music. Children's portions.

## Snows on the Green
**Chic neighbourhood restaurant**
166 Shepherd's Bush Road, W6 7PB
Tel no: (020) 7603 2142
www.snowsonthegreen.co.uk
⊖ Goldhawk Road, Shepherd's Bush
**Modern European | £30**
**Cooking score: 4**

Sebastian Snow has been cooking at this well-liked neighbourhood restaurant on Brook Green (hence the title) since 1990, and continues to deliver carefully crafted, unshowy food in a setting of soft lights, arty photos and considerate table spacings. His signature dish is foie gras with fried egg and balsamic vinegar, which he describes as 'eccentrically eclectic'. Other seasonal ideas are closer to the modern European mainsteam, witness a 'spring green' risotto with peas, broccoli and fava beans, baked fillet of cod with chorizo, clams, wild garlic leaves and leek purée or roast corn-fed chicken breast with asparagus and morels. The Italian old guard also gets a look in with fritto misto, vitello tonnato and osso buco. Desserts put hot treacle tart and steamed chocolate pudding alongside espresso crème caramel with poached fruits, and fans of unpasteurised Italian cheeses won't be disappointed by the selection served with toasted walnut bread and pickled grapes. The wine list offers a broad spread of fine bottles from around the globe. Fourteen are available by the glass, and bottle prices start at £12.50.

**Chef/s:** Sebastian Snow. **Open:** Mon to Fri L 12 to 3, Mon to Sat D 6 to 11. **Closed:** 4 days Christmas, bank hol Mon. **Meals:** alc (main courses £13.50 to £16). Set L and D £13.25 (2 courses) to £16.50. Cover 95p. **Service:** optional charge 12.5%. **Details:** Cards accepted. 70 seats. 8 seats outside. Air-con. No mobile phones. Wheelchair access. Music. Children's portions.

## READERS RECOMMEND
### Blah Blah Blah
**Vegetarian**
78 Goldhawk Road, Shepherd's Bush, W12 8HA
Tel no: 020 8746 1337
**'Inventive vegetarian offerings and BYO'**

## ▊ South Kensington
### Bibendum
**A balance of elegance and informality**
Michelin House, 81 Fulham Road, SW3 6RD
Tel no: (020) 7581 5817
www.bibendum.co.uk
⊖ South Kensington
**Modern British | £66**
**Cooking score: 4**
🍷

Bibendum's great quality is the light – day or night –and the integrated Michelin-contoured design makes it a compelling and gratifying space, well suited to the food's reassuring foundation of approachable, unfussy modern British and French dishes. Materials and treatments are impressively varied; start with ,perhaps, a warm salad of smoked eel, Jersey Royals and crisp pancetta and watercress velouté. At inspection a sauté of rabbit with new season garlic, basil and white wine was 'wonderfully tender and well-flavoured', its counterpart, a slow-cooked, crisp pork belly with caramelised onions, apple sage and calvados sauce 'succulent and with a sweet earthiness'. Desserts such as chocolate tart with chocolate malt ice cream show 'lightness of touch in the kitchen'. Wines may be a tad expensive but the extensive global list is worth exploring. There's a decent choice of half bottles under £20 and well-chosen offerings by the glass. But it's the house wines that stand out and a lot of care has been taken in choosing an extensive selection mostly under £25.

**Chef/s:** Matthew Harris. **Open:** all week 12 to 2.30 (12.30 to 3 Sat and Sun), 7 to 11 (10.30 Sun). **Closed:** D 24 Dec to 26 Dec. **Meals:** alc D (main courses £16.50 to £26). Set L £24 (2 courses) to £28.50. **Service:** 12.5% (optional). **Details:** Cards accepted. 80 seats. Air-con. No music. Wheelchair access. Children's portions.

# Brasserie St Quentin

**A dynamic Knightsbridge eaterie**
243 Brompton Road, SW3 2EP
Tel no: (020) 7589 8005
www.brasseriestquentin.co.uk
⊖ Knightsbridge, South Kensington
French | £49
Cooking score: 3

Evoking traditional French brasserie style, this long-running west London restaurant none the less moves with the times, inspired by a youthful kitchen team with fresh ideas. Among starters on the regularly changing menu, classic fish soup with aïoli and croûtons might rub shoulders with linguini with foie gras and peas, or a pigeon terrine with pear chutney. Main courses show similarly broad scope, ranging from good old-fashioned ribeye of Buccleuch beef with béarnaise and chips, or calf's liver with port-glazed shallots and mash, to dishes with a more contemporary feel, such as crab-crusted halibut with baby leeks, lemongrass and ginger broth. End perhaps with hot chocolate fondant with burnt orange ice cream, or caramelised banana terrine. A predominantly French wine list opens with house selections at £14.50.

**Chef/s:** Gary Durrant. **Open:** all week 12 to 3, 6 to 10.30 (10 Sun). **Closed:** 23 to 30 Dec. **Meals:** alc (main courses £10.50 to £25). Set L and D 6 to 7.30 to £18 (3 courses). **Service:** 12.5% (optional). **Details:** Cards accepted. 55 seats. Air-con. No music.

# L'Etranger

**Ambitious fusion of French and Japanese cuisine**
36 Gloucester Road, SW7 4QT
Tel no: (020) 7584 1118
www.circagroupltd.co.uk
⊖ Gloucester Road
Modern European | £56
Cooking score: 2

Muted grey and aubergine colours mark out the interior of this smartly attired Kensington restaurant. It may be French by name, but the 'strangeness' of the menu often befuddles first-timers. A few Gallic fixtures such as Charolais beef tartare or confit shoulder of Pyrénean lamb with grilled aubergine remain, although a tide of Japanese-influenced fusion has overrun just about everything else: even roast duck and orange is tweaked with white miso paste. Elsewhere, Chilean sea bass is served with black bean sauce and green tea soba noodles, while lime leaves and 'mi sancho' pepper are used to flavour-enhance roast Côte de Veau 'Blonde Aquitaine'. Desserts go with the flow, offering Nashi pear tarte Tatin as well as mango soufflé with yuzu and tofu sorbet. The deeply serious wine list majors in Burgundy and the rest of the world receives exhaustive coverage (sake included). A cut-price selection is offered at lunchtime and everything can be purchased from the adjacent wine shop. Prices start at £22 and there are plentiful options available by the glass.

**Chef/s:** Jerome Tauvron. **Open:** Mon to Fri and Sun L 12 to 3, all week D 6 to 11 (10 Sun). **Meals:** alc (main courses L £16.50 to £29, D £16.50 to £49). Set L Mon to Fri £14.50 (2 courses) to £16.50, Sun brunch £16.50 (2 courses) to £19.50, set D £65. **Service:** 12.5% (optional). **Details:** Cards accepted. 75 seats. Air-con. Music.

## Launceston Place

**Simple, well-judged British dishes**
1A Launceston Place, W8 5RL
Tel no: (020) 7937 6912
www.egami.co.uk
⊖ Gloucester Road
British | £50
Cooking score: 2

There's reassuring continuity at this decent, no surprises, neighbourhood restaurant. With no intention to astonish with expansive flourishes, dishes are kept simple and flavours stick to classic combinations; expect the likes of confit of duck with sweet potatoes and bacon terrine, red mullet with sautéed potatoes and broad bean coulis or, simple steak with béarnaise and fries. Strawberries and cream, a brûlée with biscuits or a praline tart with maple syrup ice cream maintain the unfussy policy. Wines show greater adventure; sets of chardonnays and cabernet sauvignon from the world over, including seriously big drinks at matching prices, 'aromatic whites' and decent regional varieties, a few by the glass, start at £16.00.
**Chef/s:** Phillip Reed. **Open:** Sun to Fri L 12.30 to 2.30, all week D 6 to 11 (10 Sun). **Closed:** 24 Dec to 4 Jan, 14 to 18 Apr, Aug bank hol weekend. **Meals:** alc (not Sun or 14 Feb; main courses £14.50 to £18). Set L £16.50 (2 courses) to £18.50, Set L Sun £24.50, Set D (Mon to Fri 6 to 7) £15.50 (2 courses) to £18.50 (2 courses). **Service:** 12.5% (optional). **Details:** Cards accepted. 75 seats. Air-con. No music. Wheelchair access.

## Lundum's

**Modern take on Danish cooking**
119 Old Brompton Road, SW7 3RN
Tel no: (020) 7373 7774
www.lundums.com
⊖ Gloucester Road, South Kensington
Scandinavian | £55
Cooking score: 3

London's 'only Danish restaurant' takes place behind a delightful terracotta Edwardian façade, reflected inside in nostalgic Danish design; afficianados of minimal Scandinavian will be disappointed. Many ingredients are sourced from northern Denmark so Aquavit served with marinated herrings is no surprise. But these are set alongside more modern takes on tradition; gravad lax with a mustard–dill foam or roast-cured duck with white asparagus and oyster mushrooms bring the worthiness of Denmark bang up to date in reliably stylish manner. Try Sunday lunch, drifting on into the afternoon starting with herrings with egg and caviar and a lavish buffet of north sea fish, meatballs and pig in many transformations. Puddings command respect and pleasure as does the wine list, a range of classic Europeans; prices start at £18.50 but rise inexorably including the best of Piedmont, Medoc and Rioja.
**Chef/s:** Kay Lundum and Torben Lining. **Open:** all week L 12 to 4, Mon to Sat D 6 to 11. **Closed:** 22 Dec to 4 Jan. **Meals:** alc Mon to Sat (main courses L £13 to £18.50, D £14.50 to £28). Set L Mon to Sat £13.50 (2 courses) to £16.50, Sun buffet brunch £21.50, Set D £19.50 (2 courses) to £24.50. **Service:** 13.5% (optional). **Details:** Cards accepted. 80 seats. 28 seats outside. Air-con. Wheelchair access. Music.

### Cooking score

A score of 1 is a significant achievement. The score in any review is based on several meals, incorporating feedback from both our readers and inspectors. As a rough guide, 1 denotes capable cooking with some inconsistencies, rising steadily through different levels of technical expertise, until the scores between 6 and 10 indicate exemplary skills, along with innovation, artistry and ambition. If there is a new chef, we don't score the restaurant for the first year of entry. For further details, please see the scoring section in the introduction to the Guide.

## ▌Westbourne Park

### Ledbury
**European master settling into its niche**
127 Ledbury Road, W11 2AQ
Tel no: (020) 7792 9090
www.theledbury.com
⊖ Westbourne Park
Modern European | £44
Cooking score: 6

♭ ⋎

Tucked away in a quiet corner of Westbourne Grove, the Ledbury is an oasis of calm civility amid the bustle of W11. It's a high-ceilinged dining-room with a diverting black-beaded chandelier and, although the floor is uncarpeted, it somehow doesn't get too rackety. The fixed-price menus offer a broad spectrum of culinary thinking, from some once off-beat ideas that have become established fixtures (scallops roasted in liquorice is a stayer), to simply conceived, but skilfully rendered, pasta dishes. A pasta option might be tender ravioli of chicken and morels, in a white asparagus fondue with caramelised onion, a dish that was well-delivered at inspection, gaining extra depth from its frothy Parmesan velouté. Crab with green asparagus (it was spring, after all) came with a perfectly apposite citrus dressing combining pink grapefruit and pomelo. Pigeon has always impressed as a main course, and was good again, the various bits treated separately and sensitively, the breast resting on soft spinach, the legs properly timed, and the various accoutrements including a sausage of the offals and the liver presented on a skewer. Artichoke purée and a tarte fine of ceps added to the sense of occasion. Fish is handled with equal confidence, as witness the monkfish roasted in rosemary that came with the cheek meat schnitzel-battered and truffled. Only a slightly underwhelming sauce of mushrooms and capers, not quite achieving the intensity of the rest, fell a little short here. Cheeses offer a wide, mostly French selection, some being in better nick than others on inspection night, but desserts inspire unalloyed respect, in the form of a complex citrus terrine with a trio of

rhubarb and vanilla beignets, a Sauternes anglaise and rocket-fuelled passion-fruit sorbet. The wine list is substantial, and very well compiled. There are no fewer than 15 German wines, good Italian choices, and gems from Burgundy and Alsace. Six reds and six whites come by the glass. Bottles prices start comfortably north of £20.
**Chef/s:** Brett Graham. **Open:** all week 12 to 2.45, 6.30 to 10.30. **Closed:** 24 and 25 Dec, 1 Jan, Aug bank hol. **Meals:** Set L Mon to Sat £24.50 (2 courses) to £55, Set L Sun £30 to £55, Set D £45 to £55. **Service:** 12.5% (optional). **Details:** Cards accepted. 64 seats. Air-con. No music. No mobile phones. Wheelchair access.

## ALSO RECOMMENDED
### ▲ Cow Dining Room
89 Westbourne Park Road, Westbourne Park, W2 5QH
Tel no: (020) 7221 0021
www.thecowlondon.co.uk
⊖ Royal Oak

The Saloon Bar downstairs is quite often packed, with everyone supping Guinness and slurping on Irish rock oysters (£7.75 a dozen). Upstairs, the dining room offers a simple but tasty menu of dishers such as foie gras, lentil and French bean salad (£7.50) or smoked eel with potato salad and bacon (£9). Mains include roast halibut with leeks, laverbread toasts and an orange butter sauce (£16.50), and loin of rabbit with black pudding, fennel and celeriac (£18.50). There's a popular weekend brunch and and wines from £13.75. The dining room is open Sat and Sun L and all week D.

## ▌Barnes

### Sonny's
**A well-established consistent local**
94 Church Road, SW13 0DQ
Tel no: (020) 8748 0393
www.sonnys.co.uk
⊖ Hammersmith
**Modern European | £30**
**Cooking score: 3**

Part of the neighbourhood for long enough that locals cannot imagine life without it, Sonny's is the epitome of a good London 'village' restaurant. Its well-heeled clientele are not short of choice for decent dining, but Sonny's has won their loyalty – half the customers are regular enough to be known by name; those who are not are welcomed with equal politeness and ushered into the reassuringly unchanging, comfortabe and relaxed dining room. The menu is a seasonal affair featuring modern classics; a fragrant broad bean and thyme soup and a generous plate of zesty endive & smoked trout salad were both winners from a list of seven starters; a a terrific, hearty chunk of monkfish with a rich borlotti bean stew to follow outshone a more pedestrian duck leg with new season turnips. Typical modern British puddings: tarte Tatin and lemon tart are worth saving room for. To accompany, there's an eclectic wine list ranging from £3.50 for a glass of house white to £100 Corton Charlemagne, but there's plenty in between, and the staff are confident and knowledgable enough to recommend unusual but clever pairings.
**Chef/s:** Ed Wilson. **Open:** all week L 12 to 2.30, Mon to Sat D 7 to 11. **Closed:** bank hols. **Meals:** alc (main courses £11.50 to £16.50). Set L Mon to Sat £15.50 (2 courses) to £17.50, Set D Mon to Thur £18.50 (2 courses) to £21.50.. **Service:** 12.5% (optional). **Details:** Cards accepted. 100 seats. Air-con. No music. Wheelchair access. Children's portions.

## ▌Chiswick

### Fish Hook
**Eclectic seafood in downtown Chiswick**
6-8 Elliott Road, W4 1PE
Tel no: (020) 8742 0766
www.fishhook.co.uk
⊖ Turnham Green
**Seafood | £32**
**Cooking score: 2**

Michael Nadra's bright, unfussy neighbourhood restaurant plies its trade in a tall Victorian house on one of Chiswick's residential streets. An emphatic piscatorial moniker spells out the kitchen's intentions and allegiances: fish from far and wide is the main business and Nadra rings the changes each day depending on the market. Red mullet might be turned into escabèche with broccoli 'micro leaves' and crostini as accompaniments, while soft shell crabs are given the tempura treatment. Global themes also point up main courses of grilled sea bream with chorizo, peppers and couscous, or monkfish with Alsace bacon, salsa verde and summer-bean salad. Meat fanciers are offered aged, Scotch fillet steak with shiitake mushrooms, while desserts could feature blueberry and almond sponge with Greek yogurt and honey sorbet. Fish-friendly French whites are the pick of the wine list, with prices starting at £10.
**Chef/s:** Michael Nadra. **Open:** Tue to Sun 12 (12.30 Sun) to 2.30 (3.30 Sat and Sun), 6 to 10.30 (6.30 to 10 Sun). **Meals:** alc (main courses £16). Set L £10 (2 courses) to £13.50. **Service:** 12.5% (optional). **Details:** Cards accepted. 52 seats. Air-con. Wheelchair access. Music. Children's portions.

## Sam's Brasserie and Bar

All-singing, all-dancing favourite
11 Barley Mow Passage, W4 4PH
Tel no: (020) 8987 0555
www.samsbrasserie.co.uk
⊖ Chiswick Park, Turnham Green
Modern European | £29
Cooking score: 4

Ⅴ ⚑£30

Sam Harrison's lively Chiswick venue aims to be a neighbourhood hot-spot and is big enough for a diverse range of neighbourhood needs, with a large bar and eating area, along with a brasserie on ground-floor and mezzanine levels. It's an infectiously buzzy place, and there is good eating to be had. Pasta dishes in two sizes include orecchiette with courgettes, tomatoes, basil and capers, while starters bring on rare tuna with bean salad, or grey shrimps with endive and bacon. Robust fish main courses take in seared monkfish with parsley mash and caper butter, or there is the tri-nations composition of Italian sausages with bubble and squeak and sauerkraut. Finish with chocolate pithiviers, cooked to order, or blood orange and mango jelly with mint syrup. Wines are a pleasing international jumble, the whites majoring in Sauvignon and Chardonnay, the reds ascending to the full-throttle glory of Penfold's Grange at £165. Prices start at a distinctly gentler £12.50 (£3.50 a glass).
Chef/s: Rufus Wickham. Open: all week 12 to 3 (4 Sat and Sun), 6.30 to 10.30 (10 Sun). Closed: 24-26 Dec. Meals: alc (main courses £8.75 to £17.50). Set L Mon to Fri £11.50 (2 courses) to £15. Set D £13.50 (2 courses). Set D Sun £19.50. Bar menu available.
Service: 12.5% (optional). Details: Cards accepted. 100 seats. Air-con. Separate bar. Wheelchair access. Music. Children's portions.

## La Trompette

A buzzing neighbourhood restaurant
5-7 Devonshire Road, W4 2EU
Tel no: (020) 8747 1836
www.latrompette.co.uk
⊖ Turnham Green
French | £35
Cooking score: 6

♦ Ⅴ

Don't underestimate this tasteful restaurant on its leafy Chiswick side street. Fans say it's more than just a good local; it's a 'destination restaurant' in its own right. The French-style fixed price (£35 for three courses) approach garners praise, as do the menus that offer an enticing range of seven or so starters, mains and pudds that 'reflect the season'. The cooking is French with a Mediterranean touch; simple dishes with flavours that sing out loud. All our dishes at inspection had an endearingly split personality: a Salad Lyonnaise charmed us with its neat celeriac remoulade, petite croutons and delicate slices of duck breast, then wham!, shards of crisped-up duck skin, hunks of gutsy confit leg meat, and an orange globe of runny poached egg yolk made a mockery of the dish's affectation of refinement. A gilthead bream main course was a dream of soft white flesh and crispy skin, enhanced by subtly lemony gremolata. Puddings showed well too in the form of a Brillat Savarin cheesecake and a Valhrona fondant. The 'fabulous' Cheese board comes at a £5 supplement but certainly warrants it. There's a lot of fun to be had with the wonderful wine list. Vinous thrills abound, starting low (at £16) with wines plucked from all corners of the world including Georgia, Lebanon, Canada and Switzerland.
Chef/s: James Bennington. Open: Mon to Sat 12 to 2.30, 6.30 to 10.30, Sun 12.30 to 3, 7 to 10. Closed: 24 to 26 Dec, 1 Jan. Meals: Set L Mon to Fri £23.50, Set L Sat £25, Set L Sun £29.50, Set D £35.
Service: 12.5% (optional). Details: Cards accepted. Air-con. No music. Wheelchair access. Children's portions.

## Le Vacherin

Chiswick's Parisienne enclave
76-77 South Parade, W4 5LF
Tel no: (020) 8742 2121
www.levacherin.co.uk
⊖ Turnham Green
French | £31
Cooking score: 4

Ⅴ

A little dollop of Paris is an unlikely find on a Chiswick thoroughfare, but that is what Chef/Patron Malcolm John has striven to create and the resulting restaurant has the feel of one that has been part of the neighbourhood for years. Locals treat it as a place to sup or to celebrate and the hubbub of happy diners is all pervading. The French, bistro décor, complete with piles of Vacherin cheeses, leaves little room for mistaking the style of the food – escargots, foie gras, truffled, baked Vacherin (in season) abound as do steaks (avec frites), grilled fish and rich, carefully made stews, followed by ile flotante and tarte aux amandes. The menu may seem nostalgic, but John knows what he's about and he cooks well within his limits. A well-annotated all French wine list and friendly, if rather harrassed, service complete the picture. House wines start at £3.50 a glass.
**Chef/s:** Malcolm John. **Open:** Tue to Sun L 12 to 3, all week D 6 to 10.30. **Closed:** Bank hols. **Meals:** alc (main courses L £10 to £12, D £13 to £19). **Service:** 12.5% (optional). **Details:** Cards accepted. 80 seats. 10 seats outside. Air-con. No music. No mobile phones. Children's portions.

## READERS RECOMMEND

## Budsara

Thai
99 Chiswick High Road, Chiswick, W4 2ED
Tel no: (020) 8995 5774
'Above-average cooking in a relaxed setting'

## High Road Brasserie

Modern French
162 Chiswick High Road, Chiswick, W4 1PR
Tel no: 020 8742 7474
'A fantastic Parisian-style bistro'

## Roebuck

Gastropub
122 Chiswick High Road, Chiswick, W4 1PU
Tel no: 020 8995 4392
'Simple, decent cooking'

# ▌Crystal Palace

## Numidie

Laid-back dining
48 Westow Hill, SE19 1RX
Tel no: (020) 8766 6166
www.numidie.co.uk
North African | £21
Cooking score: 2

Ⅴ £30

With a name that harks back to ancient Algeria and a room filled with an eclectic mix of old mirrors, stone floor tiles and traditional wooden chairs, you would expect a menu boasting a range of North African dishes, but there's a much wider feel to the food. Alongside merguez in harissa and vegetable tagine, there might be courgette and Roquefort fritter with black cherry sauce as well as bouillabaisse. Sadly, some of the Mediterranean dishes try too hard and tend to disappoint. The Algerian couscous and slow-cooked lamb, on the other hand, are more reliable and should not be missed. From the short list of desserts, stuffed pear with almond, pistachio and yoghurt has distinct flavours and wonderful textures. Service is delightful and the wine list offers good value with several wines by the glass and plenty of interest under £20.
**Chef/s:** Serge Ismail. **Open:** Wed to Sun L 12 to 4, Tue to Sun D 6 to 10.30. **Meals:** alc (main courses £9.50 to £15.50). Set D Tue to Thur £14.50 (2 courses), £18.50 (3 courses). **Service:** not inc. **Details:** Cards accepted. 35 seats. Air-con. Separate bar. Music.

## Ealing

### Ealing Park Tavern
**Victorian gastropub with friendly staff**
222 South Ealing Road, W5 4RL
Tel no: (020) 8758 1879
⊖ South Ealing
Gastropub | £30
New Chef

A thoroughly modern gastropub, the Ealing Park Tavern is as much a drop-in drinking establishment as a destination local restaurant. The kitchen is an open-plan affair, lively and animated, offering an attractively simple, daily changing, market-led menu, with light salad based starters and heavier mains of seared calf's liver with trimmings or fillet of mullet with white bean stew and harissa to follow. The cooking is surprisingly good – a chargrilled chilli squid salad was punchy but not overwhelming; a plump and tender roast chicken breast given a richness from its accompaniment of tomatoes, sultanas, pinenuts and citrus dressing. However, one reader felt that the 'raft of garnishes' was excessive. Puddings; sticky toffee pudding, poached pear, apple and rhubarb pancake are an Anglophile's dream but, given the portion sizes, possibly surplus to requirements. House wines start at £3.25 a glass.
**Chef/s:** John O'Riordan. **Open:** Tue to Sun L 12 to 3 (3.45 Sun), all week D 6 to 10 (9 Sun). **Closed:** 25 Dec to 1 Jan. **Meals:** alc (main courses £9 to £16). Bar tapas menu available Thur to Sat D.
**Service:** not inc. **Details:** Cards accepted. 75 seats. 40 seats outside. No music. Children allowed.

## East Sheen

★NEW ENTRY★

### La Saveur
**A short menu of French classics**
201 Upper Richmond Road, SW14 8QT
Tel no: 020 8876 0644
⊖ North Sheen Rail
French | £25
Cooking score: 1
V £30

This latest restaurant from the Lawrence Hartley/Bruce Duckett partnership (see entries for Brula Bistro and La Buvette) sees an expansion into Sheen. The long, narrow site lacks the quirkiness of their other restaurants but they make the most of the space with a lining of smoked mirror along the full length of the dining room proper, lending an illusion of airiness and space and the big wooden bar at the front which gives a proper continental feel. The short, very French menu is a parade of all time greatest hits – pâté of foie gras, escargots, onglet steak frites and coquilles St Jacques – all dishes simple enough for the kitchen to be able to cope very well. The equally brief but unashamedly French wine list, with wines by the glass from £3.25 to decent burgundies at £50 a bottle, make it useful whatever the occasion. A well-priced lunch and early evening menu add to the appeal though the breakfast and tea sessions have yet to make a proper impact.
**Chef/s:** Steven Gupta. **Open:** Mon to Sun 9 to 10.30. **Meals:** alc (main courses £11.50 to £18.75), Set L and early D £9 to £14. **Service:** 12.5% (optional). **Details:** Cards accepted. 60 seats. 10 seats outside. No music. Wheelchair access. Children's portions.

## Forest Hill

### Babur Brasserie

**Tradition meets innovatation**
119 Brockley Rise, SE23 1JP
Tel no: (020) 8291 2400
www.babur.info
**Modern Indian | £25**
**Cooking score: 2**

£5 OFF  V  £30

Traditional Indian arts and crafts form the decorative focal points at this long-established venue, set against a backdrop of exposed brick walls and bare, walnut tables. Though the mood is relaxed, the kitchen takes a serious approach, with starters taking in murgh pattice (a Delhi street snack of minced chicken with potato and crispy sev) and tandoor-roasted lamb chops with ginger, alongside modern inventions such as ostrich infused with fenugreek and sandalwood. Main courses are similarly varied, ranging from Parsee chicken with apricots and straw potatoes to pan-fried barbary duck breast with honey and coriander, or red snapper with a Himalayan berry sauce on an Indian version of risotto. Alongside the more familiar side dishes are intriguing creations such as green banana with sweet potato, baby aubergine and shallot. Traditional Indian desserts round off the meal, and wines have been cleverly chosen to match the food, priced from around £13.
**Chef/s:** Enam Rahman and Jiwan Lal. **Open:** all week 12.15 to 2.15, 6.15 to 10.30. **Closed:** 25 and 26 Dec. **Meals:** alc exc Sun L (main courses £8 to £17). Sun buffet L £10.95. **Service:** not inc. **Details:** Cards accepted. 72 seats. Air-con. Wheelchair access. Music. Children's portions.

---

## Please send us your feedback

To register your opinion about any restaurant listed in the Guide, or a new restaurant that you wish to bring to our attention, please visit the web address at the bottom of the page. Your feedback informs the content of the book and will be used to compile next year's reviews.

---

## Hackney

★NEW ENTRY★

### Empress of India

**Outstanding addition to the Hackney scene**
130 Lauriston Road, E9 7LH
Tel no: (020) 8533 5123
www.theempressofindia.com
**Gastropub | £28**
**Cooking score: 3**

£30

Close to Victoria Park, this is not a tandoori but a smart new brasserie from Tom and Ed Martin (see entries for the Gun and White Swan) – reincarnated from a former existence as a florist and nightclub. In twenty-first-century 'gastro' style, the restaurant, all wood floors and cream fabric blinds, elides into the long zinc bar cooled by vast brass fans above. Menu choices are sensibly selective and simple, ingredients are excellent including breads, unsalted butter and proper espresso. Starters range from Vichysoisse with soft boiled quail egg and battered monkfish with aïoli; lunchtime specials span old Irish favourites like boiled gammon with colcannon and parsley sauce, to fish and chips with minted purée. At dinner Cornish fish stew with samphire or roast suckling pig raises the kitchen's game. Cooking is very competent. The attractive wine list trawls the world from classic champagnes and burgundies to the stars of southern Italy, Iberia and the New World. A fine choice of wines by the glass from £3.30; bottles from £14.00
**Chef/s:** Tim Wilson. **Open:** L Mon to Fri 12 to 2.30 (Sat all day), D 7 to 10 (Sat 10.30). **Closed:** Christmas, Boxing day. **Meals:** alc main courses £9.50 to £15.50. **Service:** 12.5%. **Details:** Cards accepted. 60 seats. 35 seats outside. Air-con. Wheelchair access. Music. Children's portions.

# GREATER LONDON

## Harrow
### Golden Palace
**Authentic Chinese food in an unlikely setting**
146-150 Station Road, HA1 2RH
Tel no: (020) 8863 2333
⊖ Harrow-on-the-Hill
Chinese | £23
Cooking score: 2

V £30

A neighbourhood restaurant with a national reputation, the Golden Palace flies the flag for authentic Chinese food in suburban Harrow. The action takes place in a cheerful dining room where crowds can choose from a long menu based on skilled renditions of the core repertoire. Around 200 dishes are regularly on show, with earthy, peasant-style hotpots such as braised beancurd with shredded pork sharing the limelight with other Cantonese and Peking-style staples ranging from scallops with spicy salt and chilli, or baked lobster with ginger and spring onion, to crispy aromatic duck. Our inspector found service to be laconic at best, obnoxious at worst. On Sundays, all-day dim sum extravaganzas are the star attraction: expect a selection that might range from steamed, stuffed baby squid in shrimp paste to five-spiced pork belly with Chinese turnip.
**Chef/s:** Mr G. Ho. **Open:** Mon to Sat 12 (11 bank hols) to 11.30, Sun 11 to 10.30. **Closed:** 25 Dec. **Meals:** alc (main courses £5.50 to £30). Set L and D £16.50 to £24 (all min 2). **Service:** 10%. **Details:** Cards accepted. 160 seats. Air-con. No music. Wheelchair access.

### Symbols

🛏 Accommodation is available.

£30 Three courses for less than £30.

V More than five vegetarian dishes.

£5 OFF £5-off voucher scheme.

🍷 Notable wine list.

## Kew
### Glasshouse
**A gastronomic highlight**
14 Station Parade, TW9 3PZ
Tel no: (020) 8940 6777
www.glasshouserestaurant.co.uk
⊖ Kew Gardens
British | £32
Cooking score: 5

🍷 V

Glasshouse shines literally and metaphorically in this quaint, leafy corner of the world. The awkward, high-ceilinged room is given a smart, understated glamour with an interior of creams, beiges and golds surrounded by huge plate glass walls (retractable in good weather), which enlarge the space with their reflections by use of clever lighting during the evening and flood the room with natural light during the day. The ambiance is pleasant enough but the draw here is the food. Out of the same mould as Chez Bruce in Wandsworth (see entry), Glasshouse serves fine British cooking refined by classical technique, and embracing modern ingredients and flavours. The menu, which is a set price affair, changes every service but never fails to interest. The sweet meatiness of a starter of rare grilled tuna with carrot salad and shrimps is balanced with a gremolata sauce; the richness of a foie gras and chicken-liver parfait is mitigated by a covering of dressed lentils, while a main of roast middlewhite pork with morteau sausage and choucroute is a real restaurant marriage of high art and peasant cookery. The 500-bin strong wine list is an oenophile's delight, but the sommelier seems to find as much pleasure in matching tastes and budgets – house wine starts at £15.
**Chef/s:** Anthony Boyd. **Open:** Mon to Sat L 12 to 2.30, D 7 (6.30 Fri and Sat) to 10.30, Sun L 12.30 to 3, D 7.30 to 10. **Closed:** 24 to 26 Dec, 1 Jan. **Meals:** Set L Mon to Sat £23.50 (3 courses), Set L Sun £27.50 (3 courses), Set D £35 to £50. **Service:** 12.5% (optional). **Details:** Cards accepted. 65 seats. Air-con. No music. Wheelchair access. Children's portions.

## Ma Cuisine

French nostalgia
9 Station Approach, TW9 3QB
Tel no: (020) 8332 1923
www.macuisinekew.co.uk
⊖ Kew
French | £23
Cooking score: 3
Ⓥ £30

Expense has been spared on the décor of this French bistro — plastic tablecoths and laminated menus are in evidence, along with cheap banqueting chairs. Yet, somehow, these features enhance the atmosphere. To be fair, the money that Ma Cuisine appears to have saved on interior decoration seems to have been spent on raw ingredients .The restaurant is on the cusp of becoming a chain, with an establishment in Twickenham and another opening due in Barnes. The formula at each restaurant is much the same — French bistro classics. Begin with Mediterranean crab soup with rouille or assiettes de charcuterie. Main courses include crisp pork belly with choucroute, moules marinières or steak tartare. Apart from a few blips, everything was well prepared and served quickly (with a smile). House wines start at £12.50.
**Chef/s:** Tim Francis. **Open:** all week 9 to 3, 6.30 to 10.30 (all day Sat and Sun). **Meals:** alc (main courses £12.50 to £15). Set L £12.95 (2 courses) to £15.50, Set D (exc Sat) £18.50. Light L menu available Sat. **Service:** 10% (optional).
**Details:** Cards accepted. 60 seats. 20 seats outside. Wheelchair access. Music. Children's portions.

## Readers recommend

A 'readers recommend' review is a genuine quote from a report sent in by one of our readers. We intend to follow up these suggestions throughout the year to come.

## ▌Richmond

## La Buvette

Comfortable and elegant
6 Church Walk, TW9 1SN
Tel no: (020) 8940 6264
www.brula.co.uk
French | £27
Cooking score: 3
£30

Before the entrance is a courtyard filled with tables and a huge canvas parasol, which sets a continental tone for this agreeably appointed French restaurant. Start with a rich, hearty fish soup (with rouille and Gruyère), or a chunky terrine de campagne layered with prunes and served with gherkins and chutney. For mains, the generous steak grillé has been described as 'rare and tender', carré d'agneau roti has 'loads of flavour' and comes with merguez sausage, baby broad beans and harissa, while desserts include a classic crème brûlée and strawberry tart. The exclusively French wine list ranges from £12.75 to £50, with many available by the glass, from £3.25. Under same ownership as Brula Bistrot in Twickenham (see entry).
**Chef/s:** Bruce Duckett and Buck Carter. **Open:** all week 12 to 3, 6 to 10:30. **Closed:** 25 and 26 Dec, 1 Jan, Good Fri. **Meals:** alc exc Sun L (main courses £10 to £18.75). Set L and early D (6 to 7) Mon to Sat £12 (2 courses) to £14.50, Set L Sun £15.75.
**Service:** 12.5% (optional). **Details:** Cards accepted. 50 seats. 30 seats outside. No music. Wheelchair access. Children's portions.

## Petersham Nurseries Café

Straight from the kitchen garden
Church Lane, off Petersham Road, TW10 7AG
Tel no: (020) 8605 3627
www.petershamnurseries.com
Modern British | £32
Cooking score: 3
Ⓥ

The potholed lane and the sleepiness of this pseudo-rural neighbourhood aren't great augurs but any misgivings are quickly dispelled when diners finally arrive at this extraordinary establishment. A working nursery, the restaurant area occupies the back of one glasshouse with a tea and coffee area in another, but the surroundings are more like a Fellini film set than a plant-selling business. The kitchen relies greatly on local producers and farmers as well as its own kitchen garden and though the daily changing menu is brief, offering around five starters and five main courses at the beginning of service, rather less by the end, dishes tend to be inventive and well thought out; a beautifully balanced Thai influenced salad of crab with a light Nam Jim dressing might sit next to lamb served with sprouting broccoli, anchovies and harissa. Choices from the Old-World-led wine list (glasses from £4.50) are limited but there's a relatively wide choice of juices and infusions including a delightful old fashioned home-made Amalfi lemonade. The only drawback is the service which, though charming, is rather inefficient, and the poor parking which at this distance from main transport links is fairly essential.

**Chef/s:** Skye Gyngell. **Open:** Wed to Sun L only 12.30 to 3. **Meals:** alc (main courses £14 to £24). **Service:** 12.5% (optional). **Details:** Cards accepted. 80 seats. No music. Car parking.

## Restaurant at the Petersham Hotel
**Fine food matched by superb views**
Nightingale Lane, TW10 6UZ
Tel no: (020) 8940 7471
www.petershamhotel.co.uk
**Modern British | £34**
**Cooking score: 4**

🛏 V

This Gothic-style hotel, perched on the side of a hill just outside Richmond, is home to a fabulous view of the River Thames, clearly one of the main draws to this many-windowed venue. The food produced by Alex Bentley and his team is equally impressive. Probably best described as modern British but with evident influences from classic French cooking, starters include the likes of split-pea soup with the unusual addition of deep-fried

cubes of feta; brown shrimp cocktail on rocket and little gem with Marie Rose sauce; and terrine of foie gras and green peppercorns. Great care is taken with presentation, illustrated in a colourful main course of baked sea bass with seaweed on saffron-scented celeriac mash, accompanied by sauce vierge and slithers of courgette. The kitchen's expertise in pastry shines through in the desserts, such as pineapple tarte Tatin with coconut sorbet and apple galette with yoghurt and honey ice cream. Wines are mainly French but with a smattering from other European growers and the New World. Prices start at £19.50, £5 for a glass, and half-bottles are plentiful.

**Chef/s:** Alex Bentley. **Open:** Mon to Sat 12.15 to 2.15, 7 to 9.45, Sun 12.30 to 3.30, 7 to 8.45. **Closed:** D 24 to 27 Dec. **Meals:** alc exc Sun (main courses £6 to £24). Set L Mon to Sat £18.50 (2 courses) to £25, Set L Sun £29.50, Set D Sun £20 (2 courses) to £25. **Service:** 10% (optional). **Details:** Cards accepted. 65 seats. Air-con. No mobile phones. Wheelchair access. Music. Children's portions. Car parking.

## Victoria
**Packed gastropub with tapas offerings**
10 West Temple Sheen, SW14 7RT
Tel no: (020) 8876 4238
www.thevictoria.net
⊖ Richmond
**Gastropub | £32**
**New Chef**

🛏 V

This well-established gastropub has little competition in the smart, sleepy streets of Sheen Common. Securing a table, especially on sunny weekends when its bright white conservatory, garden and children's play area have extra appeal to the well-heeled families of the area, can be very hard. There is plenty to please at other times too: a comfortable bar; a relaxed attitude and an up-to-the-minute fully traceable and seasonal menu featuring excellent tapas (evening only), estofada of squid and morcilla, grilled sea bream with wild garlic mash, sauce ravigote and huge, tender Berkshire-bred Charolais steaks; a

decent wine list starts at £13.95. If only the service were a little sharper and the cooking a touch tighter, this would be exemplary.
**Chef/s:** Stephen Paskins. **Open:** all week 12 to 2.30 (3 Sat, 4 Sun), 7 to 10 (9 Sun). **Closed:** 4 days Christmas. **Meals:** alc (main courses £9 to £20). **Service:** 12.5% (optional). **Details:** Cards accepted. 70 seats. 50 seats outside. No music. Wheelchair access. Children's portions. Car parking.

## ALSO RECOMMENDED
### ▲ Chez Lindsay
11 Hill Rise, Richmond, TW10 6UQ
Tel no: (020) 8948 7473
www.chezlindsay.co.uk

This is the place to come for authentic Breton cuisine. The organic buckwheat galettes range from those simply filled with cheese (£4.75) to speciality combinations like onion sauce, celery, walnuts and Roquefort sauce (£7.45). Fresh seafood is also something of a speciality or you can choose from enticing salads and 'grand plats' like braised lamb shank with red-wine sauce, gratin dauphinois and seasonal vegetables (£13.75). For desserts there are filled crêpes (from £3.50), ices (£5.50) or crème brûlée (£5.25). The set lunch is two courses for £14.50, dinner £17.50. Breton cider is served in ceramic 'boles' (litre jug £9.95); French wines start from £13.95. Open all week.

## ▌Southall
### Brilliant
Revamped local stalwart
72-76 Western Road, UB2 5DZ
Tel no: (020) 8574 1928
www.brilliantrestaurant.com
⊖ Southall
Indian/Pakistani/Bangladeshi | £22
Cooking score: 3
£5 OFF   V   £30

After over 30 years, Brilliant continues to accumulate awards and this Guide has long recognised the qualities that set it apart. The main dining room has finally been completely

refurbished to include plasma screens showing Bollywood films, and the overall look is 'modern and tasteful'. Details like crisp, vibrantly spiced onion bhaji and 'terrific' romali bread contribute as much to the experience as more substantial dishes. These draw largely from Northern India but aspects of East Africa, as in chicken dishes cooked and served on the bone, reflect the Anand family's journey to Britain via Kenya. Lengthy menus can bring on the unsettling uncertainty, if not plain disbelief, in a kitchen's abililty to deliver. But, here, the sheer size of the restaurant provides assurance that dishes are properly prepared and not the result of a last minute pick-and-mix operation. Newly introduced 'healthy options' unsurprisingly do not extend to the sweet section that includes kulfi with pistachio and almond. Wines start at £9 but the usual range of beers or one of the several versions of lassi might provide more appropriate accompaniment.
**Chef/s:** Davinder Anand. **Open:** Tue to Fri L 12 to 2.30, Tue to Sun D 6 to 11.30. **Meals:** alc (main courses £4.50 to £13). Set L and D £17.50. **Service:** not inc. **Details:** Cards accepted. 225 seats. Air-con. Wheelchair access. Music. Children's portions. Car parking.

### Madhu's
Unerring service
39 South Road, UB1 1SW
Tel no: (020) 8574 1897
www.madhusonline.com
North Indian | £28
Cooking score: 3
£5 OFF   V   £30

More than 25-years old, Madhu's popularity is part-founded on impressively professional service, but it's the food that really counts. The care and attention on timing and the retention of texture and distinct flavours across the board is notable. On inspection, well-marinated tandoori salmon allowed 'subtle hints of spice' while preserving excellent texture in the fish. Dishes, drawn from the entire sub-continent and East Africa, are described accurately; 'you get to know the

## Scores on the Doors

To find out more about the Scores on the Doors campaign, please visit the Food Standard's Agency website: www.food.gov.uk or www.which.co.uk.

spices in the range of rice preparations'. Several dishes for six people encourage sharing. Vegetarians are looked after with a tantalising range of dishes that go well beyond the usual. For less chilli-rich dishes, wines from £9 are fairly priced and might be worth considering, but beers or lassi would be better matches for the more fiery offerings.

**Chef/s:** J.P. Singh. **Open:** Mon and Wed to Fri L 12.30 to 2.30, Wed to Mon D 6 to 11.30. **Closed:** 25 Dec. **Meals:** alc (main courses £6 to £12). Set L and D £17.50 to £20. **Service:** not inc. **Details:** Cards accepted. 104 seats. Air-con. Wheelchair access. Music. Children's portions.

## ALSO RECOMMENDED

### ▲ Gifto's Lahore Karahi

162-164 The Broadway, Southall, UB1 1NN
Tel no: (020) 8813 8669

This Pakastani restaurant stands out among the throng on Southall's Broadway. Expect crowds, noise and action in the vast ground-floor eating area, and contemporary Pakastani cooking with an authentic punch – it really is the real thing. In the snack department (£1.50 to £3) you will find pani puri, onion bhaji and dahi bhalla (lentil doughnuts with tamarind sauce). Follow with a tandoori dish (from £4.20), or go for a tawa special cooked on a hotplate, perhaps ginger chicken (£7.20) cooked with green chillies and onions, or one of the Lahore dishes – king fish curry (£6.90). Bread and rice dishes are plentiful, while desserts include kheer (rice pudding, £1.80). Unlicensed but bring your own (no corkage). Open all week.

## ▮ Tottenham Hale

### The Lock Dining Bar

Riverside dining
Heron House, Hale Wharf, Ferry Lane, N17 9NF
Tel no: (020) 8885 2829
www.thelock-diningbar.com
⊖ Richmond
Modern European | £23
Cooking score: 5
Ⓥ £30

Maybe the 2012 effect is heading up the Lea Valley? The Lock Dining Bar has now established itself in this unlikely industrial riverside location in N17. The gamble by chef Ade Adeshina and partner/front-of-house manager Fabrizio Ruso appears to have paid off. The menu changes with the seasons – it was due to move from winter/spring to spring/summer at inspection. Other changes include a new alfresco seating area, and new furniture for the light, bright, wooden-floored main restaurant. The à la carte treats vegetarians, pescatarians and meat lovers equally, with vegetarian options no afterthought. Meat and fish are sourced as locally as possible. Starters may include pan-fried polenta fritter, baked goat cheese with mushroom tapenade crust, dressed with truffle emulsion. Alternatively, there may be a pan-fried scallop, alongside a perfectly timed mackerel fillet, and a small square of pungent Cheddar cheese pasta bake with a herby tomato sauce. Terrines, pâtés and foie gras often also feature as opening options. Technical skill is demonstrated with a main course dish of well-timed pan-roasted fillet of freshwater pink trout with a garlic and vanilla foam, sautéed potatoes, caramelised onions and warm tomato dressing. Alternatively, there may be roast Barberry duck on a bed of braised cabbage and mushrooms and wine reduction. Desserts do not disappoint, and may include tarte Tatin for sharing. Expect top-notch amuse-bouche – an intense cauliflower soup, for instance – and pre-desserts. Service is efficient, knowledgeable and welcoming. The Lock has a lighter lunch menu and a Sunday lunch menu. The wine list focuses on Italy and France, along with 'the rest'. Sicilian house wines start at a reasonable £13.50, with four red and four white options by the glass from £3.50.

**Chef/s:** Ade Adeshina. **Open:** Sun to Fri L 12 to 2pm, Mon to Sat D 6 to 10pm. **Closed:** 1 and 2 Jan, 1 to 10 Jun. **Meals:** alc exc Sun L (main courses £10.25 to £16). Set L £12 (2 courses), Set D £25 (3courses). **Service:** 10% (optional). **Details:** Cards accepted. 60 seats. 30 seats outside. Wheelchair access. Music. Children's portions. Car parking.

# Twickenham

## A Cena

**Simple Italian dining in the suburbs**
418 Richmond Road, TW1 2EB
Tel no: (020) 8288 0108
www.acena.co.uk
**Italian | £45**
**Cooking score: 2**

𝖸

A Cena sits pretty on a row of chichi boutiques at the foot of Richmond Bridge. Candles in bottles illuminate a mismatch of wooden chairs, tables and church pews, suggesting relaxed charm. But the chasm between bench (fixed to the floor) and table (at least a foot away) will have the average-sized customer 'hailing a taxi to get to their plate'. The seasonal menu features beef carpaccio or asparagus with fried egg and Parmesan – safe choices, simply presented and well-executed. Slow-roast rabbit bruschetta or Parmesan frittella catch the more intrepid diner's eye. Main courses tread a well-beaten path: grilled ribeye steak, pan-fried corn-fed chicken or veal chop arrive with mash and seasonal vegetables. Desserts are a lip-smacking dairy-fest: vanilla cheesecake, rhubarb and custard trifle or mocha tartufo with cream. Portions are generous. Service is discreetly attentive. A Merlot Corvina 2006 opens the all-Italian wine list at £13.50.

**Chef/s:** Nicola Parsons. **Open:** Tue to Sun L 12 to 2.30pm, Tue to Sat D 7 to 10.30pm. **Meals:** alc (main courses L £8 to £15, D £11.50 to £20). Set L

Sun £22.50. **Service:** not inc. **Details:** Cards accepted. 55 seats. Air-con. Wheelchair access. Music. Children's portions.

## La Brasserie McClements

**A renaissance for Twickenham?**
2 Whitton Road, TW1 1BJ
Tel no: (020) 8744 9610
www.labrasserietw1.co.uk
**French | £33**
**Cooking score: 4**

It's all change again at Brasserie McClements. Having dumbed down from his glory days last year and seemingly put the concept of grand French cooking firmly in the past, John McClements has had a change of heart. The shortened menu is now a set-price affair, with the likes of 'Fantasy of Oysters' (oysters prepared five ways) and assiettes Landaise (a tasting of foie gras and confit duck) offered as two of the five starters. Mains include turbot with lobster, or sausage and veal chop (with sweetbread and loin, little gem and pommes purée). McClements demonstrates his assured technique throughout. The aforementioned turbot was excellent, delivering the great fish cooked perfectly; it was well contrasted with a rich, bean cassoulet. The wine list (starting at £17.50 for house wine) is well chosen, and given the classicism of the food, has a surprisingly broad scope.

**Chef/s:** John McClements. **Open:** Mon to Sat L 12 to 3, D 7 to 11. **Closed:** 1 Jan. **Meals:** alc (main courses £15 to £25). Set L (exc Sat) £20. Set D £30 (2 courses) to £35. **Service:** 10% (optional). **Details:** Cards accepted. 45 seats. Air-con. Music. Children's portions.

> Average price
>
> The average price listed in main-entry reviews denotes the price of a three-course meal, without wine.

## Brula Bistrot
**Gallic delight**
43 Crown Road, St Margaret's, TW1 3EJ
Tel no: (020) 8892 0602
www.brulabistrot.com
French | £31
New Chef

A real comfort spot for St Margaret's, Bistrot Brula is reliable, familiar and unchallenging in equal measure. The first of the mini restaurant empire from Bruce Duckett and Laurence Hartley which includes La Saveur in East Sheen and La Buvette in Richmond (see entries), Brula remains the best of the bunch. The cooking has a very French accent, featuring escargots and foie gras as well as onglet steak, grilled fish and confit duck, and the kitchen has a confidence of long practice and competence. The wine list is similarly Gallic but kindly priced, starting at £12.75 and offering plenty of choice by the glass or 50cl pichet. If in a celebratory mood the final bill can stack up, but locals tend to be drawn to the very good value set lunches and early evening dinners.
**Chef/s:** Bruce Duckett, Toby Williams. **Open:** all week L 12 to 3, D 6 to 10.30. **Closed:** 25 and 26 Dec, 1 Jan,. **Meals:** alc (main courses £11.50 to £18.50). Set L £11 (2 courses) to £13.50. **Service:** 12.5% (optional). **Details:** Cards accepted. 45 seats. 12 seats outside. No music. No mobile phones. Wheelchair access. Children's portions.

★NEW ENTRY★
## Tapas Y Vino
**Modern and traditional tapas**
111 London Road, TW1 1EE
Tel no: 020 88925417
www.elvinotapas.co.uk
⊖ Twickenham
Modern European | £20
Cooking score: 2
Ⅴ £30

John McClements seems to be taking over this corner of Twickenham, but this latest string to his bow takes his cooking out of the grand

French tradition and into tapas. He hasn't splashed out on the interior: tables and chairs are basic and the looped Gypsy Kings on the sound system might grate, but the food is fun and relatively cheap. A generous plate of Jabugo is unmissable, but there is plenty else on offer: from clams with chickpeas and chorizo, or perfect deep-fried squid with a properly pungent aïoli, to hare royal, here served as a slice of deep, rich pâté. Portions are small, so multiple ordering is de rigueur, but at £4.50 or less per portion, there is little chance of a massive bill at the end. Fill up on the savouries: desserts are not a strong point and nor, despite its name, is the wine list. Note: no children under 10 after 9pm.
**Chef/s:** Michael Jackson. **Open:** Mon to Sun, L 12pm to 3pm, D 7pm to 10.30pm. **Closed:** Sun. **Meals:** alc (main courses £12 to 15). **Service:** 10% (optional). **Details:** Cards accepted. 45 seats. Wheelchair access. Music. Children's portions.

## READERS RECOMMEND
## Tangawizi
**Indian**
406 Richmond Road, Richmond Bridge, Twickenham, TW1 2EB
Tel no: (020) 8891 3737
'The menu mixes the familiar with the more ambitious'

## Jeevan
**Indian**
381 High Road, Wembley, HA9 6AA
Tel no: 020 8900 0510
'Pleasant tandoori dishes'

## Monty's
**Nepalese**
54 Northfield Avenue, West Ealing, W13 9RR
Tel no: 020 8567 6281
www.montys-restaurant.com
'Speedy food and generous portions'

# Wood Green

## Mosaica @ The Factory
**Reliable results**
Chocolate Factory, Clarendon Road, N22 6XJ
Tel no: (020) 8889 2400
www.mosaicarestaurants.com
⊖ Wood Green
Modern European | £26
Cooking score: 3

ⓥ £30

The former factory has an open kitchen, an eclectic mix of old tables and chairs, wooden floors, local artists' work on the walls, and friendly and welcoming service. After a period of change in the kitchen and some inconsistencies, a new chef is now producing more reliable results. Some Mosaica menu staples remain, joined by some imaginative additions. Chilled cucumber soup made a refreshing opening at inspection, while charred English asparagus with rocket and Parmesan shavings was 'simple and just right'. Pan-fried chicken was well handled with great flavour, and came set a bed of spinach with roasted baby potatoes and jus, while roasted halibut was presented on a bed of good, fresh pappardelle pasta with an inventive cockle beurre noisette. Desserts were a notable highlight, including a lime and lychee cheesecake with an intense pineapple ice cream. House wines start from £12, with four or five choices by the glass from £3.30.
**Chef/s:** Phil Ducker. **Open:** Tue to Fri and Sun L 12 to 2.30, Tue to Sat D 7 to 9.30. **Closed:** 2 weeks Christmas. **Meals:** alc (main courses L £5 to £15, D £10 to £16). **Service:** 10% (optional). **Details:** Cards accepted. 100 seats. Air-con. Wheelchair access. Music. Children's portions. Car parking.

## Tom Aikens

**Why did you become a chef?**
I was exposed to fantastic food from an early age, mainly due to my father's trade as a wine merchant.

**Who was your main inspiration?**
Professionally, David Cavalier and Pierre Koffman helped me become who I am today.

**Which of today's chefs do you admire?**
Unfortunately, not many of the 'well known' chefs still cook in their kitchens. Admiration though has to go to Michel and Albert Roux, for their dedication and consistency in their commitment to the industry.

**Where do you eat out?**
Close to home, either the Wolseley or Tom's Kitchen. When I am away, I try to eat at local top restaurants to pick up ideas and trends.

**Where do you source your ingredients?**
We have a great number of suppliers, but working for Lady Bamford when she was developing Daylesford farm has meant that organic produce has been a firm principle of mine ever since.

**What's the best dish you've ever eaten?**
A simple, but exquisite, grilled chicken with summer truffles at Eugenie les Bains in South-West France.

**If you could only eat one more thing, what would it be?**
My brother Rob's freshly baked muffins.

# ENGLAND

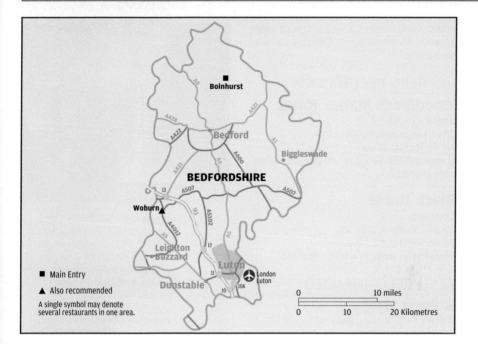

## Bolnhurst

★ READERS' RESTAURANT OF THE YEAR ★
SOUTH EAST

### The Plough
**Impeccable sourcing and accomplished cooking**
Kimbolton Road, Bolnhurst, MK44 2EX
Tel no: (01234) 376274
www.bolnhurst.com
Gastropub | £28
Cooking score: 5

Standing well apart from its neighbours, the Plough is a beautiful and very old building. The place has been superbly restored both inside and out. Chef-proprietor Martin Lee has an impressive track record, though his style is not outlandish or flashy. Instead he makes his mark with attention to detail, sourcing of raw materials (especially local), and sound culinary intelligence. Seared scallops with cauliflower purée and a caper and sultana dressing is a typical starter, as is grilled home-made black pudding with Montgomery Cheddar hash and smoked bacon, though there might also be something utterly simple such as smoked Western Isles salmon with capers and lemon. Main courses, meanwhile, might include slow-cooked shoulder of lamb with chickpea purée, spinach, tomato and onion; roast calves' sweetbreads and kidney with rösti potato, girolle mushrooms and Madeira sauce; or chargrilled monkfish with Jersey potatoes and asparagus. To end the meal, choices could include lemon tart with crème fraîche or rhubarb crumble with vanilla ice cream. The wine list lives up to the standards set by the cooking, with a broad and varied selection from around the world, carefully chosen to balance quality and price, with house selections from £12.95 and a page of 17 offerings by the glass.

**Chef/s:** Martin Lee. **Open:** Tue to Sun L 12 to 2 (2.30 Sun), Tue to Sat D 6.30 to 9.30. **Closed:** first 2 weeks Jan. **Meals:** alc (main courses £10.95 to £21). Set L £12.50 (2 courses) to £16. **Service:** not inc.

**Details:** Cards accepted. 80 seats. 30 seats outside. No music. Wheelchair access. Children's portions. Car parking.

## READERS RECOMMEND
### Woodlands Manor Hotel
British
Green Lane, Clapham, MK41 6EP
Tel no: (01234) 363281
**'A secluded manor house, serving traditional English dishes'**

### Black Horse
Gastropub
Ireland, Shefford, SG17 5QL
Tel no: (01462) 811 398
**'Imaginative menu in a traditional pub'**

## ALSO RECOMMENDED
### ▲ Paris House
Woburn Park, Woburn, MK17 9QP
Tel no: (01525) 290692

A black and white timbered house in the Duke of Bedford's Woburn Park estate is the fine setting for a sophisticated restaurant where chef-proprietor Peter Chandler offers classic French cooking. Dining options include a midweek lunch (£25). Chandler's dinner menu (£55) might start with foie gras and prune terrine, go on to delice of salmon in champagne sauce, and finish with prune and Armagnac cheesecake for dessert. The wine list is pricey but house selections are £17 to £19. Closed Sun D and Mon.

## READERS RECOMMEND
### Inn at Woburn
British
George Street, Woburn, MK17 9PX
Tel no: (01525) 290441
www.theinnatwoburn.com
**'Contemporary cuisine in elegant surroundings'**

English sparkling wine

Since its rebirth in the 1950s, English wine-making has been hard going. In 1992 Jim Ainsworth of *Punch* wrote tellingly that, 'As marginal climates go, England's is nearly off the scale. Only a moderate maritime effect makes wine-growing in England possible.' Production was erratic. In a Burgundian summer like 1989, the Breaky Bottom Vineyard near Lewes made 27,000 bottles but in a poor year it might have produced just one thousand.

However, 21st century climate change has helped English wine growers to survive and raise their game. Some exceptional sparkling wines are now being made from classic champagne grapes – most success-fully on the chalky South Downs. The soil is similar to Champagne's, high in the acids which give the fizz its verve and bounce. The weather is similar, too. Crucially, warmer autumns have allowed producers to achieve decent ripeness in their grapes.

The most prestigious is the Nyetimber Vineyard at West Chiltington, specifically designed and planted to make fizz to rival the finest champagne. In Sussex, Ridgeview Wine Estate at Ditchling creates subtle blends showing a restrained exuberance uncannily like the real thing. Peter Hall, the inspired maverick at Breaky Bottom, also makes the excellent Cuvée Rémy Alexandre, the 1999 now fully mature. Or for a fresher Cornish sparkling style, Camel Valley Vineyards near Bodmin is a racy winner.

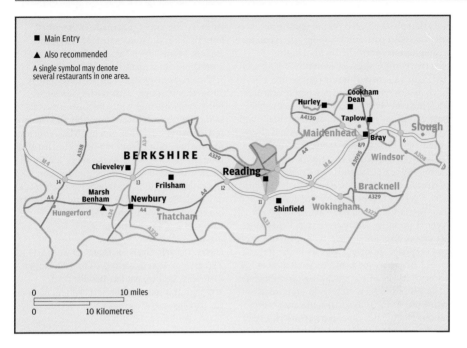

■ Main Entry

▲ Also recommended

A single symbol may denote
several restaurants in one area.

BERKSHIRE

Cookham Dean
Hurley
Taplow
Maidenhead
Bray
Slough
Windsor
Chieveley
Reading
Bracknell
Frilsham
Marsh Benham
Newbury
Thatcham
Shinfield
Wokingham
Hungerford

0          10 miles
0          10 Kilometres

## ▮ Bray

### The Fat Duck

**White-hot gastronomic alchemy**
1 High Street, Bray, SL6 2AQ
Tel no: (01628) 580333
www.fatduck.co.uk
**Modern European | £80**
**Cooking score: 9**

It requires a full measure of courage, audacity and real talent to put on public display the results of biochemical experimentation and culinary alchemy, but that is exactly what Heston Blumenthal Ph.D OBE has achieved at this converted pub in an affluent Thames-side village. Inside, the Fat Duck feels cosily charming rather than overtly luxurious and maître d' Eric Doerr goes about his work with low-key courtesy. The stage is set, but a 'wizard's' experimental needs its props, and these come in the form of extraordinary crockery inspired by the natural world: white bone china with concentric 'tree rings' slate slabs, even grass-topped boxes with hydrogen mist wafting out of them. Diners are offered a choice of a three-course carte or an eight-course tasting menu (plus all manner of extras), which now weighs in at £115. This is the best way to get your money's worth out of the show, especially if a full quota of 'oohs and aahs' is required: marvel at the nitro-green tea and lime mousse, be amazed by the bacon and egg ice cream (even though this has already entered the realms of culinary folklore). The whole spectacle could seem like Harry Potter's box of tricks, were it not for the fact that it is also supremely fine cooking defined by astonishing curiosity, daring and consummate technique. The Fat Duck really does venture boldly where few other UK restaurants dare to tread. Amuse bouche prove that it's showtime from the very outset, and one creation in particular continues to set the senses racing: a beautifully textured quail's egg jelly layered with rich, silky foie gras, some langoustine mousse and pea purée adding an extra dimension of colour and taste. Many dishes stay on the menu for a considerable time and fully deserve their place in the repertoire, witness sweet pan-fried scallops, sliced on to scallop tartare, garnished with a highly effective combination of white chocolate and caviar plus a few pea shoots for texture. The kitchen also works miracles when it ventures back into the world of classic haute cuisine. Sole véronique is ingeniously reinvented with champagne jelly containing grapes and slivers of radish, a little parsley foam, fried onions fashioned into a trellis and a stack of 'genuinely top class' chips, while tarte Tatin is perfect in every detail. Elsewhere, desserts can have a very different sensory impact: an exquisitely fashioned chocolate délice has a layer of popping candy at its base. Petits fours are tantalising, jokey, tiny explosions of taste and surprise: chocolate appears in the style of an old Aero bar, apple and caramel mousse comes with an edible 'wrapping', and there are little jellies spiked with five different malt whiskies. As for wine, mark-ups may 'verge on the absurd', but there is an astute choice of producers across the board. The classic French regions are covered exhaustively and it is worth delving into the high-end vintages from Spain and Italy if money is no constraint. Bottles prices do not dip below £30, and even selections by the glass will set you back at least £11.

**Chef/s:** Heston Blumenthal. **Open:** Tue to Sun L 12 to 1.45 (2.30 Sun), Tue to Sat D 7 to 9. **Closed:** 2 weeks Christmas. **Meals:** Set L and D £80 to £115. **Service:** 12.5% (optional). **Details:** Cards accepted. 46 seats. Air-con. No music. No mobile phones. Children allowed.

## Hinds Head Hotel

**The burgeoning Blumenthal empire**
High Street, Bray, SL6 2AB
Tel no: (01628) 626151
**British | £31**
**Cooking score: 4**

Viewers of Heston Blumenthal's TV series will have seen him dashing to and fro between the Fat Duck and this neighbouring old inn at the centre of the village, which he has owned since 2004. But don't expect to find the whizz-bang culinary fireworks that made Blumenthal famous here; the tone is instead set by the ancient beams, open fires and lively atmosphere that mark this place out as a traditional village inn. The cooking style is altogether earthier, with starters taking in potted shrimps and watercress, tea-smoked salmon with soda bread, or rabbit and bacon terrine with cucumber pickles. Main courses, meanwhile, range from whole sea bream with fennel, and skate wing with capers, lemon and parsley, to oxtail and kidney pudding, and Lancashire hotpot. Sandwiches and bar snacks are available at weekday lunchtimes, and there is a compact wine list headed up by Argentine varietals at £13 a bottle, or £3.35 to £4.75 a glass.

**Chef/s:** Dominic Chapman. **Open:** all week L 12 to 2.30 (3 Sun), Mon to Sat D 6.30 to 9.30. **Closed:** Bank hols. **Service:** not inc. **Details:** Cards accepted. 160 seats. No music. Children's portions. Car parking.

## Waterside Inn

Ferry Road, Bray, SL6 2AT
Tel no: (01628) 620691
www.waterside-inn.co.uk
**French | £120**
**Cooking score: 8**

🍴 ⟊

The Waterside Inn has been in transition from Michel Roux to his son Alain, but the head chef Russell Holborn has been a constant for several years now. The magical location does not change. For despite the necessary removal of the famous weeping willow tree which framed the restaurant, this is still one of the loveliest riverside settings in southern England; you can take drinks in the little summer house, there's a jetty to tie up boats. Flashes of the old Michel Roux brilliance are still there, as in a superb amuse of deep-fried ravioli of crab, resting in a little pool of red pepper sauce, and in heavenly desserts like the lemon parfait on a biscuit base, and the wonderful tiramisu. But reports have highlighted a disappointing starter of courgette flowers stuffed with wild mushrooms and a medley of other vegetables. Such a dish, simple in nature, requires perfect ingredients and exact timing: the vegetables looked tired and frankly past their best. Breads, too, baked by the restaurant, can sometimes lack that nth degree of flavour one would expect here. The menu has a fairly wide selection of generally classic dishes with some modern twists, like breast of pigeon and quail served with a lime jus. Sole is served as two fillets, with a mousse of broad beans in between the pieces. A main course of fillet of Scotch beef is praised for its simplicity, nicely cooked, with a beautiful flavour. French cheeses are immaculate and there is a particularly good English blue from Bracknell. Passion fruit tart has lovely moistness, a fine piece of nougat, a delicate chocolate marshmallow, orange jelly, a lemon tart, a crisp caramelised almond tuile, and a stunning but simple arrangement of almond pastry. Petits fours are superb. Service is from formally dressed, mostly French staff, who are very attentive. The only real blemish on one occasion 'was that the sommelier had no idea what we had ordered when he came to discuss the wine, something that would be almost unthinkable in France'. The wine list, vast in scale with page after page in a green leather binder, is exclusively French (except for sherry and port). House wine is a stiff £37. Growers are, however, top drawer: Guigal's Côte Rôtie La Mouline 1995, priced at £550 a bottle, but also his Condrieu 2004 at £98 and Château Simone from Provence 2004 comes in at a fair £48.

**Chef/s:** Alain Roux. **Open:** Wed to Sun 12 to 2 (2.30 Sun), 7 to 10; also Tue D 1 June to 31 Aug. **Closed:** 26 Dec to 1 Feb. **Meals:** alc (main courses £38 to £52). Set L Wed to Sat £40 to £89.50, Set L Sun £56 to £89.50, Set D £89.50. **Service:** 12.5% (optional). **Details:** Cards accepted. 75 seats. No music. No mobile phones. Wheelchair access. Car parking.

## ▌Chieveley
## The Crab at Chieveley
**Seafood scuttles inland**
Wantage Road, Chieveley, RG20 8UE
Tel no: (01635) 247550
www.crabatchieveley.com
**Seafood | £40**
**Cooking score: 3**

The name makes it no surprise that this relaxed restaurant-with-rooms deals in the bounty of the sea, but the land-locked Berkshire location comes as a bit of a surprise. Still, the décor makes up for it with a nautically themed look that extends to a fish-netted ceiling in the restaurant, filled with crab shells and the like. The Cornish kin of those crabs are featured on the menu, along with Carlingford Loch oysters, native lobster, turbot, rouget, the humble herring and even the occasional meat or vegetarian dish. A characteristic starter might be butter-poached lobster, mango and pak choi, with a main course of, say, John Dory, Parmesan gnocchi, English asparagus, langoustine and tarragon sabayon, while desserts include crowd pleasers such as pear tarte Tatin with caramel Crunchie ice cream. Staff are 'cheerful and well informed'; especially good are wine recommendations from a respected and likeable sommelier. In addition, there is a decent range of bottles for pockets of varying depth and ten wines come by the glass at £4.75.

**Chef/s:** David Horridge. **Open:** Mon to Sat, 12 to 2.30, 6 to 9.30. Sun, 12 to 3, 6 to 9. **Meals:** alc (main courses £15.95 to £37.50).. **Service:** not inc. **Details:** Cards accepted. 130 seats. 50 seats outside. Air-con. Separate bar. No music. Wheelchair access. Children's portions. Car parking.

## Cookham Dean
### Inn on the Green
Traditional setting and approach
The Old Cricket Common, Cookham Dean,
SL6 9NZ
Tel no: (01628) 482638
www.theinnonthegreen.com
Modern British | £38
Cooking score: 4

Ｖ

Standing by the green in a quintessentially English village, this could be any rural inn. Inside, its more serious ambitions as a stylish 'boutique hotel' become apparent. In the main dining room the tone is set by an impressive chandelier, while rich wood panelling gives a Swiss chalet look to the Stublie room. The inn is under the same ownership as the Embassy in London (see entry), with menus overseen by executive chef Gary Hollihead, and accordingly, the cooking is founded on classical principles while showing modern sensibilities and an intelligent, unpretentious approach. Starters of venison carpaccio with poached egg, crispy parsnips and Parmesan, or roast scallops with piccalilli and mixed leaf salad, might be followed by rump of Devon lamb with white bean and shallot purée; confit of duck with dauphinoise potatoes, dates and Merlot jus; or Dover sole meunière with mussels, clams, tomatoes and capers. Steaks from the grill come with crispy onion rings, onion marmalade and béarnaise, and to finish there might be dark chocolate and mocha tart with pistachio ice cream, or tarte Tatin with Granny Smith sorbet. An extensive wine list aims to suit all palates and budgets, opening with house French at £14.50.
**Chef/s:** Garry Hollihead. **Open:** Sun L 1 to 4, Tue to Sat D 7 to 10. **Meals:** alc exc Sun L (main courses £12 to £22). Set D Tue to Fri £17.95 (2 courses) to £21.95. **Service:** 12.5% (optional). **Details:** Cards accepted. 100 seats. 64 seats outside. Air-con. No mobile phones. Wheelchair access. Music. Children's portions. Car parking.

## Frilsham
### Pot Kiln
Daily changing menus
Frilsham, RG18 0XX
Tel no: (01635) 201366
www.potkiln.co.uk
Gastropub | £25
Cooking score: 3

£5 OFF  Ｖ  £30

Thoroughly rooted in its countryside, this glorious red-brick pub with evolving gardens encouragingly focuses on local produce. What chef/patron Mike Robinson doesn't shoot or catch comes from a nearby dealer. Expect constant changes; responses to what comes through the kitchen door are as likely to drive inspiration as the earthy European recipes that dominate the menu: pigeon with bacon and black pudding; prunes and hazelnuts with venison terrine; or mains like cassoulet or slow-cooked rabbit with lemon are typical, while braised red cabbage and garden kale characterise the vegetable accompaniments. Puddings steer a safely solid course with classics like sticky toffee pudding, apple crumble and brownie with poached pear. At its best this is 'serious country cooking', soundly based and of worthy ambition, but not all reporters have gone away happy. Beers from the West Berkshire Brewery, literally from over the garden wall, supplement the 60-bottle wine list that starts at £12.50 with a Pays d'Oc.
**Chef/s:** Mike Robinson. **Open:** all week L 12 to 2, Mon to Sat D 7 to 9. **Closed:** 25 Dec. **Meals:** alc (main courses £12 to £17.50). Set L Mon to Fri £13.50 (2 courses) to £16.50, Set L Sun £15.50 (2 courses) to £19.50.. **Service:** 10% (optional). **Details:** Cards accepted. 48 seats. 120 seats outside. No music. No mobile phones. Wheelchair access. Children's portions. Car parking.

## ▌Hurley

### Black Boys Inn
**Smartly refurbished restaurant-with-rooms**
Henley Road, Hurley, SL6 5NQ
Tel no: (01628) 824212
www.blackboysinn.co.uk
**Modern British | £23**
**Cooking score: 5**

🛏 £30

With its polished wood surfaces and well-upholstered feel, the transformation of this country pub may be swish rather than personal, but chef Simon Bonwick has set the kitchen off to a rollicking good start. He oversees a short menu built around local produce in which technical challenges are met with ease. Rillettes of smoked trout and fresh crayfish comes with a vibrant-tasting watercress purée to produce a refined and enjoyable starter, while another starter, a tartare of bluefin tuna served with an intense liquorice and saffron dressing, has become something of a signature dish. There is a welcome restraint to the cooking, too; note a contemporary take on the classic combination of black bream fillets teamed with a light provençale stew and pesto – nothing explosive but a simple success. Desserts are done with equal care and presentational agility, from griottine cherry and marzipan fritter with cherry and yoghurt smoothie to chocolate sablé with bitter chocolate mousse and pistachio sauce. Reports on service have been mixed this year. The wine list is an enterprising global collection with plenty of variety for those on a relatively modest budget. A whopping 39 wines are by the glass (from £3.65), with bottles from £16.50.
**Chef/s:** Simon Bonwick. **Open:** Tue to Sun L 12 to 2, Tue to Sat D 7 to 9. **Closed:** 2 weeks Christmas, 2 weeks Aug. **Meals:** alc (main courses £10.50 to £15). **Service:** not inc. **Details:** Cards accepted. 45 seats. 20 seats outside. Wheelchair access. Music. Car parking.

## ALSO RECOMMENDED

### ▲ Red House
Marsh Benham, RG20 8LY
Tel no: (01635) 582017

This off-the-beaten-track, old-beamed hostelry in leafy surroundings is more restaurant than pub, delivering Anglo-French food in a traditional setting. Start with brochette of scallops with kumquat confit, followed by cod fillet with chargrilled potatoes and a lime and coriander dressing, or sea bass on wild mushroom risotto with a cep velouté, and finish with cinnamon-and-vanilla-infused rice pudding with caramel sauce. Set L £19.95, D £25. House wine £14. Closed Sun D.

## ▌Newbury

### The Vineyard at Stockcross
**Culinary and aesthetic contrasts**
Newbury, RG20 8JU
Tel no: (01635) 528770
www.the-vineyard.co.uk
**Modern European | £65**
**Cooking score: 8**

🍷 🛏 ⋎

The dramatic fire and water display outside is a striking introduction to a meal at this slick, modern temple to fine wines and classy food. John Campbell has perfected a personal style with painstaking attention to detail in the way he thinks about food, mixing lightness and intensity so that textures are well balanced and flavours lingeringly powerful. His energy is apparent in an appealing and luxury-strewn menu that might take in wild mushroom risotto with truffle jelly, slow-cooked organic salmon with spiced lentils and foie gras ballottine, and fillet of beef, again slow cooked, served alongside its braised rib and beetroot. Despite their apparent simplicity, dishes can involve a lot of work, many stages of preparation and several components, but these are done without losing sight of the point of the dish. Indeed, the kitchen's clear focus has produced some interesting and

intelligent combinations, in particular, a 'stunning, intensely flavoured' dessert of cucumber, lime, mango and yoghurt. On a simpler level, easy mastery of technique came through in a very fine rendition of classic fish and chips from a Sunday lunch, a meal that also took in a summer salad of very fresh baby leaves, a few pickled morels, baby artichokes, little pieces of roast potato and sun-dried tomatoes with a balsamic dressing, and a 'virtually perfect' lemon posset with a fresh blueberry centre. There is little wrong with lesser details, either – excellent bread and petits fours, for example – while service is fully in keeping, quietly professional and not given to rushing. The wine list must be one of the most extensive in the UK, with 2,000 bottles in all. As befits owner Sir Peter Michael's unimpeachable credentials as a wine producer in California, the list has particularly extensive coverage of wines from that state. Back in the Old World, growers are carefully chosen, even Germany gets a look-in, and there is a great selection from France, and not just the classics. There is no house wine as such, though one bottle, listed at £25, is possibly the cheapest, but more than 20 wines come by the glass.
**Chef/s:** John Campbell and Peter Eaton. **Open:** all week L 12 to 2, D 7 to 9.30. **Meals:** alc £55 (2 courses) to £65, Tasting menu £85. **Service:** not inc. **Details:** Cards accepted. 80 seats. 30 seats outside. Air-con. No mobile phones. Wheelchair access. Music. Children's portions. Car parking.

## Reading

### London Street Brasserie
Riverside brasserie with popular appeal
2-4 London Street, Reading, RG1 4SE
Tel no: (01189) 505036
www.londonstbrasserie.co.uk
**Modern European | £35**
**Cooking score: 3**
V

Overlooking the River Kennet, in a building dating from the 1700s, this bustling brasserie offers an informal, relaxed setting as well as a riverside terrace. An eclectic menu of inspired

combinations can include a starter of butternut squash, thyme and feta risotto, with zesty garlic parsley gremolata, followed by pink, carved venison fillet with Macsween haggis, figs, baby spinach and a port, redcurrant and juniper sauce. The set-price menu supplies an admirable multicultural mix. A selection of British and Irish cheeses provides an alternative to the dessert menu, although for the sweet-toothed, white chocolate and raspberry cheesecake with raspberry sorbet may prove too tempting to resist. The decent globe-trotting wine list starts at £13.95, with a scattering served by the glass from £3.95.
**Chef/s:** Paul Brotherton. **Open:** all week, 12 to 11. **Closed:** Christmas Day. **Meals:** alc (main courses £12 to £20). Set L and D, 12 to 7, £13.50 (2 courses). **Service:** not included. **Details:** Cards accepted. 70 seats. 20 seats outside. Separate bar. No mobile phones. Wheelchair access. Music. Children's portions. Car parking.

## Shinfield

### L'Ortolan
Top-end cuisine with a serious pedigree
Church Lane, Shinfield, RG2 9BY
Tel no: (0118) 988 8500
www.lortolan.com
**Modern French | £60**
**Cooking score: 6**
V

In the depths of moneyed Berkshire, this classically designed red-brick residence is now widely regarded as one of the region's most affluent fine-dining destinations. Alan Murchison's kitchen keeps its finger on the culinary pulse, fusing fashionable themes from East and West while keeping faith with the core modern French repertoire. A starter of crab and fennel salad with mango salsa, lemongrass jelly and wasabi yoghurt has eclecticism in abundance, while another salad – this time involving Périgord truffles, artichokes and asparagus with crispy quails' eggs – is much closer to the classic tradition. To follow, there might be saffron-marinated fillet of John Dory with mussel pistou, polenta and rouille, or a tasting plate of rabbit accompanied by lettuce ravioli, peas and carrots. Desserts are pointed up with clever accompaniments: champagne and elderflower jelly with poached peach; wild strawberry sorbet and toasted marshmallow alongside vanilla parfait, for example. The comprehensive wine list has the expected big runs of classy Bordeaux and Burgundies. Bottle prices start at £18, with selections by the glass from £5.50. NB Alan Murchison bought Hibiscus in Ludlow early in 2007 and was about to reopen it as Le Becasse as the Guide went to press. L'Ortolan will continue as before, although some minor changes in the kitchen are expected.

**Chef/s:** Alan Murchison. **Open:** Tue to Sat 12 to 2.30, 6.45 to 9.30 (10 Sat). **Closed:** Christmas. **Meals:** Set L £18 (2 courses) to £60, Set D £49 (2 courses) to £99 (inc wine). **Service:** 12.5% (optional). **Details:** Cards accepted. 60 seats. No music. No mobile phones. Wheelchair access. Children's portions. Car parking.

## ▌Taplow
## Cliveden, Waldo's
**Refined cuisine in a glorious stately home**
Taplow, SL6 0JF
Tel no: (01628) 668561
www.clivedenhouse.co.uk
**Modern European | £68**
**Cooking score: 5**

⇌ ⋎

A roll-call of distinguished visitors has graced this grand Italianate mansion since Georgian times, although it is best known as the family home of the Astors. The house sits amid 376 acres of grounds and formal gardens maintained by the National Trust, and diners are obliged to contribute £1 to the organisation (charge levied on bill). Waldo's restaurant is a stately basement room festooned with portraits and manned by a brigade of impeccably turned-out French staff. Daniel Galmiche aims to 'tantalise and excite' with luxurious starters like roasted langoustines with caramelised cauliflower, seaweed cracker and shellfish sabayon. Main

courses are neatly categorised into 'sea and river', 'farm and field' and 'grain and seed' (for vegetarians). Line-caught sea bass is served colourfully with ravioli of spinach, confit of tomato and baby squid finished with lemon and olive dressing, while pan-roasted Anjou pigeon arrives with poached foie gras, some simple buttered spinach and a jus tinged with sherry vinegar. When it comes to desserts, the kitchen sets out to surprise by offering black cherry and Kirsch soup served with a white chocolate parfait, cherry beignets and black cherry sorbet. The monumental 800-bin wine list is, predictably, dominated by pedigree clarets and Burgundies but there is also some gilt-edged drinking from other sources. Prices are not for the faint-hearted, with the cheapest house selections weighing in at £30 (£8 a glass).

**Chef/s:** Daniel Galmiche. **Open:** Tue to Sat D only 7 to 9.30. **Meals:** Set D £68. Cover £1. **Service:** not inc. **Details:** Cards accepted. 28 seats. Air-con. No music. No mobile phones. Jacket and tie required. Car parking.

## READERS RECOMMEND
## Ruchetta
**Italian**
6 Rose Street, Wokingham, RG40 1XU
Tel no: (0118) 978 8025
www.ruchetta.com
**'Interesting menu in an intimate setting'**

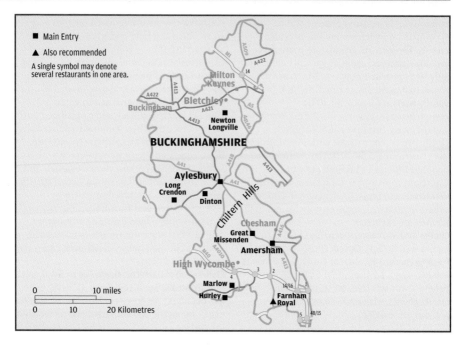

Main Entry ■

Also recommended ▲

A single symbol may denote several restaurants in one area.

BUCKINGHAMSHIRE

0      10 miles
0    10    20 Kilometres

## ▌Amersham

## Artichoke

**Formidable talent in sixteenth-century conversion**
9 Market Square, Amersham, HP7 0DF
Tel no: (01494) 726611
www.theartichokerestaurant.co.uk
**Modern European | £40**
**Cooking score: 4**

The Artichoke sits on the market square of the old part of town. Beams and a huge open fireplace announce the venerability of the surroundings, and there is a charming courtyard at the back for aperitifs and coffee when the sun is out. Laurie Gear is a formidable talent, mobilising tradition and contemporary fashion to productive effect. The scallop-and-bacon idea is given fresh legs in a pairing of braised belly pork with sautéed Skye scallops and celery purée. Another opener sees quail presented in a salad and in ravioli with toasted hazelnuts, sauced with a sage beurre noisette. Well-sourced main

ingredients might be brill, with razor clams, a plethora of vegetables and a bacon vanilla foam, or English veal with celeriac rösti in a citrus dressing, the sweetbread given a voguish crusting of pollen. Desserts maintain the pace with compositions such as pistachio meringue, lemon sherbet, limoncello truffle, white chocolate and a foam scented with basil. The wine list leads with France, without being quite top-heavy in that department, but prices throughout are on the stiff side. Glasses start at £6.50, bottles at £19.50 for a Trentino Pinot Grigio.
**Chef/s:** Laurie Gear. **Open:** Tue to Sat 12 to 2, 6.30 to 9.30 (9.45 Fri and Sat). **Closed:** 1 week Christmas, 1 week Easter, 2 weeks from Aug bank hol.
**Meals:** alc L (main courses £12 to £18). Set L £18.50 (2 courses) to £22.50, Set D £28 (2 courses) to £49 (whole table only). **Service:** 12.5% (optional).
**Details:** Cards accepted. 24 seats. 4 seats outside. Music.

## ▮ Aylesbury

### Hartwell House
Historic stately home
Oxford Road, Aylesbury, HP17 8NR
Tel no: (01296) 747444
www.hartwell-house.com
Modern European | £38
Cooking score: 4

🍴 ⋎

Jacobean and Georgian features vie for attention with impeccable historical credentials at this grand stately home and its intrinsic splendour is more than matched by the extravagant 90 or so acres in which it sits. There's a charm to the old-fashioned feel of the place, but the dining room is a light and airy, and gives out a cheerful, welcoming feel. If there's a sense that the kitchen hasn't quite moved with the times in culinary terms (they still offer a sorbet at dinner) there's no doubt that the grasp of technique is unquestioned, sourcing is impeccable, and the cooking is sound. The lunchtime set menu may take in starters of home-cured gravad lax with a citrus salad and orange vinaigrette, followed by breast of duck with dauphinoise potato, leek and asparagus truffle jus. Evenings are à la carte, say shellfish bisque followed by squab pigeon with poached turnips, globe artichokes and a lemon and ginger orange chutney sauce, and banana soufflé with caramelised bananas and honeycomb ice cream for pudding. France dominates on the wine front but no region is neglected and even English wines get a look-in. House selections are £17.50.
Chef/s: Daniel Richardson. Open: all week 12.30 to 1.45, 7.30 to 9.45. Meals: alc (main courses £22 to £28). Set L Mon to Sat £19.50 (2 courses) to £29, Set L Sun £32, Set D £48 to £65. Buttery L menu available. Service: net prices. Details: Cards accepted. 90 seats. 25 seats outside. No mobile phones. Wheelchair access. Music. Car parking.

## READERS RECOMMEND

### Ivy House
Gastropub
London Road, Chalfont St Giles
Tel no: (01494) 872 184
www.theivyhouse-bucks.co.uk
'Exciting menu in a cosy atmosphere'

## ▮ Dinton

### La Chouette
Belgian adventures
Westlington Green, Dinton, HP17 8UW
Tel no: (01296) 747422
Modern European | £34
Cooking score: 4

🍷

A village green, the air thick with birdsong, a converted pub full of old beams and unforced charm: it's most people's idea of a quality day out. The whole show is run by Belgian Frédéric Desmette, whose tireless culinary intelligence and sound instinct for the kind of European food that England enjoys have made the place a success. Fillet of Scottish salmon is paired with bacon in the Ardennes fashion, while a Flemish spin is given to the first of the new season's asparagus. Otherwise, expect grilled scallops in a saffron beurre blanc, with perhaps duck and morels, or gigot d'agneau with spring vegetables, to follow. Vanilla ice cream may well come topped with a sauce of fine Belgian chocolate, in another nod to the best of the proprietor's homeland. The wine list is a thriller. As you turn its pages, it will remind you why you ever got excited about French wines in the first place, with glorious runs of Chablis and Châteauneuf-du-Pape among the many treasures. House wines are £14, or £3.50 a glass.
Chef/s: Frédéric Desmette. Open: Mon to Fri L 12 to 2, Mon to Sat D 7 to 9. Meals: alc (main courses £13 to £17). Set L £11 to £37.50, Set D £27.50 to £37.50. Service: 12.5% (optional). Details: Cards accepted. 30 seats. No mobile phones. Music. Children's portions. Car parking.

## ALSO RECOMMENDED

### ▲ King of Prussia

Blackpond Lane, Farnham Royal, SL2 3EG
Tel no: (01753) 643006
www.thekingofprussia.com

Tucked down a leafy lane in affluent Farnham Royal, this sensitively modernised Victorian pub draws diners from afar for confident cooking. Menus blend traditional classics with more adventurous modern ideas. At lunch, tuck into ham, egg and chips (£7.95) or fresh cod in beer batter with chunky chips and minted pea purée (£10.50) with a pint of London Pride. Menus and dishes are a tad more imaginative in the evenings, so linger over roast pheasant served with sweet red cabbage and bubble and squeak (£14.95) and follow with bitter chocolate tart (£4.95). Wines start at £14.95. Décor is simple and understated – polished wooden floors, original beams and crackling log fires. Open daily L and D (exc D Sun).

## ▮ Great Missenden

### La Petite Auberge

Classic French cooking
107 High Street, Great Missenden, HP16 0BB
Tel no: (01494) 865370
French | £34
Cooking score: 3

Great Missenden continues to appreciate Hubert Martel's welcoming bistro, now nearing 20 years of service. Menus written in both languages deal in such classics as artichoke heart with forest mushrooms, or courgette flower stuffed with crab in brandy-rich sauce armoricaine, to start. After that, it's on to turbot with anchovies and capers, or meats such as Gressingham duck in port, or beef fillet with Roquefort. You know you'll want a mousse au chocolat at the end of it all, and you won't be disappointed. Otherwise, there is crème brûlée or lemon tart. Wines stick to the principal French regions, opening at £14.50 for Muscadet.

Chef/s: Hubert Martel. Open: Mon to Sat D only 7.30 to 10. Closed: 2 weeks Christmas, 2 weeks Easter. Meals: alc (main courses £16.80 to £18.90). Service: not inc. Details: Cards accepted. 28 seats. No music. Children's portions.

## ▮ Long Crendon

### Angel Restaurant

Classic British dishes with a twist
47 Bicester Road, Long Crendon, HP18 9EE
Tel no: (01844) 208268
www.angelrestaurant.co.uk
Modern British | £32
Cooking score: 1

£5 OFF ▯ ▱ ∨

From the main road through the village the distinct, gabled coaching inn looks old and this is even more apparent inside, where there are low beams. Trevor Bosch presides over a menu that offers many traditional British dishes. Twice-baked cheese soufflé and spicy fish cakes with lime and ginger mayonnaise are typical starters. Among mains there could be poached smoked halibut on leek and mustard mash with poached egg and cheese sauce, or breast of guinea fowl with pea bonne femme, wild mushrooms and tarragon from the evening carte. If you can, follow that with lemon meringue pie, or iced white and dark chocolate parfait. A dozen wines come by the glass (from £4.50) or 500ml pichet (£12.50), with bottles on the global list arranged by style and opening at £15.50

Chef/s: Trevor Bosch and Donny Joyce. Open: all week L 12 to 2.30, Mon to Sat D 7 to 10. Closed: 1 and 2 Jan. Meals: alc exc Sun L (main courses £14.50 to £25). Set L £18.50 (3 courses). Service: not inc. Details: Cards accepted. 70 seats. 40 seats outside. Air-con. Music. Children's portions. Car parking.

## ■ Marlow

### Danesfield House, Oak Room
**Dazzlingly inventive menu**
Henley Road, Marlow, SL7 2EY
Tel no: (01628) 891010
www.danesfieldhouse.co.uk
French | £55
Cooking score: 5

£5 OFF 🍷 🚗

The sweeping vistas of the sun-dappled Thames at its bucolic best from the wisteria-clad terrace of Danesfield House make a visit to the Anoushka Hempelised white-limed panelling and linen-elegant Oak Room alluring, but what a shame not to bask in such views from the dining room. The entirely unnecessary muzak makes it difficult to concentrate fully on the daringly creative and complex menu of Adam Simmonds, fresh from Ynyshir Hall in Wales (see entry), who offers a tantalising insight into futurist cuisine, mostly executed with considerable intricacy and consummate flair. A still trembling 62-degree slow-cooked duck egg emphasises the exquisite delicacy of pea soup with truffle crème. Simmonds is evidently fond of haute surf'n'turf typified by refined langoustine and veal sweetbreads remarkably well partnered with tart rhubarb purée, pickled cauliflower and coffee caviar spheres, which burst into liquid in the mouth. Palate-challenging inventive main dishes include the likes of roasted loin of hare with beetroot purée, ultra-light celeriac choucroute, bitter chocolate pearl barley and chocolate jelly, which just succeeds in not trying too hard. The joyfully abundant, well-kept cheese trolley demands sampling and is accompanied by excellent home-made biscuits and the pleasing extra of celery and apple sorbet shots. To finish, desserts are equally palate broadening, with much textural complexity without compromising delicate nuances of wild strawberry mousse, nettle pannacotta, meringue and crystallised nettle leaves. The head sommelier knowledgeably steers guests through an impressively quirky, if Franco-centric, wine list.

**Chef/s:** Adam Simmonds. **Open:** all week 12 to 1.45, 7 to 10. **Meals:** Set L £15.50 (2 courses) to £29.50 (3 courses), Set D £55 (5 courses).. **Service:** 12.5% (optional). **Details:** Cards accepted. 36 seats. 20 seats outside. Air-con. No mobile phones. Wheelchair access. Music. Children's portions. Car parking.

### Hand & Flowers
**Hugely appealing pub-restaurant**
126 West Street, Marlow, SL7 2BP
Tel no: (01628) 482277
Modern British | £31
Cooking score: 6

It may have regulation beams, real ales and undressed tables, but the cooking at this whitewashed pub on the outskirts of Marlow is more sophisticated than the country-casual interior suggests. This is down to Tom Kerridge, whose cooking exudes deceptive and effortless flair, and is founded on a bedrock of fine ingredients. The food straddles both traditional and contemporary – potted Dorset crab with cucumber and dill chutney, for example, or warm smoked salmon with beetroot purée, frozen horseradish and blini pancake among starters. Equally well considered have been fish main courses like generously proportioned plaice fillet served with baby artichokes, mustard leaves, potato gnocchi and beurre noisette. Meats might include impressive braised belly of Middle White pork accompanied by broad beans, squash and sage, or slow-cooked veal with roast onions, beetroot linguine and lemon oil. A selection of cheeses offers outstanding quality, or there are desserts like praline parfait with compressed pineapple and pineapple sorbet, and vanilla peach with Amaretto savarin, curd ice cream and honey. Service is smiling, genuine and helpful. An individual, international line-up of wines at fair prices (starting at £15.50) hits just the right note.
**Chef/s:** Tom Kerridge. **Open:** All week L 12 to 2.30, all week exc Sun D 7 to 9.30. **Closed:** D 24 Dec to 26 Dec. **Meals:** alc (main courses £10 to £21).

**Service:** not inc. **Details:** Cards accepted. 50 seats. 28 seats outside. Music. Children's portions. Car parking.

## Vanilla Pod
**Sharp modern ideas**
31 West Street, Marlow, SL7 2LS
Tel no: (01628) 898101
www.thevanillapod.co.uk
**Modern British | £39**
**Cooking score: 5**
Y

This small restaurant in the centre of Marlow may look the epitome of tradition from the outside, but a total refurbishment since the last edition of the Guide has given a welcome contemporary look to match the up-to-date culinary skills of Michael Macdonald. Top quality produce is at the heart of the cooking, which constructs dishes carefully around simple but forthright flavour combinations using accomplished technique. How about warm potted salmon with pickled cauliflower, lemon risotto with garden peas and tiger prawns, or perhaps a salad of baby leeks, walnuts and Bleu d'Auvergne cheese with a fig syrup, for starters? Follow that with loin of venison with poached pear and bitter chocolate sauce, or brill with cep gnocchi and hazelnut duxelles. Vegetarians are well catered for with their own menu, while dessert highlights have included Tahitian vanilla crème brûlée with raspberry jelly, and vanilla polenta cake with pineapple salsa. Service is well drilled, and a short, mainly French wine list opens at £18, with five by the glass at £3.50.
**Chef/s:** Michael Macdonald. **Open:** Tue to Sat 12 to 2, 7 to 10. **Meals:** Set L £15.50 (2 courses) to £19.50, Set D £40 to £45. **Service:** not inc. **Details:** Cards accepted. 36 seats. No music. No mobile phones. Wheelchair access.

## ▮ Newton Longville
## Crooked Billet
**Intelligent cooking with a modern edge**
2 Westbrook End, Newton Longville, MK17 0DF
Tel no: (01908) 373936
www.thebillet.co.uk
**Modern British | £45**
**Cooking score: 2**
🍷 Y

The Crooked Billet is a delightfully quaint-looking village inn, with a thatched roof and bare beams inside. John Gilchrist heads up the bar and dining room, while his wife Emma takes care of the cooking. Her menus cater for every eventuality, from a quick bite (sandwiches, wraps, burgers, and things on toast) to an engrossing six-course tasting menu. Typical choices include (from the starters) a crab burger with crispy squid, shredded courgette and mild chilli mayonnaise; or carpaccio of seared smoked beef fillet with Parmesan shavings and celeriac rémoulade. Mains might be fish bourride; rack of lamb with deep-fried sweetbreads, broad bean, pea and mint cream, fondant potato, cooking juice and red wine; or saddle of rabbit with prune and pistachio stuffing, pea purée, baby carrots and leg shepherd's pie. The lovingly compiled wine list includes recommendations for individual dishes and opens at £14 a bottle.
**Chef/s:** Emma Gilchrist. **Open:** Sun L 12 to 2, Mon to Sat D 7 to 9.30. **Meals:** alc (main courses £8 to £25). Set D £45 to £75 (inc wine). Bar L menu available. **Service:** not inc. **Details:** Cards accepted. 50 seats. 40 seats outside. No music. Children's portions. Car parking.

## READERS RECOMMEND
## Betsey Wynne
**British**
21 Mursley Road, Swanbourne, MK17 0SH
Tel no: (01296) 720825
www.thebetseywynne.co.uk
'Village pub serving fresh, local produce'

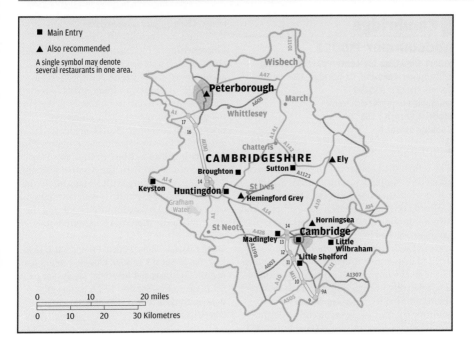

■ Main Entry

▲ Also recommended

A single symbol may denote several restaurants in one area.

# ▌Broughton

★NEW ENTRY★

## The Crown Inn

**Popular country pub-restaurant**
Bridge Road, Broughton, PE28 3AY
Tel no: (01487) 824428
www.thecrownbroughton.co.uk
Gastropub | £26
Cooking score: 2
£30

With a wealth of experience at the Old Bridge in nearby Huntingdon (see entry), chef-proprietor Simon Cadge and several of his team have brought their Huntsbridge talents to this proper village hostelry. The pub is upbeat and modishly rustic in a twenty-first-century fashion, where a jaunty smiling welcome greets newcomers, regulars and villagers alike (most of the latter with a share in the freehold). Expect robust, well-executed modern fare from the varied carte and specials board. Simpler tastes are met by the likes of chicken Caesar salad or smoked Scottish salmon but the majority of the gutsy dishes show ambitious flair. A typically exuberant meal could start with an Asian-inspired warm salad of marinated tuna with chilli, ginger and coriander with fancy leaves, roasted red pepper and aubergine, be followed by chargrilled Scotch beef bavette ('well flavoured and just the right amount of texture') cooked rare on horseradish crushed Jersey Royals, spring greens and a red wine gravy, and finish with a 'perfectly wobbly' vanilla bean pannacotta with sweet-sour rhubarb compote. Interesting smaller producers appear on the delightfully succinct wine list, with 36 bins from £14.95.
**Chef/s:** Simon Cadge. **Open:** L 12 to 2 (3 Sun), D 6.30 to 9 (9.30 Sat). **Closed:** Mon and Tue. **Meals:** alc (main courses £9.50 to £17.50). Set L £11 (2 courses). **Service:** not inc. **Details:** Cards accepted. 50 seats. 40 seats outside. Children's portions. Car parking.

# Cambridge

## Midsummer House

**Smart showcase for contemporary cooking**
Midsummer Common, Cambridge, CB4 1HA
Tel no: (01223) 369299
www.midsummerhouse.co.uk
Modern French | £55
Cooking score: 6

The refurbished conservatory dining room is all stylistic simplicity, with neutral, natural colours forming a backdrop to Daniel Clifford's cooking. There's a sense of space and airiness, though one visitor thought an opportunity had been missed to make more use of upstairs for dining where the under-utilised first-floor bar makes the most of views of the river Cam and Midsummer Common. The relatively unchanging menu is a showcase for contemporary cooking, which sees multiple flavours jostle for attention despite simple menu descriptions. A straightforward sounding veal kidney cooked in its own fat (and served with snails, parsley, onions and spinach), saw the kidney encased in unadvertised potato rösti which rather overpowered the whole dish, and the components of poached and grilled squab pigeon, with cherries, sweet potato, spinach, pistachios and Valhrona never quite pulled together. Indeed, we worry that the ambitious chef's quest to express his indisputable talents can sometime conjure one flavour too many. Then again, when things work, they work stonkingly well ('you feel you are really having an experience') with an amuse-bouche of pink grapefruit and champagne froth – squirted at table from a soda siphon – giving just the right acidic hit ahead of the rich creamy flavours of a stunning pea and sea water velouté. This reflects an innovative streak that has also produced a masterful starter of maple-caramelised sweetbreads with ribbons of ox tongue and dots of turnip, pistachio and maple jelly, an astonishing pre-dessert of candied fennel and pineapple with a pastis sorbet, and a witty deconstruction of a classic lemon meringue pie – delivered as a zingy, citrussy tart with separate lemon meringue and crystallized ginger. Unsurprisingly, the experience does not come cheap, which puts focus on the impersonal, anonymous service found at inspection. Although drinkers on a budget will find their choice somewhat restricted, there's no denying the quality and appeal of the wines. An unexpected find of an Alois Lageder Italian Alto Adige Gewürztraminer at £45 proved a positive lunchtime choice in contrast to the richer counterpart from the Alsatian selection. The latter, in keeping with all regions on the worldly vinous selection, is well covered with a good eye and palate for interest among the great and godly therein. House wines start at £25.

**Chef/s:** Daniel Clifford. **Open:** Fri and Sat L 12 to 1.30, Tue to Sat D 7 to 9.30. **Closed:** 2 weeks April, August, Christmas and New Year. **Meals:** Set L £55, Set D £55 to £75. **Service:** 12.5% (optional). **Details:** Cards accepted. 44 seats. No music. Wheelchair access.

## Restaurant 22

**Tiny terrace-house restaurant**
22 Chesterton Road, Cambridge, CB4 3AX
Tel no: (01223) 351880
www.restaurant22.co.uk
Modern European | £26.50
Cooking score: 2

David Carter's restaurant is positively crammed into this small terrace house, with photographs on display of his triumphs at Cambridge Regional College, apparently the source of his brigade. On the plate, the modern style extends to experimentation, not always successfully – 'bland' cubes of fruit jelly added little to an excellent crab tian with streaks of mango sauce at inspection. However, roast cod did team well with glazed chicken winglets, and, more traditionally, just off-pink roast pork loin was matched with soft fennel, sautéed apples and cider sauce, with batons of parsnip, green beans and carrots on the side. Assiette of rhubarb illustrated seasonal skill with desserts. The wine list is extensive, with expanding New World offerings, stickered updates of vintages and a list of unusual bin ends. House wines offer value for money at £14.95 a bottle or £3.95 per glass.

**Chef/s:** Martin Cullum and Seb Mansfield. **Open:** Tue to Sat D 7 to 9.45. L by prior arrangement. **Closed:** Christmas to New Year. **Meals:** Set D £26.50 (3 courses). **Service:** not inc. **Details:** Cards accepted. 40 seats. Air-con. No mobile phones. Music.

## ALSO RECOMMENDED
### ▲ Cotto
183 East Road, Cambridge, CB1 1BG
Tel no: (01223) 302010

The dedication to sustainably sourced seasonal produce is refreshing at this restaurant above a diminuitive deli-bakery (in the same ownership). A modern wood-filled interior and revolving exhibitions of contemporary art for sale set the scene, and there is a distinct dinner-party feel to the operation, due in part to the simple 'no frills, no choice' three-course set menu plus optional cheese. An inspection meal started with home-made wood-fired sourdough and unpasteurised butter to accompany Greek feta, cherry tomato, lentil and pesto salad, followed by baked line-caught mackerel with a hot mooli ribbon and chive cream and ended with an indulgent Valrhona chocolate and hazelnut brownie and Suffolk vanilla crème fraîche. Diners should phone beforehand to discuss the menu. Among the concise wine selection (from £12.75) are some interesting dessert and digestif oddities.

## READERS RECOMMEND
### Al Casbah
**North African**
62 Mill Rd, Cambridge, CB1 2AS
Tel no: (01223) 579500
**'Busy restaurant with Algerian-inspired menu'**

## ALSO RECOMMENDED
### ▲ Boathouse
5-5a Annesdale, Ely, CB7 4BN
Tel no: (01353) 664388
www.cambscuisine.com

A converted boathouse overlooking the Great Ouse is the setting for this smart gastropub-cum-restaurant. A new chef recently took over the helm, although the food is much as before. Expect a lively mix of modern British and European dishes, kicking off with starters like locally smoked eel and potato salad (£7) or baked duck parcels with Asian slaw. Home-made sausages and mash (£10) are a speciality, but main courses also move into the realms of sea bass fillets with chorizo, tomato and butter beans. Desserts (£5) might feature passion-fruit mousse with red-grape coulis. Wines from £12 (£2.90 a glass). Open all week. Reports please.

### ▲ The Cock
47 High Street, Hemingford Grey, PE28 9BJ
Tel no: (01480) 463609
www.cambscuisine.com

Just north of the frenetic A14 between Cambridge and Huntingdon and in a pretty white-washed thatched village high street, the Cock (the sister establishment of the Boathouse, Ely – see entry above) makes a good gastro-pubby bolthole. Specials boards offer interesting fresh fish selections, such as seared scallops with clam, samphire and pea chowder or crab and lobster linguine, as well as an array of home-made sausages with quartets of mash and sauce choices. The printed menus more than satisfy carnivores, with nut-crusted lamb's liver and bacon (on the two-course lunch menu for £9.95), herb-marinated sirloin steak or sautéed lamb (both £14.95). More than half the great value 45-bin wine list comes in at less than £20; bottles from £12. L 12 to 2.30 all week. D Mon to Thu 6.30 to 9, Fri and Sat 6.30 to 9.30, Sun 6.30 to 8.30.

## ▲ The Crown & Punchbowl

High Street, Horningsea, CB5 9JG
Tel no: (01223) 860643

Just north-east of Cambridge, this capacious seventeenth-century restaurant-with-rooms delivers an eclectic carte that is exuberantly put together, featuring lavender jus and beetroot with rack of lamb (£14.95) or kumquat and Cointreau jus alongside spinach and confit duck (£13.95). Specials boards feature the day's fresh fish dishes (from £5.95 to £13.95) and mix'n'match sausages (bangers, mash and sauce for £9.95). The simpler set lunch proves good value, and may feature dishes such as crisp pork belly with bacon, cabbage, apple and mustard cream (two courses for £9.95). The reliable, quite classic wine list starts at £12.50. Closed Sun D.

## ▋ Huntingdon

## Old Bridge Hotel

**High-calibre food and impeccable wines**
1 High Street, Huntingdon, PE29 3TQ
Tel no: (01480) 424300
www.huntsbridge.com
**Modern British | £29**
**Cooking score: 4**

🍴 ⇆ V £30

John Hoskins, the consummate restaurateur behind the Huntsbridge name, has sold the three sister restaurants in his enterprising company to concentrate solely on this smart town-house hotel overlooking the River Ouse. Exciting plans are afoot for a wine shop and new courtyard, but the Terrace, with its light, arty conservatory, remains a popular good-value destination, unsurprising given the calibre of the food and wine. Chef Gareth Thorpe mixes the Mediterranean and modern British styles, dipping into the Orient for added effect. Zesty dishes, such as roast Anjou pigeon breast with baby gem lettuce, spring peas, salsify and tarragon, followed by veal saltimbocca with linguine, salsa verde and a green bean, watercress and hazelnut salad, demonstrated technical care and seasonal consideration at inspection, while a nutmeg custard tart with pouring cream proved a simple finale. If the Old Bridge is an oenophile's oasis, then Mr Hoskins must be their best friend, not just for the extent and quality of his highly individual list of 300-odd wines but also for its sheer value. Descriptions are informative and it takes several pages to list those by the glass and under £20. Early cellarage and fixed mark-ups mean top-class bottles can be tried at cheaper prices than from some wine merchants. Alluring house wines, such as Italian Garganega or Chianti, Austrian Riesling and South Australian Shiraz Viognier, start at £13.75.
**Chef/s:** Gareth Thorpe. **Open:** all week 12 to 2, 6.30 to 9.30, Set L and D Mon to Fri 6.30 to 7.30. **Meals:** alc (main courses £11 to £24). Set L £14.50 (2 courses) exc. Sun. **Service:** not inc. **Details:** Cards accepted. 80 seats. 30 seats outside. Air-con. No music. No mobile phones. Wheelchair access. Children's portions. Car parking.

## ▋ Keyston

## Pheasant

**Quintessential thatched pub**
Loop Road, Keyston, PE28 0RE
Tel no: (01832) 710241
www.huntsbridge.com
**Modern European | £30**
**Cooking score: 2**

🍴 V

Jay and Taffeta Scrimshaw have bought the old thatched and beamed pub they ran for the enterprising Huntsbridge Group for the last two years. But little else has changed. Winter visitors are still welcomed with a crackling log fire, drinkers crowd the bar, and diners flock in for food that is a bedrock of modern British ideas with additions from France, Italy and beyond. The kitchen's success lies in sourcing fine ingredients across the board with fish from Cornwall a particular strength – say John Dory with olive mashed potato, gremolata, courgette and tomato. Beef is Aberdeen Angus crossed with Limousin or Belgian Blue (perhaps a sirloin with mushrooms en persillade, watercress purée, chips and red-wine sauce); otherwise there is grilled quail with radicchio, fennel and blue cheese salad to start, then local lamb paired with chickpea, pea and mint purée, gazpacho salad and mint pesto, and chocolate fondant with lemon curd ice cream to follow. John Hoskins has been retained as a consultant to the wine list and it remains a delight, opening with a dozen characterful, affordable house wines by the bottle (from £13.75) and glass (from £3.65), before moving on to a mixture of classy global bins with non-greedy markups.

**Chef/s:** Jay Scrimshaw. **Open:** all week 12 to 3 (4 Sun), 6.30 to 9.30. **Meals:** alc (main courses £9.50 to £23.50). **Service:** not inc. **Details:** Cards accepted. 87 seats. 30 seats outside. No music. No mobile phones. Wheelchair access. Children's portions. Car parking.

## Little Shelford
### Sycamore House
**Assured cooking**
1 Church Street, Little Shelford, CB2 5HG
Tel no: (01223) 843396
**Modern British | £25**
**Cooking score: 2**

£5 OFF | 🍷 | V | £30

Michael and Susan Sharpe's ambitions are clear in the fixed-price four-course menu (£25) and simple style reflected in the two dining rooms with plain white walls and tableclothes. Serving dinner only, the menu can play to seasonal strengths and short order: a leek and Gruyère tart made with soft olive oil short pastry was fresh and warm, the leeks melting in the cheese sauce. Imagination perked up a velvety butter bean soup, with dots of red oil from chorizo slices providing a spicy contrast, while sweet chilli livened up a crisp mixed-leaf salad, with shards of green beans and mixed nuts. Main courses can include grilled pigeon breast with black bean sauce, with accompanying sauté potatoes and vegetables. Desserts and cheese continue the theme of simplicity, and a relatively short and inexpensive wine list provides house wines by the bottle, 50cl carafe or glass,

including a white Bordeaux Château Nicot 2005 and a red Côtes du Rhône Guigal 2003 (bottle £13, 50cl carafe £9).
**Chef/s:** Michael Sharpe. **Open:** Wed to Sat D 7.30 to 9. **Closed:** Christmas to New Year. **Meals:** Set D £25. **Service:** not inc. **Details:** Cards accepted. 24 seats. No music. No mobile phones. Car parking.

## Little Wilbraham
### Hole in the Wall
**Assured cooking in a traditional village pub**
2 High Street, Little Wilbraham, CB1 5JY
Tel no: (01223) 812282
**Modern British | £30**
**Cooking score: 4**

Christopher Leeton and Jenny Chapman (with Stephen Bull giving behind the scenes support) run this fifteenth-century village hostelry as a genuine 'free house', with locally brewed real ales on draught and garlands of dried hops draped around the heavily beamed bar. Diners sit at bare wooden tables and food is served courteously without undue fuss or ceremony. The kitchen chooses its ingredients with care and takes an openminded approach to things gastronomic. Twice-baked local asparagus and watercress soufflé with orange-butter sauce is a typically seasonal starter, which might line up alongside Denham Estate cured venison with beetroot and potato salad. The menu changes every ten days, but main courses could range from chump of Hartest spring lamb with onion and mint purée, lemon and thyme sauce, to gilthead bream with cucumber, dill, crème fraîche and brown shrimp butter. A blackboard of daily specials provides even more choice. To finish, consider warm lemon polenta cake or elderflower pannacotta with mint syrup and orange shortbread. Four dozen wines provide plenty of enjoyable drinking at very realistic prices. Vins de pays open the show at £12.50, and eight are available by the glass (from £2.95).

**Chef/s:** Christopher Leeton. **Open:** Tue to Sun and bank hol Mon L 12 to 2, Tue to Sat D 7 to 9. **Meals:** alc (main courses £10 to £15). **Service:** not inc. **Details:** Cards accepted. 70 seats. 15 seats outside. No music. Children's portions. Car parking.

# ▮ Madingley

## Three Horseshoes

Assured Italian cooking
High Street, Madingley, CB3 8AB
Tel no: (01954) 210221
www.huntsbridge.com
**Modern Italian | £36**
**Cooking score: 3**

🍷 ⋎

The Three Horseshoes team has been hard at work sprucing up the garden in 2007. Richard Stokes has now bought the Three Horseshoes from Huntsbridge, but continues in the successful country-pub culinary idiom that had made the Huntsbridge group so popular. Rare-breed meats, salmon from Loch Duart, Tuscan olive oils and Spanish almonds are among the gastronomic fare. Pea soup with mint and prosciutto sounds good whatever its mother tongue, and main courses run a gamut from grilled Dover sole with braised borlotti beans, spinach and pine nuts, to tempting spring lamb with an array of its offal (liver, kidneys and sweetbreads) with truffle oil, mint and garlic. Finish in keeping with affogato (vanilla ice cream with hot espresso poured over it), or white chocolate pannacotta with raspberries doused in grappa. The Italian centre of gravity is in evidence on the wine list, too, which is presented by wine style with helpful shorthand notes. Prices start at £13.75, or £3.65 a glass.

**Chef/s:** Richard Stokes. **Open:** all week L 12 to 2 (Sat and Sun 12 to 2.30), Mon to Sat D 6.30 to 9.30. **Closed:** 1 and 2 Jan. **Meals:** alc (main courses £9.50 to £23.95). Bar/grill menu available. **Service:** not inc. **Details:** Cards accepted. 110 seats. 60 seats outside. Separate bar. No music. Children's portions. Car parking.

READERS RECOMMEND

## Cherry House

Modern European
125 Church Street, Peterborough, PE4 6QF
Tel no: (01733) 571721
'Intimate atmosphere and consistent cooking'

# ▮ Sutton

## The Anchor Inn

An island of gastronomy in the Fens
Sutton, CB6 2BD
Tel no: (01353) 778537
www.anchorsuttongault.co.uk
**Modern British | £27**
**Cooking score: 2**

£5 OFF 🍷 ⊨ ⋎ £30

The young couple who managed this 'island' of gastronomy next to the Hundred Foot Drain in the Fens for the past five years are now the owners. Very much a restaurant, pine tables, chairs and pews are the setting for imaginative cooking, with nods to the traditional, evidenced in large portions. Four thick slices of superb just-past-pink rump of English lamb comes with a large slab of dauphinoise, thick with cream, and a mound of al dente purple sprouting broccoli. Suffolk chicken breast stuffed with mozzarella and sun-blushed tomatoes, tightly wrapped in Parma ham, drizzled with red pesto, emerges tender. The monthly menu and 'today's specials' provide seven or eight options at each course, plus a trio of British cheeses. The list of 62 wines from around the world includes a large selection by the glass, arranged by style, with both house wines falling into the light character. Prices start at £13.50 per bottle or £3.35 the glass.

**Chef/s:** Adam Pickup and William Mumford. **Open:** all week 12 to 2 (3 Sun), 7 to 9 (6.30 to 9.30 Sat). **Meals:** alc, exc Sun L (main courses £9.50 to £16.50). Set L Mon to Fri, £10.95 (2 courses), Set L Sun, £17 (2 courses) to £21. **Service:** not inc. **Details:** Cards accepted. 60 seats. 30 seats outside. No music. No mobile phones. Wheelchair access. Children's portions. Car parking.

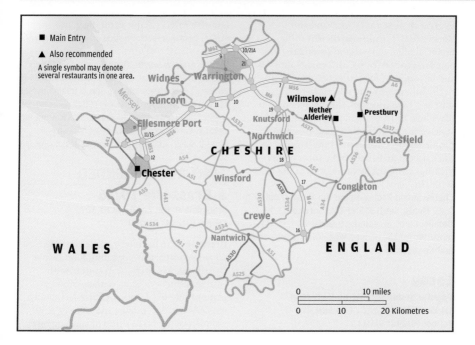

# ▪ Chester

## Chester Grosvenor, Arkle
**Modern food in grandiose surroundings**
Eastgate, Chester, CH1 1LT
Tel no: (01244) 324024
www.chestergrosvenor.com
**Modern European | £60**
**Cooking score: 7**

Built in 1865 and owned by the Dukes of Westminster, the majestic Grosvenor is Chester's pride and joy – a mighty edifice right in the centre of the city. At its heart is the hotel's hotshot restaurant, a moneyed luxury-strewn dining room named after the legendary racehorse that belonged to the late Anne, Duchess of Westminster. Everywhere there are equine prints and echoes of the 'sport of kings'. Chef Simon Radley deals in the kind of ultra-complex cooking that is perfectly at home in such unashamedly sleek surroundings. He exploits the current fashion for meat/fish pairings to the full, offering seared scallops with crispy pig's foot, partnering 'fingers' of John Dory with confit of chicken wings, and studding fillet of Welsh Black beef with native oysters. There are jokes, too: a starter of frogs' legs, English snails, wild cress and crayfish tails is dubbed 'pond life'. Elsewhere, the kitchen goes about its business with deadly serious intent, witness the 24-hour, slow-braised leg of mutton with Scottish langoustines, Jerusalem artichokes and shaved truffle or line-caught turbot 'Caesar' (a neat parody involving grilled lettuce hearts, smoked bacon emulsion, croûtons and Parmesan froth). Needless to say, this is food that never fights shy of luxury trimmings. Desserts encompass everything from a truly wacky 'leguminous assemblage' involving vanilla squash with fondant chocolate, Hass avocado with pomello sorbet plus duck egg brûlée with beetroot, to the refreshing, unadorned simplicity of raspberries with vanilla cream and a shot of eau de vie. The monumental 600-bin wine list shows its true colours and old-school pedigree with a seemingly endless procession of great champagnes, Bordeaux and Burgundies. Thankfully, there is some financial relief to be found among the big names recruited from California, South Africa and beyond. A few bottles below £25 might fit the bill; otherwise, selections by the glass start at £5. In addition, the Grosvenor also plays host to La Brasserie, a Parisian-style venue open for breakfast, lunch and dinner. Expect dishes like bouillabaisse or duck mixed grill, backed by some choice pickings from the lower regions of the full wine list.

**Chef/s:** Simon Radley. **Open:** Tue to Sat D only 7 to 9.30. **Meals:** Set D £55 to £65. **Service:** 12.5%. **Details:** Cards accepted. 50 seats. Air-con. No music. No mobile phones. Wheelchair access. Jacket and tie required.

## Locus

**Popular venue serving no-frills food**
111 Boughton, Chester, CH3 5BH
Tel no: (01244) 311112
www.locustheplace.co.uk
**Modern British | £37**
**Cooking score: 1**
£5 OFF **V**

Andrew and Sally Smyth's clever conversion of a local pub has proved a hit with Chester locals, especially those who appreciate live jazz: regular Sunday night sessions attract an enthusiastic crowd. The interior has been stylishly transformed, with floors of wood and African slate, subdued lighting and contemporary art on the walls. It makes a stylish setting for Andrew Smyth's cooking, which offers mainstream grills alongside more modern dishes with a smattering of exotic influences. Stilton and walnut pâté with citrus salad or smoked duck breast with sesame egg noodles might precede rack of lamb with oregano mash or 'lemon crumb' salmon with sautéed butter beans, asparagus and watercress dressing. Raspberry and crème de Cassis mousse is a typical dessert and the Anglo-Irish cheeseboard is worth exploring. The

wine list offers reliable drinking across the range; house selections start at £11.95 (£4.50 a glass).

**Chef/s:** Andrew Smyth. **Open:** Tue to Sun D only 6.30 to 10 (6 to 10 Sat, 5.30 to 9 Sun). **Closed:** 24 to 26 Dec, 1 Jan. **Meals:** alc exc Sun D (main courses £13 to £16). Set D Tue to Thur £11.95 (2 courses), Set D Sun £13.95 (2 courses) to £15.95. **Service:** not inc. **Details:** Cards accepted. 42 seats. Wheelchair access. Music. Children's portions. Car parking.

## ALSO RECOMMENDED
### ▲ Brasserie 10/16
Brookdale Place, Chester, CH1 3DY
Tel no: (01244) 322288

Brasserie 10/16 is a buzzy modern venue, serving consistently appealing food fusing British and Mediterranean cuisine with eastern influences. Start with an oriental platter to share (£9.50), or Parma ham with roasted beetroot, orange and mint (£5.50) before moving on to rump of lamb niçoise (£15.95), or wild mushroom risotto (£12.50). Pastas and salads can be ordered as starters, or main courses. Wines are well priced, with several between £9.95 and £12.95. There is also a stylish lounge bar 'packed with *Hollyoaks* types' sipping cocktails. Open all week.

## READERS RECOMMEND
## Swettenham Arms
**Modern British**
Swettenham Village, Near Congleton, CW12 2LF
Tel no: (01477) 571284
www.swettenhamarms.co.uk
**'Sixteenth-century inn with fantastic real ales'**

## ▌Nether Alderley
### The Wizard
**Former pub with wide-ranging menu**
Macclesfield Road, Nether Alderley, SK10 4UB
**Tel no:** (01625) 584000
**Modern European | £30**
**Cooking score: 2**

What appears to be a pub on the outside turns out to be 'one hundred per cent restaurant' inside with plenty of plain wood tables, beams and 'old pictures' creating a cottagey feel to the three dining areas. Paul Beattie continues to man the stoves, his wide ranging and approachable style taking in salmon rillette with tempura smoked salmon and butter sauce, sea bass with chargrilled asparagus, salsa verde and baby new potatoes, and roast cannon of lamb with bubble and squeak and rosemary jus. Sound materials are evident in the good-value set menu, which has turned out chicken liver parfait with walnut bread and plum and pear chutney, steak and ale pie, and crème brûlée. The wine list is on the ball and kicks off with Australian Shiraz and Italian Pinot Grigio at £14.50.
**Chef/s:** Paul Beattie. **Open:** Tue to Sun L 12 to 2, Tue to Sat D 7 to 9.30. **Closed:** Bank hols. **Meals:** alc (main courses £12 to £21). Set L Tue to Fri and Set D Tue to Thu £10 (2 courses) to £15. **Service:** 10%. **Details:** Cards accepted. 80 seats. 20 seats outside. Music. Children's portions. Car parking.

## ▌Prestbury
### White House
**Sophisticated offerings**
The Village, Prestbury, SK10 4DG
**Tel no:** (01625) 829336
www.thewhitehouseinprestbury.com
**British | £32**
**Cooking score: 3**

This immaculately styled former farmhouse feels relaxed, modern and unpretentious. Begin with canapés and drinks in the bar, then settle down to starters such as crispy lemon sole with plum tomato, gem salad and tartare sauce or duck liver and foie gras parfait with pickled pears and warm brioche. Follow with best end of Welsh lamb with crushed peas, olive mash, redcurrant and mint; or cod fillet with parsley, crab linguine, asparagus and tapenade. Round it off with a chocolate fondant with mascarpone ice cream; or lemon curd tart with sherry sabayon and raspberry sorbet. A reasonable set-price menu is also available at lunch or dinner, offering the likes of braised ham hock and potato salad with beetroot and thyme followed by glazed salmon with English asparagus and new potatoes, and then pecan pie for dessert. The wine list starts at £14.95 a bottle, and includes a decent selection of half-bottles.
**Chef/s:** Dominic Davallou. **Open:** all week L 12 to 2, Mon to Sat D 7 to 10. **Closed:** 24 to 26 Dec, 1 Jan. **Meals:** alc (main courses £12 to £27). Set L £16.95, Set D Mon to Fri £16.95 (2 courses) to £19.45. Bar menu available. **Service:** not inc. **Details:** Cards accepted. 80 seats. 12 seats outside. Wheelchair access. Music. Children's portions. Car parking.

## ALSO RECOMMENDED
### ▲ Heddy's
100-102 Water Lane, Wilmslow, SK9 5BB
**Tel no:** (01625) 526855

Eat here once and you will feel like a local. Heddy Ghazizadeh's Wilmslow restaurant serves up perfectly cooked Middle Eastern and Mediterranean dishes with admirable consistency. A mezze for two (£15) is a generous ten dishes including tabbouleh and spicy lamb kibbeh. Otherwise, there are feta cheese börek parcels for £3.50. Scan a long list of charcoal-grilled kebabs (from £10.95 to £15.50) or couscous dishes, with several vegetarian options. Bring your appetite (the portions are pretty large), but do save room to finish with the sticky-sweet baklava (£3.50). A banquet menu of mezze, mixed kebabs, baklava and coffee comes in at a very reasonable £20. Wines are from £12.50 and take-away is also available. Open for dinner Mon to Sat.

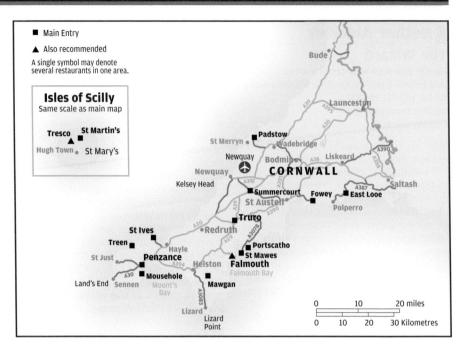

## East Looe

### Trawlers on the Quay

**Striking culinary imagination**
The Quay, East Looe, East Looe, PL13 1AH
Tel no: (01503) 263593
www.trawlersrestaurant.co.uk
**Seafood | £30**
**Cooking score: 3**

£5
OFF

Ensconced in their quayside restaurant, with the eponymous trawlers moored nearby, this front-of-house/cook partnership is busily extending the kitchen's cheerful influence with a range of preserves and other goodies. As well as fine fish, Cornish cider, cheese, black pudding and beef – carnivores, veggies and pescophiles continue to be equally charmed – find their way on to the sensibly brief dinner-only menu. Local ingredients are treated to a range of techniques and are often thrust into untraditional marriages: scallops, parsnip purée and black pudding; goats' cheese coated in polenta with orange and hazelnut;

monkfish wrapped in pancetta with butternut squash and balsamic. Timing, especially of fish, is immaculate. Skills carry over into classic crème brûlée and neatly balanced combinations such as orange and chocolate custard. A succinct wine list ranges from the Camel to the Hunter valleys and all are fairly priced. House wines start at £13.75.
**Chef/s:** Mark Napper. **Open:** Tue to Sat D only 6.15 to 10. **Closed:** 25 and 26 Dec. **Meals:** alc Easter to Nov (main courses £14 to £18). Set D Nov to Easter £23.50 (2 courses) to £28. **Service:** not inc. **Details:** Cards accepted. 40 seats. 12 seats outside. Wheelchair access. Music.

## ALSO RECOMMENDED
### ▲ Three Mackerel
Swanpool Beach, Falmouth, TR11 5BG
Tel no: (01326) 311886
www.thethreemackerel.com

In a glorious location overlooking Falmouth Bay, this lively café's winning formula takes in plenty of outdoor seating, a suitably relaxed atmosphere, and a global approach to cooking locally caught fish. A light lunch of seafood chowder (£8.50) or mackerel fillets with Bombay potatoes, coriander and curry oil (£8.05) is typical, while dinner might bring scallops and crevettes with minted pea purée and sauce vierge (£7.95) and seafood laksa with coconut milk, lemon grass, lime ginger and coriander (15.95). There's meat, too, in the form of steaks and rack of lamb, a separate children's menu and house wine at £10.95. Open all week.

## READERS RECOMMEND

### Sticky Prawn

**Modern British**
Flushing Quay, Flushing, TR11 5TY
Tel no: (01326) 272734
www.thestickyprawn.co.uk
'Local produce served on the quayside'

## ▌Fowey

### Old Quay House

**Waterside dining**
28 Fore Street, Fowey, PL23 1AQ
Tel no: (01726) 833302
www.theoldquayhouse.com
**Modern British | £29**
**Cooking score: 2**

🛏 V £30

This restaurant surely has one of the best views in the county, overlooking Fowey estuary. You would expect the menu to reflect the proximity to the sea, so crab ravioli, sautéed spinach and sauce vierge doesn't disappoint, nor the classic moules marinière. Moving on to mains, pan-fried lemon sole à la Grenobloise with potatoes hits the mark, whilst roast whole red guernard, fennel and potato salad, though at the pricey end of the menu, fulfills its promise. Carnivores get a look-in too, in the shape of roast breast of Terras Farm duck with cocotte potatoes, sauce albafuera and carrot purée. Puddings lean towards the conventional, with knickerbocker

glory and chocolate brownie with malted ice cream making an appearance. Wine starts at £14 a bottle, with 5 by the glass at £4.60.
**Chef/s:** Ben Bass. **Open:** all week 12.30 to 2.30, 7 to 9. **Closed:** L Nov to Apr. **Meals:** alc (main courses L £10 to £12, D £12.50 to £21). **Service:** 10% (optional). **Details:** Cards accepted. 38 seats. 38 seats outside. No mobile phones. Wheelchair access. Music.

## ★NEW ENTRY★

★ RESTAURANT NEWCOMER OF THE YEAR ★

### Restaurant Nathan Outlaw

**A new star in Cornwall's firmament**
Marina Villa Hotel, Esplanade, Fowey, PL23 1HY
Tel no: (01726) 833315
www.themarinahotel.co.uk
**Modern European | £42**
**Cooking score: 8**

£5 OFF 🍶 🛏

The arrival of Nathan Outlaw has transformed the Marina Villa Hotel. His refined, beautifully crafted cooking is worth travelling some distance for, and there probably isn't a better or more committed chef for miles around. The newly refurbished dining room is striking – the best seats in the house have fabulous views over the Fowey estuary – but simply laid tables and approachable service ensure a relaxed ambience. In the kitchen, painstaking attention to detail offers the seasonal best of the region alongside carefully sourced meat and fish. Classical technique informs pleasant dishes that have a fresh modern edge: an amuse-bouche, for example, was a small cup of cep soup, simple in composition, but revealing an exquisite depth of flavour. Starters proper included ox tongue teamed with anchovies as well as capers, tarragon and mint, which harmoniously blended a spectrum of stunning flavours from sweet to salty, typical of Outlaw's fresh, innovative and well-balanced approach, while cured salmon with marinated beetroot risotto, horseradish and dill has also impressed. Often succinct and always vibrant, the cooking uses elegantly matched ingredients to achieve the most wonderful flavours, with a main course of tender pork finding its perfect partner in black pudding, apple and cider, while another's sea bass is so fresh it could satisfy on its own, although accompaniments of leeks and mustard and brown shrimps lift it still further. A pre-dessert of gin and tonic (lime sorbet and gin jelly with a juniper syrup) was a perfectly balanced taster, and set up the recipient for a simple dessert of plum tart with bay leaf ice cream. Fruits are certainly favoured at pudding stage: rhubarb sponge with stem ginger ice cream is another enticing seasonal choice. Readers are wholly impressed. The wine list takes a commendably user-friendly approach, grouping wines by style and offering fair prices throughout – even the more modest bottles make good drinking. Prices start at £17.

**Chef/s:** Nathan Outlaw. **Open:** Wed to Sun L 12 to 1.30, Tue to Sun D 7 to 9.30. **Closed:** 1 week Jan, Valentines weekend. **Meals:** alc (main courses £20 to £22). Set L £27.50 (3 courses), Set D £40 (3 courses). **Service:** not inc. **Details:** Cards accepted. 36 seats. 10 seats outside. No music. No mobile phones. Car parking.

## READERS RECOMMEND

### Sam's
**Seafood**
20 Fore Street, Fowey, PL23-1AQ
Tel no: (01726) 832273
www.samsfowey.co.uk
'Fresh fish served in informal surroundings'

## ■ Mawgan

### New Yard
**Straight from the boat**
Trelowarren, Mawgan, TR12 6AF
Tel no: (01326) 221595
www.trelowarren.com
Modern British | £32
Cooking score: 2

A converted coach house within the courtyard of Trelowarren House is the setting. There is a local feel to the cooking, with raw materials

mostly sourced from within 30 miles, and everything from bread to ice cream made on the premises. This approach results in a menu of interesting yet unfussy dishes such as a warm tartlet of local Toppenrose cheese with onion relish to start. Sautéed venison loin might appear as a main course with roasted vegetables and a cinnamon and red-wine sauce, while the fish of the day – delivered every morning direct from the fishing boats – might be simply grilled and served with lemon, garlic and parsley sauce. Plum and almond tart with cinnamon cream is among tempting dessert options. Simpler lunch menus offer the likes of twice-baked cheese soufflé with smoked ham, or fresh crab salad with beetroot and citrus dressing. The wine list is organised by grape variety, with prices starting at £13.50.

**Chef/s:** Greg Laskey. **Open:** Tue to Sun L 12 to 2, Tue to Sat D 7 to 9; also open Mon L and D June to Aug. **Meals:** alc (main courses L £8 to £12.50, D £11.50 to £17). Set L £13.50. Set D £20 (Oct to May only). **Service:** not inc. **Details:** Cards accepted. 48 seats. 25 seats outside. No mobile phones. Wheelchair access. Music. Children's portions. Car parking.

## ■ Mousehole

★NEW ENTRY★
### 2 Fore Street
**Smart bistro with harbour views**
2 Fore Street, Mousehole, TR19 6QU
Tel no: (01736) 731164
www.2forestreet.co.uk
Modern European | £21
Cooking score: 2

Large shopfront windows mean diners enjoy unrivalled views over this picturesque fishing village's medieval harbour, while distressed wooden tables, white walls and nautical artwork set the scene within. The menu offers an eclectic range of dishes including open crab sandwiches, home-smoked mackerel pâté or pan-fried ray wing with brown butter, capers and hand-cut chips. These are all brilliantly simple and well-executed lunch dishes. The supper menu might offer shell-roasted

scallops with sweet tomato and basil butter, or steamed mussels with chilli, garlic and coriander for starters, followed by mains of sea-fish casserole with saffron and fennel-cream sauce, or cider-braised ham hock with white beans. Service is friendly and attentive and the chef 'darting from table to table, chatting about the menu, makes for a relaxed and convivial environment'. Extra seating can be found in the rear walled garden. The wine list is as succinct as it is well chosen, the only drawback might be that the selection offers only one variety by the glass (at £3.25).
**Chef/s:** Joe Wardell. **Open:** 10 to 10 daily.
**Meals:** Main courses £10 to £14. **Service:** 10%.
**Details:** Cards accepted. 38 seats. 20 seats outside. Music. Children's portions.

## ALSO RECOMMENDED
### ▲ The Old Coastguard
The Parade, Mousehole, TR19 6PR
Tel no: (01736) 731222
www.oldcoastguardhotel.co.uk

Formerly a coastguard's lookout lodge, this hotel has spectacular views over Mount's Bay, which the spacious, contemporary bar and dining room make the most of. The menu celebrates its seaside location with a bistro-led daytime menu offering handpicked Newlyn crab sandwiches (£9.95), or sea bass with new potatoes and salad (£12), while in the evening the modern piscine ideas extend to lobster ravioli with spiced guacamole and tomato and tarragon consommé, and bouillabaisse with saffron potato and garlic rouille. Back on land the choice extends to osso bucco, or breast of duck. Dinner is £35 for three courses including dessert – such as hot chocolate fondant with pistachio ice cream. Decent wines by the glass (from £3.70) on an impressive list. Open daily.

## ▮ Padstow
### No. 6
**Ambition and fiery enthusiasm**
6 Middle Street, Padstow, PL28 8AP
Tel no: (01841) 532093
www.number6inpadstow.co.uk
**Modern European | £38**
**Cooking score: 6**

With the builders now gone from this Georgian town house in a tiny street in the heart of Padstow, Paul Ainsworth and his team have finally settled into their groove. Even on the small sample of dishes reported on this year, consistency appears to be a strength. There are foams, veloutés and jellies and stock bases are first-class. Modish combinations have included spice-roast scallops with black pudding, carrots and foraged herbs, alongside monkfish with crab, orange couscous, pickled beetroot and smoked aubergine. Dishes can be complex, requiring a range of high-level skills to prepare, but what is promised is delivered – notably a pillow of perfectly timed turbot of outstanding flavour, a mini oxtail cottage pie, creamed cabbage and spring peas forming an almost impeccable bond with it. Flavouring partnerships are well conceived, and dishes deftly executed. Among starters, poached and roast pork belly has come with pickled tongue, rhubarb and foie gras salad, while a luxuriant and grown-up pudding could take the form of a warm chocolate moelleux served with pistachio nougatine, Pansal de Calas wine jelly and cherry sorbet. Vegetarians are well catered for with their own tasting menu. 'Attention to detail, pleasant surroundings, friendly knowledgeable staff and the food was fantastic', says it all for one reader. Exciting wines by the glass (£4.75 to £7.25) introduce a confident wine list that offers plenty of scope for experimentation. With prices from £17, diners on a budget aren't excluded, but the action really starts above £25.
**Chef/s:** Paul Ainsworth. **Open:** all week 6.30 to 10.
**Closed:** Jan, 25 and 26 Dec, Mon and Tue Nov and Dec. **Meals:** alc (main courses £13 to £20). Set D

£38 (2 courses). **Service:** 10% (optional).
**Details:** Cards accepted. 50 seats. Wheelchair access. Music.

## Rick Stein's Café
**Relaxed, buzzy bistro**
10 Middle Street, Padstow, PL28 8BQ
Tel no: (01841) 532700
www.rickstein.com
**Seafood | £29**
**Cooking score: 2**

The name ensures the place is always heaving and is a sound bet for reliable fish and seafood. With bookings not taken for lunch, do arrive early whatever the time of year or weather. Aptly set in an old fisherman's cottage, it comes bright and welcoming in modern vogue, decked out with white-painted wood-clad walls and plain lightwood furniture. Tables are packed in, so expect a degree of bustle and chatter, while the simple, compact bistro-style menu is the expectedly − though not exclusively − fishy affair. Think goujons of plaice with tartare sauce and chips jostling for selection alongside whole grilled lemon sole served with lemongrass butter. Straightforward desserts − like sunken chocolate cake and pouring cream − continue the theme, while the short, well-chosen wine list has a seafood-friendly tilt, starting out at £14.50. Breakfast is also available.
**Chef/s:** David Sharland and Luke Taylor. **Open:** all week 12 to 3, 7 to 9.30. **Closed:** Call ahead for details. **Meals:** alc (main courses £10 to £17). Set D £19.95 (3 courses). **Service:** not inc. **Details:** Cards accepted. 60 seats. 10 seats outside. Wheelchair access. Music. Children's portions.

## St Petroc's Bistro
**Light alternative to the Seafood Restaurant**
4 New Street, Padstow, PL28 8EA
Tel no: (01841) 532700
www.rickstein.com
**Modern Seafood | £33**
**Cooking score: 2**

One of the oldest buildings in Padstow, and a long-standing fixture in Rick Stein's stable of ventures in the town, this smart white-painted hotel is bright, airy and contemporary. The bistro, in particular, has lots of pale wood and white walls hung with striking modern canvasses. The emphasis is on the celebrated fish, although there is warm salad of pigeon breast with watercress, potatoes and walnut oil dressing, and escalopes of veal with a crisp fennel and green bean salad. Whole grilled scored lemon sole with shrimps and mushrooms, Moroccan fish tagine, and starters such as mackerel fillets with sun-dried tomatoes and fennel seeds, or moules marinière, are where the heart is. Vegetables are charged extra. Desserts are nothing fancy, perhaps a passion-fruit pavlova, or a chocolate truffle torte with mango sorbet. Unstuffy, friendly service is a plus, as is the fish-friendly wine list with prices from £16.50 and plenty by the glass.
**Chef/s:** David Sharland and Alistair Clive. **Open:** all week 12 to 2, 7 (6.30 school hols) to 10. **Closed:** 24 to 26 Dec, May Day. **Meals:** alc (main courses £14 to £18). **Service:** not inc. **Details:** Cards accepted. 55 seats. 20 seats outside. Air-con. Wheelchair access. Music. Children's portions.

## Seafood Restaurant

**Rick Stein's celebrated restaurant**
Riverside, Padstow, PL28 8BY
Tel no: (01841) 532700
www.rickstein.com
**Seafood | £51**
**Cooking score: 5**

The mothership of the 'Padstein' fleet, the Seafood Restaurant still proves a magnet, the personality of the man and the popularity of his TV series and books ensuring the crowds of culinary pilgrims continue to beat a path to its door. Although Stein himself is no longer at the kitchen's helm, the food bears his hallmark – sea-fresh fish (much straight from the boats on the quayside and in through the kitchen door) treated with intelligent simplicity and the occasional nod to foreign climes. The narrow conservatory at the front of the restaurant offers an informal setting for pre-meal drinks, while the spacious dining room comes decked out with block flooring or flagstones and fresh, white-painted walls enlivened by bold modern art. It may be a white-linen zone, but it is buzzy and unbuttoned. Fish and shellfish remain the menu drawcard (albeit a little wallet-bruising), perhaps delivering a braised fillet of turbot teamed with fresh summer truffles, slivers of potato, mushrooms and truffle oil, or maybe local cod with a traditional partnership of chips, tartare sauce and mushy peas. Desserts, like a hot chocolate fondant with coffee ice cream, maintain standards through to the end. Wines are a serious globetrotting affair well matched to the piscatorial menu, with an 18-strong house selection from £18.75, though the main list makes for interesting reading and there are also good selections by the half-bottle and glass.
**Chef/s:** David Sharland and Stéphane Delourme.
**Open:** all week L 12 to 2, D 7 to 10. **Closed:** 24 to 26 Dec, 1 May. **Meals:** alc (main courses £17.50 to £45). Set L and D £65. **Service:** not inc. **Details:** Cards accepted. 110 seats. Air-con. No music. Wheelchair access. Children's portions.

## ▌Penzance

## Abbey Restaurant

**Seafood with swagger**
Abbey Street, Penzance, TR18 4AR
Tel no: (01736) 330680
www.theabbeyonline.com
**Modern European | £34**
**Cooking score: 4**

Tucked away down a nondescript alley in the quieter part of Penzance, Ben and Kinga Tunnicliffe's small restaurant occupies a once renowned nightclub. This is very much a restaurant of two halves. The downstairs bar boasts a vibrant red colour scheme and resembles a psychedelic 60s club, while the upstairs dining room is all calming stone colours and clean modern lines. At inspection, grilled fillets of accurately timed mackerel were incredibly fresh and any richness was cut by the fiery horseradish cream, earthy roasted beetroot and well-dressed leaves. Similarly, a grilled whole lemon sole was well handled and served with creamed potato and a velvety chervil and chive beurre blanc. Everything is made in house, from bread and chutneys through to marmalade and ice cream. No-nonsense desserts include chocolate mousse with hazelnut macaroons and a very good apple and rhubarb crumble tart. The short, functional wine list includes the highly prized Cornish sparkling wine (Camel Valley 2003 at £26 a bottle or £5.95 a glass). House wine kicks off at £14.50.
**Chef/s:** Ben Tunnicliffe. **Open:** Fri to Sun L 12 to 1.30, Tue to Sat D 7 to 9.30. **Closed:** Tue D Oct to May, Wed D Nov to Feb, Jan. **Meals:** alc D (main courses £16 to £22). Set L £18 (2 courses) to £23. **Service:** not inc. **Details:** Cards accepted. 30 seats. Air-con. No mobile phones. Music. Children's portions.

## Bay Restaurant
**Room with a view**
Mount Prospect Hotel, Britons Hill, Penzance,
TR18 3AE
Tel no: (01736) 366890
www.bay-penzance.co.uk
**Modern European | £25**
**Cooking score: 3**

£5 OFF ⊨ V £30

With magnificent views over the rooftops towards Penzance harbour and Mount's Bay, this stylish hotel dining room doubles up as an art gallery. There may be pictures on the walls, but the kitchen here produces modern British masterpieces of its own, many with far-reaching influences. Line-caught pickled tuna loin with a fennel and radish salad and white crabmeat aïoli is a typically inspired starter, or there might be the more classic steamed River Exe mussels in a white wine, garlic, shallot and watercress sauce. Main courses range from oven-baked fillet of hake with saffron bisque and local, hand-picked white crab meat and watercress pesto or braised free-range loin of pork with sweet potato purée and a mango and red chilli salsa. To finish, Cornish farmhouse cheeses are an alternative to desserts such as balsamic vinegar and black peppercorn flambéed strawberries with dark chocolate sorbet. A varied wine list kicks off with house selections at £13.75.
**Chef/s:** Ben Reeve and Katie Semmens. **Open:** Wed to Fri L 11.30 to 1.30, all week D 6.15 to 9. **Meals:** Set L £11 (2 courses) to £14.50. Set D £22 (2 courses) to £27. **Service:** not inc. **Details:** Cards accepted. 60 seats. 10 seats outside. Air-con. No mobile phones. Wheelchair access. Music. Children's portions. Car parking.

## Harris's
**Predominantly Cornish produce**
46 New Street, Penzance, TR18 2LZ
Tel no: (01736) 364408
www.harrissrestaurant.co.uk
**Anglo-French | £35**
**Cooking score: 2**

Open since 1972, Roger and Anne Harris's bistro offers a good-value light lunch alongside a generous carte. Duck terrine and green tomato chutney or cornets of smoked salmon with fresh white crab meat could be followed by roast monkfish with wild mushroom risotto and white wine sauce or guinea fowl breast grilled with Cornish brie on spinach with a lime and basil sauce. Desserts might include chocolate torte with a vanilla and Amaretto sauce and fresh blackcurrant sorbet. From the 50-plus wines listed by country, it should not be hard to find a good match, even with the large number of half-bottles. House wines are £13.50 to £14.95. NB Children must be over 5.
**Chef/s:** Roger Harris. **Open:** Tue to Sat L 12 to 2, Mon to Sat D 7 to 9.30. **Closed:** 3 weeks in winter, 25 and 26 Dec, 1 Jan. **Meals:** alc (main courses L £7.50 to £15, D £17 to £25.50). **Service:** 10%. **Details:** Cards accepted. 40 seats. Music. Children allowed.

## Summer House
**Opulent decoration**
Cornwall Terrace, Penzance, TR18 4HL
Tel no: (01736) 363744
www.summerhouse-cornwall.com
**Italian | £41**
**Cooking score: 2**

⊨

Set in a quiet lane 50 metres from the sea, this stylish Regency house may look quintessentially English, but step inside and you are transported to the sun-drenched Mediterranean. The elegant dining room opening out to an attractive walled garden replete with terracotta pots and palm trees. Chef proprietor Ciro Zaino sticks to the tried and tested regional Italian cuisine he grew up

with and fish and shellfish arrive direct from the local boats. Start, perhaps, with seared local Newlyn scallops served with a langoustine sauce and move on to the more rustic triglie portofino fillets of red mullet with tomatoes, black olives and fresh basil. The kitchen can also deliver the more French-inspired rack of lamb aux herbes de Provence which has become something of a speciality of the house. Coffee crème brûlée or summer fruits layered in grappa-infused aspic with mango purée may end a meal. The 40-strong wine list is equally Italian, opening at £14.
**Chef/s:** Ciro Zaino. **Open:** Thur to Sun D only 7.30 to 9.30. **Closed:** Nov to Feb. **Meals:** Set D £29.50 (3 courses). **Service:** 10%. **Details:** Cards accepted. 22 seats. 22 seats outside. Music.

## Portscatho

### Driftwood

**Seaside hotel with seasonal menus**
**Rosevine, Portscatho, TR2 5EW**
**Tel no: (01872) 580644**
**www.driftwoodhotel.co.uk**
**Modern European | £39**
**Cooking score: 5**

Dazzling panoramic views are one of the attractions at this privately run hotel perched above the sea at Rosevine. Seaside colours evoke sun, sand and sky in the prettily decorated dining room, and huge expanses of plate glass provide clear views of the maritime scene. New chef Chris Eden has picked up where his predecessor left off, focusing on seasonal fixed-price dinner menus with a modern European accent. He takes full advantage of abundant Cornish seafood, serving scallops with asparagus, morels and golden raisins as well as partnering John Dory with squid, leek fondue, cocoa beans and white onion. Fresh lobsters can be ordered with 24 hours' notice (minimum two persons), although a sizeable supplement is added to the bill. Elsewhere, the kitchen pleases meat fans with saddle of lamb and Mediterranean accompaniments or roast Terras Farm duck breast with a pastilla of leg meat, endive, orange and port jus. To conclude, customers can look forward to prune and Armagnac soufflé with Earl Grey ice cream or chilled strawberry rice pudding with mango sorbet. The helpfully annotated, 60-bin wine list has some fine bottles from the southern hemisphere, although the rest of the world is also well represented. Prices start at £15 (£3.75 a glass).
**Chef/s:** Chris Eden. **Open:** all week D only 7 to 9.30. **Closed:** Dec and Jan. **Meals:** Set D £39. **Service:** not inc. **Details:** Cards accepted. 34 seats. No mobile phones. Music. Car parking.

## READERS RECOMMEND

### Whitsand Bay Hotel

**Modern British**
**Portwrinkle, PL11 3BU**
**Tel no: (01503) 230276**
**www.whitsandbayhotel.co.uk**
**'Contemporary yet classic, top-quality food'**

## St Ives

### Alba

**Modern cuisine by the harbour**
**Old Lifeboat House, Wharf Road, St Ives, TR26 1LF**
**Tel no: (01736) 797222**
**www.thealbarestaurant.com**
**Modern European | £45**
**Cooking score: 3**

What was once this gentrified coastal town's old lifeboat building is now a thoroughly modern restaurant with highly prized window seats overlooking the harbour. As with many of the buildings in St Ives, it makes use of the incredible natural light, and this is echoed in the bright and airy style of the dining room, with its clean, contemporary lines. Despite its white napery, this is an informal dining experience and service is relaxed and friendly. Line-caught local fish has a major role to play in the kitchen and can be seen in starters such as Japanese Cornish crab salad or pan-fried diver-caught scallops with home-made merguez sausages and Puy lentils. Flavour combinations can be bold – bourride of monkfish and mussels with aïoli and confit of fennel and orange, perhaps – and meat and game are also well handled, as in pan-fried Barbary duck breast with date purée, apple and saffron compote. Finish with rich chocolate truffle cake with tangerine ice cream. Plenty of wines are served by the glass from a global list. House Australian is £12.95. **Chef/s:** Grant Nethercott. **Open:** all week L 11.30 to 2, D 5 to 10 (6 to 9 low season). **Closed:** 25 and 26 Dec. **Meals:** alc (main courses £9 to £19). Set L and D until 7.30 £13 (2 courses) to £16. **Service:** not inc. **Details:** Cards accepted. 65 seats. Air-con. Wheelchair access. Music. Children's portions.

## Porthminster Beach Café
**Outstanding location**
Porthminster Beach, St Ives, TR26 2EB
Tel no: (01736) 795352
www.porthminstercafe.co.uk
**Seafood | £33**
**Cooking score: 4**

A striking white Art Deco building standing proud on one of the finest beaches in Cornwall, it would be hard to beat the location of this perennially popular Beach Café. Now open all year round to meet the demand of locals, tourists and the increasing number of second home owners who have decamped to this delightful town, the panoramic views of the sea and harbour from the Mediterranean-style terrace is breathtaking. Aussie Michael Smith has been chef since 2002, and he has become something of a TV celebrity in that time. A reasonably priced lunch can range from Cornish mussels steamed with sweet-and-sour Thai sauce and crispy shallots to crab linguine with chilli, garlic, parsley and Fowey mussels. The dinner menu moves up a gear in both complexity and price. Typical starters include spiced Cornish scallops with chorizo foam, fennel and Parmesan crisps and star turns among the main courses include monkfish curry with the addition of tiger prawns, Fowey mussels, sweet potato, tamarind and turmeric. Desserts might offer orange and bergamont brûlée

with Valhrona chocolate sorbet or rhubarb crumble with lavender and cream cheese ice cream. The lively wine list starts at £11.95. **Chef/s:** Michael Smith. **Open:** all week 12 to 3.45, 6 to 10. **Meals:** alc (main courses L £7 to £13, D £17 to £20). **Service:** not inc. **Details:** Cards accepted. 57 seats. 70 seats outside. No mobile phones. Music. Children's portions.

## ★NEW ENTRY★
## St Andrews Street Bistro
**Eclectic flavours and local ingredients**
16 St Andrews Street, St Ives, TR26 1AH
Tel no: (01736) 797074
**Modern European | £28**
**Cooking score: 1**

The colourful ceiling roses and teardrop-shaped chandeliers hanging from the high ceiling are gentle reminders that this was once an Indian restaurant. Tucked away down a narrow street behind the harbour, this popular addition to the St Ives scene feels more London gastropub than Cornish bistro. Antique standard lamps and candelabras on the tables ensure a suitably low-light ambience in the bohemian, two-floor restaurant, which is dotted with Persian rugs and and esoteric artwork. To a backdrop of jazz and soul, scan the blackboards and choose from starters such as mussels with harissa and lemon or the lamb koftas with cumin-flavoured tsatsiki and rocket. A main course roast haddock came with a broth of clams, fennel and peas with a punchy salsa verde, while the meal ended with a retro Black Forest gâteau. Readers have commented on 'poor service', giving up after a lack of acknowledgement and going elsewhere. The short wine list is a whistlestop tour of the world, with everything under £25 and five available by the glass. **Chef/s:** Adam Collier. **Open:** All week 12 to 3.30, 6 to 9.30. **Meals:** alc (main courses £13 to £17). **Details:** Cards accepted. 60 seats. Music.

## ALSO RECOMMENDED

### ▲ Porthgwidden Beach Café

Porthgwidden Beach, St Ives, TR26 1NT
Tel no: (01736) 796791
www.porthgwiddencafe.co.uk

Sister to the Porthminster Beach Café (see
entry above), this whitewashed, Aussie-
style seaside café occupies a fabulous spot in a
secluded beach overlooking St Ives Bay. The
simple, uncluttered décor is mirrored in the
menu which majors on local seafood:
mackerel fillets with new potatoes and red-
onion jam (£8.95) or whole local bream en
papillote with olive oil, lemon, thyme and
white wine (£13.95). Full English breakfasts
(£5.95) and light lunches such as scrambled
egg and smoked salmon (£4.95) are also
served. Wines from £10.95. Open all week
Apr to Oct.

## READERS RECOMMEND

### Blas Burgerworks

Modern European
The Warren, St Ives, TR26 2EA
Tel no: (01736) 797272
www.blasburgerworks.co.uk
'High-quality burgers to eat in or take away'

## ▮ St Mawes

### Hotel Tresanton

Vibrant food on the Cornish coast
27 Lower Castle Road, St Mawes, TR2 5DR
Tel no: (01326) 270055
www.tresanton.com
Modern European | £39
Cooking score: 4

🛏 Ⴝ

Designed as a yachtsmens' club in the 1940s,
this distinctive cluster of old Cornish
dwellings is now reaping the benefits of a
sharp Olga Polizzi makeover. Inside, the feel is
'smart casual', rather than glamorous. The
lounge is done out in seaside shades of blue
and yellow, while the restaurant puts on a
cool, contemporary look with mosaic floors

and plate-lined walls. Above all there is
the view, which is best observed from the
terrace. Paul Wadham's food has a sophisticated
brasserie style and sunny Mediterranean
accent designed to please the fashionable set.
Cornish seafood and local organic meat figure
prominently on the fixed-price menus, and
the results look suitably photogenic on the
plate. Red mullet with salsa rosa, asparagus
and virgin olive oil is a typical first course, and
it precedes dishes like turbot with crispy
potato, Puy lentils, peas and ceps or sea bass
with mash, broccoli, green beans, broad beans
and pancetta. Meat fans might steer a course
towards chump of Alenick lamb served with
an assemblage of roast peppers, courgettes,
aubergines and olives, while desserts keep it
simple with, say, burnt English custard with
strawberries or lemon posset with shortbread
and raspberries. Italian regional bottles head
the modern wine list, with prices starting at
£18 (£4.50 a glass) for Pinot Grigio.
**Chef/s:** Paul Wadham. **Open:** all week 12.30 to 2.30,
7 to 9.30. **Closed:** 6 to 15 Jan. **Meals:** Set L £23 (2
courses) to £30, Set D £39. Snack L menu available.
**Service:** not inc. **Details:** Cards accepted. 50 seats.
50 seats outside. No music. No mobile phones.
Wheelchair access. Children's portions. Car parking.

## ▮ Summercourt

### Viners Bar and Restaurant

Modern food in casual surroundings
Carvynick, Summercourt, TR8 5AF
Tel no: (01872) 510544
www.vinersrestaurant.co.uk
Modern European | £30
Cooking score: 4

A one-time pub among the timeshare cottages
of Carvynick is the unlikely setting for Kevin
and Jane Viner's all-purpose restaurant and bar.
The interior is spread over two floors, and it
has a gentrified farmhouse style with
chunky bare tables, exposed beams and
varnished floorboards. Like the décor, there is
nothing cluttered or fancy about the food,
which aims to please with its mix of casual
bistro favourites and more elaborately worked
restaurant dishes based on West Country

produce. Helford river crab comes as a salad with lemon and Noilly Prat, Fowey oysters are grilled and tweaked with a chilli dressing, while pot-roast shoulder of Cornish lamb is accompanied by thyme and port jus. The kitchen might also send out classic moules marinière and chargrilled fillet steak with rosemary and wild mushroom jus. Viner's legendary bread-and-butter pudding still figures among the desserts, along with iced berry soufflé and lemon tart with blackcurrant sorbet. The wine list does its job by offering a broad global choice at prices that are kind to the wallet. Six house selections are £13.95 a bottle (£3.65 a glass).

**Chef/s:** Kevin Viner, Neill Farrelly, Ross Pitman. **Open:** Sun L 12.30 to 3, all week D 6.30 to 9.30. **Closed:** 4 weeks winter. Possible reduced opening hours winter; phone to enquire. **Meals:** alc D (main courses £16 to £19). Sun Set L £16.95 (three courses). **Service:** not inc. **Details:** Cards accepted. 90 seats. 40 seats outside. Wheelchair access. Music. Children's portions. Car parking.

## Treen
### Gurnard's Head
**Simplicity is a virtue**
Treen, TR26 3DE
Tel no: (01736) 796928
www.gurnardshead.co.uk
Gastropub | £25
Cooking score: 3
🛏 £30

The Inkin brothers have something of the Midas touch when it comes to transforming forlorn and remote pubs into stylish, welcoming gastropubs-with-rooms. Run along similar lines to the Felin Fach Griffin (see entry, Wales), this rambling pub on the windswept coastal road between St Ives and Penzance lives up to the owners' 'simple is best' mantra. This shows in everything from the bright yet homely décor in the bar, dining room and bedrooms, to the daily changing menus. A starter of smoked Cornish pilchards with pickled beetroot and horseradish ice cream is a triumph of simplicity and ingredient intelligence. The ethos of no-fuss

cooking continues with the signature Gurnard's fish stew served with new potatoes and aïoli, and duck breast with peas, carrots and bacon. Well-kept local cheeses are served with a sweet apple jelly and soda bread, while the chocolate torte with rum and raisin ice cream and biscotti has won many admirers. The good wine selection comes from around the globe, starting at £11.75, with 11 choices by the glass.

**Chef/s:** Mathew Williamson. **Open:** all week 12.30 to 2.30, 6.30 to 9.30. **Meals:** alc (main courses D £9 to £13). **Service:** not inc. **Details:** Cards accepted. 65 seats. 35 seats outside. No music. Children's portions. Car parking.

## ALSO RECOMMENDED
### ▲ Island Hotel
Tresco, TR24 0PU
Tel no: (01720) 422883
www.tresco.co.uk

A flagship, family-run hotel blessed with gorgeous views on the sub-tropical 'Island of Flowers'. Dinner menus (£38 for three courses) change daily and the kitchen delivers modern European food. Starters of niçoise salad or confit salmon with saffron mascarpone might precede seared sea bream with Bryher crab cake and pea purée. Strawberry parfait with warm berry compote is a typical dessert. International wines from £15. Bar menu available. Open all week D only; closed Nov to end Jan.

## Truro

★NEW ENTRY★
### Saffron
**Well-judged, with a bright outlook**
5 Quay Street, Truro, TR1 2HB
Tel no: (01872) 263771
www.saffronrestauranttruro.co.uk
British | £25
Cooking score: 3

A passion to promote the very best in seasonal Cornish produce is the mantra for Nik and Traci Tinney at this charming café/restaurant in the heart of Truro. The L-shaped dining room is decorated head to toe in a cheery custard yellow and orange, the chunky, scrubbed pine tables are unclothed and fishy paintings and artwork adorn the walls. The owners' desire to source the majority of produce from within a few miles of the kitchen shows in the menu, which even has potted histories of the local suppliers. Occasional specialist menus highlight seasonal treats, such as asparagus in May. The daily changing carte could start with a salad of grilled ox heart served with watercress, parsley-flecked gnocchi and Parmesan or cured Newlyn pilchard with black olive and tomato risotto. A main of precisely cooked bream arrived on a bed of excellent home-made tagliatelle and gently wilted spinach. Dessert might be warm rhubarb meringue tart or bread pudding with Barwick Farm clotted cream. The nicely weighted wine list opens at £11.70. NB Children welcome before 7pm. **Chef/s:** Nik Tunney. **Open:** Mon to Sat 12 to 2, Tue to Sat 5 to 10 (NB D June to Dec only). **Closed:** 25, 26 Dec, bank hols. **Meals:** alc L (main courses £7.50 to £10.50), D (main courses £10.50 to £14.50) Set D £19.50 (3 courses). **Service:** not inc. **Details:** Cards accepted. 40 seats. Wheelchair access. Music. Children's portions.

## Tabb's

**Comfortable, contemporary niche**
85 Kenwyn Street, Truro, TR1 3BZ
Tel no: (01872) 262110
www.tabbs.co.uk
**Modern British | £31**
**Cooking score: 4**

£5 OFF  V

Since moving their operation from Portreath to Truro, Melanie and Nigel Tabb have won the support of the locals with their stylish and intimate restaurant, housed in what was once the Royal Standard pub. The pale lilac walls and slate floors create a calming environment in which to enjoy the assured, modern cooking. The Tabbs are passionate advocates of using local produce and the menu boasts a separate page in order to give their suppliers a

well-deserved name-check. Nigel believes in robust flavours: as demonstrated in pan-fried monkfish with smoked bacon, fresh ginger, lemongrass, tomato and a little chilli or a full-flavoured provençale fish soup with chilli relish and basil oil. Main courses show an international attitude in braised belly of pork with star anise, pink peppercorns and stir-fried pak choi. Baked breast of Terra Farm Cornish duck with celeriac purée and tarragon just shows that the rest of the menu is firmly anchored in French classics with a twist. Desserts have included a dark chocolate marquise served alongside a scoop of white chocolate ice cream and a solid chocolate coffee spoon. Very good service accentuates the opulence of the place, and the wine list, starting at £12.95, offers a fairly priced international selection. **Chef/s:** Nigel Tabb. **Open:** Tue to Fri L 12 to 2, Tue to Fri D 5.30 to 9, Sat D 6.30 to 9.30. **Closed:** 26 Dec, 1 Jan. **Meals:** alc (main courses £13.75 to £20). **Service:** not inc. **Details:** Cards accepted. 30 seats. Music. Children's portions.

## READERS RECOMMEND

### Fifteen

**Modern British**
On the beach, Watergate Bay, TR8 4AA
Tel no: 01637 861000
'Stunning views, with food to match!'

## Symbols

| | |
|---|---|
| 🛏 | Accommodation is available. |
| £30 | Three courses for less than £30. |
| V | More than five vegetarian dishes. |
| £5 OFF | £5-off voucher scheme. |
| 🍾 | Notable wine list. |

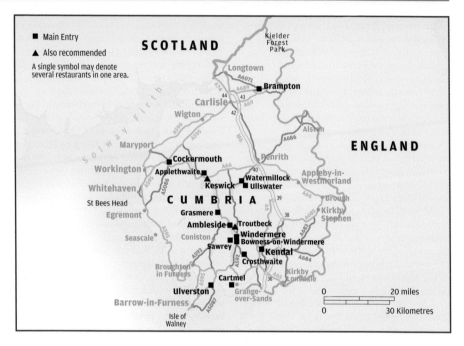

Map legend:
■ Main Entry
▲ Also recommended
A single symbol may denote several restaurants in one area.

## ■ Ambleside

### Drunken Duck Inn

Handsome, rambling pub
Barngates, Ambleside, LA22 0NG
Tel no: (015394) 36347
www.drunkenduckinn.co.uk
Gastropub | £33
Cooking score: 4

For some time, this pub has been a destination for foodies, despite its remote location, but since the arrival of chef Neil McCue there's even more reason to struggle to find it. This is high-end cuisine in what must be one of the most attractive spots in the North of England – in fine weather enjoy an aperitif outside, overlooking jaw-dropping views of the Ambleside fells. Despite the sophisticated starched linen and leather-seated dining room, informality is the watchword, but there's nothing casual about the food. An asparagus amuse-bouche arrives with a perfect miniature brown loaf. Rillettes of Morecambe Bay shrimp, crab and avocado with passion-fruit dressing to start is a triumph. Goosnargh duck breast with wilted endive and mango is perfectly cooked, while turbot fillet with Savoy cabbage, roasted ceps and grapes hits the spot. And just when you think it can't get any better, there is some serious wizardry in the pudding department – from the first mouthful of thyme brûlée to the Stilton cheesecake. At lunchtime, seriously good sandwiches are on offer, teamed with a pint of Barngates brewed on the premises. A well-rounded wine list includes good, affordable options starting at £12.95, and a choice of 14 by the glass from £3.95. NB No children under 14 after 8pm.
**Chef/s:** Neil McCue. **Open:** all week 12 to 2.30, 6 to 9. **Closed:** 25 Dec. **Meals:** alc (main courses L £9.50 to £25, D £14.50 to £25). Bar L menu available. **Service:** not inc. **Details:** Cards accepted. 60 seats. 30 seats outside. No music. Wheelchair access. Children's portions. Car parking.

★NEW ENTRY★
## Lucy's on a Plate
**Deli and restaurant with cookery courses**
Church Street, Ambleside, LA22 0BU
Tel no: (01539) 431191
www.lucysofambleside.co.uk
**Modern British | £28**
**Cooking score: 2**

V £30

Set on a quiet side street, Lucy's is long established, and something of a brand these days – as well as the deli, the main restaurant and Lucy4 bistro, you can also enroll on cookery courses. The main eatery is easy on the eye, with bare floorboards, mismatched furniture, tiny twinkling lights and candles everywhere; interesting, comfortable and rustic, which pretty well describes the food too. Starters include grilled scallops and big fat prawns in coriander, lime and lemon alongside chunky and spicy fishcakes, while substantial mains are along the lines of a dense and fragrant lamb tagine or chilli salmon marinated in soya sauce, garlic, spring onions and ginger and served with mini dim sum. Puddings are famous, and there are over 30 to choose from, ranging from chocolate almond torte with lime cream via Westmorland toffee apple crumble tart to Lancashire lemon tart. House wine is £13.95.
**Chef/s:** Darren McGuigan. **Open:** Daily 10 to 9. **Closed:** Christmas Day and Boxing Day. **Meals:** Main courses £9.95 to £21. **Details:** Cards accepted. 80 seats. 16 seats outside. No mobile phones. Wheelchair access. Music. Children's portions.

## Rothay Manor
**Country house with landscaped gardens**
Rothay Bridge, Ambleside, LA22 0EH
Tel no: (015394) 33605
www.rothaymanor.co.uk
**British | £39**
**Cooking score: 3**

å ᄅ V

Despite an imposing appearance, there are no airs and graces about this listed Georgian house. Dinner is up to five courses, rich and elaborate in the country-house style. Smoked salmon, halibut and prawn terrine with herb mayonnaise, or chicken liver and truffle parfait with Madeira jelly might open proceedings. Then an intermediary soup or sorbet is followed by a main course of perhaps braised fell-bred lamb shoulder with root vegetables on red cabbage, broad beans, sweet potato mash and a rich rosemary-infused sauce; or a roulade of belly pork with sage and onion stuffing partnered with pork tenderloin, asparagus, glazed carrots, sweet potato mash and sage gravy. End on an indulgent note with chocolate marquise or a tangy baked lemon tart with meringue topping and berry compote. Eight varied house selections open the wine list, by the bottle (£15), half-bottle or glass. Beyond that, fans of Bordeaux and Burgundy will be just as well satisfied as those with more adventurous tastes, who might look to the excellent Australian and North American sections.
**Chef/s:** Jane Binns and Colette Nixon. **Open:** all week L 12.30 to 1.45, D 7.15 to 9. **Closed:** 3 to 20 Jan. **Meals:** Set L Mon to Sat £18.50, Set L Sun £20, Set D £36 (3 courses) to £40. Light L menu available Mon to Sat. **Service:** not inc. **Details:** Cards accepted. 65 seats. Air-con. No music. No mobile phones. Wheelchair access. Children's portions. Car parking.

## ■ Applethwaite
## Underscar Manor
**Country-house hotel with spectacular views**
Applethwaite, CA12 4PH
Tel no: (01768) 775000
**Anglo-French | £38**
**Cooking score: 5**

ᄅ V

Sweeping views down to Derwentwater make this one of the more dramatic settings in Cumbria, especially with Skiddaw's bulk looming behind. Not to be outdone, the Italianate villa delivers a stunning ornate plasterwork ceiling in the drawing room, and the conservatory dining room makes much of the view and lush grounds. Menus offer around half a dozen options per course, with dishes having broad appeal. Starters may be relatively old-fashioned creations such as cheese soufflé, or ravioli of lobster and seared king scallops with spinach and brandy and elderflower butter sauce, but beer-battered prawns are given a decidedly fashion-conscious accompaniment of spiced couscous with beetroot and a sweet-and-sour sauce. Luxuriant main courses typically feature Lakeland beef fillet with a confit of beef, horseradish, spinach, fondant potato and a red-wine sauce, alongside roasted rack of fell-bred lamb with a moussaka gâteau, mixed bean tartlet and a port-wine sauce with olives, and to finish there may be strawberry shortcake with strawberry pannacotta. There is good drinking to be had under £25 on a wine list that majors in France but doesn't neglect the rest of the world.

**Chef/s:** Robert Thornton. **Open:** all week 12 to 1, 7 to 8.30. **Meals:** alc (main courses L £16 to £17, D £22 to £23). Set L £28, Set D £38. **Service:** not inc. **Details:** Cards accepted. 55 seats. 12 seats outside. No mobile phones. Music. Car parking.

## Bowness-on-Windermere

### Linthwaite House

**Fine views and polished cooking**
Crook Road, Bowness-on-Windermere, LA23 3JA
Tel no: (015394) 88600
www.linthwaite.com
**Modern British | £61**
**Cooking score: 4**

£5 OFF  🍴 🛏 ⋎

The B5284 leads upwards from the edge of Windermere to this traditional country-house hotel located high up on the fell. Public rooms command breathtaking views and it is the sort of place where relaxed, informal comfort are very much the key words. The drawing room is deep-cushioned and the 'delightfully old-fashioned' dining room has highly polished mahogany tables and a collection of curios – Victorian toys, stuffed animals, books, hat boxes – but modern cooking is what's on offer. The kitchen makes good use of regional

materials such as Mansergh Hall asparagus with truffle and hollandaise, or Herdwick lamb cooked at 60 degrees and served with braised neck kataif and a cep and kidney risotto. Desserts range from a homespun damson crumble tart with ripple ice cream to vanilla rice pudding with roasted rhubarb, poppy seed tuile and rhubarb cordial. Service is 'lovely and attentive'. The list of well-reviewed wines is arranged by style and starts at £21.

**Chef/s:** Simon Bolsover. **Open:** all week 12.30 to 2, 7 to 9. **Meals:** alc L (main courses £8 to £16). Set L Mon to Sat £13.95 (2 courses) to £16.95, Set L Sun £18.95, Set D £46. Bar menu available. **Service:** not inc. **Details:** Cards accepted. 60 seats. 25 seats outside. No mobile phones. Wheelchair access. Music. Children's portions. Car parking.

## Brampton

### Farlam Hall

**Splendid country-house hotel**
Brampton, CA8 2NG
Tel no: (016977) 46234
www.farlamhall.co.uk
**Modern British | £33**
**Cooking score: 3**

🛏

The heart of this elegant country-house hotel dates from the mid-sixteenth century. The current owners, who have been here over 30 years, have restored the place to its Victorian splendour, while the kitchen has at least one foot planted firmly in the present. Dinner is four courses, kicking off perhaps with smoked prawns with lemon mayonnaise, or lamb pastrami with potato salad and rocket. Among main courses, boned quail filled with chicken and herb mousseline served on bacon and red-wine sauce with crisp pancetta is typical of the elaborate style, while grilled lemon sole fillet with banana and coconut on buttered spinach with cream, herb and white-wine sauce shows an inventive streak. A selection of English cheeses precedes dessert, which might be pannacotta with rhubarb compote, ginger cheesecake, or orange marmalade jelly with orange and Grand Marnier ice cream. House selections from £19.95 open the wine list, which also offers good choice by the glass. **Chef/s:** Barry Quinion. **Open:** all week D only 8 to 8.30. **Closed:** 26 to 30 Dec. **Meals:** Set D Sun to Fri £37.50, Set D Sat £39 (4 courses). **Service:** not inc. **Details:** Cards accepted. 45 seats. No music. No mobile phones. Wheelchair access. Car parking.

# █Cartmel
## L'Enclume
**Astonishing avant-garde food**
Cavendish Street, Cartmel, LA11 6PZ
Tel no: (015395) 36362
www.lenclume.co.uk
**Modern European | £45**
**Cooking score: 8**
£5 OFF 🍷 🚆 ✔

It may be in the 'backwoods of Cumbria', but Simon Rogan and Penny Tapsell's extraordinary restaurant-with-rooms is now a world-class destination serving some of the most radical and risqué food in the UK. The location for this gastronomic wizardry is just about as unlikely as they come: 'enclume' is French for anvil and the building once served as Cartmel's local smithy. Some tiny windows and old beams remain, but the place now has a brand-new look with plate-glass doors, twenty-first-century artwork and a conservatory extension for drinking and chatting. Simon Rogan has placed himself at the outer limits of modern British gastronomy and his cooking is a dangerous, roller-coaster ride taking in extraordinary flavours, bizarre combinations and unlikely textures. Dishes are tiny masterpieces and they come in waves, with some of the tasting menus running to a dozen courses or more. Much of the food is now designed for 'the whole party', although a modest carte is also available for those who are happy to be bound by convention. Dish descriptions can seem bewildering, but staff are knowledgeable and sympathetic to requests and queries. Some ideas are easy to grasp ('five-flavoured monkfish, pimento, lentils, hazelnut' gives the basic information); others are word-play fantasies

('expearamenthol frappé' is a stroke of linguistic genius). At the front end of these extravaganzas there might be 'egg drop hot and sour soup', pork cheeks with pink grapefruit, Brussels sprout and pine nut or 'cold and colder' foie gras paired with blood orange, pistachio and quinoa. This is a kitchen that loves playing with extreme temperatures. Towards the finishing line, diners might be offered thrilling temptations like 'liquid chocolate, peanut, cherries, pepper, malt', or Sticky Tacky pudding (a deliberate parody of a Lakeland cliché, no doubt). Rogan also revels in the flavours and fragrances of wild flowers and herbs, many of which have fallen by the wayside over the centuries: he has been known to make use of hyssop, balm of Gilead and many other rare species in his multi-layered, experimental compositions. It is all done in the name of excitement and surprise, often with a sprinkling of tongue-in-cheek humour along the way. Compared to the wild eccentricity that defines everything else, L'Enclume's wine list might seem slightly straight-laced. That said, it is a strong and impressive selection with a big contingent of high-quality labels from France and beyond. Eight house wines start at £24 (£5 a glass) for Alsatian Pinot Noir. NB Simon Rogan is planning a move to the Home Counties (probably Henley-on-Thames) at the end of 2007, although it seems likely that L'Enclume will continue to operate normally. **Chef/s:** Simon Rogan. **Open:** Thur to Sun 12 to 1.45, Tue to Sun 7 to 9.30. **Meals:** alc (main courses £23 to £27). Set L £18 (2 courses) to £25, Set D £39 to £70. **Service:** not inc. **Details:** Cards accepted. 40 seats. No music. No mobile phones. Wheelchair access. Children's portions. Car parking.

# Cockermouth

## Quince & Medlar

**Appealing vegetarian restaurant**
11-13 Castlegate, Cockermouth, CA13 9EU
Tel no: (01900) 823579
**Vegetarian | £23**
**Cooking score: 4**

V £30

Great attention to detail and considerable expertise in the construction of 'appealing and original' vegetarian dishes mark out Colin and Louisa Le Voi's long-standing restaurant. Dishes are mainly Mediterranean based, but take in North African, South-East Asian and Indian influences, in a well-conceived cooking style. To start, savour the aromatic kick of spiced leaf spinach and chilli pepper globes on dressed pumpkin seed leaves, or try broad bean, caper berry and green olive pâté. To follow might be roasted aubergine, chickpeas and sun-dried tomatoes topped with saffron couscous and pine nuts and served with a sweet pepper sauce, or butternut squash filo parcels with a tarragon sauce. Appealing desserts have included a citrussy lime tart and chocolate orange torte. The all-organic wine list has broad appeal and reasonable prices; house wines from France and Italy are £11.60 and £12.60 respectively. NB Children must be over 5.
**Chef/s:** Colin and Louisa Le Voi. **Open:** Tue to Sat D only 7 to 9.30. **Closed:** 24 to 26 Dec. **Meals:** alc (main courses £14). **Service:** not inc. **Details:** Cards accepted. 26 seats. Wheelchair access. Music. Children allowed.

# Crosthwaite

## Punch Bowl Inn

**Contemporary, uncluttered atmosphere**
Lyth Valley, Crosthwaite, LA8 8HR
Tel no: (015395) 68237
www.the-punchbowl.co.uk
**Modern European | £33**
**New Chef**

This Cumbrian stalwart has lots of local support, a simple, uncluttered interior and a smart dining room. High standards are obvious, from the locally brewed ale, via the excellent atmosphere, to the good service. Despite a change at the stoves, the sourcing of good raw materials remains a priority, and the kitchen distinguishes itself with enthusiasm and honest effort. The menus centre on appetising combinations: baked Cumbrian cheese with spring onion soufflé, wilted spinach and Parmesan cream, and Morecambe Bay shrimps served with lemon-dressed watercress, while a cassoulet of summer beans and rosemary accompanies herb-crusted rack of lamb. It's also worth checking out fish dishes, which could include sea bass with crab and chilli mash or halibut teamed with braised oxtail and served with buttered spinach and lemon oil. To round off the meal, try a selection of northern cheeses, from Kendal Creamy to Appleby's Cheshire, or the ginger crème brûlée with toffee-grilled figs and shortbread. The wine list opens with a wide range available by the glass. Bottles from £14.50 are an international mix with many options under £20.
**Chef/s:** Craig McMeekin. **Open:** all week 12 to 3, 6 to 9. **Meals:** alc (main courses £9.50 to £18.50).. **Service:** not inc. **Details:** Cards accepted. 70 seats. 50 seats outside. No music. Wheelchair access. Car parking.

## Grasmere

### Jumble Room

**Colourful and eclectic food in a friendly
environment**
Langdale Road, Grasmere, LA22 9SU
Tel no: (015394) 35188
www.thejumbleroom.co.uk
Global | £38
Cooking score: 2

£5 OFF ✔

'This informal eatery offers honest, tasty food
of the highest quality, with a smile and
humour. Long may it prosper,' says one
satisfied customer of this quirky little
restaurant which has drawn a huge amount of
praise from diners this year. You could start
with fresh oven-baked sardines served with a
rich tomato sugo; carpaccio of Grizedale
venison with dressed salad and Parmesan; or
roasted vegetables served on hummus with
olives and dressed leaves. The wholesome,
unpretentious style continues into main
courses such as beer-battered fresh haddock
and chips with mushy peas; Cambodian fish
curry; Herdwick lamb casserole with soused
vegetables, roasted parsnips and herb
dumplings; or tomato and mozzarella ravioli
with roasted sweet potatoes, basil pesto and
Parmesan. Chef Chrissie Hill's home-made
pasta is 'the best I have tasted outside Italy and
beats a lot within as well', while Andy Hill is
'fantastic, very welcoming and laid-back in his
approach'. His knowledge of the wine list has
also garnered praise. Bottles start at just
£10.95 and there is plenty to choose from for
under £20.
**Chef/s:** Chrissy Hill, and David and Trudy Clay.
**Open:** Easter to end Nov Wed to Sun 11 to 4, 6 to
10; also open Sat and Sun Jan (phone for times).
**Closed:** 11 to 27 Dec. **Meals:** alc (main courses L £8
to £15, D £11 to £20). **Service:** not inc.
**Details:** Cards accepted. 50 seats. Wheelchair
access. Music. Children's portions.

### White Moss House

**Historic house, classic cooking**
Rydal Water, Grasmere, LA22 9SE
Tel no: (015394) 35295
www.whitemoss.com
British | £39
Cooking score: 5

🍷 🛏 ✔

This homely 1730 house with Victorian
additions was bought by William Wordsworth
for his son and it remained in the family until
the 1930s. Peter and Susan Dixon have been
here for nearly three decades and have created
an unstuffy, informal atmosphere in the log-
fired lounge, the oak-panelled hall with its
grandfather clock, and the cottagey dining
room. The kitchen buys carefully, often
locally, and these prime raw materials set the
tone for the five-course dinners (no choice
until dessert stage) that draw inspiration from
English tradition. Dinner opens with a soup,
say leek and lovage, before going on to a light
fish course, which might be sea bass poached
in the Aga with champagne and served with a
sorrel and saffron sauce. Rack of Lakeland
lamb, for the main course, could come with a
herb crust, a blueberry-blackberry enriched
Bordeaux sauce, as well as new Charlotte
potatoes, beetroot with redcurrant and mint,
steamed cauliflower and stir-fried baby
turnips. Finish with a good traditional bread-
and-butter pudding with Calvados and
marmalade, ahead of a plate of English
cheeses. Wines are a contemporary
international mix, smartened up by some
serious Bordeaux and Burgundy. Bottles start
at £13.95.

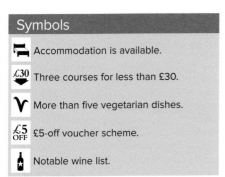

### Symbols

🛏 Accommodation is available.

£30 Three courses for less than £30.

✔ More than five vegetarian dishes.

£5 OFF £5-off voucher scheme.

🍷 Notable wine list.

Chef/s: Peter Dixon. Open: Mon to Sat D only 8 (1 sitting). Closed: Dec and Jan. Meals: Set D £39.50. Service: not inc. Details: Cards accepted. 18 seats. No music. No mobile phones. Wheelchair access. Car parking.

# ▌Kendal

## Bridge Street Restaurant

**Fresh and modern British cooking**
1 Bridge Street, Kendal, LA9 7DD
Tel no: (01539) 738855
www.one-bridgestreet.co.uk
**Modern British | £29**
**New Chef**
£5 OFF   £30

Julian and Liz Ankers have taken over the restaurant formerly known as Bridge House and are quickly setting about stamping their own personality on the place. Julian's cooking goes in for lively flavours with inspiration taken from far and wide. Warm Blacksticks Blue cheese tart with a soft herby crust, or aromatic duck parcels with glass noodle salad and a plum and star anise dipping sauce might open proceedings; while main courses typically range from poached sea trout on crushed new potatoes with asparagus cream sauce to poached chicken breast on wild mushroom risotto with thyme cream sauce, or a casserole of shin of beef in Black Sheep ale with horseradish dumplings and celeriac purée. Finish with warm cherry and almond tart or white chocolate cheesecake. House selections at £10.95 open a varied, international wine list.
Chef/s: Julian Ankers. Open: Tue to Sat L 12 to 2, D 6.30 to 9. Closed: 25 and 26 Dec. Meals: Set L £10 (2 courses) to £13. Set D £22 (2 courses) to £25. Bar menu available. Service: not inc. Details: Cards accepted. 44 seats. 10 seats outside. Wheelchair access. Music. Children's portions.

## Déjà-vu

**Cheery and flexible bistro**
124 Stricklandgate, Kendal, LA9 4QG
Tel no: (01539) 724843
www.dejavukendal.co.uk
**Modern European | £27**
**New Chef**
£5 OFF   V   £30

A brightly painted exterior sets exactly the right tone for this laid-back bistro. The approach is informal, with a tapas menu for grazers, taking in everything from patatas bravas to smoked chicken breast with paprika mayonnaise, as well as a good-value set-price dinner and à la carte choices. Starters from the latter take in deep-fried prawn beignets with aïoli, as well as pan-fried polenta fritters with warm tomato salsa, or smoked duck breast with toasted brioche and Calvados apple compote. Pan-fried sesame-coated sea bass with olive mash and sauce vierge might follow, or there could be pan-roasted duck breast with star anise, orange and honey sauce and parsnip mash. Most of the bottles on the compact wine list are under £20, with house selections from £12.
Chef/s: Fran Wood. Open: Wed to Mon L 12 to 2, D 5.30 to 9 (9.30 Fri and Sat). Closed: 25 and 26 Dec, 1 Jan, bank hol Mon. Meals: alc (main courses £10 to £16). Set D (until 7.30 Fri and Sat) £9.95 (3 courses). Tapas menu only Wed to Sat L. Service: not inc. Details: Cards accepted. 34 seats. No mobile phones. Wheelchair access. Music.

## ALSO RECOMMENDED

### ▲ Swinside Lodge

Grange Road, Newlands, Keswick, CA12 5UE
Tel no: (017687) 72948

Overlooking Derwentwater in a tranquil setting at the foot of Cat Bells, a few miles west of Keswick, this Georgian hotel is a fine place to get away from it all. Elaborate country-house cooking is what to expect from the four-course dinner (£35) served at 7.30pm every evening. Meals typically open with a salad of seared scallops and black pudding, before soup, then a main course comprising roast Cumbrian lamb fillet with rosemary, a parcel of braised shoulder and a sun-dried tomato risotto rösti with kumquat relish. Finish perhaps with rum pannacotta with pineapple and passion-fruit compote. The wine list consists mostly of French wines, with prices starting at £15.95. Open all week D only.

## Sawrey
### Ees Wyke
**Elegant Georgian country-house hotel**
Sawrey, LA22 0JZ
Tel no: (015394) 36393
www.eeswyke.co.uk
**Modern British | £35**
**Cooking score: 2**

Richard and Margaret Lee's hotel is hidden away in Beatrix Potter's home hamlet with glorious views across meadows to Esthwaite and sheep-grazed fells. Guests are asked to convene in the lounge at 7.30pm for pre-dinner drinks with their hosts. In true Lakeland style, dinner revolves around Richard's daily changing, fixed-price menu that runs to five courses. Good local sourcing is evident and the kitchen balances traditional favourites with some more modern ideas. Begin with roasted tomato soup, follow with grilled salmon and garlic pea mash with lemon butter sauce, before the main course, perhaps pot-roasted Goosnargh chicken with tarragon cream sauce, or monkfish wrapped in pancetta with rosemary and thyme. Comforting desserts extend to apple and plum crumble and strawberries in Cassis jelly with raspberry coulis, before a plate of regional farmhouse cheeses rounds things off. Six house wines at £16 open an uncomplicated list to please simple tastes.
**Chef/s:** Richard Lee. **Open:** all week D only 7.30 (1 sitting). **Meals:** Set D £31. **Service:** not inc. **Details:** Cards accepted. 20 seats. 20 seats outside. No music. Wheelchair access. Car parking.

## ALSO RECOMMENDED
### ▲ Queens Head Hotel
Townhead, Troutbeck, LA23 1PW
Tel no: (01539) 432174

The views over Troutbeck and the Garburn Pass must rank as some of the finest in the Lake District, and this 400-year-old coaching inn makes the most of them. Tradition reigns supreme in the bustling bar, but food is bang up to date, with an excellent-value set menu (£18.50) and an ambitious evening carte offering sustenance in the form of foie gras, rabbit and ham hock terrine with spiced apple jelly (£6.95), Holker Hall venison with plum jus and espresso coffee foam (£15.95), and warm chocolate pudding with mango sorbet (£5.25). Locally brewed beers and wines from £12.95. Open 12 to 9 daily.

## Ullswater
### Sharrow Bay
**The original country-house hotel**
Ullswater, CA10 2LZ
Tel no: (01768) 486301
www.sharrowbay.co.uk
**British | £47**
**Cooking score: 6**

2008 sees the original country-house hotel celebrating its sixtieth season. Visitors still come for the whole Sharrow Bay experience, which begins with a view that is second to none – down Ullswater to the fells beyond. Inside there is a feeling of comfort verging on luxury, overseen by staff imbued with a tradition of courtesy and care. This is not a place for casual eating and although nothing truly startling emerges from the kitchen, there a sense of time-warp about the menus. Starters and main courses offer plenty of alternatives, while no-choice sorbet and a soup or fish course (perhaps a fried fillet of plaice with shallot, bacon and thyme mash) are slotted in between. Against the full-on country-house look ('as befits the hotel which begat this manner'), the food is surprisingly modern,

taking in anything from salad of smoked duck breast with poached pear, grilled goats' cheese and walnut dressing to a dish of noisette of venison with red onion marmalade and butternut squash purée served with a glazed apple and Grand Veneur sauce. An impressive array of desserts includes a strawberry and lemongrass jelly with pink champagne granita, but the selection of British cheeses is worthy of attention, if only to continue one's acquaintance with the lengthy, all-embracing wine list. This is commendably high on quality (the Sharrow Selection offers a helpful shortcut), is strongest in French classics, but includes interesting, mature New World bottles too. Prices start just below £20 and there is an interesting range by the glass.
**Chef/s:** Mark Teasdale and Colin Akrigg. **Open:** all week 1, 8 (1 sitting). **Meals:** Set L £39.50, Set D £52.50. Light L menu available. **Service:** not inc. **Details:** Cards accepted. 60 seats. Air-con. No music. No mobile phones. Wheelchair access. Car parking.

## Ulverston

### Bay Horse
**Complicated basics and rich puds**
Canal Foot, Ulverston, LA12 9EL
Tel no: (01229) 583972
www.thebayhorsehotel.co.uk
British | £35
Cooking score: 3

This eighteenth-century former coaching inn with impressive views over Morecambe Sands shows a loyalty to locally sourced ingredients (air-dried Cumbrian ham and Lancashire cheese, for example). A tendency to complexity, as in chicken marinated in lime and wine, filled with cheese and herb pâté, coated with savoury breadcrumbs, then baked and served with bacon, can be matched with excellent basics like lamb shank braised with mushrooms and rosemary. Either the simpler lunch menu or the 'Lite Bites' list offer genuine choice at relatively low cost. A vegetarian menu is a nice touch. Seriously rich desserts like chocolate mascarpone cheesecake with

passion-fruit custard or brandy pudding with cream cater for the sweet-toothed. Wines start at £16.50 and modestly priced glasses are offered, too.
**Chef/s:** Robert Lyons. **Open:** Tue to Sun L 12 to 2, all week D 7.30 for 8 (1 sitting). **Meals:** alc (main courses L £10.50 to £25.50, D £22.50 to £25.50). Set D £30.50. Bar L menu available. **Service:** not inc. **Details:** Cards accepted. 50 seats. 20 seats outside. No mobile phones. Wheelchair access. Music. Children allowed. Car parking.

## Watermillock

### Rampsbeck Country House Hotel
**Smooth service and confident cooking**
Watermillock, CA11 OLP
Tel no: (017684) 86442
www.rampsbeck.fsnet.co.uk
Anglo-French | £42
Cooking score: 3

Wonderful views over Ullswater make this eighteenth-century manor house a pleasant place to linger. The décor is a little staid, but well suited to the setting (think candelabra, high ceilings and walls decorated with paintings and plates). The cooking is classically based, but starters wear some international flavours – brandade of cod with Sakura cress, curry oil and toasted almonds, for example, or pan-fried hand-dived scallops with water chestnuts, courgettes, bean sprouts and a soy dressing. Typical main courses include roasted fillet of beef with shallot confit, celeriac fondant, pan-fried sweetbreads wrapped in Cumbrian air-dried ham and a Madeira wine sauce; and pan-fried fillet of turbot with langoustine tortellini, roasted langoustine, caramelised apple and a cider emulsion. Round it off with a hot plum soufflé with rum and raisin ice cream and a raisin drop scone; or Bourbon vanilla crème brûlée with braised plums and plum sorbet. The extensive, good-value wine list begins at £12.50.

**Chef/s:** Andrew McGeorge. **Open:** all week 12 to 1, 7 to 8.30. **Closed:** 5 Jan to 10 Feb. **Meals:** Set L £28, Set D £39.50 to £47. Bar L menu available. **Service:** not inc. **Details:** Cards accepted. 40 seats. No music. No mobile phones. Car parking.

## ■ Windermere

## Gilpin Lodge

**Impressive hotel dining in Lakes oasis**
Crook Road, Windermere, LA23 3NE
Tel no: (015394) 88818
www.gilpinlodge.co.uk
**Anglo-French | £35**
**Cooking score: 6**

A family-run country-house hotel, Gilpin Lodge basks in 20 acres of majestic, leafy tranquility and, though it swaggers with all the stylish trappings of a luxury hotel, still maintains an endearing friendly, cheerful and homely atmosphere. Brightly coloured lounges welcome with blazing winter fires, fresh flowers, magazines and books, though, with no fewer than four smartly attired, intimate dining rooms, there is no doubting food takes centre stage here. Decked out in their best white linen, sparkling glasses and gleaming cutlery, each of the rooms has their own individual character. Chris Meredith, at the helm in the kitchen, shows off his fine pedigree, his modern approach underpinned by a classical theme and driven by top-notch local produce. This is fine-tuned, sophisticated cooking of precision and passion, its deft, simple approach allowing clean, clear flavours to shine in harmony. Lunch menus change weekly, while dinner is a daily changing affair offering, say, pan-fried sea bass combined with saffron boulangère potatoes, a gazpacho sauce and cucumber linguine, or perhaps a fillet of veal teamed with a sweetbread ravioli, spaghetti of vegetables and Madeira sauce. Desserts, like the first-rate petits fours, maintain standards through to the end, with maybe a date and orange soufflé vying for selection alongside a classic Valrhona chocolate fondant with pistachio ice cream. A fittingly accomplished globetrotting wine list is built on interest rather than ancient vintages, with France in the ascendancy. The house wine kicks off proceedings at £19.75 (white) or £23.50 (red), with fourteen offered by the glass and an admirable selection by the half-bottle.

**Chef/s:** Chris Meredith. **Open:** all week L 12 to 2, D 6.45 to 9.15. **Meals:** Set L £20 (2 courses) to £25, Set D £47. Light L menu available. **Service:** not inc. **Details:** Cards accepted. 60 seats. 25 seats outside. No music. No mobile phones. Car parking.

## Holbeck Ghyll

**Breathtaking views, destination food and wines**
Holbeck Lane, Windermere, LA23 1LU
Tel no: (015394) 32375
www.holbeckghyll.com
**Modern British | £55**
**Cooking score: 7**

We say so every year, but the views from Holbeck Ghyll are scintillating. You climb about half a mile from the main road to a commanding vista that embraces not only Lake Windermere in the middle distance, but the backdrop of the Langland Fells and the Old Man of Coniston too. Inside, there is a period feel, but not a fusty one, more a pleasing evocation of the kind of domestic peace people took for granted before the Great War. Service fits in well with the amiable tone, and knows what the menus are about. David McLaughlin maintains productive working relations with Cumbrian suppliers, and aims to treat their wares with respect. A tripartite terrine might feature rabbit, corn-fed chicken and foie gras, offset with a sharp gribiche dressing, while a fascinating fish starter fashions salt cod into a 'pannacotta', served with salmon beignets and pickled vegetables. Technique is assured and combinations precisely judged, so that roasted turbot might be teamed with creamed leeks, crisped ham and a red-wine sauce for one main course, while another (from a spring menu) made the most of seasonal veg, putting broad beans and baby leeks with veal fillet and butternut squash. Vegetarians have their own menu to peruse, but all are reunited for irresistible desserts like nougat glâcé with warm mango parcels, a salad of tropical fruits and passion-fruit sorbet. It all comes with a wine list worth the journey in itself. Page after page of thrilling bottles flash by, the section called 'Fantastic Finds' worth making a beeline for. Organic offerings, plenty of half-bottles and enough classics to satisfy well-heeled Francophiles are all thoroughly commendable. The Personal House Selection starts at £19.50, or £4.95 a glass.

**Chef/s:** David McLaughlin. **Open:** all week 12 to 2, 7 to 9.30. **Meals:** Set L £29.50, Set D £49 and £60. Light L menu available. **Service:** not inc. **Details:** Cards accepted. 50 seats. 30 seats outside. Separate bar. No music. No mobile phones. Wheelchair access. Car parking.

## Jerichos
**Confident, creative cooking**
Birch Street, Windermere, LA23 1EG
Tel no: (015394) 42522
www.jerichos.co.uk
**Modern British | £31**
**Cooking score: 5**

Husband-and-wife team Chris and Jo Blydes celebrate a decade at their atmospheric, evening-only town-centre restaurant in 2008. The rich, bold décor still catches the eye, with its striking plum colour scheme, subdued lighting and Toulouse Lautrec-style pictures that add an endearing nod of classic Parisian brasserie. Chris continues to man the stoves in the open-to-view kitchen, cooking as confidently as ever with a creative modern approach, the spotlight on simplicity and flavour to make the very best of quality local and seasonal produce. The menu comes sensibly compact, perhaps kicking off with butter-glazed new season Formby asparagus accompanied by crispy smoked pancetta, soft-boiled local bantam egg and hollandaise dressing. Main courses might tempt with roasted Gressingham duck breast served on baked provençale red pepper with smoked sausage, sun-dried tomato couscous and glazed beans, or perhaps a poached fillet of

line-caught sea bass — teamed with herb-roasted vegetables, glazed spinach, shrimp butter and a lemon vinaigrette — could rock your boat. Desserts provide temptation too strong to resist, like an almond, pecan and popcorn cheesecake served with pear and orange sorbet, or raspberry and strawberry jelly accompanied by shortbread, pistachio ice cream and crème anglaise. The menu also offers a couple of wine suggestions, while the varied list itself is helpfully set out on food-matching lines, with house wine rolling out at a reasonable £13.50.

**Chef/s:** Chris Blaydes and Tim Dalzell. **Open:** Tue to Sun D only 6.45 to 10. **Closed:** last 2 weeks Nov, first week Dec, 25 and 26 Dec, 1 Jan. **Meals:** alc (main courses £14.50 to £18.50). **Service:** not inc. **Details:** Cards accepted. 36 seats. Music.

## Samling
**Lilliputian-scale country house**
Ambleside Road, Windermere, LA23 1LR
Tel no: (015394) 31922
www.thesamling.com
**Anglo-French | £38**
**Cooking score: 4**

The Samling is the former home of John Benson, Wordsworth's landlord — it was here that the poet would come to pay his rent for Dove Cottage in nearby Grasmere. The house is now a luxury hideaway with majestic views over distant Lake Windermere. The menu offers a well-balanced and interesting selection of dishes in an ambitious, modern style. Among starters, a confit chicken, ham and foie gras mosaic could be served with celeriac remoulade and tarragon mustard dressing, while slow-cooked belly of Gloucester Old

## Anthony Demerre

**Why did you become a chef?**
My grandmother's cooking inspired me.

**Which of today's chefs do you admire?**
Gordon Ramsay; a great chef, but above all a great business man.

**Where do you eat out?**
Galvin and Racine – but otherwise locally.

**What's the best dish you've ever eaten?**
My Grandmother-in-law's slow-cooked veal with carrots.

**Do you have a favourite local recipe?**
Arbutus's warm pig's head (a variation on the classic English brawn dish).

**What's your guilty food pleasure?**
Krispy Kreme doughnuts.

**If you could only eat one more thing, what would it be?**
Spit-roasted chicken.

**Which are your proudest achievements?**
The success of Arbutus in such a short time.

**What's coming up next for you?**
The opening of our new restaurant, Wild Honey in Mayfair.

**What does The Good Food Guide mean to you?**
Real people giving honest opinions.

Spot is teamed with langoustines. Presentation means that dishes look the part, whether a colourful spring chicken with fresh peas, Jersey Royals, roasted ceps and tarragon, or a pairing of breast of duck and confit duck 'hash brown' with creamed leeks and crispy bacon. Desserts include the likes of warm chocolate and toffee pudding with banana ice cream and caramelised banana, or iced Bramley apple crumble with blackberries and custard. The wine list is wide ranging, with a good selection in both Old and New Worlds, but with prices zooming up from £32, value is more debatable; diners on a budget might want to stick to the good range of wines by the glass from £9.

**Chef/s:** Nigel Mendham. **Open:** all week 12 to 2.30, 7 to 10. **Meals:** Set L £38, Set D £55. **Service:** not inc. **Details:** Cards accepted. 22 seats. No mobile phones. Music. Children's portions. Car parking.

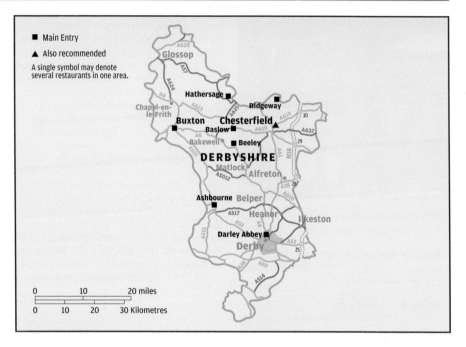

- ■ Main Entry
- ▲ Also recommended

A single symbol may denote several restaurants in one area.

## ■ Ashbourne
## Callow Hall

**44 acres of rural loveliness**
Mappleton Road, Ashbourne, DE6 2AA
Tel no: (01335) 300900
www.callowhall.co.uk
**Modern British | £32**
**Cooking score: 3**

The setting is as pleasant as the welcome at this Victorian country-house hotel. Relaxed and relaxing, it is an ideal place to hole up for the evening over a leisurely five-course dinner. The kitchen does not cut corners, so expect home-made everything (pretty much) and a wealth of the best local ingredients. Begin with home-smoked organic salmon with a smoked haddock and tarragon fishcake, salad leaves and horseradish dressing or provençale roast vegetable and herb leaf salad with a hot Gruyère beignet and aged balsamic dressing. After a palate-cleansing sorbet or perhaps roast monkfish with fennel and Pernod-scented fish fumet, move on to main courses such as pan-fried veal striploin steak with spinach and wild mushroom risotto and a rich red-wine sauce; or halibut steak with lobster and samphire and a bisque sauce. Finish with English and Continental cheeses or a home-made dessert, followed by coffee and petits fours. A good selection of wines starts at £13.50.

**Chef/s:** David and Anthony Spencer. **Open:** Sun L 12.30 to 1.30, Mon to Sat D 7.30 to 9. **Closed:** 25 and 26 Dec. **Meals:** alc (main courses £17.50 to £21). Set L £25, Set D £42. **Service:** not inc. **Details:** Cards accepted. 60 seats. 20 seats outside. No music. No mobile phones. Wheelchair access. Children's portions. Car parking.

### Average price

The average price listed in main-entry reviews denotes the price of a three-course meal, without wine.

## The Dining Room
**Tiny, sixteenth-century building**
33 St John Street, Ashbourne, DE6 1GP
Tel no: (01335) 300666
www.thediningroomashbourne.co.uk
**Modern British | £35**
**Cooking score: 4**

Booking is advisable to ensure bagging one of six tables in Peter and Laura Dale's restaurant. Simple, contemporary furnishings blend well with the old oak beams, limestone lintels and massive cast-iron kitchen range. The setting may be old-worldly but Peter's cooking is ardently cosmopolitan and highly inventive, infused with fashionable round-the-world treatments and top-notch locally sourced ingredients. Dishes are meticulously described on the short menu of three choices per course. Begin with smoked organic salmon, served with asparagus, puffed saffron rice, lemon and lime sorbet, capers, cucumber, yoghurt and avocado. Follow with peppered Ellastone steak with pickled tongue and warm green peppercorn jelly, accompanied with roasted new potatoes, asparagus and café au lait sauce. The food's strongly seasonal feel extends to desserts like roast rhubarb with strawberry jam sponge, vanilla buttermilk foam and spice-bread ice cream. Menus may take some reading but Peter's skill matches his ambition. Wines are well chosen and fairly priced, from £16.
**Chef/s:** Peter Dale. **Open:** Tue to Sat 12 to 1.30, 7 to 8.30. **Closed:** 2 weeks after 25 Dec, 1 week Mar, 1 week Sept. **Meals:** alc (main courses L £13, D £20). Set L £22. Set D (needs booking) £40. **Service:** not inc. **Details:** Cards accepted. 16 seats. No mobile phones. Wheelchair access. Music.

## ▌Baslow

## Cavendish Hotel, Gallery Restaurant
**A tranquil, pastoral view**
Baslow, DE45 1SE
Tel no: (01246) 582311
www.cavendish-hotel.net
**Modern European | £35**
**Cooking score: 3**

Sitting close by the grandeur of the Chatsworth estate, the Cavendish is quite grand enough in itself; oils and watercolours crowd the walls. Ben Handley's menus present a considered tour of contemporary taste, unafraid to try new combinations but without jarring the sensibilities. Anything up to five courses may be taken. Start perhaps with citrus-cured salmon with cucumber tagliatelle and oyster tempura, and follow it with a salad or soup (maybe clam and sweetcorn chowder). Main courses run from halibut poached in red wine with pancetta, to venison loin with Derbyshire black pudding and a foie gras butter sauce. If you've a sweet tooth, opt for honeycomb parfait with milk chocolate mousse, but leave room for the great British cheeses, which are carefully described on the menu. House Sauvignon and Cabernet are £15.50, or £3.95 a glass. Simpler fare is served in the Garden Room.
**Chef/s:** Ben Handley and Chris Allison. **Open:** all week 12 to 2, 6.30 to 10. **Closed:** Dec 25. **Meals:** alc (main course £5.95 to 18.95) Set L and D £29.50 (2 courses) to £51.50 (5 courses). **Service:** 5%. **Details:** Cards accepted. 50 seats. No mobile phones. Wheelchair access. Music. Car parking.

## Fischer's Baslow Hall

**Delightful gardens and graceful decoration**
Calver Road, Baslow, DE45 1RR
Tel no: (01246) 583259
www.fischers-baslowhall.co.uk
**Modern European | £46**
**Cooking score: 7**

Right on the edge of the Chatsworth Estate, Baslow Hall is a grand Derbyshire pile, reached along a driveway lined with mature chestnut trees. Max Fischer is tireless in his pursuit of quality raw materials, sourcing organic meats locally, including spring lamb, Chatsworth venison and Derbyshire pork, and reaching into neighbouring Yorkshire for that must-have contemporary ingredient, rhubarb. The six-course Prestige Menu is an inviting way to test the range, taking you perhaps from a terrine of foie gras and butternut squash, roast scallops with pea foam, and slow-cooked monkfish tail with oxtail carpaccio, through herb-crusted lamb chump with aubergine caviar and thyme jus, to arrive at the pair of desserts that conclude. On one spring occasion, they were raspberry soufflé, or blood orange and nougat parfait with blood orange sorbet. For a slightly higher outlay, you get to please yourself from the main carte, which might take in seared bluefin tuna and swordfish dressed in wasabi, honey-glazed duck breast with rhubarb, sauced with Sauternes, and strawberry consommé with basil ice cream. A corker of a wine list does a dizzying global spin, sweeping up many good producers, both familiar and not, and with plenty of half-bottles in evidence. House wines start at £18, or £5.25 a glass.
**Chef/s:** Max Fischer and Rupert Rowley. **Open:** Tue to Sun L 12 to 1.30, Mon to Sat D 7 to 9.30 (residents only Sun D). **Closed:** 25 and 26 Dec. **Meals:** Set L Tue to Sat £20 (2 courses) to £24, Set L Sun £35, Set D Mon to Fri £30 (2 courses) to £65, Set D Sat £60 to £65. **Service:** not inc. **Details:** Cards accepted. 70 seats. No music. No mobile phones. Wheelchair access. Car parking.

## Rowley's

**Bold brasserie**
Church Lane, Baslow, DE45 1RY
Tel no: (01246) 583880
www.rowleysrestaurant.co.uk
**Modern European | £28**
**Cooking score: 3**

Light lunches, early evening deals and children's menus are part of the package at this town-centre bar-brasserie, a branching out by Susan and Max Fischer of Baslow Hall (see entry) and chef Rupert Rowley. Wooden floors and a soft purple colour scheme lend the place a contemporary appeal and the food follows on with confidence. Ingredients are first-class – local suppliers are used wherever possible – with a trio of duck (potted, smoked and sausage) and hot smoked salmon with capers, quails' eggs and fine beans typical of the style. A main course of whole lemon sole comes with a rarebit glaze. On the meat side there could be stuffed and rolled loin of rabbit wrapped in Parma ham and served with mixed bean cassoulet and Noilly Prat sauce, while, with an eye to the casual 'brasserie' ethos, there are always chargrilled steaks with béarnaise sauce. Satisfying desserts have taken in cinnamon rice pudding fritters with home-made jam or banana bread-and-butter pudding with custard. Service has been described as 'professional, and yet friendly and attentive', while the wine list dashes hither and yon in its search for quality and reasonable prices, with house Italian and Australian opening proceedings at £13.95.
**Chef/s:** Robin Allison. **Open:** Mon to Fri L 12 to 2.30 (Sat and Sun 3), Mon to Fri D 5 to 9 (Sat 6 to 10). **Meals:** alc (main courses L £6.40 to £16, D £9 to £18) Sun L £12 (2 courses) to £16. **Service:** not inc. **Details:** Cards accepted. 64 seats. 12 seats outside. Wheelchair access. Children's portions. Children allowed. Car parking.

# Beeley

★NEW ENTRY★
## Devonshire Arms

**Country pub for the twenty-first century**
Devonshire Square, Beeley, DE4 2NR
Tel no: (01629) 733259
www.thedevonshirearms.co.uk
**Gastropub | £20**
Cooking score: 3

V £30

Built as a row of cottages in the mid-eighteenth century, this relaxed and friendly inn on the Chatsworth Estate is now enjoying the benefits of a stylish, twenty-first century revamp. Creature comforts may have been refined but the charm is undisturbed and in the bar there remains a down-to-earth ambience lent by stone walls, low beams and several open fires. Admittedly, the restaurant would be at home in smarter cosmopolitan surroundings: it's brasserie mode certainly, with lots of plate glass, bright colours and modern furniture, while the menu is of the same ilk. Ideas are unfussy and dishes are given some neat tweaks – roast beef fillet comes with white asparagus, peas, ox tongue and truffle sauce – and classics such as bangers and mash and shallot red-wine gravy keep faith with pub credentials. Seafood is well handled, witness a starter of cold-poached salmon ballottine with herbs and grain-mustard sauce and main of sea trout with Jersey Royals, spring greens and caviar sauce. A citrussy lemon tart has been the pick of the desserts. House wines start at £11.
**Chef/s:** Alan Hill. **Open:** Open all week L 12 to 3, D 6 to 9.30. **Meals:** alc (main courses £9.95 to £19.50). **Service:** optional. **Details:** Cards accepted. 70 seats. 20 seats outside. Separate bar. Wheelchair access. Music. Children's portions. Car parking.

# Buxton
## Columbine

**Popular value-for-money venue**
7 Hall Bank, Buxton, SK17 6EW
Tel no: (01298) 78752
www.buxtononline.net/columbine
**Modern British | £21**
Cooking score: 2

V £30

'Licensed Restaurant with Cellars' trumpets the Columbine – and indeed that's where you will end up on a busy night. Don't worry, they are not damp and musty, just vaulted. Start with local Derbyshire oatcake with mushrooms and baked ham in a mild mustard-seed sauce, or choose pâté of Hartington white Stilton and walnuts with red onion compote. Mains include leg steak of Derbyshire lamb, casseroled with red wine and roast veg, under herb crumble – wholesome and substantial – while fillet of sea bass with parsley crust and lemon-butter sauce is lighter and subtle. Desserts are along the treacle tart, bread-and-butter pudding lines, or there's brandy-snap spilling over with fruit salad. A short but adequate wine list has house wine starting at £9.95, with glasses from £2.65.
**Chef/s:** Steve McNally. **Open:** Mon to Sat D only 7 to 9.30; also open Thur to Sat L during July Festival. **Closed:** Tue Nov and Jan to Apr, 2 weeks from 24 Dec. **Meals:** alc (main courses £10 to £13.50). **Service:** not inc. **Details:** Cards accepted. 45 seats. No mobile phones. Music. Children's portions.

## ALSO RECOMMENDED
### ▲ Old Post
43 Holywell Street, Chesterfield, S41 7SH
Tel no: (01246) 279479

At Hugh Cocker's ambitious restaurant you could start with twice-baked haddock and Gruyère soufflé with poached quails' eggs (£6.65), before moving on to roast Cornish hake with white asparagus and roasted langoustines (£20.95). Prices are high, but there is a good-value set menu at £25.50 for three courses and a three-course Sunday lunch

(£20.50). House wine is £12.95. Booking is essential as there are only eight tables. Closed Sat lunch, Sun dinner and Monday.

## Darley Abbey
### Darleys
**Fine dining by the Derwent**
Darley Abbey Mills, Haslams Lane, Darley Abbey, DE22 1DZ
Tel no: (01332) 364987
www.darleys.com
**Modern British | £32**
**Cooking score: 4**

Part of an old cotton mill in a pretty setting overlooking a fast-flowing weir, Darleys lays on the nineteenth-century charm and delivers a relaxed and friendly ambience, yet the restaurant has an elegant, contemporary feel in terms of design and cooking. A seasonally changing menu is based on local supplies and manages to push all the right buttons, with Jonathan Hobson's dishes accurately timed and reassuringly consistent. An up-to-the-minute menu at lunch might offer starters such as mushroom risotto with red-wine foam and chicken and pistachio roulade, and a main course of confit duck leg with vanilla mash and blackberry sauce. At dinner, the carte may produce sweet potato soup with smoked haddock rarebit, followed by ribeye steak with onion Tatin and Guinness sauce, or free-range chicken breast with seared scallops and watercress sauce. For dessert, try the dark chocolate tart with banana ice cream. The short wine list is a mixed bag from around the world, opening with 'personal recommendations' from £14.
**Chef/s:** Jonathan Hobson. **Open:** all week L 12 to 2, Mon to Sat D 7 to 9.30. **Closed:** bank hols.
**Meals:** alc D (main courses £16.50 to £19). Set L £13.95 (2 courses) to £15.95. **Service:** not inc.
**Details:** Cards accepted. 60 seats. 12 seats outside. Air-con. No mobile phones. Wheelchair access. Music. Children's portions. Car parking.

## Hathersage
### George Hotel
**Smart, stylish and modern**
Main Road, Hathersage, S32 1BB
Tel no: (01433) 650436
www.george-hotel.net
**Modern British | £31**
**Cooking score: 4**

This 500-year-old grey stone coaching inn has been brought up to date with more than just a lick of paint, providing an ideal setting for the contemporary cooking that is Ben Handley's forte. A note on the menu proudly states, 'we are proud of the ingredients we use and wherever possible we use suppliers and produce from in and around Derbyshire,' and this commitment to quality is evident throughout the meal. Starters typically include confit of duck and prune rillettes with sweet cured breast and toasted caramelised onion bread. Follow with herb-stuffed slow-roasted free-range pork belly with Bramley apple mash, pancetta, roasted red onions and cider gravy, or sautéed fillet of halibut with butternut squash tortellini, baby leaf spinach, sage butter and Madeira glaze. For dessert, perhaps a dark chocolate delice with toasted orange ice cream and an orange tuile. Wines start at £14.95 a bottle with a decent selection under £20.
**Chef/s:** Ben Handley and Helen Heywood. **Open:** all week 12 to 2.30, 6.30 to 10. **Meals:** alc (main courses £12 to £19). Set L 12.30 to 1.30 and D 6.30 to 7.30 Mon to Fri £13.50 (two courses) to £16. Lounge L menu available. **Service:** not inc.
**Details:** Cards accepted. 50 seats. No mobile phones. Wheelchair access. Music. Children's portions. Car parking.

# ▮ Ridgeway

## Old Vicarage

**Excellent food in a lush country setting**
Ridgeway Moor, Ridgeway, S12 3XW
Tel no: (0114) 247 5814
www.theoldvicarage.co.uk
**Modern British | £50**
**Cooking score: 7**

£5 OFF 🍾 V

Surrounded by a wild-flower meadow and woodland walks, this superlative restaurant could be a world away from Sheffield's urban sprawl, yet it is less than ten miles from the city centre. For many, Tessa Bramley remains not only the quintessential host, but also an inspired presence in the kitchen and one of the senior campaigners for local and regional British food. She is a genuine expert, who understands the workings of her productive garden and the traditions of wild food as well as the intricacies of top-end modern British cuisine. At its best, her food is boldly innovative without being disconnected or outlandish. Ideas really do work on the plate, with dazzling combinations and kaleidoscopic flavours setting the tone. Faultless ingredients are the key, and the kitchen manages to fuse local materials with exotica and gilt-edged luxuries. Slow-braised pork belly tinged with star anise and carrot purée is accompanied by langoustines, while roast fillet of Whitby cod appears in a complex assemblage with Sevruga caviar, steamed mussels, crispy polenta cake and oven-dried tomatoes, all set off by honey and chive foam. Earthier themes also surface in meat dishes such as roast fillet of beef with cinnamon-braised shin, Seville orange and horseradish mash or tarragon-roasted saddle of lamb on a rösti with caramelised sweetbreads and sautéed morels. To follow, there are delights aplenty: sweet woodruff from the garden adds its special fragrance to ice cream, which is served alongside 'old-fashioned tipsy trifle' and a raspberry shortbread tart. Alternatively, follow the well-trodden savoury path with devils on horseback. Unpasteurised cheeses are sourced from across the British Isles; the bespoke selection of coffees and teas is also worth investigating, along with the exquisite chocolates. The wondrous wine list is an exhaustive, intelligently chosen selection, arranged by style and culminating in a roll-call of fabulous names and rare vintages. One reporter bemoaned the apparent lack of half-bottles, although the splendid collection of two dozen 'cheap and cheerful' everyday gluggers more than makes amends (prices start at £15 and all are available by the glass).
**Chef/s:** Tessa Bramley and Nathan Smith. **Open:** Tue to Fri L 12.30 to 2, Tue to Sat D 7 to 9.30 (6.30 to 9.45 Sat). **Closed:** 26 Dec to 4 Jan, first 2 weeks Aug, bank hol Mon and Tue. **Meals:** Set L £30 to £40, Set D £55 to £65. **Service:** not inc. **Details:** Cards accepted. 46 seats. 16 seats outside. No mobile phones. Wheelchair access. Music. Children's portions. Car parking.

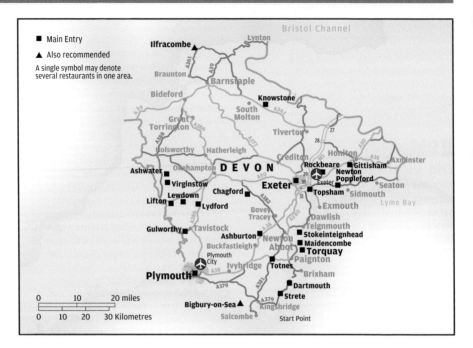

- ■ Main Entry
- ▲ Also recommended

A single symbol may denote several restaurants in one area.

Bristol Channel

Lynton
Ilfracombe ▲
Braunton ■
Barnstaple
Bideford
Knowstone ■
South Molton
Great Torrington ■
Tiverton ● 27
28
Holsworthy Hatherleigh
Crediton
Honiton Axminster
Ashwater ■ Okehampton ■ **DEVON** Rockbeare ■ Gittisham
29 Newton Poppleford ■
■ Virginstow Exeter ■ 30 Exeter ● Seaton
Lydford ■ Chagford ■ Topsham ● Sidmouth
Lifton ■ Lewdown 31
Lydford ■ Bovey Exmouth
Tracey Lyme Bay
Gulworthy ■ Tavistock Dawlish
Ashburton ■ Newton Teignmouth ■ Stokeinteignhead
Buckfastleigh Abbot ■ Maidencombe
Plymouth Ivybridge ■ Totnes ■ Torquay
City Paignton
Plymouth ● Brixham
A379 ■ Dartmouth
■ Strete
Bigbury-on-Sea ▲ Kingsbridge
Salcombe ● Start Point

0   10   20 miles
0   10   20   30 Kilometres

## ■ Ashburton

## Agaric

**Unpretentious cooking and surroundings**
30 North Street, Ashburton, TQ13 7QD
Tel no: (01364) 654478
www.agaricrestaurant.co.uk
**Modern British | £31**
**Cooking score: 4**

🛏 ⋎

Behind the unprepossessing dark shopfront – easily spotted in the middle of town – is this charming, rustic, single-roomed restaurant with a husband-and-wife team at the helm and a real home-from-home vibe. Nick Coiley does the cooking while Sophie runs front-of-house. The best local and seasonal Devon produce is championed here, alongside own-grown garden produce and home-made breads and pastries, jams, preserves and cured meat and fish. The result is imaginative, and dishes are confident, delivering well-balanced, emphatic flavours without over-elaboration. Take roasted best end of local

lamb with herb crust served with celeriac, a garlic and rosemary tart and rosemary gravy, or perhaps grilled turbot teamed with marsh and pickled rock samphire and a nettle chive sauce. A rhubarb and elderflower oaty crumble with clotted cream might catch the eye at dessert, as could the selection of West Country cheeses, while the short but well-chosen wine list sets out on its global journey with Argentinean house at £14.95.
**Chef/s:** Nick Coiley. **Open:** Wed to Fri L 12 to 2, first and last Sun L, Wed to Sat D 7 to 9. **Closed:** 2 weeks at Christmas, 2 weeks Aug. **Meals:** alc (main courses £15 to £18). Set L £14.95 (2 courses). **Service:** not inc. **Details:** Cards accepted. 28 seats. 12 seats outside. No music. No mobile phones. Wheelchair access. Children's portions.

# ■ Ashwater

## Blagdon Manor

**Refreshing country-house hotel**
Ashwater, EX21 5DF
Tel no: (01409) 211224
www.blagdon.com
**Modern European | £36**
**Cooking score: 2**

Liz and Steve Morey have clocked up six years at their Grade II-listed manor with its airy décor, splendid views and resident chocolate brown Labradors. They succeed in their aim to provide quality food and wine without pretension, using generally simple treatments to bring out the best of their well-sourced produce. Lunch offers a cheaper and lighter selection than the dinner menu, say baked field mushroom with beetroot relish and Cornish Blue, then rump of lamb with macaroni gratin and Parmesan and carrot emulsion, while dinner delivers tian of crab with smoked salmon roulade and caviar dressing, and sea bream with squid tempura, aubergine purée and ratatouille jus. A meatier route might begin with duck three ways (pressed foie gras and ham hock, rillettes, and smoked, with grapefruit salad), and proceed to breast of guinea fowl and pancetta with black pudding, caramelised pears and Gewürztraminer juices. West Country cheeses are the savoury alternative to desserts such as hot cinnamon and pear soufflé with Drambuie ice cream. An enterprising and fairly priced wine list from around the world opens at £13.50.
**Chef/s:** Steve Morey. **Open:** Wed to Sun 12 to 2, Tue to Sat 7 to 9 (residents only Sun D and Mon D). **Closed:** 2 weeks Jan, 2 weeks Oct. **Meals:** Set L £17 (2 courses) to £20 (3 courses), Set L Sun £23.50, Set D £32 (2 courses) to £35 (3 courses). **Service:** not inc. **Details:** Cards accepted. 24 seats. No music. No mobile phones. Wheelchair access. Car parking.

## ALSO RECOMMENDED

## ▲ Oyster Shack

Milburn Orchard Farm, Stakes Hill, Bigbury-on-Sea, TQ7 4BE
Tel no: (01548) 810876
www.oystershack.co.uk

The 'shack' itself is decorated with seaside bric-à-brac and, unsurprisingly, oysters are the thing here. Farmed in the River Avon, they come either au naturel (at £1 each) or in a variety of styles, including with spicy sausage (£5.95 for six) or garlic butter and Parmesan (£6.95 for six). There's an impressive seafood menu offering chilli-fried crab claws (£5.95) or local moules marinière (£4.95) ahead of grilled gilthead bream fillets with a lemon, tomato and parsley vierge (£13.95) or local sea bass baked with fennel, dill and white wine (£15.95). House wine is £12.50. Open all week, closed Mon from Nov to June.

# ■ Chagford

★NEW ENTRY★
## Gidleigh Park

**Exemplary country-house dining**
Chagford, TQ13 8HH
Tel no: (01647) 432367
www.gidleigh.com
**Modern European | £50**
**Cooking score: 7**

Closed for refurbishment for most of 2006 (and absent from last year's Guide), with building work completed it is clear that this elegant, civilised and eminently likeable country house has lost none of its distinct Englishness – 'rooms, décor and ambience remain superb'. The half-timbered Edwardian building emerges at the end of a long and winding Devon lane with the moor at its back and the waters of the Upper Teign tumbling past the front. It is in an enchanted place, retaining the presence of a grand establishment with impressive standards – as they might be at the price. Eating takes place at generously spaced tables in one of the two interconnecting panelled dining rooms. Michael Caines' take on French cooking is contemporary and clearly focused, producing food that is as easy to understand as it is to enjoy. Tastes are rounded, with no sharp edges, and among highlights have been a delicate tartlet of poached quails' eggs and rich onion confit dotted with slithers of smoked bacon and truffle and teamed with roast quail in a light quail jus, and main courses of lamb with fondant potato – a perfect piece of meat perfectly matched by classic Mediterranean flavours of onion and thyme purée, tomato fondue and tapenade jus – and slow-roast local venison and braised pork belly served with red cabbage and fig and chestnut purée. Fine, unflamboyant craftsmanship creates deep satisfaction maybe via an amuse-bouche of rich foie gras and lentil soup, or miniature desserts served with coffee: lemon tart, crème brûlée, chocolate mousse. Desserts proper, perhaps a coconut pannacotta with sorbets of coconut milk, pineapple and chilli, just about keep pace, but first-rate cheeses, a mix of French and British, are very fine. Sometimes portions are thought small, but 'the generous quantities of beautiful breads' saved the day for one reporter. The broad-minded wine list with its lively explorations of both classic and regional France is a gem. It contrives to be both very serious and wholly approachable – due in large part to fairly reasonable prices for the quality and a decent selection by the glass. Intelligent selections from other regions, both European and New World, include top names from California, and some smart choices from Italy. Prices open at £25.

**Chef/s:** Michael Caines. **Open:** All week L 12 to 2.,30 D 7 to 9.45. **Meals:** Set L Mon to Thu £27 (2 courses) £35 (3 courses), D £75 and tasting menu £85. **Service:** optional. **Details:** Cards accepted. 52 seats. Separate bar. Wheelchair access. Car parking.

# ▌Dartmouth

## New Angel
Historic foodie destination
2 South Embankment, Dartmouth, TQ6 9BH
Tel no: (01803) 839425
www.thenewangel.co.uk
**Modern Anglo-French | £39**
**Cooking score: 4**

🍷 ✙

'You are not obliged to eat three courses, but of course you may if you wish,' states the menu at John Burton Race's New Angel, a user-friendly structure that admirably demonstrates the flexibility of this harbourside operation. Indeed, one visitor, surprised to find the restaurant open mid-morning, popped in for coffee and a croissant and headed back for lunch later, taking the menu at its word and ordering just half a grilled lobster with Café de Paris butter, new potatoes and tarragon salad. Menus are a sensible length and keep things simple without thereby sacrificing interest, focusing on showing off the good raw materials. Sourcing is taken seriously: grilled mackerel fillets with marinated root vegetables, horseradish cream and aged balsamic, or chump of lamb with a herb crust, served with garlic creamed potato, baby aubergine, vine cherry tomatoes and red-wine sauce typify the marriage of local ingredients with carefully controlled flavourings. The restaurant is split over two floors. At ground level is a 'relaxed, modern eating area (with an open-to-view kitchen) that can be noisy at peak times; upstairs is a quieter, more 'traditional in character' dining room. House wine starts at £13.

**Chef/s:** John Burton-Race, Robert Spencer. **Open:** Tue to Sun L 12 to 2.30, Tue to Sat D 6.30 to 10; also open bank hol Mon. **Closed:** Jan. **Meals:** alc (main courses £16 to £29). **Service:** not inc. **Details:** Cards accepted. 80 seats. Air-con. Wheelchair access. Music. Children's portions.

# Exeter

## Royal Clarence Hotel, Michael Caines at ABode

**Excellent showcase for local produce**
Cathedral Yard, Exeter, EX1 1HD
Tel no: (01392) 223638
www.michaelcaines.com
**French | £43**
**Cooking score: 4**

The fine fourteenth-century building is now a vibrant venue in Michael Caines'ABode group. In the chic restaurant, polished boards, big mirrors and bold pictures on white-cream walls provide the backdrop for Ross Melling's modern repertoire of French-inspired dishes. Menus showcase local produce: Brixham scallops and Roswell's Farm confit violet potatoes (with lemon purée, and niçoise olive rounds) and best end shoulder of Devon lamb (with crushed potatoes, ratatouille and gremolata), while locally landed fish appears as a main dish of monkfish épinard pain perdu, glazed salsify, roasted garlic and red-wine butter. Sophisticated desserts have included coconut pannacotta with a pineapple sorbet, caramelised pineapple and ginger butterscotch. For the quality, the set-lunch menu is exceptionally good value; a perfectly cooked breast of guinea fowl served with a creamy broad bean and spring onion risotto has been given an enthusiastic thumbs-up. The wine list runs to 65 bins; house red and white wines from £17.
**Chef/s:** Ross Melling. **Open:** Mon to Sat 12 to 2.30, 7 to 10. **Meals:** alc (main courses £19 to £25). Set L £12.50 (2 courses), Set D £20 (2 courses). **Service:** not inc. **Details:** Cards accepted. 80 seats. Air-con. No music. No mobile phones. Wheelchair access. Children's portions.

# Gittisham

## Combe House

**A wonderful country retreat**
Gittisham, EX14 3AD
Tel no: (01404) 540400
www.thishotel.com
**Modern British | £40**
**Cooking score: 4**

The drive through sweeping countryside – across three cattle grids and along a snaking mile-long drive of a 3,500-acre estate – makes for an impressive curtain raiser to this country-house hotel. The lounge has lots of warm colours, cushioned comforts and lovely views, all in predictable traditional-English fashion, while the intimate dining room's dominant feature is its elaborate ceiling plasterwork. The accomplished kitchen's strength lies in the quality of its suppliers, with chef Hadleigh Barrett dedicated to sourcing the finest seasonal ingredients, with herbs, fruit and vegetables from the hotel's own potager in season. His fixed-price menus admirably list the provenance of said local suppliers, with traditional breeds of meat delivered as carcasses and hung and butchered in-house. Take a roast loin of lamb served with a braised-shoulder suet pudding and garlic and rosemary dauphinoise, or maybe halibut from the day-boat catch at Brixham, delivered with a foie-gras crust, creamed celeriac and Jerusalem artichoke velouté. The hundred-or-so-bin global list is well chosen, with France in ascendancy but there is plenty of New World and European support. Bottles kick off from £17, while halves are laudably plentiful.
**Chef/s:** Hadleigh Barrett and Stewart Brown. **Open:** all week L 12 to 2, D 7 to 9.30. **Meals:** Set L £20 (2 courses) to £26, Set D £39.50 to £49.. **Service:** not inc. **Details:** Cards accepted. 60 seats. 30 seats outside. No mobile phones. Wheelchair access. Music. Children's portions. Car parking.

# ▌ Gulworthy

## Horn of Plenty

Hugely ambitious kitchen
Gulworthy, PL19 8JD
Tel no: (01822) 832528
www.thehornofplenty.co.uk
**Modern British | £40**
**Cooking score: 6**

£5 OFF ⬧ 🍷 ⤬ Ⅴ

The creeper-clad, grey-stone building in the heart of the verdant Tamar valley certainly enjoys a fabulous setting. Tranquillity reigns, as indeed it must have done pretty much since the house was built in Victorian times for one of the Duke of Bedford's officials. You could be forgiven for thinking the surroundings would inspire a sleepy version of country-house cooking, but Peter Gorton's sights have always been trained higher than that. Ideas come thick and fast, as in first courses such as grilled sea bass on a potato blini with tahini sauce, or braised lamb shank squeezed into tortellini and sauced with a mushroom beurre noisette. Mains command attention for the quality of materials like the local lamb that comes with spinach and garlic, all done up in a leek wrapping and sauced with Madeira. Fish are the often overlooked species – brill and lemon sole, the latter with gnocchi and a sauce of white wine and saffron. Vegetarians will enjoy a right royal assiette of various concoctions. At meal's end, you might like to relax into one of the trad British puddings, like steamed ginger sponge with vanilla ice cream, or light out into pastures new in the shape of pineapple fritters with Indian-spiced ice cream and lime and caramel sauce. Ten house selections from £15 head up a wine list that does the French regions in solicitous detail, before essaying a brief *tour d'horizon* of elsewhere.

**Chef/s:** Peter Gorton. **Open:** All week L 12 to 2, D 7 to 9. **Closed:** 24, 25 and 26 Dec. **Meals:** Set L £26.50, Set D £45. **Service:** not inc. **Details:** Cards accepted. 60 seats. 15 seats outside. Air-con. No mobile phones. Wheelchair access. Music. Children's portions. Car parking.

## ALSO RECOMMENDED

## ▲ Quay

11 The Quay, Ilfracombe, EX34 9EQ
Tel no: (01271) 868090
www.11thequay.co.uk

Part-owned by Brit-Art main man Damien Hirst, this good-looking venue is now a big player on Ilfracombe's trendy quayside development. Formal meals are served in the upstairs Atlantic Room, which has great views and a menu that promises contemporary starters like ham hock cannelloni with crushed peas and summer truffle (£9) ahead of halibut 'Wellington' with red onion confit and cauliflower purée (£20.50). Desserts could include Baileys crème brûlée with pistachio biscotti (£7). Casual snacks and brasserie-style dishes are served in the ground-floor bar. Reasonably priced wines with a French bias from £12 (£3.20 a glass). Open Wed to Sun L, Wed to Sat D.

# ▌ Knowstone

## Mason's Arms

Complex modern food
Knowstone, EX36 4RY
Tel no: (01398) 341231
www.masonsarmsdevon.co.uk
**Modern British | £31**
**Cooking score: 6**

A neatly thatched, medieval cottage pub hidden away in an Exmoor backwater, the Mason's Arms provides an unlikely setting for serious restaurant food with high aspirations. Mark Dodson learned his culinary craft at Cliveden and the Waterside Inn, Bray (see entry) before bringing his family down to Devon, which explains why customers are now presented with diminutive portions of pan-fried foie gras and citrus fruits or red mullet with crushed new potatoes and saffron bouillon. Make no mistake: Dodson can deliver the goods and he has made the Mason's Arms a serious contender in the Devon food stakes since his arrival. The fact that there is a rich larder of local produce on his doorstep must help, and he transforms what is on offer with a sure touch, clarity and impeccable timing. A salad of crab is dressed with tomato vinaigrette, basil oil and fennel as a starter, while main courses aim for a rustic, earthy impact: roulade of pork belly comes with braised red cabbage and apple compote, while fillet of Devon beef and 'rich oxtail' are paired with parsnip purée and red wine jus. This is emphatically not 'gastropub' food. To finish, farmhouse cheeses from Devon and Somerset sit alongside impressively executed desserts such as iced aniseed parfait with blackcurrant coulis and caraway biscuit or a shortbread mille-feuille of pineapple and coconut cream. The wine list is a modest, unshowy slate of carefully chosen bottles, with France and the New World sharing the honours. House wines start at £11.75 and several are served by the glass (from £3.75).

**Chef/s:** Mark Dodson. **Open:** Tue to Sun L 12 to 2, Tue to Sat D 7 to 9. **Closed:** first 2 weeks Jan. **Meals:** alc exc Sun L (main courses £13 to £17.50). Set L Sun £29.50. **Service:** not inc. **Details:** Cards accepted. 25 seats. 20 seats outside. No music. Wheelchair access. Children's portions. Car parking.

## ▌Lewdown

## Lewtrenchard Manor

**Vibrant contemporary food**
Lewdown, EX20 4PN
Tel no: (01566) 783222
www.lewtrenchard.co.uk
**Modern British | £36**
**Cooking score: 6**

£5 OFF  ▪  ☷  ⋎

On the site of a dwelling recorded in the Domesday Book, Lewtrenchard Manor proudly displays its many-gabled Jacobean credentials – in fact, the whole house is etched with architectural embellishments. Inside, there are stunning ornate ceilings and granite window-frames, superb carvings and swathes of dark oak panelling. At one time, this was home to Victorian hymn writer Sabine Baring Gould (who penned *Onward, Christian Soldiers* in the front hall) and his portraits are everywhere. Despite the hotel's remote

location on Dartmoor, chef/patron Jason Hornbuckle garners an impressive array of home-grown and local produce: regular supplies of seafood come from the West Country ports and the hotel's walled garden satisfies much of the kitchen's needs. Fixed-price menus are written around what is currently available and dishes are delivered with razor-sharp precision and clarity. Vibrant modernism colours just about everything, from starters such as John Dory with squid ragoût, chorizo, sweet peppers and feta cheese salsa to wacky desserts like Horlicks and white chocolate tart with milkshake and Guinness ice cream. In between, the kitchen puts together assiettes of rare breed pork and serves confit of organic salmon with crushed potatoes, sautéed scallops and basil sauce. A separate, nine-course tasting menu (with wine recommendations) is also available in the hotel's Library dining room. Britain's youngest Master of Wine, Liam Stevenson, is the driving force behind the superlative wine list, which must rank as one of the most outstanding slates in the West Country. Pages of glorious stuff from Burgundy, Bordeaux and the Rhône are bolstered by bold choices from the New World; half-bottles are plentiful and a dozen house recommendations start at £16 (£3.75 a glass).

**Chef/s:** Jason Hornbuckle. **Open:** Tue to Sun L 12 to 1.30, all week D 7 to 9. **Meals:** Set L £15 (2 courses) to £19. Set D £40 (3 courses) to £99 (inc wine). Bar menu available. **Service:** not inc. **Details:** Cards accepted. 45 seats. 16 seats outside. Wheelchair access. Music. Car parking.

## ■ Lifton

### Arundell Arms

**Simple, uncomplicated class**
Lifton, PL16 0AA
Tel no: (01566) 784666
www.arundellarms.com
Modern British | £33
Cooking score: 5

£5 OFF ♦ ⊨ Ⅴ

The reputation of this eighteenth-century coaching inn, a first-rate venue for shooting and fishing parties, spreads far beyond its immediate locale (a tiny village on the old A30). Anne Voss Bark's dependable hand on the tiller is much appreciated, while the kitchen is headed by Steven Pidgeon. His cooking demonstrates an impressive range of skills, applied to impeccable raw materials. Indeed, the great strength here lies in the quality of the supplies, many local, from meat and game right down to the courgette flowers served in a summer salad, and the front page of the menu lists the provenance and suppliers of the fish, meat, vegetables and dairy produce. This is cooking that achieves what it sets out to do, be it a comforting dish of properly cooked lamb's kidney's with bacon, mushrooms and excellent chips served in the bar, or coarse pheasant, pigeon and duck terrine with pistachio, prunes and red onion marmalade or poached chicken breast with creamed leeks, tarragon and white wine, in the elegant dining room. The carte is supplemented by daily changing set-price deals, which in spring might mean starting with fillet of turbot and scallops served with English asparagus and hollandaise sauce, then marinated fillet of lamb with honey and lavender and a sauce of broad beans, garden peas and white wine, with a gratin of strawberries, champagne sorbet and a sweet wine sabayon for dessert. Other seasonal items have included a couple of well received winter specialities – a warm wood mushroom salad with garlic croûtons, Parmesan shavings and truffle oil, and wild venison with baby vegetables and a red wine sauce. Wines are well chosen, offering good value drinking from around the world. Seven house wines, red, white and rosé, start at £15. **Chef/s:** Steven Pidgeon. **Open:** all week 12.30 to 2, 7.30 to 9.30. **Closed:** 24 Dec, D 25 Dec. **Meals:** Set L £23 (2 courses) to £27.50, Set D £38 to £42. Bar menu available. **Service:** not inc. **Details:** Cards accepted. 70 seats. 20 seats outside. Wheelchair access. Music. Children's portions. Car parking.

## ■ Lydford

### Dartmoor Inn

**High-class comfort food**
Lydford, EX20 4AY
Tel no: (01822) 820221
www.dartmoorinn.com
Modern British | £30
Cooking score: 3

£5 OFF ⊨ Ⅴ

Despite outward appearances, this is one country pub where food definitely takes precedence over pints of beer. Set in the Dartmoor National Park, the stylishly decorated building exudes a feeling of sincerity and goodwill, which counts for a lot. It consists of a series of tiny dining rooms – and some space for just drinking and sitting – with wood or stone floors, open fires and a rustic look that's straight out of the pages of Country Living. Philip Burgess cooks a menu of high-class comfort food in keeping with the tone, executed to a degree that inspires confidence. Braised oxtail with root vegetable sauce, and fish and chips, give a good solid British dimension to modern cooking with its feet on the ground, but there's a Mediterranean feel to the evening menu, which could deliver avocado and asparagus salad with pea shoots and balsamic wine vinegar, and scallops with wild garlic cream. The 'easy dining' menu (served in the bar) is particularly good value, perhaps offering roasted tomato soup with pesto, lamb's liver with bacon and herb butter, and caramelised rhubarb cake. Karen Burgess oversees 'friendly and efficient' staff and there's a grown-up wine list, too. House wines from £12.95.

Chef/s: Philip Burgess and Andrew Honey. **Open:** Tue to Sun L 12 to 2.30 (3 Sun), Tue to Sat D 6.30 to 9.30. **Meals:** alc (main courses £13 to £18.50). **Service:** not inc. **Details:** Cards accepted. 80 seats. 25 seats outside. No mobile phones. Music. Children's portions. Car parking.

# Maidencombe

## Orestone Manor
**Intrepid cooking and imperial exoticism**
Rockhouse Lane, Maidencombe, TQ1 4SX
Tel no: (01803) 328098
www.orestonemanor.com
**Modern British | £38**
**New Chef**

£5 OFF 🍷 🍽 V

This exotic colonial-style hideaway perched on the hills running down to Babbacombe Bay, is discreetly tucked away from Torquay's hustle and bustle and enjoys fabulous sea views from its verandah, terrace and dining room. Expect elegance and comfort, especially in the drawing room, which has a distinct Raffles-like ambience. But the big draw is Chris May's ambitious modern British cooking, which makes good use of top-notch regional ingredients. This translates as Start Bay crab trifle, or chargrilled scallops with roasted cauliflower purée, followed by poached fillet of South Devon beef with confit onion and horseradish emulsion, or halibut with white bean cassoulet and ham hock beignet on the carte. Desserts may take in white chocolate soup with dark chocolate and lemongrass ravioli. A summer lunch on the verandah is a real treat, especially the excellent value set lunch menu, or try something light from the terrace menu, perhaps avocado risotto or fishcake with spinach, poached egg and a chive beurre blanc. The wine list is arranged by style and offers plenty of interest at all price levels from £14.95.
Chef/s: Chris May. **Open:** all week 12 to 2, 7 to 9. **Closed:** Jan. **Meals:** alc (main courses £18.25 to £23.50). Set L £15 (2 courses) £17.50 (3 courses). **Service:** not inc. **Details:** Cards accepted. 50 seats. 46 seats outside. No mobile phones. Wheelchair access. Music. Children's portions. Car parking.

# Newton Poppleford

## Moores'
**Relaxed, formal dining**
6 Greenbank, High Street, Newton Poppleford, EX10 0EB
Tel no: (01395) 568100
www.mooresrestaurant.co.uk
**Modern British | £25**
**Cooking score: 1**

£5 OFF 🍽 V £30

New at Moores' this year is the addition of afternoon coffee and cakes, served in the conservatory. The restaurant, where fresh flowers on crisp white linen add a touch of elegance, is reserved for more formal dining, though the mood remains relaxed. Three-course fixed-price menus offer good choice from a repertoire of straightforward modern British cooking, which translates as starters of sautéed squid and chorizo with mango dressing, or pea and rocket risotto with Parmesan, perhaps followed by confit duck leg on pearl barley and spring vegetable casserole, or pan-fried wild sea bass on pak choi with vegetable linguine and Gewürztraminer cream. Lavender and honey crème brûlée, or rhubarb and pear butterscotch compote with walnut crumble and yoghurt sound like good ways to finish. A well-presented, unpretentious wine list opens with Spanish house at £12.95 a bottle.
Chef/s: Jonathan Moore. **Open:** Tue to Sun L 12 to 2.30, Tue to Sat D 7 to 9.30. **Closed:** First two weeks Jan. **Meals:** Set L Tue to Sat £13.95 (2 courses), Set D Fri and Sat £24.50. **Service:** not inc. **Details:** Cards accepted. 32 seats. 12 seats outside. No mobile phones. Wheelchair access. Music. Children's portions.

## ■ Plymouth

### Tanners

Modern cooking in a historical setting
Prysten House, Finewell Street, Plymouth,
PL1 2AE
Tel no: (01752) 252001
www.tannersrestaurant.com
**Modern British | £30**
**Cooking score: 3**

The Tanner brothers' popular restaurant may be tucked away down a back street but it is well worth seeking out. It occupies one of the city's oldest buildings, a former merchant's house built around a courtyard at the end of the fifteenth century. Décor plays on the historical theme, while the cooking takes a more up-to-date approach. Inventive starters combine glazed pork belly with roast monkfish and caramel dressing, or place seared haddock on a bed of thyme-infused lentils with cauliflower velouté. Main courses, meanwhile, typically feature seared wild sea bass with crab, crushed potatoes and braised baby gem lettuce, alongside a rack of lamb with spring greens, sauté artichokes and almond tarragon dressing, and to finish there might be dark chocolate fondant, malted milk ice cream and toffee foam, or saffron pears with lemon pannacotta and natural yoghurt sorbet. Lunch options are in a similar vein but slightly simpler, taking in risottos, salads and noodle dishes. An extensive wine list is well annotated and arranged by style, prices starting at £13.95 for house Merlot and Sauvignon Blanc.
**Chef/s:** Christopher and James Tanner, Jay Barker-Jones. **Open:** Tue to Sat 12 to 2.30, 7 to 9.30. **Closed:** 24 to 26 and 31 Dec, first week Jan. **Meals:** Set L £19.50, Set D £32. Light L menu available.
**Service:** not inc. **Details:** Cards accepted. 45 seats. 40 seats outside. No mobile phones. Wheelchair access. Music. Children's portions.

## ■ Rockbeare

### Jack in the Green

Roadside pub showcases local produce
Rockbeare, EX5 2EE
Tel no: (01404) 822240
www.jackinthegreen.uk.com
**Global | £30**
**Cooking score: 3**

While there's a sophisticated, contemporary feel to this white-painted roadside pub, leather chairs and a focus on food have not obscured its original function. Well-kept hand-pumped beers, such as Otter Ale, are still served for those who only want to pop in for a pint. Once ensconced, however, your attention may well be drawn to the bar menu with its offers of locally smoked fish, Devon cheeses and items such as lamb and vegetable hotpot. The kitchen takes full account of Devon produce from its established network of local suppliers – name-checked throughout – and in the smart restaurant asparagus tart with morel mushrooms, baby leaf spinach and a cep vinaigrette or lambs' sweetbreads with chicken mousse, puff pasty and morels, sound a more metropolitan note than may be expected in a Devon pub. Main courses might be typified by pepper lemon sole fillets with a lemon and sorrel mayonnaise, or pork tenderloin with sage and anchovies, five-spiced onion confit, potato fondant and white onion and thyme velouté. To finish there's homely sticky toffee pudding or bitter chocolate tart with lime ice cream. Eight house wines are served by the glass, from £3.60, with £13.50 the baseline for bottles on the pleasing individual wine list.
**Chef/s:** Matt Mason and Craig Sampson. **Open:** Mon to Sat 12 to 2 (2.30 Fri and Sat), 6 to 9.30 (10 Fri and Sat). Sun 12 to 9.30. **Closed:** 25 Dec to 6 Jan. **Meals:** alc (main courses £17.50 to £19.50). Set L and D Mon to Sat £25 (3 courses). Set L and D Sun £18.95 (2 courses) to £24.45. Bar menu available.
**Service:** not inc. **Details:** Cards accepted. 150 seats. 25 seats outside. Air-con. Wheelchair access. Music. Children's portions. Children allowed. Car parking.

# Stokeinteignhead

★NEW ENTRY★
## Chasers
**Darren Bunn's latest enterprise**
Stoke Road, Stokeinteignhead, TQ12 4QS
Tel no: (01626) 873670
www.thechasers.co.uk
**Gastropub**
**Cooking score: 4**
£5 OFF ✔

Having put Torquay's Orestone Manor Hotel firmly on Devon's gastronomic map, chef Darren 'Bunny' Bunn headed two miles inland with wife, Hayley, in August 2006 to take on this thatched and cob-built, sixteenth-century Devon longhouse. The pub-restaurant may be tricky to locate, as it's hidden down tortuously narrow lanes in a sleepy village, but the journey is well worth the effort for Bunn's inspired cooking. He takes a modern approach: his seasonal British carte, with classical roots, is sensibly compact and appealing, and utilises well-sourced local produce, particularly meat and game, but there's first-rate fish too. Expect accomplished, well-presented dishes, from a signature starter of fishcake with free-range egg and a light, well-flavoured chive beurre blanc, to main courses of roast monkfish with sweet pepper sauce, and crispy roast pork belly with braised red cabbage and roasted cauliflower purée. Classic chocolate terrine with orange marmalade ice cream makes a rich finish. In keeping with the informal pub atmosphere, Bunn offers a pleasing choice of light dishes, salads and sandwiches, and a great-value set-lunch menu. Service from Hayley is informal and efficient. Wines kick off at £11 for a decent house selection.
**Chef/s:** Darren Bunn. **Open:** Tue to Sun, 12 to 2, (Fri, Sat to 2.30, Sun to 3) Tue to Sat D 7 to 9 (Fri, Sat to 9.30). **Closed:** 25 Dec, last week Feb. **Meals:** alc (main courses £11.50 to 16.95) Set L £15.95 (3 courses) Set D £19.95 to £26.50 (3 courses). **Service:** not inc. **Details:** Cards accepted. 45 seats. 20 seats outside. Wheelchair access. Music. Children's portions.

# Strete
## Kings Arms
**Seafood gastropub by the sea**
Dartmouth Road, Strete, TQ6 0RW
Tel no: (01803) 770377
www.kingsarms-dartmouth.co.uk
**Seafood | £33**
**Cooking score: 2**

A pebble's throw from the coastal path, this splendid eighteenth-century pub is hard to miss because of its ornate, cast-iron balcony which overlooks the main road outside. Although this is still very much a pub for locals to have a pint of ale and gossip, it has become a gastronomic destination because of its seafood. The bar and terrace menu features Thai fishcakes with mango and coconut salad, and soft herring roes on toast with bacon, capers and nut brown butter, while the carte might start with the likes of seared local scallops with braised Puy lentils and Pedro Ximenez syrup and move on to local sand sole with lemon and pistachio butter. South Devon ribeye steak with Portabello mushroom, hand-cut chips and Café de Paris butter is an alternative meat dish, and West Country cheeses make a savoury ending, with lemon and lime tart or poached pear with pear sponge and pear sherbet for dessert. The wine list is an intelligent, and reasonably priced, selection from around the world. Over a dozen bottles are all served by the glass. House wines start at £11.95.
**Chef/s:** Rob Dawson. **Open:** Tue to Sun L 12 to 2, Tue to Sat D 6.30 to 9.30. **Closed:** last week Jan, first week Feb, first week June. **Meals:** alc (main courses £13.50 to £22). Bar L menu available. **Service:** not inc. **Details:** Cards accepted. 30 seats. 30 seats outside. No music. No mobile phones. Children's portions. Car parking.

## Topsham

### La Petite Maison

**Personable family-run restaurant**
35 Fore Street, Topsham, EX3 0HR
Tel no: (01392) 873660
www.lapetitemaison.co.uk
Anglo-French | £33
Cooking score: 4

The name just about sums up the mood, style and intimacy of this endearing family-run restaurant, which runs along happily with Douglas and Elizabeth Pestell at the helm. It occupies a centuries-old building not far from the river in trendy Topsham, and pleases visitors with a distinctive brand of modern Anglo-French cooking. The owners put great store by top-notch West Country produce, with pigeon, outdoor-reared Somerset pork and free-range Devon duck all receiving a name-check on the menu. Local seafood also gets a good airing in dishes such as fillet of mackerel with fennel and English pea salad or sea bass and monkfish with a chive potato cake, asparagus and crab bisque. Elsewhere, there are sound mainstream ideas like chump of lamb with garlic mash and ratatouille or fillet steak with sarladaise potatoes, wild mushroom and red-wine jus. Desserts stay with the classics for chocolate truffle torte, apple and walnut crumble or crème brûlée, then it's back to the West Country for farmhouse cheeses with home-made chutney. A few wines from Devon vineyards show up on the well-spread wine list. Prices are eminently fair, with house selections weighing in at £14.95.
**Chef/s:** Douglas Pestell and Sara Bright. **Open:** Tue to Sat 12.30 to 2, 7 to 10. **Meals:** Set L £19.50 (2 courses) to £22.50, Set D £26.95 (2 courses) to £32.95. **Service:** not inc. **Details:** Cards accepted. 30 seats. Music.

## Torquay

### Elephant

**Ambition and affordability**
3-4 Beacon Terrace, Torquay, TQ1 2BH
Tel no: (01803) 200044
www.elephantrestaurant.co.uk
Modern British | £29
Cooking score: 6
£5 OFF  V  £30

In a location on Torquay's sea front opposite 'a Brewer's Fayre and just round the corner from several lively bars', Simon Hulstone has struggled to attract that level of spend, especially at lunchtime, for the high level of cooking for which he is known. So, since the last edition of the Guide, he has turned the ground floor of the restaurant into an informal brasserie, creating a menu that will pull in ordinary folk for just a big bowl of mussels and a glass of wine, or potted shrimps and slow-braised beef with truffle mash. The longer-established fine dining side of the business has decamped to the more intimate confines of The Room upstairs, with its spectacular views of the illuminated bay outside; walls decorated with framed menus gathered during gastronomic travels give notice of the culinary ambition at work here. The cooking utilises a finely honed network of local suppliers to provide the very best raw materials. Such startling freshness can be found in a starter of risotto of squid ink and cuttlefish with crispy chicken wings and roast onion foam, while pan-roasted day-boat John Dory was an eyebrow-raising main course at inspection, the precisely cooked fish being served with the silkiest parsnip purée, a delightful verjus and spring onion butter sauce and some unadvertised pieces of veal sweetbread. Desserts like dark chocolate and malt tart with milk ice cream show the top form in the pastry section. A short, punchy wine list starts at £14.50 and has a fair few by the glass, from £3.50.
**Chef/s:** Simon Hulstone. **Open:** Tue to Sat, 7 to 9.30. **Closed:** First two weeks Jan. **Meals:** Set D £32.50 (2 courses) to £39.50 (3 courses). **Service:** not inc.

**Details:** Cards accepted. 24 seats. Air-con. No mobile phones. Wheelchair access. Music. Children's portions.

## ALSO RECOMMENDED
### ▲ No. 7 Fish Bistro
7 Beacon Terrace, Torquay, TQ1 2BH
Tel no: (01803) 295055
www.no7-fish.com

Long-established and very much part of the scenery on the harbour side at Torquay, this converted Regency house has barely changed since it opened. Family-run and friendly, the dark wooden floors, seafaring knick-knacks and colourful oilcloths on the tables are as traditional as the wide-ranging menus. Seafood broth or hot and cold shellfish platters are followed by lobster and crab freshly boiled or grilled with garlic and brandy, or a fillet of plaice filled with peeled prawns and baked with a thermidor sauce. Scallops simmered with mushrooms, vermouth and lemon, and monkfish baked with black pepper and sea salt expand the repertoire. Desserts include home-made apple crumble, a selection of local cheeses and the well-priced wine list sets sail at £12.

## ■ Totnes
### Effings
**Food emporium**
50 Fore Street, Totnes, TQ9 5RP
Tel no: (01803) 863435
**Modern European | £30**
**Cooking score: 2**

With the branch in Exeter now closed, focus is firmly on the original venue, an Aladdin's Cave of a restaurant/deli in the heart of Totnes. As well as charcuterie, cheeses, savoury and sweet tarts, and home-made meals to take away, a few modest tables are in demand throughout the day for light dishes and snacks, peaking at lunchtime when a blackboard menu offers dishes with the emphasis on seasonal and locally sourced produce. Lambs' sweetbreads with asparagus

salad and a green peppercorn sauce, then steamed local and organic trout with fennel and tomato, new potatoes and local vegetables, or a French country plate with Bayonne ham, saucisson, terrine and cornichons are typical offerings. Simple desserts include mango and strawberry gratin with own-made vanilla ice cream. A compact wine list opens with house wine at £13.75.
**Chef/s:** Karl Rasmussen. **Open:** Mon to Sat L only 12 to 2.15. **Closed:** bank hols. **Meals:** alc (main courses £11 to £17). **Service:** net prices. **Details:** Cards accepted. 12 seats. Air-con. No music. No mobile phones. Wheelchair access. Children's portions.

### Wills
2/3 The Plains, Totnes, TQ9 5DR
Tel no: (01803) 865192
www.willsrestaurant.co.uk
**Modern European | £28**
**Cooking score: 3**
V £30

A Georgian town house by the River Dart is the setting for this stylish restaurant. The downstairs has a relaxed, café atmosphere while the upstairs dining rooms are spacious with linen-clad tables. A meal might begin with a salad of pan-fried halloumi, cherry tomatoes, pine nuts and rocket; home-made spicy duck spring rolls with chillies, noodles, coriander and ginger served with a spicy plum sauce and a salad garnish; or a Caesar salad served with local crab. Typical main courses include pan-fried scallops with salad, guacamole and sweet chilli sauce; pan-fried duck breast with sautéed potatoes, cauliflower purée and a port jus; or a spring vegetable risotto with peas, chervil and asparagus topped with Parmesan crackling. Round it off with an individual banoffi pie, a summer fruit tartlet, or a rich chocolate tart with tropical fruit sorbet. The international wine list opens at £13.50 and includes a selection from the nearby Sharpham vineyard.

**Chef/s:** Craig Purkiss. **Open:** all week L 12 to 2.30, Tue to Sat D 7 (6.30 summer) to 9.30. **Meals:** alc (main courses L £10 to £14, D £10 to £18). Set L £9.95 (2 courses). **Service:** not inc. **Details:** Cards accepted. 42 seats. Music. Children's portions.

## ▌Virginstow

### Percy's
**Home-reared organic produce**
Coombeshead Estate, Virginstow, EX21 5EA
Tel no: (01409) 211236
www.percys.co.uk
**Modern British | £40**
**Cooking score: 4**

The thing that makes Percy's stand out from the crowd is that, unlike most other restaurants, it is located at the heart of an accredited organic farm. The Bricknell-Webb's (Tony and Tina) grow (and rear) much of their own produce on the tranquil 130-acre country estate (as well as offering accommodation), and supply much of the kitchen's needs, while fish comes from the day boats at Looe. A modern extension to the 400-year-old building includes a zinc bar, while the dining room in the older part of the house comes with a low ceiling, crisp linen and high-backed chairs. Tina's cooking takes a relaxed modern approach, her straightforward, unfussy style allowing the quality and freshness of ingredients to shine. Think seared squid and scallops with dill, honey and mustard dressing to start, then roasted home-reared lamb, cooked pink, and served with a rosemary jus, or perhaps a grilled duo of John Dory and turbot with a béarnaise sauce, while desserts might deliver a chocolate, prune, hazelnut and Armagnac tart with cassia-bark ice cream. As you would expect, wines are carefully chosen with plenty of organic bottles and fair pricing. Prices start at £16.
**Chef/s:** Tina Bricknell-Webb. **Open:** Mon to Sat D only 7 to 9. **Meals:** Set D £40. **Service:** not inc. **Details:** Cards accepted. 20 seats. 16 seats outside. No mobile phones. Wheelchair access. Music. Car parking.

Michael Caines

*Why did you become a chef?*
I had a passion for food as a young man encouraged by the enjoyment of cooking at home with my mum.

*Who do you most admire amongst today's chefs?*
I have an admiration for a lot of today's chefs - far too many to name them all individually - but people such as Raymond Blanc, Gordon Ramsay, Heston Blumenthal and The Roux Brothers.

*Where do you eat out?*
Unfortunately I do not get much spare time to dine out but when I do I like to dine in the restaurants of the aforementioned chefs. I have an interest in ethnical food and I also have a few local favourites I visit when the opportunity arises.

*Who is your favourite producer?*
I work with so many local producers that it would be unfair to name just one. They are all so different and artisan and I feel very privileged to have them in this region.

*What's the best dish you've ever eaten?*
The most memorable is a truffle tart made by Jöel Robuchon.

*What's your guilty food pleasure?*
It is loving all food! And at the same time trying to keep my weight down. Chefs love to taste all the time but it sometimes has its consequences!

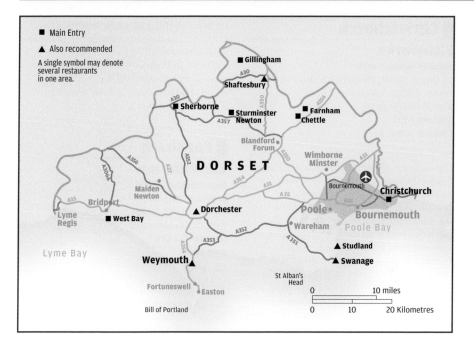

- ■ Main Entry
- ▲ Also recommended

A single symbol may denote several restaurants in one area.

## READERS RECOMMEND
### Hive Beach Café
**Seafood**
Burton Bradstock, Bridport, DT6 4RF
Tel no: (01308) 897070
www.hivebeachcafe.co.uk
**'Fresh fish and chips on a National Trust beach'**

## ■ Chettle
### Castleman Hotel
**Generous portions and British ingredients**
Chettle, DT11 8DB
Tel no: (01258) 830096
www.castlemanhotel.co.uk
**Modern British | £28**
**Cooking score: 2**

Understated and gently aging elegance combine with relaxed informality in this old stone building. British ingredients such as Loch Fyne smoked salmon, Denhay ham and Dovedale Blue cheese are brought in as main and supporting characters to many dishes. Menus may be brief but they provide real choices; the cautious will be happy with steak while the more adventurous can have a great time with pigeon breasts with poivrade or guinea fowl stuffed with cheese – meat and fish eaters as well as vegetarians are looked after. Generous puddings are constructed lovingly with fresh and well-judged flavours. Enthusiasm for decent wine shows itself with very fair pricing, a range of half-bottles and a list that encompasses well-made modest bottles to very grand vintages from the Medoc. House wine starts at £12 a bottle.
**Chef/s:** Barbara Garnsworthy and Richard Morris.
**Open:** Sun L 12.30 to 1.30, all week D 7 to 9.30.
**Closed:** 25, 26 and 31 Dec, Feb. **Meals:** alc D (main courses £9 to £17.50). Set L Sun £20. **Service:** not inc. **Details:** Cards accepted. 40 seats. No music. Wheelchair access. Children's portions. Car parking.

## ▌Christchurch

### FishWorks

Popular seafood chain
10 Church Street, Christchurch, BH23 1BW
Tel no: (01202) 487000
www.fishworks.co.uk
Seafood | £33
Cooking score: 3

Set in a pedestrianised cobbled street next to Christchurch Priory, this branch of Mitchell Tonks' 'fishmonger's with tables' chain (see entries in Bath, Bristol and London) is proving as popular as ever. Deliveries arrive daily, and diners can choose from the day's catch chalked up on the specials board – served simply grilled or fried – or take the option to share a whole fish roasted with herbs and garlic. The printed carte features fishy classics, anything from a simple bowl of mussels via smoked haddock fishcakes with spinach and hollandaise, to dishes with a more lively global approach, say squid piri-piri style or zuppa del pescatore, which arrives at the table in its rustic cooking pot. Plateau de fruits de mer is another option. The atmosphere is suitably relaxed, and the wine list is a good, reasonably priced selection from £15.
**Chef/s:** Nick Davies. **Open:** Tue to Sat 12 to 2.15, 6 to 9.45. **Closed:** bank hols and day after bank hols. **Meals:** alc (main courses £13 to £50). **Service:** not inc. **Details:** Cards accepted. 44 seats. Music. Children's portions.

## ALSO RECOMMENDED

### ▲ Sienna

36 High West Street, Dorchester, DT1 1UP
Tel no: (01305) 250022
www.siennarestaurant.co.uk

A husband and wife double act serving the denizens of Dorchester with a high standard of food and drink. Reports suggest that the kitchen is on the up, turning out consistently satisfying results from appealing menus that take account of local produce, e.g. roast cutlet and poached loin of new season Dorset lamb with pan-fried polenta, roasted vine tomatoes,

lamb jus and olive oil foam. Start with pea, broad bean and ricotta risotto with pea shoot salad and salted ricotta and finish with Valhrona milk chocolate and salted caramel mousse with almond praline and orange sorbet. Lunch is from £16.50, dinner is £33.50. Wines from £12.

## ▌Farnham

### Museum Inn

Sophisticated dining
Farnham, DT11 8DE
Tel no: (01725) 516261
www.museuminn.co.uk
Gastropub | £24
New Chef

A venerable, red-brick, thatched inn facing the village green, the Museum now houses a fully fledged gastropub operation of the most sophisticated stamp. Clive Jory is a busy man, overseeing a kitchen that is on duty for all fourteen sessions in the week, and the effort pays off handsomely. Lunch might be a steak, mushroom and onion sandwich that uses excellent Longhorn beef, and comes with thin chips. In the evenings, things go up a gear, with a starter of lightly pickled Chesil Beach mackerel, served with aïoli and a potato salad made with Pink Fir apples, or sautéed chicken livers in a pastry case with mushrooms and sherry vinegar. Some appetising combinations inform main courses such as venison loin with butternut mash, honey-glazed parsnips and a sour cherry jus, or a substantial Portland fish stew with rouille croûtes and saffron potatoes. Rhubarb in season makes a fine trio of pannacotta, jelly and compote. France leads the charge on the wine list. If you're lucky (and rich), you might be in time to bag one of the run of vintages of Mouton-Rothschild before they go. Otherwise, prices are level-headed, and open at £14 (£3.50 a glass).
**Chef/s:** Clive Jory. **Open:** all week 12 to 2 (2.30 Sat and Sun), 7 to 9.30 (9 Sun). **Closed:** 25 Dec. **Meals:** alc (main courses £14 to £17.50).

Service: not inc. Details: Cards accepted. 70 seats. 40 seats outside. Separate bar. No music. No mobile phones. Wheelchair access. Car parking.

# Gillingham

## Stock Hill

**Dorset mansion with Austrian hosts**
Stock Hill, Gillingham, SP8 5NR
Tel no: (01747) 823626
www.stockhillhouse.co.uk
**Modern European | £32**
**Cooking score: 5**

A beech-lined drive leads up to Peter and Nita Hauser's affluent-looking Victorian residence set in 11 acres of pleasant parkland and landscaped gardens. Inside, it is country-house comfort personified, with William Morris wallpaper in the bar and chintzy colour schemes setting the tone in the spacious, very proper dining room. The Hausers have been in residence for more than two decades and Peter's Austrian roots continue to have an impact on his cooking. Native specialities from his homeland sit alongside more broadly based dishes, even though the bulk of the fixed-price menu changes each day. European flavours dominate the choice of starters, whether it's home-cured ox tongue and garden horseradish salad with pumpkin oil dressing or julienne of calf's liver with raspberry vinegar served in a puff pastry case. Main courses usher in seared fillet of Dorset roe deer 'Baden Baden' with chive polenta and braised red cabbage, medallions of veal with sorrel, and (from further afield) whole roast John Dory accompanied by Mediterranean vegetable risotto. By contrast, desserts belong emphatically to the Viennese school of apfelschbeiterhaufen and Salzburger hönig nockerl. The substantial wine list is international in scope, with a cluster of Austrian bottles making their mark alongside big names from France and elsewhere. House selections start at £17.10 (£4.95 a glass).

Chef/s: Peter Hauser and Lorna Connor. Open: Tue to Fri and Sun L 12.15 to 1.45, all week D 7.15 to 8.45. Meals: Set L £27 (3 courses), Set D £39 (4 courses). Service: not inc. Details: Cards accepted. 36 seats. 8 seats outside. No music. No mobile phones. Children's portions. Car parking.

## ALSO RECOMMENDED

## ▲ La Fleur de Lys

Bleke Street, Shaftesbury, SP7 8AW
Tel no: (01747) 853717
www.lafleurdelys.co.uk

Anglo-French cuisine is well presented at La Fleur de Lys, and is worth the slight price stretch. Start with pan-fried veal sweetbreads served with a salad of roquette lettuce, apples, spring onions and raspberries in a raspberry dressing (£7). Follow with roasted fillet of monkfish served on English asparagus and samphire with a light lemon butter sauce (£16.50) or settle in with the huge Sunday roast (Sunday lunch only). There are some tantalising dessert options, such as lychee mousse between honey pastry leaves served on a fresh strawberry crush or a warm creamy caramel and banana tart served with almond ice cream (both £6). House wines start at £15. Open Wed to Sun L and Mon to Sat D.

# Sherborne

## The Green

**Husband-and-wife team at the helm**
The Green, Sherborne, DT9 3HY
Tel no: (01935) 813821
**Modern European | £31**
**Cooking score: 2**

After six or so years there is a comfortable sense that the Rusts are here to stay. Good news for Sherborne since this is cooking that sets its sights absolutely in tandem with the available, very decent, skills. Good ingredients, like poultry from the Quantocks, are given what has become standard modern treatment: grounded in tradition but spiced up with Eastern promise and flavours of the Mediterranean. West Bay scallops accompanied neatly with aloo bhaji or

carpaccio of beef with soy sauce sit alongside sound classics such as bass with mussels and saffron. Home-made ices may be part of a trio joining jellies and fools or there are English cheeses. House wines start at £15.25.
**Chef/s:** Michael Rust. **Open:** Tue to Sat 12 to 2, 7 to 9. **Closed:** 2 weeks Feb, 1 week June, 1 week Sept, bank hols. **Meals:** alc L (main courses £9 to £17). Set D £22.50 (2 courses) to £28.95. **Service:** not inc. **Details:** Cards accepted. 50 seats. 10 seats outside. No music. Wheelchair access.

## ALSO RECOMMENDED
### ▲ Shell Bay
Ferry Road, Studland, BH19 3BA
Tel no: (01929) 450363
www.shellbay.net

Wonderfully situated looking out towards Brownsea Island, this well-loved seafood restaurant is enjoyed by diners who arrive there both by land and by sea (the Sandbanks Ferry is just 200 metres away). The menu displays a global touch: chargrilled Moroccan-spiced skewered scallops with taboulleh (£8.95) or soused herrings (£5.95) might be followed by a similarly international swordfish and marlin duo with wok-charred vegetables and hoisin sauce (£9.95), or baked whole sea bass with Thai-scented crab meat wrapped in nori seaweed and served with French fries (£18.95). Wines start at £12.50. Closed Sun D.

## ■ Sturminster Newton
### Plumber Manor
Relaxed and unpretentious
Sturminster Newton, DT10 2AF
Tel no: (01258) 472507
www.plumbermanor.com
Anglo-French | £27
Cooking score: 2

🛏 V £30

In the heart of gentle Dorset countryside, the Prideaux-Brunes genuinely share their comfortable, rather than grand, home that has been in the family for 400 years plus.

Ostentation is avoided; there are few departures from tried-and-tested combinations. Gravlax with smoked trout or asparagus with hollandaise, and for mains, lemon sole with grapes and white wine, loin of pork with the expected apples and sage, and beef Wellington with béarnaise, show loyalty to an age when French cooking, and menus, dominated. But with expert timing and decently sourced ingredients, the intention and inspiration of such staid marriages become clear and they sing. Reasonably priced wines pursue the same ethos; some concessions are made to the New World, but the sense is that the heart remains solidly in Europe with impressive lists from the classic regions, including even neglected Mosel, and a fair sprinkling of half-bottles. House wines start at £14.50.
**Chef/s:** Brian Prideaux-Brune and Louis Haskell. **Open:** Sun L 12 to 1.30, all week D 7.30 to 9.30. **Meals:** Set L Sun £22, Set D £24 (2 courses) to £27. **Service:** not inc. **Details:** Cards accepted. 60 seats. No music. Wheelchair access. Children's portions. Car parking.

## ■ West Bay
### Riverside Restaurant
Popular seafood veteran
West Bay, DT6 4EZ
Tel no: (01308) 422011
www.thefishrestaurant-westbay.co.uk
Seafood | £30
Cooking score: 3

Traverse the walkway over the river to reach this long-serving seafood restaurant surrounded on all sides by water. Since 1964, the Watson family has been dispensing top-notch local fish to an appreciative crowd, who pack into the bare-boarded, chalet-style dining room and sun themselves on the terrace. The West Bay boats provide ample supplies, which the kitchen transforms into uncluttered dishes ranging from dressed Lyme Bay crab and bourride to John Dory with sweet potato mash and mango salsa or fillet of brill with crispy spinach and sorrel sauce. Seafood platters are a sure-fire hit, while fish-free alternatives could include roast chicken breast stuffed with Applewood cheese and prosciutto or wild mushroom risotto. Finish with Manuka honey custard tart with apricot and blood orange compote or seek comfort in an old faithful like banana split. The re-cast wine list is a well-chosen slate brimming with useful information. Fish-friendly whites top the bill and house selections start at £14.95 a litre (£2.95 a glass). **Chef/s:** Nick Larcombe, George Marsh and Anthony Shaw. **Open:** Tue to Sun L 12 to 2.15, Tue to Sat D 6.30 to 9. **Closed:** 2 Dec to 9 Feb. **Meals:** alc (main courses £12 to £33.50). Set L Tue to Fri £17.50 (2 courses) to £21.50. **Service:** not inc. **Details:** Cards accepted. 90 seats. 30 seats outside. No mobile phones. Wheelchair access. Music. Children's portions.

## ALSO RECOMMENDED

### ▲ Crab House Café

**Fleet Oyster Farm, Ferryman's Way, Weymouth, DT4 9YU**
**Tel no: (01305) 788867**

To call it a crab 'house' is almost an exaggeration; it's really just a wooden shack by Chesil Beach, but it has a real charm, and the atmosphere on the outside tables on a sunny day is a joy. The menu is more varied than the name suggests, changing once or twice daily according to the day's catch: try squid Singapore-style or Thai fishcakes to start (from £5.25 to £8.50) with skate with chorizo and spring onions to follow (£14.50). The wine list starts at £12.95. Open Wed to Sun L and Wed to Sat D year round, and Mon and Sun D in the summer. Closed Tue.

Gary Rhodes

**Why did you become a chef?**
Cooking from the age of 13 became a necessity at home. However, it was also a complete obsession and one which I still have today – 30 years later!

**Who was your main inspiration?**
Without doubt, the godfathers of our culinary world – Albert and Michel Roux.

**Where do you eat out?**
Le Gavroche and The Waterside Inn, but I'm also a big fan of Chris Galvin's, and my local Chinese restaurant, Xi'ans, as well as one of the best Indians in London – The Painted Heron on Cheyne Walk.

**Where do you source your ingredients?**
We always endeavour to take advantage of great British produce, but also utilise many flavours from all over the world.

**Do you have a favourite local recipe?**
I love supporting Kent, as I've lived there for many years, so the perfect Kentish apple pie would always be a winner, with lashings of custard or cream.

**If you could only eat one more thing, what would it be?**
The largest bowl of braised oxtails and creamy mashed potatoes.

**What's your proudest achievement?**
Being awarded an OBE; it's something you just don't ever dream of receiving.

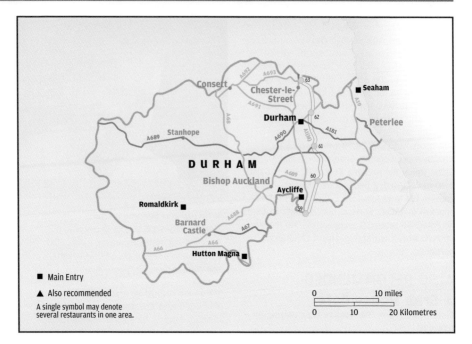

- ■ Main Entry
- ▲ Also recommended

A single symbol may denote several restaurants in one area.

| 0 | | 10 miles |
| 0 | 10 | 20 Kilometres |

## ▌Aycliffe

### County

**Pub grub and haute cuisine**
13 The Green, Aycliffe, DL5 6LX
Tel no: (01325) 312273
www.the-county.co.uk
**Modern European | £35**
**Cooking score: 2**

£5 OFF  V

Overlooking the village green, this popular gastropub boasts fresh contemporary décor, a relaxed and friendly atmosphere, regularly changing modern menus, real ales and a short wine list. Oh, and a blue plaque at the door, commemorating Prime Minister Tony Blair dining there with French President Jacques Chirac. Cooking is unfussy, as befits the pub setting, but you can still expect quality ingredients, confidently handled with a touch of *je ne sais quois*. A flavour-packed starter of baked field mushroom with goats' cheese, aubergine and courgette has been well received, as was a main course of fillet of halibut poached in a shellfish velouté, served with fettucine egg pasta and fresh mussels. Red berry cheesecake with (very boozy) marinated cherries is a typical dessert. House wines start at £12.95.
**Open:** Mon to Sun L 12 to 2, Mon to Sat D 5.30 to 9.
**Closed:** 25 and 26 December, 1 January. **Meals:** alc (main courses £12.50 to £19.95). **Service:** not included. **Details:** Cards accepted. 75 seats. Music. Children's portions. Car parking.

## ▌Durham

### Bistro 21

**Relaxed bistro serving French-style dishes**
Aykley Heads House, Aykley Heads, Durham, DH1 5TS
Tel no: (0191) 384 4354
**Modern European | £40**
**Cooking score: 2**

A solid, seventeenth-century building in leafy surroundings on the northern edge of Durham is the location for Terry Laybourne's relaxed country-style bistro. Décor is clean and simple with cream walls, rustic chairs, white-clothed tables and a log-burning stove. The menu is strongly French-influenced, so expect to find classics such as confit of duck with lyonnaise potatoes, fillet steak au poivre, and sole meunière, with a few modern inclusions – rare tuna spring rolls with soy, lime and coriander, for example – providing variety. Start perhaps with carefully constructed terrine of duck, corn-fed chicken and foie gras, progress through the robust flavours of slow-cooked shoulder of lamb with Mediterranean vegetables and confit garlic, and finish with a subtle dessert of tropical fruits with coconut, chilli and lime sorbet. Unfussy presentation carries through to foil-wrapped butter pats, sugar in paper tubes and a limited but reasonably priced wine list, which starts at £12.50.

**Open:** Mon to Sat 12 to 2, 7 to 10.15. **Meals:** alc (main courses £13.50 to £22.50). **Service:** 10%. **Details:** Cards accepted. 24 seats. Separate bar. No music. No mobile phones. Children's portions. Car parking.

## ▌ Hutton Magna

### Oak Tree Inn
**Imaginative cooking of local produce**
Hutton Magna, DH11 7HH
Tel no: (01833) 627371
**Modern European | £30**
**Cooking score: 2**

Before moving north Alistair Ross worked at top-class London addresses. He has brought this experience to the row of modest cottages that have become the Oak Tree Inn. While much is made of local sourcing of ingredients, inspiration for dishes comes from wider-spread European roots. A May menu included: grilled goats' cheese with asparagus and pesto; spaghetti with mussels and leeks; and a salad of pork belly and black pudding. Main courses were sea bass, king prawn, pea and lettuce risotto or chicken breast with olive oil mash, asparagus and cep sauce. These epitomise the blending of proper seasonality with broader gastronomic intentions with the Mediterranean especially getting the upper

hand. Wines are a short but generous list; the £12 starting price reflects generally low mark-ups for decent bottles. There is also a good collection of halves.

**Chef/s:** Alastair Ross. **Open:** Tue to Sun D only 6.30 to 9. **Closed:** 25 and 26 Dec, 1 Jan. **Meals:** alc (main courses £14.50 to £17.50). **Service:** not inc. **Details:** Cards accepted. 25 seats. No mobile phones. Music. Car parking.

## ▌ Romaldkirk

### Rose and Crown
**Upmarket country inn**
Romaldkirk, DL12 9EB
Tel no: (01833) 650213
www.rose-and-crown.co.uk
**British | £28**
**Cooking score: 2**

£5 OFF 🛏 £30

At the heart of an unspoilt village of grey stone cottages, overlooking the green with its old stocks, the Rose and Crown is an eighteenth-century coaching inn that continues to cheer visitors with its very civilised blend of cosy bar, relaxed brasserie and traditional oak-panelled restaurant, with picnic tables outside for fine weather. The cooking style is confidently unfussy, as in a lunch dish of salmon fishcakes with wilted spinach and chive cream sauce: 'simple but tasty comfort food'. More stops are pulled out for the fixed price four-course dinners which might begin with rich duck liver pâté with plum chutney, followed by celeriac and apple soup, before roasted fillet of monkfish with leek and smoked bacon purée and red wine and balsamic jus. Walnut and syrup tart with Amaretto ice cream could be a good way to finish. The wine list starts at £14.50 a bottle, with fourteen available by the glass.

**Chef/s:** Christopher Davy and Andrew Lee. **Open:** Sun L 12 to 1.30, all week D 7.30 (6.30 in the brasserie) to 9. **Closed:** 24 to 26 Dec. **Meals:** Set L Sun £17.25 (3 courses), Set D all week £28 (4 courses). **Service:** not inc. **Details:** Cards accepted. 24 seats. 24 seats outside. No music. No mobile phones. Wheelchair access. Car parking.

## ▌Seaham

### Seaham Hall, White Room

Upmarket seaside hotel
Lord Byron's Walk, Seaham, SR7 7AG
Tel no: (0191) 516 1400
www.seaham-hall.com
**Modern European | £45**
**Cooking score: 5**

🍷 ⊨ ⋎

'It really ought to be in the heart of a major city instead of by the coast next to a seaside village,' noted one reader of this large, clifftop-located spa hotel overlooking the North Sea. The approach is impressive, with a giant glass water feature out front, and the interior is seriously modern with shades of beige and brown in the lounge bar and crisp white in the dining room. Steven Smith's subtly inventive food sits well with the surroundings. Sea bream comes with braised fennel and a bouillabaisse sauce as one way to start. A just-seared foie gras has a slick of pear purée and gingerbread and foie gras ice cream for company. Fish shows up well at main-course stage, with a grilled piece of salmon served with Savoy cabbage, carrot purée, bacon and red wine and horseradish foam. Balmoral Estate venison loin might be served with pumpkin purée together with chestnuts and crosnes and bitter chocolate sauce. Finish with banana parfait and pistachio ice cream. A commendable wine list covers a fair amount of ground, giving slight, but not undue prominence to the French regions. It's not short of premier league players, but there's good drinking in the £25-plus range and around 10 by the glass.
**Chef/s:** Steven Smith. **Open:** all week 12 to 2.30, 7 to 10. **Meals:** alc (main courses £20 to £34). Set L Mon to Sat £17.50 to £65, Set L Sun £27.50, Set D £30 to £65. Bar L menu available. **Service:** not inc. **Details:** Cards accepted. 50 seats. 50 seats outside. Air-con. No mobile phones. Wheelchair access. Music. Car parking.

Bjorn van der Horst

**Why did you become a chef?**
Life's circumstances really, but I also find profound joy in pleasing others, teaching and training.

**Which of today's chefs do you admire?**
Alain Passard and Alain Ducasse for very different reasons. The first for passion and elegance, the latter for leadership and business sense.

**What's the best dish you've ever eaten?**
I had a Zarzuela sort of Catalan-style bouillabaisse in a village called Cadaques just north of Barcelona once. One of those magical moments when everything was just right. The food, the company and the setting. It doesn't happen often, but when it does even a New York slice could be the best thing in the world and rival any top restaurant.

**What's your guilty food pleasure?**
Overstuffed bagels.

**Who is your favourite producer?**
Mother nature.

**Which are your proudest achievements?**
Seeing the chefs that have worked with me grow and prosper. Two chefs in New York now own their own restaurants.

**What's coming up next for you?**
Peace. I think I've finally found myself.

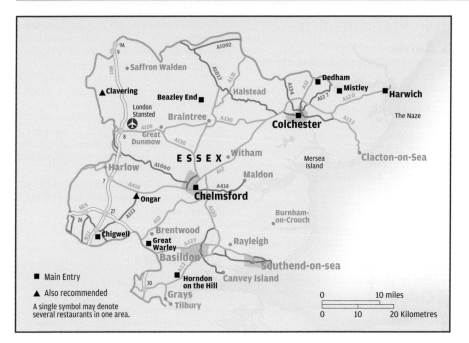

## ▊ Beazley End

★NEW ENTRY★
## Cock Inn

**Modern Italian from Jamie Oliver's trainee**
Nr Braintree, Beazley End, CM7 5JH
**Tel no:** (01371) 850566
**www.thecock-inn.com**
**Italian | £29**
**Cooking score: 2**
£30

Take an inner-city couple, one of whom went through Jamie Oliver's chefs' training school at Fifteen (see entry, London), and give them the keys to their own country pub – oh, and show their trials and tribulations on the telly. The mentor's 'fantastic funky' food has come to deepest rural Essex – good robust Italian-style cooking, lots of fresh local and imported seasonal ingredients in simple dishes, home-made pasta a big thing. Undoubtedly, the music, art and interiors might be 'louder and groovier than the locals are used to in your

average 400-year-old Essex pub', but the warm friendly staff bring it all together. 'It works for me,' declared one contented reporter. Lunch brings Big Al's home-made pasta (perhaps delicious savoury lasagnette with wild boar ragù or tagliatelle al funghi) and classic pub grub (chicken and mushroom pie with Gorgonzola or Priors Hall Farm ham with truffle-scented eggs and rosemary-salted chips). Dinner might offer bresaola with beetroot and horseradish or spring lamb chops with spinach, creamy borlotti beans and mint pesto. A simple Italian-dominated wine list has Prosecco on tap to join Peroni lager; and wines are from £11.95 a bottle.

**Chef/s:** Aaron Craze. **Open:** Tue to Sat L 12.30 to 3.30, D 6.30 to 9.30, Sun L 12.30 to 3.30. **Closed:** Mon, Sun eve, Christmas Eve and Christmas Day. **Meals:** alc main courses £14 to £17. **Service:** optional. **Details:** Cards accepted. 96 seats. Separate bar. Wheelchair access. Music. Children's portions. Car parking.

## ALSO RECOMMENDED
## ▲ Barda
30-32 Broomfield Road, Chelmsford, CM1 1SW
Tel no: (01245) 357799
www.barda-restaurant.com

Stranded in a gastro wasteland in the west end
of Chelmsford, Barda lights a beacon amid the
office buildings and kebab shops near the
railway station. A modern wood-panelled
restaurant, it offers 'friendly' service and solid,
seasonal food. A starter of figs, blue cheese and
Parma ham, for example, is well matched by
monkfish, roasted peppers and 'stunningly
good' spring onion mash or mackerel with
orange and chilli. Desserts, such as a well-
constructed iced berry pudding, are notable.
Wine starts at £13.

# ▮ Chigwell
## Bluebell
**Eclectic mixture of contemporary and classic**
117 High Road, Chigwell, IG7 6QQ
Tel no: (020) 8500 6282
www.thebluebellrestaurant.co.uk
**Modern European | £30**
**Cooking score: 3**

A range of ambiences is on offer at the
Bluebell. The room at the front looks to have
been transported from the set of a Jane Austen
costume drama, but the further back you
penetrate, the more contemporary things get
until, in the bustling bar area, you arrive in
modern-day Essex. The culinary style doesn't
settle for any particular orientation either, but
essays a global span that takes in roast
monkfish in Thai green curry with lime-leaf
rice, Welsh lamb with ratatouille, spinach and
a potato and Gruyère gratin, and roasted
piquillo peppers stuffed with Mediterranean
vegetables, served with couscous and harissa,
and a feta salad. The world at once indeed. That
most dishes are brought off with notable
aplomb is testament to the kitchen's
confidence. Start with Ragstone goats' cheese
soufflé with poached pear, braised celery and
red onion and port chutney, and make your

way sedately towards one of the seductively
calorific desserts – perhaps Valhrona chocolate
tart with peanut-butter ice cream. A modern
jumble of wines is well presented, with
notable producers including Tesch from
Germany's Nahe region and the little-seen
Cloudy Bay Pinot Noir. Prices start at £13.95
(or £3.95 a glass) for a Languedoc Merlot.
**Chef/s:** Paul Korten. **Open:** Tue to Fri and Sun L 12
to 2, Tue to Sat D 6.45 to 10. **Meals:** alc D (main
courses £16.50 to £21.95). Set L Tue to Fri £12.95 (2
courses) to £18.95, Set L Sun £22.95.
**Service:** optional. **Details:** Cards accepted. 95 seats.
Air-con. Separate bar. Wheelchair access. Music.
Children's portions.

## ALSO RECOMMENDED
## ▲ Cricketers
Clavering, CB11 4QT
Tel no: (01799) 550442

Busy, busy, busy. It's not just the Jamie O
connection that brings the crowds flooding in
to his parents' traditional country inn a few
miles north of Stansted. You're unlikely to
catch a glimpse of Oliver Jr, superstar chef and
saviour of school dinners, so settle for one of
his cookbooks on the way out. Good, simple,
hearty cooking is the appeal here, plus the
English hostelry setting – think bedwarmers,
horse brasses, red-brick fireplaces and lots of
dark woodwork. Daily specials might be pan-
fried pigeon breasts with port jus (£10.25) or
halibut fillet with creamy cep sauce (£13.50),
while the carte can feature oriental stuffed
chicken with aubergine mash and soy
(£14.50) or half roast duck with star anise,
orange and honey (£15.50). A 65-bin wine
list, priced from £12.30, includes some good
Lay and Wheeler names.

### Scores on the Doors

To find out more about the Scores on the
Doors campaign, please visit the Food
Standard's Agency website:
www.food.gov.uk or www.which.co.uk.

# ▌ Colchester

## The Lemon Tree
**British menu under a Roman wall**
48 St Johns Street, Colchester, CO2 7AD
Tel no: 01206 767337
www.the-lemon-tree.com
**Modern European | £25**
**New Chef**

£5
OFF

With a recent refurbishment taking it from bistro-style wrought-iron chairs to contemporary leather seats and whitewashed walls, The Lemon Tree 'may have lost a little of its charm', but the focal point of an exposed Roman wall helps retain the cosy, romantic feel. The menu is a diverse and eclectic mix of traditional British fare, ranging from bangers and mash, and liver and bacon, to European-inspired halloumi with a French bean and sundried tomato salad. A changing menu and a policy for local sourcing 'where possible' make free-range chicken a regular option, alongside rump of lamb with rosemary-scented risotto and redcurrant jus – 'a real triumph' – and quality seafood mainly from local shores. The wine list encompasses a favourable selection from around the world. House wine starts at £12.55.
**Chef/s:** Paul Wassan. **Open:** Mon to Sat L 12 to 2, D 5 to 9, (10 Fri and Sat). **Closed:** 25 Dec to 4 Jan, bank hols. **Meals:** alc (main courses £10.50 to £15.95). Set L £13.50 (3 courses), Set D £16.50 (3 courses). **Service:** not inc. **Details:** Cards accepted. 85 seats. 60 seats outside. Air-con. Wheelchair access. Music. Children's portions.

# ▌ Dedham

## milsoms
**Quirky restaurant-with-rooms**
Stratford Road, Dedham, CO7 6HW
Tel no: (01206) 322795
www.milsomhotels.com
**Global | £25**
**Cooking score: 1**

🛏 ❦ £30

The Vale of Dedham's well-known restaurateur family have galvanised their fifty-plus years of experience with their eponymous, relaxed contemporary bar-restaurant set in a pretty Georgian house and gardens (great for alfresco eating). Most striking is the house formula (no bookings, grab a table, order food at the bar before ferrying one's drinks back); it evidently has its fans, being incredibly busy. But it can come across as somewhat processed, and service – and the mix of Western and oriental dishes – have not always impressed this year. Among menu choices could be prawn cocktail and simple Suffolk sausages with bubble and squeak, or more exotic feta and bulgar aubergine cannelloni, Asian spring rolls, and deep-fried squid with cucumber sambal. Some interesting affordable wines from £13.50.
**Chef/s:** Stas Anastasiades and Sarah Norman. **Open:** all week 12 to 9.30 (10 Fri and Sat). **Meals:** alc (main courses £8.50 to £22). **Service:** not inc. **Details:** Cards accepted. 80 seats. 80 seats outside. Separate bar. Wheelchair access. Music. Children's portions. Car parking.

## Sun Inn

Anglo-Italian cuisine in Constable country
High Street, Dedham, CO7 6DF
Tel no: (01206) 323351
www.thesuninndedham.com
**Modern European | £25**
**New Chef**

 £30

Owner Piers Baker is passionate about the
provenance of the seasonal produce served in
his busy and stylish fifteenth-century
coaching inn. His restaurant menu is a
showcase for what's in season, at a meal in May
delivering roasted lambs' sweetbreads with
globe artichokes, watercress, pine nuts,
Parmesan and a white-wine cream, and
chargrilled ribeye with sweet, juicy beets and
their leaves, alongside horseradish cream,
balsamic and sautéed new potatoes. Local
early hot-house strawberries with mint, black
olives and pouring cream proved an unusual
finale. Great local real ales as well as 'proper'
soft drinks join an impressive very personal
wine list. Food notes assist choice. Bottles
from £12; many wines come by the 500ml
carafe as well as the half-bottle, not forgetting
30 by the glass.
**Chef/s:** Ugo Simonelli. **Open:** all week L 12 to 2.30
(3 Sat and Sun), Mon to Sat D 6.30 to 9.30 (10 Fri
and Sat). **Closed:** 25 to 26 Dec, New Year's Eve.
**Meals:** alc (main courses £8.50 to £15). Bar L menu
available. **Service:** not inc. **Details:** Cards accepted.
80 seats. 100 seats outside. Separate bar. Music.
Children's portions. Car parking.

## READERS RECOMMEND

## The Starr

British
Market Place, Great Dunmow, CM6 1AX
Tel no: (01371) 874321
www.the-starr.co.uk
'Family-run restaurant-with-rooms'

# ■ Great Warley

★NEW ENTRY★
## The Headley

A new venture specialising in classic fare
Headley Common, Great Warley, CM13 3HS
Tel no: 01277 216104
www.theheadley.co.uk
**British**
**Cooking score: 3**

The former Chef & Brewer pub by the village
green, close to Brentwood and the M25 (J28
& 29), is the unlikely location for Daniel
Clifford (see entry Midsummer House,
Cambridge) to open his first pub venture.
With Scott Wade (ex-The Gun, London, see
entry) at the stove, the Headley opened in May
2007 and Essex diners have been beating a path
to the door to sample the classy modern
British cooking. Set across two floors, it's a
big, informal place with deep leather sofas
fronting the downstairs bar, and acres of
wooden tables beyond and in the open-plan
upstairs dining room – it can easily seat 180.
Lunch and dinner menus offer an inspired
choice of classic dishes with a distinctive
contemporary edge, and good use is made of
local produce, such as a starter of local
asparagus with truffle vinaigrette or Farmer
Sharp's mutton loin on anchovy crushed
potatoes for main course. Interesting
alternatives may include a chou farci with
smoked black pudding and ham with a rich
tomato sauce, and a 'beautifully cooked' cod
fillet served with Savoy cabbage, cockles and
bacon. Along with a selection of cheeses,
desserts include vanilla pannacotta with
rhubarb soup, and dark chocolate brownie
with milk ice cream. Service is friendly and
efficient and the carefully chosen and wide-
ranging list of wines start at £12.50.
**Chef/s:** Scott Wade. **Open:** all week 12 to 3 (8 Sun),
Mon to Sat 6 to 9.30. **Meals:** alc (main meals £12 to
£16.75). **Service:** not inc. **Details:** Cards accepted.
120 seats. 50 seats outside. Air-con. Wheelchair
access. Music. Children's portions.

## Harwich
### Pier Hotel, Harbourside Restaurant
**Drink in the marine view**
The Quay, Harwich, CO12 3HH
Tel no: (01255) 241212
www.milsomhotels.com
**Seafood | £35**
**Cooking score: 2**

Slap-bang on the quayside, the Pier Hotel is master of all it surveys (the Stour estuary, mostly). It's an utterly apposite setting for a restaurant that naturally specialises in freshest fish and seafood. The menu cleverly mixes up traditional fare, such as smoked haddock fishcakes with a poached egg, lobster thermidor and moules mariniére, with some speculative efforts, along the lines of roast monkfish in pancetta with wild rice and a sauce of green peppercorns. For confirmed meat-eaters, there's the option of a steak, or maybe calf's liver and smoked bacon, and if you're determined not to stray from the straight and narrow, a footnote suggests, 'If you would like fish and chips, please ask'. You can't say fairer than that. Finish with passion-fruit and mango cheesecake, or cheeses and fruit. The wine list has a surprising degree of choice in reds for a fish restaurant, with prices opening at £14. This operation also includes the Ha'penny Pier, where the food is generally cheaper and simpler.
**Chef/s:** Chris Oakley. **Open:** all week 12 to 2, 6pm to 9.30. **Closed:** D 25 December. **Meals:** alc (main courses £9 to £31). Set L £17.50 (2 courses) to £23. **Service:** 10%. **Details:** Cards accepted. 70 seats. 30 seats outside. Air-con. Wheelchair access. Music. Children's portions. Car parking.

## Horndon on the Hill
### Bell Inn
**Cosmopolitan food in an historic pub**
High Road, Horndon on the Hill, SS17 8LD
Tel no: (01375) 642463
www.bell-inn.co.uk
**Modern European | £26**
**Cooking score: 2**

The Bell Inn, a large, ancient coaching inn, ably fills the role of traditional village pub, but also attracts outsiders for its jolly atmosphere and excellent food. Eat in the lively bar or in the calmer, more formal restaurant, from a contemporary menu that offers a broadly European flavour spectrum. Quiet ingenuity is the stock-in-trade, producing a starter of scallops with sea bass tortellini, chorizo and fennel vanilla cream, and a main course of honey roast suckling pig on creamed baby sweetcorn and garlic mash. Flavour combinations may not always be wholly successful, but meals are marked by first-rate ingredients and a good grasp of technique. The juxtaposition of flavours helps to spark some fizz at dessert stage, as crème brûlée and honey mango are teamed with pineapple sorbet and biscotti, and brandy coffee parfait with Chantilly cream and almond fudge. There's also a bar menu of simpler main dishes and lunchtime sandwiches. Wines offer good value with house Australian opening proceedings at £11.75.
**Chef/s:** Stuart Fay. **Open:** all week 12 to 1.45 (2.15 Sun), 6.30 to 9.45 (7 Sun). **Closed:** 25 and 26 Dec, bank hol Mon. **Meals:** alc (main courses £10.50 to £16). **Service:** not inc. **Details:** Cards accepted. 80 seats. 36 seats outside. No music. No mobile phones. Children's portions.

# Mistley

## Mistley Thorn
**Simple style and a focus on clear flavours**
High Street, Mistley, CO11 1HE
Tel no: (01206) 392821
www.mistleythorn.com
**Modern European | £21**
**Cooking score: 2**

This large, solid building overlooking the
Robert Adam-designed Swan Basin remains a
pub that attracts the locals, but has also become
a restaurant that is a destination for people
who care about food. It has a bright and warm
modern feel and is run with aplomb and well-
honed professionalism. Bar lunch sandwiches
are a cut above average and while the menu
disregards geography, drawing on ideas from
around the world, everything manages to
seem in place due to the quality sourcing of
ingredients – from local lamb and beef, via
oysters from Mersea Island, to Harwich
lobster. Delicate flavours in a scallop salad
complemented by a pea purée, lemon olive oil
and organic leaves, outstandingly fresh
pollack, and proper chips and tempura onion
rings accompanying ribeye steak epitomize
the careful buying and unfussy approach.
Desserts end on a high note with a Jack
Daniel's pecan tart with crème fraîche and hot
fudge sundae. Excellent home-made bread,
too. House wines start at £11.95.
**Chef/s:** Sherri Singleton. **Open:** all week L 12 to 3 (5
Sun), D 6.30 to 9.30. **Closed:** Christmas. **Meals:** alc
(main courses £9 to £16.50). Set L £11.95 (2 courses)
to £14.95. **Service:** not inc. **Details:** Cards accepted.
75 seats. 12 seats outside. Wheelchair access. Music.
Children's portions. Car parking.

## ALSO RECOMMENDED
### ▲ Smith's
Fifield Road, Ongar, CM5 0AL
Tel no: (01277) 365578
www.smithsbrasserie.com

Smith's marks its fiftieth anniversary in 2008,
the key to its longevity being daily supplies of
first-rate fish and seafood. Menus reveal a
preference for classic fish cookery, with
starters taking in pan-fried sardines with salsa
verde (£7) or traditional fish soup (£5.80),
while mains range from salmon with
hollandaise (£14) to lobster thermidor (£25).
There's also a fair choice of meat dishes and
desserts such as apple tart with caramel sauce
(£6). House wines £14. Closed Mon.

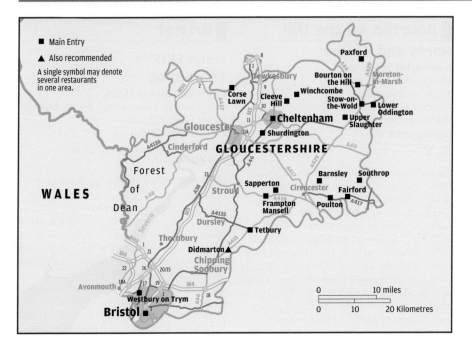

■ Main Entry

▲ Also recommended

A single symbol may denote several restaurants in one area.

Paxford

Tewkesbury
Bourton on the Hill
Moreton-in-Marsh

Corse Lawn
Cleeve Hill
Winchcombe
Stow-on-the-Wold
Lower Oddington

**Cheltenham**
Upper Slaughter

Gloucester
Shurdington

Cinderford
**GLOUCESTERSHIRE**

Forest
of
Dean

**WALES**

Barnsley Southrop

Sapperton
Cirencester
Fairford

Stroud
Frampton Mansell
Poulton

Dursley

**Tetbury**

Thornbury

Didmarton ▲

Chipping Sodbury

Avonmouth

Westbury on Trym

**Bristol** ■

| 0 | | 10 miles |
| --- | --- | --- |
| 0 | 10 | 20 Kilometres |

## ▌Barnsley
### Barnsley House
**Modern-day Italian-influenced cooking**
Barnsley, GL7 5EE
Tel no: (01285) 740000
www.barnsleyhouse.com
**Modern European | £38**
**Cooking score: 5**

Built at the end of the seventeenth century, this Cotswold manor house was formerly the home of the great Rosemary Verey. The dining room affords a fine view of her famed 'acres' of garden and the whole house has been tastefully and sympathetically made over to create a relaxed but upmarket hotel. Graham Grafton heads the kitchen, his cooking built on admirable principles, both in sourcing materials from local specialists (as well as home-grown produce from the kitchen garden), and in the execution. Puntarella salad with poached egg and anchovy dressing as a first course gives a hint to the Italian strand that runs through the repertoire, while crayfish bisque or salted duck with pickled damsons are interesting alternatives. Vincigrassi is a never-off-the menu house speciality – an eighteenth-century baked pasta dish containing Parma ham, porcini and truffles – but seasons are conscientiously observed elsewhere, so a June dinner brought peas and mint to accompany a plate of lamb, while asparagus and citrus butter partnered sea trout. Desserts, too, garner high praise: chocolate tart with fior di latte (a fresh, mozzarella-style cheese) or mascarpone brûlée with fresh rhubarb. Service is spot on, but it is a shame the wine list offers nothing under £21 for the spread is wide, the quality good.
**Chef/s:** Graham Grafton. **Open:** all week 12 to 2, 7 to 9.30. **Meals:** Set L £19.50 (2 courses) to £25.50, Set D £39.50 to £46. **Service:** 12.5% (optional). **Details:** Cards accepted. 50 seats. 24 seats outside. No mobile phones. Wheelchair access. Music. Children's portions. Children allowed. Car parking.

## ▌Bourton on the Hill

### Horse and Groom
**A self-styled 'proper pub'**
Bourton on the Hill, GL56 9AQ
Tel no: (01386) 700413
www.horseandgroom.info
**Modern British | £25**
**Cooking score: 2**

ᗙ Ⅴ

No frills – that goes for the décor, menu and food – just about sums up this old Cotswold stone inn run by Will and Tom Greenstock. The bar dispenses real ale and drinkers are made very welcome, but value-for-money cooking is the thing, and people come from miles around to eat here. The straightforward menu might see the likes of home-made Scotch quails' eggs with mustard cream sauce, or crab cake with garden leaves and salsa verde mayo to start. To follow, griddled Old Spot pork chop with apple compote and cider cream sauce vies for attention with locally reared Dexter rump steak with green peppercorn and tarragon butter. For dessert, the River Café's chocolate nemesis is a rich finish, as is vanilla pannacotta with home-grown raspberries. Service is 'young, enthusiastic and efficient'. The compact, reasonably priced wine list opens with French Muscadet and Australian Shiraz at £15.25 and £15.50 respectively.
**Chef/s:** Will Greenstock. **Open:** Tue to Sat L 11 to 3, Sun L 12 to 3.30, Mon to Sat D 6 to 11. **Closed:** 25 Dec. **Meals:** alc (main courses £9.50 to £15). **Service:** not inc. **Details:** Cards accepted. 75 seats. 54 seats outside. No music. Wheelchair access. Children's portions. Car parking.

### Please send us your feedback

To register your opinion about any restaurant listed in the Guide, or a new restaurant that you wish to bring to our attention, please visit the web address at the bottom of the page. Your feedback informs the content of the book and will be used to compile next year's reviews.

## ▌Bristol

★NEW ENTRY★
### The Albion
**Sturdy gastropub in Clifton**
Boyces Avenue, Clifton Village, Bristol, BS8 4AA
Tel no: (0117) 973 3522
www.thealbionclifton.co.uk
**Gastropub | £30**
**Cooking score: 1**

Renovated some two years ago from a very run-down boozer to its present trendy state, this dining pub shows off reclaimed wooden floors, comfy leather chairs and solid wooden tables. Jake Platt's menu focuses on the seasonal and the hearty, illustrated by rustic dishes such as rillettes of Gloucester Old Spot with onion jam and pickles, roast organic chicken in a fresh and generous Caesar salad, and rich and spicy baked duck egg with chorizo and new potatoes. For afters, you'll find favourites like Eton Mess, with occasional touches of the Med, such as the 'truly irresistible' olive oil pistachio cake with roast black figs. Nine house wines available by the small or large glass from £3.80/£5.40 and bottles start at £14.50.
**Chef/s:** Jake Platt. **Open:** Tue to Sun 12 to 3, Tue to Sat 7 to 10. **Meals:** alc (main courses £15 to £22) Set L £16 (3 courses) Set D £35 (3 courses). **Service:** 10% optional. **Details:** 120 seats. 50 seats outside. Separate bar. Wheelchair access. Music. Children's portions.

### Bell's Diner
**Ambitious kitchen**
1-3 York Road, Montpelier, Bristol, BS6 5QB
Tel no: (0117) 924 0357
www.bellsdiner.com
**Modern European | £31**
**Cooking score: 5**

The unassuming frontage gives nothing away – the long windows on two sides of the dining room retaining the feel of shopfronts from a generation ago. Yet inside, the place has a civilised, urbane look in keeping with Christopher Wicks's sophisticated modern cooking. His innovative concepts are supported by sound techniques, impeccable sourcing and unusual flavourings that bring vigour and surprise. Combinations vary from classical to novel, but none is contrived or attention-grabbingly outlandish. There are variations on familiar themes, such as the combination of Gressingham duck three ways – confit leg, roast breast, neck sausage – with sweet potato purée, pear jelly, pommes Anna and duck reduction, and turbot teamed with the classic Mediterranean flavours of tomato, roast peppers, rainbow chard, borlotti beans and courgette flower fritter, alongside rump of lamb with onion soubise and coffee-bean infusion. Interesting twists and turns among starters include teaming oysters with strawberry gazpacho and Serrano ham dust, and one-and-a-half-hour poached duck egg with Serrano ham, braised peas, gem lettuce and pea sorbet. Gentle invention is also applied to desserts, which might turn up a vinadaloo ice cream cornet with mango, lime, mint and a poppadom cone, or a pear pudding with Roquefort ice cream and walnut syrup. The enthusiasm of the staff contributes to the 'most enjoyable experience'. The food-friendly modern wine list is wide ranging, and keeps prices within reason, opening with French country wines at £13.

**Chef/s:** Christopher Wicks and Johnny Hazel. **Open:** Tue to Fri L 12 to 2.15, Mon to Sat D 6.30 to 10.30. **Closed:** 24 to 30 Dec. **Meals:** alc (main courses £14.50 to £19.50). Set D £45 (Mon to Thur, whole table only, max 6). **Service:** 10% (optional). **Details:** Cards accepted. 50 seats. No mobile phones. Wheelchair access. Music. Children's portions.

## ★NEW ENTRY★
## Bordeaux Quay
**Organic food haven**
V-Shed, Canons Way, Bristol, BS1 5UH
Tel no: (0117) 9431200
www.bordeaux-quay.co.uk
**Modern European | £30**
**Cooking score: 3**

The dream made real of Barny Haughton who also runs Quartier Vert, this ambitious project opened in September 2006 and includes a fine dining restaurant, brasserie, bar, cooking school, bakery and deli all under one ecologically sound roof. Indeed the building – too minimalist looking for some  has been designed to make the most of natural light and ventilation with rainwater flushing toilets and recycling in the kitchen. BQ's ethos also includes a commendable commitment to organic and local suppliers. The menu in the restaurant, with fine views over the harbour, reveals an à la carte and set menu with Mediterranean-style dishes such as Chew Valley beef sirloin with stewed red onions, peppers, chard and black olive relish followed by cheeses from Somerset, Berkshire and Pembrokeshire. The brasserie dishes are more straightforward, with moules marinière and roast mackerel and warm potato salad, olive and capers. The wine list shows intelligence, with a wide range of grapes and, wonderfully, every single one available by the 175ml or 250ml glass. Prices start at £13.50.

**Chef/s:** Liz Payne. **Open:** Mon to Sat 12.30 to 3, 6.30 to 10. **Closed:** Christmas Day & Boxing Day, New Year's Day. **Meals:** alc (main courses £12.50 to £19.50). **Service:** 10% (optional). **Details:** Cards accepted. 190 seats. 64 seats outside. Separate bar. Wheelchair access. Music. Children's portions.

## Café Maitreya

**Vegetarian food with attitude**
89 St Mark's Road, Easton, Bristol, BS5 6HY
Tel no: (0117) 951 0100
www.cafemaitreya.co.uk
**Vegetarian | £20**
**Cooking score: 4**

'Maitreya' is the Sanskrit word for 'universal love', but don't be fooled: this is no finger-cymbal, hippie hideaway. Instead, it serves dazzling vegetarian food with attitude and edge in an unshowy setting of pine tables, tiled floors and abstract artwork on grey/mauve walls. Mark Evans sets about plundering the world larder for quinoa, smoked ricotta, nori seaweed and other fashionable provisions; he also uses traditional herbs and gleanings from the wild for dishes that are light, vibrant, full of contrasts and decidedly left-field. It takes nerve – and considerable skill – to transform samphire into crispy beignets and serve them with baby fennel marinade and wood-smoked pepper dressing. Likewise, a meatless 'shank' fashioned from slow-cooked 'wet' garlic and pistachio nuts or a tarte Tatin of 'pied bleu' mushrooms and baby turnips with asparagus and nasturtium dressing are also guaranteed to raise eyebrows. To round things off, there might be a cherry and macaroon tartelette served with rhubarb and thyme ice cream or passion-fruit parfait with nougatine, passion-fruit tuile and sauce. The all-organic wine list doesn't venture outside Europe ('to avoid unnecessary transport'). House French is £12.50 (£4.25 a glass).
**Chef/s:** Mark Evans. **Open:** Tue to Sat D only 6.45 to 9.45. **Closed:** 24 Dec to 2 Jan. **Meals:** Set D £17.50 (2 courses) to £20.95. **Service:** not inc. **Details:** Cards accepted. 50 seats. Wheelchair access. Music.

★ READERS' RESTAURANT OF THE YEAR ★
SOUTH WEST

## Culinaria

**Unpretentious and consistently excellent**
1 Chandos Road, Bristol, BS6 6PG
Tel no: (0117) 973 7999
www.culinariabristol.co.uk
**French | £29**
**Cooking score: 4**

Stephen and Judy Markwick continue to do what they do best; serving up Elizabeth David-inspired classics that make the most of seasonal, top-quality ingredients in an informal, friendly setting. At Culinaria it's possible to browse the shelves of cookery books at your table or buy pastries, fresh soups, precooked meals and their own signature ice creams and sorbets from the deli. Stephen's experience behind the stoves is shown by a deep understanding of flavour and combinations and, with the emphasis on fresh, vibrant colours, he's not afraid to keep it simple and let the ingredients speak for themselves. The handwritten, weekly changing menu features classics such as Provençale fish soup with aïoli and sauce rouille and pan-fried scallops with pea and mint purée and air-dried ham to start. Following up are dishes such as roast guinea fowl with apples, Somerset brandy and cream or a vegetable tagine with saffron quinoa. Desserts stick to classic lines with St Emilion au chocolat or lime and ginger cheesecake with chocolate crust. Underpinning the food is the relaxed patter of a neighbourhood bistro with service that strikes the fine balance between attentive and discreet. The Markwicks' passion and integrity for Culinaria is also revealed by their short but well-constructed wine list from France (with Argentina and Italy edging in too). Prices begin at £14. NB. The restaurant is open Fri to Sat L and Wed to Sat D until Jan 2008, when new opening times, detailed below, take over.

**Chef/s:** Stephen Markwick. **Open:** Thu to Sat L 12 to 2, Thu to Sat D 6.30 to 9.30. **Meals:** alc (main courses £11.50 to £14.50). **Service:** not inc. **Details:** Cards accepted. 30 seats. No music. Wheelchair access. Children's portions.

## FishWorks

**Modern and classic British seafood**
128 Whiteladies Road, Clifton, Bristol, BS8 2RS
Tel no: (0117) 974 4433
www.fishworks.co.uk
**Seafood | £30**
**Cooking score: 2**

Seaside prints, ocean-blue walls and wooden flooring give the impression of relaxed coastal chic at this branch of Mitch Tonks' seafood chain. Although the penchant is for regional produce, European and Mediterranean influences are thoughtfully integrated in starters such as whitebait with aïoli or grilled swordfish with Moroccan spices and tomato salad. Mains could include easy-going dishes such as prawn, langoustine and fish pie, or the distinctive sea bream baked in salt. The well-conceived daily specials board showcases seasonally fresh catches such as pan-fried langoustines with garlic butter, and at its best the cooking style is thoroughly enjoyable, with dishes sparkling in their simplicity. Dessert brings classics such as sticky toffee pudding. Wines start at £3.75 a glass, with bottles from £16.
**Chef/s:** Neil Roach. **Open:** Tue to Sat 12 to 2.30 (soon to be extended to 3), 6 to 10.30. **Closed:** Bank hols and day after bank hols. **Meals:** alc (main courses £11.50 to £25). Set L £17. **Service:** Not inc. **Details:** Cards accepted. 48 seats. Air-con. Music. Children's portions.

★NEW ENTRY★

## Greens' Dining Room

**Welcoming neighbourhood diner**
25 Zetland Road, Bristol, BS6 7AH
Tel no: (0117) 924 6437
www.greensdiningroom.com
**Modern British | £25**
**Cooking score: 2**

With its 1950s-green exterior and awning Greens' has something of an American diner feel about it. The first solo venture by brothers Simon and Andrew Green, it's where you can expect to find a cosy interior of white walls, colourful modern art and a warm atmosphere, where the closely packed tables hardly seem to matter. Influenced by their culinary heroines Elizabeth David, Claudia Roden and Jane Grigson, the brothers' cooking style ranges widely from a very British starter of wood pigeon and rabbit terrine 'en croûte' with Cumberland sauce to a Mediterranean style main of seafood stew with fennel and aïoli. Eastern flavours also make an appearance with a starter of deep-fried Thai fishcakes with soy and pickled ginger. Desserts keep it simple with rhubarb fool and hot chocolate fondant. Service is confident with often-helpful advice on the interesting and reasonably priced wine list. It features a number of bottles from Greece, Germany and Austria as well as the French, Italian, Australian and New Zealand staples. A bottle of house white or red starts at £10.95.
**Chef/s:** Andrew and Simon Green. **Open:** Tue to Sun L 12.30 to 3, Tue to Sat D 6.30 to 10.30. **Closed:** Christmas week and last two weeks in Aug. **Meals:** alc L (main courses £6.50 to £9.50), D £19.50 (2 courses) £25 (3 courses). **Service:** not inc. **Details:** Cards accepted. 40 seats. 12 seats outside. Children's portions. Children allowed.

## Hotel du Vin & Bistro

**Wine-focused hotel and brasserie**
The Sugar House, Narrow Lewins Mead, Bristol,
BS1 2NU
Tel no: (0117) 925 5577
www.hotelduvin.com
**Modern European | £32**
**Cooking score: 3**

Part of an ever-expanding group that also
includes outlets in Birmingham, Brighton,
Harrogate, Henley-on-Thames, Tunbridge
Wells and Winchester (see entries), Bristol's
Hotel du Vin inhabits a spectacularly restored
sugar warehouse. The listed building
dates back to the eighteenth century, but it is
now reaping the benefits of a thorough
modern-day makeover. Classically inclined,
French brasserie cooking is the order of the
day, with dishes such as salad lyonnaise with
poached duck egg, rump of lamb with
provençale vegetables, and fillet of sea bass
with sauce vierge on offer. The kitchen also
tips its hat to the Mediterranean (chargrilled
swordfish, harissa mash and crayfish
gremolata, for example), while desserts
embrace everything from elderflower mousse
to chocolate and pecan brownie. Wine is a
major theme and the list makes impressive
reading, with champagnes aplenty and a vast
contingent of classy stuff from the French
regions. The rest of the world is also explored
in detail, with strong showings from
New Zealand, California and elsewhere
(including name-checks for Uruguay and
Slovenia). House vins de pays are £14.50.
**Chef/s:** Marcus Lang. **Open:** all week 12 to 2 (2.30
Sun), 6 to 10. **Meals:** alc exc Sun L (main courses
£12.50 to £20). Set L Mon to Sat £15 (2 courses), Set
L Sun £22.50. Bar menu available 2 to 5.
**Service:** 10%. **Details:** Cards accepted. 80 seats.
Wheelchair access. Music. Children's portions.

★NEW ENTRY★

## The Kensington Arms

**Newly restored pub**
35-37 Stanley Road, Redland, Bristol, BS6 6NP
Tel no: (01179) 446 4444
www.thekensingtonarms.co.uk
**Gastropub | £24**
**Cooking score: 3**

Where once was a scruffy and neglected
boozer is now a pub with a wooden-topped
bar, a chalkboard wine list and a separate
dining room. Serving real ales on draught,
Brothers bottled cider, Luscombe soft drinks
and a range of snacks such as dripping and
toast at the bar, is as integral here as the kitchen
and its fine dining room. Head chef Simon
Bradley, who sharpened his knives for eight
years at Odette's in Primrose Hill, sticks to a
repertoire of solid British classics. Dinner
might kick off with wild boar, veal and pork
meatballs or a dozen Mendip wallfish poached
in local cider. To follow are equally sturdy
dishes such as braised oxtail, steak and kidney
pie with suet pastry and Guinness gravy or a
chargrilled quail with a ham and cheese potato
cake. Desserts stay in the vein of 'like mother
used to make it' with rhubarb crumble and
custard, or apple and raison almond cake with
real vanilla ice cream. House wines start
at £13.50.
**Chef/s:** Simon Bradley. **Open:** Mon to Sun 12 to 3
(10 to 3 Sat) Mon to Sat 6 to 9.30 (6 to 10, Wed to
Sat). **Closed:** Christmas. **Meals:** alc (main courses
£11 to £12.75). **Service:** not inc. **Details:** Cards
accepted. 40 seats. 35 seats outside. Separate bar.
Music. Children's portions. Children allowed.

## One30

**Laid-back Mediterranean dining**
130-132 Cheltenham Road, Bristol, BS6 5RW
Tel no: (0117) 944 2442
www.one30.co.uk
**Spanish/Portuguese | £21**
**Cooking score: 2**
Ⓥ £30

With its leather sofas, low-slung tables and
terracotta walls, a relaxed Mediterranean
approach pervades the bar of One30. In
keeping is its tapas menu with spiced
aubergine salad and palourde clams with
Serrano ham, chilli and sherry. In the
restaurant a set menu kicks the cooking up a
notch as starters include provençale fish soup
with Gruyère, rouille and croûtons and pan-
fried chicken livers with tomato and bayleaf
sauce. Mains could be a colourful gnocchi
with roast squash, broad beans and Parmesan
or seared red mullet with sautéed ratte potato
and anchovy sauce. Desserts find their voice
with raisin and Earl Grey ice cream with warm
Pedro Ximenez and almond tuile or a plate of
Spanish artisan cheese (£1.50 supplement). It's
left to Portugal and Spain to slug it out on the
compact wine list that starts at £12.50 for a
bottle.
**Chef/s:** Johnny Evans and Chris Wicks. **Open:** Mon
to Thu 4 to 12, Fri to Sat 11 to 1, Sun 11 to 4 (D Mon
to Sat 6 to 10.30). **Closed:** 25 and 26 December.
**Meals:** alc (tapas £2.50 to £6.50). Set £16 (2
courses) to £21.50 (3 courses). **Service:** not inc.
**Details:** Cards accepted. 40 seats. 30 seats outside.
Separate bar. Wheelchair access. Music. Children's
portions.

## riverstation

**British dishes with European inspiration**
The Grove, Bristol, BS1 4RB
Tel no: (0117) 914 4434
www.riverstation.co.uk
**Modern European | £29**
**Cooking score: 3**
🍾 Ⓥ £30

It's not only the harbourside setting of this
modernist two-storey establishment that
makes a strong visual statement, but also the
ambitious cooking with its leaning towards
modern European ideas. Broadly appealing,
with the menu options changing daily, there is
undoubtedly culinary flair in dishes such as
Scottish scallops, 'glossy, light as pillows' offset
by aubergine caviar and saffron vierge, or a
delicately flavoursome pea pod and asparagus
soup. Consider finishing with chocolate St
Emilion – a cocoa, lemony and amaretti
sensation with 'soothing, dense layers'. Light
lunches and suppers include smoked haddock
beignets for mains or various mezze, which
can be taken in the lower-level bar. The global
wine list is reasonably priced, with ten house
wines available by the glass (from £3.50) and
by the bottle (from £13.50).
**Chef/s:** Peter Taylor & Tom Green. **Open:** Mon to
Fri, L 12 to 2.30, D 6 to 10.30 (11 Fri), Sat, L 10.30 to
2.30, D 6 to 11, Sun, L 12 to 3, D 6 to 9. **Closed:** 24 to
26 Dec, 1 Jan. **Meals:** alc (main courses £13.50 to
£20). Set L Mon to Fri £12 (2 courses) to £14.50, Set
L Sun £15.50 (2 courses) to £18.75. **Service:** not inc.
**Details:** Cards accepted. 120 seats. 28 seats
outside. Separate bar. No music. Children's
portions.

## ▌ Cheltenham

### Le Champignon Sauvage

**Modest, but capable of big statements**

24-26 Suffolk Road, Cheltenham, GL50 2AQ

Tel no: (01242) 573449

www.lechampignonsauvage.co.uk

**French | £48**

**Cooking score: 8**

£5 OFF 🍷

Occupying the ground floor of two small houses on a terrace just outside Cheltenham, Le Champignon Sauvage could hardly be lower key if it tried. Owners David and Helen Everitt-Matthias – he in the kitchen, she front-of-house – have run the restaurant almost like a small family-run French restaurant since 1987. 'David and Helen' (as their business card says) are confident enough to do things their way rather than follow restaurant fashion. The refit of two years ago has brightened up the relaxed blue and cream dining room, providing space enough for all to enjoy the generously proportioned tables. Bold modern art adorns the walls. Service is smooth and friendly, never overbearing. The idea is to relax, to be at the perfect point where enjoying food, drink and old-fashioned hospitality achieves near bliss. The restaurant has no truck with the business of tasting menus, wine flights and all that jazz. Instead, there is an à la carte menu, and a menu du jour that is available for lunch and from Tuesday to Friday for dinner. Everitt-Matthias goes where other, prissier chefs dare not. His highly technical, modern French cooking embraces wild, rootsy flavours – a forager's hand is much in evidence – where lesser chefs would shun them. A first course of 'cannelloni' of kid goat must have taken hour after hour of slow-cooking to reach a toothsome tenderness. A garnish of goats' milk curd, curls of landcress, and a vivid landcress purée complete the countryside tableau. Pressed terrine of rabbit, ham hock, and foie gras was similarly impressive. A main course of roasted Winchcombe venison, beetroot and horseradish purée was a celebration of the humble beetroot, offering subtle flavours and

textures paired with lightly pickled sauerkraut to set off the tender meat. Fillet of zander, Jerusalem artichoke cream, globe artichokes with liquorice, red wine and liquorice emulsion had a sweetness and depth to the emulsion, to which the unannounced samphire lent a contrasting saltiness. Desserts show the kitchen's even-handed way with taste, texture and temperature in balance: bitter chocolate and salted caramel délices, served with malted milk ice cream took a fashionable flavour pairing to new heights, soothing the salt, sweet and bitter with the cool ice cream. Chicory cheesecake with chicory ripple ice cream came with a bold nutty sweep of sauce. The wine list is short for a restaurant competing at this level, but all the choices are serious, food-friendly wines, guaranteed to set off the the kitchen's artistry. It is a very well-priced, predominantly French list – with a couple of pages apiece of Burgundy and Bordeaux – with choices from California, Australia and New Zealand. House wine starts as low as £11.

**Chef/s:** David Everitt-Matthias. **Open:** Tue to Sat 12.30 to 1.30, 7.30 to 9. **Closed:** 10 days Christmas, 3 weeks June. **Meals:** Set L £22 (2 courses) to £47, Set D Tue to Fri £22 (2 courses) to £47, Set D Sat £38 (2 courses) to £47. **Service:** not inc. **Details:** Cards accepted. 40 seats. No music. No mobile phones. Wheelchair access.

### Lumière

**Husband-and-wife team at the helm**

Clarence Parade, Cheltenham, GL50 3PA

Tel no: (01242) 222200

www.lumiere.cc

**Global | £35**

**Cooking score: 5**

🍷

Occupying a small Regency terrace just off the Promenade in the centre of Cheltenham, Lumière goes for a calm and soothing look, its deep mulberry and pale-green walls hung with abstract canvases. The place is owned by husband and wife team, Geoff and Lin Chapman. Lin runs a smooth operation front-of-house, and is a friendly and attentive host, while Geoff works hard in the kitchen to produce his inventive modern cooking. The Pacific Rim is the focus of his culinary attentions, though he takes his inspiration from wherever he finds it. Thus starters range from warm salad of grilled quail and crispy belly pork with cider dressing to seared foie gras with pan-fried baked potato, sweet apple dressing and aged balsamic. There are four or five choices per course, mains typically featuring seared brill fillet with sweet chilli tiger prawns and coriander potato pavé, or cashew-dusted rack of lamb with mustard tarragon sauce and curried leek potatoes. For dessert, choices might extend to coconut rice pudding with mango cream and coconut ginger sorbet, or pecan torte with caramel mousse and Jack Daniel's whiskey ice cream. The wine list, arranged by style, is updated 'almost daily', as regularly changing specials make way for new discoveries. Lin Chapman has compiled the list expertly and is always on hand to offer sensible advice. Prices start around the £20 mark.

**Chef/s:** Geoff Chapman. **Open:** Tue to Sat D only 7 to 8.45. **Closed:** first 2 weeks Jan, 2 weeks late summer. **Meals:** Set D Tue to Thur £31 (2 courses) to £38, Set D Fri and Sat £38 (3 courses). **Service:** not inc. **Details:** Cards accepted. 30 seats. Air-con. No music. No mobile phones.

## ALSO RECOMMENDED

### ▲ Brosh
8 Suffolk Parade, Cheltenham, GL50 2AB
Tel no: (01242) 227277
www.broshrestaurant.co.uk

In a street of fancy shops Brosh achieves an understated, refreshing calm with its white walls, wooden and slate floors and bare tables. Israeli cooking in the UK has tended to be dominated by kosher cooking; Sharon and Raviv Hadad, with long Israeli pedigrees including kibbutz living, remind us that it is first and foremost a Mediterranean country. Supported by good sourcing of local ingredients where appropriate, expect mezze, minced lamb with yoghurt, sardines with tomatoes and mains of vine leaves stuffed with feta, spinach and aubergine or caramelised garlic and capers alongside roast gilthead bream. Levantine accents are maintained with haroset ice cream. Two-dozen wines are well documented, cleverly chosen and start at £12.95. Open Wed to Sat, 12 to 2.30, 7 to 9.30

### ▲ Mayflower
32-34 Clarence Street, Cheltenham, GL50 3NX
Tel no: (01242) 522426

This long-running family-owned Chinese restaurant in Cheltenham now has a younger sibling in Cirencester. The formula must work; it's been serving the restaurant's faithful Cheltenham customers for over 25 years now, with a wide choice of set meals and an extensive à la carte. House specials like paper-wrapped prawns (£6.50) and Szechuan chicken (£8.50) are good options. The wine list starts at £12.95. Open all week.

## ■ Cleeve Hill
### Malvern View Hotel
**Refurbished and comfortably appointed**
Cleeve Hill, GL52 3PR
Tel no: (01242) 672017
www.malvern-viewhotel.co.uk
**Modern British | £34**
**Cooking score: 3**

Paul and Anna Hackett's smart restaurant-with-rooms commands stunning views over the Severn Valley from its lofty position on the flanks of Cleeve Hill near Cheltenham. The focal point is the bright dining room, where generous, well-spaced tables look on to the garden. Paul sources his raw materials conscientiously from local suppliers, with fish making a longer journey from Cornwall. His confident modern British cooking delivers largely straightforward dishes, the daily carte perhaps kicking off with potted salmon, prawns, spring onion and dill butter, or Evesham asparagus with chive butter. Follow with beef fillet with dauphinois and horseradish sauce, or monkfish wrapped in spinach. and turbot mousseline with mussels,

lobster and basil cappuccino. To finish, try the panaché of lemon desserts, or banana pannacotta with hazelnut baklava and orange glaze. Service from Anna is welcoming and enthusiastic and the wine list offers good variety, excellent value and plenty of choice, with prices starting at £13.75.
**Chef/s:** Paul Hackett. **Open:** Wed to Sun L 12 to 2, Tue to Sat D 7 to 9. **Meals:** alc (main courses L £10 to £18, D £18 to £22). Set L £15.95 (2 courses), Set D (exc Sat) £25. **Service:** not inc. **Details:** Cards accepted. 35 seats. 16 seats outside. Wheelchair access. Music. Children's portions. Car parking.

## READERS RECOMMEND

### The Albion
**Modern British**
Boyces Avenue, Clifton, BS8 4AA
Tel no: (0117) 973 3522
www.thealbionclifton.co.uk
'High-end gastropub'

## ▌Corse Lawn

### Corse Lawn House
**Inspired traditional cooking**
Corse Lawn, GL19 4LZ
Tel no: (01452) 780771
www.corselawn.com
French | £34
Cooking score: 3

🍷 ╤ V

The dignified Queen Anne building is separated from the village green by an expanse of water. It has belonged to the Hine family (as in cognac) since the 1970s, and is still personably and professionally run by Baba Hine with her son Giles. The dining room business is in the capable hands of Andrew Poole. The lengthy à la carte menus appear determined to promise all (or most) that earth, river and sea have to offer. It might be as traditional as a bowl of fish soup with rouille, or as modern as roast breast of duckling with braised lentils and quince glazed in honey and cider. Within that compass, though, dishes tack to readily comprehensible and appealing ideas, perhaps accompanying chargrilled

squid with a stew of beans and chorizo, or braising ox tongue in a red wine liquor and offsetting it with puréed beetroot. At the end comes banana tempura with pineapple crisp and coconut ice cream, or a vibrant sorbet selection. A very fine wine list is strong in classical France, but also shows evidence of pains taken elsewhere, with Iberia showing up enterprisingly. House wines are a Castilian red and a Muscadet at £13.70, or £3.80 a glass.
**Chef/s:** Andrew Poole and Martin Kinahan. **Open:** all week L 12 to 2, D 7 to 9.30. **Closed:** 24 to 26 December. **Meals:** alc (main courses £14.95 to £18.95). Set L £20.50 (2 courses) to £23.50 (3 courses), Set D £30.50. Bistro menu available. **Service:** not included. **Details:** Cards accepted. 100 seats. 60 seats outside. No music. No mobile phones. Wheelchair access. Children's portions. Car parking.

## ALSO RECOMMENDED

### ▲ Kings Arms
The Street, Didmarton, GL9 1DT
Tel no: (01454) 238245

This close to Badminton Estate, game is the order of the day at this seventeenth-century Cotswolds coaching inn. Seasonal specials crop up on the blackboard menu and weekly changing carte throughout the year. Few will resist the likes of roast haunch of Badminton venison and butter onion mash with red wine and juniper berry jus (£10.95). Lighter options could be a starter of goats'cheese and red onion charlotte (£5.10) or a pan-seared sea bass fillet on a sweet tomato and prawn risotto (£10.95). The lunch menu includes sandwiches and lighter dishes. There's a short wine list (from £13.75) plus local beers and cask ales. Open all week.

## ▌Fairford

### Allium

**Accomplished seasonal cooking**
1 London Street, Fairford, GL7 4AH
Tel no: (01285) 712200
www.allium.uk.net
**Modern European | £32**
**Cooking score: 6**

V

A pair of centuries-old, listed stone houses at the bottom of Fairford market square provides the setting for this immensely welcoming restaurant. Erica Graham's pleasant manner defines proceedings in the spacious dining room, while her partner holds sway in the kitchen. There is a vivid sense of seasonality about James Graham's cooking, and he is never shy about showing off his local allegiances. In summer, expect to see Claydon crayfish (served as a starter with pepper-cured salmon and gazpacho) as well as main courses involving roast Great Farm chicken, which needs nothing more elaborate than braised onions, leeks and cauliflower. Poached wood pigeon with snail-stuffed cabbage and St George's mushrooms has a pungent earthy ring to it, and the fondness for game also extends to haunch of roebuck with blackcurrants and morels. By contrast, fish is given clear, precise treatment, witness steamed red mullet with summer vegetables and herb nage. Presentation is a strong point, and it reaches its peak with finely honed desserts such as strawberry soufflé with strawberry meringue ice cream or peach and basil gâteau with champagne sorbet. The trolley of artisan British and Irish cheeses is 'out of this world', according to one satisfied correspondent, while the well-considered wine list puts France centre stage, with in-depth exploration of the major regions (notably Languedoc and the South-west). Global coverage extends to Oregon, Austria and Greece, and dessert wines are given special treatment. Almost 20 house selections are available by the carafe or glass (from £3), and bottle prices start at £16.50.

**Chef/s:** James Graham. **Open:** Wed to Sun L 12 to 2, Wed to Sat D 7 to 9. **Meals:** Set L £16 (2 courses) to £18.50, Set D Wed to Fri £20 (2 courses) to £50, Set D Fri and Sat £28.50 (2 courses) to £50, Set L Sun £22.50. **Service:** not inc. **Details:** Cards accepted. 34 seats. No mobile phones. Music. Children's portions.

## ▌Frampton Mansell

### White Horse

**Good-value menus**
Cirencester Road, Frampton Mansell, GL6 8HZ
Tel no: (01285) 760960
**Gastropub | £26**
**Cooking score: 2**

V £30

The White Horse's credentials as a slightly idiosyncratic gastropub are retained, and it continues to draw a chic young crowd. The fixed-price menu (two courses for £15.25) might include salmon and dill fishcakes with tartare sauce, followed by pan-fried kidneys with roasted shallots and garlic, crisp bacon and Madeira jus. The main menu, which changes monthly, offers oysters with red wine and shallot vinegar to start, then the likes of bream fillet with saffron risotto, lemon, dill, cream and capers. Desserts are mostly of the comforting variety – in evidence are bread-and-butter pudding with cream, and hot sugared beignets with toffee sauce. The wine list is expansive, but not necessarily expensive, with twenty or so under £20, with a good house white for £13.75. Glasses come in at £3.50 to £5.75.

**Chef/s:** Howard Matthews. **Open:** all week L 12 to 2.30 (3 Sun), Mon to Sat D 7 to 9.45. **Closed:** 25 to 26 Dec, 1 Jan. **Meals:** alc (main courses £11 to £16.50). **Service:** not inc. **Details:** Cards accepted. 45 seats. 50 seats outside. Music. Children's portions. Car parking.

## Lower Oddington

### Fox Inn

**Elegant and civilised dining pub**
Lower Oddington, GL56 0UR
Tel no: (01451) 870555
www.foxinn.net
**Modern British | £24**
**Cooking score: 1**

Among the pretty, mellow stone buildings in this quintessential Cotswold hamlet stands the Fox. The rambling interior has been kitted out with style and flair, the succession of intimate beamed rooms sporting exposed stone, attractive colour schemes, old pine tables on polished stone floors, fresh flowers, classical music and evening candlelight. On sunny days dine alfresco in the walled garden. Food is consistently good and the short, daily-changing modern menu makes good use of local produce. Begin with roasted butternut squash risotto or a simple crab mayonnaise with toast, then follow with casserole of rabbit with bacon, shallots and Dijon mustard or lamb shank braised with rosemary, red wine and whole roast garlic. Round off with rice pudding with plum jam. House wines are priced from £12.
**Chef/s:** Ray Pearce. **Open:** all week 12 to 2 (3 Sun), 6.30 to 10 (9.30 Sun). **Closed:** 25 Dec. **Meals:** alc (main courses £9.50 to £14). **Service:** not inc. **Details:** Cards accepted. 80 seats. 80 seats outside. Music. Children's portions. Car parking.

## Paxford

### Churchill Arms

**Continental cuisine in the Cotswolds**
Paxford, GL55 6XH
Tel no: (01386) 594000
www.thechurchillarms.com
**Modern European | £23**
**Cooking score: 4**

In essence this enchanting, mellow-stone inn, set in a pretty hamlet with glorious views over a stone chapel and rolling hills, looks no different in appearance from any other Cotswold village local. However, what sets it apart from your humble boozer is the well-heeled clientele, the 'vibrant' dining atmosphere and, most importantly, Sonya Brooke-Little's sophisticated cooking. In a setting of wooden floors, rough stone walls and a motley collection of old furnishings, she delivers simple, modern and robustly flavoured dishes that rely on quality ingredients, including properly reared meats and local seasonal vegetables. Look to the chalkboard menus on the thick central pillar for the day's choice, perhaps a hearty pea and ham soup or a peppered loin of tuna with horseradish, lemon and parsley for starters. Main courses may take in assiette of rabbit (leg confit, saddle and faggot) with Madeira; black bream with herb polenta and creamed fennel; and a 'gorgeous' rack of lamb. There are some pubby sounding dishes too, perhaps honey roast ham with egg and chips. Desserts run from triple chocolate torte with raspberry parfait to maple and mascarpone baked cheesecake with pineapple. The 'comprehensive, reasonably priced' wine list roves around the world and stays mostly below £20, with eight available by the glass. Note: best to arrive early as no bookings are taken.
**Chef/s:** Sonya Brooke-Little and David Toon. **Open:** all week L 12 to 2, D 7 to 9. **Meals:** alc (main courses £8 to £14). **Service:** not inc. **Details:** Cards accepted. 60 seats. 40 seats outside. No music. Children's portions.

## Poulton

### Falcon Inn

**Modern cooking in an informal pub setting**
London Road, Poulton, GL7 5HN
Tel no: (01285) 850844
www.thefalconpoulton.co.uk
**Modern European | £35**
**Cooking score: 4**

The Falcon continues to fly high on the food front. Behind a traditional white-painted façade lies a stylish and contemporary interior, with low ceilings, beams, a large fireplace guarded by a pair of stone falcons, and three intimate dining areas with chunky wooden furnishings, modern artwork on the walls, and subdued lighting. The monthly changing menu might open with crab cakes with home-made mayonnaise alongside smoked salmon and dill terrine, before roast cod on olive oil mash with pipérade, pan-fried duck with spiced red cabbage, or Old Spot pork chop served with a sage and apple jus. Skilfully crafted desserts span anything from sticky toffee pudding to vanilla crème brûlée. At lunchtime, there's a shorter menu of similar dishes and a great-value set menu. The well-chosen and well-described wine list offers plenty of interest, with wines by the bottle from £13.95 for white, and a Merlot for £14.95.

**Chef/s:** Willham Abraham and Jeremy Lockley. **Open:** all week L 12 to 2, Mon to Sat D 7 to 9. **Closed:** 25 and 26 Dec, 1 Jan. **Meals:** alc (main courses £9 to £17). Set L Mon to Fri £12 (2 courses), Set L Sun £15 (2 courses) to £20. **Service:** not inc. **Details:** Cards accepted. 50 seats. Wheelchair access. Music. Children's portions. Car parking.

## ▊Sapperton
### Bell at Sapperton
**Gentrified Cotswold pub**
Sapperton, GL7 6LE
Tel no: (01285) 760298
www.foodatthebell.co.uk
**Modern European | £30**
**Cooking score: 4**

The very model of a reinvigorated, prosperous Cotswold country inn, the Bell goes about its business diligently. Much of the focus is now on good-looking restaurant-style food, and the owners' allegiance to local produce can be judged by the list of trusted suppliers printed on the back of their menus. Meat and game dominate the monthly printed menu, and the kitchen sends out dishes such as breast of wood pigeon on warm black pudding and potato ahead of chump of Lighthorne lamb with root vegetables and rosemary. Daily deliveries of West Country fish ensure that the specials

board is also brimming with interesting possibilities like pan-fried wild sea bass with roasted globe artichoke, vanilla and red wine. To finish, there are well-crafted desserts such as ginger bavarois with poached rhubarb or chocolate and hazelnut torte with white chocolate sorbet. 'Grazing boards' and lighter dishes are the mainstays at lunchtime. Real ales from small Cotswold breweries are taken seriously (as befits a bona fide pub) and the thoughtfully chosen wine list includes some noteworthy Italian selections. Prices start at £14.50 for vins de pays and around 20 are available by the glass (from £4).

**Chef/s:** Ivan Reid. **Open:** all week 12 to 2, 7 to 9.30 (9 Sun). **Closed:** 25 and 26 Dec (evening). **Meals:** alc (main courses £13 to £17). **Service:** not inc. **Details:** Cards accepted. 75 seats. 50 seats outside. No music. No mobile phones. Wheelchair access. Children's portions. Car parking.

## ▊Shurdington
### The Greenway
**Well-appointed dining room**
Shurdington, GL51 4UG
Tel no: (01242) 862352
www.thegreenway.co.uk
**French | £43**
**Cooking score: 5**

🍴 ۷

The creeper-clad manor house dates from the reign of the first Elizabeth, and presents a honey-hued, essence-of-Cotswold face to the world. Marc Hardiman arrived in the summer of 2006, and aims to continue the style of gently contemporary cooking for which the place has been renowned. Crisp pork belly and braised cheek are partnered in a first course that is robustly bolstered with broad beans, caramelised onions and a Madeira jus. If you've room after that, main courses span the range from a modern classic pairing of turbot and oxtail (the meat stuffed into tortellini), accompanied by braised lettuce, to stuffed rabbit saddle with braised lambs' tongues, served with sweet carrots and parsley. More mainstream tastes might plump for a breast of corn-fed chicken with mash and truffled green

beans. The house speciality is a selection of chocolate and orange desserts, or you may opt for a plate of cheeses with fruit and nut bread, quince jelly and apricots. The weighty wine list essays a global trek from Champagne to the Cape, concentrating on breadth rather than depth. Eight house wines at £25.50 bring up the rear.
**Chef/s:** Marc Hardiman. **Open:** all week L 12 to 2, D 7 to 9.30. **Meals:** Set L £16.50 (2 courses) to £22.50, Set D £46.50 (3 courses). Bar menu available. **Service:** not inc. **Details:** Cards accepted. 36 seats. 24 seats outside. No mobile phones. Wheelchair access. Music. Car parking.

## Southrop
### Swan at Southrop
**Metropolitan dining in a rustic setting**
Southrop, GL7 3NU
Tel no: (01367) 850205
www.theswanatsouthrop.co.uk
**Modern British | £30**
**Cooking score: 2**

The handsome, creeper-clad Swan has been the jewel in the Cotswolds' crown for quality pub food since ex-Bibendum chef James Parkinson took control of the kitchen back in 2005. Having trained under Simon Hopkinson, his cosmopolitan menus reflect his mentor's classic ideas, with such simple dishes as steak tartare, langoustine mayonnaise, grilled entrecôte with béarnaise and pommes frites, and crab vinaigrette. More adventurous offerings may come in the form of guinea fowl with confit cabbage, lardons and thyme, and fillet of bream on crushed potatoes with grilled fennel, peppers, olives and parsley. Hot chocolate fondant with vanilla ice cream and lemon and cardamom parfait are typical desserts. Thick beams, uneven tiled floors, bare tables and roaring fires set the informal scene in the dining room. Head next door and you'll find a bustling bar and skittle alley for the locals. The wine list is a well-chosen slate favouring the Old World, with house French £12.50.

**Chef/s:** James Parkinson. **Open:** all week L 12 to 2.30, D 7 to 9.30. **Closed:** 25 and 26 Dec. **Meals:** alc (main courses £9.50 to £22). Set L Mon to Fri £12.50 (2 courses) to £16.50. **Service:** not inc. **Details:** Cards accepted. 75 seats. 24 seats outside. No mobile phones. Music. Children's portions.

## Stow-on-the-Wold
### Old Butcher's
**Quality ingredients and cooking impress**
7 Park Street, Stow-on-the-Wold, GL54 1AQ
Tel no: (01451) 831700
www.theoldbutchers.com
**Modern British | £24**
**Cooking score: 3**
£30

When Peter and Louise Robinson took over this stylish conversion of a former butcher's shop, everyone nodded approvingly – the couple had built up a loyal local following at the King's Arms across town. Two years on and the Robinsons have settled in, bringing a noticeably cosmopolitan edge to the brasserie-style operation while a modern outlook with local and seasonal materials helps to give the food its particular identity. Typical of the fine British food on offer is excellent organic bread from Daylesford, and Severn and Wye smoked eel with horseradish and bacon alongside home-bred Old Spot pork chop with fennel, garlic and parsley, although other ingredients come from further afield: seafood from Cornwall includes roast Fowey cockles with garlic and Ricard, for example, and turbot served with capers. A trio of fine farmhouse cheeses – perhaps Cashel blue, Saint Eadburgh and Saval, a Welsh artisan cheddar – is the savoury alternative to desserts such as Venetian rice pudding and chocolate tart. The short wine list spans both Old and New Worlds, with a clutch of house wines from both starting at £13.
**Chef/s:** Peter Robinson. **Open:** all week 12 to 2.30, 6 to 9.30 (7 to 9 Sun). **Closed:** 1 week May, 1 week Oct. **Meals:** alc (main courses £11 to £15). **Service:** not inc. **Details:** Cards accepted. 45 seats. 12 seats outside. Air-con. Wheelchair access. Music. Children's portions.

## Unicorn Hotel

**Traditional uncomplicated food**
Sheep Street, Stow-on-the-Wold, GL54 1HQ
Tel no: (01451) 830257
www.birchhotels.co.uk
**Modern European | £25**
**Cooking score: 2**

Standing proud between the Fosse Way and the local parish church, the stone-built Unicorn Hotel feels reassuringly English to a T. It makes a suitably traditional setting for food that takes due account of seasonal supplies and Cotswold produce. In the evening, the kitchen gets to work on uncluttered modern ideas in the mould of roast rump of lamb with minted courgettes, roast garlic gravy and olive oil mash or grilled fillet of halibut with local asparagus, salsa verde and Jersey Royals. Start with seared scallops and green pea guacamole or a salad of broad beans and locally smoked bacon, and close proceedings with chocolate marquise or rhubarb fool. At lunchtime, the emphasis is on simpler, light dishes. Three-dozen reasonably priced wines promise dependable drinking from £14 (£3.60 a glass). **Chef/s:** Michael Carr. **Open:** all week 12 to 1.45, 7 to 8.45. **Meals:** alc (main courses L £8.50 to £13, D £10.50 to £15.50). **Service:** not inc. **Details:** Cards accepted. 40 seats. Wheelchair access. Music. Children's portions.

## ▮ Tetbury

## Calcot Manor

**Ambitious modern food**
Tetbury, GL8 8YJ
Tel no: (01666) 890391
www.calcotmanor.co.uk
**Modern British | £39**
**Cooking score: 3**

Surrounded by a courtyard of ancient barns and stables, Calcot Manor has come a long way from its humble origins as a Gloucestershire farmhouse. These days it is a sleek country hotel complete with its own spa and the aptly named Conservatory restaurant. Slate floors, wooden blinds and candelabras provide a contemporary backdrop to Michael Croft's serious modern cooking. An ambitious streak runs through starters such as rabbit and lovage rillettes with marinated aubergine and toasted campaillou, while main courses often feature Highgrove organic beef and Duchy spring lamb (perhaps served with pea cappelletti, baby leeks and mint oil). Elsewhere, fish has its say with Dorset crab salad and pomegranate dressing, while liquorice crème brûlée with blackberry sorbet might feature among the list of vivid desserts. The wine list roams far and wide, with much of the space devoted to fine French vintages. House selections start at £16.75 (£4.20 a glass). In the grounds of the Manor is the Gumstool Inn, a family-friendly pub serving good-value food and real ales. **Chef/s:** Michael Croft. **Open:** all week 12 to 2, 7 to 9.30. **Meals:** alc (main courses L £9 to £14, D £17 to £19). Bar meals available. **Service:** not inc. **Details:** Cards accepted. 100 seats. 30 seats outside. Air-con. No mobile phones. Wheelchair access. Music. Children's portions. Car parking.

## ▮ Upper Slaughter

## Lords of the Manor

**Classy cooking in secluded surroundings**
Upper Slaughter, GL54 2JD
Tel no: (01451) 820243
www.lordsofthemanor.com
**Modern European | £48**
**Cooking score: 6**

Situated just upstream from Lower Slaughter, this honey-coloured Cotswold stone manor spreads itself comfortably amid eight acres of parkland running down to the banks of the River Eye. The grand building began life as a rectory around 1650, but has been extended over the centuries. It now flourishes as a luxurious and moneyed country-house hotel, much favoured by American tourists. Formal meals are served in a bijou dining room, which has numerous portraits on the walls and

a pleasing prospect of the walled garden from its French windows. Les Rennie's cooking is totally in keeping with the auspicious surroundings: it touts the obligatory quota of luxury ingredients, but also deploys the native regional produce to telling effect. Foie gras is pan-fried and served as a signature starter with tamarind ice cream and aged balsamic vinegar, while a main course of roast Gloucester Old Spot tenderloin keeps earthier company with pasta garganelli, broad beans and vanilla. Fish also makes its presence felt in different ways: eclectic Mediterranean influences work their way into a dish of seared bream with couscous, chorizo and matchstick chips, while monkfish receives exemplary modern British treatment with purple sprouting broccoli and wild garlic. Desserts are fancy creations like warm carrot cake with orange pannacotta and buttermilk sorbet or Valhrona chocolate tart accompanied by macadamia nut ice cream and black sesame. The heavyweight international wine list gives a lot of space to the French and Italian regional classics. Casa du Pedra house wines start the ball rolling at £19.50 (£4.50 a glass), and half-bottles also show up well.
**Chef/s:** Les Rennie. **Open:** Sun L 12 to 2.30, all week D 7 to 9.30 (10 Fri and Sat). **Meals:** Set L £25.50 (4 courses), Set D £49 (3 courses) to £59. Bar/terrace L menu available (exc Sun). **Service:** 10% (optional). **Details:** Cards accepted. 50 seats. 25 seats outside. No music. No mobile phones. Children allowed. Car parking.

## Symbols

🛏 Accommodation is available.

£30 Three courses for less than £30.

V More than five vegetarian dishes.

£5 OFF £5-off voucher scheme.

🍶 Notable wine list.

## ▌ Westbury on Trym

★ BEST UP-AND-COMING CHEFS ★ PETER AND JONRAY SANCHEZ-IGLESIAS

### Casamia
**Inspiring Italian in a traditional setting**
38 High Street, Westbury on Trym, BS9 3DZ
Tel no: (0117) 9592884
www.casamiarestaurant.co.uk
**Italian | £30**
**Cooking score: 5**

£5 OFF  V

A genuinely exciting newcomer on the scene since Peter and Jonray Sanchez-Iglesias recently returned home to cook at their parents' previously sleepy Italian restaurant. The interior of white linen, wrought iron and scenes of Venice may still be comfortably traditional but the menu reveals daring variations on classics and wholly contemporary Italian dishes. From a lengthy menu the starters might include a 'deconstructed Caesar salad' or a pear and walnut salad with Parmesan Reggiano dribbled with white truffle oil. Mains also show innovation with roast breast of chicken served with confit of its wings, Amaretto flavours and carrots in different textures. From here, move on to pasta and risotto dishes such as ten hour ragù of venison with tubular pasta followed by desserts of hazelnut dark chocolate truffle cake or strawberry soup with balsamic caramel ice cream. This is cooking constructed with real passion and beautifully presented. Produce is sourced from the surrounding area and Milan market, with herbs and exotic fruit grown in the courtyard. Meanwhile, parents Paco and Susan run front-of-house with all the friendly familiarity of a local restaurant. The wine list is mostly Italian, starting at £13.50 for a bottle of house red, with a full range of sherry and grappas planned.
**Chef/s:** Peter and Jonray Sanchez-Iglesias. **Open:** Mon to Sat D 6 to 11. **Closed:** Bank Hols, 25 and 26 Dec. **Meals:** alc (main courses £9.95 to £19.50).

Taster £35 (9 courses). **Service:** not inc.
**Details:** Cards accepted. 45 seats. 8 seats outside.
Wheelchair access. Music. Children's portions.

# ▌Winchcombe

## 5 North Street
**Intricate contemporary cuisine**
5 North Street, Winchcombe, GL54 5LH
**Tel no: (01242) 604566**
**Modern European | £33**
**Cooking score: 6**
ᐁ

A centuries-old, slightly crooked, half-
timbered exterior marks out Marcus and Kate
Ashenford's pint-sized restaurant, which
comprises two cosily rustic rooms with
ancient beams, bare varnished tables and a
tiled fireplace. It may feel endearingly
homespun, yet the food on offer is
emphatically up-to-the-moment, with bold
ideas and fashionable European flavours in
abundance. Menus are fixed-price and there is
no choice in the evening, although the kitchen
provides a full work-out for vegetarians.
Marcus Ashenford is an assured chef and his
cooking shows impressively high levels
of skill, technique and confidence. He also
works very hard. A great deal of effort and
precision is required for a starter that brings
together half a roast Cornish lobster with
pasta, ginger vegetables and a sauce of
champagne and lemongrass, although breasts
of local wood pigeon with apricot chutney and
watercress salad shows that the kitchen is also
at ease with less intricate notions. Big, bold
flavours ooze out of main courses like loin of
Old Spot pork with stuffing, caramelised
apples and black pudding sauce or duck breast
with lentils and smoked bacon, paired with
baby beetroots, spring onions and cassis sauce.
Imaginative touches have also been noted in
straightforward dishes like rhubarb mousse
pointed up with lemon and thyme; otherwise,
the chosen dessert might be something more
involved such as lemon polenta cake with
strawberry compote and chocolate sorbet. The
60-bin wine list gives preference to France and
the Old World, although there are keenly
priced, reputable pickings from around the
globe. Prices start at £17 for a pair of
Argentinians.
**Chef/s:** Marcus Ashenford. **Open:** Wed to Sun L
12.30 to 1.30, Tue to Sat D 7 to 9. **Closed:** 2 weeks
Jan, 1 week Aug. **Meals:** Set L £19.50 (2 courses) to
£23.50, Set D £30 to £50. **Service:** not inc.
**Details:** Cards accepted. 26 seats. No mobile
phones. Wheelchair access. Music. Children's
portions.

## Wesley House
**Energetic conviviality**
High Street, Winchcombe, GL54 5LJ
**Tel no: (01242) 602366**
**www.wesleyhouse.co.uk**
**Modern British | £33**
**Cooking score: 3**
🛏

Could this be anywhere other than England?
A resounding 'no' is the answer, as you survey
the half-timbered building and take in the fact
that the founder of Methodism, who once
stayed here, has unwittingly bequeathed his
name to the place. The air of energetic
conviviality with which it is run is a great
draw, as is Martin Dunn's pleasing culinary
style. Roast halibut with chorizo makes a
hearty main course, or there could be saddle of
rabbit with gnocchi, leeks and mushrooms, all
sauced with mustard and tarragon. Bookending the meal might be a plate of Isle of
Lewis smoked salmon with dill crème fraîche
and capers, and the sumptuous conclusion of
Calvados bavarois with apple jelly and sorbet.
Wine is taken seriously, the list adorned with
helpful notes and the selections frequently
imaginative. Drink by the glass from £4.50,
or the bottle from £16.50. A new wine bar
and grill under the same ownership has now
opened next door.
**Chef/s:** Martin Dunn. **Open:** all week L 12 to 2, Mon
to Sat D 7 to 9 (Sat 9.30). **Closed:** 25 and 26 Dec.
**Meals:** Set L £19.50 (2 courses) to £24.50, Set D
£29.50 (2 courses) to £35. **Service:** not inc.
**Details:** Cards accepted. 80 seats. Air-con.
Separate bar. No mobile phones. Music. Children's
portions.

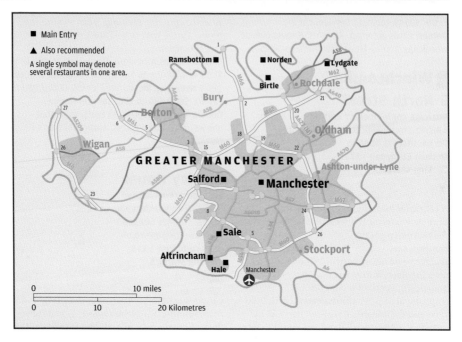

**Map legend:**
- ■ Main Entry
- ▲ Also recommended

A single symbol may denote several restaurants in one area.

0 — 10 miles
0 — 10 — 20 Kilometres

## ▍Altrincham

### Juniper

**At the cutting edge of experimentation**
21 The Downs, Altrincham, WA14 2QD
Tel no: (0161) 929 4008
www.juniper-restaurant.co.uk
**Modern French | £50**
**Cooking score: 7**

Behind an unprepossessing green and white frontage, on an Altrincham street lined with estate agents, lies the somewhat prosaic home to arguably one of the UK's most innovative chefs, Juniper's Paul Kitching. Based on a solid foundation of classic French cookery, there is evidence of technical excellence aplenty. But perhaps greater than all of these elements is the fact that Kitching seems to be the chef who is having the most fun. On arrival at the table the standard grandeur of the linen and cutlery is punctured by an incongruous plastic spoon. The bread arrives in a plastic sandwich case, for this night at least (themes seem to come and go): this is fine dining as imagined by Easyjet. There is no definitive explanation forthcoming but it works with the menu and makes for an excellent talking point. Experimentation and innovation is everywhere. Only at Juniper could you get a genuinely amusing amuse-bouche (one table dissolved into a fit of giggles on its arrival). The exquisite sliver of bitter chocolate tart that comes with the slow-cooked beef confounds the tastebuds by triumphing as a partnership. A starter of plain white scallops is served on a glorious technicolour oil slick of pimento colours. The pre-dessert is milk sweetened with oatmeal and crushed Love Hearts. Here is a chef who pours his ideas straight on to his plates but, essentially, never forgets the principle that the food should taste good. 'Unexpected and delicious', opined one reader, which neatly encapsulates the Juniper experience. There are areas for improvement – a relatively short wine list tends towards safer French choices (from £17) and a better selection by the glass would be welcome. Service is smart, knowledgeable and efficient but somehow doesn't seem to marry with the fun that's being had in the kitchens. However, a visit to Juniper represents a chance to witness one of the best chefs at work in the UK having the time of his life.

**Chef/s:** Paul Kitching. **Open:** Fri and Sat L 12 to 2, Tue to Sat D 7 to 10. **Closed:** Christmas, 1 week Feb, 2 weeks Aug. **Meals:** alc L (main courses £17 to £20). Set L £20 to £45, Set D £40 to £60. **Service:** not inc. **Details:** Cards accepted. 34 seats. Air-con. Music.

## ■ Birtle

## The Waggon at Birtle

Solid pub grub
131 Bury and Rochdale Old Road, Birtle, BL9 6UE
Tel no: (01706) 622955
www.thewaggonatbirtle.co.uk
Gastropub | £21
Cooking score: 3
£5 OFF  V  £30

If it weren't for the sign it would be difficult to detect the Waggon's former life as a pub. The claim that 'we are a neighbourhood restaurant that seves good food with an attention to detail' is amply supported by the evidence – shepherd's pie and venison stew for example, and the week-day market menu, a snip at £12.50 for two courses, might include chicken and black pudding terrine and pork, apple and sage sausage. Ingredients are carefully sourced with meat especially noted. Good English cooking is the mainstay but expect the odd bit of exotica such as smoked haddock risotto cakes or chorizo might pal up with roasted salmon and new potatoes. Boundaries are also crossed in the pudding zone; hot chocolate pudding and ginger sponge sit alongside praline parfait and crema catalana. Decent wines are available at fair prices (from £12.50).

**Chef/s:** David Watson. **Open:** Wed to Fri L 12 to 2, Wed to Sat D 6 to 9.30, Sun 12.30 to 7.45. **Closed:** 10 days from 1 January, first 2 weeks in August. **Meals:** alc (main courses £8 to £15.50). Set L and D Wed to Fri £12.50 (2 courses) to £14.50. **Service:** not included. **Details:** Cards accepted. 70 seats. Wheelchair access. Music. Children's portions. Car parking.

## ■ Hale

### ★NEW ENTRY★
### Earle

Omnivorous venture from Simon Rimmer
4 Cecil Road, Hale, WA15 9PA
Tel no: (0161) 929 8869
Modern British | £30
New Chef
V

Earle is proof, if proof were needed, that Simon Rimmer is one of the safest pair of hands on the Manchester restaurant scene. After setting high standards with his vegetarian operation, Greens, in nearby West Didsbury, new opening Earle shows that Rimmer is equally capable with other ingredients. The restaurant boasts polished wood floors, exposed brickwork and clean white walls. Although the décor may not break new ground it is comfortable, functional and displays a restrained style, befitting the monied environs of Hale. The menu doesn't take too many chances, indeed, it imports a few of the coveted dishes from Greens, including the signature starter of oyster mushroom pancakes. As you would expect, vegetarians are well catered for and there is even a vegetarian improvisation on the Lancashire hotpot which works beautifully. Elsewhere the menu sticks to safe ground, such as grilled salmon with new potatoes, burgers, crème brûlée and apple crumble, but this is several steps beyond standard brasserie fare.

**Chef/s:** Steve McLaughlin and Craig Kirk. **Open:** Tue to Fri L 12 to 2.30, Mon to Fri D 5.30 to 10.30, Sat and Sun 12 to 4.30, 5.30 to 10.30. **Closed:** Bank hol Mons. **Meals:** Set L £12.95 (2 courses) Set D £12.95 (2 courses). **Service:** not inc. **Details:** Cards accepted. 68 seats. 20 seats outside. Air-con. Separate bar. Music. Children's portions.

## Lydgate

### The White Hart Inn
Charming restaurant and country pub
51 Stockport Road, Lydgate, OL4 4JJ
Tel no: (01457) 872566
www.thewhitehart.co.uk
Modern British | £29
Cooking score: 4
£5 OFF ⊨ V £30

It may not be far from Manchester, but the setting of this old coaching inn is distinctly rural, with the village church opposite and views of the Pennines all around. The cooking style is straightforward and unpretentious, but not lacking in imagination, as demonstrated by starters of duck rillettes with mulled wine gooseberries and melba toast, or herb hash brown with poached egg and curry sauce. To follow, main courses take in braised lamb shoulder with rocket mint pesto and Anna potatoes, and roast rabbit leg stuffed with cured ham, black pudding and colcannon potatoes. There's also a range of locally made sausages served with a choice of flavoured mash, and to finish, desserts such as sticky toffee pudding with butterscotch sauce and cream. A hefty wine list makes room for ample notes and opens with a page of favourites, all available by the glass or bottle, priced from £15.

Chef/s: John Rudden. Open: Mon to Sat L 12 to 2.30, D 6 to 9.30, Sun and bank hol Mon 1 to 7.30. Closed: 26 and 27 Dec. 1 to 3 Jan. Meals: alc (main courses £15 to £20). Set L Mon to Sat and D Mon to Thur 6 to 6.45 £14.25 (2 courses) to £17.75. Set L Sun £19.75 (2 courses) to £23.50. Service: not inc.
Details: Cards accepted. 46 seats. 20 seats outside. No mobile phones. Wheelchair access. Music. Children's portions. Car parking.

## Manchester

★NEW ENTRY★
### Chaophraya
Stylish city-centre Thai dining
Chapel Walk, Manchester, M2 1HN
Tel no: (0161) 832 8342
www.chaophraya.co.uk
Thai | £22
Cooking score: 4
£30

Although discussing the various ways that this restaurant's name could be pronounced makes for a diverting dinnertime discussion, the prosaic answer is that it's 'Chow-pie-a'. It's an unfamiliar word that is beginning to be used with increased frequency as this triumphant new arrival sets the standards for Thai cuisine in the city. Chaophraya's décor falls just the right side of opulence without straying into OTT territory and the setting matches the quality of the service. The restaurant offers diners two options, the Yee Rah Sizzler Grill, which offers a tapas-style lunch option, and the 120-seat à la carte restaurant upstairs with its stately table settings. The menu runs to around 100 items with ample choice for vegetarian diners and in-depth seafood, curry and stir-fry options. With dishes like skewered king prawns of the goong yang BBQ, the flavoursome chicken of the gai nutty, and a consummately spiced tom yum gai soup all proving the skill and experience of the kitchens, it seems Chaophraya is an essential addition to your vocabulary.

Chef/s: Thanyanan Phuaknapo. Open: Daily 12 to 12. Meals: alc (main courses £8 to £26).
Service: not inc. Details: Cards accepted. 130 seats. Music. Children allowed.

## Glamorous Chinese

**Popular Chinese specialising in dim sum**
Wing Yip Business Centre, Oldham Road, Ancoats,
Manchester, M4 5HU
Tel no: (0161) 839 3312
www.glamorous-restaurant.co.uk
**Chinese | £30**
**Cooking score: 2**

The not so glamorous entry to this busy Chinese is hidden on the first floor amid a vast business centre and car park. Nevertheless the place fills up fast and serves up a wide-ranging menu from 11am, seven days a week. Dim sum seem to be the highlight with a vast array to choose from, such as steamed beef or pork dumplings, scallop dumplings, deep-fried oysters or perhaps 'light as a feather' salt and pepper squid with chilli. The remainder of the menu is more straightforward Cantonese fare: duck with black bean and green pepper, or perhaps steamed king prawns with ginger. The wine list provides well-chosen wines for the cuisine at fair prices. Bottles start at £10.25. **Chef/s:** Piu Hung. **Open:** all week 11 to 11 (to 11.45 Fri and Sat). **Meals:** alc (main courses £6.50 to £13). Set L £5.95 (2 courses) to £9.95, Set D £15.50 (min 2) to £22 (min 2). **Service:** not included. **Details:** Cards accepted. 400 seats. Air-con. Wheelchair access. Music. Car parking.

## Greens

**Delightful modern bistro**
43 Lapwing Lane, West Didsbury, Manchester,
M20 2NT
Tel no: (0161) 434 4259
www.greensrestaurant.net
**Vegetarian | £25**
**Cooking score: 2**

♈ £30

Thanks to Simon Rimmer's exciting way with vegetables, there is no chance that you will need coercion to eat your greens; indeed, it will be a pleasure. Several menu items take their inspiration from notable meat dishes but gratifyingly they often improve on the original, as with Green's signature oyster mushrooms with pancakes and plum sauce.

The herb and Cheshire cheese sausages are excellent, as is the risotto with fennel and roasted tomatoes. Dessert tends to be a more mainstream affair with crème brûlée, chocolate pudding and spotted dick all featuring. The cheeses are worth investigating as they are often local. This is only a relatively small restaurant and its ongoing popularity means booking early is advisable. If you prefer privacy ask for a table away from the front, as passing pedestrians often peek through the window, plus it avoids the occasional draft from the door. House wines start at £11. **Chef/s:** Simon Rimmer. **Open:** Tue to Fri and Sun L 12pm to 2pm (12.30pm to 3.30pm Sun), all week D 5.30pm to 10.30pm. **Closed:** bank hols. **Meals:** alc (main courses £10.95). Set L Sun and D Sun to Fri 5.30 to 7 £12.95 (2 courses). **Service:** not inc. **Details:** Cards accepted. 48 seats. 8 seats outside. Air-con. Music. Children's portions.

## Lime Tree

**Crowd-pleasing modern British menu**
8 Lapwing Lane, West Didsbury, Manchester,
M20 2WS
Tel no: (0161) 445 1217
www.thelimetreerestaurant.co.uk
**Global | £26**
**Cooking score: 3**

♈ ♈

Every suburb deserves a restaurant like the Lime Tree, where you can get excellent-quality food without any of the ego that you sometimes have to suffer in city-centre restaurants. Patrick Hannity's modern British restaurant has quality built into every element from the light and airy dining room to the excellent local produce that features on the constantly changing menu. Starting with oysters Rockefeller, carpaccio of beef fillet or a spatchcocked quail served with a rich port jus, the kitchen wisely avoids being over-fussy with simple, honest ingredients. Mains are mostly a mix of roast meats and fish, and while the menu may not startle you with originality, it does deliver consistently excellent food. A fillet steak with fat chips is faultless and a halibut steak with Welsh rarebit crust proves the chef has a winning way with fish. Desserts include rich chocolate torte and a startlingly good sticky toffee pudding. With wines starting from £12.95 and a rota of frequently changing wines to match the menu the Lime Tree is well worth a detour.

**Chef/s:** Jason Parker and Jason Dickenson. **Open:** Tue to Fri and Sun L 12 to 2.30, all week D 5.45 to 10.15. **Meals:** alc, exc Sun L (main courses £7 to £16.50). Set L Tue to Fri £14.95, Set L Sun £16.95, Set D 5.45 to 6.30 £14.95. **Service:** not inc. **Details:** Cards accepted. 90 seats. 24 seats outside. Wheelchair access. Music. Children's portions.

## Little Yang Sing

**Classic Cantonese dishes**
17 George Street, Manchester, M1 4HE
Tel no: (0161) 228 7722
www.littleyangsing.co.uk
**Cantonese | £25**
**Cooking score: 1**
£5 OFF  V  £30

While it may not necessarily deserve the adjective 'Little', the titular link with Yang Sing is a worthy indicator of the quality that can be found inside this George Street Cantonese restaurant. The selection is extensive and ranges from classics such as fried wontons, spring rolls and sui mai to more adventurous, but still resolutely delicious, dishes, like coconut chicken samosas and prawn bauble with almond flakes. A special selection of vegetarian dim sum is also available. The carte offers a range of Cantonese dishes like steamed duck with seasonal green vegetables and seafood dishes such as pan-fried scallops with ginger and spring onion and oysters in black pepper sauce. House wines start from £11.95.

**Chef/s:** Kui Keung Yeung. **Open:** all week 12 to 11.30 (till 12 Fri, 12.30 Sat, 10.45 Sun). **Closed:** 25 December. **Meals:** alc (main courses £8 to £13). Set L £9 (2 courses) to £11, Set D £17.50 to £27.95 (min 2). **Service:** 10%. **Details:** Cards accepted. 220 seats. Air-con. Wheelchair access. Music. Children's portions.

## Moss Nook

**An intriguing French restaurant**
Ringway Road, Manchester, M22 5WD
Tel no: (0161) 437 4778
**Anglo-French | £42**
**Cooking score: 4**

If you struggle to find Moss Nook then simply follow the rapidly descending planes, as their landing gear almost grazes the roof of this South Manchester restaurant. Despite its proximity to the 747s of Manchester Airport there are no problems with noise from the aircraft once inside the restaurant. The interior here feels somewhat dated and indeed the menu could best be described as having a classical French focus but with its ongoing popularity – Moss Nook has been open since 1973 and chef Kevin Lofthouse has been in situ since 1983 – suggesting that there's nothing broken, it would be foolish to make any attempt to fix it. Starters might include hot foie gras on a potato rösti or pan-seared scallops with vegetables. Some excellent cuts of meat grace the main menu and again display Lofthouse's passion for French cuisine – medallions of fillet beef served with a Café de Paris sauce and roast breast of duck with dauphinoise potatoes. The Menu Surprise represents the best value, with several tasting courses demonstrating the capabilities of the kitchen. Naturally, the wine list focuses largely on French wines and the house wines start at £16.50. Overall, Moss Nook is an enjoyable blast from the past.

**Chef/s:** Kevin Lofthouse. **Open:** Tue to Fri L 12 to 1.30, Tue to Sat D 7pm to 9.30. **Closed:** 2 weeks Christmas. **Meals:** alc (main courses £19.50 to £23). Set L £19.50 (whole table only), Set D £37 (whole table only). **Service:** not included. **Details:** Cards accepted. 65 seats. 20 seats outside. Air-con. No music. No mobile phones. Jacket and tie required. Children allowed. Car parking.

## Pacific

**High-profile Chinatown restaurant**
58-60 George Street, Manchester, M1 4HF
Tel no: (0161) 228 6668
www.pacificrestaurant.co.uk
Cantonese/Thai | £28
Cooking score: 2

V £30

As well as keeping standards high, the novelty of this restaurant is that it is really two operations in one, with a Chinese restaurant on the ground floor and a Thai kitchen serving the first floor. The two separate aspects of Pacific even have different opening times, so be sure to check that your preferred part of the restaurant is open when you go. Pacific Chinese offers a largely standard Cantonese menu, although it does have an excellent range of seafood, such as the whole steamed eel, abalone and a superb Dover sole steamed with garlic sauce. Pacific Thai is arguably the better half of the restaurant with a popular lunchtime buffet and an extensive menu covering curries, noodle dishes and a decent selection for vegetarians. House wines start at £11.50.
**Chef/s:** Tim Wong. **Open:** Thai: Mon to Sat 12 to 3, 6 to 11, Sun 12 to 10; Chinese: all week 12 to 12 (11.30 Sun). **Meals:** alc (main courses £8 to £18). Set L and D £19 to £35.50 (some min 2). **Service:** 10%.
**Details:** Cards accepted. 250 seats. Air-con. Wheelchair access. Music.

## Red Chilli

**Excellent Cantonese cooking**
70 Portland Street, Manchester, M1 4GU
Tel no: (0161) 236 2888
www.redchillirestaurant.co.uk
Chinese | £22
Cooking score: 2

V £30

Whilst the majority of Manchester's Chinatown restaurants serve Cantonese food, the appeal of Red Chilli is its focus on the delights of Beijing and Szechuan cooking. Evocatively named dishes like Mountain City Pork Duet, Crystal Layers and Crispy Yellow Croaker with sweet and sour sauce mean that

even if you're not quite sure what they are, it sounds like they might be interesting to try. Even if the décor is a bit flat, the presentation of the food couldn't be more exciting – flashes of colour grace each dish and some of the fish dishes, such as the deep-fried sea bass, look stunning and are worthy of a visit alone. House wines start at £11.50.
**Chef/s:** Mr Zhang. **Open:** all week 12 to 10.30 (11.30 Fri and Sat). **Meals:** alc (main courses £6.50 to £14). Set L £8 (3 courses) Set D £18 to £26 (min 2). **Service:** not inc. **Details:** Cards accepted. 90 seats. Air-con. Music. Children allowed.

## Restaurant Bar & Grill

**Solid choice for familiar grub**
14 John Dalton Street, Manchester, M2 6JR
Tel no: (0161) 839 1999
www.individualrestaurants.com
Global | £27
Cooking score: 2

V £30

It will be interesting to see how the arrival of other grill restaurants in the city centre affect this perenially popular brasserie. With the busy bar downstairs and the light and bustling restaurant upstairs, Restaurant Bar and Grill is the sort of venture that does exactly what it says on the tin. With a crowd-pleasing menu featuring all the dishes like burgers, grilled steaks and fish and chips that you might expect, the only deviation is in a light scattering of global influences such as the lamb tagine or the mushroom cannelloni. The dessert menu continues to bring few surprises with sticky toffee pudding, crème brûlée and cheesecake all in evidence. A shorter than expected list of wines starts from £13.95.
**Chef/s:** Alan Earle and Dave Bright. **Open:** all week 12 to 3, 6 to 11 (10.30 Sun). **Closed:** 25 Dec.
**Meals:** alc (main courses £9.50 to £20). Bar menu available. **Service:** not inc. **Details:** Cards accepted. 185 seats. Air-con. No mobile phones. Wheelchair access. Music. Children's portions.

## Second Floor

Fine dining with outstanding views
Harvey Nichols, Exchange Square, Manchester, M1 1AD
Tel no: (0161) 828 8898
www.harveynichols.com
**Modern European | £34**
**Cooking score: 5**

�♈ ✙

With its floor-to-ceiling windows and stark interior there is something almost clinical about Second Floor. Following the departure of Robert Craggs, the new head chef is Alison Seagrave, who has been with the restaurant since 2003. Her tenure has been fêted by press and customers alike, leading to awards for best chef and Manchester's Food Hero of the Year. With the closure of fine dining restaurants The Establishment and Le Mont, you would imagine Seagrave would be playing it safe, but there is no sign of nerves in her French-inspired menus. Starters of fillet of red mullet with salsa verde and slow-cooked ham hock with pease pudding show a remarkable way with flavours, and mains of braised beef bourguignon and horseradish dumplings and curried aubergine risotto confirm that Seagrave is one of the best chefs currently working in the city. Her humour also shines through with desserts such as an assiette of pick and mix desserts, which takes sweetshop flavours into new areas, and the dark chocolate and peanut butter ice cream profiteroles deserve a much wider audience. House wines start at £13.50.
**Chef/s:** Alison Seagrave. **Open:** all week L 12 to 3 (5 Sun), Tue to Sat D 6 to 10. **Closed:** 25 and 26 December, 1 January, Easter Sunday. **Meals:** alc (main courses £11 to £21). **Service:** 10%. **Details:** Cards accepted. 100 seats. Air-con. Wheelchair access. Music. Children allowed.

## Simply Heathcotes

Modern brasserie offering eclectic food
Jackson Row, Deansgate, Manchester, M2 5WD
Tel no: (0161) 835 3536
www.heathcotes.co.uk
**Modern British | £26**
**Cooking score: 2**

✙

This large, friendly modern brasserie in the heart of Manchester is the forerunner of a small Northern chain (see Leeds, Liverpool and Wrightington) which offers an eclectic menu with fixed pricing. Start with a crispy soft-shell crab, chilli, lime and coriander, or golden beetroot with shallot and parsley dressing and sour cream. Mains are wide ranging, with offerings such as citrus-seared sea bass with braised fennel or, perhaps, a simply grilled rump steak with Marmite butter. Finish with a wonderfully creamy goats' milk pannacotta with mixed berries and basil sugar. Service is 'excellent'. A substantial selection on the wine list provides some interesting drinking, with more than a dozen by the glass. House wine is an Italian duo at £14.95 and £3.85 per glass.
**Chef/s:** Eve Worsick. **Open:** all week 12 to 2.30, 6 to 10 (11 Sat, 9 Sun). **Closed:** 25 and 26 December, 1 January. **Meals:** alc (main courses £9.50 to £22). Set L Mon to Sat £12.95 (2 courses), Set D Mon to Sat 6 to 7, £12.95 (2 courses), Set D Mon £15 (inc wine). **Service:** not included. **Details:** Cards accepted. 150 seats. Air-con. Wheelchair access. Music. Children's portions.

## The French at the Midland Hotel

Belle Epoque splendour
16 Peter Street, Manchester, M60 2DS
Tel no: (0161) 236 3333
www.qhotels.co.uk
**Modern European | £44**
**New Chef**

🍽 ✙

To say that the Midland French is an institution is almost an understatement. This lavish Belle Epoque-style venue has been open since 1903 and Bruno, the maître d', has presided over the restaurant for nearly 40 years. As one might expect, the service is the efficient and gracious old-fashioned kind, but the food has been modernised – which does not please everyone. First courses of intensely flavoured mushroom risotto with truffle oil or tortellini of chicken might be followed by Scottish organic salmon with beetroot risotto and cauliflower beignets, or a more daring wild brill with an oxtail jus, but inspection found that good ideas were not always consistently well executed. Desserts found favour in the form of a stem ginger pudding with mango sorbet and an assiette of all things chocolate. A selection of 'gutsy' home-made loaves also impressed. The now reigned-in but representative wine list holds some very decent drinking; prices reflect the quality. House wine is less than £20, with a number of labels available by the glass.

**Chef/s:** Paul Beckley. **Open:** Tue to Sat D 7 to 10.30. **Closed:** 25 to 30 Dec, Bank Hols. **Meals:** alc (main courses £29.95 to £28.95). Set D Tue to Thu £25 (2 courses) to £41 (4 courses). **Service:** not inc. **Details:** Cards accepted. 50 seats. Air-con. Separate bar. No mobile phones. Wheelchair access. Music.

## Yang Sing
**Leading Cantonese restaurant**
34 Princess Street, Manchester, M1 4JY
Tel no: (0161) 236 2200
www.yang-sing.com
**Chinese | £28**
**Cooking score: 4**
V £30

Make no mistake: the Yang Sing is a Manchester institution. In recent years, expansion has been on the agenda and now the Princess Street restaurant feels more like the hub of an empire. Fortunately, the main

restaurant has not been neglected and a recent renovation has been successful in brightening the corners, transforming shady-looking nooks into fantastic bright booths. With the dim sum menu running to 60 items and the à la carte menu offering close to 200 dishes, menu blindness can be a real problem, so it is wise to enlist the help of your waiter. Cantonese cuisine ranges from the predictable to the innovative. Try chicken and sweetcorn parcels, bamboo boxes crammed full of steamed prawn dumplings, roast pork with soy-drenched jellyfish, pigs' trotters steeped in a rich broth or ostrich fillets in a piquant lemongrass sauce. House wines start at £18.90.

**Chef/s:** Harry Yeung. **Open:** all week 12 to 10.45 (11.15 Fri and Sat, 9.45 Sun). **Closed:** 25 December. **Meals:** alc (main courses £8 to £15.50). Set L and D from £27.50 (min 2). **Service:** net prices. **Details:** Cards accepted. 230 seats. Wheelchair access. Music.

## ALSO RECOMMENDED
### ▲ Bridgewater Hall, Charles Hallé Room
Lower Mosley Street, Manchester, M2 3WS
Tel no: (0161) 907 9000

The Charles Hallé restaurant opens 276 nights a year. That's not a random number: it's the number of performances at this stunning Manchester concert venue – before each one of which concert-goers can enjoy a pre-performance dinner in the in-house restaurant (last orders at 6.45pm). Creative, but agreeably balanced menus change daily (£20 or £25 for 2 or 3 courses plus coffee and petits fours) are French with a twist, as seen in such dishes as pork rillettes, quenelle of potted goose, confit of spiced red cabbage and beetroot; mille feuille of salmon and crayfish, baby vegetables, tomato and star anise sauce; and coupelle of raspberry bavarois, blackberry compôte, white chocolate sauce. Wine from £11.95.

## ▲ Koh Samui

16 Princess Street, Manchester, M1 4NB
Tel no: (0161) 237 9511

Koh Samui is a colonial-style, airy basement restaurant close to Manchester's Chinatown, priding itself on high-quality Thai cuisine. Seafood is a strong suit, with a menu that strives to offer more than the same old British Thai standards. Hot and sour fish samui-style (from £12.95), stir-fried morning glory and crispy belly pork (£7.95) or the winningly named, 'the drunk's cure' (from £7.95) sit alongside a good choice of stir-fries, hot soups, noodles and Thai curries (with anything from chicken or pork to sea bass or halibut). Vegetarians are very well catered for. The weekday business lunch starts at just £7, with the wine list opening at £10. Closed Sat and Sun L.

## ▲ Market Restaurant

104 High Street, Manchester, M4 1HQ
Tel no: (0161) 834 3743
www.market-restaurant.com

Although the décor of this Northern Quarter cornerstone might be frozen in the past, its modern British menu is anything but dated, which explains why the restaurant has got to the point where it can celebrate its 20th birthday. The menu created by gifted chef Mary-Rose Edgecombe changes every five to six weeks to make the most of seasonal produce and can feature chorizo with a butter-bean and tomato salad (£6.25) or roast duck with potato and sorrel pancakes (£16.95). Inspiration comes mainly from France and Italy but relies on produce from much closer to home. Desserts are a house speciality – to the extent that they run Sweet Meets, an occasional pudding club where for £25 you can indulge in a light main followed by five puddings. Refreshingly, the wine list starts at £9.95 for a carafe of house white and is augmented by a speciality beer list.

## ▲ Palmiro

197 Upper Chorlton Road, Manchester, M16 0BH
Tel no: (0161) 860 7330
www.palmiro.net

Some might struggle with a menu that shuns Italian crowd-pleasers such as garlic bread or pizza, but when even choosing blindly, Palmiro will reward the diner with dishes like grilled mushroom with caciocavallo (£4.95), fennel and salsiccia risotto (£6.25) and seared duck breast with orzo and spinach (£13.95), comprehension comes at a different level. An expansive wine list focusing appropriately on regional Italian wines, with prices starting at £8.75.

## ▲ That Café

1031 Stockport Road, Levenshulme, Manchester, M19 2TB
Tel no: (0161) 432 4672
www.thatcafe.co.uk

It seems unlikely that anything good can possibly exist on the A6, but That Café is proof that great restaurants sometimes turn up in unlikely places. The cooking is handled by Alison Eason who creates a constantly changing menu of Modern British dishes which wear their Mediterranean influences lightly. A roulade of smoked fish served on wild garlic leaves (£6.95) and a salad of avocado, feta, pea and celery (£6.95) show that despite the name this is not the sort of food you'd expect from a standard café. Mains might be an inventive seafood lasagne which somehow gets salmon, monkfish and shrimps to work together (£15.75) or stuffed chicken served on spicy chickpeas (£15.25). Finish with desserts such as blueberry and marscapone cheesecake or the chocolate truffle tart. House wines start at £10.50.

# ▌Norden

## Nutters

**Friendly outfit with a loyal fan club**
Edenfield Road, Norden, OL12 7TT
Tel no: (01706) 650167
**Modern British | £36**
**Cooking score: 3**

One of the interesting things about Andrew Nutter's operation, sited in an eighteenth-century manor house overlooking Ashworth Moor, is the rabid loyalty that it engenders from its clientele. Customers seem to be converted into Nutter missionaries in the space of one visit. It's easy to see why customers feel such a strong connection with the restaurant. Even though this is a grand venue it is always welcoming and there is a real warmth in the service. Perhaps it is the fact that this is a family operation (Nutter's mother and father are integral to the running of the operation) or maybe it's simply because it offers consistently high-quality food in pleasant surroundings. Even the menu seems to befriend you: offering comforting choices which are innovative enough to excite (the black pudding wontons being a case in point) without risking alienation. Some solid work has gone into sourcing the produce and the meats are excellent. The pork medallions served with ginger and soy dumplings are absolutely ripe with flavour and perfectly cooked. With an excellent range of wines (including half a century of bottles under £20) even those who find selecting wines onerous should find themselves feeling at home at Nutters.

**Chef/s:** Andrew Nutter. **Open:** Tue to Sun 12 to 2 (4 Sun), 6.30 to 9.45 (9 Sun). **Closed:** Christmas, New Year, bank hol Mon. **Meals:** alc exc Sun L (main courses L £13.50 to £15.50, D £16.50 to £19). Set L Tue to Sat £12.95 (2 courses) to £15.95, Set D £35. **Service:** not inc. **Details:** Cards accepted. 154 seats. No mobile phones. Wheelchair access. Music. Children's portions. Car parking.

# ▌Ramsbottom

**★ READERS' RESTAURANT OF THE YEAR ★
NORTH WEST**

## Ramsons

**An Anglo-Italian-inspired treasure**
18 Market Place, Ramsbottom, BL0 9HT
Tel no: (01706) 825070
www.ramsons.org.uk
**Anglo-Italian | £35**
**Cooking score: 4**
£5 OFF ♦ Ⅴ £30

Chris Johnson is an evangelist, totally committed to preaching the message about sourcing traceable and seasonal ingredients. This admirable commitment permeates the Anglo-Italian menu, which offers a choice of two to five courses or the chef's special 'surprise' nine-course affair. Whatever you choose, there are still revelations, such as a tiny cup of leek and potato soup preceding, perhaps, brown shrimp ravioli in a lobster bisque or an intensely flavoured and perfectly executed squid ink risotto with pepper salami. Vegetables or salad are served as a separate course 'to aid digestion' before following with organically reared Inglewhite veal served with cremini mushroom sauce, say, or grilled fillet of turbot teamed with sautéed spinach and fennel sauce. Dishes are assured and uncluttered, enabling the complexity of flavours to show through. Skill and attention is also evident in the sweet department. A little taste of England in a pre-dessert custard tart might be followed by buttermilk pannacotta with rhubarb compote or the now signature Amalfi lemon quartet. The 'informal friendly atmosphere, but dedicated approach to good food and service' impresses many readers, while the exclusively Italian and fully annotated wine list is a real treat, with Chris on hand to offer advice. Prices start at about £15, with some by the glass at £3.50. NB As the guide went to press we were told that chef Amy Bicknell is to leave after 14 years, to be replaced by Mary-Ellen McTague (formerly of the Fat Duck). Abdullah Naseem continues in the kitchen.

**Chef/s:** Abdulla Naseem and Mary-Ellen McTague.
**Open:** Wed to Sat L 12 to 2.30 (1 to 3.30 Sun), Wed
to Sat D 7 to 9.30. **Closed:** 2 weeks in May.
**Meals:** Set L £15 to £20 (2 courses), Set L Sun
£22.50 (2 courses) to £27.50, Set D £25 to £50.
**Service:** not inc. **Details:** Cards accepted. 34 seats.
No music. No mobile phones. Children's portions.

## Sale
### Hanni's
**Good-value food from the Middle East**
4 Brooklands Road, Sale, M33 3SQ
Tel no: (0161) 973 6606
**Eastern Mediterranean | £23**
**Cooking score: 2**
£5 OFF  V  £30

Mohammed Hanni has moved on and new
owners are now at the helm of this popular
neighbourhood restaurant, although the name
remains the same. It is also business as usual in
the kitchen, where the team continues to serve
up a colourful mix of authentic Eastern
Mediterranean and Middle Eastern dishes.
Appetising meze are one of the star turns:
expect a varied hot and cold assortment
ranging from grilled halloumi cheese, börek
pastries and yershig (chunks of garlicky lamb
sausage) to hummus, tabbouleh and fasuliya (a
salad of white and red beans with peppers and
mint). High-protein kebabs dominate the
main courses, although the choice is fleshed
out with specialities such as lamb kleftiko and
couscous in various guises. Meals end in
traditional fashion with sticky baklava,
Turkish delight and halva. The wine list is a
short international slate, with Chilean house
selections opening at £12.95 (£3 a glass).
**Chef/s:** Hovanan Hoonanian and Mehmet Eken.
**Open:** Mon to Sat D only 5.30 to 10 (6 to 10.30 Sat).
**Closed:** 25 and 26 Dec, Easter Mon. **Meals:** alc
(main courses £11.50 to £17.50). Set D £22 to £25
(min 2 persons). **Service:** not inc. **Details:** Cards
accepted. 40 seats. Air-con. Wheelchair access.
Music. Children's portions.

## Salford
### Lowry Hotel, River Restaurant
**Contemporary chic with British classics**
50 Dearmans Place, Chapel Wharf, Salford,
M3 5LH
Tel no: (0161) 827 4041
www.roccofortehotels.com
**Modern European | £38**
**Cooking score: 4**
🍷 ⊨ V

Located on the banks of the Irwell, the River
Restaurant has been criticised in the past for
feeling impersonal and it should be noted that
it is the restaurant of a large hotel. The
criticism seems especially harsh, though, as
the brilliance of executive head chef Eyck
Zimmer's menu has more than enough
identity to overcome any quibbles over the
interior design. Zimmer is a multi-award-
winning chef whose most recent prize is the
National Chef of the Year award, formerly
held by Gordon Ramsay. Since taking over in
2005 he has refined his mainly modern
European menu and fine-tuned the service
and the River Restaurant now has a strong
claim for offering the best dining experience
in the city centre. Starters might be a minted
pea soup with pear or oyster ravioli with
smoked bacon foam. Thereafter, the menu
splits into risottos and pastas, fish, meat and a
bonus menu of classic British dishes – a
peerless Lancashire hotpot among the latter
choices. Desserts include five spice crème
brûlée, custard tart and a chocolate brownie.
The extensive wine list has a global pedigree
and house wines start at £26.
**Chef/s:** Eyck Zimmer. **Open:** Mon to Sat 12 to 2.30, 6
to 10.30, Sun 12.30 to 4, 7 to 10.30. **Meals:** alc
(main courses £15.50 to £34.50). Set L and D £20 (2
courses) to £42. **Service:** 10% (optional).
**Details:** Cards accepted. 110 seats. 40 seats
outside. Air-con. Wheelchair access. Music.
Children's portions.

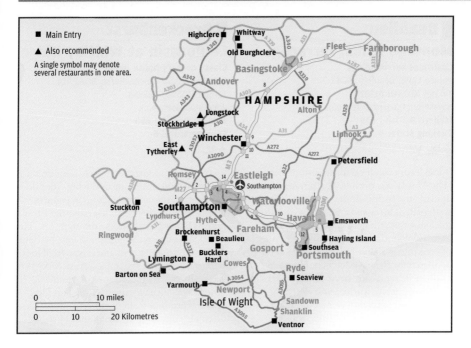

Map legend:
- ■ Main Entry
- ▲ Also recommended

A single symbol may denote several restaurants in one area.

## ■ Barton on Sea

### Pebble Beach

**Stunning cliff-top location**
Marine Drive, Barton on Sea, BH25 7DZ
Tel no: (01425) 627777
www.pebblebeach-uk.com
**Modern Seafood | £32**
**Cooking score: 3**

Exceptional views from the modern dining room and terrace extend across Christchurch Bay to the Needles and the western tip of the Isle of Wight. Add the culinary talents of Pierre Chevillard, who spent many years at Chewton Glen (see entry, New Milton), and you have a seriously good seafront café/brasserie. Expect Breton-style fish soup, Gigas rock oysters, or crayfish and French bean salad to feature among the starters, with main courses run along the lines of bouillabaisse, or pan-fried monkfish with tomato confit and white wine and rosemary jus. Carnivores get a good choice, too, perhaps duck with sweet-

and-sour cherry sauce, or assiette of pork – tenderloin, confit belly and black pudding – served with Savoy cabbage, and Burley apple cider sauce. Impeccable desserts may include warm chocolate brownie with crème anglaise and peanut ice cream. Most bottles on the short, French-led wine list are in the £20-plus range, but house wines start at £12.95.
**Chef/s:** Pierre Chevillard. **Open:** all week 12 to 2 (2.30 Sun), 6.30 to 9.30 (10 Fri and Sat). **Closed:** D 25 Dec, D 1 Jan. **Meals:** alc (main courses £10 to £25). Light menu available exc Sat D. **Service:** not inc. **Details:** Cards accepted. 70 seats. 40 seats outside. Air-con. No mobile phones. Wheelchair access. Music. Children's portions. Car parking.

### Average price

The average price listed in main-entry reviews denotes the price of a three-course meal, without wine.

## ▌Beaulieu

### Montagu Arms, Terrace

Luxurious surroundings
Palace Lane, Beaulieu, SO42 7ZL
Tel no: (01590) 612324
www.montaguarmshotel.co.uk
**Modern British | £38**
**Cooking score: 4**

🍷 ╪ Ⅴ

If you have a fondness for traditional luxury, 'The Monty' fits the bill. The Terrace is a large, opulent and formal dining room and service is well drilled, brisk and attentive with 'a slight tendency towards hard-sell'. The kitchen's gastro-credentials are impressive: the 'director of cooking' is Shaun Hill. While the Terrace is no match for the old Merchant House in Ludlow, its repertoire bears the hallmarks of Hill's considered, forthright style. The highlight at inspection was an intensely flavoured (and 'impressively wobbly') pannacotta-style scallop mousse, topped with pea shoots and served on a warmly spiced carrot and ginger purée. Plaudits were also due for an interesting quail and rabbit pudding filled with morel cream, set on a vibrant, orange-flavoured jus. An overly sweet gravy and a wad of coarse greens lowered the tone of an otherwise creditable trio of pork loin, belly and black pudding. Desserts take an innovative spin on traditional favourites: witness sticky toffee pudding with banana-split parfait. Wines are grouped by style, rather than grape or origin, with bottles from £17.
**Chef/s:** Shaun Hill and Scott Foy. **Open:** all week 12 to 2.30, 7 to 9.30. **Meals:** Set L Mon to Sat £19 (2 courses) to £22, Set L Sun £25, Set D £42. **Service:** not inc. **Details:** Cards accepted. 70 seats. 30 seats outside. No mobile phones. Wheelchair access. Music. Children allowed. Car parking.

## ▌Brockenhurst

### Le Poussin at Whitley Ridge

Classy country-house dining
Beaulieu Road, Brockenhurst, SO42 7QL
Tel no: (01590) 622354
www.lepoussin.co.uk
**Modern British | £50**
**Cooking score: 6**

🍷 ╪

Two huge stone watchdog-style hounds, set sentry-like on either side of the big front door of this wisteria-covered Georgian country house, have no chance of deterring the savvy crowds beating a path to the dining room. The menu picks up on the poussin theme, perhaps delivering stuffed breast and crispy fried legs with a cassoulet of vegetables. Alex Aitken's classically based modern cooking continues its innovative journey, driven by the best local seasonal produce from the forest and sea. Ideas often play out on the plate as duos or trios: pink loin of lamb served with slow-cooked kidney and roast sweetbreads, while a signature hot passion-fruit soufflé comes teamed with a 'wonderfully intense' passion-fruit sauce with an accompanying passion-fruit sorbet and passion-fruit curd delivered 'cornet style' in a tuille cone perched in a shot glass. The wine list is a cracker, a sublime classical collection with plenty of starry names, but plenty of easy-going drinking too (house from £15 and there's plenty by the glass). Note: Parkhill, Le Poussin's real home at Lyndhurst, is undergoing major refurbishment, and is currently expected to reopen in the spring of 2008.
**Chef/s:** Alex Aitken and Shane Hughes. **Open:** all week L 12.30 to 2, D 6.30 to 9.30. **Meals:** alc (main courses £25.50 to £27.50). Set D £45 (3 courses). **Service:** 12.5% (optional). **Details:** Cards accepted. 55 seats. 36 seats outside. No music. No mobile phones. Wheelchair access. Children's portions. Car parking.

## Simply Poussin
**Gutsy flavours**
The Courtyard, Brookley Road, Brockenhurst,
SO42 7RB
Tel no: (01590) 623063
www.simplypoussin.co.uk
**Modern British | £30**
**New Chef**

Alex Aitken's other restaurant is a thriving town-centre brasserie. Open with the signature starter, a rich, creamy, twice-baked cheese soufflé; or maybe go for the chicken terrine with figs poached in red wine, or smoked pigeon breast on a mango and pine-nut salad with optional foie gras. To follow, rare beef fillet is topped with sticky oxtail and served with wild mushrooms, horseradish mash and red-wine sauce; and a 'trio of lamb' comprises the best end, braised shoulder and kidney on ratatouille with rosemary dumplings. Round off the meal with passion-fruit soufflé, or an 'assiette of chocolate' comprising hot chocolate fondant, white chocolate mousse, chocolate brûlée and sorbet. House wines start at £14.50.
**Chef/s:** Martin Dawkins. **Open:** Tue to Sat 12 to 2, 6.30 to 9.45. **Meals:** alc (main courses £10.50 to £16). Set L 12 to 1.30 and Set D Tue to Thur 6.30 to 8.30 £10.50 (2 courses). **Service:** 10% (optional). **Details:** Cards accepted. 36 seats. No mobile phones. Wheelchair access. Music.

## ▌Bucklers Hard
## Master Builder's House Hotel, Riverview Restaurant
**Historic maritime settings**
Bucklers Hard, SO42 7XB
Tel no: (01590) 616253
www.themasterbuilders.co.uk
**Modern European | £31**
**Cooking score: 2**

⇔ ⋎

With a magical setting on the River Beaulieu estuary, this smart hotel's Riverview Restaurant certainly lives up to its name. The dining room is relaxed and modern, offering a subtle nod to the nautical with its blond-wood floors and ceiling. The straightforward, appealing cooking charts a crowd-pleasing course enhanced by quality ingredients and a nod to foreign climes. Think barramundi served with crushed potatoes, tomato concassé, black olives and spinach, while a peach tarte Tatin teamed with a peach sorbet might head up desserts. The wine list's French-led global mix is all perfectly shipshape too, with some interesting choices and a dozen or so house offerings to kick things off, starting at £14.75.
**Chef/s:** Denis Rhoden. **Open:** all week L 12 to 3, D 7 to 10. **Meals:** alc (main courses £10 to £22). Set L £16.50 (2 courses) to £22.50, Set D £29.95. **Service:** not inc. **Details:** Cards accepted. 70 seats. 30 seats outside. Music. Children's portions. Car parking.

## READERS RECOMMEND
## The Baker's Arms
**Gastropub**
High Street, Droxford, SO32 3PA
Tel no: (01489) 877533
**'A family-run pub with a warm welcome'**

## ALSO RECOMMENDED
## ▲ Star Inn
East Tytherley, SO51 0LW
Tel no: (01794) 340225
www.starinn-uk.com

Tucked away in the picturesque Test valley, this former seventeenth-century brick-built coaching inn's setting provides that quintessential English idyll. Nevertheless, this is no timeless rustic local, rather a country inn and restaurant-with-rooms. Lunch is a light affair while dinner ratchets up the output, driven by quality local seasonal produce. The kitchen's accomplished traditional approach is given modern spin and eye-catching presentation; take baked fillet of cod served with bubble and squeak, crispy vegetables and red-wine sauce, and perhaps a glazed lemon tart teamed with raspberry coulis to finish.

The compact wine list is grouped by old and new worlds and sets off globetrotting from £13.95.

# ▮ Emsworth

## Fat Olives

**Harbourside location**
30 South Street, Emsworth, PO10 7EH
Tel no: (01243) 377914
www.fatolives.co.uk
**Modern British | £25**
**Cooking score: 3**

Ⅴ £30

Whether the name or the olives came first they certainly have fat ones at this former fisherman's cottage. Since 2000 (when the Murphys went it alone) Lawrence has applied his learning, picked up the hard way in hotel kitchens, to a surprisingly ambitious menu that would defeat lesser cooks. While influences reflect the ubiquitous plundering of European cooking, there is healthy regard for local sourcing; from South Downs' pork with curly kale and apple sauce, via local mutton served with a robust accompaniment of black olives and red wine, to braised shin of beef from the Rother Valley. Puddings often seem to come as trios of this and that; ice creams have been particularly noted. A succinct wine list is fairly priced (from £12.75).
**Chef/s:** Lawrence Murphy. **Open:** Tue to Sat 12 to 2, 7 to 9.15. **Closed:** 2 weeks Christmas, 1 week in Oct, Tue after Bank Hols. **Meals:** alc (main courses £13 to £19). Set L £15 (2 courses) to £16 (3 courses). **Service:** not included. **Details:** Cards accepted. 28 seats. 10 seats outside. Wheelchair access. Music.

## 36 On The Quay

**Restaurant-with-rooms by the harbourside**
47 South Street, Emsworth, PO10 7EG
Tel no: (01243) 375592
www.36onthequay.com
**Modern European | £35**
**Cooking score: 6**

🍷 🛏

Down beside the cobbled quayside, among the old cottages, bobbing boats and the shrill of seagulls, one could almost be in Devon rather than overlooking Chichester Harbour. While 36 is housed in a seventeenth-century building, proprietor's Ramon and Karen Farthing have their eyes firmly set on current trends. Ramon's confident, complex and sophisticated cooking adds contemporary spin to classical French underpinning, perhaps delivering roast honey-spiced duck breast alongside a confit leg pastry, poached Agen prunes, caramelised peppered swede and a 'cracking' duck and cumin sauce. Wife Karen at front-of-house marshalls her team with equal efficiency, though the mood is friendly, relaxed and unbuttoned for a South Coast culinary big-hitter. Ramon's fixed-price repertoire is a stylish affair driven by the freshest produce, flavour and originality, combined with head-turning presentation. Portions are on the generous side, even desserts (like the iced peanut parfait coated in crisp chocolate and decked out with warm mini-butterscotch doughnuts and a coffee-and-white-chocolate foam), so do break out those loose-fitting gladrags. A serious wine list comes ordered mainly by style, with house from a wallet-friendly £14.50, while both Italian and French selections catch the eye.
**Chef/s:** Ramon Farthing. **Open:** Tue to Sat 12 to 1.45, 6.45 to 9.45. **Closed:** 3 weeks Jan, 1 week May. **Meals:** Set L £18.95 (2 courses) to £22.95, Set D £45 (5 courses) to £60. **Service:** not inc. **Details:** Cards accepted. 45 seats. 10 seats outside. Wheelchair access. Music. Children's portions. Car parking.

## ▌Hayling Island

### Marina Jaks

**Local seafood is the star**
Sparkes Boatyard, 38 Wittering Road, Hayling
Island, PO11 9SR
Tel no: (02392) 469459
www.marinajaks.co.uk
**Modern British | £28**
**Cooking score: 2**
£5 OFF  V  £30

This former chandler's in a marina at the
entrance to Chichester harbour may not be the
easiest restaurant to find, but it is well worth
making the effort. Starters take in everything
from gazpacho soup with a crab cocktail
garnish to red mullet with butter-poached
tiger prawns on lemon and chive risotto, while
main courses feature roasted salmon with
citrus-braised endive, crab, crushed potatoes
and lobster broth, or mussels with creamy
cider and smoked bacon sauce. Finish perhaps
with lemon posset or white chocolate mousse
with Baileys. French house selections at
£10.95 open a compact, accessible wine list.
**Chef/s:** Leicester Kettlety. **Open:** all week 12.30 to
3, 7 to 10. **Closed:** Mon Nov to June. **Meals:** alc
(main courses £8 to £30). **Service:** not inc.
**Details:** Cards accepted. 80 seats. 50 seats outside.
Air-con. Wheelchair access. Music. Children's
portions. Car parking.

## ▌Highclere

### Marco Pierre White's Yew Tree

**Gastropub with classic French food**
Hollington Cross, Andover Road, Highclere,
RG20 9SE
Tel no: (01635) 253360
**Modern Anglo-French | £40**
**Cooking score: 5**
🍴 V

Marco Pierre White has stamped his identity
on to this attractive roadside inn (literally). It's
a class act, decorated with lashings of good
taste and a dollop of humour. Highclere is

many miles from the sea, but there's
something fishy going on at the Yew Tree. The
embossed cutlery and some of the artwork
have all been 'recycled' from Wheeler's, an
iconic London fish restaurant that the astute
Mr White bought when it ceased trading.
Indeed, several of the restaurant's signature
dishes (the excellent gravad lax, say) have
joined MPW stalwarts on a menu where no-
nonsense dishes worthy of Mrs Beeton sit
alongside classic French fodder straight out of
*Larousse Gastronomique* (which you need to
decipher the menu). Traditional favourites run
from shepherd's pie, via venison 'Pierre
Koffmann' served with a bitter-chocolate
bordelaise sauce, to a very boozy sherry trifle
credited to Wally Ladd (one of MPW's cohorts
at the Connaught). Fresh, perfectly cooked
fillets of sardines impressed at inspection,
stacked on toasted sourdough and topped with
a vibrant tomato coulis; likewise an utterly
classic lobster thermidor. The perfectly
rendered raspberry soufflé is a star among the
puddings. The wine list majors on France and
features some canny selections. Bottle prices
range upwards from £14.50.
**Chef/s:** Neil Thornley. **Open:** all week 12 to 3, 6 to
10 (9 Sun). **Meals:** alc exc Sun (main courses £10.50
to £27.50). Set L Mon to Sat £13.50 (2 courses) to
£16.50, Set L Sun £17.50 (2 courses) to £19.95, Set D
Sun £12.50 (2 courses) to £14.50. Cover £2.
**Service:** not inc. **Details:** Cards accepted. 90 seats.
30 seats outside. Children's portions. Car parking.

## ▌Isle of Wight

### George

**Straight off the ferry**
Quay Street, Yarmouth, Isle of Wight, PO41 0PE
Tel no: (01983) 760331
www.thegeorge.co.uk
**Anglo-French | £34**
**Cooking score: 3**
🍴 V

The location could hardly be more convenient
for mainland folk – step off the ferry, turn left
and walk ten metres along the pavement. But
the George has charms besides convenience.
Gone is the serious and sombre restaurant, but

the brasserie is still going great guns with new chef Jose Graziosi at the helm. There's a very strong emphasis on local ingredients, which the Isle of Wight does rather well, but the cuisine is fundamentally French, albeit with a few English touches (colcannon with your confit duck, perhaps). Potted salmon, a mixture of poached and smoked fish set in clarified butter, made the grade at inspection, along with a richly truffled duck salad and a first-rate rib steak, served on the bone. The wine list is unashamedly (and appropriately, perhaps) about three-quarters French, but very much geared to the British palate, with an emphasis on Châteauneuf and other familiar favourites. House offerings start at £15.25.
**Chef/s:** Jose Graziosi. **Open:** Mon to Sat L 11 to 4, D 6 to 12, Sun L 12 to 3, D 7 to 10.30. **Meals:** alc (£40 to £50 for three courses). **Service:** not inc. **Details:** Cards accepted. 60 seats. Air-con. No music.

## Hambrough Hotel
**Stylish boutique hotel**
Hambrough Road, Ventnor, Isle of Wight, PO38 1SQ
Tel no: (01983) 856333
www.thehambrough.com
**Modern European | £36**
**Cooking score: 4**
£5 OFF ⇌ V

On the Isle of Wight's southern fringe, this stylish boutique hotel affords stunning views over the bay at Ventnor. The cooking is in tune with the times, delivering a dish of scallops, fashionably teamed with cauliflower, pancetta and curry oil, or a crispy goats' cheese with Mediterranean vegetable pressé, tomato sorbet and aged balsamic. Good raw materials are more often than not improved by the treatment they receive: a fine fillet of beef with a creamed garlic, wild mushroom tortellini, spinach, truffled gnocchi and Maderia jus had been accurately roasted, and a sparkling fresh brill successfully combined with braised fennel, sautéed morels, stuffed courgette flower, shallots and a flavourful

bisque-style sauce. Meals end on a high note with praline parfait, Italian meringue and roasted peach, or a plate of rhubarb desserts (mousse, jelly, fennel and rhubarb salad) with stem ginger ice cream. The global wine list is arranged by style and opens with house Chilean at £14.
**Chef/s:** Craig Atchinson. **Open:** all week 12 to 2, 7 to 9.30. **Meals:** Set L £17.95, D £38. 50 (3 courses). **Service:** not inc. **Details:** Cards accepted. 30 seats. No mobile phones. Music.

## Seaview Hotel
**Captain Walker at the helm**
High Street, Seaview, Isle of Wight, PO34 5EX
Tel no: (01983) 612711
www.seaviewhotel.co.uk
**Modern British | £31**
**Cooking score: 3**
⇌ V

The culinary ambition of this pretty, ivy-clad boutique hotel has been racheted up a couple of notches with the arrival of chef Graham Walker. Dining is now an altogether more formal experience, with full-on French service, and there's a smart new setting, too. Think sharp modern styling with a vaguely nautical theme. The modern British menu screams its seasonal and local credentials with complex-sounding creations to the tune of Sandown Bay black bream, toasted rice water, white beans, fennel and lemon oil. At inspection, slow-cooked duck was a novel riff on the classic chou farci: three medallions cut from a cylinder of rich meat encased in Savoy cabbage, resting upon artful smears of prune compote and vanilla-flavoured parsnip purée. To finish, desserts are mostly updated versions of traditional classics, from a solid but flavoursome sticky toffee pudding to a pear crumble with pear sorbet and compote. Bottle prices on the international wine list kick off in the mid-teens, but the real action starts just over £20.
**Chef/s:** Graham Walker. **Open:** all week L 12 to 2.30, D 6.30 to 9.30. **Closed:** 24 to 26 Dec. **Meals:** alc (main courses £14 to £22). **Service:** not inc.

**Details:** Cards accepted. 80 seats. 25 seats outside. Air-con. Separate bar. No mobile phones. Wheelchair access. Music. Car parking.

## ALSO RECOMMENDED

### ▲ Peat Spade Inn
Village Street, Longstock, SO20 6DR
Tel no: (01264) 810612
www.peatspadeinn.co.uk

Andrew Clark and Lucy Townsend have created an upbeat country retreat that oozes relaxed, unbuttoned charm and character. Service is friendly, while Andrew's straightforward modern British food 'hits all the right notes'. Driven by quality seasonal produce, his intelligent, 'less-is-more' cooking comes with clean flavours; perhaps seared calf's liver teamed with white asparagus and shallot marmalade, while desserts such as Eton mess or rhubarb crumble have a high comfort factor. House wines start at £13.50.

## ▪ Lymington

### Egan's
**New Forest favourite**
24 Gosport Street, Lymington, SO41 9BE
Tel no: (01590) 676165
Modern British | £30
Cooking score: 2

A crowd-pleasing formula of reliable food coupled with a relaxed atmosphere proves a winning combination at John and Deborah Egan's modest bistro-style restaurant. Confit of bacon with pickled lentils, or scallops with marinated cucumber and tomato dressing, for instance, may precede a choice of seven main courses ranging from roast hake with smoked haddock risotto and a white port and lemongrass sauce, and wild sea bass with chorizo, potatoes and pesto to herb-crusted rack of lamb. Simple desserts include pear and Amaretto cheesecake and warm chocolate fondant with Cointreau anglaise. The good-value wine list concentrates on France, Italy and the New World. House offerings start at £13.95.

**Chef/s:** John Egan. **Open:** Tue to Sat 12 to 2, 6.30 to 10. **Closed:** 26 Dec to 9 Jan. **Meals:** alc D (main courses £12.50 to £18). Set L £11.95 (2 courses). **Service:** not inc. **Details:** Cards accepted. 50 seats. 20 seats outside. Wheelchair access. Music. Children's portions.

## ▪ Old Burghclere

### Dew Pond
**Glorious views**
Old Burghclere, RG20 9LH
Tel no: (01635) 278408
www.dewpond.co.uk
Anglo-French | £30
Cooking score: 4

Keith and Julie Marshall's sixteenth-century house is located on a narrow lane with glorious views of the countryside. Inside, the two interlinked dining rooms are comfortably furnished and the atmosphere is cool, relaxed and unstuffy. Uncomplicated cooking of mostly local ingredients, including game supplied by a farm that is within sight across the fields, is Keith Marshall's forté, and his nightly set-price menus offer a generous choice of six items per course, with a supplement here and there for perhaps a starter of seared scallops with pea purée, truffle oil and chorizo or main course of Orkney beef fillet with Madeira sauce. Finish with the vanilla pannacotta. Wines start at £12.95, with a dozen by the glass from £3.50.
**Chef/s:** Keith Marshall. **Open:** Tue to Sat D only 7 to 9.30. **Closed:** 2 weeks Christmas to New Year, 2 weeks early Aug. **Meals:** Set D £28. **Service:** not inc. **Details:** Cards accepted. 50 seats. No music. Wheelchair access. Children's portions. Car parking.

## ▌Petersfield

### JSW

**Simple, stylish dishes**
20 Dragon Street, Petersfield, GU31 4JJ
Tel no: (0871) 4265950
**Modern Anglo-French | £35**
**Cooking score: 6**

🍷 ⋎

JSW has moved across town from a cramped little shopfront into larger premises in an attractive old town house with parking at the rear. Save for the oak beams overhead, the interior is as plain, uncluttered and monochrome as ever. What's new is the feeling of space. Jake Watkins' strongest suit is his brace of tasting menus – each a well-composed and logical progression of deceptively simple dishes. Fish comes straight from small, Solent-based boats. Typical creations are simple presentations that capture the essence of three main ingredients: three plump scallops, seared with pin-point accuracy, sitting on an unctuous pillow of sharp-tasting but silky-textured cauliflower cheese custard and topped with ephemerally thin Parmesan tuiles, say, or the highlight at inspection, a combo of beef fillet and ox cheek, the latter meltingly tender and sticky, propped up on exquisitely textured mashed potato and sauced with a well-flavoured bordelaise. Puddings have frequently impressed, none more so than Watkins' signature salt-caramel mousse, although the stridently flavoured rhubarb feuillantine comes close. The wine list, featuring some 600 bins, is priced fairly from £16.50. France is covered comprehensively (with an exceptional range from Alsace).
**Chef/s:** Jake Watkins. **Open:** Tue to Sat 12 to 1.30, 7 to 9.30. **Meals:** Set L £23.50 (2 courses) to £35, Set D £34.50 (2 courses) to £45. **Service:** not inc. **Details:** Cards accepted. 40 seats. No music. No mobile phones.

## ▌Southampton

### The White Star Tavern

**A short hop from Ocean Village**
28 Oxford Street, Southampton, SO14 3DJ
Tel no: (023) 8082 1990
www.whitestartavern.co.uk
**Gastropub | £28**
**Cooking score: 3**

£5 OFF ⋎ £30

The design-conscious, contemporary, Oxford Street bar-cum-restaurant was once a hotel for ocean-going passengers. The formula, based on a flexible aim to please, ranges from bar bites and sandwiches to broadly familiar brasserie dishes such as 'a lusciously creamy and rich' scrambled duck eggs with aromatic smoked salmon topped with fresh chives and a little garlic-infused oil. Elsewhere, expect beer-battered fish and chips with pea purée, and breast of free-range chicken accompanied by dauphinoise potatoes, wilted spinach and wild mushrooms in a rich gravy. Bread-and-butter pudding with sauce anglaise or a vanilla crème brûlée make an accomplished finale. House wines start at £12.75.
**Chef/s:** Gavin Barnes. **Open:** Mon to Thu 12 to 2.30, 6.30 to 9.30, Fri and Sat 12 to 3, 6 to 10, Sun 12 to 9. **Closed:** 25 and 26 December, 1 January. **Meals:** alc (main courses L £9 to £17, D £9 to £17). **Service:** not included. **Details:** Cards accepted. 75 seats. 25 seats outside. Air-con. Music. Children's portions.

## ▌Southsea

### Montparnasse

**Gastronomic experimentation**
103 Palmerston Road, Southsea, PO5 3PS
Tel no: (023) 9281 6754
www.bistromontparnasse.co.uk
**Modern European | £30**
**Cooking score: 4**

⋎

Bistro Montparnasse has morphed simply into Montparnasse; bold and brassy giving way to muted and classy. The cooking has stepped up a notch, too, with Kevin Bingham pushing culinary boundaries by introducing Fat Duck tried, tested and ace methods; meat and other well-chosen local ingredients cooked at an über-low temperature for increased depths of flavour and succeeding. Lunch and dinner menus are virtually copycats, with perhaps a tomato and sherry broth with aubergine pesto ravioli, seared scallops with chilli noodles or home-smoked duck with a potato confit and roasted tomato mayonnaise, the latter a masterful dish of unalloyed pleasure. As was the local skate with cubed pork belly, sautéed prawns and capers, both courses demonstrating this chef's skyward confidence. An aged ribeye, partnered with a sweet garlic and lemon butter and home-cured pork fillet with apple and onion marmalade, could also find favour on the short, evolving menu. Neither puds nor service are found wanting either, with twists to old sweet favourites, such as trifle with champagne, blackberries and a raspberry sorbet. The 60-plus wine list has a pleasing mix of mainly European wines, with a smattering of global labels opening at £12.95.

**Chef/s:** Kevin Bingham. **Open:** Tue to Sat 12 to 1.45, 7 to 9.30. **Closed:** 25 and 26 Dec, 1 Jan, 2 weeks Mar, 2 weeks late Sep to early Oct. **Meals:** alc (main courses £11.50 to £16.50). Set D £22.50 (2 courses) to £27.50. **Service:** not inc. **Details:** Cards accepted. 32 seats. Wheelchair access. Music.

## ▮ Stockbridge

### Greyhound

**Modern food in a classy village pub**
31 High Street, Stockbridge, SO20 6EY
Tel no: (01264) 810833
**Modern British | £32**
**Cooking score: 4**

🍷 ⇌ V

Remodelled with a sense of style some time ago, the Greyhound oozes rustic sophistication. Angling is a big thing hereabouts and the bar is suitably decked out with mementos and paraphernalia relating to the sport. The kitchen works to a concise modern British repertoire, with confident results and more than a touch of artistic intent. A few dishes, like the fishcake with poached

egg and chive beurre blanc are never taken off the menu; just about everything else changes with the market and the seasons. Centrepieces might range from Greenfield organic pork chop with white pudding, spring greens and mustard velouté to seared salmon with provençale vegetables, saffron potatoes and balsamic dressing. To close, consider something like dark chocolate marquise or poached peach with a soup of summer berries. France gets top billing on the astutely chosen wine list. Good drinking abounds and prices are realistic: regularly changing house selections start at £16.

**Chef/s:** Helene Schoeman. **Open:** all week L 12 to 2 (2.30 Fri, Sat and Sun), Mon to Sat D 7 to 9 (9.30 Fri, Sat and Sun). **Closed:** 25, 26 and 31 Dec, 1 Jan. **Meals:** alc (main courses £11.50 to £23). Bar menu available. **Service:** 10% (optional). **Details:** Cards accepted. 48 seats. 30 seats outside. No music. Children's portions. Car parking.

## ▮ Stuckton

### Three Lions

**Long-standing eccentric gastropub**
Stuckton, SP6 2HF
Tel no: (01425) 652489
www.thethreelionsrestaurant.co.uk
**Anglo-French | £36**
**Cooking score: 5**

£5 OFF 🍷 ⇌

Mike Womersley's appealing restaurant with rooms on the western fringe of the New Forest may no longer be breaking new ground with its cooking – indeed, one might venture that the Three Lions' cuisine is the epitome of the gastropub style, perfectly preserved in aspic – but the dishes themselves are as appealing, and the execution as reliable, as ever. Cottagey pine dressers loaded with undistinguished knick-knacks line the salmon-pink, woodchip-textured walls while a rather loud carpet and tomato-coloured, patterned curtains vie for attention. The fashion police be damned; this is a quirky and comfortable dining room. A recent inspection dinner teed off with sautéed kidneys, liver and faggot, the offal flash-fried to just-pink perfection and the faggot smothered in a first-rate sticky gravy. A generous slab of foie gras was studded with ceps and served with home-made brioche toast. 'Loin of lamb and crispy bits' was just that – and the quality of the meat was beyond reproach. There's a good choice of fish from Solent day-boats and perhaps a wild trout with samphire and saffron. Puddings carry on the theme of simplicity with the likes of poached pears and verbena ice cream, or strawberry gratin and custard. An enlightened, medium-weight wine list features some interesting choices and name-checks a lot of highly regarded independent producers. There's limited choice under £20, but prices are fair and the mid-range bottles tend to impress.

**Chef/s:** Mike Womersley. **Open:** Tue to Sun L 12 to 2, Tue to Sat D 7 to 9. **Meals:** alc (main courses £16.50 to £21.50). Set L £18.50 (3 courses). **Service:** not inc. **Details:** Cards accepted. 60 seats. No mobile phones. Wheelchair access. Music. Children's portions. Car parking.

## READERS RECOMMEND

### Keepers Arms
**Gastropub**
Trotton, GU31 5ER
Tel no: (01730) 813724
'A great pub with ambition'

## ▌Whitway

### Carnarvon Arms
**Well-judged cooking**
Winchester Road, Whitway, RG20 9EL
Tel no: (01635) 278222
www.carnarvonarms.com
**Modern European | £39**
**Cooking score: 2**

⊟ ⋎

The Carnarvon Arms is in tiptop condition at the moment, basking in a new lease of life under the guidance of executive chef Robert Clayton. He ensures the rambling building lives up to its title as an inn, dispensing real ales and pub hospitality, but also puts on a stylish show for customers in search of food.

Sensibly planned menus comprise a short, sharp assortment of modern dishes. Wood pigeon breasts with crispy mushroom tart and shallot sauce typifies the starters, while main courses could run from Berkshire Black pork cutlet served with slow-roasted butternut squash, sautéed potatoes and cider sauce to double-cooked shoulder of lamb with goats' cheese gratin, greens and a rosemary jus. Honest pub cooking can be found in the bar, classics such as local sausages and mash, or beer battered cod and chips with crushed peas, say, while desserts range from sticky toffee pudding to raspberry crème brûlée. The short wine list is accessible and varied, with house wines from £13.95.

**Chef/s:** Robert Clayton and Simon Pitney-Baxter. **Open:** all week L 12 to 2. 30 (3 Sun), D 6 to 9.30 (8.30 Sun). **Meals:** alc (main courses £10 to £19). Set L Mon to Fri £9.95 (2 courses) to £14.95. Bar menu available. **Service:** not inc. **Details:** Cards accepted. 80 seats. 20 seats outside. Wheelchair access. Music. Children's portions. Car parking.

## ▌Winchester

### Chesil Rectory
**Modern dining in a period setting**
1 Chesil Street, Winchester, SO23 0HU
Tel no: (01962) 851555
www.chesilrectory.co.uk
**Modern French | £45**
**Cooking score: 5**

⋎

This striking half-timbered gem – said to be the city's oldest house – dates back to the early fifteenth century and certainly stands out from the crowd on bustling Chesil Street. Stepping down through the front door is like 'turning back the pages of history', the place just 'oozes atmosphere and period charm'; think dark beams and timbers, whitewashed walls, floorboards and a huge inglenook for openers. Tables come dressed in their best whites and high-backed chairs are comfortably upholstered, the uncluttered décor offering a stylish informality and intimacy. Upstairs is laid out in a similar vein. Chef Robert Quéhan shows his pedigree background via an appealing modern French repertoire dotted with its 'wish-list of luxury' (Périgord truffles, foie gras) among classy seasonal produce and locally sourced fish and meat. Portioning is light and there is plenty of finesse and ambition, with dishes clean-cut and well balanced: line-caught Solent sea bass teamed with crushed ratte potato, wild leek, ceps, new-season asparagus and a lobster vinaigrette, or perhaps milk-fed Pyrénées lamb (slow-cooked shoulder and medium-rare saddle) served with a Périgueux sauce. Service is suitably relaxed but attentive, while the French-led and -dominated wine list kicks off with house from £16.

**Chef/s:** Robert Quéhan. **Open:** Wed to Sat L 12 to 1.30, Tue to Sat D 7 to 9.30. **Closed:** first 2 weeks Aug. **Meals:** Set L £19 (2 courses) to £23, Set D £45. **Service:** not inc. **Details:** Cards accepted. 45 seats. No mobile phones. Wheelchair access. Music. Children's portions.

## Hotel du Vin & Bistro

**Stylish town-house hotel**
Southgate Street, Winchester, SO23 9EF
Tel no: (01962) 841414
www.hotelduvin.com
**Modern European | £32**
**New Chef**

The original launch pad of the thriving boutique hotel chain, this early Georgian town house strikes an elegant pose in the heart of the city. Wine continues to play a leading role, inspiring both the décor and trademark wine list, which is a corker. Starry names and vintages are backed by house offerings from £15 and there are some 17 by the glass. The kitchen's confident, straightforward approach rides in tandem with the easy-going surroundings. There is something for everyone, including 'simple classics' like chargrilled ribeye with pommes frites and béarnaise, otherwise more gentle innovation delivers in combinations like roast monkfish teamed with pak choi, artichokes and wild mushrooms. The upbeat atmosphere and

service spill over into the adjoining bar, also decked out with a few dining tables, while side and rear gardens beckon for alfresco drinks.

**Chef/s:** Marcela Morales. **Open:** all week 12 to 1.30, 7 to 9.45. **Meals:** alc exc Sun L (main courses from £15.50). Set L Sun £23.50. **Service:** not inc. **Details:** Cards accepted. 72 seats. 40 seats outside. No music. No mobile phones. Children's portions. Car parking.

## Wykeham Arms

**Brimming with atmosphere**
75 Kingsgate Street, Winchester, SO23 9PE
Tel no: (01962) 853834
**Global | £26**
**Cooking score: 3**

A cracking location it may be – hidden away among the cobbled streets of the old quarter – yet the Wykeham certainly lives up to the billing. Its labyrinth of rooms come decked out with roaring winter fires and rustic wood furniture (including school desks), while a myriad of interesting memorabilia jostles for attention with characterful locals. Daily-changing menus combine traditional fare with gentle innovation. Lunch is a light affair, while dinner cranks up the ante; perhaps roast rack of new season Hampshire lamb served with dauphinoise potato, panaché of market vegetables and redcurrant and mint jus, while a lychee cheesecake with blackberry syrup might provide the finale. Table service is suitably relaxed and friendly, while the hefty wine list offers a good selection by glass and house from £12.50.

**Chef/s:** William Spencer. **Open:** all week L 12 to 2.30 (12.15 to 1.45 Sun), Mon to Sat D 6.30 to 9. **Closed:** 25 Dec. **Meals:** alc (main courses L £6.50 to £10, D £11 to £20). Set L Sun £15.50 (2 courses) to £19.50. **Service:** not inc. **Details:** Cards accepted. 80 seats. 60 seats outside. No music. No mobile phones. Children allowed. Car parking.

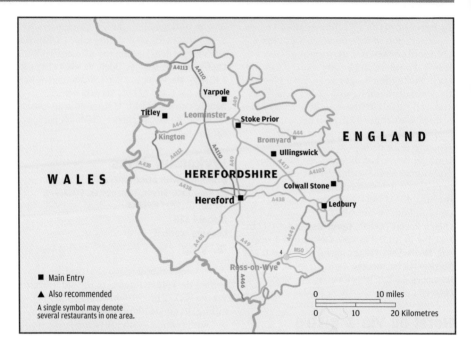

- ■ Main Entry
- ▲ Also recommended

A single symbol may denote several restaurants in one area.

0          10 miles
0     10     20 Kilometres

## ■ Colwall Stone

### Colwall Park
**Understated stalwart**
Walwyn Road, Colwall Stone, WR13 6QG
Tel no: (01684) 540000
www.colwall.com
**Modern British | £32**
**Cooking score: 3**

£5 OFF  🍴

The food here couldn't really be expected to outshine the scenery – this corner of the Malvern hills is particularly stunning – but it gives it a pretty good run for its money. Whether cooking for the oak-panelled Seasons restaurant or the Lantern bar, chef James Garth takes great ingredients – local organic lamb and chicken, prime Scottish beef – and gives them the treatment they deserve. More likely than not, that will be something quite simple, such as chargrilling a beef fillet and serving with grain mustard mash or pot-roasting chicken in a light broth of potato, wild mushrooms and leeks. But there are nice imaginative touches too, as in the Pernod and sesame dressing with a salad of fresh lobster, new potatoes and asparagus, or the tomato and basil sauce vierge enriching a delicious goats' cheese ravioli. The restaurant is an appealing blend of old and new and rather formal. For more relaxed eating, try the bar with its crowd-pleasers such as fish pie but also slightly more unusual dishes, perhaps a Moroccan mutton tagine. Everything is prepared with the same high level of care and service is friendly and attentive. House wines start at £14.95.

**Chef/s:** James Garth. **Open:** all week 12 to 2, 7 to 9. **Meals:** alc D (main courses £17.50 to £21.50). Set L £16.95 (2 courses). **Service:** not inc. **Details:** Cards accepted. 40 seats. Air-con. Wheelchair access. Music. Children's portions. Car parking.

### Average price

The average price listed in main-entry reviews denotes the price of a three-course meal, without wine.

## Hereford
### Castle House
Inventive contemporary food
Castle Street, Hereford, HR1 2NW
Tel no: (01432) 356321
www.castlehse.co.uk
**Anglo-French | £40**
**Cooking score: 5**

£5 OFF ▮ ☱ ⋎

A change of ownership in 2006 resulted in a new name for the restaurant, but nothing else has been affected. The formally appointed dining room makes an auspicious backdrop for Claire Nicholls' innovative modern food. A starter of Asian-spiced pressing of pork with gooseberry and chilli jam and bean sprout salad sets the tone, ahead of ambitious main courses that are typified by expert sourcing. Pan-fried organic Shetland salmon receives the simplest of accompaniments in the form of creamed cauliflower, samphire and tarragon butter, while fillet of Hereford beef sits well with ceps, sautéed new potatoes and watercress purée. Grand design and impeccable execution are the hallmarks of intricately wrought desserts such as caramel pannacotta with ginger poached rhubarb and grenadine syrup or carrot and cardamom cheesecake with dark chocolate ice and orange wafers. Big names from the grand vineyards of Bordeaux and Burgundy are at the heart of the helpfully annotated wine list, although the rest of the world receives plenty of serious coverage: in particular, there are some stunners from Italy and Australia. Prices open at £16.95 (£4.20 a glass) for baseline house selections.
**Chef/s:** Claire Nicholls. **Open:** all week 12.30 to 2, 7 to 10 (9 Sun). **Meals:** alc exc Sun L (main courses £13 to £20). Set L Sun £24 (3 courses), Set D £49.95 (7 courses). **Service:** not inc. **Details:** Cards accepted. 36 seats. 24 seats outside. Air-con. No mobile phones. Wheelchair access. Music. Children's portions. Car parking.

## Ledbury
### Malthouse
Ambitious food in a historic part of town
Church Lane, Ledbury, HR8 1DW
Tel no: (01531) 634443
www.malthouse-ledbury.co.uk
**Modern British | £30**
**Cooking score: 3**

Tucked away up a cobbled lane just behind Ledbury's historic Market Square, this discreet, family-run restaurant occupies two floors of a converted barn. Ken Wilson's cooking aims for intricacy, with lots of components jostling for attention on the plate. Lasagne of braised rabbit, crayfish and asparagus is served as a starter with Cajun-spiced cream sauce, while main courses might run from herb-crusted rack of lamb with braised shoulder, smoked garlic, potato purée and spinach to poached fillet of lemon sole rolled with tomato and basil, served with langoustines, spring vegetables and tomato herb butter sauce. Desserts maintain the creative momentum with, perhaps, glazed passion-fruit and lemon tart with mango sorbet and orange crisp. House wines are from £12.50 (£3.25 a glass).
**Chef/s:** Ken Wilson. **Open:** Sat L 12 to 1.30, Tue to Sat D 7 to 9.30. **Closed:** 25 Dec, 1 to 7 Jan. **Meals:** alc (main courses L £9 to £14.50, D £15 to £19). Set D Tue to Thu £18.75 (2 courses) to £24.50. **Service:** not inc. **Details:** Cards accepted. 30 seats. 16 seats outside. No mobile phones. Wheelchair access. Music. Children's portions.

## Stoke Prior
### Epicurean Restaurant
Understated dining
68 Hanbury Road, Stoke Prior, B60 4DN
Tel no: (01527) 871929
www.epicbrasseries.co.uk
**Modern European | £30**
**Cooking score: 5**

The elegant tone of this converted pub, running on two fronts as both brasserie and restaurant, makes a fine showcase for the talents of Jason Lynas. As befits the seriousness of his culinary ambition, local produce forms the backbone of the menus. Younger patrons are not neglected either. If the Nintendo Gameboy is your thing, kids, just ask for one. Elders will find plenty to distract them on the plate, starting perhaps with lobster and basil ravioli in shellfish cappuccino, a modish dish if ever there was one. Seared red mullet makes a first-course appearance, too, perhaps paired with duck tortellini and pommes mousseline. Mains offer some original ideas, such as a spin on cassoulet that matches lamb rump with chorizo in a tarragon sauce. To finish, there are British and Continental cheeses, served with a warm pear tartlet in case you don't want to miss out on something sweet, as well as full-dress desserts like prune and Armagnac parfait with coffee pannacotta. House wines are a Merlot and a Chardonnay at £18, or £5 a glass.

**Chef/s:** Jason Lynas. **Open:** Tue to Sat 12 to 2, Tue to Thu 7 to 9, Fri to Sat 7 to 9.30. **Meals:** Set L £17.50 (2 courses) to £22.50, D alc (main courses £17.75 to £23.75) Set D £45. **Service:** 10% optional.
**Details:** Cards accepted. 45 seats. 60 seats outside. Separate bar. Wheelchair access. Music. Children allowed. Car parking.

## ■ Titley
### Stagg Inn
**A traditional village pub**
Titley, HR5 3RL
Tel no: (01544) 230221
www.thestagg.co.uk
**Modern British | £27**
**Cooking score: 5**
♦ ➦ ◭30

This Herefordshire pub is a perfect example of a village local. Nicola Reynolds runs the front-of-house, winning praise for the friendly atmosphere, and her husband, Steve, delivers consistently precise cooking with the emphasis on quality local ingredients presented as simply as possible – a board in the bar proudly lists all the Stagg's suppliers. Fruit and vegetables come from the garden and eggs are supplied by the resident hens. A starter of

pan-fried foie gras is served with Pembridge apple jelly to cut through the richness and pigeon breast comes with a comforting combination of pearl barley and roast root vegetables. As a main course, fillet of Herefordshire beef may be served with mustard glaze and wasabi mashed potato or with béarnaise sauce and chips. Dauphinoise potatoes also accompany sea bass fillet with mushroom duxelles and herb oil. There is an impressive choice of over 20 local and Welsh cheeses, and seriously good puddings include treacle tart with local clotted cream, and cinnamon pannacotta with caramelised apples. The helpfully annotated wine list offers good value. House wines (including Broadfield Court from Herefordshire) start at £12.90 a bottle and there is a good choice of half-bottles.

**Chef/s:** Steve Reynolds and Mathew Handley. **Open:** Tue to Sun L 12 to 2, Tue to Sat D 6.30 to 9.30. **Closed:** first week of Nov and Feb, 25 to 26 Dec, 1 Jan. **Meals:** alc exc Sun L (main courses £12.50 to £17). Set L Sun £14.90. Bar menu available Tue to Sat L, Tue to Fri D. **Service:** not included.
**Details:** Cards accepted. 70 seats. 20 seats outside. No music. Children's portions. Car parking.

## ■ Ullingswick
### Three Crowns
**A perfect country pub**
Ullingswick, HR1 3JQ
Tel no: (01432) 820279
www.threecrownsinn.com
**Modern British | £27**
**Cooking score: 4**
➦ ◭30

Tucked away down Herefordshire country lanes, the Three Crowns is not the easiest place to find. Flagstones floors, scrubbed tables, log fires and hop-festooned beams make the bar welcoming. The recent restaurant extension is more modern and less atmospheric. The short menu has a sensible pricing structure – one price for starters, one for mains and one for puddings – while the prix fixe lunch menu is good value. Starters might include ultra-fresh Cornish squid in a light tempura batter with a

## Cooking score

A score of 1 is a significant achievement. The score in any review is based on several meals, incorporating feedback from both our readers and inspectors. As a rough guide, 1 denotes capable cooking with some inconsistencies, rising steadily through different levels of technical expertise, until the scores between 6 and 10 indicate exemplary skills, along with innovation, artistry and ambition. If there is a new chef, we don't score the restaurant for the first year of entry. For further details, please see the scoring section in the introduction to the Guide.

butter bean salad, or mussels and clams in a subtle masala sauce. A huge sirloin steak of Risbury Court beef is a robust main course and the horseradish and lovage butter an inspired accompaniment. Puddings are uncomplicated and include glazed lemon tart with vanilla ice cream or raspberry cranachan. Shaky and amateurish service can spoil an otherwise faultless experience. House wines are £14.50 a bottle.

**Chef/s:** Brent Castle. **Open:** Tue to Sun 12 to 2.30, 7 (6 Sat July and Aug) to 10. **Closed:** L 2 weeks from 24 Dec. **Meals:** alc (main courses £14.50). Set L £12.95 (2 courses) to £14.95. Bar menu available. **Service:** not inc. **Details:** Cards accepted. 75 seats. 24 seats outside. No music. Wheelchair access. Children's portions. Car parking.

## ▮ Yarpole

### Bell Inn

**Traditional country pub**
Green Lane, Yarpole, HR6 0BD
Tel no: (01568) 780359
Modern British | £30
Cooking score: 2

Claude and Claire Bosi have taken Hibiscus to pastures new in Mayfair, but their pub remains in the capable hands of Claude's brother Cedric. Although the food might suggest otherwise, this is no gastropub. Horse brasses hang from the beams and locals still drink at the bar. The monthly changing carte always shows a choice of first-class fish, maybe Cornish pollack with spring vegetable risotto. Plump crisp smoked haddock fishcakes wallow in a pool of intense pea velouté and meaty choices include Toulouse cassoulet, though vegetarians are well served, too. Generally, the cooking is skilled and accurate but some carelessness, such as 'overcooked beef, leathery Yorkshire pudding and school dinner-type vegetables' at one Sunday lunch, can disappoint. However, desserts are a high point, whether you decide on a simple apple crumble or the more exotic caramelised pineapple. House wine is £12.50.

**Chef/s:** Mark Jones. **Open:** Tue to Sun 12 to 2.30, 6.30 to 9.30. **Meals:** alc (main courses £9.50 to £17). Snack menu available. **Service:** not inc. **Details:** Cards accepted. 90 seats. 50 seats outside. Music. Children's portions.

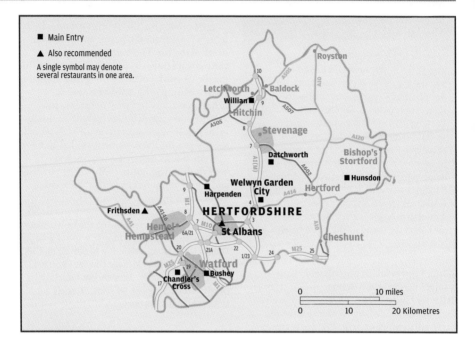

- ■ Main Entry
- ▲ Also recommended

A single symbol may denote
several restaurants in one area.

## ▍Bushey

### St James

**Convivial neighbourhood restaurant**
30 High Street, Bushey, WD2 3DN
Tel no: (020) 8950 2480
www.stjamesrestaurant.co.uk
**Modern British | £30**
**Cooking score: 1**

This is an easy restaurant to find, opposite the
church that shares the same name. Stripped
wooden floors, bare brick walls and an
abundance of white linen on the tables are
tempered with clever lighting, creating a
convivial place to eat. Starters, such as smoked
salmon with sour cream on a blini or king
prawns and avocado gâteau, don't quicken the
pulse, but they're good clean dishes of food
that sate rather than surprise. Mains take in a
flavoursome fillet of beef with potato rösti and
horseradish creamed spinach. Fish options are
plentiful, such as turbot with a caper and
parsley potato cake and sea bass with fennel.
Among the half-dozen desserts, the cold
mixed berry soufflé was convincing and there's
a generous and satisfying pear and apple tarte
Tatin. Both Italian red and white wines start at
£12.95 a bottle.
**Chef/s:** Simon Trussell. **Open:** Mon to Sat 12 to 2.30,
6.30 to 9.30. **Closed:** Christmas Day, Bank hols.
**Meals:** alc (main courses £17 to £26). Set L £13.95 (2
courses), Set D Mon to Fri £15.95 (2 courses).
**Service:** 12.5% (optional). **Details:** Cards accepted.
100 seats. Air-con. Separate bar. No mobile phones.
Wheelchair access. Music. Children's portions.

## Symbols

🛏 Accommodation is available.

£30 Three courses for less than £30.

V More than five vegetarian dishes.

£5 OFF £5-off voucher scheme.

🍾 Notable wine list.

## ▌Chandler's Cross

### The Grove, Colette's

**Modern thinking and astute technique**
Chandler's Cross, WD3 4TG
Tel no: (01923) 296015
www.thegrove.co.uk
**Modern European | £54**
**Cooking score: 5**

🍴 ⅋

The Grove is sufficiently grand to have tempted both Queen Victoria and Edward VII to dine here successively with one or other of its ancestral owners, the Earls of Clarendon. Chris Harrod seeks out the best of domestic produce to fashion dishes that are full of up-to-the-minute culinary thinking, refracted through the prism of classical technique. Slow-cooked squab pigeon makes a robust starter, served with foie gras parfait, poached rhubarb and juniper. Main courses offer a good balance of fish and meat, the former in neat pairings (such as John Dory and clams), the latter showcasing such prime materials as Denham Estate venison. Fine pastrywork sets off desserts such as plum tart with vanilla ice cream and an Amaretto yoghurt milkshake. Smaller mark-ups on the ritzier wines should encourage adventurous drinking. Wines by the glass start at £7, bottles at £24.
**Chef/s:** Chris Harrod. **Open:** Sun L 12.30 to 2.30, Mon to Sat D 7 to 10.30. **Closed:** bank hol Mon. **Meals:** Set D £49 (2 courses) to £54. **Service:** not inc. **Details:** Cards accepted. 45 seats. Air-con. Separate bar. No mobile phones. Wheelchair access. Music. Children's portions. Car parking.

## READERS RECOMMEND

### The Tilbury

**British**
Watton Road, Datchworth, SG3 6TB
Tel no: (01438) 815550
www.thetilbury.co.uk
'Fresh ingredients at good, honest prices'

## ALSO RECOMMENDED

### ▲ Alford Arms

Frithsden, HP1 3DD
Tel no: (01442) 864480
www.alfordarmsfrithsden.co.uk

Follow the tourist signs to Frithsden Vineyard to track down this out-of-the-way gastropub in the depths of Ashridge Estate (National Trust). Crowds make the trip to enjoy its convivial buzz and the generous, robust food on offer. 'Small plates' such as Szechuan peppered squid with chilli dipping sauce (£6) head up a regularly changing menu that might also feature braised local lamb shank on basil mash with broad beans and smoked garlic cream (£14) or cider-soused organic salmon fillet. To finish, elderflower crème brûlée with spiced plum jam (£5) strikes a seasonal note. Around 30 quaffable wines from £11.50. Open all week.

## ▌Harpenden

### A Touch of Novelli at the White Horse

**Well-heeled gastropub in leafy Harpenden**
Hatching Green, Harpenden, AL5 2JP
Tel no: (01582) 469290
www.atouchofnovelli.com
**Gastropub | £31**
**Cooking score: 2**

🍾 ⅋

Culinary zeitgeist Jean-Christophe Novelli took over this likeable gastropub in 2006, but Wesley Smalley heads up the kitchen, offering some confident, although not always entirely consistent, output. Prudent selection from the carte can still deliver the goods, however, there are irksome issues, including bread as a menu option at £2.25 and the autumn/winter menu still running at the back end of March. A good ragoût of Aylesbury duck teamed with a corpulent slice of foie gras sets the standard and an interesting rabbit pasty with celeriac purée holds together well, lightening the mood. Cold and hot Jaffa chocolate fondant with orange ice cream ups the ante with its oozy molten textures. If you're still in a savoury disposition then there's a respectable British cheese plate on offer, too. Service can seem pushed, even confused at times, but is perfectly affable. A laconic wine list offers a safe selection from France and the New World, and there's a generous selection of wines by the glass, starting at £4, and by the bottle at £12. **Chef/s:** Wesley Smalley. **Open:** Mon to Sat, 12 to 3, 6 to 10, Sun, 12 to 5. **Closed:** 24 and 25 Dec, 1 January. **Meals:** alc (main courses £14.50 to £18.50). **Service:** not inc. **Details:** Cards accepted. 50 seats. 50 seats outside. Separate bar. Wheelchair access. Music. Children allowed. Car parking.

## ■ Hunsdon
### Fox & Hounds
**Stylish hamlet pub**
2 High Street, Hunsdon, SG12 8NH
Tel no: (01279) 843999
www.foxandhounds-hunsdon.co.uk
**Gastropub | £26**
**Cooking score: 2**
£5 OFF ♦ V £30

'This is how country pub dining should be – palpable food savvy coupled with big-hearted portions and beaming smiles from the genial staff' enthused one reporter of James Rix's homely yet stylish pub. A mound of 'melting' chicken livers with a coddled egg and seasonal watercress is a lesson in content over style. Mains, such as Black Angus côte de boeuf with 'almost perfect' chips and a splendid béarnaise, show that simplicity wins out, and fish is also shown a deft hand with a whole lemon sole and brown shrimp butter light and über-fresh. A fun raspberry and vanilla ice cream sundae evoked memories of childhood seaside Knickerbocker Glories for one reporter, but without the 'ersatz cream and saccharine syrup', and there's a good farmhouse cheese plate. House red and white kick off at £11.55 and there's a selection of 12 by the glass, from £2.95. NB Children under 12 are not allowed in the dining room on Saturday evenings.

**Chef/s:** James Rix. **Open:** Tue to Sun L 12 to 4 (5pm Sun), Tue to Sat D 6 to 11. **Closed:** Mondays. **Meals:** alc (main courses £10 to £17). Set L Tue to Fri £11 (2 courses), Set D Tue to Thur £13.50 (2 courses). **Service:** 10% (opt). **Details:** Cards accepted. 80 seats. 40 seats outside. Separate bar. Wheelchair access. Music. Children allowed. Car parking.

## ALSO RECOMMENDED
### ▲ The Restaurant at Sopwell House
Cottonmill Lane, Sopwell, St Albans, AL1 2HQ
Tel no: (01727) 864477
www.sopwellhouse.co.uk

An auspicious Georgian country mansion, Sopwell House was once the country home of Lord Mountbatten and is now one of Hertfordshire's big-name hotels. The restaurant (formerly Magnolia) recently underwent a thorough makeover, and it now puts the emphasis on modern British dishes inspired by indigenous seasonal ingredients. Start with a Brixham crab plate at £8.50, move on to wild sea trout with samphire at £17.50 and conclude with, perhaps, buttermilk and vanilla pannacotta with a mint granita at £7. Vast global wine list, featuring a decent selection of Old- and New-World wines, with prices starting at £17.50. Closed L Mon.

## ■ Welwyn Garden City
### Auberge du Lac
**Swish country setting**
Brocket Hall, Welwyn Garden City, AL8 7XG
Tel no: (01707) 368888
www.brocket-hall.co.uk
**Modern French | £75**
**Cooking score: 5**
♦ ⇄ V

Sitting pretty within the gated grounds and verdant pastures of Brocket Hall estate, Auberge du Lac is a grand eighteenth-century hunting lodge transformed into a hospitality venue for all occasions. Phil Thompson's

cooking aims for modern French intricacy backed by impressive technique and visual impact. To begin, there might be honey-poached crown of quail with a foie gras crêpe, spring pea mousse and roasted peanuts or marinated ballotine of mackerel with pickled beetroot and crème fraîche ice cream. 'Assiettes principales' have featured seasonal dishes like grilled fillet of red mullet with spring broad bean risotto, new season's garlic and chervil or sweet-and-sour slow-roast pork belly with Chardonnay pomme purée, buttered Hispi cabbage and pickled apple. Desserts are picture-perfect, elegantly assembled creations such as warm treacle tart with a prune and pear samosa and pear sorbet or coconut parfait with pineapple sorbet and coconut foam. The illustrious 700-bin wine list naturally takes it cue from France, although there is plenty for everyone, from platinum-tagged vintage clarets to more affordable bottles (£30 upwards) gleaned from top growers around the globe. Wines by the glass start at £5.50.
**Chef/s:** Phil Thompson. **Open:** Tue to Sun L 12 to 2.30, Tue to Sat D 6.30 to 10. **Meals:** alc (not Sun L; main courses £21 to £32). Set L Tue to Sat £29.50, Set L Sun £35, Set D £45 (Tue to Fri) to £65. **Service:** 10% (optional). **Details:** Cards accepted. 60 seats. 54 seats outside. Air-con. No mobile phones. Music. Children's portions. Car parking.

## Willian

### The Fox
**Fish delivered daily from Norfolk**
Willian, SG6 2AE
Tel no: (01462) 480233
www.foxatwillian.co.uk
**Gastropub | £26**
**Cooking score: 2**
£30

Standing by the village pond, opposite the church, the Fox is a stylish modern gastropub. Starters of Brancaster oysters are served au naturel, or in tempura batter with a sweet chilli sauce. Main courses encompass a broad range, from seared sea bass fillet with star anise and clove-pickled apples, to roasted cod fillet with clams on coconut, lemon and saffron linguini. Sticky toffee pudding with vanilla ice cream, or spiced chocolate pot, might end the meal. Wines are arranged by style, with crisp dry house white and light, fruity house red at £12.
**Chef/s:** Hari Kodagoda. **Open:** all week L 12 to 2 (3 Sun), Mon to Fri D 6.45 to 9.15, Sat D 6.30 to 9.30. **Meals:** alc (main courses L £9 to £15.50, D £11 to £16.50). **Service:** not inc. **Details:** Cards accepted. 70 seats. 16 seats outside. Air-con. No mobile phones. Wheelchair access. Music. Children's portions. Car parking.

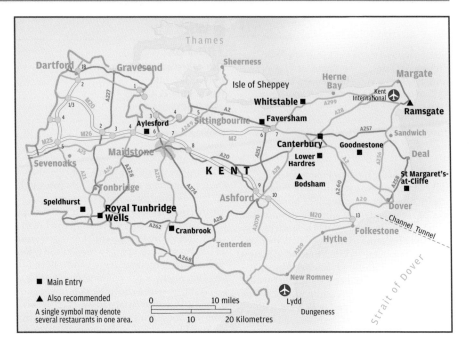

# Aylesford

## Hengist

**Austere Georgian façade**
7-9 High Street, Aylesford, ME20 7AX
Tel no: (01622) 719273
www.hengistrestaurant.co.uk
**Modern French | £34**
**Cooking score: 3**

Ⴘ

Aylesford is an extremely pretty village of great age, reputedly one of the oldest villages in England. Owned by the team behind Thackeray's (see entry, Tunbridge Wells), with chef Jean-Marc Zanetti at the stove, expect a modern French menu that makes good use of top-notch local and regional raw materials. A meal from the carte might open with quail, onion confit and truffle tartlet with wild mushrooms and chicken jus, or marinated mackerel and confit potato terrine with dill and aubergine caviar, before following with roast best end of Kentish lamb with lamb and thyme jus, or pan-fried cod with butternut

squash risotto and bouillabaisse sauce. Seville orange soufflé with suzette sauce is one way to finish, a traditional iced nougat with gingerbread and fig sauce, another. France is at the heart of the intelligently composed wine list, with a good range under £20 and bottles starting at £12.95.

**Chef/s:** Jean-Marc Zanetti. **Open:** Tue to Sun L 12 to 2.30, Tue to Sat D 6.30 to 10.30. **Closed:** 25 to 27 Dec, 1 Jan. **Meals:** alc exc Sun L (main courses £14 to £18). Set L Tue to Sat £10.95 (2 courses) to £12.95, Set L Sun £16.50 (2 courses) to £18.50, Set D Tue to Thur £19.95, Set D Tue to Sat £42.50. **Service:** 11% (optional). **Details:** Cards accepted. 73 seats. Air-con. Wheelchair access. Music. Children's portions.

## Scores on the Doors

To find out more about the Scores on the Doors campaign, please visit the Food Standard's Agency website: www.food.gov.uk or www.which.co.uk.

## ALSO RECOMMENDED

### ▲ Froggies at the Timber Batts

School Lane, Bodsham, TN25 5JQ
Tel no: (01233) 750237
www.thetimberbatts.co.uk

Located deep in the countryside south of Canterbury, the Timber Batts is the picture of a traditional English country inn, dating from the fifteenth century. French owners remain true to their roots in the kitchen, producing a menu of classic dishes ranging from coquilles St Jacques with bacon to warm goats' cheese salad for starters, with main courses taking in confit duck salad, roast herbed rack of lamb, or fillet steak with Roquefort sauce. Profiteroles, tarte Tatin and crème brûlée are among desserts, and bar snacks feature croque monsieur alongside various filled baguettes. House wine £14. Closed Mon and D Sun.

## READERS RECOMMEND

### Ginny's Kitchen

**Chinese**
2 West Street, Bromley, BR1 1RF.
Tel no: (020) 8313 3343
'Quality food, atmosphere and good service'

## ▌Canterbury

★NEW ENTRY★

### ABode Canterbury

Ambitious contemporary cooking
High Street, Canterbury, CT1 2RX
Tel no: (01227) 766266
www.abodehotels.co.uk
**Modern European | £37**
**Cooking score: 4**
⊨

ABode Canterbury is the third boutique hotel to open in Michael Caines' expanding empire, joining Exeter and Glasgow (see entries), and gives a welcome contemporary look to the faded building that was once the city's County Hotel. The cooking, under Mark Rossi, keeps

in tune with the times by offering novel combinations, but a gentle, toned-down style. Quality home-made bread and the de rigueur creamy velouté amuse- bouche in a coffee cup all post notice of culinary intent. A starter of pan-fried veal sweetbreads might be accompanied by shallot, mustard and Xeres vinegar sauce, while choice at main course might be monkfish wrapped in Parma ham with creamed leeks, mussels and saffron cream sauce or sirloin of Kent beef with braised salsify, roasted shallots, wild mushrooms and Madeira sauce. Desserts generally lack firepower, although a pre-dessert shot glass of home-made yoghurt topped with apple purée and a mini doughnut, and dessert proper of a trio of cherries with Valhrona chocolate have hit the spot. The good-value fixed-price lunch menu inhabits less high-flown territory, but the room, despite 'sophisticated colours and napery', feels very much a hotel's restaurant with the staff 'correct rather than committed'. House wine is £16.50.

**Chef/s:** Mark Rossi. **Open:** L Mon to Sat 12 to 2.30, Sun 12.30 to 2.30, D Mon to Sat 7 to 10. **Meals:** alc (main courses £13 to £18). **Service:** optional.
**Details:** Cards accepted. Separate bar. Wheelchair access. Car parking.

### Goods Shed

Local produce shines
Station Road West, Canterbury, CT2 8AN
Tel no: (01227) 459153
**Modern British | £32**
**Cooking score: 1**
ᐯ

Britain's first (and currently only) all-week farmers' market, housed in a listed Victorian railway shed next to Canterbury West Station, is where lucky Kent foodies flock to buy locally grown produce. Benefiting from all this is the simply styled on-site restaurant. Blackboard menus live up to the setting, not surprisingly paying proper attention to produce available from the stalls that day and showing touches of class within the modern British framework. Simple treatments are apparent in starters such as slow-roast

tomatoes and goats' cheese with sweet onions on toast, or skate cheek with tartare sauce and grilled lemon, while main courses take in leg of spring lamb, pot-roast chicken with asparagus, tarragon and cream or a simple dish of mackerel fillets served with tomato, olive and lemon. House wines start at £13.
**Chef/s:** Rafael Lopez. **Open:** Tue to Sun L 12 to 2.30 (3 Sat and Sun), Tue to Sat D 6 to 9.30. **Closed:** 25 and 26 Dec, 1 Jan. **Meals:** alc (main courses £10 to £18). **Service:** not inc. **Details:** Cards accepted. 80 seats. No music. Children's portions. Car parking.

## READERS RECOMMEND
### Due Amici
Italian
11 Royal Parade, Chislehurst, BR7 6NR.
Tel no: (020) 8467 4496
'Run by Italians who care deeply about their food'

## ▌Cranbrook
### Apicius
Rustic charm
23 Stone Street, Cranbrook, TN17 3HE
Tel no: (01580) 714666
Modern European | £41
Cooking score: 4

ⱴ

Named after the famous Roman gastronome of the first century AD, this intimate little restaurant retains much of its rustic charm. With just six tables in the smart but unpretentious dining room and with the short, set-price menus, which highlight Tim Johnson's impressive classically based modern cooking, proving such excellent value, it's advisable to book ahead. Local and seasonal ingredients are a mainstay of the menus and fresh, clear flavours shine through in starters such as warm buttered Frogshole Farm asparagus with Parmesan and black truffle cream, or deep-fried veal sweetbreads with white onion purée, followed perhaps by roast pork belly with caramelised apples and confit shallots. To finish there may be iced banana and liquorice mousse with rum-poached

banana and caramel sauce, or a plate of British and French cheeses. The short wine list has been thoughtfully compiled with an eye for interesting names and good value. Prices start at £17.
**Chef/s:** Tim Johnson. **Open:** Wed to Fri and Sun L 12 to 2, Tue to Sat D 7 to 9. **Meals:** Set L £18.50 (2 courses) to £22.50, Set D £22.50 (2 courses) to £26.50. **Service:** 10% (optional). **Details:** Cards accepted. 22 seats. No music. No mobile phones. Wheelchair access. Children allowed.

## ALSO RECOMMENDED
### ▲ George Hotel
Stone Street, Cranbrook, TN17 3HE
Tel no: (01580) 713348
www.thegeorgehotelkent.co.uk

At the heart of this bustling little town, the revamped fourteenth-century former coaching inn successfully blends striking period features (fine inglenook fireplace and magnificent wooden staircase) with a contemporary décor. The modern feel extends to the informal brasserie menu, which draws on quality ingredients from a network of local producers and suppliers. Dishes take in broad bean and mascarpone salad with rocket salad (£9.50), rump of Park Farm lamb with salsa verde (£16.50), wild sea bass with a warm salad of spinach and peas (£14.50), and dark chocolate and rum tart with orange sorbet (£6). Wines kick off at £13 for vins de pays; 15 by the glass from £3.25. Open daily.

# Faversham

★NEW ENTRY★

## Dining Room at the Railway Hotel
Informal town-centre dining
Preston Street, Faversham, ME13 8PE
Tel no: (01795) 533173
Modern British | £25
Cooking score: 4
£30

As names go, this one accurately sums up the operation in the Railway Hotel, just across the road from Faversham Station. The light, airy dining room is casually decked out with an assortment of wooden tables and feels just right, while Anthony North and Jonny Butterworth bring pedigree backgrounds to the kitchen. One of the strengths of the cooking is its foundation on carefully sourced materials. Local suppliers come up with Kent marsh lamb and Sussex beef. Fish arrives from the coast a few miles away, nearby farms supply vegetables and fruit in season, and a forager fills in the gaps. There's admirable restraint in the kitchen and while the techniques employed are generally straightforward, timing is good and saucing fundamentally sound – witness a main course of roast and braised marsh lamb with a flavourful but not over-reduced sticky ale and rosemary jus. Other favourable results have included mackerel with horseradish, pickled beetroot and a lively tangle of foraged leaves, and an intensely flavoured roast pepper and tomato soup with a hint of basil pesto. Desserts impress, too, if an apple tarte Tatin served with an unusual beer crème anglaise is anything to go by. Home-made bread and charming service are extra brownie points, and there's a short global wine list with prices opening at £11.
Chef/s: Anthony North and Jonny Butterworth.
Open: Wed to Sat L 12 to 2.30 D 6.30 to 9, Sun L 12 to 3.30. Closed: Mon, Tue. Meals: alc (main courses £12 to £18). Service: optional. Details: Cards accepted. 35 seats. Separate bar. Children allowed. Car parking.

## Read's
Fine-tuned cooking
Macknade Manor, Canterbury Road, Faversham, ME13 8XE
Tel no: (01795) 535344
www.reads.com
Modern British | £48
Cooking score: 6
£5 OFF

A rather beautiful red-brick Georgian house of classic proportions with guest rooms, Read's is set in pretty grounds and run with consummate, yet unstuffy, professionalism. It is the kind of welcoming place where the door is opened as you approach, and where you are ushered to the bar first to peruse the menus (there is also a lovely sheltered terrace for summer aperitifs). The interior is very English in a quiet sort of way, while the uncluttered, comfortable, dining room (two interconnecting rooms) comes with well-spaced tables impeccably turned out in their best whites. David Pitchford's modern approach comes underpinned by a classical theme, his carefully crafted dishes allowed to evolve rather than chase fashion, the emphasis on consistency and flavour, with the use of high-quality, local, seasonal produce at the cooking's heart; the manor's own walled kitchen garden providing much summer produce. Thus a warm salad of rocket, broad beans and new potatoes might provide the accompaniment for pan-fried local black bream served with a lobster sauce, while a dish of Kentish lamb cooked four ways (rack, loin, rolled breast and shepherd's pie) could be teamed with celeriac and buttered spinach. Desserts seduce even those without a sweet tooth; take a Valrhona chocolate and caramel tart teamed with salted almond ice cream. The extensive, well-chosen wine list tours the globe and rolls out some 300 bins, though there is a user-friendly, condensed version of 60 'Best Buys' up front for those on more of a budget, which sets out at £16 and plateaus off at £28. There is quality throughout, but the list's heart is lost to France.

**Chef/s:** David Pitchford and Ricky Martin. **Open:** Tue to Sat L 12 to 2, D 7 to 9.30. **Closed:** 25 and 26 Dec, first week Jan. **Meals:** Set L £23, Set D £48. **Service:** not inc. **Details:** Cards accepted. 50 seats. 24 seats outside. No music. Wheelchair access. Children's portions. Car parking.

## Goodnestone

★NEW ENTRY★
### Fitzwalter Arms
**Unpretentious village local**
The Street, Goodnestone, CT3 1PJ
Tel no: (01304) 840303
Gastropub | £22
Cooking score: 2
£30

Nearby Goodnestone Park is famous for its gardens and Jane Austen connection, but the centuries-old Fitzwalter Arms can be described as a true village local, nothing fancy. Decoration is basic, a philosophy that applies to the food too extras are conspicuous by their absence, helping to keep prices down and focus the kitchen's attention on essentials. Simplicity is a feature. A short blackboard menu, perhaps starting with lightly grilled pigeon breast on Puy lentils, makes the most of local materials, in flavourful roast lamb, for example, or roast Kentish ranger chicken breast (served with bread sauce and gravy) and a 10-hour slow-roast pork belly, which comes with tart rhubarb and perfect crackling. Chocolate terrine is a pleasurable way to finish. Meals begin with first-class home-baked bread and the service is characterised by 'lots of smiles, help and cheerfulness'. A short wine list offers fair choice from £11.50.
**Chef/s:** David Hart. **Open:** Mon to Sun L 12 to 2, Mon to Sat D 7 to 9. **Closed:** Sun D. **Details:** Cards accepted. 25 seats. 25 seats outside. Separate bar. Music. Children's portions.

## Locksbottom

### Chapter One
**Accomplished dining at refreshing prices**
Farnborough Common, Locksbottom, BR6 8NF
Tel no: (01689) 854848
www.chaptersrestaurants.co.uk
Modern European | £28
Cooking score: 5
♈

The suburban half-timbered exterior of Chapter One belies the glamorous new interior with shimmering silver window treatments, dramatic red lampshades and chic chocolate walls, yet the restaurant remains astonishingly – shout-from-the-rooftops – good value for food and service of such verve and finesse. Both a furiously busy yet impressively calm Sunday lunch, with many multi-generation celebratory tables, and a more sedate dinner, confirm chef Andrew McLeish's accomplished cooking. He draws on his classical Ritz training to offer dishes that will appeal to all. Sophisticated twists to modish ingredients and more familiar classics, such as exemplary crisp fishcakes with avocado-enriched tartare sauce. Notable dishes include a starter of stuffed cabbage with venison and celeriac purée with unctuous sticky jus, and beautifully judged braised pork cheek subtly infused with cardamom, with buttered asparagus and modish micro-greens. Desserts are outstanding, notably a tangy refreshing early summer pudding with plums, strawberries, raspberries and espuma of iced yoghurt. Significantly, the details are memorable too: exemplary bread and quirky fine twists of puff pastry with warm lemon curd made for a playful riff on the petits fours ritual. The impressive glass wine cellar within the restaurant concentrates on smaller, quality producers, and is fairly priced with plenty of halves and glasses. House offerings start at £15.50.
**Chef/s:** Andrew McLeish. **Open:** All week 12 to 2.30 (2.45 Sun), 6.30 to 10 (11 Fri and Sat, 9.30 Sun). **Closed:** First few days Jan. **Meals:** Set L £19.95 (3 courses), £18.95 Sun L, Set D £28.50. Brasserie

menu available. **Service:** 12.5% (opt). **Details:** Cards accepted. 120 seats. 20 seats outside. Air-con. Children's portions. Children allowed. Car parking.

# ■ Lower Hardres

## Granville

Country dining pub
Street End, Lower Hardres, CT4 7AL
**Tel no:** (01227) 700402
Modern European | £30
Cooking score: 4

ᐯ

The Granville is one of those solidly built country pubs that lends itself so well to conversion to a dining pub – the large double dining room with the kitchen partially to view sports the usual kit of large wood tables, bare floors and regularly changing artists' work on the walls. Ingredients are mainly British and local at that, the skill is in the impeccable sourcing and the ability of the kitchen to leave well alone and let natural flavours shine through. Bouillabaise sauce, served with a 'very fresh, meaty' red mullet is absolutely correct with a rich, deep flavour, and there are some robust meat main courses, such as pork belly with crackling and apple sauce, and a seemingly never-off-the-menu crispy duck with crème fraîche and smoked chilli salsa. In addition, the home-made focaccia is unmissable, and if it's on, the richly caramelised tarte Tatin is the dessert to have. Otherwise, expect a separate drinkers' bar – this remains a good local with Shepheard Neame ales on tap – a blackboard wine list offering reasonable price and choice, and lovely laid-back service. House wines start at £11.50. Related to the Sportsman at Seasalter, Whitstable (see entry).
**Chef/s:** Jim Shave, Ezra Gaynor and Natalie Toman.
**Open:** Tue to Sun L 12 to 2 (2.30 Sun), Tue to Sat D 7 to 9. **Closed:** 25 and 26 Dec. **Meals:** alc (main courses £11 to £19). **Service:** not inc. **Details:** Cards accepted. 60 seats. Air-con. Wheelchair access. Music. Children's portions. Car parking.

## ALSO RECOMMENDED

### ▲ Surin

30 Harbour Street, Ramsgate, CT11 8HA
**Tel no:** (01843) 592001
www.surinrestaurant.co.uk

Located in the harbour town of Ramsgate, Surin is named after the home town of chef-owner Damrong Garbutt. It specialises in three types of Asian cuisine – Thai, Cambodian and Lao. Steamed sea bass in lime juice (£12.95), beef in oyster sauce (£8.50), mixed vegetable tom yum soup (£3.95) and classic Thai desserts (£4.25) are just a few examples of what to expect. Among a selection of beers is one from a local micro-brewery. Closed Sun (except D in summer), Mon L.

# ■ St Margaret's-at-Cliffe

## Oakley and Harvey at Wallett's Court

An air of remote tranquillity
Westcliffe, St Margaret's-at-Cliffe, CT15 6EW
**Tel no:** (01304) 852424
www.wallettscourt.com
Modern European | £36
Cooking score: 3

£5 OFF  ♦  ➖

This venerable manor house sits in landscaped gardens, the scene enlivened to the senses by the distinct touch of ozone-fresh sea air that tells you you're in White Cliffs country. Together, Gavin Oakley and head chef Stephen Harvey have created a wholly contemporary dining idiom, drawing on the vogue for childhood tastes. First might come terrine of Kentish wild boar dressed fragrantly with lemon and elderflower, or there could be crab gazpacho revved up with bird's-eye chilli. Lobster from St Margaret's Bay might top a puff-pastry pizza, and share the billing with pomodorini tomatoes, tapenade and truffled foie gras, while double rib pork chop arrives in more traditional guise, with a rösti of Bramley apple, and sauced with honey and grain mustard. Crème brûlée, is flavoured with

Amalfi lemon and comes with basil sorbet. A truly exciting wine list jumbles nationalities together, and is bursting at the seams with fine growers. Bottles start from £14.95 for Guigal Côtes du Rhône and Sauvignon Blanc from Torres. NB Children under 8 are not permitted after 8pm.
**Chef/s:** Stephen Harvey. **Open:** Sun L 12 to 2, all week D 7 to 9. **Closed:** Christmas. **Meals:** Set L £23, Set D £40. Bar menu available. **Service:** 10% (optional). **Details:** Cards accepted. 70 seats. No mobile phones. Wheelchair access. Music. Car parking.

## READERS RECOMMEND
### Brasserie St Nicholas
**French**
61 London Road, Sevenoaks, TN13 1AU
Tel no: (01732) 456974
www.brasseriestnicholas.com
'Sophicated cooking and seasonal produce'

## ▌Speldhurst
### George & Dragon
**Ancient pub, modern food**
Speldhurst, TN3 0NN
Tel no: (01892) 863125
www.speldhurst.com
**Modern British | £30**
**Cooking score: 2**

The very ancient George & Dragon (it dates from the thirteenth century) is a thriving timber-framed pub at the very heart of a charming Kent village. In the bar, the large flagstones, massive inglenook fireplace and simple wooden furniture keep up traditional appearances, while the short menu is decidedly modern. The kitchen's repertoire is forever changing, reflecting the seasons as much as a prodigious talent for sourcing prime raw materials, many from local suppliers. Thus a spring menu might feature Groombridge asparagus with poached duck egg and hollandaise, and Rye Bay dressed crab with lemon, onion relish and aïoli. Rye Bay also supplies wild sea bass (with caper and brown shrimp dressing) at main course stage, while

meat dishes run to braised Black pork with butter beans and cider. The same menu is offered in the magnificent, heavily timbered dining room upstairs. A dozen or so wines are served by the glass from £3.25, with £13 the starting price for a short, global selection.
**Chef/s:** Max Leonard. **Open:** all week L 12 to 2.45 (to 4.30 Sun), Mon to Sat D 7 to 10.30. **Meals:** alc (main courses £8 to £20). Light L menu available Mon to Sat. **Service:** 12.5%. **Details:** Cards accepted. 100 seats. 55 seats outside. Wheelchair access. Music. Children's portions. Car parking.

## ▌Tunbridge Wells
### Hotel du Vin & Bistro
**Classy comfort food and first-class wines**
Crescent Road, Tunbridge Wells, TN1 2LY
Tel no: (01892) 526455
www.hotelduvin.com
**Modern European | £30**
**Cooking score: 4**

🍷 ⊑ ✌

Sharing a successful formula with its sister operations in a chain of bespoke hotels that stretches from Bristol to Harrogate, this is a lively, informal bistro within a Georgian town house. The dining room is hung with wine pictures, candles flicker on dark wooden tables and the army of staff march in unison. Begin with warm black pudding and pancetta salad, or salmon fishcake with herb beurre blanc, and follow with roast halibut with braised baby gem, or chargrilled aged rib-eye steak with garlic butter and hand-cut chips, or perhaps saffron and pea risotto. Lemon tart with raspberry sorbet, vanilla and honey cheesecake with glazed bananas, or a choice of home-made ice creams should round things off nicely. The cracking wine list includes some interesting global vintages and opens with own-label house selections from £14.50.
**Chef/s:** Jason Horn. **Open:** all week 12.30 to 2, 7 to 10. **Meals:** alc (main courses £12.50 to £17.50). Set L Sun £14.50. Bar menu available. **Service:** 10% (optional). **Details:** Cards accepted. 84 seats. 20 seats outside. No music. Wheelchair access. Children's portions. Car parking.

## ★NEW ENTRY★
## Thackeray's
**Cool and elegant surroundings**
85 London Road, Tunbridge Wells, TN1 1EA
Tel no: (01892) 511921
www.thackeraysrestaurant.co.uk
French | £40
Cooking score: 6

Tucked in an unassuming corner plot along the greener stretch of the London Road, the neat, whitewashed exterior of Thackeray's restaurant does little justice to its cool and tastefully converted Tardis-like interior. The bright and elegant Grade II-listed building sports low ceilings and dark, slightly skew-whiff antique floorboards, polished to a patent-leather shine. Outside, to the rear, the tranquil Japanese Terrace, with its soothing water feature and heated canopy, will delight fans of alfresco dining. Following stints in the kitchens of the Roux Brothers and Marco Pierre White, chef and co-proprietor Richard Phillips spent time with the Schrager hotel group before coming to Tunbridge Wells to 'deliver a unique dining experience'. Starters might include pan-seared scallops with roasted langoustine, scallop mousse and vanilla velouté, or confit chicken roulade with poached rhubarb salad and hazelnut dressing. Philllips' aims to source the best possible produce, while supporting local producers and dishes such as roast saddle of local rabbit, reflect this. Dedicated followers of fish might appreciate butter-poached lobster with saffron linguine, sautéed baby vegetables and tomato, carrot and cumin cream sauce, while desserts might include the ever-changing Thackeray's sharing plate for two, although the more single-minded diner might opt for a pretty apple soufflé with Biddenden apple juice jelly and Granny Smith sorbet. A comprehensive and eclectic wine list complements the menu; with a good range available by the half-bottle and a wide selection by the glass. House wine is £12.95 a bottle.

**Chef/s:** Richard Phillips. **Open:** Tue to Sat 12 to 2.30, 6.30 to 10.30. Through Dec Mon to Sat 12 to 2.30, 6.30 to 10.30 Sun. **Meals:** alc (main courses £19 to £26). **Service:** 12.5% (discretionary). **Details:** Cards accepted. Air-con. Separate bar. Music.

## ■ Whitstable
## JoJo's
**Contemporary tapas restaurant**
209 Tankerton Road, Whitstable, CT5 2AT
Tel no: (01227) 274591
Modern European | £30
Cooking score: 4

There's a touch of Mediterranean warmth about Nikki Billington and Paul Watson's likeable and informal tapas-style restaurant, with its simple, understated décor, open-plan kitchen, and wide glass doors opening on to the front terrace. The kitchen sources a fine range of raw materials, from Kentish wild venison to salad leaves grown in the garden at the back, although fish from local day boats is the top attraction judging by reports: haddock goujons with beer batter and tartare mayonnaise, and specials such as spicy mackerel fillet with a spicy tomato sauce have both been endorsed. Other high points have included lamb and feta koftas, patatas bravas, deep-fried courgettes and a superb selection of charcuterie. The strength here lies in the fact that everything is 'simply prepared, perfectly cooked, beautifully served, at sensible prices'. Baklava is the pick of desserts, though chocolate torte has its fans. The restaurant is unlicensed, but you can bring your own bottle for a token corkage charge.
**Chef/s:** Nikki Billington and Sarah Hannell. **Open:** Wed to Sun L 12.45 to 2.30, Wed to Sat D 6.30 to 10. **Meals:** alc (main courses £3 to £7.50). Unlicensed; BYO £1. **Service:** not inc. **Details:** 35 seats. 15 seats outside. No mobile phones. Wheelchair access. Music.

## Sportsman

**Local food, simple surroundings**
Faversham Road, Seasalter, Whitstable, CT5 4BP
Tel no: (01227) 273370
www.thesportsmanseasalter.co.uk
**Modern European | £30**
**Cooking score: 5**

In a remote spot, sheltered by a sea wall, stands this white painted pub with a simple interior. But this is no backwoods watering hole but a strongly rooted enterprise. Dishes are detailed on blackboards, orders taken at the bar and the kitchen deals in well sourced local and seasonal materials. While dishes may appear quite simple in concept, the level of technique brought to bear on them is what dazzles: you may eat Steve Harris's own air-dried ham, home-churned butter and own salt ('from the seawater by the pub') surely the sign of an enthusiastic chef. Combinations are soundly judged, pairing oysters with chorizo, Thornback ray with cockles, goose with chestnuts and bacon, and quantities don't overwhelm. Reporters have praised an intense beetroot soup, the crispy duck with chilli salsa (one of a handful of dishes in common with sibling, the Granville (see entry, Lower Hardres), the 'superb' home-made focaccia, and declared the fish cookery 'perfect'. An eight-course tasting menu brings many of these strands together – oysters, ham and bread, alongside Horn of Plenty (mushroom) agnolotti, steamed wild sea bass fillet with Avruga caviar sauce and Seasalter marsh lamb. The intense chocolate mousse with salted caramel and soured ice cream has become something of a signature dish. Service, led by Phil Harris, is welcomingly casual, the blackboard wine list wide ranging and affordable; prices start at £13.95.
**Chef/s:** Stephen Harris and Dan Flavel. **Open:** Tue to Sun L 12 to 2 (3 Sun), Tue to Sat D 7 to 9. **Meals:** alc (main courses £10 to £19). **Service:** not inc. **Details:** Cards accepted. 50 seats. Wheelchair access. Music. Children's portions. Car parking.

## Wheelers Oyster Bar

**A Whitstable institution**
8 High Street, Whitstable, CT5 1BQ
Tel no: (01227) 273311
**Seafood | £31**
**Cooking score: 2**

This tiny seafood restaurant has been in the same family since it was established in 1856 – you pass through the original Victorian oyster bar, with just four counter stools, to reach the dining room. This is an old-fashioned, predominantly brown room with five cramped tables – the place does not set out to impress with smart décor, or indeed trimmings of any kind. Rather, it goes in for starters of tempura of salt and pepper squid with oriental couscous and sweet chilli dressing, followed by meatier fish for the main course, say roast monkfish teamed with a baked pistou tart of baby mozzarella, basil sun-blushed tomatoes and red onion marmalade. Or there may be local smoked haddock three ways: with prawns in a fish pie, on bubble and squeak with grainy mustard sauce, or as a fishcake with wilted spinach and poached quails' egg – the cooking pays allegiance to no obvious style. Booking is essential and BYO; the restaurant is unlicensed.
**Chef/s:** Mark Stubbs, Gavin Kember and Sid Phillips. **Open:** Thur to Tue 1 to 7.30 (7 Sun). **Meals:** alc (main courses £15 to £18.50). Light menu available. **Service:** not inc. **Details:** 16 seats. Air-con. No music. Wheelchair access. Children's portions.

## Williams & Brown Tapas

**Understated modern tapas**
48 Harbour Street, Whitstable, CT5 1AQ
Tel no: (01227) 273373
**Spanish/Portuguese | £35**
**Cooking score: 2**

Ⅴ

With its low-key décor and open-to-view kitchen, Williams & Brown presents a cool setting for some understated modern Spanish tapas. You can graze your way through a constantly changing blackboard menu, mixing classics with up-to-date ideas, so albondigas (meatballs), escalivada, excellent mini chorizo baked in cider, or morcilla with chickpeas, stand alongside chicken livers in cognac, paper-thin Cecina smoked beef, and Catalan honeyed chicken. Specials are scrawled on a mirrored wall and take in lamb cutlets with chickpeas and cucumber salsa and a vegetarian paella of spinach, tomatoes and pine nuts, while a short dessert selection can deliver a first-rate pear frangipane tart. Reporters approve of the concept and service wins points for its friendliness. House wine is £13.95.

**Chef/s:** Christopher Williams and Matt Sibley. **Open:** Wed to Mon L 12 to 2 (2.30 Sat, 2.45 Sun), Wed to Sat and Mon D (also Sun June to Aug) 6.30 to 9 (9.30 Fri and Sat). **Closed:** D 24 Dec, 26 and 27 Dec, 1 and 2 Jan. **Meals:** alc (main courses £7 to £10). **Service:** 10% (optional). **Details:** 33 seats. Air-con. No mobile phones. Music.

## ALSO RECOMMENDED

### ▲ Whitstable Oyster Fishery Co.

Royal Native Oyster Stores, Horsebridge Road, Whitstable, CT5 1BU
Tel no: (01227) 276856

The décor remains unchanged at this Whitstable institution, with the bare-floored, check-clothed restaurant making the most of its rough-edged warehouse setting and seaside ambience. Seafood is the draw, with shellfish piled on ice in the bar and the time-honoured style taking in smoked eel and creamed horseradish (£8.50) to start and mains of grilled whole local Dover sole (£18.50) or baked grey mullet with lemon and thyme (£14.50), although separately priced sides of chips or mixed leaf and fine bean salad (£3) can push up the price. Straightforward desserts (£5.95) run from sticky toffee pudding to white chocolate cheesecake with raspberry coulis. House wines start at £15. Closed Mon.

Child-friendly restaurants

**National Dining Rooms**, London
A varying selection of regional dishes, a children's menu and an all-day bakery.

**Simply Heathcote**, Leeds
Sunday lunch is a good family day with a sensible and proper children's menu.

**Melton's Too**, York
Welcome touches include a stock of daily papers and a genuine attention to families.

**Valvona and Crolla**, Edinburgh
Long-standing Edinburgh Italian with a warm welcome for children.

**White Horse**, Brancaster Staithe, Norfolk
Fabulous coastal setting equalled by high standards of hospitality, food and drink.

**Magpie Café**, Whitby, Yorkshire
Harbourside café that continues to draw praise for the best traditional fish and chips.

**Anchor**, Walberswick, Suffolk
Super, family orientated seaside dining pub.

**Rick Stein's Café**, Cornwall
Bright, breezy bistro popular with families (fish fingers and chips are a favourite).

**The Three Pigs**, Norfolk
Proper pub with a real family bias. Piglets (under 12 years) get their own tasty real food.

**Felin Fach Griffin**, Wales
Does relaxed, modern-rustic style to devastatingly good effect – families love it.

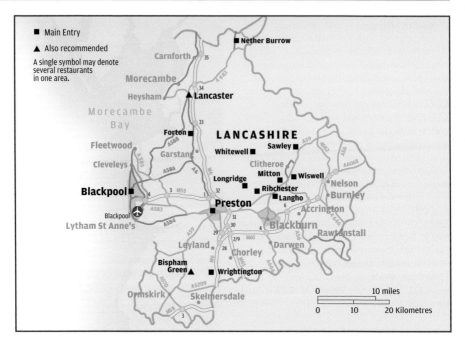

- ■ Main Entry
- ▲ Also recommended

A single symbol may denote several restaurants in one area.

(Map of Lancashire showing: Nether Burrow, Carnforth 35, Morecambe, Heysham, Lancaster ▲ 34, Forton ■ 33, LANCASHIRE, Fleetwood, Garstang, Whitewell ■, Sawley ■, Cleveleys, A586, Clitheroe, Longridge, Mitton ■, Wiswell ■, Nelson, Blackpool ■ 4, 3 MS5 1, 32, Ribchester ■, Burnley, Preston ■, Langho ■ 6, Accrington, Blackpool, Lytham St Anne's, A584, 31, 30, Blackburn, Rawtenstall, 29, 2/9, Darwen, Leyland 28, Chorley, Bispham Green ▲ ■ Wrightington, Ormskirk, Skelmersdale, 0 10 miles, 0 10 20 Kilometres)

## ■ Blackpool

### Kwizeen

**Eccentric spelling and seaside cuisine**
47-49 King Street, Blackpool, FY1 3EJ
Tel no: (01253) 290045
www.kwizeen.co.uk
**Modern European | £28**
**Cooking score: 2**

£5 OFF  V  £30

A bistro big on style without being precious or pretentious about it. Jury still out on the name – Kwizeen? – but the cuisine's fun, cheeky, and chic. Small wonder conference delegates, businessfolk, ladies-who-lunch and tourists-in-the-know beat a path here by day. Who can blame them at £6.50 for a two-course lunch and 'a pretty palatable' Spanish house white and red at a tenner a bottle from a short but select wine list. Kwizeen then courts theatricals with inventive tapas (6 to 7) before slipping gracefully into 'relaxed dining'. Inventive starters include Lancashire hot pot, main courses dare you to try liquorice sauce with savoury pheasant (maybe next time...) and strawberry pepper sauce goes down a storm with venison, pork and beef fillets and bacon mash. Desserts include offerings such as glazed lemon tart and basil ice cream. House wines start at £10.

**Chef/s:** Marco Callé-Calatayud. **Open:** Mon to Fri L 12 to 1.30, Mon to Sat D 6 to 9. **Closed:** Sat lunch, Sunday. **Meals:** alc (main courses £12.50 to £20). Set L £6.50 (2 courses). **Service:** not inc. **Details:** Cards accepted. 40 seats. No mobile phones. Music. Children's portions.

## READERS RECOMMEND

### Yu and You
**Chinese**
500 Longsight Road, Copster Green, Blackburn, BB1 9EU
Tel no: (01254) 247111
www.yuandyou.com
**'Quality food in a trendy setting'**

## Forton

### Bay Horse Inn
**Dining pub that relishes regional produce**
Bay Horse Lane, Forton, LA2 0HR
Tel no: (01524) 791204
www.bayhorseinn.com
**Modern British | £28**
**Cooking score: 3**

The Bay Horse's rural location is highlighted by the fact that it is only minutes from the M6. The place can still be used as an inn (note the open fire and draught ales) and it maintains a home-from-home atmosphere in the bar, but the dining room deals in modern cooking with its feet on the ground: say grilled black pudding with soused onions and English mustard. Craig Wilkinson's modest and straightforward approach is much appreciated by reporters, as is the fact that he cares about the provenance of his supplies, with the Forest of Bowland, Lakeland fells and local farms supplying the building blocks of the menu. Thus, slow-cooked Goosnargh duck with potato purée and boozy prunes could appear among main courses at dinner, while lunch in the bar has delivered Lancashire hotpot and Cumbrian mutton shank braised in red wine and thyme. Sticky toffee pudding is the dessert of choice. The wine list is a model of playing it straight, delivering a sound international selection at sensible prices. Chilean house wine is £12.95. NB No children allowed in the dining room after 9.
**Chef/s:** Craig Wilkinson. **Open:** Tue to Sun L 12 to 2 (3 Sun), Tue to Sat D 7 to 9.30. **Closed:** 25 Dec, 1 Jan. **Meals:** alc exc Sun L (main courses £11.50 to £18.50), Set L Sun £13.95 (2 courses) to £17.90. **Service:** not inc. **Details:** Cards accepted. 40 seats. 30 seats outside. Wheelchair access. Music. Children allowed. Car parking.

## ALSO RECOMMENDED

### ▲ Quite Simply French
27A St Georges Quay, Lancaster, LA1 1RD
Tel no: (01524) 843199
www.quitesimplyfrench.co.uk

Offering exactly what is says on the tin, this simple but stylishly decorated French restaurant overloooking the River Lune delivers dishes such as warm home-made aubergine and fromage frais gâteau (£4.80), oven-baked corn-fed chicken with a mushroom and Madeira jus (£12.85) and Belgian white-and-dark chocolate fondue for two (£7). A lobster tank is a focal point. Open daily for dinner, plus Sunday lunch; early-bird discounts.

## Langho

### Northcote Manor
**Ever-evolving regional cuisine**
Northcote Road, Langho, BB6 8BE
Tel no: (01254) 240555
www.northcotemanor.com
**Modern British | £45**
**Cooking score: 6**

Nigel Haworth's menus have raised eyebrows with the trendy turn they've taken of late. But the lime caramel with seared British White beef and bone marrow, and the lemon jelly accompanying Lytham sea bass tempura aren't so alarming really. Such quirky touches turn out to be minor details, counterpoints of texture and flavour on dishes as balanced and elegant as ever. The trendy dots and dashes send a message we can't miss, however; time doesn't stop at Northcote. This extends to the handsome Ribble Valley property itself, the whole of which has undergone a refurbishment in the last couple of years. It can still feel slightly muted in the spruced-up dining room but the neutral backdrop lets the food shine. Haworth's strong suit is harnessing the quality of produce from the North West's forests, seas, and pastures, and grafting it onto a classical base. His beliefs shine through, so when he gets into something – be it Langdale mutton or Ascroft's cauliflowers, he really gets into it, taking his customers along on the ride. Heaps of options including set, vegetarian, and tasting menus make choosing tough. The wine list is super, with around 80 half bottles (from £9.95), house wine at £17.50, and a good selection from Chile and Portugal as well as Burgundy and Bordeaux.

**Chef/s:** Nigel HawortH, Lisa Allen. **Open:** all week 12 to 1.30 (2 Sun), 7 to 9.30 (10 Sat). **Closed:** Christmas and New Year. **Meals:** alc (main courses £19.50 to £26.50). Set L £20, Set D £50 to £85. **Service:** not inc. **Details:** Cards accepted. 60 seats. No mobile phones. Wheelchair access. Music. Children's portions. Car parking.

## ▌Longridge

## Longridge Restaurant

Confident, contemporary cooking
104-106 Higher Road, Longridge, PR3 3SY
Tel no: (01772) 784969
www.heathcotes.co.uk
**Modern British | £35**
**Cooking score: 5**

It's been all go at the Longridge Restaurant this year. Not only has the nineteenth-century cottage been given a smart new look, it's also got itself a brand-new head chef in James Holah. An assured performance at inspection suggests this north-west favourite is in safe hands. The duck hash brown with black pudding, crispy bacon and poached egg remains a winner, and small wonder, each ingredient was the best of its type, cooked to perfection. Foie gras ballottine with a crusting of roast hazelnuts proved to be an inspired pairing with the aid of just a lick of apple purée for sweetness. The newly confident, subtle approach benefits the sparkling local ingredients enormously. Flavours are clean and clear, in presentations that take you by surprise. A pickled turnip slice secreted under soft, pink roast Goosnargh duck breast was a nice touch; a baked sea bream main came carefully layered, terrine-style, on top of lemony, shaved fennel. Stopping short of playing whale music, everything is done to aid relaxation. Muted eau de nil and taupe tones, set-price menus (bar a £5 supplement on the beef fillet), a straightforward wine list (from £15.95 for a well-chosen Sicilian house white or red), charming service from sunny, on-the-ball staff... it's all so blissfully straightforward, and it feels fresher than ever.

**Chef/s:** James Holah. **Open:** Tue to Fri and Sun L 12 to 2.30, Tue to Sun D 6 (5 Sat) to 10 (9 Sun). **Closed:** bank hols. **Meals:** alc (main courses £12.50 to £25). **Service:** not inc. **Details:** Cards accepted. 85 seats. Air-con. Wheelchair access. Music. Car parking.

## Thyme

Friendly neighbourhood bistro
1-3 Inglewhite Road, Longridge, PR3 3JR
Tel no: (01772) 786888
**Modern European | £26**
**Cooking score: 2**
£5 OFF **V** £30

This welcoming contemporary space on the high street in Longridge is a good backdrop to chef Alex Coward's easy-eating brand of Modern European cuisine. The kitchen does very well with safe fare – like the beefy cup of onion soup and the sirloin steak with exemplary chips enjoyed at inspection – but comes unstuck when it tries too hard. The à la carte's hotchpotch of influences from Italian to Indian is slightly muddled; the vertical stack approach to presentation only works if dishes reach the table untoppled. The simple, fairly-priced lunch and early evening menus provide better value than the ambitious à la carte. Wine to accompany comes from a wallet-friendly, pocket-sized international list starting at £12.75. Regrettably, an air of carelessness coloured proceedings on inspection: grubby, creased menus and distracted waiters did not inspire confidence. A second branch is at the Sirloin Inn, Station Road, Hoghton, Preston; tel: (01254) 852293

**Chef/s:** Michael Law. **Open:** Tue to Sat 12 to 2, 6 to 9.30, Sun 1 to 8. **Meals:** alc (main courses £13 to £18). Set L Tue to Sat £8.95 (2 courses) to £10.95, Set D 6 to 7.30 £9.95 (2 courses) to £11.95. Light L menu available Tue to Sat. **Service:** not inc.

**Details:** Cards accepted. 50 seats. Air-con. No mobile phones. Wheelchair access. Music. Children's portions.

## Mitton

### Three Fishes

**Punters angle for a table**
Mitton Road, Mitton, BB7 9PQ
Tel no: (01254) 826888
www.thethreefishes.com
**Modern British | £21**
**Cooking score: 5**

V

Three years in, the Three Fishes in peaceful Mitton has worn in and warmed up very nicely, and is even more popular than ever. Sunday lunch is an institution, hence the rammed car park and queues at the bar. Don't expect the rest of the week to be much quieter; the old whitewashed inn is always alive with customers piled around the wooden tables by the fires – reservations are for eight or more only. The array of starters, sandwiches and platters, plus regional classics like Lancashire hotpot and cheese and onion pie, tells of a relationship with the farmer, not the freezer. The regular menu is packed with local goodies like Morecambe Bay shrimps and Goosnargh chicken and often there are seasonal specials, maybe Formby asparagus or Westmorland damsons. Reports praise owner Nigel Haworth and chef Richard Upton's resurrection of 'largely ignored traditional British delicacies', like mutton, offal and pigs' trotters 'presented in a totally modern way'. The interesting wine list, from £12.50, is not your typical pub list, hitting £50 at the top end, so it's a shame more aren't offered by the glass. A second pub, the Highwayman at Nether Burrow, is new this year (see entry).
**Chef/s:** Richard Upton. **Open:** Mon to Sat 12 to 2, 6 to 9 (9.30 Fri and Sat), Sun 12 to 8.30. **Meals:** alc (main courses £7.50 to £15). **Service:** not inc. **Details:** Cards accepted. 60 seats. No music. Wheelchair access. Children's portions. Car parking.

## Nether Burrow

★NEW ENTRY★

★ PUB NEWCOMER OF THE YEAR ★

### The Highwayman

**Banging the drum for quality produce**
Nether Burrow, LA6 2RJ
Tel no: (01524) 274249
**Modern British | £20**
**Cooking score: 3**

V £30

The second Lancastrian pub from Craig Bancroft and Nigel Haworth, the duo behind the Three Fishes in Mitton (see entry), the Highwayman bangs the same drum as its sibling for top-quality produce from the north-west. If the pub's refurbishment feels just a little bit too polished to make it a genuinely atmospheric local, the quality of food and terrific value for money more than merit a journey from those who live further afield. Prominence given to provenance can make the menu read a little like a family tree: Peter Gott's potted wild boar might be followed by Farmer Sharp's Herdwick mutton pudding. But there's more to the Highwayman than name-dropping and the kitchen knows how to get the best out of its scrupulously sourced ingredients: slow-cooked leg of Goosnargh corn-fed duckling falls off the bone into a hearty casserole of Howbarrow organic vegetables, with a dinky bowl of gratin potatoes on the side adding a creamy dollop of comfort. Elsewhere are platters of Cumbrian hams and smoked fish, grilled steaks and sausages, salads and sandwiches, cheese and home-made ice cream and a 'young person's menu'. House red and white by the glass are £3.15.
**Chef/s:** Mike Ward. **Open:** Mon to Sat L 12 to 2, Mon to Fri D 6 to 9, Sat 5.30 to 9, Sun 12 to 8.30. **Closed:** Christmas Day. **Meals:** alc (main courses £7 to £16). **Service:** optional. **Details:** Cards accepted. 120 seats. 70 seats outside. Wheelchair access. Children allowed.

## ALSO RECOMMENDED

### ▲ Eagle & Child

Malt Kiln Lane, Bispham Green, Ormskirk,
L40 3SG
Tel no: (01257) 462297

This eighteenth-century inn is worth seeking out, set as it is in a tiny village in beautiful countryside. Open fires, a flagstone floor and beamed ceilings create a cosy and friendly atmosphere, a suitable setting for some good, homely cooking. Local ingredients feature in dishes such as roast Bury black pudding with mash and onion gravy (£5), loin of lamb with chorizo mash (£11) and spiced rhubarb served with warm butter cake (£4). Real ales, a decent wine list. Open all week.

## ▌Preston

### Winckley Square Chop House

A town-centre British brasserie
23 Winckley Square, Preston, PR1 3JJ
Tel no: (01772) 252732
www.heathcotes.co.uk
**Modern British | £26**
**Cooking score: 3**

Pitched somewhere between the fine-dining heights of his Longridge Restaurant and the high-street vibe of pizza-pasta chain the Olive Press, comes Paul Heathcote's modern British brasserie, Winckley Square Chop House. The philosophy of good ingredients, simply done, extends from fish and chips to more exciting international dishes like soft-shell crab and Asian-spiced pork belly. A vast veal escalope with warm potato salad (£17) found favour with us, as did al dente pappardelle with Southport tomatoes and Parmesan foam. A rare beef salad with celery à la grecque (£5.50) was over-salty, but improved immeasurably once the sweetly apologetic waiter retrieved the missing one-day curd cheese from the kitchen. Puddings – trifle and ice cream with Pedro Ximénez – were terrific. The £15 set menu is rightly popular with local business

types and exhausted shoppers, as is the wine list, with its baseline price of £14.95 and extensive range under £30.
**Chef/s:** David Crabtree. **Open:** all week 12 to 2.30, 6 to 10 (11 Sat, 9 Sun). **Closed:** bank hols. **Meals:** alc (main courses £9.50 to £22). Set L Mon to Sat and D Mon to Sat 6 to 7 £12.95 (2 courses, inc wine), Set D Mon £15 (inc wine). **Service:** not inc. **Details:** Cards accepted. 90 seats. Air-con. Wheelchair access. Music. Children's portions.

## READERS RECOMMEND

### Bangla Fusion

Indian
Liverpool Old Road, Much Hoole, Preston,
PR4 5JQ
Tel no: (01772) 610 800
'Indian with a modern slant – out of this world'

## ▌Ribchester

★NEW ENTRY★
### White Bull

Village pub with lots of promise
Church Street, Ribchester, PR3 3XP
Tel no: 01254 878303
whitebullrib.co.uk
**Gastropub | £20**
**Cooking score: 3**
£5 OFF £30

The White Bull, now under the ownership of Chris and Kath Bell, in partnership with butcher Martin Carefoot, is off to a promising start. The Bells have previous form – as chef and manager respectively – at Paul Heathcote's Longridge Restaurant, so this village pub is quite a departure. It's a proper local, with fruit machines, pool table and chirpy staff, just one with a rather good kitchen. The menu is British, not local, so haggis, neeps and tatties rubs shoulders with Irish stew while more adventurous – if sometimes slightly incongruous – specials appear on the blackboard. The steaks (c/o Mr.Carefoot) are particularly good, and the accompanying chips aren't too shabby either. All 20 or so wines are under £20, with house wine at £2.85 a glass. Cask ales – Copper Dragon or Black Sheep, say – change monthly. **Chef/s:** Chris Bell. **Open:** Tue to Sat L 12 to 2, D 6 to 9, Sun L 12 to 8. **Closed:** Christmas. **Meals:** Set L and D £10 (2 courses). **Service:** not inc. **Details:** Cards accepted. 80 seats. 30 seats outside. Wheelchair access. Music. Children's portions.

## ▌Sawley
### Spread Eagle
**Handsome, solid pub**
Sawley, BB7 4NH
Tel no: (01200) 441202
www.the-spreadeagle.co.uk
**Gastropub | £24**
**Cooking score: 4**
£5 OFF  V  £30

The Spread Eagle sits at the crossroads of sleepy Sawley, opposite the atmospheric ruined abbey and bang next door to the River Ribble. 'Not my idea of an absolute gem' reports one reader of the traditional interior: swirly carpets, piped popular classics, fussy wall lamps and 'too much' dark wood panelling. But don't judge just yet, because anachronism stops sharp at the kitchen door. Paul Heathcote-trained chef Greig Barnes produces thoughtful, inventive dishes using local ingredients. The likes of cured salmon gravadlax, smooth potato purée, beetroot, dill and smoked trout rillette appear on your starched linen tablecloth 'sweet, smoky and beautifully proportioned'. Pan-fried salmon, with chicory marmalade, braised beef shin and carrot and tarragon veal stock is a triumph, as is the roast fillet of pork with apple purée, pancetta and smooth piccalilli velouté. For a great ending, the bread-and-butter pudding with vanilla custard and apricot compote is possibly 'one of the best puds you'll have this year'. An exhaustive wine list starts at £10.80, with 12 by the glass starting at £3.05. **Chef/s:** Greig Barnes. **Open:** Tue to Sun L 12pm to 2pm, Tue to Sat D 6pm to 9pm. **Meals:** alc (main courses £9.50 to £16.50). Set L Tue to Sat £13.50 (2 courses). **Service:** not inc. **Details:** Cards accepted. 80 seats. Separate bar. Wheelchair access. Music. Children's portions. Car parking.

## ▌Whitewell
### The Inn at Whitewell
**Upper-tier pub grub**
Whitewell, BB7 3AT
Tel no: (01200) 448222
www.innatwhitewell.com
**Modern British**
**Cooking score: 3**
⊨ V

The journey seems endless as you venture deeper and deeper into the Forest of Bowland, but finally, you're rewarded by the sudden appearance of this handsome, rambling inn. The open fires, stone floors and richly polished furniture restore the sense of place. You can choose to eat in any of the bar areas or more formal dining room, but if you want to gaze at the astounding views over the River Hodder towards the Trough of Bowland, the bar is best. Much of the food is locally sourced: grilled Bury black pudding, grain mustard mash and home-made baked beans is an earthy and fitting start. Roast loin of Bowland lamb, minted pease pudding and cocotte potatoes vies for flavour with Whitewell fish pie, bursting with smoked haddock and prawns. Puddings are described as 'wholesome, traditional and sometimes nursery-like', and indeed, 'you had better have a walk in mind after as portions are generous to a fault'. The wine list is global and comprehensive, with 14 by the glass, starting at £2.50, while the house red and white come in at £11.50. **Chef/s:** Jamie Cadman. **Open:** Daily D 7.30 to 9.30. **Meals:** alc (main courses £14 to £23). **Service:** not inc. **Details:** Cards accepted. 65 seats. 30 seats outside. Children's portions. Car parking.

## ▌Wiswell

### Freemasons Arms

**Three separate dining areas**
8 Vicarage Fold, Wiswell, BB7 9DF
Tel no: (01254) 822218
www.freemasonswiswell.co.uk
**Modern British | £23**
**Cooking score: 3**

£5 OFF  £30 ♨

Small is beautiful. Tucked down a ginnel in a picture-perfect village outside Clitheroe is this bijou boozer dishing up great food. An ever-changing menu is chalked up on the wall this part of Lancashire produces great ingredients. Witness Goosnargh duck pâté with foie gras, which arrives in a dinky Kilner jar with cherry chutney, and baked figs wrapped in pancetta stuffed with Blacksticks Blue cheese. Slow roast shoulder of local lamb, potato purée and rosemary jus arrives dark and sticky. Finish with apple and Kirkham Lancashire cheese tartlet with ale syrup. The wine list has extraordinary breadth and variety. House wine is £14.
**Chef/s:** Ian Martin. **Open:** Wed to Sat L 12 to 3 D 6 to 9.30. **Closed:** Mon, Tue. **Meals:** alc (main courses £9.50 to £16.95). Set D before 7 £11.95 (two courses). **Service:** optional. **Details:** Cards accepted. 36 seats. 16 seats outside. No music. Wheelchair access.

## ▌Wrightington

### Mulberry Tree

**A gentrified inn**
9 Wood Lane, Wrightington Bar, Wrightington, WN6 9SE
Tel no: (01257) 451400
**Modern British | £32**
**Cooking score: 4**

From the outside it looks like a large, traditional pub, but the Mulberry Tree has a smart, contemporary bar area; food is served here and in the restaurant. The menus are slightly different in each, allowing for a range of food that runs from sandwiches all the way to such luxuries as caviar or oysters. Start with

dressed Brixham crab salad with melba toast, olives with caper berries and sun-blushed tomatoes. Main courses include lobster with seasonal vegetables, new potatoes and a champagne and herb sauce; 'lighter dishes' such as a warm salad of Morteaux sausage with crushed new potatoes, a soft poached egg and hollandaise sauce; and, from a separate list headed 'larger dishes', roast rack of lamb with savoyarde potatoes. A separate vegetarian menu offers an impressive selection of meat-free options, while dessert might be a hot melting chocolate pudding with vanilla ice cream. A globe-trotting list of seventy-plus wines starts at £14.25 a bottle.
**Chef/s:** Mark Prescott. **Open:** all week 12 to 2, 6 to 9.30 (10 Fri and Sat). **Closed:** 26 Dec, 1 Jan. **Meals:** alc exc Sun L (main courses £9.50 to £21.50). Set L Mon to Sat £12.50 (2 courses), Set L Sun £19.50, Set D 6 to 7 £14.50 (2 courses). Bar menu available exc Sat D. **Service:** 10% (optional). **Details:** Cards accepted. 75 seats. 20 seats outside. Air-con. Wheelchair access. Music. Children's portions. Car parking.

### Simply Heathcotes

**Nostalgic dishes**
Wrightington Hotel, Moss Lane, Wrightington, WN6 9PB
Tel no: (01257) 478244
www.heathcotes.co.uk
**Modern British | £28**
**Cooking score: 2**

🍽 V £30

The youngest branch of Paul Heathcote's brasserie chain (see entries in Leeds, Liverpool and Manchester) occupies the first floor of a modern hotel complex. Like its siblings, it deals in seasonal produce and modern flavours, all served in a casual setting that positively encourages families (note the children's menu). Heathcote's Lancastrian trademarks are easy to spot (a springtime salad of black pudding and ham hock with boiled egg and chive hollandaise, for example). Crispy soft shell crab with chilli, lime and coriander could line up ahead of honey- and ginger-spiced pork belly or

**Fergus Henderson**

pappardelle with Southport tomatoes, wild mushrooms and English Parmesan foam. Desserts are equally eclectic, ranging from goats' milk pannacotta to trifle with rosewater and strawberry jelly and elderflower custard. The concise global wine list kicks off with house Italians at £14.95.

**Chef/s:** Michael Noonan. **Open:** all week 12 to 2.30, 6 to 10 (11 Sat, 9 Sun). **Closed:** 27 and 28 Dec, 1 Jan. **Meals:** alc (main courses £9.50 to £22). Set L £15 (2 courses), Set D Mon to Sat 6 to 7 £15 (2 courses), Set D Mon £15 (2 courses, inc wine). **Service:** not inc. **Details:** Cards accepted. 81 seats. Air-con. Wheelchair access. Music. Children's portions. Car parking.

*Why did you become a chef?*
The fickle finger of fate.

*Who was your main inspiration?*
Mum.

*What's your favourite cookery book?*
Marcella Hazan's *Classical Italian Cooking*.

*What's the best dish you've ever eaten?*
That rather depends on the spirit of the time and place.

*What's your guilty food pleasure?*
Eating the Toblerone from the mini bar at three in the morning.

*If you could only eat one more thing, what would it be?*
Sea urchins.

*Who would you invite to your ideal dinner party?*
Audrey Hepburn, Isambard Kingdom Brunel, Glenn Miller and Kate Moss. It should make for a lively evening.

*What's the hardest thing about running a restaurant?*
What's easy?

*Which are your proudest achievements?*
In my small way, helping British produce.

*What's coming up next for you?*
I still leave that to the fickle finger of fate.

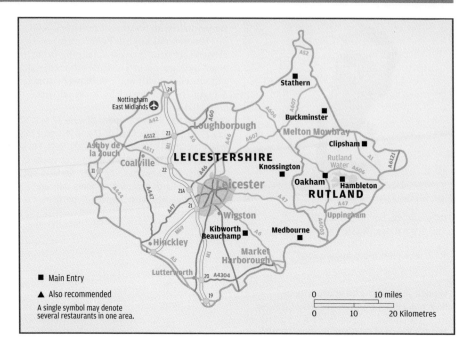

## Buckminster

### Tollemache Arms

**Comfortable country inn**
48 Main Street, Buckminster, NG33 5SA
Tel no: (01476) 860007
www.thetollemachearms.com
**Modern British | £29**
**Cooking score: 4**

£5 OFF 🍽 ♈ £30

Owned by the Tollemache estate, this converted country inn is a short hop from the A1. Mediterranean vibrancy informs dishes such as a salad of grilled mozzarella with avocado and chorizo, or freshwater crayfish risotto. Menus are written straightforwardly, eschewing the bizarre metaphorical turns of much modern cookery, so that you have an accurate idea of what you'll get when ordering. Grilled chicken with sauté potatoes and Swiss chard, confit duck leg with Puy lentils and creamed chicory, or sea bream with basil mash, are the kinds of preparations to expect. Crowd-pleasing desserts have included hot chocolate pudding with pistachio ice cream, while several bases are covered in the form of strawberry vodka champagne milkshake. There is a menu of simpler bar snacks too. A short but serviceable list has informative notes, and starts with house wines from Gaillac in Southwest France at £12.95.

**Chef/s:** Mark Gough. **Open:** Tue to Sun L 12 to 2, Tue to Sat D 7 to 9. **Meals:** alc (main courses £9.50 to £17.50). Set L £10 (2 courses) to £14.50, Set D Tue to Thurs £10 (2 courses) to £14.50. Bar menu available. **Service:** not inc. **Details:** Cards accepted. 50 seats. 30 seats outside. Wheelchair access. Music. Children's portions. Car parking.

## ▮ Clipsham

### Olive Branch
**Quirky informality**
Main Street, Clipsham, LE15 7SH
Tel no: (01780) 410355
www.theolivebranchpub.com
Modern British | £24
Cooking score: 3

The rambling interior of the Olive Branch is suitably shabby-chic, with crackling log fires and soft lamplight. The real attractions are the blackboards listing wonderful bin-end wines and the diverse modern British menus, listing soups, sandwiches and an excellent value two- or three-course lunch menu. Both these and the daily printed carte overflow with local ingredients. Menus proudly identify the produce source, be it Northfield Farm chargrilled rib-eye with béarnaise, or Grasmere Farm sausages with mustard mash and braised red cabbage. The feel of the place may be down-to-earth but the cooking is accomplished and notable for its flair and simplicity, in dishes like pan-fried scallops with beetroot and blood orange salad, roast duck with chilli gratin and stir-fry vegetables, and caramelised lemon tart with lemon sherbet sorbet. Exemplary value distinguishes the wine list, which darts about the globe in search of interesting flavours, kicking off with house wines from France at £13.50.
**Chef/s:** Sean Hope. **Open:** all week 12 to 2 (3 Sun), 7 (6 Fri) to 9.30 (9 Sun). **Meals:** alc (main courses £7.50 to £19). Set L Mon to Sat £14 (2 courses) to £16.50, Set L Sun £19. Snack L menu available Mon to Sat. **Service:** not inc. **Details:** Cards accepted. 48 seats. 24 seats outside. Wheelchair access. Music. Children's portions. Car parking.

## READERS RECOMMEND

### Ashfield's Restaurant
**Modern British**
High Street, Earl Shilton, LE9 7DG
Tel no: (01455) 841556
www.ashfieldsrestaurant.com
'Quality English produce'

## ▮ Hambleton

### Hambleton Hall
**Excellent classical cuisine**
Hambleton, LE15 8TH
Tel no: (01572) 756991
www.hambletonhall.com
Modern British | £70
Cooking score: 7

Tim and Stefa Hart's Hambleton Hall Hotel and Restaurant is at the top of the superleague of country-house restaurants. It manages, quite effortlessly, to exude both sophistication and a chintzy country feel. Prepare to be cosseted, whether you start off with drinks in the drawing or – on a sunny day – in the beautiful, mature gardens offering wonderful views over Rutland Water. There's a host of menus spanning a broad price range from 'lunch for less', to the tasting menu and the a la carte. But note one inspector's caveat: portions on the tasting menu are on the large side, so 'some will find it heavy-going'. At inspection, a Waldorf salad from the lunch menu transpired to be a relatively loose interpretation of this popular classic, but made a fresh, yet luxurious opener. A main course of Shetland salmon was a very natural dish accompanied by a frothy dill-flavoured nage and perfect, tender asparagus tips. This sums up long-term chef Aaron Patterson's style – in tune with the seasons and with the environment. Patterson's philosophy manifests itself in well-composed classics incorporating thoughtful exploratory twists, or, as one reader put it, 'assiettes – the main ingredient in different ways – are a preoccupation'. A mosaic of chicken, black pudding and sweetbreads with apple and blackberry compôte, or breast of Goosnargh duck, caramelised endive and pan-fried foie gras show off the kitchen's technical accomplishment with a nod to pure English country flavours. The tranquil dining room is textbook country house, in muted shades of ochre, rust, and cream, decorated with abundant cut flowers. Service is seamless, with the excellent sommelier on hand to advise – at all price points. The wine list is high end, with plenty of classic French wines but there are well-priced and well-chosen house selections too (from £16) plus a decent list of half bottles. Finish with good coffee and petits fours (white chocolate with star anise or green olive, for example) then disappear for a nap or a stroll round the gardens if you can manage it. It's that kind of place.

**Chef/s:** Aaron Patterson. **Open:** all week 12 to 1.30, 7 to 9.30. **Meals:** alc (main courses £25 to £39). Set L £18.50 (2 courses) to £35, Set L Sun £37.50 to £50, Set D £40 to £60. Snack menu available. **Service:** not inc. **Details:** Cards accepted. 64 seats. 20 seats outside. No music. No mobile phones. Wheelchair access. Children's portions. Car parking.

## Kibworth Beauchamp
### Firenze
**Sophisticated food in a friendly setting**
9 Station Street, Kibworth Beauchamp, LE8 OLN
Tel no: (0116) 279 6260
www.firenze.co.uk
**Modern Italian | £32**
**Cooking score: 3**

£5 OFF 🍷

Lino and Sarah Poli's pretty village restaurant pays loving homage to Florence with Florentine pictures on the wall and a Tuscan red colour scheme. The seasonally changing menu draws from all over Italy. All fish 'secondi' are ultra-fresh specials and not on the menu as such: a good move in landlocked Leicestershire. The kitchen clearly has a taste for vivid colours and equally bright flavours. At inspection perfectly al dente asparagus risotto was enlivened visually by an egg yolk tucked inside; raviolo of goats' cheese came with traffic-light-bright pepper purée; halibut with mussels and saffron sauce was another multi-coloured and flavour-charged stunner. The wine list is a pleasure: not only about big names but about hand-selected bottles (from £13.50) from all over Italy, from Alto Adige to Sicily. A range of a dozen or so sweet wines makes pudding – in liquid form at the very least – hard to resist. A pannacotta with licquorice went wonderfully with a glass of

Barolo Chinato; coffee came with plentiful home-made biscotti – a typically generous touch.

**Chef/s:** Lino Poli and Stuart Batey. **Open:** Mon to Sat L 12 to 3, D 7 to 11. **Closed:** 10 days from 23 Dec, bank hols. **Meals:** alc (main courses £7.50 to £30). Set L £12 (1 course), Set D Tue to Thur £15 (2 courses) to £25 (4 courses). **Service:** not inc. **Details:** Cards accepted. 60 seats. No mobile phones. Wheelchair access. Music. Children's portions.

## Knossington
### Fox & Hounds
**Handsome building, covered in creepers**
6 Somerby Road, Knossington, LE15 8LY
Tel no: (01664) 454676
**Modern British | £33**
**New Chef**

˅

Behind the thick stone walls of this creeper-covered village inn locals, hikers and visiting diners can be found happily ensconced. In fine weather, they overflow into the large garden at the rear. 'Standards are high' says one reporter of the food, which is definitely the highlight of any visit. Dishes from the daily-changing blackboard menu include starters of pan-fried lambs' kidneys with Puy lentils, chilli and garlic; crab bruscetta with fennel and lemon; and Swiss chard and ricotta ravioli with sage butter, followed by pan-roasted rib-eye steak with wild garlic butter, pan-fried turbot fillet with crushed potatoes, wilted spinach and lemon oil; or Italian sausages with cannellini beans, spring greens and salsa verde. Finish with dark chocolate truffle cake and espresso ice cream; or Lowna Dairy Bluestones goats' cheese with cherries and oatcakes. The short, simple wine list starts at £12.

**Chef/s:** Robert Wendlant. **Open:** Tue to Sun L 12 to 2.30, D 7 to 9.30. **Meals:** alc (main courses £9.95 to £14). Set L £10.95 (2 courses) to £16.95. **Service:** not inc. **Details:** Cards accepted. 40 seats. 40 seats outside. No mobile phones. Music. Children's portions. Car parking.

## ▮ Medbourne

### Horse & Trumpet

**Modern cooking in a rural setting**
Medbourne, LE16 8DX
Tel no: (01858) 565000
www.horseandtrumpet.com
**Modern British | £34**
**Cooking score: 5**

The Horse & Trumpet is a small restaurant with a low-key ambience, its reputation being founded on high-quality cooking. It's a former village pub that has been sympathetically converted to give several small dining rooms. Gary Magnani heads the kitchen and there is a vigorous streak of culinary daring running through his menus. An intensely flavoured celeriac and apple velouté with truffle oil followed by a rich but delicate Parmesan crème caramel with Parmesan air opened the evening tasting menu, the highlights of which were yoghurt and lemon noodles with pea shoots, vegetable bouillon and Avruga caviar, and sweet, perfectly timed halibut teamed with intensely flavoured beef cheek as well as salsify and parsnip. Desserts included Valhrona chocolate iced double cream with morello cherries, followed by a tiny piece of Colston Bassett Stilton with pear chutney, then outstanding petits fours. Alongside the evening tasting menu (there's a truncated version available at lunch) there are good-value fixed price lunches and à la carte dinners. 'Child friendly' service neatly balances formality and informality, and wines are a competently chosen collection with a decent slate by the glass from £3.25, with bottles starting at £16.95.
**Chef/s:** Gary Magnani. **Open:** Tue to Sun L 12 to 1.45 (2.30 Sun), Tue to Sat D 7 to 9.30. **Meals:** alc exc Sun L (main courses L £9, D £15.50 to £21). Set L Tue to Sat £16 (2 courses) to £20, Set L Sun £17 (2 courses) to £23, Set D £45. **Service:** not inc. **Details:** Cards accepted. 45 seats. 20 seats outside. Wheelchair access. Music. Children allowed.

## ▮ Oakham

### Lord Nelson's House Hotel, Nick's Restaurant

**A quirky family-run restaurant**
11 Market Place, Oakham, LE15 6DT
Tel no: (01572) 723199
www.nelsons-house.com
**French | £41**
**Cooking score: 3**

Lord Nelson's House, a quirky hotel in a former coaching inn, has been taken over by Simon and Kasia McEnery. The restaurant, Nick's, remains as family-friendly and charming as ever with brightly painted brick walls, beams, and artful clutter creating a relaxing place to settle down for dinner after an apertif in the lounge. The menu exploits local ingredients and seasonal produce, with a few – not always successful – nods to fashion, eg savoury ice creams, foams and truffle oil. A table d'hôte starter of cauliflower velouté with roast scallops boasted natural flavours and sweet fleshy scallops; a vegetarian main of wild mushroom lasagne was a robust choice paired with a well-flavoured though huge scoop of Parmesan ice cream. Dessert of fried custard with rhubarb sorbet and vanilla foam was a contrast of texture and temperature, but the foam contributed little. One reader commented on 'uncomfortable seats' and described service as 'indifferent' The predominantly French wine list has been pepped up with a few interesting bottles from the New World, mostly under £30. House wine is £14.50. Reports please.
**Chef/s:** Dameon Clarke. **Open:** Tue to Sat 12 to 2.30, 7 to 9.30. **Closed:** 2 weeks Christmas, 2 weeks Aug. **Meals:** alc (main courses L £8 to £21, D £14 to £22). Set L £20 (2 courses) to £25, Set D £30 (2 courses) to £35. **Service:** not inc. **Details:** Cards accepted. 46 seats. No mobile phones. Music. Children's portions. Car parking.

## Stathern

### Red Lion Inn

**Culinary eclectism in a village local**
2 Red Lion Street, Stathern, LE14 4HS
Tel no: (01949) 860868
www.theredlioninn.co.uk
**Modern British | £30**
**New Chef**

True to its pub roots, this rambling white painted building has tables in the garden, a relaxed country auction room feel to the décor, and real ales on draught in the flag-floored bar. Eat here or make your way to the dining room, one menu serves the whole place and displays an admirable commitment to local produce along with a feel for combining diverse flavours. Beetroot, for example, is a foil to ox tongue terrine, and sea bream might be served with potato and chorizo Parmentier. You might also find chicken breast with Moroccan-style couscous and saffron dressing, or smoked haddock with champ mash and grain mustard sauce. Desserts focus on tradition —apple crumbles, rhubarb and custard — and contrasting ideas like hot chocolate fondant with Irish liqueur cream. The thoughtfully chosen wine list sports succinct tasting notes; house wine is £12.50. Younger sibling of the Olive Branch at Clipsham (see entry, Rutland).
**Chef/s:** Edward Leslie. **Open:** all week L 12 to 2 (4 Sun), Mon to Sat D 7 (6 Sat) to 9.30. **Closed:** 1 Jan.
**Meals:** alc (main courses £10 to £20). Set L Mon to Sat £12.95 (2 courses) to £15.95, Set L Sun £16.50.
Bar L menu available. **Service:** not inc.
**Details:** Cards accepted. 50 seats. 54 seats outside. No music. Children's portions. Car parking.

## READERS RECOMMEND

### The Baker's Arms

Main Street, Thorpe Langton, Market Harborough, LE16 7TS
Tel no: (01858) 545201
www.thebakersarms.co.uk
**'Consistently good quality and variety'**

Tom Parker Bowles

***Where do you eat out?***
Blueprint Café, Locanda Locatelli, Scotts, Caprice, Greens, Rivington Grill, Kiasu, Que Tre, The Fat Badger, St John, Royal China, Bar Shu, Chisou, Inahao and Assagi.

***Who's your favourite chef?***
Jeremy Lee or Rowley Leigh.

***What's your favourite cookery book?***
*Food in England* by Dorothy Hartley, *Thai Food* by David Thompson, *The Prawn Cocktail Years* by Simon Hopkinson and Lindsey Bareham and *Modern Cookery* by Eliza Acton

***What's the best dish you've ever eaten?***
Veal sweetbreads stuffed with truffle at Le Grand Vefour in Paris or a bowl of buffalo pho soup in a small roadside stall just outside Luang Prabang in Laos.

***What's your guilty food pleasure?***
McDonalds cheeseburger.

***If you could only eat one more thing, what would it be?***
Colchester No 2 native oysters.

***What's your favourite wine?***
1982 Leoville Barton.

***Who would your ideal dinner guests be?***
I suppose I should be learned and say Proust, Gandhi or Voltaire. But in truth, it's my wife and friends.

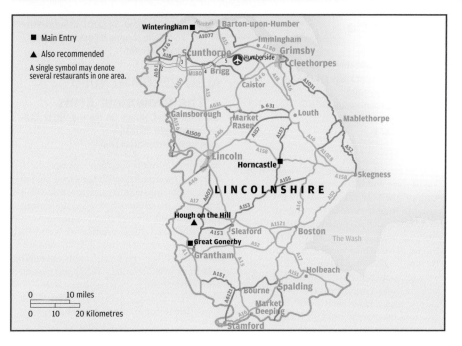

- ■ Main Entry
- ▲ Also recommended

A single symbol may denote several restaurants in one area.

Winteringham ■
Barton-upon-Humber
Humber
Immingham
Scunthorpe
A1077
A161
A18
A159
M180
Brigg
Humberside
Grimsby
Cleethorpes
Caistor
A631
Gainsborough
Market Rasen
A631
Louth
Mablethorpe
A1500
A46
A158
Lincoln
Horncastle ■
A155
Skegness
L I N C O L N S H I R E
A17
A153
Hough on the Hill ▲
A153
Sleaford
A1121
Boston
■ Great Gonerby
A52
The Wash
Grantham
A151
A151
Holbeach
Bourne
Spalding
Market Deeping
Stamford

0    10 miles
0   10    20 Kilometres

## ■ Great Gonerby

### Harry's Place
**Long-standing culinary delight**
17 High Street, Great Gonerby, NG31 8JS
Tel no: (01476) 561780
**Modern French | £49**
**Cooking score: 7**

£5
OFF

Going from strength to strength, the Hallams are entering their third decade in charge here. Harry and Caroline do everything between them, and always have. He cooks, she runs the front-of-house, and it all feels like being invited into a private home for a particularly grand gastronomic occasion. Regulars return repeatedly for the highly polished, ingredient-led cooking, presented in the form of short menus offering two choices at each stage. Spring might see the simplicity of a bowl of chilled asparagus soup to start, or perhaps Orkney scallops in a spicy marinade with julienne of red pepper and orange. The engaging straightforwardness continues into the fish or meat mains, the first perhaps Scottish monkfish in a sauce of Sauternes, with shallots, leeks, spring onions, chives and basil, the latter roe deer loin stuffed with onion and herbs, richly sauced with white wine and Madeira. The pair of dessert options – caramel mousse brûlée with strawberries and raspberries, or prune and armagnac ice cream with passion fruit – is supplemented by a glorious, international cheese selection that may go from Epoisses to Cropwell Bishop Stilton. The single-page, handwritten wine list kicks off with red Reserva and white Crianza Riojas, and stops when it gets to the wonderful 1995 Ch. Cos d'Estournel. Prices start at £20, or £4.50 a glass, for that white Rioja.

**Chef/s:** Harry Hallam. **Open:** Tue to Sat 12.30 to 2, 7 to 8.30. **Closed:** bank hols, 1 week at Christmas. **Meals:** alc (main courses £32). **Service:** not inc. **Details:** Cards accepted. 10 seats. No music. Wheelchair access. Children's portions. Car parking.

## Horncastle

### Magpies

**Homely and comfortable**
73 East Street, Horncastle, LN9 6AA
Tel no: (01507) 527004
www.eatatthemagpies.co.uk
**Modern European | £31**
**Cooking score: 5**

🍷 ⋎

Horncastle is a small town in the heart of the Lincolnshire Wolds conservation area, and Magpies is at its centre, occupying a row of terraced cottages. A wood-burning stove provides warmth in cooler months, while a courtyard with shrubs and olive trees is a pleasant place to take aperitifs in summer. Owners Caroline Ingall and Andrew Gilbert lend a personal touch to the operation, with Caroline overseeing front-of-house while Andrew cooks. His style is a self-assured and ambitious take on the modern British theme. Among starters, carrot and cardamom soup is served with king scallops and a vanilla truffle foam, while sautéed sea bass fillet is set on a crunchy vegetable herb salad with pomegranate dressing. To follow, adventurous diners might opt for baked cod fillet on cabbage with pancetta, king prawn wontons and rhubarb butter sauce, while relatively safe – yet no less appealing – choices could include Lincolnshire Red beef fillet on horseradish mash with a mini steak and wild mushroom pie. Dark chocolate fondant with pistachio ice cream and dark chocolate sauce features for dessert alongside passion fruit soufflé with goats' cheese semifreddo. Lunchtime menus are shorter and the dishes are slightly simpler but equally accomplished. The wine list scores particularly well for its illustrious bottles from Bordeaux and Burgundy, but also does well in other countries and regions, and value is excellent throughout, with plenty of good drinking under £15.
**Chef/s:** Andrew Gilbert. **Open:** Wed to Fri and Sun L 12 to 2.30, Wed to Sun D 7 to 9.30. **Meals:** Set L £21 (2 courses) to £25, Set D £32. **Service:** not inc.

**Details:** Cards accepted. 34 seats. 10 seats outside. Air-con. No mobile phones. Wheelchair access. Music. Children allowed.

## ALSO RECOMMENDED

### ▲ The Brownlow Arms

Grantham Road, Hough on the Hill, NG32 2AZ
Tel no: (01400) 250234
www.thebrownlowarms.com

In summer months you can eat out on the terrace, in winter in front of an open log fire – this seventeenth-century country inn with the ambience of a country house has the seasons nicely covered. Expect classic cooking, typically baked cheese soufflé with Roquefort, celery, walnuts and cream (£7.50), wild sea bass with saffron and lovage mash and lemon and chive beurre blanc (£16.95) and passion fruit crème brûlée, with raspberry and strawberry sorbet (£5.25). Accommodation. Open Tue to Sat dinner and Sun lunch.

## Winteringham

### Winteringham Fields

**Provincial champion continues to shine**
Winteringham, DN15 9PF
Tel no: (01724) 733096
www.winteringhamfields.com
**Anglo-French | £75**
**Cooking score: 8**

🍷 ⊨ ⋎

It's been two years since Colin McGurran took over Winteringham Fields from Annie and Germain Schwab, the couple who turned a tumbledown farmhouse in the flatlands of North Lincolnshire into one of the country's most outstanding restaurants. Inevitably, diners are still comparing the old and new regimes but the transition has been astonishingly seamless under the wisely retained services of wunderkind Robert Thompson as head chef. There are cheaper menus, but do not shy from the six course gourmet menu or the à la carte because it is at the top end that Thompson truly soars, sending out extraordinary dishes that are deeply involved and complex, but so skilfully synthesized that the ultimate point is never muddied: 'eating his food is the headiest of pleasures'. An inspection lunch began with ballottine of smoked eel and foie gras with apple and slow cooked belly pork, the sweetness of the apple cutting through the richness of the foie gras, the pork complementing the subtle smokiness of the eel, while a pavé of turbot was perfectly judged, set on truffled globe artichoke and seasonal asparagus and topped with wafer-thin mini discs of crisp potato slices. Desserts exhibit similar panache if not quite the flourish, on this showing, of Germain Schwab at his most playful. A selection of six in miniature included among others a delicate crème brûlée, an immaculate chocolate fondant played off against a plate of seven blobs of intensely flavoured ice creams and sorbets. Along the way are some 'divine' extras: an amuse of potato mousse topped with lovage oil; a duck egg filled with scrambled egg and truffle; seven breads and four butters. If there are quibbles – surely the décor is ready for an overhaul. The wine cellar remains as rewarding and exciting as your wallet allows. House wines start at £28.

**Chef/s:** Robert Thompson. **Open:** Tue to Sat 12 to 1.30, 7 to 9. **Closed:** 24 Dec to 6 Jan, last week Apr, 2 weeks Aug. **Meals:** alc (main courses £22 to £36.50). Set L £39, Set D £79. **Service:** not inc. **Details:** Cards accepted. 50 seats. No music. No mobile phones. Car parking.

## Cookery books

*Moro*, Samuel and Samantha Clark
Supremely cookable, making this far more than a restaurant cookbook.

*Mediterranean Food*, Elizabeth David
Britain's love affair with Italian and rustic French food can be traced back to David.

*The Art of Eating*, M.F.K. Fisher
An anthology of five of Fisher's genre-defying food books, first published in 1954.

*Vegetable Book*, Jane Grigson
Grigson's books are thorough and erudite, yet companionable and encouraging.

*Roast Chicken and Other Stories*, Simon Hopkinson with Lindsay Bareham
Filled with recipes devoted to the pure pleasure of eating.

*Middle Eastern Food*, Claudia Roden
A fascinating slice of food and culture with a generous and meticulous guide.

*The Independent Cook*, Jeremy Round
An eclectic collection of recipes (including one for Noah's pudding, said to have been prepared on the Ark).

*Japanese Cooking*, Shizuo Tsuji
Tsuji's uncomplicated, elegant style animates this detailed, encyclopaedic work.

*Good Things in England*, Florence White
White's project of collecting English household recipes from 1399 to 1932 was years ahead of its time.

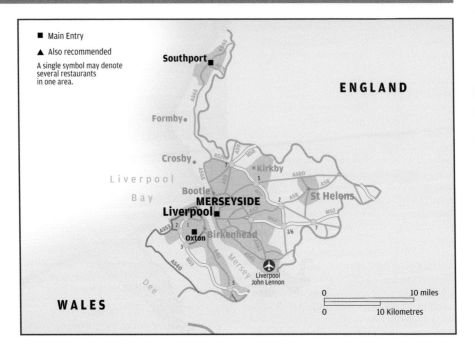

- ■ Main Entry
- ▲ Also recommended

A single symbol may denote several restaurants in one area.

Southport

ENGLAND

Formby

Crosby

Liverpool Bay

Kirkby

Liverpool

Bootle

MERSEYSIDE

Liverpool

St Helens

Oxton

Birkenhead

Liverpool John Lennon

Mersey

Dee

WALES

0          10 miles
0          10 Kilometres

# ■ Liverpool

## London Carriage Works

**Ambitious, well-conceived cooking**
Hope Street Hotel, 40 Hope Street, Liverpool,
L1 9DA
Tel no: (0151) 705 2222
www.tlcw.co.uk
**Modern British | £45**
**New Chef**

Built in the grand Venetian palazzo-style in
1860, and impressively renovated in 2003, the
Hope Street Hotel houses two impeccably
modern restaurant and brasserie operations.
While the brasserie deals in the likes of confit
of duck, or calf's liver with garlic mash,
sharing plates and deli sandwiches, the weekly
changing menu in the London Carriage
Works is more ambitious, offering starters of
braised pork cheek with pea purée and broad
bean herb salad, and mains of medallions of
monkfish with buttered celery, red wine fish
sauce and summer salad on the good-value

two-or-three course set menu. The cooking is
refined and presentation artistic but not overly
fussy and there's a flair for good flavour
combinations, as can be seen in a starter (from
the multi-course 'Menu Excellence') of just
seared foie gras served with confit of carrot,
carrot cubes and ginger sauce. Among
impressive main courses have been loin of
iron-age rare-breed Duroc pork served with
its shoulder, white radish, morel mushrooms
and rosemary beurre blanc, while dessert
might be an attractively presented
combination of toffee roasted pears with pear
crisps, coulis and salted caramel ice cream. A
contemporary, international collection of
wines bursts with good names. Prices start at
£13.95 and there's an interesting selection by
the glass from £5.50.
**Chef/s:** David Brewitt. **Open:** Mon to Sun L 12 to
3.30, D 5.30 to 9.30. **Meals:** Set L £19 (2 courses),
Set D £45 (2 courses) to £55. Brasserie menu
available. **Service:** not inc. **Details:** Cards accepted.
60 seats. Air-con. No mobile phones. Wheelchair
access. Music. Children's portions.

## The Side Door

Friendly and cosy
29a Hope Street, Liverpool, L1 9BQ
Tel no: (0151) 707 7888
www.thesidedoor.co.uk
Eclectic global menu | £16
Cooking score: 2

£5 OFF  V  £30

This relaxed and friendly bistro in the heart of the city near the theatre neighbourhood offers a menu of small yet global choice of dishes, simply cooked using top-quality ingredients. Starters include a fresh, tasty pea and mint soup, and wild mushroom, rocket and pine-nut linguine, while main courses feature a light goats' cheese and red onion tart in crisp pastry with new potatoes and fresh green salad, chamoula-marinated pork steak, and confit of shredded duck with noodles. Desserts include chocolate brownie and lemon posset. A modest but good wine list opens at £11.95 for the pleasant Italian house (also sold by the glass at £3.50).
**Chef/s:** Sean Millar, Alex Navarro, Jay Brown. **Open:** Mon to Sat 11.30 to 2.30, 5.30 to 10.30. **Closed:** 25 to 28 Dec, 31 Dec to 2 Jan. **Meals:** alc (main courses L £5.95 to £8.95) D £14.95 (2 courses) £16.95 (3 courses). **Service:** not included. **Details:** Cards accepted. 60 seats. Air-con. Music. Children's portions.

## Simply Heathcotes

Brasserie food from the Paul Heathcote stable
Beetham Plaza, 25 The Strand, Liverpool, L2 0XL
Tel no: (0151) 236 3536
www.heathcotes.co.uk
Modern British | £30
Cooking score: 2

A striking structure with swathes of curving plate glass, granite walls and slate floors, this branch of Paul Heathcote's brasserie chain still looks as pristine as the day it opened. In keeping with the group's ethos, seasonal produce from local North Country sources is the basis for a choice of menus tailored to just about everyone (including children). Springtime offerings might include green

vegetable minestrone or radish-cured salmon with pickled cucumber as starters, while the choice of main courses could extend from crispy duck confit with baby onions and smoked bacon to citrus-seared sea bass with braised fennel, spinach and garlic butter. Heathcote's legendary bread-and-butter pudding with a compote of apricots and clotted cream is an ever-present dessert; otherwise, try meringue with lemon curd and red berries. The wine list is a lively global slate with prices from £14.95 (£3.85 a glass). Other branches are in Leeds, Manchester and Wrightington (see entries).
**Chef/s:** Philip Sinclair. **Open:** all week 12 to 2.30, 6 to 10 (11 Sat, 9 Sun). **Closed:** bank hols. **Meals:** alc (main courses £9.50 to £22). Set L Mon to Sat £12.95 (2 courses, inc wine), Set D Mon £15 (inc wine), Set D Mon to Sat 6 to 7 £12.95 (2 courses, inc wine). **Service:** not inc. **Details:** Cards accepted. 110 seats. Air-con. Wheelchair access. Music. Children's portions.

## 60 Hope Street

Confident, contemporary cooking
60 Hope Street, Liverpool, L1 9BZ
Tel no: (0151) 707 6060
www.60hopestreet.com
Modern European | £37
Cooking score: 4

🍷 V

The end-terrace, double-fronted Georgian house, not far from the Philharmonic Hall, contains a basement café bar and ground-floor restaurant, where pale wood and white walls are offset by large mirrors, period fireplaces and odd splashes of colour. A great deal of confidence is built around the contemporary style of cooking, which draws inspiration from English and European repertoires, as seen in close-to-home Cumbrian beef fillet with mustard glaze, confit onion and red-wine jus, or cannon of fell lamb with slow-cooked shoulder cannelloni, red pepper purée and olive jus, which gives more than a nod to the shores of the Mediterranean. Starters may take in peppered tuna carpaccio with beetroot granita or asparagus tart with Cumbrian ham and poached egg, while accomplished desserts could include pine nut and chestnut honey parfait with ginger biscuit. Service is of the good, no-nonsense but friendly variety. The wine list is refreshingly straightforward; mark-ups are not greedy and house wines kick off at £13.95.

**Chef/s:** Sarah Kershaw. **Open:** Mon to Fri L 12 to 2.30, Mon to Sat D 6 to 10.30. **Closed:** bank hols. **Meals:** alc (main courses £10.50 to £26). Set L and D 6 to 7 £13.95 (2 courses) to £16.95. **Service:** not inc. **Details:** Cards accepted. 90 seats. 15 seats outside. Air-con. Music. Children's portions.

## ★NEW ENTRY★
# Spire

**High quality at reasonable prices**
1 Church Road, Liverpool, L15 9EA
Tel no: (0151) 734 5040
www.spirerestaurant.co.uk
**Modern European | £25**
**Cooking score: 4**

£5 OFF ▯ ∀ £30

This busy restaurant located in south Liverpool offers superb, well-cooked food in a welcoming and friendly atmosphere. Service is efficient and friendly, with staff keen to explain dishes. Everything is made on the premises and the inspiring menu uses regional British produce in several dishes, such as starters of Cornish crab and spring pea risotto, and mains of chump of Cumbrian lamb, fondant potato, spring peas and pancetta with natural lamb jus, and roasted fillet of Whitby cod with broad bean and smoked garlic purée, crispy onion rings and red-wine sauce. Desserts include Toblerone soufflé and apple and vanilla samosa with vanilla ice cream and butterscotch sauce. At inspection an amuse-bouche of cappuccino of pale green spring pea soup was 'terrific', as was the freshly made herb focaccia with basil oil; Chef Matt Locke's cooking is 'first class'. A well-chosen wine list offers an interesting selection, including French and Italian red and white house wines at £11.95 per bottle or £2.35 per glass. There's an outstanding number of labels

from around the world, including Canada and Chile, plus a selection of dessert wines and champagnes.

**Chef/s:** Matt Locke. **Open:** Mon to Thu D 6 to 9, Fri to Sat D 6.30 to 9.30, Tue to Fri L 12 to 3. **Closed:** Sun. **Meals:** Set L £12.95 (3 courses), D £14.95 (three courses). **Service:** not inc. **Details:** Cards accepted. 68 seats. Air-con. Wheelchair access. Music. Children's portions. Car parking.

# Ziba

**A fusion of flavours**
Hargreaves Buildings, 5 Chapel Street, Liverpool, L3 9AG
Tel no: (0151) 236 6676
www.racquetclub.org.uk
**Modern European | £32**
**Cooking score: 4**

£5 OFF ▯ ⊨ ∀

Once a private club for the local judiciary, now contemporary tables and chairs preside over the spacious elegant dining room. Keeping up standards, impeccable service is knowledgeable, helpful and friendly, and there's also a simpler all-day menu available in the adjacent bar. An imaginative menu offers a fine choice, including local produce, such as farm asparagus and Goosnargh chicken, while inspired cooking allows the taste of the ingredients to shine. Starters include oak-smoked Cecina de León beef with beetroot carpaccio and horseradish crème fraîche and cream of Jersey Royal soup. Mains might include an innovative roast chicken breast with crushed Bombay potatoes, local asparagus and cardamom and vanilla jus, with desserts ranging from Pimm's summer berry terrine and crème fraîche sorbet to classics, such as apple crumble with a very good vanilla ice cream. Australian house wines are £14, (£3.50 per glass).

**Chef/s:** Neil Dempsey. **Open:** Mon to Fri L 12 to 2.30, Mon to Sat D 7 to 11. **Closed:** bank hols. **Meals:** alc (main courses L £14.75 to £16.65, D £11.25 to £20). Set L £17 (3 courses).. **Service:** not inc. **Details:** Cards accepted. 80 seats. Air-con. Music. Children's portions.

## Oxton

# Fraiche

**A Merseyside high-flyer**
11 Rose Mount, Oxton, CH43 5SG
Tel no: (0151) 652 2914
www.restaurantfraiche.com
**Modern French | £40**
**Cooking score: 6**

Marc Wilkinson's stylish little restaurant has brought a taste of top-end modern French cuisine to the Wirral and it has staked its place as one of the region's high-flyers. The location is a terraced house in a conservation village close to Birkenhead: it's an area that the energetic chef/patron considers to be his gastronomic home patch. An intimate 20-cover dining room done out in pastel shades is the setting for a succession of beautifully worked dishes shot through with invention and challenging possibilities. The format is a brief fixed-price menu with generally four choices at each stage, but the sheer range and diversity of ideas and accumulated flavours is remarkable. A torchon of foie gras regularly appears among the starters, perhaps partnered by an extract of pistachio and crushed 'ginger bread'; another intriguing opener might be roast butternut squash with morels and Parmesan ice cream. Main courses often look to Europe for their core ingredients, witness Loire guinea fowl served with Umbrian lentils, hazelnut dressing and lime extract. Fish is generally from British waters: fillet of sea bream might be presented with asparagus and crispy wild rice or with wilted spinach and a shellfish-infused risotto. Anglo-French cheeses 'with contrasting flavours' can be ordered as a plate of five; also look for Mrs Bourne's Cheshire, which is given a North Country tribute with beer jam and fruit cake. Otherwise, sweetness prevails in the shape of tiramisu or apple pastilla with rosemary ice cream. Marc Wilkinson's wine list is a prestigious and imaginative selection of the great and the very good from Europe, bolstered by wise choices from exciting New World growers. Strictly controlled mark-ups are a real bonus. House wines were being reorganised as we went to press, but expect good drinking from around £15 (£4 a glass).
**Chef/s:** Marc Wilkinson. **Open:** Fri and Sat L 12 to 1.30, Tue to Sat D 7 to 9.30. **Closed:** 25 Dec, 1 to 8 Jan. **Meals:** Set L £25, Set D £40 (3 courses). **Service:** not inc. **Details:** Cards accepted. 20 seats. 10 seats outside. No mobile phones. Wheelchair access. Music.

## Southport

# Warehouse Brasserie

**Glamorous setting**
30 West Street, Southport, PR8 1QN
Tel no: (01704) 544662
www.warehousebrasserie.co.uk
**Global | £36**
**Cooking score: 3**

The Warehouse's generously proportioned warm-coloured dining room with hints of Art Deco is not quite the all-day affair promised by its name, opening as it does strictly for lunch and dinner. The good value 'lunch specials' nod to tradition with mushrooms on toast and grilled lamb's liver and bacon, but strike more modern notes with roasted peppers with feta or chilli fried prawns with jasmine rice. Mains bring a similar mix with fish'n'chips, black pudding with poached egg, and standards like fillet steak and béarnaise alongside Mexican spiced chicken, and sticky plum and ginger-glazed duck breast. Baked Alaska for dessert fits the surroundings. The wine list is a succinct well chosen business spreading itself geographically as well as economically. House wines £13.95.
**Chef/s:** Marc Vérité and Darren Smith. **Open:** Mon to Sat 12 to 2, 5.30 to 10.30. **Closed:** 25 and 26 Dec. **Meals:** alc (main courses L £7 to £17.50, D £11 to £17.50). Set L £11.95 (2 courses) to £13.95, Set D Mon and Tue to Thur 5.30 to 6.45 £13.95 (2 courses) to £15.95. **Service:** not inc. **Details:** Cards accepted. 110 seats. Air-con. Wheelchair access. Music. Children's portions.

## Cooking score

A score of 1 is a significant achievement. The score in any review is based on several meals, incorporating feedback from both our readers and inspectors. As a rough guide, 1 denotes capable cooking with some inconsistencies, rising steadily through different levels of technical expertise, until the scores between 6 and 10 indicate exemplary skills, along with innovation, artistry and ambition. If there is a new chef, we don't score the restaurant for the first year of entry. For further details, please see the scoring section in the introduction to the Guide.

## ALSO RECOMMENDED
### ▲ Tyndall's
23 Hoghton Street, Southport, PR9 ONS
Tel no: (01704) 500002

This is a converted brick and bay-windowed town house located opposite the Little Theatre in the town centre. Expect a friendly and informal atmosphere in the two intimate dining areas, a separate bar area for pre-dinner drinks, and sound French-style and European cooking. The two-course midweek deals are a steal at either £8.95 before 7pm, or £12.50 between 7pm and 8pm. 'Gourmet' menus take in steamed mussels with wine, thyme and garlic (£6.95), whole baked bass on fennel (£14.75), and rack of lamb with mint and redcurrant gravy (£14.75). Two-dozen drinkable wines from £12.95. Open Tue to Sat D only.

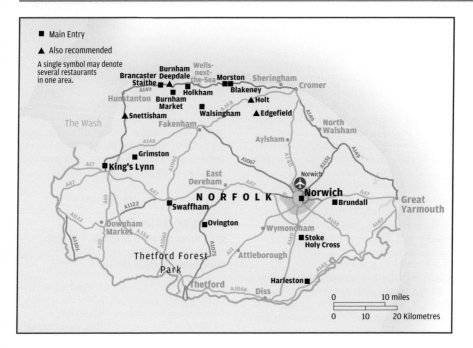

- ■ Main Entry
- ▲ Also recommended

A single symbol may denote several restaurants in one area.

# Blakeney

## White Horse Hotel

**A firm local favourite**
4 High Street, Blakeney, NR25 7AL
Tel no: (01263) 740574
www.blakeneywhitehorse.co.uk
**Modern British | £36**
**New Chef**

£5 OFF ╤ ⅄

Located on the narrow High Street, just a few strides from the quayside, this seventeeth-century former coaching inn is Blakeney's oldest hotel. Chris Hyde's imaginative dinner menu is served in the sunny yellow-painted restaurant. He taps into the rich local supply lines: all the shellfish and much of the fish come from fishermen along the coast, game is from local estates and seasonal asparagus and soft fruits are sourced from nearby farms. This translates as fish soup with rouille, pan-fried brill with a warm lentil and bacon salsa and a red pepper coulis, or roast saddle of lamb with

an aubergine, spinach and pine nut stuffing. For pudding, try the vanilla poached pear and custard tartlet. The wine list starts at £11.50. **Chef/s:** Duncan Philp. **Open:** Tue to Sat D only 7 to 9. **Closed:** 25 Dec. **Meals:** alc (main courses £13 to £17). Bar menu available L and D. **Service:** not inc. **Details:** Cards accepted. 100 seats. 40 seats outside. No mobile phones. Music. Children's portions. Car parking.

# Brancaster Staithe

## White Horse

**Stunning coastal views**
Main Road, Brancaster Staithe, PE31 8BW
Tel no: (01485) 210262
www.whitehorsebrancaster.co.uk
**Modern British | £23**
**Cooking score: 3**

╤ ⅄ £30

From the outside it may seem plain and easy to overlook, but reporters consider this a 'truly special' pub, its fabulous coastal setting equalled by high standards of hospitality, food and drink. Head for the rear conservatory dining area, which opens on to a large terrace – both give unrivalled views across a vast expanse of salt marsh towards Scolt Head Island. Nick Parker's monthly menu and daily specials both feature the best available fish and seafood, notably oysters from the 'beds' at the bottom of the garden. Risotto of local brown shrimps might be among starters, cod, line-caught sea bass, skate wing and Dover sole may all make an appearance at main course stage, the last-named served, perhaps, with a fricassee of broad beans. Norfolk duck, with sautéed potatoes and a port sauce could represent meat, while white chocolate and coffee parfait with coffee syrup could round off the meal. There's a decent line-up of ales and a concise international wine list opening at £12 for their house wines.

**Chef/s:** Nicholas Parker. **Open:** all week; 12 to 2, 6.30 to 9. **Meals:** alc (main courses L £4.50 to £13.95, D £9.25 to £17). **Service:** not inc. **Details:** Cards accepted. 90 seats. 90 seats outside. No mobile phones. Wheelchair access. Music. Children's portions. Car parking.

## Brundall

★NEW ENTRY★
### Lavender House
**A modern country-house dining experience**
39 The Street, Brundall, NR13 5AA
Tel no: (01603) 712215
www.thelavenderhouse.co.uk
**Modern British | £38**
Cooking score: 2

£5 OFF V

Richard Hughes has unstoppable enthusiasm for Norfolk's produce, demonstrated in the suppliers' role of honour adorning his charming thatched restaurant. With a forward-thinking brigade behind him, the cooking is gradually embracing the twenty-first century, but keeps its idiosyncratic homeliness (citrus and thyme espuma as an inter-course signature freebie now replacing outmoded sorbet). Good bread rolls come in various flavours straight from the oven,

preceding a little appetiser (perhaps asparagus velouté with truffle oil). Next a 'delicate well made' rabbit and foie gras terrine, perhaps, then a trio of lamb, including 'perfect' loin and kidney. For dessert, a 'wonderful' prune, almond and Armagnac tart or dark chocolate marquise. Attractive varied selection of small production wines from £14.95.

**Chef/s:** Richard Hughes and Richard Knights. **Open:** Tue to Sat D 7 to 9. **Meals:** Set D £38.50 (6 courses). **Details:** Cards accepted. 45 seats. 10 seats outside. No music. Wheelchair access. Car parking.

## ALSO RECOMMENDED

### ▲ Deepdale Cafe
Main Road, Burnham Deepdale, PE31 8DD
Tel no: (01485) 211055
www.deepdalecafe.co.uk

Young families, older couples and walkers of the Norfolk Coastal Path (across the road) have flocked to this modern, unassuming-looking café since it opened behind a garage forecourt in 2006. As well as salads, sandwiches and all-day breakfasts, they can order the likes of vegetable soup (£3.95) enhanced by a croûton and a curl of sour cream, fillets of precisely cooked sea bass on crushed new potatoes (£11.25), or a selection of Mediterranean tapas (£7.95). Don't miss such puddings as apple and winterberry crumble (£3.25). Bring your own alcohol, sample the large choice of teas and coffees, or order a glass of local apple juice.

## Burnham Market

### Fishes
**The finest from Anglia's anglers**
Market Place, Burnham Market, PE31 8HE
Tel no: (01328) 738588
www.fishesrestaurant.co.uk
**Seafood | £34**
Cooking score: 4

Big bay windows overlook fashionable Burnham Market's green from this light and airy restaurant, which has a relaxed, bistro feel

and, as its name suggests, is devoted to fish and seafood. Chef-patron Matthew Owsley-Brown is a keen advocate of locally available ingredients and the success of Fishes relies on the steady supply of fresh fish, much of it delivered by local fisherman – oysters, lobsters and mussels from Brancaster – which he cooks in a general Mediterranean style with the odd Asian twist. An intensely flavoured fish stew of John Dory, red gurnard, smoked cod and mussels, perhaps, or roast wild turbot with caramelised fennel, oranges and hollandaise, or grilled tuna with Bombay spiced vegetable curry, cumin pao and coconut and lime chutney. Start with fish soup, or smoked eel with piquillo pepper and foie gras terrine, chilli salt and brioche, and round off with carrot and walnut cake with Indian vanilla and cinnamon ice cream, or rhubarb and elderflower soup with mascarpone. On the wine list, fish-friendly whites outnumber reds with prices from £17.50, and a few good choices by the glass (from £5).
**Chef/s:** Matthew Owsley-Brown. **Open:** Tue to Sun L 12 to 2.15, Tue to Sat D 6.45 to 10. **Closed:** 1 week Christmas. **Meals:** Set L £22 (2 courses), Set D £32 (2 courses) to £37. **Service:** not inc. **Details:** Cards accepted. 42 seats. Wheelchair access. Music.

## Hoste Arms

**A successful mix of pub, restaurant and upmarket hotel**
The Green, Burnham Market, PE31 8HD
Tel no: (01328) 738777
www.hostearms.co.uk
**Modern British | £29**
**Cooking score: 2**
🛏 ⋎

Paul Whittome's handsome seventeenth-century inn overlooks the green in this affluent village. It's a rare combination that appeals to a broad mix of customers, be it local fishermen or celebrities. Beyond the rustic, unpretentious bar, the tardis-like Hoste extends into numerous dining areas, including an extensive alfresco terrace. Fish and seafood – much of it local – is the star attraction. Brancaster oysters get top billing, perhaps

with tomato chutney and Emmental, but the kitchen gets straight to the heart of some eclectic cooking that trawls the world for inspiration, with tuna sashimi with lemon confit, and oriental beef broth among the starters. Similar treatment is given to the main courses, say, mixed Thai seafood stew, although rack of lamb with glazed beetroot and port jus and rib-eye steak with hand-cut chips will satisfy more conservative tastes. Desserts may include banana tart Tatin with liquorice ice cream. Expect good home-made bread, attentive service, and an impressive wine list that kicks off at £12.50.
**Chef/s:** Rory Whelan. **Open:** L 12 to 2 , D 7 to 9 all week. **Meals:** alc (main courses £10.75 to £24.25). **Service:** not inc. **Details:** Cards accepted. 140 seats. 100 seats outside. Air-con. No music. Wheelchair access. Children's portions. Car parking.

## READERS RECOMMEND

### The Dabbling Duck
**Gastropub**
King's Lynn, Great Massingham,, PE32 2HN,
Tel no: (01485) 520827
'Like a London gastropub in a country setting'

## ▌Grimston

## Congham Hall, Orangery
**Accomplished modern British cuisine**
Lynn Road, Grimston, PE32 1AH
Tel no: (01485) 600250
www.conghamhallhotel.co.uk
**Anglo-French | £50**
**Cooking score: 4**
🛏 ⋎

A quintessential country-house hotel, Congham Hall holds particular allure on a sunny day, when diners can take post-prandial coffee and petits fours on the terrace overlooking sublime lawns and woodland. Whatever the weather, the Orangery restaurant, with its classical Georgian dimensions, chandeliers, peach-hued walls and large windows, makes an enjoyable setting. Polite, low-key staff add to the relaxed atmosphere. Jamie Murch has devised various menus. The great-value set lunch is marked by exquisite presentation and talented preparation: witness a boldly flavoured rabbit and quail terrine, enlivened by garlic and parsley, and well-matched with fig compote. Main course might be a fillet of black bream, its flavour outshining that of the modest portion of pea risotto on which it rested, though its fennel, cream and mussel sauce had tang aplenty. A more elaborate dish from the carte or menu gourmande might be roast chump of lamb, confit potatoes, salsify, sautéed kidney with parsley and shallot and a lamb jus dressing. Picture-perfect puddings might include a cone-shaped Cassis parfait with mascarpone and Agen prunes soaked in Armagnac. Red wine costs from £17 a bottle, white from £19.50.

**Chef/s:** Jamie Murch. **Open:** all week 12 to 1.45, 7 to 9.15. **Meals:** Set L £15.50 (2 courses) to £33, Set L Sun £22.50, Set D £35 (2 courses) to £57.50. Bar L menu available Mon to Sat. **Service:** not inc. **Details:** Cards accepted. 40 seats. 24 seats outside. No music. No mobile phones. Wheelchair access. Children's portions. Car parking.

## Harleston

★NEW ENTRY★

### Momiji Japanese Restaurant

A rare provincial find

3 Redenhall Road, Harleston, IP20 9EN
Tel no: (01379) 852243
www.momiji-japanese-restaurant.co.uk
Japanese | £22
Cooking score: 2

£5 OFF  V  £30

This charming timbered town house with open-partition walls separating split-level dining is mixed with gentle Japanese touches such as bamboo, oriental porcelain, silk floral wall hangings and, of course, chopsticks (cutlery for the inexperienced). Novices to Japanese cuisine do well here, as the understanding staff recommend set menus, there are lots of helpful explanations, and dish spicing is varied accordingly. Sushi-lovers are not disappointed if they time their visit with

the one advertised week a month that fresh, expertly made nigiri patties, maki rolls and te maki cones are on offer, as well as an array of sashimi slivers. At other times, enjoy a huge variety of hot and chilled dishes, including textbook tempura, savoury yaki soba noodles, kara age marinated fish, stuffed gyouza dumplings and teriyaki meats, all accompanied by refreshing miso soup and sticky rice. Thought is given to worldly wines to match the dishes, and there's an impressive variety of ume shu plum wine, shochu sweet potato vodka and saké as well as quaffable Asahi beer. Wines from £11.50.

**Chef/s:** Taka Nakamoto. **Open:** Fri and Sat L 12 to 2, Tue to Sat D 6.30pm to 9pm. **Closed:** Sun, Mon, 25 Dec, 26 Dec, 1 Jan, 2 Jan. **Meals:** Set L £18.95 (3 courses), Set D £19.95 (3 courses). **Service:** not inc. **Details:** Cards accepted. 46 seats. Wheelchair access. Music. Children allowed.

## Holkham

### Victoria

Jewel-in-the-Crown-style décor
Park Road, Holkham, NR23 1RG
Tel no: (01328) 711008
www.victoriaatholkham.co.uk
Modern British | £26
Cooking score: 3

⇆ V £30

The Victoria is an imposing brick-and-flint building. The colonial theme that extends through the bar, restaurant and bedrooms comes as a surprise for a building owned by the Earl of Leicester. Expect carved wooden furnishings and a wealth of unusual Indian artefacts. But culinary inspiration is rooted closer to home, with game from the estate, perhaps venison loin with braised red cabbage and root vegetable casserole, or local Thornham mussels served with linguine, garlic and herb cream. For starters, try the antipasto – Holkham smoked venison, Binham blue cheese, Suffolk salami – then follow with cod on crushed potatoes with a delicious shellfish chowder. Desserts could

feature pineapple tarte Tatin with lemongrass ice cream. A well-chosen wine list is organised by style, with prices starting at £12.95.
**Chef/s:** Neil Dowson. **Open:** all week 12 to 2.30, 7 to 9.30. **Meals:** alc (main courses £7 to £16). Bar menu available.. **Service:** not inc. **Details:** Cards accepted. 70 seats. 100 seats outside. Wheelchair access. Music. Children's portions. Car parking.

## ALSO RECOMMENDED
### ▲ Cookies Crab Shop
The Green, Salthouse, Holt, NR25 7AJ
Tel no: (01263) 740352

For the past 50 years three generations of the McKnespiey family have been selling quality shellfish from their tiny, brick-and-cobbled cottage that overlooks the village green and acres of salt marsh. It continues to thrive, drawing foodies from afar for the best crab, smoked fish and seafood for miles. The menu is pleasingly simple and incredibly good value, so arrive early to bag a table in the shop, the garden shed or under the gazebo and order the crab salad (£4.90) or the special lobster salad (£8.50). Wash down with a cup of tea or BYO – there's no corkage charge. Open daily.

### ▲ The Three Pigs
Norwich Road, Edgefield, Holt, NR24 2RL
Tel no: (01263) 587634

This is a friendly country pub full of proper pubby ephemera – shove ha'penny, bar billiards – as well as a slate of real ales, open fires, barrel tables and a real family bias. Piglets (under 4, 6 or 12 years, below shoe size 1) get their own tasty real food. Indeed, proper gutsy British food is the thing here, starting with mulligatawny (£4.50), corned beef hash cakes (£5.95) or omelette Arnold Bennett (£5.95), with mains of suet game pudding (£10.95) or fish pie (£10.95). Robust desserts include Horlicks double-cream rice pudding with strawberry jam or spiced prunes with Earl Grey and vanilla tapioca (£4.95). Adnams wines from £12.50 a bottle.

## ■ King's Lynn
## Maggie's Restaurant
**Modern British cuisine in an old town house**
11 Saturday Market Place, King's Lynn, PE30 5DQ
Tel no: (01553) 771483
www.rococorestaurant.org.uk
**Modern British | £36**
**Cooking score: 3**

The kerfuffle following Gordon Ramsay's televised makeover has died down, leaving Nick Anderson's restaurant with a new name (Rococo becoming Maggie's, after St Margaret's Church opposite) and a simpler menu. Located in Lynn's oldest quarter, Maggie's occupies a venerable town house full of cosy nooks. Whitewashed walls match the crisp white table linen, pleasingly offset by wooden floorboards and bright artworks. The efficient French waiter is as cool as the background French jazz. A daily-changing menu offers the choice of five dishes for each course. At inspection, the best dish was a starter of warm confit of rabbit salad with watercress and green beans, the strips of meat boosted by fresh herbs in an appetising dressing. A neighbour's deep-fried salt pollack cakes with tartare sauce also gained praise. To follow, pan-roasted halibut with butter beans and chive butter sauce was more notable for excellent (if unfilleted) fish than the timidly flavoured accompaniments. Puddings such as tart rhubarb matched with an exemplary pannacotta show Anderson's fondness for simplicity and seasonality. The French house white is £10.95 a bottle.
**Chef/s:** Nick Anderson and Tim Sandford. **Open:** Tue to Sat 12 to 2, 7 to 9 (6.30 to 10 Sat). **Meals:** alc (main courses £14.50 to £21). Bistro menu available exc Sat D. **Service:** not inc. **Details:** Cards accepted. 40 seats. Wheelchair access. Music. Children's portions.

## READERS RECOMMEND

### Titchwell Manor

**Modern British**
Titchwell, Kings Lynn, PE31 8BB
Tel no: (01485) 210221
www.titchwellmanor.com
'Fantastic seafood, near a nature reserve'

## ▌Morston

### Morston Hall

**Personal charm in a seductive setting**
Morston, NR25 7AA
Tel no: (01263) 741041
www.morstonhall.com
**Modern British | £39**
Cooking score: 6
🍷 ⇌

Galton and Tracy Blackiston run this delightful brick-and-flint residence with personal charm and good humour. Of course, it helps that the Hall is in a nigh-perfect spot, on the edge of the North Norfolk salt marshes close to the sea. This is an industrious set-up, with monthly cookery courses, home-made provisions for sale and a new conservatory now tacked on to the dining room. True to the domesticity of the setting, Galton Blackiston puts his faith in a daily-changing no-choice menu that it totally dependant on seasonal and local supplies. There is only one sitting and meals proceed at a measured pace, beginning with at least three home-baked breads before, say, celeriac soup with parsley and bacon foam. One course is always fish from the coast, perhaps crisp, lightly spiced sea bass with tomato chutney, or roast monkfish on peperonata with lemongrass beurre blanc. Meat tends to be treated with enviable restraint, thus roast loin of 'well-hung' lamb might appear simply with fondant potato and rich jus. To conclude, diners are given the option of dessert (warm banana soufflé, perhaps) or British farmhouse cheeses. 'There is a very good team in the Morston,' concluded one visitor; others have singled out the 'professional and soothing' service by young, clued-up staff. The Blackistons' dazzling wine list is clearly a labour of love: choice is impeccable, notes are informative and prices are drinker-friendly; the layout by grape variety is also immensely helpful. Two 'wines of the month' take the place of conventional house selections: typically these have included Kumeu River Pinot Noir from New Zealand and Gavi de Gavi, Cortese, both at £25 (£5 a glass).
**Chef/s:** Galton Blackiston and Sam Wegg. **Open:** Sun L 12.30 for 1 (1 sitting), all week D 7.30 for 8 (1 sitting). **Closed:** 1 Jan to first week Feb. **Meals:** Set L £30, Set D £44. **Service:** not inc. **Details:** Cards accepted. 40 seats. No music. No mobile phones. Wheelchair access. Children's portions. Car parking.

## ▌Norwich

### Mad Moose Arms and 1Up Restaurant

**Refined edge-of-city brasserie**
2 Warwick Street, Norwich, NR2 3LD
Tel no: (01603) 627687
**Modern British | £27**
Cooking score: 2
Ⅴ £30

Just over the ring road from the fashionable St Giles, sits the Mad Moose Arms, a pretty, leafy hostelry in a residential quarter off Unthank Road. Upstairs (1UP) is more refined and slower paced than the lively pub-restaurant on the ground floor. High ceilings, carver chairs and period touches gave one reader an impression of a 'rectory drawing room', albeit with an avant-garde edge (such as silvery tree-printed wallpaper). The lengthy menu combines reassuring comfort with ambitious zeal; for example, in a tian of Cromer crab with white bean purée, Bloody Mary sorbet, tomato and shallot dressing. There is no doubting Eden Derick's culinary ability, with properly cooked quail and melting pork belly demonstrating good timing. Commendable local brasserie company Animal Inns' hallmarks include good-value pricing, especially on the well-chosen wine list, where

bottles start at £12.50 (see also Mackintosh's Canteen, Norwich and Wildebeest Arms, Stoke Holy Cross).
**Chef/s:** Eden Derick. **Open:** Sun L 12 to 3, Mon to Sat D 7 to 10. **Meals:** alc (main courses £10 to £14.50). Bar menu available. **Service:** not inc. **Details:** Cards accepted. 45 seats. Music. Children's portions.

## Tatlers
**In the lively Tombland quarter**
21 Tombland, Norwich, NR3 1RF
Tel no: (01603) 766670
www.tatlers.com
**Modern British | £32**
**Cooking score: 3**
£5 OFF  V  £30

Finding somewhere to park nearby in trendy Tombland can be quite a task, but the effort is well rewarded at this period town house where black-clad waiting staff hover by the door to welcome you in. Different dining rooms are painted in heritage hues and sport stripped floorboards and scrubbed tables (as well as ones covered in crisp linen). Well known locally, chef Brendan Ansbro used to work at the Crown and Castle, Orford (see entry). His gutsy cuisine is hard to define, competently going from European classics, such as roasted pepper and mozzarella bruschetta, or coq au vin, to complex ethnic palate-warmers, such as hot and spicy Thai beef salad or chicken and prawn kedgeree with soft egg, chilli sauce and crispy onions. Comforting puddings follow similarly diverse paths; perhaps a glazed passion-fruit tart with mango compote and mascarpone or, at inspection, a vibrant pomegranate jelly, sesame ice cream and cardamom biscotti. House wines start at £14.65.
**Chef/s:** Brendan Ansbro. **Open:** Mon to Sat 12 to 2, 6.30 to 10. **Closed:** Bank hols. **Meals:** alc (main courses £11.95 to £16.95). Set L £11.95 (1 course) to £19.95 (3 courses).. **Service:** not inc. **Details:** Cards accepted. 70 seats. Air-con. Separate bar. Music.

## ALSO RECOMMENDED
## ▲ Delia's Restaurant and Bar
Norwich City Football Club, Carrow Road, Norwich, NR1 1JE
Tel no: (01603) 218705
www.deliascanarycatering.com

Food and football are two subjects that invoke great passion. Here Delia Smith, one of Britain's best-loved chefs, has brought the two together, although you don't have to be a Norwich City fan to eat here. The weekly-changing menu takes advantage of local, seasonal produce, with a three-course meal with coffee and chocolates costing £29.50 per person – say Jersey Royal potato soup with wilted greens, Thai fish curry with mango, and fresh peaches baked in marsala with vanilla mascarpone cream. Open Fri and Sat dinner.

## ▲ Mackintosh's Canteen
Unit 410, Chapelfield Plain, Norwich, NR2 1SZ
Tel no: (01603) 305280
www.mackintoshscanteen.co.uk

Easily spooked diners won't fail to miss the gravestones from the huge glass windows, but this voguish first-floor gallery brasserie certainly affords atmospheric views of city life below. This is part of the local restaurant group Animal Inns, and Henry Watts knows what his urbane diners like in all three of his diverse eateries (Wildebeest Arms, Stoke Holy Cross and 1UP at the Mad Moose Arms, Norwich – see entries), joined by the house style of modern relaxed restaurants. Choices here cover some ground, from tasty simplicities, such as chicken satay or spiced lamb burger with tsatsiki and flatbread, to the more complex duck liver pâté with pickled girolles and celeriac rémoulade, and ambitious specials, such as seared scallops with samphire or pan-fried sea bass with minted pea purée and a crayfish caper beurre noisette. Complementing the experience are some choice gutsy wines, starting at £13.50.

## Ovington

### Brovey Lair
**Bold approach to seafood**
Carbrooke Road, Ovington, IP25 6SD
Tel no: (01953) 882706
www.broveylair.com
**Fusion/Pan-Asian | £42**
**Cooking score: 5**

£5 OFF

Blink for a second as you pass through the art-strewn hallway into the cool, contemporary kitchen-cum-dining room and you could be forgiven for thinking you had been transported to another country. There's a feel of warmer climes about the view from the plate-glass windows over the terrace, swimming pool and lush garden. But it is the air of confidence that strikes visitors, so unusual in such a rural spot, combined with Mike and Tina Pemberton's understanding of that elusive cosset factor, which makes eating here rather like attending a rather civilised dinner party. It's a unique experience. Lack of choice is always a high-risk strategy, partly because expectations are naturally high – visitors can expect something wonderful in return for giving up their right to choose and Tina's blending of ideas from the Mediterranean and Asia cooked in front of you on a teppan grill is a success. Fish and seafood are the main inspiration, a meal opening, perhaps, with sesame-coated Chinese five-spice scallops on mixed leaves with a lime, coriander, ginger and spring onion vinaigrette, before a soup of carrot and coriander with ginger, turmeric, fresh orange juice and toasted pine nuts. Monkfish and tiger prawns on squid ink noodles and a salad of mixed leaves with a wasabi, mustard and honey dressing is a typical main course, before dessert of Caribbean brioche-and-butter coconut pudding with rum-soaked raisins. Booking is essential, and breakfast for those staying is outstanding. Wines on the brief, fish-friendly list start at £19.95.
**Chef/s:** Tina Pemberton. **Open:** all week D only 7.45 (1 sitting). L by arrangement. **Closed:** 25 Dec. **Meals:** Set D £42.50. **Service:** 10%. **Details:** Cards

accepted. 20 seats. 16 seats outside. Air-con. Wheelchair access. Music. Children allowed. Car parking.

## ALSO RECOMMENDED

### ▲ Rose and Crown
Old Church Road, Snettisham, PE31 7LX
Tel no: (01485) 541382

A mix of familiar reworked British classics and more cosmopolitan oriental novelties, it's not just the food that is a clever blend of old and new at this wonderful fourteenth-century inn; expect confit lamb ravioli (£5.85) and hot sour scallop and sweet pork salad(£7.50) alongside seared calf's liver and bacon (£12.95) or rib-eye steak with fries and a feta mizuna salad (£13.75). Rambling rooms, uneven floors, beamed ceilings, open fires, it's got period feel by the pint (as well as real ale in the well stocked bars), combined with child-friendly gardens and an array of eating areas (both more formal and more family-friendly). Wines start at £11.50. Open all week.

## Stoke Holy Cross

### Wildebeest Arms
**Civilised country pub**
82-86 Norwich Road, Stoke Holy Cross, NR14 8QJ
Tel no: (01508) 492497
**Modern European | £28**
**Cooking score: 2**

Planned refurbishment at the time of going to press may see changes in the décor at this pub, though the cooking is expected to continue in the same lively, contemporary vein as before. Chargrilled smoked salmon with king prawns and guacamole is a typically forthright starter, while to follow there might be pan-seared haunch of venison with fondant potato, Parma ham and dark chocolate sauce. To finish, choose from a selection of fine cheeses or a dessert such as warm treacle tart with coconut sorbet, lemon curd and lime syrup. The wine list is a fine example, frequently going off the beaten track to pluck interesting bottles from the wine world's less familiar regions, and a policy of low mark-ups across the board encourages experimentation. The list opens with a page of varied house selections, all at a very reasonable £12.95 a bottle. NB As the Guide went to press, we were informed of refurbishment plans for autumn. Reports please.

**Chef/s:** Daniel Smith. **Open:** all week 12 to 2, 7 to 10. **Meals:** alc exc Sun L (main courses £12 to £22). Set L £12.95 (2 courses), Set D Sun to Fri £15 (2 courses) to £18.50. **Service:** not inc. **Details:** Cards accepted. 70 seats. 30 seats outside. Air-con. Wheelchair access. Music. Children's portions. Car parking.

## Swaffham

### Strattons

**Hidden, quirky Palladian bolthole**
4 Ash Close, Swaffham, PE37 7NH
Tel no: (01760) 723845
www.strattonshotel.com
**Modern European | £40**
**Cooking score: 3**

Few hotels could boast better green credentials than Vanessa and Les Scotts' environmentally friendly 'country house in town'. Relaxed and with the right kind of homeliness, it means slipping off one's shoes or dozing after a good meal might just be positively encouraged. Vigour was evident in the gutsy cooking of seasonal and often very local ingredients. A 'light and savoury' pork and pigeon terrine came with whole roasted plum, fancy leaves and a split fruit-oil dressing while wild mushroom dumplings, lentils, spring onion mash and fat olives bolstered 'surprisingly toothsome tender' spring rabbit casserole. The taster cheese course – four perfectly ripe British specimens including Mrs Temple's Binham Blue and Feltwell ewe's milk White Lady – were explained with expert flair. Turkish delight with a twist" comprised a shotglass of sweet rosewater jelly and a chocolate biscotti. The style-categorised wine list is well versed with bottles from £13.

**Chef/s:** Vanessa Scott, Maggie Cooper and Sam Bryant. **Open:** Mon to Sat D only 7 to 8.30 (9 Fri and Sat) (residents only Sun D). **Closed:** Christmas one week. **Meals:** Set D £40 (4 courses). **Service:** not inc. **Details:** Cards accepted. 22 seats. 12 seats outside. No mobile phones. Music. Children's portions. Car parking.

## Walsingham

★NEW ENTRY★
### Norfolk Riddle Restaurant
**Owned by a partnership of local farms**
2 Wells Road, Walsingham, NR22 6DJ
Tel no: (01328) 821903
**British | £17**
£30

Jettison all preconceptions about chip shops as you walk through the takeaway section of this newly converted cottage, into the stylish L-shaped restaurant. Born out of the Walsingham Farms Shop enterprise, Norfolk Riddle uses local ingredients of the highest order. Nearby farms supply meat, vegetables, and the Maris Piper potatoes for frying; smoked food hails from the Cley smokehouse; drinks comprise Norfolk cider and beer, and wine (starting at £7 a bottle) from a Burnham Market merchant. Daily specials (served by friendly, slowish staff) might include fresh, vibrant tomato and basil soup followed by tender mutton in rich red wine jus. Fish and chips, though, steals the show: moist, flaky, brilliant white haddock, clothed in light crisp batter, with golden chips and thick mushy peas. Prices are divertingly low for such quality. To finish: an exemplary dark chocolate, almond and Norfolk-honey tart. In heaven, all chippies are like this.

**Chef/s:** Samantha Halls. **Closed:** Tuesdays. **Details:** Cards accepted. 34 seats. 40 seats outside. Children's portions. Car parking.

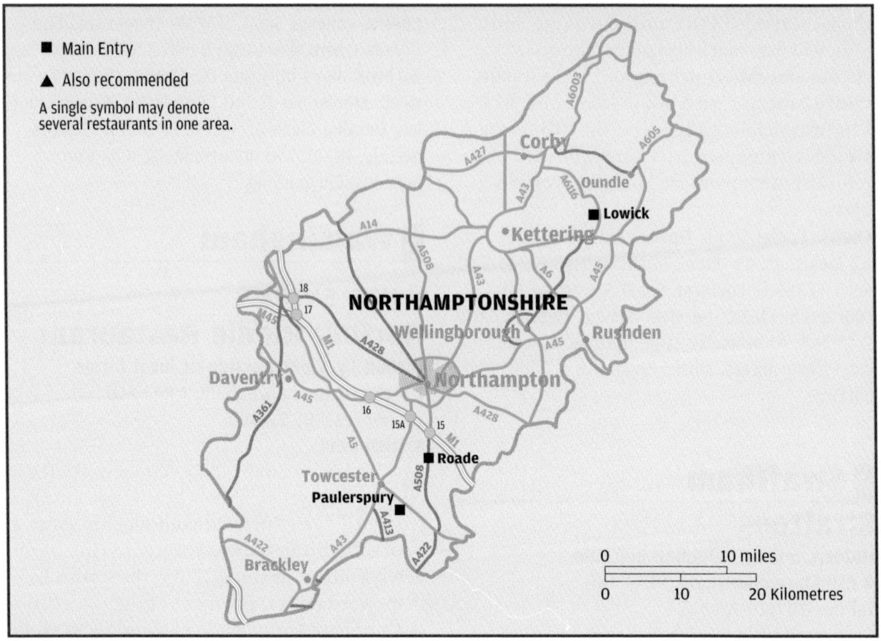
■ Main Entry
▲ Also recommended
A single symbol may denote several restaurants in one area.
Corby
Oundle
Lowick
Kettering
NORTHAMPTONSHIRE
Wellingborough
Rushden
Daventry
Northampton
Roade
Towcester
Paulerspury
Brackley
A6003
A605
A427
A43
A6116
A14
A508
A6
A45
M45
M1
A428
A361
A5
A413
A422
18
17
16
15A
15
0
10 miles
0
10
20 Kilometres

## Lowick

### Snooty Fox

**Superior pub food in a middle-England manor**
**16 Main Street, Lowick, NN14 3BH**
**Tel no: (01832) 733434**
**Modern British | £37**
**Cooking score: 3**

V

Hidden away in a verdant Northamptonshire backwater, the many-gabled Snooty Fox started life as a sixteenth-century manor house, although it is now a gentrified country pub/restaurant dealing in forthright, no-frills food. A rotisserie/grill is at the centre of things and it is put to good use: cut-to-order steaks from dry-aged Aberdeen Angus beef are a speciality and they come with fat chips, peppercorn sauce, watercress and red onion salad. Elsewhere, the kitchen tackles an assortment of gastropub favourites running from garden pea soup with crème fraîche or gravlax with dill potato salad via Jimmy Butler's bangers and grilled Brixham plaice with Jersey Royals to cherry and mascarpone tart or 'artisan' cheeses. Sandwiches and pub-grub standards are also available in the bar. The Snooty Fox holds a decent stock of real ales and it also provides wine drinkers with plenty of choice at reasonable prices. House selections start at £12.95 (£3 a glass).

**Chef/s:** Clive Dixon. **Open:** all week 12 to 2, 6.30 to 9.30. **Closed:** D 25 Dec, 1 and 2 Jan. **Meals:** alc (main courses £8 to £15). Set L Mon to Sat £9.95 (2 courses) to £14.50. Bar menu available. **Service:** not inc. **Details:** Cards accepted. 50 seats. Music. Children's portions. Car parking.

**Please send us your feedback**

To register your opinion about any restaurant listed in the Guide, or a new restaurant that you wish to bring to our attention, please visit the web address at the bottom of the page. Your feedback informs the content of the book and will be used to compile next year's reviews.

## ▌Paulerspury

### Vine House
**Charming restaurant-with-rooms**
100 High Street, Paulerspury, NN12 7NA
Tel no: (01327) 811267
www.vinehousehotel.com
**Modern British | £30**
**Cooking score: 3**
£5 OFF 🛏

This rambling old stone house is run with personal style by owners Marcus and Julie Springett. The atmosphere is informal and homely, with Julie taking charge front-of-house while Marcus reigns in the kitchen. His inventive cooking showcases fashionable flavours. With compact menus offering three choices per course, starters might include home-smoked salmon or rillettes of local Dexter beef with sourdough toast. To follow, Cornish brill with salted almonds, tomatoes and chive sauce typically appears alongside roast confit of Gloucester Old Spot belly pork with garlic and mushroom sauce, and breast of Goosnargh duck with caper sauce and chips. To finish, there might be hot apricot bread pudding with clotted cream, or chilled champagne and rhubarb soup with honey and orange jelly. Four house wines at £13.95 open a French-dominated list.
**Chef/s:** Marcus Springett. **Open:** Tue to Sat L 12 to 2, all week D 6.30 to 10. **Meals:** Set L and D £26.95 (2 courses) to £29.95. **Service:** 12.5%. **Details:** Cards accepted. 33 seats. 8 seats outside. No music. Wheelchair access. Children's portions. Car parking.

## ▌Roade

### Roade House
**Close to the roar of Silverstone**
16 High Street, Roade, NN7 2NW
Tel no: (01604) 863372
www.roadehousehotel.co.uk
**Modern British | £30**
**Cooking score: 4**
🛏

The stone-built former pub is to be found in a village that manages to combine serenity and proximity to the M1. Its frontage, once a blushing red, is now a more sedate creamy white. Meanwhile, within, Chris Kewley maintains a culinary pace that, if not Silverstone, is certainly capable of holding its own in the fast lane of modern bistro fashion. There's chorizo in the parsnip soup, for starters, or a warm salad of roasted quail dressed in honey and mustard. Menus keep a weather eye on the seasons and produce some satisfying combinations, as of grilled sea bass with prawn and fennel risotto and tomato salsa, or blade of beef gently braised in red wine and served with colcannon. Finish up classically with apple strudel and vanilla ice cream, or brandy-snap baskets of raspberries with lime ice cream. The wine list is arranged stylistically in a way that makes sense, and prices are pretty reasonable. It all starts at £14, or £4 a glass.
**Chef/s:** Chris Kewley and Debbie Richardson. **Open:** Mon to Fri L 12 to 2, Mon to Sat D 7 to 9.30. **Closed:** 1 week Christmas and New Year, bank hol Mon. **Meals:** Set L £20 (2 courses) to £23, Set D £26 (2 courses) to £31. **Service:** not inc. **Details:** Cards accepted. 48 seats. Air-con. No music. Wheelchair access. Children's portions. Car parking.

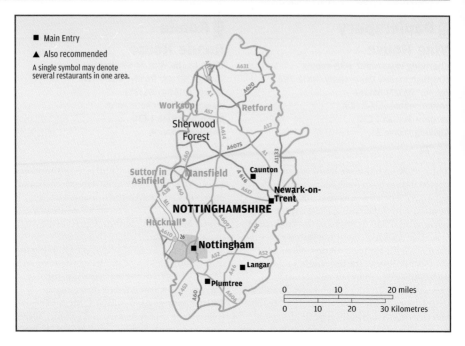

- ■ Main Entry
- ▲ Also recommended

A single symbol may denote several restaurants in one area.

# Caunton

## Caunton Beck
Welcoming and diverse
Main Street, Caunton, NG23 6AB
Tel no: (01636) 636793
Modern European | £23
Cooking score: 2

£5 OFF  Ⅴ  £30

Caunton Beck defies categorisation. An all-week brasserie in a quiet country setting no music, birdsong instead – it opens at 8am for breakfast with an energetic determination to please all sorts, including children. A range of sandwiches with a generally Mediterranean slant is complemented by sophisticated starters like sardines on toast with oven dried tomatoes and twice baked cheese soufflé with broccoli and Stilton. Basics like grilled salmon with warm potato salad or more exotic gremolata marinated red mullet with rice noodles and bok choi laksa each have recommended wines, by the bottle or the glass. Ever-so-grand, highly priced clarets and champagnes vie with more modest careful selections, and with house wine at £12.55 this is a place for most pockets.

**Chef/s:** Andrew and Katie Pickstock. **Open:** all week 8 to 11. **Meals:** alc (main courses £9.50 to £19). Set L Mon to Sat £11 (2 courses) to £13.95. Set D Sun to Fri £11 (2 courses) to £13.95. **Service:** not inc. **Details:** Cards accepted. 90 seats. 40 seats outside. No music. Wheelchair access. Children's portions. Car parking.

# Langar

## Langar Hall
Attractive country house
Langar, NG13 9HG
Tel no: (01949) 860559
www.langarhall.com
Modern British | £34
Cooking score: 4

£5 OFF  ⌁  Ⅴ

The advice is to roll up the long drive in early-evening sunlight to get the best view of this attractive house and its gardens. Inside, it is gracious, albeit with a friendly, homely feel and public rooms, including the dining area off the hall, are domestic in scale. Game is a regular feature, local supplies include meat, eggs, cheese, fruit and vegetables (some home-grown), and pea, wild garlic and ham soup might set the ball rolling on the short, daily-changing menu. Roast breast of duck and confit leg with petits pois bonne femme and blood orange sauce, or shank of lamb with roast new potatoes and confit garlic are typical main courses. Although many dishes are turned out well – ham hock and parsley terrine with home-made piccalilli, for example – standards and timing do slip from time to time as the kitchen, enthusiastic as it is, struggles to meet all its commitments. This is true at dessert stage where reporters have praised a refreshing vanilla pannacotta with caramelised oranges but found ice-coffee parfait too sweet and the accompanying walnut ice cream 'over-egging the pudding'. Home-made bread has been praised, and service is competent. The wine list plays safe with a selection from France before moving on to cover key points on the wine compass.

**Chef/s:** Garry Booth, Rick Woolfsen and Peter Carr. **Open:** all week 12 to 2, 7 to 9.30. **Meals:** alc D (main courses £13.50 to £20). Set L Mon to Thur £13 (2 courses) to £16.50, Set L Fri and Sat £16.50 (2 courses) to £20, Set L Sun £27.50. Set D Sun and Mon £20 (2 courses) to £25, Set D Sat £34.50 (2 courses) to £39.50. **Service:** 10% (optional). **Details:** Cards accepted. 60 seats. 20 seats outside. No mobile phones. Wheelchair access. Music. Children's portions. Car parking.

## ■ Newark

### Café Bleu
Inviting bistro
14 Castle Gate, Newark, NG24 1BG
Tel no: (01636) 610141
www.cafebleu.co.uk
**Modern European | £27**
**Cooking score: 1**
V £30

The vibe is friendly and warm at this bustling bistro; the interior is all oak floors, mismatched furniture and distressed paint-effect walls, with huge contemporary canvases hither and thither – you can eat outside, too, in the charming walled courtyard. Good, local ingredients are pressed into service – warm Lincolnshire asparagus with fruit, vanilla hollandaise, pea shoots and beetroot crisps makes a cracking starter. Of the six or so mains on offer, a good choice might be roast rump of Lincolnshire lamb with braised Puy lentils, shoulder of lamb hash and slow-dried tomatoes – a dense, substantial dish. There's no parsimony here, so check you've got room before you plump for rhubarb bavarois or warm chocolate pudding with almond ice cream. A shortish but perfectly adequate wine list offers house starting at a very reasonable £10.95, with five by the glass, starting at £2.95.

**Chef/s:** Mark Cheseldine and Mark Osborne. **Open:** all week L 12 to 2.30 (2 Sat, 3 Sun), Mon to Sat D 7 to 9.30 (6.30 to 10 Sat). **Closed:** 25 and 26 Dec. **Meals:** alc (main courses £8.50 to £15). **Service:** not inc. **Details:** Cards accepted. 80 seats. 50 seats outside. Wheelchair access. Music. Children's portions.

## ▌Nottingham

★NEW ENTRY★
### French Living
**Rustic French bistro in the heart of town**
27 King Street, Nottingham, NG1 2AY
Tel no: (0115) 958 5885
www.frenchliving.co.uk
**French | £23**
**Cooking score: 2**
£30

Check tablecloth, Van Gogh chair, old paintings in wonky frames on yellowing walls, the traditional English take on a French city bistro is alive and well in this bustling basement. Husband and wife team Stephane and Louise Luiggi, he Corsican, she English, set up a shop and café in 1994 expanding into a restaurant that serves honourable, home cooked, seasonal French dishes at reasonable prices. A rustic provençal tart at lunch was not picture perfect, but rang bells with the flavours of onion, tomato, basil and thyme. Sardines come filleted and grilled with a touch of chilli. A spring main course of pork fillet with an onion and mushroom sauce and sauté potatoes was robust and satisfying. Puddings were less successful, but the service, relaxed vibe and overall value explain its popularity.
**Chef/s:** Jeremy Tourne. **Open:** Tue to Sat 12 to 2, 6 to 10 (12 to 2.30 Sun). **Meals:** alc (main courses £9.50 to £17.50) Set L £6.50 to £12 (2 courses), £15.50 to £20 (3 courses), Set D 15.50 (2 courses) to £20 (3 courses). **Service:** not inc. **Details:** Cards accepted. 80 seats. 42 seats outside. Air-con. Music. Children's portions.

## Hart's
**Classy, modern, professional operation**
1 Standard Court, Park Row, Nottingham, NG1 6GN
Tel no: (0115) 911 0666
www.hartsnottingham.co.uk
**Modern British | £49**
**Cooking score: 5**
♀ ⌐ V

Hart's has earned its place in the affections of Nottingham's gastronomes. Occupyng part of the former Nottingham General Hospital, it was converted in 1997. The contemporary yet informal interior has a distinct brasserie feel, with its shiny woodwork and glass, splashes of bright colour, abstract art, and buzzy atmosphere. The food is deceptively simple, with no unnecessary fuss or trimmings, just high-quality ingredients lightly and confidently handled by Alan Gleeson. His expansive, yet very appealing menus blend the traditional, say beef fillet served with Koffman cabbage, rösti potato and béarnaise, with modern touches in such dishes as rack of lamb with minted potato mash, pea purée and crispy sweetbreads, or John Dory with parsley and smoked bacon risotto. Typically, start with smoked chicken and foie gras terrine with spiced pear chutney, or pea soup with ham hock tortellini, and finish with hot chocolate pudding with nougat ice cream or mille-feuille of banana parfait and cocoa biscuit with lime froth. The set-price lunch menu gets the thumbs-up and the service is impeccable from attentive, polite and well-drilled staff. Wines are an easy-going mix of classic and modern, arranged by style to make navigation and choice easier, and there are some classy, interesting bottles at sensible mark-ups; prices start at £14.50.
**Chef/s:** Alan Gleeson. **Open:** all week 12 to 2, 7 to 10.30 (9 Sun). **Closed:** 26 Dec, 1 Jan. **Meals:** alc (main courses £13.50 to £22.50). Set L Mon to Sat £12.95 (2 courses) to £15.95, Set L Sun £18, Set D Sun to Thur £21. **Service:** 12% (optional). **Details:** Cards accepted. 80 seats. 20 seats outside. No music. Wheelchair access. Children's portions. Car parking.

## Restaurant Sat Bains
**A brilliantly eccentric establishment**
Old Lenton Lane, Nottingham, NG7 2SA
Tel no: (0115) 986 6566
www.restaurantsatbains.net
**Modern European | £50**
**Cooking score: 7**

The converted farmhouse and outbuildings in the Lenton area of Nottingham has been home, since 2005, to the Bains' highly idiosyncratic restaurant-with-rooms. It is all impressively elegant, and the evidence of total commitment is clear throughout. Sat Bains is aiming high, and getting there. There is a wealth of seriously ambitious, labour-intensive and intelligent effort going on in every dish, amply justifying the avant-garde conceptions and the terse and tantalising menu descriptions. Start perhaps with 'raw-cooked' scallop and its accompaniments of butternut squash, yuzu and pickled cauliflower. Milk-fed rabbit turns up almost traditionally with morels and asparagus in a truffle vinaigrette, but the riot of flavours that accompanies Goosnargh duck reads almost like free association: melon, feta, mint, carrot, chocolate and grapefruit. That these dishes succeed is indicative of the fact that this isn't just novelty for its own sake. An eight-course tasting menu will take you through the repertoire, from a duck egg cooked at 62 degrees centigrade, all the way to rhubarb with pistachio and vanilla, via a main course of Cumbrian lamb cooked sous-vide, with confit tomato, anchovy and couscous. There is a pretty nifty wine list too, albeit an expensive one. Grouped in style categories, with organics listed separately, it has many fine, world-class growers. Think £25 and head upwards.
**Chef/s:** Sat Bains and John Freeman. **Open:** Tue to Sat D only 7 to 9.30. **Closed:** 2 weeks Dec to Jan, 2 weeks Aug. **Meals:** Set D £47 to £65.
**Service:** 12.5%. **Details:** Cards accepted. 34 seats. 10 seats outside. Air-con. No mobile phones. Music. Car parking.

## World Service
**East meets West**
Newdigate House, Castle Gate, Nottingham, NG1 6AF
Tel no: (0115) 847 5587
www.worldservicerestaurant.com
**Global | £34**
**Cooking score: 4**

Newdigate House, the seventeenth-century Georgian building that is home to World Service, is hidden away down a narrow lane that leads to the castle and is a real find. Inside, a contemporary décor fuses colonial grandeur with a chic oriental look (patterned fabrics, ornate mirrors, Indonesian artefacts). As its name suggests, food is international fusion, happily embracing West and East without being fussy; from the former you might encounter pressed duck and pistachio terrine with chicory and pomegranate salad or rack of lamb with butternut squash tarte Tatin and spring garlic, while the latter could reveal a starter of cured salmon with oriental salad and yuzo miso sauce. Ingredients are top-notch and flavours are vibrant, especially through the use of colourful relishes and accompaniments, such as freshly made piccalilli with smoked pork Kassler, and red pepper mousse with pan-fried halibut. Exceptional desserts include warm dark chocolate fondant with white chocolate mousse. Service is professional and courteous. The wine list is eclectic and comprehensive, with house recommendations from £13.50.
**Chef/s:** Chris Elson and Preston Walker. **Open:** all week 12 to 2.15 (2.30 Sun), 7 to 10 (9 Sun). **Closed:** 1 to 6 Jan. **Meals:** alc (main courses £13.50 to £19.50). Set L £12 (2 courses) to £16.50. **Service:** 10% (optional). **Details:** Cards accepted. 80 seats. 40 seats outside. Music. Children's portions.

## READERS RECOMMEND

### Cast

**Modern British**
Nottingham Playhouse, Wellington Circus,
Nottingham, NG1 5AN
Tel no: (01158) 523898
www.castrestaurant.co.uk
**'Try the butternut squash brioche'**

### Cock and Hoop

**Gastropub**
25 High Pavement, Lace Market, Nottingham,
NG1 1HE
Tel no: (0115) 8523232
www.cockandhoop.co.uk
**'Strong British cooking with hearty real ales'**

## ▌Plumtree

★ READERS' RESTAURANT OF THE YEAR ★
MIDLANDS

### Perkins

**A country restaurant of some class**
Station House, Station Road, Plumtree, NG12 5NA
Tel no: (0115) 9373695
www.perkinsrestaurant.co.uk
**Anglo-French | £30**
**Cooking score: 2**

This unaffected restaurant, located in a
Victorian railway station (the single track
remains in use as an occasionally test line),
continues to be a safe bet for a good meal in a
pleasant, welcoming environment. The
Perkins family has chalked up some 25 years of
bonhomie, offering a straightforward menu to
an appreciative Nottinghamshire crowd. The
kitchen makes the most of its strong roots,
typically featuring smoked fish from their
own smokehouse and local asparagus (with a
rich hollandaise sauce) alongside George
Stafford's black pudding and rump of Stathern
lamb. Notable successes have included scallops
with curried apple and a well-timed fillet of
cod served atop a fresh tasting pea, bacon,
tomato and tarragon fricassée. Desserts might
include poached pear stuffed with vanilla
cream and served with toffee sauce and

brioche, and service is always friendly and
timely. A helpful, varied, good value wine list
includes plenty of bottles under £20 with
house French at £12.95.
**Chef/s:** Sarah Newham, David Perkins. **Open:** Tue to
Sun L 12 to 2 (2.30 Sun), Tue to Sat D 6.45 to 9.45.
**Closed:** 25 and 26 Dec, 1 Jan. **Meals:** alc (exc Sun L;
main courses £12.95 to £17.50). Set L Tue to Sat
£11.25 (2 courses), Set L Sun £13.50 (2 courses), Set
D Tue to Thu £21.50 (3 courses). **Service:** not inc.
**Details:** Cards accepted. 72 seats. 24 seats outside.
Air-con. Music. Children's portions. Car parking.

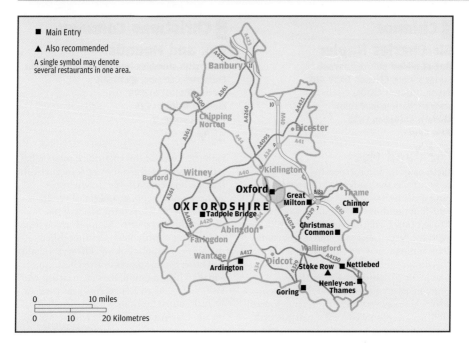

■ Main Entry

▲ Also recommended

A single symbol may denote several restaurants in one area.

0          10 miles

0     10        20 Kilometres

## █ Ardington

### Boar's Head
**Hearty village local**
Church Street, Ardington, OX12 8QA
Tel no: (01235) 833254
www.boarsheadardington.co.uk
Gastropub | £38
Cooking score: 3

£5 OFF ⊨

The Boar's Head's modern exterior belies its ancient origins – it dates back some 150 years. It's still very much the village local, and the restaurant is the rustic setting for Bruce Buchan's ambitious style of modern cooking. He works with the seasons and sourcing is a strength – lamb and pork are from local farms, game from the Lockinge Estate, and vegetables come from with five miles of the pub. This could translate to seared foie gras with brioche and rhubarb, venison with fondant potato and mustard sauce, and red mullet with ratatouille and chorizo on the short, simply described menu. To finish are farmhouse cheeses with sticky malt bread, or hot pistachio soufflé with chocolate ice cream. The wide-ranging wine list favours France and prices open at £12.50.

**Chef/s:** Bruce Buchan. **Open:** all week 12 to 2.15, 7 to 9.30 (10 Fri and Sat). **Meals:** alc exc Sun (main courses £14.50 to £19.50). Set L Mon to Sat £14.50 (2 courses) to £17.50, Set L Sun £22 (3 courses). Bar menu available. **Service:** not inc. **Details:** Cards accepted. 40 seats. 30 seats outside. No mobile phones. Music. Children's portions. Car parking.

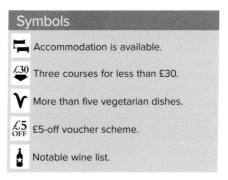

## Symbols

⊨  Accommodation is available.

£30  Three courses for less than £30.

V  More than five vegetarian dishes.

£5 OFF  £5-off voucher scheme.

🍾  Notable wine list.

## Chinnor

### Sir Charles Napier

One-of-a-kind pub/restaurant
Sprigg's Alley, Chinnor, OX39 4BX
Tel no: (01494) 483011
www.sircharlesnapier.co.uk
**Modern European | £35**
**New Chef**

£5 OFF 🍷 ❤ V

'Very original décor, especially all the metal sculptures in the garden' is how one reader described this assortment of ancient brick-and-flint buildings tucked into a wooded fold. Owner Julie Griffiths celebrates her 40th year with the Napier this year, and if you take a look at the longest-serving list, you'll see that this unique pub–restaurant has been in the Guide for 27 consecutive years. Raw ingredients are first-class and the kitchen makes almost everything from scratch. Early summer has produced local asparagus with own free-range eggs perched on top, and a soup of wild garlic (picked from the surrounding woods) and broccoli. Fish is a strength, whether 'very fresh' scallops on a celeriac purée accompanied by a cup of 'frothy fishy broth' and a tortellini containing another scallop, or fillet of sea trout with crushed potatoes, red chard, pine nuts and sorrel. Elsewhere, deftly judged combinations have included loin of wild rabbit teamed with ravioli, white bean and truffle purée, and traditional roasts for Sunday lunch have been endorsed. The wine list is a well-thought-through global affair with fair choice under £20 and a decent selection by the glass. Bottle open at £14.95.
**Chef/s:** Sam Hughes. **Open:** Tue to Sun L 12 to 2.30 (3.30 Sun), Tue to Sat D 6.30 to 10. **Closed:** 3 days Christmas. **Meals:** alc (main courses £15.50 to £21). Set L Tue to Fri £14.50 (2 courses), Set D Tue to Fri £16 (2 courses). **Service:** 12.5% (optional). **Details:** Cards accepted. 70 seats. Air-con. Wheelchair access. Music. Children's portions. Car parking.

## Christmas Common

### Fox and Hounds

Gastropub stumbles into the media limelight
Christmas Common, OX49 5HL
Tel no: (01491) 612599
**Modern British | £25**
**Cooking score: 3**

£5 OFF V £30

Fame beckons for this traditional inn – it has recently been used as a filming location by the BBC, who were no doubt drawn by the authentic old fireplaces and smart yet down-to-earth décor. Hopefully, this will not distract chef-proprietor Kieron Daniels from continuing to turn out his accomplished modern gastropub cooking. His style is bold and hearty, as in starters of roast butternut squash with red onion, Parmesan tartine and a fashionable 'micro' salad accompaniment, or Danish soused herrings with horseradish cream. Guernsey crab soufflé with thermidor sauce is another dish guaranteed to pack a flavour punch, while Aberdeen Angus ribeye hash topped with a fried egg, or roast Gressingham duck breast with potato gratin, green beans and apple gravy should satisfy those of a carnivorous bent. Lunch dishes are slightly simpler – but no less appealing – and to finish, roast rhubarb semifreddo or panettone bread-and-butter pudding are typical. Prices on the compact wine list start at £14 a bottle, £3.75 a glass.
**Chef/s:** Kieron Daniels. **Open:** all week 12 to 3, 5.30 to 11. **Closed:** 25 Dec, D 31 Dec. **Meals:** alc (main courses £11 to £18). **Service:** not inc. **Details:** Cards accepted. 70 seats. 50 seats outside. Wheelchair access. Music. Children's portions. Car parking.

## ▌Goring-on-Thames

### Leatherne Bottel

The Bridleway, Goring-on-Thames, RG8 OHS
Tel no: (01491) 872667
www.leathernebottel.co.uk
**Modern European | £33**
**Cooking score: 3**

Ⓥ

The charming rural riverside setting evokes a relaxed mood at this long-standing restaurant. The cosy dining room features with homely décor and generously proportioned tables. Chef Julia Storey's imaginative cooking lives up to the setting, whether in the form of a simple, comforting starter such as flat mushrooms on black olive toast, or a lively modern creation such as sesame-crusted tuna carpaccio with pickled carrot and cucumber and wasabi crème fraîche. Similarly varied main courses range from honey and apple glazed duck breast with spinach and apple tart and parsnip cream, to venison saddle roasted with ginger and cardamom, with braised chicory, trompette mushroom jus and fondant potatoes, while desserts encompass sticky toffee pudding and caramelised lime tart with mango and ginger salad. The wine list is an impressive catalogue of fine bottles, with prices starting at £17.50.

**Chef/s:** Julia Storey. **Open:** all week L 12 to 2 (2.30 Sat, 3.30 Sun), Mon to Sat D 7 to 9 (9.30 Sat). **Meals:** alc (main courses £18 to £22). Set L £17.95 (2 courses).. **Service:** 10% (fixed). **Details:** Cards accepted. 42 seats. 8 seats outside. No music. No mobile phones. Wheelchair access. Children allowed. Car parking.

## ▌Great Milton

### Le Manoir aux Quat' Saisons

**Rejuvenated excellence**
Church Road, Great Milton, OX44 7PD
Tel no: (01844) 278881
www.manoir.com
**French | £95**
**Cooking score: 9**

🍷 🛏 Ⓥ

In a sixteenth-century manor house of honeyed Cotswold stone, Le Manoir has the most beautiful setting of manicured lawn, terrace and ornamental gardens. Behind a stone wall is one of the finest English kitchen gardens devoted to growing vegetables and herbs for the restaurant. Compared with Mediterranean markets, getting really top-quality produce in Brtiain is a challenge – not here, for the tremendous quality of the vegetables is obvious on every plate.

The comfortable classic dining room has a section inside the house and a large plant-filled conservatory, which now sensibly has blinds added as shade from the summer sun. There are two tasting menus (culminating in the 'discovery' at £110 each), a short à la carte and two nice touches: a full vegetarian version of the tasting menu, and a children's menu at £18. The menus draws heavily on seasonal ingredients and generally have an almost Mediterranean lightness of style. They are fairly classical, though steadily evolving. At inspection, an excellent little piece of tuna on a sesame tuile preceded superb cod brandade of delicate texture. A real strength here is the selection of breads, all made on the premises, uniformly magnificent. Praised dishes this year range from a confit of Landais foie gras, served simply with a little pile of rhubarb purée, to perfect cheese soufflé made from Vieux Lille cheese, with a salad of walnut and apple. Also found to be exceptional was fillet of halibut from Iceland, resting on a bed of fregola Sardinian pasta made from semolina, and wilted rocket, served with a red wine and star anise sauce. Gressingham duck comes in two generous pieces of breast cooked pink, with a superb garlic and shallot purée and tender pak choi (grown in the garden). The tagliatelle of summer vegetables is a stunning dish. Sumptuous desserts include a carpaccio of blood orange topped with a scoop of blood orange sorbet – technically perfect. There's no doubt Le Manoir is on a surge of rejuvenated excellence. The wine list is 42 pages long, covering France thoroughly, this year with more regional wines. Spain fares well, sporting classics such as Torres Mas la Plana 1999 at £85. There is a page of wines by the glass, with some astute choices, such as the excellent Mas de Daumas Gassac red.

**Chef/s:** Raymond Blanc. **Open:** all week 12.15 to 2.30, 7.15 to 9.45. **Meals:** alc (main courses £36 to £38). Set L Mon to Fri £45 to £95, Set L Sat and Sun £95, Set D £95. **Service:** not inc. **Details:** Cards accepted. 90 seats. Air-con. No music. Wheelchair access. Jacket and tie required. Children's portions. Car parking.

## ▊ Henley-on-Thames

### Hotel du Vin & Bistro
Lively addition to the Hotel du Vin family
New Street, Henley-on-Thames, RG9 2BP
Tel no: (01491) 848400
www.hotelduvin.com
Modern European | £30
Cooking score: 3

This striking Georgian building, once the Brakspear brewery, seems very comfortable in its stylish new boutique-hotel garb. It stands in the heart of historic Henley-on-Thames, some 50 yards from the river, and is decked out in the trademark Hotel du Vin style. The bistro menu opens with starters such as salad Lyonnaise with a poached egg or confit duck, guinea fowl and foie gras terrine with toasted brioche. Follow with local Gloucester Old Spot pork belly with rhubarb tart, watercress purée and Scottish balsamic dressing or salmon and prawn lasagne with confit cherry tomato and dill velouté. A pleasing mix of side orders includes fat-cut chips and chargrilled courgettes. Dessert continues in the same unfussy-classic vein with the likes of crème brûlée, vanilla panacotta with berry compote,

and lemon tart. As you would hope, there is an impressive wine list, supported by a dedicated team of sommeliers. Bottles start from £14.50.

**Chef/s:** Matt Green-Armytage. **Open:** all week 12.30 to 2.30, 7 to 9.45 (10 Fri and Sat). **Meals:** alc (main courses £12.50 to £20). Set L Mon to Fri £15 (2 courses), Set D £17.50 (3 courses). **Service:** 10%. **Details:** Cards accepted. 90 seats. 50 seats outside. No music. Wheelchair access. Children's portions.

## READERS RECOMMEND

### Nut Tree Inn
Modern British
Main Street, Murcott, OX5 2RE
Tel no: (01865) 331253
'Exemplary cooking from Michael North'

## ALSO RECOMMENDED

### ▲ White Hart
28-30 High Street, Nettlebed, RG9 5DD
Tel no: (01491) 641245
www.whitehartnettlebed.com

A centuries-old, brick-and-flint pub in the centre of an affluent village, the White Hart is full of promise and possibilities. Crowds now populate the airy, pastel-hued bistro that spreads over much of the original bar. Sharp modern cooking is the prevailing theme, from starters like tuna tartare with fennel and cucumber salad (£7) to main courses of roast veal fillet with broad bean and morel risotto (£18.50) or seared duck breast with pear tarte Tatin and spiced orange jus. House vins de pays are £12.95 (£3.50 a glass). Open all week.

# Oxford

## Branca

**Buzzing atmosphere**
111 Walton Street, Oxford, OX2 6AJ
Tel no: (01865) 556111
www.branca-restaurants.com
Modern Italian | £26
Cooking score: 1

Ⅴ £30

Friendly service from tireless staff, all-day opening and early evening deals make this live-wire, modern Italian brasserie a favourite with the under-30 crowd. A long, light and airy room, with a high glass ceiling and grand chandeliers, is the setting for a wide-ranging repertoire of dishes, from stone-baked pizzas, pasta and risottos (such as seared king scallops, tomato and basil), to more contemporary offerings like roast lamb rump with chargrilled vegetables and mint crème fraîche. For dessert, try the pannacotta with spiced fig compote. The Italian wine list is brief but good value, from £12.95.
**Chef/s:** Michael MacQuire. **Open:** all week 12 to 11. **Closed:** 24 and 25 Dec. **Meals:** alc (main courses £9 to £17). Set L Mon to Fri 12 to 5 £5.95 (1 course, inc wine), Set D Mon to Fri 5 to 7 £10 (2 courses, inc wine). **Service:** not inc. **Details:** Cards accepted. 125 seats. Air-con. No mobile phones. Wheelchair access. Music. Children's portions.

## Cherwell Boathouse

**Oxford landmark with a patrician wine list**
50 Bardwell Road, Oxford, OX2 6ST
Tel no: (01865) 552746
www.cherwellboathouse.co.uk
Modern British/French | £25
Cooking score: 1

£5 OFF Ⅴ £30

For almost 40 years, Anthony Verdin and family have been captivating visitors with their riverside restaurant overlooking the Cherwell. The Boathouse is famed for its terrace, although the premises also includes an airy conservatory, which sits cheek-by-jowl with the original bare-boarded dining room.

Anglo-French food is the kitchen's business and it sends out confit duck rilletes with potato beignet and poached duck egg ahead of rack of new season's lamb with purple potatoes, curly kale, white truffle oil and morel jus. Exotic touches also keep visitors on their toes (chocolate oil provides the final flourish for breast of duck with honey and rosemary) and desserts aim to surprise with baked popcorn cheesecake. Anthony Verdin is serious about wine and his aristrocratic list shows its strength in the classic French regions, with Chile also starting to make an impact elsewhere. Around 20 house selections start at £12.50 (£3.25 a glass).
**Chef/s:** Carson Hill and Clive Rogers. **Open:** all week 12 to 2 (2.30 Sat and Sun), 6.30 to 9.30 (10 Fri and Sat). **Closed:** 25 to 30 Dec. **Meals:** alc (main courses £15.50 to £19). Set L Mon to Fri £12.50 (2 courses) to £22.50, Set D £24.50 (3 courses). **Service:** not inc. **Details:** Cards accepted. 70 seats. 40 seats outside. No music. Wheelchair access. Children's portions. Car parking.

## Chiang Mai Kitchen

**Side-street gem**
130a High Street, Oxford, OX1 4DH
Tel no: (01865) 202233
www.chiangmaikitchen.co.uk
Thai | £26
Cooking score: 1

You will find this restaurant tucked down a tiny alley just off the High Street. Expect competently cooked, largely familiar Thai dishes made with decent ingredients; perhaps Thai toast with minced pork and Thai herbs, served with a sweet chilli relish or crispy fried rolls stuffed with vermicelli and mixed vegetables and served with a sweet and sour plum sauce, followed by whole fresh fish cooked in coconut curry with lime leaves and Thai herbs, garnished with fresh chillies. There is a lengthy, separate vegetarian menu, while desserts range from ice cream (including several organic options) to steamed sticky rice with cashew nuts and banana. Wines from £12.50 a bottle.

Open: all week 12 to 2.30, 6 to 10.30. Closed: Christmas, New Year, Easter. Meals: alc (main courses £7.50 to £12.50). Service: not inc. Details: Cards accepted. 65 seats. Air-con. No music. Wheelchair access.

## Gee's
Modern food and glitz in the conservatory
61 Banbury Road, Oxford, OX2 6PE
Tel no: (01865) 553540
www.gees-restaurant.co.uk
Modern British | £30
Cooking score: 2

Housed in a dramatic Victorian conservatory that was originally the Gee family's floristry business, this restaurant has become an Oxford landmark over the years. Contemporary style defines the interior, with vivid modern art on the walls, live jazz every Sunday night and a mood that is modishly cosmopolitan. The kitchen makes use of meat from owner Jeremy Mogford's Oxfordshire farm as well as seafood sent over from his brother's business in Jersey. Menus ring the seasonal changes with pea and goats' cheese risotto ahead of veal burger with seared foie gras, fried egg and chips or roast skate with lyonnaise potatoes and caper butter. There is also a weekly 'star dish' (grilled lobster with wilted spinach and tomato compote, for example), and proceedings conclude with desserts such as vanilla pannacotta with strawberry consommé. The trendily eclectic wine list opens with a fistful of house selections from £10.50 (£3.95 a glass).
Chef/s: Michael Wright. Open: Mon to Fri 12 to 2.30, 6.30 to 11.30, Sat 12 to 11.30, Sun 12 to 10.30. Closed: 27 and 28 Dec. Meals: alc (main courses L £10 to £20, D £14 to £20). Set L (exc Sun) £12.95 (2 courses) to £14.95, Set D £22. Service: not inc. Details: Cards accepted. 80 seats. 40 seats outside. Air-con. Wheelchair access. Music. Children's portions.

## Lemon Tree
Lively brasserie with Mediterranean overtones
268 Woodstock Road, Oxford, OX2 7NW
Tel no: (01865) 311936
www.thelemontreeoxford.co.uk
Mediterranean | £30
New Chef

Sunny Mediterranean echoes waft through this animated brasserie in the Summertown district of the city. Wicker chairs, verdant horticultural displays and mustard-yellow walls set the tone in the split-level dining room, and there's a gravelled courtyard garden for alfresco meals. Ross Duncan is the new man at the stoves and he is not about to make any major changes in the kitchen. Carefully sourced produce (especially fish) remains the starting point for concise menus with a cosmopolitan drift. Seared pigeon with violet potatoes and chorizo oil could open proceedings ahead of fillet of sea bass with mussels, clams and white wine butter sauce or slow-roast free-range duck leg with Asian vegetables and spiced noodle broth. A fistful of desserts promises exoticism in the shape of, perhaps, coconut and lemongrass rice pudding with fresh mango. Australian house wines are £10.90 (£2.95 a glass).
Chef/s: Ross Duncan. Open: All week 12 to 11. Closed: 25 Dec. Meals: alc (main courses £9 to £18). Set L Mon to Sat and Set D Sun to Thu £10 (2 courses). Service: 12.5% (optional). Details: Cards accepted. 95 seats. 45 seats outside. Wheelchair access. Music. Children's portions. Car parking.

## ALSO RECOMMENDED
## ▲ Crooked Billet
Newlands Lane, Stoke Row, RG9 5PU
Tel no: (01491) 681048

This ancient pub-restaurant, hidden down a single track lane, is horrendously difficult to find, yet crowds pack in for the atmosphere, regular live music, and the food. The handwritten menu says it all: tuna sashimi with avocado, chilli salsa, crispy capers and oriental dressing (£6.80) is a typical starter, while mains take in grilled local Old Spot pork chop with black pudding, seared foie gras, home-cured pickled cabbage and red wine jus (£17.50). Desserts include homely rhubarb crumble and custard or rich dark Belgian chocoalte mousse with clotted cream. Around 50 wines from £15.95. Open all week.

## ▌Tadpole Bridge
### Trout at Tadpole Bridge
**Glamorous revamp**
Tadpole Bridge, SN7 8RF
Tel no: (01367) 870382
www.troutinn.co.uk
Gastropub | £25
Cooking score: 2
🛏 £30

The setting – on the banks of the river Thames – may be traditional but the food at this recently refurbished pub fizzes with fashionable flourishes. Experienced hoteliers, Gareth and Helen Pugh, took over in 2006 and have worked wonders with the seventeenth-century stone building, upgrading the bedrooms, revamping the restaurant and reinvigorating chef Robbie Ellis. Expect starters like sautéed king scallops with pan-fried chorizo, puréed shallots and rosemary jus or carpaccio of seared beef with horseradish crème fraîche, before roast rump of lamb with herb lentils and red wine jus or roast suckling pig with braised root vegetables, baked apple and black pudding. Look also to the chalkboard for Cornish-sourced seafood specials like baked whole bream with warm green bean and rocket salad. Finish with rich chocolate tart or a plate of local cheeses. A serious wine list opens with good-value bottles from £12
**Chef/s:** Robert Ellis. **Open:** Mon to Sun L 12 to 2, D 7 to 9. **Closed:** 25 Dec and 1 Jan. **Meals:** alc (main courses £11.25 to £17.95). **Service:** not inc. **Details:** Cards accepted. 70 seats. 40 seats outside. No music. Children's portions. Car parking.

## Cooking score

A score of 1 is a significant achievement. The score in any review is based on several meals, incorporating feedback from both our readers and inspectors. As a rough guide, 1 denotes capable cooking with some inconsistencies, rising steadily through different levels of technical expertise, until the scores between 6 and 10 indicate exemplary skills, along with innovation, artistry and ambition. If there is a new chef, we don't score the restaurant for the first year of entry. For further details, please see the scoring section in the introduction to the Guide.

## READERS RECOMMEND
### Feathers Hotel
**Modern British**
Market Street, Woodstock, OX20 1SX
Tel no: (01993) 812291
www.feathers.co.uk
**'Excellent use of local organic ingredients'**

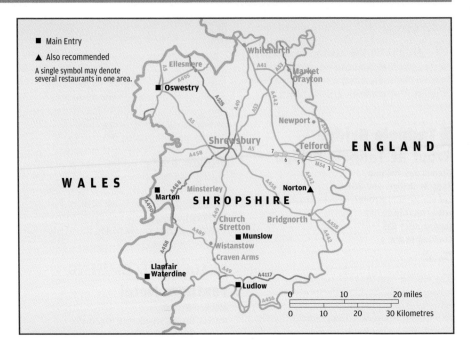

■ Main Entry

▲ Also recommended

A single symbol may denote
several restaurants in one area.

Whitchurch

Ellesmere

Oswestry

Market Drayton

Newport

Shrewsbury

Telford

**ENGLAND**

**WALES**

Minsterley

Norton ▲

Marton ■

**SHROPSHIRE**

Church Stretton

Bridgnorth

■ Munslow

Wistanstow

Craven Arms

Llanfair Waterdine ■

■ Ludlow

0        10        20 miles

0        10        20        30 Kilometres

## ■ Llanfair Waterdine

### Waterdine

**Peaceful views of rolling hills**
Llanfair Waterdine, LD7 1TU
Tel no: (01547) 528214
www.waterdine.com
**Modern British | £31**
**Cooking score: 4**

Standing across from the church, the
sixteenth-century longhouse was originally
built as a drover's inn, the River Teme barely
visible at the bottom of the garden marking
the English-Welsh border at this point.
Although it still has the feel of a pub, with real
ale on tap in the homely bar, Ken Adams
operates it as a country restaurant-with-
rooms. Dinner is three courses from an
ambitious modern menu in which top-quality
local produce is to the fore (beef and lamb
come from surrounding farms) but influences
come from all over. Starters of terrine of Old
Spot pork with black fig and raspberry

chutney, or Cornish crab cannelloni with
chive sauce might be followed by roast turbot
on leek confit with girolle mushrooms, or
pan-fried beef fillet with Dijon mustard sauce.
Accomplished desserts may include Valhrona
chocolate mousse or iced apricot parfait. Wines
are a global selection starting at £15.50, with a
handful by the glass from £2.25.
**Chef/s:** Ken Adams. **Open:** Wed to Sun L 12 to 1.30,
Tue to Sat D 7 to 9. **Closed:** 1 week autumn, 1 week
spring. **Meals:** Set L Tue to Sat £23.50 (2 courses) to
£30. Set L Sun £20 (3 courses). Set D £30 (3
courses). **Service:** not inc. **Details:** Cards accepted.
24 seats. No music. Car parking.

## Ludlow
# Mr Underhill's
**Consistently high standards**
Dinham Weir, Ludlow, SY8 1EH
Tel no: (01584) 874431
www.mr-underhills.co.uk
**Modern European | £57**
**Cooking score: 7**

Overlooked by Ludlow Castle, this riverside restaurant is in an idyllic location. Described as 'enchanting', from the dining room, guests are privy to captivating views of the tumbling weir and on warm evenings, the courtyard garden provides a fragrant setting for pre-dinner drinks. Chris Bradley continues to win praise for 'food cooked to a consistently high standard'. The seven-course, no-choice (until the dessert) menu demonstrates the care taken with the meal's overall balance of flavour and texture. A canapé of marinated salmon in a delicate cone hones the appetite, while from a spring menu, a vibrant asparagus velouté with chive cream may precede a silky foie gras custard with sweetcorn cream and cep glaze. Fish follows, with maybe a thick chunk of brill encased in a featherlight, crisp spring roll-type wrapper and spiked with ginger and coriander. The main course majors on red meat, such as Mortimer Forest venison, local lamb or butter-soft rosy slices of slow-roasted Marches beef fillet served with an intense braised beef sauce, a miniature ox-cheek cottage pie and a tangle of finely shredded vegetables. A choice of sweets, after a tiny fruit sponge pre-dessert, follows with a deeply dark hot chocolate tart exactly living up to its name, while the accompanying roasted sweet pepper ice cream works surprisingly well. Excellent bread and unusual fruit 'marmalades' are served with the cheese. Impeccable service is under the watchful eye of Judy Bradley who runs the front-of-house with a self-assured efficiency. She also shares knowledgeable advice about a carefully selected list of wines, including an impressive selection of dessert and half-bottles. House wines start at £14.50.

**Chef/s:** Chris Bradley. **Open:** Wed to Sun D only 7.15pm to 8.15pm. **Closed:** Christmas, 1 week summer, 1 week autumn. **Meals:** Set D £45. **Service:** not inc. **Details:** Cards accepted. 32 seats. 32 seats outside. No music. No mobile phones. Children allowed. Car parking.

## ALSO RECOMMENDED
## ▲ The Clive
Bromfield, Ludlow, SY8 2JR
Tel no: (01584) 856565

Originally an eighteenth-century farmhouse, the Clive is now a popular pitstop on the A49 just north of Ludlow. The bright contemporary interior houses a bar with adjoining family-friendly dining room and a more formal restaurant. The menu might start off with Wenlock Farm cured beef with baby beets (£5.95) followed by roast pork fillet and Hereford apples with butter mash, turnips and cider cream (12.95). House wines start at £11.85. Open for lunch and dinner every day.

## ▲ Old Downton Lodge
Downton on the Rock, Ludlow, SY8 2HU
Tel no: (0845) 838 6334
www.olddowntonlodge.co.uk

Martyn and Jayne Emson have swapped the higgledy-piggledy Jolly Frog at nearby Leintwardine for a group of stylishly converted farm buildings set around a kitchen garden. Typical dishes are tender roast rabbit with apples and Calvados, and pink roast rack of lamb with a hotpot garnish (root vegetables). Seared scallops with roasted asparagus and chive butter sauce featured on a spring menu and were perfectly cooked. Desserts might include an Amaretto crème brûlée with lavender biscuits, and banoffee pannacotta with ristretto sauce and chocolate ice cream. House wine is £13.95 a bottle and all wines on the list are available by the glass.

## ∎ Marton
### Sun Inn
Calm and contemporary
Marton, SY21 8JP
Tel no: (01938) 561211
www.suninn.biz
**Modern British | £23**
Cooking score: 2

Ⅴ £30

Helen Short's menu is centred around comfortable favourites and classic flavour combinations, with the occasional less familiar offering (a starter of crab brik with tomato and chilli sauce, for example) thrown in for good measure. Or there could include double-baked blue cheese soufflé followed by butter-roast fillet steak with wild mushrooms and shallots or calf's liver and bacon with sage and onion gravy. Desserts continue in a similar vein: perhaps baked blueberry cheesecake or pannacotta with strawberry and black pepper soup. Wash it down with wines sourced from small, independent growers around the world, priced from £11.90.
**Chef/s:** Helen Short. **Open:** Wed to Sun L 12 to 2, Tue to Sat D 7 to 9.30. **Meals:** alc exc Sun L (main courses £10.50 to £16). Set L Sun £10.50 (2 courses) to £13.50.. **Service:** not inc. **Details:** Cards accepted. 50 seats. 8 seats outside. No music. Wheelchair access. Children's portions. Car parking.

## ∎ Munslow
### The Crown
Sound cooking in a Tudor inn
Munslow, SY7 9ET
Tel no: (01584) 841205
www.crowncountryinn.co.uk
**Modern British | £28**
Cooking score: 3

£5 OFF ⊨ Ⅴ £30

Standing beneath Wenlock Edge in the Corve valley, this Grade II listed building boasts a wealth of original features. The kitchen is a champion of local produce, though it looks across Europe and beyond for culinary inspiration, coming up with starters of black pudding crostini with tomato fondue and dry-cured bacon from Wenlock Edge Farm, or griddled monkfish medallions with fennel and orange marmalade. Mains, meanwhile, feature griddled loin of Muckleton Old Spot pork with rösti potato, chorizo and a creamy basil and red onion sauce alongside home-smoked chicken breast with mustard creamed leeks, fondant potato and balsamic jus, or Devon sea bass served on a fricassée of rice-grain pasta, crayfish and basil with sun-dried tomato pesto and salsa verde. To finish, there's layered chocolate pavé with fruit compote, or pecan and treacle tart with bitter orange ice cream and Herefordshire clotted cream. Prices on the straightforward wine list start at £12.50.
**Chef/s:** Richard Arnold. **Open:** Tue to Sun L 12 to 2, Tue to Sat D 6.45 to 9 (6.30 to 7.45 Sun). **Closed:** 25 Dec. **Meals:** alc (main courses £10.50 to £17). Bar and light L menu available. **Service:** not inc. **Details:** Cards accepted. 70 seats. 20 seats outside. No music. Wheelchair access. Children's portions. Car parking.

## ALSO RECOMMENDED
### ▲ Hundred House Hotel
Bridgnorth Road, Norton, TF11 9EE
Tel no: (01952) 730353

The Philips family run this bar, brasserie, restaurant and hotel with convincing aplomb, delivering dishes such as rich chicken liver pâté (£4.95) and grilled beef fillet served with smoked bacon, blue cheese risotto and beef jus (£18.95). Daily specials may include casserole of monkfish, and salmon and scallops with lobster and tarragon bisque (£18.95). In addition, there's a fine selection of beers, a children's menu and even a herb garden. Wines from £13.95. Accommodation. Open all week.

## Oswestry

### Sebastians

Gallic delight
45 Willow Street, Oswestry, SY11 1AQ
Tel no: (01691) 655444
www.sebastians-hotel.co.uk
French | £32
Cooking score: 3

Tina Pemberton

Sebastian Fisher delivers a thoroughly French experience. The four-course menu provides sensible choices within a small range. Kicking off with a soup, which might be cauliflower with truffle oil, a dinner offered roast monkfish, magret de canard or steak as main courses – vegetarians are especially invited to ask to be catered for, a nice touch not too common in the *patrie*. Sadly, unavailable on Saturdays, the no-choice Menu du Marche is excellent value and, with a dessert like 'Brownie' au chocolat, sorbet au gin, there seems to be no holding back on complexity or interest on this economy option. Apart from having to turn a blind eye to odd seasonal infelicities – during May, rhubarb good, strawberries bad - what appears on the plate consistently shows good technical skills and originality. Understandably, France receives greatest exposure in *nos vins* but there is also surprising global reach; prices are fair, from £15.95.

**Chef/s:** Mark Sebastian Fisher. **Open:** Tue to Sat D 6.30 to 9.30. **Meals:** Set D £32, Set D Tue to Fri £16.95. **Service:** not inc. **Details:** Cards accepted. 35 seats. 20 seats outside. No mobile phones. Wheelchair access. Music. Children's portions. Car parking.

### Where do you eat out?

Amaya, Zuma, Hakkasan or any new fusion Asian restaurant I hear good things about. There really is no point in going out for pasta or steak so I seek out places that are modern and challenging. Seafood is a test even for the best chefs, so if I know there's a star in the kitchen, that's what I order.

### Who's your favourite chef?

Antipodean or California chefs who specialise in the east-meets-west equation, such as Peter Gordon and Wolfgang Puck.

### What's your favourite wine?

'I need a holiday!'. Joking aside, I would choose an excellent Pinot Noir from the Pemberton Estate (sadly I'm not related) in Western Australia for its aromatic nose and versatility. For coiffing nightly, an Albarino from Galicia in Spain is unbeatable with its gorgeously tropical and fragrant bouquet. Finally, as a Sauvignon person I just love a Pouilly Fumé from one of France's top growers, Patrice Moreux.

### Who would your ideal dinner guests be?

I like people who are entertaining and make me laugh so I would gather some big personalities who, I am positive, are epicureans as well as great raconteurs. Here, in my opinion, are four of the best to be going on with – Matt Lucas, David Walliams, Woody Allen and Ruby Wax. I might even include my husband, who still makes me laugh after 25 years!

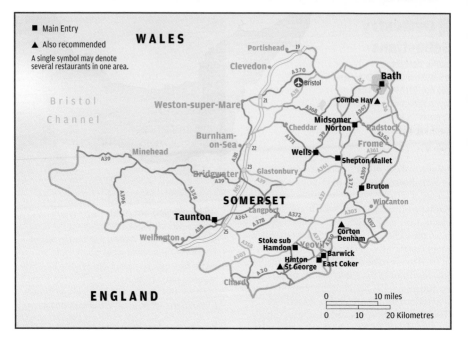

## Barwick

### Little Barwick House

**Exquisitely crafted food**
Barwick, BA22 9TD
Tel no: (01935) 423902
www.littlebarwickhouse.co.uk
**Modern British | £36**
**Cooking score: 6**

Tim and Emma Ford are long-serving custodians of this Georgian dower house, which they continue to run as an enchanting restaurant-with-rooms. Inside it feels serene, ever-so-English and refined in a domestic sort of way. Views of the impressive garden and grounds may temporarily divert diners from the essential business in the elegant dining room, where Tim Ford's confident cooking is the main attraction. Regular visitors value the reassuring consistency of the food and its highly skilled execution. Local ingredients and produce from other corners of the West Country form

the backbone of each day's menus: pan-fried Lyme Bay scallops are served as a starter with roast butternut squash purée, crispy bacon and truffle oil, while a pressed terrine of local ham hock and foie gras is accompanied by pear chutney. Moving on, there might be rump of Somerset lamb with girolles, asparagus and rosemary jus or a medallion of Cornish sea bass in company with basil crushed potatoes and chive sauce. Desserts are impressively crafted assemblages along the lines of coffee crème caramel partnered by dark chocolate sponge, chocolate and Dalwhinnie whisky ice cream. Emma Ford oversees front-of-house with a degree of sharp, self-assured professionalism. The wine list is a glorious collection of mouthwatering names to tempt oenophiles and everyday drinkers alike. Bottles are grouped together by style ('zesty, crisp and refreshing whites') and there are prime pickings to be had from France, Italy and Australia in particular. Half-bottles are plentiful, and house selections start at £15.95 (£5 a glass) for a pair of little gems from the Languedoc.

Chef/s: Tim Ford. Open: Wed to Sun L 12 to 2, Tue to Sat D 7 to 9 (9.30 Sat). Closed: 2 weeks after Christmas. Meals: Set L Wed to Sat £19.95 (2 courses) to £23.95, Set L Sun £25.95, Set D £36.95. Service: not inc. Details: Cards accepted. 40 seats. 12 seats outside. Air-con. No music. No mobile phones. Children's portions. Car parking.

## ▌Bath

# Bath Priory

**Understated elegance**
Weston Road, Bath, BA1 2XT
Tel no: (01225) 331922
www.thebathpriory.co.uk
**Modern French | £52**
Cooking score: 6

🍷 🚗 V

Built in 1835, in a beguiling mix of Gothic styling and Bath stone, the Priory makes an inviting retreat from the city centre. The dining room, with its plush seating and hunting prints, doesn't seem to have changed for decades – in marked contrast to the thoroughly modern spirit of Chris Horridge's innovative and refined cooking. There's a definite hedgerow theme going on – lamb is served with layers of different roots and 'hedge herbs and flowers of the moment'; foie gras with sycamore sap and cow parsley purée; grilled bass with St John's wort emulsion – but it's not mere whimsy. Slow-poached saddle of fallow deer, for example, is bolstered by the intense, jammy flavours of a liquorice reduction and the sweetness of lightly caramelised fennel, while rhubarb and pain d'épices add an elegant, sweet-sharp edge to pork belly. The attention to detail carries through to desserts: a deep-amber caramel soufflé, made with a proper bittersweet caramel and served with a sharp lime sorbet, delivered some knockout flavours, while 'sorbets and ices – cones, wafer, pollen and paper' is a tour de force in itself. The wine list is exceptional, with a decent selection of organically produced bottles and a wide range of half-bottles. Unusual producers with an idiosyncratic approach to oenology are championed. House selections start at £17.50.

Chef/s: Chris Horridge. Open: all week 12 to 1.45, 7 to 9.30. Meals: Set L Mon to Sat £20 (2 courses) to £25, Set L Sun £30, Set D £55 to £70. Service: not inc. Details: Cards accepted. 64 seats. 20 seats outside. Separate bar. Wheelchair access.

★NEW ENTRY★
# Blackstones

**Modern, city-centre restaurant**
2-3 Queen Street, Bath, BA1 1HE
Tel no: (01225) 444403
www.blackstonefood.co.uk
**British | £26**
Cooking score: 1

£5 OFF  £30 ⬇

Clean, modern simplicity is the theme at the Blackstones' pretty Georgian town house looking on to a quaint cobbled street (and opposite their now well-established epicurean take-away). The subtle grey and wood décor is enlivened by splashes of acid green and fuschia pink tabletops, while a team, led by Rebecca Blackstone, delivers familiar classics with a twist. Pan-fried bream comes with mushy peas, tartare sauce and, of course, proper chips, and puddings are as homely as a hearty seasonal fruit crumble with a freshly made creamy vanilla custard. A balanced selection of 24 reasonably priced wines starts at £12.50 (£3.50 by the glass), or check out the Somerset Pomona, a blend of juice and cider brandy that proves a fine partner for some choice West Country cheeses.

Chef/s: Rebecca Blackstone. Open: Tue to Fri L 12 to 3, D 6 to 10, Sat L 10 to 4, D 6 to 10, Sun L 11 to 4. Closed: Mondays. Meals: alc (main courses £12 to £15.50), Set L £14.50 (2 courses), £16.50 (3 courses) Set D £25 (3 courses). Service: 10%. Details: Cards accepted. 55 seats. Music. Children's portions.

## Cavendish Restaurant, Dukes Hotel

Grade-I-listed Palladian town house
Great Pulteney Street, Bath, BA2 4DN
Tel no: (01225) 787963
www.dukesbath.co.uk
**Modern British | £32**
**Cooking score: 3**

Dukes Hotel epitomises the grand Georgian style for which Bath is famous. Not that the building's original occupants would recognise much about the menus offered in the hotel's Cavendish restaurant: starters of quail breast with spring onion hash, dandelion salad and poached egg, or seared hand-dived scallops with crisp black ham, pea and shoot salad and pea purée showcase the kitchen's inventive, modern style. Main courses continue in similar vein with wild sea bass on a fricassee of samphire and spring vegetables with native lobster; beef fillet with young turnips, leeks and onions; or poached-then-roasted spring chicken with morels, asparagus, Jersey Royals, foie gras and sultanas with a chicken jus. Dessert might be exotic coconut pannacotta with lychee sorbet and roasted banana tart, or perhaps a rhubarb themed creation comprising cannelloni, jelly and a rhubarb and custard ice cream. The compact wine list opens with French house selections at £16.
**Chef/s:** Richard Allen. **Open:** Tue to Sat L 12 to 2.30, D 6.30 to 10. **Meals:** Set L £12.95 (2 courses) to £15.95. Set D £42.95 (3 courses). **Service:** not inc. **Details:** Cards accepted. 40 seats. 40 seats outside. No mobile phones. Music. Children's portions.

★NEW ENTRY★

## Demuths

International inspiration for veggie dishes
2 North Parade Passage, Bath, BA1 1NX
Tel no: (01225) 446059
www.demuths.co.uk
**Vegetarian | £20**
**Cooking score: 1**

Set in a tiny Georgian townhouse, just round the corner from the Abbey, Demuth's is Bath's typically refined answer to the problem of where to eat if you're vegetarian. Cool, calm colours, high ceilings and big windows help give it a spacious feel. The menu, running from breakfast through to dinner, plunders the Middle East and Asia for its inspiration, producing vibrant, colourful dishes that are naturally vegetarian – and in many cases vegan. Hence you might find Marrakesh tagine with saffron herb couscous, charred brinjal with tomato and mango chutney or a beautifully composed mezze plate of labneh balls, fuls Mesdames, quinoa salad and marinated olives. Puddings are equally inventive and include a showstopping dark chocolate fudge cake that, remarkably, turns out to be vegan. Service is willing but can be slow. A good range of organic wines and beers rounds things off.
**Chef/s:** Helen Lawrence. **Open:** all week 12 to 3.30, 6 to 10. **Closed:** 24 to 26 Dec, 31 Dec, 1 Jan. **Meals:** Set L £9.95 (2 courses, Mon to Wed only), Set D £16.95 (2 courses, Mon to Wed only). **Service:** not inc. **Details:** Cards accepted. 40 seats. No mobile phones. Music. Children's portions.

## The Dower House, Royal Crescent

**A luxurious elegant atmosphere**
16 Royal Crescent, Bath, BA1 2LS
Tel no: (01225) 823333
www.royalcrescent.co.uk
**Modern British | £50**
**New Chef**

🍷 🍴 ✓

One of the most elegant locations in Bath, The Dower House (formerly Pimpernel's) is a beautiful Georgian stone building in the gardens of the Royal Crescent Hotel. At the time of inspection, the kitchen was in the middle of change with the departure of Steven Blake, to be replaced in a matter of weeks by Phil Dixon – too late for us to make a return visit. This left sous chefs in temporary charge, but the standard of food did not appear to have suffered. The food perfectly fits the surroundings (revamped since our visit) with modern, predominantly English, classics in intricate and innovative style, with starters including a delicate cannelloni of crab with a rich shellfish sauce. Main choices, at inspection, included a 'meltingly tender' best end of lamb under a well-flavoured herb crust, with red onion Tatin and glazed baby turnips. Familiar classics dominate the desserts, but the presentation is stunning – a perfect rhubarb crumble soufflé given a fashionable edge by a mascarpone smoothie, grenadine compote and a ring of light-as-air macaroon. An extensive and impressive wine list comes with prices to match, but with several under £30 there's enough choice at all levels.
**Chef/s:** Phil Dixon. **Open:** all week L 12.30 to 2, D 7 to 10. **Meals:** Set L £20 (2 courses) to £25 (3 courses), Set D £45 (2 courses) to £55 (3 courses). Light L and bar menus available. **Service:** not inc. **Details:** Cards accepted. 70 seats. 45 seats outside. Air-con. Separate bar. Wheelchair access. Music. Children's portions. Car parking.

## FishWorks

**Nautical dining room**
6 Green Street, Bath, BA1 2JY
Tel no: (01225) 448707
www.fishworks.co.uk
**Seafood | £32**
**Cooking score: 2**

✓

Ten years on, the first of Mitchell Tonks' seafood chain is still turning out some exemplary cooking. A printed menu features every kind of fishy classic, from smoked salmon to fish stew, but it's the blackboard specials that offer the most interest. Here the emphasis is on the day's catch, simply grilled or fried, and there's always the sociable option of ordering a whole large fish to share. It's a simple formula, well executed. Fried squid with aïoli had real character and flavour at inspection, while grilled sea bass with rosemary and sea salt had been perfectly timed for a succulent, crisp-skinned result. Puddings are more than just an afterthought, as a well-made lemon tart testified. Although the focus of the short, well-chosen wine list is on whites, there are a few fish-friendly reds too. House wines start at £15.95.
**Chef/s:** Neil Roach. **Open:** Tue to Sat 12 to 2.30, 6 to 10.30. **Closed:** bank hols and day after bank hols. **Meals:** alc (main courses £13 to £50). **Service:** not inc. **Details:** Cards accepted. 50 seats. 12 seats outside. Air-con. Music. Children's portions.

## The Garrick's Head

**A gastropub that puts on a performance**
7-8 St Johns Place, Bath, BA1 1ET
Tel no: (01225) 318368
**Modern British | £30**
**Cooking score: 3**

Following on from the success of the King William (see entry), Charlie and Amanda Digney's historic city centre inn has a similar feel and simple style. Charlie Digney is constantly striving to source as much local produce as possible, even growing some of his own vegetables for his pubs, and goes to great lengths to buy in whole animals so he can do his own butchery and utilise every part of the beast by slow cooking. Comforting cauliflower cheese with greens, fiery devilled kidneys on toast, and ox tongue served with Puy lentils and a piquant green sauce are typical choices, but increasingly popular are dishes to share – rib of beef with greens, anchovy and roast potatoes being one of the most requested. Traditional English desserts of treacle tart with cream bring things to a reassuringly old school finish, as does a splendid cheeseboard containing up to five truckles from West Country cheesemakers. Almost 20 wines by the glass will encourage mixing and matching, although a pint of well-kept local real ale is a fine alternative. The list takes its lead from France, but Italy, Spain and the southern hemisphere get a look in too. Prices open at £11.50.

**Chef/s:** Hugh Dennis-Jones, Rufus Hanson and Charlie Digney. **Open:** all week L 12 to 3, Mon to Sat D 6 to 11.30. **Closed:** 25 and 26 Dec. **Meals:** alc (main courses £10 to £17). Set L Sun £27.50 (4 courses). Bar menu available. **Service:** not inc. **Details:** Cards accepted. 50 seats. 24 seats outside. Music. Children's portions.

## King William

**Seasonal specialities and intelligent cooking**
36 Thomas Street, Bath, BA1 5NN
Tel no: (01225) 428096
www.kingwilliampub.com
**British | £25**
**Cooking score: 3**

£5 OFF  🍷  £30

This tiny pub on Bath's busy London Road may seem an unlikely place of pilgrimage but people come from all over, squeezing round a table in the bar or eating in the small, elegant upstairs dining rooms. The draw is Charlie Digney's take on British cooking. Based on a proper appreciation of our culinary heritage and an uncompromising devotion to local ingredients, it delivers food that feels absolutely right for the time and place: in winter perhaps soused fish with kale, beetroot and horseradish, or pot-roast partridge with goose-fat roast potatoes; in summer, Cornish

crab with fennel and rocket, or wood pigeon with potato gratin and runner beans. This close focus on what's in season delivers big flavours on the plate. English asparagus with spring herb salad was an object lesson in culinary minimalism, the warmth of the asparagus breathing life into a scattering of young herbs. Slow-roast shoulder of lamb combined crisp skin, tender meat and a refreshing broad bean and leek broth. Puddings sometimes lack refinement, though a well-made lemon posset hits the spot. Well-kept local beers are supplemented by a keenly priced wine list.

**Chef/s:** Adie Ware. **Open:** all week L 12 to 3, Mon to Sat D 6 to 10. **Closed:** 24 and 25 Dec. **Meals:** alc (main courses £9 to £18). Set D £22.50 (2 courses) to £26.50. Bar menu available. **Service:** not inc. **Details:** Cards accepted. 60 seats. Music. Children's portions.

## Olive Tree at The Queensberry Hotel

**Modern British food in a stylish, urban setting**
4-7 Russel Street, Bath, BA1 2QF
Tel no: (01225) 447928
www.thequeensberry.co.uk
**Modern British | £41**
**Cooking score: 3**

£5 OFF  🍷  🍽  ♈

Olive Tree is the stylish basement restaurant below the Queensberry Hotel, in a typical Georgian Bath terrace, just minutes from the famous Royal Crescent. Cool, neutral colours, oak floors, white linen and subtle lighting give an air of calm and gentle formality, matched by a team of attentive staff. Chef Marc Salmon's predominantly modern English menu is also splashed with Mediterranean touches and makes imaginative use of local, seasonal produce in modern dishes with classic combinations. Starters may include a ham hock and apple cake with mushy peas and cider dressing; while the mains focus on traditional meats, such as West Country lamb and Aberdeen Angus beef, plus excellent local seafood – though a fillet of Cornish sea bass on risotto of crab, basil and leeks, tried at inspection, showed a rather heavy touch and was lacking in flavour. Typical desserts are fashionable classics, such as a faultless white chocolate pannacotta with pomegranate jelly paired with a rhubarb and hazelnut shortcake. An extensive wine list, grouped by flavour for easy food matching, has pricey peaks but house wines start at £15, with more than 30 by the small or large glass (from £3.75 to £10.50).

**Chef/s:** Marc Salmon. **Open:** Tue to Sun L 12 to 2, all week D 7 to 10. **Meals:** alc (main courses £15.75 to £25). Set L £15 (2 courses) to £17.50. **Service:** not inc. **Details:** Cards accepted. 60 seats. Air-con. No mobile phones. Music. Children's portions.

## ALSO RECOMMENDED

### ▲ Yak Yeti Yak

12a Argyle Street, Bath, BA2 4BQ
Tel no: (01225) 442299
www.yakyetiyak.co.uk

The name might raise a smile, but with chefs from Nepal, natural ingredients and vegetarians catered for properly, Yak Yeti Yak takes it food very seriously. Start with spiced potato and sesame salad served in a poppadom basket (£3.90) or grilled strips of lamb marinated in traditional spices and served with chutney (£4.50), then chicken or pork stir-fried in a blend of spices with a light gravy (£6.90) and finish with creamed saffron yogurt with marined oranges (£3.50). Set menus for a minimum of six people start from £12.50 per head. House wines are £11.50. Open all week.

### Please send us your feedback

To register your opinion about any restaurant listed in the Guide, or a new restaurant that you wish to bring to our attention, please visit the web address at the bottom of the page. Your feedback informs the content of the book and will be used to compile next year's reviews.

## ■ Bruton

### Bruton House

**A likeable young team**
2-4 High Street, Bruton, BA10 0AA
Tel no: (01749) 813395
www.brutonhouse.co.uk
**Modern British | £35**
**Cooking score: 6**

It's hard to miss this striking, blue-painted house in the centre of Bruton, although the 'nasty' one-way system might mean another lap of the town to find a parking space. Once inside, a sympathetic modern makeover has created a light look of creams and whites, offsetting the odd dark beam, and it makes a fitting backdrop to James Andrews and Scott Eggleton's ambitious cooking. Their repertoire moves along gently, changing with the seasons and offering plenty of original ideas and novel presentations. The focus, however, is on sound culinary principles and traditional cooking methods, backed up by well-sourced raw materials – much of them local. There are plenty of attention grabbing ideas among the choices offered, though. Starters have included chilled rock oysters and pickled walnuts, or warm Somerset goats' cheese with red beetroot sorbet, as well as simple asparagus with soft-boiled quails' eggs. You might come across main courses of loin of rabbit with smoked bacon, ravioli and consommé, or red mullet and Mediterranean vegetables, with peanut parfait served alongside caramelized banana and peanut brittle a well-considered dessert. It that's too sweet, there are West Country cheeses. The combination of good-value lunchtime carte and set menu priced for two, three and four courses at dinner is worthy of note. Service is 'friendly and cheerful' and a delightfully straightforward wine list is full of good ideas and reasonable prices. Some 15 come by the glass from £3 to £6, and by the bottle from £13.50.

**Chef/s:** Scott Eggleton and James Andrews. **Open:** Tue to Sat L 12 to 2, D 7 to 9.30. **Closed:** 2 weeks Dec, 2 weeks Aug. **Meals:** alc L (main courses £12 to

£15). Set D £31 (2 courses) to £46.50. **Service:** not inc. **Details:** Cards accepted. 34 seats. No music. No mobile phones. Wheelchair access. Children's portions.

## ALSO RECOMMENDED
### ▲ The Wheatsheaf
Combe Hay, BA2 7EG
Tel no: (01225) 833504
www.wheatsheafcombehay.com

The pretty village of Combe Hay is really on the map thanks to the Wheatsheaf – a classy restaurant carved out of a former down-at-heel country pub. Reports have been consistently good, although the appointment of a new chef after our inspection has resulted in an Also Recommended entry this year – 'the new owners have certainly been doing all the right things up till now'. Previously, the kitchen was noted for a lively, seasonally changing menu, using local produce where possible, delivering 'tender' slices of pigeon breast with bean sprouts and a raspberry jus dotted with fresh raspberries, and a perfectly cooked turbot fillet served with a creamy herb mash, salsify and sorrel. A lively wine list has an appealing mix of largely European wines and a wide price range, with house wines from £12.95 and 13 wines by the glass from £3.50. More reports please.

### ▲ Queens Arms
Corton Denham, DT9 4LR
Tel no: (01963) 220317
www.thequeensarms.com

It's location deep within the heart of the countryside means this is perfect for those who've built up an appetite while walking or cycling, or those looking for traditional meals from local produce. Start your evening with the seared duck with orange and pear salad (£5) then move on to the Queens Arms jugged hare with roasted winter root vegetables and mash (£10.90). End on a high note with the gooey chocolate pudding with chocolate-chip cream (£4.20) Sunday lunch options include roast rib of beef, Yorkshire pudding, winter roasties, garden veg and

trimmings (£12.70). A generous kids menu is also available. Wines start at £10.90. Accommodation. Open all week.

## ■ East Coker
## Helyar Arms
Hunting, catching or growing?
Moor Lane, East Coker, BA22 9JR
Tel no: (01935) 862332
www.helyar-arms.co.uk
**Gastropub | £26**
**Cooking score: 1**
🍴 ✔ £30

The food at the Helyar Arms demonstrates devotion to the locality, summarised in the current owners' request, 'If you're great at hunting, catching or growing things... we'll be glad to take them off your hands in exchange for a few drinks'. So, you'll find rabbits and pigeons, vegetables, eggs and cider all coming from the Somerset countryside. A great range of basic grills, home-made ice creams and West Country cheeses add up to that still relatively rare find, a pub with real food, all reinforced by the wines. Starting at £12.50, forty-plus carefully chosen bottles are offered in two glass sizes, a fine example to be followed and to be cherished. The Guide has been told that the pub is currently up for sale, so we'd like to hear about any changes from readers.
**Chef/s:** Mathieu Eke. **Open:** Mon to Sat 12 to 2.30, 6.30 to 9.30, Sun 12 to 4.30, 6.30 to 9. **Closed:** 25 Dec. **Meals:** alc (main courses L £7 to £10, D £8 to £16). Bar menu available. **Service:** not inc. **Details:** Cards accepted. 95 seats. 40 seats outside. Wheelchair access. Music. Children's portions. Car parking.

## ALSO RECOMMENDED

### ▲ Lord Poulett Arms

High Street, Hinton St George, TA17 8SE
Tel no: (01460) 73149
www.lordpoulettarms.com

The tiny village of Hinton St George can take some finding, but when you get there this revitalised restaurant-cum-pub with rooms is a pleasant surprise. It delivers a skilful blend of the old and the new with the décor period and the food contemporary. Purple sprouting broccoli and Devon blue cheese soup (£4.40) and wild nettle and Somerset smoked streaky bacon risotto (£6) reveal the strong seasonal bias of the kitchen, as does port braised local hare with parsnip purée (£14.75). End with a selection of West Country cheeses (£6) or dark chocolate tart with orange mousse (£5.75). Open daily. More reports please.

## ▌Midsomer Norton

### Moody Goose at the Old Priory

Assured modern cooking in a medieval priory
17-19 Church Square, Midsomer Norton, BA3 2HX
Tel no: (01761) 416784
www.theoldpriory.co.uk
**Modern European | £35**
**Cooking score: 4**

🍽 ∀

Stephen and Victoria Shore's current home is this refashioned twelfth-century priory in the centre of prosperous Midsomer Norton. It is a delightful warren of a place, with flagstone floors, ancient windows and original watercolours in the dining room. Menus follow the seasons and Stephen Shore draws heavily on local supplies as well as making fruitful use of pickings from the hotel's walled kitchen garden. A lot of care and effort is clearly involved in each dish and presentation is classy — but never at the expense of intrinsic natural flavour or cohesion. The combination of scallops with parsnip purée is one of Shore's favourite culinary devices, but other ideas seek to surprise: foie gras parfait takes on a distinctly oriental complexion when partnered by a pineapple spring roll and sweet soy sauce, while roast brill could be served as a main course with braised borlotti beans, chorizo and truffle cream. Other star turns have included an assiette of lamb involving braised shoulder, roast rump and pan-fried sweetbreads served with Scotch broth and rosemary potatoes. The concise dinner menu concludes enticingly with sweet offerings like passion-fruit and vodka pannacotta with poached kumquats or a trio of caramel desserts. Victoria Shore heads a friendly team out front, and the well-spread global wine list kicks off with nine decent house selections from £15 (£4 a glass).
**Chef/s:** Stephen Shore. **Open:** Mon to Sat 12 to 1.30, 7 to 9.30. **Closed:** Christmas, bank hols exc Good Fri. **Meals:** alc D (main courses £19 to £21). Set L £16 (2 courses) to £20, Set D £25. **Service:** not inc. **Details:** Cards accepted. 32 seats. No mobile phones. Music. Children allowed. Car parking.

## ▌Shepton Mallet

### Sharpham Park, Charlton House Hotel

Fresh, fashionable and fastidiuous
Shepton Mallet, BA4 4PR
Tel no: (01749) 342008
www.charltonhouse.com
**Modern British | £50**
**Cooking score: 5**

£5 OFF 🍷 🍽 ∀

Comfort and seemingly effortlessly vintage chic is what Charlton House is all about. Not so surprising when you realise it is owned by Roger Saul, founder of Mulberry, who is now a Somerset farmer specialising in the UK's only organically produced spelt. Spelt features ingeniously on the menu at Charlton House's conservatory restaurant, where nonchalantly placed antiquarian cookery books jostle for position with plants and intriguing objets d'art. Elisha Carter brings a refreshingly original blend of the highly seasonal, avant-garde technique and a certain West Indian insouciance, along with his classical training at

Le Manoir aux Quat' Saisons. Head to tail, field to fork dining is very much to Carter's taste: own-made prosciutto of venison served with carpaccio of venison, pickled mushrooms and the delectable detail of venison Scotch egg with quail's egg, say, slow-roasted loin of Sharpham Park lamb with braised artichoke and cassoulet beans made deeply savoury with house-cured bacon. Spelt sceptics should try fragrant herb-infused pearl spelt risotto with impeccable bite. Stand-out dessert is fig tart with warm fig purée and tobacco ice cream, though the more cautious might prefer mandarin cheesecake with orange curd and roasted pine nuts. The wine list flags up a seasonal selection of wines, an appealing approach, and caters well to both novices and oenophiles willing to spend seriously on good vintages; though prices are steep, with house selections from £22.

**Chef/s:** Elisha Carter. **Open:** all week L 12.30 to 2 (2.30 Sun), D 7.30 to 9.30. **Meals:** Set L £22 (2 courses) to £27. Set D £52.50 (3 courses) to £68 (7 courses). **Service:** not inc. **Details:** Cards accepted. 70 seats. 20 seats outside. Air-con. No music. No mobile phones. Wheelchair access. Children's portions. Car parking.

## ALSO RECOMMENDED

### ▲ Blostin's

29-33 Waterloo Road, Shepton Mallet, BA4 5HH
Tel no: (01749) 343648
www.blostins.co.uk

Chef-proprietor Nick Reed's restaurant may not be the biggest in town, but it more than makes up for it with its unique ambience and excellent variety. Two set-price menus (£15.95/£17.95) give plenty of choice. Kick things off with a warm salad of chicken and smoked bacon with olive oil and balsamic vinegar dressing, then honey roasted loin of pork with apple and cider brandy sauce, and finish with crème brûlée. Vegetarians can take advantage of the same set menu deals (roasted fennel and tomatoes with couscous and broad beans, say). House wine is £9.95. Open Tue to Sat D only.

## ■ Stoke-sub-Hamdon

### Priory House Restaurant

**Assured cooking, especially pastries**
1 High Street, Stoke-sub-Hamdon, TA14 6PP
Tel no: (01935) 822826
www.theprioryhouserestaurant.co.uk
**British | £31**
**Cooking score: 5**

A former clergyman's residence, as the name denotes, this charming restaurant is built of the same ochre-coloured stone as the rest of the village. Entering their fifth year of operations here, Peter and Sonia Brooks have built up an impressive head of steam. Linking up with the South Somerset Food Festival in the autumn, and working the local supply lines, produces menus of forthright West Country appeal. Start with Somerset goats' cheese in filo with crispy leeks and blackberry coulis, or a soufflé of smoked haddock and Lyme Bay scallops with rich thermidor sauce. Mains favour prime cuts of meat over fish (which might be limited to just the one, such as turbot with spinach, pine nuts, chanterelles and hollandaise). The local venison is well-reported, perhaps appearing as the loin with puréed sweet potato and roasted baby onions. Confidence in pastrywork is such that there may be three kinds of tart on the dessert menu: blackberry and apple, apricot and almond, or chocolate soufflé tart with clotted cream. A range of Somerset Royal cider brandy backs up an enterprising wine list that is strong in France, and opens with a house range from £14.

**Chef/s:** Peter Brooks. **Open:** Sat L 12.30 to 2.30, Tue to Sat D 7 to 9.30. **Closed:** last 2 weeks Nov, last 2 weeks May, all bank hols. **Meals:** alc D (main courses £17.50 to £19.50). Set L £16 (2 courses) £22 (3 courses).. **Service:** not inc. **Details:** Cards accepted. 20 seats. 8 seats outside. Wheelchair access. Music. Children allowed.

# █ Taunton

## Castle Hotel

**Contemporary food in an historical setting**
Castle Green, Taunton, TA1 1NF
Tel no: (01823) 272671
www.the-castle-hotel.com
**Modern British | £35**
**Cooking score: 7**

🍷 ⇌ Ⴤ

The site was once a Norman fortress, but history does not weigh heavily here. The interior impresses without overpowering and the restaurant, a magnificent room with an ornately moulded ceiling, delivers well-spaced impeccably set tables and a welcoming feel. Into it, from Richard Guest's industrious kitchen, pour fresh fish from Brixham, smoked fish from Brown and Forest, South Devon beef, Old Spot pork, poultry, eggs and cheese from Somerset farms, fruit and vegetables from local growers and seasonal game. Ideas are well defined and skill levels are high. Seasonality is all. Dishes are never fussy and flavours are fine-tuned so that they balance rather than compete with each other: for example, in a starter of fillet of John Dory with a spring vegetable broth, or an impressive main course of rib-eye with button mushroom purée and sauce Choron. Contrasts are well handled: crab comes with marinated vegetables and rhubarb jelly, while loin of deer is served alongside prune purée and spring greens. Desserts shine too, in the forms of almost teasingly straightforward apple charlotte with clotted cream or rhubarb trifle. Selecting from a pedigree range of West Country cheeses is the alternative. Lunch is a simpler affair, priced at one, two or three courses (including bread and a glass of house wine) and could include home-cured boar and Coppa ham with pickled cucumber and Spenwood cheese to start, then skate wing with rosemary gnocchi. The wine list is a match for the surroundings, with a depth that offers real fascination for lovers of classical appellations, and a nose for subtle, food-friendly style among global pretenders. A page of well-selected wines by the glass (from £4.50) offers a short cut and house bottles kick off at £16.

**Chef/s:** Richard Guest. **Open:** all week L 12.30 to 2, Mon to Sat D 7 to 9.30. **Meals:** Set L and D £22.50 (2 courses) to £47. **Service:** not inc. **Details:** Cards accepted. 70 seats. 20 seats outside. No music. No mobile phones. Wheelchair access. Children's portions. Car parking.

## Willow Tree

**Warm and inviting**
3 Tower Lane, Taunton, TA1 4AR
Tel no: (01823) 352835
www.thewillowtreerestaurant.co.uk
**Modern European | £29**
**Cooking score: 6**

£30

The beamed ceiling and cottagey interior make for a snug, welcoming ambience. This is restaurateuring in the old style, and none the worse for that. Things move more sharply up to date in Darren Sherlock's attractive menus, in which British and Mediterranean modes mingle productively. Start with oxtail and fondant potato ravioli with celeriac and parsley purée and wild garlic, or Cornish smoked salmon dressed in crème fraîche, cucumber and caviar. There is plenty of fish around in main courses, possibly including steamed bream with crayfish and ginger risotto and red pepper coulis, as alternative options to the likes of roast duck breast with a gâteau of smoked bacon, potato and Gruyère, served with cabbage and broccoli. Desserts live on in the memory when they are as imaginative as the warm chocolate tart that comes with beetroot ice cream, or as pretty as the summer berries set in champagne jelly, alongside a red berry sorbet. Amiable and charming service wins many friends. Wines are a serviceable international bunch, with house wines – a Chilean Chardonnay and a French red blend – leading the charge at £13.95, or £3.75 a glass.

**Chef/s:** Darren Sherlock. **Open:** Tue to Sat D only 6.30 to 10. **Closed:** Jan, Aug. **Meals:** Set D Tue and Wed £24.95, Thu to Sat £29.95. **Service:** not inc.

**Details:** Cards accepted. 35 seats. 10 seats outside. No mobile phones. Wheelchair access. Music. Children allowed.

# ▊ Wells

## Goodfellows

**Contemporary seafood restaurant**
5 Sadler Street, Wells, BA5 2RR
Tel no: (01749) 673866
www.goodfellowswells.co.uk
**Seafood | £30**
**Cooking score: 5**

The presence of this seafood restaurant isn't immediately apparent to the casual observer, as you have to weave your way through the well-populated patisserie-cum-delicatessen to get to the dining room. Tables are arranged along the walls and you get a centre-stage view of Adam Fellows and his team at work. There is, however, a further dining room at the top of a spiral staircase. Concise lunch menus of two choices at each stage broaden to a wealth of options from a short-choice carte and a six-course tasting menu, and the culinary style imaginatively reinvents the classic provincial French repertoire. It's mostly fish, sourced from day boats off the Devon and Cornish coasts (there's just the occasional nod to carnivores), and starters include the likes of skate terrine with purple potato, chilled anchovy essence and anchovy straw. For main course, choices might include fillet of sea bass with samphire, spring vegetables and a light shellfish nage, or fillet of turbot with a ricotta and spinach cannelloni, crispy Parma ham, artichoke and rosemary oil. Equally impressive are details such as good bread – the organic spelt is excellent – fruit tarts for dessert, and the selection of local and French farmhouse cheeses. The global wine selection starts at £13 with some 13 by the glass.
**Chef/s:** Adam Fellows. **Open:** Tue to Sat L 12 to 2, Thur to Sat D 6.30 to 9.30. **Closed:** 1Jan to 15 Jan. **Meals:** alc D (main courses £14.50 to £23). Set L £14 (2 courses) to £17, Set D £33 to £49.. **Service:** not inc. **Details:** Cards accepted. 40 seats. 12 seats outside. Air-con. No mobile phones. Wheelchair access. Music. Children's portions.

★NEW ENTRY★
## Old Spot

**Relaxed restaurant with seasonal offerings**
12 Sadler Street, Wells, BA5 3TT
Tel no: (01749) 689099
**British | £30**
**Cooking score: 4**

A quick look at the framed menus on the walls of this bistro reveals a lot about chef/proprietor Ian Bates's background. He has spent most of his cooking career in London, most prominently working under Simon Hopkinson at Bibendum. A passionate devotee of Elizabeth David, Bates cooks from the head and the heart. Start with the classic brasserie dish of frisee salad with black pudding, fried egg and bacon or a brilliantly executed version of Richard Olney's chicken liver terrine. Main courses might include roast wood pigeon with lentils and butternut squash or lambs' kidneys with parsley mash and green peppercorn butter. Finish with rhubarb fool and brown butter shortbread or baked chocolate mousse with crème fraîche. Located in the heart of Wells, grab one of the tables on the upper level with their stunning views of the cathedral. A notable wine list from merchant Bill Baker contains a number of vinous treats. House offerings start at £13.95.
**Chef/s:** Ian Bates. **Open:** Tues 6.30 to 10.30, Weds to Sat 12.30 to 2.30, 6.30 to 10.30, Sun 12.30 to 2.30. **Closed:** Monday. **Meals:** Set L £17.50 (three courses), Set D £25 (three courses). **Service:** Optional. **Details:** Cards accepted. 50 seats. No music. No mobile phones.

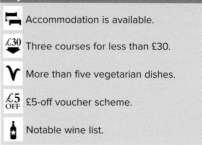

## Symbols

🛏 Accommodation is available.

£30 Three courses for less than £30.

V More than five vegetarian dishes.

£5 OFF £5-off voucher scheme.

🍾 Notable wine list.

## Widcombe

★NEW ENTRY★
### White Hart Inn
**Off the beaten path**
Widcombe Hill, Widcombe, BA2 6AA
Tel no: (01225) 338053
www.whitehartbath.co.uk
**Gastropub | £20**
**Cooking score: 2**

A two-minute walk from Bath's railway station, this much-improved gastropub just seems to get busier and busier. Popular with locals, rugby fans and tourists who have left the beaten path, this large, detached pub doubles up as a busy youth hostel, but downstairs the food is much more than travellers' fare. Chef Rupert Pitt has been cooking around the city for years and his simple, modern European food is bold and refreshingly simple. The menu is short and to the point. Starters may include a game terrine with red onion, pear and date chutney or crab and potato cakes with pickled cucumber. A meltingly tender slow-braised pork belly is served simply with mashed potato and cider gravy, with other main courses including whole baked sea bass with lemon and saffron butter. The short wine list is well balanced, but the real ales may prove too much of a distraction. House wines start at £12.90.
**Chef/s:** Rupert Pitt. **Open:** All week 12 to 3, 6.30 to 9.30. **Meals:** alc (main courses £9.50 to £11.50). **Service:** Optional. **Details:** Cards accepted. 50 seats. Separate bar. Wheelchair access. Children allowed.

### Seasonal produce by month

**January** – beetroot, fennel, spinach, chard, oranges, venison, cod, mackerel, scallops.

**February** – cress, chives, parsley, chicory, shallots, wild rabbit, hare, lemon sole.

**March** – purple sprouting broccoli, spring onions, halibut, wild salmon and sea trout.

**April** – morel, tarragon, leeks, Welsh lamb, mullet, first crabs and lobster.

**May** – first asparagus, sorrel, rhubarb, poussin, spring lobster, haddock, prawns.

**June** – broad beans, new potatoes, watercress, strawberries, radishes, sardines.

**July** – peas, runner beans, dill, garlic, raspberries, blueberries, herring.

**August** – courgettes, peppers, plums, apricots, peaches, grouse, crayfish.

**September** – calabrese, rocket, wild mushrooms, figs, blackberries, grapes, Kentish cobnuts, wild duck, oysters, mussels.

**October** – fungi, broccoli, English apples, pears, quinces, walnuts, guinea fowl, squid.

**November** – squash, parsnips, turnips, celeriac, almonds, sea bream.

**December** – clementines, curly kale, pumpkin, swede, goose, carp.

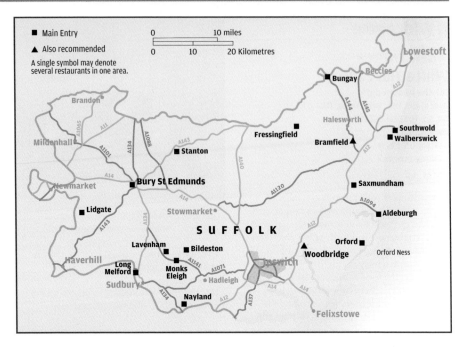

**Main Entry**
▲ **Also recommended**

A single symbol may denote several restaurants in one area.

0 _____ 10 miles
0 ____ 10 ____ 20 Kilometres

Lowestoft
Beccles
■ **Bungay**
Brandon
Halesworth
Mildenhall
Southwold
■ **Fressingfield**
**Bramfield** ▲
■ **Walberswick**
■ **Stanton**
Newmarket
■ **Bury St Edmunds**
■ **Saxmundham**
■ **Lidgate**
Stowmarket
■ **Aldeburgh**
S U F F O L K
**Lavenham**
Orford ■
**Haverhill**
■ **Bildeston**
▲ **Woodbridge**
Orford Ness
**Long Melford** ■
■ **Monks Eleigh**
Ipswich
Hadleigh
Sudbury
■ **Nayland**
Felixstowe

## ▌Aldeburgh

### The Lighthouse Restaurant
**A beacon for good eating**
77 High Street, Aldeburgh, IP15 5AU
Tel no: (01728) 453377
www.lighthouserestaurant.co.uk
**Modern British | £24**
**Cooking score: 2**

**V** £30

The Lighthouse is linked to a town stable of exciting gastro enterprises, including a wine merchant, exotic greengrocer, cookery school and café-bar. With a fresh coastal-Scandinavian feel (think light wood, mirrors, pastels with bright blue and yellow accents), this revamped bistro-style fish restaurant positively hums 'come highdays and holidays', growing more restful outside 'the silly season'. The blackboard seafood specials make full use of the day's catch from the beach's fish sheds, perhaps crab or lobster served cold with herb mayo and new potatoes or local seasonal treat, Middleton asparagus with butter and

Parmesan. Other piscine favourites, such as tiger prawn bisque and tuna niçoise, come from further afield. Carnivores eat well off duck confit with spinach, crème fraîche and chilli jam or rack of lamb with minted spring vegetables. A 90-odd bin wine list (starting at £11.95) offers fish-friendly choices, such as delightful Viogniers, the iconic Bonny Doon Malvasia and interesting Sicilian and Sardinian labels.

**Chef/s:** Sara Fox and Guy Welsh. **Open:** all week 12 to 2 (2.30 Sat and Sun), 6.30 to 10. **Closed:** 1 week Jan, 1 week Oct. **Meals:** alc (main courses £8.45 to £15.75). **Service:** not inc. **Details:** Cards accepted. 90 seats. 12 seats outside. Air-con. No music. No mobile phones. Wheelchair access. Children's portions.

# 152 Aldeburgh

**Bright modern restaurant**
152 High Street, Aldeburgh, IP15 5AQ
Tel no: (01728) 454594
www.152aldeburgh.co.uk
**Modern European | £26**
**Cooking score: 2**

£5
OFF

A relaxed, informal atmosphere prevails at this light, modern restaurant just off the High Street and only yards from the pebbly beach. As you'd expect in this seaside location, seafood is a key feature, both in the classic form of a satifying Aldeburgh fish soup with rouille and in the more contemporary style of monkfish and tiger prawns with vegetable ribbons and lemongrass dressing. Meat-lovers and vegetarians are also catered for with dishes such as rump of lamb with garlic, anchovies, capers and boulangère potatoes for the former, and warm puff pastry tart with spring vegetables, port and truffle dressing for the latter. The freshness of 'lovely moist cod in perfect crispy batter' has been praised, though at inspection minimal vegetables and unimpressive chips let the side down. Warm pear and almond tart with praline ice cream is typical of desserts, and Adnams of Southwold supply a useful wine list.
**Chef/s:** Garry Cook. **Open:** all week 12 to 3, 6 to 10. **Meals:** alc (main courses £10.95 to £15.95). Set L and D (exc Sat D) £14 (2 courses) to £17.50. **Service:** not inc. **Details:** Cards accepted. 54 seats. 24 seats outside. Air-con. Wheelchair access. Music. Children's portions. Children allowed.

## ALSO RECOMMENDED
## ▲ Regatta Restaurant and Wine Bar

171-173 The High Street, Aldeburgh, IP15 5AN
Tel no: (01728) 452011
www.regattaaldeburgh.com

A sunny blue and yellow façade marks out this long-serving Aldeburgh favourite, which has a cheery, nautically inclined interior and a menu majoring in fresh local seafood. Daily blackboard specials flesh out a choice of unpretentious dishes that might include Mediterranean fish soup with rouille and croûtons (£5) and spaghetti with blue swimmer crab and pesto. Home-smoked salmon is a house speciality and other well-tried brasserie favourites might include confit of duck on potato and horseradish purée or roast corn-fed chicken breast on Caesar salad (£12). Reasonably priced global wines from £12.50 (£3.75 a glass). Open all week.

# ▋ Bildeston

## ★NEW ENTRY★

**★ BEST UP-AND-COMING CHEF ★ CHRIS LEE**

# The Bildeston Crown

**Glamour in a former coaching inn**
High Street, Bildeston, IP7 7EB
Tel no: (01449) 740510
www.thebildestoncrown.com
**Modern British | £29**
**Cooking score: 5**

🛏 £30

A picture-pretty coaching inn, the Crown's simple High Street exterior belies the wow factor within (the result of a facelift with no expense spared over the past few years). Rococo interiors are combined with an excess of beams and period feel, think huge paintings, rich red walls, mirrors, stripped boards, hunting prints. But it is still a locals' hostelry of sorts, albeit grander than your average Suffolk pub. It's a luxurious restaurant-with-rooms in essence, and Chris Lee is an ambitious self-taught chef. His 'intricate cuisine gastronomique' is definitely showy but backed up by sound technique. Subtle flavours, complementary textures and dish combinations are analytically thought out, as in a melting braised oxtail in delicate horseradish foam served fashionably alongside baked turbot on vanilla-scented butter beans, pancetta and tomato. Elsewhere pumpkin cannelloni might come with cinnamon and hazelnuts, or cauliflower and spiced date chutney with seared scallops and lobster. At inspection, a main course of 'pork head to toe' with its eight different miniature cuts of 'piggy delight' demonstrated ability and intent, starting with crispy cigarillos from the ear, five more individually garnished body parts, ending with a parcel of the trotters with spring vegetables, topped off with a salty brittle whisker of crackling. A seven-course tasting menu gives an impressive culinary insight while Crown Classics, its simpler bar food selections, are a step up from the norm. Welcoming staff could do with more polish and élan to match this level of cooking, as could the mostly prosaic selections on the wine list, lacking much of the expected depth and prestige in its 100-odd bottlings (from £14).

**Chef/s:** Chris Lee. **Open:** all week 12 to 3, 7 to 10 (9.30 Sun). **Meals:** alc (main courses £10 to £19) Set L and D £20 (3 courses). **Service:** not inc. **Details:** Cards accepted. Separate bar. Car parking.

## ALSO RECOMMENDED
### ▲ Queen's Head

The Street, Bramfield, IP19 9HT
Tel no: (01986) 784214
www.queensheadbramfield.co.uk

Exposed beams, a large fireplace and pine tables have their olde-worlde charm, but luckily the food is considerably more up-to-date. The ever-changing menu is completely seasonal and local organic produce features heavily in the repertoire. Standout starters include chicken kebabs marinated in soy, ginger and garlic (£5.50) and egg and prawns with dill mayonnaise (£4.95). Mains are 'unpretentious but pleasant', liver, bacon and onion casserole (£9.95) may feel like it belongs on a pub menu but the quality is above and beyond most bar fare. All the ice cream is home-made and the brown-bread variety (£3.95) is a particular delight. Wines from £11.50. Open daily.

## ▌ Bungay

★NEW ENTRY★
### Earsham Street Café
**A popular, buzzy neighbourhood brasserie**
11-13 Earsham Street, Bungay, NR35 1AE
**Tel no: (01986) 893103**
**Modern British | £29**
**Cooking score: 2**
V £30

If the level of custom and the queues at the Earsham's door are a good benchmark, then you're on to a winner here. Only open for supper the last weekend of each month, but seven days a week for lunch, this rustic, chic yet unpretentious brasserie positively buzzes between 11am and 3pm, come rain or shine (it also doubles as an excellent all-day café). The combination of consistently proficient, simple cooking of fresh ingredients, partnered with affable service and good-value prices epitomises everything a neighbourhood restaurant should be. Reassuring comfort food on the lengthy eclectic menu might include starters of sticky pork belly and mango salad or treacle-cured salmon with ripped mozzarella, baked beets and horseradish, followed by herb-roasted chump of Suffolk lamb with braised chicory, lentils, baby leeks and tapenade or oriental fishcakes with stir-fried pak choi and ginger. Soul-satisfying puds finish a praiseworthy meal, such as sticky toffee pudding or oozing chocolate fondant. A snappy worldwide wine list mixes cosmopolitan smaller producers with established big names. Wines start at £12.50 a bottle and £3 a glass.

**Chef/s:** Christopher Rice. **Open:** Mon to Sat L 11 to 4, Sun L 12 to 2.30. Last weekend every month D 6.30 to 9.. **Closed:** 25 Dec, Bank holidays. **Meals:** alc (main courses L £8.25 to £13.95, D £9.50 to £19.50). **Service:** not inc. **Details:** Cards accepted. 55 seats. 26 seats outside. Wheelchair access. Music. Children's portions.

## ▌Bury St Edmunds
## Maison Bleue
Consistent, contemporary restaurant
30-31 Churchgate Street, Bury St Edmunds,
IP33 1RG
Tel no: (01284) 760623
www.maisonbleue.co.uk
**Seafood | £30**
**Cooking score: 2**

'It is always excellent, and the service is first class' notes a visitor to this sophisticated seafood restaurant. With its exposed brick walls, plushly upholstered banquettes and fresh white table linen, Maison Bleue is a little haven of tranquility away from the busy streets in the centre of Bury St Edmunds. From the carte, choose from a dozen or so starters, say terrine of duck foie gras and sultanas. Mains are naturally mostly fishy, and might include whole roasted sea bass with fennel, lemon and olive oil dressing – but again there are options for carnivores and vegetarians. To finish, pain perdu is served with butterscotch and chocolate sauce. The wine list is predominantly French, though the New World gets a look-in. House wine starts at £11.95 a bottle, £8.40 a carafe, and glasses at £2.40.
**Chef/s:** Pascal Canévet. **Open:** Tue to Sat 12 to 2.30, 7 to 9.30 (10 Fri and Sat). **Closed:** 2 weeks Jan, 2 weeks summer. **Meals:** alc (main courses £9.95 to £22.95). Set L £13.95 (2 courses) to £16.95, Set D £25.95. **Service:** not inc. **Details:** Cards accepted. 65 seats. Wheelchair access. Music. Children's portions.

## ▌Fressingfield
## The Fox and Goose Inn
Historic setting for ambitious cuisine
Church Road, Fressingfield, IP21 5PB
Tel no: (01379) 586247
www.foxandgoose.net
**Modern British | £23**
**Cooking score: 1**

£30

As village restaurants go, the Fox and Goose has a distinct edge on quaintness, with its idyllic setting beside an imposing fourteenth-century church. The slightly tongue-in-cheek sign (of a goose with a beakful of fox) is a hint that things might not be as traditional as this atmospheric former guildhall with its timbered interior might suggest. Cooking is distinctly 'in the present', with ambitious combinations of flavours – mandarin jelly, creamy foie gras mousse and a rich walnut vinaigrette embellishing a rocket and Parma ham salad. Much effort is put into the trappings, a prelude of good bread and appetiser, such as a frothy demi-tasse of langoustine bisque, and a finale of petits fours, perhaps chocolate fudge and honeycomb, make for quite a gentrified experience, but substance doesn't always match the intricate style. A complex main course of lime, thyme and honey marinated pork fillet with apples, celeriac Parmentier, chorizo creamed potato and a shallot jus muted on the eye and palate at inspection.
**Chef/s:** Paul Yaxley and Matt Wyatt. **Open:** Tue to Sun L 12 to 2 (1.45 Sat), D 7 to 8.30 (9 Sat), Sun 6.30 to 8.15. **Closed:** 2 weeks Jan. **Meals:** alc (main courses £8 to £17.50). Set L Mon to Sat £11.95 (2 courses) to £14.50 (3 courses), Set D £38 (7 courses). **Service:** not inc. **Details:** Cards accepted. 50 seats. 18 seats outside. Wheelchair access. Music. Children's portions. Car parking.

## Lavenham

### Great House

**A taste of France in one of Suffolk's oldest wool towns**
Market Place, Lavenham, CO10 9QZ
Tel no: (01787) 247431
www.greathouse.co.uk
French | £35
Cooking score: 2

Set on the old town square of a quintessential Suffolk wool town, the Great House sits seamlessly alongside its neighbours, but step across the threshold and the Gallic accents, baguette on the table and the traditional cuisine française soon transport you spiritually across 'La Manche'. Full of atmosphere, history oozes from the timbers. Hidden to the rear, the verdant courtyard is similarly laid for alfresco dining, all napery, candles and silver cutlery. It's a real French experience. The classically inspired carte can appear pricey to some, with simple main courses, such as veal kidneys with mustard, rack of lamb with thyme jus or poached turbot with hollandaise sauce. An extensive wine list with a naturally French bias starts at £11.50. The sister venue is Maison Bleue at Bury St Edmunds (see entry).
**Chef/s:** Regis Crépy. **Open:** Tue to Sun L 12 to 2.30, Tue to Sat D 7 to 9.30 (10 Sat). **Closed:** Jan. **Meals:** alc (main courses £16 to £21). Set D Tue to Fri (and Sun L) £25.95 (3 courses). **Service:** not inc. **Details:** Cards accepted. 45 seats. 30 seats outside. Wheelchair access. Music. Children's portions.

## ALSO RECOMMENDED

### ▲ Star Inn

The Street, Lidgate, CB8 9PP
Tel no: (01638) 500275

In the somewhat paradoxical setting of a classic Suffolk-pink hostelry, the Star's authentic taste of Iberia is as celebrated in these well-heeled equine parts as the inimitable charisma of its Spanish landlady, Maria Teresa Axon. It's not just wealthy racing types who flock to this unassuming but welcoming historic pub to

tuck into hearty cooking of cassoulet-style fabadas asturianas (£5.90), zarzuela of fish with its red pepper and almond enriched nage (£16.50) or wild boar with strawberries (£16.50). Boquerones, piquillo peppers, oxtail casserole and suckling pig, too, all play their part in enticing diners to this venue. Wines start at £12.50. Closed Sun D.

## Long Melford

### Scutchers

**Informal village dining**
Westgate Street, Long Melford, CO10 9DP
Tel no: (01787) 310200
www.scutchers.com
Modern British | £29
Cooking score: 2

'Everything is freshly prepared and of the highest quality,' wrote one fan of the food at this pretty, beamed village house decked out in homely wooden furniture. Nick Barrett's 'simple, delicious' bistro-style cooking is underpinned by well-sourced ingredients and a sound knowledge of the classics – as in a starter of smoked salmon with a cucumber, spring onion and asparagus salad and a soy and lime dressing. Mains could include loin fillet of new season Suffolk lamb with a minty gravy and a rösti; or fillets of lemon sole in crispy crumb with hand-cut chips. Pudding might be a crème brulée with a compote of caramelised pineapple or steamed chocolate pudding with chocolate custard. A well-balanced wine list begins at £15.
**Chef/s:** Nick Barrett and Guy Alabaster. **Open:** Tue to Sat 12 to 2, 7 to 9.30. **Closed:** Christmas, 10 days early Mar, 10 days late Aug. **Meals:** alc (main courses £14 to £22). Set L Tue to Fri £15 (2 courses), Set D Tue to Thur £15 (2 courses). **Service:** not inc. **Details:** Cards accepted. 65 seats. 35 seats outside. Air-con. No music. Wheelchair access. Children's portions. Car parking.

## Monks Eleigh

### Swan Inn
**Well-executed modern classics**
The Street, Monks Eleigh, IP7 7AU
Tel no: (01449) 741391
www.monkseleigh.com
Modern European | £25
Cooking score: 3

There's much to praise about this village pub, not least long-standing owners Nigel and Carol Ramsbottom, who are likeable people, and modest with it, though they have much to be proud of. The thatched, timber-framed pub is what most people hope to find in a Suffolk village, and the kitchen is equally integrated with its surroundings with meat, game, fish, fruit and vegetable all meticulously sourced. The formula is simple. Nigel's blackboard menus deal in well-wrought dishes that are fresh and flavourful. Among starters there could be dressed Cromer crab with lemon and mayonnaise, and a main course of pan-fried guinea fowl breast is served with wild mushrooms, grapes and tarragon sauce, as well as swede and carrot purée and new potatoes. Desserts keep up the standards, a creamy rice pudding and date sticky toffee pudding with sticky toffee sauce proving the point for several readers. Real ales are on draught and the thoroughly accessible wine list offers plentiful options by the glass from £3; bottles from £12.
**Chef/s:** Nigel Ramsbottom. **Open:** Wed to Sun 12 to 2, 7 to 9.30. **Closed:** 25 and 26 Dec, 1 Jan. **Meals:** alc (main courses £9 to £17). **Service:** not inc. **Details:** Cards accepted. 40 seats. 20 seats outside. No music. Children's portions. Car parking.

## Nayland
### The White Hart Inn
**Elegant restaurant-with-rooms**
11 High Street, Nayland, CO6 4JF
Tel no: (01206) 263382
www.whitehart-nayland.co.uk
Modern European | £28
Cooking score: 3

This fine old-beamed coaching inn has been cleverly reworked into an elegant restaurant-with-rooms; enjoy aperitifs in a comfortable seating area with plump sofas while perusing the menu – the more inquisitive can investigate the glass floor over the White Hart's cellar. In late May the carte offered a simple selection of mainly classically inspired French and Italian dishes. A variety of wild greenery, such as pea shoots, garlic and dandelion leaves underlines distinct interest in seasonality, while the likes of Caesar salad, home-smoked salmon with granary bread or mackerel piri-piri make rather simple starters. A textbook chicken liver parfait came garnished with dressed celery leaf, brioche toast and a powerfully strong dark chutney, while an unctuous crispy pork belly main was presented with a rustic golden-crusted black pudding and potato hash, buttered greens and velvety Bramley apple sauce. A reliable wine list of about fifty bins starts at £15.
**Chef/s:** Marcus Verberne. **Open:** All week L 12 to 2.30, D 7 to 9.30. **Closed:** 2 weeks Jan. **Meals:** alc (main courses £9.70 to £21.60). Set L £12.90 (2 courses). **Service:** not inc. **Details:** Cards accepted. 40 seats. 20 seats outside. Wheelchair access. Music. Children's portions. Car parking.

# Orford

## The Trinity, Crown and Castle

Bags of atmosphere
Orford, IP12 2LJ
Tel no: (01394) 450205
www.crownandcastle.co.uk
**Modern British | £29**
**Cooking score: 4**

〓 V £30

Despite its tiny size and remote location on the Suffolk coast, Orford is a vibrant fishing village. At its centre is the Victorian hotel run by David and Ruth Watson, whose friendly, welcoming personality is stamped on every aspect of the place. Food is a key part of the operation, and a flexible approach means plenty of choice for customers, whether they opt for a simple, light lunch or a full three-course dinner. At lunchtime, dual-priced starter/light dishes include the likes of home-smoked trout with beetroot and potato salad, while main courses take in seared black bream with warm white bean, orange and watercress salad. Evening menus extend choice further with slow-roast pork belly on celeriac, rosemary and sweet potato fricassee, or guinea fowl on gently curried pea ragôut and pak choi, and to finish there might be a sparkling prosecco, mango, physalis and passion-fruit jelly. A lengthy and extensively annotated wine list features a good few interesting and unusual bottles, and value is fair throughout (prices start at £14.50), with a good choice by the glass.
**Chef/s:** Ruth Watson and Max Dougal. **Open:** all week 12 to 2.15, 6.45 to 9.15 (10 Sat). **Closed:** 7 to 11 Jan. **Meals:** alc (main courses L £9.50 to £15, D £14 to £19.50). Set D Sat £35. **Service:** not inc. **Details:** Cards accepted. 52 seats. No music. No mobile phones. Wheelchair access. Children's portions. Car parking.

## ALSO RECOMMENDED

## ▲ Butley-Orford Oysterage

Market Hill, Orford, IP12 2LH
Tel no: (01394) 450277
www.butleyorfordoysterage.co.uk

How many restaurants can guarantee the freshness of their fish? No such problems at Butley Orford as they catch it, smoke it and serve it to you as quickly as they can. Oysters are at the heart of the menu and you can have them in a soup (£4.50), in a cocktail (£4.50), on horseback (£5.40) or you can order then by the half-dozen (£6.50). The dishes are cooked simply to allow the seafood to shine: grilled prawns (£7.90) are sweet and juicy, the fish pie (£9.80) hearty and warming. Blackboard specials add an element of surprise and there's usually a dish or two for anyone who isn't a fan of fish, although frankly when it tastes this good it could convert anyone. A selection of wines start from £12.75. Open all week except Nov- March (closed D Sun-Thu) and April-May (closed D Sun-Tue).

# Saxmundham

## The Bell Hotel

Foraged food
31 High Street, Saxmundham, IP17 1AF
Tel no: (01728) 602331
www.bellhotel-saxmundham.co.uk
**Anglo-French | £23**
**Cooking score: 2**

〓 V £30

With a seemingly particular interest in local and wild provender – jack-by-the-hedge pannacotta, grey mullet with hop shoots and Adnams bitter sauce, plus a wild garlic mousse stuffing a roasted poussin – paired with a quite classical French-inspired cuisine, Andrew Blackburn's calming town centre bolthole could be a good reason to turn off the bypass. A late spring meal didn't quite hit the lofty heights of previous visits for one regular, but rich starters might include tarte fine of figs and goats' cheese with a rocket salad, and foie gras terrine with beetroot, silverskin onions and

truffle vinaigrette, perhaps followed by horseradish-crusted fillet of beef with red cabbage and rösti, or roasted monkfish with parsnip purée, clams, broad beans and a chive butter sauce. Sheep's milk mousse proved an excellent refresher to end the meal (albeit with poor flapjack instead of the expected ginger butter biscuit), alternatively, bitter chocolate délice, with white chocolate ice cream, or farmhouse cheeses may also be available. Awkward close table arrangements and grating modern muzak – spoiling the otherwise elegant dining room in this handsome coaching inn have been noted. However, a good value and reliable Lay and Wheeler wine list starts at £10.95 a bottle.
**Chef/s:** Andrew Blackburn. **Open:** Tue to Sat L 12 to 2, D 6 to 9.30. **Closed:** 26 Dec, 1 Jan, spring and autumn half-term. **Meals:** alc (main courses £9.50 to £16.50). Set L £12.50 (2 courses) to £15.50 (3 courses). Set D £18.50 (3 courses). Bar menu available. **Service:** not inc. **Details:** Cards accepted. 26 seats. 15 seats outside. Separate bar. No music. Wheelchair access. Music. Car parking.

## READERS RECOMMEND

## The Crown Inn
Gastropub
The Street, Great Glemham, Saxmundham, IP17 2DA
Tel no: (01728) 663693
'Home-cooked fare using Alde Valley produce'

## ∎ Southwold

## Crown Hotel
**One of the original gastropub-hotels**
90 High Street, Southwold, IP18 6DP
Tel no: (01502) 722186
www.adnams.co.uk/hotels
**Modern British | £27**
**Cooking score: 2**

🍷 🍴 ♈

While guests can choose to sit in the quieter red-and-pistachio-hued dining room across the hallway, the hum and bustle of the Crown is to be found in the front bar of what was one

of the UK's first gastropubs. An auction lot of window-side tables and creaky chairs entertains chic promenader-watching up and down the High Street, while the menu delivers a modern European array of gutsy flavours and local ingredients in enthusiastic combinations; but results can be hit and miss. Start with spicy Mediterranean fish soup or potted duck confit, followed with East Coast sardines with grain mustard dressing and pesto or lamb's liver with red cabbage and bacon-sage bread pudding. Indulgent puddings include olive oil and pistachio cake with Marybelle clotted cream or chocolate mousse, honeycomb and toffee ice cream (the best dish at inspection). Adnams' flagship hotel and restaurant, this venue comes with all the liquid pedigree expected of possibly East Anglia's finest brewer and wine merchant. From an impressively informative wine list, you can drink particularly well by the glass or choose from all manner of esoteric gems, especially the good value French Country and Italian selections (bottles from £11.50).
**Chef/s:** Ian Howell. **Open:** all week 12 to 2, 6.30 to 9. **Meals:** alc (main courses £10.50 to £17.95). **Service:** not inc. **Details:** Cards accepted. 100 seats. 12 seats outside. Separate bar. No music. No mobile phones. Wheelchair access. Children's portions. Car parking.

★NEW ENTRY★

### ★ BEST USE OF LOCAL PRODUCE ★

## Sutherland House
**Besotted with local ingredients**
56 High Street, Southwold, IP18 6DN
Tel no: (01502) 724544
www.sutherlandhouse.co.uk
**Modern British | £27**
**Cooking score: 2**

🍴

It's been a nostalgic return to their favourite seaside haunt for Peter and Anna Banks, who recently acquired this once-faded restaurant-with-rooms. Now fully revamped, in the most part, the house dates, reputedly, from 1455 (with Georgian and Victorian additions) and delivers accents of rich natural colours in fabrics, distinctly funky light fittings and abstract coastal art, all complementing open fireplaces, exposed beams, and ornate plaster ceilings. Chef Alan Paton's food is indulgent, forward-thinking and generally restrained. Local produce is everything; food miles are listed by each dish and if the boats can't leave the harbour, don't expect fresh fish for supper. An obsessive focus on doorstep produce means a foodie trail around Suffolk on the appetising menu, with the Salisburys' excellent Suffolk Gold cheese fondue style with Aspall cyder, Jimmy Butler's impressive Blythburgh pork as a slow-roasted belly, and plenty of locally dug veggies. Everything is home-made, including the bacon and black pudding. The good-value, reliable wine list purposefully sources wines from other parts to bring customers something different on Adnams' home turf; bottles start at £12.50.

**Chef/s:** Alan Paton. **Open:** Tue to Sun L 12 to 2.30, Tue to Sun D 7 to 9.30. **Closed:** Mondays, 25 Dec, 2 weeks Jan. **Meals:** alc (main courses £9 to £14). **Service:** not inc. **Details:** Cards accepted. 50 seats. 30 seats outside. Wheelchair access. Music. Children's portions.

## Stanton

### Leaping Hare
Informal café and rustic restaurant
Wyken Vineyards, Stanton, IP31 2DW
Tel no: (01359) 250287
www.wykenvineyards.co.uk
Modern British | £22
New Chef
£30

The Carlisles' country estate appeals on many fronts: the beautiful gardens and architecture of the grand house, the stylish country store, the regular Saturday farmers' market, the 'very quaffable delights of the vineyards' and the striking timbered space of the huge barn, which houses a laidback, family friendly café and a more formal restaurant. This year inspection took place just as Peter Harrison was handing over the reins to new chef Jon Ellis and there is every indication that Ellis

will continue the accomplished, simple, yet classical cooking for which the Leaping Hare is known. That meal produced a 'light savoury' pressed Suffolk ham terrine with celeriac rémoulade and 'caramelised hash-style' salt beef stovies with braised Savoy cabbage and a beetroot horseradish relish, with a wedge of peach and almond tart served with thick local Jersey cream for dessert. An enjoyable if short wine list, priced from £14.50, naturally features (but not exclusively) produce from the Leaping Hare Vineyard.

**Chef/s:** Jon Ellis. **Open:** all week L 10 to 6, Fri and Sat D 7 to 9.30. **Closed:** 1 week Christmas. **Meals:** alc (main courses £11 to £16). Set L £16.95 (2 courses) to £19.95 (3 courses).. **Service:** not inc. **Details:** Cards accepted. 50 seats. 20 seats outside. No music. No mobile phones. Wheelchair access. Children's portions.

## Walberswick

### The Anchor
A real find for food and beer afficionados
The Street, Walberswick, IP18 6UA
Tel no: (01502) 722112
www.anchoratwalberswick.com
Modern British | £20
Cooking score: 2

Having left the White Horse at Parson's Green early in 2007, beer guru Mark Dorber is now full-time at the Anchor, helping wife (and chef) Sophie in developing this Adnams-owned 1920s Arts & Crafts pub. Refurbishing continues in the bar and dining areas, which now sport soothing sand, stone and aqua tones as befits its seaside location, but the real passion and draw here is the fresh seasonal food and the first-class beer and wine. Sophie sources the best local or home-grown produce, much of it organic, and uses it to good effect on simple, daily menus. Follow a big bowl of moules marinière, served with home-made bread, with a hearty and full-flavoured lamb tagine or beer battered local haddock with hand-cut chips and pease pudding. Straightforward puddings include steamed syrup sponge and apple tart Tatin.

Tim Wilson

**Why did you become a chef?**
In Dorset, I loved that fishermen came to the door selling fresh produce – it hooked me. Mum also teaches home economics, so I was cooking before I could walk.

**Who was your main inspiration?**
David Bourke and Rick Stein.

**Who do you most admire among today's chefs?**
Fergus Henderson and the guys at the Anchor & Hope.

**Where do you eat out?**
Ethnic restaurants in East London, such as Vietnamese places. I also enjoy Fino.

**What's your favourite cookery book?**
*Roast Chicken and Other Stories* by Simon Hopkinson and Lindsey Bareham.

**What's the best dish you've ever eaten?**
Sea urchin ragu at the Gramercy Tavern in New York.

**What's your guilty food pleasure?**
Spicy squid with purple basil dressing from the Green Papaya, Mare Street, Hackney.

**What is your proudest achievement?**
Making a 45-minute speech to the Oxford University Gastronomy Society, with 90 people in the audience, or cooking at the Oscars and the Cannes Film Festival.

Menus also recommended a beer from Mark's impressive bottled beer list to accompany each dish, and there's a wide-ranging list of wines from £11.25.
**Chef/s:** Sophie Dorber. **Open:** all week L 12 to 3, D 6 to 9. **Closed:** 25 Dec. **Meals:** alc (main courses £10 to £15). **Service:** not inc. **Details:** Cards accepted. 85 seats. 160 seats outside. Wheelchair access. Children's portions. Car parking.

## ALSO RECOMMENDED
### ▲ Riverside
Quayside, Woodbridge, IP12 1BH
Tel no: (01394) 382587
www.theriverside.co.uk

If you're tired of having to coordinate a night out around a meal and a trip to the cinema, the Quayside kills two birds with one stone. Behind the façade of an old-fashioned cinema you will find a modern restaurant serving either light tapas dishes such as marinated olives in rosemary olive oil (from £3) at lunch, or deep-fried goats' cheese, crème fraîche and chilli jam, and oriental free-range pork (mains from £10) at dinner. To enjoy the best value there is a three-course dinner and a film package for £25, with a similar scheme involving lunchtime tapas for £15. Wines from £12. Closed Sun L.

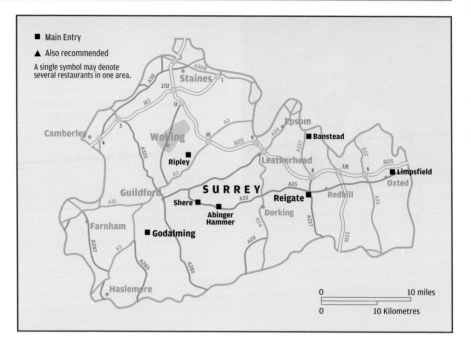

Legend:
- ■ Main Entry
- ▲ Also recommended

A single symbol may denote several restaurants in one area.

Staines, Camberley, Woking, Ripley, Banstead, Leatherhead, Limpsfield, Oxted, Epsom, Guildford, SURREY, Shere, Abinger Hammer, Reigate, Redhill, Dorking, Farnham, Godalming, Haslemere

0    10 miles
0    10 Kilometres

# ▌Abinger Hammer

## Drakes on the Pond

**Colourful interior and magnificent views**
Dorking Road, Abinger Hammer, RH5 6SA
Tel no: (01306) 731174
www.drakesonthepond.com
**Modern European | £33**
**Cooking score: 5**

The Pond on which Drake's (almost) sits has more the dimensions of a small lake, but the place itself is compact and trim. There is much evidence of exciting culinary intelligence at work in John Morris's creations, seen in a serving of sautéed king scallops with potato rösti and a sauce of orange, tarragon and star anise. More scallops might turn up in a risotto to which strips of confit squid are added. Main courses balance prime materials with a lightness of touch, offering halibut on crushed new potatoes with spinach, asparagus and a foam flavoured with bacon and peas, while slow-cooked pork belly is partnered with Ireland's Clonakilty black pudding and a cream sauce infused with pancetta. Modish desserts have included almond and treacle tart with salt caramel ice cream, or honey-glazed figs with brown sugar parfait and coconut tuiles. Confident staff serve it all forth with genuine enthusiasm. Wines kick off with a French Viognier and a Spanish red at £18.
**Chef/s:** John Morris. **Open:** Tue to Fri L 12 to 1.30, Tue to Sat D 6.45 to 9.30. **Closed:** Between Christmas and New Year, last week Aug. **Meals:** alc D (main courses £21 to £24). Set L £19.50 (2 courses) to £23.50. **Service:** not inc. **Details:** Cards accepted. 32 seats. Air-con. No music. No mobile phones. Wheelchair access. Children allowed. Car parking.

## Banstead

★NEW ENTRY★
### Post
**Slick mini gastrodome**
28 High Street, Banstead, SM7 2LQ
Tel no: 01737 373839
www.postrestaurant.co.uk
**Modern British | £45**
**Cooking score: 1**

Post is the latest opening from Tony 'Ready, Steady, Cook' Tobin, who also owns the well-established Dining Room in Reigate (see entry). A stylishly converted village post office comes with plenty of blue and chrome, a well-stocked deli (coffees and breakfasts are served here) and informal brasserie (no table reservations during the day, a wood-fired oven for pizzas and classic comfort food), with 'covetable white leather swivel chairs' and modern British food offered in the smart, low-ceilinged upstairs dining room. The menu plays it safe. Sunday lunch, for example, runs to fishcakes spiked with lime; kangeroo fillet, and a 'faultless' sea bream on crushed lemon potatoes alongside the usual roast beef with towering Yorkshire pudding, which was sadly 'all crust and no substance'. However, a retro brandy snap basket, which accompanied strawberries and clotted cream, was 'delicious'. House wines start at £14.95.
**Chef/s:** Tony Tobin. **Open:** Dining room open all week except Sat L and Sun D. **Closed:** Dec 26.
**Meals:** Set D £34 (two courses, Mon to Thu), Sun lunch £35 (4 courses and petits fours).
**Details:** Cards accepted. Air-con.

## Godalming

★NEW ENTRY★
### La Luna
**A real gem in Godalming's crown**
10-14 Wharf Street, Godalming, GU7 1NN
Tel no: (01483) 418286
www.lalunarestaurant.co.uk
**Italian | £30**
**Cooking score: 4**
£5 OFF

Bright and white on the outside, light and airy within, this Italian eatery oozes feelgood factor. Stylish, contemporary furnishings complement innovative food, and front-of-house staff are cheery, efficient – clearly proud of the food and wines they serve. A perfectly seasoned two-sip-sized gazpacho and a crunchy crumb-coated ball of risotto made an impressive opening at inspection, while starters, including home-made tortelli filled with slow-cooked Welsh lamb shank and served with pecorino cheese gratin and broad bean purée, use the pick of the season's ingredients. Perfectly cooked fish and beautifully balanced accompaniments made baked red snapper fillet served with sautéed sea asparagus and home-pickled vegetables a memorable main course, while roast noisettes of new season Welsh lamb stuffed with spring onion and provolone cheese with sweet and sour Mediterranean vegetables delivered fabulous gutsy flavour. A dense chocolate mousse or featherlight ricotta tart are just a couple of the desserts on offer, but centre-stage must be shared with the sensational all-Italian wine list comprising 150 carefully selected wines ranging in price from £14 to £350 – it includes some real gems.
**Chef/s:** Valentino Gentile. **Open:** Tue to Sun 12 to 2, Tue to Sat 7 to 10. **Meals:** alc (main courses £16.50 to £18.50) Set L £12.95 (2 courses). **Service:** not inc.
**Details:** Cards accepted. 50 seats. Air-con. No mobile phones. Wheelchair access. Music. Children's portions.

## ▊ Limpsfield

★NEW ENTRY★
### Alexander's at Limpsfield
**New restaurant with ambitious intentions**
The Old Lodge, High Street, Limpsfield, RH8 ODR
Tel no: (01883) 714365
www.alexanders-limpsfield.co.uk
**Modern British | £40**
**Cooking score: 4**

Alexander's, on a quintessential English
village high street, has all the makings of a
restaurant of serious gastronomic intent.
Inside, it's clearly a former sixteenth-century
schoolroom and chapel with an unusual
barrel-shaped roof, elaborate carved fireplace
and decorative wooden panelling, enhanced
with contemporary chic fabrics. Simon
Attridge has worked with both Gordon
Ramsay and Heston Blumenthal and their
influence is apparent in dishes notable for
thoughtful, dextrous contrasts of textures and
flavours. Stand-out dishes have included surf
'n' turf reinvented as sublimely unctuous pork
macaroni with roasted langoustines and
seaweed tartare and impeccable roast sea bass
'blissfully partnered' with Serrano ham, bone
marrow, crispy croûtons and cepes.
Impressive, too, has been Cornish lamb
cooked medium-rare with agrodolce lentils
and a wondrously rich reduction, a witty pre-
dessert of dill jelly and mango foam and the
ubiquitous hot chocolate fondant given an
edge with salted caramel sauce and ice cream.
Just occasionally dishes try too hard: pain
d'epice crumble did nothing to enhance seared
scallops and the addition of yoghurt jarred,
despite lightning roasted foie gras. Service
'could be a little more relaxed', though
manager Bruno Cicco's stint with Alain
Ducasse in Monaco perhaps explains its
grander gestures. An expansive wine list starts
at £17 and rises steeply.
**Chef/s:** Simon Attridge. **Open:** Tue to Sat D 7 to
11.30. **Closed:** Mon and Sun D. **Meals:** Set L £23.50
Sun, Set D £40 (3 courses). **Service:** 12.5%

## ▊ Reigate
### Dining Room
**Metropolitan cooking in a suburban setting**
59A High Street, Reigate, RH2 9AE
Tel no: (01737) 226650
www.tonytobinrestaurants.co.uk
**Modern British | £40**
**Cooking score: 3**

Tony Tobin joined the ranks of TV celeb chefs
a while back, but he hasn't neglected his duties
as a man of the stoves. His public profile no
doubt helps to drive this upbeat contemporary
brasserie, which is done out in relaxing
colours and soft tones. Fixed-price menus are
the order of the day, with lots of sharp modern
ideas and eclectic influences on show. Honey-
seared salmon and Asian spiced noodle salad
lines up alongside sweet leek and Stilton tart,
while mains explore the enticing possibilities
of cinnamon-smoked guinea fowl breast with
quinoa tabbouleh, orange and cinnamon
vinaigrette or deep-fried baby John Dory
with girolles, broad beans and pancetta.
Desserts tend to be given slick names: 'Choux
fit for Jimmy Choo' is iced cream filled
profiteroles with chocolate sauce. The modern
wine list kicks off with a dozen house
selections from £15.95 (£4.50 a glass); there
are also some classier bottles on the 'library
list'. Tony Tobin's latest venture is Post, a
family-friendly brasserie housed in what was
Banstead village post office (see entry).
**Chef/s:** Tony Tobin. **Open:** Mon to Fri L 12 to 2, Sun
L 12.30 to 2.30, Mon to Sat D 7 to 10. **Closed:**
Christmas, Easter Sun, bank hols. **Meals:** Set L Mon
to Fri £19.50 (2 courses), Set L Sun £28.50, Set D
Mon to Thur £28.50 (2 courses) to £42, Set D Fri
and Sat £34 to £42. **Service:** 12.5% (optional).
**Details:** Cards accepted. 78 seats. Air-con. Music.
Children's portions.

★NEW ENTRY★
## Westerly
Unpretentious bistro de luxe
2-4 London Road, Reigate, RH2 9AN
Tel no: (01737) 222733
Modern British | £28
Cooking score: 4

£5 OFF 🍷 £30

The Westerly is a refreshing and likeable antidote to most high street eateries – low-key and comfortable with a robustly seasonal and quirky menu and charming service. Its chef-proprietor Jon Coombe doesn't believe in short-cuts: starters can include own hot-smoked salmon of superlative texture with fennel, apple and soured cream. The frequently changing menus are peppered with seasonal ingredients and rarer specialities such as Amalfi lemons (used in a fantastic ice-cream) which suggests considerable dedication to sourcing. The food more than lives up to expectations in every detail from impeccable sourdough bread with definitive crust to the snails giving textural garnish to a wonderfully green and intense wild garlic soup. Many regulars return just for the bourride of monkfish, red mullet, bream, prawns, mussels and clams. Among straightforward posh comfort desserts, a wonderful wobbly Sauternes custard with caramelised blood oranges stands out. The Cave de Pyrene wine list is concise and modestly priced too (starting from £9) with plenty by glass and pot lyonnais, besides some rarer more pricey gems .

**Chef/s:** Jon Coomb. **Open:** L Wed to Fri 12.30 to 2 , D Tue to Fri 7 to 10.30. **Closed:** Sun, Mon, Tue L. **Meals:** Set L £19.50 (three courses). **Service:** 12.5%. **Details:** Cards accepted. 45 seats. No music. Children allowed.

## ■ Ripley
## Drake's Restaurant
Elegant fine dining
The Clock House, High Street, Ripley, GU23 6AQ
Tel no: (01483) 224777
www.drakesrestaurant.co.uk
French | £36
Cooking score: 6

£5 OFF V

The exquisite, very proper and elegantly understated Queen Anne house with an impressive illuminated clock above the pillared entrance, certainly stands out on this immaculate village High Street. Inside, first impression is the luxury of well-spaced tables elegantly laid and, weather permitting, the beautiful walled garden with terrace for pre-prandial drinks. Steve Drake, a one-time Roux scholar, trained with Marc Veyrat and Tom Aitken and his accomplished, technically demanding and original approach is clear evidence of such haute echelon credentials. It rather belies his own disingenous description of his cooking as 'artisan'. Drake delights in complex construction, yet never over-adorns and flavours remain fresh and clear. Take roasted scallops with the zing of seaweed tartare, the richness of cauliflower purée, the acidity of Granny Smith and the warmth of sherry – 'risk-taking, yet accessible to savour'. Perfectly flaky sea bass is poached and partnered with flawless crab risotto, roasted cumin aubergine 'caviar', grilled fennel and frothy fennel velouté. Meat dishes often involve several complementary cuts and techniques: crispy pork belly, cheek cooked in white port, roasted carrot purée and seared scallop. Vegetarian dishes are superb, too, say ratte potato wrapped in spinach with rich and juicy roasted cepes. Drake's signature dessert is the lightest of crème reversée (a French take on pannacotta) partnered with Granny Smith sorbet and artfully arranged dried apple tuiles. 'Mesmerising' petits fours include tiny lemon muffins, 'exquisite' passion-fruit and apricot truffles and roasted hazlenut gianduja. Wine prices incline steeply, but good, measured advice is always on hand. Many glasses sit around the £6 marker. NB Children must be over 12.

**Chef/s:** Steve Drake. **Open:** Tue to Fri L 12 to 1.30, Tue to Sat D 7 to 9. **Closed:** Christmas, 2 weeks Aug. **Meals:** Set L £19.50 (2 courses), Set D £42.50 (3 courses). **Service:** not inc. **Details:** Cards accepted. 42 seats. No music. No mobile phones. Wheelchair access. Children allowed. Car parking.

# Shere
## Kinghams
**Sound food at reasonable prices**
Gomshall Lane, Shere, GU5 9HE
Tel no: (01483) 202168
www.kinghams-restaurant.co.uk
**Modern British | £32**
**Cooking score: 3**
£5 OFF  V

At the centre of the pretty village of Shere, Kinghams occupies a seventeenth-century red-brick house where chef-proprietor Paul Baker has held the reins for 15 years. Starters on the à la carte might feature venison carpaccio with port-glazed grapes and a quince and rosemary compote; smoked haddock topped with lime and crayfish butter, spinach purée and lemon oil; or fresh langoustine with watercress mousse and keta caviar dressing. Main courses show similar scope, taking in pan-fried duck breast flavoured with five-spice and served with crispy chilli noodles, bok choi and a water chestnut, ginger and soy sauce, alongside rolled lamb loin with fresh pesto on a bed of chargrilled aubergines and red pepper coulis. Daily fish specials are listed on a blackboard, and for dessert there might be crème brûlée with cherry and kirsch compote, or butterscotch and mint crisp torte. Wines from £14.95.

**Chef/s:** Paul Baker. **Open:** Tue to Sun L 12 to 2.30 (3.30 Sun), Tue to Sat D 7 to 9.30. **Closed:** 25 Dec to 5 Jan. **Meals:** alc (main courses £13 to £22). Set L Tue to Sat £16.50 (2 courses), Set L Sun £18.95 (2 courses) to £22.95, Set D Tue to Thur £16.50 (2 courses). **Service:** not inc. **Details:** Cards accepted.

48 seats. 20 seats outside. No music. No mobile phones. Wheelchair access. Children's portions. Car parking.

# Surbiton
## The French Table
**Great-value restaurant**
85 Maple Road, Surbiton, KT6 4AW
Tel no: (020) 8399 2365
www.thefrenchtable.co.uk
**French | £30**
**Cooking score: 3**

In the short leafy parade of restaurants and pubs that serve smart Surbiton and Kingston folk, The French Table stands out. Chef/ proprietor Eric Guignard's cooking is French at heart but uses complex combinations of flavours and ideas to create an inventive menu. The results are generally good, if a little fussy – a starter of mackerel and smoked aubergine delivered the fish freshly cooked and absolutely fresh, a basil pesto, aubergine chutney as a great foil for the oiliness of the fish; a dish of pork belly prepared three ways, including a mini pork burger with foie gras and a deep fried pork spring roll, was interesting and clever without losing the unctuous sweet richness of the cut. However, Brixham crab prepared as a savoury sundae, with cardamom rice at the bottom, seafood froth on the top, avocado cream and a crab mixture somewhere in between was less than the sum of its parts and a mille feuille of exotic fruits oversweet and over-prepared. Long waits between courses can be tiresome but with a decent wine list (house wines start at £3.50 per glass and fine wines are available for those who want them) and a lightish bill at the end, there are few complaints.

**Chef/s:** Eric and Sarah Guignard. **Open:** Tue to Sun L 12 to 2.30, Tue to Sat D 7 to 10.30. **Closed:** 25 and 26 Dec, 1 to 10 Jan. **Meals:** alc D (main courses £10.50 to £17.50). Set L Tue to Fri £15.50 (2 courses) to £18.50 (3 courses), Set L Sun £19.50 (3 courses). **Service:** 12.5% (optional). **Details:** Cards accepted. 50 seats. Air-con. No mobile phones. Wheelchair access. Music. Children's portions.

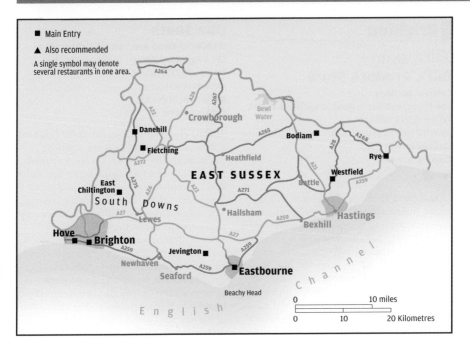

# Bodiam

## Curlew

**Country pub with exceptional wines**
Junction Road, Bodiam, TN32 5UY
Tel no: (01580) 861394
www.thecurlewatbodiam.co.uk
**Modern European | £34**
**Cooking score: 2**

£5 OFF 🍷 𝗬

Functioning primarily as a restaurant, this quintessential white-clapboarded Wealden inn thrives with patronage from well-heeled locals and visitors to nearby Bodiam Castle. The exposed beams and patterned carpet contrast with the contemporary cooking. Wild mushroom risotto, for example, served with truffle oil, tasted of the ancient oak woodlands that dominate the county, and red mullet with herb mash and wilted spinach presented fresh, subtle sea flavours. The extensive wine list, drawn from more than 200 bins, is mostly from France, Italy and Australia. English wines feature from the local Sedlescombe and Sandhurst vineyards and prices begin at £12.95, with seven by the glass from £3.75.
**Chef/s:** Robert Leeper. **Open:** all week L 12 to 2, Tue to Sun D 7 to 9. **Meals:** alc exc Sun and Mon (main courses £13 to £19). Set L Mon to Sat £19.95 (3 courses), Set D Tue to Fri £19.95 (3 courses). **Service:** not inc. **Details:** Cards accepted. 60 seats. 12 seats outside. Air-con. Separate bar. No mobile phones. Music. Children allowed. Car parking.

## Please send us your feedback

To register your opinion about any restaurant listed in the Guide, or a new restaurant that you wish to bring to our attention, please visit the web address at the bottom of the page. Your feedback informs the content of the book and will be used to compile next year's reviews.

# ▌Brighton

★NEW ENTRY★
## Bill's Produce Store

**Colossal portions**
The Depot, 100 North Road, Brighton, BNY 1YE
Tel no: 01273 692894
www.billsproducestore.co.uk
**Modern British | £23**
**Cooking score: 3**
V £30

Here is the very image of a modern British eatery. Bill's originated in Lewes (see entry), its successful formula that of a fresh produce store and deli, plentifully stocked with organic and speciality ingredients and wines, with an eating-area attached. In Brighton, the premises are a converted bus depot, and the vibe is something like eating in the middle of a food market. As this is a shop, weekday eating stops at 8pm, but the evening session brings on supper dishes such as a soft frittata bulging with its filling of salmon and smoked haddock, and piled high with rocket, dried tomatoes and spring vegetables. Other dishes recall the tapas menu, as in a hearty pot of stewed chorizo, butter beans and peppers, alive with cumin, coriander, chilli and paprika. To advise leaving room for desserts is to under-egg the pudding: how about a brick-sized wedge of chocolate, cashew and cardamom mousse, piped with cream and hedged about with mango, raspberries, blood orange and gouts of chocolate sauce? A list of barely half-a-dozen organic wines complements the food. Expect to pay around £13 for a bottle, £3.95 a glass. Another branch is situated in Lewes.
**Chef/s:** Bill Collison. **Open:** Mon to Sat 8 to 8; Sun 10 to 4. **Service:** not inc. **Details:** Cards accepted. Air-con. No music. Children allowed.

## Due South

**Wonderful views and fantastic atmosphere**
139 Kings Road Arches, Brighton, BN1 2FN
Tel no: (01273) 821218
www.duesouth.co.uk
**Modern British | £31**
**Cooking score: 2**

Tucked into one of the arches under Brighton promenade with the beach just a pebble's throw away, Due South relies on a 'crowded, jolly' atmosphere for impact, rather than fancy décor. Simple wooden furniture and wood floors reflect the unfussy tone of the cooking. The restaurant's green credentials are proudly trumpeted on the menu, where the words 'organic', 'free-range' and 'biodynamic' all make a showing. The bulk of the ingredients come from within a 35-mile radius of Brighton beach, so seafood is a strength – perhaps starters of mussels marinière or the Due South fish soup, followed by grilled fish of the day with garlic, lemon and thyme and dressed leaves. The straightforward approach extends to other options such as local asparagus with poached garlic sauce and home-made focaccia followed by pan-fried wood pigeon breast with confit legs and creamed broad beans, bacon and mustard. For dessert, perhaps a generous slab of warm chocolate brownie with chocolate sauce and ice cream. Wines (local, European and often organic) start at £13.
**Chef/s:** James Jenkins. **Open:** all week L 12 to 3.30, D 6 to 10. **Meals:** alc (main courses £11.50 to £18). Set L £14.95 (2 courses). **Service:** 10% (optional). **Details:** Cards accepted. 40 seats. 40 seats outside. Air-con. Wheelchair access. Music. Children's portions.

## Gingerman

**Small and unpretentious**
21A Norfolk Square, Brighton, BN1 2PD
Tel no: (01273) 326688
www.gingermanrestaurants.com
**Modern European | £32**
**Cooking score: 2**

Located just off the square, this is a long, narrow room with bare wooden floors, tables set with white linen and simple artwork on warmly painted walls. Owner and executive chef Ben McKellar now heads up Gingerman at Drakes (see entry) but his original eatery remains a popular, relaxed venue for modern food presented with skill and assurance by David Keats. Kick off with a robust starter, say, pig's head with home-made piccalilli, move on to sea trout with brown shrimp croquette, pea purée and tartare dressing, and finish with steamed chocolate and blueberry pudding with blueberry sauce. A short wine list of well-chosen bottles opens with house Chilean and Italian at £13 or £3.50 a glass.
**Chef/s:** David Keates. **Open:** Tue to Sun 12.30 to 1.45, 7 to 9.45. **Meals:** Set L £13.95 (2 courses) to £16.95, Set D £24 (2 courses) to £27. **Service:** not inc. **Details:** Cards accepted. 36 seats. Air-con. Music. Children's portions.

## Gingerman at Drakes

**Seriously impressive cooking**
44 Marine Parade, Brighton, BN2 1PE
Tel no: (01273) 696934
www.gingermanrestaurants.com
**Modern British | £30**
**Cooking score: 6**

In just a few short years, Ben McKellar's restaurant in the basement of the ultra-chic Drakes hotel, opposite the seafront on Marine Parade, has become established as the number one choice for fine dining in Brighton. Soothing neutral tones dominate the décor, which creates an appropriately refined mood for cooking with an undeniable wow factor. Confit of Tamworth pork belly is served with cauliflower purée and roast langoustine for a starter, or there might be foie gras, chicken 'oyster' and smoked eel terrine with roast figs, intelligently counterpointing rich, luxuriant flavours. No less appealing is an altogether earthier dish of roast veal kidneys on dripping-fried bread with truffle sauce. To follow, an assiette of rabbit with wild garlic, fondant potato and braised Savoy cabbage lines up alongside grilled Pyrenean pork loin with boulangère potatoes, Madeira sauce and baby leeks, while fish dishes might include sea trout on crushed potatoes with wild leeks, potato galette and red wine sauce. End with a choice of savoury or sweet – hot port and Stilton toast, or blood orange and pink grapefruit terrine with passion-fruit sorbet. As well as the comfortable main dining room, there is a private dining room where small groups can eat at the chef's table. A regularly changing choice of wine specials from around £15 a bottle, £4 a glass, is offered alongside a relatively short but well chosen main list.
**Chef/s:** Ben McKellar and Andrew McKenzie. **Open:** all week 12.30 to 2 (2.30 Sun), 7 to 10. **Closed:** 25 Dec. **Meals:** Set L £15 (2 courses) to £18, Set D £27 (2 courses) to £32. **Service:** not inc. **Details:** Cards accepted. 50 seats. Air-con. Music. Children's portions.

## Hotel du Vin & Bistro

**Formula continues to thrive**
2-6 Ship Street, Brighton, BN1 1AD
Tel no: (01273) 718588
www.hotelduvin.com
**Modern European | £30**
**Cooking score: 1**

It's no surprise that the blend of comfortable accommodation and unpretentious, informal bistro dining is still popular – though one reporter thought the kitchen might show a little more ambition. Still, a starter of pink-cooked pigeon breast with balsamic reduction made the right impression. Choice extends to ham hock and foie gras terrine, and to follow there might be pork belly, or perhaps a 'simple classic' such as chargrilled ribeye with fries and béarnaise. Layered rice pudding with lime blueberries might end the meal. A serious wine list groups its offerings by region, with impressive offerings across the board. While there are plenty of bottles with three-figure price tags, there's also good drinking under £20.

**Chef/s:** Rob Carr. **Open:** all week L 12.30 to 1.45 (2.30 Sun), D 7 to 10 (10.30 Fri and Sat). **Meals:** alc exc Sun L (main courses £12.50 to £20). Set L Mon to Fri £14.50 (2 courses) to £19.95, Set L Sun £23.50. **Service:** 10% (optional). **Details:** Cards accepted. 90 seats. No music. Wheelchair access. Children's portions.

## La Marinade

**Neighbourhood restaurant**
77 St Georges Road, Kemp Town, Brighton, BN2 1EN
Tel no: (01273) 600992
www.lamarinade.co.uk
**Modern European | £28**
**Cooking score: 1**

£5 £30
OFF

Eating at La Marinade feels a bit like going to dinner at a friend's house. Visitors to this homely neighbourhood restaurant are welcomed by warm, helpful staff, while Nick Lang sometimes pops out from his kitchen for a quick chat. Back at the stove, he cooks up dishes with a Southern European influence that include starters such as pan-fried chicken livers on spring onion mash or roasted artichoke heart with a plum tomato, palm heart and pine nut salad. Main courses range from Barbary duck with sweet potato mash to pan-fried fillet of sea bass with anchovies, capers and olives in beurre noisette. To finish, choose from desserts such as banana and sesame flambé or home-made amaretti biscuit ice cream. The surprisingly full wine list starts at £11.95.

**Chef/s:** Nick Lang. **Open:** Thu to Sat, L 12 to 3, Tue to Sat, D 6 to 11. **Meals:** alc (main courses £15.50 to £16.50). Set L and D (not Sat) £15. **Service:** not inc. **Details:** Cards accepted. 42 seats. Air-con. Music.

## ★NEW ENTRY★
## Pintxo People

**Contemporary Catalan cooking**
95-99 Western Road, Brighton, BN1 2LB
Tel no: (01273) 732323
www.pintxopeople.co.uk
**Spanish/Portuguese | £30**
**Cooking score: 4**

🍷 🅥 £30

Once the dining-room of a department store, as the architecture attests, now transformed into a two-storey shrine to modern Spanish eating, Pintxo People speaks – like much in Brighton – of sleek, metropolitan fashion. On the ground floor is a wood-floored café where pintxos (the Catalan version of tapas) are served. Climb the curving staircase to a room with white-clothed tables and extravagantly friendly staff and the cooking moves up through several gears. Prices may seem high once you've accumulated a few dishes, but the quality of materials and level of skill they buy are impressive. Fish is excellent, with juicy-fresh prawns finding their way into a salad with apple and avocado, while beautifully timed monkfish is adorned with a dressing of beetroot-purple seaweed and a roll of Serrano ham. Meats offer vibrancy too, in the form of lime-dressed lamb loin of deliquescent tenderness. Banana parcels with Earl Grey ice cream is one way to finish, or there are fine Spanish cheeses with membrillo. The wine list leads with a good Spanish selection, before lighting out for foreign climes. Choice by the glass is wide, including a range of unmissable sherries. Bottles start at £15.50 for a Rueda.

**Chef/s:** Miguel Jessen. **Open:** Tue to Thu D 6 to 12, Fri to Sat L 12 to 4, D 6 to 1, Sun L 12 to 4. **Meals:** Dishes £3 to £14 Set D £28 and £35. **Service:** 12% (included). **Details:** Cards accepted. Air-con. Separate bar. Music. Children's portions.

## Real Eating Company
**All-in-one brasserie, restaurant and deli**
86-87 Western Road, Brighton, BN3 1JB
Tel no: (01273) 221444
www.real-eating.co.uk
Modern European | £30
Cooking score: 2

All-day eating in a relaxed and casual environment is the modus operandi of this Hove deli-cum-restaurant. Ingredients are sourced principally from local suppliers, the range extended with specialities from around the world, to provide breakfast, lunch and dinner with coffee and cakes to fill the gaps in between. The day might start with a full cooked breakfast, eggs benedict, or even French toast with banana and maple syrup, while the lunch menu features simple, hearty fare such as fishcakes with mayonnaise, ribeye steak sandwich with aïoli and chips, or seared tuna niçoise. In the evening, the kitchen pulls out the stops to offer seared scallops with sauté potatoes, or ballotine of rabbit with blueberries, followed by lamb rump with spring greens, fondant potato and tomato fondue, or bream with gem lettuce, potato gallette and blackberry shallots, with bread-and-butter pudding with custard to finish. Wines from £14. Branches in Lewes and Horsham.
Chef/s: Chris O'Brien. Open: all week L 12 to 3, Wed to Sat and bank hol Sun D 6.30 to 9.30. Closed: 25 and 26 Dec, 1 Jan. Meals: Set D £18 (3 courses). Service: not inc. Details: Cards accepted. 40 seats. 12 seats outside. Air-con. Wheelchair access. Music. Children's portions.

## Sevendials
**Spacious informality**
1 Buckingham Place, Brighton, BN1 3TD
Tel no: (01273) 885555
www.sevendialsrestaurant.co.uk
Modern European | £31
Cooking score: 3

The red-brick premises look like a prime piece of Brighton real estate, sitting as they do on the Seven Dials intersection. The menu is modern brasserie through and through, majoring in such dishes as sautéed garlic prawns with celeriac coleslaw and roasted cherry tomatoes, or duck wonton with sweet-and-sour dressing and a crisp salad, to start, maybe followed by monkfish in Parma ham wrap with endive tart and chive butter. This is the kind of unfiddly food, big on flavour, that Brighton likes to eat, seen at its proudest perhaps in a main course of chargrilled pork loin chop with apple and date chutney, mustard mash and spring greens. You finish with the likes of rhubarb and macadamia fool, or – since this is the seaside – a 'magic ice cream sundae'. Wines are arranged by price and colour only, starting with French Sauvignon and Merlot at £13.
Chef/s: Sam Metcalfe. Open: all week L 12 to 3 (12.30 to 4 Sun), Mon to Sat D 7 (6.30 Fri and Sat) to 10.30. Closed: Christmas. Meals: alc (main courses £10 to £16), Set L Mon to Sat £12.50 (2 courses) to £15, Sun £15 (2 courses) to £20. Service: 12% (optional). Details: Cards accepted. 60 seats. 50 seats outside. Air-con. Wheelchair access. Music. Children's portions. Car parking.

## Terre à Terre

**Vegetarian trail-blazer**
71 East Street, Brighton, BN1 1HQ
Tel no: (01273) 729051
www.terreaterre.co.uk
**Vegetarian | £29**
**Cooking score: 3**

V £30

It is the happy fate of Terre à Terre to have garnered a solid local following of customers who are possibly only vegetarian when they eat here. Space barely permits a comprehensive roll-call of dishes that might take in 'Baked Golden Cross ash crottin and whole roast garlic, served with black onion-seed fried cracker breads, fresh pea shooter, lemon mint creamcino and pea-shoot Cox's Pippin tangle'. By the time you've untangled yourself from the puns and esoterica, the result on the plate is more often than not a glorious melange of vivid flavours, fascinating textures and great ideas. Starters might include bruschetta with garlicked squash and an olive 'cassoulet', while desserts tempt with rhubarb and rosehip trifle with orange crackle and ginger syrup ripple. Wines are an organic and biodynamic bunch, in keeping with the philosophy, with prices from £16.85 (glasses from £4.85).
**Chef/s:** Glen Lester. **Open:** Tue to Sun L 12 to 6, Tue to Sun D 6 to 10.30, (11 Sat, 10 Sun). **Closed:** 25 and 26 Dec, 1 Jan. **Meals:** alc (main courses £10.50 to £13.95). **Service:** not inc. **Details:** Cards accepted. 100 seats. 12 seats outside. Air-con. No music. Wheelchair access. Children's portions.

## ALSO RECOMMENDED

### ▲ Moshi Moshi

Bartholomew Square, Brighton, BN1 1JS
Tel no: (01273) 719195

The Brighton outpost of this popular chain of sushi restaurants occupies a glass box of a building, wherein the familiar conveyor belt snakes its way about bearing plates of Japanese delicacies. As well as a range of raw fish, there are cooked dishes such as chicken yakitori, or vegetable and pork gyoza dumplings. Dishes are priced according to a colour-coding

system, ranging from £1.50 to £3. Just sit at the counter and grab what you fancy as it trundles past, or place special orders with the chef. Drink green tea, Japanese beer, hot or cold saké, or wines from £13.80 a bottle. Closed Mon.

## ■ Danehill
## Coach & Horses

**Rural pub and restaurant with gardens**
School Lane, Danehill, RH17 7JF
Tel no: (01825) 740369
**Modern British | £25**
**Cooking score: 2**

£30

This cosy country pub, complete with dartboard, retains regulars while serving modern European food in the adjoining converted beamed stables. There is a pretty front garden with an 'adults only' preserve at the rear. In season, start with 'faultless' asparagus soup, or stuffed Portobello mushrooms, with strong feta cheese. Tender ribeye steak is cooked this side of medium rare and comes topped with a bitter-sweet red-onion marmalade accompanied by cherry tomatoes on the vine with a full shovel of fries. Sea bass, caught in Seaford Bay, is perfectly timed. Puddings, like the rest of the menu, vary with the seasons, and can include white chocolate pannacotta. Vin de pays on the global wine list starts at £12.50, with 13 wines by the glass from £3.30.
**Chef/s:** Jason Tidy. **Open:** all week L 12 to 2 (2.30 Sat and Sun), Mon to Sat D 7 to 9 (9.30 Fri and Sat). **Closed:** D 24 Dec, 25 and 26 Dec, D 1 Jan. **Meals:** alc (main courses £10.95 to £15.50). **Service:** not inc. **Details:** Cards accepted. 70 seats. 30 seats outside. Separate bar. Wheelchair access. Music. Children's portions. Car parking.

## East Chiltington

### Jolly Sportsman

**Quality cooking at this updated country pub**
Chapel Lane, East Chiltington, BN7 3BA
Tel no: (01273) 890400
www.thejollysportsman.com
**Modern European | £25**
**Cooking score: 3**

V £30

This rural pub feels more contemporary than rustic and the kitchen's busily inventive menus transcend the sleepy setting. The modern feel is reflected in the food, which is built around fresh, carefully sourced ingredients. Starters such as salt cod and leek tagliolini, or a rich crab bisque, set the tone and combine exemplary freshness with sound technique. Flavour is built up robustly in main courses, partnering a crisp, confit duck leg with a plum and ginger compote, or fashioning an aubergine stew to go with herbed lamb rump. There are more homely dishes too, such as fish and chips, or an Angus beef bourguignonne offered alongside duck rillettes on the good-value set lunch menu. Puddings are generally variations on traditional themes: orange marmalade steamed pudding with fresh custard, or date and almond tart with clotted cream. Courteous and efficient staff add to the sense of well being. France is at the heart of the global wine list, with around nine offered by the glass (from £3.25), and bottle prices starting at £12.85.
**Chef/s:** Richard Willis. **Open:** Tue to Sun 12.30 to 2.15 (3 Sun), Tue to Sat 7 to 9.15 (10 Fri and Sat). **Closed:** 4 days Christmas. **Meals:** alc (main courses £9 to £17.50). Set L Tue to Sat £12.50 (2 courses). **Service:** not inc. **Details:** Cards accepted. 80 seats. 40 seats outside. Air-con. No music. Wheelchair access. Children's portions. Car parking.

## Eastbourne

### The Mirabelle at The Grand Hotel

**Grand by name and grand by nature**
King Edwards Parade, Eastbourne, BN21 4EQ
Tel no: (01323) 412345
www.grandeastbourne.com
**Modern European | £32**
**Cooking score: 5**

🍾 🍴 V

The Mirabelle has, for years, been a small but important part of this archetypal seaside hotel, with its era-driven rouched curtains and pile carpet; trolleys and domes; hushed, attentive and knowledgeable service and a pianist tinkling through old show tunes. But the food, under Gerald Röser, a master of flavouring, is thoroughly modern. From a small pile of deeply accented crab meat on toast to the concluding petits fours – the dinner menu price includes coffee *and* service - everything confirms you are in skilled hands. Until the desserts, don't expect elaboration. A fresh springtime parsley and thyme soup and a chunky salade niçoise supporting a generous steak of accurately cooked tuna share essential simplicities. An inspection meal showed sharply defined flavours; in a main course of immaculately timed fillets of black bream on light, subtle coriander and lemon couscous complemented in texture and colour by small mounds of tender samphire, followed by rhubarb terrine (a parfait) with hints of ginger, sporting arches of thin strips of dried rhubarb, everything tasted as good as it looked. A careful selection of twenty wines by the glass, in two sizes, are matched by fine bottles at big prices.
**Chef/s:** Keith Mitchell and Gerald Röser. **Open:** Tue to Sat 12.30 to 2, 7 to 10. **Closed:** first 2 weeks Jan. **Meals:** Set L £17.50 (2 courses) to £20, Set D £36.50 to £55. **Service:** net prices. **Details:** Cards accepted. 48 seats. Air-con. No mobile phones. Wheelchair access. Music. Jacket and tie required. Children's portions. Car parking.

## Fletching

### The Griffin Inn
Sweeping views across the Weald
Fletching, TN22 3SS
Tel no: (01825) 722890
www.thegriffininn.co.uk
Modern European | £30
Cooking score: 1

£5 OFF 🍷 🍴 ∀

The hamlet of Fletching is home to a Norman church and the four-century-old Griffin Inn, which sits in a row of intriguing early Victorian 'medieval' houses and shops. Locals, both drinkers and diners, tend to reflect the prosperity of this corner of Sussex. Ambitious menus have a modern feel, provide a good balance of fish and meat, much of it locally sourced – Rye Bay sea bass, Romney Marsh lamb – and give some recognition to seasonality. Carefully timed red mullet fillets and decent pastry for an apricot tart demonstrate sound technique; but equal attention needs to be given to the odd lack of flavouring and signs of items emerging with the chill of the refrigerator about them. Wines, however, are taken seriously, with several available by the glass. House wine from £12.50

Chef/s: Andrew Billings. Open: all week, L 12 to 2.30, Mon to Sat, D 7 to 9.30. Closed: 25 Dec. Meals: alc exc Sun L (main courses £11 to £19.50). Set L Sun £25.. Service: not included. Details: Cards accepted. 60 seats. 35 seats outside. No mobile phones. Wheelchair access. Music. Children's portions. Car parking.

## Hove

★NEW ENTRY★
### Ginger Pig
Comfort cooking with intelligence
3 Hove Street, Hove, BN3
Tel no: (01273) 736123
www.gingermanrestaurants.com
Gastropub | £30
Cooking score: 3

Those not paying due attention might just mistake Ben McKellar's latest seaside venture, just off the Hove promenade, for a restaurant rather than the no-frills dining pub it aims to be. A smart bar area fronts a spacious room, with laminate wood tables, a no-booking policy, and the kind of friendly, unpretentious staff that make Brighton a welcome escape from metropolitan shrugginess. Presentations look distinctly cheffy, and the celebration of local materials and seasonality are in the mode of best restaurant practice, but the menu is structured around homely pub dishes. These might be chicken liver terrine, followed by steak with roasted tomato and garlic butter. Boyton Farm supplies fine pork products, whether they be sausages or belly, which comes slow-cooked to crackly perfection, with crunchy green beans and apple sauce. Fish pie presents a huge bowl of smouldering cream sauce containing white fish, salmon, prawns and mussels under a puff pastry lid, its expected buttery mash topping served separately. Finish with a delightfully creamy, lemon and vanilla pannacotta with raspberry compote. The short wine list is a succinct collection of the kinds of bottles Britain like to drink these days. Prices start at £12.

Chef/s: Ben McKellar and Simon Neville Jones. Open: Mon to Fri 12 to 2, 6.30 to 10; Sat 12 to 4, 6.30 to 10; Sun 12.30 to 4, 6.30 to 10. Closed: Christmas Day. Service: not incl. Details: Cards accepted. 55 seats. 35 seats outside. Air-con. Separate bar. Music. Children's portions.

## ▌Jevington

### Hungry Monk
**Welcoming and intimate**
Jevington, BN26 5QF
Tel no: (01323) 482178
www.hungrymonk.co.uk
**Anglo-French | £32**
**Cooking score: 2**
£5 OFF ✌

The ancient house can trace its lineage back to the 1300s. Nigel Mackenzie hasn't been running the Hungry Monk quite that long, but the operation exudes the confidence that comes from long practice anyway. What they return for is proficient cooking that moves with the times, without chasing after breathless innovation for its own sake. Spring menus saw halibut roasted in a prosciutto wrap with new season's asparagus for company, or duck breast accompanied by a peppery sauce of tropical fruits. Pasta works its way into quite a few dishes, as in the luganega sausage ravioli starter, with chilli-spiked tomato sauce, while desserts might take in rhubarb and mascarpone soufflé. Be it noted, though, that this is where the banoffi pie originated, which everybody should try at least once. French house wines from £14.50 head a substantial list that makes room for a handful of home-grown whites, and there are plenty of half-bottles.
**Chef/s:** Gary Fisher and Matt Comben. **Open:** Sun L 12 to 2.30, all week D 6.45 to 9.30. **Closed:** 24 to 26 Dec, 1 Jan, bank hols. **Meals:** Set L £29.95 (3 courses), Set D £32.95 (3 courses). **Service:** not inc (12.5% for parties of 7+). **Details:** Cards accepted. 38 seats. Air-con. No mobile phones. Wheelchair access. Music. Children's portions. Car parking.

## READERS RECOMMEND

### Pailin
**Thai**
19-20 Station Street, Lewes, BN7 2DB
Tel no: (01273) 473906
**'Lively and authentic approach'**

## ▌Rye

★NEW ENTRY★
### The George in Rye
**Ancient inn, modern food**
98 High Street, Rye, TN31 7JT
Tel no: (01797) 222114
www.thegeorgeinrye.com
**Modern European | £30**
**Cooking score: 1**
£5 OFF 🍷 🛏 ✌ £30

After a spell in decline, this classic Tudor coaching inn has been turned into a stylish hotel. The enterprise is split into two parts: a pubby, beamed bar and a simply dressed modern restaurant – 'too modern' say some locals who feel the owners should have run to a pair of solid doors between the dining area and the bar, which, on a Saturday night, can 'disturb gourmet satisfaction'. On the day menu (available in both the bar and restaurant) it's a delight to see goujons of Rye Bay plaice, shrimps and scallops. The evening menu (served in the restaurant) can bring dressed crab with excellent sourdough toast and local leaf salad, then chargrilled Romney Marsh lamb with patatas a los pobres and watercress salad and an an 'intensely flavoured' chocolate almond and Armagnac cake. At inspection, however, it was felt that while the ideas and the ingredients are all there, 'flavours need to be sharpened and deepened'.
**Chef/s:** Rod Grossman. **Open:** all week, 12 to 3, 6.30 to 10. **Meals:** alc (main courses £13 to 16.50) Set L £13 (2 courses) to £16. **Service:** not inc.
**Details:** Cards accepted. 30 seats. 35 seats outside. Separate bar. No mobile phones. Wheelchair access. Music. Children's portions.

## ★NEW ENTRY★
## Landgate Bistro
**Traditional farmhouse country cooking**
5-6 Landgate, Rye, TN31 7LH
Tel no: (01797) 222829
www.landgatebistro.co.uk
**Modern British | £23**
**Cooking score: 3**
V ₤30

The Landgate menu evokes food from a
Victorian farmhouse kitchen and makes rich
use of the varied and distinctive local
ingredients: game, Romney Marsh lamb,
scallops, crab and shrimps from Rye Bay, and
cream and butter from a dairy down the road.
The small dining room, with its exposed
beams and brickwork, has a reassuring rustic
charm and the food pays more than a nod to
traditional English fare (potted rabbit, jugged
hare). Home-made soda bread is 'light,
flavoursome and crusty', and a perfect foil to
the nettle soup, served with a lightly poached
egg – a neat twist on *bouillon mit ei* – and
scallops in bacon with sherry and shallot sauce
is served both as starter and main. Local fish is
used extensively; Dover sole, for example, is
baked in Vermouth, after which, the cooking
liquor is used to flavour a beurre blanc:'it
looked a bit of a mess but tasted heavenly'.
Puddings are just as seductive and include a
moist chocolate cake, a sharp lemon tart and a
Muscat-flavoured trifle. House wines start
at £10.90.
**Chef/s:** Martin Peacock. **Open:** Tue to Sat 7 to close.
**Closed:** Bank hols. **Meals:** alc (main courses £10.50-
£14.40). Set L £13.50 (2 courses). **Service:** inc.
**Details:** Cards accepted. 37 seats. Music. Children's
portions.

## Webbe's at the Fish Café
**Popular with visitors and locals alike**
17 Tower Street, Rye, TN31 7AT
Tel no: (01797) 222226
www.thefishcafe.com
**Modern Seafood | £24**
**Cooking score: 4**
£5 OFF ♦ V ₤30

This century-old venue proudly presents a
ground-floor café, built around an open-plan
kitchen. Upstairs, Webbe's restaurant offers a
more formal setting and is open for dinner. A
diverse range of ten dishes in each of the three
courses includes fried local scallops, poached
or steamed black bream or bass, and
chargrilled squid. But not all the fish comes
from Rye Bay or even nearby: the sardines,
salmon and prawns did not swim the Channel,
while the lobster came from Canada.
Nevertheless, the menu caters for all tastes,
from deep-fried cod in a beer batter with chips
to a lobster seafood platter, while carpaccio of
monkfish with salsa verde, pork and black
fungus rillette with preserved apple or
asparagus mousse with pickled pear could be
designed for the more discerning guest and
also ensure that both carnivore and vegetarian
are considered. Homely dishes include
smoked haddock with spinach and poached
egg and, inevitably, the ubiquitous fishcakes.
Vegetables tend towards the chic pak choi,
rocket, pea and bean shoot brigade, stir-fried
but slightly caramelised. The desserts fulfil
their role of ultimate temptation and house
wines are all highly drinkable (from £13.25).
**Chef/s:** Paul Webbe. **Open:** all week, D 6 to 9.30.
**Meals:** alc (£14 to £18). Set D £12 (2 courses) to £16
(3 courses). **Service:** not inc. **Details:** Cards
accepted. Air-con. Music. Children allowed.

## Westfield

# Wild Mushroom
**Modern menus**
Woodgate House, Westfield Lane, Westfield,
TN35 4SB
Tel no: (01424) 751137
www.wildmushroom.co.uk
**Modern European | £24**
**Cooking score: 2**

£5 OFF  V  £30

A converted farmhouse behind an ancient
wooden fence, with an almost equally antique
lamp-post in front of it, the Wild Mushroom
is in the same ownership as its junior sibling,
Webbe's at the Fish Café (see entry, Rye).
Dishes are given a one-word headline, so that
'Pork' translates as rillettes of pork and black
fungus mushrooms with apricot chutney, or a
main course of 'Bream' is grilled fillets of
black bream with brandade, pak choi,
asparagus, red pepper and a shellfish sauce.
Old-fashioned puddings such as pear and
blackcurrant crumble then rub shoulders with
the more exploratory likes of dark chocolate
and kirsch fondue with biscotti,
marshmallows and soft fruits for dunking.
The wine list settles for offering a small
handful from most regions (not forgetting
Mexico). Glass prices start at £3.50, bottles
at £13.95.
**Chef/s:** Matthew Drinkwater. **Open:** Tue to Fri and
Sun L 12 to 2, Tue to Sat D 7 to 9.30. **Closed:**
Christmas, first 2 weeks Jan. **Meals:** alc D (main
courses £11.95 to £18.95). Set L £15.95 (2 courses) to
£18.95. Set D £32. **Service:** not inc. **Details:** Cards
accepted. 44 seats. Wheelchair access. Music.
Children's portions. Car parking.

Pascal Sanchez

**Why did you become a chef?**
I was inspired by my mother's passion
for cooking.

**Which of today's chefs do you admire?**
Pierre Gagnaire.

**Where do you source your ingredients?**
I source my shellfish locally from Premier
Shellfish in London, along with fresh
ingredients from France, Spain and Italy.

**Who is your favourite producer?**
Bastellica – they are based in South-West
France and I consider their organic herbs
to be the best.

**What's the best dish you've ever eaten?**
A Gruyere soup in Switzerland. It was from
a small family-run establishment located in
the Swiss Alps.

**Do you have a favourite local recipe?**
Fish soup from Marseille.

**What's your guilty food pleasure?**
Sweet pastries, especially the ones filled
with chocolate cream.

**If you could only eat one more thing,
what would it be?**
Kobe beef.

**What's coming up next for you?**
Fine-tuning our menus and our style
at Sketch.

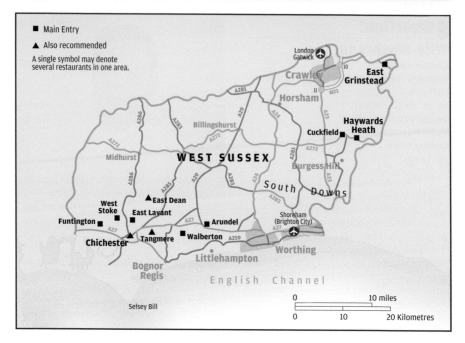

- ■ Main Entry
- ▲ Also recommended

A single symbol may denote several restaurants in one area.

## ▌Arundel

### Arundel House
**An oasis in a culinary desert**
11 High Street, Arundel, BN18 9AD
Tel no: (01903) 882136
www.arundelhouseonline.co.uk
**Modern British | £28**
**Cooking score: 2**

🍷 ⊨ Ⅴ ₤30

'This is a lovely place, beautifully decorated and nicely furnished: plenty of room between tables' notes a visitor to this bow-windowed house at the bottom of the High Street hill. The service is excellent and the set lunch value for money. Wild mushroom soup, laced with cream and served with hot bread, was a triumph, 'palpably fresh' seared salmon and halibut fillets with champ potatoes and pesto dressing were also excellent, puddings delicious (despite the hot caramelised satsuma defying cutting into smaller portions, and the banana and honeycomb parfait still 'almost frozen in the middle'). The à la carte is

impressively ambitious – 'a bonus mark for offering Scotch woodcock as an alternative to sweet desserts'. The wine list is equally notable, with some 150 wines eclectically sourced from around the world and just enough description to be helpful. Prices start at £16 and there are half-a-dozen wines by the glass from £4 to £6. NB Children must be over 5.
**Chef/s:** Luke Hackman and Claire Small. **Open:** Tue to Sat, L 12.30 to 2, Mon to Sat, D 7 to 9.30. **Closed:** Christmas. **Meals:** Set L £16 (3 courses). **Service:** not inc. **Details:** Cards accepted. 34 seats. Music. Children allowed.

## ALSO RECOMMENDED

### ▲ Comme Ça
67 Broyle Road, Chichester, PO19 6BD
Tel no: (01243) 788724
www.commeca.co.uk

The proximity of this French restaurant to the adjacent Chichester Festival Theatre may scream pre-theatre food fix, but others may want to take their time and savour every mouthful. Favourites include loin of venison on a bed of red cabbage (£16.95) and free-range French guinea fowl with Madeira jus and Puy lentils (£14.95). Desserts vie for atention with a selection of the best cheeses France has to offer. House wine is £12.95. Open Wed to Sun L and Tue to Sat D.

## ▲ Dining Room at Purchases

31 North Street, Chichester, PO19 1LY
Tel no: 01243 537352
www.thediningroom.biz

A useful pitstop for tapas or Danish open sandwiches pre- or post-theatre (Chichester's Festival Theatre is a hop, skip and a jump away), the Dining Room, in a converted Georgian house with secluded garden, also offers à la carte. Local Selsey crab in filo (£8.95) with a pungent curry sauce, Irish Oysters (£8.95), chargrilled calf's liver with bubble and squeak galette and a shallot sauce (£14.50) or Omelette Arnold Bennett (£11.95) are possibles. This is foie gras, caviar and game territory too with a selection of well-chosen cheeses, lemon tart or home-made ice creams (£5.50) to follow. Thirteen wines by the glass and half-bottles galore from well-sourced wine list. Open all week.

## ▮ Cuckfield

## Ockenden Manor

Sixteenth-century manor house
Ockenden Lane, Cuckfield, RH17 5LD
Tel no: (01444) 416111
www.hshotels.co.uk
Modern French | £40
Cooking score: 6

£5 OFF ▬ ✔

Ockenden is enviably situated. Its nine acres of grounds include a walled garden, and the interiors are awash with gilt-framed paintings and an air of formal gentility. Two contrasting dining rooms form the setting for Stephen Crane's technically polished, ambitious cooking. This works within the soft-centred country-house idiom, but

manages to encompass some inventive touches while maintaining a sense of balance. A Gallic pairing of breaded frogs' legs and snail persillade turns up with garlic mayonnaise and pickled mushrooms among starters, or there might be the deceptive simplicity of a raviolo of langoustine served in matching velouté. Pork and duck are sourced from South-west France, but the lamb at least is local, from Ditchling, and might be the saddle served with a stew of flageolet beans, crisp sweetbreads and minted hollandaise. For fish-lovers, the choice on a spring menu included an escalope of brill with button mushrooms, purple sprouting broccoli and a crab velouté. Finely wrought desserts make the most of seasonal fruits, instead of majoring in chocolate, so that April turned up poached rhubarb with ginger, shortbread biscuits and fromage blanc ice cream (but there was also chocolate fondant for those with the hankering). A cheese trolley offers savoury relief. Without a blush for anachronism, the seven-course tasting menu turns around a mid-point sorbet, such as pink grapefruit and champagne, while vegetarians have their own short menu. An extensive wine list makes commendable efforts outside Europe, although the centre of gravity is Bordeaux and its various districts. Eleven house wines are all pegged, hearteningly, at the one price: £19.50 a bottle, £4.75 a glass.

**Chef/s:** Stephen Crane. **Open:** all week 12.30 to 2, 7 to 9.30. **Meals:** Set L £13.95 (2 courses), Set D £47.50 (3 courses). Bar menu available.
**Service:** not inc. **Details:** Cards accepted. 48 seats. 20 seats outside. No mobile phones. Wheelchair access. Children's portions. Car parking.

## ALSO RECOMMENDED

## ▲ Star & Garter

East Dean, PO18 0JG
Tel no: (01243) 811318
www.thestarandgarter.

It is easy to dismiss the Star and Garter as just another refurbished old inn which sells decent food. But leave your preconceptions at the door and enjoy the finest seafood and the kind of atmosphere you can only get in a country pub. Traditional cod in a crispy beer batter with chips and chef's tartare (£8.50) sits well with fresh shellfish delivered every day. Non-fish choices can include rib-eye steak or roast rump of lamb (both £15.50). Wines from £12. Open all week. Accommodation.

## East Grinstead
### Gravetye Manor
**Exquisite dishes and high standards**
Vowels Lane, East Grinstead, RH19 4LJ
Tel no: (01342) 810567
www.gravetyemanor.co.uk
**Modern French | £40**
**Cooking score: 5**

Stunning gardens and oak panelled rooms mark Gravetye out from many places that share its high culinary aspirations. It is possible to get more than the gist of this quality through the limited – two dishes for each course – good value, set menu. At inspection outstanding flavouring was eptimised in two starters: a powerfully gamey duck terrine, its richness complemented by ribbons of acidified minty jelly; or softer, accurately defined, marine flavours in a charlotte of evenly textured smoked salmon mousse wrapped delicately in lemon sole fillets surrounded by an elegant smooth lobster sauce, each element contribute to a perfect *menage a trois*. Timing, as in a superb hunk of moist halibut and a dish of tender pork loin, compares well with other skills; on the periphery the range of fresh, soft breads, crispy nibbles and the not-too-sweet petits

### Please send us your feedback

To register your opinion about any restaurant listed in the Guide, or a new restaurant that you wish to bring to our attention, please visit the web address at the bottom of the page. Your feedback informs the content of the book and will be used to compile next year's reviews.

fours confirm a confident kitchen working within achievable ambition. Service is young, efficient and skilful and not expected to execute arcane rituals such as dome raising. A leather bound wine list provides an afternoon's reading; more practical is the excellent selection of wines by the glass at relatively modest prices. NB Children must be over 7.
**Chef/s:** Mark Raffan. **Open:** all week 12.30 to 1.45, 7.30 to 9.30. **Closed:** Christmas Day. **Meals:** Set L £26, Set D £35. **Service:** 12.5% (optional). **Details:** Cards accepted. 45 seats. 25 seats outside. No music. No mobile phones. Jacket and tie required. Children allowed. Car parking.

## East Lavant
### Royal Oak
**Open fires in winter**
Pook Lane, East Lavant, PO18 0AX
Tel no: (01243) 527434
www.thesussexpub.co.uk
**Modern European | £31**
**Cooking score: 3**

Lisa and Nick Sutherland's empire has four inns including this highly sought-after one in the flint-cottaged village of East Lavant, two miles north of Chichester. It's a must-book place with clattering wood floors and white, scrubbed pine tables in the original pub area and conservatory. A basket of 'superb', rustic bread soon hits the table, and the kitchen mixes very British fish and chips with Thai sea bass with pak choi and lime butter, while French influences are felt with such dishes as ham hock and foie gras terrine (served too chilled at inspection, but with all the 'hallmarks of a stunning dish') but calf's liver with a red-wine sauce redressed the balance, as did a lemon posset tart. Service can be 'utterly delightful'. An accessible 60-plus wine list has 13 by the glass.
**Chef/s:** Malcolm Goble and Oz Whatson. **Open:** all week 12 to 2.30, 6 to 9. **Meals:** alc (main courses £11.50 to £18). **Service:** not inc. **Details:** Cards accepted. 30 seats. Air-con. Wheelchair access. Music. Children's portions. Car parking.

## Funtington

### Hallidays

**Wood-fired oven for breads and roasting**
Watery Lane, Funtington, PO18 9LF
Tel no: (01243) 575331
www.halidays.com
**Modern European | £20**
**Cooking score: 2**

Set in a terrace of ancient thatched cottages, in a village near Chichester, this place is very much a tribute to the missionary zeal of one man, Andy Stephenson. He is an avowed believer in local sourcing, and to that end has built up an unimpeachable network of local contacts among smallholders, day-boats and suppliers of seasonal produce. Dinner might open with soft-shell crab tempura, served with pickled vegetable relish and chilli jam. Proceedings then continue with honey-roast guinea fowl with Puy lentils and sherry vinegar, or with line-caught sea bream served with a roasted pepper salsa, basil oil and lemon. Scotch beef fillet is royally treated, hung for three weeks and accompanied with girolles and garlic leaves. To finish, there may be a thin apple tart with rosemary ice cream and caramel sauce, or citrus buttermilk mousse with rhubarb compote and toasted almonds. An international selection of wines opens with a house listing from £12, or £3.30 a glass.
**Chef/s:** Andy Stephenson. **Open:** Wed to Fri and Sun L 12 to 1.30, Wed to Sat D 7 to 9.15 (Sat 9.30). **Closed:** 2 week Mar, 1 week Aug. **Meals:** alc L Wed to Fri (main courses £18.50 to £19.50). **Service:** not included. **Details:** Cards accepted. 26 seats. No music. Wheelchair access. Children allowed. Car parking.

## Haywards Heath

### Jeremy's

**Bright dining room**
Borde Hill, Balcombe Road, Haywards Heath, RH16 1XP
Tel no: (01444) 441102
www.jeremysrestaurant.com
**Modern European | £31**
**Cooking score: 4**

The low brick building, arranged around a courtyard at the entrance to Borde Hill Gardens, welcomes with a dining room decorated with colourful artwork. When the sun shines, the expanse of terrace overlooking a Victorian walled garden is a splendid alfresco spot. Jeremy Ashpool is a confident and skilful chef, serving up an eclectic range of dishes based on impressive local produce, from asparagus (with tarragon butter sauce) and Rye Bay fish ragôut, to loin of Balcombe venison with red wine and majoram sauce. Further choices on the monthly carte and set-price menus may include a seared squid starter, served with leek vinaigrette and roasted tomatoes, and a main course of rack and braised neck of Romney Marsh lamb, served with spring vegetables, dauphinois and mint jus. Do leave room for dessert, perhaps chocolate torte with rosewater marinated raspberries and buttermilk ice cream. A list of monthly recommendations heads up the short wine list, with house wines from £14.50.
**Chef/s:** Jeremy Ashpool. **Open:** Tue to Sun L 12.30 to 2.30, Tue to Sat D 7.30 to 10. **Meals:** alc exc Sun L (main courses £13.50 to £20). Set L Tue to Sat £17.50 (2 courses) to £23, Set D Tue to Thur £17.50 (2 courses). **Service:** not inc. **Details:** Cards accepted. 55 seats. 35 seats outside. Wheelchair access. Music. Children's portions. Car parking.

## ALSO RECOMMENDED

### ▲ Cassons

Arundel Road, Tangmere, PO18 0DU
Tel no: (01243) 773294
www.cassonsrestaurant.co.uk

Popular with locals, this rural restaurant is two miles east of Chichester. There's an eclectic feel to the menu, with starters taking in Arbroath smokies with beetroot salad and quail's eggs (£8.95) and oysters in champagne (£9.95 for six). Mains are simple and hearty with Scottish prime fillet of beef served in various sauces, ranging from truffles and foie gras (£29.50) to blue cheese (£21.50), while mille-feuilles of goats' cheese and Mediterranean vegetables (£15.95) is a good vegetarian choice. If it's hard to choose at dessert stage, take the chef's quartet (£8.95). House wines start at £13.95. Open all week.

## ■ Walberton

### Oaks Restaurant

**Unfussy food in friendly surroundings**
Yapton Lane, Walberton, BN18 0LS
Tel no: (01243) 552865
www.kencancook.com
**Modern British | £28**
**Cooking score: 2**

£5 OFF ⊨ V £30

Occupying a primrose yellow painted Georgian house, the Oaks aims to be 'the perfect neighbourhood restaurant'. The Browns are hands-on owners, running the place enthusiastically, and on Sundays Ken comes out of the kitchen to carve the Sunday roast on his antique carving trolley. Bold, gutsy flavours are a key feature of the cooking, as demonstrated in starters such as smoked goose with piccalilli and venison rillettes with pickled cabbage. Equally forthright main courses typically include crispy slow-roasted pork belly served on apple bubble and squeak with a creamy cider sauce, and to finish, there might be Chichester tart, a traditional delicacy of baked egg custard with ground almonds and cinnamon. A selection of fine British

cheeses makes an appealing savoury alternative. A well-chosen and well-annotated wine list kicks off with house French at £12.50.

**Chef/s:** Ken Brown. **Open:** Tue to Sun L 12 to 2.30, Tue to Sat D 7 to 10. **Meals:** alc (main courses £13 to £20). Set L Tue to Sat £12 (2 courses) to £15, Set L Sun £16.95 (2 courses) to £20.95. **Service:** not inc. **Details:** Cards accepted. 66 seats. 30 seats outside. Music. Children's portions. Car parking.

## ■ West Stoke

★ MOST-IMPROVED RESTAURANT ★

### West Stoke House

**French flair with English precision defines this restaurant**
Downs Road, West Stoke, PO18 9BN
Tel no: (01243) 575226
www.weststokehouse.co.uk
**Anglo-French | £40**
**Cooking score: 5**

🍷 ⊨

Darren Brown, late of the Lanesborough Hotel and Monsieur Max, has joined forces with Mary and Rowland Leach, new owners of this effortlessly civilised restaurant-with-rooms surrounded by Sussex countryside near Goodwood. He cooks bang up-to-date modern British dishes with a few French influences thrown in for excellent measure. Brown's lightness of touch is found in a rabbit and spring baby vegetable terrine or seared South Coast scallops with a cauliflower purée and beignet. One reporter felt a dish of English asparagus with hen's egg and hollandaise reached new highs thanks to well-sourced ingredients handled with style and simplicity. Fish is a highlight, say fillet of bream with a mussel cream sauce, or mackerel with an orange and horseradish risotto, while confit belly of Sussex pork with braised pork cheek and celeriac purée confirms Brown's all-round approach to cooking. Gressingham duck, cooked to more French rareness than English doneness, was deemed a fine dish, too, alongside its celeriac purée and sculpted mound of Savoy cabbage. The kitchen wasn't

## Shannon Whitmore

**Why did you become a chef?**
Throughout my childhood I enjoyed cooking odd things; I also thought I could cook something better than my brother could serve me.

**Who was your main inspiration?**
As a kid growing up, it would have been Peter Russell-Clarke. Then as I started my trade, I loved the tension Gordon Ramsay would give at boiling point.

**Which of today's chefs do you admire?**
Heston Blumenthal; not for his chemistry techniques but for the way that he treats his younger peers.

**Who is your favourite producer?**
Denham Estate would be one of the best.

**Do you have a favourite local recipe?**
Fresh English asparagus, dipped into a soft-boiled duck egg.

**What's your guilty food pleasure?**
The smell of caramelising a banana, then tossing it in hot, butterscotch sauce.

**What's the hardest thing about running a restaurant?**
Trying to have a life outside work hours, and making a happy working environment.

**What's coming up next for you?**
Well, the next step is to make all this money for myself and to have a happy life!

found wanting either with a well-judged lemon sabayon tart with home-made dense raspberry sorbet, a more quirky chocolate brownie with banana milkshake showing a sense of humour. Sour dough brown bread deserves a mention, as does the mainly French wine list, opening with a Côtes du Tarn at £13.50.
**Chef/s:** Darren Brown. **Open:** Wed to Sun L 12.30 to 2, Wed to Sat D 7 to 9. **Closed:** Mon, Tue, Christmas. **Meals:** Set L £22.50 (3 courses), Set D £39 (3 courses). **Service:** not inc. **Details:** 30 seats. 10 seats outside. No mobile phones. Wheelchair access. Music. Children's portions. Car parking.

## READERS RECOMMEND

## The Fish Factory
**British**
51 Brighton Rd, Worthing, BN11 3EE.
Tel no: (01903) 207123
**'Simple seafood with a twist'**

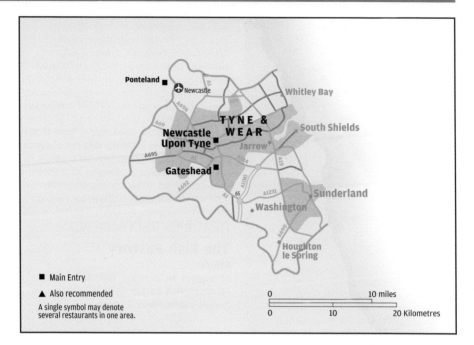

■ Main Entry

▲ Also recommended

A single symbol may denote several restaurants in one area.

0            10 miles

0     10     20 Kilometres

## ■ Low Fell, Gateshead

### Eslington Villa

**Modern dishes amidst finery**
8 Station Road, Low Fell, Gateshead, NE9 6DR
Tel no: (0191) 487 6017
www.eslingtonvillaltd.co.uk
**Modern European | £30**
**Cooking score: 3**

£5 OFF ⊨ ⋎

A sense of the fragility of 'all being right with the world' extends to the modern-day cooking emerging from this Victorian villa. Properly honed skills set to work on an international array; on a single menu, four starters take in gravad lax and Caesar salad, mozzarella, Parmesan, Gruyère and truffle cheeses alongside anchovies and Parma ham. Main courses resist such a global catch with black pudding mash and apple and sage accompanying slow roast pork, smoked haddock with mustard or just plain ribeye with chips. Things finally settle with the homely delights of sticky toffee, chocolate truffle and a range of decent ice creams. A house selection of seven wines starts at £12.50 with each offered by the glass.
**Chef/s:** Andrew Moore. **Open:** Sun to Fri L 12 to 2, Mon to Sat D 7 to 10. **Meals:** alc exc Sun L (main courses £13.50 to £19.50). Set L Mon to Fri £14 (2 courses) to £16, Set D Mon to Fri £20. **Service:** not inc. **Details:** Cards accepted. 85 seats. 20 seats outside. Wheelchair access. Music. Children's portions. Car parking.

## ■ Newcastle upon Tyne

### Black Door

**Enormous flair**
32 Clayton Street West, Newcastle upon Tyne, NE1 5DZ
Tel no: (0191) 261 6295
www.blackdoorrestaurant.co.uk
**Modern European | £40**
**Cooking score: 6**

For nigh on three years David Kennedy has been cooking at this 'fairly intimate' restaurant in a Georgian terraced house close to the

cathedral. Now it's all change. As the Guide went to press, the restaurant informed us that they were moving 'in the near future' to a bigger site. Details may be sketchy, but Kennedy will remain at the helm offering his imaginative twists on French classics. Dishes can be as straightforward as home-made black pudding with poached egg, pea purée and toasted broche, or along the lines of a more imaginative blue cheese pannacotta with Iberico ham, pea cream and pea shoots, while main courses range from fillet of turbot with wilted lettuce and risotto of new season's greens to stuffed saddle of rabbit with roasted langoustines, asparagus and herb gnocchi. At dessert stage, there may be tiramisu with Amaretto jelly, spiced crème brûlée and fig purée, or a selection of British and French cheeses with pickled celery and oat cakes, while the well-rounded, soundly chosen wine list opens with house French at £14.
**Chef/s:** Dave Kennedy. **Open:** Tue to Sat 12 to 2.30, 7 to 10. **Meals:** Set L £15.50 (2 courses) to £17.50, Set D £39.50 (2 courses) to £42.50. **Service:** not inc. **Details:** Cards accepted. 34 seats. Music.

## Blackfriars Restaurant
**A Dominican friary with a catholic menu**
Friars Street, Newcastle upon Tyne, NE1 4XN
Tel no: (0191) 261 5945
www.blackfriarsrestaurant.co.uk
**Global | £30**
**Cooking score: 3**
£5 OFF ⊨ V

In the hustle of central Newcastle upon Tyne it is a shock, albeit a pleasant one, to turn off the main streets and find a tiny medieval quarter, originally the site of a thirteenth-century Dominican friary. Taking pride of place here is Blackfriars, built as the Dominicans' refectory so authentically antique in both look and atmosphere – particularly with its wooden tables and exposed stone walls. The proprietors certainly capitalise on the space with medieval banquet nights and even decent picnics for sale that can be eaten directly outside on the grassy courtyard, but the restaurant really comes into its own at night

when the candles are lit. Then diners are looking at starters like Gressingham duck breast fritters with carrot and orange salad, or neat goats' cheese and walnut 'truffles' with apricot and thyme jam. The mixed grill main is a full-on trencherman experience (fillet steak, lamb chop, garlic prawns, and chips) but it sits on the menu alongside organic celeriac risotto with smoked apple, toasted hazelnuts, and Ribblesdale Cheddar. Desserts might include vodka pannacotta or pistachio sundae while wines kick off at £3.60 a glass. A deservedly popular venue, not least because of the care taken in sourcing ingredients. NB As the Guide went to press, we heard rumours of a new chef arriving at Blackfriars. Reports please.
**Chef/s:** Simon Brown. **Open:** All week L 12 to 2.30, Mon to Sat D 6 to 10. **Closed:** D 25 and 26 Dec, bank hol Mon. **Meals:** alc (main courses L £11.50 to £18.50, D £11.50 to £24.50). Set L £10.50 (2 courses) to £12.50, Set D before 7pm Mon to Sat £12.50 (2 courses) to £15. Afternoon tea available. **Service:** not inc. **Details:** Cards accepted. 70 seats. 20 seats outside. Air-con. Music. Children's portions.

## Brasserie Black Door
**Eclectic eating for culture vultures**
Biscuit Factory, Stoddart Street, Newcastle upon Tyne, NE2 1AN
Tel no: (0191) 260 5411
www.blackdoorrestaurant.co.uk
**Modern European | £32**
**Cooking score: 4**
V

Brasserie Black Door may have its own separate and quite distinct entrance but it is effectively inside Newcastle upon Tyne's most accessible art emporium, the Biscuit Factory. This makes for interesting moments as unsuspecting Geordie art lovers turn a corner and discover tables of people tucking into chargrilled beef rump instead of seeing yet another shelf of baffling ceramics; it also explains the contemporary if populist art on the brasserie's walls. New on the scene in 2006, and part of the same group as the Black Door

Restaurant (see entry, Newcastle upon Tyne), it is spacious, with neat décor, often buzzing, and takes very much a brasserie approach to cooking with an odd nod to the Far East (a starter like king prawn tempura, Asian salad, and red chilli jam, for example). A more typical three-course lunch could involve warm beetroot and potato salad with shallot dressing to start; pan-fried black bream, olive oil potatoes, spiced ratatouille and cumin oil as a main; rhubarb and almond tart with clotted cream for dessert. Dinner is a little more elaborate with mains like slow-cooked pork shoulder, salmon choucroute, or that chargrilled beef rump. Wines start at £3.50 per glass, £14 per bottle, and the list runs to around 60, including bin ends.

**Chef/s:** David Kennedy. **Open:** Mon to Sat 12 to 2, 7 to 10. **Meals:** alc D (main courses £11 to £15). Set L £15 (2 courses) to £16.50. **Service:** not inc. **Details:** Cards accepted. 100 seats. Air-con. Wheelchair access. Music. Car parking.

## Café 21

**On the move...**
Trinity Gardens, Quayside, Newcastle upon Tyne, NE1 3UG
Tel no: (0191) 222 0755
www.cafetwentyone.co.uk
French | £30

After 19 distinguished years, Terry Laybourne has moved Café 21 from Queen Street to larger premises in nearby Trinity Gardens, the change over taking place too late for the Guide to review – hence no score this year. The restaurant tells us that the team remains the same, with Chris Dobson continuing to run the kitchen, and the same appealing mix of upmarket brasserie dishes appearing on the menu. Thus, starters might feature foie gras terrine or double salmon rillettes, with mains offering crowd pleasers such as steak au poivre, and deep-fried fillet of haddock with minted pea purée, tartare sauce and chips. But there are imaginative offerings too, say, leeks vinaigrette with Cashel Blue and candied walnuts to start, followed by rare breed pork belly with French green lentils and braised

chicory. To finish there's classic crème brûlée or custard tart with nutmeg ice cream. In addition, an all-day bar menu delivers popular dishes along the lines of fishcakes, minute steak, omelette, or a charcuterie plate. House Georges Duboeuf is £13.

**Chef/s:** Chris Dobson. **Open:** Mon to Sat 12 to 2.30, 6 to 10.30. **Closed:** bank hols. **Meals:** alc (main courses £12.50 to £22.50). Set L £14 (2 courses) to £16.50. **Service:** 10% (optional). **Details:** Cards accepted. 60 seats. Air-con. Wheelchair access. Music. Children's portions.

## Fisherman's Lodge

**Still the tops in the city**
Jesmond Dene, Jesmond, Newcastle upon Tyne, NE7 7BQ
Tel no: (0191) 281 3281
www.fishermanslodge.co.uk
Modern Seafood | £34
Cooking score: 6

The setting feels remote – a Victorian lodge by a stream reached via a single-track road through 'quite dense woodland' – yet it is 'but a few minutes from town'. A colour scheme of muted neutrals sets a rather rarified tone in the interior, but it makes a fitting backdrop for Jamie Walsh's mix of familiar and gently inventive cooking. The skill in the execution brings out the best in the quality of the materials to produce 'first-class food', such as a warm tart of feta cheese with red onion marmalade and pumpkin or spring cabbage velouté with crumbled bacon. Fish remains a strong suit, the perfect timing and lightness of olive and pesto-crusted halibut wowed one reporter, while others have been impressed by a classic dish of sea bass, pomme purée and creamed leeks. Among meat dishes there may be roast pork belly wrapped in Parma ham, teamed with pork fillet and served with ceps and mustard sauce, or roast loin of Northumberland lamb, served alongside its confit shoulder with provençale vegetables and truffle jus. It's worth the 20-minute wait for Valhrona chocolate soufflé (with an accompanying mille feuille of bitter chocolate and raspberry), but the warm Calvados cake with Bramley apple compote, cider jelly and cream cheese ice cream has its fans too. For many readers this is 'still the tops in the city', with ambience and service both described as 'excellent'. The international wine list opens at £17, and if the markings seem a trifle keen thereafter, the options by the glass at around £4.75 to £7.95 are worth enquiring about. **Chef/s:** Jamie Walsh. **Open:** Mon to Sat 12 to 2, 7 to 10. **Closed:** Christmas, bank hols. **Meals:** Set L £22.50 to £50, Set D £40 (2 courses) to £50. **Service:** not inc. **Details:** Cards accepted. 114 seats. Wheelchair access. Music. Children's portions. Car parking.

## Jesmond Dene House

**Grand residence, dating back to 1822**
Jesmond Dene Road, Newcastle upon Tyne, NE2 2EY
Tel no: (0191) 212 3000
www.jesmonddenehouse.co.uk
British | £42
Cooking score: 5

Jesmond Dene House only opened as a hotel as recently as 2005 and now carries all the hallmarks of an elegant, modern country house, despite sitting foursquare in one of Newcastle-upon-Tyne's more chichi suburbs. Stylewise it successfully combines old with new; the restaurant is bright and airy with refined décor, while outside, weather permitting, tables overlook a well-kempt lawn. Service is friendly and efficient, while the kitchen goes about its work with admirable enthusiasm. Andrew Richardson is now in charge, replacing Jose Graziosi (who has taken over the kitchens at the George, Yarmouth – see entry). He presents a lively dinner menu, quite content to throw a little blood orange zing into a starter comprising smoked salmon, mâche salad, olive oil and caviar. Mains could involve line-caught sea bass, roast venison or an organic Aberdeen Angus plate of specific provenance (Steve Ramshaw from West Woodburn, Northumbria) comprising shoulder slow-cooked in red wine, rare fillet, bone-marrow

topping, braised celery and celeriac cream. To complete, the blueberry and thyme jelly with candied apple ice cream for dessert is a fine choice, while wines start at £14.50 a bottle and £4 a glass. **Chef/s:** Andrew Richardson. **Open:** all week 12 to 2.30 (4.30 Sun), 7 to 10.30. **Meals:** alc D (main courses £19 to £24.50). Set L £18.50 (2 courses) to £22.50, Set L Sun £21.50. Bar menu and afternoon tea available. **Service:** 10%. **Details:** Cards accepted. 85 seats. 30 seats outside. Wheelchair access. Music. Children's portions. Car parking.

# ▌Ponteland

## Café Lowrey

**Easy-going bistro**
33-35 The Broadway, Darras Hall, Ponteland, NE20 9PW
Tel no: (01661) 820357
Modern British | £22
Cooking score: 4

Ian Lowry's modest bistro-style restaurant scores with a pleasingly simple décor and capable service, and it's also prepared to invest in decent raw materials, particularly fish. There's little doubt that the kitchen can deliver unfussy dishes with skill and dexterity: to start you might choose scallops with gremolata and lemon oil, or Cheddar cheese and spinach soufflé. Confit of duck is served with black pudding mash, confit tomato and peppercorn sauce, and monkfish is wrapped in Parma ham and served with Puy lentils and red wine sauce. Desserts could vary from passion-fruit crème brûlée to banoffee crumble tart with crème anglaise. Wines are a contemporary international mix opening with house Duboeuf at £12.95. **Chef/s:** Ian Lowrey. **Open:** Sat L 12 to 2, Mon to Sat D 5.30 (6 Sat) to 10. **Closed:** 25 and 26 Dec, bank hols. **Meals:** alc (main courses £9.50 to £20). Set L £13.50 (2 courses) to £16.50, Set D 5.30 to 7 £12.50 to £15.50. **Service:** not inc. **Details:** Cards accepted. 70 seats. Air-con. Wheelchair access. Music. Children's portions. Car parking.

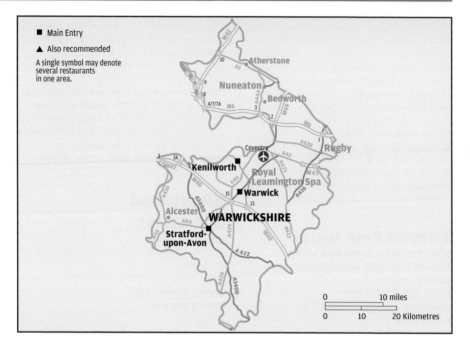

# Kenilworth

## Restaurant Bosquet

**Modern and welcoming**
97A Warwick Road, Kenilworth, CV8 1HP
Tel no: (01926) 852463
www.restaurantbosquet.co.uk
**French | £32**
**Cooking score: 4**

It takes a keen eye to spot this small, terraced restaurant on the main road through Kenilworth; its narrow façade comprises just the front door and a small window. But once found, the modern dining room makes a good impression, as does Jane Lignier's friendly and chatty front-of-house style and Bernard Lignier's classical French cooking. His conscientious, quality-first approach to sourcing and cooking upmarket ingredients, notably Scottish beef, Brixham shellfish, lamb sweetbreads, foie gras and fine French cheeses, play their part in the enticing menus, which are either à la carte or prix fixe. Typically, start with warm scallop terrine, follow with beef fillet served with confit shallots and a mustard sauce, and finish with blueberry and almond tart with home-made vanilla ice cream. The all-French wine list is divided into regions and starts at £15.50.

**Chef/s:** Bernard Lignier. **Open:** Tue to Fri L (bookings only) 12 to 1.15, Tue to Sat D 7 to 9.30. **Meals:** Set L and D Mon to Fri £29.50. **Service:** not inc. **Details:** Cards accepted. 30 seats. No music. No mobile phones. Wheelchair access. Children's portions.

## Symbols

🛏 Accommodation is available.

£30 Three courses for less than £30.

V More than five vegetarian dishes.

£5 OFF £5-off voucher scheme.

🍷 Notable wine list.

## ▌ Stratford-upon-Avon

### Malbec

**Bistro with an ambitious streak**
6 Union Street, Stratford-upon-Avon, CV37 6QT
Tel no: (01789) 269106
www.malbecrestaurant.co.uk
**Modern European | £26**
**Cooking score: 2**

£5 OFF ∀ £30

A relaxed mood prevails at this popular bistro, which occupies a terraced property in the town centre. Chef/proprietor Simon Malin comes up with some interesting ideas on his lively, modern menu, such as a starter of honey-roast quail with parsley risotto , which might appear alongside home-cured salt beef with new potato, caper and gherkin salad. Main courses, meanwhile, encompass Brixham plaice with brown shrimps, parsley and lemon couscous; roast rump of lamb with creamy garlic potatoes, ratatouille and rosemary jus; and poached cornfed poussin with fresh pasta, spinach and truffle sauce. Lemon syllabub with almond shortbread, or warm ginger sponge with rhubarb compote and sorbet might be among desserts. Prices on the short international wine list start around £14.
**Chef/s:** Simon Malin. **Open:** Tue to Sat 12 to 2, 7 to 9.30. **Closed:** 1 week Christmas, 1 week May, 1 week Oct, bank hol Tue. **Meals:** Set L £15 (3 courses). **Service:** not inc. **Details:** Cards accepted. 40 seats. Music. Children's portions.

## ▌ Warwick

### Findons

**Bold modern flavours**
7 Old Square, Warwick, CV34 4RA
Tel no: (01926) 411755
www.findons-restaurant.co.uk
**Modern European | £31**
**Cooking score: 2**

£5 OFF ∀

Standing in the corner of a square in the town centre, opposite St Mary's church, Findons aims for a refined, elegant look. Potato

gnocchi with warm herb butter, aubergine and cannellini beans appears among half a dozen starter options alongside terrine of duck and black pudding with beetroot and orange salad. Main courses show similarly broad scope, taking in cannon of Welsh lamb with spring onion and ginger ragôut, as well as sea bass fillet with fennel and olives, cardamom and star anise jus, and calf's liver on wilted spinach, balsamic onions and pancetta. To finish, there might be crème brûlée with rhubarb and biscuit crumble, or bread-and-butter pudding with crème Chantilly. An uncomplicated wine list gets the ball rolling with house Italian red and white at £14.95.
**Chef/s:** Michael Findon. **Open:** Mon to Sat D only 6 to 9.30. **Closed:** 18 to 25 Oct. **Meals:** alc (main courses £11 to £26). Set D £15.95 (2 courses). **Service:** 10% (fixed). **Details:** Cards accepted. 40 seats. 20 seats outside. Wheelchair access. Music.

### Rose and Crown

**Former coaching inn**
30 Market Place, Warwick, CV34 4SH
Tel no: (01926) 411117
www.roseandcrownwarwick.co.uk
**French | £27**
**New Chef**

🛏 ∀ £30

The Rose and Crown now looks every inch the modern city dining pub, with lots of bare wood and a light, open, airy feel. The menu is traditional British in the sense that it assimilates many ideas from around the world, so starters typically feature mushroom and Taleggio bruschetta with tomato oil, sizzling prawns in lemon and garlic, and spicy lamb kofta with mint yoghurt dressing; while prawn and sesame-crusted sea bass with coriander noodles and light Thai broth lines up alongside sausages and mash with onion gravy among main courses. Desserts range from rum and raisin fudge parfait to star anise baked baby pineapple. There's also a deli board with small snacky dishes to nibble or share over a drink, plus a range of breakfast items for early starters and sandwiches and snacks at

Hamish Watt

lunchtime. The uncomplicated wine list offers eight by the large or small glass, and good-value bottles from £12.50.

**Chef/s:** Gavin Alcock. **Open:** all week L 12 to 2.30, D 6.30 to 10 (9.30 Sun). **Meals:** alc (main courses £8.75 to £16.50). Bar menu available. **Service:** not inc. **Details:** Cards accepted. 70 seats. 30 seats outside. Air-con. Music. Children's portions.

**Why did you become a chef?**
I was the eldest of four in a single-parent home, so I was the cook. My father was the most adventurous domestic cook that I have known. While my friends at school were eating take-away for dinner I was cooking a seven-course Chinese banquet or a South-Asian curry.

**Which of today's chefs do you admire?**
Rowley Leigh for bringing seasonal food to the table and inspiring many young chefs from all over the world.

**Where do you eat out?**
Hakkasan for the flavours and textures, and Brindisa because their tapas menu is always changing, with fresh flavours and amazing ingredients.

**Where do you source your ingredients?**
Cove for fish; Secrets for herbs and amazing veg; Cheeseaholics; Macken Brothers butchers.

**If you could only eat one more thing, what would it be?**
Lorraine Godsmark's date tart at the Yellow Bistro, Sydney.

**What is your proudest achievement?**
Having customers coming up to the chefs during service and thanking the team for a lovely meal. It makes everyone feel great and proud about what they are cooking.

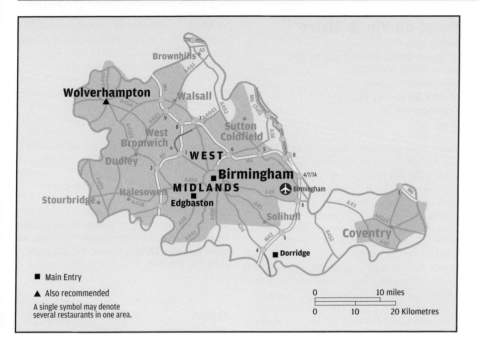

■ Main Entry

▲ Also recommended

A single symbol may denote
several restaurants in one area.

0          10 miles

0        10        20 Kilometres

# ▌Birmingham

## Bank

**Dependable, contemporary food**
4 Brindley Place, Birmingham, B1 2JB
Tel no: (0121) 633 4466
www.bankrestaurants.com
Modern European | £30
Cooking score: 2

£5
OFF

Something about Bank restaurant and bar hits
exactly the right spot and year in, year out, it
remains one of the city's most popular venues.
It is as busy and buzzy at lunch as it is at dinner
(breakfast is also available) and it has the space
to cope – a large and airy dining room with
views of the canal and a long bar alongside the
open kitchen for those with just a liquid
appetite. There are no airs and graces about the
easy yet efficient service and certainly none
about the food yet it's all very well done. Both
lunch and dinner menus offer lots of choice,
whether homely (the perennial favourite
is fish and chips) to the more exotic (confit

belly pork with celeriac purée, Szechuan
pepper-crusted tuna). It may be a well-worn
path but Bank never fails to please and its
reliability is probably its greatest asset.
**Chef/s:** Steven Woods. **Open:** all week 12 (11.30 Sat
and Sun) to 3 (3.30 Sun), 5.30 (5 Sun) to 11 (11.30
Sat, 10 Sun). **Closed:** 26 Dec and 1 Jan. **Meals:** alc
(main courses £12 to £19). Set L and D (exc 7 to
10pm) £12.50 (2 courses) to £15. Bar menu
available. **Service:** 12.5% (optional). **Details:** Cards
accepted. 250 seats. 90 seats outside. Air-con.
Wheelchair access. Music. Children's portions.

## Hotel du Vin & Bistro

Gallic chain
25 Church Street, Birmingham, B3 2NR
Tel no: (0121) 200 0600
www.hotelduvin.com
Modern European | £32
Cooking score: 3

♨ ⊨ ✔

There is, not too surprisingly, a strong French feel to the bistro at the Hotel du Vin. With its dark wood flooring, picture-packed walls and soft (almost too soft) lighting, it offers not only an authentic brasserie ambience but also one of the few genuinely romantic dining venues in the city. There are no cheffy bells and whistles, just straightforward, homely winners from both sides of the Channel – confit duck or steak and kidney pudding, perhaps. Or even a French twist on fish and chips – beer-battered cod with pont neuf potatoes and pea purée. The bistro's easy yet urbane feel coupled with sure-footed cooking and a highly knowledgeable wine list ensures a broad appeal. One of its most winning aspects, in fact, is that the dining room will be busy with everyone from families to businessmen to love-struck couples.
Chef/s: Nick Turner. Open: all week 12 (12.30 Sun) to 2, 6 (7 Sun) to 10. Meals: alc exc Sun L (main courses £12.50 to £22). Set L Mon to Sat £14.50 (2 courses), Set L Sun £32.50. Service: not inc. Details: Cards accepted. 94 seats. 25 seats outside. No music. Wheelchair access.

## Metro Bar & Grill

Sleek, modern watering hole
73 Cornwall Street, Birmingham, B3 2DF
Tel no: (0121) 200 1911
www.metrobarandgrill.co.uk
Modern European | £30
Cooking score: 2

✔

Suits may come and suits may go but one thing is for sure – they'll probably all eat and drink in the Metro bar. Round the corner in the atrium-lit restaurant, things are a little less hectic but odds are there'll be a roaring trade

for Metro's trademark, imaginative yet no-nonsense menu which offers a range of crowd-pleasers from fish and chips to slow-roast collar of bacon with pea mash and parsley sauce. Grills are eternally popular but seafood is also a big player – not surprising with lively stuff such as Thai-spiced scallop and noodle broth or squid encrusted with fennel seed and coriander, which makes a punchy starter or 'light plate'. The menu states a commitment to using local growers and suppliers but gives little hints as to provenance apart from Scotch beef and Cornish crab. House wines start at £13.95.
Chef/s: Andrew Twigg. Open: Mon to Fri L 12 to 2.30, Mon to Sat D 6 to 10. Closed: 25 Dec to 2 Jan, bank hols. Meals: alc (main courses £10 to £18). Bar menu available. Service: not inc. Details: Cards accepted. 120 seats. Air-con. Wheelchair access. Music.

## Opus

Simple confidence
54 Cornwall Street, Birmingham, B3 2DE
Tel no: (0121) 2002323
www.opusrestaurant.co.uk
Modern British | £38
Cooking score: 2

£5 OFF ✔

Floor to ceiling windows provide a bright outlook at this confident large-scale brasserie. It's a well-designed space, the dining area spacious and comfortable and filled with 'energetic atmosphere'. The kitchen favours a predominantly modern British approach and has the good sense to keep things simple, be it caramelised onion and Sharpham cheese tart, simply grilled fillet steaks, slow-braised venison, or steamed fillet of halibut with crushed potatoes and purple sprouting broccoli. Seafood embraces the posh end of the spectrum – oysters, lobsters, scallops – but the value of the set lunch remains astonishingly good. Typical of the output has been cream of forest mushroom soup followed by free-range coq au vin with buttermilk mousseline, and warm chocolate Valhrona cake with Black Forest ice cream. Service is attentive and friendly and wines are varied and full of interest with fair choice. House wines open at £12.95.

**Chef/s:** David Colcombe and Dean Cole. **Open:** Mon to Fri L 12 to 2.30, Mon to Sat D 6 to 10.30 (10 Mon). **Closed:** 24 Dec to 2 Jan, bank hols. **Meals:** alc (main courses £12.50 to £21). Set L and D Mon to Fri £15.50 (2 courses) to £17.50. **Service:** 12.5% (optional). **Details:** Cards accepted. 85 seats. Air-con. Wheelchair access. Children's portions.

## ALSO RECOMMENDED

### ▲ Itihaas
19 Fleet Street, Birmingham, B3 1JL
Tel no: (0121) 212 3383
www.itihaas.co.uk

Modern meets traditional not only in the food at Itihaas but with the décor, too. Cooking influences vary from North India to Kenya, ensuring there will be dishes that will not come across on a conventional Indian restaurant menu, such as king prawns cooked with chillies, roasted garlic and lemon (£9.95). Traditionalists can sample the whole chicken marinated in yoghurt, mixed with herb paste and seared over charcoal (£12.95) – or one of three thalis (£16.95). A large selection of decent wines starts at around the £15 mark. Open Monday to Friday L. Open daily D.

### ▲ Lasan
3-4 Dakota Buildings, James Street, Birmingham, B3 1SD
Tel no: (0121) 212 3664
www.lasan.co.uk

Knowledgeable staff, a relaxed atmosphere and cooking that marries traditional and experimental to good effect – can be found at Lasan. Extensive choices for seafood, too, and vegetarians could opt for the vegetarian platter for two (£9.25) followed by bhindi dopiaza, a spicy okra and onion curry (£6.95). Otherwise, expect lightly spiced traditional potato cakes served with tamarind and ginger chutney (£4.25) and a Rajput delicacy, lal mans pitika, which is cardamom- and clove-

smoked tender lamb chops, cooked in spicy curry (£12.95). Wine starts at £12.95 with several bottles available to order by the glass. Closed Sat L.

## ▮ Dorridge
## The Forest
Contemporary styling
25 Station Approach, Dorridge, B93 8JA
Tel no: (01564) 772120
www.forest-hotel.com
Modern French | £26
Cooking score: 2
£5 OFF 🍴 ▼ £30

The Forest has been here since 1870, when it opened to serve rail travellers passing through Dorridge. A riot of gables and scalloped roof tiles, it has an agreeably raffish air, which makes a modern brasserie kind of statement, complete with assertive music track. In keeping with this, Dean Grubb has brought new-fangled brasserie cooking to Dorridge, frying tiger prawns with spring onions and giving them a mango and green curry sauce, or poaching sea bass in a basil-scented bouillon, and partnering it with peas and bacon. Eastern touches surface again in duck breast with noodles, pak choi and coriander, and meals might conclude with egg custard tart, jollied up with Earl Grey ice cream, or dark chocolate fondant and orange curd. A briskly efficient wine list, arranged by style, kicks off with listings by the glass from £3.60. Bottle prices are from £12.95.

**Chef/s:** Dean Grubb. **Open:** Mon to Sat L 12 to 2.30, Sun L 12 to 3; Mon to Sat D 6.30 to 10. **Closed:** 25 Dec. **Meals:** alc (main courses £11 to £17.50). Set L and D Mon to Fri £12 (2 courses) to £15, Set L Sun £14.50 (2 courses) to £17.50 (3 courses). **Service:** 10% (optional). **Details:** Cards accepted. 90 seats. 60 seats outside. Air-con. Wheelchair access. Music. Children's portions. Car parking.

## ▌Edgbaston

## Simpsons

**A Birmingham institution**

20 Highfield Road, Edgbaston, B15 3DU

Tel no: (0121) 454 3434

www.simpsonsrestaurant.co.uk

**Modern French | £50**

**Cooking score: 6**

♦ ⇆ Ⅴ

Simpsons bestrides the Birmingham restaurant scene like a colossus. Owner Andreas Antona now tends to leave the cooking to the talented double act of Luke Tipping (executive chef) and Adam Bennett (head chef) but the cooking remains as sophisticated and meticulous as always. A name check is also due to one of the most talented pastry chefs in the business, Simon Morris, whose section provides stunning desserts, breads and petits fours. The food here is strongly rooted in classical French cuisine but allows ample breathing space for innovation and imagination. Lunch and evening menus offer plenty of accomplished, reassuringly high quality choice. Start, perhaps, with a quail bonbon with green bean and hazelnut salad and apricots − or maybe a torte of Salcombe crab with Loch Fyne smoked salmon − and follow up with loin of French rabbit in Parma ham or monkfish fillet with Indian spices and cumin basmati rice. Unsurprisingly, there are plenty of takers and the dining room is inevitably busy.

**Chef/s:** Andreas Antona and Luke Tipping. **Open:** all week 12 to 2 (2.30 Sun), 7 to 9.30 (10 Fri and Sat). **Closed:** 24 to 27 and 31 Dec, 1 and 2 Jan, bank hol Mon. **Meals:** alc (main courses £21 to £32.50). Set L £22.50 (2 courses) to £27.50, Set D £30. **Service:** 12.5% (optional). **Details:** Cards accepted. 75 seats. 40 seats outside. Air-con. No music. No mobile phones. Wheelchair access. Children's portions. Car parking.

## ALSO RECOMMENDED

## ▲ Bilash

2 Cheapside, Wolverhampton, WV1 1TU

Tel no: (01902) 427762

www.thebilash.co.uk

Situated in the middle of Wolverhampton town centre, Bilash is a smart Bangladeshi eatery. Chicken chat (£3.90) may seem familiar territory, but here is elevated to new levels of taste, and one reporter notes that Goan tiger prawn masala (£13.90) is 'one of the many dishes that gives this restaurant a lot of repeat business'. Wines from £18.90. Closed Sun.

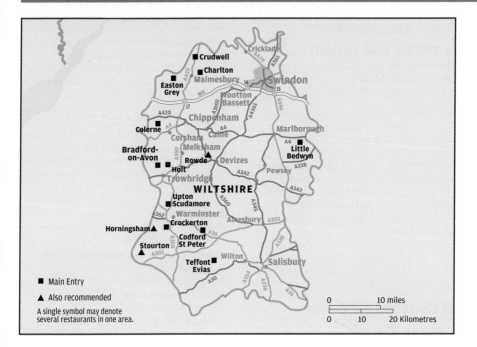

- ■ Main Entry
- ▲ Also recommended

A single symbol may denote several restaurants in one area.

| 0 | 10 miles |
|---|---|
| 0 | 10     20 Kilometres |

## ■ Bradford on Avon

★NEW ENTRY★
### Swan Hotel
**Delightful market town**
1 Church Street, Bradford on Avon, BA15 1LN
Tel no: (01225) 868686
www.theswan-hotel.com
**British | £21**
**Cooking score: 2**

Veteran West Country hoteliers and restaurateurs Stephen and Penny Ross have injected new life into this historic sixteenth-century inn-with-rooms. Completely refurbished in 2006, the light, airy dining room boasts an enormous fireplace and there are freshly cut flowers on unclothed tables. The menus bear all the hallmarks of Ross's Jane Grigson and Elizabeth David-inspired seasonal food and local suppliers are listed on the menu. Start, perhaps, with Looe Bay spider crab and artichoke salad with herb mayonnaise or omelette Arnold Bennett. Lighter options include cured Orkney salmon with crème fraîche and watercress salad. Main courses take on a more bistro attitude – fish pie with Cheddar mash and buttered carrots and grilled Aberdeen Angus ribeye with hand-cut chips being typical examples. Desserts are of the comforting, nursery variety with seasonal fruit crumble and sticky toffee pudding being particular crowd pleasers. The carefully chosen, French-biased wine list includes 12 by the glass.
**Chef/s:** Tom Bridgeman. **Open:** Mon to Sat 12 to 2.30 (Sun 12 to 3), all week 6.30 to 9. **Meals:** alc (main courses £9.50 to £14) Set L £10.50 (2 courses). **Service:** not inc. **Details:** Cards accepted. 50 seats. 20 seats outside. Wheelchair access. Music. Children's portions.

### Average price

The average price listed in main-entry reviews denotes the price of a three-course meal, without wine.

## ALSO RECOMMENDED
### ▲ Horse and Groom
The Street, Charlton, SN16 9DL
Tel no: (01666) 823904
www.horseandgroominn.com

The solidly elegant Cotswold stone house stands in its own paddock and dates from the sixteenth century when it was a thriving coaching inn. In a setting of rug-strewn wooden floors, solid oak tables and chairs and open log fires within informal beamed bar and dining areas, you can tuck into sandwiches, classic pub dishes and more imaginative meals, perhaps roast belly pork with sage mash and apple and cider sauce, and grilled sea bream with basil cream sauce. Home-made puddings take in vanilla pannacotta with poached rhubarb. House wines from £13.95.

## ▌Codford St Peter
### George Hotel
Showcasing local produce
High Street, Codford St Peter, BA12 0NG
Tel no: (01985) 850270
Modern British | £24
Cooking score: 4
🛏 £30

This village inn-with-rooms puts a homely face on its simple but tastefully decorated interior – walls are cream and terracotta, there are scatter cushions, polished tables and candles – and it all adds up to a pleasant ambience. Real ales draw the locals, but the cooking is the main focus here – even bar lunches are a cut above the norm. Boyd McIntosh buys locally and sets great store by the provenance of his raw materials (his beef is exceptional) and the results on the plate have pleased most reporters. Typically you might find guinea fowl and duck rillette served with green beans and a gooseberry chutney alongside venison steak with confit of garlic and wild mushroom jus, although other ingredients come from further afield: Brixham plaice is served with caper, lemon and garlic butter, for example, and meals can

open with Indian-spiced lamb spring rolls with mango and mint crème fraîche. Desserts encompass caramelised Brayburn apple tart and soft poached William pear with passion fruit and mango sorbet. An international line-up of wines at fair prices hits just the right note. A sheltered terrace for alfresco dining is a new addition this year.
Chef/s: Boyd McIntosh and James King Cole. Open: Wed to Mon L 12 to 2, Mon and Wed to Sat D 7 to 9. Meals: alc (main courses £8 to £17). Service: not inc. Details: Cards accepted. 50 seats. 24 seats outside. Music. Children's portions. Car parking.

## ▌Colerne
### Lucknam Park
Innovative cuisine and unashamed luxury
Colerne, SN14 8AZ
Tel no: (01225) 742777
www.lucknampark.co.uk
Modern European | £60
Cooking score: 6
🛏 �V

Occupying 500 acres of prime Wiltshire real estate, Lucknam Park is a massive undertaking with a corporate persona. The mansion itself, built in 1720, is Palladian splendour set in stone: orginally a long-standing family residence, it has only functioned as an elite country hotel for a mere twenty years. Along the way, it has been kitted out in moneyed fashion with all manner of facilities ranging from a health spa to a world-class equestrian centre. The sumptuous Park Restaurant occupies what was the original ballroom, an overtly grand, lofty space with full-length windows, pink drapes and Venetian glass mirrors. As one visitor noted, it 'oozes elegance'. Hywel Jones is very much his own man in the kitchen, and he seems determined to break free from the shackles of soft-centred country-house cooking. Diners can expect confident, innovative food, with carefully sourced British produce at its heart. Steamed fillet of sea bass is paired with chicken confit, spring peas, broad beans, wild garlic and morels, while loin of Brecon venison sits on the plate with chicory Tatin, carrot purée,

braised oxtail and sloe gin sauce. Among the starters, Norfolk duckling 'three ways' vies for attention with ballottine and carpaccio of blue fin tuna with smoked haddock, sweet potato fritters and ginger dressing, while desserts inhabit the technically assured world of iced honeycomb parfait with banana tart and chocolate sorbet or apple tarte fine with prune and Armagnac ice cream. This is attention-grabbing stuff, delivered with real panache and guaranteed to make an impact. The patrician wine list majors in top-end French classics aimed at those with deep pockets. Prices start at £20 for house selections and there are several affordable options by the glass (from £5). NB Children must be over 5.
**Chef/s:** Hywel Jones. **Open:** L 12.30 to 2.30, all week D 7 to 10.15. **Meals:** Set L £25, Set D £60 (3 courses). **Service:** not inc. **Details:** Cards accepted. 80 seats. No mobile phones. Wheelchair access. Music. Children's portions. Car parking.

## Crockerton
### Bath Arms
**Quintessential English pub**
Clay Street, Crockerton, BA12 8AJ
Tel no: (01985) 212262
www.batharmscrockerton.co.uk
**Modern British | £24**
**Cooking score: 3**

This whitewashed pub on the Longleat Estate plays host to tourists, walkers and locals in equal measure and looks every inch the old-fashioned English country pub with its rambling interior, open fires and wood floors. The cooking, more modern than you would expect from the traditional surroundings, responds to the seasons and sourcing is a strength. Fillet of John Dory with fried egg and pancetta, or breast of chicken with mushroom risotto are the kind of Mediterranean inspired main courses to expect, and meals are bookended with the likes of tomato terrine with Cornish crab mayonnaise, and chocolate brownie with malt ice cream. But chef-cum-landlord Dean Carr has not lost sight of the fact that he's running a

pub, offering gammon with poached eggs, mixed grills and breaded pollack and chips alongside the selection of real ales. There's a short, good value wine list, too; house wine is £11.70.
**Chef/s:** Dean Carr and Mark Payne. **Open:** all week 12 to 2.30 (3 Sun), 6.30 to 9.30 (9 Sun). **Meals:** alc (main courses £10 to £15). **Service:** not inc. **Details:** Cards accepted. 80 seats. 120 seats outside. Wheelchair access. Music. Children's portions. Car parking.

## Crudwell
### Rectory Hotel
**Traditional hotel promoting local produce**
Crudwell, SN16 9EP
Tel no: (01666) 577194
www.therectoryhotel.co.uk
**Modern British | £30**
**Cooking score: 3**

A quiet Cotswold village not far from Malmesbury is the setting for this timeless hotel, which has the bonus of a three-acre walled garden in the shadow of the local church. Inspired by the ethos of the Slow Food Movement, the kitchen is proud of the fact that much of its produce ('with the exception of fish') is sourced from within a 30-mile radius. A fixed-price 'menu rapide' now operates at lunchtime, promising burgers with fries, Gloucester Old Spot sausages with bubble and squeak, wild mushroom risotto and the like. The evening menu features similar dishes, although the repertoire is fleshed out with a few more ambitious choices including ravioli of braised chicken, lentils and wild mushrooms with parsnip purée and truffle dressing ahead of slow-cooked skirt of beef with Hereford oxtail and horseradish mash. To finish, try the British and French farmhouse cheeses or settle for something sweet like dark chocolate and raspberry tart with fennel ice cream. House wine is £12 a bottle (£4.50 a glass).
**Chef/s:** Peter Fairclough. **Open:** all week 12 to 2, 7 to 9 (9.30 Fri and Sat). **Meals:** alc (main courses £13.50 to £18.50). Set L £14.50 (2 courses) to

£18.50. **Service:** not inc. **Details:** Cards accepted. 35 seats. 24 seats outside. Wheelchair access. Music. Children's portions. Car parking.

## ▌Easton Grey
## Whatley Manor
**Complex cuisine in an opulent manor**
Easton Grey, SN16 0RB
Tel no: (01666) 822888
www.whatleymanor.com
**Modern European | £80**
Cooking score: 6

£5
OFF ⏳ 🛏 Ⅴ

A meandering tree-lined drive through herb-scented gardens and landscaped grounds provides the perfect introduction to this spectacular, opulently restored Costwold country house. Whatley Manor has been given the full treatment by its current owner, who has installed a state-of-the-art spa and remarkable leisure facilities as part of the top-end package. Furnishings and fittings are as sumptuous as can be, with hand-made wallpapers, all manner of ornate woodwork and fabulous Venetian chandeliers. Formal meals are served in the prosaically titled Dining Room, which provides a softly lit backdrop to Martin Burge's highly complex cuisine. A starter of scallop carpaccio with oyster mayonnaise and shoots acidulated with lime sits near the cutting edge, likewise a Parmesan cassonade dressed with courgette flowers and fennel foam. As for main courses, the mainstream reinvents itself with the likes of caramelised veal kidney accompanied by braised snails and potato crisps or fillets of John Dory topped with Sauternes gel, its juices lightly creamed and infused with truffle oil. Foie gras is ever-present: as a mousse it adorns roast fillet of Scotch beef, and in its cured form it might sit alongside warm duck breast and pistachio purée. To conclude, there are confections of many parts – perhaps an assortment of nuts 'prepared in different ways' or a tasting of chocolate desserts 'combined and infused with various flavoured peppercorns'. Otherwise, lemon 'ravioles' served with pink grapefruit, lime jelly and

vanilla foam might tempt. The wine list is breathtaking in its scope, with an explosion of champagnes, glorious classic French vintages and fascinating stuff gleaned from unlikely sources. Prices start at £21 (which says a great deal about the list); half-bottles provide welcome relief and there is a goodly assortment by the glass (from £5.50).
**Chef/s:** Martin Burge. **Open:** Wed to Sun D only 7 to 10. **Meals:** Set D £65 to £80. **Service:** 10%. **Details:** Cards accepted. 40 seats. No mobile phones. Wheelchair access. Music. Car parking.

## ▌Holt

★NEW ENTRY★
## The Tollgate Inn
**A charming, traditional country pub**
Ham Green, Holt, BA14 6PX
Tel no: (01225) 782326
www.tollgateholt.co.uk
**Gastropub | £27**
Cooking score: 3

£5
OFF 🛏 £30

The Tollgate is as traditionally English as it gets, warm, welcoming, with beams, comfy leather armchairs, a woodburner and stone-flagged floors. Dining is divided into a cosy tranquil area downstairs, where a curved wooden staircase leads up to the larger former weaver's chapel, home to a roaring fire in winter, a high-beamed ceiling, tall leather chairs and impressive windows overlooking the village green. Alexander Venables cooks a wide-ranging menu of British dishes, with occasional Mediterranean touches. Hearty is the keyword here as notably well-cooked and honestly presented dishes are very generous. Daily specials feature the best of seasonal produce, such as wild garlic and ricotta tart or a tender fillet of local venison on bubble and squeak, and a selection of very fresh seafood direct from Brixham. Finish with traditional favourites such as proper rice pudding with caramelised Bramleys and home-made vanilla ice cream. A reasonably priced wine list includes ten by the glass (from £3.20); by the carafe or bottle from £11.50.

Chef/s: Alexander Venables. Open: Tue to Sun 12 to 2, Tue to Sat 7 to 9. Meals: alc (main courses £14.50 to £17.50) Set L £11.95 (2 courses) £13.95 (3 courses). Service: not inc. Details: Cards accepted. 60 seats. 38 seats outside. Wheelchair access. Music. Children's portions.

## ALSO RECOMMENDED

### ▲ Bath Arms
Longleat Estate, Horningsham, BA12 7LY
Tel no: (01985) 44308
www.batharms.co.uk

Standing by the gates to Longleat Estate and fronted by 200-year-old pollarded lime trees, the impressive, estate-owned Bath Arms has been on the up since Christoph Brooke took over in 2006. From the set dinner menu a starter of plump and juicy scallops comes with a coriander cream dressing, and could be folowed by pork tenderloin wrapped in prosciuitto with chorizo potato and aubergine purée. Leave room for a gooey sticky toffee pudding served with lashings of clotted cream. Excellent bar meals and the set lunch menu is great value for money. The well-balanced global wine list kicks off at £12.50.

## ▌ Little Bedwyn

★NEW ENTRY★
### The Harrow at Little Bedwyn
Pedigree country restaurant
Little Bedwyn, SN8 3JP
Tel no: (01672) 870871
www.theharrowatlittlebedwyn.co.uk
British | £40
Cooking score: 5

It is hard to believe that one could find such a hidden gem at the heart of an upmarket, out-of-the-way village on the Kennet and Avon Canal, but the much-acclaimed Harrow certainly 'ticks all the right epicurean boxes'. Inside comes 'bursting with sunny, modern Mediterranean colour', the intimate dining room split in two by a central fireplace. Tables come 'dressed in their best whites', while chairs are high-backed dark-brown leather, set against polished floorboards or pale blue carpet. Sue Jones leads the friendly, relaxed but informed service, while the other half of the duo, husband Roger, is found at the stove. His 'fine-tuned' modern repertoire comes driven by fresh, quality, seasonal ingredients and natural free-range produce. There is a strong emphasis on fish, too, with day-boat catches landed at Brixham, perhaps delivering a grilled fillet of line-caught turbot simply accompanied by grilled courgettes, lime and rock cress, while meats are supplied from specialist farmers and butchers. Take a breast of Llanllwni hillside duck (specially bred for the Harrow and 10-day hung), served with Indian spices, yoghurt and lentils. The cooking style is skilfully straightforward and clean cut with emphatic flavours, while the medley of menus all come with useful by-glass recommendations for each course. The list itself is an 'absolute corker' and displays Roger's other love: 'bursting with enthusiasm, passion and interest' with a 'stunning' selection by bottle from £18 and glass from £5. A rear terrace offers the opportunity for fair-weather aperitifs.

Chef/s: Roger Jones and John Brown. Open: Wed to Sun L 12 to 2, Wed to Sat D 7 to 9. Closed: 23 Dec to 16 Jan. Meals: alc (main courses £24). Set L £30 (3 courses inc wine). Set D £40 (4 courses) to £70. Service: not inc. Details: Cards accepted. 32 seats. 26 seats outside. Wheelchair access. Music. Children's portions.

## ALSO RECOMMENDED

### ▲ George & Dragon
High Street, Rowde, SN10 2PN
Tel no: (01380) 723053

Inspired, inventive and realistically priced cooking emanates from the kitchen at this rather plain looking seventeenth-century pub in the village centre. This is landlocked Wiltshire, yet copious supplies of fresh fish are delivered from Cornwall and find their way on to a blackboard menu of vivid modern dishes. Typically, follow creamy baked potted crab (£8) with roast monkfish with a green peppercorn cream (£13.50) or simply grilled skate wing with caper butter (£15). Meat-eaters are not forgotten – try the roast rack of lamb with mustard mash (£17.50). The setting is rustic, so expect bare boards, simple, unclothed tables and a roaring log fire. Wines from £14.

## ▲ Spread Eagle Inn

Stourton, BA12 6QE
Tel no: 01747 840587
www.spreadeagleinn.com

At the entrance to Stourhead House and Garden and popular with the many visitors drawn to this National Trust property, this inviting old inn features a stone floor, open fires, a comfortably appointed bar and an attractive restaurant. One reader has praised bar lunches, enjoying beef and ale casserole with root vegetables and bubble and squeak mash. Restaurant meals, too, are notable for high quality ingredients. Warm blue cheese fritters with vine tomato, beetroot and tarragon salad is a favourite, and could be followed by lamb shank with pickled cabbage, or cod fillet with wilted red chard, tomato and shallot dressing. Desserts might include dark chocolate and brandy pot with vanilla cream.

## ■ Teffont Evias
### Howard's House

Traditional feel with a French accent
Teffont Evias, SP3 5RJ
Tel no: (01722) 716392
www.howardshousehotel.co.uk
**Modern British | £33**
**Cooking score: 3**

£5
OFF 🛏

You'll find this seventeenth-century dower house down a winding country lane, with a tiny stream trickling alongside. Seared scallops with sauce vierge and crab mayonnaise is a typically indulgent starter, or there might be a somewhat earthier roast saddle of rabbit with wild mushrooms and parsley purée. Main courses show a fondness

for intense flavours in well-balanced combinations: roast cannon of lamb comes with truffled potatoes and wild garlic; while John Dory fillet is partnered with Parma ham, Parmesan gnocchi and capers; and roast Scottish beef fillet is set on crushed peas with braised oxtail. To finish, choices might include rhubarb crumble with champagne jelly and vanilla ice cream, or chocolate feuilletine with chocolate and cherry cannelloni. The major French regions make up about half of the wine list, though house Chilean at £15.50 is among a good choice of bottles from elsewhere.
**Chef/s:** Nick Wentworth. **Open:** Tue to Thu and Sun L 12.30 to 2, all week D 7 to 9 (8.30 Sun). **Closed:** 5 days Christmas. **Meals:** Set £21.50 (2 courses) to £25, Set D £25.95 (3 courses) to £42. **Service:** not inc. **Details:** Cards accepted. 30 seats. 20 seats outside. No music. No mobile phones. Wheelchair access. Children's portions. Car parking.

## ■ Upton Scudamore
### Angel Inn

Modern dining pub
Upton Scudamore, BA12 0AG
Tel no: (01985) 213225
www.theangelinn.co.uk
**Modern British | £25**
**Cooking score: 3**

🛏 V £30

Hidden away in a hamlet north of Warminster, the sixteenth-century Angel is a neat-looking, white-painted building. The interior is equally spick-and-span, a series of linked rooms on slightly different levels, including a high, narrow and light-filled bar area with boarded floors and terracotta walls, and a sizeable dining area with bare tables, a tasteful décor and a civilised atmosphere. Chef Paul Suter takes care with good ingredients and offers a printed menu backed up by blackboards of desserts and daily specials (mainly Brixham fish). His cooking is simple and unpretentious, with modern twists to some classic ideas, as in herb-crusted rack of lamb on courgette provençale with sauce niçoise, or sea bass with ginger cream sauce on tomato and basil linguini. Precede with steamed River Exe mussels with white wine, parsley and garlic cream sauce and round off with warm fig and almond tart with clotted cream. Global wines from £12.95.

**Chef/s:** Paul Suter. **Open:** all week 12 to 2, 7 to 9.30. **Closed:** 25 and 26 Dec, 1 Jan. **Meals:** alc (main courses L £8 to £12, D £12 to £20). **Service:** not inc. **Details:** Cards accepted. 60 seats. 40 seats outside. Wheelchair access. Music. Children's portions. Car parking.

## Cooking score

A score of 1 is a significant achievement. The score in any review is based on several meals, incorporating feedback from both our readers and inspectors. As a rough guide, 1 denotes capable cooking with some inconsistencies, rising steadily through different levels of technical expertise, until the scores between 6 and 10 indicate exemplary skills, along with innovation, artistry and ambition. If there is a new chef, we don't score the restaurant for the first year of entry. For further details, please see the scoring section in the introduction to the Guide.

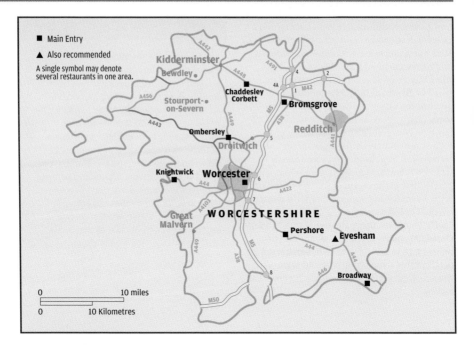

## ■ Broadway

### Russell's

**Modern brasserie showing flair**
20 High Street, The Green, Broadway, WR12 7DT
Tel no: (01386) 853555
www.russellsofbroadway.com
**Modern British | £28**
**Cooking score: 4**

£5 OFF ☰ V £30

At the heart of one of the most popular
villages in the Cotswolds, this modern
restaurant-with-rooms is an all-round
polished affair. Housed in a mellow stone-
built former furniture factory, the bar and
dining room, with big glass doors opening on
to a courtyard, is a cool, informal space. Young
and enthusiastic staff serve accurately rendered
modern food with the emphasis on freshness.
Start perhaps with a well composed salad of
marinated beetroot and Chantenay carrots
with feta cheese and a honey sherry vinegar
dressing. Precisely timed fish is impressive
(maybe sea bass with creamed salsify, buttered
spinach and curried mussel broth), while a
meat dish might feature braised collar of pork
with garlic mash, braised bok choy and a soy,
honey and spring onion sauce. Side orders of
garlic and rosemary roasted new potatoes are
excellent and rhubarb crumble crème brûlée
with a rhubarb compote, gingersnap biscuits
and iced custard parfait makes a great finish. A
short, international list of wines opens at
£14.95 with around a dozen choices by the
glass from £4.50.

**Chef/s:** Matthew Laughton. **Open:** all week L 12 to
2.30, Mon to Sat D 6 to 9.30. **Meals:** alc D (main
courses £13 to £23). Set L and D before 7pm £10.95
(1 course) to £16.95, Set D £17.95 (2 courses) to
£22.95 (no set meals after 7pm Fri and Sat).

### Scores on the Doors

To find out more about the Scores on the
Doors campaign, please visit the Food
Standard's Agency website:
www.food.gov.uk or www.which.co.uk.

Service: not inc. **Details:** Cards accepted. 55 seats. 40 seats outside. Air-con. Wheelchair access. Music. Children's portions. Car parking.

## Bromsgrove
## Grafton Manor

**A strong sense of history**
Grafton Lane, Bromsgrove, B61 7HA
Tel no: (01527) 579007
www.graftonmanorhotel.co.uk
**Modern Indian | £25**
**Cooking score: 3**

🍴 V £30

This imposing sixteenth-century manor, which stands in extensive gardens and is fitted out in luxurious style. And the kitchen aims to live up to the setting with some ambitious and elaborate cooking. Dinner is four courses, perhaps opening with spicy Goan crab soup. First course proper might be potted oak-smoked salmon, or braised blade of beef with beetroot purée and shallot foam, while inventive main course options take in cod with sorrel, spinach and caviar sauce; home-salted monkfish with confit chicken wings, served on a nettle emulsion and carrot purée; or sali Goa chicken caffrael with Indian vegetables. To finish, there might be whisky steamed pudding with whisky cream, or jasmine crème brûlée with green apple sorbet and pain d'épice toast. The main thrust of the wine list is the major French regions, but there is also a page of good-value house selections from around the world, priced from £11.40.
**Chef/s:** Tim Waldren and Adam Harrison. **Open:** all week L 12 to 2, D 7 to 9.30. **Closed:** first week Jan. **Meals:** Set L £20.50 (3 courses), Set D £32.75 (4

### Please send us your feedback

To register your opinion about any restaurant listed in the Guide, or a new restaurant that you wish to bring to our attention, please visit the web address at the bottom of the page. Your feedback informs the content of the book and will be used to compile next year's reviews.

courses). **Service:** not inc. **Details:** Cards accepted. 60 seats. No music. No mobile phones. Wheelchair access. Children's portions. Car parking.

## Chaddesley Corbett
## Brockencote Hall

**French cooking with zeal and finesse**
Chaddesley Corbett, DY10 4PY
Tel no: (01562) 777876
www.brockencotehall.com
**Modern French | £40**
**Cooking score: 4**

£5 OFF 🍴 V

Brockencote was Didier Philipot's springboard before setting up his independent venture La Toque d'Or in Birmingham's jewellery quarter six years ago. And in 2006, when he was exhausted by the demands of chef-patronage, Brockencote welcomed him back. His considerable gifts are allowed full rein in these gracious surroundings. A sweeping, tree-lined drive takes guests right to the door and, once inside, all is comfort if not cutting edge design. The sun-filled conservatory or elegant terrace overlooking the large grounds make ideal settings for aperitifs and the procession of amuse-bouches and nibbles that inevitably arrive. The elegant, chintzy restaurant with its French windows and scenic views is a perfect backdrop for food which combines a strong French influence with a passion for prime English ingredients, local wherever possible. Alongside the roll-call of luxury – Brixham turbot, Perigord foie gras et al – there are plenty of imaginative twists and turns, as well as such Anglo-French combinations as a gigolette of frogs' legs with local asparagus and wild garlic foam (they're quite keen on foams). A perfect symbol, perhaps, of a Gallic-looking English country seat owned by a Frenchman and his English wife – Joseph and Alison Petitjean. Wines are, unsurprisingly, French dominated and include the usual suspects in the expected price range. Service is razor-sharp yet friendly and obliging and as French as the chef and patron. House wines start at £16.

**Chef/s:** Didier Philipot. **Open:** Sun to Fri L 12.30 to 1.30, all week D 7 to 9.30. **Closed:** 2 to 17 Jan. **Meals:** alc exc Sun L (main courses £15.50 to £22.50). Set L Mon to Fri £14 (two courses) to £18, Set L Sun £24.50, Set D £32.50 to £48. **Service:** not inc. **Details:** Cards accepted. 60 seats. 20 seats outside. No mobile phones. Wheelchair access. Music. Children's portions. Car parking.

## ALSO RECOMMENDED
### ▲ Evesham Hotel
Cooper's Lane, Evesham, WR11 1DA
Tel no: (01386) 765566
www.eveshamhotel.com

The Tudor farmhouse was modernised in Georgian times and the hotel has been in the Jenkinson family since 1975. Much of its vitality derives from John Jenkinson's spirited – or, as reporters put it, 'eccentric' – approach. He's a friendly force in the dining room, overseeing a menu that is global in inspiration. There may be chilli chicken (£6) or Lancashire cheese and vegetable soup (£4.25) to start, with main courses ranging from cod with a cranberry and orange salsa (£15) to sweet chilli ostrich (£15.50). End with rhubarb fool (£5.20) or a selection of British cheeses. The wine list is a French-free zone with house Spanish £15.40. Open all week.

## Knightwick
### The Talbot
Traditional country inn
Knightwick, WR6 5PH
Tel no: (01886) 821235
www.the-talbot.co.uk
British | £40
New Chef

The Clift family show admirable devotion to seasonal and local produce at their large fourteenth-century black-and-white inn by the River Teme. It's an industrious set-up: what they can't produce themselves (beer, preserves, bread, black pudding, pies, vegetables) or gather from the wild, they buy

from local farmers, the only exception to the rule being fresh fish, which is delivered from Cornwall and Wales. Slow roasted shoulder of lamb with caper and preserved lemon velouté sauce and rabbit fricassee with a lovage butter sauce and pea shoots are the kind of gutsy main courses to expect, and meals are bookended with the likes of homecured salmon, smoked mackerel and cured wild brown trout served with dressed leaves and a chive and horseradish soured cream dressing, and apple, rhubarb and ginger fool with an almond and pistachio biscotti. Peckish drinkers, in for the home-brewed beers, can tuck into faggots with mash and gravy or pig's head brawn with salad and pickles from the bar menu. House wine is £11.25.
**Chef/s:** Mark Lloyd. **Open:** Sun L 12 to 2, all week 6.30 to 9.30 (9 Sun). **Closed:** D 25 Dec. **Meals:** alc (main courses £13 to £15). Set D £25 (2 courses) to £30. Set L Sun £23 (3 courses). **Service:** not inc. **Details:** Cards accepted. 36 seats. 24 seats outside. No music. Wheelchair access. Children's portions. Car parking.

## Ombersley
### Venture In
Confident cooking in a timbered building
Ombersley, WR9 0EW
Tel no: (01905) 620552
British | £42
Cooking score: 3

Ⅴ

Venture in, and why wouldn't you? This is the oldest building in the village, dating from 1430 and, behind its ancient black and white timbered exterior, is a cottagey restaurant with comfy sofas and giant inglenook. The small dining room follows the theme, with plenty of mellow beams and exposed stone or pastel-painted plastered walls. The cooking is driven by quality local produce, with a confident kitchen displaying skilful preparation, carefully considered combinations and consistency. The fixed-priced repertoire features a stand-alone fish menu, perhaps delivering pan-fried fillet of monkfish served with a mushroom risotto and

red wine and star anise sauce at mains, while the carte could seduce with more traditional pan-fried calf's liver combined with a shallot sauce and crispy bacon. Desserts have a classic ring, perhaps a rich chocolate tart with pistachio ice cream, while the wine list ventures far and wide to ensure interest, striking out with a short house selection at £14.
**Chef/s:** Toby Fletcher. **Open:** Tue to Sun L 12 to 2, Tue to Sat D 7 to 9.45. **Closed:** 1 week Christmas, 2 weeks Feb, 2 weeks Aug. **Meals:** Set L £19.50 (2 courses) to £23, Set D £33. **Service:** not inc. **Details:** Cards accepted. 32 seats. Air-con. Music. Car parking.

## Pershore
## Belle House
**Quality food in an unusual setting**
5 Bridge Street, Pershore, WR10 1AJ
Tel no: (01386) 555055
www.belle-house.co.uk
**Modern European | £26**
**Cooking score: 3**
Ⅴ

They keep things simple yet elegant at Belle House that goes for the décor as well as the food. Yet one reader drove 415 miles to celebrate his 60th birthday here, so there must be something special going on. A starter of Brixham crab and prawns with gazpacho sauce, artily arranged in two timbales, was a winning mix of fresh-from-the-sea tastes, while breast of well-cooked duck went perfectly with braised cabbage, rösti potato and puréed celeriac. Homely flavours are well combined and executed with care. Vegetarian options are innovative – perhaps crispy-fried discs of polenta sandwiched with sweet roast pepper with smoked garlic or a mushroom and shallot tart spiked with horseradish. House wines start at £13.95.
**Chef/s:** Stephen Waites, Sue Ellis. **Open:** Tue to Sat 12 to 2, 7 to 9.30. **Closed:** 2 weeks Jan, 1 week Aug. **Meals:** Set L £18 (3 courses) Set D £20.50 (2 Courses) to £26 (3 courses). **Service:** not inc. **Details:** Cards accepted. 80 seats. Air-con. Wheelchair access. Music. Children's portions.

## Worcester

★NEW ENTRY★
## The Glasshouse
**A new contender on the scene**
Danesbury House, 55 Sidbury, Worcester, WR1 2HU
Tel no: (01905) 611120
www.theglasshouse.co.uk
**Modern European | £30**
**Cooking score: 3**
£5 OFF

Ludlow's loss promised to be Worcester's gain when Shaun Hill and his business partner opened this city brasserie. The building is unremarkable from outside, but a design fest within features barcode-striped banquettes, which positively discourage slouching. There were hits and misses at inspection, but highlights included a 'stunning' starter of mousse-like pheasant pudding with fried sage and bacon, while a Hill classic of calves' sweetbreads with potato and olive cake was as good as it ever was at the Merchant House. Breads, too, were 'impressive', as was treacle tart for dessert. Additionally, the bar menu offers a selection of tapas-style platters of charcuterie, fish, vegetables or cheese, for sharing. All wines listed are available by the carafe - one third of a bottle at exactly one third of the price, while a bottle of house wine is £15.
**Chef/s:** Shaun Hill. **Open:** Mon to Sat 12 to 2.30, 6 to 10, Sun 11 to 3. **Closed:** bank hols. **Meals:** alc (main course £13 to £18). **Service:** not inc. **Details:** Cards accepted. 100 seats. 20 seats outside. Air-con. Separate bar. Music. Children's portions.

## ALSO RECOMMENDED
## ▲ Brown's
24 Quay Street, South Quay, Worcester, WR1 2JJ
Tel no: (01905) 26263
www.brownsrestaurant.co.uk

Housed in a red brick building almost completely obscured by creeping vines and set on the River Severn, Brown's location alone makes it a tempting dining location. A strong lunch menu offers two courses for £17.50 or three for £21.50. On offer are temptations such as roast ballotine of local pigeon wrapped in Parma ham with a light spring vegetable broth. The set-price dinner menu (two courses £27.50, five £39.50) features starters of double-baked blue cheese and spinach soufflé with braised apple, celery and sultana salad. Main courses include vanilla-infused, corn-fed duck breast, sautéed greens, spiced fruits, coconut and soy sauce. A solid wine list opens at £15.95. Closed Sat L, Sun D and Mon.

## Cooking score

A score of 1 is a significant achievement. The score in any review is based on several meals, incorporating feedback from both our readers and inspectors. As a rough guide, 1 denotes capable cooking with some inconsistencies, rising steadily through different levels of technical expertise, until the scores between 6 and 10 indicate exemplary skills, along with innovation, artistry and ambition. If there is a new chef, we don't score the restaurant for the first year of entry. For further details, please see the scoring section in the introduction to the Guide.

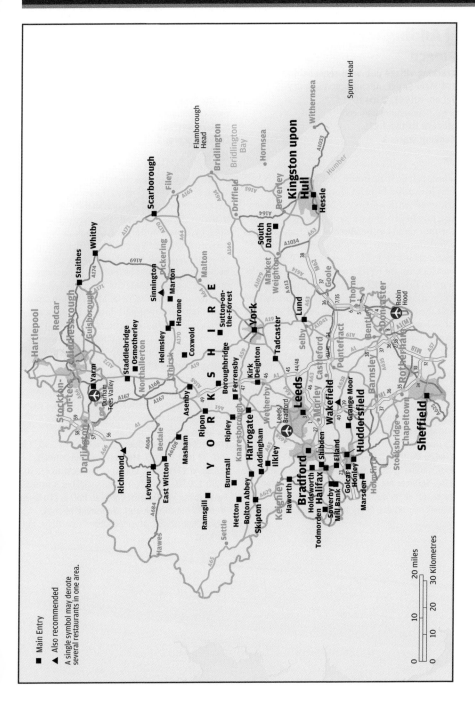

Main Entry
▲ Also recommended
A single symbol may denote
several restaurants in one area.

0    10    20 miles
0    10    20    30 Kilometres

## ▌Addingham

### Fleece

Cracking village pub with seasonal food
154 Main Street, Addingham, LS29 0LY
Tel no: (01943) 830491
www.fleeceaddingham.com
Modern British | £21
Cooking score: 3

£30

There can be little doubt that the Fleece is still emphatically a North Country hostelry, complete with a drinkers' bar and real ales on tap, low beams and a blazing fire to keep out the moorland chills. Much of the food also has a Yorkshire accent, with local ingredients given their full due in the kitchen. Whitby haddock might be sent to the deep-fryer or used to fill fish pies (along with woof and salmon); meat and potato pie is another fixture and the menu also extends to braised shoulder of Wharfedale lamb or roast pork belly with honey mustard glaze and savoury red cabbage. Sandwiches, omelettes and exciting salads (confit mallard with roast plums, for example) flesh out the menu, the specials board is replete with possibilities. Twenty house wines from £12.15 (£3.20 a glass) provide the prospect of decent drinking and a separate list offers some more prestigious options – particularly from France.
Chef/s: Matthew Brown. Open: all week 12 to 2.15, 6 to 9.30 (Sun 12 to 8). Meals: alc (main courses £8 to £16). Service: not inc. Details: Cards accepted. 70 seats. 60 seats outside. Air-con. No music. Wheelchair access. Children's portions. Car parking.

## ▌Asenby

### Crab & Lobster

Eclectic ephemera
Dishforth Road, Asenby, YO7 3QL
Tel no: (01845) 577286
www.crabandlobster.co.uk
Modern Seafood | £33
Cooking score: 3

What appears to be a charming thatched inn – albeit with lobster pots on the roof – turns out to contain a kind of 'French shabby chic with a maritime tang'. Seafood takes centre stage – ranging from traditional haddock in beer batter or fish pie to green Thai fish curry with sweet potato with honey and fig naan. In between there could be 'plump and delicate' queenie scallops, baked on the half shell with shallots and Gruyère, or wild sea bream stuffed with crab, pine nuts and raisins. Elsewhere, honey and Dijon ice cream is an unusual accompaniment to goats' cheese and onion marmalade tart, and a 'superb' risotto of peas, greens, broad and French beans served alongside a courgette and Parmesan fritter is available as a starter or main course. Portions are more than generous, but try to make room for fudge and pecan cheesecake. House Georges Duboeuf is £17.
Chef/s: Steve Dean. Open: all week 12 to 2.30, 7 to 9 (6.30 to 9.30 Sat). Meals: alc (main courses £13.50 to £37). Set L £14.50 (2 courses) to £17.50, Set D £29.50. Afternoon menu available 3 to 6. Service: not inc. Details: Cards accepted. 140 seats. 70 seats outside. Air-con. No mobile phones. Wheelchair access. Music. Children's portions. Car parking.

## ▌Bolton Abbey
# Devonshire Arms
**Breathtaking modern food**
Burlington, Bolton Abbey, BD23 6AJ
Tel no: (01756) 710441
www.devonshirehotels.co.uk
**Modern British | £40**
**Cooking score: 5**

🍷 ⊨ Ⅴ

In case you didn't know who your hosts were, the Devonshire Arms belongs to the Duke and Duchess of that ilk. There are two operations here, the first a lively, colourful modern brasserie, the second the Burlington Restaurant, where smartly attired tables set the scene. In the restaurant, Michael Wignall offers dishes that take an average three lines on the menu to explain, all headed up in the fashion imported from elsewhere with their main ingredient, today's longer cooking times in evidence through regular appearance of the word 'braised'. 'Pig' might start, and turn out to be a salad of roast and slow-cooked Lancashire porker, with apple crème fraîche, a pressing of the braised leg and lavender honey jus. Some recherché ingredients steal in under those terse headings, such as the cock's comb that shares the billing with poached langoustines, warm cep jelly and a boudin of salt cod. The vogue for dishes that combine fish and meat elements is given a new twist with a pairing of John Dory and veal shin in a curry velouté with caramelised foie gras. A more mainstream combination might be slow-poached poussin with violet asparagus and a quail's egg. Desserts are equally intricately wrought, in the manner of pavé of strawberry, lime and yoghurt with Sauternes and vanilla jelly, marinated strawberries and passion-fruit sorbet. Vegetarians have their own menu, with a pair of choices at starter and main. This year, the Devonshire Arms has spared us the labour of poring over all 169 pages of the wine list, but past inspections have confirmed it is a masterpiece of the genre. Wines by the glass start at £4.50, bottle prices from £13.50.

**Chef/s:** Michael Wignall. **Open:** Sun L 12.30 to 2.30, Tue to Sun D 7 to 10. **Meals:** Set L £35, Set D £58 to £73. Snack and brasserie menus available.
**Service:** 12.5% (optional). **Details:** Cards accepted. 70 seats. Wheelchair access. Music. Children's portions. Car parking.

## ▌Boroughbridge
# Dining Room
**Seasonal food in a quiet Georgian square**
20 St James Square, Boroughbridge, YO51 9AR
Tel no: (01423) 326426
**Modern British | £23**
**Cooking score: 4**

£5 OFF   £30

Once a stage of the Great North Road, Boroughbridge is now bypassed, but the Dining Room has no problem attracting a regular clientele. It provides accomplished cooking in a cosseted environment, where the restrained neutrals of the downstairs dining room contrast well with the exuberance of the deep-red drawing room upstairs. Dinner offered a seasonal asparagus and Parmesan risotto, pretty in green and yellow, and fat Cajun prawns circling crisp cucumber, mint and crème fraîche and topped with über-trendy micro leaves; local lamb shank, plump and slow-cooked tender, stood on a dais of nearly mashed minted new potatoes; and a sea bass of delicate, layered butter-browned fillets with a sweet chilli and coconut sauce. The kitchen missed its footing with the vegetarian option - an over-thick filo wrapped a crudely unsubtle filling of feta and olive, but the extravagantly vanilla-bespeckled crème brûlée and pannacotta were well executed. An 11-page wine list covers all the bases, with a selection starting at £13.95.

**Chef/s:** Christopher Astley. **Open:** Sun L 12 to 2, Tue to Sat D 7 to 9.15. **Closed:** 25 and 26 Dec, 1 Jan, Bank hol Mon. **Meals:** alc L (main courses £13.50). Set L £24.25 (3 courses). Set D £25.00 (3 courses). **Service:** not inc. **Details:** Cards accepted. 32 seats. 20 seats outside. Separate bar. No mobile phones. Wheelchair access. Music. Children's portions. Car parking.

## ▌Bradford

### Mumtaz

**Karahi dining on an epic scale**
386-400 Great Horton Road, Bradford, BD7 3HS
Tel no: (01274) 571861
www.mumtaz.co.uk
**Karahi | £24**
**Cooking score: 2**
£30

Twenty years ago Mumtaz occupied a small
front room in a terraced house, now it's grown
into a glass and granite high-end bling-fest,
which has spread to occupy the whole row.
There's a massive car park, too, with the odd
Porsche or Ferrari giving every indication that
you need deep pockets to eat here. Not so.
Value for money is the watchword, although
these days you don't choose the curry by
weight (it was a bit of a gimmick but it
worked). Start with the pickle tray – the garlic
is so good 'you'll want to take a jar home'.
Karahi dishes make up most of the menu –
lamb, chicken and vegetable, fresh and
fragrant, with naan 'the size of small
spaceships'. Karahi fish anari is succulent,
cooked with ginger, garlic, pomegranate and
lime juice, the subtle Kashmiri spices not
shouting down the fish at all. Desserts are
traditional – barfi, rass malai – but take time
to have a cup of Kashmiri tea – creamy,
perfumed, and great to finish with. Mumtaz is
alcohol-free, but the sweet lassi is so good you
won't notice.
**Open:** all week 11am to 12am (1am Fri and Sat).
**Meals:** alc (main courses £6 to £14.50). **Service:** not
inc. **Details:** Cards accepted. 500 seats. Air-con.
Wheelchair access. Music. Children's portions. Car
parking.

### Prashad

**Take-away snacks and homely cooking**
86 Horton Grange Road, Bradford, BD7 2DW
Tel no: (01274) 575893
www.prashad.co.uk
**Indian/Pakistani/Bangladeshi | £26**
**Cooking score: 2**
Ⅴ

A 'friendly, relaxed' atmosphere prevails in this
small restaurant on the Bradford ring road. At
the front is the shop, selling ready-prepared
sweets, snacks and take-aways. A side door
leads to the restaurant at the rear. The
vegetarian cooking at Prashad reflects the
street snacks and traditional cooking of
Gujarat. The menu includes starters of pea
kachori (spiced ground pea and garlic balls
deep-fried in chapatti); and pethis (spiced
coconut, deep fried in a fluffy potato coating).
More substantial starters, typical of the
roadside snacks found in Gujurati cities,
include bhel supreme (puffed rice, potato and
chickpeas with tamarind sauce) and dhal vada
(lentil balls marinated in sweet yoghurt and
garnished with tamarind and coconut). Main
dishes include Bombay bataka (potatoes
cooked in a rich tangy sauce and served in a
balti); butter paneer masala; and idli sambar
(steamed rice flour dumplings with a spicy
lentil soup and coconut and yoghurt chutney).
Finish with traditional Indian sweets such as
barfi. Alcohol is not served, but an inspector
noted that 'a salt lassi with a pronounced
flavour of cumin made an ideal
accompaniment.'
**Chef/s:** Kaushy Patel. **Open:** Tue to Sun 11 to 2.30, 6
to 9.30 (10 Sat). **Meals:** alc (main courses £7 to £12).
Set L £7.50 (2 courses), Set D £10. **Service:** not inc.
**Details:** Cards accepted. 30 seats. Air-con. Music.
Children's portions.

## READERS RECOMMEND

### Great Victoria

Modern British
Bridge Street, Bradford, BD1 1JX
Tel no: (01274) 728706
www.tomahawkhotels.co.uk
'A beautiful dining room'

## ▌Burnsall

### Devonshire Fell

Stylish contemporary conversion
Burnsall, BD23 6BT
Tel no: (01756) 729000
www.devonshirehotels.co.uk
Modern British | £28
Cooking score: 3

£5 OFF 🛏 V £30

Set high on a hill overlooking the River
Wharfe, this little brother of the Devonshire
Arms, Bolton Abbey (see entry), started life as
a 'club for gentlemen mill owners'. Bistro-style
meals are served in the bar, but most attention
focuses on the conservatory dining room
tacked on to the front of the hotel, which also
has stunning views. Paul Deakins offers a mix
of British classics with slightly more
ambitious dishes drawn from the
modern repertoire. Die-hard traditionalists
might opt for Bury black pudding with a
toasted spinach croûte and hollandaise or
Lancashire hotpot with spiced red cabbage.
Elsewhere, there are more intriguing
possibilities: scallops are served with smoked
salmon and endive salad, Gressingham duck
breast is paired with elderflower sauce, while
beetroot purée is used to complement rump of
lamb. To finish, expect desserts like pistachio
and nougat parfait with raspberry coulis.
More than two dozen house selections (from
£13.95 a bottle, £3.50 a glass) top the wide-
ranging wine list.
Chef/s: Paul Deakins. Open: all week 12 to 2.30 (3
Sun), 6.30 to 9.30 (9 Sun). Meals: alc (main courses
£13 to £18). Bistro menu available. Service: 12.5%.
Details: Cards accepted. 50 seats. 18 seats outside.
Wheelchair access. Music. Children's portions. Car
parking.

## ALSO RECOMMENDED

### ▲ Abbey Inn

Byland Abbey, Coxwold, YO61 4BD
Tel no: (01347) 868204
www.english-heritage.org.uk/bylandabbey

This attractive ivy clad restaurant with rooms
and a pretty garden stands opposite the Byland
Abbey. It is the first and only inn owned by
English Heritage and the décor reflects the
owners. They serve a suitably traditional
English heritage menu, too. Main courses
deploy the likes of shin beef and kidney
pudding, calf's liver, lamb shank and stuffed
chicken breast matched with worthy and
seasonal root vegetables, cooked with solidity
and substance. They source good bread and
offer four named house wines (£12.95) along
with a specially brewed local ale: Byland
Brew.

## ▌East Witton

### Blue Lion

A gastropub with a lived-in feel
East Witton, DL8 4SN
Tel no: (01969) 624273
www.thebluelion.co.uk
Modern British | £24
Cooking score: 3

🍾 🛏 V £30

Sitting handsomely at one end of a picture-
perfect village, this reassuringly solid pub
'opens its arms widely and delivers a big hug as
you walk in' – high ceilings, stone floors and a
huge fire reflected in the glass and brass adding
to the sense of being in the right place.
Smartly dressed, cheerful staff guide you
through the menu which is chalked up above
the bar and round the walls, 'and what choices
you have'. Parma ham and Yorkshire blue
cheese tart is piquant, with perfect pastry,
while terrine of ham hock is a doorstep of
sweet tenderness, offset by a subtle yellow split
pea purée. The mains list is long – often not a
good thing – but the quality of dishes coming
from the kitchen is not compromised; smoked
haddock with new potatoes, poached egg, leek

and mushroom sauce with toasted Gruyère is delicately assembled and works well, and the braised masala mutton with cumin sweet potato mash is dense and fragrant. Puddings are a triumph too – lemon posset with raspberries and lemon-curd shortbread is 'dangerously creamy with a zing', and the iced liquorice terrine 'mind-bending – in a good way'. A short but well thought out selection of wines from Argentina to Australia cater for most pockets and all can be had by the glass, starting at £3.75.

**Chef/s:** John Dalby. **Open:** Sun L 12 to 2.15, all week D 7 to 9.30. **Closed:** Christmas. **Meals:** alc (main courses £10 to £19). **Service:** not inc. **Details:** Cards accepted. 70 seats. 30 seats outside. No music. Wheelchair access. Children's portions. Car parking.

## Elland
### La Cachette
**Good-value brasserie menu**
31 Huddersfield Road, Elland, HX5 9AW
**Tel no: (01422) 378833**
**Modern European | £22**
**Cooking score: 3**

A welcoming bustle and buzz is one part of this bistro's charm; attentive service makes up the rest of the winning formula. The atmosphere is modern and informal, and the choice of dishes should please all-comers. A European influence runs through starters of ham hock terrine with pineapple chutney and melba toast or deep-fried Brie with apple, cinnamon and sultana chutney through to main courses such as butternut squash risotto with Gorgonzola; cheese-glazed fillet of haddock with spinach, creamed potato and white wine sauce; or pan-fried Cumbrian venison with honey-roast parsnips, buttered cabbage and port sauce. Finish with apple tart Tatin and vanilla ice cream or iced strawberry parfait with red fruits. A lengthy, well-chosen wine list starts at £11.95.

**Chef/s:** Jonathan Nichols. **Open:** Mon to Sat 12 to 2.30, 6 to 9.30 (10 Fri and Sat). **Closed:** 10 days Christmas, last 2 weeks Aug, bank hol Mon. **Meals:** alc (main courses £9 to £18). Set L £9.95 (2

courses), Set D Mon to Thur and 6 to 7 Fri and Sat £16.95 (inc wine). **Service:** not inc. **Details:** Cards accepted. 85 seats. Air-con. Wheelchair access. Music. Children's portions.

## Ferrensby
### General Tarleton
**Cosy pub and upmarket restaurant**
Boroughbridge Road, Ferrensby, HG5 0PZ
**Tel no: (01423) 340284**
www.generaltarleton.co.uk
**British | £33**
**Cooking score: 4**

The sudden appearance of this beautifully restored coaching inn on the very edge of the main road might make for a rather jarring arrival, but once inside the warm welcome and effortlessly comfortable interior will put you very much at ease. Pass through the cosy but surprisingly expansive bar to reach the far more refined but no less welcoming restaurant and you'll experience local star John Topham at his very best. A veritable showcase for local produce, the menu abounds with regional delights: Knaresborough asparagus needs no more than the accompanying hollandaise; Whitby crab is paired with Nidderdale hot oak-smoked salmon; and a trio of brûlée, crumble and compote pays homage to the 'Rhubarb Triangle' of Bradford, Wakefield and Leeds. All dishes, whether locally sourced or not, are delicious and presented with the perfect amount of flair. Service is so good you might question whether you are still in Britain. Much like the restaurant with its beautiful new garden terrace, the already broad range of the wine list, which starts at £12.95, has been further expanded and now features some great choices from vineyards as far and wide as Lebanon and Kent.

**Chef/s:** John Topham and Robert Ramsden. **Open:** Sun L 12 to 2, Mon to Sat D 6 to 9.15. **Meals:** Set L £22.95 (3 courses), Set D £32.50 (3 courses). Bar/ brasserie menu available all week L and D. **Service:** not inc. **Details:** Cards accepted. 145 seats. 80 seats outside. Separate bar. No music. Wheelchair access. Children's portions. Car parking.

## Golcar

### Weavers Shed

Slick, regional cooking
86-88 Knowl Road, Golcar, HD7 4AN
Tel no: (01484) 654284
www.weaversshed.co.uk
**Modern British | £42**
**Cooking score: 5**

£5 OFF 🍴 ➡ 𝖸

The close-by kitchen garden of this textile
mill turned accomplished restaurant-with-
rooms, plays a major role in Stephen Jackson's
fine modern regional cooking, supplying
virtually all the fruit, herbs and vegetables.
Sensibly compact menus proudly identify
those dishes created with pickings from the
kitchen, orchard, and wild, while fish and
seafood is guaranteed from sustainable stocks.
So a main-course dish of chargilled calf's liver
might come with wilted spinach, sautéed
artichoke and salsify, plus parsley mash and
veal jus, while farmed black-cod fillet, roasted
and served with a cassolette of carrots,
potatoes and prawns, might be finished with
dill and cream. 'Sublime puddings' could
feature a vanilla crème brûlée accompanied by
oven-poached Yorkshire rhubarb and rhubarb
syrup. Tracy Jackson at front-of-house is an
affable, calm and informed host, and, while
her dining room may have undergone a
contemporary face-lift, it retains many
original features like wooden beams and stone
arches alongside its relaxed buzz. The carefully
selected wine list has France in the ascendancy
on its global tour, includes some helpful
tasting notes, and, in line with the kitchen
garden-driven philosophy, focuses on smaller,
lesser-known producers, while crediting its
wine merchants. A six-house collection kicks
things off at £13.95.
**Chef/s:** Stephen Jackson, Ian McGunnigle and Cath
Sill. **Open:** Tue to Fri L 12 to 2, Tue to Sat D 7 to 9.
**Closed:** 25 Dec to 1 Jan. **Meals:** alc (main courses
£17 to £23). Set L £12.95 (2 courses) to £15.95.
**Service:** not inc. **Details:** Cards accepted. 24 seats.
No mobile phones. Music. Children allowed. Car
parking.

## Grange Moor

### Kaye Arms

Traditionally decorated, popular gastropub
29 Wakefield Road, Grange Moor, WF4 4BG
Tel no: (01924) 848385
**Modern British | £30**
**Cooking score: 3**

This isolated but popular old black and white
pub is a well-established, well-oiled, food-
focused affair. Inside there are two main
dining areas with a bar in the middle, but the
emphasis is on eating rather than pints of beer.
It has an open-plan arrangement with an
honest, traditional, slightly old-fashioned
slant, but dressed tables, friendly and helpful
service, and a crowd-pleasing, up-tempo carte
offer plenty of modern-day interest, bolstered
by daily specials and a simple lunch offering.
Grilled fillet of sea bass served with pesto,
tapenade, roast provençale vegetables and new
potatoes might jostle for selection alongside
four-hour crispy roast pork belly
accompanied by mustard mash, braised red
cabbage with apple and roasting juices. There
are simple classics options too, while puddings
come down on the familiar, waistband-
extending side (bread-and-butter pudding
with whisky and honey cream), but there are
lighter options too, like a house speciality
raspberry soufflé. Wines are an easy-going,
interesting, globetrotting selection, offering
plenty of drinking under the £20 threshold,
starting out at £12.50.
**Chef/s:** Adrian Quarmby. **Open:** Tue to Sun 12 to 2,
7.15 to 9.30. **Closed:** 25 Dec to 4 Jan. **Meals:** alc
(main courses £10 to £22). Light L menu available
Tue to Sat. **Service:** not inc. **Details:** Cards
accepted. 90 seats. Wheelchair access. Music.
Children allowed. Car parking.

## ▌Harome

### Star Inn

**Championing local suppliers**
High Street, Harome, YO62 5JE
Tel no: (01439) 770397
www.thestaratharome.co.uk
**Modern British | £30**
**Cooking score: 5**

♦ ═ Υ

The very model of an English country pub, the Star Inn has everything. As well as a smart restaurant (the only area where bookings are taken), there is a cheering, friendly main bar and outdoor eating in the garden. Menus change frequently to make the most of good seasonal produce, and there is a separate vegetarian menu available on request. Meals start as they mean to go on, with complex but successful assemblages such as grilled black pudding with foie gras, watercress salad, apple and vanilla chutney and a scrumpy reduction, or perhaps dressed white crabmeat with plum tomato and basil, a green herb mayonnaise and Bloody Mary dressing. Local suppliers are proudly credited on the menus, in main courses such as haunch of Duncombe Park roe deer with venison cottage pie, girolles and tarragon, or Helmsley belly pork with a fried duck egg and devilled sauce. The selection of miniature desserts is the option of those who are spoiled for choice, while the more decisive might plump for caramelised lemon tart with raspberry sauce. A sensational wine list is priced with restraint, and will disgorge superb growers and great vintages wherever you happen to land. The house selection alone, beginning with Australian blends at £14.75, or £3.85 a glass, is hard to tear yourself away from.
**Chef/s:** Andrew Pern. **Open:** Tue to Sat 11.30 to 2, 6.30 to 9.30, Sun 12 to 6. **Meals:** alc (main courses £15.25 to £22.50). **Service:** not inc. **Details:** Cards accepted. 70 seats. 50 seats outside. Separate bar. Wheelchair access. Music. Children's portions. Children allowed. Car parking.

## ▌Harrogate

### Hotel du Vin & Bistro

**Boutique dining at this solid hotel chain**
Prospect Place, Harrogate, HG1 1LB
Tel no: (01423) 856800
www.hotelduvin.com
**Modern European | £31**
**Cooking score: 3**

♦ ═ Υ

This hotel and bistro occupies a converted row of solid-looking Georgian-style houses overlooking the 200-acre common in the heart of Harrogate. The bistro's good reputation is built around quality ingredients and the kind of unfussy, modern-classic cooking style that guarantees a broad appeal. Begin with rabbit ballottine with frisée and orange and apricot chutney; mackeral tartare with sorrel, celery and radish or snail, bacon and mizuna salad. Main courses could include sea bream with crushed new potatoes and watercress; roast squab pigeon with swede purée, pancetta and thyme sauce; and 'simple classics' such as Hereford cross ribeye steak with home-made chips or veal Holstein. Side orders include mixed greens, gratin dauphinoise, and hand-cut chips cooked in duck fat. Desserts range from the homely comforts of sticky toffee pudding to tweaked classics like pineapple tart Tatin, while an impressive cheese selection showcases finds from Britain and France. The extensive wine list is another highlight, and opens at £14.50.
**Chef/s:** Gareth Longhurst. **Open:** all week 12 to 2 (12.30 to 2.30 Sun), 7 to 10. **Meals:** alc (main courses £12.50 to £21.50). Set L Mon to Fri £12.50 (2 courses) to £17.50 (inc wine). **Service:** not inc. **Details:** Cards accepted. 85 seats. No music. Wheelchair access.

★NEW ENTRY★
## Oxford Street Brasserie
**Much-needed contemporary outing**
34 Oxford Street, Harrogate, HG1 1PP
**Tel no: (01423) 505 300**
**Modern British | £25**
**Cooking score: 4**

£5 OFF  **V**  £30

Swapping a stellar riverside restaurant in Leeds for a space above a Carphone Warehouse in Harrogate may seem a bad move, but as David Robson is now working for himself, both as head chef and owner, that changes things somewhat. Having worked under Jeff Baker at Pool Court for so long, the urge to break out and assert his individual style must have been strong indeed, as there is a real sense – both from the menu and the feel of the place – of a man who has been dying to express himself freely. The result is a youthful brasserie that, though not yet at the top of its game, has gone down extremely well in this traditional town. The menu suggests a classical background, but everything is delivered with a boldness that might feel cocky if it wasn't so charming. Starters like king prawns fried with beansprouts and chilli sit alongside more traditional choices like a Gruyère soufflé, but all bear the same vibrant, contemporary hallmarks. In many cases simplicity is made a virtue, with mains like a seared beef fillet with hand-cut chips and a fried duck egg getting it spot-on. A large range of daily vegetarian specials has got the town talking, as have the desserts. The wine list echoes this blend of classic and contemporary and starts at a very reasonable £12.
**Chef/s:** David Robson. **Open:** Mon 12 to 2.30, Tue to Sat 12 to 2.30 and 5.30 to 9.30. **Closed:** 25 and 26 Dec. **Meals:** alc (main courses £10.95 to £14.95). Set D £30 (3 courses). **Service:** not inc. **Details:** Cards accepted. 40 seats. Air-con. Music. Children's portions.

★NEW ENTRY★
## Sasso
**Low-key Italian restaurant**
8-10 Princes Square, Harrogate, HG1 1LX
**Tel no: (01423) 508838**
www.sassorestaurant.co.uk
**Italian | £30**
**Cooking score: 5**

🍾 **V**

Tucked away in a simple, uncluttered basement on Princes Street, Sasso looks modest, somewhere between a new-wave Italian and a candle-in-the-Chianti-bottle trattoria. But do not mistake the middle ground for mediocre because Stefano Lancelotti's instinct for excellence, his way with ingredients, and the precision in his cooking goes from strength to strength. He comes from Bologna and if modern Bolognese cooking is a blend of rustic and metropolitan, he has mastered it. Home-made ravioli (he makes all his own pasta) brought three gorgeous parcels filled with lobster, courgettes, shallots and tarragon sitting in a light lobster broth. Another perfectly composed and thoroughly delicious dish was wild sea bass fillets given a porcini mushroom crust, topped off with a herby, garlic butter and served on Parmesan and rocket mash, with roast potatoes, baby carrot and chargrilled baby corn. Other highly tempting items from a generous main menu were warm octopus salad with bacon, shallot, roasted peppers and rocket with sweet chilli sauce and truffled taglioline served with tiger prawn, scampi, lobster, crabmeat and asparagus. But Lancelotti does not depend on exotic ingredients to make a show. His £7.50 bargain lunch menu produced an exemplary risotto made simply from tomatoes, Italian sausage and a splash of caramelised balsamic vinegar. Then came sautéed cod fillet in thick flakes and a crisped skin, served on wilted spinach and a prawn, cream and white wine sauce. Desserts of pannacotta and tiramisu are the real thing. The walnut and white chocolate semifreddo with a toffee and Amaretto sauce is a 'divine version' of a frozen Crunchy bar.

Drink from a 50-strong list of Italian wines that begins at £12.50 for Villa Moranda, majors between there and £20, and peaks at £420 for a Dal Forno Armarone 2000, with a fair cross-section by the glass. Good bread and sensitive service rounded off an operation at the top of its game.

**Chef/s:** Stefano Lancelotti. **Open:** Tue to Sat L 12 to 2, Mon to Thu D 6.30 to 10 (to 10.30 Fri and Sat). **Closed:** bank hols. **Meals:** alc (main courses 13.50 to 19.75) Set L 7.50 (2 courses). **Service:** 10% (parties of six or more). **Details:** Cards accepted. 56 seats. 20 seats outside. Air-con. No mobile phones. Music. Children allowed.

## ▌Haworth

## Weavers

Local produce sourced from Brontë country
13-17 West Lane, Haworth, BD22 8DU
Tel no: (01535) 643822
www.weaversmallhotel.co.uk
**Modern British | £24**
**Cooking score: 3**

🚬 V £30

Three terraced cottages have been knocked together to make this rambling, cosy restaurant. Big on personality, with quirky décor and warm lighting, it provides an ideal backdrop for the characterful modern British cooking that is its forte. Starters could include ham hock and shredded duck terrine with piccalilli sauce or baked English goats' cheese with spinach, shallots and spelt toast. Move on to slow-cooked shoulder of Dales lamb with creamy sliced potatoes, rosemary-infused juices and cranberries; a meat and potato pie made with Pennine beef, rich gravy and shortcut pastry with white onion relish and a jug of gravy; or crisp-skinned breast of local farm chicken with creamy leek mash and a wild mushroom sauce. Lunch brings 'big soups' and snacks such as a traditional roast beef sandwich with horseradish cream and salad, alongside the mains. Wines from £13.95.

**Chef/s:** Tim, Jane and Colin Rushworth. **Open:** Wed to Fri and Sun L 12 to 2, Tue to Sat D 6 to 9. **Closed:** 10 days from 25 Dec. **Meals:** alc (main courses L £8

to £14, D £11 to £18). Set L Wed to Fri £9.95 (2 courses), Set L Sun £16.95, Set D Tue to Fri £13.95 (2 courses) to £16.95. **Service:** not inc. **Details:** Cards accepted. 65 seats. Air-con. No mobile phones. Music. Children's portions.

## READERS RECOMMEND

## Restaurant Anise

British
Hazlewood Castle, Paradise Lane, Hazlewood, LS24 9NJ
Tel no: (01937) 535317
www.hazlewood-castle.co.uk
**'Impressive building and excellent food'**

## ▌Helmsley

## Feversham Arms Hotel

Modern designer hotel
Helmsley, YO62 5AG
Tel no: (01439) 770766
www.fevershamarmshotel.com
**Modern European | £40**
**Cooking score: 4**

£5 OFF 🚬 V

Tucked away beside the church in a traditional market town beloved of ramblers (it's at the start of the Cleveland Way), this stylish modern hotel serves up an elegant carte in a dining room that might remind some of a drill hall if it weren't for the rosy glow of the deep red walls. Classic Anglo-French cuisine forms the basis for most dishes, though influences from elsewhere in Europe add a contemporary note, as in a starter of pan-fried foie gras with pink grapefruit, beansprouts and lime dressing. At inspection, wild mushroom consommé with truffle ravioli combined rich flavours with a delicacy of touch, while Whitby smoked salmon was deftly matched with new potato salad, caviar and shallot sauce. A main course of 12-hour braised shin of beef with spring cabbage and horseradish crème fraîche may have looked like a standard beef stew but the flavours were exemplary. Desserts, however, were not a strength at inspection. Thumbs up to the lengthy wine list, though – covering a good range and including a welcome choice of half-bottles as well as wines by the glass. Prices start reasonably but if you want to push the boat out, a £750 champagne is ready and waiting. **Chef/s:** Simon Kelly. **Open:** all week 12 to 2 (1 to 3 Sun), 7 to 9.30. **Meals:** alc (main courses L £12.50 to £13.95, D £17.50 to £22.50). Set D £32. **Service:** not inc. **Details:** Cards accepted. 55 seats. 30 seats outside. No mobile phones. Wheelchair access. Music. Children's portions. Car parking.

## ▌Hessle

## Artisan

**Dedicated to first-class food**
22 The Weir, Hessle, HU13 0RU
Tel no: (01482) 644906
www.artisanrestaurant.com
**Modern British | £34**
**Cooking score: 4**

£5
OFF

This small and contemporarily decorated restaurant is situated near the Humber Bridge. The menu makes a virtue of simplicity, and Richard Johns is proud of his top-quality materials provided by a well-established network of suppliers, which might show up as a straightforward salad of Lowna Dairy goats' cheese with fresh mango, avocado and fig, or a ballottine of chicken with foie gras, bacon and Puy lentils. The choice at main course might be between wild sea bass with fondant potato, buttered spring greens and citrus beurre blanc sauce and 15-hour braised free-range pork with seasonal greens, potato and cider apple reduction. Finish perhaps with an indulgent Belgian white chocolate and Cointreau chocolate pot with raspberries, chocolate sauce and white chocolate ice cream. Reports have highlighted the excellent service from Lindsey Johns. The nicely judged wine list (not too long, not too short) holds plenty of interest, but with an entry level of £19.50. **Chef/s:** Richard Johns. **Open:** Wed to Sun D 7 to 9.30. **Meals:** Set L £14.50 (2 courses) to £18.95, Set D £29.95 (2 courses) to £33.95. **Service:** not inc. **Details:** Cards accepted. 18 seats. Air-con. No mobile phones. Wheelchair access. Music. Car parking.

## ▌Hetton

## The Angel Inn

**Culinary delight in the Dales**
Hetton, BD23 6LT
Tel no: (01756) 730263
www.angelhetton.co.uk
**Modern British | £32**
**Cooking score: 3**

▲ ᕦ Ψ

Over the years The Angel has evolved into a destination dining pub, one where you are amply rewarded for the up-hill and down-dale drive along narrow lanes. Parts of the building are hundreds of years old, so there are plenty of quiet corners as well as flagged floors, open fires and a magnificent, gleaming black range at one end of the comfy bar – where tables are unbookable and fill up quickly. You can book tables in the smart restaurant. In the kitchen sous chef Mark Taft has been promoted (former head chef Bruce Elsworth is now the overall manager of the inn), but little else has changed. Both bar and restaurant menus continue to reveal commitment to top-class local produce, finely illustrated by earthy and flavoursome home-made black pudding with spiced roasted pear and Puy lentils, and roasted chump of Yorkshire lamb, pink and dense, served with crushed Jerusalem artichokes and trompette mushrooms. Elsewhere you'll discover duck from Goosnargh, Dales-reared pheasant and beef, as well as fish delivered daily from Fleetwood. Vegetarians are also exceptionally well catered for. Puddings are along the lines of sticky toffee pudding or a glorious rhubarb brûlée that's sharp and sweet all at once. Wines are predominantly French, with a generous nod to the New World. House wines start at £14.95. **Chef/s:** Mark Taft. **Open:** Mon to Sat, L 12 to 2, D 6 to 9.30, Sun L 12 to 2,. **Meals:** alc exc Sat D and Sun L (main courses £11 to £19). Set L Sun £23.95, Set D Mon to Fri £14 (2 courses) to £17, Set D Sat £34.50.. **Service:** not inc. **Details:** Cards accepted. 60 seats. 40 seats outside. Air-con. No music. Wheelchair access. Children's portions. Car parking.

## ▌Holdsworth

### Holdsworth House

**Fine dining in a Jacobean mansion**
Holdsworth, HX2 9TG
Tel no: (01422) 240024
www.holdsworthhouse.co.uk
**Fusion/Pan-Asian | £32**
**Cooking score: 3**

The surrounding landscape is all mills and moors, and this beautiful building, with its grey stone walls and leafy garden is every inch a part of it. Behind the mullioned windows is all the timeless charm you could hope for: roaring fires, candlelight and wood-panelling, for example. Against this historical backdrop, the menu is surprisingly modern, pulling together a diverse range of dishes that runs from fish poached in a Thai-spiced broth or Indian butter chicken with a timbale of spinach basmati and a miniature almond naan through to pan-fried salmon with wilted baby spinach, sautéed queen scallops and garlic and lemon butter; or noisette of Kendall Fell lamb with spinach and Pommery mustard stuffing and sweet potato purée. Finish with mini cinnamon doughnuts with pistachio kulfi and rosewater syrup or orange and passion- fruit cheesecake with marmalade ice cream. The wine list includes a good selection by the glass. Bottles from £13.95.
**Chef/s:** Gary Saunders. **Open:** Mon to Fri L 12 to 2, Mon to Sat D 7 to 9.30. **Closed:** 24 Dec to 3 Jan exc L 25 and 26 Dec, D 31 Dec. **Meals:** alc D (main courses £14.50 to £19.50). Set L £13.95 (2 courses) to £16.95. **Service:** not inc. **Details:** Cards accepted. 50 seats. 10 seats outside. No mobile phones. Wheelchair access. Music. Children's portions. Car parking.

## ▌Honley

### Mustard and Punch

**Fashionably bold flavours**
6 Westgate, Honley, HD9 6AA
Tel no: (01484) 662066
www.mustardandpunch.co.uk
**Modern European | £25**
**Cooking score: 3**

This former shop in the centre of the village aims for a relaxed atmosphere. But behind the low-key façade is an industrious kitchen that produces breads, ice creams and pretty much everything else on the premises. Cured venison salad with quince paste, spiced sultana and caper dressing appears among starters alongside king scallops on bean cassoulet with brown shrimp vinaigrette; while main courses typically feature pork fillet with potato gnocchi, poached apples and a light curry and sultana sauce, or sea bass with crayfish tails, basil spaghetti and a tomato and caper dressing. To finish try iced lime parfait with grilled plums, pear cheesecake with walnut ice cream or a selection of fine British cheeses. Half a dozen wines are available by the large or small glass, while bottle prices on the compact list start at £11.95.
**Chef/s:** Richard Dunn and Wayne Roddis. **Open:** Mon to Sat D 6 to 9.30. **Closed:** Bank hol Mon. **Meals:** alc (main courses £10.50 to £18.50). Set D Mon to Fri and before 6.30 Sat £17.95 (3 courses inc wine).. **Service:** not inc. **Details:** Cards accepted. 55 seats. Air-con. Music. Children's portions.

## ▌Huddersfield

### Bradley's

**Eclectic entertainment and dining**
84 Fitzwilliam Street, Huddersfield, HD1 5BB
Tel no: (01484) 516773
**Modern European | £24**
**Cooking score: 2**

Latin jazz, Elvis impersonators and 'Ozzie night' are among the themed events that liven up proceedings at this city centre brasserie.

Menus show a wide range of influences, apparent in starters that range from grilled sardines with lemons and capers to tempura of king prawns with sweet chilli jam, via pappardelle pasta with chargrilled vegetables. To follow, rack of new season lamb with roast sweet potato, pancetta and basil pesto, and Gressingham duck breast with griottine cherries line up alongside pan-fried sea bass and king scallops with shellfish risotto and saffron foam. Meals might end with dark chocolate soufflé with five-spice syrup. A compact, value-conscious wine list offers good choice by the glass and bottles from £12.50.

**Chef/s:** Eric Paxman. **Open:** Mon to Fri L 12 to 2, Mon to Sat D 6 to 10 (5.30 Fri and Sat). **Closed:** 27 Dec to 3 Jan, bank hols. **Meals:** alc (main courses £11 to £17). Set L £5.50 (2 courses) to £8.95, Set D £17.95 (3 courses inc wine). **Service:** not inc. **Details:** Cards accepted. 120 seats. Air-con. Wheelchair access. Music. Children's portions. Car parking.

## Dining Rooms @ Strawberry Fair

**Fresh, innovative brasserie-style lunches**
14-18 Westgate, Huddersfield, HD1 1NN
Tel no: (01484) 513103
Modern European | £18
Cooking score: 2

V £30

Bare floorboards, high-backed leather chairs, subtle lighting and a pale colour scheme give a cool, modern feel to the Dining Rooms, located on the first floor of the posh home-accessories shop Strawberry Fair. It's open for breakfast, sandwiches and afternoon tea. Locals flock in for the excellent value two-course menu or tuck into home-made fishcakes with sauce verde, followed by pork loin chop served with Jersey Royals, curly kale and gooseberry sauce, or chicken breast with black olives and mozzarella on buttered gnocchi. Finish with rum and caramel crème brûlée. A short wine list opens with Chilean red and white at £10.65.

**Chef/s:** Glenn Varley and Rachel Miller. **Open:** Mon to Sat L only 11.30 to 3 (breakfast 9 to 11.30, afternoon tea 2 to 4). **Closed:** bank hol exc Good Fri. **Meals:** alc (main courses £6.50 to £7.50). **Service:** not inc. **Details:** Cards accepted. 48 seats. Air-con. No mobile phones. Wheelchair access. Music. Children's portions.

## Vanilla

**Ambitious, confident cooking**
75 Lidget Street, Lindley, Huddersfield, HD3 3JP
Tel no: (01484) 646474
Modern European | £34
Cooking score: 2

£5 OFF V

In the centre of town, above a row of shops in a Victorian terrace, Vanilla is a bright, modern kind of restaurant with no shortage of ambition and confidence. The long menu offers plenty of variety, with starters ranging from cucumber and ricotta cheese cannelloni with pickled vegetables, mango and vanilla-scented sauce vierge to roast chicken risotto with home-made black pudding, white onion velouté and Bramley apple confit. To follow, five-spice sea bass fillet with 'scorched' king scallop, king prawn wonton, stir-fried pak choi and sweet and sour pineapple sauce lines up alongside roast Gressingham duck breast with a 'pasty' of confit leg, honey and black pepper, plus 'squash crush potato pie' and roasting juices flavoured with Grand Marnier. Peach crumble with vanilla ice cream sounds like a good way to finish. Vegetarians have their own separate menu and the wine list is helpfully annotated to aid choosing, with prices starting at a very reasonable £13.50.

**Chef/s:** Chris Dunn, Alex Knott and Floyd Holden. **Open:** Tue to Fri L 12 to 2, Tue to Sat D 5.30 to 9.30 (10 Sat). **Closed:** Jan 1. **Meals:** alc (main courses £7 to £18). Set D 5.30 to 8 (6 Fri and Sat) £15.50 (3 courses). **Service:** not inc. **Details:** Cards accepted. 50 seats. Music. Children's portions.

## ▊ Hull

### Boars Nest

Traditional Northern cooking
22 Princes Avenue, Hull, HU5 3QA
Tel no: (01482) 445577
www.theboarsnest.co.uk
British | £23
Cooking score: 2

Ⅴ £30

Loving preservation of this fomer butcher's shop is all of a piece with the cooking, which brings new life to old flavours. Open seven days a week, there are serious attempts to develop a modern northern accent to food; from brawn with watercress, soft boiled duck egg with crispy pig's ear 'soldiers' to Bury black pudding with onions and mash there's a refreshing lightness of touch and even humour. Earthy flavours in Swaledale mutton with tattie and neeps suet pudding or peppered skate, fat chips and creamed peppercorn meat juices confirm a vigorous urge to experiment combined with respect for the past. Puddings get drawn into the party; 'my mother's Manchester tarte' or rice pudding with medjool date ice cream might veer towards different forms of pretention but they seem to get away with it here. A neat list of thirty or so wines to match these robust flavours starts at £13.
**Chef/s:** Simon Rogers, Richard Bryan and Andy Young. **Open:** all week 12 to 2, 6.30 to 10. **Meals:** alc (main courses L £5 to £10, D £8 to £15). **Service:** not inc. **Details:** Cards accepted. 40 seats. 10 seats outside. No music. Wheelchair access. Children's portions.

## ▊ Ilkley

### Box Tree

Outstanding cooking in a legendary restaurant
35-37 Church Street, Ilkley, LS29 9DR
Tel no: (01943) 608484
www.theboxtree.co.uk
Anglo-French | £50
Cooking score: 6

🍾

Simon and Rena Gueller have certainly given the legendary Box Tree – once regarded as a British culinary institution and whose kitchens were the inspiration for a young Marco Pierre White – restored status since they took over in 2004. The refurbished 300-year-old building has a restrained contemporary edge, and there is a warm, intimate and welcoming atmosphere. Smart, comfortable high-backed chairs partner tables donning their best whites, while service is 'knowledgeable, friendly and attentive' without being stuffy. Simon's refined and elegant approach to modern cooking comes underscored by classical French technique, with dishes refreshingly uncluttered and driven by flavour and taste, all backed by a serious commitment to sourcing top-notch seasonal ingredients. Take a terrine of foie gras pressed with Armagnac and soaked Agen prunes matched with an orange salad, which opens a meal in classic style. Main courses make an impact, perhaps a roast rack of spring lamb partnered by a provençale ratatouille, pomme fondant and a jus of olives, tomato and basil, while a pavé of wild turbot with viennoise breadcrumbs might be delivered with buttered spinach and a velouté of grain mustard and chives. Desserts promote an equal agony of choice, perhaps a white peach sorbet and chocolate sauce vying for attention alongside a pineapple tart Tatin teamed with black pepper ice cream and a pineapple cigarette. Ancillaries like breads, petits fours and coffee do not disappoint either, while the extensive global wine list comes not unsurprisingly strong on French classics (in tandem with the food), but offers fine bottles from all quarters too. The house selection kicks off at £25 (£6 by glass), and there is also an admirable choice by half-bottle.

**Chef/s:** Simon Gueller. **Open:** Fri to Sun L 12 to 2, Tue to Sat D 7 to 9.30 (10 Sat). **Meals:** alc (main courses £22 to £30). Set L £18 (2 courses) to £25. **Service:** not inc. **Details:** Cards accepted. 60 seats. Air-con. No mobile phones. Wheelchair access. Music.

## Farsyde
**Straightforward, yet modern**
1-3 New Brook Street, Ilkley, LS29 8DQ
Tel no: (01943) 602030
www.thefarsyde.co.uk
**Modern British | £23**
**Cooking score: 4**

V £30

Bare floorboards, polished tables and a peachy colour theme set the tone at Gavin Beedham's breezy, brasserie-style restaurant opposite the parish church. His wide-ranging contemporary ideas are incorporated into a menu that shows respect for good materials and a dedication to offering value for money across the board. The lunchtime menu satisfies a range of appetites, from bagels and sandwiches to pasta and risotto dishes and more substantial main courses like cod cake on pea purée with shallot beurre blanc. At dinner, follow crispy duck leg on a sweet potato and wild rice fritter with sweet and sour dressing, with herb-crusted lamb served on spring pea, broad bean and pancetta cassoulet with red wine sauce. Fish dishes appear on the specials board and straightforward desserts like warm chocolate and cherry shortcake or apple and blackberry crumble round things off nicely. A well-chosen list of wines rarely strays over £20, starting with house French at £10.50.

**Chef/s:** Gavin Beedham. **Open:** Tue to Sat 11.30 to 2, 6 to 10. **Closed:** 25 and 26 Dec, 1 Jan. **Meals:** alc (main courses L £5 to £9, D £12.50 to £15.50). Set L £12.95, Set D 6 to 7.15 £13.45 (2 courses). **Service:** not inc. **Details:** Cards accepted. 82 seats. Air-con. Wheelchair access. Music.

## Kirk Deighton
### Bay Horse Inn
**Solid pub grub**
Main Street, Kirk Deighton, LS22 4DZ
Tel no: (01937) 580058
**Modern British | £20**
**Cooking score: 3**

🍾 V £30

Strung with hops and filled with miscellaneous furniture, this busy pub can feed as many as 130 on a Saturday night. The menu changes every six weeks, and on a visit in May, specials chalked up offered mainly fish, bouillabaisse, crab salad and fresh Whitby fish. A terrine of home oak-smoked salmon with king prawns, pea and mint purée was strong on flavour, more delicate though equally good was the poached plaice in crayfish sauce. Local Yorkshire beef is cooked in a variety of ways, and Dales saddle lamb comes with pearl barley, honey roast garlic and pickled red cabbage. Desserts of fruit jelly, crème brulée, bread-and-butter pudding and chocolate brownie are well presented and moorish. With 26 wines on the list priced from £13.95 to £39.95, Chilean house wine is served by the glass for £3.50.

**Chef/s:** Stephen Ardern, Annette Brassey. **Open:** Tue to Sun L 12 to 2.15, Mon to Sat D 6 to 9.15. **Meals:** alc (main courses £8 to £14). Set L and D 6 to 7 £13.95 (2 courses). **Service:** not inc. **Details:** Cards accepted. 55 seats. 20 seats outside. Wheelchair access. Music. Children's portions. Car parking.

## Leeds

### Anthony's at Flannels

**Elegant dining under the Flinn umbrella**
68-78 Vicar Lane, Leeds, LS1 7JH
Tel no: (0113) 242 8732
www.anthonysatflannels.co.uk
**British | £25**
**Cooking score: 4**

Ⴤ

Epitomising modern Leeds' bottomless appetite for upmarket shopping and cool eateries, this branch of Anthony's is perfectly pitched in the pure white, airy attic space above the upmarket Flannels clothing emporium. Its leather chairs, changing exhibitions of contemporary art, and immaculately dressed tables offer a soothing refuge for brunch, lunch, afternoon tea or whenever the Harvey Nichols bags are weighing heavy. The deceptively spare and simple lunchtime menu might consist of a warm goats' cheese tart with caramelised onions, duck breast with champ and pak choi followed by chocolate and almond cake served with rum and raisin ice cream. Elsewhere on the menu there could be grilled sea bass with crisp pancetta or vegetable chilli with pilau rice. Anthony Flinn's exacting standards obviously inform the cooking but it is less high church and less finessed than the original Anthony's on Boar Lane and correspondingly more formal than Anthony's Patisserie in the Vic Quarter across the road. Wines start at £3.99 a glass, and from a bottle of Georges Duboeuf a modest £11.95 can escalate sharply but intriguingly. An enterprising beer list, too. One duff note involves getting the drinks in: service can be painfully slow.
**Chef/s:** Christopher Kelly. **Open:** Tue to Sat 10 to 6, Sun 11 to 5. **Meals:** alc (main courses £6.50 to £10). Set L £12.95 (2 courses) to £15. **Service:** 10% (optional). **Details:** Cards accepted. 75 seats. Air-con. Wheelchair access. Music. Children's portions.

### Anthony's Restaurant

**Cutting-edge creations**
19 Boar Lane, Leeds, LS1 6EA
Tel no: (0113) 245 5922
www.anthonysrestaurant.co.uk
**Modern European | £55**
**Cooking score: 7**

🍾

Anthony Flinn bowled almost everybody over with his innovative, provocative cooking when he exploded on the scene in 2004. Since then he has opened Anthony's at Flannels (see entry), but his focus and creativity remain firmly rooted in the kitchen at Anthony's. From a menu that offers just four choices per course, a riot of ingredients and tastes burst out. Baby squid comes with mango sorbet, mozzarella rolled in coconut and pink candy floss. John Dory finds itself with pea and green olive sorbet and chicken popcorn. In less accomplished hands it might be a pretentious disaster, but Flinn invariably makes it work stunningly well. If there is a plot, it is that sweet sits with savoury, salt with sour, crunch with softness, hot with cold. Each item earns its place so that essential individual flavours and textures bounce off one another. For example, shredded crab on Jabugo ham with salted peanut foam and pickled cucumber culminated in a pure sea-fresh flavour that was a revelation. Pork cooked in a water bath 'sous-vide' was a wonderful deconstruction of roast pork and all the trimmings. The pork looked unsettlingly pink ('like tinned luncheon meat') but tasted as sweet, and tender as pork gets. Deep fried crisp chitterlings (pigs' intestines) and slivers of pigs' ears were the 'crackling', cubes of honey jelly were the glaze. Then there were tiny sweet sage macaroons and a foaming shot glass of elderflower. Fun, crazy even, but absolutely delicious. At dessert, more familiar dishes are rethought. A pear crumble lovingly paired two miniature baby pears, given a crunchy sugar coating, with a smoked brie ice cream. Flinn's take on chocolate mousse brings chocolate truffles and a peanut foam. Service is attentive and informed. The pre-starter – an eggy foam –

and a pre-dessert – chocolate sorbet with hazelnuts, the traditional white loaf with flyaway Parmesan butter – were all masterly. There are rewards and surprises at every turn, even before taking on the £60 tasting menu. Criticism comes in for Flinn's over-reliance on foams, the décor that is a pale companion to the exuberance of the food, and a wine list that is high-priced and provides only one red and one white by the glass. Try instead the more enlightened beer list.

**Chef/s:** Anthony James Flinn. **Open:** Tue to Sat 12 to 2, 7 to 9.30. **Meals:** alc (main courses £20 to £25). Set L £18.95 (2 courses) to £55, Set D £55. **Service:** not inc. **Details:** Cards accepted. 40 seats. Air-con. Wheelchair access. Music.

## Brasserie Forty Four
**A dependable city-centre favourite**
44 The Calls, Leeds, LS2 7EW
Tel no: (0113) 234 3232
www.brasserie44.com
**Modern European | £29**
**Cooking score: 3**

£5 OFF ☗ ⊟ Ⅴ £30

Though it owes much of its success to former head chef Jeff Baker, who used one kitchen to service this restaurant and, incredibly, its neighbouring sister, the late Pool Court, we're happy to report that the new kitchen team haven't let standards slip. Of course, the menu at the less formal Brasserie 44 was always rather less ambitious than Pool Court's, and while Baker's skeleton crew somehow wore both hats at once, this team have only the brasserie to worry them. But what they achieve is still very respectable. The menu comprises classic dishes served unashamedly simply with few 'witty' twists, so expect choices like carpaccio of beef, pepped up by a horseradish and celeriac rémoulade, or even a well-judged coq au vin. This mostly straightforward approach serves them well, creating something that is more safe than staid. A bottle of house wine, considering the size and range of the list, is a surprisingly decent £11.75, and the large choice of wines by the glass deserves a mention. Given their

reputation and enviable city-centre riverside location, it would be very easy for Brasserie 44 to get complacent. Thankfully things here are as solid as ever. NB Children must be over 2.
**Chef/s:** Antoine Quentin. **Open:** Mon to Fri L 12 to 2, Mon to Sat D 6 to 10 (10.30 Fri and Sat). **Closed:** bank hols. **Meals:** alc (main courses £9.50 to £19.50). Set L £13.50 (2 courses) to £17, Set D 6 to 7.15 £19.95 (inc wine). **Service:** 10% (optional). **Details:** Cards accepted. 130 seats. 24 seats outside. Air-con. Separate bar. Wheelchair access. Music. Children's portions.

## Fourth Floor Café and Bar
**Style and substance**
Harvey Nichols, 107-111 Briggate, Leeds, LS1 6AZ
Tel no: (0113) 204 8000
www.harveynichols.com
**Modern British | £30**
**Cooking score: 4**

☗ Ⅴ

You might think staff in a kitchen catering to fashionistas would spend most of their time waiting for someone to eat something. This is not the case at Harvey Nic's swanky upstairs space, where the clinking sound of cutlery being used is ever present. Does this mean the northern beau monde somehow defy the usual style set stereotypes? Hardly. It's more likely a reflection on the good work of Walton-Allen's team. A quick scan on your average day reveals that the claret-coloured banquettes and linen covered chrome tables are occupied by customers of all types, from the painfully trendy to simple folk who know a good thing when they eat it. This is mirrored in the menu, which is as sophisticated and luxurious as you would expect but makes good use of seasonal local produce, and is clearly aimed at people who want content as well as style. Hence a ribeye from award-winning Ilkley butcher Lishman's with sweet potato wedges and wild garlic butter appears alongside seared scallops with coconut dhal, and a sweet pork wonton. From a starting point of £13.50 for a house-label bottle, the wine list stretches far and

wide, and the potential of buying bottles from their adjacent food-market to take home is an added bonus.
**Chef/s:** Richard Walton-Allen. **Open:** all week L 12 to 3 (4 Sat and Sun), Thur to Sat D 5.30 (7 Sat) to 10. **Closed:** 25 and 26 Dec, Easter Sun. **Meals:** alc (main courses £10 to £17). Set L and D £15 (2 courses) to £18. Bar menu available Mon to Sat. **Service:** 10% (optional). **Details:** Cards accepted. 80 seats. 14 seats outside. Air-con. Separate bar. Wheelchair access. Music. Children's portions.

★NEW ENTRY★
## Mill Race
**Organic pioneers**
2/4 Commercial Road, Kirkstall, Leeds, LS5 3AQ
Tel no: (0113) 275 7555
www.themillrace-organic.com
**Modern British | £27**
**Cooking score: 3**
£5 OFF ♦ V £30

It's easy to forget that the organic movement has only recently entered the mainstream. Then there's the current popularity of using 'local produce'. But if it now seems a bit of a bandwagon, we shouldn't let that steal the glory of trailblazers like The Millrace. They have been promoting the benefits of locally sourced organic food and drink since well before it became trendy and they're still leading the way now: not only is the menu organic, but their wine list is, too. As if that doesn't confirm their green credentials, note the fact that most of the fixtures and fitting are made from recycled or reclaimed materials. Thankfully, eating here does not mean 'favouring your conscience over your tastebuds'. The local produce is extremely well chosen, following the seasons to give dishes such as chargrilled venison steak from Barnsley (served with chilli and ginger roasted squash), or a rack of lamb from Bolton Abbey, while a summer broth of artichokes with asparagus and pistou sauce typifies their bold attitude to the often under-exploited potential of the humble vegetable. House wines start at £12.95.

**Chef/s:** Rob Black. **Open:** Tue to Sun, L 12 to 3, D 5.30 to 12. **Closed:** Christmas and New Year. **Meals:** alc (main courses £8.75 to £17.50). **Service:** 10%. **Details:** Cards accepted. 60 seats. 20 seats outside. Separate bar. Music. Children's portions.

## No. 3 York Place
**Good-value high-end French cuisine**
3 York Place, Leeds, LS1 2DR
Tel no: (0113) 245 9922
www.no3yorkplace.co.uk
**Modern European | £29**
**Cooking score: 5**
£30

News that this Leeds institution was making an array of cost-cutting changes caused great concern amongst its devotees, but they needn't have worried. The loss of the pre-starters, amuse-bouches, hand-made chocolates and the heavy white linen certainly strips the experience of a great deal of its luxury, but food and service are as good as ever. Perhaps more remarkable is that the savings generated by this overhead reduction exercise have been fully passed on to the customer, meaning that dining here need no longer be reserved for very special occasions only. Courses are still immaculately presented, and range from perfectly turned out classics such as confit duck leg with buttered Savoy cabbage and pomme purée with a red wine sauce, to more unexpected combos like roast monkfish paired with curried mussels. Desserts are a strong point, particularly when it comes to soufflés. That this quality is now available at far lower prices is miraculous. The wine list has taken a big hit with far fewer options than before, but what remains is still well chosen and far from dull, with prices starting at £14 per bottle. Add to this the service, which is no less friendly, intuitively discreet and competent than before, and you're unlikely to find many who mourn the loss of No 3's more indulgent days.
**Chef/s:** Martel Smith. **Open:** Mon to Fri L 12 to 2, Mon to Sat D 6.30 to 10. **Closed:** 25 Dec to 4 Jan. **Meals:** alc (main courses £11 to £18). Set L and D

6.30 to 7.30 Mon to Fri £14.50 (2 courses) to £18.50 (3 courses). **Service:** 10% (optional). **Details:** Cards accepted. 46 seats. Air-con. Wheelchair access. Music. Children's portions.

★NEW ENTRY★

## Plush

**Sophisticated basement restaurant**
10 York Place, Leeds, LS1 2DS
Tel no: (0113) 234 3344
www.plush-bar-restaurant.com
**Modern British | £23**
**Cooking score: 3**
£5 OFF  V  £30

Martin Spalding was in the vanguard of the Leeds restaurant renaissance with seminal ventures like the original much-loved Paris in Horsforth and the recently closed Leodis, an early excursion into canal-side conversions before they were commonplace. That was 14 years ago, however, and his latest preoccupation is in the commercial quarter in this expensively fitted out bar/basement restaurant at the outer end of York Street – a street that has been heavily boarded up, but is clearly ripe for rich future pickings. Starters range through crayfish salad, stuffed Portabella mushrooms, and smoked Wensleydale and cauliflower tart. Follow up with reliable steaks and lamb chops, grilled sea bass and market fish, or vegetable filo parcel. Desserts feature strawberry cheesecake, raspberry brûlée and French apple tart. There is a pleasing set menu at £15.95 and a bar menu of plates to share and snack. House wines start with Chilean Sauvignon Blanc at £13.95 and plenty of named wines by the glass at £3.50.
**Chef/s:** Ruth Adamcheck. **Open:** Mon to Fri 12 to 2, Mon to Thu 6 to 10, Fri to Sat 6 to 10.30. **Closed:** Christmas and New Year. **Meals:** alc (main courses £10.50 to £18.90) Set L £12.95 (2 courses) Set D £15.95 (3 courses). **Service:** 10% (optional). **Details:** Cards accepted. 70 seats. Air-con. Wheelchair access. Music. Children's portions.

## Simply Heathcotes

**Modish mill conversion**
Canal Wharf, Water Lane, Leeds, LS11 5PS
Tel no: (0113) 244 6611
www.heathcotes.co.uk
**Modern European | £42**
**Cooking score: 3**
V

This spacious, contemporary grain mill conversion with views out to the canal basin and the city centre's ever-rising skyline, is part of Paul Heathcote's northern empire to go with his 'Simply' branches in Liverpool, Manchester and Wrightington (see entries). The interior is modish and spare with an impressive curving staircase to the upstairs cocktail bar. It all suggests upmarket fineries from the kitchen but the menu is rooted reliably in seasonal, British bistro dishes. Black pudding and ham hock salad or English cured meats with piccalilli jump out from the starters. Typical main courses are grilled sea bass with braised fennel and garlic butter or calf's liver and bacon with mashed potatoes and onion gravy. Desserts, too, are given an original spin: try goats' milk pannacotta and berries with basil sugar or vanilla ice cream with aged caramelised sherry. The wine list is predominantly Italian and New World starting at £14.95 with plenty by the glass (£3.85). Sunday lunch is a good family day with a sensible and proper childrens' menu. Good value lunch and early evening deals include a cracking cod and chips with mushy peas.
**Chef/s:** Luke Culkin. **Open:** all week 12 to 2.30, 6 to 10 (11 Sat, 9 Sun). **Closed:** Bank hols. **Meals:** alc (main courses £9.50 to £22). Set L £15 (2 courses), Set D pre-7 Mon to Sat £15 (2 courses). **Service:** not inc. **Details:** Cards accepted. 120 seats. Air-con. Wheelchair access. Music. Children's portions. Car parking.

## Sous le Nez en Ville

**French style meets Yorkshire portions**
The Basement, Quebec House, Quebec Street,
Leeds, LS1 2HA
Tel no: (0113) 244 0108
www.souslenez.com
**Modern European | £27**
**Cooking score: 4**
£5 OFF ♦ ￥ £30

Thanks to its basement location and windows
that peek up on to a busy city centre street, this
place is quite literally 'under the nose'. Perhaps
more resonant is the idea that despite this
prominence, and its reputation, Sous Le Nez is
overlooked in a second way – as Leeds has
boomed many other restaurants have stolen
the limelight. Not that business is quiet, but
rather that with an overall experience this
good, getting a table ought to be much harder.
Directors Robert Chamberlain and Andrew
Carter have changed little over the years, and
for this they deserve much credit. The dark
wood and cream walls are as good a fit today as
they were fifteen years ago. Service is still
swift and efficient, if not over-friendly. Old
faves like the deep-fried brie with red pepper
and mango chutney, the roast black pudding,
or the fillet-steak gâteau continue to please.
The reputation for excellent fish dishes is still
very much deserved, one reporter
commending some perfectly roasted cod, and
a generous monkfish tail on a creamy smoked
haddock risotto supports this. Despite the
French bias, portions are more traditional
Yorkshire than nouvelle cuisine, something
they are rightly proud of. Starting at £11.95,
the wine list has continued to grow, making it
one of the very best in the region.
**Chef/s:** Andrew Carter, Andrew Lavender. **Open:**
Mon to Sat 12 to 2.30, 6 to 10 (11 Sat). **Closed:** 24
Dec to 3 Jan, bank hols. **Meals:** alc (main courses
£10.50 to £19.50). Set L Sat £21.95, Set D 6 to 7.30
(7 Sat) £21.95 (inc wine). Bar menu available.
**Service:** not inc. **Details:** Cards accepted. 85 seats.
Air-con. Music.

## ALSO RECOMMENDED

### ▲ Hansa's

72-74 North Street, Leeds, LS2 7PN
Tel no: (0113) 244 4408

This vegetarian Gujurati restaurant, just off
the main city centre thoroughfares, has earned
its place as a modest Leeds institution, having
operated here for twenty years. Standard
Indian curry fans may need some guidance
through an unfamiliar menu but for
vegetarians and especially vegans Hansa's is a
blessing. From starters of stuffed and stir fried
colocasia leaves or pastry stuffed with dhal, to
every sort of vegetable curry: bottle gourd and
chickpea, black-eye beans and chickpea kofta,
and stuffed aubergines. For pudding try hot
sweet vermicelli with almond, sultanas and
cardamon.

### ▲ Little Tokyo

24 Central Road, Leeds, LS1 6DE
Tel no: (0113) 243 9090
www.littletokyo.co.uk

Enterprising little Japanese café complete with
hand-made wooden tables and a coal-fired
Yakatori grill. Good-value bento boxes are at
the heart of the extensive menu, each
containing a complete meal based around a
main course such as spicy mackerel teriyaki
(£11.25), chicken ginseng (£12.35) or duck
with mango (£15.35). Other options include
sushi and sashimi platters (£10.55 for 12 pieces
of nigiri) and soup noodles (chicken ramen
£6.25). House wines at £12.

### ▲ Salvo's

115 Otley Road, Headingley, Leeds, LS6 3PX
Tel no: (0113) 2755017
www.salvos.co.uk

This neighbourhood restaurant opened back
in August 1976 and is now a Leeds institution,
with a strong crowd of regulars. So what keeps
them coming back? A devotion to
authenticity and a continuing passion for what
they're doing certainly helps. But it's the food
that seals the deal: both traditional and
contemporary Italy are well represented with

excellent pizzas and pastas (starting at £7.50 and £9 respectively), imaginative antipasti, like grilled black tiger prawns with rose harissa and lime (£7.50), and hearty large plates like the chicken dia vola (£13.95), half a free range bird marinated in herbs, chillies and garlic.

## ▲ Sukhothai

8 Regent Street, Chapel Allerton, Leeds, LS7 4PE
Tel no: (0113) 237 0141
www.thaifood4u.co.uk

When it opened in 2002, Sukhothai was no bigger than your average greasy spoon. Much like the rather cosmopolitan urban village it's situated in, Sukhothai has expanded rapidly since then, having taken over some of the neighbouring business premises. The usual suspects are all present – tentative types would do well with any of the delicious pad thai noodle dishes (from £6.95) – but there are tons of more unusual options for the connoisseur, like tab gata lon (£8.50), sizzling chicken and duck livers fried in lime leaves, chilli and lemongrass. Everything, across the board, is top-notch.

## READERS RECOMMEND

### Oliver's Paris
Modern British
Calverley Bridge, Leeds, LS13 1NP
Tel no: (0113) 258 1885
www.oliversparis.com
'Suburban fine dining'

### Room
Modern British
Boar Lane, Leeds, LS1 5DE
Tel no: (0113) 242 6161
www.roomrestaurants.com
'Kitsch food reborn with a witty twist'

## ▌ Leyburn

## Sandpiper Inn
Laid-back family feel
Market Place, Leyburn, DL8 5AT
Tel no: (01969) 622206
Gastropub | £24
Cooking score: 3

Harrison's substantial stone-built building is reputedly Leyburn's oldest pub, standing in the town's market square. Meals can be eaten in the rustic bar or amid the attractive olive-green walls, oak floorboards and bare tables in the adjacent restaurant. Food is taken seriously and Jonathan Harrison works to a menu of enticing modern dishes that uses top-notch local ingredients and takes in all corners of Europe. In the evening start with crab and salmon cake with dill and chive mayonnaise, before continuing with pressed shoulder of Dales lamb with summer vegetables and redcurrant and mint sauce, roast cod with lemon balm and crayfish risotto, or Moroccan-spiced chicken with couscous. Desserts range from sticky toffee pudding with butterscotch sauce to terrine of three chocolates with pistachio sauce. Jo Harrison leads the attentive and cheerful service. The well considered wine list is good value, with house selections at £13.50.
Chef/s: Jonathan Harrison. Open: Tue to Sun 12 to 2.30 (2 Sun), 6.30 (7 Sun) to 9 (9.30 Fri and Sat). Closed: 25 Dec, 1 Jan. Meals: alc (main courses £10 to £17). Light L menu available. Service: not inc. Details: Cards accepted. 40 seats. 20 seats outside. No mobile phones. Music. Children's portions.

## Lund

### Wellington Inn
Smart, upmarket gastropub
19 The Green, Lund, YO25 9TE
Tel no: (01377) 217294
Gastropub | £25
Cooking score: 3

Russell and Sarah Jeffrey have created a pub
that successfully combines the roles of village
inn and restaurant. Traditional features
abound, but for all its flagstones and beams
there is nothing cobwebby about this
operation. Polished tables, candlelight and
white walls provide a peaceful backdrop for
the evenings-only menu, cooked up by Sarah
while Russell handles front-of-house. Expect
a sophisticated take on hearty, traditional
dishes – devilled lambs' kidney and
mushroom hotpot or Lancashire black
pudding with foie gras, Muscat and mixed
peppercorn reduction among the starters; and
then perhaps traditional suet pudding filled
with beef, red onions and mushrooms or
roasted chicken breast with roasted winter
vegetables and tarragon jus. Finish with
British cheeses; a chocolate brownie with
vanilla ice bream; or a warm pecan and
almond tart with maple cream. An interesting,
personally compiled wine list opens at £11.95.
**Chef/s:** Sarah Jeffery. **Open:** Tue to Sat D only 7 to
9.30. **Meals:** alc (main courses £14 to £19). Bar
menu available. **Service:** not inc. **Details:** Cards
accepted. 42 seats. No mobile phones. Music.
Children allowed. Car parking.

## Marsden

### Olive Branch
Informal dining
Manchester Road, Marsden, HD7 6LU
Tel no: (01484) 844487
www.olivebranch.uk.com
British | £28
Cooking score: 4

There's a certain pub atmosphere to this
friendly place on the edge of Marsden Moor
Estate. Menus live up to the setting, showing
touches of class within an imaginative range
that mixes English modes with hints of
warmer climes. The raw materials are good
and timings are accurate for vegetables as they
are for fish and meat. Ideas, too, are generally
well conceived. Starters might include a wild
forest mushroom risotto, or smoked haddock
fish cakes with creamy tarragon sauce. Main
courses have some equally robust dishes, such
as beef bourguignonne with braised ox cheek,
or crispy belly pork with spicy oriental sauce,
sultanas, chilli and white cabbage. The quality
of meat in an aged local beef fillet served with
four peppercorn and brandy sauce has
impressed, and fish dishes could include wild
sea bass fillet served with an olive crust,
creamy mash, fennel and white wine cream, or
whole lemon sole simply served with a herb
and lemon butter. House wine is £13.95.
**Chef/s:** Paul Kewley. **Open:** Wed to Fri L 12 to 2,
Mon to Sat D 6.30 to 9.30, Sun all day 12.30 to 8.30.
**Closed:** first 2 weeks Jan. **Meals:** alc (main courses
£11.50 to £19.50). Light L menu available.
**Service:** not inc. **Details:** Cards accepted. 68 seats.
Music. Car parking.

## Marton

### Appletree

**A warm, welcoming pub**
Marton, YO62 6RD
Tel no: (01751) 431457
www.appletreeinn.co.uk
**Modern British | £35**
**Cooking score: 3**

Tucked away in a peaceful little village, this solid stone inn has warmth and charm to spare. From the welcoming friendliness of Melanie front-of-house to the multiple freebie courses added to your meal by chef TJ, a feeling of real hospitality pervades. A forest of glowing candles and deep squishy sofas add to the relaxing atmosphere. The menu makes the most of local produce, giving it a modern twist. Whitby crab fishcakes come with sweet chilli sauce and crème fraîche, while roast rump of Ryedale lamb is served pink with black olive soft polenta, rosemary and lamb jus. At inspection, confit belly of pork with mustard mash and apple sauce came in for special praise, as did goose fat Marton crispies (very moreish roast potatoes). Desserts include mini versions at £3 each. Real ales, a well-chosen wine list and complementary mineral water ensure the drinks side is equally well catered for. NB No children under 8 after 9pm.
**Chef/s:** T.J. Drew. **Open:** Wed to Sun 12 to 2, 6 (6.30 Sun) to 9.30 (9 Sun). **Closed:** 25 Dec, 2 weeks Jan. **Meals:** alc (main courses £10 to £16). **Service:** not inc. **Details:** Cards accepted. 26 seats. 8 seats outside. Wheelchair access. Music. Children's portions. Car parking.

## Masham

### Swinton Park, Samuel's

**Majestic pile with an unstuffy approach**
Masham, HG4 4JH
Tel no: (01765) 680900
www.swintonpark.com
**Modern British | £40**
**Cooking score: 4**

£5 OFF 💺 ❤

The 200-acre grounds of this towered and turreted pile bought by Samuel Cunliffe-Lister in the 1880s include a four-acre walled garden growing a wealth of fresh produce, and the surrounding estate plays its part in supplying the kitchen with game and lamb. Andy Burton's modern British cooking uses pinpoint accuracy of timing, careful balance and pretty much faultless composition to make an impact. He rings interesting changes on the set lunch and dinner menus, opening perhaps at dinner with breast of quail with a hazelnut crust, creamed artichokes and a spring cassoulet, followed by a trio of lamb (cannon, slow-braised neck, rillettes of shoulder) with rosemary jus, or an interesting combination of breast of Goosnargh duck, confit of pork belly, mini toffee apple and sage and onion jus. Desserts seem to be a particular strength: witness spiced orange and olive oil cake with a blood orange shot and gingerbread ice cream. While Swinton Park puts some emphasis on corporate entertaining, reporters feel that the place has always had an unstuffy approach. House wine is £17.95.
**Chef/s:** Andy Burton. **Open:** all week 12.30 to 2, 7 to 9.30 (10 Fri and Sat). **Meals:** Set L Mon to Sat £17 (2 courses) to £21.50, Set L Sun £24, Set D £43 to £50. Bar menu available. **Service:** not inc. **Details:** Cards accepted. 60 seats. 20 seats outside. Wheelchair access. Music. Children's portions. Car parking.

## Vennell's Restaurant

**Informal dining with ship-shape service**

7 Silver Street, Masham, HG4 4DX
Tel no: (01765) 689000
www.vennellsrestaurant.co.uk
**Modern British | £24**
**Cooking score: 5**

The aubergine-coloured frontage announces the continuing presence of a serious restaurant on this site. The Vennells hit the ground running when they bought the place in 2005.ṗ Themed evenings of food and wine pairing, or showcases for local artists in paint and pottery, help to bring in custom, but the truth is that Jon Vennell's cooking could do that all on its own. Deftly presented and carefully conceived, these are dishes that raise the culinary bar. Home-smoked sea trout benefits from an apposite accompaniment of raisin and caper compote, while roast quail sits alongside artichoke hearts and beetroot in a daring passion-fruit dressing. Main courses typically offer one fish – perhaps sea bass with spinach, roasted chickpeas and a red pepper sauce – and three meats. These might encompass rabbit done three ways (as cassoulet, in a sausage, and the saddle), or roast Gressingham duck breast, with the leg meat fashioned into a cake with potato, all richly sauced with port. Yorkshire cheeses are a roll-call of the great and the really great, and offer savoury relief to those not in the market for rhubarb trifle containing Armagnac-soaked sponge and passion-fruit custard. Wine prices start at £13.95, or £3.30 a glass.

**Chef/s:** Jon Vennell. **Open:** Fri to Sun L 12 to 2, Tue to Sat D 7.15 to 9.15. **Closed:** first 2 weeks Jan, bank hols, 26 to 30 Dec. **Meals:** Set L £16.95 (2 courses) to £21.95, Set D £21 (2 courses) to £26.50. **Service:** not inc. **Details:** Cards accepted. 30 seats. No mobile phones. Music. Children's portions.

## ■ Osmotherley

★NEW ENTRY★
## Golden Lion

**Simple, well-cooked homely dishes**

6 West End, Osmotherley, DL6 3AA
Tel no: (01609) 883526
www.goldenlionosmotherley
**British | £25**
**Cooking score: 3**

This gently upgraded pub-with-rooms has few pretensions beyond providing substantial, homely, well-cooked dishes and it consistently delivers on all points. A comprehensive menu reads with deceptive simplicity: starters include tomato and basil soup, mussels in wine and cream or deep fried squid; for mains choose from the likes of fish cakes and sorrel sauce, a suet crusted steak and kidney pudding or non-meat spicy lentil enchiladas. But this is not mere nursery food but a menu that celebrates trusty sourcing, relishable cooking and gutsy flavours. A recent innovation is a blackboard menu extending the choice still further. Recent chalk-ups have introduced game terrine with onion and apricot relish; and a cream and brandy laden pork strogonoff. Desserts stay dependably in the comfort zone of sticky toffee pudding, crème brûlée and real ice cream. The art of doing simple things well extends to the décor of whitewashed walls, dark wood furniture, lots of candlelight, a glowing peat fire and a generous show of fresh flowers.

**Chef/s:** Chris Wright, Judith Wright, Sam Hind, Lucy Corner. **Open:** all week 12 to 3, 6 to 9. **Closed:** 25 Dec. **Meals:** alc (main courses £10.95 to £16.50). **Service:** not inc.. **Details:** Cards accepted. 130 seats. 20 seats outside. Music. Children's portions.

## Ramsgill

**★ READERS' RESTAURANT OF THE YEAR ★
NATIONAL WINNER**

### Yorke Arms

**Proud demonstration of Yorkshire roots**
Ramsgill, HG3 5RL
Tel no: (01423) 755243
www.yorke-arms.co.uk
Modern European | £41
Cooking score: 6

£5 OFF 🍷 🍴 ✔

It's hard to miss the Yorke Arms as you pass through this tiny Yorkshire village. The creeper-covered eighteenth-century former shooting lodge overlooks a tiny village green, and the atmospheric interior combines the best of both worlds. The small bar is ideal for those just wanting a drink, plus excellent bar food, ranging from black pudding cooked in brioche with a poached egg, bacon and rocket to Nidderdale mutton pie with chive mash, while the elegant dining room has its own more ambitious menu. Frances Atkins' cooking, although based on simple ideas and well-tried combinations, contrives to introduce new twists and original touches. Raw materials are typically first class, portrayed by roast fillet of Yorkshire beef with wild mushrooms, foie gras and truffle jus, while presentation shows imagination and finesse throughout. Dishes aim to entice rather than baffle, with fine renditions of cheese soufflé (made with Wensleydale) served with scallops, vanilla and tomato, or wild trout and Whitby crab with a tartare of avocado. A spring main course that combined loin and shoulder of Nidderdale lamb with lovage impressed for its technical polish; its counterpart, a sparkling fresh piece of roast turbot, was served with a truffled leek cannelloni and asparagus. Desserts, too, garner high praise: rhubarb and ginger crumble brûlée and chocolate delice say, or basil pannacotta with curd tart and marinated raisins. Service is 'friendly and attentive', and breakfast is soundly endorsed if you're staying the night. A well-rounded global collection of wines is strongest in France but includes interesting New World bottles too; there's a strong South African and Australian range and some 14 wines come by the glass from £3.75. House wines are priced from £16. As we went to press, the Yorke Arms was hit by the floods in the north of England. We hope to see a triumphant return to form in the near future.

**Chef/s:** Frances Atkins. **Open:** all week L 12 to 2, D 7 to 9. **Meals:** alc (main courses £17.50 to £26). Set L Mon to Sat £21 (3 courses), Set L Sun £29 (3 courses), Set D £60 (6 courses). Bar menu available Mon to Sat L, Mon to Fri D. **Service:** not inc. **Details:** Cards accepted. 50 seats. 20 seats outside. No mobile phones. Wheelchair access. Music. Car parking.

## ALSO RECOMMENDED

### ▲ Charles Bathurst Inn

Arkengarthdale, Richmond, DL11 6EN
Tel no: (01748) 884567
www.cbinn.co.uk

An eighteenth-century inn that offers accommodation, fine ales and good food. While the menu puts emphasis on local and seasonal produce, the kitchen spans the globe for inspiration: breast of duck with stir-fry vegetables, noodles, confit duck leg spring roll (£12.85), and fillet of beef on oxtail terrine with green peppercorn sauce and foie gras (£16.50). Desserts are aimed squarely at reviving fatigued moor walkers with sticky toffee pudding, caramel sauce and ice cream (£3.95) being the most likely to suceed. House wine is £9.95 Open all week.

## ▌Ripley
### The Boar's Head Hotel
Consistent former coaching inn
Ripley, HG3 3AY
Tel no: (01423) 771888
www.boarsheadripley.co.uk
British | £37
Cooking score: 3

🍷 ⌐ ⋎

The picturesque village of Ripley is such a perfect little piece of Olde England that you almost feel if you shook it, you could make it snow. Clearly, Sir Thomas and Lady Ingilby are attuned to this, as the only way the Boar's Head could be any more traditional would be if they handed out ruffs to all who entered. Not that this is a bad thing. The whole of this sixteenth-century coaching inn (and that means bar, bistro, restaurant and hotel) offers the perfect escape from the modern world and nowhere more so than in the restaurant. Deep-red walls and centuries-old art marry with a menu that proudly takes you back in time, to dishes such as Yorkshire beef fillet with pommes Anna and braised shallots, plus an array of decadent desserts, among which a chocolate and bread fondant stands tall. Some dishes subtly employ modern tricks to give these grand old plates an edge: the chicken liver tempura that surrounds the sautéed wood pigeon with glazed beetroot and fig purée being a very tasty case in point. The wine list (which starts at £11.95 for a bottle) is a big one, as you might by now expect, giving them room enough to offer plenty of New World alongside the 'Olde'.
**Chef/s:** Andy Flockhart. **Open:** all week 12 to 2, 7 to 9 (9.30 Fri and Sat). **Meals:** Bistro: alc (main courses £10 to £16). Restaurant: Set L £16.95 (2 courses) to £19.95, Set D £34 to £40. **Service:** not inc. **Details:** Cards accepted. 60 seats. Separate bar. No mobile phones. Wheelchair access. Music. Children's portions. Car parking.

## ▌Ripon
### Old Deanery
Stylish renovations in a Georgian setting
Minster Road, Ripon, HG4 1QS
Tel no: (01765) 600003
www.theolddeanery.co.uk
Modern British | £34
Cooking score: 2

⌐ ⋎

Although the owners have sympathetically restored many of the Georgian features, including window shutters and beautiful panelled walls, this striking stone building by Ripon Cathedral has a contemporary interior; in the dining room bare dark floorboards, leather chairs and stylish chandeliers reflect the thoroughly modern cooking. There's much thought and inventiveness in the kitchen with crab cake, baby spinach and tarragon vichyssoise jostling for position mong starters with roast pigs' cheeks with blood orange and beetroot tart. Mains are similarly innovative, and might include fillet of pollock, tomato fondue, smoked paprika and tempura squid, and braised ox tongue and black pudding with Dijon mustard. It's worth leaving some room for dessert, when milk chocolate truffle, Horlicks foam and tiramisu sorbet is on offer. House wine starts at £13.95, and 10 come by the glass from £3.25. There's a stunning garden at the back where aperitifs can be taken on a warm day.
**Chef/s:** Barrie Higginbotham. **Open:** all week L 12 to 2, Mon to Sat D 7 to 9.30. **Meals:** alc (main courses L £7 to £10, D £16 to £19.50). Set L £9.50 (2 courses) to £11.75. **Service:** not inc. **Details:** Cards accepted. 50 seats. 28 seats outside. Wheelchair access. Music. Car parking.

## ∎ Scarborough

### Lanterna

**A must for truffle devotees**
33 Queen Street, Scarborough, YO11 1HQ
Tel no: (01723) 363616
www.lanterna-ristorante.co.uk
**Italian | £30**
**Cooking score: 3**

A fixture of Scarborough's restaurant scene since the mid-1990s, Giorgio and Rachel Alessio's cosy venue proudly pats itself on the back, with press cuttings and glitzy signed photographs lining the walls of the cheery dining room. The owners hail from Piedmont and native traditions prevail on the menu. Ingredients are also robustly authentic, witness a dish of steamed Monferrato salami with a fondue of Val d'Aosta cheese and black truffles. Seafood is procured from early-morning trips to Scarborough market, and the kitchen puts it to good use for dishes like fillet of ling in Piedmontese batter with tomato vinegar or red mullet stew. White truffles from Moncalvo make a treasured seasonal appearance and are methodically shaved over everything from beef carpaccio to risotto with Fontina cheese. To conclude, try Giorgio's legendary nettle cream dessert or York Minster Pale Ale ice cream; otherwise watch the man himself producing zabaglione 'a la lampada'. The wine list is an Italian heavyweight with many bottles imported direct from Piedmont (including Barolo dating back to 1990). House selections are £12.50.
**Chef/s:** Giorgio Alessio. **Open:** Mon to Sat D only 7 to 9.30. **Closed:** 2 weeks end of Oct. **Meals:** alc (main courses £16 to £45). **Service:** not inc. **Details:** Cards accepted. 35 seats. Air-con. Wheelchair access. Music. Children allowed.

## ∎ Sheffield

### Artisan and Catch

**Two operations lowbrow and highbrow**
32-34 Sandygate Road, Crosspool, Sheffield, S10 5RY
Tel no: (01142) 666096
www.artisancatch.com
**Modern European | £29**
**Cooking score: 5**
£5 OFF  £30

The two-part name denotes the fact that there are two distinct operations here. Catch is an informal fish and seafood set-up, with a blackboard menu, majoring in the likes of crab risotto with red pepper compote and Moroccan seafood stew with couscous and yoghurt, while Artisan is a more obviously high-toned 'bistrot de luxe'. Executive chef Simon Wild cooks in the kind of idiom familiar to anyone schooled in the ways of metropolitan food fashion. A truffled chicken boudin is dressed with braised lentils and pancetta, and sauced with an almond and redcurrant jus, to make an inventive starter dish, but then you might equally well go on to fish and chips, or Lancashire hotpot with pickled red cabbage. Mini crab cakes are the unusual garnish for a bowl of minted pea soup, while sea bass might be given an off-the-wall Spanish treatment, with a ragoût of chickpeas, clams and chorizo, salt-and-pepper squid and smoked paprika. Straightforward puds have included pot au chocolat and crème brûlée. A concise modern wine slate opens with French vins de pays at £13. Glass prices go from £3.75.
**Chef/s:** Simon Wild and Daniel Smith. **Open:** all week L 12 to 2.30, D 6 to 10. **Closed:** Christmas. **Meals:** alc (main courses £12 to £40). Set L £16 (3 courses) and set D £24 (3 courses). **Service:** not inc. **Details:** Cards accepted. 90 seats. 8 seats outside. Air-con. No mobile phones. Wheelchair access. Music. Children's portions.

## Greenhead House

Sixteenth-century setting
84 Burncross Road, Chapeltown, Sheffield,
S35 1SF
Tel no: (0114) 2469004
Modern European | £37
Cooking score: 2

Away from the city centre, this restaurant offers a touch of country house style, and has been run personally by husband-and-wife owners Neil and Anne Allen for over 20 years. Anne plays the charming hostess, while Neil works the stoves, his cooking style grounded in traditional techniques but informed by contemporary ideas. Trout fillet is served as a starter with courgette tagliatelle, while seared sesame-coated pork fillet is partnered with a borlotti bean and rosemary cake. Up next in the four-course dinner might be white onion soup, before a main course of perhaps poached plaice paupiettes on a clam and champagne risotto, or osso buco with cognac, sultanas, pine nuts and myrtle. Inventive desserts might feature blood orange and blueberry salad with violet jelly and yoghurt foam, and prices on the international wine list start at £16.50.
Chef/s: Neil Allen. Open: Fri L 12 to 1, Wed to Sat D 7 to 9. Closed: 1 week Christmas to New Year, 2 weeks Easter, 2 weeks Aug. Meals: Set L £24, Set D £43. Light L menu available. Service: not inc. Details: Cards accepted. 34 seats. 10 seats outside. No music. No mobile phones. Wheelchair access. Car parking.

## Shibden, Halifax

### Shibden Mill Inn

Seventeenth-century setting
Shibden Mill Fold, Shibden, Halifax, HX3 7UL
Tel no: (01422) 365840
www.shibdenmillinn.com
Modern British | £20
Cooking score: 3

On the outskirts of Halifax, close to Shibden Hall, this inn is a rabbit warren of cosy rooms inside, with a lively, informal atmosphere throughout. The bar menu offers pub grub with a difference, including king prawn and crab fishcakes, or venison burger, as well as more traditional fare such as meat and potato pie or battered haddock and chips. The first-floor dining room takes a more ambitious tack, kicking off with starters of seared king scallops on butternut squash cannelloni with lime hollandaise, or broad beans and spaghetti of vegetables with tomato sorbet and basil foam. Main courses continue in similar vein with salmon on Thai-spiced lentils and crispy pancetta; guinea fowl breast marinated in lime and coriander and served on sweetcorn pancake with a rhubarb reduction; or pan-fried plaice and John Dory with horseradish rémoulade and beetroot dressing. Apple and fruit jelly with toffee ice cream or rhubarb cheesecake with pink ginger might end the meal. The roving wine list opens with a dozen house selections from £11.95, all available by the small, medium or large glass.
Chef/s: Steve Evans. Open: Mon to Fri L 12 to 2, D 6 to 9.30, Sat D 6 to 9.30, Sun 12 to 7.30. Closed: 25 and 26 Dec. Meals: alc (main courses £10 to £17). Mon to Fri Set L and D 6 to 7 £9.95 (2 courses). Bar menu available. Service: not inc. Details: Cards accepted. 100 seats. 50 seats outside. Music. Children's portions. Car parking.

## ALSO RECOMMENDED
### ▲ Fox and Hounds

Main Street, Sinnington, YO62 6SQ
Tel no: (01751) 431577
www.thefoxandhoundsinn.co.uk

The setting – on the fringes of the North Yorks Moors – may be agreeably off the beaten track, but the cooking at this genteel eighteenth-century country pub/restaurant aims high. The kitchen mixes modern ideas with tradition, putting crab cakes with red pepper pesto (£5.95), smoked salmon blinis with horseradish and shallot cream (£5.95) and slow-cooked shoulder of lamb with roast root vegetables and rosemary and garlic mash (£13.25). Desserts are typically traditional with treacle and butterscotch tart (£4.65) a perennial favourite. House wine is £11.75. Open all week.

## ▋Skipton

### Le Caveau

Intriguing basement dining
86 High Street, Skipton, BD23 1JJ
Tel no: (01756) 794274
www.lecaveau.co.uk
**Anglo-French | £24**
**Cooking score: 2**
£30

Descend steep stairs from the street beneath a shop in the town centre to find this small cellar restaurant, with stone walls and a barrel-vaulted ceiling, which once served as a prison. Richard Baker cooks a simple, fairly priced menu supplemented by blackboard specials, and makes good use of locally sourced ingredients: 21-day aged beef (sirloin steak with horseradish mash and red wine jus) from the Yorkshire Dales and fresh fish, perhaps halibut with lemon butter sauce, landed at Fleetwood. His repertoire may also take in duck confit salad, rack of lamb with fresh mint jus, and dark chocolate truffle cake with pineapple sauce. The wine list is strong in the southern hemisphere, although it starts in France with George Duboeuf at £11.95.
**Chef/s:** Richard Barker. **Open:** Tue to Fri L 12 to 2, Tue to Sat D 7 (5.30 Sat) to 9.30. **Meals:** alc (main courses L £8 to £11, D £10 to £20). Set D Tue to Thur £18.95. **Service:** not inc. **Details:** Cards accepted. 28 seats. Music. Children's portions.

## READERS RECOMMEND

### The Red Lion

British
By the bridge at Burnsall, Skipton, BD23 6BU
Tel no: (01756) 720204
www.redlion.co.uk
'Top-notch food in a gorgeous riverside pub'

## ▋South Dalton

### Pipe and Glass Inn

Rural pub given a culinary facelift
West End, South Dalton, HU17 7PN
Tel no: (01430) 810246
www.pipeandglass.co.uk
**Modern British | £23**
**Cooking score: 4**
£30

This modest centuries-old pub-turned-restaurant makes an informal yet upmarket stage for chef-patron James Mackenzie's impressive cooking. Refurbished interiors are light and modern; cream walls, leather chesterfields, bare floorboards, well-spaced wood tables, as well as the odd dark beam and an inglenook, create a relaxed, unpretentious atmosphere. The menu, too, is appealing and modern, flavours are clear and well defined, and portioning and presentation are spot-on. Raw ingredients are decidedly local: sea trout from Mapplethorpe, for instance, which may appear in fishcakes with Cullen skink stew, or Harome duck breast (with Scrumpy braised potato, crispy black pudding and apple sauce). Cold pressed terrine of locally shot hare and foie gras with pease pudding might head the starters, alongside salt beef hash with fried egg, devilled sauce, ox tongue and caper salad, while mains could feature braised lamb with champ potato and a pot of mutton and kidney Turbigo casserole. To finish, maybe coconut cream with sticky peppered pineapple. The nicely judged wine list is arranged by style and holds plenty of interest. Prices start at £11.95.
**Chef/s:** James Mackenzie. **Open:** Tue to Sun L 12 to 2 (4 Sun), Tue to Sat D 6.30 to 9.30. **Closed:** 2 weeks Jan. **Meals:** alc (main courses £6 to £16). **Service:** not inc. **Details:** Cards accepted. 90 seats. 40 seats outside. Wheelchair access. Music. Children's portions. Car parking.

## ▌Sowerby

# Millbank

**Innovative, daliy-changing menu**
Mill Bank Road, Sowerby, HX6 3DY
Tel no: (01422) 825588
www.themillbank.com
**Modern European | £26**
**Cooking score: 5**

£5 OFF  V  £30

Sometimes the best places are the hardest to find. Clinging to a steep verdant Calderdale valley, this former pub goes from strength to strength, defying both gravity and the recent proliferation of places to eat in these parts. The pubby vibe remains, with proper hand-pulled Yorkshire ales if you just fancy a pint, but the continental feel of the restaurant draws you in. Owner/chef Glen Futter is not one to rest on his laurels; the ever-changing menu delights at every turn – is there a 'Yorkshire/European' genre? If not, there should be, because that's what's on offer. Ox tongue fritter with horseradish coleslaw and red chard sounds improbable, but tastes terrific, smooth and punchy at the same time. Loin of Yorkshire lamb with shepherd's pie of the shoulder, roast pimento, pea purée and mint oil is a cacophony of tastes without any element of it shouting too loud – and then there's honest, straightforward veal and ham pie and mash – a simple enough dish, but hard to pull off well, as this one is, with pastry 'light as angel's wings'. Iced honeycomb parfait with caramelised bananas is a worthy finish. The comprehensive wine list is categorised with headings like 'fruit driven whites' and 'Mediterranean-style reds', with house wines from £12.95, and 12 by the glass, starting at £2.40.
**Chef/s:** Glen Futter. **Open:** Tue to Sun L 12 to 2.30 (4.30 Sun), all week D 6 to 9.30 (10 Fri and Sat, 8 Sun). **Closed:** first week Jan, first 2 weeks Oct. **Meals:** alc exc Sun (main courses £9 to £19). Set L Tue to Sat and D Mon to Thu and Fri 6 to 7 £12.95 (2 courses), Set L and D Sun £12.95 (2 courses). **Service:** not inc. **Details:** Cards accepted. 58 seats. 25 seats outside. Air-con. Separate bar. Wheelchair access. Music. Children's portions.

# Travellers Rest

**Flagstone floors and a roaring log fire**
Steep Lane, Sowerby, HX6 1PE
Tel no: (01422) 832124
www.travellersrestsowerby.co.uk
**Modern British | £28**
**New Chef**

£5 OFF  V  £30

A remote moorland location with fine views all around is one of the main attractions of this eighteenth-century inn. Menus play it fairly safe, aiming for popular appeal with starters such as confit duck salad with tangy pear and salted walnuts, or smoked salmon roulade with dill and lemon crème fraîche and cucumber salad. Main courses include steak with all the traditional trimmings, as well as pan-fried lamb fillet with crushed new potatoes and braised root vegetables, or pan-fried chicken breast with tomato risotto and roast asparagus, while a blackboard lists daily fish specials. The bar menu offers hearty fare such as steak and ale pie, or chicken curry, and for dessert there might be jam roly-poly with custard, or iced orange parfait with dark chocolate mousse. Hand-pulled Yorkshire ales are the thing to drink, though there is also a short wine list with bottles priced from £9.75.
**Chef/s:** Garry Saunders. **Open:** Sat and Sun L 12 to 2.30 (3.30 Sun), Wed to Sun D 5.30 to 8.30 (10 Sat). **Meals:** alc (main courses £12.50 to £19.50). Set L Sun £17.95 (3 courses). Bar menu available. **Service:** not inc. **Details:** Cards accepted. 90 seats. 50 seats outside. No mobile phones. Wheelchair access. Music. Children's portions. Car parking.

## Staddlebridge

### McCoy's at the Tontine

**Charming old stager moving with the times**
Staddlebridge, DL6 3JB
Tel no: (01609) 882671
www.mccoysatthetontine.co.uk
**Modern British | £38**
**Cooking score: 5**

Brothers Eugene and Tom McCoy have been presiding over this rambling, idiosyncratic venue since 1976 and it remains a delightfully oddball destination on the A19 between York and Newcastle. The orginal stone inn dates back to Victorian times and comprises a maze of distinctively decorated little rooms and passageways, with a bistro-style restaurant downstairs. It reminded one correspondent of 'an olde-worlde Parisian café', with its dim lights and mirrors, candles on the tables and a plaster vine motif over the ceiling. The whole place certainly has a faded, 'slightly eccentric' charm all of its own. 'Classic' prawn cocktail shows up incongruously among the starters, alongside twenty-first-century offerings like scallops with celeriac and fennel purée. Chargrilled fillet steak and Dover sole add their weight to the main courses, which also extend to rack of lamb with spiced aubergine, tarragon and tomato jus or pan-fried sea bass with asparagus and lobster sauce. A sizeable contingent of desserts calls into play some old-school favourites like ginger sponge, 'squidgy' chocolate pudding and crêpe San Lorenzo (filled with Chantilly cream, Grand Marnier and crushed amaretti biscuits). Sunday lunch is reckoned to be 'good value', and France finds favour on the 80-bin wine list. Other major producing countries provide brief contributions, while house selections kick off at £16.95 (£5.50 a glass).
**Chef/s:** Stuart Hawkins. **Open:** all week 12 to 2, 7 to 9 (6.30 to 9.45 Fri and Sat). **Closed:** 25 and 26 Dec, 1 to 3 Jan. **Meals:** alc (main courses L £12 to £17, D £18 to £24.50). Set L £16.95 (3 courses), Set L Sun £19.95 (3 courses). **Service:** not inc. **Details:** Cards accepted. 50 seats. Music. Children's portions. Car parking.

## Staithes

### Endeavour

**Cosy fish-lovers haven**
1 High Street, Staithes, TS13 5BH
Tel no: (01947) 840825
www.endeavour-restaurant.co.uk
**Modern Seafood | £23**
**Cooking score: 4**

Set in the heart of one of the most atmospheric fishing villages of the Yorkshire coast, the Endeavour has long been an intimate haven for fish lovers. There's only room for half a dozen tables in a candlelit downstairs dining room but a full and changing menu always nets a seductive catch of wild fish and seafood. Brown crab, langoustines, razorshells, cod, halibut, turbot and ray can be on the plate within hours of landing at Whitby or Staithes itself. Local lobster is available with 24 hours notice. Chef Brian Kay brings out the best of his prime raw material, with dishes like mousse of home-salted cod, grilled langoustines with olive oil and Pernod dressing, or turbot with apple wafers and a Calvados sauce. Fillet steak is always on as well as a non-meat dish or two. Commitment to quality sustains through home-made breads, fudge and a fulsome dessert menu that has featured fresh berries with mascarpone and flaked almonds, chocolate mousse, pannacotta, spiced plums or an elaborate 'assiette' of five different puddings. A judicious wine and beer list includes some notable organic wines. Prices start at £12.75 and reach £25.95 for the Domaine Begude Chardonnay.
**Chef/s:** Charlotte Willoughby and Brian Kay. **Open:** Tue to Sat D 7 to 11, Thu to Sat L 12.30 to 1.30. **Closed:** 25 and 26 Dec, 1 Jan. **Meals:** alc (main courses £13 to £16). **Service:** not inc. **Details:** Cards accepted. 20 seats. Music. Children's portions. Car parking.

## ALSO RECOMMENDED
### ▲ Blackwell Ox Inn
Huby Rd, Sutton-on-the-Forest, YO61 1DT
Tel no: (01347) 810328

There is laudable ambition in this former
village pub now morphing into a full-blown
restaurant-with-rooms. A bar remains for
drinkers and informal dining but the linen
cloths and polished silver of the dining room
is where the serious eating takes place. Chef
Steven Holding confesses to an affection for
the food of South West France and Catalan
Spain, borne out by the confits and cassoulets
on his menu. Lovingly slow-cooked lamb,
excellent crisp-skinned belly pork and a
definitive Whitby cod and chips showed his
talent; an over-ripe goats' cheese starter and a
tough nugget of treacle and raisin bread
betrayed inconsistencies. One to watch.

## ■ Tadcaster
### Singers
**Reasonable prices and excellent service**
16 Westgate, Tadcaster, LS24 9AB
Tel no: (01937) 835121
www.singersrestaurant.co.uk
**Modern European | £22**
**Cooking score: 2**
£30

The décor of this bow-windowed restaurant
has a musical theme and a smart, modern-
classic feel. The early evening menu (available
Tuesday to Thursday) is especially good value,
and typically includes fresh crab beignets with
a sweet chilli dressing followed by roast loin of
pork with apple tart topping and cider gravy,
and a dessert of dark chocolate and orange tart
with vanilla ice cream. A meal from the
evening menu could take in terrine of confit
pork, duck and honey-roasted shallots with
sweet piccalilli, a main course of breast and
thigh of local pheasant over beer-braised
cabbage with bacon dumplings, and lemon
and cinnamon rice pudding with pear and
pomegranate compote for dessert. Wines
from £12.75.

**Chef/s:** Adam Hewitt and John Appleyard. **Open:**
Tue to Sat D only 6 to 9.30. **Closed:** 1 week
Christmas. **Meals:** Set D Tue to Thur 6 to 7 £14.95 to
£22.95, Set D Tue to Thur £18.95 (2 courses), Set D
Fri and Sat £22.95. **Service:** not inc. **Details:** Cards
accepted. 38 seats. Air-con. Wheelchair access.
Music.

## ■ Todmorden
### Old Hall
**Sample ingredients from the local area**
Hall Street, Todmorden, OL14 7AD
Tel no: (01706) 815998
**Modern British | £30**
**Cooking score: 2**
£5 OFF V

Mullioned windows, flagstone floors, wood
panelling and huge fireplaces make the
interior of this Elizabethan manor house as
interesting as its imposing exterior. The main
thrust is towards reworked classics: perhaps
eggs Benedict incorporating Bury black
pudding and a potato cake or twice-baked Mrs
Bell's Yorkshire Blue cheese soufflé with a
walnut and rocket salad, followed by pan-
fried fillet of haddock with a butter bean and
chorizo cassoulet; grilled Curwin Hill beef
with sautéed fine beans and a pink and green
peppercorn sauce; or poached supreme of
chicken filled with Parma ham, spinach and a
Parmesan mousse. Dessert might be Yorkshire
parkin with plum sauce and gingerbread ice
cream or Baileys crème brûlée. A
comprehensive wine list starts at £13.25.
**Chef/s:** Chris Roberts and Peter Windros. **Open:**
Sun L 12 to 2:30, Tue to Sat D 7 to 9.30. **Closed:** First
10 days in Jan, last 12 days in Aug. **Meals:** alc (main
courses £14 to £22). Set L Sun £18 (3 courses).
**Service:** not inc. **Details:** Cards accepted. 70 seats.
20 seats outside. Music. Children's portions. Car
parking.

## ALSO RECOMMENDED

## ▲ Wolski's

Monarch House, George Street, Wakefield,
WF1 1NE
Tel no: (01924) 381252
www.wolskis.co.uk

Seafood (some from Wolski's own boat) is a strong suit at this vast bar/restaurant occupying three floors of a converted wine merchant (circa 1910). Expect anything from marinated seafood salad of cockles, mussels, baby octopus and prawns (£4.50) to sea bass fillet served with celeriac and sweet potato dauphinoise (£11.95) with token meat dishes such as grilled fillet steak with mushrooms, grilled tomatoes, chunky chips and a rich shallot gravy (£16.50). Finish with jam roly-poly (£2.95) Wines from £11.95. Closed Sun.

# ▮ Whitby

## Greens

Subtle and sophisticated
13 Bridge Street, Whitby, YO22 4BG
Tel no: (01947) 600284
www.greensofwhitby.com
**Modern British | £30**
Cooking score: 3

'Consistently superb' is the view of one regular of the town's most sophisticated dining experience, especially since Rob and Emma Green expanded upstairs to offer 'fine dining'. Rob Green has shifted up a couple of gears from the bistro food still served downstairs (chicken liver parfait, daily fish specials, steaks), delivering, at inspection, a delightful Thai amuse 'coconutty and fragrant' with a fat prawn at its centre. Crispy Whitby langoustines with lime, chilli oil and watermelon continued the aromatic theme, while belly pork with apples, chorizo and black pudding wonton was sticky and rich. Fillets of Whitby turbot with cauliflower purée, pickled onion bhaji, king scallop and a light curried cream was restrained, and a trio of prime Yorkshire lamb – chop, noisette and a little shepherd's pie – worked well. A pre-

dessert thimble of champagne jelly and strawberry heralded the arrival of a 'spectacularly dense and gooey' date and ginger pudding with rhubarb and custard ice cream. Staff are considered 'very accommodating' – certainly 'the cheerful Yorkshire lasses pull Greens back from being pretentious'. Wine starts at £12.95, with 14 by the glass from £3.30.
**Chef/s:** Rob Green. **Open:** Fri to Sun L 12 to 2 (3 Sun), all week D 6.30 to 9.30 (6 to 10 Sat). **Closed:** 25 and 26 Dec, 1 Jan. **Meals:** alc (main courses £12.50 to £20). **Service:** not inc. **Details:** Cards accepted. 50 seats. Air-con. No mobile phones. Music. Children's portions.

## Magpie Café

Food straight from Whitby Fish Market
14 Pier Road, Whitby, YO21 3PU
Tel no: (01947) 602058
www.magpiecafe.co.uk
**Seafood | £24**
Cooking score: 2
Ⓥ £30

'Always consistent; we've never had a disappointing meal,' says one reporter of this seaside café. Its sterling reputation means that it is reliably busy, but an extension has cut the queues, and the 'friendly, efficient' staff do not rush you once seated. The menu offers something for everyone, with dishes ranging from deep-fried cheese (goats' or Camembert) to vegetarian shepherd's pie or locally reared fillet steak with all the trimmings. Fish and shellfish are the main attraction and Magpie sources the freshest local ingredients. The café continues to draw praise for making the 'best traditional fish and chips', but other choices include mussels steamed in wine, cream and garlic and Whitby crab among the starters, and main courses such as seafood chowder; Whitby lemon sole and chips; and oven-baked wild sea bass. The wine list includes a decent selection by the glass or carafe, with bottles priced from £11.95.
**Chef/s:** Ian Robson and Paul Gildroy. **Open:** all week 11.30 to 9. **Closed:** 25 and 26 Dec, 1 Jan, 8 Jan to 8 Feb. **Meals:** alc (main courses £7 to £19).

Service: not inc. Details: Cards accepted. 130 seats.
Air-con. Wheelchair access. Music. Children's
portions.

# ▎Yarm
## Chadwick's
Continental style café
104B High Street, Yarm, TS15 9AU
Tel no: (01642) 788558
Modern European | £24
Cooking score: 3

Ⓥ £30

This café-restaurant now opens throughout
the day, serving breakfasts until 11.30 and an
all-day menu, including cream teas, from
11.30 until 5.30. Its modern frontage is
unmissable among Yarm's more historical
buildings. Inside, light wood tables and
yellow walls provide an attractive setting for
the unfussy cooking which brings together
French, British and Mediterranean influences,
plus the occasional touch of Asian spice.
Starters could include a bruschetta of garlic
mushrooms and goats' cheese; sautéed chicken
livers with pancetta and Marsala cream; and
linguine with king prawns, chilli and garlic.
Follow with fillet of halibut with braised
fennel, saffron potatoes, fine beans and
mustard cream; Asian chicken with sag aloo,
harissa and raita; chargrilled sirloin steak au
poivre with salad and fries; or grilled lamb
cutlets with crushed potatoes and peas, black
pudding and minted béarnaise. Wines
from £11.95.
Chef/s: David Brownless and Steven Conyard.
Open: Mon to Sat 12 to 2.30, 5.30 to 9.30 . Closed:
24 and 25 Dec, third week Oct, bank hols.
Meals: alc (main courses L £6.50 to £10.50, D £12 to
£21.50). Service: not inc. Details: Cards accepted.
70 seats. Air-con. No mobile phones. Music.
Children's portions.

# ▎York
## J. Baker's
Top-class cooking in a relaxed setting
7 Fossgate, York, YO1 9TA
Tel no: (01904) 622688
www.jbakers.co.uk
Modern British | £24
Cooking score: 5

£5 OFF  Ⓥ  £30

Jeff Baker had done ten years straight at Leeds'
top rated restaurant Pool Court when he
arrived in York last spring to go it alone and hit
the ground running. His lunchtime and early
evening 'grazing menu' of small plates has
become an immediate institution. The £25.50
dinner menu is another hot ticket. Baker can
cook with real panache and top-end dining in
a relaxed setting was just what city centre York
needed. Discarding the foie gras and amuse-
gueule formalities of Pool Court, Baker has
plumped for cheaper ingredients and big, bold
British flavours like black pudding dumpling
and spiced fruit mustard; soused mackerel and
rhubarb; ham pie; fish and chips. It doesn't
come as rumbustiously as it sounds. Crab trifle
brought brown and white crabmeat, served in
a Kilner jar and topped with an intense
seafood foam. Carefully refined cooking and
precision plating-up were evident again with
almond crusted lemon sole roasted on the
bone and served with brown butter and
celeriac, a simple and effective main course.
Ham pie, a little pastry parcel of meltingly
sweet ham hock, served with carrot, parsnip
and lemony juices, was terrific. Playfulness
runs through the menu to desserts like Bounty
Bar Revisited and Lemon Tops. The 'Bounty'
was Manjari chocolate, toasted coconut; and
dark rum 'Lemon Tops' updated a childhood
dream of jelly, ice cream, lemon curd and
biscuit. House wines start at £10.95.
Chef/s: Jeff Baker and Steve Smith. Open: Tue to
Sat L 12 to 2.30, D 6 to 10. Meals: alc L (main
courses £4 to £6). Set D £21.50 (2 courses) to
£25.50 (3 courses). Service: not inc. Details: Cards
accepted. 66 seats. Wheelchair access. Music.
Children's portions.

# Melton's

**Evergreen York champion**
7 Scarcroft Road, York, YO23 1ND
Tel no: (01904) 634341
www.meltonsrestaurant.co.uk
Modern European | £30
Cooking score: 5

£5 OFF V

This modest terraced house just outside the city walls has been sending out good food, indeed York's most consistently satisfying food, for nearly two decades. Through their own high standards and with growing quality opposition, the husband and wife team of Michael and Lucy Hjort have not rested on their laurels. Their style is modern and British with ingredients firmly rooted in the region. Carpaccio of Whitby smoked halibut with fennel seed sets the tempo. So, too, the buckwheat blini topped with sweet and earthy local beetroot, finished with crème fraîche. Mains offer more well-composed plates: a selection of Yorkshire-landed fish, brown crab and black pasta is served with braised fennel. Belly pork comes with pease pudding, turnips in port and curly kale. There are properly thought out non-meat dishes too: savoury red pepper custard with borlotti beans, purple sprouting broccoli and chilli and lemon salsa; or a Melton's favourite – ravioli of butternut squash served with sage butter and curly kale. The regional bias continues with a Yorkshire influenced cheeseboard and puddings that feature white chocolate parfait served with Yorkshire rhubarb compote. While the cooking stays fresh and contemporary, the décor is more suburban. A fun mural depicts local worthies in a romanticised York setting, but heavy carpets and plodding furniture weigh the room down. The comprehensive wine list is arranged by region starting at £14 with many half-bottles. Service is easy-going but attentive. There are numerous good value offers: early bird menus, Saturday lunches, monthly gourmet dinners, and, on race days, champagne brunch.

**Chef/s:** Michael Hjort and Annie Prescott. **Open:** Tue to Sat L 12 to 2, Mon to Sat D 5.30 to 9.45. **Closed:** 2 weeks Christmas. **Meals:** alc (main courses £12.50 to £18.20). Set L and D £21. **Service:** not inc. **Details:** Cards accepted. 42 seats. Air-con. Wheelchair access. Music. Children's portions.

# Melton's Too

**All-purpose all-day bistro**
25 Walmgate, York, YO1 9TX
Tel no: (01904) 629222
www.meltonstoo.co.uk
Modern European | £18
New Chef

V £30

A busy, laid back bistro in the rapidly expanding 'restaurant quarter' of Walmgate and Fossgate. Dining is on three floors in an agreeably rustic set of rooms, featuring exposed brick, rickety staircases, old beams and uneven wood floors. The old York ropemaker who once worked here provided for both church bells and hangman's nooses. Melton's Too is much breezier in feel and food to its founding father, Melton's. The cooking is satisfactory rather than special but the ingredients are invariably well-sourced. Drop in all day for full English breakfast, the works or vegetarian; mid-morning coffee and cake, then lunch as light or heavy as you fancy: soup, sandwich or tapas – chorizo and butter bean ragoût, belly pork with chick peas. Dinner could be potted prawns, steak and chips or vegetable tagine with couscous followed by rhubarb crumble and home-made custard. A modest wine list begins with house Australian at £11.95. Welcome touches include a stock of daily papers and a genuine attention to families.

**Chef/s:** Martin Hewitt , Andy Battson. **Open:** all week 10.30 to 10.30. **Closed:** 25 and 26 Dec, 1 Jan. **Meals:** alc (main courses £7.50 to £13.50). **Service:** not inc. **Details:** Cards accepted. 120 seats. Air-con. Wheelchair access. Music. Children's portions.

## Middlethorpe Hall

**Luxurious setting, aspirational menu**
Bishopthorpe Road, York, YO23 2GB
Tel no: (01904) 641241
www.middlethorpe.com
**Modern British | £39**
**Cooking score: 3**

A fine William and Mary house of mellow brick close to the racecourse promises luxurious stabling and top-end dining in the grandest of settings. Sober suited staff sweep guests through a marbled hallway to a country house drawing room and on to a fine-panelled dining room where the food is on-message. A marinated wild mushroom salad with a creamy garlic dressing was a simple but winning dish at inspection, and pan-fried salmon and scallop was given an intense shellfish foam. A main dish of cod came neatly balanced by cocotte potatoes, baby spinach, smoked bacon and foam (again). Elsewhere, duck breast with beetroot, sherry-vinegar glazed onions and crisp duck canelloni was 'impeccably executed'. Desserts have scored well too, notably a rich chocolate tart beside a sharp passion-fruit sauce and fromage blanc sorbet, and a banana and pecan parfait, with caramelised bananas. Readers have been impressed by a wine list that majors in the French classic regions, although prices are high. House wines start at £23.50. NB Children must be over 6.
**Chef/s:** Nick Evans. **Open:** all week 12.30 to 1.30, 7 to 9.45. **Meals:** Set L £17 (2 courses) to £23, Set D £39 to £55. **Service:** inc. **Details:** Cards accepted. 56 seats. 20 seats outside. No music. No mobile phones. Wheelchair access. Children allowed. Car parking.

## Tasting Room

**Pleasing British menu in the city centre**
13 Swinegate Court East, York, YO1 8AJ
Tel no: (01904) 627879
www.thetastingroom.co.uk
**Modern British | £30**
**Cooking score: 3**

Tucked away in a courtyard in the boutique Swinegate Quarter, the Tasting Room is an attractive option for a shopper's lunch or a night-out dinner. Painted in muted green and filled with Scandinavian-style furniture, it has a clean-cut air that is reflected in its menu and uncluttered cooking. Lunch graduates from soups, sandwiches and salads to more substantial plates such as calf's liver with champ or a generous and well flavoured tomato and goats' cheese risotto. In the evening the mood – and price – changes with the candlelight. Seasonal variations have brought turbot with cucumber confit, spinach and crushed potatoes for fish lovers' and lamb cutlets and devilled kidneys served with potato mille-feuille and green beans for meat lovers. Desserts have a simple elegance through a classic crème brûlée, treacle tart and walnut ice cream, and roast plums with orange and cardamom cream.
**Chef/s:** Russell Johnson. **Open:** all week L 12 to 2.30, Mon to Sat D 6 to 10. **Closed:** Sun Jan to Apr, bank hol Mon. **Meals:** alc (main courses L £9.50 to £18, D £13 to £20). Set D Mon to Thur £17.95 (2 courses) to £20.95. Light L menu available Mon to Sat. **Service:** not inc. **Details:** Cards accepted. 38 seats. 20 seats outside. Wheelchair access. Music. Children allowed.

# SCOTLAND

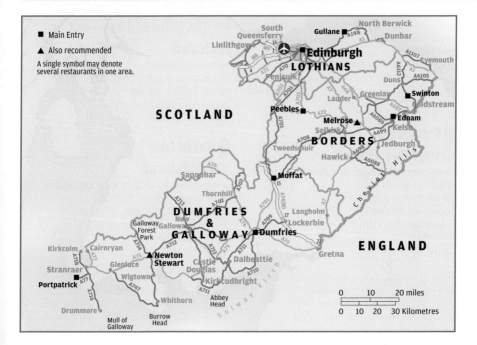

Legend:
■ Main Entry
▲ Also recommended
A single symbol may denote several restaurants in one area.

## Ednam

### Edenwater House

**A magical country setting for home cooking**
Ednam, TD5 7QL
Tel no: (01573) 224070
www.edenwaterhouse.co.uk
British | £37
Cooking score: 4

The enchanting landscape of the Scottish borders unfolds around this converted manse. The interior has plenty of period charm, and husband and wife team Jacqui and Jeff Kelly can be relied upon to make visitors feel welcome and comfortable. Jacqui is a 'super, imaginative home cook', whose unpretentious cooking draws on many of the excellent ingredients available locally. 'Our meal had no weak links', wrote one happy visitor. The four-course, no-choice dinner menu could include pan-fried red mullet with a warm salad of cannelloni beans, smoked tomato and fennel and a fennel emulsion followed by rack of Border lamb with fondant butternut squash, minted sugar snap peas, Dunbar Rover potatoes sautéed in olive oil and garlic, with a natural jus. Next might come griddled Forelle pears with farmhouse Gorgonzola, rocket and local wildflower honey. While the kitchen is Jacqui's domain, Jeff composes the wine list. Wines are chosen with the menus in mind, and are priced from £12.50 a bottle.
**Chef/s:** Jacqui Kelly. **Open:** Wed to Sat D only 8pm (1 sitting). **Closed:** first 2 weeks Jan. **Meals:** Set D £37.50. **Service:** not inc. **Details:** Cards accepted. 16 seats. No music. No mobile phones. Children's portions. Children allowed. Car parking.

## ALSO RECOMMENDED

### ▲ Burt's Hotel

Market Square, Melrose, TD6 9PL
Tel no: (01896) 822285

Impressively set in Melrose's eighteenth-century Market Square, Burt's has been run by the Henderson family for over 30 years. Sound British cooking is served in the smart restaurant. Set lunch is £25.75, dinner is £32.75, and might feature Teviot smoked salmon with lemon and caperberries, roast guinea fowl with black pudding ravioli and grain-mustard sauce, and perhaps pain perdu with rum and raisin ice cream to finish. House wines £13.75. Open all week.

## ▌Peebles
### Cringletie House

France meets Scotland in a shooting lodge
Peebles, EH45 8PL
Tel no: (01721) 725750
www.cringletie.com
**Franco-Scottish | £51**
New Chef

£5 OFF 🍽 V

Built in 'lairdly' baronial style around 1861, this grandiose Borders' mansion sits amid 28 acres of grounds complete with a listed dovecote, a waterfall and one of the oldest walled gardens in Scotland. New chef Jimmy Desrivieres makes use of seasonal pickings and draws on local produce for an elaborate Franco-Scottish menu. Proceedings might begin with a white boudin of pig's trotter and wild mushroom fricassee or globe artichoke velouté with foie gras ice cream and bacon cake. A French accent also points up main courses of sautéed lobster with an étuve of vegetables, saffron and ginger, or rack of lamb with pistachio croûte, aubergine caviar and boulangère potatoes. Desserts look elsewhere for griottine tiramisu with mocha ice cream and a duo of orange and rose soup with Glenkinchie whisky sorbet. Regional French classics vie with young pretenders from the New World on the well-spread wine list, which opens with six house selections at £18 (£4.75 a glass).
Chef/s: Jimmy Desrivieres. **Open:** Sun 12 to 2, all week 7 to 9. **Meals:** Set Sun L £20, Set D £43.50 (5 courses). **Service:** not inc. **Details:** Cards accepted. 35 seats. No mobile phones. Wheelchair access. Music. Children's portions. Car parking.

## READERS RECOMMEND
### Halcyon

**Modern European**
39 Eastgate, Peebles, EH45 8AD
Tel no: (01721) 725 100
www.halcyonrestaurant.com
'Best food in town'

## ▌Swinton
### Wheatsheaf

A reputation for quality local ingredients
Main Street, Swinton, TD11 3JJ
Tel no: (01890) 860257
www.wheatsheaf-swinton.co.uk
**Modern Scottish | £30**
Cooking score: 3

£5 OFF 🍽 V

This attractive stone building – part upmarket inn, part country hotel – has a reputation for using quality ingredients from local suppliers. Dishes range from classic combinations such as chicken liver parfait with grape and apple chutney or sautéed lamb's liver with onions and bacon on a spring onion mash, to more modern, internationally inspired options such as hot-smoked salmon with avocado and Greenland prawns on a mango and chilli salsa. An impressive vegetarian selection could include beetroot and tarragon risotto; or slow-roast aubergine with oregano, coriander, white peppercorns and garlic. Finish with warm bramble and almond tart with cardamon custard or hot sticky ginger and pear pudding with fudge sauce and vanilla-pod ice cream. The lengthy, good-value wine list opens at £11.95.
Chef/s: John Keir. **Open:** all week 12 to 2, 6 to 9 (8 Sun). **Closed:** Sun D Dec to Feb, 25 to 27 Dec. **Meals:** alc (main courses L £8.50 to £13, D £14.50 to £19). **Service:** not inc. **Details:** Cards accepted. 45 seats. No mobile phones. Wheelchair access. Music. Children's portions. Car parking.

## Dumfries

### Linen Room
Daring innovation and bold gestures
53 St Michael Street, Dumfries, DG1 2QB
Tel no: (01387) 255689
www.linenroom.com
**Modern European | £39**
Cooking score: 4

Russell Robertson hit the ground running when he opened his thoroughly modern restaurant. Since then, the Guide has been overwhelmed by reader endorsements and plaudits from all quarters. Sleek fittings and bold monochrome décor provide a fitting backdrop to cooking that 'would take a big city by storm'. Périgord foie gras is subjected to a 'seven-stage process' and served with 'oriental-influenced' cherries, balsamic and frisée; elsewhere, there is talk of 'hazelnut manipulation' and 'Tanzanie chocolate escalation'. Any flashes of gastromonic sorcery are, however, tempered with sound respect for native raw materials. Robertson's way with Scottish ingredients shows in Fred Ballard's local lamb in company with Weetabix purée, veal sweetbreads, parsnip silk and that much-neglected wild plant 'Good King Henry'. Proceedings reach a climax with culinary pyrotechnics in the form of '4 corners, 6 flavours, 8 techniques, 1 result!!' (the 'flavours' in question being banana, vanilla, lemon, meringue, coffee and toffee). The wine list impresses with its comprehensive coverage of the French regions. It is also refreshing to see that the best drinking is not necessarily the most expensive. Bottle prices start at £17, with selections by the glass from £5.
**Chef/s:** Russell Robertson. **Open:** Tue to Sun 12.30 to 2.30, 7 to 9.30. **Closed:** 2 weeks Jan, 2 weeks Oct. **Meals:** alc D (main courses £13 to £18), Set L £14.95 to £15.95, Set D £39.50 to £45. **Service:** not inc. **Details:** Cards accepted. 32 seats. No mobile phones. Wheelchair access. Music. Car parking.

## Moffat

### Limetree
Simple food using the freshest ingredients
High Street, Moffat, DG10 9HG
Tel no: (01683) 221654
www.limetree-restaurant.co.uk
**British | £24**
Cooking score: 2

Located at the top end of the high street, the Limetree is a converted two-storey house, with an immaculate interior and a simple, set-price menu that continues to please locals and tourists alike. Matt Seddon's philosophy of simple food using fresh local ingredients works well here; he cooks with skill and flair, delivering dishes along the lines of pan-fried pigeon with honey, ginger and pancetta with mustard-dressed leaves, or salt and chilli squid with squid ink risotto, spring onion and dill. After a main course of maybe roast duck with shallot and red-wine sauce, or red snapper with slow-roasted vine tomatoes, olive oil and basil dressing, there might be chocolate marquise with Amaretto ice cream. A compact wine list includes six by the glass and house French at £12.50.
**Chef/s:** Matt Seddon. **Open:** Sun L 12.30 to 2.30, Tue to Sat D 6.30 to 9. **Closed:** 2 weeks Oct. **Meals:** Set L £14.75 (2 courses) to £18.50, Set D £18.50 (2 courses) to £23.50. **Service:** not inc. **Details:** Cards accepted. 26 seats. No mobile phones. Wheelchair access. Music. Children's portions.

### Well View
Communal dining in a family-run Victorian villa
Ballplay Road, Moffat, DG10 9JU
Tel no: (01683) 220184
www.wellview.co.uk
**Franco-Scottish | £28**
Cooking score: 4

The Schuckardts run Well View as a family affair, and their peaceful Victorian villa has accumulated all the virtues of a 'superior B&B' since opening its doors in 1984. Endearing personal touches abound. Communal dining around one long table is the order of the day, giving proceedings the feel of a civilised house party, where guests are offered a short fixed-price menu with no choice until desserts. Meals generally begin with a canapé designed to give the palate a wake-up call; then comes a simply crafted starter such as home-cured gravlax with melon, rocket and a honey and lemon dressing. For the main course, expect something robust and meaty, perhaps roast breast of partridge on a compote of red cabbage with 'solferino' of vegetables and red-wine jus. A trio of desserts brings up the rear with a selection that might include rhubarb fool, pear and almond tart, and cinder toffee ice cream in a tuile basket. Well View is no longer licensed, but complimentary glasses of appropriate wines are offered as a matter of courtesy.

**Chef/s:** Janet and Lina Schuckardt. **Open:** Sun L 1 (1 sitting), all week D 7.30 (1 sitting). **Meals:** Set L £22 (3 courses), Set D £35 (4 courses). **Service:** not inc. **Details:** Cards accepted. 12 seats. No music. No mobile phones. Wheelchair access. Children allowed. Car parking.

## ALSO RECOMMENDED
## ▲ Kirroughtree House
Newton Stewart, DG8 6AN
Tel no: (01671) 402141

Grand country house hotel with an impressive pedigree, two smart dining rooms and a connection with Robert Burns. Three-course dinners (£32.50) and à la carte lunches rely on local Galloway produce. Lunch dishes include a rabbit, wild mushroom and pistachio terrine (£3.50), then loin of Kirroughtree venison with braised red cabbage and Valhrona chocolate sauce (£14.75). For dinner, try carpaccio of Castle Mey beef, Scottish lamb with gratin dauphinois, followed by local cheeses or a Drambuie parfait with Glayva anglaise. House wine is £15.75. Open all week, with a set lunch on Sunday for £16.

## ▌Portpatrick
## Knockinaam Lodge
**Refined cooking in remote surroundings**
Portpatrick, DG9 9AD
Tel no: (01776) 810471
www.knockinaamlodge.com
**Modern European | £50**
**Cooking score: 5**

£5 OFF ♦ ⟷ V

At the end of a track in the back of beyond, this Victorian hunting lodge stands in its own grounds, leading down to a beach by the Atlantic Ocean. On clear evenings, the lights of Belfast harbour are visible in the far distance. It may be remote, but nothing detracts from the genuine family welcome. Knockinaam's format is a fixed-price four-course deal with no choice apart from the option of dessert or cheese. Tony Pierce's food is cleverly balanced, with precise seasoning and spot-on timing across the board. In April, he might offer a ceviche of 'native' scallops with a small leaf salad and citrus vinaigrette ahead of beef and wild mushroom consommé flavoured with tarragon and sherry. As a centrepiece, there could be grilled fillet of Luce Bay sea bass served on chive pomme purée with champagne sauce or roast 'poulet de Bresse' accompanied by a ravioli of its leg, parsnip purée and a Madeira and lime reduction, while hot rhubarb soufflé with raspberry sorbet is a typical dessert. David Ibbotson's 450-bin wine list bears all the hallmarks of a real enthusiast and knowledgeable oenophile. He cites the wines of Pauillac and Brunello di Montalcino among his personal favourites, although there is ample to enjoy from other mature Gallic vintages, Mediterranean gems and splendid offerings from Australia. House selections start at £24 (£6 a glass).

**Chef/s:** Tony Pierce. **Open:** all week 12 to 2, 7 to 9. **Meals:** Set L Mon to Sat £37.50, Set L Sun £25, Set D £50 (5 courses). Bar L menu available. **Service:** not inc. **Details:** Cards accepted. 22 seats. Wheelchair access. Music. Car parking.

# █ Edinburgh

## Atrium

**The obvious choice for the theatre crowd**
10 Cambridge Street, Edinburgh, EH1 2ED
Tel no: (0131) 228 8882
www.atriumrestaurant.co.uk
**Modern European | £36**
Cooking score: 4

The Atrium has been around since 1993 and still looks essentially the same now as then, with its chunky wooden tables, slighty dated modishness, and almost crepuscular mood (although a wash and brush-up scheduled for after the Guide goes to press should remove any frayed edges). Start with something like wild mushroom pavé, served with truffle mash, grain-mustard ravioli, and a garnish of rock chive and purple shizu. Typical mains involve the likes of perfectly cooked fillet of halibut with shimeji, sea kale and parsley froth or a straightforward saddle of Perthshire lamb with lyonnaise potatoes, roast fennel and parsnip. Desserts can be adventurous in context (grapefruit and coriander seed cheesecake with pink grapefruit and mint salad) or orthodox (apple tarte Tatin with Calvados ice cream). An engaging and thoughtful wine list makes everything available by the glass, while house bottles start at £17. Excitement in the local restaurant scene may have long moved elsewhere, but this remains a destination diner.
**Chef/s:** Neil Forbes. **Open:** Mon to Fri 12 to 2.30, Mon to Sat 6 to 10. **Closed:** 25, 26 Dec, 1, 2 Jan. **Meals:** alc (main courses £19.50 to £23.50). Set L £15.50 (2 courses) to £19.50 (3 courses), Set D £27.00. **Service:** not inc. **Details:** Cards accepted. 100 seats. 100 seats outside. Air-con. No music. Wheelchair access. Children's portions.

## Balmoral, Number One

**Serious French restaurant in a civilised setting**
1 Princes Street, Edinburgh, EH2 2EQ
Tel no: (0131) 556 2414
www.roccofortehotels.com
**Modern European | £50**
Cooking score: 6

🍷 ⊨ Ⅴ

Number One offers the kind of menu where even a fairly experienced diner needs to seek the guidance of waiting staff, or the *Larousse Gastronomique*. It throws around words like 'ventreche', 'cromesque', 'gribiche' and 'gaufrette' with what could once have been termed gay abandon. It is quite French, then, in a manner that only the flagship diner of a stately Edwardian railway hotel – owned by Rocco Forte – could possibly be. Under the direction of chef Jeff Bland, Number One is multiple award-winning, relatively iconic and just horribly civilised. You will enjoy going down the stairs from a busy end of Princes Street, you will enjoy the sense of space in the restrained dining room, and you will certainly enjoy the food. The experience might start with peanut-crusted scallops with curried oxtail and parsnip mousse, then hare en crépinette could follow with cocotte potato, braised cabbage and game jus. The gingerbread soufflé dessert with prune and Armagnac tartlet and vanilla ice cream is mercifully comprehensible, as restaurant French goes (ditto the almond financier). There is a good selection of heavyweight wine to accompany the food; glasses start at £7.50, bottles of French red start at £22 and sail unashamedly to £850 for a Château Le Pin 1988.
**Chef/s:** Jeff Bland. **Open:** Wed to Fri L 12 to 2, all week D 6.30 to 10. **Closed:** first 2 weeks Jan. **Meals:** alc D (main courses £25.50 to £27). Set L £24 (2 courses) to £28, Set D £65. **Service:** not inc. **Details:** Cards accepted. 50 seats. Air-con. No mobile phones. Wheelchair access. Music.

## The Bonham

Contemporary Caledonian chic
35 Drumsheugh Gardens, Edinburgh, EH3 7RN
Tel no: (0131) 274 7444
www.thebonham.com
**Modern European | £32**
Cooking score: 4

The Bonham is a self-avowed boutique hotel, billing itself as 'the coolest in Edinburgh'. Compared to some of the nouveaux vulgarians elsewhere in the city, it may have a case. The fabric of the premises comprises converted Victorian town houses, while the dining room is spacious and light with wooden panelling and contemporary artworks. Pop in for dinner and Michel Bouyer's menu could bring seared, hand-dived scallops to start ,with smoked haddock tortellini and watercress coulis – fresh, sweet shellfish nicely offset by the other flavours on the plate. Mains could involve partridge, venison, halibut or a deft fillet of Scotch beef with roasted cep risotto and tarragon jus; vegetarians could opt for baked, stuffed artichoke with goats' cheese crumble, wilted greens and red pesto. Desserts are mostly kept simple (mousse, tarte Tatin, crème brûlée) although the kitchen may run to a hot caramel soufflé. The wine list is around 50 strong with a fair selection at £25 or under – glasses of house wine from £4.50.
**Chef/s:** Michel Bouyer. **Open:** all week 12 to 2.30 (12.30 to 3 Sun), 6.30 to 10. **Meals:** alc D (main courses £13 to £22.50). Set L £13.50 (2 courses) to £16, Set L Sat and Sun £65 for 4 people (inc wine). **Service:** not inc. **Details:** Cards accepted. 65 seats. Wheelchair access. Music. Children's portions. Car parking.

## Café St Honoré

Popular French restaurant
34 NW Thistle Street Lane, Edinburgh, EH2 1EA
Tel no: (0131) 226 2211
www.cafesthonore.com
**French | £30**
Cooking score: 3

There are a limited number of ways to pronounce 'Mâcon Villages Blanc', but when you try for the third time, then give up and just point at the wine list, you know you're in a proper French restaurant. Three courses at dinner could start with a simple watercress and lovage soup, or pigeon breast with colcannon and lentils. Boeuf bourguignon with mash is a popular main, other options including duck breast or a fine lemon sole with prawns, samphire, capers and chillies. Desserts are simple (chocolate truffle cake, crème brûlée or rhubarb crumble), and the wine list is split roughly half and half between France and 'the rest' with some interesting bargains among the house wines; by the glass from £3.40.
**Chef/s:** Chris Colverson and Bob Cairns. **Open:** all week 12 to 2.15, 5.30 (6 Sat and Sun) to 10. **Closed:** 3 days Christmas, 3 days New Year. **Meals:** alc (main courses L £9 to £15, D £16 to £20.50). Set D Mon to Fri 5.30 to 6.45, Sun 6 to 7.15 £14.95 (2 courses) to £19.95. **Service:** not inc. **Details:** Cards accepted. 44 seats. Music. Children's portions.

## David Bann

Vegetarian fare flourishes
56-58 St Mary's Street, Edinburgh, EH1 1SX
Tel no: (0131) 556 5888
www.davidbann.co.uk
**Vegetarian | £19**
Cooking score: 2

The fact that David Bann's eponymous restaurant has now been around for more than five years is testament to its local popularity – his unique selling point has been to promote vegetarian food. The operation is fairly flexible, so the people on the next table might just be having coffee or snacks, but a full exploration of the menu brings much more.

Starters range from a simple hummus, with olive tapenade and bread, to steamed asparagus with watercress soup and a poached egg. Mains could entail anything from tofu and noodles to a crêpe provençale. Try a rhubarb cheesecake to finish, or a Glenmorangie pannacotta with orange sorbet perhaps, while the wines are mostly under £15 a bottle.

**Chef/s:** David Bann. **Open:** all week 11 to 10 (10.30 Fri and Sat). **Closed:** 25 and 26 Dec, 1 and 2 Jan. **Meals:** alc (main courses £7.50 to £12). **Service:** not inc. **Details:** Cards accepted. 86 seats. Air-con. No music. Wheelchair access. Children's portions.

## Forth Floor

**High-flying fare**
Harvey Nichols, 30-34 St Andrews Square, Edinburgh, EH2 2AD
Tel no: (0131) 524 8350
www.harveynichols.co.uk
**Modern European | £31**
**Cooking score: 3**

Named for its Forth views, and fourth-floor location, this venue comprises an informal brasserie plus a more premium-priced restaurant. The more ambitious restaurant lunch could start with pan-fried pigeon breast, Puy lentils, goats' cheese and a poached pear, then comes top-notch roast venison as a main with oxtail and foie gras tortellini, and caramelised shallots. Chilled melon and Midori soup with yoghurt parfait is a novel dessert. The brasserie's simpler offerings would typically involve mains like steak frites or pasta. Service is attentive throughout, the wine list is good, and a prix fixe lunch menu in the brasserie is an economical way to get a glimpse of the high life. House wines start at £14.50.

**Chef/s:** Stuart Muir. **Open:** all week L 12 to 3 (3.30 Sat and Sun), Tue to Sat D 6 to 10. **Meals:** alc D (main courses £15 to £20). Set L Mon to Sat £24.50 (2 courses). **Service:** 10%. **Details:** Cards accepted. 55 seats. 32 seats outside. Air-con. Wheelchair access. Music. Children's portions.

## Haldanes

**French cooking takes a Highland fling**
13B Dundas Street, Edinburgh, EH3 6QG
Tel no: (0131) 556 8407
www.haldanesrestaurant.com
**French/Scottish | £33**
**Cooking score: 3**

The entrance to Haldanes is down a few steps from street level, then there are narrow interior stairs to a smart basement dining area. For anyone with walking difficulties, or divas who don't do stairs, there is access from the lane to the rear. Chef George Kelso continues to pursue a mature Franco-Scottish style which still finds an appreciative local audience. Starters like haggis in filo with mustard mash and whisky sauce, or a splendid tartlet filled with scallops, leeks and bacon are typical. Monkfish as a main might come with mussels and crayfish on a saffron and chive butter sauce while the menu regularly features Scottish lamb, salmon and beef. Try banana and cardamon crème brûlée, or lemon tart with a sorbet-filled brandy basket for dessert. The wine list has a good French regional selection, with house offerings starting at £14.

**Chef/s:** George Kelso. **Open:** Tue to Fri L 12 to 1.45, Tue to Sat all week D 5.30 to 10. **Closed:** 25 and 26 Dec. **Meals:** alc D (main courses £17 to £26). Set L and D 5.30 to 6.30 £15 (2 courses). **Service:** not inc. **Details:** Cards accepted. 60 seats. Music.

## Kalpna

**Popular veggie Indian in central Edinburgh**
2-3 St Patrick Square, Edinburgh, EH8 9EZ
Tel no: (0131) 667 9890
**Indian/Vegetarian | £20**
**Cooking score: 2**

Kalpna holds a special place in many people's affections, both in Edinburgh and further afield. Its many fans might see criticism as sacrilegious, but for first-time customers there are caveats. Service can vary from effusive to morose, the décor is on the sparse side and the food registers hits and misses. Among the

starters, aloo firdoshi (sesame-coated potato barrels stuffed with nuts, paneer and sweetcorn) is good and so is the hara bara kebab (fried spinach patties stuffed with paneer and herbs), while a main course such as saam savera (spinach stuffed with paneer, saffron, ginger and nuts) provokes interest for both its taste and presentational aesthetics. Kalpna also offers dosas and thalis as well as a short wine list with a couple of Fair Trade bottles. Wines by the glass start at £2.75.
**Chef/s:** Ajay Bhartdwaj. **Open:** Mon to Sat 12 to 2, 5.30 to 10.30 (11 Sat); also open Sun D 6 to 10 Apr to Sept. **Closed:** 25 and 26 Dec, 1 Jan. **Meals:** alc (main courses £5.50 to £12.50). Set L £6, Set D £12.95 to £16.95. **Service:** 10%. **Details:** Cards accepted. 65 seats. Wheelchair access. Music.

rabbit is stuffed with spinach, kidneys and shallots, and comes with pipérade basquaise, with each constituent of the dish enjoying suitable care and attention. The dessert involves a considered ensemble of vanilla and Calvados bavarois, apple sorbet, elderflower jelly and cream. Service is attentive without being fussy, wines by the glass start at £3.50, and there is a decent choice of bottles under £25.
**Chef/s:** Tom Kitchin. **Open:** Tue to Sat 12.30 to 2.30, 7.30 to 10.00 (6.45 to 10.30). **Closed:** 1 to 17 Jul, 1 to 21 Jan. **Meals:** alc (main courses £23 to £25) Set L £19.50 (3 courses). **Service:** not inc. **Details:** Cards accepted. 45 seats. 32 seats outside. No mobile phones. Wheelchair access. Music. Jacket and tie required.

## ★NEW ENTRY★
## Kitchin
**Classy cooking in a converted warehouse**
78 Commercial Quay, Leith, Edinburgh, EH6 6LX
Tel no: (0131) 5551755
www.thekitchin.com
**Modern European | £43**
New Chef

Run by Tom Kitchin and his wife, Michaela, the Kitchin occupies a ground-floor unit in a converted Leith warehouse. You enter through a light, modern conservatory, while the more enclosed dining space, with its funky patterned wallpaper, is to the rear. One reader described the layout as 'awkward' but this is a rare criticism among general praise. Lesser venues may sell on atmosphere or fashion but the focus here falls definitively on food. Tom Kitchin's CV is littered with spells at illustrious establishments in London, Monte Carlo and Paris, while his mission statement 'from nature to plate' makes explicit an interest in well-sourced, seasonal ingredients. Dishes are described in fashionable minimal headline terms, so three courses could entail halibut followed by rabbit, then apple, but the devil is most certainly in the detail. That starter is actually carpaccio of wild halibut, beetroot, pickled garlic, capers and lemon dressing: 'an excellent flavour combination'. Saddle of

## ★NEW ENTRY★
## Plumed Horse
**Small venue for solid French cooking**
50 Henderson Street, Edinburgh, EH6 6DE
Tel no: (0131) 5545556
www.plumedhorse.co.uk
**Modern French | £38**
Cooking score: 4

Tony Borthwick is a man bedevilled by expectation. After running the Plumed Horse for some years in Crossmichael, a move to the Scottish capital attracted pre-publicity long before the relocated restaurant managed to open. This gave local foodies and journalists time to whip themselves into a frenzy over a new venue that they felt should parachute, effortlessly, into Edinburgh's upper echelon. But the available location on a downmarket Leith street corner was not the most salubrious, while the actual operation is homely in scope. Diners who expect well-oiled perfection on all fronts may be disappointed – and it is hardly cheap – but the Plumed Horse still has much to recommend it. Borthwick is a capable chef, in that traditonal French style, and you have to admire someone who offers a starter like new-season garlic and potato soup with mini cheese soufflés and braised snails. Mains could involve organic pork, salmon or roast loin of rabbit, while a sampled dish of nage-poached monkfish with langoustine, parsley pomme purée, and purple broccoli was of a high standard, complemented by a classy sauce Chateauneuf Du Pape. Dark chocolate tart for dessert comes with a pistachio ice cream that is cool in all senses. The wine list is decent for the size of establishment, while glasses start at £4.25. Great staff, too, once you break the ice.

**Chef/s:** Tony Borthwick and Malcolm Kirkpatrick. **Open:** Tue to Fri L 12.30 to 1, Tue to Sat D 7 to 9; also open one Sun L per month. **Closed:** 25 and 26 Dec, 1 and 2 Jan, 2 weeks Jan, 2 weeks Sept. **Meals:** alc exc Sun L (main courses £19 to £21). Set L Tue to Fri £23, Set L Sun £25. **Service:** not inc. **Details:** Cards accepted. 28 seats. Air-con. No mobile phones. Wheelchair access. Music.

## Prestonfield, Rhubarb

**A classic choice**
Priestfield Road, Edinburgh, EH16 5UT
Tel no: (0131) 225 1333
www.prestonfield.com
**Modern European | £40**
**New Chef**

There is no rule that says you must have the rhubarb dessert here, but since this was the first place in Scotland where rhubarb was cultivated, it seems impolite not to. It involves mini rhubarb spring rolls, rhubarb mousse wearing a biscuit shawl, a fantastically light rhubarb soufflé topping, also an impossibly white and soft meringue with rhubarb ice cream inside. You might have started lunch with hearty leek and potato soup enlivened by some Arbroath smokie and unusual chive spätzli, then gone on to perfectly cooked wild sea bass with curried onion purée, langoustine tortellini, and chive buerre blanc. Vegetarians could have a delicate mille-feuille stacked with spinach, intense mushrooms and shallots with red pepper purée. Sitting in its own grounds in the city's southern suburbs, the main part of this building was completed in 1687 as the home of Edinburgh's Lord Provost. Service is excellent and the hefty wine 'encyclopedia' runs to over 800 bins,

covering all bases; by the glass from £4.50. Once again Rhubarb has a new chef (John McMahon) but on current evidence his cooking forms a central part of the multi-sensory Prestonfield experience.

**Chef/s:** John McMahon. **Open:** all week 12 to 3, 6 to 10.30 (11 Fri and Sat). **Meals:** alc (main courses £16 to £28). Set L and D 6 to 7 and 10 to 10.30 (11 Fri and Sat) £16.95 (2 courses). **Service:** not inc. **Details:** Cards accepted. 100 seats. 20 seats outside. Wheelchair access. Music. Car parking.

## Restaurant Martin Wishart

**Dazzling creativity from Scotland's top chef**
54 The Shore, Leith, Edinburgh, EH6 6RA
Tel no: (0131) 553 3557
www.martin-wishart.co.uk
**Modern French | £50**
**Cooking score: 8**

'I would forego eating anywhere else all year in order to have one meal here,' typifies the popular response to Martin Wishart's eponymous restaurant on Leith's re-invigorated waterfront. It is a venue that generates fond affection, awe and excited anticipation in equal measure. A contemporary design makeover has resulted in clean lines, mirrors and wood panels, but the special atmosphere remains. Wishart is a hands-on chef/proprietor *par excellence,* cooking with supreme confidence and dazzling creativity while ensuring that the wheels of his restaurant run like clockwork. He follows the seasons meticulously, cherry-picking the very best from Scotland's native resources for a choice of menus with a bold contemporary slant. Eating here is a cavalcade of delights and surprises. Canapés are designed to give the palate a wake-up call: haggis bonbons, smoked organic salmon with white radish, crispy risotto rice with tomato fondue and more besides, arrive right on cue. After that, diners can expect a succession of daring ideas and possibilities, often involving fashionable meat/fish partnerships: consider, for example, crab and potato cannelloni accompanied by veal tartare and warm crab mayonnaise or poached Anjou pigeon paired with squid risotto, oyster 'rissolée' and Savoy cabbage. Meat is often given more robust treatment, as in braised shin and shortrib of beef with veal sweetbreads and mushroom ravioli or a gutsy, peasant assemblage of roast loin of pork with choucroute, saucisson de Morteaux and braised trotter, which is luxuriously finished off with a sauce of champagne and grain mustard. Events proceed to a climax with impeccably fashioned desserts in the shape of strawberry soufflé with basil cappuccino or passion fruit, apricot and yoghurt terrine. This is 'food as art', observed one correspondent, although it is also food that emphatically deserves to be eaten with gusto. The whole experience is heightened by personable yet totally professional service that 'makes you feel special'. An aristocratic French presence lords it over the wine list, which provides countless temptations despite the lack of descriptive notes. There is fine drinking to be had wherever you look, with plenty of bottles weighing in at around £25 and some very impressive, affordably priced selections by the glass. Alternatively, throw financial caution to the wind and explore the three-figure vintage Bordeaux and glorious Tuscan rarities.

**Chef/s:** Martin Wishart. **Open:** Tue to Sat L 12 to 2, Tue to Sat D 6.45 to 9.30. **Closed:** Christmas and New Year. **Meals:** Set L £22.50 (3 courses), Set D £50 (3 courses) to £60 (7 courses). **Service:** not inc. **Details:** Cards accepted. 54 seats. No mobile phones. Wheelchair access. Music.

## ★NEW ENTRY★
# Scotsman Hotel, Vermilion
**Discreetly situated restaurant**
20 North Bridge Street, Edinburgh, EH1 1YT
Tel no: (0131) 622 2814
**British | £35**
**Cooking score: 4**

Vermilion is the flagship dining room at the Scotsman, which changed the benchmark for the top end of Edinburgh's hotel trade when it

opened in 2001. Housed in the former offices of the *Scotsman* newspaper, fixtures and fittings have an Edwardian opulence and you reach the restaurant down an impressive marble staircase. With a relatively small dining room, though, and no street-front presence, Vermilion does not have the highest profile compared to its upmarket peers in the city. Enclosed and discreet, the décor is dominated by wall cabinets filled with wine bottles back-lit to create silhouettes: a subtle *coup de théâtre*. Dinner could kick off with dressed crab from Buckhaven, tian of roasted tomatoes and shallots – or Angus asparagus with poached duck egg, organic Parmesan, and truffle mayonnaise. Vegetarians get a good deal with mains such as artichokes three ways, which features Jerusalem artichoke risotto, globe artichoke tart, and Jerusalem artichoke crisps in a salad. Alternatively, diners could have loin of venison, wild garlic tart, gratin potatoes and ceps and, perhaps, rhubarb clafoutis with clotted cream for dessert. Wines by the glass start at £5, and the list runs to over 100 bins. NB Vermilion's sister venue in the hotel is the buzzier and more informal North Bridge Brasserie.

**Chef/s:** Geoff Balharry. **Open:** Wed to Sun D 7 to 10. **Meals:** alc (main courses £16 t0 £24). Set D Wed, Thur and Sun £35 (3 courses). **Service:** not inc. **Details:** Cards accepted. 32 seats. No mobile phones. Wheelchair access. Music.

# Skippers
**A long-standing Leith favourite**
1A Dock Place, Leith, Edinburgh, EH6 6LU
Tel no: (0131) 554 1018
www.skippers.co.uk
**Seafood | £26**
**New Chef**
£5 OFF ✓ £30

A pillar of the local restaurant scene for more than quarter of a century – and early Leith resident before the gentrification of the docks – this establishment has a seafood bistro format and sticks to it with commendable dedication. The lunchtime-favourites menu offers two light dishes at a bargain price (mussels in marinière sauce, then whole grilled sardines with garlic and lemon oil, perhaps), but the ever-changing à la carte has some real treats. Shellfish enthusiasts could start with excellent chargrilled crevettes, or oysters with shallot vinegar. There's duck or steak for meat fans, and polenta with goats' cheese for vegetarians. The kitchen knows its strengths, so desserts are simple: brioche bread-and-butter pudding, or boozy chocolate pot. The wine list is functional, weighted towards whites; by the glass from £2.95.

**Chef/s:** Ian Carlisle. **Open:** all week 12.30 to 2, 6 to 10. **Closed:** 25 and 26 Dec, 1 Jan. **Meals:** alc (main courses L £7.50 to £16, D £12 to £22.50). Set L £8.45 (2 courses) to £11.45, Set D Sun to Fri £19.95. **Service:** not inc. **Details:** Cards accepted. 60 seats. 12 seats outside. Wheelchair access. Music. Children's portions.

## Valvona & Crolla Caffè Bar

**The bread and butter of Italian eateries**
19 Elm Row, Edinburgh, EH7 4AA
Tel no: (0131) 556 6066
www.valvonacrolla.com
**Italian | £20**
**Cooking score: 3**
£5 OFF | V | £30

The story is well rehearsed, but to recap: leading Italian delicatessen dating from 1934, much loved, opened its Caffè Bar in a refurbished stable block to the rear of the shop in 1996. Not open in the evenings, it does breakfast until 11.30am, coffee and snacks all day, but the lunch menu (noon to 3pm) is where things really get going. From the antipasti list comes a bruschetta involving sourdough bread made in the deli's very own bakery, Italian fennel and prosciutto di Parma, all dressed with extra virgin olive oil and lemon juice. The primi piatti selection can offer a great penne puttanesca (with anchovies, capers, Taggiasche olives and tomato sugo) while the piatti principali may centre on free-range chicken breast, marinated squid or Italian artichoke. The Gorgonzola dolce with honey, roasted pine nuts and

oatcakes is wonderful – and the lemon polenta cake legendary. Wine policy allows you to pick a bottle off the shelf for £6 corkage, a decent deal given the award-winning Italian selection; house wine by the glass from £3.50.
**Chef/s:** Mary Contini. **Open:** Mon to Sat 8 to 6, Sun 10.30 to 4.30 (L served 12 to 3). Also open Thu to Sat D during Festival. **Closed:** 25 and 26 Dec, 1 and 2 Jan. **Meals:** alc (main courses L £9 to £15, D £9 to £19.50). **Service:** not inc. **Details:** Cards accepted. 64 seats. Air-con. Wheelchair access. Music. Children's portions.

## Vintners Rooms

**Historic setting**
The Vaults, 87 Giles Street, Leith, Edinburgh, EH6 6BZ
Tel no: (0131) 554 6767
www.thevintnersrooms.com
**French | £29**
**Cooking score: 4**
£5 OFF | £30

If a restaurant has been around for more than two decades, with several chefs at the helm during that period, it will have ups and downs. But with Patrice Ginestière well established in the kitchen here and local legend Silvio Praino (formerly of Silvio's, Scalini, and more) front-of-house, the Vintners may well be on 'career best' form right now. Housed on the ground floor of an eighteenth-century wine warehouse, diners have the choice of the atmospheric bar area, or the old auction room with its delicate stucco work – excellent at night when candlelit. Starters can kick off simply with half a dozen oysters from Scotland's West Coast, or a rather richer guinea fowl terrine with fig chutney. Ginestière's mains are a full-flavoured joy, from the roast Buccleuch beef fillet with Perigord truffle sauce to roast venison with braised cabbage and chocolate sauce. Sea bass with fennel and sauce antiboise is a lighter alternative, and there is coffee crème brûlée with iced whisky truffle to finish. You would expect a decent wine list in these historic

surroundings, and there certainly is, with a fair whack under £30 but most over; by the glass from £3.95.
**Chef/s:** Patrice Ginestrière. **Open:** Tue to Sat 12 to 2, 7 to 10. **Meals:** alc (main courses £16 to £22). Set L £15.50 (2 courses) to £19. **Service:** 10% (optional). **Details:** Cards accepted. 70 seats. Wheelchair access. Music. Car parking.

## Witchery by the Castle
**Hubble, bubble...**
Castlehill, Royal Mile, Edinburgh, EH1 2NF
Tel no: (0131) 225 5613
www.thewitchery.com
**Modern European | £38**
**Cooking score: 3**

🍴 ⅴ

The Witchery is almost on Edinburgh Castle Esplanade and in tourist season the footfall past its door has to be seen to be believed. There are two dining rooms: the original Witchery with its red leather and old wood, which dates from 1979, while the adjacent Secret Garden (added in 1989) is even more impossibly romantic. The Witchery and Secret Garden operate the same menu and at dinner this could involve seared Skye scallops to start, served with crisp pork belly and a spiced aubergine compote, or a steak tartare with celeriac remoulade and a fried quail's egg. Mains might bring a saddle of rabbit in Parma ham with couscous, caramelised fennel, and grain mustard, with passion fruit and mascarpone custard trifle for dessert, perhaps. The gargantuan wine-o-pedia offers everything you can think of and represents hours of reading for enthusiasts; by the glass from £3.95.
**Chef/s:** Douglas Roberts. **Open:** all week 12 to 4, 5.30 to 11.30. **Closed:** 25 and 26 Dec. **Meals:** alc (main courses £14 to £50). Set L £12.50 (2 courses), Set D 5.30 to 6.30 and 10.30 to 11 £12.50 (2 courses). **Service:** not inc. **Details:** Cards accepted. 90 seats. 20 seats outside. Air-con. Music.

## ALSO RECOMMENDED
### ▲ Fishers
1 Shore, Leith, Edinburgh, EH6 6QW
Tel no: (0131) 554 5666

Fishers sells seafood by the sea shore, or at least beside the docks, and has done so since 1991. Nautically nice on the inside, there is a daily-changing menu. Tempura plaice is a pale but interesting starter, on a bed of samphire with a salsa comprising pineapple, passion fruit and chilli. The hot shellfish platter (everything you can imagine on a big dish) needs 24 hours' notice but is quite the show-stopper. Desserts are an afterthought (crème brûlée, sticky toffee pudding). An economical wine list starts at £3.15 per glass. Fishers in the City is the central Edinburgh branch (added in 2001) with updated décor and similar menus.

## READERS RECOMMEND
### Centotre
**Italian**
103 George Street, Edinburgh, EH2 3ES
Tel no: (0131) 225 1550
www.centotre.com
'A modern Italian brasserie run with a smile'

### Iglu
**Modern European**
2B Jamaica Street, Edinburgh, EH3 6HH
Tel no: (0131) 476 5333
www.theiglu.com
'Commendable commitment to organic food'

### Saffrani
**Indian/Pakistani/Bangladeshi**
11 South College Street, Edinburgh, EH8 9AA
Tel no: (0131) 667 1597
'Small and homely with seriously interesting dishes'

## Cooking score

A score of 1 is a significant achievement. The score in any review is based on several meals, incorporating feedback from both our readers and inspectors. As a rough guide, 1 denotes capable cooking with some inconsistencies, rising steadily through different levels of technical expertise, until the scores between 6 and 10 indicate exemplary skills, along with innovation, artistry and ambition. If there is a new chef, we don't score the restaurant for the first year of entry. For further details, please see the scoring section in the introduction to the Guide.

## Shapes

**Modern European**
Bankhead Avenue, Sighthill, Edinburgh, EH11 4BY
Tel no: (0131) 453 3222
www.shapesrestaurant.co.uk
**'Extravagant décor; a really eccentric restaurant'**

## ▍Gullane

### Greywalls Hotel

**Sophisticated cuisine in a unique Lutyens house**
Muirfield, Gullane, EH31 2EF
Tel no: (01620) 842144
www.greywalls.co.uk
**Modern British | £45**
Cooking score: 3

£5 OFF 🍴 ∀

Purchased by the Weaver family in 1924 and run by them as a hotel since 1948, Greywalls is famous as the only surviving Edwin Lutyens-designed house in Scotland. The distinctive crescent-shaped building (golden-honey in colour, despite the name) has a sunken garden designed by Gertrude Jekyll and stands almost within putting distance of Muirfield golf course. Diners get a glimpse of the tenth tee from the windows of the formally attired restaurant, where David Williams's cleverly worked modern food is the major attraction.

Keenly sourced Scottish produce shows up strongly, whether it's organic Shetland sea trout partnered by crushed cocoa beans and grain-mustard cream or East Lothian pork belly, slow-cooked for four hours then served with roast fillet, purple sprouting broccoli and beetroot. The cheese menu boasts a fascinating collection of Scottish natives, while desserts add a touch of exoticism in the shape of coconut parfait with mango and passion-fruit syrup. The lengthy, French-biased wine list opens with 13 house selections from £18.
**Chef/s:** David Williams. **Open:** Fri to Sun 12 to 2, all week 7 to 9.30. **Closed:** Jan and Feb. **Meals:** Set L £20 (2 courses) to £25 (3 courses), Set D £45 (6 courses). **Service:** not inc. **Details:** Cards accepted. 50 seats. No music. Wheelchair access. Children's portions. Car parking.

## La Potinière

34 Main Street, Gullane, EH31 2AA
Tel no: (01620) 843214
www.la-potiniere.co.uk
**Modern British | £38**
Cooking score: 6

The entrance is discreet, décor in the small, elegant dining room restrained, and the style is low-key, offering a couple of choices at each stage on the fixed price lunch (very good value) and dinner menus. But combinations are interesting – Mary Runciman and Keith Marley are scrupulous about the origins of their raw materials, and they set out their stall with some skill, offering from the lunch menu a starter of carrot and ginger mousse matched with a carrot and sauternes jelly, carrots pickled in a salad and served as a sorbet as well as a yoghurt and coriander dressing. Craftsmanship and attention to detail are evident: for example, in an intermediate course of smoked salmon terrine served with warm smoked salmon, smoked salmon soup and a cucumber salad, or a main course of roast and slow-cooked new season lamb with rosemary mash, seasonal vegetables and a lamb and redcurrant jus. Contrasts also tend to be pronounced, thanks to an artful relish here and there, as in baked aromatic monkfish with

### Best for breakfast

Early birds may like to make time to stop off at one of the two branches of **Bill's Produce Store**, in Lewes and Brighton. Egg and soldiers, buttermilk pancakes, home-made flatbread topped with bacon and egg, organic smoothies; open at 8am.

The **Wolseley** on Piccadilly in London may be one of the few places open in these parts at 7am, when eggs Benedict, smoked salmon or prunes with orange and ginger, might tempt.

If you've a healthy appetite first thing, the breakfasts at **Smith's** in Smithfield Market await to sustain Londoners with proper porridge and doorstop bacon butties.

Edinburgh's **Valvona and Crolla** offers a taste of Italy at breakfast, with the likes of lemon polenta cake, and coffee that will keep you motoring through till mid-morning.

'Slap-up breakfasts' are a powerful lure in the **London Carriage Works Brasserie** at the Hope Street Hotel, Liverpool, and there is no stinting on quantity or quality of ingredients.

Readers who stay at the **Corse Lawn House Hotel** in Gloucestershire rarely fail to mention the breakfasts, which offer a heartening array of sublime local produce.

Gargantuan platters of all that we like to see first thing are on offer at **Well House** at St. Keyne, near Liskeard in Cornwall.

crushed Jersey Royals, crème fraîche and chives with local asparagus, and a Lanarkshire tomato, fennel and dill dressing. Meals might finish with a raspberry medley of jelly, compote and sponge served alongside white chocolate and raspberry ice cream. The wines on the short list have been carefully selected and are fairly priced from £16 for a Spanish white and Argentinian red.

**Chef/s:** Mary Runciman and Keith Marley. **Open:** Wed to Sun 12.30 to 1.30, 7 to 8.30. **Closed:** Sun D Oct to Apr, last 2 weeks Jan. **Meals:** Set L £17 (2 courses) to £20, Set D £38. **Service:** not inc. **Details:** Cards accepted. 30 seats. No music. No mobile phones. Wheelchair access. Children's portions. Car parking.

## READERS RECOMMEND

### The Boat House
**Seafood**
19B High Street, South Queensferry, EH30 9PP
Tel no: (0131) 331 5429
www.the-boathouse.info
**'Excellent fish, unique view'**

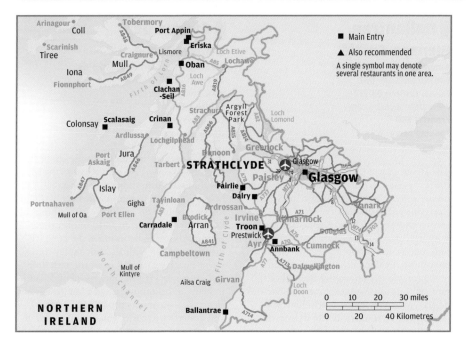

## ■ Annbank

### Enterkine House

**Welcoming country-house hotel**
Annbank, KA6 5AL
Tel no: (01292) 520580
www.enterkine.com
Modern European | £26
Cooking score: 4

'I was completely charmed by Enterkine House,' wrote one satisfied visitor. You drive along a long, winding avenue lined with trees and rhododendron bushes to reach this luxurious country house. The hotel itself – a white, square, 1930s building – still feels like the private residence it once was. The kitchen is fuelled by top-notch Scottish ingredients and turns out modern-looking, classically based dishes that are 'impeccably cooked, elegantly presented and full of delicious flavours'. A meal from the four-course dinner menu could begin with ravioli of diver-caught Kintyre Bay scallops with spinach soubise and a roast garlic and thyme cappuccino, followed by butternut squash velouté with braised ham hock, and a main course of loin of wild red deer with red cabbage, roast salsify, fondant potatoes and morel jus. Finish with an iced, praline pyramid with nougatine glace, white chocolate praline and macerated golden raisins. The wine list majors in French wines and starts at £20.50.

**Chef/s:** Paul Moffat. **Open:** all week 12.30 to 2 (3 Sun), 7 to 9. **Meals:** Set L £16.50 (2 courses) to £18.50, Set D Sun to Thu £21.95 (2 courses) to £29.50, Set D Fri and Sat £40. **Service:** not inc. **Details:** Cards accepted. 70 seats. No mobile phones. Music. Children's portions. Car parking.

### Average price

The average price listed in main-entry reviews denotes the price of a three-course meal, without wine.

## Ballantrae

### Glenapp Castle

**Atmospheric Victorian pile**
Ballantrae, KA26 0NZ
Tel no: (01465) 831212
www.glenappcastle.com
**French | £50**
Cooking score: 6

£5 OFF 🛏

The Deputy Lord Lieutenant of Ayrshire was the first person to call this Scots baronial pile home, when it was built for him in 1870. Everyone will appreciate the air of calm civility that pervades the elegant dining room, with its battery of silverware and almost indecently comfortable chairs. Menus continue to evolve, the six-course dinner menu (previously no-choice throughout) now offering alternatives at main course and dessert. Matt Weedon is a confident chef, putting on the country-house style with considerable panache. A spring menu opened with celeriac velouté with poached scallops, and followed it up with a terrine of foie gras garnished with leeks in a truffle dressing, before proceeding to the seafood course, in this case, local Ballantrae crab dressed with smoked salmon and lemon. The main-course choice of meats was between Angus fillet with braised onions, mushroom duxelles and a red-wine sauce, or roast pork wrapped in Parma ham, with a serving of the braised belly, apple purée and a sauce of the roasting juices. After Scottish cheeses, the evening closed with either a cheesecake of strawberry, rhubarb and white chocolate with almond croquant, or hot passion-fruit soufflé with matching sorbet. Suggested wines – a white, a red and something sweet – accompany the menu, or you may choose to delve headlong into the broadly based wine list, which has plenty of good growers. Wines by the glass are a fairly hefty £6.50. Bottle prices start at around £25. **Chef/s:** Matt Weedon. **Open:** all week D only 7 to 10. **Closed:** 22 to 30 Dec, 2 Jan to 1 Apr. **Meals:** Set D £55. Light L menu available. **Service:** not inc. **Details:** Cards accepted. 34 seats. No music. No mobile phones. Wheelchair access. Car parking.

## Carradale

### Dunvalanree

Port Righ Bay, Carradale, PA28 6SE
Tel no: (01583) 431226
www.dunvalanree.com
**British | £26**
Cooking score: 2

£5 OFF 🛏 V £30

Dunvalanree sits in a clifftop eyrie above Port Righ Bay, keeping a watchful eye on the Isle of Arran. The Milsteads have created a real home-from-home atmosphere here, with no undue standing on ceremony, just lashings of cosy, welcoming cheer, and a single dinner sitting. Alyson cooks in much the same style, kitting out fresh sardines with a spicy tomato sauce, poaching salmon in cream with lime and ginger, or crusting rack of Ifferdale lamb in herbs and anointing it with Madeira gravy. Vegetarian menus are thoughtfully offered, and desserts will cosset you with the likes of chocolate brownies with vanilla ice cream and Drambuie sauce. The tiny wine list always opens with a couple of short-stay listings of mature wines in small quantities. The rest runs from £11.95 up to the dizzy heights of £18. **Chef/s:** Alyson Milstead. **Open:** all week D only 7.30 (1 sitting). **Meals:** Set D £22.50 (2 courses) to £26 (3 courses). **Service:** not inc. **Details:** Cards accepted. 24 seats. No music. Children's portions. Car parking.

## Clachan-Seil

### Willowburn Hotel

**Carefully tended waterside hotel**
Clachan-Seil, PA34 4TJ
Tel no: (01852) 300276
www.willowburn.co.uk
**Modern Scottish | £33**
Cooking score: 3

🛏 V

Travellers need to traverse the historic 'Bridge over the Atlantic' to reach Seil Island and the delights of Willowburn Hotel. This is a busy set-up, with an ever-expanding smallholding and a productive on-site smokery supporting the kitchen's efforts. Local boats provide shellfish, other seafood comes from Oban and lamb is bought direct from a nearby farm. Chris Wolfe puts all of this to good use use, offering four-course dinners with trademark horticultural flourishes. Fillet of halibut is dressed in crispy potato 'scales' and accompanied by a sauce perfumed with lemon myrtle; grilled goats' cheese is marinated in lavender, while Barrichbeyan pork might be roasted with fennel pollen then served with a sweet potato and apple rösti and roast pear. Warm gingerbread pudding with walnut ice cream and gingersnaps could close the show. House wine prices start at £14.

**Chef/s:** Chris Wolfe. **Open:** all week D only 7 (1 sitting). **Closed:** 17 Nov to mid-Mar. **Meals:** Set D £35 (5 courses). **Service:** not inc. **Details:** Cards accepted. 20 seats. No mobile phones. Music. Car parking.

## Colonsay
### Isle of Colonsay Hotel
**Sophisticated home to modern menus**
Scalasaigh, Colonsay, PA61 7YP
Tel no: (01951) 200316
www.thecolonsay.com
**Modern Scottish | £22**
**Cooking score: 2**

It would be hard to get more 'away-from-it-all' than this. But while the remote location might suggest a weather-worn refuge, this place is in fact decked out in true boutique-hotel style, with bold, uncluttered décor. The menu makes commendable use of local (and island) produce, as typified by a supper dish of half a Colonsay lobster with salad from the garden of Colonsay House and lime mayonnaise. Other dishes from the modern, unpretentious menu might include starters of Colonsay spinach and Taleggio tart or falafel with mint and yoghurt dressing; and main courses such as the Colonsay burger with coleslaw and tomato relish; lamb chump with rhubarb compote; or baked haddock with thick-cut chips and tartare sauce. This is

simple, straightforward cooking using excellent raw materials. House wines start at £10.

**Chef/s:** Annabel Taylor and Simon Wallwork. **Open:** all week D only 6 to 9. **Meals:** alc (main courses £8.50 to £14). Bar meals available L and D. **Service:** not inc. **Details:** Cards accepted. 30 seats. Wheelchair access. Music. Children's portions. Car parking.

## Crinan
### Crinan Hotel, Westward Restaurant
**Beautiful location**
Crinan, PA31 8SR
Tel no: (01546) 830261
www.crinanhotel.com
**Scottish/French | £40**
**Cooking score: 4**

Loch Crinan is a small dent in the Argyll coast, spilling into the Sound of Jura and backing up against the Moine Mhor, a flat expanse noted for its prehistoric monuments. At its southern edge is the Crinan Canal and at the canal's western terminus, in a truly beautiful setting, the Crinan Hotel. An architectural pot pourri on the outside, owners Nick and Frances Ryan have provided a consistency of approach on the inside for over 35 years. In the polite Westward dining room chef Scott Kennedy pursues a four-course Franco-Scots menu where local seafood is undoubtedly the star. Starters might involve pan-fried mackerel with a ravioli of Loch Etive mussels and chive velouté, or scallop brochettes with a balsamic reduction. The soup course could be cauliflower velouté with cockles, while mains entail the likes of stunning Loch Crinan prawns, lemon sole with pommes purée, or pan-fried cod with many trimmings. (Fish-averse diners could try terrine of local rabbit and foie gras to start, then a roast saddle of local venison as a main.) Parfait of vanilla, slow-roasted figs and plums, and raspberry ice cream is a grand way to finish. The wine list is varied and international; by the glass from £4.10.

**Chef/s:** Scott Kennedy. **Open:** all week D only 7 to 8.30 (9 summer). **Closed:** Christmas. **Meals:** Set D £45. Bar menu available. **Service:** not inc. **Details:** Cards accepted. 40 seats. 20 seats outside. No music. Wheelchair access. Children's portions. Car parking.

## ▌Dalry
# Braidwoods

**A charming restaurant with character**
Drumastle Mill Cottage, Dalry, KA24 4LN
Tel no: (01294) 833544
www.braidwoods.co.uk
**Modern Scottish | £35**
Cooking score: 6

Surrounded by rolling countryside, Keith and Nicola Braidwood's cottagey restaurant is an unusual place. Blessed with a well-stocked natural larder on their doorstep, the Braidwoods focus on local produce in their cooking, and having worked under top chefs at some of Britain's most illustrious restaurants, Keith Braidwood brings plenty of quality experience to the kitchen. Among starters on the four-course dinner menu might be seared hand-dived scallops from Wester Ross on a fragrant cardamom-infused lentil dhal, or fresh Skye crab and avocado salad with a gently spiced Bloody Mary dressing. To follow, perhaps a choice between spring fennel soup with a hint of lovage, or warm Parmesan tart, before a main course of roast Lanarkshire pork stuffed with black pudding and served with lemon thyme-scented Savoy cabbage. Farmhouse cheeses from Iain Mellis would round off a meal nicely, while the sweet of tooth might opt for chilled caramelised rice pudding with rhubarb compote.
Unpretentious notes and fair mark-ups make for a highly accessible wine list, and even at the more modest end of the spectrum, quality is high. Prices start around £18.

**Chef/s:** Keith Braidwood. **Open:** Wed to Sun L 12 to 1.30 (Sun L Sept to Apr only), Tue to Sat D 7 to 9. **Closed:** 25 and 26 Dec, first 3 weeks Jan, first 2 weeks Sept. **Meals:** Set L Wed to Sat £21 (3 courses), Set D £36 to £40. **Service:** not inc. **Details:** Cards accepted. 24 seats. No music. No mobile phones. Car parking.

## ▌Eriska
# Isle of Eriska

Ledaig, Eriska, PA37 1SD
Tel no: (01631) 720371
www.eriska-hotel.co.uk
**Scottish | £39**
Cooking score: 4

Sitting proud and alone on its island, the Buchanan-Smith family's castellated Victorian house is a sight for sore eyes. The surrounding landscape is bare and rugged, the lush furnishings within creating quite the opposite impression. Robert MacPherson has notched up 20 years of service in the kitchens here, and his classically informed dinner menus have continued to move gracefully with the times. Five courses are the norm, with a soup in second place, and a handsome cheese trolley following dessert. An April dinner kicked off with ravioli of witch sole with pea purée, gazpacho coulis and avocado oil. After a bowl of white onion soup, it was on to Angus beef fillet with celeriac purée, sauced in red wine and shallots, or roast stuffed turkey carved at the table and served with all the expected accoutrements. A range of international house wines starts at £12.50 for an Ardèche Chardonnay and a Rioja. Prices are eminently reasonable throughout.

**Chef/s:** Robert MacPherson. **Open:** all week D only 8 to 9 (L residents only). **Closed:** Jan. **Meals:** Set D £39.50 (6 courses). **Service:** not inc. **Details:** Cards accepted. 50 seats. Air-con. No music. No mobile phones. Wheelchair access. Car parking.

## Fairlie

### Fins

**Enterprising family-run set-up**
Fencefoot Farm, Fairlie, KA29 OEG
Tel no: (01475) 568989
www.fencebay.co.uk
**Seafood | £30**
**Cooking score: 2**

For more than a decade, Bernard and Jill Thain have been nurturing their passion for fish in this fascinating set-up. The whole business takes in a smokehouse, farm shop and a regular farmers' market, in addition to Fins restaurant. Bernard Thain's own boat brings in a useful haul, and printed menus are topped up with a slate of blackboard specials inspired by the day's catch. The kitchen keeps things simple, offering gravlax, moules marinière and Cumbrae oysters ahead of grilled sea bass fillets with warm Mediterranean dressing or seared scallops with dill and smoked salmon sauce. Ginger and Grand Marnier parfait is a typically appealing dessert. The fish-friendly wine list kicks off with house selections at £13.40.
**Chef/s:** Jane Burns and Paul Harvey. **Open:** Tue to Sun L 12 to 2.30, Tue to Sat D 6.30 to 9. **Closed:** 25 and 26 Dec, 1 Jan. **Meals:** alc (main courses L £10 to £18, D £14 to £23). **Service:** not inc. **Details:** Cards accepted. 50 seats. No mobile phones. Wheelchair access. Music. Children's portions. Car parking.

## Glasgow

### Brian Maule at Chardon d'Or

**Classy French restaurant**
176 West Regent Street, Glasgow, G2 4RL
Tel no: (0141) 248 3801
www.brianmaule.com
**French | £40**
**Cooking score: 3**

🍷 ❦

Mr Maule moved home to Scotland after a spell as head chef at Le Gavroche in London and opened the Chardon d'Or back in 2001. Brian and his kitchen brigade are still doing a grand job keeping diners happy and collecting plaudits especially for the bargain that is the pre-theatre menu (Mon to Sat). The dining room is quietly classy and contemporary, and three à la carte courses could start with the simple genius of pea and ham soup, or asparagus with Parmesan and white truffle dressing. Then come mains featuring the likes of pan-fried Scotch sirloin, lamb with saffron-flavoured jus, or roast guinea fowl with ceps. An alternative would be poached mixed fish with choucroute which arrives with leeks and the lift of a neat juniper butter sauce. For dessert the cheese plate is usually acclaimed (French and British) although you could opt for a white chocolate mousse with blueberry compote. Professional service and a good international wine list, with some offerings by the glass from £5.85.
**Chef/s:** Brian Maule. **Open:** Mon to Fri L 12 to 2.30, Mon to Sat D 6 to 10. **Closed:** first 2 weeks Jan, last week July, first week Aug, bank hols. **Meals:** alc (main courses £19.50 to £22.50). Set L and D 6 to 7 £15.50 (2 courses) to £18.50, Set D £48.50. **Service:** not inc. **Details:** Cards accepted. 110 seats. Air-con. Music. Children's portions.

### étain

**Tucked-away venue for a terrific kitchen**
The Glasshouse, Springfield Court, Glasgow, G1 3JX
Tel no: (0141) 225 5630
**Modern European | £30**
**Cooking score: 4**

One of the welcome things about étain is that there is nothing to distract from the food. It may be upstairs in a shopping mall and it may have one wall completely made of glass (giving a view of backstreet Glasgow), but the restaurant still manages to feel tucked away and the décor – modern and discreet – allows due concentration on the output of Neil Clark's kitchen. Having undergone a change of ownership in late 2005, then a change of chef in 2006, Scottish foodies were worried that étain might fade, but this is not the case. Service is slick and Clark's lightness of touch shines through even with the bargain lunch menu. This could bring a simple Bradan

Orach smoked salmon to start with quails' eggs, fennel and lemon emulsion. Mains could involve cod, twice-cooked pork belly, duck, vegetarian risotto, or a perfect fillet of seared sea bream on wilted baby gem lettuce and brandade, with poached leeks. Rhubarb parfait for dessert is highly accomplished and comes with a long shot glass layered with rhubarb and honey mousse; tiny and geometrically perfect cubes of rhubarb to one side hold up a skateboard-shaped biscuit. The wine list has over 150 bins but interest is accompanied by some premium prices and there is little under £20; by the glass from £4.75.

**Chef/s:** Neil Clark. **Open:** Sun to Fri L 12 to 2.30 (3 Sun), Mon to Sat D 5.30 to 10 (10.30 Sat). **Closed:** 25 Dec, 1 Jan. **Meals:** Set L £16 (2 courses) to £29, Set D £26 (2 courses) to £39. **Service:** 12.5% (optional). **Details:** Cards accepted. 60 seats. Air-con. Wheelchair access. Music.

# Gamba

**Signature seafood cooking**
225A West George Street, Glasgow, G2 2ND
Tel no: (0141) 572 0899
www.gamba.co.uk
**Seafood | £39**
**Cooking score: 3**

Alan Tomkins and Derek Marshall are among the most successful restaurateurs in Glasgow. Tomkins himself owns Manna in Bath Street, while the duo also have the Urban Bar & Brasserie in nearby St Vincent Place and the Urban Grill south of the Clyde in Shawlands. The longevity prize among their restaurants goes to Gamba, however, the city's premier seafood destination, described by one reader as 'the ideal venue for that special occasion'. You could start with six oysters on the half-shell, or tuna sashimi with the expected accompaniments (soy, ginger and wasabi). Signature Gamba fish soup with crab, ginger, and prawn dumplings is perhaps the most popular way to kick off a meal. Main courses have the same range and could bring anything from roast monkfish with mussels, lemon and thyme, to Cajun-spiced red mullet with

honey, ginger, and jasmine rice. An effort is made with dessert as anyone who samples their iced lemon parfait with basil-soaked blueberries will testify. The fairly international wine list has a small selection of half-bottles that all come in under £18; wines by the glass from £4.75.

**Chef/s:** Derek Marshall and John Gillespie. **Open:** Mon to Sat 12 to 2.30, 5 to 10.30. **Closed:** 25 and 26 Dec, 1 and 2 Jan **Meals:** alc (main courses £11 to £24). Set L and D 5 to 6 £15.95 (2 courses) to £17.95. **Meals:** Pre-theatre D 5 to 6.15 £16 (3 courses) Set D £39 to £44 (three courses). **Service:** not inc. **Details:** Cards accepted. 66 seats. Air-con. No mobile phones. Music.

# Michael Caines at ABode

The Arthouse, 129 Bath Street, Glasgow, G2 2SZ
Tel no: (0141) 572 6011
www.michaelcaines.com
**Modern European | £40**
**Cooking score: 5**

£5 OFF ⊨ V

A stylish dining room done in restful autumnal hues provides the backdrop for the Scottish outpost of the gastronomically pace-setting ABode hotel group (see Royal Clarence Hotel, Exeter). The modern approach reigns throughout, from the varietally arranged wine list to the separate vegetarian and multi-course tasting menus, the latter of which are in the talented hands of Martin Donnelly. Good Scots ingredients and classical technique combine to produce dishes such as scallop salad with endive marmalade and a reduction of port, or roast quail with a fricassée of artichokes, ceps and spinach. Main courses bring on salmon from Loch Duart, boldly sauced with a horseradish velouté, while wild red deer gets the regal treatment, with caramelised swede, kohlrabi, braised salsify and mixed berries in attendance. There is evidence of genuine culinary innovation on the plate, but equally no reluctance in offering something much more mainstream, in the shape of sirloin steak with fondant potato, mushrooms in cream and a full-throttle Madeira sauce. Sweet wines by the glass are suggested with desserts like caramelised apple mille-feuille with apple sorbet, and there is a highly tempting, predominantly Scottish cheese menu. Nine wines by the glass from £3.95 lead off an adventurous list that is full of inspiration and value. Even the fine wines are not as painfully marked up as they might be. Bottle prices open at £16.50.

**Chef/s:** Martin Donnelly. **Open:** Mon to Sat L 12 to 2.30, D 7 (6.30 Fri and Sat) to 10. **Closed:** 1 Jan, Sundays. **Meals:** alc D (main courses £17.50 to £22.95). Set L £13 (2 courses), Set D £55. **Service:** optional. **Details:** Cards accepted. 40 seats. Air-con. No music. Wheelchair access.

## Rococo

**Sleek and stylish restaurant**
202 West George Street, Glasgow, G2 2NR
Tel no: (0141) 221 5004
www.rococoglasgow.co.uk
**Modern European | £39**
**Cooking score: 3**

£5
OFF

If ever a restaurant begged to be described as 'nice', it is Rococo. This city-centre basement has sparkling ceiling lights, fresh flowers, tasteful artworks and a calming blue theme in its décor. Wine glasses shine and table linen exudes freshness. Pop in for lunch and you might start with mushroom velouté with white truffle oil and thyme croûtons, or perhaps a relatively adventurous carpaccio of tuna crusted with sesame. A main course of pasta with mushrooms and asparagus in herb and mascarpone cream is 'hearty'; other mains could involve blanquette of veal; cured and roasted loin of Ayrshire pork; or cod with a sweet pepper pipérade, vine tomatoes, rocket pesto, lemon and black olive dressing. Desserts include 'a very well crafted' caramelised apple tart, crème Chantilly, and Calvados syrup. The wine list of over 100 bins has some stunning bottles at equally stunning prices; by the glass from £5.50.

**Chef/s:** Mark Tamburrini. **Open:** all week 12 to 2.30, 5 to 10 (10.30 Fri and Sat). **Closed:** 26 Dec, 1 Jan. **Meals:** alc (main courses £11.50 to £18.75) Set L £19.50 (3 courses) Set D £19.50 (3 courses).

**Service:** not inc. **Details:** Cards accepted. 70 seats. Air-con. Wheelchair access. Music. Children's portions. Children allowed.

## 78 St Vincent

**A Parisian-style eaterie that's keen to please**
78 St Vincent Street, Glasgow, G2 5UB
Tel no: (0141) 248 7878
www.78stvincent.com
**Modern Scottish | £27**
**New Chef**

£5
OFF £30

This spacious restaurant retains the 1912 period – soaring vertical columns, marble staircase, and saucy fish tiles – and the ambience is 'enjoyable', its central location 'useful'. It caters with efficient Glaswegian friendliness for all ages: the £5.95 children's menu offers proper chicken goujons and Arran ice cream, while the three-course lunch and pre-theatre menu at £15.95 is excellent value. Choose spanking fresh codling, ribeye steak or lamb's liver with proper hand-cut chips. The sticky toffee pudding and apple pie win plaudits, as does the 'amiable and prompt service'. House wines come by the glass at £3.95.

**Chef/s:** Robbie O'Keefe. **Open:** all week 12 to 4, 4 to 10 (10.30 Fri and Sat). **Meals:** alc (main courses L £7.50 to £11.50, D £12.95 to £23.95). Set L £12.95 (2 courses) to £15.50, Set D Sat £24.95 (2 courses) to £29.95. **Service:** not inc. **Details:** Cards accepted. 120 seats. No music. No mobile phones. Wheelchair access. Children's portions.

## Stravaigin

**A whistle-stop culinary tour**
28 Gibson Street, Glasgow, G12 8NX
Tel no: (0141) 334 2665
www.stravaigin.com
**Global | £28**
**Cooking score: 2**

£5
OFF   V £30

The refurbished Stravaigin, with more comfortable seating and open kitchen, changes menus monthly. Scottish staples – such as haggis – are authentic, but soup of the day may be a glossy wine-red apple and

beetroot served with granary and chilli bread, and West Coast fishcakes are enlivened by a crispy polenta crust. Lovers of fusion cookery should sample the richly spiced Indian Rajastani red lentil dhal, or Marrakesh vegetable tagine with tangy minted couscous. For desserts eschew the steamed puddings and try a hot Scottish rhubarb soup with vanilla snow eggs, or zingy jackfruit and lemongrass jelly with pineapple. An intelligent, keenly priced wine list includes an interesting English selection. House wines start at £13.95. NB Stravaigin 2, operating along similar lines, can be found at 8 Ruthven Lane.
**Chef/s:** Daniel Blencowe. **Open:** all week 12 to 5, 5 to 11. **Closed:** 25 Dec, 1 Jan. **Meals:** alc (main courses £12 to £24). Set L and D 5 to 7 (6.30 Sat) £11.95 (2 courses) to £13.95. Café/bar menu available. **Service:** not inc. **Details:** Cards accepted. 70 seats. Air-con. Music. Children's portions.

## Ubiquitous Chip
**Long-standing**
12 Ashton Lane, Glasgow, G12 8SJ
Tel no: (0141) 334 5007
www.ubiquitouschip.co.uk
**Scottish | £30**
**Cooking score: 4**

The Chip is not simply a restaurant but more a complex of interconnected venues including a main diner (with indoors area as well as covered, cobbled courtyard), an upstairs brasserie (with seating indoors and on the courtyard mezzanine) and at last count three separate bars. An icon of Scottish cuisine since 1971, it long ago earned its status as 'an institution'. You could sit in one of the bars and opt for food like beef stovies or crayfish cocktail, but most people want to sample that unique courtyard with its foliage, water feature and Bohemian garden atmosphere. At dinner, its menu offers starters such as venison haggis with mashed potato and garlic (vegetarian version available), pan-fried scallops on rösti, or oxtail sausage with yellow split pea pudding. The sheer Scottishness level is cranked up on main courses like Scrabster-landed lythe on clapshot with chilli roasted red pepper and grape sauce, or Perthshire pigeon roasted in bacon, wild mushroom sauce, game sauce and barley risotto. The cheese selection swings by Caledonian classics (Lanark Blue, Isle of Mull Cheddar, goats' milk cheeses from Gigha and Ayrshire, and more), while dessert could entail a signature oatmeal ice cream with fruit compote, or a whisky mac parfait with rhubarb. The wine list is wide, deep and frankly astonishing, in a good way; by the glass from £4.
**Chef/s:** Ian Brown. **Open:** all week 12 to 2.30 (12.30 to 3 Sun), 5.30 (6.30 Sun) to 11. **Closed:** 25 Dec, 1 Jan. **Meals:** Set L Mon to Sat £22.80 (2 courses) to £28.65, Set L Sun £17.95 (inc wine), Set D £33.80 (2 courses) to £38.95. Bar and brasserie menus available. **Service:** not inc. **Details:** Cards accepted. 180 seats. Air-con. No music. Wheelchair access. Children's portions.

## READERS RECOMMEND

### Dakhin
**Indian/Pakistani/Bangladeshi**
89 Candleriggs, Glasgow, G1 1NP
Tel no: (0141) 553 2585
www.dakhin.com
'South Indian cooking in Glasgow, with dosas!'

### Kember & Jones
**Modern European**
134 Byres Road, Glasgow, G12 8TD
Tel no: 0141 337 3851
www.kemberandjones.co.uk
'Brilliant delicatessen with a knockout café'

### The Sisters Kelvingrove
**Scottish**
36 Kelvingrove Street, Glasgow, G3 7RZ
Tel no: (0141) 564 1157
www.sistersrestaurant.com
'Chic but informal in the West End'

# Oban

## Ee-Usk
A harbourside favourite
North Pier, Oban, PA34 5QD
Tel no: (01631) 565666
www.eeusk.com
Seafood | £30
Cooking score: 1

'Fantastic fresh fish cooked to perfection,' was one reporter's straightforward assessment of this waterfront restaurant. The kitchen keeps things simple, allowing the top-quality seafood to speak for itself. This means starters of dressed local crab, sweet-tasting langoustines with chilli and ginger, or smoked haddock pot, while mains typically include a platter of halibut, monkfish and sea bass with parsley sauce and mash, or baked halibut with creamed leeks and sautéed potatoes. Classic battered haddock and chips is a regular option, and non-fish eaters are offered steak. Desserts are comforting favourites such as sticky toffee pudding or hot clootie dumpling. Good value wines from £11.95.
Chef/s: Wayne Keenan. Open: all week 12 to 3, 6 to 9.30 (9 in winter). Closed: 25 and 26 Dec, 1 Jan. Meals: alc (main courses £9 to £29.50). Service: not inc. Details: Cards accepted. 104 seats. 24 seats outside. Air-con. No mobile phones. Wheelchair access. Music.

## ALSO RECOMMENDED
## ▲ Waterfront
1 The Railway Pier, Oban, PA34 4LW
Tel no: (01631) 563110
www.waterfrontoban.co.uk

Chef Alex Needham now doubles as one of the owners of this lively seafood restaurant. A new seafood bar below stairs is open for daytime meals and extra seats have been added outside. The owners' boats provide much of the catch, and the kitchen sends out a lively assortment of dishes along the lines of scallops with beetroot risotto and tarragon olive oil (£8.75), haddock and chips, and sea bass fillet with shellfish minestrone (£17.50). Finish

with sticky toffee pudding (£4.25). Good-value wines from £13.50. Open all week; closed 25 Dec to early Feb.

# Port Appin

## Airds Hotel
Rigorously rendered meals in a remote location
Port Appin, PA38 4DF
Tel no: (01631) 730236
www.airds-hotel.com
Modern Scottish | £45
Cooking score: 5
£5 OFF  🍷  ⊨  V

This restaurant is set in an upmarket hotel in the tiny hamlet of Port Appin. You can look out over the Lynn of Lorne to the island of Lismore, the mountains of Mull and Morvern beyond. If that fails to make you happy, chef Paul Burns cranks up the assault of sheer loveliness with his skilled Franco-Scots cooking, making this one of Scotland's great all-round foodie excursions (or neighbourhood eateries if you live between Oban and Fort William). The hotel dining room is a polite affair and also has great views from the window seats, while dinner involves four courses. Local Lismore oysters are an obvious starter (au naturel or with herb velouté) but an alternative would be a deft confit of duck leg with parsnip purée, potato wafer, prune and apple. Then comes an intense tomato and rosemary soup, followed by sea bass, lamb or halibut perhaps – the latter lightly grilled in citrus juices with wilted wild leeks and garlic. Warm date pudding with butterscotch sauce could finish. Under the ownership of the McKivragans, service still combines professionalism and the personal touch. The ample wine list is good on France; by the glass from £4.95.
Chef/s: Paul Burns. Open: all week 12 to 1.45, 7.30 to 9. Closed: 2 days each week Dec to Jan, 5 to 22 Jan. Meals: alc L (main courses £16 to £17.50). Set D £49.50 (7 courses).. Service: not inc. Details: Cards accepted. 32 seats. 12 seats outside. No music. No mobile phones.

## John Campbell

**Why did you become a chef?**
I've never wanted to do anything else, and I feel I've never worked a day in my life. I'm very lucky.

**Which of today's chefs do you admire?**
The obvious Heston Blumenthal, also Phil Howard. Anyone who doesn't chase accolades.

**Where do you eat out?**
Home mostly. You can't beat it.

**Where do you source your ingredients?**
Good suppliers who guarantee provenance, livestock husbandry etc. We also take as many products directly from the wild as we can; we shoot deer, trap crayfish, collect flowers and berries, watercress, and wild mushrooms. The list is endless.

**What's your favourite cookery book?**
I don't have one, my inspiration comes from author Paulo Coelho.

**What's the best dish you've ever eaten?**
My Nan's red lentil soup.

**Who would you invite to your ideal dinner party?**
Winston Churchill, Tony Blair, Marco Pierre-White, Simon Cowell, Jonathan Ross, and my father.

**Which are your proudest achievements?**
My son and daughter.

## READERS RECOMMEND
## The Russian Tavern
**Eastern European**
37 Marine Road, Port Bannatyne, PA20 0LW
Tel no: (01700) 505073
www.butehotel.com
'Blinis and latkas on Bute!'

## The Sorn Inn
**Modern European**
35 Main Street, KA5 6HU, Sorn, KA5 6HU
Tel no: (01290) 551305
www.sorninn.com
'Amazing standards for a roadside inn'

## ▌Troon
## MacCallums Oyster Bar
**No-frills seafood restaurant on the quay**
The Harbour, Troon, KA10 6DH
Tel no: (01292) 319339
**Seafood | £42**
**Cooking score: 2**

Set a course for Troon harbour to find the MacCallum brothers' oyster bar in a sympathetically converted building close to where the fishing boats tie up. A bowl of Cullen skink or a plate of langoustines with garlic butter could start things off in simple fashion, before seared king scallops with celeriac purée and truffle dressing or grilled fillet of halibut with squat lobster and tarragon sauce. Fish and chips features at lunchtime, while a 'catch of the day' is added in the evening. To finish, there are homespun desserts in the raspberry crème brûlée/sticky toffee pudding mould. House wines start at £12.65.
**Chef/s:** Ewan and Craig McAllister. **Open:** Tue to Sun L 12 to 2.30 (3.30 Sun), Tue to Sat D 6.30 to 9.30.
**Meals:** alc (main courses £9.50 to £26.50).
**Service:** not inc. **Details:** Cards accepted. 43 seats. Wheelchair access. Music. Car parking.

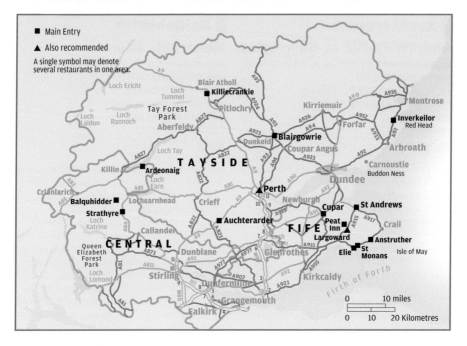

- ■ Main Entry
- ▲ Also recommended

A single symbol may denote several restaurants in one area.

# ■ Ardeonaig
## Ardeonaig Hotel
**A multi-cultural mixture**
Ardeonaig, FK21 8SU
Tel no: (01567) 820400
www.ardeonaighotel.co.uk
**South African/Scottish | £26**
Cooking score: 4

£5 OFF | ⊨ V £30

A bumpy ride along a single-track road on the southern shore of Loch Tay brings you to the vision in white that is the Ardeonaig. Across the loch, Ben Lawers glowers, but within, all is as comfortable as can be, the armchairs in the lounge as soft as the dining-room linen is crisp. The deal is prime Scottish fare, lightly filtered through the prism of chef-proprietor Pete Gottgens's native South Africa. Extensive local fishing rights bring plenty of lake and river fare on to the menu, and there are rare delights, such as local hare with shallots and Puy lentils, or braised shoulder of hogget (the elder sibling of lamb) with sweet potato and a rosemary jus. Bookending these enterprising main courses might be a salad of hand-picked spider crab, or smoked Scrabster haddock with braised leeks in mustard, and the house speciality, chocolate mielie pudding. A Franco-Scottish cheese selection comes with home-made walnut bread. Staff are exceedingly personable, yet professional. The wine list is exclusively South African a bold, persuasive initiative. Sparkling wines made by the champagne method, a roll-call of fine producers – many of them unavailable elsewhere – and some of the Cape's best sticky-pudding wines (all offered by the glass), add up to quite a treasure-trove. Prices start at £19.50.

**Chef/s:** Pete Gottgens. **Open:** all week L 12 to 2.30, D 7 to 8.45. **Meals:** Set L and D £26.50. Bistro menu available (main courses £5 to £16). **Service:** not inc. **Details:** Cards accepted. 60 seats. 50 seats outside. Air-con. No mobile phones. Wheelchair access. Music. Car parking.

## ▌Auchterarder

### Andrew Fairlie at Gleneagles

Highly accomplished cooking in a luxury hotel
Auchterarder, PH3 1NF
Tel no: (01764) 694267
www.andrewfairlie.com
French | £55
Cooking score: 7

Fully refurbished in January 2007, Andrew Fairlie's eponymous restaurant within the opulent confines of the luxury Gleneagles Hotel remains a calming and professionally run operation. All around may speak of expense-account corporatism, but the restaurant remains a must-go destination. What awaits you is sleek, imaginative cooking presented with great artistry and gloss. Dishes are headlined in the now familiar way with their main ingredient — lobster, lamb, pineapple — and there are tasting and market menus for those who find themselves unable to choose. Scallops baked in the shell are teamed with caramelised garlic and a lemongrass velouté, or there could be the relative simplicity of wild mushroom ravioli dressed in black truffle butter. Fish come dressed to impress, the sea bass in a crusting of pistachios, for example, while meats are a full roll-call of various parts of their respective anatomies. Pork comes as roasted fillet, braised cheek, confit belly and black pudding, while lamb consists of roasted loin and kidney and braised shoulder. That pineapple for dessert is sliced carpaccio-thin, and dressed with iced coconut and a lychee sorbet. A plate of citrus variations embraces soufflé, mille-feuille, sorbet and salad. Uniformed staff do well to dispel any over-formality. Wines are energetically marked up high from the get-go, with nothing below £25, although there is a range by the glass.
Chef/s: Andrew Fairlie and Stephen McLaughlin. Open: Mon to Sat D only 6.30 to 10. Closed: 24 and 25 Dec, 3 weeks Jan. Meals: Set D £65 to £85. Service: not inc. Details: Cards accepted. 52 seats. Air-con. No mobile phones. Wheelchair access. Music. Car parking.

## ▌Balquhidder

### Monachyle Mhor

Cosmopolitan food in a remote setting
Balquhidder, FK19 8PQ
Tel no: (01877) 384622
www.monachylemhor.com
Modern Scottish | £46
Cooking score: 5

Follow the single-track road that winds along the fringes of Loch Voil and through the Braes of Balquhidder to find the Lewis family's remote country house. Monachyle Mhor is part of a 2,000-acre estate including a working farm and two lakes frequented by anglers. Tom Lewis revels in abundant supplies of home-grown organic produce and the generosity of Balquhidder's natural larder. His cooking is full of clever twists, neat touches and deft gestures: a Kyle of Tongue oyster topped with crème fraîche appears as an amuse-bouche; a spring truffle boudin accompanies Gressingham duck breast; while loin of red deer is partnered by a chicory and walnut gratin, chard, red cabbage and Madeira sauce. Other dishes have noticeable Far Eastern overtones (Thai vegetable spring rolls with carrot and ginger purée and pineapple chilli chutney, for example), while desserts revert to the deep-rooted European tradition of chocolate terrine 'Negus' with Glenturret whisky ice cream. The varietally arranged wine list is supplemented by a cluster of self-styled 'oddballs' (Massaya Classic 2004 from Bekaa Valley, Lebanon, for example). House recommendations start at £17 (£4 a glass).
Chef/s: Tom Lewis and Shaun Hall. Open: all week 12 to 1.45, 7 to 8.45. Closed: Jan. Meals: alc L (main courses £15 to £17). Set L Sun £31, Set D £46 (5 courses). Service: not inc. Details: Cards accepted. 40 seats. 16 seats outside. No mobile phones. Wheelchair access. Music. Children's portions. Car parking.

## READERS RECOMMEND

### The Inn At Kippen

Gastropub
Fore Road, Kippen, FK8 3DT
Tel no: (01786) 871010
www.theinnatkippen.co.uk
'The pub grub you get in heaven'

 **Strathyre**

### Creagan House

Enthusiastic cooking and warm hospitality
Strathyre, FK18 8ND
Tel no: (01877) 384638
www.creaganhouse.co.uk
French | £23
Cooking score: 4

Aiden Byrne

A welcoming restaurant-with-rooms converted from a one-time seventeenth-century farmhouse, Creagan is run with enthusiasm by the Gunns. Their mock-baronial dining room – with grand fireplace and vaulted ceiling – can seem a little echoey with just 14 covers, but there's simply no doubting the dedication here. Proceedings kick off with everyone arriving in the lounge for drinks at 7.30 for dinner at 8pm. But, in contrast to all the convention, Gordon's cooking takes an unexpected modern approach. The repertoire is driven by quality produce from the abundant Scottish larder. Take the likes of a collop of Glen Artney venison teamed with a sandwich of black pudding, apple and passion-fruit purée, foie gras and a juniper and port-wine sauce. The French-led and inspired globetrotting list has plenty of drinking under £20, a commendable range of halves, plus eight house wines available by bottle (from £11.25), carafe and glass.
**Chef/s:** Gordon Gunn. **Open:** Fri to Wed (Fri to Mon from 24 Nov to 24 Dec) D only 7.30 (1 sitting). **Closed:** 5 to 23 Nov, 21 Jan to 9 Mar. **Meals:** Set D £22.50 to £29.50. **Service:** not inc. **Details:** Cards accepted. 14 seats. No music. No mobile phones. Wheelchair access. Car parking.

*Why did you become a chef?*
It was the first thing I fell in love with.

*Which of today's chefs do you admire?*
Tom Aikens.

*Where do you eat out?*
The Square, Tom Aikens, Sketch, the Fat Duck.

*Where do you source your ingredients?*
Mainly from the British Isles, and my favourite producer is Richard Vine from R.V. Salads.

*What's your favourite cookery book?*
I would have to say *L'Encyclopedia Culinaire du XXIe Siecle* by Marc Veyrat.

*What's the best dish you've ever eaten?*
Probably Heston Blumenthal's salmon with liquorice.

*Do you have a favourite local recipe?*
Being based in London you don't really get local recipes, but I do love the asparagus season.

*What's the hardest thing about running a restaurant?*
Keeping the staff motivated 18 hours a day.

*What's coming up next for you?*
A cookery book and hopefully more accolades.

# Anstruther

## Cellar

**Skilled simplicity with impeccable sourcing**
24 East Green, Anstruther, KY10 3AA
Tel no: (01333) 310378
**Modern Seafood | £27**
Cooking score: 6

Little seems to have changed during the 26 years that Peter Jukes has been serving up fresh fish at his stone-built restaurant by the harbour. Seafood has its seasons and this gives structure to menus. Combinations are well-considered and perfectly balanced, with shellfish and smoked fish permeating starters, whether diver-caught sea scallops served simply with leaves and herb and garlic butter or dressed local crab with lemon mayonnaise. Main courses revolve around the likes of grilled halibut with greens, smoked bacon, pine nuts and basil mash (something of a signature dish), or seared fillet of John Dory on crushed olive, oregano and mint potatoes, served with pak choi and niçoise dressing. A pavlova, filled with local soft fruit and served with a pink champagne purée, sums up the Cellar's ethos – exemplifying the simple, fresh, seasonal approach to the entire menu. The wine list highlights excellent producers throughout France and the global tour that follows. Reasonable prices start at £5.50 for a glass and £18.50 for a bottle.
**Chef/s:** Peter Jukes. **Open:** Wed to Sat L at 1, Tue to Sat D 7 to 9.30. **Closed:** 24 to 27 Dec. **Meals:** Set L £17.50 (2 courses) to £22.50, Set D £31.50 (2 courses) to £36.50. **Service:** not inc. **Details:** Cards accepted. 40 seats.

## READERS RECOMMEND

### The Anstruther Fish Bar

**Seafood**
42-44 Shore Street, Anstruther, KY10 3AQ
Tel no: (01333) 310518
www.anstrutherfishbar.co.uk
'Fantastic fish and chips'

# Cupar

## Ostlers Close

**Neighbourhood restaurant with deep roots**
25 Bonnygate, Cupar, KY15 4BU
Tel no: (01334) 655574
www.ostlersclose.co.uk
**Modern Scottish | £32**
Cooking score: 5

In the centre of this small market town lies a stone-built cottage-restaurant. Here, for 27 years, husband and wife team Jimmy and Amanda Graham have produced food that is underpinned by fine local and regional ingredients, including their own-grown herbs, soft fruits and vegetables and foraged wild food. According to one regular visitor, everything is 'very precisely cooked but not served in a pretentious way'. Ideas are straightforward and well-conceived, and dishes can be dead simple, say a starter of scallops with sultanas, pine nuts and crispy Serrano ham. Roast saddle of lamb, a main course, might be served with its shoulder done as a confit with rosemary lyonnaise potatoes and roast root vegetables, or there could be a selection of Pittenween seafood with boulangère potatoes, buttered leeks and a champagne butter sauce. Desserts, such as steamed apricot syrup sponge served with a cream custard don't let the side down either. The focus on quality sourcing carries on to the drinks list, where a host of good producers mingles under the banners of Europe and the New World. Prices are very fair, with house Chilean at £16. NB Children must be over 6 to have dinner.
**Chef/s:** Jimmy Graham. **Open:** Sat L 12.15 to 1.30, Tue to Sat D 7 to 9.30. **Closed:** 25 and 26 Dec, 1 and 2 Jan, 2 weeks Easter, 2 weeks Oct. **Meals:** alc (main courses L £10.50 to £15, D £18 to £19.50). **Service:** not inc. **Details:** Cards accepted. 26 seats. No music. No mobile phones. Wheelchair access.

# Elie

## Sangster's
**Idiosyncratic cooking**
51 High Street, Elie, KY9 1BZ
Tel no: (01333) 331001
www.sangsters.co.uk
British | £32
Cooking score: 5

Bruce Sangster is used to commanding large brigades and competing at high culinary levels. Today, he cooks on his own in this small yet spacious restaurant. In recent years, he has been taken by the 'water bath' method of cooking, so when he offers slow-cooked fillet of salmon, it's cooked for an hour at 46°C. There is a nod to the combination of prime and tougher cuts in one dish, but the cooking method is anything but conventional, with the prime cuts cooked for a long period, such as roast rump and braised shoulder of lamb. The accompanying vegetables may not carry the same concentration of the main idea, but are flavorsome none the less. Convention returns with a light chocolate and maple syrup tart and a quivering pannacotta with strawberries. The wine list is reasonable. Bruce's mark-up of £10 a bottle makes a bargain of Cloudy Bay at £30. House wines start at £15.
**Chef/s:** Bruce Sangster. **Open:** Wed to Fri and Sun L 12.30 to 1.45, Tue to Sat D 7 to 9.30. **Closed:** 25 and 26 Dec, first 3 weeks Jan. **Meals:** Set L £16.75 (2 courses) to £18.75, Set D £25 (2 courses) to £32.50. **Service:** not inc. **Details:** Cards accepted. 28 seats. No music. No mobile phones. Wheelchair access.

## ALSO RECOMMENDED

### ▲ Inn at Lathones
Largoward, KY9 1JE
Tel no: (01334) 840494
www.theinn.co.uk

Chef Marc Guibert has returned to this former coaching inn, which dates from 1603. However, as the Guide went to press the inn was in 'serious expansion' mode with the building of some 15 decidedly upmarket bedrooms, doubling the number of rooms offered. Tartare of cured trout served on toast with crème fraîche and caviar (£7.50) and grilled lamb cutlets with celeriac purée (£24) are typical choices, or there's the more complicated 'trilogy' menu with tripartite dishes at each course, finishing perhaps with dark chocolate truffle sorbet with iced honey nougat and chilled fennel parfait. 'Personal, friendly' service has been praised. House wine is £14. Open daily. More reports please.

## READERS RECOMMEND

## The Wee Restaurant
**Modern European**
17 Main Street, North Queensferry, KY11 1JG
Tel no: (01383) 616263
www.theweerestaurant.co.uk
'Small is definitely better in this instance'

# Peat Inn

★NEW ENTRY★
## Peat Inn
**A new lease of life**
Peat Inn, KY15 5LH
Tel no: (01334) 840206
Modern British | £32
New Chef

A new broom in the shape of Geoffrey Smeddle has taken over the Peat Inn. The fire now burns instead of smoulders. Menus are inventive and seasonally aware; a late-May menu of the day brought risotto of asparagus garnished with pea sprouts and a well-executed braised daube of pork, wilted greens, glazed onions and Puy lentil dressing. First courses brought a soft-poached duck egg with globe artichokes, with a sprightly salad including sweet cicely; all beautifully judged. A main course of roast and braised lamb, polenta and broad beans reflected the trend of prime cuts along with cheaper cuts cooked in different ways. Puddings were not a strong

point at inspection, but the cheese trolley, from Iain Mellis, is excellent. A choice of house wines are available from £5.50 a glass.
**Chef/s:** Geoffrey Smeddle. **Open:** Tue to Sat L 12.30 to 2, D 7.30 to 9. **Meals:** Set L £16, Set D £32. **Service:** not inc

## St Andrews
## Seafood Restaurant
**Dramatic setting**
The Scores, Bruce Embankment, St Andrews, KY16 9AB
Tel no: (01334) 479475
www.theseafoodrestaurant.com
**Modern Seafood | £45**
**Cooking score: 4**
🍶

Younger sibling to the Seafood Restaurant at St Monans (see entry), this high-roller is perched dramatically like a glass box on the St Andrews' sea wall overlooking the waters of the North Sea. The kitchen takes a fashion-conscious view of things, offering crab and salmon sushi with wasabi, pickled mooli and red pepper syrup as a first course. Main courses are in similar modish vein; witness grilled fillet of John Dory with braised oxtail, wilted greens, truffle and pea foam or seared monkfish partnered by curried lentils, braised celery and curry cream. Desserts have included praline parfait with pineapple sorbet as well as dark chocolate torte with vanilla emulsion and fennel ice cream. The comprehensive wine list does an extensive trek across the European regions before a whistlestop tour of the New World. Rare 'cellar wines' add some extra weight to the list and eight house selections start at £18 (£5 a glass).
**Chef/s:** Craig Millar, Neil Clarke and Scott Miller. **Open:** all week 12 to 2.30 (12.30 to 3 Sun), 6.30 to 10. **Closed:** 25 and 26 Dec, 1 Jan. **Meals:** Set L £22 (2 courses) to £26, Set D £45. **Service:** not inc. **Details:** Cards accepted. 25 seats. Air-con. No music. No mobile phones. Wheelchair access. Children's portions.

## St Monans
## Seafood Restaurant
**Stunning views**
16 West End, St Monans, KY10 2BX
Tel no: (01333) 730327
www.theseafoodrestaurant.com
**Seafood | £36**
**Cooking score: 5**
🍶

Overlooking the rocky harbour entrance, with vistas looking out across the water to Bass Rock and the Isle of May, this classy venue has made the leap from fisherman's cottage to chic contemporary bar/restaurant. Diligently sourced seafood is at the centre of things here. Warm crab tart might be served as a starter with herb salad and sweetcorn purée, while the kitchen's take on traditional Cullen skink involves gilding it with pink peppercorn and coriander butter. Main courses pick up the theme by offering collops of monkfish with leek and pancetta risotto or giving roast fillet of cod a shot in the arm with crayfish mash and spring onion velouté. Those who prefer meat ought be be assuaged by the prospect of roast fillet of beef with a ragoût of mushrooms and Savoy cabbage. Desserts are rich confections in the comforting mould of dark chocolate tart with caramelised oranges, baked lime cheesecake with blueberries and flaked almonds or warm vanilla sponge. The premier-league wine list has been astutely tailored to the piscine thrust of the menu, with particular strong showings from France, Spain and Germany (note the remarkable Riesling 'Dönnhoff', Schlossböckelheim 2004). House selections start at £17 a bottle (£4.50 a glass).
**Chef/s:** Craig Millar and Andrew Simpson. **Open:** all week L 12 (12.30 Sun) to 3, D 6.30 to 10. **Closed:** 25 and 26 Dec, 1 Jan, Mon and Tue Oct to May. **Meals:** Set L £24 (3 courses). Set D £35 (3 courses). **Service:** not inc. **Details:** Cards accepted. 40 seats. 20 seats outside. No music. No mobile phones. Wheelchair access. Car parking.

## ■ Blairgowrie

### Kinloch House Hotel

Elaborate modern cooking
Blairgowrie, PH10 6SG
Tel no: (01250) 884237
www.kinlochhouse.com
**Modern European | £37**
Cooking score: 5

Built in 1840 for a 'nouveau riche' family in the once-fashionable jute trade, this creeper-clad mansion stands in 25 acres of wooded grounds. The kitchen makes ample use of local game, Angus beef and produce from the hotel's enclosed Victorian garden. Straightforward lunches of, say, fillet and belly of pork with leeks, fondant potato and Madeira sauce give way to more elaborate fixed-price dinner menus fronted by dishes like seared scallops with lemon purée, herb tortellini and salsa verde. A mid-course soup might precede mains with a red-blooded, carnivorous tendency: roast loin of lamb with seared kidney, spinach, roast garlic and rosemary sauce, or Gressingham duck breast with rösti, plum tarte Tatin, prune and apple sauce, for example. Desserts are in the classic mould of caramel parfait with orange syrup or date and walnut pudding with toffee sauce. The prestigious wine list has something to please most palates and preferences, with vintage Burgundies dating back to 1990 leading the pack. House selections are from £20.50 a bottle, with other options from £6.50 a glass.
**Chef/s:** Andrew May. **Open:** all week 12 to 2, 7 to 9. **Closed:** 15 to 29 Dec. **Meals:** Set L £18.50 (2 courses). Set D £45 (4 courses). Light bar L menu available. **Service:** not inc. **Details:** Cards accepted. 40 seats. No music. No mobile phones. Wheelchair access. Jacket and tie required. Children's portions. Car parking.

## ■ Inverkeilor

### Gordon's

Finely crafted, modern food
32 Main Street, Inverkeilor, DD11 5RN
Tel no: (01241) 830364
www.gordonsrestaurant.co.uk
**Modern Scottish | £34**
Cooking score: 5

Three members of the Watson family run the show at this inviting restaurant-with-rooms in a tiny village not far from Lunan Bay. Maria oversees the front-of-house with welcoming good humour, while Gordon and son Garry work the stoves. One correspondent was particulary impressed by the owners' willingness to share culinary ideas; in fact, the whole set-up feels rather like an informal French auberge. Dinner might begin with a twice-baked soufflé of Isle of Mull Tobermory Cheddar or tender wood pigeon, cooked pink and served on a textbook cep and chive risotto with Pinot Noir jus. Next comes an expertly crafted little soup, perhaps cauliflower and Maris Piper velouté with white truffle foam. Main courses show off the kitchen's loyalty to Scottish produce, as in slow-cooked fillet of Black Faced lamb with pea and mint mousse, truffle mash and onion marmalade or wild sea trout on a potato galette with sweetcorn and mussel fricassee. A pleasantly surprising pre-dessert of, say, lemon mousse and raspberry sorbet, might precede comforting Baileys croissant butter pudding with crème anglaise. The well-chosen, helpfully annotated wine list is arranged by grape. House selections are £12.95 (£4.25 a glass) and most bottles will leave change from £25.
**Chef/s:** Gordon and Garry Watson. **Open:** Wed to Fri and Sun L 12 to 1.45, Tue to Sat D 7 to 9. **Closed:** 2 weeks Jan. **Meals:** Set L £26 (3 courses), Set D £39 (4 courses). **Service:** not inc. **Details:** Cards accepted. 24 seats. No music. No mobile phones. Wheelchair access. Children's portions. Car parking.

## ▌Killiecrankie

### Killiecrankie House
**Dependable modern food**
Killiecrankie, PH16 5LG
Tel no: (01796) 473220
www.killiecrankiehotel.co.uk
**Modern European | £31**
Cooking score: 3

£5 OFF 🍷 ⊨ V

Set in secluded grounds at the entrance to the
Pass of Killiecrankie, Tim and Maillie Waters'
converted Victorian manse has beautiful views
over wooded valleys and the River Garry.
Mark Easton has been running the kitchen for
more than a decade and has honed a style that
depends on reliable Scottish supply lines. A
terrine of duck, hare and port is served with
onion chutney. Crisp-skinned fillets of sea
bass come with an asparagus tartlet, saffron
potatoes and sunblush tomato butter sauce,
while roast boned quail is stuffed with apricot
and pine-nut mousse. Warm raspberry and
frangipane flan is a typical dessert. Tim Waters
spent many years in the wine trade and has
assembled a dazzling personal list. Prices start
at £14.90 (£3.90 a glass).
**Chef/s:** Mark Easton. **Open:** all week D only 6.15 to
8.15. **Closed:** Jan. **Meals:** Set D £31 (3 courses). Bar
L and D menu available. **Service:** not inc.
**Details:** Cards accepted. 30 seats. No music. No
mobile phones. Wheelchair access. Car parking.

## ALSO RECOMMENDED
### ▲ 63 Tay Street
63 Tay Street, Perth, PH2 8NN
Tel no: (01738) 441451
www.63taystreet.co.uk

A new team headed by chef/co-proprietor,
Graeme Pallister, is now at the helm of
this neighbourhood restaurant close to the
river, but exciting modern food with global
influences is still the order of the day. Fixed-
price menus (from £15 lunch, from £28
dinner) promise challenging dishes such as
aromatic pig's belly and chilli-fried squid salad
with crab butter tortellini, 'poach-roast' corn-
fed chicken with wild garlic and foie gras
boudin and a spring pea risotto, plus desserts
including roast pineapple pannacotta with
passion fruit and lime sorbet. Well-chosen
wines from £12.45. Open Tue to Sat. Reports
please.

## READERS RECOMMEND
### Apron Stage
**Modern British**
5 King Street, Stanley, PH1 4ND
Tel no: (01738) 828 888
**'Small, but perfectly formed, riverside
restaurant'**

## Symbols

⊨ Accommodation is available.

£30 Three courses for less than £30.

V More than five vegetarian dishes.

£5 OFF £5-off voucher scheme.

🍷 Notable wine list.

## ■ **Aberdeen**

### **Silver Darling**

A beacon for culinary dexterity
Pocra Quay, North Pier, Aberdeen, AB11 5DQ
Tel no: (01224) 576229
**Seafood | £41**
**Cooking score: 6**

The Silver Darling has an iconic position both as a place to eat and because of its harbour location. The dining room occupies a modern conservatory on the first floor of the old customs house on the landward side of the north pier. The only drawback may be the dubious aspects of its neighbourhood, which has raised comment from readers. Either way, Silver Darling is an affectionate old name for herring, so seafood is the main attraction, in chef Didier Dejean's accomplished French style. The dining room has smart but simple décor, with a central bar feature, and dinner could start with seared king scallops with a barigoule of baby vegetables and green pesto on toast. Mains could bring grilled beef with mascarpone polenta or more appropriately a steamed fillet of halibut with fondue of leeks and cockles, squid-ink tagliatelle, champagne velouté, and a poached oyster with Avruga. Roast monkfish, steamed sea bass, or pan-fried swordfish regularly feature and there is usually a catch of the day. Whisky iced parfait, or dark chocolate delice with salted caramel and caramel ice cream might be for dessert. The wine list is good on France, has over 50 bins and is sold by the glass from £4.20.
**Chef/s:** Didier Dejean. **Open:** Mon to Fri L 12 to 1.30, Mon to Sat D 7 to 9.30. **Closed:** 2 weeks Christmas to New Year. **Meals:** alc (main courses L £10.50 to £11.50, D £19.50 to £21.50). **Service:** not inc, 10% for parties of 10 or more. **Details:** Cards accepted. 50 seats. Music.

## ALSO RECOMMENDED

## ▲ Archiestown Hotel

Archiestown, AB38 7QL
Tel no: (01340) 810218

Right on the Whisky Trail, the Archiestown
Hotel is an elegant eighteenth-century stone
manor house. There is local produce in
evidence on the menu, combined with the odd
Asian influence. For lunch, start with coconut
crab cakes with chilli and lime (£6.50), then
cottage pie with a herbed cheese crust (£8.50);
at dinner, venison terrine with local oatcakes
(£7.50), and fillet steak with mushroom and
tarragon compote (£22). Puddings include
golden syrup sponge with custard (£5.50).
House wines are £17. Accommodation. Open
all week.

## ▎Ballater

## Balgonie Country House

Refined setting and food in the Dee valley
Braemar Place, Ballater, AB35 5NQ
Tel no: (013397) 55482
www.balgonie-hotel.co.uk
Modern Scottish | £40
Cooking score: 4

This grand, ivy-clad Edwardian country
house in the splendid setting of the Dee valley
is a true haven of peace and tranquillity, and is
fitted out in luxurious style. Four-course
dinners in the restaurant are in tune with the
refined mood of the place, with daily-
changing menus making good use of first-rate
local materials in a modern, international style
of cooking. Start perhaps with a creamy,
lightly curried parsnip and apple soup or
maybe game terrine with cranberry chutney,
before a fish course, typically collops of
monkfish on black pudding with blood
orange oil. A trio of main course options
might feature Aberdeen Angus beef fillet with
sautéed potatoes, wild mushrooms and red-
wine jus, alongside Gressingham duck breast
with glazed beetroot, roast sweet potato and
game jus. To finish, try hot chocolate fondant

with Amaretto ice cream, or choose from an
impressive range of Scottish and Irish cheeses,
from Isle of Gigha Cheddar to Babbity blue
and soft, creamy Wee Wummle. The major
French regions account for around half the
wine list, though there are also interesting
bottles from other countries. Prices start just
under £20.
Chef/s: John Finnie. Open: all week 12 to 2
(reservations only), 7 to 9. Closed: 6 Jan to mid Mar.
Meals: Set L £25, Set D £40. Service: not inc.
Details: Cards accepted. 30 seats. Wheelchair
access. Music. Children allowed. Car parking.

## Darroch Learg

Assured modern cooking
Braemar Road, Ballater, AB35 5UX
Tel no: (013397) 55443
www.darrochlearg.co.uk
Modern Scottish | £45
Cooking score: 6

A fixture of the Royal Deeside landscape since
it was built in 1888, Darroch Learg is a fine-
looking baronial edifice perched on high
ground overlooking Ballater and
Craigendarroch. It is a substantial house full of
spacious panelled rooms, with much attention
focused on the conservatory-style restaurant.
David Mutter has been cooking here for more
than a decade and has developed a reliable
network of local suppliers over the years. He
serves wood pigeon as a starter with fig jam
and a foie gras and shallot pie, and sends out
loin of Deeside venison with caramelised red
cabbage, Scottish black pudding and goats'
cheese gnocchi. His fixed-price dinner menus
also highlight fish from Aberdeen market in
the shape of, say, pan-fried scallops with
cauliflower, smoked salmon and capers or
roast monkfish with peas, pomme purée,
chorizo, garlic and parsley velouté. Fillet of
Aberdeen Angus beef often takes pole position
among the main courses, perhaps served in
true country-house fashion with celeriac,
asparagus and oxtail sauce. The choice of well-
tried desserts ensures that proceedings end on
a high: expect anything from sticky toffee

pudding to warm chocolate fondant with hot chocolate sauce and mango ice cream. A separate multi-course tasting menu offers the prospect of an enticing tour through David Mutter's repertoire. The heavyweight wine list is sure of its ground when it comes to seeking out the cream of the crop from Bordeaux and Burgundy, while Italy, South Africa and the Antipodes provide impressive back-up. The page of one-off curiosities titled 'brief encounters' is also worth a flutter. Bestsellers start at £22, and there are several selections at £5 a glass.

**Chef/s:** David Mutter. **Open:** Sun L 12.30 to 2, all week D 7 to 9. **Closed:** Christmas, last 3 weeks Jan. **Meals:** Set L £23, Set D £40 (3 courses) to £45 (7 courses). **Service:** net prices. **Details:** Cards accepted. 48 seats. 8 seats outside. No music. Wheelchair access. Children allowed. Car parking.

## Green Inn
**Dazzling innovation**
9 Victoria Road, Ballater, AB35 5QQ
Tel no: (013397) 55701
www.green-inn.com
**Modern | £33**
Cooking score: 4

£5 OFF 🍴 ✌

Hard by the village green, the Inn is altogether a little grander than its modest designation might suggest. The O'Hallorans' son Chris heads up the kitchen, and is producing some innovative cooking that blends the most dazzling of Scots produce with refined French technique. Dishes at all stages are comprised of a multiplicity of ingredients, but it all makes sense. A fillet of sea bass is grilled as a starter, tricked out with sweet parsnip purée, spinach and wild garlic, and sauced with saffron and vanilla. To follow, there may be braised cheeks of Perthshire boar with caramelised baby shallots, button mushrooms and lardons, or else roast Gressingham duck with pak choi, glazed apple, celeriac purée and a sauce of honey and cracked pepper. Desserts maintain the creative pace, with lemon and pine nut tart, accompanied by warm marinated cherries and honeyed mascarpone cream.

Cheeses are given their own individual treatments, as in the red plum and clove oil combination that offsets a serving of Strathdon Blue. The French-led wine list has a sprinkling of good offerings from the southern hemisphere, a page of halves, and house wines at £17.95 and £18.95.

**Chef/s:** Chris O'Halloran. **Open:** Tue to Sat D only 7 to 9. **Closed:** Christmas Day. **Meals:** Set D £29.50 (2 courses) £36 (3 courses). **Service:** not included. **Details:** Cards accepted. 30 seats. Wheelchair access. Music.

## ▌Dufftown
## La Faisanderie
**Accomplished cooking and convincing flair**
2 Balvenie Street, Dufftown, AB55 4AD
Tel no: (01340) 821273
www.dufftown.co.uk/lafaisanderie.htm
**French | £36**
Cooking score: 3

A corner site on a rugged town square is home to Eric Obry's and Amanda Bestwick's successful restaurant. Regulars note that the menu options are getting steadily more adventurous. Mussels and langoustines are richly sauced and gratinated under an Emmenthal topping to make a handsome seafood starter, which might be followed up by today's fish, cooked according to 'how the chef's feeling', as the menu has it. Meat main courses have included duck breast on a fricassee of Puy lentils and pancetta in a sauce of sage and port. With most dishes replicated between the carte and the fixed-price menu, it isn't easy to see why you would choose one over the other, but while you figure that one out, you can look forward to the prospect of rhubarb fool with mango coulis when you get to the other end. House French is £10.90 a bottle, £2.95 a glass.

**Chef/s:** Eric Obry. **Open:** Thur to Mon L 12 to 1.30, Wed to Mon D 6 to 8.30 (7 to 9 Fri and Sat). **Closed:** D Oct to Apr, 23 Oct to 6 Nov, 25, 26 and 31 Dec, 1 and 2 Jan. **Meals:** alc (main courses £15.50 to £18). Set L £13.50 (2 courses) to £16.80, Set D £24.50. **Service:** not inc. **Details:** Cards accepted. 26 seats. Wheelchair access. Music. Children's portions.

Henrietta Green

It wasn't long ago that 'British' on a menu meant York ham, Aylesbury duck or Scottish salmon – and that was as good as it got.

It is patently evident that what and where to buy is important to any kitchen, but nowadays sourcing has become a top priority. Restaurants are looking for that point of difference, something customers might talk about or might 'lift' the menu. Cooking is part of this equation, the ingredients another.

The trend for local and regional sourcing makes huge sense. Working directly with farmers, growers and producers within the area brings advantages to everyone concerned. The kitchens benefit from fresh, traceable ingredients in season with low food miles, the producers have new outlets on their doorsteps, income stays within their locale and the customers are served a slice of local distinctiveness. At last what has always struck me as a reasonable expectation of being served, say, Hereford beef while in Herefordshire, is satisfied.

This appetite for anything local may be relatively new, but is to be encouraged. It is perhaps less to do with cooking local recipes and more about the judicious use of the produce. At its best, it focuses on what is available at that time and encourages chefs to make the most of the seasons. This, in turn, has given rise to a more grounded style of cooking. It may be a lessdazzling style of food but it is nonetheless satisfying and fulfilling - in all senses of the word.
*www.foodloversbritain.com*

## ALSO RECOMMENDED
### ▲ Minmore House
Glenlivet, AB37 9DB
Tel no: (01807) 590378

Set in the 90-square-mile Glenlivet Estate, Minmore House Hotel is run with dedication by Lynne and Victor Janssen. There is a smart dining room serving three-course set lunches at £25 and four-course set dinners for £39. The traditional French-influenced food might include a soufflé followed by tournedos of Highland venison with juniper and foie gras. House wines start at £17.95.

## Udny Green
### Eat on the Green
Modern restaurant in a rural setting
Udny Green, AB41 7RS
Tel no: (01651) 842337
www.eatonthegreen.co.uk
**British | £30**
Cooking score: 2

It may be just a 20-minute drive from Aberdeen Airport but this old stone-built former pub overlooking the village green has a remote, peaceful setting. Eat on the Green has quickly earned itself a dedicated following for 'unfussy, delicious food'. Talent and ambition are at work here. Dishes are straightforward and the quality of raw materials consistently high: assiette of seafood (Thai crab cake, gateau of hot smoked salmon, marinated sea bass, rollmop herring), followed by slow-roast belly and pan-fried fillet of pork served alongside black pudding, an apple stack, Savoy cabbage, bacon, fondant potatoes and cider jus; finish with summer berry pavlova and passion-fruit coulis. The short, good-value global wine list opens at £12.50.
**Chef/s:** Craig Wilson. **Open:** Wed to Fri and Sun L 12 to 1.45, Wed to Sun D 6.30 to 9. **Closed:** first 2 weeks Jan. **Meals:** alc (main courses £13 to £19). Snack L menu available. **Service:** not inc. **Details:** Cards accepted. 65 seats. Wheelchair access. Music. Children's portions. Car parking.

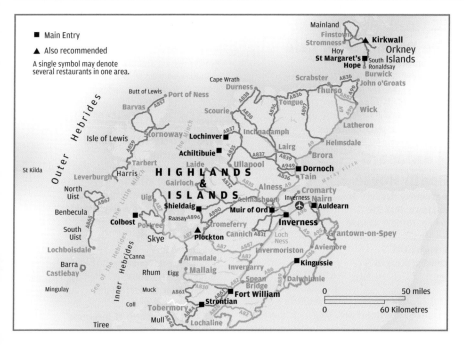

- ■ Main Entry
- ▲ Also recommended

A single symbol may denote several restaurants in one area.

## ■ Achiltibuie

### Summer Isles Hotel
**Legendary Highland hideaway**
Achiltibuie, IV26 2YG
Tel no: (01854) 622282
www.summerisleshotel.co.uk
**Modern European | £40**
**Cooking score: 5**

This is not only one of the most distinctive and remarkable hotels in Scotland, it is also the Guide's longest-serving Scottish restaurant (now in its 38th consecutive year). Lunch is a light repast of fresh seafood, locally smoked salmon and the like, but dinner is the big attraction. Daily menus take full advantage of the local catch and the harvest from the hotel's hydroponicum for a deceptively simple assortment of dishes with clear, bright flavours. To start proceedings, there might be a warm flan of asparagus with leeks, chives and goats' cheese dressing, always accompanied by a home-baked loaf. Next, young quail breast

on wilted spinach with mushroom purée, which gives way to fillet of Lochinver halibut with steamed saffron mussels, anchovy-roasted purple sprouting broccoli and black olives. After that, a trolley of desserts is wheeled round, with ample delights such as chocolate roulade or bread-and-butter pudding. Finally, guests are offered cheeses, mostly from elite Scottish producers. As a fillip to the evening's food, specially selected wines are available by the glass from the stellar 400-bin list. The full tome is a heady selection with inspired choices from all quarters of France, backed up by gems from Germany, California and elsewhere. Prices start at £14.50 for white Bergerac, with plenty of excellent drinking for under £25.

**Chef/s:** Chris Firth-Bernard. **Open:** all week 12.30 to 2, 8 (1 sitting). **Closed:** 15 Oct to Easter. **Meals:** alc L (main courses £15 to £30). Set D £51 (5 courses). Bar menu available. **Service:** net prices.
**Details:** Cards accepted. 30 seats. No music. No mobile phones. Wheelchair access. Car parking.

READERS RECOMMEND
## The Potting Shed Café
**Modern British**
The Walled Garden, Applecross House,
Applecross, Wester Ross, IV54 8ND
Tel no: (01520) 744440
www.eatinthewalledgarden.co.uk
'It really is a shed; fantastic'

## Auldearn
## Boath House
A stunning Regency house
Auldearn, IV12 5TE
Tel no: (01667) 454896
www.boath-house.com
French | £45
Cooking score: 5

'I always enjoy eating here,' remarks a regular
visitor to this impressive Regency house. The
setting, too, draws praise – 20 acres of gardens,
which include a lake – as does the welcoming,
attentive service, especially from the chatty
host Don Matheson. In the kitchen Charles
Lockley prepares a five-course dinner with
choice only at main course and dessert stage,
but this doesn't appear to be a problem for
anyone. After canapés in the lounge might
come soup, perhaps Jerusalem artichoke with
sea relish (made from seaweed, giving a nice
salty touch) and Parmesan crisp. Then a confit
of salmon with beetroot salad, jelly and orange
powder precedes main-course choices of
organic cod with buckwheat and crab salad,
asparagus and sweet cicely foam, or cannon of
roe deer with spelt, bacon, salsify and roasted
onion purée. Desserts – after a trio of Irish and
British cheeses – run to Alpaco chocolate and
cocoa-nib cake with tonka bean ice cream, or
spiced bread parfait with roasted rhubarb and
sorbet. Knowledgeable advice is dispensed
about the wine list, which, while centred on
France, features some astute selections from
the New World. House wines are £18
to £19.50.

Chef/s: Charles Lockley. **Open:** Thur to Sun L 12.30
to 1.15, all week D 7 to 8.15. **Closed:** 1 week at
Christmas. **Meals:** Set L £32.50, Set D £45.
**Service:** not inc. **Details:** Cards accepted. 28 seats.
No mobile phones. Wheelchair access. Music.
Children's portions. Car parking.

READERS RECOMMEND
## The Mountain Café
**Modern Scottish**
111 Grampian Road, Aviemore, PH22 1RH
Tel no: (01479) 812473
www.mountaincafe-aviemore.co.uk
'Excellent cakes and a fine breakfast'

## Sutor Creek
**Italian**
21 Bank Street, Cromarty, IV11 8EY
Tel no: (01381) 600855 (Limited opening, please
call ahead for further details)
www.sutorcreek.co.uk
'The best pizza north of Inverness'

## Dornoch
## 2 Quail
A welcoming restaurant-with-rooms
Castle Street, Dornoch, IV25 3SN
Tel no: (01862) 811811
www.2quail.com
**Modern European | £39**
Cooking score: 4

This small two-storey town house has been
converted into a restaurant-with-rooms, but
retains the feel of the family home it used to
be. Begin proceedings with drinks and olives
in the cosy lounge, tended by the 'busy,
efficient and pleasant' Kerensa Carr. Her
husband, Michael, is the chef, and he handles
his well-sourced ingredients with confidence
and accuracy. There are no choices (until
dessert) on the four-course dinner menu, a
typical example of which opens with a salad of
curly endive, mushrooms, crispy bacon,
artichoke crisps and a creamy grain-mustard
dressing, followed by supreme of salmon with
cucumber and a nut brown butter sauce. Next
comes a roast Gressingham duck breast with

provençale vegetables and rösti potatoes, after which you could plump for cheeses with biscuits and oatcakes or a caramelised raspberry tart with Drambuie ice cream. Wines start at £14.50.

**Chef/s:** Michael Carr. **Open:** Tue to Sat D only 7.30 to 9.30. **Closed:** Only open Fri and Sat in winter, 1 week at Christmas, 2 weeks Feb/Mar. **Meals:** Set D £39. **Service:** not inc. **Details:** Cards accepted. 12 seats. No mobile phones. Wheelchair access. Music.

## ▮ Fort William

## Crannog

**Honest cooking with local ingredients**
Town Pier, Fort William, PH33 6DB
Tel no: (01397) 705589
www.crannog.net
**Seafood | £25**
**New Chef**

£30

Open every day, this unpretentious place draws inspiration from the wonders of its local produce – mostly fish direct from boats, although venison, Aberdeen Angus beef and single malt also get a look in. The cooking reflects the best of Scotland's no-fuss approach to the stove: Cullen skink, a creamy soup of smoked haddock and potato, basic steamed mussels and so on. But culinary interests range beyond the traditional, with trios of sauces, rocket salads and chilli cream, albeit served with salmon and haddock fishcakes. Puds are basic and Scottish cheeses are well selected. House wine starts at £14.75.

**Chef/s:** Deep Vengurlekar. **Open:** all week 12 to 2, 6 to 9.30. **Closed:** D 24 Dec, 25 Dec, 1 Jan. **Meals:** alc (main courses £11.50 to £20). **Service:** not inc. **Details:** Cards accepted. 60 seats. Wheelchair access. Music. Children's portions.

## Inverlochy Castle

**Magnificent Victorian pile**
Torlundy, Fort William, PH33 6SN
Tel no: (01397) 702177
www.inverlochycastlehotel.com
**Modern European | £58**
**Cooking score: 6**

Past the ruins of its namesake – the thirteenth-century castle – the nineteenth-century pastiche is quite a pile. It has an entrance hall two storeys high, crystal chandeliers, antique paintings, real fires and a dining room with views over the hotel's own lake. Against such surroundings, in the plumpest and most enjoyable grand taste, the food served is surprisingly modern. Matthew Gray's menus showcase an ambitious but well-conceived cooking style. To start, veal sweetbread ravioli is served with its own marinated fillet, watercress purée and a red-wine butter; alternatively, there might be impeccably fresh Scottish blue lobster teamed with cauliflower salad, yoghurt beignets and a bisque mousseline. The wow factor is equally present in main courses of slow-cooked pork belly with foie gras and petits pois. Or there could be crispy breast of Gressingham duck with an onion risotto and Parmesan. And to finish, there might be perfect hot raspberry soufflé with a pistachio and olive oil cake that is well worth the ten-minute wait. Wine buffs can enjoy plenty of top-quality bottles from the classic French appellations before moving into the rest of Europe and the New World. By the glass there's some nine (including champagne) with wines opening at £32 and rising rapidly thereafter.

**Chef/s:** Matthew Gray. **Open:** all week 12.30 to 1.15, 6.30 to 10. **Meals:** Set L £28.50 (2 courses) to £35, Set D £58. Light L menu available. **Service:** not inc. **Details:** Cards accepted. 50 seats. No music. No mobile phones. Wheelchair access. Jacket and tie required. Children's portions. Car parking.

## Inverness

### Glenmoriston Town House, Abstract Restaurant

Minimalist chic and intricate cuisine

20 Ness Bank, Inverness, IV2 4SF

Tel no: (01463) 223777

www.glenmoristontownhouse.com

**Modern French | £42**

**Cooking score: 4**

Sitting on the east bank of the River Ness, the ground floor of this three-storey town-house hotel is home to Abstract, a high-fashion, minimalist restaurant. Geoffrey Malmedy has taken on the mantle of head chef and continues to explore the intricacies of the modern French repertoire. Judiciously sourced Scottish produce remains the inspiration for dishes such as West Coast langoustines with confit of lemongrass butter, fresh coriander salad and lobster bisque or red mullet with Japanese bouillon, white radish, and wasabi emulsion. Meat and game are also overlaid with some esoteric components: smoked potatoes, marinated tempura of anchovies, and vinegary sauce accompany Aberdeen Angus beef. To finish, the kitchen rides high with complex creations such as pear mille-feuille pointed up with a sorbet, jelly, and white pear spirit emulsion. France dominates the lengthy wine list, which bulges with posh names at serious prices. House selections, from £18 a bottle, provide some light relief. The second branch of Abstract is at 33–35 Castle Terrace, Edinburgh, tel: (0131) 229 2398. Head chef is Damien Rolian, who, just as the Guide went to press, took up the reins after Loic Lefebvre's departure; Rolian formerly worked at Abstract in Inverness.

**Chef/s:** Geoffrey Malmedy. **Open:** Mon to Sat D only 7 to 9.30. **Closed:** 26 to 28 Dec, 2 to 4 Jan. **Meals:** Set D £34 (2 courses) to £75 (inc wine). **Service:** 12.5% optional charge. **Details:** Cards accepted. 47 seats. Wheelchair access. Music. Children's portions. Car parking.

### Rocpool Rendezvous

Overlooking the River Ness

1 Ness Walk, Inverness, IV3 5NE

Tel no: (01463) 717274

**Modern European | £30**

**Cooking score: 2**

The Rocpool Rendezvous knows how to draw attention to itself – 'fizz with all the buzz' is its slogan – and certainly it's a popular spot. Inside the vibe is contemporary chic, with gleaming wooden floors, panelled walls and upholstered booths. The bargain two-course lunch might include chicken and white bean soup, followed by spiced pork casserole with chorizo sausage and roasted red peppers with coriander and crisp polenta. The carte is altogether a more sophisticated affair, matching Orkney crab with avocado, crème fraîche and a sweet ginger and chilli dressing, or halibut with Parmesan creamed cauliflower, new potatoes and an egg and asparagus sauce. The comprehensive wine list covers Europe and the New World, with whites starting at £13.50.

**Chef/s:** Steven Devlin. **Open:** Mon to Sat 12 to 2.30, 5.45 to 10; also open Sun D Mar to Oct. **Meals:** alc (main courses £9 to £18.50). Set L £8.95 (2 courses). Set D £5.45 to 6.45 £10.95 (2 courses). **Service:** not inc. **Details:** Cards accepted. 55 seats. Air-con. No mobile phones. Wheelchair access. Music. Children's portions.

## READERS RECOMMEND

### The Mustard Seed

**Modern European**

16 Fraser Street, Inverness, IV1 1QY

Tel no: (01463) 220220

'Relaxed bistro-style dining'

## ▌Isle of Skye
### Three Chimneys
Skye's the limit for culinary finesse
Colbost, Dunvegan, Isle of Skye, IV55 8ZT
Tel no: (01470) 511258
www.threechimneys.co.uk
**British | £45**
**Cooking score: 5**

If you're looking for an elegant restaurant-with-rooms, you could do worse than head down the single-track road that leads to the Three Chimneys, where Eddie and Shirley Spear have offered a warm welcome for over 20 years. Unspoilt views look west across the sea to the Outer Hebrides, but equally distracting is the modern Scottish cooking of Michael Smith. With experience working under the likes of the Roux brothers, Smith's style shows a degree of refinement. So, while langoustines from Loch Dunvegan are served as a simple starter with organic leaves and a lemon and olive oil dressing, there might also be a seared saddle of rabbit with Puy lentils, celeriac purée and a bitter chocolate and cep mushroom sauce. Main dishes on the four-course dinner menu can be even more elaborate; perhaps a carnivorous treat of grilled lamb loin with kidneys, heart, shoulder and sweetbreads on Savoy cabbage, golden polenta, 'neep purry' and a good old-fashioned lamb gravy. Desserts range from hot marmalade pudding with Drambuie custard to pineapple carpaccio with lime and chilli, topped with passion-fruit jelly. The wine list provides a concise but wide-reaching tour of each of the major French regions; the only disappointment is a limited choice of bottles under £25.
**Chef/s:** Michael Smith. **Open:** Mon to Sat L 12.30 to 2, all week D 6.30 to 9.30. **Closed:** L Nov to Mar, 3 weeks Jan. **Meals:** Set L £21 (2 courses) to £27, Set D £47.50 to £55. **Service:** not inc. **Details:** Cards accepted. 30 seats. 4 seats outside. No music. Wheelchair access. Car parking.

## ▌Kingussie
### The Cross
Local produce is the star
Tweed Mill Brae, Ardbroilach Road, Kingussie, PH21 1LB
Tel no: (01540) 661166
www.thecross.co.uk
**Modern British | £40**
**Cooking score: 5**

In the heart of the Cairngorms National Park, this charming family-run restaurant-with-rooms stands in four acres of riverside grounds. Chef-proprietor David Young's menus allow local produce to take centre stage – and include 'wild' food foraged from the local area. The cooking style is apparently straightforward, somewhat belying the technical accomplishment and imagination behind it: home-smoked Shetland salmon is served for a starter with herb mayonnaise, apple and avocado. Main courses go in for multiple layers of flavour, as in Scrabster halibut fillet with spiced Shiraz, wilted spinach, pumpkin purée and Jersey Royals, while Gressingham duck breast is given an accompaniment of pickled apple and Calvados, creamed Savoy cabbage and boulangère potatoes. To finish, there might be crème caramel with poached pear, Pedro Ximenez and raisin ice cream, or hot chocolate fondant with caramelised bananas and milk sorbet. The wine list continues to be a high point here, and this year's annual shake-up has seen an increased emphasis on biodynamic wines. Sensible mark-ups mean prices are fair throughout the list, starting around £15.
**Chef/s:** Becca Henderson and David Young. **Open:** Tue to Sat D only 7 to 8.45. **Closed:** Christmas, 2 Jan to mid-Feb. **Meals:** Set D £41 to £45. **Service:** net prices. **Details:** Cards accepted. 24 seats. No music. No mobile phones. Wheelchair access. Children allowed. Car parking.

## ALSO RECOMMENDED

### ▲ Dil Se

7 Bridge Street, Kirkwall, KW15 1HR
Tel no: (01856) 875242
www.dilserestaurant.co.uk

Head chef Motin Uddin serves up traditional Indian food at this modern, glass-fronted restaurant set just behind the harbour. There is a range of grilled kebabs and chaats (£4.85) to start, followed by signature dishes like lamb Kashmiri chasni (£8.95) or sag balti (£8.45), and home-made ice creams (£3.65). House wine £11.95. Open daily.

## Lochinver

### Albannach

Fine food and Highland hospitality
Baddidarrach, Lochinver, IV27 4LP
Tel no: (01571) 844407
www.thealbannach.co.uk
**Modern Scottish | £47**
**Cooking score: 6**

🍷 🍴

Colin Craig and Lesley Crosfield's tall white house looks enticingly romantic, standing high above Lochinver with glorious Highland vistas all around. Inside, the décor is snug and heroically Scottish, right down to the tartan prints and stag antlers. The owners work as a team in the kitchen and they are fully committed to all things local. They bake their own breads and oatcakes, encourage crofters to grow organic vegetables to their requirements and procure seafood from Lochinver's inshore creelers. Dinner is a single sitting served at a leisurely pace, with a daily five-course menu as the familiar and well-tried framework. The evening might begin with a warm tartlet of Lochinver crab jazzed up with vine tomato chutney before a bowl of spiced butternut squash soup. As a centrepiece, the kitchen could pick roast saddle of wild venison served on braised red cabbage with tarragon mash and a gamey port sauce. A pair of cheeses (say, Camembert and Ireland's Gubbeen) are ushered in ahead of dessert,

which could be a hot chocolate soufflé with vanilla ice cream and plums poached in Sauternes. Colin Craig's fascinating wine list continues to evolve, although France remains the focus. House selections (from £14) are real eye-openers.
**Chef/s:** Colin Craig and Lesley Crosfield. **Open:** Tue to Sun D only 8 (1 sitting). **Closed:** 5 Jan to 1 Mar. **Meals:** Set D £47 (5 courses). **Service:** not inc. **Details:** Cards accepted. 20 seats. No music. No mobile phones. Car parking.

## Muir of Ord

### Dower House

One-sitting dinners in a former shooting lodge
Highfield, Muir of Ord, IV6 7XN
Tel no: (01463) 870090
www.thedowerhouse.co.uk
**British | £38**
**Cooking score: 2**

🍴

Originally a farmhouse, this building was converted to a dower house at the start of the nineteenth century. Robyn and Menna Aitchison bought it in 1989 and have been careful to preserve the feel of a family home, so dinner, cooked by Robyn is a simple no-choice menu. The evening begins with drinks in the drawing room, after which you settle in the traditionally styled dining room for a starter of, perhaps grilled polenta with asparagus, followed by fillet of beef with herb relish and a dessert of raspberry soufflé. On another night, the menu might offer tomato and lovage risotto followed by chicken breast braised with herbs, and finally a chocolate crème brûlée. Wines start at £18.
**Chef/s:** Robyn Aitchison. **Open:** all week D only 8 (1 sitting). **Closed:** Christmas. **Meals:** Set D £38. **Service:** not inc. **Details:** Cards accepted. 18 seats. 6 seats outside. No music. No mobile phones. Wheelchair access. Children's portions. Car parking.

## ALSO RECOMMENDED
### ▲ Plockton Inn
Innes Street, Plockton, IV52 8TW
Tel no: (01599) 544222
www.plocktoninn.co.uk

Not far from Plockton harbour, the Inn offers a menu of solid seafood favourites. A platter of items smoked in-house (£6.95) is a good way to start, or there may be gravad lax (£5.65) or moules marinière (£5.50). Move on to pesto-crusted hake (£10.50) or venison cooked in local ale (£9.50), but save room for a homely dessert such as lemon and ginger crunch pie (£3.50). A superior pub wine list starts at £10.50. Accommodation. Open all week.

## READERS RECOMMEND
### Pool House Hotel
Modern European
Poolewe, Ross-shire, IV22 2LD
Tel no: (01445) 781272
www.poolhousehotel.com
'Magical atmosphere and memorable food'

## ▮ St Margaret's Hope
### The Creel
Showcase for Orkney's seafood
Front Road, St Margaret's Hope, KW17 2SL
Tel no: (01856) 831311
www.thecreel.co.uk
Modern Scottish | £36
Cooking score: 7

An air of unaffected simplicity defines proceedings at Alan and Joyce Craigie's spellbinding restaurant-with-rooms overlooking St Margaret's Hope Bay. Since 1985, they have manintained this three-storey, cream-painted house with unerring enthusiasm and care. Inside, it is modest, humble and domestic in the best sense. The lack of fuss and pretence spills over into the kitchen, where Alan Craigie wows visitors with his harmonious, unembellished seafood cookery. He takes an eco-friendly view of things, deliberately seeking out and working wonders with some of the less familiar (but sustainable) inhabitants of Orkney's waters. Wolf fish is paired with scallops and braised brown lentils, ling is salted and transformed into a brandade, while his signature Orcadian fish stew is a cornucopia of saithe, mussels, cockles and razor clams. The kitchen also looks to the land for seaweed-fed North Ronaldsay mutton, which might be given the seven-hour treatment in company with barley broth; shoulder of beef is also slow-cooked, often with caramelised onions, black pudding and Orkney-brewed Raven Ale. There is also a wealth of domestic industry at work here, from the home-griddled bannocks served with each appetiser to the bold chutneys and relishes that add zest to many other dishes. Desserts aim for familiarity, with an assortment of tried-and-trusted favourites including glazed lemon tart with marmalade ice cream or special 'trios' involving, perhaps, apple crumble, orange pannacotta and blackcurrant ice cream. House wine selections start at £14 (£4 a glass). NB The Creel was up for sale as we went to press, so call ahead to avoid disappointment.
Chef/s: Alan Craigie. Open: Apr to Oct D only 7 to 8.45. Closed: Mon and Tue Apr, May, Sept and Oct. Meals: alc (main courses £18 to £24). Service: not inc. Details: Cards accepted. 34 seats. No music. Wheelchair access. Children's portions. Car parking.

## READERS RECOMMEND
### The Captain's Galley
Seafood
The Harbour, Scrabster, KW14 7UJ
Tel no: (01847) 894999
www.captainsgalley.co.uk
'Eat local fish with a clear conscience'

## Shieldaig

### Tigh an Eilean Hotel

Sound cooking in an enchanting setting
Shieldaig, IV54 8XN
Tel no: (01520) 755251
**Modern Scottish | £42**
Cooking score: 3

£5 OFF ⊏ Ⅴ

Originally a Highland watering hole, Tigh an Eilean (literally 'the house opposite the island') is charmingly situated in a tiny hamlet overlooking the waters of Loch Torridon. Christopher and Cathryn Field have run the place as an appealing hotel since 1999. Daily deliveries from the local boats form the backbone of their dinner menus, witness feuilleté of langoustines with saffron and vermouth cream or gratin of Shieldaig crab with pink grapefruit. On the meat front, medallions of Highland beef might appear with a truffled-scented risotto or with cep, olive and Manchego butter and sauce spiked with Pedro Ximenez sherry, while desserts could run to a trio of new season's rhubarb or flambéed bananas served with lime and butterscotch sauce. House wine starts at £13.95.

**Chef/s:** Christopher Field. **Open:** all week D only 7 to 8.30. **Closed:** end Oct to mid-Mar. **Meals:** Set D £42.50. Bar menu available. **Service:** not inc. **Details:** Cards accepted. 30 seats. No music. No mobile phones. Children's portions. Car parking.

## READERS RECOMMEND

### Kishorn Seafood Bar

**Seafood**
Kishorn, Strathcarron, Ross-shire, IV54 8XA
Tel no: (01520) 733240 (Seasonal opening, call ahead)
www.kishornseafoodbar.co.uk
**'Simple shellfish on the far edge of nowhere'**

## Strontian

### Kilcamb Lodge

Small-scale country house in a grand location
Strontian, PH36 4HY
Tel no: (01967) 402257
www.kilcamblodge.co.uk
**French/Scottish | £40**
New Chef

⊏ Ⅴ

Kilcamb Lodge is a stone-built country house set on the shores of Loch Sunart and surrounded by 22 acres of meadow and woodland. It's a dream location. Sally and David Ruthven Fox continue to provide hospitality, but there have been changes in the kitchen this year, with Gordon Smillie now in charge. We are told the new man is introducing 'more innovative dishes'. This typically translates into starters of scallops with a cauliflower timbale and a citrus butter sauce, or guinea fowl and cep roulade with wild mushrooms and raspberry vinaigrette, followed by main courses ranging from simple roast loin of local venison with celeriac and potato dauphinoise, braised red cabbage, caramelised vegetables and rich game jus, to more involved dishes such as fillets of lemon sole with langoustine mousseline, stuffed langoustine tails and a herb potato gnocchi and shellfish bisque velouté. A wine list was not available as the Guide went to press, but if it is similar to last year's, there will be a good range of bottles from France and the New World.

**Chef/s:** Gordon Smillie. **Open:** Tue to Sun L 12.30 to 2.30, all week D 7.30 to 9. **Closed:** Jan. **Meals:** alc L (main courses £9.50 to £18.50). Set D £42. Snack menu available. **Service:** not inc. **Details:** Cards accepted. 24 seats. 8 seats outside. No mobile phones. Music. Car parking.

# WALES

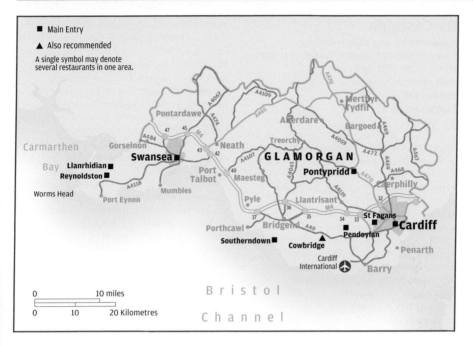

- ■ Main Entry
- ▲ Also recommended
- A single symbol may denote several restaurants in one area.

# Cardiff

## Armless Dragon
**Comfy showcase for local ingredients**
97-99 Wyeverne Road, Cathays, Cardiff, CF24 4BG
Tel no: (029) 2038 2357
www.armlessdragon.co.uk
Modern Welsh | £35
Cooking score: 2

£5 OFF ⓥ

This comfortable yet modern restaurant (deep red walls, modern artwork, wooden furniture) showcases some of the best ingredients Wales can offer. You could begin with a platter of miniature starters themed around 'land', 'sea' or 'earth' – the 'land' selection might include Monmouthshire smoked chicken with avocado and Carmarthen ham crisps, while the 'sea' starters could feature Pembrokeshire spider crab tart and sewin pancakes with dill yoghurt. Move on to best end of Brecon lamb with a faggot, lamb and rosemary cake and spring greens or skate wing with a cockle and leek sauce and

Pembrokeshire new potatoes. The Welsh theme extends to desserts such as caramelised lemon and Welsh honey tart with Bower farm clotted cream; or bara-brith-and-butter pudding. You will even find a Welsh wine among the offerings on the well-annotated wine list, which opens at £9.25.

**Chef/s:** Paul Lane. **Open:** Tue to Fri L 12 to 2, Tue to Sat D 7 to 9 (9.30 Fri and Sat). **Closed:** 1 week Christmas, 1 week Easter, 1 week August. **Meals:** alc (main courses £12 to £18). Set L £12 (2 courses) to £14. **Service:** not inc. **Details:** Cards accepted. 45 seats. No mobile phones. Wheelchair access. Music. Children's portions.

## Average price

The average price listed in main-entry reviews denotes the price of a three-course meal, without wine.

## Da Castaldo
Italian cuisine in a stylish setting
5 Romilly Crescent, Canton, Cardiff, CF11 9NP
Tel no: (029) 2022 1905
www.dacastaldo.com
Italian | £38
Cooking score: 2
£5 OFF ⓥ

Expect simple, clear-flavoured Italian cooking at this welcoming neighbourhood restaurant. The menu is as comfortable as the surroundings, offering many much-loved favourites such as spaghetti Napolitana, saltimbocca alla Romana or traditional lasagne. A good selection of meat-free dishes could include home-made ravioli of broccoli and pine nuts with a Gorgonzola sauce or risotto Milanese (with saffron, white wine and asparagus). Even the most commonplace ingredients, such as carrots and leeks in a creamy soup, are deftly spiced and seasoned to creating flavourful, thoroughly enjoyable food. An inspection dish of sea bass, served in the foil parcel in which it was baked with fennel and potatoes, is typical of the unfussy style. Finish with the likes of tiramisu or pistachio pannacotta. The interesting list of Italian wines opens at £12.50, with a good selection available by the glass.
**Chef/s:** Antonio Castaldo and Rodrigo Gonzalez. **Open:** Tue to Sat 12 to 1.45, 7 to 9.45. **Closed:** 24 to 26 and 31 Dec. **Meals:** alc (main courses £8 to £16). Set L £13.50. **Service:** not inc. **Details:** Cards accepted. 40 seats. Air-con. Wheelchair access. Music. Children's portions.

## Le Gallois
Family-run restaurant
6-10 Romilly Crescent, Canton, Cardiff, CF11 9NR
Tel no: (029) 2034 1264
www.legallois-ycymro.com
Modern European | £35
Cooking score: 5

Chef Padrig Jones is still at the helm and the modern, clear-flavoured cooking that was the trademark of Le Gallois remains, but otherwise it's all change at this city restaurant.

Many of the ingredients that have long been staples of Jones's repertoire now crop up on the tapas menu, where cured ham, gazpacho, foie gras crostini and chorizo with squid in a chilli sauce are all players. The push towards informal all-day dining continues with the addition of a morning breakfast menu, allowing you to start the day on a 'full Welsh' breakfast; eggy bread with crispy bacon and maple syrup or scallops and black pudding with crispy cockles and seaweed relish. For those still attached to the old Le Gallois formula, a regular restaurant menu remains (including a carte and an excellent value express lunch). An inspection visit made amid all the change revealed that Jones' accuracy and ability to balance textures and flavours remain strong: a generously proportioned starter of foie gras with Calvados-glazed apples, wild rocket and lentil dressing hit all the right notes, while a main course of crispy confit of duck with cabbage Koffman, fondant potatoes, roast onions and red- wine sauce was marred only by the toughness of some mouthfuls of duck. In another starter, delicate slices of marinated salmon were almost swamped by a strong citrus dressing. A dessert of chocolate fondant teamed the dark delights of decent cocoa with the sweetness of pistachio ice cream. Diners remain charmed by the 'excellent service and friendly atmosphere' and by the 'fine wine list', which starts at £13.95. NB As we went to press, we heard of plans to rename the restaurant as 'Canna Canteen', but these details have yet to be confirmed.
**Chef/s:** Padrig Jones. **Open:** Tue to Sun tapas 12 to 7, D Tue to Thu 7 to 9, Fri to Sat 7 to 10. **Closed:** 23 Dec to 4 Jan. **Meals:** Set L £16.95 (2 courses) to £19.95, Set D £30 (2 courses) to £35. **Service:** Not inc. **Details:** Cards accepted. 60 seats. Air-con. Wheelchair access. Music. Children's portions. Car parking.

## Gilby's

Comfort food in an eighteenth-century barn
Old Port Road, Culverhouse Cross, Cardiff,
CF5 6DN
Tel no: (029) 2067 0800
www.gilbysrestaurant.co.uk
Modern European | £45
Cooking score: 2

Ⴗ

The impeccable conversion of this eighteenth-century barn has given it a carpeted, domestic look while retaining its high-beamed ceiling and exposed stonework. A generous lounge and bar area adds to the homely feel but the brightly lit open kitchen leaves you in no doubt about the real focus of this well-established operation. Here the aim is to comfort rather than challenge, but there are some interesting modern flourishes. You might begin with grilled sardines with chilli and apricot glaze or a feuilleté of lambs' kidneys with mustard and Armagnac. Typical main courses range from pork tenderloin with apple boulangère, crispy leeks and mushroom sauce to good old British fish and chips with yeast and beer batter and mushy peas. Desserts are in the same vein: perhaps raspberry pavlova with a soft-centred meringue or bread-and-butter pudding with crème anglaise. The short but comprehensive wine list starts at £13.95.
**Chef/s:** Anthony Armelin and Michael Jones. **Open:** Tue to Sun L 12 to 2.30 (3.30 Sun), Tue to Sat D 5.45 to 10. **Closed:** 10 days Christmas, 1 week Whitsun, 2 weeks Sept. **Meals:** alc exc Sun L (main courses £13 to £20). Set L Tue to Sat £14.50 (2 courses), Set D 5.45 to 7.15 (6.30 Sat) £18.50. **Service:** Not inc. **Details:** Cards accepted. 30 seats. No mobile phones. Wheelchair access. Music. Children allowed. Car parking.

## Woods Brasserie

Dining room looks on to the bay
The Pilotage Building, Stuart Street, Cardiff,
CF10 5BW
Tel no: (029) 2049 2400
www.woods-brasserie.com
Modern European | £35
Cooking score: 2

Ⴗ

Cardiff Bay has changed drastically in recent years, emerging as a stylish waterfront development bursting with bars and restaurants. Woods' setting – the landmark Pilotage building – seems all the more distinctive set against the new buildings that now surround it. The restaurant offers pre-theatre meals from 5.30 to 7pm, as well as lunch and dinner. Begin with crab and avocado spring roll with mango and lime salsa or pressed terrine of guinea fowl with poached pear. Main courses could include pot-roasted corn-fed chicken breast with spiced broth and egg noodles or roasted fillet of brill wrapped in crispy potato with baby leeks and Madeira jus. Desserts, each listed with a wine recommendation, might be chocolate terrine with light grapefruit mousse and sweet vinaigrette; or raspberry parfait. Wines from £15.95.
**Chef/s:** Sean Murphy. **Open:** all week L 12 to 2 (3 Sun), Mon to Sat D 7 to 10. **Closed:** 24 to 27 Dec. **Meals:** alc (main courses £10.95 to £19.95). Set L £13.95 (2 courses) to £16.95, Set pre-theatre D 5.30 to 7pm £16.95 (2 courses) to £19.95, Set D £35 (min 6). **Service:** not inc. **Details:** Cards accepted. 100 seats. 60 seats outside. Air-con. Wheelchair access. Music. Children's portions.

## ALSO RECOMMENDED

### ▲ Le Monde

60-62 St Mary's Street, Cardiff, CF10 1FE
Tel no: (029) 2038 7376
www.le-monde.co.uk

At the heart of this lively eatery is a tantalising display of fresh meat, fish and salads. The concept is simple and popular: you choose what you want from the display, and it is cooked in the bustling open kitchen. Typical starters are deep-fried whitebait; provençale fish soup; asparagus with hollandaise sauce; and home-made game pâté. Main courses include Scottish beef fillet steak; and medallions of venison in a port wine sauce. The extensive fish selection, which is mostly sold by weight, might feature sea bass baked in rock salt; red snapper; and lobster. Everything is simply served, with chips, jacket or new potatoes. Wines from £11.95.

## READERS RECOMMEND
## Casanova
**British**
13 Quay Street, Cardiff, CF10 1EA
Tel no: (029) 2034 4044
'Tiny Italian restaurant serving authentic food'

## Patagonia
**Modern European**
11 Kings Road, Cardiff, CF11 9BZ
Tel no: (029) 2019 0265
www.patagonia-restaurant.co.uk
'French cooking with an Argentinian twist'

## ▌Llanrhidian
## Welcome to Town
**Culinary excellence on the Gower Peninsula**
Llanrhidian, SA3 1EH
Tel no: (01792) 390015
www.thewelcometotown.co.uk
**Classical/Modern Welsh | £46**
**Cooking score: 3**
**V**

Before it became a country bistro the 'Welcome' was an historic inn. In the early nineteenth century it was the meeting place for the Gower Association for the Prosecution of Felons. These days it may be all carpets, crisp linen and fresh paintwork but there is no mistaking the old world atmosphere. Ian Bennett's sharply seasonal, classically rooted cooking is, as ever, both engaging and satisfying. The good-value lunch menu might offer garden pea and prawn risotto with

lobster oil followed by free-range chicken breast with vegetable consommé and saffron tagliatelle. Dinner could include artichoke heart with field mushroom duxelles, topped with a poached free-range egg and chive hollandaise, followed by roast best end of Gower lamb with celeriac purée, broad beans, garlic confit and port and tarragon sauce. Finish with vanilla pannacotta with rhubarb compote and orange sorbet; or cheese with handmade oatcakes. A good selection of wines starts at £13.50.

**Chef/s:** Ian Bennett and Nigel Bissett. **Open:** Tue to Sun L 12 to 2, Tue to Sat D 7 to 9.30; also open Mon July and Aug. **Closed:** last 2 weeks Feb, last week Oct. **Meals:** Set L Tue to Sat £13.50 (2 courses) to £15.95, Set L Sun £14.95 (2 courses) to £19.95, Set D £27 (2 courses) to £32.50. **Service:** not inc. **Details:** Cards accepted. 40 seats. 20 seats outside. Wheelchair access. Music. Children's portions. Car parking.

## READERS RECOMMEND
## Hurrens Inn on the Estuary
**Modern British**
13 Station Road, Loughor, SA4 6TR
Tel no: (01792) 899 092
www.hurrens.co.uk
'Honest home cooking'

## ALSO RECOMMENDED
## ▲ Llys Meddyg
East Street, Newport, SA42 0SY
Tel no: (01239) 820008
www.llysmeddyg.com

This striking, creeper-clad stone building positively oozes boutique-hotel style and understated sophistication. From the jute-floored dining area with its vivid blue walls to the cosy cellar bar, which spills on to a small terrace beside a tumbling stream, everything is beautifully, sympathetically (and no doubt expensively) done. The menu sits comfortably with the relaxed, old-new setting, offering a twice-baked Welsh cheese soufflé (£6.50) or pan-seared king scallops on a laverbread and bacon galette with chilli jam (£6.95) followed by best end of Welsh lamb with colcannon and a Penderyn Welsh whisky sauce (£17.50) or pork belly confit cured in maple syrup and star anise with spicy red cabbage and a chilli and plum sauce (£18). Wines from £12.50.

## █ Pontypridd

## ★NEW ENTRY★
## Bunch of Grapes
**Unpretentious, imaginative gastropub**
**Ynysangharad Road, Pontypridd, CF3 4DA**
**Tel no: (01443) 402 934**
**www.bunchofgrapes.org.uk**
**Gastropub | £23**
**Cooking score: 1**
£5 £30
OFF

Prepare to be surprised. Drive down the dead-end road towards a row of traditional Welsh Valley terraced houses to encounter this uncelebrated culinary find a pub offering an imaginative menu using local ingredients. The creative seasonal menu is supplemented with plenty of blackboard specials. Starters might include a rich home-made crayfish bisque with citrus crème fraîche or deep-fried breaded lambs' sweetbreads. For mains you could opt for a risotto of squid ink and crab with Welsh cockles. Popular desserts include crème brûlée or a lemongrass and coconut pannacotta with spicy pineapple. Portions are robust. Service is friendly and attentive. House wine is £10.75.
**Chef/s:** Nick Otley, Sebastien Vanoni. **Open:** Mon to Sat L 12 to 2.30pm, D 6.30 to 9.30pm, Sun L 12 to 3.30pm. **Meals:** alc (main courses start at £13.50, desserts at £4.50). **Service:** optional. **Details:** Cards accepted. 6 seats. 18 seats outside. Separate bar. Wheelchair access. Music. Children's portions. Car parking.

## █ Reynoldston

## Fairyhill
**Imaginative use of local produce**
**Reynoldston, SA3 1BS**
**Tel no: (01792) 390139**
**www.fairyhill.net**
**Modern Welsh | £53**
**Cooking score: 4**
£5 🍷 ⎌ 𝖸
OFF

This secluded country-house hotel and restaurant stands in 24 acres of wooded grounds. The beauty of Gower is all around, and it is also on the plate – perhaps as battered cockles among the canapés in the relaxing, traditionally furnished lounge, or in starters such as organic egg and laverbread frittata or carpaccio of Welsh Black beef with home-grown rocket and radish and Parmesan shavings. The cooking is simple and classically inspired, with a few winning modern touches. Typical main courses include steamed Gower lobster with garlic and lemon butter; supreme of free-range chicken with streaky Welsh bacon and Thai coconut broth; and loin and rack of Gower lamb with mashed potato and olive jus. For dessert, perhaps a chocolate fondant with white chocolate ice cream or a mixed berry parfait with a brandy-snap biscuit. A set-price selection of lunchtime

### Cooking score

A score of 1 is a significant achievement. The score in any review is based on several meals, incorporating feedback from both our readers and inspectors. As a rough guide, 1 denotes capable cooking with some inconsistencies, rising steadily through different levels of technical expertise, until the scores between 6 and 10 indicate exemplary skills, along with innovation, artistry and ambition. If there is a new chef, we don't score the restaurant for the first year of entry. For further details, please see the scoring section in the introduction to the Guide.

classics could include Caesar salad; fish of the day with wilted greens and laverbread sauce; and chocolate tart with orange clotted cream. The extensive and much-praised wine list opens at £14.50. NB No children under 8 in evenings.
**Chef/s:** Paul Davies and James Lawrence. **Open:** Tue to Sun L 12.30 to 2, Mon to Sat D 7.30 to 9. **Closed:** first 2 to 3 weeks Jan. **Meals:** alc L (main courses £14 to £19.50). Set L £19.95 (3 courses), Set D £40.00 (3 courses). **Service:** not inc. **Details:** Cards accepted. 60 seats. 20 seats outside. Wheelchair access. Music. Children's portions. Car parking.

## St Fagans
### Old Post Office
**Unexpected sleek minimalism**
Greenwood Lane, St Fagans, CF5 6EL
Tel no: (029) 2056 5400
www.old-post-office.com
**Modern European | £25**
**Cooking score: 3**

☐ ✓ £30

From the front, the restaurant blends seamlessly with the old walls and leafy gardens of St Fagans, but drive round to the entrance at the rear and you'll find a more modern aspect, the restaurant being in a stylish, conservatory extension. Both restaurant and bar are a study in minimalist economy, with almost bare walls and (from the restaurant) a pleasingly contrary view of brushed-steel patio planters and the old church tower beyond. The interior is calming rather than sterile and the cooking (by new chef-proprietor Simon Kealy) is delightfully exact. At inspection, a starter of local asparagus with a soft poached duck egg was perfectly cooked and seasoned. The excellent Welsh ingredients continue into main courses such as chump of lamb with sweetbreads and a ragout of spring vegetables or a 10oz ribeye of Welsh beef with homemade oven chips and béarnaise sauce. A very impressive, well-annotated wine list starts at £9.95.

**Chef/s:** Simon Kealy. **Open:** L Tue to Sun 12 to 3, D Tue to Sat 7 to 9.30. **Closed:** Sun evenings, all-day Mon, Christmas and New Year. **Meals:** alc main courses £8.50 to £15, L 11.96 two courses £14.95 three courses. **Service:** not inc. **Details:** Cards accepted. 35 seats. 30 seats outside. Air-con. Separate bar. Wheelchair access. Music. Children allowed. Car parking.

## Southerndown
### Frolics
**The ingredients speak for themselves**
52 Beach Road, Southerndown, CF32 0RP
Tel no: (01656) 880127
**Modern European | £23**
**New Chef**

✓ £30

The dated-looking sign – and the name itself – are not very promising, but Frolics is full of surprises. Inside is a light, modern dining room with wood-effect floors and tastefully restrained décor. Equally pleasing are the prices; if you plump for the supper menu, three courses will set you back just £16.95. At inspection a duck and Madeira parfait with onion marmalade and toasted raisin bread revealed a delightfully balanced set of flavours and textures. A main course of slow-braised Welsh mountain lamb with Dijon mustard, mint and parsley crust and Port jus was similarly impressive. Desserts, such as a hot chocolate brownie with honey and walnut ice cream, deserve rapt attention. Service is well intentioned but not polished. A short, international wine list opens at £12.95.

**Chef/s:** Russel Clay, James Sykes. **Open:** Tue to Sun L 12 to 2.30, Tue to Sat D 6.30 to 9.30. **Closed:** 24 and 26 Dec, 1 Jan. **Meals:** alc exc Sun L (main courses £10 to £17). **Service:** not inc. **Details:** Cards accepted. 55 seats. 15 seats outside. Wheelchair access. Music. Children's portions. Car parking.

# Swansea

★NEW ENTRY★

## Bartrams at 698

A curious blend of tradition and modernity
698 Mumbles Rd, Mumbles, Swansea, SA3 4EH
Tel no: (01792) 361 616
www.698.uk.com
Modern European | £28
Cooking score: 3

♈ £30

A sleek, stylish restaurant, the modest size and understated signage of which belies the very significant contribution it has made to the Mumbles dining scene. Large, well-spaced polished wood tables, laid-back jazzy background music and a glass-fronted open kitchen set a sophisticated tone, while the cooking reveals an avid engagement with culinary trends and traditions. Crusty, warm, home-made bread is an excellent opening to a meal which could continue with starters such as carpaccio of Welsh beef with a rocket salad and truffle dressing or pan-seared scallops with laverbread linguine and saffron vinaigrette. The cooking is almost always exact and demonstrates a real flair for flavour. Main courses – perhaps roast supreme of Gressingham duck with a confit duck cake and a red-wine syrup or seared monkfish with crushed new potatoes and a lemon beurre blanc – might be followed by a perfect bread-and-butter pudding with Baileys crème anglaise. Wines start at £11.95 for a bottle and £4.65 for a glass.
Chef/s: Steven Bartram. Open: Tue to Sat, L 12 to 2.15, D 6 to 9. Closed: Sunday and Monday; Christmas. Meals: Set D, early-bird menu, £18.95 two courses. Service: Optional. Details: Cards accepted. 45 seats. Wheelchair access. Music. Children's portions. Car parking.

## Didier & Stephanie

Fluent French in a sophisticated setting
56 St Helens Road, Swansea, SA1 4BE
Tel no: (01792) 655603
French | £38
Cooking score: 4

Occupying a tall Swansea house, this is a little beacon of Gallic style and sophistication. Everything inside seems to be done with love and care, from the simple but cosy décor (palest yellow walls and a wealth of stripped wood) to the charming and efficient front-of-house team led by Stephanie. Didier is tucked away in the kitchen, where he cooks up fluently French offerings of great balance and precision. At lunch, these might include terrine of rabbit with a Cumberland sauce followed by poached skate wing with a balsamic vinegar reduction, then a dessert of pistachio crème brûlée. In the evening, you could try a salad of smoked duck breast and Granny Smith apple followed by rack of lamb in rosemary jus, and poached pear in saffron with cinnamon ice cream for dessert – though the selection of French cheese is also a worthy distraction. A decent selection of wines, many from Burgundy, Bordeaux and Champagne, opens at £10.90.
Chef/s: Didier Suvé. Open: Tue to Sat 12 to 1.30, 7 to 9. Closed: 25 Dec and 1 Jan. Meals: alc D (main courses £14 to £17). Set L £9.90 (1 course) to £14.90. Service: not inc. Details: Cards accepted. 25 seats. Air-con. No mobile phones. Music.

Symbols

🛏 Accommodation is available.

£30 Three courses for less than £30.

♈ More than five vegetarian dishes.

£5 OFF £5-off voucher scheme.

🍾 Notable wine list.

## ★NEW ENTRY★
## Hanson at the Chelsea Restaurant
**Welcoming restaurant**
17 St Mary's Street, Swansea, SA1 3LH
Tel no: (01792) 464068
**Modern Welsh | £25**
**Cooking score: 3**
£5 OFF   £30

Andrew Hanson – formerly of Hanson's restaurant on Swansea marina – has found a new mooring in this welcoming, atmospheric little restaurant. It stands on a pedestrianised side street just a whisker (but also a world) away from Wind Street with its many pubs, cafés and bars. Wood floors and wood-panelled walls set a stylish but homely scene, and the large fish board is testament to the fact that Hanson is still sought out for his deft and intelligent use of fresh fish. Examples include baked Cornish hake cutlet with parsley and lemon butter; and cod wrapped in crispy pancetta with a sauté of bacon and black pudding. Other choices could include Welsh beef fillet steak on baby leaf spinach with horseradish béarnaise and hand-cut chips. Wines from £11.50.
**Chef/s:** Andrew Hanson. **Open:** Mon to Sat 12 to 2.15, 7.30 to 9.30. **Meals:** alc (main courses £12.75 to £37.95) Set L £10.95 (2 courses) Set D £14.95 (3 courses). **Service:** not inc. **Details:** Cards accepted. 50 seats. No music. No mobile phones. Wheelchair access. Children's portions. Children allowed.

## The Restaurant @ Pilot House Wharf
**Fabulous views and a fish-centric menu**
Trawler Road, Swansea, SA1 1UN
Tel no: (01792) 466200
**Modern Seafood | £27**
**Cooking score: 3**
£30

This landmark turreted building in the heart of Swansea Marina houses a smart first-floor restaurant, reached by a winding spiral staircase. The comfortable interior has a modern edge, with bare wooden tables, high-backed chairs and a simple brown and cream colour scheme. If you can, sit by one of the windows with views of Swansea's fishing boats and the swish new SA1 development beyond. An inspection meal began with unremarkable bread but picked up pace with a generous goats' cheese filo tart with sweet fig and red onion, followed by mussels in a well-balanced white wine and parsley cream sauce. Other fish options include fillets of bream with pancetta rösti and a lemon and basil cream sauce; or a whole plaice with king prawns and parsley butter. The simple, modern-classic style carries through to desserts such as white chocolate crème brûlée or strawberry parfait. Wines start at £10.95 a bottle.
**Chef/s:** Craig Gammon. **Open:** Tue to Sat L 12 to 2, Tue to Sat D 6.30 to 9.30. **Closed:** lSun and Mon, ast week Oct, first week Nov. **Meals:** alc (main courses £11 to £29). Set L £10.95 (1 course) to £14.95. **Service:** not inc. **Details:** Cards accepted. 50 seats. Music. Children's portions. Car parking.

## ALSO RECOMMENDED
## ▲ Mermaid
686 Mumbles Road, Swansea, SA3 4EE
Tel no: (01792) 367744

A stylish refurbishment has added character and atmosphere to this seafront restaurant and lounge. A justifiably popular, excellent-value lunch could include cockle fritters with a prawn and ginger salsa followed by Dover sole with a herb crust and crayfish salsa. In the evening you might start with carpaccio of home-cured Black beef with horseradish dressing and fresh Parmesan, followed by cannon of saltmarsh lamb with a redcurrant and rosemary jus. Desserts are just as pretty and precise as the rest of the cooking; examples include plum and almond tart with vanilla cream; and fig, cherry and apricot bread-and-butter pudding. An interesting, well-balanced wine list begins at £10.05.

## ▲ No 13

13 Dillwyn Street, Swansea, SA1 4AQ
Tel no: (01792) 522950

It may look like the archetypal modern British restaurant (slate and wood-effect floors, smart wooden tables, charming staff, bold artwork on pale walls) but No. 13's menu sets the tone for a more relaxed, greedy style of eating. International flavours dominate the specials board, while regular dishes could include a Welsh Black beef burger with excellent hand-cut chunky chips or oven-roasted supreme of chicken with sautéed bacon and leeks and a rarebit cheese sauce. Desserts such as butterscotch crème brûlée or apple and berry crumble also deserve attention. A short list of mostly New World wines begins at £9.95.

## ▲ La Parilla

Unit 5, J Shed, Kings Road, Swansea, SA1 8PL
Tel no: (01792) 464530
www.laparilla.co.uk

La Parilla is the offspring of La Brasseria in Wind Street. It's set in the slick, trendy SA1 docklands development and styled accordingly; but food-wise it's a carbon copy of its daddy. As with La Brasseria, prices are high for what's on offer (moules marinière £5.25, monkfish and chips £13.50, salad £2.95, French bread £1.10) and it's more suited to a quick meal than a leisurely evening, but both are good places for a decent steak or fresh fish with chips. An interesting, French and Spanish-dominated wine list opens at £12.25.

## Best places for afternoon tea

**Betty's Café**, 6-8 St Helen's Square, York
A Yorkshire institution, with traditional teas served by frilly-aproned waitresses.

**De Wynn's**, 55 Church Street, Falmouth
This family-run tea shop serves teas grown in the nearby Tregothnan Tea Garden.

**The Dorchester**, Park Lane, London
The ultimate tea-time setting in which to watch the world go by.

**Elizabeth Botham & Sons Ltd**,
35/39 Skinner Street, Whitby
Family bakery, founded in 1865; famous for plum bread and irresistible ginger brack.

**Peacocks Tearoom**, 65 Waterside, Ely
With an encyclopaedic range of over fifty varieties, tea is taken very seriously here.

**Swinton Park**, Masham, Ripon
A fine country house hotel and cooking school, serving elegant teas.

**The Willow Tea Rooms**,
217 Sauchiehall Street, Glasgow
A splendid setting, designed by Charles Rennie Mackintosh in 1904.

**The Wolseley**, 160 Piccadilly, London
Battenburg cake and an Art Deco silver tea service are highlights at this café/brasserie.

**Yauatcha**, 15 Broadwick Street, London
A minimalist, all-day tea house with a library of China teas and infusions, served alongside stunning cakes.

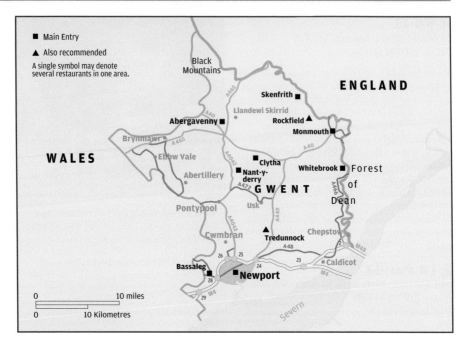

Map legend:
- ■ Main Entry
- ▲ Also recommended

A single symbol may denote several restaurants in one area.

Black Mountains

ENGLAND

Skenfrith ■

Llandewi Skirrid

Abergavenny ■        Rockfield ▲

Brynmawr                    Monmouth ■

WALES

Ebbw Vale

Clytha ■

Abertillery        Nant-y-     ■Whitebrook ■  Forest
                   derry                        of
                        GWENT              Dean

Pontypool        Usk

Cwmbran        ▲
              Tredunnock

Chepstow

Bassaleg ■        26   25     24        23    ■ Caldicot
              28        ■Newport

0        10 miles
0        10 Kilometres

Severn

## Abergavenny

### The Hardwick

**Assured straightforward cooking**
Old Raglan Road, Abergavenny, NP7 9AA
Tel no: (01873) 854220
www.thehardwick.co.uk
Gastropub | £25
Cooking score: 4

V £30

After years spent working in some of the most influential kitchens in London, Stephen Terry has put down some firm roots at this remote pub a couple of miles outside of Abergavenny. A plain-looking white building set against a backdrop of the Black Mountains, there is nothing fanciful about the interior, just quarry-tile floors, reclaimed wooden furniture and low lighting. Much is made of local sourcing, with several producers getting name-checks on the menu, whether it's the Longhorn beef from Huntsham Farm at Goodrich or cured meats from nearby Trealy Farm. Crispy, breadcrumbed belly of local

Old Spot pork is given a Cantonese twist with bok choi, soy sauce, chilli, garlic and ginger. Alternatively, you could kick things off with a salad of Colston Basset Stilton, walnuts and baked croûtons with watercress, dandelion, rocket and endive. Of the 20 or so main courses, an individual Longhorn beef, kidney, oxtail and ale pie plays a starring role and arrives with exemplary triple-cooked chips. Service is chatty and welcoming. A short choice of desserts includes rice pudding with prune d'Argent and Armagnac, with half of the puddings being available in 'small' sizes. The revised wine list starts at £11.50.
**Chef/s:** Stephen Terry. **Open:** Tue to Sun L 12 to 3, Tue to Sat D 6.30 to 10. **Closed:** 25 Dec, 26 Dec. **Meals:** alc L and D (main courses £10.50 to £16.95). **Service:** not inc. **Details:** Cards accepted. 70 seats. No mobile phones. Music. Children's portions. Car parking.

## ▌Bassaleg

### Junction 28

Eclectic menu at a culinary crossroads
Station Approach, Bassaleg, NP10 8LD
Tel no: (01633) 891891
www.junction28.com
**Modern European | £30**
**Cooking score: 2**

This is a place of comings and goings – the railway behind, the rushing river below, an old church opposite – but Junction 28 has stood solidly as a restaurant for years. Inside it's spacious but intimate – domestic, even. A typical meal could include pan-fried foie gras and lamb's sweetbreads on a bacon, potato and cheese galette, then grilled rib of veal with warm salad of beef tomatoes. Appealing side orders run from the expected chips and salads to the likes of Mediterranean-style couscous or Jerusalem artichokes in hollandaise. The presentation sometimes echoes the kitschness of the décor. Flavour-wise, simple combinations (gurnard fillets with cherry tomatoes, rosemary and garlic) are the most effective, while a lunchtime dish of duck breast in oriental broth with a prawn dumpling disappointed at inspection, having nothing to balance the overly sweet broth. Wines start at £12.95.

**Chef/s:** Jonathan West. **Open:** all week L 12 to 2, Mon to Sat D 5.30 to 9.45. **Closed:** 24 July to 8 Aug. **Meals:** alc exc Sun L (main courses £7 to £17). Set L Mon to Sat £10.95 (2 courses) to £12.45, Set D 5.30 to 7 £14.95, Set D £17.95. **Service:** not inc. **Details:** Cards accepted. 60 seats. 30 seats outside. Air-con. Wheelchair access. Music. Children's portions. Car parking.

## ▌Clytha

### Clytha Arms

Cosy restaurant with old-world charm
Clytha, NP7 9BW
Tel no: (01873) 840206
www.clytha-arms.com
**British | £42**
**Cooking score: 3**

£5 OFF 🍷 🍽 🗸

The smell of woodsmoke and a buzz of conversation greet you at this pink-washed inn which continues to deserve its reputation for great beers and proper cooking. Everything about it feels authentic, from the uncluttered old-world charm of the bar and lounge to the utterly ordinary-looking dining room, where happy diners and the food itself provide the sense of occasion. You could start with a basket of rustic breads then use them to mop the juices of a weightless Perl Las and port soufflé before following with a monkfish and scallop kebab, or, from the set-price menu, a gargantuan cassoulet of boar and duck leg. For dessert, perhaps a home-made hazelnut meringue with strawberries and cream. The style is simple and hearty with clear, confident flavours. Service from a young team is sincere but overstretched on busy nights. Good wines start at £12.50, but do try the beers too.

**Chef/s:** Andrew and Sarah Canning. **Open:** Tue to Sun L 12.30 to 2.15, Tue to Sat D 7 to 9.30. **Closed:** 25 Dec. **Meals:** alc exc Sun L (main courses £12 to £20). Set L and D Tue to Sat £16.95 (2 courses) to £19.95, Set L Sun £14.95 (2 courses) to £17.95. Bar menu available exc Sat D, Sun L. **Service:** not inc. **Details:** Cards accepted. 60 seats. 40 seats outside. No music. Children's portions. Car parking.

## ▌Monmouth

## Twenty Four

A popular and innovative new restaurant
24 Church Street, Monmouth, NP25 3BU
Tel no: (01600) 772744
**Modern British | £26**
Cooking score: 2

£5 ꝩ £30
OFF

This sophisticated little restaurant is tucked away on one of the prettiest streets in Monmouth. The building has all the charm and character that come with old age, while feeling subtly modern. Lunch brings a comforting, modern-rustic selection of grilled sandwiches and light bites (baked whole Camembert with toasted soldiers and home-made quince jelly) plus more substantial choices such as roast fillet of organic salmon with sautéed new potatoes, purple sprouting broccoli and caper, parsley and lemon butter. In the evening, you could start with roast beetroot and balsamic soup with Bower Farm crème fraîche; or Gloucester Old Spot meat loaf with crisp potato chips and warm red-onion marmalade, followed by braised shin of Welsh beef with creamy mashed potato, buttery clapshot, steamed spinach and red-wine reduction or chargrilled chicken supreme with braised Puy lentils, red-wine sauce, polenta croûtons and rocket salad. Round it off with a hot dark chocolate fondant and vanilla ice cream or Baileys semi-freddo with coffee cream. Wines from £13.95.
**Chef/s:** Wes Harris. **Open:** Tue to Sat L 12 to 2.30, D 6.30 to 9.30. **Closed:** Sun, Mon, Christmas.
**Meals:** Main courses £10.50 to £15.50.
**Service:** optional. **Details:** Cards accepted. 24 seats. Wheelchair access. Music. Children allowed.

## ▌Nant-y-derry

## Foxhunter

Traditional cooking with a modern twist
Nant-y-derry, NP7 9DN
Tel no: (01873) 881101
www.thefoxhunter.com
**Modern European | £30**
Cooking score: 4

Once a stationmaster's house, this pretty building in peaceful Nant-y-derry has undergone thorough refurbishments in the hands of chef-proprietor Matt Tebbutt and his wife, Lisa. The interior is uncluttered and sophisticated, but with a rural burr. The restaurant is 'small enough for you to feel important', says one reporter, who also took delight in the locally sourced ingredients. Matt trained under the likes of Marco Pierre White, Alastair Little and Sally Clark, and their influences have informed his cooking style, which brings a breezy modern edge to traditional European and British dishes. A typical dinner could begin with braised oxtail with tagliatelle and Parmesan; grilled sardines and squid with coriander and chilli salsa; or wood pigeon bruschetta with deep-fried artichokes and lemon dressing. Among the main courses might be braised longhorn rump with garlic, onions, parley, mash and spinach; traditionally garnished roast partridge; and duck breast with warm white beans and basil oil. Lemon posset, bread-and-butter pudding with clotted cream, or quince and apple crumble with vanilla cream are typical desserts. The wine list is full of interest, with plenty of good French finds and a decent list of half-bottles. Prices from £13.95 a bottle.
**Chef/s:** Matt Tebbutt. **Open:** Tue to Sat 12.30 to 2.30, 7 to 9.30. **Closed:** Christmas, 2 weeks Feb.
**Meals:** alc (main courses £12 to £20). Set L £17 (2 courses) to £21. **Service:** not inc. **Details:** Cards accepted. 50 seats. 12 seats outside. Wheelchair access. Music. Children's portions. Car parking.

# Newport

## Chandlery

**Tastefully converted Grade-II-listed building**
77-78 Lower Dock Street, Newport, NP20 1EH
Tel no: (01633) 256622
www.thechandleryrestaurant.com
**Modern European | £41**
**Cooking score: 4**

Originally a nineteenth-century ships' chandlery, this building has been converted with modern sensibilities and an eye for period detail. Exposed floorboards, characterful wooden furniture and a gathering of smartly upholstered sofas set the tone for a modern, classically inspired menu. At lunch, there are light bites such as Welsh rarebit or free-range sausages with mash and gravy, plus an excellent value business lunch offering the likes of smoked pork salad and piccalilli followed by bourride of seafood and a dessert of tiramisu. An evening meal might kick off with a deep fried duck egg with spring vegetable salad followed by sirloin of Welsh Black beef with champ, buttered cabbage and bordelaise sauce. Desserts include lemon meringue pie; hot chocolate fondant and organic yogurt bavarois with melon soup. A comprehensive 45-strong wine list starts at £12.95.
**Chef/s:** Simon Newcombe and Carl Hamett. **Open:** Tue to Fri L 12 to 2, Tue to Sat D 7 to 10. **Closed:** 1 week Christmas to New Year. **Meals:** alc D (main courses £9.50 to £18). Set L £12.95 (3 courses). Light L menu available. **Service:** not inc. **Details:** Cards accepted. 80 seats. Air-con. Wheelchair access. Music. Children's portions. Car parking.

## ALSO RECOMMENDED

## ▲ Stone Mill

Rockfield, NP25 5SW
Tel no: (01600) 716273
www.thestonemill.co.uk

Soft lighting on bare wood makes this converted barn an attractive prospect for an intimate meal. The menu credits an impressive list of local suppliers, and everything from pasta and breads to chutney is made on site. Carpaccio of venison with pickled chicory, crème fraîche and an orange and cardamon reduction (£7.50) and fillet of turbot with crushed new potatoes, cannelloni of langoustine and clam nage (£16.95) are typical of the style. Wines start at £11.95. Accommodation is available in the ivy-covered cottages opposite.

# Skenfrith

## Bell at Skenfrith

**Competent cooking beside the castle ruins**
Skenfrith, NP7 8UH
Tel no: (01600) 750235
www.skenfrith.co.uk
**British | £39**
**Cooking score: 1**

Original features blend seamlessly with country-style modernity in this beautifully located pub by the river Monnow. There's an inglenook fireplace, a hint of woodsmoke and a rambling dining area furnished with bare wood tables. The food is modern, but with a strong sense of place; the blackboard lists local suppliers, and much of the fruit and vegetables come from the kitchen garden. Lunch might begin with soy-marinated salmon terrine with pickled mango, followed by grilled ribeye of Welsh beef with hand-cut chips and béarnaise sauce. For dinner, perhaps pan-roasted quail with wild mushroom and truffle lasagne and chocolate port sauce followed by roast halibut with rocket crust, chorizo and basil risotto, mange-tout diamonds and sun-dried tomato pesto. Finish with passion-fruit posset with a black-pepper tuile and exotic fruit compote. Landlord William Hutchings' outstanding wine list currently reveals a passion for champagne and (as always) cognacs. Bottles from £14; lots of half-bottles.
**Chef/s:** David Hill. **Open:** all week 12 to 2.30, 7 to 9.30 (9 Sun). **Meals:** alc exc Sun L (main courses L £13 to £16, D £14 to £18). Set L Sun £18.50 (2 courses) to £21.50. **Service:** not inc. **Details:** Cards accepted. 80 seats. 20 seats outside. Wheelchair access. Music. Children's portions. Car parking.

## ALSO RECOMMENDED

### ▲ Newbridge Inn

Tredunnock, NP15 1LY
Tel no: (01633) 451000

Beautifully restored and restyled, this riverside gastropub delivers a warm welcome. Chef and management remain unchanged but a recent shift of focus has seen the arrival of a less formal menu, with choices extending from sandwiches to modern-rustic meals such as chicken liver parfait with toasted brioche and onion marmalade (£6) followed by saddle of Bwlch venison on bubble and squeak (£16). Finish with panettone bread-and-butter pudding and clotted cream (£5). Wines from £12.75 a bottle. Accommodation available. Open all week.

# Whitebrook

## Crown at Whitebrook

Roadside restaurant-with-rooms
Whitebrook, NP25 4TX
Tel no: (01600) 860254
www.crownatwhitebrook.co.uk
Modern European | £53
Cooking score: 6

This restaurant stands deep in a wood with lofty trees and birdsong all around. Internally it is just as relaxing. The food is a joy, from dainty canapés (perhaps a blue cheese samosa, smoked duck with sweet pepper, scallop roe in batter, and a shot of courgette and mint soup) to playful petits fours back in the lounge later on. In between, there might be an amuse-bouche of cabbage-wrapped crab and ginger 'cannelloni'; a starter of roast and confit quail with foie gras, beetroot and orange; a palate-cleansing apple sorbet with berry foam; and a main course of poached and seared rare breed pork with confit of celery, shallot and five spice jus – a dish which impressed at inspection with its pinpoint accuracy and glorious spectrum of flavours. Other main courses include loin of Welsh lamb with fresh morels, wild garlic, liquorice and black treacle; and slow-roasted Anjou squab on lemon pearl barley with glazed beets and camomile emulsion. Dessert might be apple pie mousse with rhubarb jelly and a cinnamon doughnut. The 'great attention to detail' noted by one reporter is evident in every aspect of the operation. Décor-wise, the place is pristine and safely middle-of-the-road, with a latte and cream colour scheme, wood floors in the lounge, and smartly framed life drawings in the carpeted restaurant. 'Wonderful service' comes from charming waitresses who bring genuine warmth to what might otherwise seem a starchy operation. The long, intelligent wine list starts at £16 and ends in the stratosphere. It is well annotated, and enhanced further by the attentions of a helpful sommelier.

Chef/s: James Sommerin. Open: Wed to Sun L 12 to 2, Wed to Sat D 7 to 9 (Sat 9:30). Closed: 25 Dec to 8 Jan. Meals: Set L £22.50 (2 courses) to £25. Set D £39.95 (3 courses). Service: not inc, 12.5% for parties of 6 or more. Details: Cards accepted. 30 seats. 18 seats outside. No mobile phones. Wheelchair access. Music. Car parking.

---

### Cooking score

A score of 1 is a significant achievement. The score in any review is based on several meals, incorporating feedback from both our readers and inspectors. As a rough guide, 1 denotes capable cooking with some inconsistencies, rising steadily through different levels of technical expertise, until the scores between 6 and 10 indicate exemplary skills, along with innovation, artistry and ambition. If there is a new chef, we don't score the restaurant for the first year of entry. For further details, please see the scoring section in the introduction to the Guide.

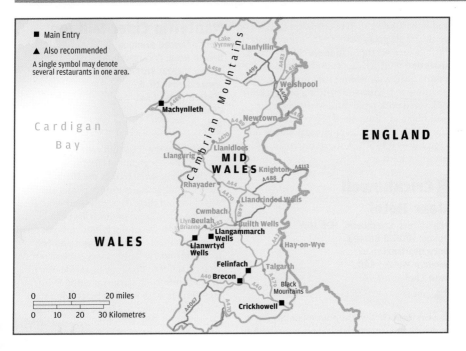

## Brecon

### Tipple'n'Tiffin

**A fitting stage for dish-sharing**
Theatr Brycheiniog, Brecon, LD3 7EW
Tel no: (01874) 611866
**Modern European | £21**
**Cooking score: 1**

Pre-theatre meals do not get much more convenient than this. The restaurant occupies the ground floor of Theatr Brycheiniog, overlooking the canal. On a sunny evening you can sit outside watching the ducks and swooping swallows. The interior is modern, informal, and has a buzz that indicates people come here specifically for the food. The menu is based around 'plates and bowls to share'; these might be deep-fried Penclawdd cockles; mussels in wine and cream with roasted garlic; pigeon breast salad with bacon and mushroom; excellent home-made bread with olives and dipping oil; game sausages with root mash, caramelised shallot and claret gravy; and crispy duck legs on kumara (a type of sweet potato) with butternut squash rösti and apple and onion compote. Home-made puddings include glazed lime tart with crème fraîche; and plum crumble with vanilla ice cream. A short wine list starts at £11.

**Chef/s:** Richard Gardener. **Open:** Mon to Sat, B 10, L 12 to 2.30; D 6/7 to 9 (last sitting). **Closed:** Sundays; Christmas and New Year. **Service:** optional.
**Details:** Cards accepted. 40 seats. 20 seats outside. Wheelchair access. Music. Children allowed. Car parking.

## ALSO RECOMMENDED

### ▲ Barn at Brynich
Brynich, Brecon, LD3 7SH
Tel no: (01874) 623480

A fine example of diversification, this barn was, not so long ago, part of a working farm. Then owners, Colin and Maureen Jones, opened a caravan park and in time the barn was converted into a smart, spacious restaurant. Food here ranges from daytime tea and cakes and light lunches such as omelettes (£5.25) or steak and ale pie (£9.50) to the evening à la carte, which might include tian of crab with sparkling wine jelly (£6.25) followed by boned quail with walnut stuffing, game potatoes, red-wine and pancetta jus (£14.50) or layered pork tenderloin with beer-batter pudding and caramelised apple with Caerphilly cheese, dauphinoise potatoes and sage sauce (£13.50). A short, international wine list starts at £9.95.

# ▌Crickhowell

## Bear Hotel

High Street, Crickhowell, NP8 1BW
Tel no: (01873) 810408
www.bearhotel.co.uk
Modern Welsh | £40
New Chef

A new head chef was appointed in 2007 at this genially run former coaching inn on the A40. The massive first-floor dining room is big enough to accommodate the press of business, and there seem to be many satisfied customers. Menus are built around winning combinations such as chicken liver parfait with toasted brioche and red-onion marmalade, or seared scallops and home-made black pudding, to start. Main courses showcase good Welsh produce, like Black beef and lamb, the latter served majestically enough with three sauces, while fish might be grilled Dover sole, garnished with prawns, pancetta and beurre noisette. Finish with variations on grape – mousse, sorbet and compote – or five different chocolate confections on one plate. Wines are varietally arranged, and kick off with house vins de pays at £11.

**Chef/s:** Steve Hodson. **Open:** Sun L 12 to 2, Tue to Sat D 7.30 to 9.30. **Closed:** Christmas Day. **Meals:** alc (main courses £14.95 to £19.95) Sun L £16.95. **Service:** not inc. **Details:** Cards accepted. 100 seats. 54 seats outside. Separate bar. No mobile phones. Wheelchair access. Music. Children's portions. Car parking.

## Nantyffin Cider Mill Inn

Family-farmed produce
Brecon Road, Crickhowell, NP8 1SG
Tel no: (01873) 810775
www.cidermill.co.uk
Modern Welsh | £41
Cooking score: 2

Dating from the sixteenth century, this old drovers' inn has plenty of charm, as well as a lovely setting at the foot of the Black Hills. As the name suggests, its former preoccupation was cider, but these days, food and wine are its twin passions. Local produce has been key to the operation since long before such concerns were fashionable, with meat and poultry sourced from the family farm just seven miles away. It is put to good use in a wide-reaching menu that features starters ranging from open ravioli filled with smoked Black Mountain chicken, Parmesan and leeks, to griddled spiced lamb kebab with hummus and herb salad filo tarts. Main courses offer confit of lamb with rosemary and garlic sauce and mash alongside more exotic offerings such as Thai-spiced pork tenderloin with coriander butter, lemongrass, chilli, ginger and coconut curry. To finish, crème brûlée with rhubarb and ginger compote, or sticky toffee pudding with Jersey cream and toffee sauce are typical. The wine list offers a good balance between value, variety and quality, with some interesting selections and plenty of choice under £20, plus eight wines by the glass.

**Chef/s:** Sean Gerrard. **Open:** Tue to Sun L 12 to 2.30, Tue to Sat D 6.30 to 9.30. **Closed:** 25 and 26 Dec. **Meals:** alc (main courses £13 to £16). Set L Tue to Fri £12.95 (2 courses) to £16.95, Set D Tue to Thur £12.95 (2 courses) to £16.95. **Service:** not inc. **Details:** Cards accepted. 100 seats. 40 seats outside. No music. Wheelchair access. Children's portions. Car parking.

## Felinfach

★ BEST FAMILY RESTAURANT ★

### Felin Fach Griffin
**Relaxed dining with local produce**
Felinfach, LD3 0UB
Tel no: (01874) 620111
www.felinfachgriffin.co.uk
British | £45
Cooking score: 3

☷ ⋎

The Felin Fach Griffin does relaxed, modern-rustic style to devastatingly good effect. It is pub enough to have excellent, well-kept ales on tap, but restaurant enough to deliver excellent service and cooking that is hearty but reliably exact.. Much of the food is rooted in the surrounding landscape (some ingredients come from the kitchen garden). Start with a Welsh goats' cheese salad with young vegetable salad and mint oil, followed by rump of local lamb with ratatouille, sweet potato purée and thyme jus. For pudding, perhaps bitter chocolate tart with blood orange or excellent home-made ice creams (look out for the delectably sweet and fiery gingerbread variety). A well-chosen international wine list with Francophile leanings starts at £11.95.
**Chef/s:** Ricardo van Ede. **Open:** Tue to Sun L 12.30 to 2.30, all week D 6.30 to 9.30. **Closed:** 24, 25 Dec. **Meals:** alc (main courses D £14 to £17). Set L £12.50 (2 courses) Set D £28.90 (3 courses). **Service:** not inc. **Details:** Cards accepted. 60 seats. 25 seats outside. Wheelchair access. Music. Children's portions. Car parking.

## Llangammarch Wells

### Lake Country House
**An arresting Victorian pile**
Llangammarch Wells, LD4 4BS
Tel no: (01591) 620202
Modern European | £32
Cooking score: 2

£5 OFF ♦ ☷ ⋎

Antique furniture and watchful old portraits lend this country-house hotel an Agatha Christie-style charm. The main event, in the hushed, carpeted and chandeliered dining room, is more modern than you might expect. A typical meal might take in yellowfin tuna with a green bean and Chinese truffle salad; loin of Bwlch venison with creamed Savoy cabbage, pancetta, roasted onion purée and truffle sauce; and camomile pannacotta with a warm poppy seed muffin, blueberry sauce and a pecan wafer. The more adventurous flavour combinations are not always successful, but the cooking is precise. The impressive 300-strong wine list is weighted towards the Old World. House wines start at £16.
**Chef/s:** Sean Cullingford. **Open:** all week 12.30 to 2, 7.15 to 9. **Meals:** Set L £24.50, Set D £39.50. **Service:** not inc. **Details:** Cards accepted. 50 seats. 12 seats outside. No music. No mobile phones. Wheelchair access. Children's portions. Car parking.

### Average price

The average price listed in main-entry reviews denotes the price of a three-course meal, without wine.

## ▌Llanwrtyd Wells

### Carlton Riverside

**Grand culinary designs**
Llanwrtyd Wells, LD5 4RA
Tel no: (01591) 610248
www.carltonrestaurant.co.uk
**Modern Welsh | £48**
**Cooking score: 6**

£5
OFF ♦ ⊨

Formerly at Carlton House, chef Mary Ann Gilchrist and her husband, Alan, have moved up the road to Carlton Riverside. The new restaurant is more spacious, and has the added benefit of views over the River Irfon from one end. Downstairs is a cavern-like cellar bar frequented by welcoming locals. Back upstairs, Alan provides delightfully affable, attentive service while clanks, sizzles and tantalising smells from the kitchen announce that Mary Ann is at work. She has a masterful grasp of flavours, and her set-price chef's menu is intelligent and well balanced. Style-wise, there is a tendency towards timeless classics, but Gilchrist is no stranger to culinary trends or invention. An inspection meal included historical (but newly fashionable) Scotch woodcock and an exemplary dessert of chilled spiced plum soup with rosewater ice cream, while the main act – roast rack of local lamb with braised shoulder, a devilled kidney, flageolet beans, buttered leeks, sweet pepper ragout and crushed Jersey Royals – was full of classical charm and subtly unfolding flavours. The décor suggests the intention to strike a modern note here, but some aspects of the experience (the cherry tomato garnish that accompanied a delicious salt-cod pâté appetiser, for example) do not yet sit comfortably with this approach. Not that this matters, as there is no doubting Mary Ann's ongoing ability to delight, nor Alan's flair for choosing (and recommending) deliciously complementary wines, starting at £16.
**Chef/s:** Mary Ann Gilchrist. **Open:** Mon to Sat D only 7 to 8.30. **Closed:** 6 to 30 Dec. **Meals:** alc (main courses £22 to £26), Set D £28 (two courses).

**Service:** not inc. **Details:** Cards accepted. 20 seats. Separate bar. No mobile phones. Wheelchair access. Children's portions.

### Lasswade Country House

**Charming country-house hotel**
Station Road, Llanwrtyd Wells, LD5 4RW
Tel no: (01591) 610515
www.lasswadehotel.co.uk
**Modern British | £36**
**Cooking score: 2**

⊨ ⋎

As Food Ambassador for Mid-Wales on behalf of the National Assembly, chef-proprietor Roger Stevens amply demonstrates his serious commitment to organic and local produce. Starters such as salmon and crème fraîche ravioli with watercress pesto, or a herb salad with artichoke hearts, smoked pine nuts and sunflower seeds, might be followed by slow-roast pork belly on caramelised onions with sautéed apple and scrumpy cider, or roast cod with chilli jam, lime couscous and sugar snap peas. To finish, choose between a dessert such as cognac crème brûlée or a selection of unpasteurised Welsh cheeses. Wines are a well-chosen and varied selection. Prices start at around £10 for house French.
**Chef/s:** Roger Stevens. **Open:** all week D 7.30 to 9. **Meals:** Set D £28 (3 courses). **Service:** not inc. **Details:** Cards accepted. 20 seats. No mobile phones. Music. Car parking.

## ▌Machynlleth

### Wynnstay

**Modern comforts**
Maengwyn Street, Machynlleth, SY20 8AE
Tel no: (01654) 702941
www.wynnstay-hotel.com
**Modern Welsh | £35**
**Cooking score: 2**

⊨ ⋎

Standing on the main road through the village, this is an imposing Georgian coaching inn. Chef Gareth Johns takes an eminently flexible approach. His cooking has a local

## Foraging – Fergus Drennan

The resurgent force of great British cuisine is enjoying a celebratory renaissance of interest for the magical culinary journeys and intoxicating possibilities afforded by our collective natural inheritance: wild foraged foods.

Traditionally foraged ingredients include: Marsh Samphire, Dulse seaweed and the apricot-scented Chanterelle, but recent additions to menus include Scarlet Elfcups, pungent Dittander, Japanese Knotweed and Bristly Ox-tongue. Rafael Lopez, head chef at The Goods Shed in Canterbury, and Blaise Vasseur of the George and Dragon in Kent have embraced this vast range of offerings with aplomb. Dishes include Pellitory of The Wall Tart with smoked trout and Sea Buckthorn hollandaise; Sweet Wood Sorrel jelly; roast squirrel with elderflower, caramelised onions and ver juice. Terrific!

But what does the future hold for wild foraged foods? We must negotiate and define an ecologically aware and sustainable relationship with nature. Can the surrounding countryside meet the voracious demands of an ever-expanding London restaurant trade? It is an exceedingly moot point. Treading softly on the land requires respect. For the continuity of our wild food heritage to sustain both our pallet and cultural imagination, we must resist profiteering and resolve never to exploit the natural world but, instead, to embrace wild foods as a uniquely intimate gateway to our culinary past and future.

character, with fine local produce at its heart, put to good use in a varied range of dishes. Spaghetti with calamari or smoked haddock brandade with crostini might be among the small options, while large plates typically run to about a dozen, perhaps including John Dory fillet with preserved lemon, tomato and olive oil, pork loin and belly with sage gravy and black pudding potatoes, and roast hake with cockles and wild garlic veloute. To finish, blueberry pannacotta with forest fruits, or poached red pear with chocolate ice cream and cream are typical. Italian house wines are £13.95.

**Chef/s:** Gareth Johns. **Open:** all week 12 to 2, 6.30 to 9. **Meals:** alc exc Sun L (main courses £9 to £16). **Service:** not inc. **Details:** Cards accepted. 80 seats. 40 seats outside. Wheelchair access. Music. Children's portions. Car parking.

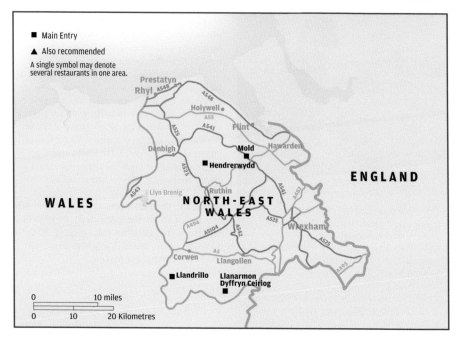

## Hendrerwydd

### White Horse Inn

**Generous portions and an extensive menu**
Hendrerwydd, LL16 4LL
Tel no: (01824) 790218
www.white-horse-inn.co.uk
Gastropub | £35
Cooking score: 2

£5 OFF ⋎

Old oak beams define this ancient country inn. Generosity is the kitchen's watchword, which applies both to the extent of the menu and the size of portions. But this is not merely trencherman fare, just honest home cooking. Bacon-wrapped rolled baked sardines with a nutty herb stuffing might be among starters. Main courses might feature venison 'Wellington', with a mushroom and smoked bacon stuffing, or halibut fillet with browned parsley butter. To finish, there's a fine selection of Welsh cheeses and desserts such as Baileys bread and butter pudding. Wines from £10.95.

**Chef/s:** Ruth Vintr, Chris Hurst and Josef Haulk. **Open:** Tue to Sun L 12 to 2.30, Tue to Sat D 6 to 9.30. **Closed:** 25 Dec, bank hols. **Meals:** alc (main courses £14 to £18). Bar menu available. **Service:** not inc. **Details:** Cards accepted. 50 seats. 60 seats outside. No music. No mobile phones. Children's portions. Car parking.

## Llanarmon Dyffryn Ceiriog

### West Arms

**Ambitious modern cooking**
Llanarmon Dyffryn Ceiriog, LL20 7LD
Tel no: (01691) 600665
www.thewestarms.co.uk
French | £33
Cooking score: 3

🛏

This gem of an 'olde-worlde' pub is hidden away in a deeply rural setting, down a winding single-track road, but is well worth a detour. Inside is a warren of slate-floored rooms with low black beams, chintzy curtains and gleaming horse brasses, making for a very comfortable setting in which to enjoy Grant Williams's ambitious modern cooking. Dinner menus offer three choices at each stage, typically opening with seared king scallops and blue crab tortellini on steamed leeks with grain-mustard sauce, or smoked duck breast on a rocket, pear and roasted red pepper salad. To follow, there might be steamed baby halibut encasing a smoked salmon and asparagus soufflé with champagne and crème fraîche sauce, or pancetta-wrapped pheasant breast on roasted apples and chestnuts with an elderberry sauce. Crème caramel with raspberries is among dessert options, or you could go for the selection of Welsh and Continental cheeses. The international wine list covers a good range of bottles at fair prices, opening with house Chilean merlot and chardonnay at £14.95.

**Chef/s:** Grant Williams. **Open:** Sun L 12 to 2, all week D 7 to 9. **Meals:** alc L (main courses £9 to £17). Set D £32.90. Bar menu available. **Service:** 10%. **Details:** Cards accepted. 50 seats. 40 seats outside. Music. Children's portions. Car parking.

## ▌Llandrillo

★ READERS' RESTAURANT OF THE YEAR ★
WALES

### Tyddyn Llan

**Personal charm and simple modern food**
Llandrillo, LL21 0ST
Tel no: (01490) 440264
www.tyddynllan.co.uk
**Modern British | £56**
**Cooking score: 7**

🍷 ⊑ ℣

A rustic Georgian house built of slate and stone is the setting for Bryan and Susan Webb's endearing restaurant-with-rooms. It stands in the shadow of the Berwyn mountains on the fringes of Llandrillo village, and is run with consummate care and personal dedication. According to one contented regular, it is a place that 'never fails to please'. A veranda looks out onto the carefully tended garden with its neat clipped hedges and ornamental fountain. Bryan Webb is a Welsh chef who understands the regional larder around him and knows instinctively how to extract the best from seasonal and local supplies. He eschews technically effete gestures in favour of bold, direct flavours and an innate simplicity, witness his long-serving signature dish of griddled scallops with tiny spoonfuls of vegetable relish around a pile of fresh rocket leaves. Other fish dishes could be as uncomplicated as dressed crab with avocado salsa or wild sea bass with laverbread beurre blanc. Meat and game are also given full-impact, native treatment with no unnecessary distractions on the plate: thus roast pigeon might appear in company with wild garlic bubble and squeak and St George's mushrooms, while leg of rabbit could be served in gutsy fashion with black pudding and mustard sauce. To finish, there is a splendid array of desserts shot through with seasonality and colour – pistachio crème brûlée or grilled pineapple with chilli syrup and coconut sorbet, for example. Alternatively, investigate the assortment of British farmhouse cheeses which comes courtesy of Neal's Yard. Reporters confirm that this is 'wondrous food' and 'unbeatable at the price'. There is also praise for Susan Webb's charm and welcoming presence out front, and applause for the 'stunning' wine list which is helpfully divided up into drinker-friendly categories like 'big scale fruity reds'. Sources and growers throughout are beyond reproach. A brilliant assortment of around 16 wines by the glass provides memorable drinking from £3.75 (£15 a bottle), and half-bottles are also in abundant supply.

**Chef/s:** Bryan Webb. **Open:** Fri to Sun L 12.30 to 2.15, all week D 7 to 9.30. **Closed:** 2 weeks Jan. **Meals:** Set L Fri and Sat £21.50 (2 courses) to £28, Set L Sun £23.50, Set D £35 (2 courses) to £60. **Service:** not inc. **Details:** Cards accepted. 40 seats. No mobile phones. Wheelchair access. Music. Children's portions. Car parking.

## Best food festivals

Drive around the UK during the summer months and it might seem that every second town is hosting a food festival. The best of them, including those listed here, are a positive reflection of closer links being forged between local people, their restaurants and food producers.

**Ludlow Marches Festival**, September
Twelve years on, the celebrated festival is still firmly centred around small suppliers.

**Whitstable Oyster Festival**, July
Great fun, even for the bivalve-ambivalent, the fair still begins with the ceremonial 'Landing of the Catch'.

**Abergavenny Festival**, September
There is always a star-studded chef line up, with events embracing food.

**Newlyn Fish Festival**, Penzance, August
Learn about the local fishing industry and sample some of Cornwall's finest catch.

**York Festival of Food and Drink**, September
Follow the Ale Trail in York's historic pubs during ten days of local food markets.

**The Dales Festival of Food and Drink**, Leyburn, Wensleydale, May
Interactive farming displays emphasise the links between community, food and soil.

**Asparagus Festival**, Bretforton, Worcestershire, May
Paying homage to the historic Vale of Evesham asparagus auctions.

## ▌Mold

## 56 High Street

Stylish fish-oriented restaurant
56 High Street, Mold, CH7 1BD
Tel no: (01352) 759225
Seafood | £35
Cooking score: 3
£5 OFF  V

By the time you read this the stylishly simple single-floor restaurant may have expanded by two floors, to meet well-deserved popular demand for its fish-oriented dishes. They don't just buy Welsh ingredients, they build close relationships with producers such as the Llandudno Smokery. A desire to please all appetites and tastes brings mussels from the Menai six ways and lobster served in a multitude of styles. Monkfish, bass and mullet may dominate but Welsh lamb with Welsh honey sauce or beef topped with chicken parfait and blue cheese keep carnivores happy. Wines start at £10.95 and, excepting the odd gesture to satisfy nearby Cheshire millionaires, the small but wide-ranging list keeps most bottles around or below £20. **Chef/s:** Karl Mitchell, Kirsten Robb and Martin Fawcett. **Open:** Tue to Sat 12 to 3, 6 to 10 (10.30 Fri and Sat). **Closed:** bank hols. **Meals:** alc (main courses £8 to £20). **Service:** not inc. **Details:** Cards accepted. 52 seats. Air-con. No mobile phones. Wheelchair access. Music. Children's portions.

## READERS RECOMMEND

## Manorhaus

**Modern British**
Well Street, Ruthin, LL15 1AH
Tel no: (01824) 704830
www.manorhaus.com
'Boutique hotel serving modern food'

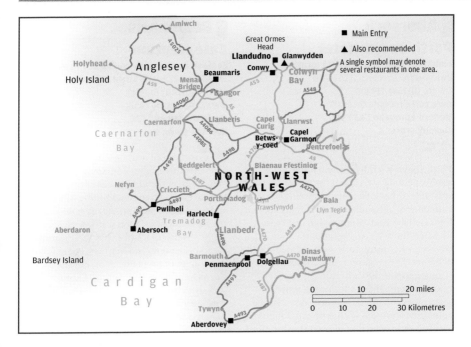

# ■ Aberdovey

## Penhelig Arms

**Outstanding sea views**
Terrace Road, Aberdovey, LL35 OLT
Tel no: (01654) 767215
www.penheligarms.com
**Modern British | £38**
Cooking score: 2

£5
OFF ♦ ⊟ ⋎

The Penhelig stands inside the boundaries of Snowdonia National Park and enjoys fine sea views, the latter providing inspiration for much of what goes on in the kitchen. 'Superbly fresh fish, simply cooked' sums up the culinary philosophy, with starters taking in grilled sardines with rosemary and lemon, or local crab simply dressed and served with a salad of chicory and apple. Main courses range from traditional battered haddock and chips to roasted whole black bream with herbs, lemon, olives and cherry tomatoes. Finish perhaps with dark chocolate brandy truffle cake, or baked vanilla and lemon cheesecake, and if all

that isn't enough to tempt you to visit, the wine list should clinch the deal. Running to over 300 bins, care has been taken to provide good drinking at all price points, as well as no fewer than 30 wines by the glass. Bottle prices start around £17.
**Chef/s:** Bronwen Shaw and Marie Kelly. **Open:** all week L 12 to 2, D 7 to 9.30. **Closed:** 25 and 26 Dec. **Meals:** alc (main courses £9 to £14.50). Set L Sun £18 (3 courses), Set D £29 (3 courses). **Service:** not inc. **Details:** Cards accepted. 36 seats. 20 seats outside. Air-con. No music. No mobile phones. Children's portions. Car parking.

## READERS RECOMMEND

## The Kinmel Arms

**British**
St. George, Abergele, LL22 9BP
Tel no: (01745) 832207
www.thekinmelarms.co.uk
**'Civilised food in civilised surroundings'**

## Abersoch

### Porth Tocyn Hotel

Ambitious food in a splendid location
Bwlchtocyn, Abersoch, LL53 7BU
Tel no: (01758) 713303
www.porth-tocyn-hotel.co.uk
Modern European | £39.50
Cooking score: 4

£5 OFF

Porth Tocyn is a fully fledged hotel, yet it retains a cottagey feel, and the personal welcome of Nick Fletcher-Brewer creates the ambience of a friendly dinner party. This year John Bell has been promoted to be Louise Fletcher-Brewer's co-chef, but the four-course dinner menu follows the same formula as before. The cooking is underpinned by a strong grasp of the technical fundamentals, and the European scope is sometimes enhanced by exotic ideas. Spiced aubergine won tons with crisp vegetable salad and balsamic reduction pleased at inspection, and another enterprising starter has been beetroot and vodka-cured gravlax with tsatsiki, pickled cucumber and cracked black pepper. A main course of Szechuan grilled monkfish was accompanied by sautéed shiitake mushrooms, red pimento noodles, sweet chilli and a spring onion and coriander dressing, yet the fish was not overwhelmed. Cannon of Welsh lamb with a petit truffle omelette, wild mushroom spring roll and a fig and blackberry compote sounds busy, but the meat was first rate. The array of Welsh, English and French cheeses is well worth exploring before going on to dessert, which might be chilled lemon soufflé with lime syrup or summer pudding. House wines on an eclectic list are £14.50.
Chef/s: Louise Fletcher-Brewer and Jonathan Bell. Open: Sun L 12.15 to 2, all week D 7.15 to 9 (9.30 high season). Closed: early Nov to 2 weeks before Easter. Meals: Buffet L Sun £22, Set D £32.50 (2 courses) to £39.50 (4 courses). Service: not inc. Details: Cards accepted. 50 seats. 30 seats outside. No music. No mobile phones. Children's portions. Car parking.

## Beaumaris

### Café Neptune

Seafood cooked with an Eastern twist
First Floor, 27 Castle Street, Beaumaris, LL58 8AP
Tel no: (01248) 812990
www.cafeneptune.co.uk
Modern Seafood | £28
Cooking score: 2

£5 OFF £30

Café Neptune is above an upmarket fish-and-chip shop on the main street of the attractive seaside town. Décor is a mixture of modern and faux-classique, and the main emphasis, as the name suggests, is on seafood, although there is Welsh Black beef and Welsh lamb for carnivores. New chef Marius Cepoiu follows in the steps of his predecessor, but the cooking shows less finesse than before. Exotic twists – such as a creamy fragrant Thai sauce with Anglesey mussels – spice up several dishes. A main course of fresh, tasty red snapper came with Puy lentils in oriental spices with feta cheese cubes, and for dessert, an unusual apple tart served with crème anglaise, toffee sauce, a refreshing apple sorbet and a small glass of Baileys Irish Cream. The wine list has a serious intent and is far from Eurocentric. House bottles start at £12.95.
Chef/s: Marius Cepoiu. Open: all week L 12 to 2, D 6 to 9.30. Closed: 25 and 26 Dec. Meals: alc (main courses £10.75 to £19.75). Light L menu available. Service: not inc. Details: Cards accepted. 48 seats. Air-con. No music. Music. Children's portions.

### Ye Olde Bulls Head

The best of Anglesey bounty
Castle Street, Beaumaris, LL58 8AP
Tel no: (01248) 810329
www.bullsheadinn.co.uk
Modern European | £37
Cooking score: 6

This is a bull of impeccable pedigree. The inn was built in 1472 as a coaching house, and has evolved sensitively over the centuries. There is a lively conservatory-style brasserie downstairs, but for fine dining head for the Loft Restaurant in the eaves of the building, where old rafters mingle with a chic décor. From the canapés in the lounge to the sweetmeats with the coffee, this is a first-class eating-out experience, punctuated by an amuse-bouche and a pre-dessert along the way. Keith Rothwell sources the best local produce from land and sea and treats it with respect. His dishes are multi-faceted, creating unity out of variety. King scallops are quickly seared so that they are light brown on the outside and translucent inside, and require little elaboration, yet they are enhanced by lovely pickled cucumber spaghetti, diced tomatoes and a shizu salad on the side (the Japanese leaves are imported from the Netherlands). Typical of main courses is duck breast paired with loin of venison, with boulangère potatoes, crisp prosciutto, fine beans, diced root vegetables and morels in a complementary port sauce. Or there might be local turbot or Menai sea bass. Desserts show an assured technique, as in a hazelnut and sweet apple semi-fredo, Bramley apple fritters and a hazelnut tuile, or a Muscavado sugar and rum parfait, fresh pineapple carpaccio and coconut crisp. The wine list focuses on France, but has a global range. The five house wines are £17.50 a bottle, £4.55 a glass.

## Cooking score

A score of 1 is a significant achievement. The score in any review is based on several meals, incorporating feedback from both our readers and inspectors. As a rough guide, 1 denotes capable cooking with some inconsistencies, rising steadily through different levels of technical expertise, until the scores between 6 and 10 indicate exemplary skills, along with innovation, artistry and ambition. If there is a new chef, we don't score the restaurant for the first year of entry. For further details, please see the scoring section in the introduction to the Guide.

**Chef/s:** Craig Yardley. **Open:** Mon to Sat D only 7 to 9.30pm; also open Sun L bank hols. **Closed:** 25, 26 Dec, 1 Jan. **Meals:** Set D £37. Brasserie menu available L and D. **Service:** not inc. **Details:** Cards accepted. 45 seats. Separate bar. No music. No mobile phones. Car parking.

## ∎ Capel Garmon
## Tan-y-Foel Country House
**Informal dining in a stunning setting**
Nr Betws-y-coed, Capel Garmon, LL26 0RE
Tel no: (01690) 710507
www.tyfhotel.co.uk
**Modern Welsh | £42**
Cooking score: 6

Perched up on a hill above the Conwy Valley, near picture-postcard Betws-y-Coed, Tan-y-Foel is Peter and Janet Pitman's pride and joy. It operates to its own rhythm, and with resonant success. The drill is dinner only, with Janet's daily-changing menus built around pairs of alternatives at each course, the two desserts supplemented by the option of pedigree Welsh cheeses. She works alone in the kitchen, and the results are evident in the highly personal cooking style that emerges. A spring evening offered either smoked salmon or Cambrian Hills organic belly pork to start, the former served with celeriac rémoulade and salsa verde, the latter with sweet chilli relish and minted piccalilli. Main courses are keyed to imaginative wine suggestions, whether for wild sea bass with roasted fennel, asparagus, tomato fondant and a dressing of mozzarella and basil, or loin of Bryn Dowsi lamb, accompanied by sautéed red onions, beluga lentils, a balsamic reduction and hazelnut oil. The sweet of tooth can then choose between roasted pistachio pear with caramel sauce and mascarpone ice-cream, or flaked rice pudding with roasted plum and almond purée. Wines are stylistically grouped, from 'crisp fresh fruity whites' to 'rich full-bodied reds'. Choices are top-drawer throughout, with Cloudy Bay and Olivier Leflaive appearing on

parade with Delas Côte-Rôtie and Fontodi Chianti. House wines open at £19, or £3.50 for a small glass.
**Chef/s:** Janet Pitman. **Open:** Tue to Sun D only 7.30 (last food orders 8.15). **Closed:** 1 Dec to 20 Jan. **Meals:** Set D £42 (3 courses). **Service:** not inc. **Details:** Cards accepted. 12 seats. No music. No mobile phones. Children allowed. Car parking.

## Conwy
### Castle Hotel, Shakespeare's Restaurant
**Modern food in traditional surroundings**
High Street, Conwy, LL32 8DB
Tel no: (01492) 582800
www.castlewales.co.uk
**Modern Welsh | £32**
Cooking score: 3

⊨ Υ

This former coaching inn was built on the site of a Cistercian abbey, but it has been brought up to date through a programme of refurbishment which blends the traditional and the modern. Graham Tinsley offers both classic and dishes based on top-quality fresh Welsh produce and enlivened by some innovative fusions. Starters such as cannelloni of Conwy crab on buttered leeks with a curried king prawn broth, or shallot tarte Tatin with sautéed chicken livers on salad leaves and a sherry vinegar dressing are indicative of his style. Main courses are carefully composed; pan-seared scallops are teamed with monkfish and served over parsley mash with tomato provençale and a leek custard. Desserts show panache, as in a raspberry crème brûlée and raspberry frangipane with sesame and raspberry crackling. The Blas ar Fwyd Welsh farmhouse cheeses with home-made chutney make a good alternative. The wine list is far from Eurocentric, and kicks off at £12.95.
**Chef/s:** Graham Tinsley. **Open:** Sun to Fri L 12.30 to 2pm, all week D 7 to 9.30pm. **Closed:** 25 Dec D, 26 Dec. **Meals:** alc D (main courses £16.95 to £18.95). Set L £12.95 (2 courses) to £15.95. Bar menu

available. **Service:** 10% (optional). **Details:** Cards accepted. 50 seats. Separate bar. Wheelchair access. Music. Children's portions. Car parking.

## READERS RECOMMEND
### Tir-a-Môr
**Modern Welsh**
1-3 Mona Terrace, Criccieth, LL52 0HG.
Tel no: (01766) 523084
www.tiramor.com
'An unpretentious gem'

## Dolgellau
### Dylanwad Da
**Long-standing bistro that's still on form**
2 Ffôs-y-Felin, Dolgellau, LL40 1BS
Tel no: (01341) 422870
www.dylanwad.co.uk
**French | £34**
Cooking score: 2

£5 OFF ♦ Υ

Dylan Rowlands marks 20 years at his eponymous bistro in 2008. Over that time, there have been few major changes to the day-to-day running of the place, and yet he keeps abreast of the times. The menu makes a nod to fashion with the inclusion of a few Mediterranean and tapas-style dishes, such as spicy meatballs with tomato, pea and mint sauce. Otherwise, starters might include smoked chicken with horseradish cream, while main courses run to pot-roast spring lamb cooked with white wine, vegetables and haricot beans, and braised loin of pork with Calvados, apple and sage. Meals might end with rhubarb and ginger crumble, or dark chocolate and Cointreau mousse. The wine list continues to be a highlight, reflecting the owner's passion for the subject. Choice below £20 is both plentiful and excellent, with house selections from £14.50.
**Chef/s:** Dylan Rowlands. **Open:** Thur to Sat D only 7 to 9; also open Tue, Wed and bank hol Sun D in high season. Open for coffee, cakes and tapas 10 to 3. **Closed:** Feb. **Meals:** alc (main courses £12 to £16).

Set D £15 (2 courses) to £19.50. **Service:** not inc. **Details:** Cards accepted. 28 seats. Music. Children's portions.

## ALSO RECOMMENDED

### ▲ Queen's Head
Glanwydden, LL31 9JP
Tel no: (01492) 546570
www.queensheadglanwydden.co.uk

This modest village inn has had an extension this year. To begin, there might be hot foie gras with black pudding (£8.50). Fresh fish is a strong suit, and might include sea bass with an orange, ginger and sultana butter (£11.75). Puddings include fresh fruit crumble of the day. House wines are £7.75 a half-litre. Open all week.

## ▌Harlech

### Castle Cottage
**Sleek restaurant-with-rooms**
Y Llech, Harlech, LL46 2YL
Tel no: (01766) 780479
www.castlecottageharlech.co.uk
**Modern Welsh | £32**
**Cooking score: 2**
£5 OFF ⊨ V

This so-called cottage is only a stone's throw from the medieval castle and houses a surprisingly modern lounge bar and restaurant. They serve a three-course dinner menu for £32. After inventive canapés in the bar, the meal might kick off with roasted quail on Puy lentils and leeks in a delicate jus, or a colourful starter of new-season asparagus with roasted cherry tomatoes, poached duck egg and Parmesan shavings. Main courses sometimes pair two cuts of meat, such as roasted loin and confit shoulder of Welsh lamb on pan-fried bubble and squeak with shallots in a red-wine sauce. Finish with lemon and lime posset with fruit compote and shortbread biscuit, or opt for Welsh farmhouse cheeses. Four wines of the month start at £14.

**Chef/s:** Glyn Roberts and Ryan Britland. **Open:** all week D only 7 to 9.30. **Meals:** Set D £32. **Service:** not inc. **Details:** Cards accepted. 40 seats. No mobile phones. Wheelchair access. Music. Children's portions. Car parking.

### Maes-y-Neuadd
**A country-house hotel of distinction**
Talsarnau, Harlech, LL47 6YA
Tel no: (01766) 780200
www.neuadd.com
**Modern Welsh | £33**
**Cooking score: 4**
£5 OFF ♦ ⊨ V

This sturdy stone mansion was renowned for its hospitality as early as the fifteenth century, when it was regularly visited by itinerant bards who sang its praises. The kitchen produces some sophisticated dishes, based on top-notch local raw materials – the finest Welsh lamb, fresh fish from Cardigan Bay and the Menai Straits, and artisan farmhouse cheeses. Last but not least are the vegetables, fruits and herbs from their own orchards and walled gardens. Dinners are normally four-course affairs. Start off perhaps with roulade of local sewin with cockles and laverbread, followed by noisettes of saltmarsh lamb topped with a leek mousse, a parcel of braised shoulder, root vegetables, fondant potatoes and rosemary jus. Cheese might come next, but keep some space for the grand finale of desserts: a mini portion each of Perl Las cheese, celery and port paté, honey and white chocolate tart with lemon and basil cream, Maes-y-Neuadd berries in sweet wine jelly and home-made ice creams and sorbets. Although the core of the wine list is French, there is a good selection from around the world, and German wines have been reintroduced. The ten house wines start at £14.25.

**Chef/s:** Peter Jackson and John Owen Jones. **Open:** all week 12 to 1.45, 7 to 8.45. **Meals:** alc L Mon to Sat (main courses £7 to £12). Set L Sun £16.50, Set D £33 to £37. **Service:** not inc. **Details:** Cards accepted. 65 seats. 20 seats outside. No mobile phones. Wheelchair access. Music. Children's portions. Car parking.

## READERS RECOMMEND

### Caban
**Global Organic**
Yr Hen Ysgol, Llanberis, LL55 3NR
Tel no: (01286) 685500
www.caban-cyf.org
**'All-day café with informal Saturday evening globetrotting buffet'**

## Llandudno

### Bodysgallen Hall
**Stunning views of Snowdonia**
Llandudno, LL30 1RS
Tel no: (01492) 584466
www.bodysgallen.com
**Modern British | £41**
**Cooking score: 5**

🍷 ⇋ ⋎

This noble seventeenth-century manor stands in over 200 acres of parkland. Inside there is a main hall, a library, drawing room and bar, as well as two dining rooms. Public rooms have a dignified air, with dark oak panelling, period furniture and oil paintings. The seemingly straightforward cooking belies a great deal of professional skill. Dishes are well composed and are not over-elaborate, yet flavours are subtle and well balanced. At a test meal, a salad of venison and figs with a red-wine dressing was a deliciously light starter, and ballotine of foie gras with honey-roasted duck and a truffle salad was a richer alternative. Top-notch locally sourced fish and meat are treated with respect, so that their innate flavours shine through, as in butter-poached turbot with roasted salsify and fennel cream, or roast cannon of lamb with braised lettuce, creamed parsnips and a Madeira and tarragon sauce. Vegetables have an earthy flavour and some bite. Finish with artistically presented chocolate marquise with raspberry ice cream, or opt for the excellent British cheeses from the trolley. Service by formally dressed waiters

and waitresses is knowledgeable and attentive. The well-compiled wine list offers some classic bottles from France and plenty of choice from the rest of Europe and the world. Prices start at £15.50. NB Children must be over 6.
**Chef/s:** John Williams. **Open:** all week 12.30 to 1.45, 7 to 9.30. **Meals:** Set L £18.50 (2 courses) to £22, Sun L £27 (3 courses), Set D £41.50. **Service:** inc. **Details:** Cards accepted. 50 seats. Air-con. No mobile phones. Wheelchair access. Music. Children allowed. Car parking.

### St Tudno Hotel, Terrace Restaurant
**Ambitious food in a Victorian town house**
Promenade, Llandudno, LL30 2LP
Tel no: (01492) 874411
www.st-tudno.co.uk
**Modern European | £34**
**Cooking score: 4**

🍷 ⇋ ⋎

This Victorian hotel by the pier doesn't stand out from the crowd from the outside, but step inside the dining room and you are transported by the murals to Lake Como. Head chef, Stephen Duffy, is back at the helm after about a year elsewhere, and judging from an inspection meal, he is in fine form. A starter of seared rare tuna with niçoise salad and confit lemon was perfectly judged, the almost-raw fish complemented by a soft-boiled quail's egg, and bits of herring and diced olives set off by the sharpness of the lemon. A main course of line-caught sea bass was charred on the outside but succulent inside, and was accompanied by crab polenta chips, white asparagus, spinach and cashew nut salad and shellfish sauce. Some dishes can seem busy, such as loin of organic rabbit with scallop mousse, pâté en croûte and a fricassee of spring greens, but on the whole the accompaniment is *sotto voce*. Desserts such as chilled tropical fruit soup with coconut ravioli and passion-fruit sorbet, or chocolate and nut cannelloni with a bitter chocolate sabayon and sugared nuts are far from run-of-the-mill. The well-annotated wine list is a pleasure to behold and starts at a modest £14.50. NB Children must be over 5.

**Chef/s:** Stephen Duffy. **Open:** all week 12.30 to 1.45, 7 to 9.30 (9 Sun). **Meals:** Set L Mon to Sat £15 (2 courses), Set L Sun £17.50 (2 courses), Set D £27.50 (2 courses). **Service:** not inc. **Details:** Cards accepted. 60 seats. Air-con. No mobile phones. Wheelchair access. Music. Children's portions. Car parking.

## ▌Penmaenpool

### Penmaenuchaf Hall
Light, imaginative food
Penmaenpool, LL40 1YB
Tel no: (01341) 422129
www.penhall.co.uk
**Modern British | £38**
Cooking score: 3

£5 OFF   🍷   🛏   V

You are greeted by an open fire in the oak-panelled entrance hall, and the same smart ambience pervades the other public rooms. There is a daily-changing, four-course dinner for £35 plus a short à la carte menu. A starter of herby smoked salmon tartare was accompanied by a complementary beetroot purée, but one reporter felt that her pan-fried scallops with celeriac purée was overwhelmed by a star anise sauce. This seems to have been a rare lapse, and confidence was restored by a main course of duo of pork with green split peas, confit garlic and sage jus, every element contributing to the well-balanced whole. A dessert of white chocolate mousse was offset by confit cherries in a cherry coulis. The core of the classy wine list is French, with a sprinkling from the New World, and the ten house bottles begin at £15.50.

**Chef/s:** Justin Pilkington assisted by Tim and Matthew Reeve. **Open:** all week 12 to 2, 7 to 9.30 (9 Sun). **Closed:** 2 to 10 Jan. **Meals:** alc D (main courses £20 to £24.50). Set L £15.95 (2 courses) to £17.95 (3 courses), Set D £35.. **Service:** not inc. **Details:** Cards accepted. 34 seats. 14 seats outside. No mobile phones. Wheelchair access. Music. Children's portions. Car parking.

## READERS RECOMMEND

### Neuadd Lwyd Country House
British
Penmynydd, Llanfairpwllgwyngyll, LL61 5BX
Tel no: (01248) 715005
www.neuaddlwyd.co.uk
'Excellent modern Welsh food'

### Yr Hen Fecws
Traditional Welsh
Lombard Street, Porthmadog, LL49 9AP
Tel no: (01766) 514 625
www.henfecws.com
'Substantial home cooking'

## ▌Pwllheli

### Plas Bodegroes
An elegant restaurant-with-rooms
Nefyn Road, Pwllheli, LL53 5TH
Tel no: (01758) 612363
www.bodegroes.co.uk
**Modern Welsh | £40**
Cooking score: 6

🍷   🛏

Reached along an avenue of 200-year-old beeches, this Grade II-listed Georgian manor is surrounded by mature grounds and gardens. It is the L-shaped dining room that is at the heart of the operation, with Welsh chef Chris Chown delivering the goods, and his elegant Faroese wife, Gunna, leading the front-of-house team with panache. The technically assured cooking has a cutting edge, but there is

## Antony De Sousa Tam

**Which of today's chefs do you admire?**
Andoni Luis Aduriz.

**What's your favourite cookery book?**
*El Bulli* from 2002 by Ferran Adria and
Juli Soler.

**What's the best dish you've ever eaten?**
Braised snake meat with Chinese medicine.

**Do you have a favourite local recipe?**
A good roast with Yorkshire puddings.

**What's your guilty food pleasure?**
Apple turnovers.

**If you could only eat one more thing, what
would it be?**
Tuna belly.

**What's the hardest thing about running a
restaurant?**
Finding good staff.

**Which are your proudest achievements?**
An *Evening Standard* review from Fay
Maschler.

**What's coming up next for you?**
I want to have my own restaurant one day.

**What does The Good Food Guide mean
to you?**
I think it's a fantastic guide, providing lots of
useful information for diners looking for all
sorts of restaurants.

no bowing to fashion. Flavours are distinctive
but they blend harmoniously, as in a starter of
seared sea bass and scallops, with the
caramelised chicory and vanilla sauce playing
second fiddle to the seafood. In a main course
of grilled breast of guinea fowl the meat was
tender and delicious; it came with an expertly
composed leg meat cannelloni in a subtle foie
gras sauce. A rosemary kebab of mountain
lamb disappointed one diner because it had
only two meagre pieces of lamb, half a kidney
and a piece of lamb burger, but it was served
with a rich minted couscous in a flavoursome
chickpea and cumin casserole. Finish off with
cinnamon biscuits with rhubarb and apple
with an elderflower custard, or bara-brith-
and-butter pudding with Welsh whisky ice
cream. The wine list offers some classic French
bottles and a good worldwide choice, with
prices starting at £16.
**Chef/s:** Chris Chown. **Open:** Sun L 12.30 to 2, Tue to
Sat D 7 to 9 (9.30 summer). **Closed:** Dec to Feb.
**Meals:** Set L £18.50, Set D £40. **Service:** not inc.
**Details:** Cards accepted. 40 seats. No mobile
phones. Wheelchair access. Music. Car parking.

## READERS RECOMMEND

### The Ship Inn
**Modern Welsh**
Nr Benllech, Red Wharf Bay, LL75 8RJ
Tel no: (01248) 852568
www.shipinnredwharfbay.co.uk
**'Quality food in a stunning setting'**

### The White Eagle Inn
**Modern European**
Rhoscolyn, LL65 2NJ
Tel no: (01407) 860267
www.white-eagle.co.uk
**'Refurbished gastropub with great seafood'**

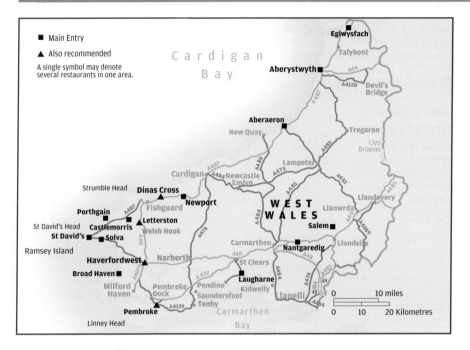

## ■ Aberaeron

## Harbourmaster Hotel
### Commanding Cambrian cuisine
2 Pen Cei, Aberaeron, SA46 OBA
Tel no: (01545) 570755
www.harbour-master.com
**Modern Welsh | £43**
**Cooking score: 3**

This landmark indigo-painted building near the mouth of Aberaeron harbour continues to be a reliable and popular destination for lunch or dinner. The stylish interior is sympathetic to the location, with bare floorboards in the dining area. The well-sourced menu features some of the best Welsh produce, from cheese to beef, lamb and, of course, fish. An inspection meal included fishcakes (compact and gloriously crisp on the outside, with a gentle lime mayonnaise and slices of fresh loaf that positively exploded with poppy seeds) followed by a blackened sea bream with a wonderfully punchy pepper crust and equally good, crunchy-fluffy chips. Other choices include chorizo and herb risotto followed by confit of duck leg with mashed potato and quince and apricot jus. Desserts such as lemon tart with crème fraîche or rhubarb, apple and ginger crumble are listed with dessert wine recommendations. The wine list itself is comprehensive and starts at £12.50.
**Chef/s:** Stephen Evans. **Open:** Tue to Sun L 12 to 2, Mon to Sat D 6.30 to 9. **Closed:** 24 Dec to 11 Jan. **Meals:** alc (main courses L £10.50 to £18.50, D £14.50 to £19.50). Set L Oct to Mar £12.50 (2 courses) to £16.50. Bar menu available.

### Please send us your feedback

To register your opinion about any restaurant listed in the Guide, or a new restaurant that you wish to bring to our attention, please visit the web address at the bottom of the page. Your feedback informs the content of the book and will be used to compile next year's reviews.

**Service:** not inc, 10% for parties of 8 or more. **Details:** Cards accepted. 40 seats. 4 seats outside. Wheelchair access. Music. Car parking.

## ▮ Aberystwyth

★NEW ENTRY★

## Ultracomida

Stylish café-bar
31 Pier St, Aberystwyth, SY23 2LN
Tel no: (01970) 630686
Modern Welsh | £20
New Chef

First and foremost this place is a delicatessen – a pristine, exciting one at that. Walk through air heavy with the scent of cheeses, past wall-to-wall olive oils, cured meats and bottled delights. Luckily nobody seems to mind sharing tables at busy times. Salads, a cheese board, tapas, filled bocatas and barras and hot panini are available from 10am to 4pm. A meal from the excellent value set-price lunch menu (three courses for £9.50) might include streaky pepper leaves with Parmesan shavings and a balsamic dressing followed by a full-flavoured cassoulet with crisp-skinned confit of duck, white beans and pork and finally a crema Catalana liqueur and croissant bread-and-butter pudding. Wines start at £9.95.
**Chef/s:** Rhodri Edwards. **Open:** Mon to Tue L 10 to 4.30 (Wed to Sat to 6.30 ). **Closed:** 25 Dec to 2 Jan, bank hols. **Meals:** Set L 9.50 (3 courses). **Service:** not inc. **Details:** Cards accepted. 32 seats. Wheelchair access. Music. Children allowed.

## Le Vignoble

Outstanding value and top-quality cooking
31 Eastgate Street, Aberystwyth, SY23 2AR
Tel no: (01970) 630800
www.orangery.uk.com
French | £26
Cooking score: 3
🍷 ⋎ £30

Table spacings are at a premium in this shopfront restaurant, but chef Cheuk Kong and his small team display considerable imagination and professionalism in cooking in semi-view of diners. Starters include a rich French onion soup or a warm and tasty leek, mascarpone and Parmesan tartlet with perfect short buttery pastry. A large juicy roasted chicken supreme stuffed with a delicate basil mousse and dauphinoise potatoes, asparagus and tomato and chive cream sauce, or confit of duck, mashed potatoes, French beans and red-wine jus, both exemplify the culinary skill of the main courses. Likewise, desserts have that extra dimension raising them well above the average – a rich custardy bread-and-butter pudding is offset with a classic vanilla ice cream and a perfectly poached pear. The selection of cheeses is impressive and there is a superb value international wine list as well as good selection of ports, Calvados and dessert wines. Wines start at £10.95.
**Chef/s:** Cheuk Kong. **Open:** Wed to Sat, L 12 to 2pm, Tue to Sat, D 6pm to 10pm. **Closed:** Closed Sun and Mon, and L Tue. **Meals:** alc (main courses £13.50 to £19) Set L £12.50 (2 courses), £16 (3 courses), Set D £16 (2 courses), £20 (3 courses). **Service:** optional. **Details:** Cards accepted. 35 seats. Music. Children's portions.

---

### Average price

The average price listed in main-entry reviews denotes the price of a three-course meal, without wine.

## ALSO RECOMMENDED

## ▲ The Orangery

10 Market Street, Aberystwyth, SY23 1DL
Tel no: (01970) 617606

The Orangery is a modern, sophisticated yet relaxed café/wine bar/restaurant with its own bakery and pizzeria. Sit in the spacious main café or the outdoor courtyard. The menu offers appetising brasserie-style snacks imaginatively prepared with local ingredients. Home-baked breads, pastry and cakes are a particular highlight. Try robust soups (£3.50), warm asparagus and goats' cheese tarts (£6.95), or a plate of charcuterie with olives and salad (£6.95). Main courses include meaty bangers and mash or seafood laden fisherman's pie. A glass of house wine is £2.95 to £3.50.

## Broad Haven

## Druidstone

**Bohemian splendour on the coast**
Druidston Haven, Broad Haven, SA62 3NE
Tel no: (01437) 781221
www.druidstone.co.uk
**Global | £36**
**Cooking score: 2**

It is hard to describe this place without using words like 'breathtaking' and 'magical'. The land plunges away from the imposing stone house to meet the Atlantic; guests can watch the waves from benches that cling to two small terraces. The house has a faded Bohemian splendour – you can imagine an older Helena Bonham Carter living in the attic. The dining areas (bare floorboards, fairy lights and yet more wonderful views) are warmed by glowing coals. A black cat materialises occasionally to greet guests, as do lovely young staff who seem to have succumbed to Druidstone's laid-back vibe. The cooking style is vibrant, full-flavoured and generous. Starters such as chicken liver parfait with chutney, or lamb, leek and rosemary soup might be followed by oak-smoked Barbary duck with braised red cabbage smothered in a

### Cooking score

A score of 1 is a significant achievement. The score in any review is based on several meals, incorporating feedback from both our readers and inspectors. As a rough guide, 1 denotes capable cooking with some inconsistencies, rising steadily through different levels of technical expertise, until the scores between 6 and 10 indicate exemplary skills, along with innovation, artistry and ambition. If there is a new chef, we don't score the restaurant for the first year of entry. For further details, please see the scoring section in the introduction to the Guide.

tangy blueberry jus; or excellent pork fillet wrapped in bacon with Calvados baked apples and chorizo mash. Desserts include banoffee pie and sticky toffee pudding. Wines start at £10.50, and there is well-kept ale in the cellar bar.
**Chef/s:** Chris Fenn, Jon Woodhouse and Angus Bell.
**Open:** all week L 12.30 to 2.30, D 7.30 to 9.30.
**Meals:** alc (main courses £12.50 to £17.50) Set L £17 (2 courses), Set D £25 (2 courses). Bar menu available. **Service:** not inc. **Details:** Cards accepted. 46 seats. 50 seats outside. Wheelchair access. Music. Children's portions. Car parking.

## Castlemorris

## Tides

**A well-hidden gem**
Llangloffan Farm, Castlemorris, SA62 5ET
Tel no: (01348) 891383
**Modern European | £27**
**Cooking score: 2**

Tides is a stylishly converted stone building whose modest size has been helped along by the addition of a conservatory; it has character enough to wear a coracle and netted glass buoys without seeming twee. The cooking is wholesome and underpinned by excellent ingredients (enormous hand-dived Porthgain scallops delighted at inspection, seared and served with a well-judged chilli sauce, crème fraîche and sprightly mixed salad leaves). While you can eat three courses at lunch, you can also opt for filled ciabatta or light meals. An evening meal might start with carpaccio of tuna with Parmesan shavings, rocket and balsamic vinegar, followed by fillet of locally reared beef with a wild mushroom gratin and béarnaise sauce; or ballottine of organic chicken stuffed with sun-dried tomato and sausage meat and served with a creamy basil sauce. Finish with vanilla crème brûlée or Baileys bread-and-butter pudding. Wines from £12.

**Chef/s:** Emma Downey. **Open:** Apr to Sep, Tue to Sat 10 to 4, D 7 to 11; Oct to Mar, Fri to Sat D 7 to 11, L Sat to Sun 10 to 4. **Closed:** Sun (summer) Mon (all year apart from bank hols) Christmas. **Meals:** alc (main courses £13.95 to £19.95). **Service:** optional. **Details:** Cards accepted. 26 seats. 30 seats outside. No mobile phones. Wheelchair access. Music. Children's portions. Car parking.

## ALSO RECOMMENDED

### ▲ The Old Sailors
Pwllgwaelod, Dinas Cross, SA42 0SE
Tel no: (01348) 811491

The Old Sailors is a traditional Pembrokeshire stone building at the back of the beach at Pwllgwaelod. A recent extension has added a bright dining room, with picture windows overlooking Cardigan Bay. The food is simple and good, and locally caught fish and seafood are a speciality. The menu usually offers half a lobster, grilled with garlic butter with new potatoes or chips and salad (£12), a pint of prawns, scallops (£13) and crab. Fish may be sea bass. Non-fish options could include steak and ale pie or traditional cawl. A short wine list starts with house wine at £3 a glass.

## ▌Eglwysfach

## Ynyshir Hall
**Stylish food in an idyllic rural retreat**
Eglwysfach, SY20 8TA
Tel no: (01654) 781209
www.ynyshir-hall.co.uk
**Modern British | £65**
**Cooking score: 5**

🍷 ⌁

This approachable country house is a tranquil retreat next to an RSPB bird sanctuary. It is now part of the von Essen collection, but Joan Reen (the previous owner) is still very much in evidence as a warm and hospitable host. The dazzling oil paintings by her husband, Rob, still dominate the dining room, but new chef Shane Hughes's food is a match for them. He was classically trained at the Connaught (under Michel Bourdin) and picked up some modish ideas while at Juniper (see entry, Cheshire). Menus are sensibly short, supplemented by a menu gourmand of six courses (no choice). A meal might begin with fresh red mullet topped with a layer of full-flavoured crusted crab, accompanied by linguine of vegetables in a delicate shellfish cappuccino. A main course of braised duck leg was bursting with flavour the meat simply melted in the mouth and was served in a rich sherry sauce with a parsnip purée, topped by a crisp potato galette. Puddings are a delight, in particular a classically made tarte Tatin with a cinnamon toffee sauce and bay-leaf ice cream. Service is not always as knowledgeable as it should be. The wine list has lots of classy bottles, but there are plenty of house wines from £4.50 by the glass and bottles from £18. NB Children must be over 9.

**Chef/s:** Shane Hughes. **Open:** all week 12.30 to 1.30, 7 to 9. **Closed:** 3 to 31 Jan. **Meals:** Set L £21 (2 courses) to £32, Set D £65. Light L menu available. **Service:** not inc. **Details:** Cards accepted. 28 seats. No mobile phones. Wheelchair access. Music. Children allowed. Car parking.

## ALSO RECOMMENDED

### ▲ Refectory at St David's

St David's Cathedral, Haverfordwest, SA62 6RH
Tel no: (01437) 721760
www.refectoryatstdavids.co.uk

The sympathetic restoration of the ruined cloisters at St David's Cathedral has created this stunning, canteen-style café. The menu is the work of Bill Sewell, who has a growing portfolio of eateries in churches. Here, smiling young staff offer up scones and cakes and 'fat little pizzas' with dressed leaves (£4.95); fish pie (£7.95); roasted fennel, potato and Perl Las cheese quiche with salad and rosemary roast potatoes (£6.75) and Mr Tudge's sausages with kidney beans in a leek and tomato broth, with bread (£6.95). A couple of wines are available from £9.95.

## READERS RECOMMEND

### George's

Modern European
24 Market Street, Haverfordwest, SA61 1NH
Tel no: (01437) 766683
'A menu anchored in Welsh produce'

### Ty Mawr Mansion

Modern British
Cilcennin, Lampeter, SA48 8DB
Tel no: (01570) 470033
www.tymawrmansion.co.uk
'Excellent use of local produce'

## ▌Laugharne

### Cors

Romantic setting and cooking to match
Newbridge Road, Laugharne, SA33 4SH
Tel no: (01994) 427219
www.the-cors.co.uk
British | £38
Cooking score: 3

⊨ Ⅴ

The setting is magical and the décor inside is all gilt mirrors, contemporary canvasses, and period features. Nick Priestland's impressive Victorian villa makes a quirky but romantic restaurant-with-rooms. Open for dinner only, the short, daily changing, hand-written menu deals in local and seasonal ingredients. A June dinner, for example, opening with starters of bruschetta of grilled Welsh goats' cheese with roasted red peppers, or hot seared smoked salmon with wild rocket and a sweet mustard sauce, then going on to fillet of local sea trout with asparagus and lemon hollandaise sauce, or rack of rosemary-crusted Welsh spring lamb and caramelised onion gravy, with home-made ice creams to finish. Although short, the wine list is well chosen and offers interest and value. House French is £11.50.
**Chef/s:** Nick Priestland. **Open:** Thur to Sat D only 7 to 9.30. **Closed:** Nov, 25 and 26 Dec. **Meals:** alc (main courses £14.50 to £19.50). **Service:** not inc. **Details:** 24 seats. 12 seats outside. Wheelchair access. Music. Children allowed. Car parking.

### Symbols

⊨ Accommodation is available.

£30 Three courses for less than £30.

Ⅴ More than five vegetarian dishes.

£5 OFF £5-off voucher scheme.

🍾 Notable wine list.

## ALSO RECOMMENDED

### ▲ Stable Door Restaurant

Market Lane, Laugharne, SA33 4SB
Tel no: (01994) 427777

Shelves of books, antique oddments, stone walls and well-worn sofas sound an eclectic, informal note but the setting is made special by the enormous sun-trap conservatory and pretty walled garden, both of which overlook the castle. The menu includes halloumi kebabs marinated with fresh coriander, flat parsley and lemon (£3.50); lamb, chilli and mint meatballs in a tomato and red-wine sauce (£3.95); and Spanish white anchovies tossed with croûtons and green leaves (£3). Desserts include rich, creamy home-made ice cream (£4). Wines start at £11.75 per bottle.

### ▲ Something's Cooking

The Square, Letterston, SA62 5SB
Tel no: (01348) 840621

There is no danger of missing this large green building, which stands smartly beside the A40. At its heart is a take-away fish and chip shop, but if you peer through the large fish tank near the main counter and bar, you'll see that the bulk of the building is a comfortable restaurant. The down-to-earth menu is exceptionally good value, and while fish and chips is the obvious option, you might be tempted by starters such as a home-made crab cake (£3.95) followed by roast chicken with onion rings, mushrooms and herb stuffing (£6.50). For dessert, try the tasty home-made banoffi pie (£3.35). A small selection of wines starts at £8.95.

## ▌Nantgaredig

### Y Polyn

The finest of Welsh ingredients
Nantgaredig, SA32 7LH
Tel no: (01267) 290000
www.ypolyn.com
**Modern British | £39**
**Cooking score: 3**

**Y**

Latterly a pub and before that a toll house, Y Polyn now confidently straddles the line between country pub and stylish modern restaurant. In the dining room is another collection, this time of cookbooks (it's enough to make the most law-abiding diner contemplate theft). Service is top-notch but genuinely relaxed and comfortable, and the menu serves up the very finest Welsh ingredients with modern-rustic panache. Regional British and retro dishes (potted shrimps with toast, coq au vin) get an airing as do classics like chicken liver parfait (with toast and plum and apple chutney); Pembrokeshire Welsh Black fillet steak with red-wine and shallot sauce; or rump of new season Pembrokeshire organic lamb with onion, garlic and thyme purée. Finish with treacle tart, crème brûlée or wonderful Welsh cheeses. A balanced, interesting wine list starts at £13.50.

**Chef/s:** Susan Manson and Maryann Wright. **Open:** Tue to Fri and Sun L 12 to 2, Tue to Sat D 7 to 9. **Meals:** alc L exc Sun (main courses £8.50 to £11.50). Set L Sun £15.50 (2 courses) to £19.50, Set D £20.50 (2 courses) to £26.50. **Service:** not inc. **Details:** Cards accepted. 40 seats. Wheelchair access. Music. Children's portions. Car parking.

## Newport

### Cnapan

East Street, Newport, SA42 0SY
Tel no: (01239) 820575
www.cnapan.co.uk
**Modern British | £38**
**Cooking score: 2**

£5 OFF ⊏ ∀

A smiling welcome sets the tone for a thoroughly relaxing meal at this pretty, pink-painted hotel and restaurant. The place has a mature, pristine domesticity, with carpeted floors, white tablecloths, and traditional ornaments. The food has a modern edge without being challenging; typical starters include a grilled goats' cheese and portabella mushroom crostini; and lime and honey-marinated pork and apricot skewers. Main courses range from pan-fried slices of local Welsh Black beef with a mushroom, fresh herb and mustard sauce to smoked haddock fish cakes on seared scallops and tiger prawns with a watercress drizzle. For dessert, perhaps sticky apricot and cinnamon shortcake with a citrus crème fraîche; or fresh plum and ginger cream with amaretti. A modest but well-chosen wine list starts at £10.75.

**Chef/s:** Judith Cooper and Oliver Cooper. **Open:** Wed to Sat and Mon L 12 to 2, Wed to Mon D 6.45 to 8.45. **Closed:** Christmas, Jan and Feb. **Meals:** alc Light L (main courses £7.50 to £12.50). Set D £22 (2 courses) to £28.50 (3 courses). **Service:** not inc. **Details:** Cards accepted. 36 seats. 30 seats outside. Wheelchair access. Music. Children's portions. Car parking.

## ALSO RECOMMENDED

### ▲ Old Kings Arms

13 Main Street, Pembroke, SA71 4JS
Tel no: (01646) 683611

Pembroke's oldest hotel continues to hold its reputation for good, straightforward food. Produce from Pembrokeshire (including fresh fish) features prominently on menus that typically include Welsh cockles with laverbread and grilled bacon (£7.95) or confit

leg of duckling on juniper cabbage (£6.95) to start, followed by pan-fried fillet steak au poivre (£18.95); seared Welsh lamb fillet on wilted greens with a port and redcurrant sauce (£15.95); or pork fillet flamed in brandy and served with caramelised apples (£14). For dessert, perhaps sticky toffee pudding; bread-and-butter pudding or lemon posset (all £4.20). An international wine list starts at £9.50 a bottle. Open all week.

## READERS RECOMMEND

### The Shed

Modern European
Porthgain, SA62 5BN
Tel no: (01348) 831518
www.theshedporthgain.co.uk
'A quirky, homespun place'

## St David's

★NEW ENTRY★

### Cwtch

**Big flavours from the little city**
22 High Street, St David's, SA62 6SD
Tel no: (01437) 720491
www.cwtchrestaurant.co.uk
**Modern British | £25**
**Cooking score: 3**

£5 OFF £30 ⬥

From hearty home-made breads to decadent desserts, the food at Cwtch is marked out by honest, unfussy presentation. Chef Matt Cox cooks with confidence and consistency, and clearly makes top-notch ingredients a priority. The quality shines through in dishes such as asparagus with pea fritters; smoked sewin with marsh samphire and Pembrokeshire new potato and chive salad. This can be followed perhaps by St Bride's Bay sea bass with sauce vierge or a shoulder of spring lamb with Puy lentils and red-wine sauce. Among the books on the floor-to-ceiling shelves is an album full of delighted feedback from customers. Staff are young and friendly, and the relaxing atmosphere encourages you to linger, perhaps over rich chocolate torte with blood orange sorbet or lemon posset with home-made shortbread and limoncello liqueur. Wines from £12.50. **Chef/s:** Matt Cox. **Open:** Tue to Sun 6 to11. **Closed:** 2nd week Jan. **Meals:** Set D £20 (2 courses) £25 (3 courses). **Service:** not inc. **Details:** Cards accepted. 44 seats. Wheelchair access. Music. Children's portions. Car parking.

## Lawtons at No 16
**A bounty of local ingredients**
16 Nun Street, St David's, SA62 6NS
Tel no: (01437) 729220
www.lawtonsatno16.co.uk
**British | £30**
**Cooking score: 2**

ϒ

Lawtons is a bright, confident-looking restaurant. While starters play with international flavours (Thai noodles with a lime and ginger sauce; couscous Greek salad; fresh scallops tempura with sweet chilli dressing), inspiration for the main courses comes from closer to home: Welsh fillet of beef might be paired with a creamed horseradish suet pudding and a green peppercorn and brandy cream sauce; local lobster with a simple garlic herb butter; and roast rack of Welsh lamb with a herb breadcrumb crust, fresh mint jelly and rich redcurrant jus. Desserts could include a hot chocolate fondant; white chocolate and Cointreau crème brûlée; and caramel profiteroles. Children eat free between five and six pm.

**Chef/s:** Stephen Lawton, Roman Modrynski. **Open:** Mon to Sat D only 6 to 9.30. **Closed:** Nov, 5 Jan to 1 Mar. **Meals:** alc (main meals £16 to £34). **Service:** not inc. **Details:** Cards accepted. 36 seats. Wheelchair access. Music. Children's portions.

## ★NEW ENTRY★
## Morgan's
**Cute restaurant specialising in fish**
20 Nun Street, St David's, SA62 6NT
Tel no: (01437) 720508
www.morgans-restaurant.co.uk
**Modern British | £32**
**Cooking score: 2**

ϒ

Morgan's is a smart, welcoming little restaurant close to the heart of this tiny city. Internally, it adheres to the pale-walled, grass-matted school of décor and feels modern yet homely. Dishes are carefully, artistically composed and make impressive use of the best local produce. The fish specials, which only use fish caught off the Pembrokeshire coast, are palpably fresh; an inspection dish of hake fillet poached in a cider and black peppercorn sauce simply delighted with its clear, balanced flavours and spot-on timing. Other typical dishes include a starter of duck liver crème brûlée with tangerine sorbet, preserved spiced pear and brioche soldiers; roast breast of Gressingham duck with Seville orange and Grand Marnier sauce and fondant potato; and perhaps a rich, warm chocolate brownie pudding with a shot glass of warm chocolate sauce and white chocolate sorbet to finish. A good choice of wines starts from £13.
**Chef/s:** Tara Pitman. **Open:** Wed to Mon, 6.30 to 11.30. **Closed:** January, Febuary. **Meals:** alc (main courses £12.95 to £20). **Service:** not inc. **Details:** Cards accepted. 38 seats. Music. Children's portions. Car parking.

## Readers recommend

A 'readers recommend' review is a genuine quote from a report sent in by one of our readers. We intend to follow up these suggestions throughout the year to come.

## ■ Salem
### Angel
**An attractive home to serious cooking**
Nr Llandeilo, Salem, SA19 7LY
Tel no: (01558) 823394
Modern European | £42
Cooking score: 4

𝒱

Set deep in deepest Carmarthenshire, the
Angel still functions as a welcoming village
inn, albeit a very attractive one with subtle
lighting and a characterful hotchpotch of
furniture including plenty of soft sofas to sink
into. The efficient front-of-house team, led by
Elizabeth Smith, strikes a fine balance
between formal and friendly. The restaurant
area (wood-floored, and with more of that
nice furniture) provides an ideal setting for
cooking of serious intent, which is what Rod
Peterson delivers at every course. The home-
made breads are not to be missed, and could be
followed by pressed ham hock terrine with
orange, honey and mustard salad; ravioli of
crayfish and dill with buttered cucumber; or
sea bass in spring-water batter with baby chips
and tartare sauce. Move on to main courses
such as braised shoulder of Welsh lamb with
sweet onion and raisin jus and Paloise sauce;
roast saddle of venison with sausage and onion
charlotte, parsnip and port jus; or steamed
salmon and John Dory with English
asparagus, crab boudin and lemon-butter
sauce. The cooking is artful and refined yet
also generous and greed-inspiring. Desserts
might include cappuccino mousse with a
chocolate sablé biscuit; glazed apple and
frangipane tart; or an assiette of mini desserts
if you find yourself spoiled for choice. A well-
chosen, helpfully annotated wine list opens
at £13.95.
**Chef/s:** Rod Peterson. **Open:** Wed to Sat L 12 to 2,
Tue to Sat D 7 to 9. **Closed:** 2 weeks Jan. **Meals:** alc
(main courses L £8 to £14, D £15 to £19).
**Service:** not inc. **Details:** Cards accepted. 70 seats.
No mobile phones. Wheelchair access. Music.
Children's portions. Car parking.

## READERS RECOMMEND
### St Brides Spa Hotel
**British**
Saundersfoot, SA69 9NH
Tel no: (01834) 812304
www.stbridesspahotel.com
'Delicious seafood, stunning sea view'

## ■ Solva
### Old Pharmacy
**Harbourside restaurant**
5 Main Street, Solva, SA62 6UU
Tel no: (01437) 720005
www.theoldpharmacy.co.uk
Modern European | £43
Cooking score: 2

£5 OFF 𝒱

This attractive old building (no prizes for
guessing what it once was) stands on the main
road that snakes through Solva. At the rear, a
secluded garden runs down to the other main
thoroughfare through this pretty village – the
river. Local seafood, including Solva lobster
and plaice from Milford Haven, is a highlight
of the menu, while other choices could
include a starter of coarse country-style pork
and herb pâté with home-made bread and
piccalilli, followed by oriental-style braised
shredded duck served in a fragrant chicken
broth with soy, spring onions and noodles.
Diners are encouraged to choose whatever
they want, in any order or quantity, so it is fine
simply to call in for a bowl of home-made
soup or perhaps a warm salad of pan-fried
potato and local free-range smoked chicken
with fresh herbs. Children are welcomed, and
while most items on the menu can be
downsized, there is also a decent 'kids' menu
offering pasta dishes, grilled free-range
chicken breast, pork sausages and the like.
**Chef/s:** Matthew Ricketts and Tom Phillips. **Open:**
all week D only 5.30 to 9.30. **Closed:** 24, 25 and 26
Dec. **Meals:** alc (main courses £12 to £24).
**Service:** not inc. **Details:** Cards accepted. 60 seats.
12 seats outside. No mobile phones. Wheelchair
access. Music. Children's portions.

## Scores on the doors

As the emphasis on local and organic produce grows, the restaurant industry has come to realise that many customers value the origins of their food as much as the taste. With the 'Scores on the Doors' campaign, food hygiene finds itself brought into the age of information.

The scheme – already being successfully piloted across the UK, including in Scotland, the East Midlands and London – allows customers access to a restaurant's last inspection results (conducted by the local authority's environmental health team) for the first time. These are available by checking online or by simply glancing at the door or the window of the outlet in question.

Which? research shows that 97 per cent of customers believe they have a right to know the scores of local establishments.

You can check whether your local council participates on the Food Standard's Agency site: www.food.gov.uk/safereating/hyg/scoresonthedoors. Even if your area isn't part of the scheme, you're entitled to make a request to your local council for results under the *Freedom of Information* Act.

The FSA is currently reviewing the best way to provide this information. Following regional successes, Which? is campaigning for this scheme to be extended nationwide. For further details on the campaign, please see: www.which.co.uk.

## READERS RECOMMEND

### Jabajak
**Modern British**
**Banc-y-Llain, Llanboidy Road, Whitland,**
**SA34 OED**
**Tel no: (01994) 448786**
**www.jabajak.co.uk**
**'Home-grown food in unusual surroundings'**

# CHANNEL
# ISLANDS

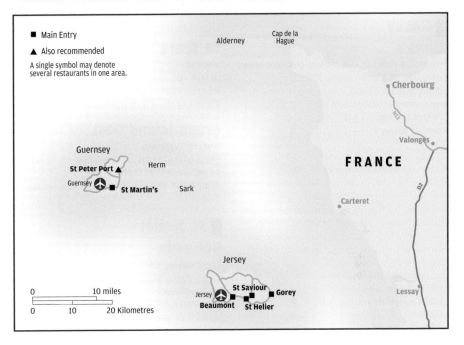

- ■ Main Entry
- ▲ Also recommended

A single symbol may denote several restaurants in one area.

# ■ Beaumont

## Bistro Soleil

**Sunny food in a seaside setting**
La Route de la Haule, Beaumont, JE3 7BA
Tel no: (01534) 720249
**Bistro/Seafood | £27**
**Cooking score: 4**

£5 OFF  ∨  £30

The sunny name seems entirely appropriate for this bright and breezy bistro overlooking St Aubin's Bay. Tables in the courtyard are at a premium when the weather obliges, and the vividly decorated L-shaped dining room is blessed with big picture windows for those who want to admire the fabulous sea views from indoors. Given the seaside location, it should come as no surprise that locally landed fish figures prominently on the lively bistro-style menus. Diver-caught scallops might be served with chive mash, a fricassee of woodland mushrooms and crispy pancetta, while whole lobsters are grilled and simply dressed with garlic butter. Other dishes pick up the colourful Mediterranean theme for example, grilled Parma ham and new season's asparagus with lemon-butter sauce or roast rump of lamb with boulangère potatoes, roast garlic and flageolet beans. Desserts keep it simple with the likes of glazed citrus tart or chocolate-brownie ice cream with chocolate and chilli sauce. The compact global wine list opens with five affordable house selections at £12.75 a bottle (£2.95 a glass).
**Chef/s:** Ian Jones. **Open:** Tue to Sun L 12.15 to 2, Tue to Sat D 6.45 to 9.30. **Closed:** 25 and 26 Dec, bank hols. **Meals:** alc exc Sun L (main courses £11 to £18). Set L £14.75 (3 courses), Set D £15 to £24.50 (5 courses). Terrace L menu available in summer. **Service:** not inc. **Details:** Cards accepted. 60 seats. 40 seats outside. Music. Children's portions. Car parking.

## ▌Gorey

### Suma's
Innovative cooking and picture-postcard views
Gorey Hill, St Martin, Gorey, JE3 6ET
Tel no: (01534) 853291
www.sumasrestaurant.com
Modern European | £41
Cooking score: 5

£5
OFF  V

The baby sister of Longueville Manor in St
Saviour (see entry), Suma's makes much of its
fantastic location and views over Gorey's
stone-walled fishing harbour and the historic
castle of Mount Orgueil. Inside, paintings and
collages by local artist Paul Kilshaw line the
walls of the clean-cut, dining room. Daniel
Ward is a chef with bags of imagination and a
confident approach to things culinary.
He plucks ideas and ingredients from the
world larder for a compendium of modern
dishes that runs from plates of Spanish nibbles
and carpaccio of beef to more complex
assemblages. Ravioli of local lobster with
tempura of baby leeks, broccoli purée and
shellfish foam is typical of his multi-
pronged approach, and the creative streak
extends to Gressingham duck breast on sweet
potato fondant with plum jam, sesame greens
and spiced confit wun tuns. To conclude, the
kitchen offers banana and hazelnut parfait
with praline sauce and hot Valhrona chocolate
fondant with Baileys ice cream, as well as an
assiette of miniature desserts. The lively
modern wine list includes a number of bottles
that are 'exclusive to Suma's'; choice is global
and prices cruise gently upwards from £9.75
for Southern Italian 'Flying Pig'.
Chef/s: Daniel Ward. Open: Sat only B 9.30 to
10.30. All week L 12 to 2, D 6.15 to 9.30. Closed:
Christmas, early Jan. Meals: alc (main courses £14
to £25). Set L and Set D 6.15 to 6.45 only Mon to Sat
£15 (2 courses) to £17.50, Set L Sun £22 (3 courses).
Set D £30 (3 courses).. Service: 10% fixed charge.
Details: Cards accepted. 40 seats. 16 seats outside.
No mobile phones. Music. Children allowed.

## READERS RECOMMEND

### La Frère
Seafood
Le Mont de Rozel, Rozel Bay, JE3 6AN
Tel no: (01534) 861000
'Classic seafood in a cliff-top location'

### Green Island Restaurant
Modern European
Green Island, St Clement, JE2 6LS
Tel no: (01543) 857787
'Busy beachside venue popular with locals'

## ▌St Helier

### Bohemia
Breathtaking cuisine in a boutique hotel
Green Street, St Helier, JE2 4UH
Tel no: (01534) 880588
www.bohemiajersey.com
Modern European | £61
Cooking score: 7

🛏

Part of the ultra-chic Club Hotel and Spa at
the heart of St Helier's financial quarter,
Bohemia seems perfectly in tune with the
prevailing mood of moneyed opulence. It
combines a fashionable bar with a richly
furnished, but refreshingly unstuffy restaurant
where Shaun Rankin's dazzling approach to
contemporary cuisine is the real star. He
often uses classic themes as the jumping-off
point for ideas that are startling and
innovative. So, a cocktail of Jersey white crab
arrives with sweetcorn and basil 'vichiçoise'
and crab jelly, while roast local suckling pig
appears not only with familiar apples and
quince, but also smoked potato and
langoustines. Ingredients from further afield
also feature strongly, and the treatment they
receive is much the same. Roast loin of
Yorkshire venison with chocolate tortellini
turns a famous pairing on its head, especially
when Medjool dates and ginger-scented
quinoa are added to the mix, while an assiette
of new season's Welsh lamb has 'Saint Maure
de Touraine' goats' cheese, rosemary and Jersey

honeycomb as companions. Given the setting and Bohemia's up-to-the-moment style, it should come as no surprise to find that the spaces between conventional courses are preceded and interspersed with canapés, shot glasses and the like. A separate dessert menu heralds a mix of effortlessly re-worked classics ('pear flavours with warm frangipane') and in-vogue creations (peanut butter with banana and Valrhona's Caraïbe chocolate). These are complex, daring but totally convincing views of the current gastronomic landscape, seen through the eyes of a chef whose cooking is streets ahead of anything else on Jersey. Wines have been garnered from small exclusive producers as well as big-name châteaux. Around 20 selections are available by the glass (from £3.95) and they are maintained in tip-top condition, thanks to 'le verre du vin' preservation system. Bottles are priced from £15.95.

**Chef/s:** Shaun Rankin. **Open:** Mon to Fri L 12 to 2.30, Mon to Sat D 6.30 to 10. **Meals:** Set L £16.50 (2 courses) to £19.50, Set D £49 (3 courses) to £95 (inc wine). Bar menu available Mon to Fri. **Service:** 10%. **Details:** Cards accepted. 40 seats. Air-con. No mobile phones. Wheelchair access. Music. Children allowed. Car parking.

## ∎ St Martin's

### Auberge
**Creative cooking in modish surroundings**
Jerbourg Road, St Martin's, GY4 6BH
Tel no: (01481) 238485
www.theauberge.gg
Modern British | £42
Cooking score: 5

£5 OFF ⋎

Fashionably redesigned in recent years, this long-serving restaurant is enviably situated high on the cliffs a few miles from St Peter Port. Inside it is modish and minimalist, with full-length windows providing spectacular views over Le Pied du Mur Bay to Guernsey's island neighbours. Locally sourced produce (especially seafood) forms the backbone of the kitchen's work and resulting dishes are characterised by a clever and sympathetic use

of interesting components. A pressed terrine of home-smoked chicken, foie gras and shiitake mushrooms is accompanied by fig and apple chutney, beef carpaccio is jazzed up with rocket pesto and red pepper sorbet, while pan-fried fillet of sea bass is served on crushed new potatoes with marinated fennel and tomato tartare. Elsewhere, a 'duo of beef' involves braised brisket pie and grilled fillet with pommes Anna and roast garlic jus; there are also some eclectic choices for vegetarians. To conclude, expect colourful flourishes in the form of lemon tart with deep-fried lemongrass ice cream or vanilla pannacotta with sweet wine jelly and raspberry sorbet. The short list of three-dozen wines is a concise global slate with six house selections at £14.95 (£3.85 a glass); a handful of posher bottles are gathered together in the 'Directors' Bin'.

**Chef/s:** Daniel Green. **Open:** all week L 12 to 2, D 7 to 9.30 (9 Sun). **Meals:** alc D (main courses £12 to £17). Set L £14.95 to £17.95. **Service:** not inc. **Details:** Cards accepted. 60 seats. 40 seats outside. Wheelchair access. Music. Children's portions. Car parking.

## ALSO RECOMMENDED

### ▲ Da Nello
46 Pollet Street, St Peter Port, GY1 1WF
Tel no: (01481) 721552

Popular Italian in a modernised fifteenth-century building with shipwreck timbers and rough stone walls. Robust trattoria cooking makes the best use of local fish and shellfish and the island's veal and dairy produce, with spring lamb brought over from Sark. A set-price three-course deal (£26.50) might include seared Guernsey scallops and brandade of smoked haddock with beetroot salad, scaloppine of veal, and orange sorbet. Italian wines stand out among a short international list from £11.50. Open all week.

## Chocolate

The Spanish conquistadors reported encountering cocoa as a form of currency and a component of Aztec sacrificial ritual, thereby establishing a European fetish that has lasted 500 years. But the substance that represented blood and gold in pre-conquest South America is not one we would recognise. The cocoa served at the court of Montezuma was a bitter, gritty drink, flavoured with chilli, cornmeal and herbs. It was only when the Spanish began to cultivate sugar that chocolate became sweet, and it was not until the factory processes of the nineteenth century that chocolate could be solid rather than liquid.

Seventeenth and eighteenth century chocolate was an exotic and expensive beverage, often consumed at home by wealthy women showing off new silver chocolate pots and china cups. It was thought to be aphrodisiac, and sold by apothecaries.

The story of the chocolate bar is not an appetising one. Slave-grown cocoa was combined with slave-produced sugar in Quaker-owned factories where the workers lived in model towns with free education and healthcare in exchange for teetotal and obedient lives. Solid chocolate was marketed mostly to children until chocolates became popular gifts from men to women in the twentieth century, and it is in the wake of this sexualisation that we find both the idea of chocolate as a sin and the recent rise of grand cru, single bean dark chocolate as a means of social discrimination.

## ▌ St Saviour

### Longueville Manor
Intricate cooking in romantic surroundings
St Saviour, JE2 7WF
Tel no: (01534) 725501
www.longuevillemanor.com
**Modern European | £65**
**Cooking score: 5**

Three generations of the Lewis family have presided over this medieval manor house in the last 50 years, and there's little doubt that the place is in very safe hands. Formal meals can be served in the sumptuous surroundings of the Oak Room with its ornate Spanish panelling or in the light, modern Garden Room. Andrew Baird has been at the stoves for nigh on 20 years and he takes full advantage of the harvest from the hotel's gardens and glasshouses. His cooking is driven by fashionable trends and impeccable technique: an assiette of oven-roast quail with a ballotine of quail and black pudding, fried egg and consommé is a signature starter. Luxury and invention also spill over into elaborately crafted main courses like grilled red mullet with sautéed langoustines, butternut squash, pak choi, spiced jus and beurre blanc, although other dishes strike a classic note. Desserts are clever and cheekily audacious, as in warm pineapple brochette cooked on vanilla with a cheese sauce and 'ten flavours' sorbet. The Longueville wine list ranks as one of Jersey's finest, and it comprises '400 perfectly conditioned' bins including pedigree vintages from Bordeaux and Burgundy, New World young bloods and a smattering of organic bottles. House vins de pays open the bidding at £19 and more than 20 are served by the glass (from £4.25).
**Chef/s:** Andrew Baird. **Open:** all week 12.30 to 2, 7 to 9.30. **Meals:** alc (main courses £28 to £30). Set L £15 (2 courses) to £20, Set L Sun £27.50. Set D £55 to £97.50 (inc wine). Light menu available.
**Service:** net prices. **Details:** Cards accepted. 70 seats. 40 seats outside. No music. No mobile phones. Wheelchair access. Children's portions. Car parking.

# NORTHERN IRELAND

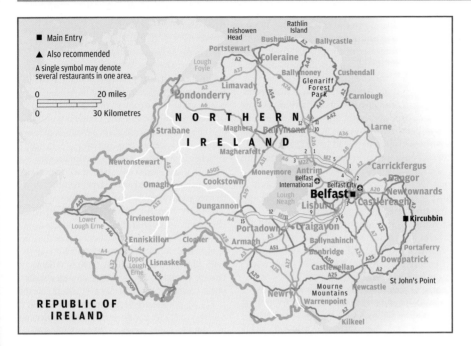

# Belfast

## Aldens

**Cosmopolitan style and vibrant food**
229 Upper Newtownards Road, Belfast, BT4 3LW
Tel no: (028) 9065 0079
www.aldensrestaurant.com
**Modern Irish | £40**
**Cooking score: 2**

Aldens' smart modern frontage helps to brighten up a rather unpromising location. The kitchen embraces a broad repertoire of modern dishes that might stretch from roast haunch of rabbit with cotechino, lentils and salsa verde to fillet of wild sea bass with prawn sauce and wild garlic. To finish, an impressive slate of Irish farmhouse cheeses holds sway alongside desserts including cinnamon-scented crème brûlée or roast pears with caramelised pecans, white chocolate and apricot ice cream. Sixteen intelligently chosen house recommendations (from £14)

head the fascinating wine list, which is peppered with intriguing and elite names from around the globe.
**Chef/s:** Denise Hockey. **Open:** Mon to Sat L 12 to 2.30, Mon to Sat D 6 to 10 (11 Fri and Sat). **Closed:** bank hols. **Meals:** alc (main courses L £6 to £10, D £9 to £21). Set D £18 (2 courses) to £22 (3 courses). **Service:** optional. **Details:** Cards accepted. 70 seats. Wheelchair access. Music. Children's portions.

## Cayenne

**Eclectic food for a fashion-conscious crowd**
7 Ascot House, Shaftesbury Square, Belfast, BT2 7DB
Tel no: (028) 9033 1532
www.rankingroup.co.uk
**Fusion/Pan-Asian | £48**
**New Chef**

Part of Paul and Jeanne Rankin's dynamic Belfast empire (see entries for Rain City and Roscoff Brasserie), Cayenne delivers punchy fusion food amid surroundings that are

irresistibly alluring to the city's urbane, fun-loving set. Live multi-media events and exhibits are a feature of the place, orange lanterns and bold design motifs point up the arty interior, and the menu hitchhikes its way across the globe. Appetisers such as hot'n'sour broth with prawn wun tuns or halibut and foie gras rice paper with pak choi and mango salad might get the trip underway, before things get serious with Indian spiced lamb shank and curried couscous or red braised short ribs with roast monkfish, Asian greens and coconut rice. Desserts quell any pangs of homeland nostalgia with the promise of warm apple, cinnamon and hazelnut pudding or rhubarb crumble with ginger cake ice cream. The trendy, top-end wine list is organised by grape and offers a tantalising mix of keenly priced everyday bottles along with more exclusive 'fine wines'.
**Chef/s:** Grainne Donnelly and Paul Waterworth. **Open:** Mon to Fri L 12 to 2.30, all week D 6 to 10.15 (11.15 Fri and Sat, 8.45 Sun). **Closed:** 25 and 26 Dec. **Meals:** alc (main courses £15.50 to £18). Set L £12 (2 courses), Set D £15.25 (2 courses). **Service:** not inc. **Details:** Cards accepted. 130 seats. Air-con. Wheelchair access. Music. Children's portions.

★ READERS' RESTAURANT OF THE YEAR ★
NORTHERN IRELAND

## James Street South
**Precise food in minimalist surroundings**
21 James Street South, Belfast, BT2 7GA
Tel no: (028) 9043 4310
www.jamesstreetsouth.co.uk
**Modern European | £47**
**Cooking score: 5**
Ⅴ

Colourful abstract artwork brightens up the white minimalism of this well-liked city-centre venue, which has made a real impact since opening in 2003. Niall McKenna's cooking receives plaudits for its well-honed techniques and precise attention to detail. He is capable of delivering a raft of exquisitely light dishes, founded on a solid bedrock of Euro-classicism (as you might expect from someone who learned the essentials of his craft

from Marco Pierre White and Nico Ladenis). Fish arrives daily from one of Belfast's top merchants and it is subjected to expert treatment: Dover sole served with brown shrimp and champagne beurre blanc is a luxuriously classic notion, while wild sea bass is equally at home with a fricassee of shellfish and artichokes. Game is well hung and the choice of meat dishes extends to lamb cutlets with apricot and fig compote, crispy aubergine and mint jus or roast quail with parsnip purée, red wine, shallot and asparagus. To finish, share the James Street fondue, or try orange pannacotta with chocolate mocha tart. The short wine list comprises astute regional choices from around the globe. Bottle prices start at £15 for Spanish Cabernet Sauvignon.
**Chef/s:** Niall McKenna. **Open:** Mon to Sat L 12 to 2.45, all week D 5.45 to 10.45 (5.30 to 9 Sun). **Closed:** 25 and 26 Dec, 1 Jan, 12 July. **Meals:** alc (main courses £14 to £20). Set L £13.50 (2 courses) to £15.50, pre-theatre Set D Mon to Thur £15.50 (2 courses) to £17.50. Bar menu available. **Service:** not inc. **Details:** Cards accepted. 70 seats. Air-con. Music. Children's portions.

## Nick's Warehouse
**Well-supported neighbourhood restaurant**
35-39 Hill Street, Belfast, BT1 2LB
Tel no: (028) 9043 9690
www.nickswarehouse.co.uk
**Modern European | £40**
**Cooking score: 3**
Ⅴ £30

Nick and Kathy Price's popular venue in Belfast's cathedral quarter started life as a bonded warehouse belonging to Bushmills Distillery. The downstairs Anix wine bar attracts big crowds, especially at lunchtime when the kitchen delivers a mixed bag of sandwiches, salads and hot dishes like Owen McMahon's steak sausages on roast garlic mash with red wine lentils. Alternatively, head up to the first-floor restaurant, where the menu promises things like roast chump of lamb with mint harissa sauce and couscous, or barramundi served on roast sweet potato and pak choi with a pickled ginger dressing. To

562

finish, there are straightforward desserts like warm orange polenta cake or chocolate mousse with fresh strawberries. The wine list nips around the world in search of value and quality. Most house selections are £13.75 (£3.70 a glass). **Chef/s:** Nick Price and Sean Craig. **Open:** Mon to Fri L 12 to 3, Tue to Sat D 6 to 9.30 (10 Fri and Sat). **Closed:** 25 and 26 Dec, Easter Mon and Tue. **Meals:** alc (main courses L £7.50 to £19, D £10.50 to £19). **Service:** not inc. **Details:** Cards accepted. 180 seats. Air-con. Music. Children's portions.

## Rain City

**All-day, American-style diner**
33-35 Malone Road, Belfast, BT9 6RU
Tel no: (028) 9068 2929
www.rankingroup.co.uk
**Modern European | £35**
Cooking score: 3
£5 OFF ✌ £30

According to owner Paul Rankin, Rain City is 'the closest you'll get to an American diner this side of the Atlantic'. Flexibility is the name of the game, with many dishes offered as 'small plates' or in medium-sized portions. Openers might include chicken Caesar salad, five-spice duck spring rolls or salt and pepper squid. After that, expect a roll call of pastas, chargrills and eclectic dishes like crispy pork belly with soft polenta and peperonata, plus best-selling burgers ranging from fish and falafel to Finnebrogue venison. Alternatively, customers can create their own three-course meals by mixing-and-matching from the menu. Weekend brunch is a popular event, cocktails hit the spot and the neat list of three dozen wines is unlikely to break the bank; prices start at £16 (£3.50 per glass). **Chef/s:** Paul Rankin. **Open:** all week 12 (10 Sat and Sun) to 5 (4 Sat and Sun), 5 to 9.30 (10 Fri, 9 Sun). **Closed:** 25 Dec. **Meals:** alc (main courses £6 to £15). **Service:** not inc. **Details:** Cards accepted. 90 seats. 25 seats outside. Air-con. Wheelchair access. Music. Children's portions.

## Roscoff Brasserie

**Iconic brasserie from Belfast's dream team**
7-11 Linenhall Street, Belfast, BT2 8AA
Tel no: (028) 9031 1150
www.rankingroup.co.uk
**Modern European | £50**
Cooking score: 5
✌

Paul and Jeanne Rankin were determined to please their legions of loyal fans when they opened this stylish brasserie behind City Hall in 2004. Many of Rankin's much-loved signature dishes remain, including his incomparable crisped-up confit of duck, which is currently being served with colcannon cake and spiced beetroot confit. Elsewhere, seafood is a perenially strong suit: pan-fried halibut keeps company with fresh clams, petits pois and tagliatelle, while roast monkfish could be paired fashionably with braised oxtail jus and fennel mash. Ideas are often deceptively simple, as in a carpaccio of new season's Finnebrogue venison with celeriac rémoulade or loin of lamb with fresh thyme and peas, but everything is delivered with consummate polish and gusto. Desserts are full of confidence and élan: consider a mille-feuille of figs and oranges accompanied by tangerine mousse or cooked-to-order caramel soufflé with banana ice cream and roast bananas, for example. The contemporary wine list hits the button, with good drinking across the board and prices that are equally kind to big spenders and those on a tight rein. Bottles from £16 (£4 a glass) lay down the marker. Paul Rankin's Belfast gastro-empire also takes in Cayenne and Rain City (see entries).

**Chef/s:** Paul Rankin. **Open:** Mon to Fri L 12 to 2.15, Mon to Sat D 6 to 10.15 (11.15 Fri and Sat). **Closed:** 25 and 26 Dec, Easter Mon and Tue. **Meals:** alc (main courses £16 to £22). Set L £15.25 (2 courses) to £19.50, Set D Mon to Thur £24.50 (3 courses). **Service:** not inc. **Details:** Cards accepted. 80 seats. Air-con. Wheelchair access. Music. Children's portions.

## ALSO RECOMMENDED
## ▲ Deanes Restaurant
36-40 Howard Street, Belfast, BT1 6PF
Tel no: (028) 9033 1134
www.michaeldeane.co.uk

Formerly Restaurant Michael Deane, this high-flying Belfast venue has recently undergone a radical makeover. Gone is the two-tiered brasserie/fine-dining approach: in its place, Deane has created a laid-back, open-plan restaurant with a purpose-built bar attached. The mood is urbane and casual; menus are short, sharp and to-the-point. Carpaccio of Irish veal with warm mushroom and bean salad and almond butter vinaigrette (£8) might precede halibut with brandade and parsley 'chlorophyll', smoked bacon and spring pea emulsion (£18), while desserts (from £7) could include spiced pineapple crumble with pineapple syllabub. Impressive wines from £18 a bottle (£4.50 a glass). Open Mon to Sat L and D. Reports please. [See also Deanes at Queens, below.]

## ▲ Metro Brasserie
13 Lower Crescent, Belfast, BT7 1NR
Tel no: (028) 9032 3349
www.crescenttownhouse.com/brasserie

Set in the heart of the Botanic Avenue district of Belfast, a little way south of the city centre, Metro is a contemporary urban brasserie with a lively ambience. The wide-ranging menu opens with crispy confit duck leg on pear chutney, foie gras parfait (£6), and goats' cheese and pine-nut galette with baked fig, Antrim honey and clove dressing (£5.50), while robust appetites will appreciate main courses such as dry aged Irish beef fillet with crispy potatoes and white wine, tarragon and foie gras butter (£22). Finish with a dark chocolate and caramel cheesecake with cherry sorbet. Wines from £13. Open Wed to Sat L and all week D.

## READERS RECOMMEND
### Beatrice Kennedy
Modern European
44 University Road, Belfast, BT7 1NJ
Tel no: (028) 9020 2290
www.beatricekennedy.co.uk
'Townhouse serving local produce'

### Deanes at Queens
Modern European
1 College Gardens, Belfast, BT7 1NN
Tel no: (028) 9038 2111
www.michaeldeane.co.uk
'Sophisticated brasserie in university grounds'

### Oriel of Gilford
Modern Irish
2 Bridge Street, Gilford, BT63 6HF
Tel no: (028) 3883 1543
'Accomplished cooking; countryside location'

## ▌Kircubbin
# Paul Arthurs
**Inventive food from a well-travelled chef**
66 Main Street, Kircubbin, BT22 2SP
Tel no: (028) 4273 8192
www.paularthurs.com
**Modern European | £40**
**Cooking score: 3**

🛏 ⴸ

Niall McKenna

Paul Arthurs' eponymous restaurant-with-rooms is rather surprisingly located on the first floor above a chippie and amusement arcade, but the dowdy setting does nothing to distract customers from the class, style or creativity of the food on offer. His take on modern European food is straight and true: he sends out seared foie gras with onion and balsamic jus, serves local spring lamb with ratatouille and offers pannacotta with raspberries to finish. Elsewhere, global influences surface in the shape of shiitake mushroom risotto with coriander, ginger and sweet sake, or tenderloin of pork teriyaki. It's also worth enquiring about the catch of the day, which might be Kirkcubbin Bay crab, steamed Strangford Lough mussels or grilled lobster. Irish farmhouse cheeses are served with quince jelly and the neat global wine list keeps its prices in check, with six house recommendations at £12.95 (£3.25 per glass). **Chef/s:** Paul Arthurs. **Open:** Sun L 12 to 2.30, Tue to Sat D 5 to 9 (9.30 Fri and Sat). **Closed:** Christmas, Jan. **Meals:** alc (main courses £15 to £17). **Service:** not inc. **Details:** Cards accepted. 45 seats. 30 seats outside. Wheelchair access. Music. Children's portions. Car parking.

## READERS RECOMMEND
## Beech Hill Country House
**Modern Irish**
32 Ardmore Road, Londonderry, BT47 3QP
Tel no: (028) 7134 9279
**'Elegant dining in a rural manor house'**

**Why did you become a chef?**
I've always had a love of food. Since the age of 15, I studied catering and worked part-time in a local restaurant.

**Who was your main inspiration?**
Early on, it would have to be my parents; both are great cooks. Professionally, it would be my first head chef, Pat Kells, as he motivated and inspired me.

**Which of today's chefs do you admire?**
Thomas Keller for his attention to detail, Guy Savoy for his continuous inspiration and Richard Corrigan for his passion for honest, quality food.

**Where do you eat out?**
A great Indian called the Bengal Brasserie, but I'm also lucky enough to have friends who love to cook and always invite me!

**Who is your favourite producer?**
My butcher is my current favourite, as he breeds his own cattle and lamb, knows the heritage of the product and has great passion.

**Do you have a favourite local recipe?**
It would have to be champ, which is mashed potato with scallions, cream, butter and eggs.

**What is your proudest achievement?**
Opening the James Street South Restaurant and sustaining it!

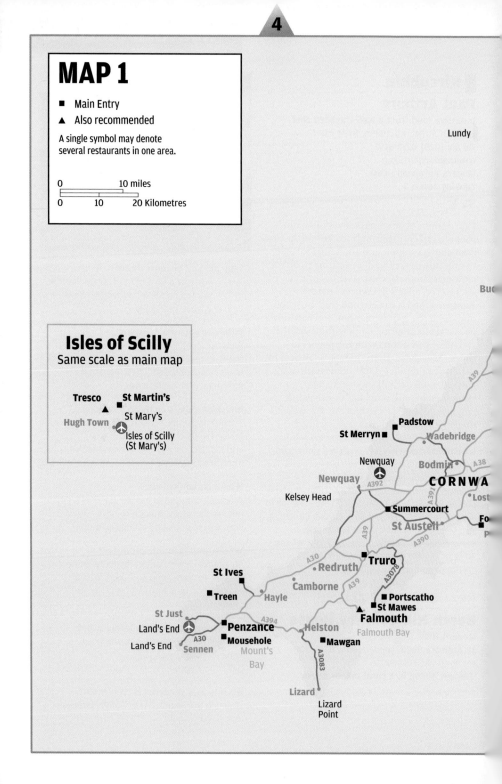

# MAP 1

- ■ Main Entry
- ▲ Also recommended

A single symbol may denote
several restaurants in one area.

0          10 miles

0     10     20 Kilometres

## Isles of Scilly
Same scale as main map

Tresco   St Martin's
▲  ■
Hugh Town   St Mary's
✈
Isles of Scilly
(St Mary's)

Lundy

Bu

St Merryn ■  Padstow
Wadebridge

Newquay
✈  Bodmin  A38
Newquay  A392  CORNWA
Kelsey Head  °Lost
■ Summercourt
Fo
St Austell °
A390  P
A30  ●Truro
St Ives ■  ●Redruth
■ Treen  Camborne  A39
Hayle
St Just  ■ Portscatho
Land's End ✈  ■Penzance  Helston  ▲ ■St Mawes
Land's End  A30  ■Mousehole  Falmouth
Sennen  Mount's  ■Mawgan  Falmouth Bay
Bay

A394

A3083

Lizard
Lizard
Point

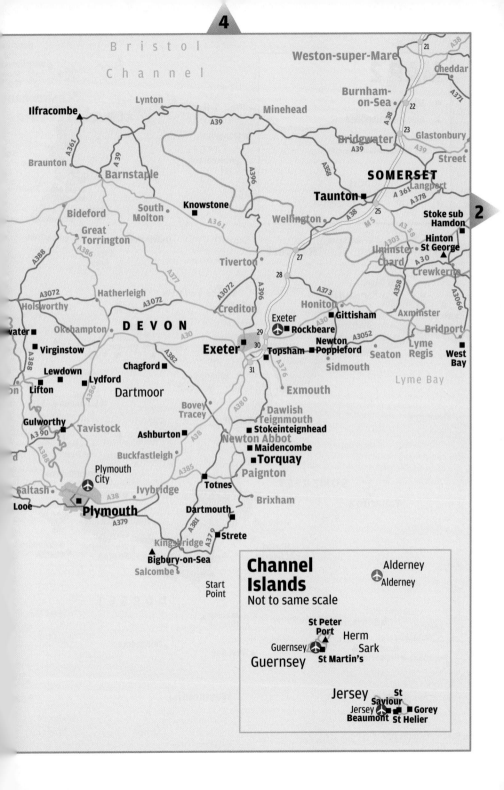

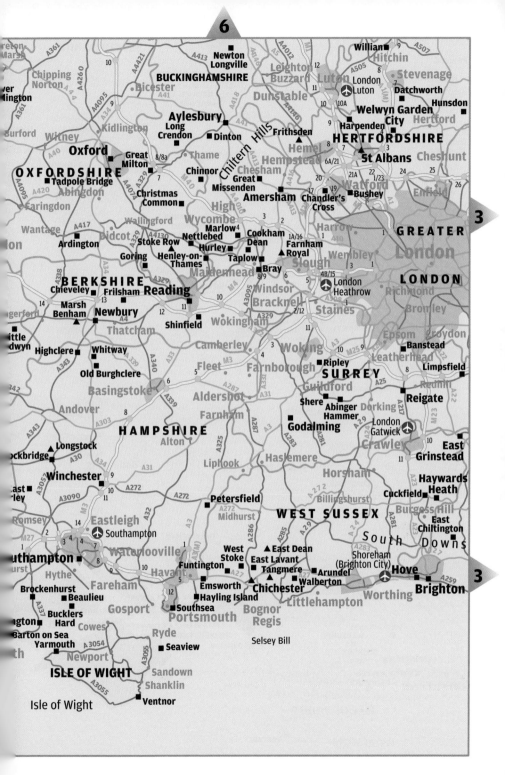

3

3

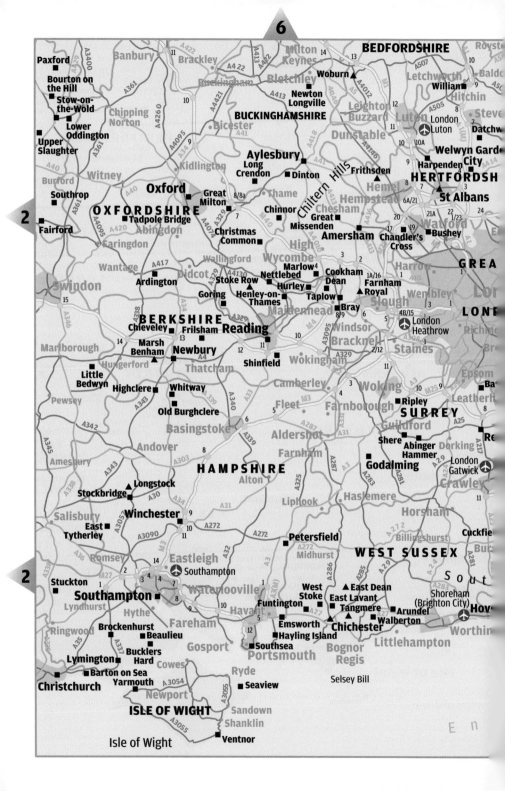

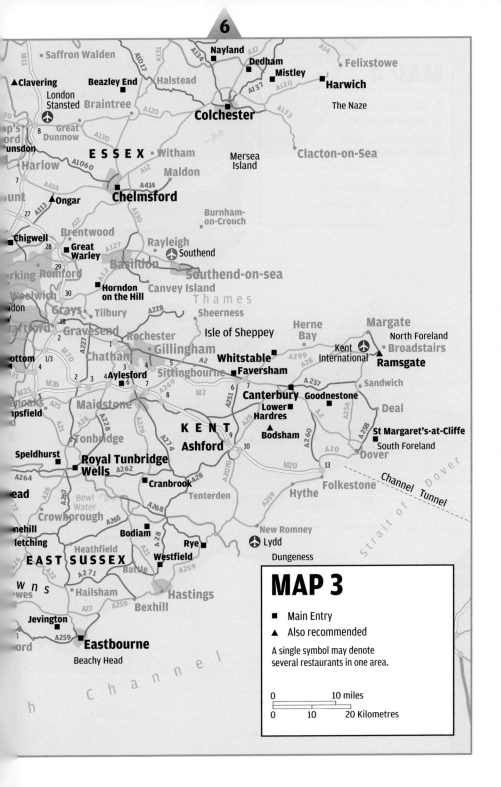

6

Saffron Walden
▲Clavering
Beazley End
Halstead
Nayland
Dedham
Mistley
Felixstowe
Harwich
London
Stansted
Braintree
A120
The Naze
Colchester
p's
ord
'unsdon
Great
Dunmow
A130
E S S E X • Witham
Mersea
Island
Clacton-on-Sea
Harlow
A1060
A12
Maldon
7
A414
A414
unt
Ongar
Chelmsford
27
A113
Burnham-
on-Crouch
Chigwell
28
Brentwood
Great
Warley
A127
Rayleigh
Southend
rking Romford
29
Basildon
Southend-on-sea
Woolwich
30
Horndon
on the Hill
Canvey Island
don
Grays
Tilbury
A228
Sheerness
T h a m e s
artford
18
Gravesend
Rochester
Isle of Sheppey
Herne
Bay
Margate
North Foreland
ottom
1/3
2
A227
Chatham
Gillingham
Kent
International
Broadstairs
4
M20
3
A2
Whitstable
A299
A28
Ramsgate
2
M26
2
3
4Aylesford
Sittingbourne
Faversham
Sandwich
M25
5
A25
Maidstone
8
M2
A251
6
7
Canterbury
Goodnestone
Deal
psfield
A26
A228
A229
Lower
Hardres
A256
A2
Tonbridge
K E N T
9
Bodsham
▲
A260
St Margaret's-at-Cliffe
Speldhurst
Royal Tunbridge
Wells A262
Ashford
10
A20
South Foreland
Dover
M20
13
A264
Cranbrook
A28
Folkestone
Channel Tunnel
ead
Bewl
Water
A268
Tenterden
A259
Hythe
Strait of Dover
Crowborough
A265
ehill
Bodiam
A28
New Romney
letching
Heathfield
Rye
Lydd
E A S T   S U S S E X
Westfield
Dungeness
A271
Battle
A259
w n s
wes
Hailsham
Hastings
A27
A259
Bexhill
Jevington
A259
Eastbourne
ord
Beachy Head

C h a n n e l

MAP 3

■  Main Entry
▲  Also recommended

A single symbol may denote
several restaurants in one area.

0                    10 miles
0          10         20 Kilometres

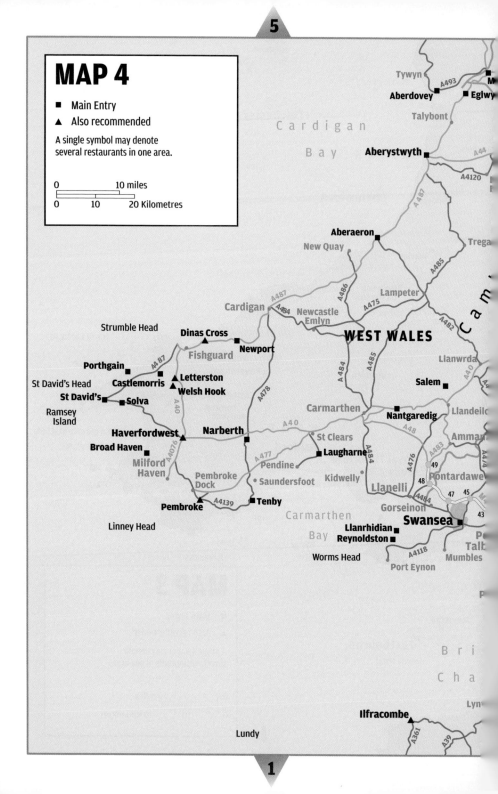

**5**

# MAP 4

- ■ Main Entry
- ▲ Also recommended

A single symbol may denote
several restaurants in one area.

```
0                10 miles
├────┼────┤
0        10        20 Kilometres
```

Tywyn
A493
Aberdovey ■ Eglwy
M

C a r d i g a n

Talybont

B a y    Aberystwyth ■
A4A
A4120

A487

Aberaeron ■
New Quay
Trega

A485

Cardigan   A484  Newcastle
Emlyn
Lampeter
A475
A482

**WEST WALES**

Strumble Head   ▲ Dinas Cross
■ Newport
Fishguard
A487
Llanwrda
A484   A485
Salem ■

Porthgain ■
St David's Head   Castlemorris ■   ▲ Letterston
▲ Welsh Hook
St David's ■
Solva ■
A40
Carmarthen
Nantgaredig ■   Llandeilo
Ramsey
Island
A48

Haverfordwest ▲   ■ Narberth
A40
St Clears
Ammar
Broad Haven ■
A4076
Laugharne ■
A484   A476
49
Milford
Haven
Pembroke   Pendine
Dock   ● Saundersfoot   Kidwelly
48   Pontardawe
47   45
Pembroke ■   A4139   ■ Tenby   Llanelli
A4484   43
Carmarthen   Gorseinon
Linney Head   Llanrhidian ■   Swansea ■
B a y   Reynoldston ■
Worms Head   A4118   Talb
Port Eynon   Mumbles   P

Camↄ

B r i

C h a

Lyn

Ilfracombe ▲
A361   A39

Lundy

**1**

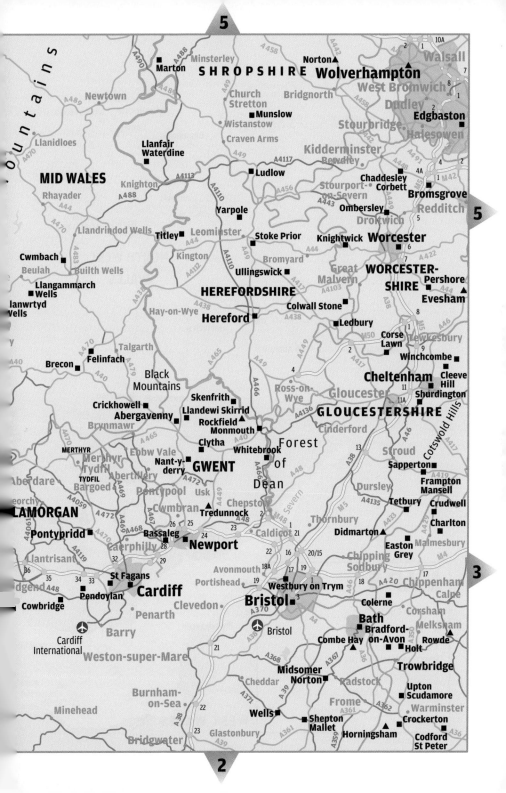

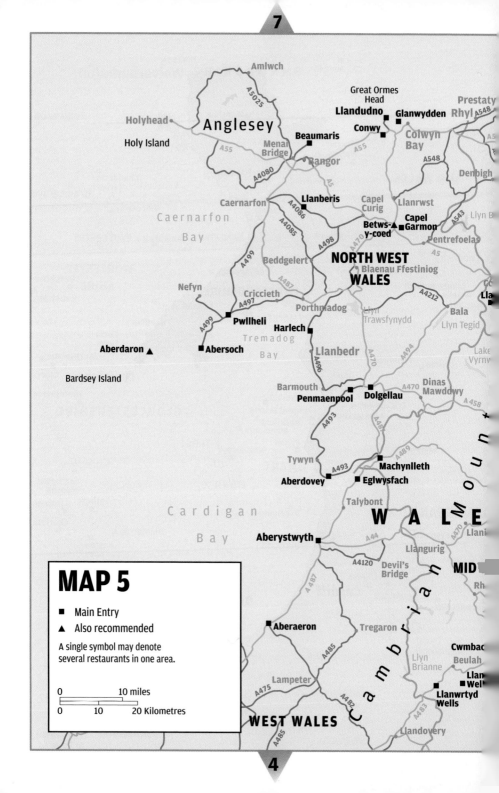

Amlwch

A5025

Great Ormes
Head

Llandudno  Glanwydden  Prestaty

Holyhead  Anglesey  Beaumaris  Conwy  Rhyl A548

Holy Island  A55  Menai  Colwyn  A5
Bridge  Bay

A4080  Bangor  A55  A548

A5  Denbigh

Caernarfon  Llanberis  Capel  Llanrwst
A4086  Curig

Caernarfon  A4085  Betws-▲  Capel  A543  Llyn B
Bay  A498  y-coed  Garmon

Pentrefoelas

A499  Beddgelert  NORTH WEST  A5
A487  Blaenau Ffestiniog

Nefyn  Criccieth  WALES  A4212  Lla
A497  Porthmadog  Llyn  Bala
A499  Pwllheli  Trawsfynydd  Llyn Tegid

Harlech  Lake
Tremadog  A494  Vyrnw

Aberdaron ▲  ■Abersoch  Bay  Llanbedr  A470

Bardsey Island  A496

Barmouth  A470  Dinas
Penmaenpool  Dolgellau  Mawddwy

A493  A458

Tywyn  A489  Machynlleth  Mount

Aberdovey  A493  Eglwysfach

Talybont

Cardigan  W  A  L  E

Bay  Aberystwyth  A44  Llani

Llangurig

A4120  Devil's  MID
A487  Bridge  Cambrian

Rh

# MAP 5

- ■ Main Entry
- ▲ Also recommended

A single symbol may denote
several restaurants in one area.

Aberaeron  Tregaron

Cwmbac

Llyn  Beulah
Brianne

Lampeter  Llan
A485  ■Well

A475  Llanwrtyd
A482  Wells

0          10 miles

0     10     20 Kilometres

WEST WALES  Llandovery

A485

# MAP 6

- ■ Main Entry
- ▲ Also recommended

A single symbol may denote
several restaurants in one area.

0             10 miles
0        10      20 Kilometres

blethorpe

Skegness

Wells-next-the-Sea

Brancaster Staithe
Burnham Deepdale
Morston
Sheringham
Cromer
Holkham
Blakeney
Munstanton
A149
▲ Holt
ash
Burnham Market
Walsingham
▲ Edgefield
North Walsham
▲ Snettisham
Fakenham
Aylsham
A148
Grimston
A1067
A17 ■ King's Lynn
A1065
East Dereham
A140
A1151
A149
Norwich
Norwich
N O R F O L K
A47
Brundall A47
Great Yarmouth
A1122
Swaffham
Downham Market
Ovington
Wymondham
A146
A143
Lowestoft
A134
A1065
Stoke Holy Cross
A1075
A11
Attleborough
A140
Thetford Forest Park
Harleston
A143
Bungay
Beccles
Brandon
Thetford
A1066
Diss
Halesworth
A144
A145
▲ Ely
A11
A134
A1088
A143
Fressingfield
Bramfield ▲
■ Southwold
Walberswick
Mildenhall
A1101
Stanton
A140
A12
A14
Bury St Edmunds
A1120
Saxmundham
ingsea
Newmarket
A14
idge
Little Wilbraham
Lidgate ■
A143
Stowmarket
A12
■ Aldeburgh
elford
S U F F O L K
Orford
A1307
Lavenham
■ Bildeston
Woodbridge
Orford Ness
Long Melford
A1141
Haverhill
A1092
Monks Eleigh
A1071
Hadleigh
Ipswich
Sudbury
A134
Nayland
A12
A14
Felixstowe
Saffron Walden
A1017
Dedham
Mistley
Harwich
ng
Beazley End
Halstead
A137
A120
Braintree
Colchester ■
The Naze

3

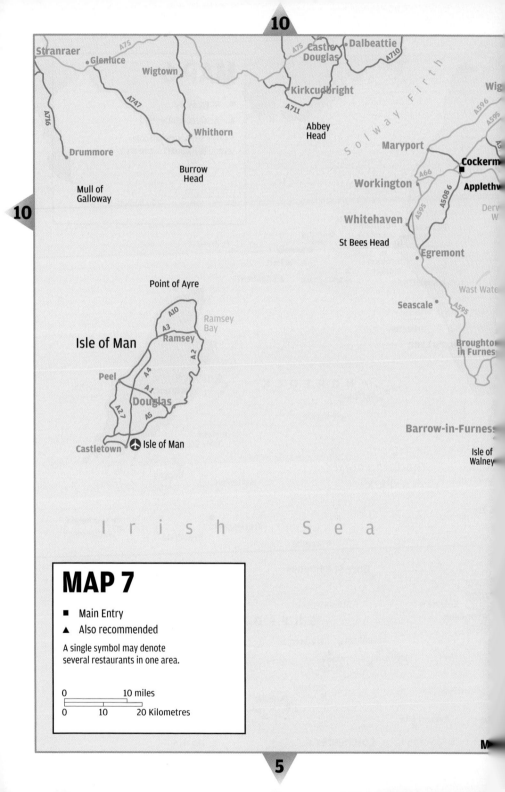

Stranraer
Glenluce
A75
Wigtown
A747
A716
Drummore
Whithorn
Burrow
Head
Mull of
Galloway

Castle
Douglas
A75
Dalbeattie
A710
Kirkcudbright
A711
Abbey
Head
Maryport
Cockerm
A66
Workington
A508 6
Applethv
A595
A595
Whitehaven
St Bees Head
Egremont
Wast Wate
A595
Seascale
Broughton
in Furnes

Wig
A596
A595
Derw
W

S o l w a y   F i r t h

Point of Ayre

A10
A3
Ramsey
Bay
Isle of Man
Ramsey
A 2
Peel
A 4
A 1
Douglas
A2 7
A5
Castletown
Isle of Man

Barrow-in-Furness

Isle of
Walney

I r i s h     S e a

# MAP 7

■  Main Entry
▲  Also recommended

A single symbol may denote
several restaurants in one area.

| 0 | | 10 miles |
|---|---|---|
| 0 | 10 | 20 Kilometres |

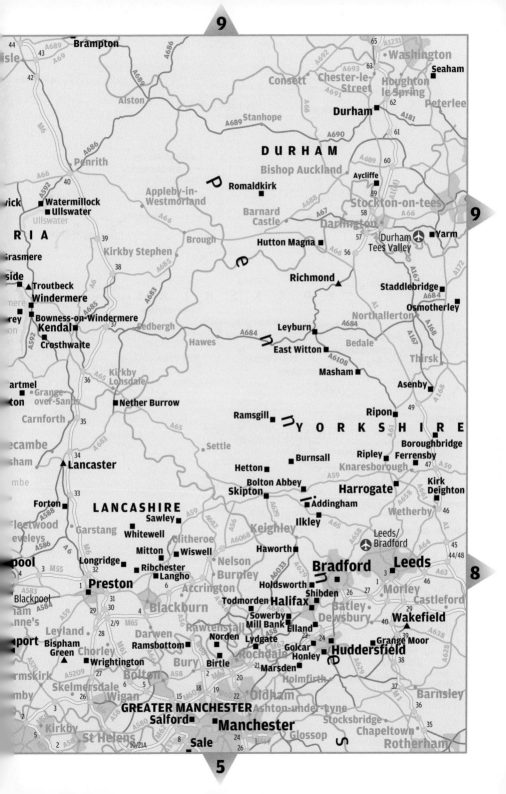

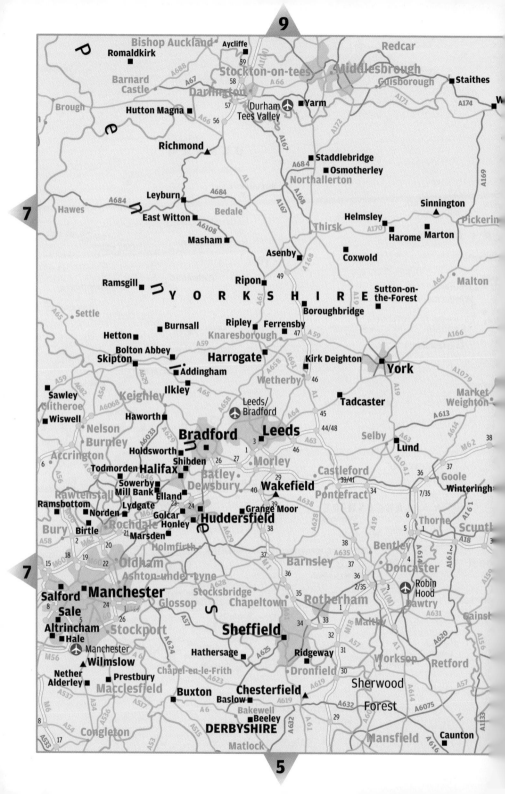

# MAP 8

■ Main Entry
▲ Also recommended

A single symbol may denote
several restaurants in one area.

0                10 miles
0        10        20 Kilometres

Scarborough

Filey

Flamborough
Head

Bridlington

riffield          Bridlington
                      Bay

Hornsea

Beverley

Kingston upon
Hull
                              Withernsea

arton-upon-
umber

Immingham          Spurn Head
Grimsby
Humberside      Cleethorpes

Caistor

A631
Market          Louth
Rasen                   Mablethorpe

A158

Horncastle    Partney
INCOLNSHIRE              Skegness

# MAP 9

- ■ Main Entry
- ▲ Also recommended

A single symbol may denote
several restaurants in one area.

```
0                10 miles
0        10       20 Kilometres
```

Holy Island

Inwick

Amble

A1

A1068

Morpeth

Ashington

Blyth

A1

Newcastle

land

Whitley Bay

Newcastle
pon Tyne

TYNE &
WEAR

South Shields

Jarrow

A695

Gateshead

65

A1231

Sunderland

A692

Washington

A693

63

Houghton le Spring

Seaham

Chester-le-
Street

A691

62

Durham

A181

Peterlee

A690

61

Hartlepool

H A M

Bishop
uckland

A689

60

A688

Aycliffe

Redcar

59

Middlesbrough

Guisborough

Staithes

Stockton-on-tees

58

A66

A67

Darlington

A174

Whitby

on

57

Durham
Tees Valley

Yarm

a

A66

56

A171

mond

Staddlebridge

A167

A171

A172

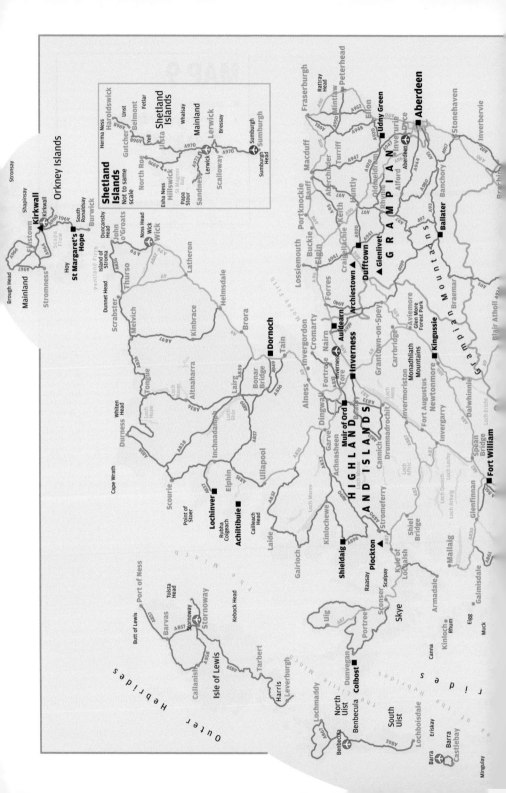

**MAP 9**

**Shetland Islands**

Not to same scale

Herma Ness
Haroldswick
Unst
Gutcher
A968
Belmont
Fetlar
Yell
A968
Whalsay
North Roe
A970
Ulsta
Mainland
Esha Ness
Hillswick
Sandness
Papa Stour
Lerwick
Bressay
Scalloway
A970
Sumburgh
Sumburgh Head

**Orkney Islands**

Stronsay
Shapinsay
A966
Finstown
A967
Kirkwall
Hoy
Stromness
Mainland
Scapa Flow
St Margaret's Hope
South Ronaldsay
Burwick
Duncansby Head
John O'Groats
Noss Head
Wick

Brough Head
Stronsay
Shapinsay

Pentland Firth
Island of Stroma
Dunnet Head
Thurso
Scrabster
Melvich
Latheron
Helmsdale
Kinbrace
Brora
Whiten Head
Durness
Cape Wrath
Scourie
Point of Stoer
Lochinver
Rubha Coigeach
Achiltibuie
Caillach Head
Elphin
Ullapool
Laide
Gairloch
Inchnadamph
Altnaharra
Loch Hope
Tongue
Lairg
Bonar Bridge
Dornoch
Tain
Invergordon
Cromarty
Alness
Dingwall
Garve
Achnasheen
Muir of Ord
Beauly
Inverness
Auldearn
Fortrose
Nairn
Forres
Elgin
Lossiemouth
Buckie
Portknockie
Portsoy
Banff
Macduff
Fraserburgh
Rattray Head
Peterhead
Turriff
Huntly
Keith
Craigellachie
Aberlour
Dufftown
Archiestown
Grantown-on-Spey
Carrbridge
Aviemore
Glen More Forest Park
Monadhliath Mountains
Newtonmore
Kingussie
Dalwhinnie
Loch Ericht
Blair Atholl
Braemar
Ballater
Banchory
Stonehaven
Inverbervie
Aberdeen
Udny Green
Inverurie
Oldmeldrum
Alford
Rhynie
Glenlivet
GRAMPIAN
Grampian Mountains

HIGHLAND AND ISLANDS

Kinlochewe
Shieldaig
Plockton
Stromeferry
Kyle of Lochalsh
Raasay
Scalpay
Stonser
Portree
Uig
Skye
Armadale
Kinloch
Rhum
Eigg
Muck
Canna
Galmisdale
Mallaig
Glenfinnan
Fort William
Spean Bridge
Invergarry
Fort Augustus
Loch Ness
Invermoriston
Drumnadrochit
Cannich
Shiel Bridge
Loch Affric
Loch Arkaig
Loch Quoich
Loch Lochy

Butt of Lewis
Port of Ness
Tolsta Head
Barvas
Stornoway
Kebock Head
Callanish
Isle of Lewis
Harris
Tarbert
Leverburgh
The Minch
The Little Minch
Lochmaddy
North Uist
Benbecula
Dunvegan
Colbost
Benbecula
Lochboisdale
South Uist
Eriskay
Barra
Castlebay
Mingulay
Outer Hebrides
Inner Hebrides
Sea of the Hebrides

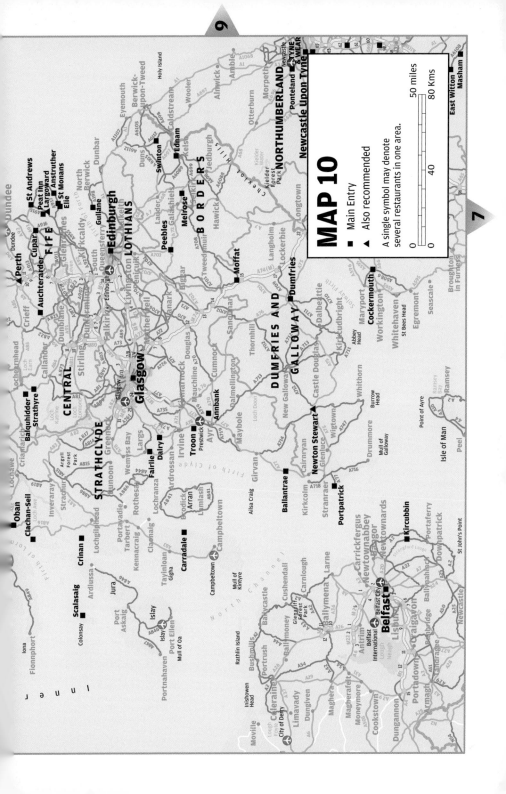

# MAP 10

- ■ Main Entry
- ▲ Also recommended

A single symbol may denote several restaurants in one area.

0          40          50 miles
0          80 Kms

# INDEX

The Good Food Guide 2008

# INDEX

The Good Food Guide 2008

# INDEX

The Good Food Guide 2008

The Good Food Guide 2008

This book couldn't happen without a cast of thousands.
Our thanks are due to the following contributors:

Mrs Sarah Aaronson
Mr Julian Abbotts
Mr V Abraham
Mr Damian Abrahams
Mrs Janet Abrahams
Miss Elaine Ackrill
Miss Victoria Ackroyd
Ms Sarah Adamczuk
Mr Chris Adams
Mr R C Adams
Mr Wayne Adams
Mrs Severine Adams
Mr Colin Adams
Mr Chris Addison
Mr David Adey
Mrs Sarah Adkins
Mr Bernard Ager
Miss L Ainsworth
Mr John Aird
Mr Les Aitkin
Mrs Anita Albone
Mr Ian Aldrich
Mrs Nicky Alexander
Mrs Gillian Alexander-Davis
Miss Kirsty Allan
Mr Robert Allen
Miss Kerry Allen
Miss Maria Aller
Mrs Carolyn Alty
Mr Daniel Ambrosioni
Mrs Karin Ament
Mr William Anderson
Mr Jovan Andjelopolj
Mr Robert Andrew
Mrs Annie Andrews
Mr Igor Andronov
Mr Gavin Ansell
Mr Dyfrig ap Dafydd
Mrs Lorna Appiah
Mr Jonathan Appleby
Mrs Cynthia Archer
Ms Hilary Armstrong
Mr Glen Armstrong
Miss Lorea Arrizabalaga
Mr Alan Arthurs
Mr Paul Ash
Mr Bernard Asher
Mr Kenneth Ashken
Mr Vidal Ashkenazi
Miss Shahida Aslam
Mrs Hannah Aspey
Mrs Dalvinder Assi
Mrs Kathryn Astley
Miss Jeannie Atha
Ms Margaret Atherton
Mr James Aufenast
Mr Nick Avery
Mr Roger Avon
Mr David Avrell
Mrs Janet Awty
Mr Michael Awty
Mrs Christina Bacon
Ms Alexandra Badwi
Mr Robin Baiden
Mrs Elizabeth Baillie
Mr james baird
Mr Michael Baker
Mr Nick Baldwin
Ms Janet Baldwin
Mrs Carol Ball
Mr John Banks
Mr Raymond Banning
Miss Sally Barber
Mr Andy Barden
Mrs Susan Barham
Mr George Barker
Mr Rebecca Barker
Mr John Barker
Mr Jason Barlow
Mr Ray Barlow
Ms Stella Barnass
Miss Sarah Barnes
Mr Michael Barratt
Mrs Judith Barrett
Mr Barry Barrett
Miss Kathryn Barry
Mrs Jane Barry
Mrs Victoria Bartlett

Ms Mels Barton
Mr John Keith Barton
Miss Sue Bates
Mr John Bates
Mr Conrad Bayliss
Ms Lesley Beach
Ms Carol Beannon
Mr George Beardow
Ms Sarah Beattie
Mr Anthony Beavan
Mr Brian Beaves
Mrs Janet Bebb
Mr Simon Beckett
Mr Bernard Bedford
Miss Julie Behan
Mrs Carol Behrens
Mr John Belfitt
Mr Rob Bell
Mr Richard Bell
Mr Gary Bell
Ms Vicky Bennison
Mr Philip Beniston
Miss Sheila E Bennett
Mrs Victoria Benning
Ms Joanne Benson
Mr Tim Bent
Mr Lloyd Bentley
Mrs Jiffy Benzie
Mr Mike Beresford
Miss Jayshri Bhana
Miss Angi Bhole
Mr Mike Bigland
Ms Betty Birch
Mrs Rosemarie Bird
Mr Bob Bishop
Mr Alister Bisset
Mr Helge Bjordal
Miss Jazz Black
Miss Deborah Black
Miss Emma Blackburn
Mr Roger Blackburn
Mr Keith Blackwell
Mr Keith Blake
Mr Timothy Blake
Mrs Debra Blakeman-barratt
Mr John Blakey
Mrs Patricia Blamey
Prof R W Blamey
Ms Christine Blancher
Mrs Bronwen Blenkin
Mrs Mavis Blow
Mr Paul Blows
Mr Ralph Blumenau
Mr Kenneth Blyth
Mr John Bolgar
Mrs Julia Bolwell
Mr Saif Bonar
Miss Julia Bond
Mr Michael Bond
Mr Fred Bone
Mrs Muriel Bonner
Mr Steve Bonnet
Mr Graham Booth
Mrs Heather Booth
Ms Annabel Bosanquet
Mr David Botsford
Mr Philippe Boucheron
Miss Maeve Bourke
Mrs Judith Bourne
Mr Richard Bourne
Miss Dee Bowker
Mrs Valerie Bowman
Mr Roger Bowring
Miss Sharan Boyal
Mr David Boyd
Mr John Boyer
Miss Rachel Boys
Mr Ken Bracey
Mr Anthony Bradbury
Mr Julian Bradley
Mr Graham Bradshaw
Mr David Bradshaw
Miss Alison Braganza
Mr Tony Bramley
Mrs Mary Bramley
Mr Andrew Brammall
Mrs Jessica Braschi
Mrs Claire Brayne

Mr Sebastian Breaks
Miss Caitlin Breewood
Mr Blair Breton
Mrs Jonica Bridge
Mrs Silvana Briers
Mr David Briggs
Mr David Briggs
Mr David Briggs
Mr David Briggs
Mr RJ Briscoe
Ms Moyra Briston
Mrs Patricia Bristow
Mrs Allison Brittain
Mrs Christine Broadhurst
Ms Annie Bromwich-
Alexandra
Mrs Susan Brookes
Mr T Brooks
Ms Celia Brooks Brown
Mrs Christine Brown
Mrs Julie Brown
Mr Adam Brown
Miss Amanda Brown
Mr Mik Brown
Mrs Nikki Brown
Mr Howard Brown
Mrs Kaye Brown
Mrs Kathleen Brown
Miss Catherine Brown
Mr Terry Brown
Mr Philip Brown
Mr Nelson Brown
Mr Richard Browne
Mr Nicky Brownell
Mr Christopher Browning
Mr Ronnie Bryant
Mr Colin Bryant
Ms Mary Bryden
Ms Katherine Bryden
Mr Douglas Bryden-Reid
Mrs Marie Brydon
Mrs Pam Buchanan
Mr Mike Buchanan
Mr Lewis Buckley
Mrs Janine Buckley-Hewing
Mr Peter Buckman
Mrs Ruth Bujack
Mr Antony Bull
Mr Steven Bullen
Mrs Nicola Buller
Miss Nicola Bullivant
Mr Chris Bulpitt
Mrs Veronica Bunyan
Miss Suzanne Burke
Mrs Julie Burkinshaw
Mr John W. Burley
Mr Ian Burnell
Mrs Sarah Burnett
Mr Terry Burns-Dyson
Mr Neil Burrows
Mr Dave Busson
Mr Jeffrey Butler
Mr John Butler
Mr Paul Butler
Mr Martin Butters
Mrs Joanne Buxton
Mr Brendan Byrne
Mrs Pauline Cade
Mrs Jane Caffrey
Mrs Emma Callery
Mr Harry Calthrop
Mr Roger Calverley
Mr Roger Calverley
Mr Martin Campbell
Mr Douglas Campbell
Mr Trevor Campbell
Mr Stuart Campbell
Mrs Philippa Camps
Mr Paul Canham
Mr Andrew Canning
Mrs Emma Canter
Ms Evelyne Canterranne
Mrs Nicola Capill
Mr Malcolm Carey
Mrs Joanne Carnell
Mrs Elinor Carr
Mrs Tina Carroll
Mrs Julie Carter

Mr John Carter
Ms Bernadette Carter
Mrs Judith Cartwright
Mrs Jacqui Cartwright
Mr Tony Caruana
Mr Paul Casella
Mr RH Cassen
Mr Dennis Casson
Mr Ian Caston
Miss Lynne Catterall
Mrs Rosie Cavies
Mr Alden Chadwick
Ms Joanne Chalcraft
Alex Chambers
Mr Steve Chambers
Mrs Samantha Chambers
Mr Vikran Chand
Mr Miles Chapman
Miss Rosalind Chapman
Mr Mark Chappels
Miss Kerri Chard
Miss Caron Chattwood
Mr Ken Cherry
Mr William Chesneau
Mr Stephen Chetrit
Mrs Marjorie Chilton
Mr David Chinery
Mr Stefan Chomka
Mr Tanni Chowdhury
Mr P chowdhury
Mr Steven Christie
Mr Richard Christopher
Ms Sarah Cielo
Mrs Eleanor Clamp
Ms Margaret Clancy
Mrs Pamela Clare
Mr Nigel Clark
Mrs Caren Clarke
Mrs Leanne Clarke
Mrs Marilyn Clayton
Mrs Carly Cleary
Mr Dave Clews
Mr Stephen Click
Ms Gilli Cliff
Mr Richard Clifford
Mr Robert Clifford
Mr J F Cobb
Mrs J F Cobb
Ms Sally Cockcroft
Mr Michaek Coe
Mr Nick Coffey
Miss Naomi Cohen
Mr Jason Colclough
Mr Andy Cole
Mrs C Cole
Mr Roger Colebrook
Mrs Deidre Coleman
Mr Martin Collier
Mr Neil Collins
Mrs Kate Collins
Mrs Fiona Collins
Mr Richard Colthurst
Mr R T Combe
Mr John Compte
Mr Flurin Condrau
Mr Dominic Conlon
Mr Pat Conneely
Ms Bridgett Cook
Mrs Karen Cook
Mr Nigel Cook
Mr Michael Cook
Mrs Anne-Marie Cook
Mr Danny Coope
Mr Andrew Cooper
Mr David Cooper
Mr Richard Cooper
Mrs Gainor Cooper
Ms Clare Corbett
Miss Alicia Corlett
Mr Jonathan Cornes
Mr Neil Cornick
Mr Paul Cottam
Mr Roger Cotterill
Mr Edward Coulson
Mrs Kate Cousins
Mrs Sarah Covey
Mr Kevin Cowan
Mr Nigel Cowdery

Ms Katharine Cowherd
Mr Ben Cox
Mrs Susan Cox
Mr Malcolm Cox
Mr Peter Craddock
Mr Carl Cramer
Mr Ronald Cramond
Mrs Helena Crawford
Mrs Vikki Crayden-Reed
Mr Colin Cregan
Mr Stephen Crick
Mr John Crisp
Ms Rosie Crook
Mr G. Crossley
Mr Les Crosthwaite
Mr William J Crouch
Mr Gary Crowe
Mr Joseph Crozier
Mr George Cruickshank
Mrs Karen Currie
Mr JOHN CURTIN
Mrs Lynne Curtis
Mrs Christine Cussans
Mr Stan Da Prato
Mr Bill Dacombe
Miss Leigh Danckert
Mr Nigel Daniels
Mrs Caroline Daniels
Ms Jacqueline Dare
Mr David Darrah
Ms Alison Davidson
Mr Keith Davidson
Mr Tom Davidson
Mr Eric Davidson
Ms Pam Davies
Ms Kirsty Davies
Mr Peter Davies
Ms Molly Davies
Mr Jonathan Davies
Mr Barry Davis
Mrs Shakti Dawadi
Mr William Dawson
Mr Peter Day
Mrs Chris Day
Mrs Katherine Dckie
Mr Gerrit de Bondt
Mr Guillaume de Brosses
Mrs Suzanne de Glanville
Mr Francis de Lima
Mr Wilf Deakin
Mrs Berenice Deakin
Mr Paul Dear
Miss Victoria Decmar
Mr Donald Decruz
Mrs Tsai Deere
Mr Alan Dell
Mr Geoffrey Dence
Ms Debbie Dennett
Mr Pete Desmond
Mr Eddie Deverill
Miss Rachael Dexter
Mr Phillip Dick
Mr J E Dickenson
Mrs Yvonne Dickinson
Mr Harry Dickinson
Mr Ian Dickson
Mrs Helen
Difrancescomarino
Mr Shaun Dillon
Mr Chris Dinning
Mr William Dobbie
Mr Bill Dobson
Mr Martin Dodd
Mr Barry Dodd
Miss Marian Doherty
Mr Fergus Donachie
Mrs Janet Donbavand
Mrs Jennifer Donnison
Miss Christina Dore
Mr George Dorgan
Miss Katharine Douglas
Miss Faith Douglas
Mrs Kelly Dowding
Mrs Christine Downes
Mrs Helen Downing-Emms
Mr Dae Drew
Mr John Ducker
Mrs Adria Duckett

Mr John Duell
Mr George M Duffus
Mr Terence Duffy
Mrs Helen Dugdale Reed
Mr Alexander Duguid
Ms Angela Dunmall
Mr Malcolm Dunmore
Mrs Lynn Dunn
Mrs Heather Dunn
Mr Jon Dunne
Miss Emily Durbidge
Mr roger durrant
Mr Dominic Dwight
Mr Kevin Dyras
Mr W Dyson
Mrs Kirsty Dyson
Mrs Sheilagh Dyson
Mrs Sylvia Eades
Ms Emily Easter
Ms Sally Easton
Mrs Zoe Eastwell
Mrs Judith Eaton
Mr Michael Edwards
Mr Osian Edwards
Mrs Denise Edwards
Mr Marc Edwards
Miss Nabila Electricwala
Mr Gary Elflett
Mrs Jan Elford
Mrs Alexandra Ellis
Mr Peter Ellwood
Mr Robert Embleton
Mr Matthew Emery
Mr Robert Emsley
Mr Stephen Engel
Mrs Marilyn Escott
Mr Santiago Eslava
Mrs Lisa Esslemont
Mr Huw Evans
Mrs Margaret Evans
Mrs Sheridan Evans
Mr Mick Evans
Mrs Nichola Evans
Mrs Ann Eve
Mrs Janet Every
Mr Steve Falder
Mr Paul Falkingham
Mr Colin Fancourt
Miss Rebbecca Farquhar
Miss Lauren Fawkes
Ms Lorraine Fearn
Mr Stephen Fellows
Mr Ian Fenwick
Ms Sarah Fergusson
Mr Brendan Ferguson
Mr Nick Fermor
Ms Polly Fernandez
Mrs Marcela Fernandez Vilar
Mr Keith Ferris
Mr Fabrizio Fiabane
Mr Adrian Field
Mrs Laura Field
Mr Nigel Fielden
Miss Katy Finch
Mr Malcolm Fincken
Mr Ted Fineran
Ms Corey Finjer
Miss Veronica Finney
Mr Roger Firman
Miss Helen Firth
Mr F Fisher
Mrs Gillian Fitch
Mrs Amanda Fitzaden-Gray
Ms Jan Fitzgerald
Mr Simon Fitz-Hugh
Mr Ian Fitzpatrick
Mr Barry Fitzpatrick
Miss Lisa Flaherty
Mr Kieran Flatt
Ms Jenni Fleetwood
Mr Simon Fleming
Mrs Debra Fletcher
Mr Roy Flitcroft
Miss Helen Ford
Miss Carrie ford
Mr Ken Forman
Mr John Formston
Mrs Pamela Forrest
Mr Brian Forrester
Ms Beatrice Forster
Mr Philip Foster
Mr Gary Fothergill
Mr Laurence Fouweather

Mrs Sylvia Foxcroft
Mr Steve Frampton
Mr Colin Francis
Ms Liz Franklin
Mr Peter Franklin
Mr Felix Franks
Mr John Franks
Mrs Emily Fraser
Miss Tabitha Frazer
Mr Cliff Free
Ms Sue Freeman
Mrs Frances Frith
Mrs Wendy Froud
Mrs Julie Fuller
Miss Julia Furley
Mr Chris Galloway
Mr Kevin Galton
Mrs Christine Gardener
Mr Matthew Gardiner
Mr Geoff Gardiner
Miss Chantal Gardiner
Mr Matthew Gardner
Mrs Christine Gardner
Ms Bridget Garner
Mr Mark Garnett
Mr Michael Garrison
Mrs Stephanie Garswood
Mrs Margaret Gash
Mrs Mary Gateley
Mr Gavin
Mrs Brenda Gayton
Mrs Julie Gearon
Mr Jeff Gee
Mr David Gee
Mr Tony Georgakis
Miss Lana George
Mrs Pamela Georgiades
Mrs Jane Geraghty
Mr Stevens Gerald
Mr Richard Gibson
Mr David Gibson
Mr John Gibson
Mr Richard Gigg
Mr Anthony Gilbert
Mrs Amanda Gilbert
Mrs Mary Ann Gilchrist
Mrs Julie Giles
Mr Michael Gilks
Mrs Gillian Gillam
Mr Paul Gillett
Mr James Gippesie
Mr Andrew Gittins
Ms Laura Gladwin
Mr Hugh Glaser
Mr John Glaze
Mr Don Glen
Mrs Claire Glendenning
Mr Neil Glew
Mr Peter Gliddon
Mr Stephen Glover
Mr Christopher Godber
Mrs Maxine Godfrey
Mrs Debra Godrich
Ms Carol Godsmark
Mr J Gold
Mr Basil Golding
Mrs Pauline Goldsmith
Mr Des Goldsworthy
Mrs Chris Goldthorp
Mr Daniel Gomm
Miss Victoria Gondzic
Mr David Goodchild
Mrs Lesley Goodchild
Mr Christopher Gooding
Mr Kenneth Goodwin
Mrs Elizabeth Gordon
Ms Anna Gordon
Mr Terry Gorman
Mr Ian Gorsuch
Mr Graham Gough
Mr David Gough
Mrs Jean Gould
Mrs Elizabeth Gould
Mr A Gower
Miss Caroline Graham
Mrs Amy Graham
Ms Doreen Grainger
Mr David Grant
Mrs Lisa Gratte
Mrs Doris Gravestock
Mr Lynton Gray
Mrs Christine Gray
Mr Iain Gray

Mr Alan Grayson
Mr James Greaves
Mrs Mavis Green
Mr Michael Green
Mrs Katherine Green
Ms Allison Greenberg
Mrs Linda Greenberg
Mr Neville Greener
Mr Chris Greenhalgh
Mr Mark Greenhalgh
Mr Duncan Greenwood
Mr Conal Gregory
Mrs Anneline Gregory
Miss Merlyn Gregory
Mr Dave Gregory
Mr Andrew Gresser
Mr George Grierson
Ms Fiona Griffiths
Mrs Linda Griffiths
Mr Peter Griffiths
Mr Graham Griffiths
Mr Clive Griffiths
Mr Ken Grimson
Mrs Gilly Groom
Mr Tom Grosvenor
Mr Howard Gudgeon
Mrs Rose Guild
Mr F Guinn
Mr Anthony Guylee
Mrs Clare Hagerup
Mr Erich Hahn
Mrs Julia Haines
Ms Yvette Hales
Mr Paul Halford
Mr Peter Hall
Mrs N J Hall
Mrs Brenda Hall
Mr Tony Hall
Mrs Mair Hall
Mr David Hall
Mrs M Hall
Mr Mark Hallam
Mr Sean Hamilton
Miss Jayne Hamilton
Mr Neil Hamilton
Mr Mike Hampson
Mrs June Hampson
Mr David Hancock
Mr Graham Handy
Mr Susan Hanley
Mr Jon Harber
Mr Mark Harding
Mr Richard Hardman
Hon Bernard Hargrove
Mrs Alison Harker
Mr Paul Harris
Mrs Iona Harris
Mr Neil Harris
Mr Mervyn Harris
Mr Paul Harrison
Mrs Diane Harrison
Mr Jonathan Harrison
Mr Daniel Harrison
Ms Lin Harrison
Ms Lindsay Harriss
Mr Phil Harriss
Mr Raymond Harrm
Mr David Harrop
Mr Timothy Hart
Mr Tony Hartnell
Mr Ross Harvey
Mrs Adele Harvey
Mr Edward Harvey
Mr Alun Harvey
Ms Louise Harvey
Mrs Sharon Harwood
Mr John Hassall
Ms Joy Hatwood
Mrs Margaret Haughey
Mrs Kathy Havercroft
Mr David Haverty
Mr Richard Haycock
Mr Andy Hayler
Mr Ronald Hayman
Mrs Sam Hazell
Mrs Sandra Healey
Ms Debbie Hearn
Mrs Patricia Hedges
Mr Terence Hefford
Miss Natalie Heidaripour
Mr Hossein Heideripoor
Mrs Valerie Hemingway
Mr Philip Hendrick

Mrs Linda Hepworth
Mr John A Hepworth
Mrs Lynn Hewitt
Ms Kirsten Hey
Mrs Amanda Heydon
Mrs Helen Heyworth
Mr Tim Hickson
Mr Keith Hickson
Mrs Jane Higginbotham
Miss Nicola Higgins
Mr Graham Hill
Mrs Patricia Hill
Mrs Nicola Hill
Ms Wendy Hillary
Mrs Jessica Hilton
Mr Angus Hinchliffe
Mr Roy Hincks
Miss Rebecca Hine
Mrs Ann Hirst-Smith
Mr Andrew Hoaen
Mr Dave Hoare
Miss Nicola Hobley
Mrs Jean Hockings
Mr Michael Hockney
Ms Caroline Hoddinott
Mr Tim Hodges
Miss Philippa Hodgkins
Mr Dermot Hogan
Ms Angela Hoh
Ms Helen Hokin
Mr D Holdsworth
Mr David Holes
Mr Clive Holland
Mr Peter Hollingsworth
Mr Steven Holmes
Mr Stephen Holt
Mrs Janet Holtby
Miss Beckie Holtham
Ms Leila Homans
Mr Keith Homewood
Mr Steve Hone
Mr Mark Hone
Mr Bernard Hood
Mr Scott Hood
Miss Julie Hooper
Mr Derek Hopes
Mr Stephen Hopkins
Mrs Jenni Hopper
Mrs Carol Horn
Mr Colin Hornby
Mr Andrew Horsler
Mr Phil Horsley
Mr Roger Horton
Mr Robin Hosking
Miss Rachel Hotchkiss
Mr Mark Houghton
Mr Dave Houldsworth
Mrs Padi Howard
Mr John Howard
Mrs Julie Howard
Miss Jessica Howard
Mrs Donna Howarth
Mrs Sally Howe
Mr Adrian Howe
Ms Clare Hubbard
Ms Rosamund Hubley
Mr David Hudson
Mrs Natasha Hughes
Mr David Hughes
Mr Steve Hughes
Mr Robert Hughes
Mr Derek Hughes
Mr Jon Hughes
Mrs Julie Hulatt
Mrs Penny Hull
Mr Allan Hull
Ms Elizabeth Hulme
Mr Matt Hulse
Ms Carolyn Humphries
Mr Neil Hunter
Mr Christopher Hunter
Mr Stewart Hunter
Mr Ian Hurdley
Mrs Emma Hurst
Miss Natalie Hurst
Mrs Pauline Hurst
Mr Syed Huss
Mr Mandy Hutchings
Mr Trevor Hutchinson
Mrs Claire Hutchinson
Mr Michael Hutchison
Mr Stuart Huxtable
Mr David Hyde

Mr Jerry Ibberson
Mr Keith Ingram
Mrs Jessica Innocenti-Lampen
Mr Gordon Irvine
Mr Andrew Irwin
Mr Stuart Isaacs
Mr Yaasiin Islam
Mrs Iuhiu Iuh
Mr Leslie Ilversen
Mrs Madeleine Jackson
Ms Kate Jackson
Mr Ben Jackson
Mr Stephen Jackson
Mrs Susan Jackson
Mrs Sheila Jackson
Mr Paul Jacques
Mr Robert Jahnke
Miss Nicky James
Mr J James
Mr Stephen James
Ms Anita James
Miss Kathy James
Mrs Rosemary James
Mr John James
Mr Robert Jamieson
Mrs Sandra Janes
Mr Jonathan Jarratt
Mrs Adina Jarvis
Mrs Janet Jarvis
Mr Anthony Jay
Mrs Brenda Jeeves
Mr Martin Jeeves
Mr Syed Yasir Jehan
Miss Louise Jenkins
Mr Philip Jenkins
Mrs Diane Jennett
Mr Michael Jennings
Mr Steve Jepson
Mrs Heather Jervis
Mr David R W Jervois
Mr Simon Jewson
Mr Alec Jezewski
Ms Rachel Johnson
Mrs Karen Johnson
Miss Nicci Johnson
Mr Derek Johnson
Miss Ruth Johnson
Mr William Johnston
Mr Edward Johnston
Ms Doreen Johnston
Mr Iain Johnstone
Mr Brenda Jolley
Ms Pamela Jones
Mr Robert Jones
Mrs C Jones
Miss Caroline Jones
Mrs Deborah Jones
Miss Sheila Jones
Mrs Penny Jones
Mrs Alison Jones
Miss Vivian Jones
Miss Anne Marie Jones
Ms Shirley Jones
Mr Andrew Jones
Mrs Jade Jones
Miss Sara Jones
Mrs Mary Jones
Mr Douglas Jones
Mr John Martin Jones
Mr Ian Jones
Miss Sarah Jowett
Mr Neil Joyce
Mr Rick Juckes
Miss Louise Judd
Mr Martin Jurasik
Mr Kevin Kane
Mrs Yasmin Karim
Ms Kawal Kaur
Mr John Kaye
Mr Richard Kaye
Mrs Sandra Keane
Mr Jac Keane
Mr Julian Keanie
Mr Barry Keates
Mr Robert Kelly
Mr Joseph Kelly
Mr Russell Kemp
Mr Robert Kendall
Mr Roger Kendall
Ms Vanessa Kendell
Mr Graham Kennedy
Mr Arthur Kennedy

# THANK YOUS

Mr David Kenning
Ms Christine Kenny
Ms Sinead Kenny
Mrs June Kent
Mr John Kenward
Mr David Kenward
Ms Emily Kerrigan
Mr & Mrs Keys
Mr Sunil Khosla
Mr Vimal Khosla
Mr Roger Kidley
Mr Terence Kidson
Mr Sascha Kiess
Miss Bernadette Kilroy
Ms Sharon King
Mr Alex King
Mr Chris King
Mrs Mary Kingston-Ford
Mr Berwyn Kinsey
Mr Remmy Kinyanjui
Mr Terry Kirby
Mr Mark Kirkbride
Mr Steve Kirkwood
Mrs Suzanne Kirkwood
Mr Michael Kitcatt
Mrs Riki Kittel
Miss Sylvia Knapp
Miss Charlotte Knapp
Miss Jane Knight
Mr Keith Knights
Mrs Rosie Knowles
Mr Marios Koulias
Mr Jack Kouwenberg
Mrs Christine Kynoch
Mr Chris Lakin
Mrs Marian Laklia
Miss Vicky Lane
Mrs Sarah Lane
Mr Anthony Langan
Mr Richard Langley
Ms Christine Last
Miss Anna Lavel
Mrs Jane Law
Mr Ashley Lawrence
Ms Ayesha Lawrence
Mr Andrew Lawrence
Mr Brian Lawrence
Mrs Charmaine Lawrence
Mrs Ginny Lawson
Miss Rebecca Leach
Mr Kim Leary
Mr Chris Leather
Ms Beverley Le Blanc
Ms Deborah Lee
Mr Alex Lee
Mr Carl Lee
Mr Adam Lee
Ms Jo Leedham
Mr Marc Lees-low
Mrs Linda Lefevre
Mr Victor Legg
Mr John Legg
Ms Nikki Lehel
Mr Steve Leighton
Ms Sharon Lennon
Mrs Susan Leonard
Miss Susan Leslie
Mrs Kate Leslie
Mr David Lesser
Professor K M Letherman
Mrs R. Letherman
Mr Malcolm Levitt
Mrs Lisa Lewis
Ms Janet Lewis
Mr Rich Lewis Jones
Mr Mike Leybourne
Mr Mark Leyland
Mrs Jenny Li
Mrs Brunhilde Liebchen
Mr Hans Liesner
Mrs Louise Lightfoot
Miss Linda Ligios
Mr Andrew Lindsay
Mrs Caroline Ling
Mr David Linnell
Mr Robert Lintonbon
Miss Alex Little
Mr William Lobo
Miss Alex Lody
Ms Tina Lofthouse
Mr David Long
Mr Jonathan Longden
Mrs Glynis Lord

Ms Jane Lorimer
Mrs Elspeth Lowe
Mrs Annabel Lowell
Mrs Avril Luke
Mr Kevin Lynch
Mr Chris Lyon
Mrs Audrey Lyon
Mrs Frances Lyons
Mr David Mabey
Mrs Fiona MacAulay-Rigby
Mr Colin Macaw
Miss Carleen Macdermid
Mr David MacDonald
Mrs Sonia Maceluch
Mr Bruce MacFarlane
Ms Catherine Mackay
Mr Jamie Mackay
Mrs E Mackintosh
Mr Hugh Mackintosh
Ms Lesley Mackley
Mrs Marcia Macleod
Mrs C Macrow
Mrs Ruth Madigan
Mr Eric Magnuson
Miss Sarah Mahoney
Miss Karine Maillard
Mr James Malcomson
Mrs Lynn Males
Mr Kaleem Malik
Ms Nicola Mallett
Mr Ian Malone
Mr Denis Maloney
Ms Wendy Maloney
Ms Beverley Mandair
Mr Paul Manley
Miss Rebecca Manning
Ms Emily Manson
Mrs Louise Markus
Mrs Louise Markus
Mr Bill Markwick
Mr Felipe Marquez
Mrs Christine Marris
Mr Chris Marsh
Mrs Linda Marshall
Mr Robert Marshall
Mr Paul Martin
Mr Gordon Martin
Mr Ian Martin
Mrs Maureen Martin
Ms Mary Martin
Ms Angela Martin
Mrs Sheila Martin
Mr Graham Martin
Mr Brian Ma Siy
Mrs Tracey Maskill
Mrs Sally Maslen
Mr Ken Mason
Mrs Jean Mason
Mrs Ilze Mason
Mr David Mason
Mr Nick Mason
Mr Don Massey
Mr Mark Massey
Mrs Diphna Mathew
Mr Stuart Mathews
Mr John Mathews
Mr David Mathewson
Mr Richard Matthews
Mr Simon Matthews
Ms Gill Maxwell
Mr Ian May
Mrs Joyce Mayhew
Miss Sharon Mayling
Miss Stephanie McAllister
Mr Peter McAndrew
Miss Helen McBay
Mr Derek McBride
Ms Andrea McCartney
Mr Neil McCole
Mr Ben McCormack
Mr Walter McCrindle
Mr Kenneth McDonald
Ms Cynthia McDowall
Mrs Anne McGilton
Mr Robert McGinty
Mrs Caroline McGoohan
Mrs Pamela McGowan
Mrs Cynthia McGowan
Miss Gemma McGowan
Ms S Y McGreavy
Mrs Susan McGrouther
Mr Patrick McGuigan
Mrs Christine McHenry

Miss Marie McHenry
Miss Sian McHenry
Mr Bill McHenry
Ms Fiona McInnes
Mr Robert McKay
Mrs Gayle McKay
Mr Craig McKay
Mrs Debra McKenna
Mr Charles McKenna
Mr Andy McKenzie
Mr William McKinlay
Mr Stuart McLaren
Mrs Karen McLaren
Mr John McLaughlin
Mr John McMillan
Miss Wendy McMillan
Miss Angela McNally
Mr Michael McNamara
Mrs Jo McNeish
Mr Richard McNulty
Mr Paul McPeake
Mr Pete McQueen
Mr Francis McSorley
Mr Deryk Mead
Mr Ranvir Mehta
Mr John Mercer
Mrs Doreen Mercer
Mr Lee Merrin
Mr Peter Messenger
Mrs Janet Messenger
Mr David Metcalf
Mr John Metcalfe
Mr Shane Metters
Mr Shahid Mian
Ms Jane Middleton
Mr John Middleton
Mr A G Milburn
Mr Douglas Miles
Mr Peter Miles
Mr Jonathan Miles
Mr James Millar
Mr Ged Millar
Miss Cara Neish Millar
Mrs Tina Millard
Miss Dahna Miller
Mr Ian Miller
Mr Luke Miller
Miss Mandy Miller
Mr Michael Miller
Mr Nic Miller
Mrs Helen Miller
Mr Roger Mills
Mr Richard Mills
Mrs C D Milne
Mr Nicoll Milne
Mrs Caroline Mitchell
Mr Mike Mitchell
Mrs Anne Mitchell
Mrs Carol Mitchell
Miss Lee Mitchell
Mr John Mitchellmore
Mr Stuart Mitchenall
Miss Tessa Mitchinson
Mr Sarang Mohinder
Ms Elizabeth Moles
Mrs Linda Montgomery
Mrs Alison Mooney
Mr David Moore
Mr Jon Moore
Mr Chris Moore
Mrs Jane Moore
Mr Francis Moran
Mr Corrado Morandi
Mr Jeremy Mordrick
Mrs Helen Morgan
Mr Brian Morgan
Mr Neil Morgan
Mrs Manisha Morjaria
Ms Jacqueline Morley
Mr Peter Morris
Mr Bernard Morris
Mrs Sara Morris
Ms Shelley Morris
Miss Rachel Morrish
Mrs Eileen Morrison
Mrs Deborah Morrissey
Ms Valerie Morrow
Mrs Emma Moscrop
Mr Robert Moss
Mr John Mott
Mr John Moy
Mr Alastair Muir
Mrs Maureen Mullins

Mr Peter Munro
Mr Charles Murch
Mr David Murdoch
Mr Mike Murphy
Mr Paul Murphy
Ms Kimberley Murphy
Mrs Janis Murphy
Mr Gordon Murray
Mr Paul Murray
Mrs Morag Murray
Mrs Sue Muspratt
Mr Colin Mutch
Mrs Jill Naylor
Mrs Ragnhild Nee
Mr John Neilson
Mrs Sara Nelson
Mrs Carolyn Neri
Mr James Netting
Mr Mathew Newman
Mrs Norma Newman
Mrs Astrid Newman
Mr Peter Newton
Mr Jeffrey Ng
Mr Timothy Niall-harris
Mr Rodney Nichols
Mrs Anne Nicholson
Mr Nicolas Nicolaides
Ms Paula Nimmo
Mr David Noble
Mr Daniel Nolan
Mr Michael Nolan
Miss Vicki Norgan
Miss Yvonne Norman
Mrs Susan Norminton
Mr J G Norris
Mrs Alison Nottle
Mr Richard Noy
Mrs Marion OBrien
Mr Alan O'Brien
Ms Jane O'Brien
Mr Keith O'Brien
Mr Alan Oddie
Ms Caroline Ogden
Mr Timothy O'Keefe
Mr David Oldham
Ms Barbara Oldham
Mrs Gayle Olsen
Mr Kevin O'Mahoney
Mrs Bree O'Neil
Mr Sian O'Neill
Mrs Lyndsey O'Neill
Mr John O'Reilly
Mr Geoffrey Ormrod
Mr Toby Orsborn
Mr Richard Osborne
Mr Martin Osborne
Mrs Lisa Osman
Mr John Oswald
Mrs Donna O'Toole
Ms Cathy Otty
Mrs Emma Oulton
Mr Graham Owen
Mr S Oxley
Mr Michael Page
Miss Rachel Page
Mrs Shelly Page
Mrs Susan Paice
Mrs Tracey Paine
Mr Vythianathan Palaniandy
Mr Richard Palframan
Mrs Clare Panton
Mr John Papadachi
Mrs Laura Park
Mr Mark Parkes
Mrs Karen Parkin
Mrs Anne Parkinson
Ms Chetna Parmar
Ms Sarah Parnaby
Mr Amol Parnaik
Mr Mike Parry
Mrs Diane Parslow
Mr Fraser Parsons
Mr Neil Partridge
Mrs Pat
Mr Michael Pater
Mr John Pattenden
Ms Caroline Pattison
Mr Michael Pawson
Mrs Janet Payne
Miss Mhairi Payne
Mr Chris Payne
Mr Nigel Peacock

Mr Brian Pearce
Mr Chris Pearson
Mr Edwin Peat
Mr Simon Peate
Mr Richard Peirce
Miss Anna Perez
Mr Anthony Perl
Miss Carlene Perris
Mr Tim Perry
Mr Brian Perryman
Ms Helen Peston
Mr Philip
Mrs Liz Phillips
Mrs Gaynor Phillips
Mr Chris Phillips
Miss Lynn Phillpots
Ms Amanda Philpott
Mrs Jennie Pickford
Mr Russell Pickup
Ms Veronica Piekosz
Mr Stuart Pierrepont
Sudi Pigott
Ms Catherine Pike
Mrs Noreen Pile
Mr David Pinchin
Miss Tia Pinnock-Hamilton
Mr John Pitt-Stanley
Mr James Pomeroy
Mrs Janine Ponsart
Mrs Lynda Pope
Ms Louise Porch
Ms Fiona Porter
Miss Lucy Powell
Mr David Powell
Mr Trevor Preston
Mr Simon Preston
Ms Victoria Prever
Ms Sandie Price
Mr David Price
Mrs Janet Price
Ms G Pritchard
Mrs Diane Proctor
Mr Ioannis Psomadakis
Mr Gavin Pugh
Mr Mike Pugh
Miss Miriam Pullar
Mrs Melanie Pullin
Miss Louise Purdie
Mr Terry Purkins
Mr Walter Purkis
Mr David Pybus
Mr Frederick Pyne
Mrs Siobhan Qadir
Miss Michelle Quance
Mr Doug Quelch
Mr John Quelch
Ms Rachel Quine
Mr John Radford
Mr Michael Raine
Miss Korina Ralph
Mrs Jane Ralston
Mr Iain Ramsay
Mrs Bridget Ramsay
Mr Euan Ramsay
Mr Jeremy Randalls
Mr Archibald Rankin
Miss Elizabeth Rattlidge
Mr John Rawlings
Mrs Jane Rawlinson-Cook
Miss Lorna Raynes
Mr Andrew Redfern
Mrs Victoria Redshaw
Mr John Reed
Mrs Anne Rees
Mrs Mary Reeve
Mrs Penny Reeves
Mr Martyn Reid
Mr Maurice Reid
Miss Jacqueline Reid
Mr Neil Renton
Mrs Caroline Repanos
Miss Lisa Reyburn
Mr A Reynolds
Ms Patricia Rhymer
Mr Peter Ribbins
Miss Kloe Rice
Mr Keith Richards
Mr Brian Richards
Miss Amy Richards
Mr David Richardson
Mr Alan Richardson
Mr Kenneth Richardson

Mr C John Richardson
Ms Sharon Richmond
Mr Mark Riddick
Mrs John Riddick
Mrs Ruth Ridge
Mr L C Ridgwell
Mrs Christine Ridley
Mr Trevor Rigby
Mrs Fiona Rigby
Mrs Anna Jo Righton
Mr Gordon Ringrose
Mr Geoff Roberts
Mr Gerald Roberts
Mr Mark Roberts
Ms Hannah Roberts
Mr Andrew Roberts
Mr Michael Roberts
Mr Keith Roberts
Ms Rebecca Robertshaw
Miss Rebecca Robertson
Ms Lynsey Robinson
Mr David Robinson
Mrs Ann Robinson
Mr Paul Robinson
Miss Cheryl Robinson
Mr Michael Robinson
Mr Alan Robinson
Mr John Robinson
Miss Jocelyn Robinson
Mr Samuel Robinson
Ms Carol Robson
Mr J Rochelle
Mrs Joanne Rockliff
Mr Will Rogers
Mr Peter Rogers
Mr Alan Roiter
Mr Andrew Root
Mrs Christine Roper
Miss Kelly Rose
Mr Phil Rose
Mrs Johann Rosser
Mrs Kay Rothwell
Mr Douglas Rounthwaite
Ms Jane Routh
Mr Christopher Row
Mr John Rowan
Mr Tony Rowed
Mr John Rowlands
Mr Richard Rowlands
Miss Mariel Roy
Miss Rebecca Royle
Mr Andy Rudd
Ms Lisa Rudrum
Mr Graham Ruff
Miss Jessica Ruiz
Mr Keith Rundle
Mrs Diana Runge
Mr Joseph Russell
Mr Hugo Russell
Mrs Bernadette Russell
Mr Peter Russell
Mr Fabrizio Russo
Mr Patrick Rutter
Mr Derek Ryder
Mr Ian Sabroe
Mr David Sainsbury
Mr Geoffrey Samuel
Ms Jayne Samuel-Walker
Mr Graham Sanderson
Mrs Ailis Sandilands
Miss Christine Sangster
Mr Gavino Sanna Smith
Miss Therese Sargent
Mr James Saunders
Ms Deborah Saw
Mr Derek K Sawyer
Mr Ian Scanlon
Mr Roger Scarlett
Mr Geoffrey Scarlett
Mrs Ruth Scarr
Mr Ronald Schwarz
Mrs Diane Scott
Mr William Searle
Mr Ken Seaton
Mr Graham Seddon
Mrs Jane Margaret Seddon
Mr Adam Sedgwick
Mr Gary Sedgwick
Ms Reshma Seeburrun
Ms Karan Sehgal
Mr Shajan Sehgal
Mr Dave Selby
Mrs Sylvie Sempala

Mr Ashim Sen
Mr Anthony Serre
Mrs Katharine Servant
Mr Andrew Shanahan
Mr John Sharp
Mrs Gill Sharpe
Mr George Shaw
Mrs Karen Shaw
Mrs Patricia Shaw
Mr Robert Shaw
Mr Matthew Shaw
Mr Peter Shearer
Mr Brian Shears
Mrs Jill Sheen
Mr Jerry Shelley
Ms Linda Shelmerdine
Mr Alan Shepherd
Mr Chris Shepherd
Mrs M L Sheppard-Bond
Miss Claire Sheridan
Mrs Emma Sherman
Mrs Sandra Sherriff
Mr Mark Sherrington
Miss Jennifer Shilliday
Miss Kirsty Shilling
Mr Trevor Shingles
Miss Becky Shipp
Mr Gilbert Short
Mr James Shotton
Mr Manoj Shrestha
Mr Peter Shrigley
Mr Chris Shrubsall
Mr Philip Sibley
Mr Peter Siddall
Mr Brian Siddall-Jones
Miss M Sidhu
Ms Mary ann Sieghart
Mrs Karen Sienkiewicz
Mr Rod Sigley
Ms Ros Simmons
Mr Niamh Simms
Mr Matt Simpson
Mrs Thelma Simpson
Miss Katherine Simpson
Ms Sue Simpson
Mr Thomas Simpson
Mr Andrew Simpson
Mr Kenny Simpson
Mrs Barbara Sims
Mr Alan Sims
Mr Nav Singh
Mr Martin Sinnott
Miss Nicola Skeffington
Mr Greg Skinner
Mrs Penny Slate
Mrs Hilda Slater
Mrs Andrea Slater
Mr David Sleight
Mrs Liz Sleith
Mr Johan Slotte
Ms Jo Small
Ms Judith Smallwood
Mr Adrian Smart
Ms Michelle Smith
Mrs Carolyn Smith
Mr Robert Smith
Mr David Smith
Mr Derek Smith
Mrs Fiona Smith
Mrs Jill Smith
Mr Jeff Smith
Mrs Joan Smith
Mr Ian Smith
Mrs Moyra Smith
Miss Anne Smith
Mr Andy Smith
Ms Julia Smith
Mr Tim Smith
Ms Juliet Smith
Mr Ivan Smith
Mr Antony Smithson
Mr Brian Smullen
Mr Alan Smythe
Ms Anita Soni
Mr Tim Soon
Mr Andy Soper
Mrs Anne Soto
Mr Ben Southam
Mr Eric Southworth
Mrs Jacqueline Southworth
Mr Pat Spadi
Mrs Norma Speller
Mr Torin Spence

Mr Colin Spencer
Mr Harry Stadler
Mr Nick Staff
Ms Pauline Stafford
Mr John Stafford
Miss Jessica Stamford
Mr R J Stancomb
Ms Alex Standen
Mrs Mandi Stansfield
Mr Richard Stansfield
Miss Elizabeth Stanyer
Mr Jonathan Stapleton
Mr Neil Stein
Mrs Barbara Steiner
Miss Marcia Stephens
Mrs Kath Stepien
Mr Keith Stevens
Mrs Chrissy Stevens
Mr Paul Stevens
Mr John Stevenson
Mrs Lindsey Stewart
Mr Alan Stewart
Mr Ian Stewart
Mr Malcolm Stewart
Ms Ann Stewart
Mr Ian Stewart
Mr John Stewart
Mr Allan Stidwell
Mr D Stirk
Mrs Laura Stocker
Mrs Minou Stoddart
Mr Martin H Stone
Mrs Christine Stone
Mr Rodney Stone
Mrs Valerie Storm
Mrs Trudie Stott
Mr Robert Strain
Mr Matthew Streeter
Mr Jonathan Strong
Mr Gerd Strophff
Mr Mark Stuart
Mr Clive Stubbs
Mrs Rosemary Sturman
Mr Andrew Stylianou
Mr Sejal Sukhadwala
Mrs Diane Sumner
Mrs Lisa Sumpton
Miss Rachel Surcombe
Mr Ken Sutton
Mr John Sutton
Mr Christopher Syer
Mr Robert Sykes
Mr Steven Symonds
Mrs Rebecca Syson
Mrs Julie Taberner
Mr Douglas Talintyre
Mr Jim Tanfield
Mrs Kate Tanfield
Mr Anne Tate
Mr D W Tate
Mr Denis Tate
Mr Mark Taylor
Mrs Jean Taylor
Mr Andy Taylor
Mr John Taylor
Mr Matt Taylor
Mrs Glennis Taylor
Mrs Chrissie Taylor
Mrs Elizabeth Taylor
Mr Jack Taylor
Ms Lesley Taylor
Miss Lisa Taylor
Miss Hannah Taylor
Mr Simon Taylor
Mr Royston Tee
Mrs Karen Terkelsen
Mrs Tina Tester
Mr Richard Thomas
Mrs Maria Thomas
Mrs Sarah Thomas
Miss Karen Thomas
Miss Kim Thomas
Mr Kevin Thomas
Miss Janet Thomas
Ms Anita Thomas
Miss Sharon Thomas
Mrs Anne Thompson
Mr Paul Thompson
Mr Christopher Thompson
Mr Alun Thompson
Mrs Tina Thompson
Ms Claire Thomson
Mr Alistair Thomson

Mr Gordon Thomson
Miss Joanne Thomson
Mrs Kate Thorley
Mrs Barbara Thornton
Mr Alan Thorpe
Mr Graeme Tickle
Mr Philip Tindal-Carill-Worsley
Mr John Titley
Mrs Susan Tomlin
Mr Roger Tomlinson
Mr Richard Tomlinson
Mr David Tonge
Mrs Jayne Towgli
Miss Katie Townsend
Mr Martin Townsend
Mrs Hylary Trayer
Ms Karen Trekelsen
Mr Matt Trott
Mr Christopher Trotter
Mrs Sally Trusselle
Mr Christopher Tuck
Mrs Susan Turley
Ms Jacquie Turner
Mrs Sandra Turner
Mrs Susan Turner
Mrs Pamela Turner
Mr Dominic turner
Mr John G. Turner
Mr Gordon Turner-Tymm
Ms Jill Turton
Mrs Lesley Tweddle
Mr Naseen Ul-Alam
Miss Ashley Underwood
Mr Peter Urquhart
Mr John Urry
Mr Paul Valentine
Ms Barbara van Amerongen
Miss Caroline van Kampen
Mr Phil Varney
Mr Anthony Vaughan
Mr Stephen Vernon
Mr Hernan Vilar
Mrs Alta Viljoen
Mr Tom Vincent
Mr Martin Vowell
Mr Jeremy Wagg
Mr Benno Wagtenveld
Mr Christopher Waite
Mr Daniels Walker
Mrs Sara Walker
Mr Matthew Walker
Miss Joan Walker
Mr Kenneth Wall
Miss Fiona Lauren Wallace
Mrs Kerrie Wallis
Ms Cathy Walsh
Ms Lorraine Walsh
Mr Mark Waltham
Mr Stuart Walton
Mrs Susanne Wang
Mr Peter Wang
Mr William Warburton
Miss Sara Ward
Mr David Ward
Mr Philip Ward
Mrs Jayne Wardell-Appleton
Mr Andrew Wardrop
Mr Stuart J.H. Waring
Mr Sanjaya Warnatilake
Mr Glynn Warner
Mr Maurice Warwick
Miss Emma Wasden
Mr Waters
Mr William Watson
Mr Ian Watson
Mrs Maria Watson
Mr William Watt
Mr John Watts
Mr Robert Weatherburn
Ms Jan Webb
Mrs Penny Webber
Mr Neil Webber
Mrs Deborah Webster
Mrs Caroline Welch
Mr Roger Weldhen
Mr Robertson Wellen
Ms Margaret West
Mr J F M West
Ms Helen West
Mr J West
Mr Graham Westgarth
Mrs Jill Weston

Mrs Carole Weston
Miss Tania Whale
Mr Peter Wheeler
Mrs Jacqueline Wheeler
Ms Hannah Whibley
Ms Jenny White
Mr Bob White
Mrs Sally White
Mr Peter White
Ms Pam White
Mr Andrew White
Miss Romney Whitehead
Mr Peter Whitehead
Mrs Ellen Whitehouse
Mrs Di Whiteley
Ms Marion Whitfield
Mrs C C Whitlock
Mr Paul Whittaker
Miss Teresa Whittaker
Mr Stephen Whittle
Ms Becky Wicks
Mr Andy Widdowson
Mrs Gemma Wiggins
Mr John Wilkinson
Mr Sandra Wilkinson
Mr Glyn Williams
Mr Steven Williams
Mr Desmond Williams
Mr Huw Williams
Mr Harold E. Williams
Mr Robert Williams
Miss Amy Williams
Miss Michelle Williams
Mrs Julie Williams
Mr Chris Williams
Mrs Kirsten Williams
Mrs Catherine Williamson
Mr Brian Williamson
Mr Phil Wills
Ms Sue Wilshere
Mrs Trish Wilson
Mr David Wilson
Mrs Carole Wilson
Mr Rob Wilson
Miss Fiona Wilson
Mrs Doreen Wilson
Mr Ralph Wilson
Mr Colin Wimble
Mr Ross Wincott
Mr John Window
Mr Terry Windsor
Ms Michelle Winslow
Mr Colin Winspear
Mr Carol Winter
Mrs Barbara Withers
Ms Lucie Wood
Mr Christopher Wood
Mr Michael Wood
Mr Chris Woodland
Miss Cheryl Woods
Mr Graham Woodward
Mr N Woodward
Miss Penny Woolford
Mrs Janet Woolliscroft
Mrs Janet Wormald
Mr John Worth
Ms Mandy Wragg
Mrs Meg Wraight
Mrs Ros Wright
Mr William Wright
Mrs Fay Wright
Miss Jayne Wright
Mr Richard Wright
Mrs Martina Wyatt
Mr R A Wyld
Mr Alex Wynter
Mrs Alison Yates
Mr John Yelland
Miss Joyce Yeung
Ms Flora York Skinner
Ms Juliette Young
Mrs Micheala Young
Mr Steven Young
Mr Morris Zwi
Mr Daniel Zylbersztajn

# Special thank yous

We'd like to extend special thanks to the following people:

Luke Block, Elizabeth Bowden, Lucy Cannon, James Cuddy, Paula Dadic, Michael Edwards, Sarah Fergusson, Good Impessions in Redruth, Alan Grimwade, Ros Mari Grindheim, Alex Hall at Charterhouse, Andy Hayler, Alan Jessop at Compass, Simone Johnson, Cadence Kinsey, Michelle Lyttle, David Mabey, Simon Mather at AMA, Angela Newton, Jeffrey Ng, Isobel Roberts, Katharine Servant, Kelly Smith, Oliver Smith, Judi Turner, Stuart Walton, Chris White, Blanche Williams and Emma Wilmot.

## Picture credits
Mateusz Atroszko, Linda B, Anna Byckling, Romina Chamorro, Michel Collot, Guy Drayton, Erik Dungan, Rachel Gilmore, Neil Gould, Steve Gould, Manu M, Jacob Metzler, Anthony Mahieu, Jacob Metzelder, Paul Raeside, Karen Rennie, Mr Sasvari, Stephanie Schleicher, Manjari Sharma, Karen Sparrow, Marcin Szczepanski, Michal Szydlowski, Manuel Trejo, John Trenholm, Steve Woods.

## Map credits
Maps designed and produced by Cosmographics, www.cosmographics.co.uk
UK digital database © Cosmographics 2007, Greater London map © Cosmographics 2006, North and South London Maps © Collins Bartholomew 2007, West, Central and East London maps © BTA (trading as VisitBritain) 2007 produced by Cosmographics and used with the kind permission of VisitBritain.

Please send updates, queries, menus and wine lists to:
goodfoodguide@which.co.uk